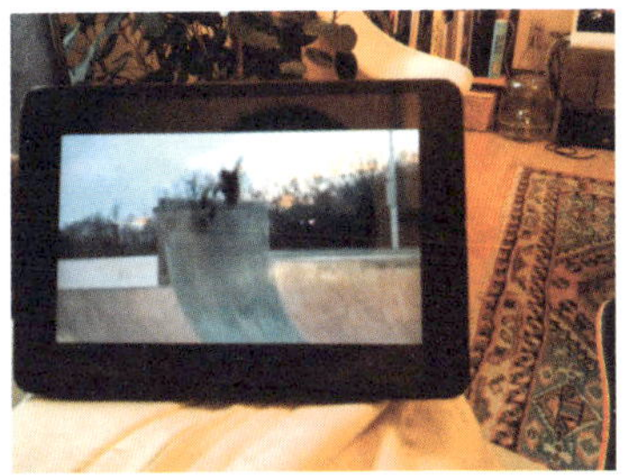

03:51

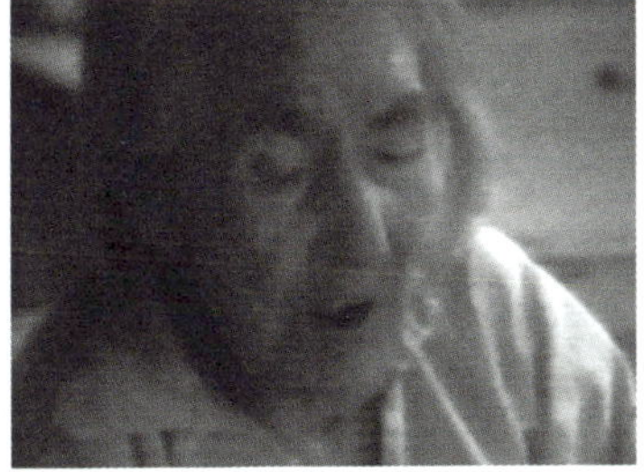

14:22

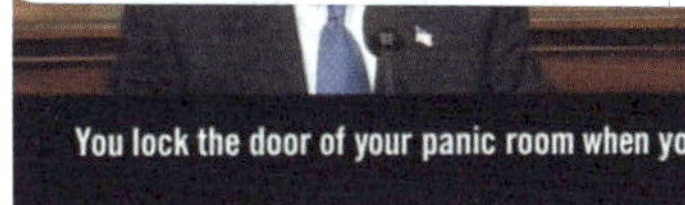

04:24

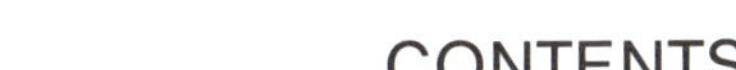

CONTENTS

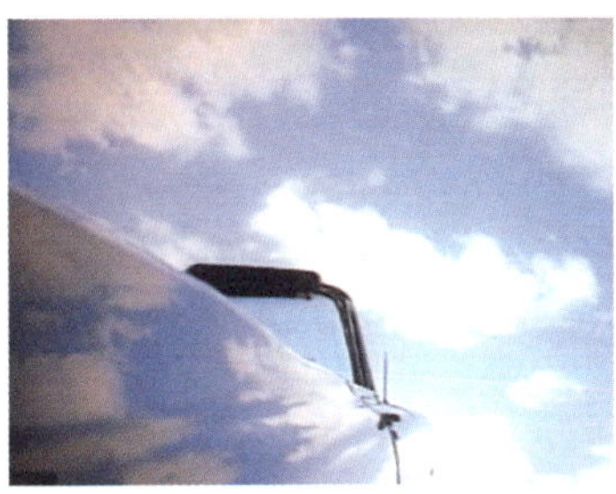

00:11

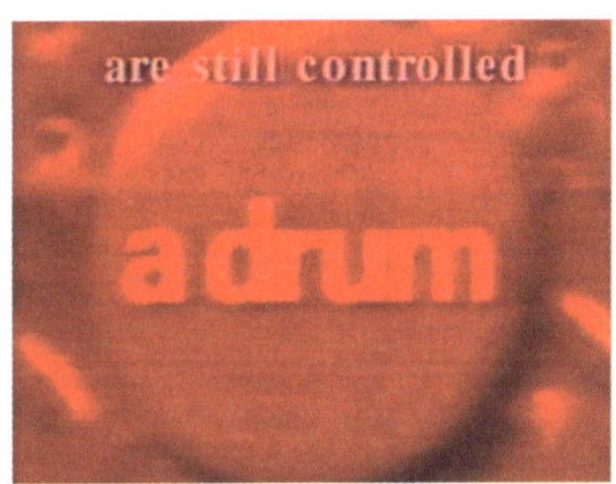

00:28

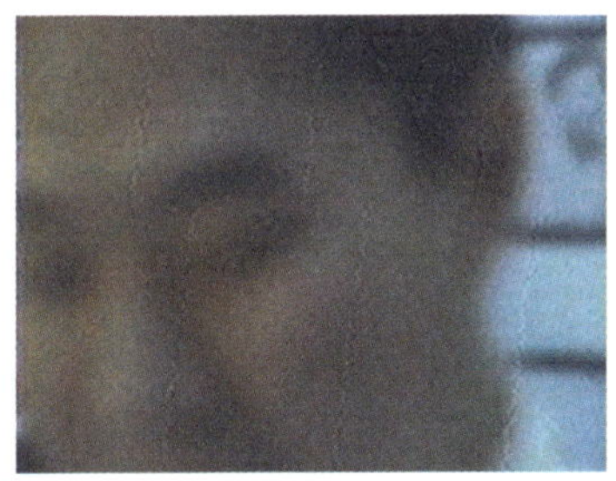

21:05

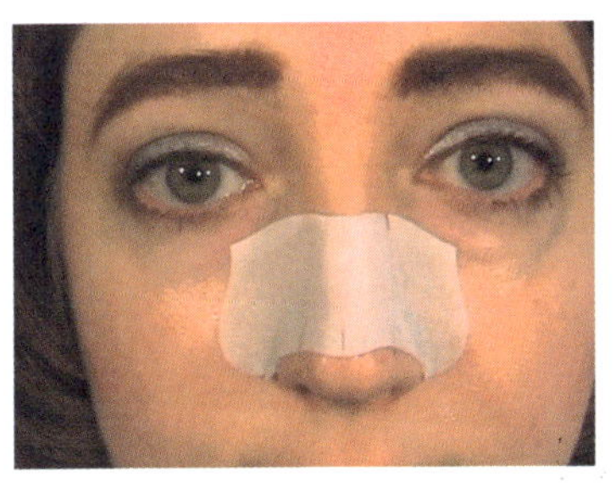

01:17

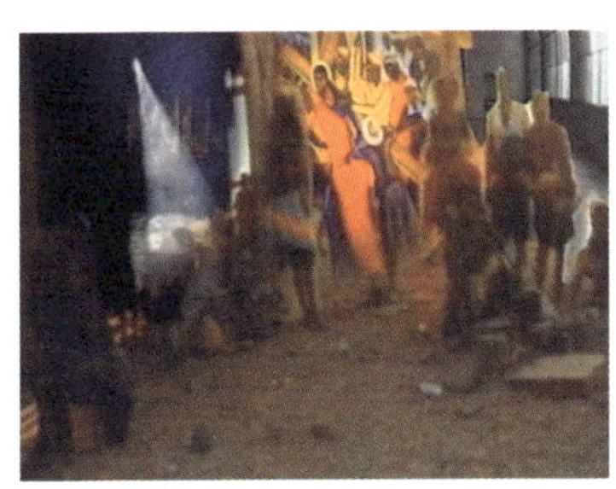

00:14

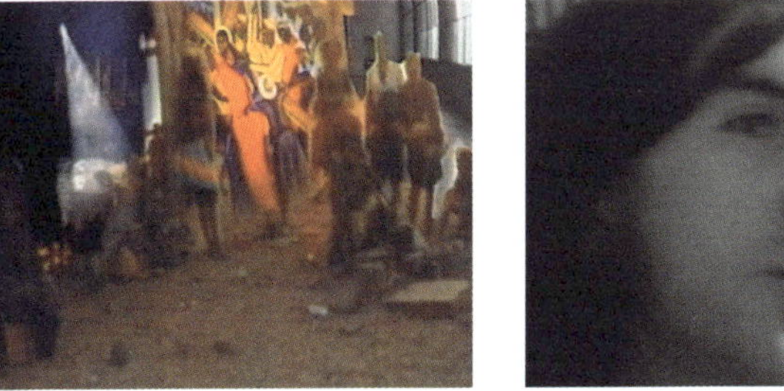

04:17

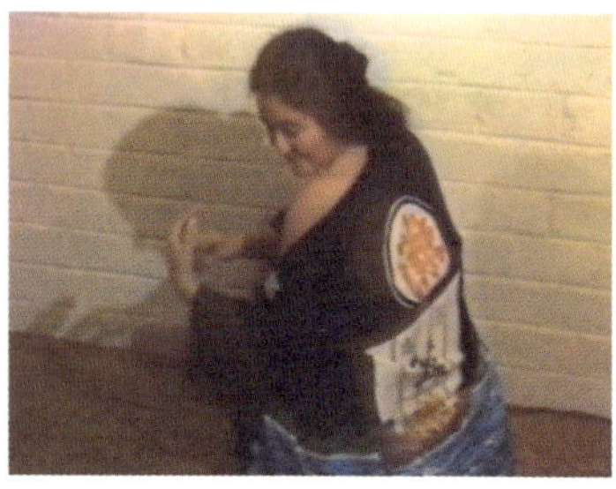
01:33

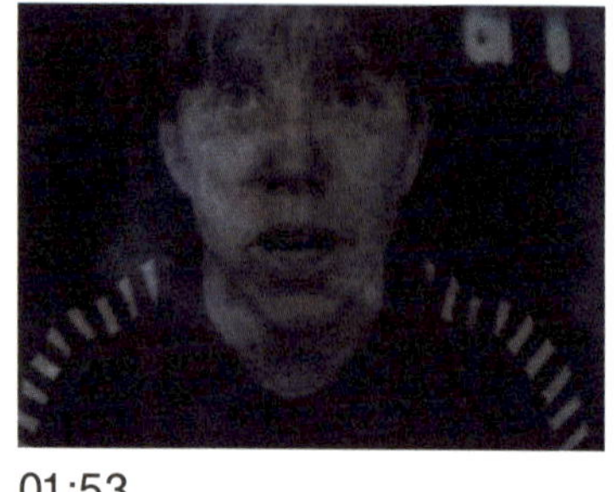
01:53

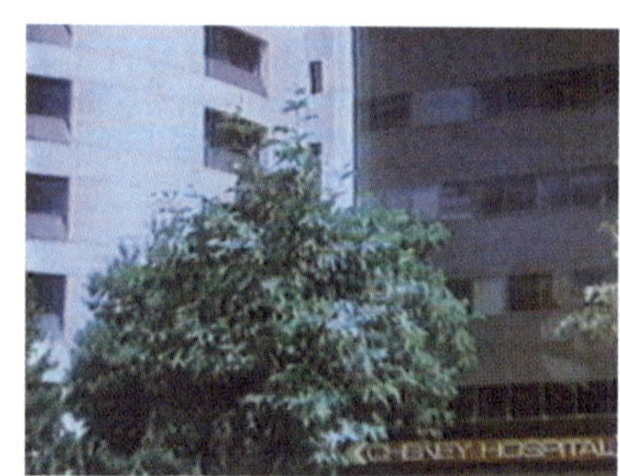
06:08

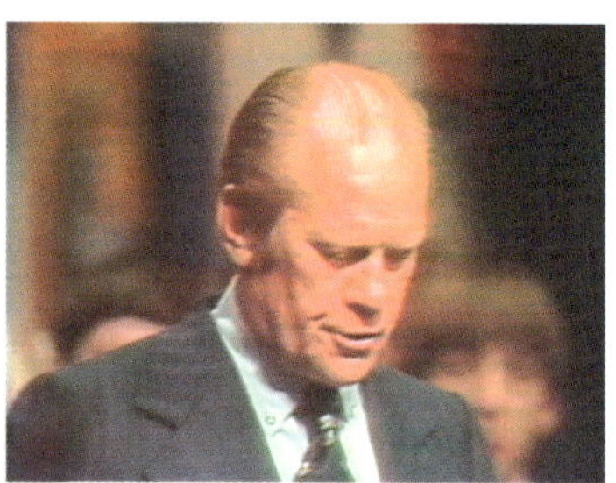
14:17

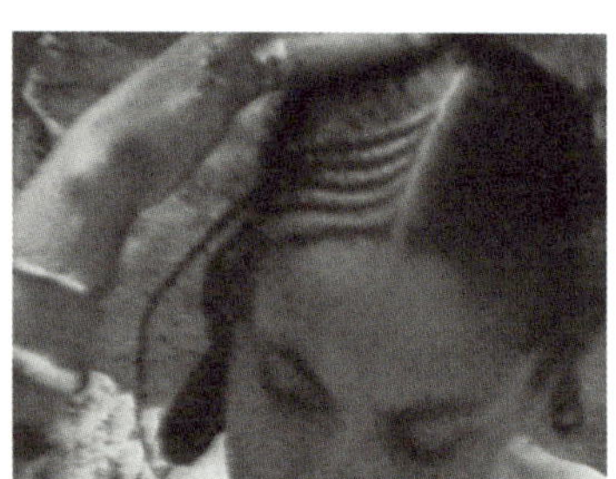
17:41

DIRECTOR'S FOREWORD
ZOË RYAN

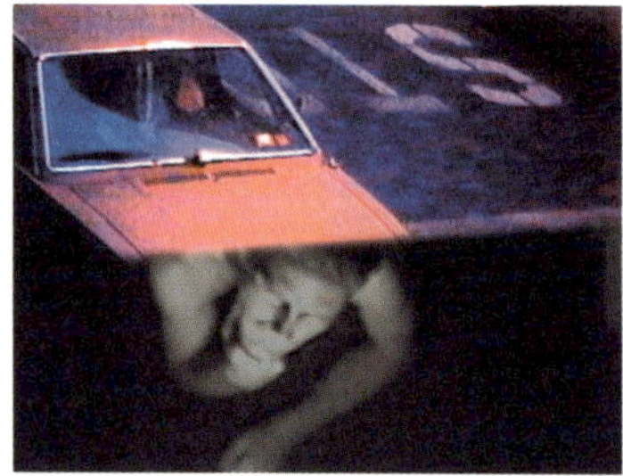
07:29

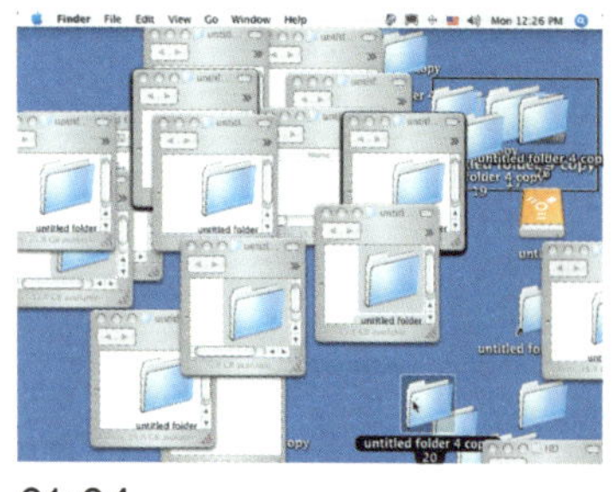
01:04

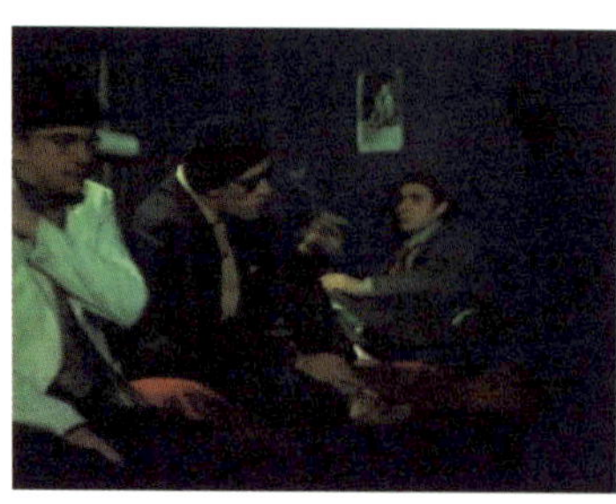
08:35

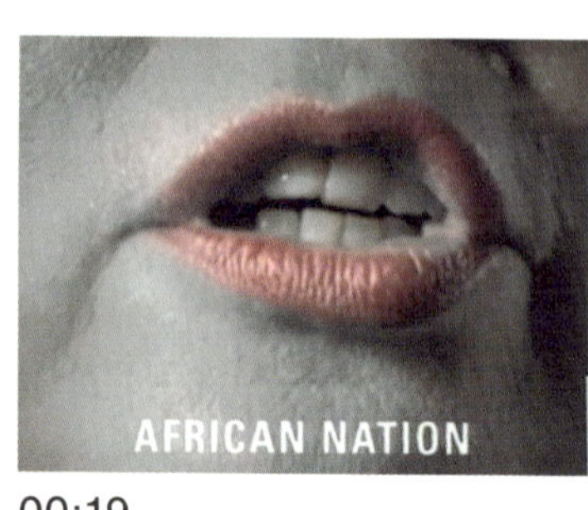

00:19

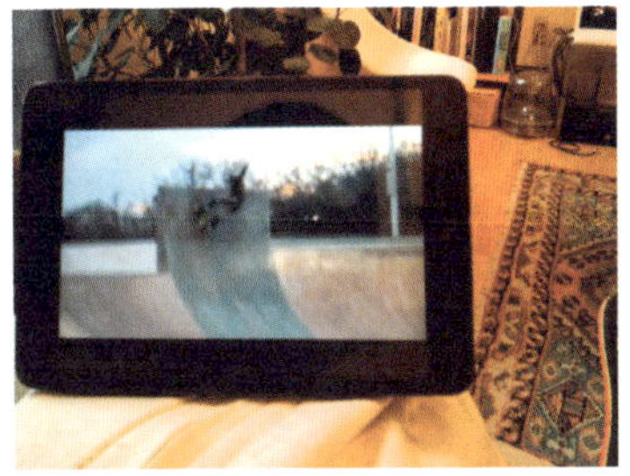
03:51

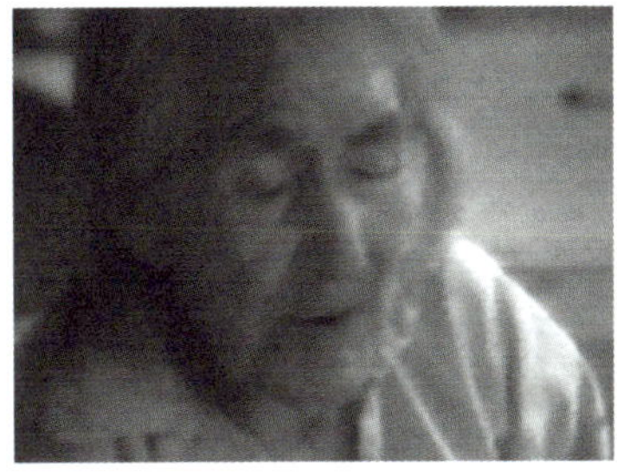
14:22

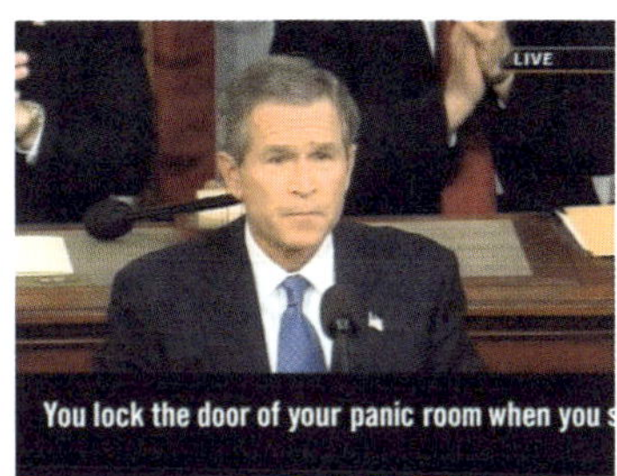

04:24

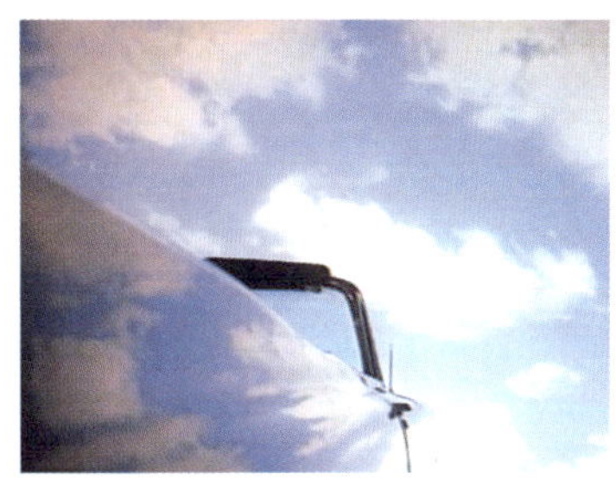
00:11

In this time of enormous global change, broadcasting has experienced a seismic shift. The Big Three networks that ruled the American airwaves when Electronic Arts Intermix (EAI) was created in 1971 have given way to the unfiltered, live-streaming universe of Twitch, Periscope, Vimeo, and myriad other new media outlets. *Broadcasting: EAI at ICA* could not come at a more prescient time. It explores the artists who have continuously shaped, exploited, and redefined the leading edge of the broadcast medium at every stage of its development.

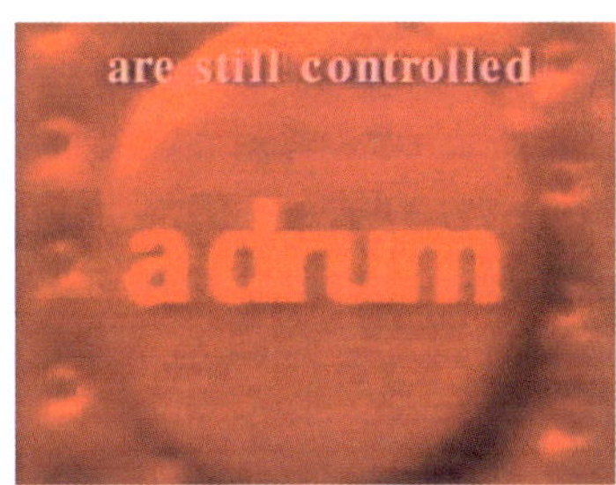

00:28

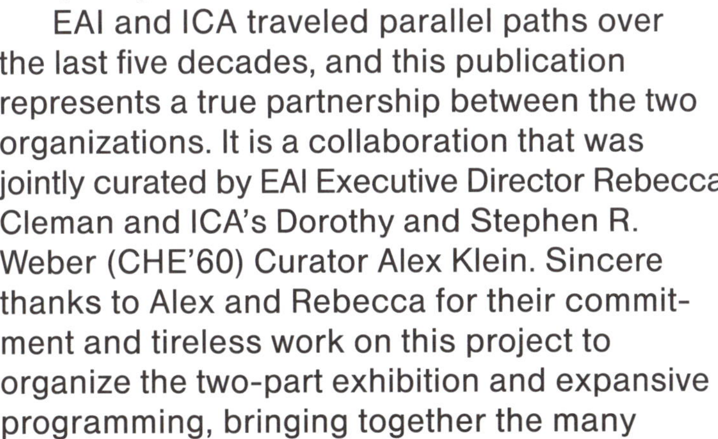

EAI and ICA traveled parallel paths over the last five decades, and this publication represents a true partnership between the two organizations. It is a collaboration that was jointly curated by EAI Executive Director Rebecca Cleman and ICA's Dorothy and Stephen R. Weber (CHE'60) Curator Alex Klein. Sincere thanks to Alex and Rebecca for their commitment and tireless work on this project to organize the two-part exhibition and expansive programming, bringing together the many

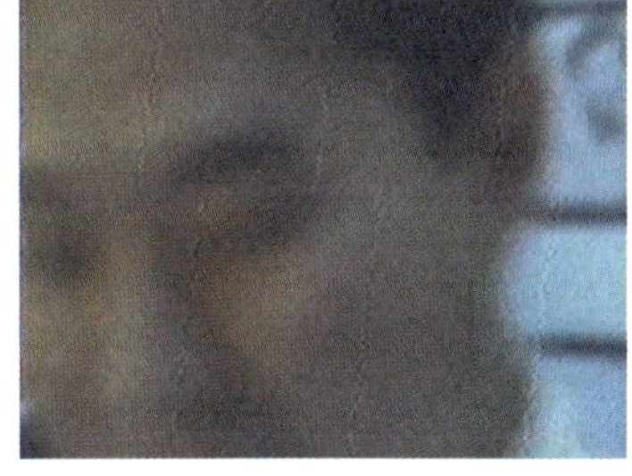
21:05

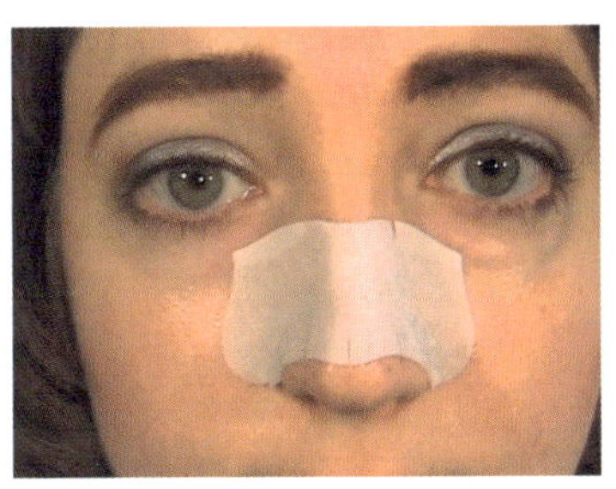
01:17

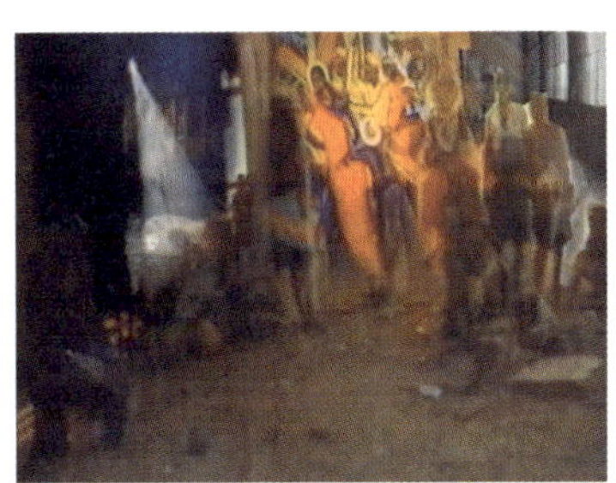
00:14

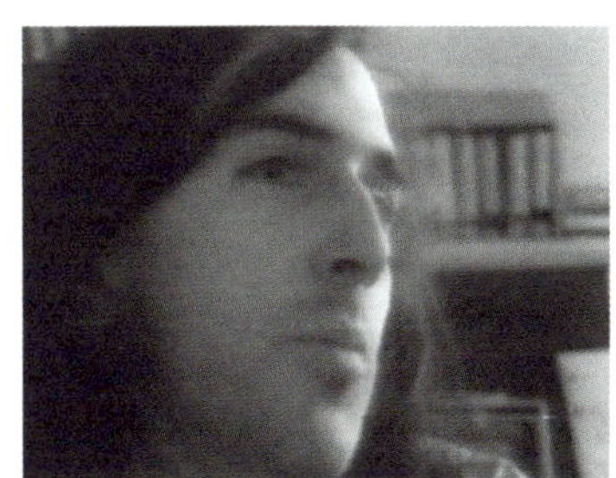
04:17

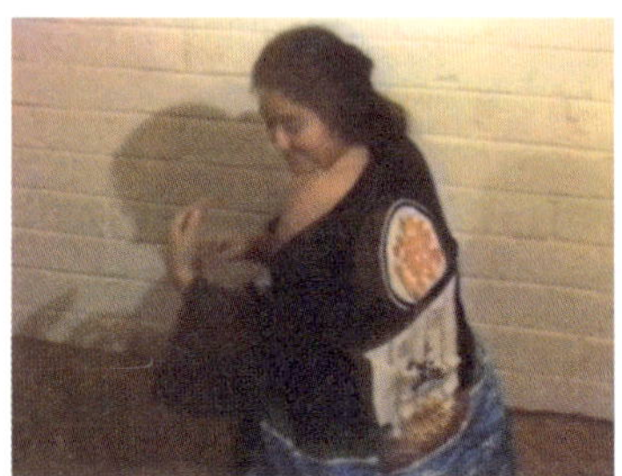
01:33

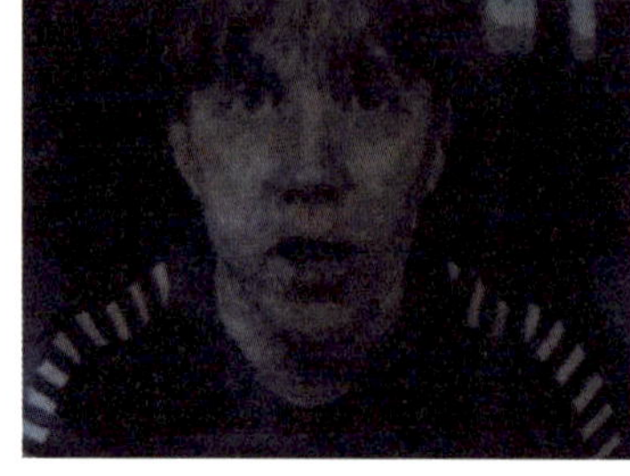
01:53

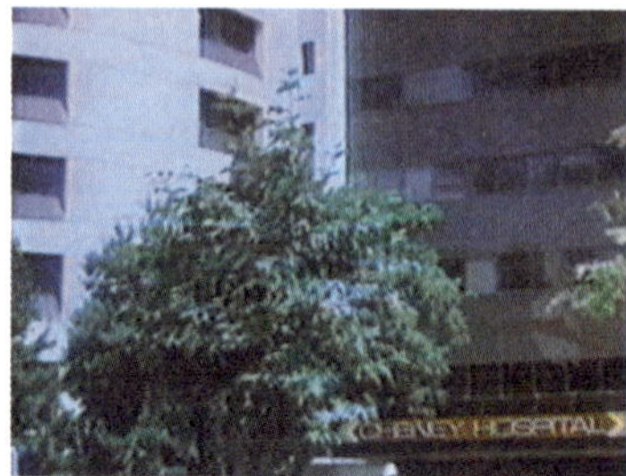
06:08

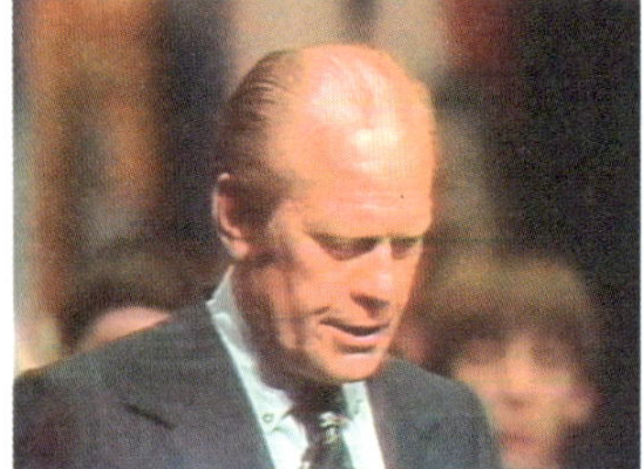

14:17

17:41

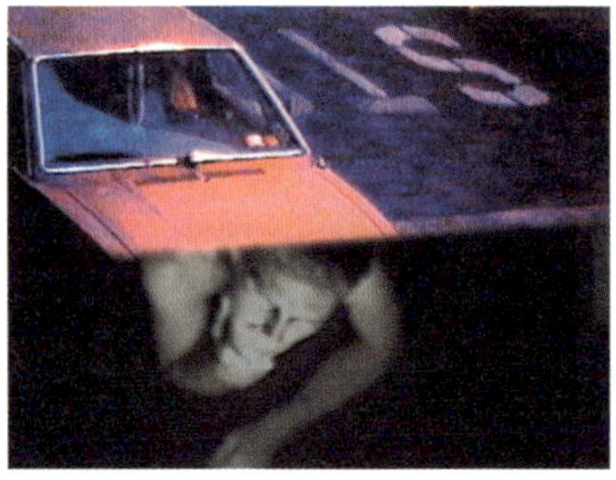
07:29

collaborators and partners, and to produce this beautiful publication.

Broadcasting: EAI at ICA highlights a range of intergenerational artists working in time-based media. Our deep gratitude goes to the artists in the ICA exhibition: Beth B, Robert Beck/Buck, Dara Birnbaum, Tony Cokes, Ulysses Jenkins, JODI, Philip Mallory Jones, Tom Kalin, Shigeko Kubota, Kristin Lucas, Victor Masayesva, Jr., Shana Moulton, Nam June Paik and Paul Garrin, Trevor Shimizu, and Bruce and Norman Yonemoto.

Special thanks are due to everyone at EAI in New York, including Director Emerita Lori Zippay, whose enthusiasm and support for this project were unwavering. Her extensive oral history of EAI produced for this publication will prove invaluable for future scholars. Thank you as well to all of the other EAI staff members who had a role in making the exhibition and this publication happen, including Karl McCool, Tyler Maxin, Jon Dieringer, Michael Blair, and Keisha Husain.

The exhibition spanned two physical venues in Philadelphia: ICA and Slought. We are grateful to

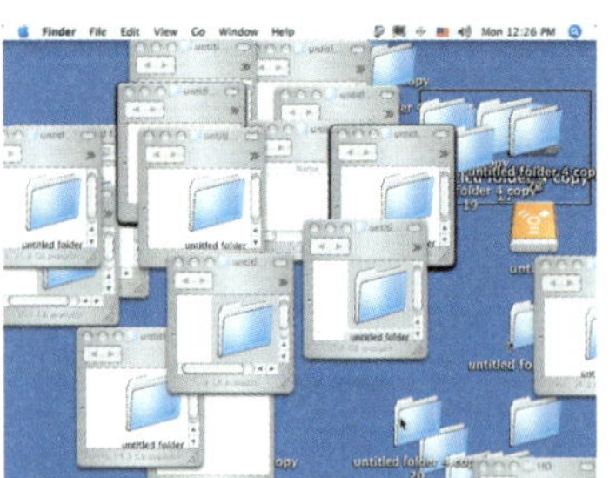
01:04

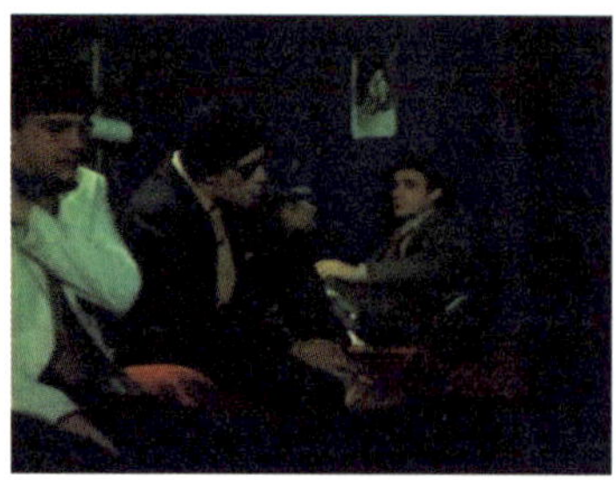
08:35

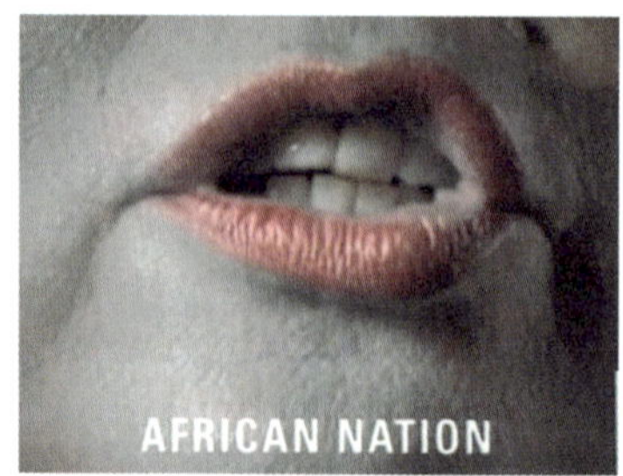

00:19

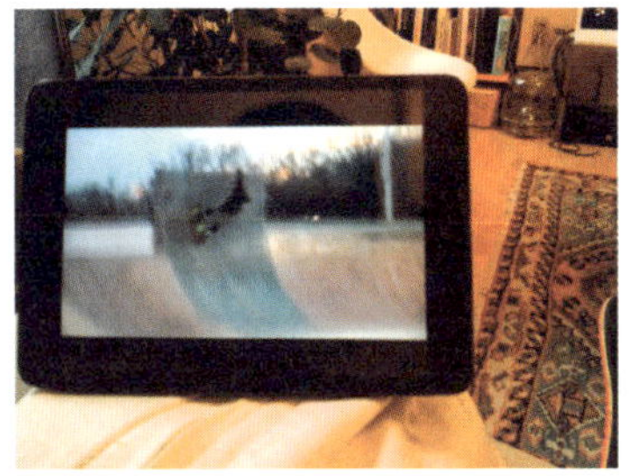
03:51

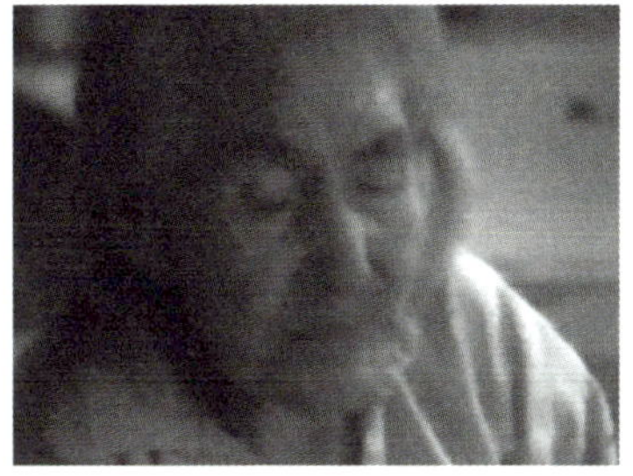
14:22

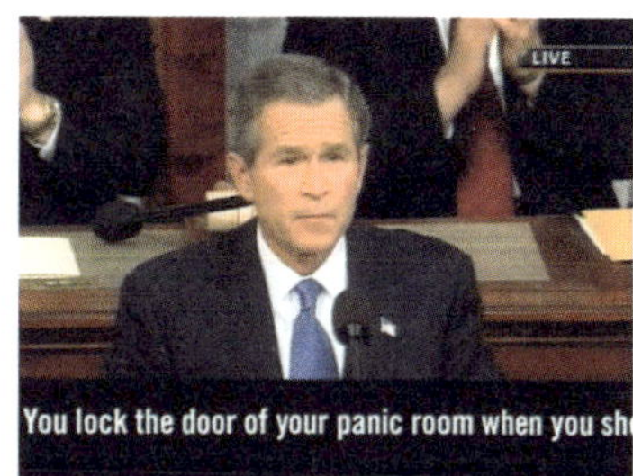

04:24

Slought Director Aaron Levy and his colleague Tung Chau who hosted *Broadcasting: Guerilla Media* at Slought. This extension of ICA's exhibition featured the work of DCTV, Robert Beck/Buck and DIVA TV, Martha Rosler and Paper Tiger Television, Radical Software Group (RSG), Squat Theatre, TVTV, Video Venice News, and X-PRZ. We also wish to thank Karl McCool for organizing the complementary screening program and discussion *Video Interference: Guerrilla Media in the 1990s*.

Our thanks go as well to Lightbox Film Center Director and Curator Jesse Pires and master projectionist Robert Cargni Mitchell, who hosted related screenings of work by Alex Bag, Dara Birnbaum, Jaime Davidovich, Ulysses Jenkins, Josh Mills, Ernie Kovacs (thank you Ediad Productions), Cynthia Maughan, Jayson Musson, Nam June Paik, Sondra Perry, Stan VanDerBeek, and William Wegman.

Programming happened across multiple venues and formats. We are particularly grateful to PhillyCAM, who turned ICA's gallery into a

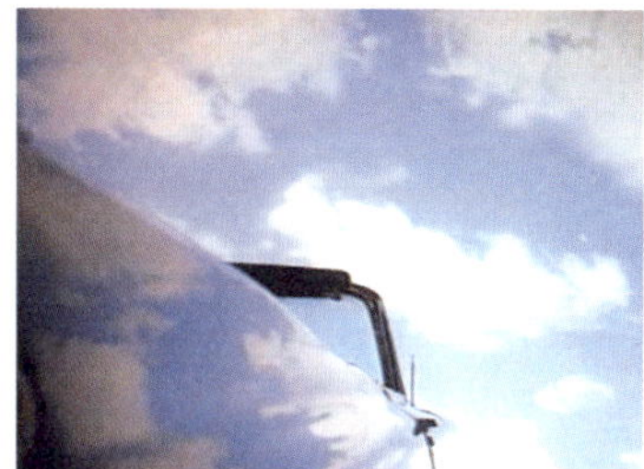
00:11

00:28

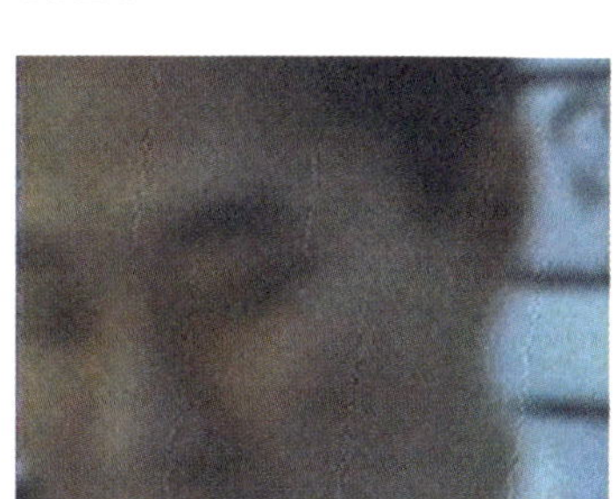
21:05

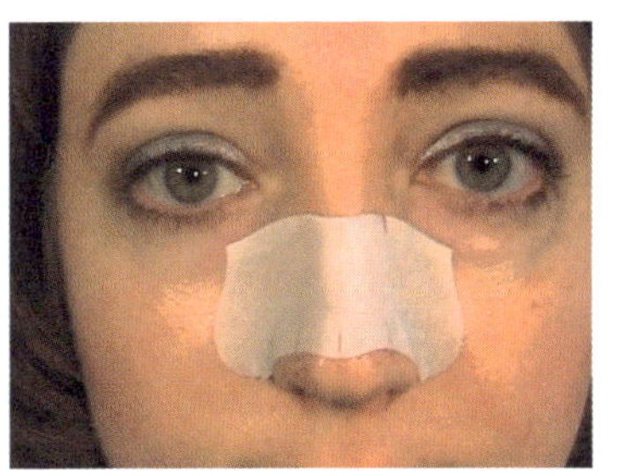
01:17

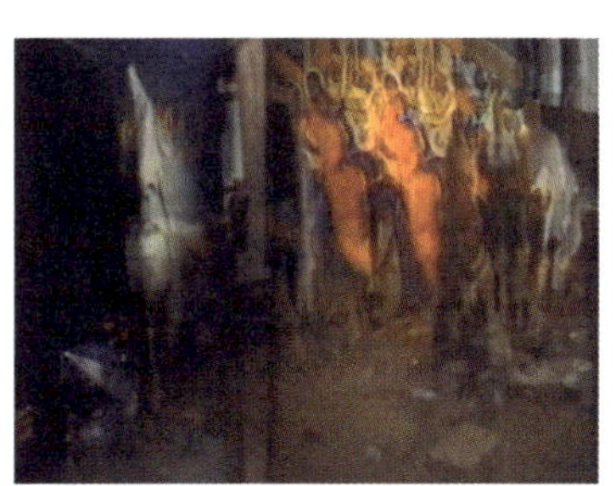
00:14

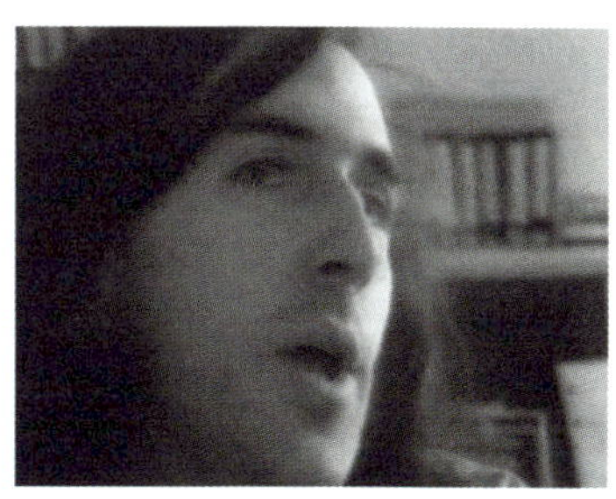
04:17

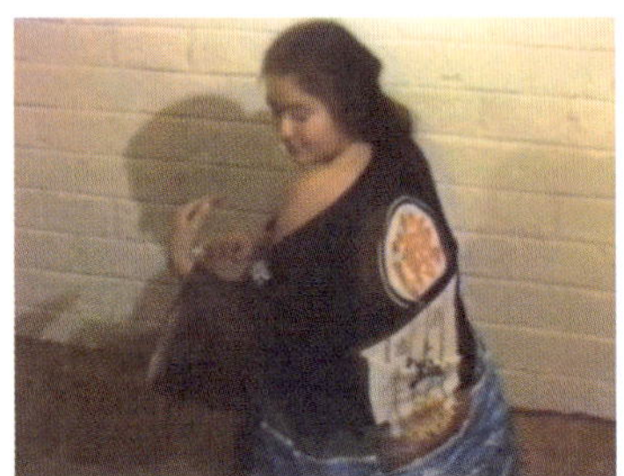

01:33

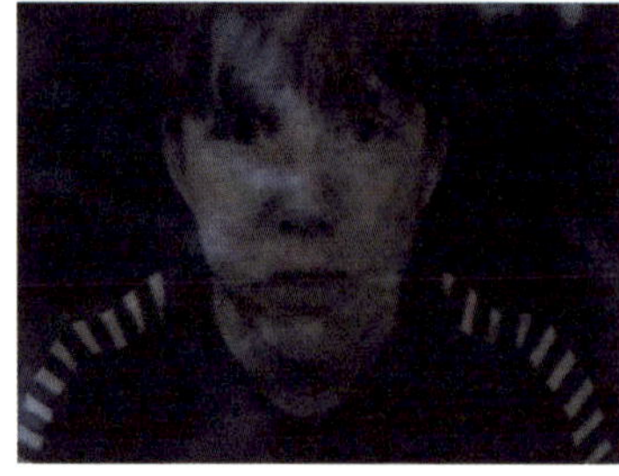

01:53

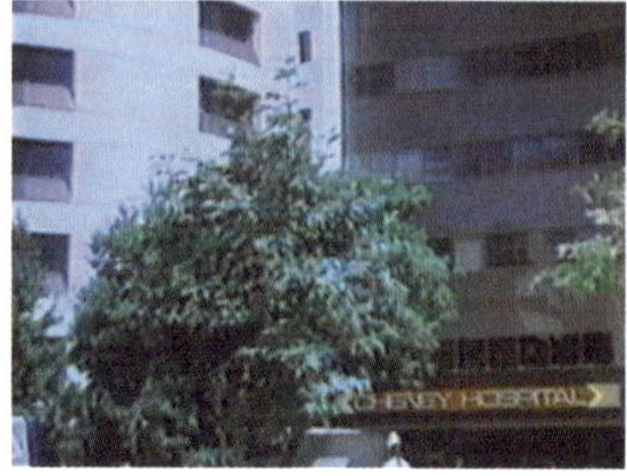

06:08

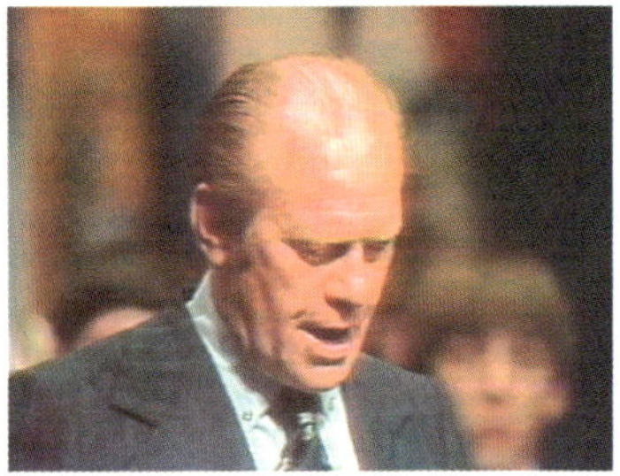

14:17

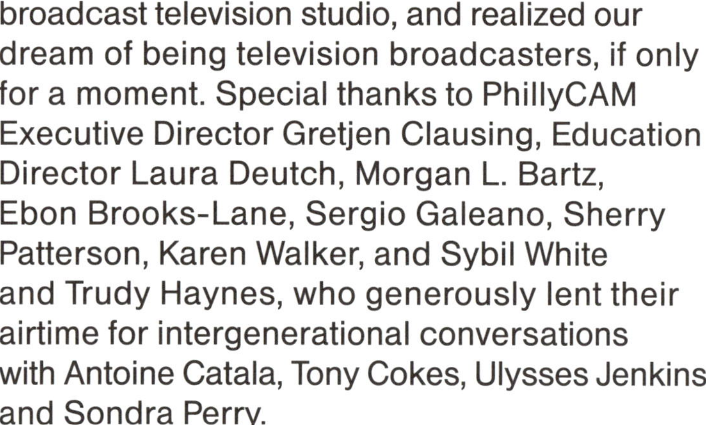

broadcast television studio, and realized our dream of being television broadcasters, if only for a moment. Special thanks to PhillyCAM Executive Director Gretjen Clausing, Education Director Laura Deutch, Morgan L. Bartz, Ebon Brooks-Lane, Sergio Galeano, Sherry Patterson, Karen Walker, and Sybil White and Trudy Haynes, who generously lent their airtime for intergenerational conversations with Antoine Catala, Tony Cokes, Ulysses Jenkins, and Sondra Perry.

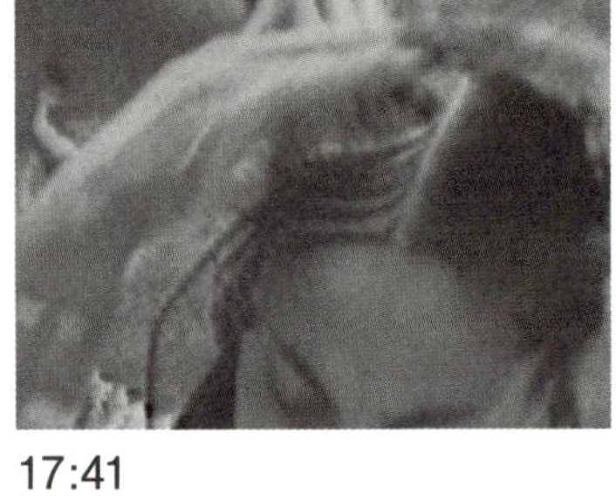

17:41

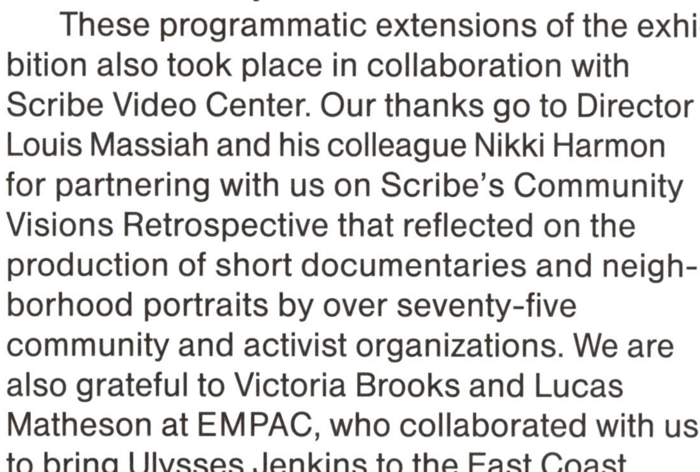

These programmatic extensions of the exhibition also took place in collaboration with Scribe Video Center. Our thanks go to Director Louis Massiah and his colleague Nikki Harmon for partnering with us on Scribe's Community Visions Retrospective that reflected on the production of short documentaries and neighborhood portraits by over seventy-five community and activist organizations. We are also grateful to Victoria Brooks and Lucas Matheson at EMPAC, who collaborated with us to bring Ulysses Jenkins to the East Coast

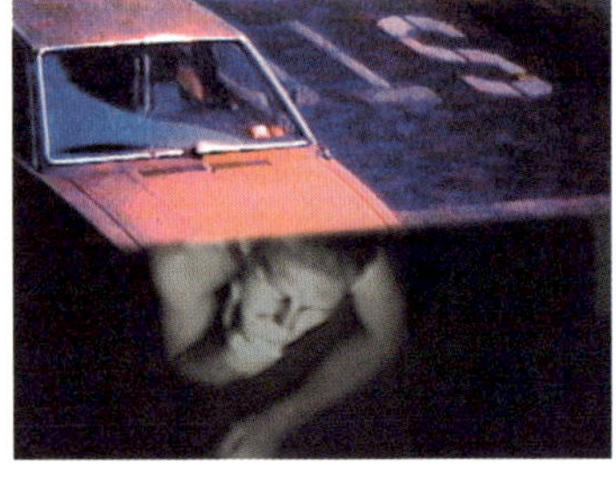

07:29

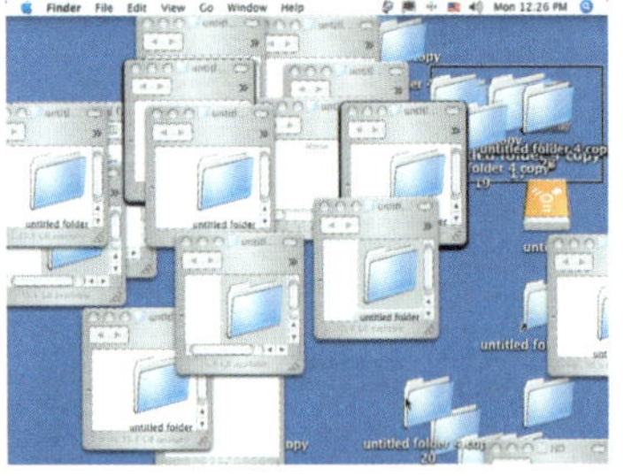

01:04

08:35

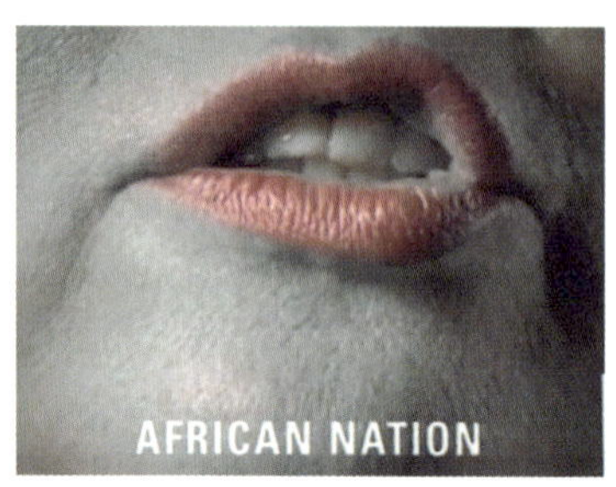

00:19

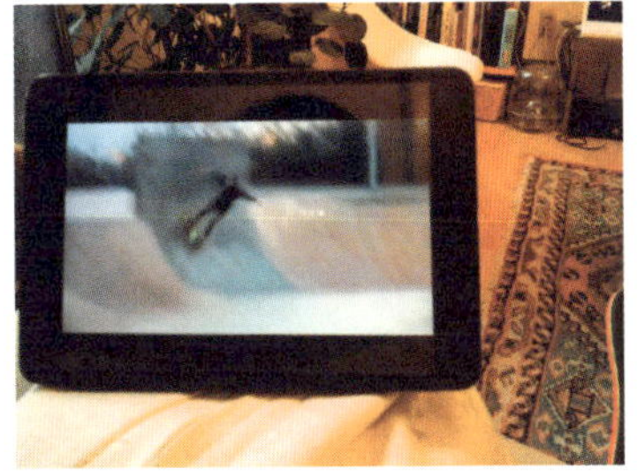
03:51

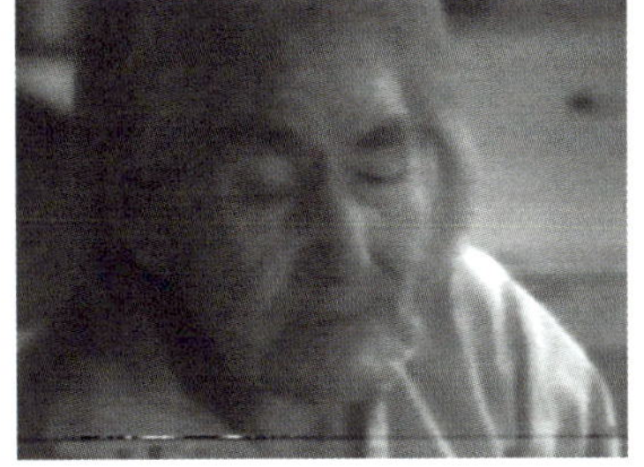
14:22

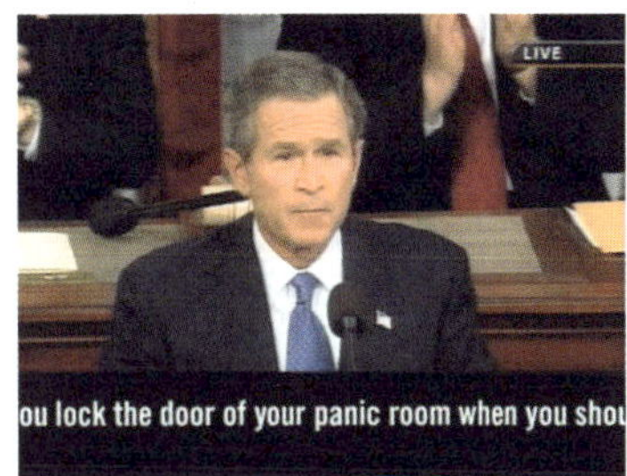

04:24

to participate in the programs at ICA, EAI, and EMPAC. We would also like to acknowledge Wendy Dorsett, John Mhiripiri, Jed Rapfogel, and Ava Tews at Anthology Film Archives in New York for hosting a related screening. And additional thanks go to Ava Tews for contributing a critical text to ICA's website that expanded on many of the ideas in the exhibition.

Lastly, this broad range of exhibitions, programs, and screenings would not have been possible without the thoughtful, creative, and inspiring staff at ICA. We are grateful to everyone involved, beginning with our crew, led by the indefatigable Paul Swenbeck, Chief Preparator, and including Julia Policastro, Preston Link, Emily B. Elliott, Sophie White, Emilia Brintnall, Isaac Lin, Adam Lovitz, Lydia Smith, Jay Roselius, Patrick Maguire, and Aaron Carrol. Special thanks to Tausif Noor, Spiegel-Wilks Curatorial Fellow (2017–2020), for his close collaboration on programming, and to Robert Chaney, Marc J. Leder Director of Curatorial Affairs, for video sourcing, exhibition logistics, and all-around

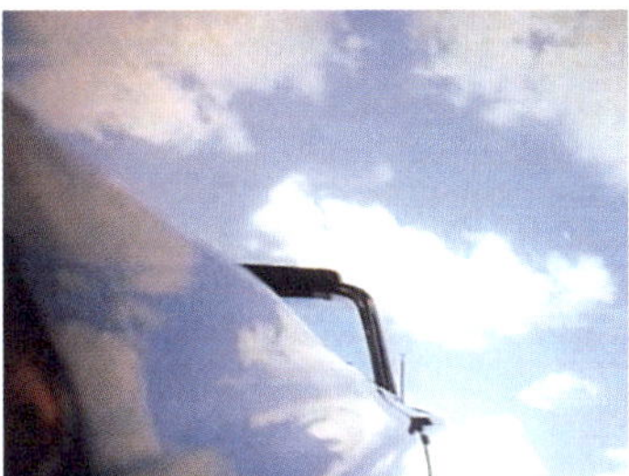
00:11

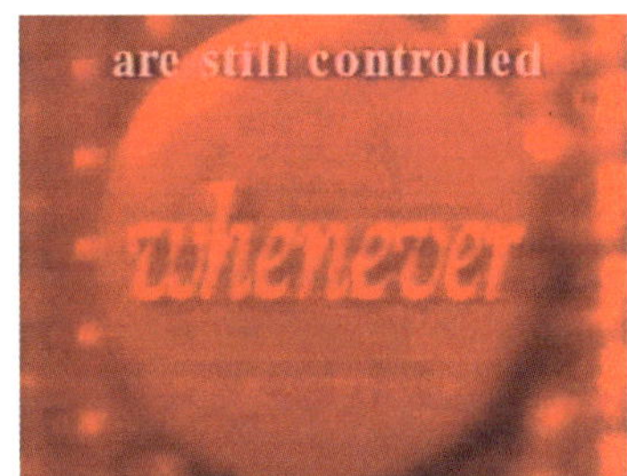

00:28

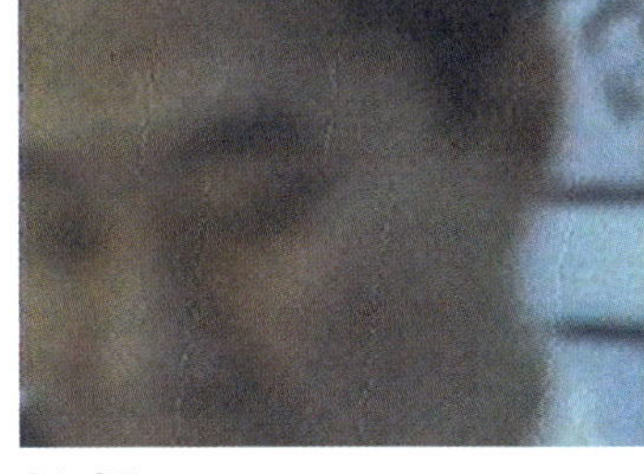
21:05

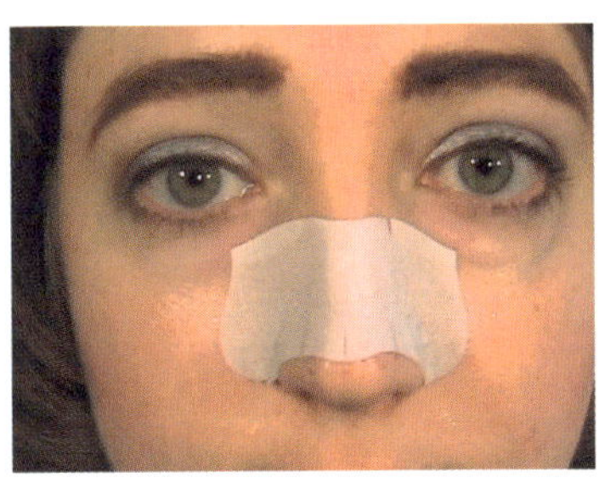
01:17

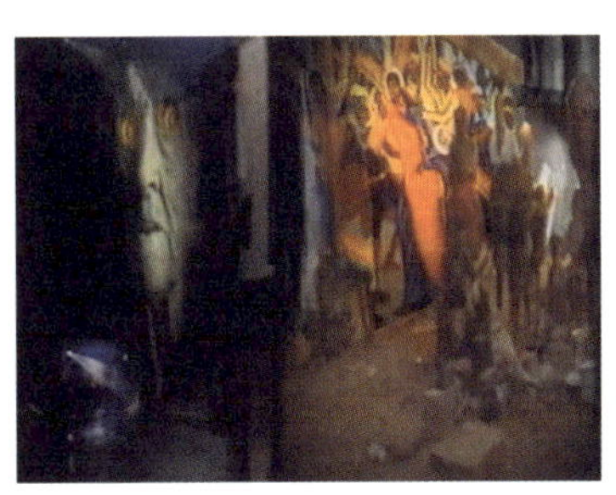
00:14

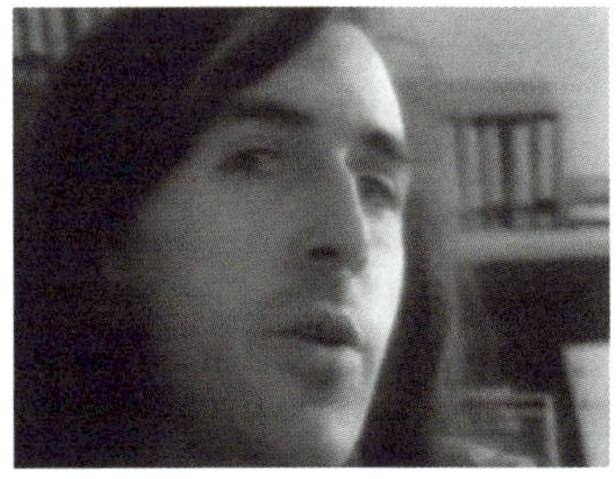
04:17

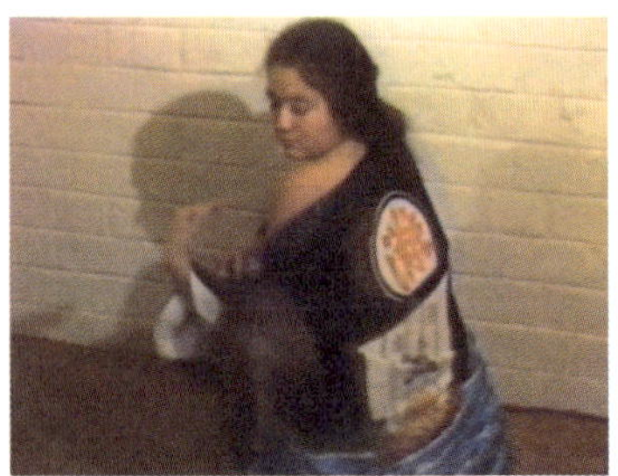
01:32

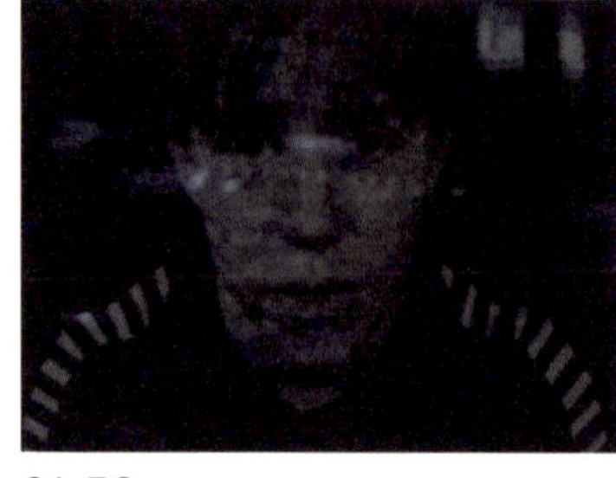
01:52

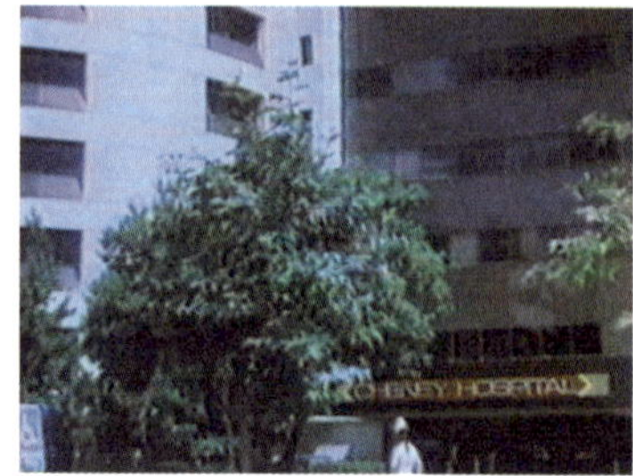
06:07

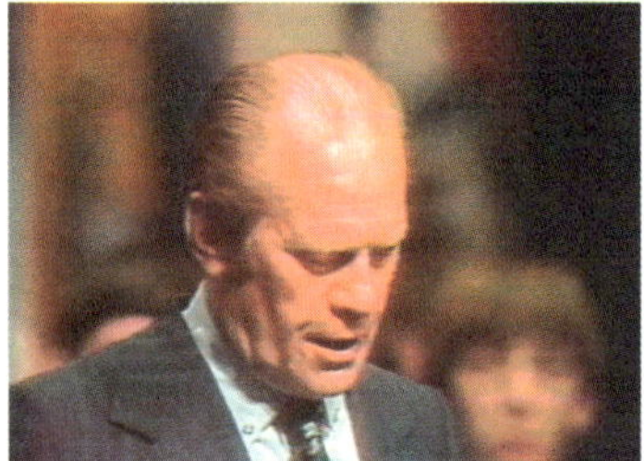
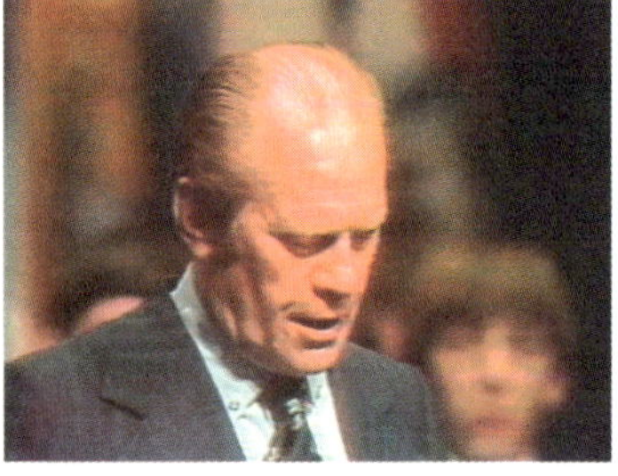
14:16

17:40

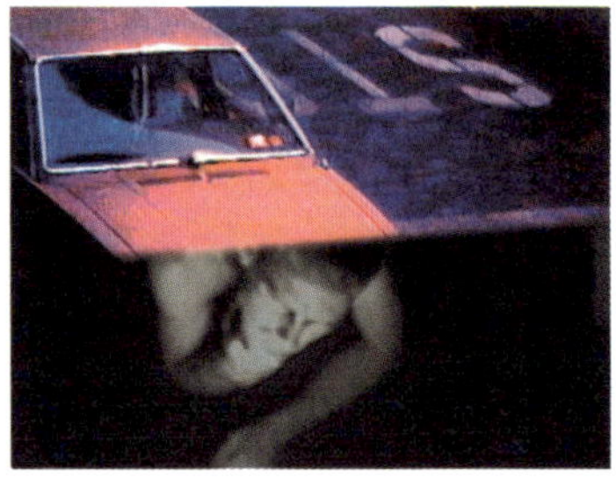
07:28

problem solving, assisted by Caitlin Palmer, former Curatorial Administrative Coordinator, who also provided an expert pair of proofreading eyes. We are also grateful to ICA's interns Laurel McLaughlin (Bryn Mawr College Ridgway Curatorial Fellow), Amalia Wiatr Lewis, and Caitlin Vitalo for their research assistance.

Design has played a crucial role in this project. We thank Other Means for bringing EAI and ICA together graphically throughout the exhibition, in the related printed materials, and over the airwaves. We are incredibly appreciative of Geoff Han and Anna Feng for this engaging and unique catalog, which manages to make media works in a book animate for the reader. The publication does a beautiful job of capturing the experience of the viewers in the show as a result of Constance Mensh's wonderful photography. Our thanks are also reserved for Gretchen Dykstra for her thorough edit.

This exhibition would not have been possible without the support of our Board of Advisors and the University, including the Office of the Provost

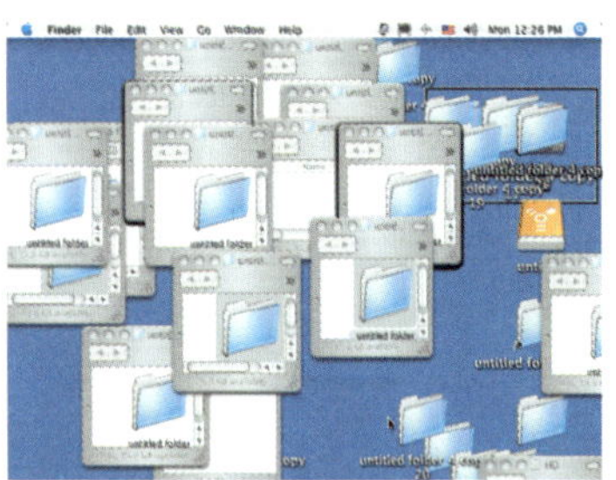
01:03

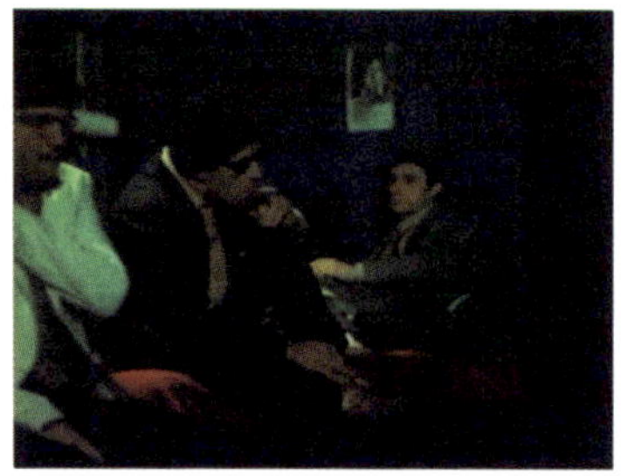
08:34

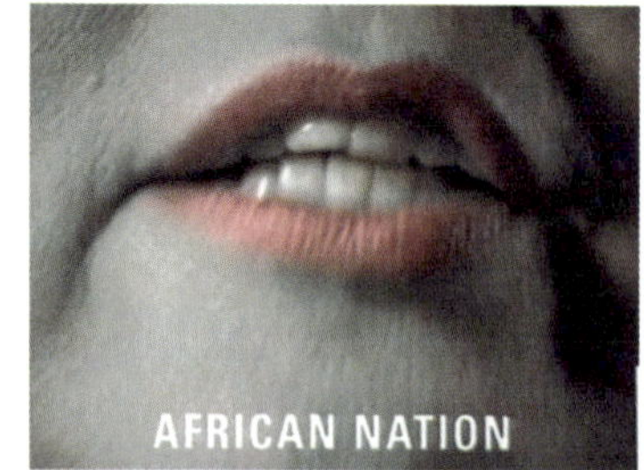

00:18

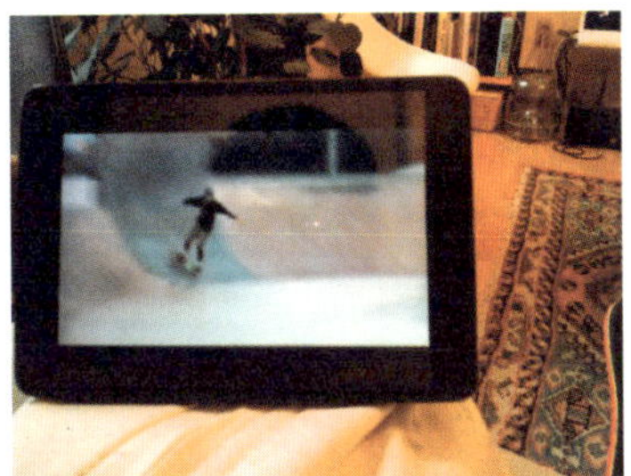

03:51

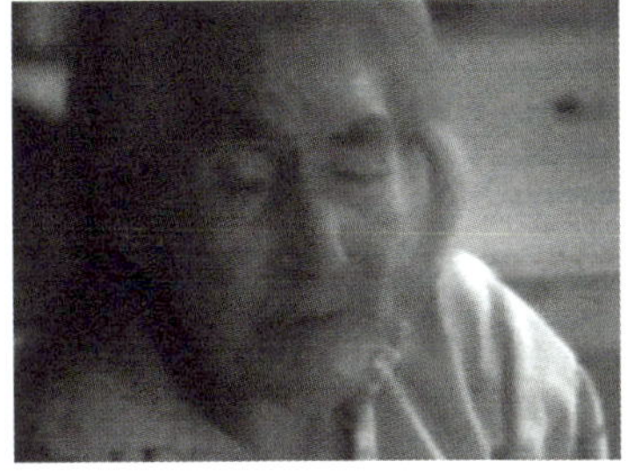

14:22

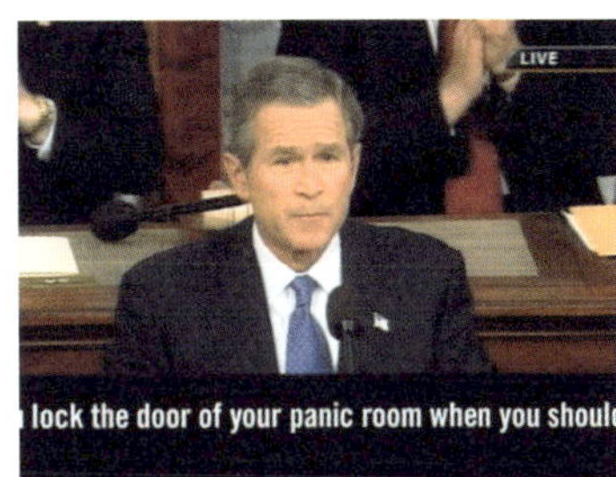

04:24

and the leadership and vision of University of Pennsylvania President Amy Gutmann. We also wish to acknowledge the crucial support of the Keith L. and Katherine Sachs Program in Contemporary Art and the Sachs Program for Arts Innovation lead by John McInerney, Executive Director, and Chloe Reison, Associate Director. In every respect, *Broadcasting: EAI at ICA* and its related catalog are the result of a true collaboration. We wish to reiterate our sincere gratitude to Electronic Arts Intermix and congratulate them on their fiftieth anniversary celebration, which coincides with the release of this publication.

Zoë Ryan
Daniel W. Dietrich, II Director

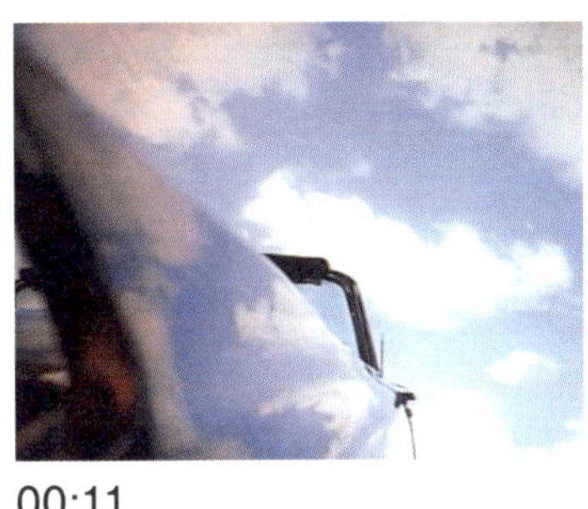

00:11

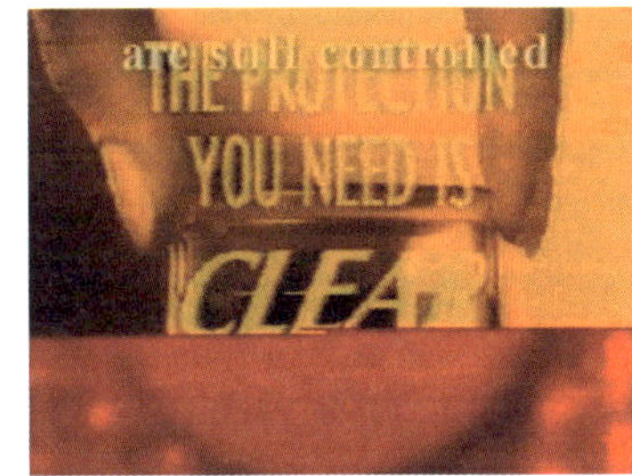

00:28

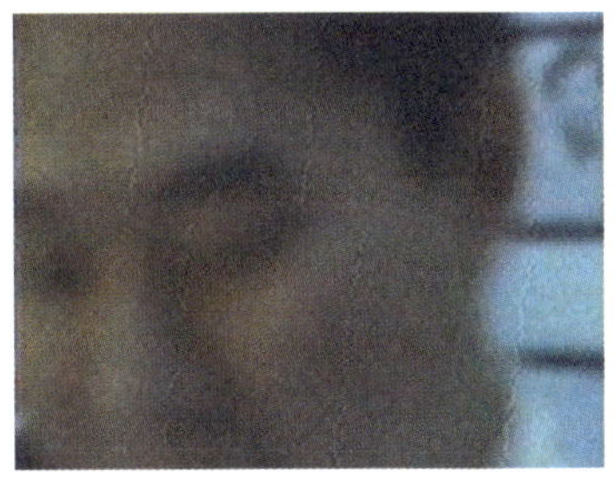

21:05

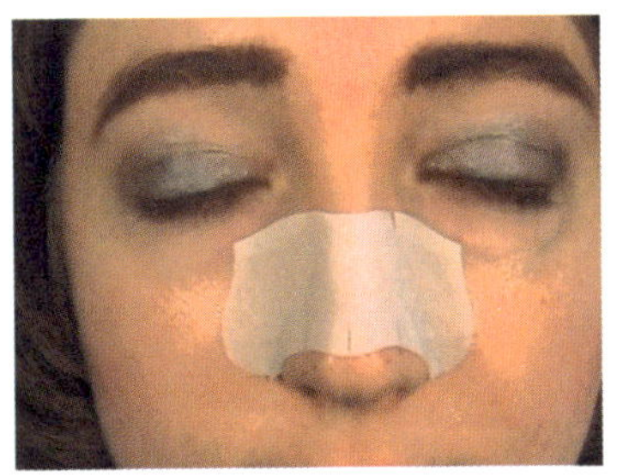

01:17

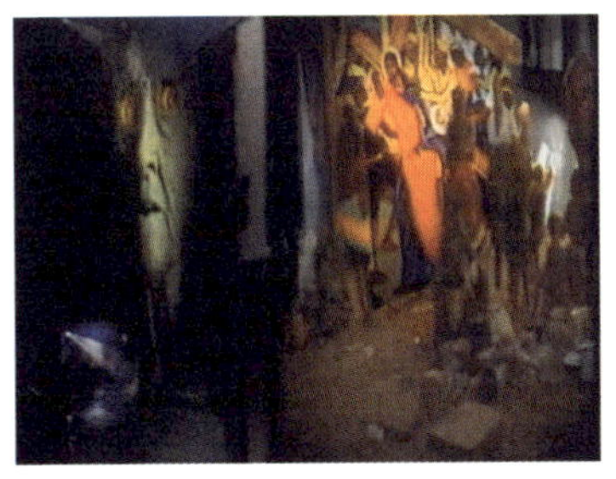

00:14

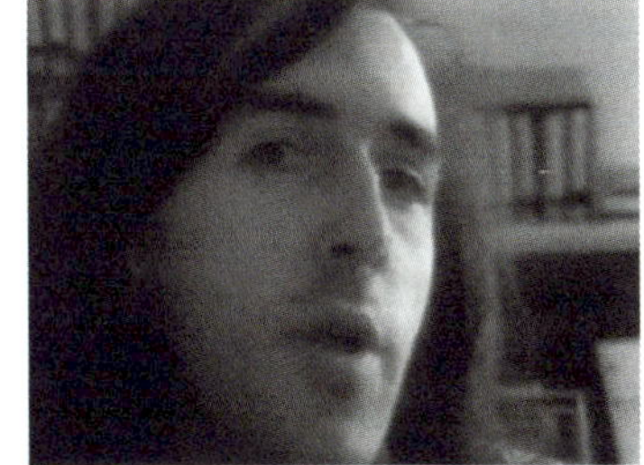

04:17

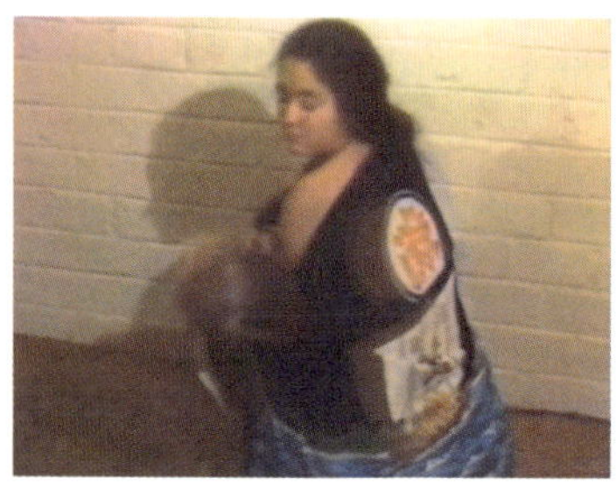

01:32

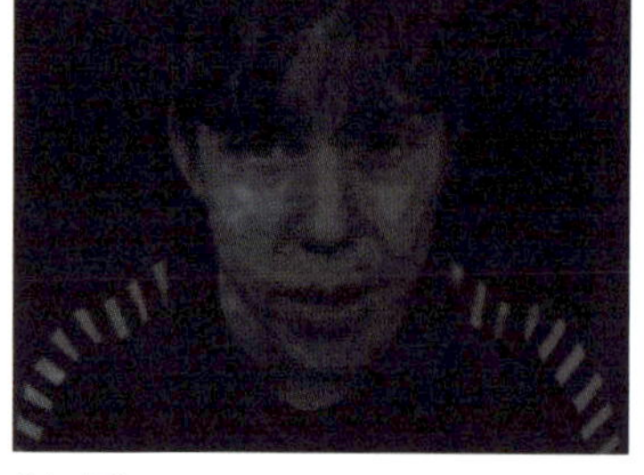

01:52

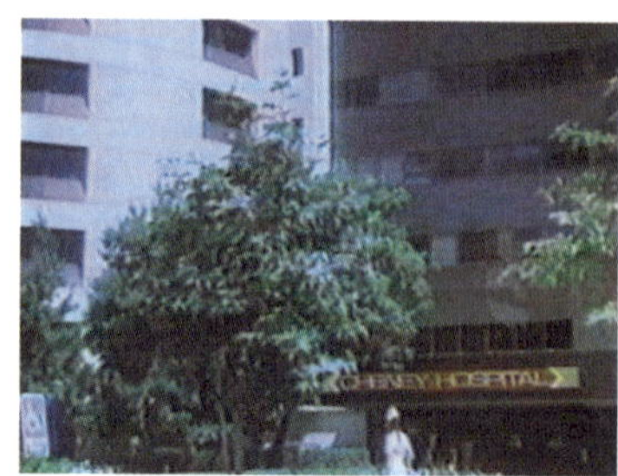

06:07

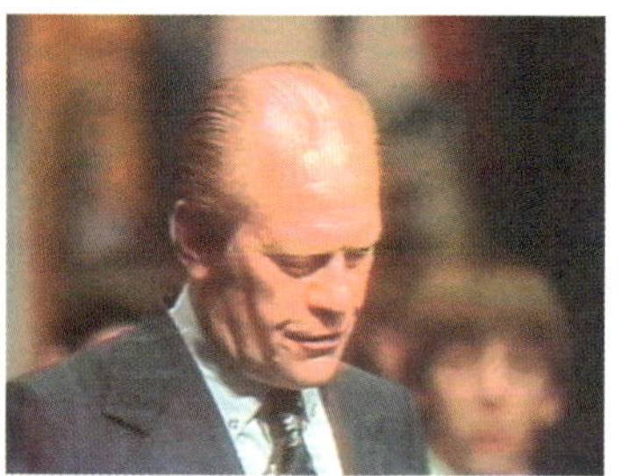

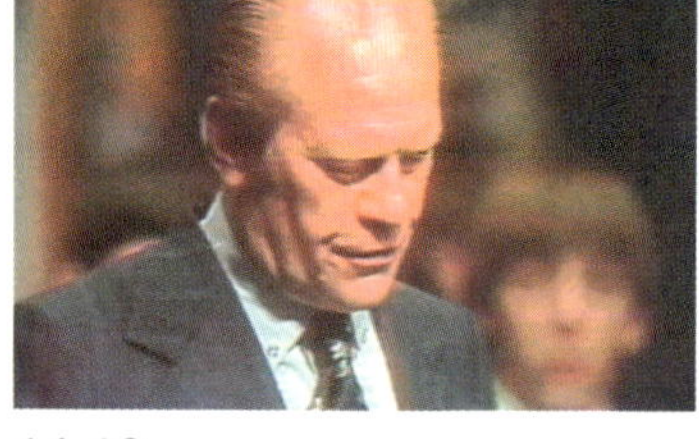

14:16

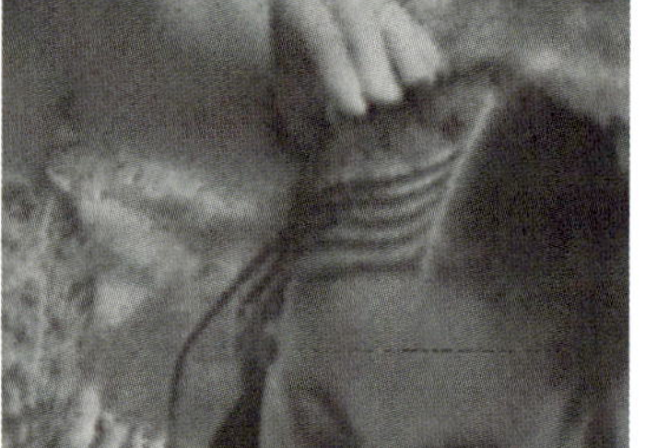

17:40

CURATORS' INTRODUCTION
REBECCA CLEMAN & ALEX KLEIN

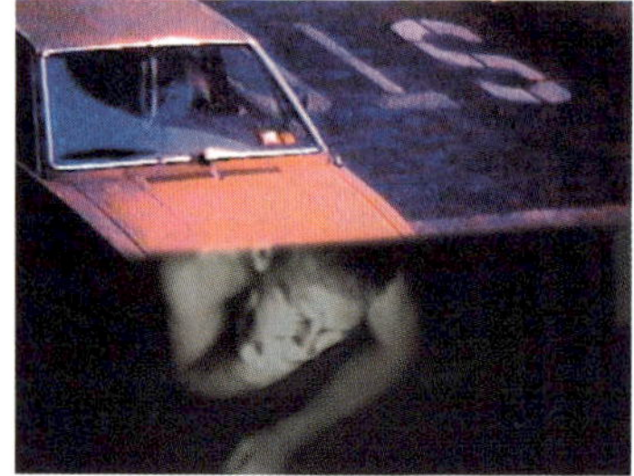

07:28

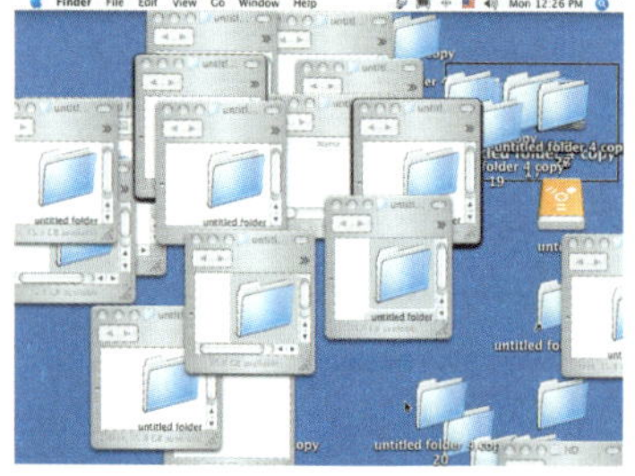

01:03

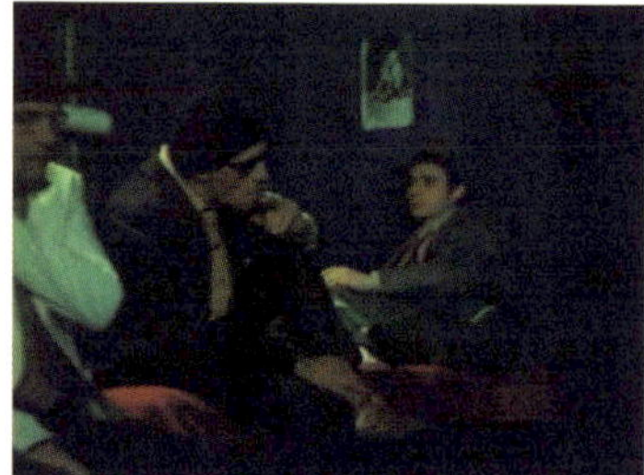

08:34

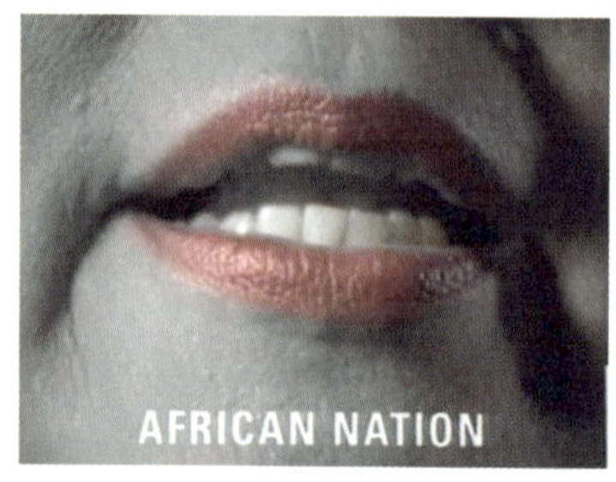

00:18

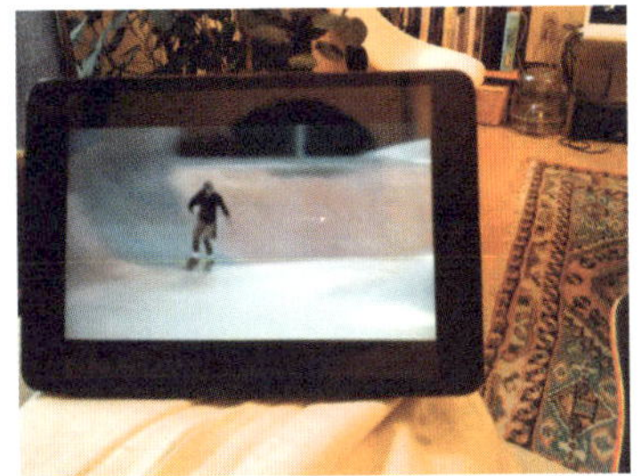

03:51

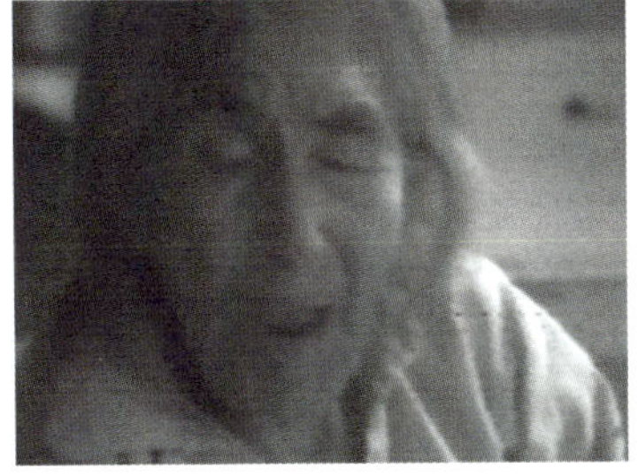

14:22

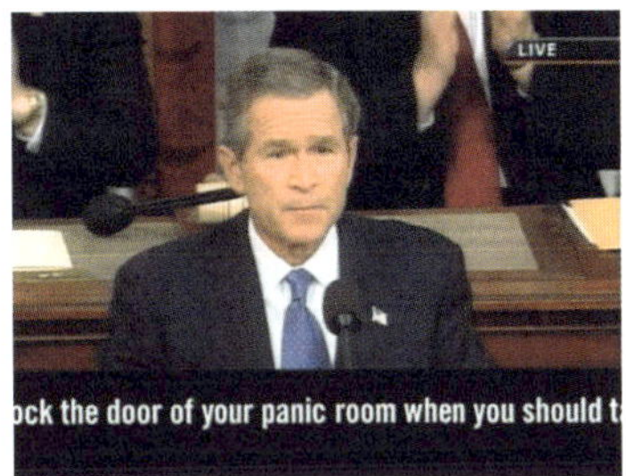

04:24

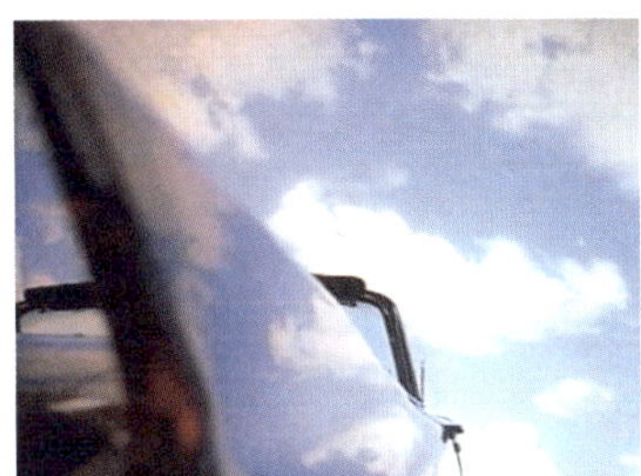

00:11

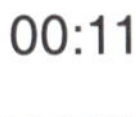

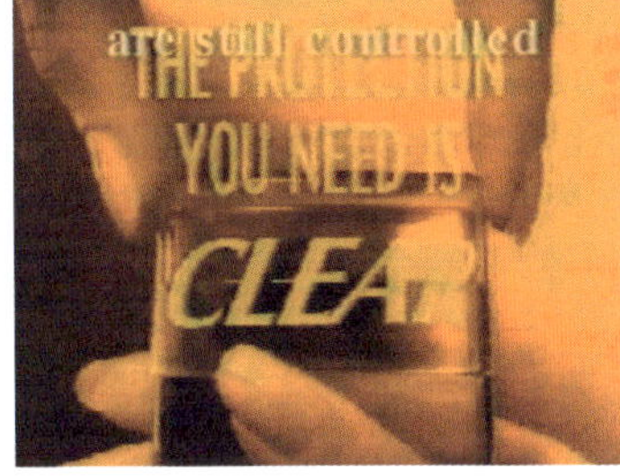

00:28

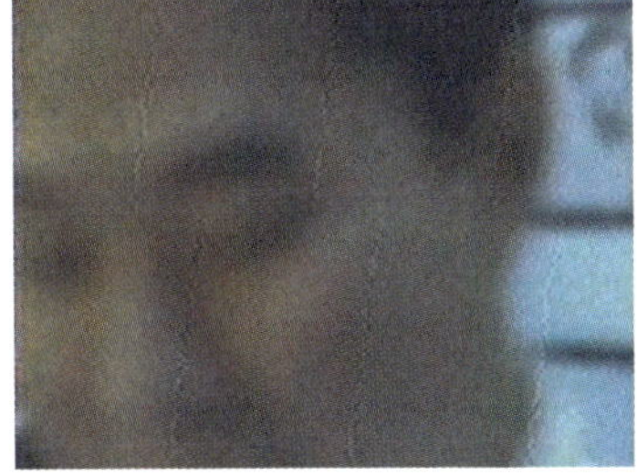

21:05

Electronic Arts Intermix (EAI) is one of the first nonprofit organizations dedicated to the advocacy and development of video as an art form, providing a crucial space for production and distribution. *Broadcasting: EAI at ICA* assembled an intergenerational group of artists whose time-based artworks were produced in concert with their means of circulation, from the democratic platform of public access television to the instantaneity of social media. Drawing on EAI's extraordinary archive and ICA's history of engagement with media art, *Broadcasting* fostered a dialogue between early innovators and contemporary practitioners through an installation, screenings, and a series of live programs. Featuring works by Beth B, Robert Beck/Buck, Dara Birnbaum, Tony Cokes, Ulysses Jenkins, JODI, Philip Mallory Jones, Tom Kalin, Shigeko Kubota, Kristin Lucas, Victor Masayesva, Jr., Shana Moulton, Nam June Paik and Paul Garrin, Trevor Shimizu, TVTV, and Bruce and Norman Yonemoto, the exhibition focused on how artists exploit the act of broadcast as a subject, as a

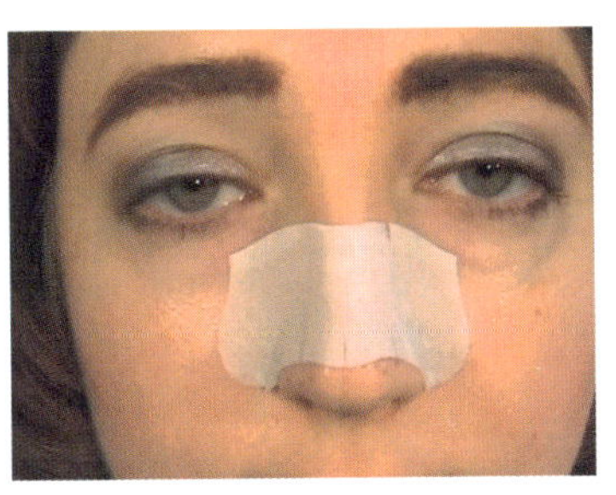

01:17

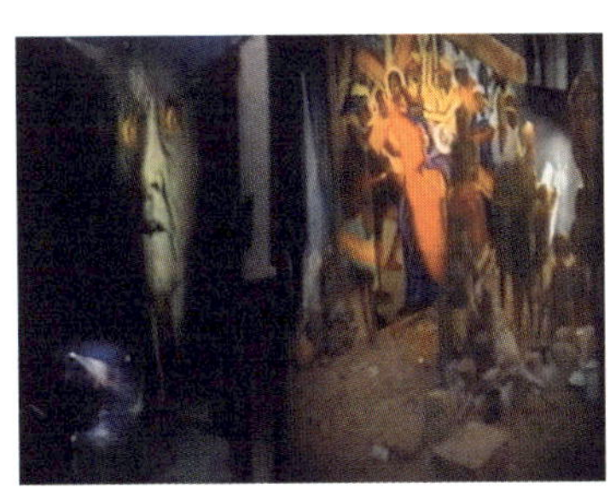

00:14

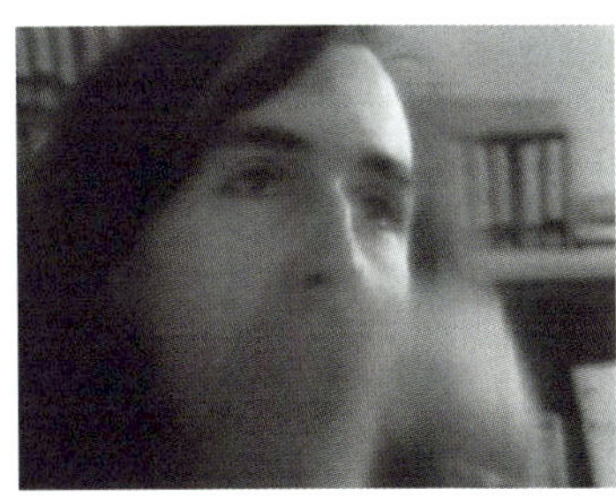

04:17

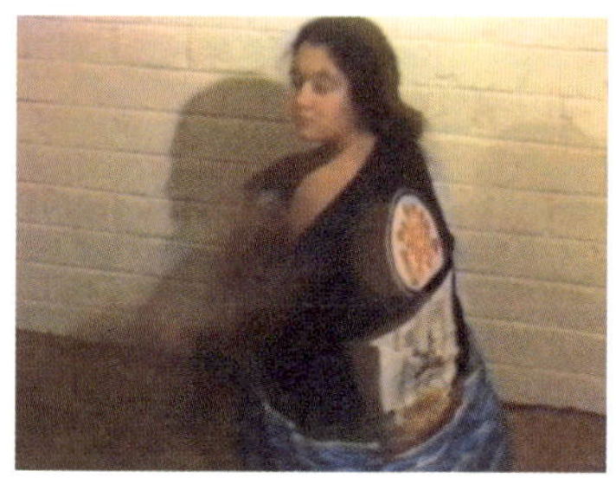

01:32

01:52

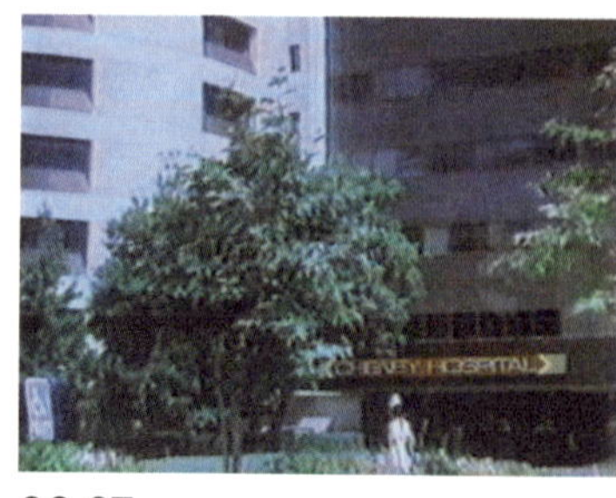

06:07

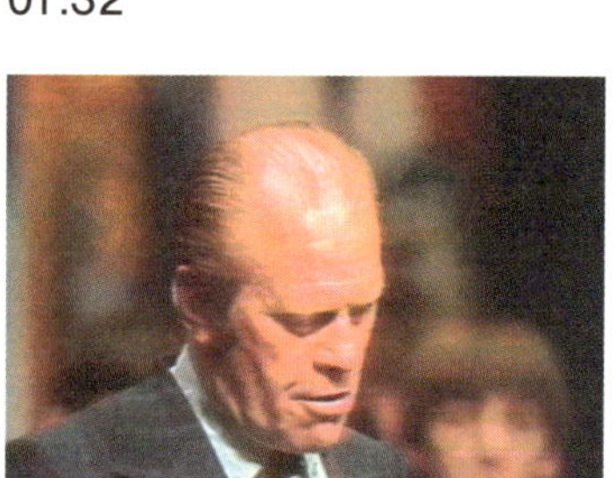

14:16

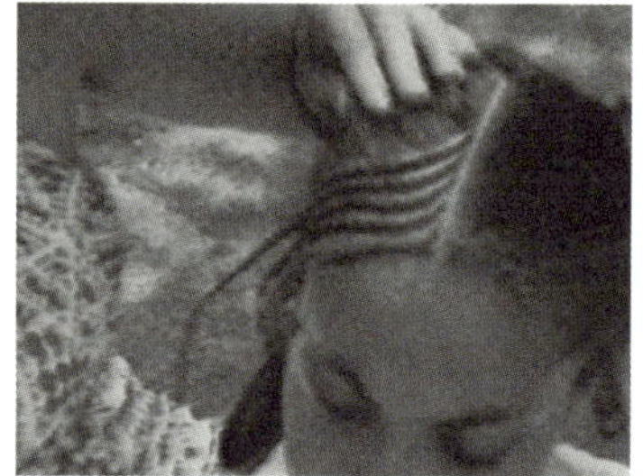

17:40

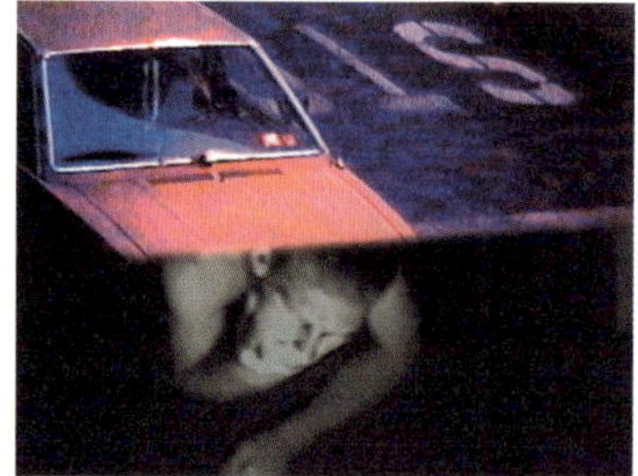

07:28

means of intervention, and as a form of participation across a variety of displays. Furthermore, the temporal nature of broadcast television was emphasized within the gallery, which doubled as an event space for public discussions to be transmitted online and via cable access during the run of the exhibition.

The word *broadcast* originated as an agricultural term meaning to disperse seeds widely, but became a figurative description for communications technology in the radio age. In the television era, with which broadcasting is most synonymous, the introduction of personal video equipment fostered a more dynamic interpretation, facilitating a two-way flow of information that resonates with contemporary participatory media. In this spirit, the physical walls of the gallery were extended through a series of collaborations with Lightbox Film Center, PhillyCAM, Scribe Video Center, Anthology Film Archives, EMPAC, and Slought. The exhibition continued at Slought in the complementary installation *Broadcasting: Guerrilla Media*. This extension focused on activist

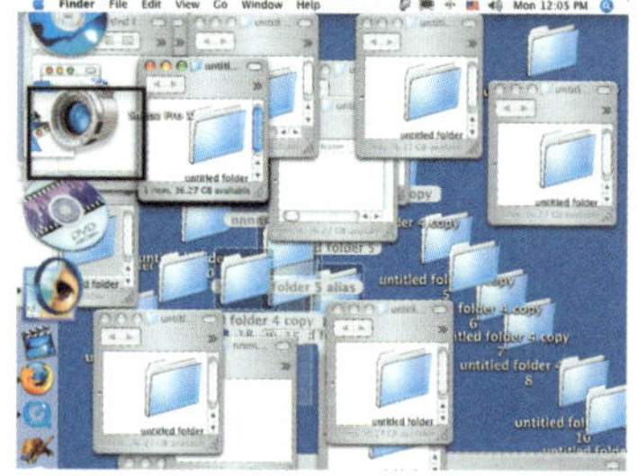

01:03

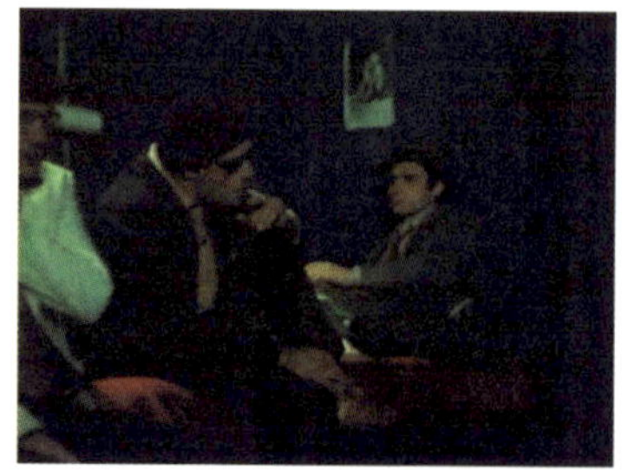

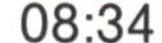

08:34

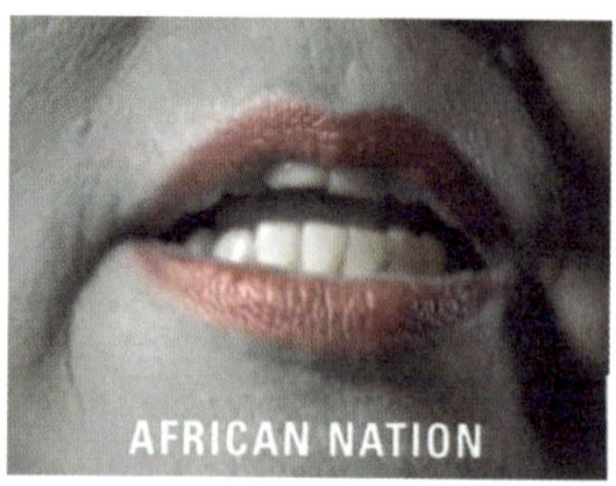

00:18

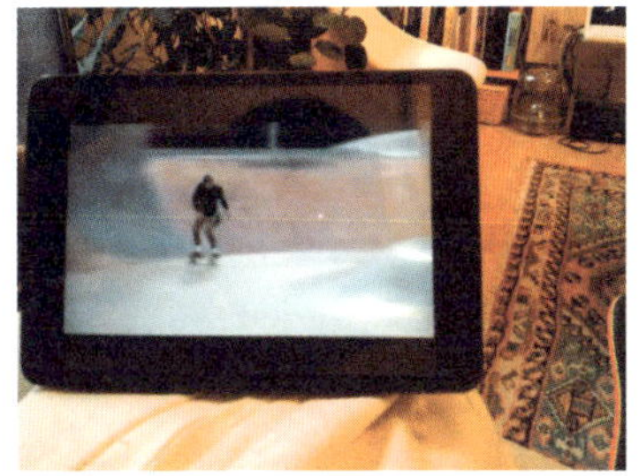
03:51

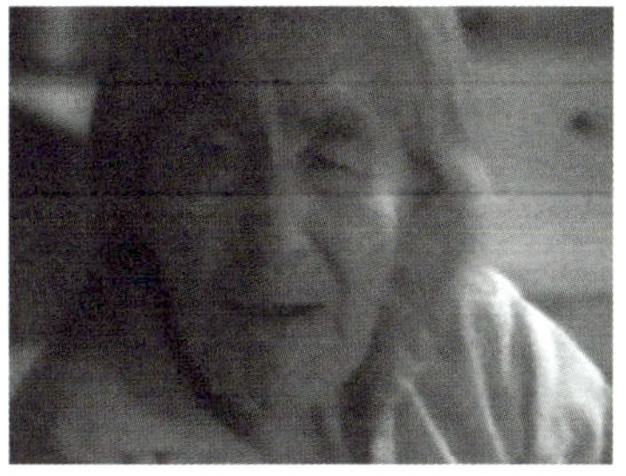
14:22

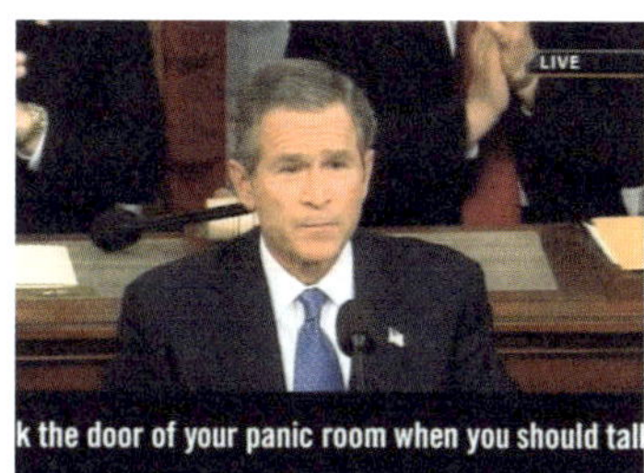

04:24

strategies undertaken by collectivist media from the 1970s to the present and included works by DCTV, DIVA TV, Martha Rosler and Paper Tiger Television, Radical Software Group (RSG), Squat Theatre, TVTV, Video Venice News, and X-PRZ.

The title, *Guerrilla Media*, is a nod to the Raindance Foundation's *Guerrilla Television*. Published in 1971, just a few years after the introduction of the first consumer-grade video equipment and the advent of personal video, the group described it as a "meta-manual" for gaining agency in an information-saturated, corporately determined "Media-America." Michael Shamberg, who authored the book, coined the term *guerrilla television* more as a new way of relating to television than as a militant action against it. In his introduction, he writes:

> *This Meta-Manual is here to lay out why the information environment is a good and verifiable reality model; why we must perceive media structures biologically (media-ecology); and why videotape, particularly portable video systems, can enhance survival and generate power in Media-America.*[1]

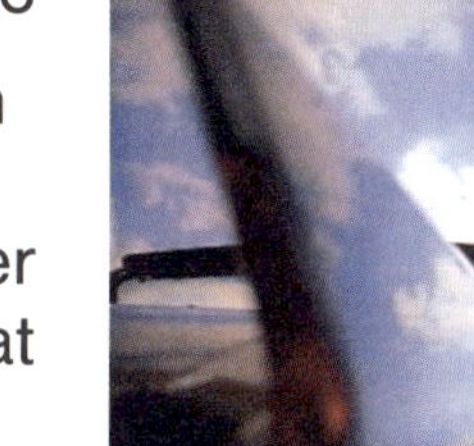
00:11

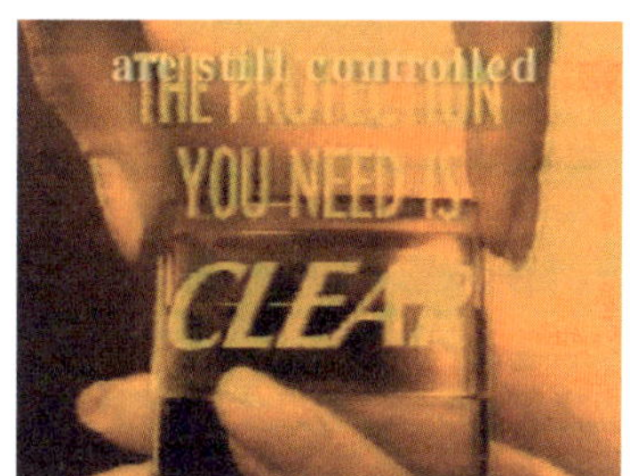

00:28

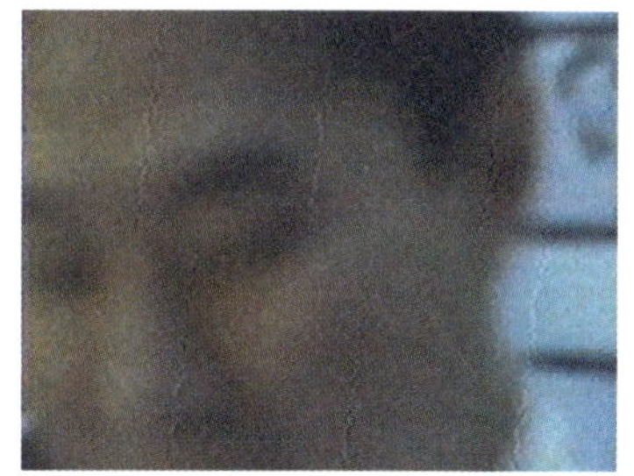
21:05

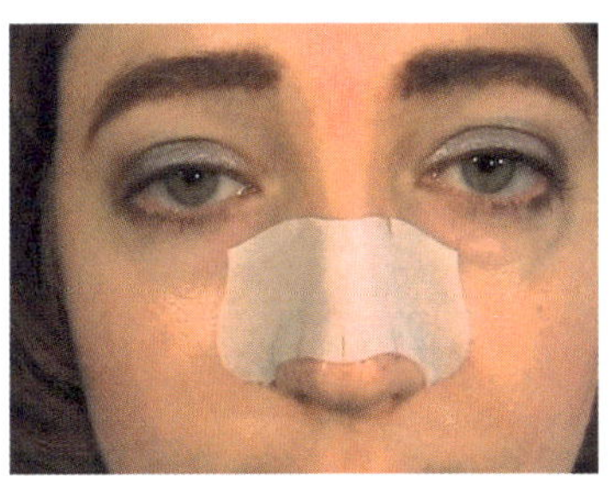
01:17

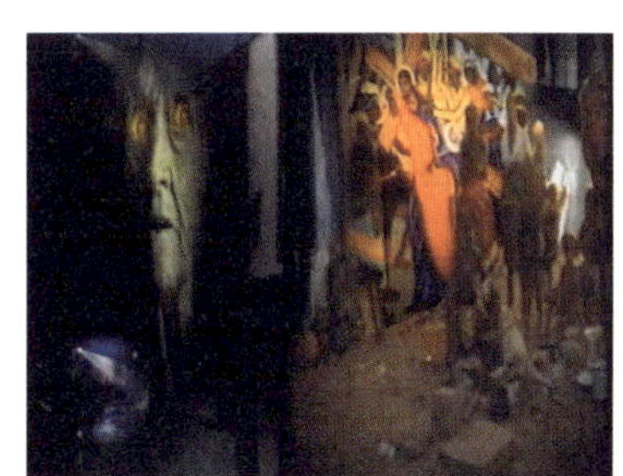
00:14

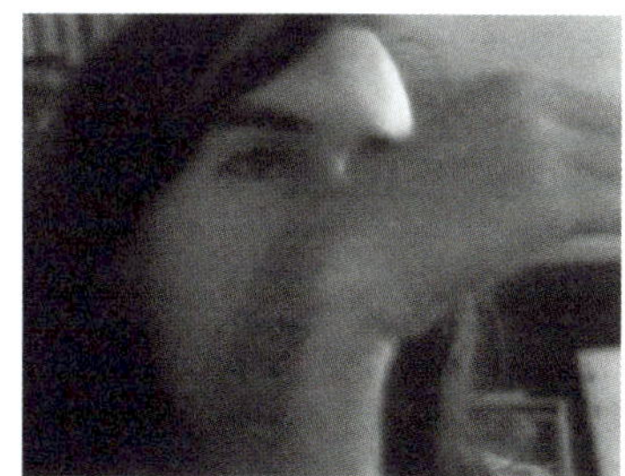
04:17

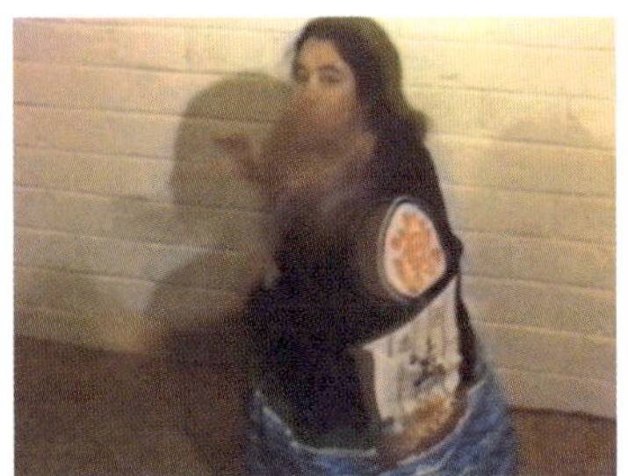
01:32

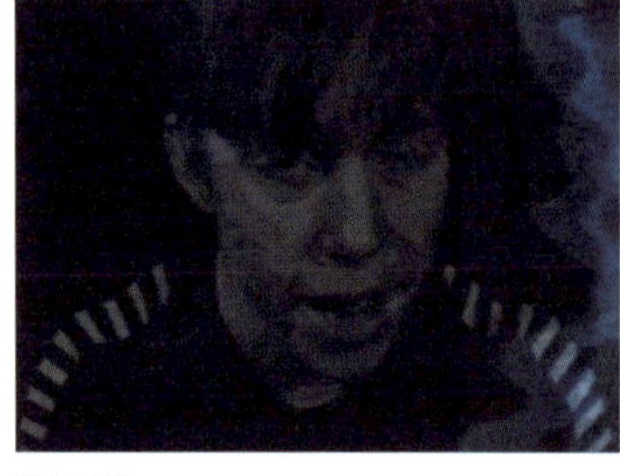
01:52

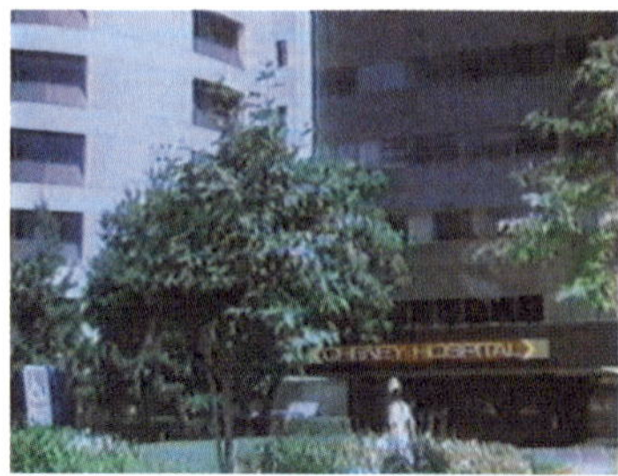

06:07

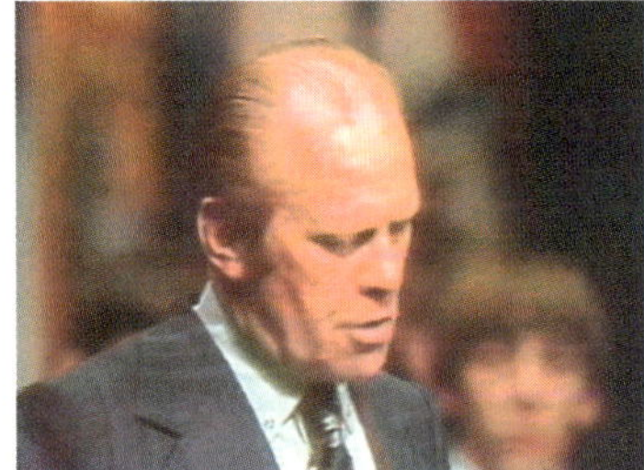
14:16

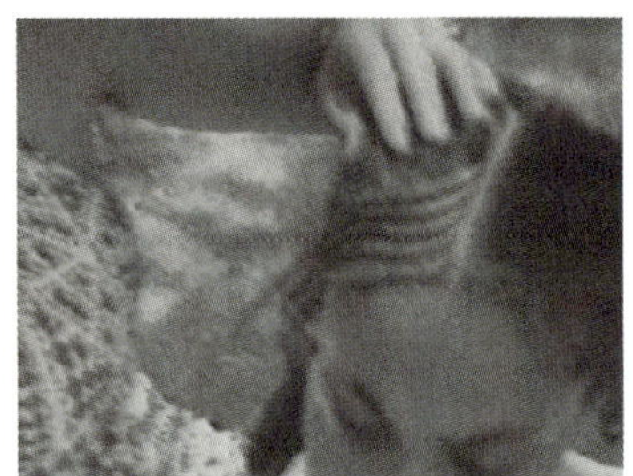
17:40

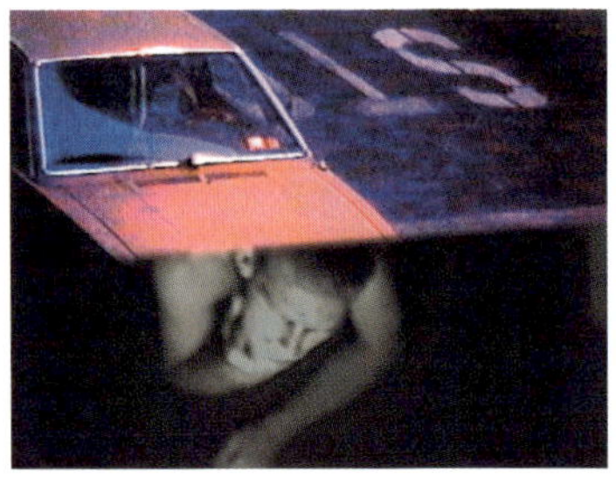
07:28

The year 1971 also marked gallerist Howard Wise's founding of EAI, with the intent to create a non-commercial context for video experimentation by offering access to media production, distribution, and education. In a 1970 letter announcing the simultaneous closure of his gallery, Wise wrote:

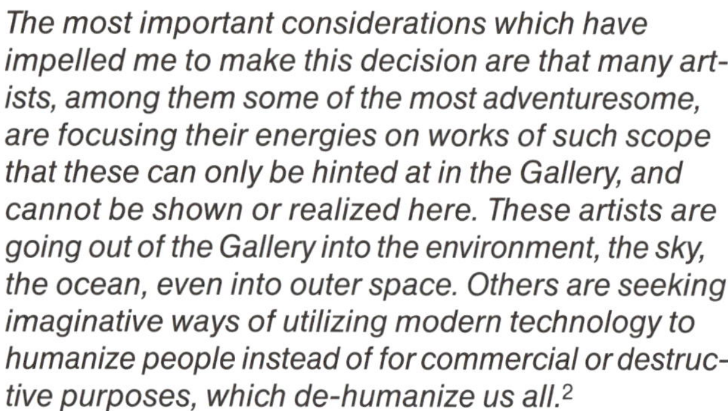
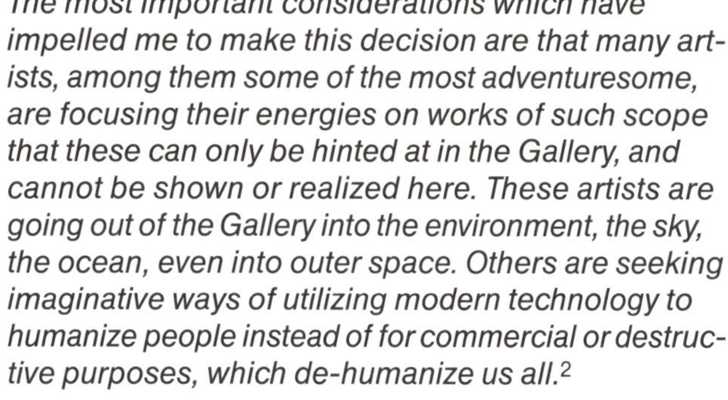
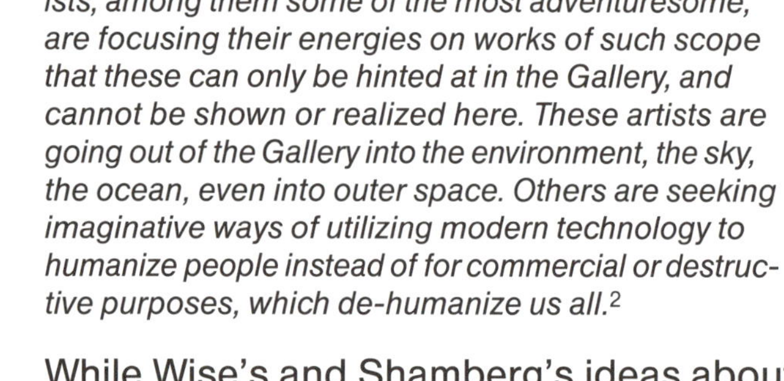

> *The most important considerations which have impelled me to make this decision are that many artists, among them some of the most adventuresome, are focusing their energies on works of such scope that these can only be hinted at in the Gallery, and cannot be shown or realized here. These artists are going out of the Gallery into the environment, the sky, the ocean, even into outer space. Others are seeking imaginative ways of utilizing modern technology to humanize people instead of for commercial or destructive purposes, which de-humanize us all.*[2]

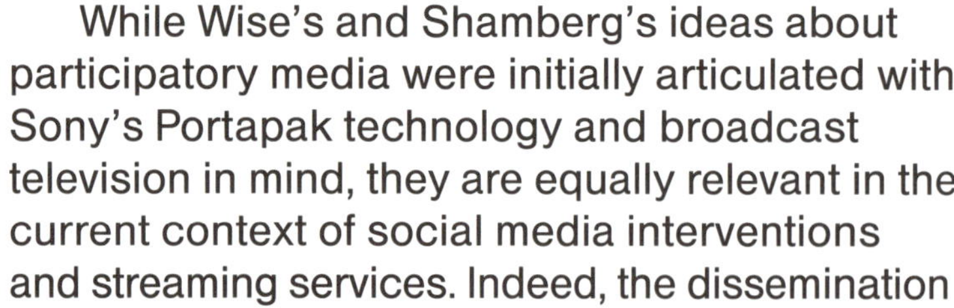

While Wise's and Shamberg's ideas about participatory media were initially articulated with Sony's Portapak technology and broadcast television in mind, they are equally relevant in the current context of social media interventions and streaming services. Indeed, the dissemination

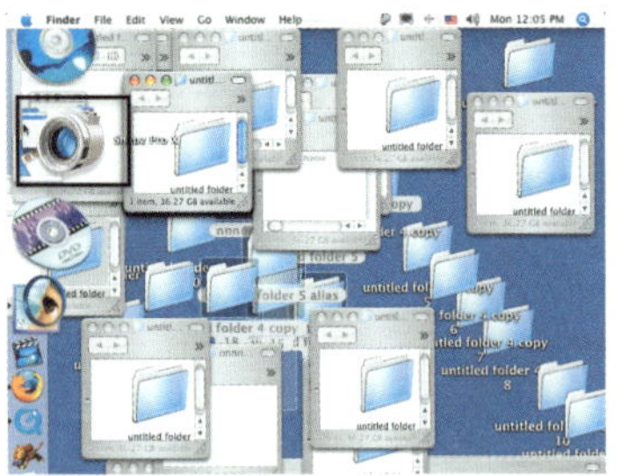
01:03

08:34

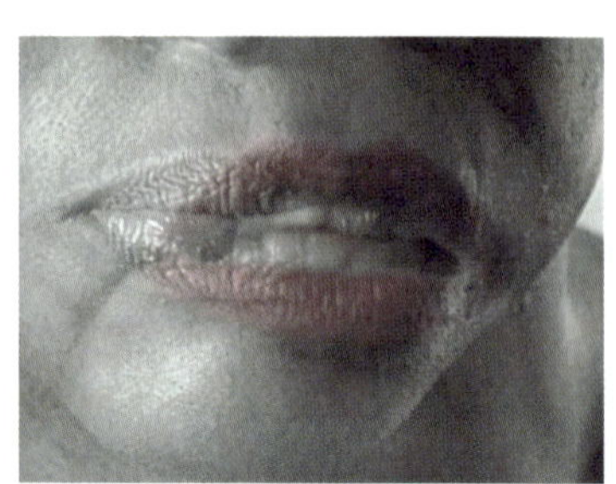
00:18

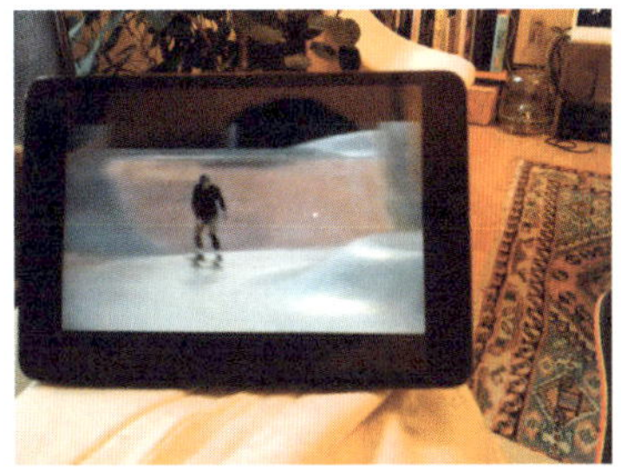

03:52

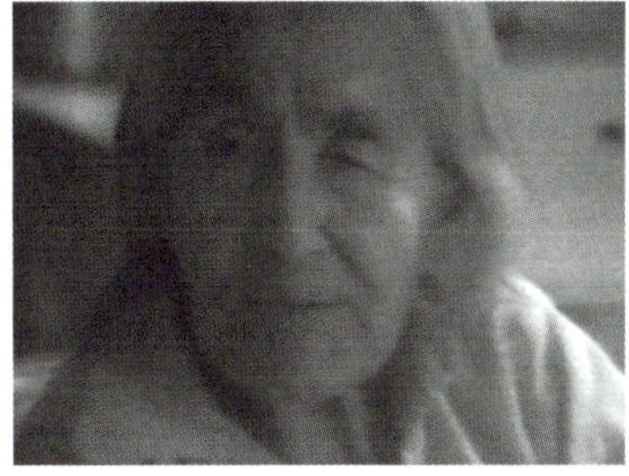

14:23

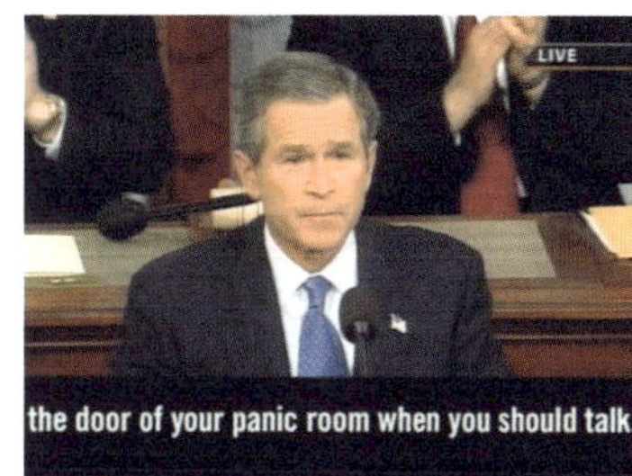

04:25

of media art beyond the confines of a gallery space and the reclamation and repurposing of the tools of mass media are at the core of the artists' work in this multifaceted exhibition.

As EAI celebrates its fiftieth anniversary in 2021, our media landscape has become increasingly corporatized, even as the mechanisms of broadcast itself have become more democratized. Against this backdrop, this volume attempts to document the temporal experience of the exhibition alongside the history of EAI as an organization. Admittedly, this publication includes only a small selection of the many artists and individuals who have engaged with EAI over five decades. In place of an exhaustive archive we have thus attempted to trace an ethos and to evoke the communal space of exchange and critical intervention that are inextricable features of EAI's legacy as an editing facility and international distributor.

Rebecca Cleman, Executive Director, EAI and Alex Klein, Dorothy and Stephen R. Weber (CHE'60) Curator, ICA

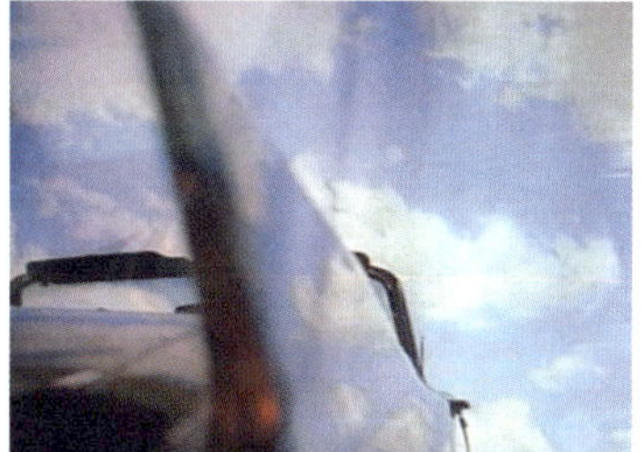

00:12

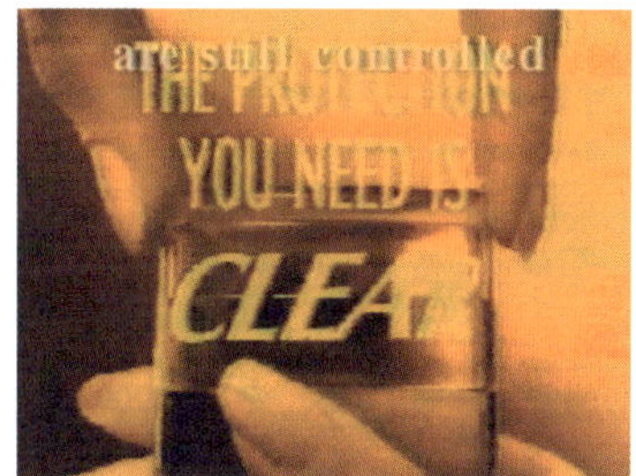

00:29

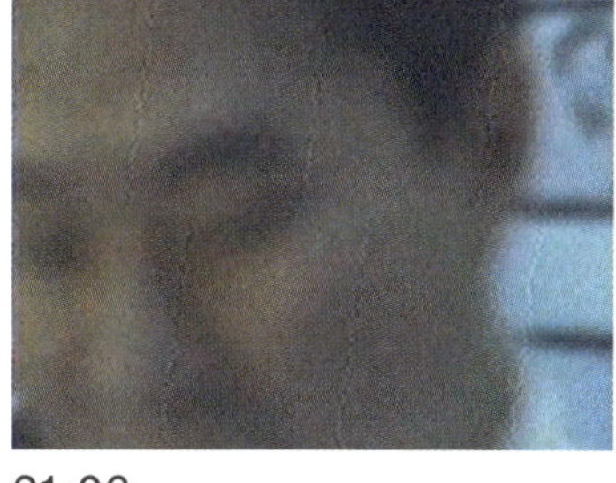

21:06

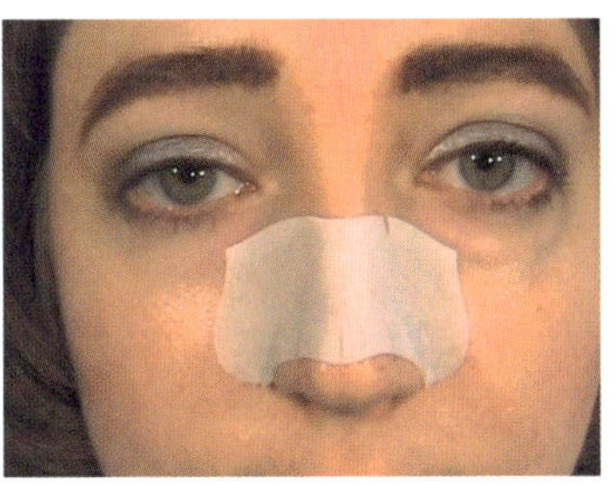

01:18

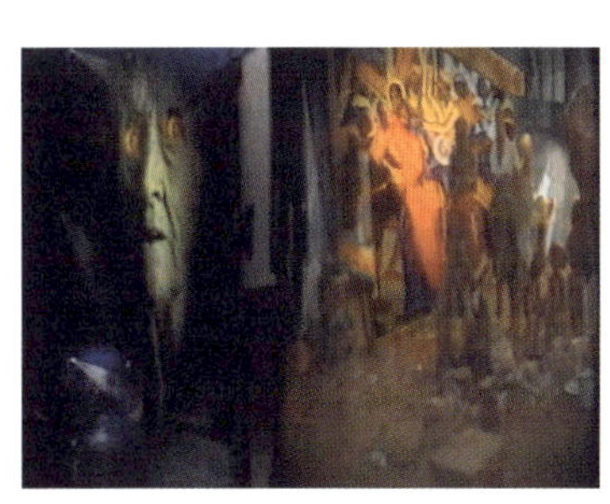

00:15

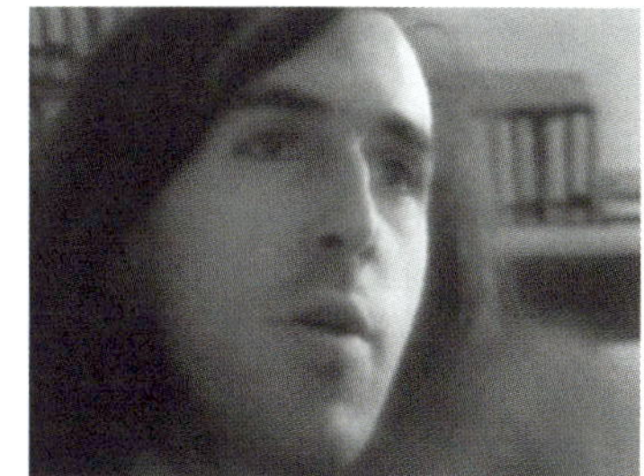

04:18

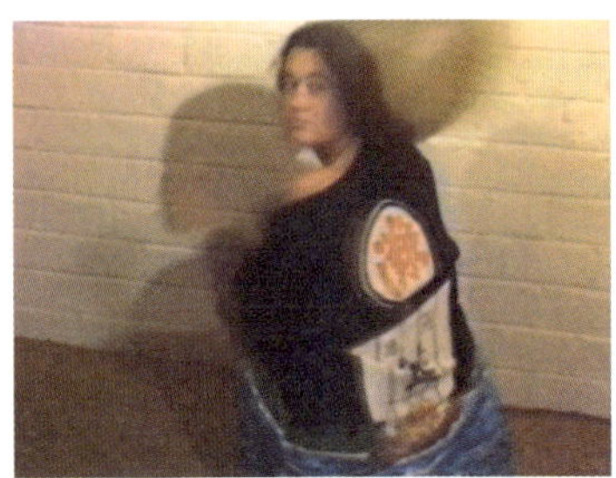

01:32

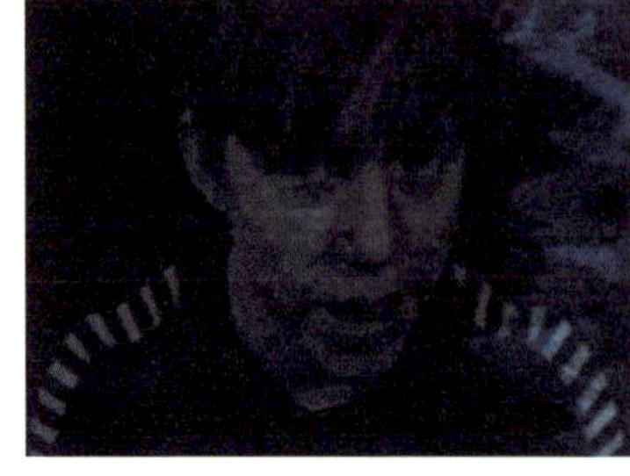

01:52

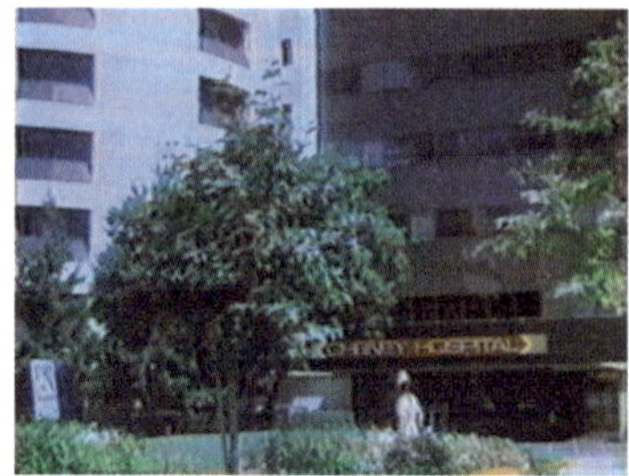

06:07

1 Michael Shamberg, *Guerrilla Television* (New York: Holt, Rinehart and Winston, 1971), 2.

2 Howard Wise to the friends of the Howard Wise Gallery, New York, NY, December 16, 1970.

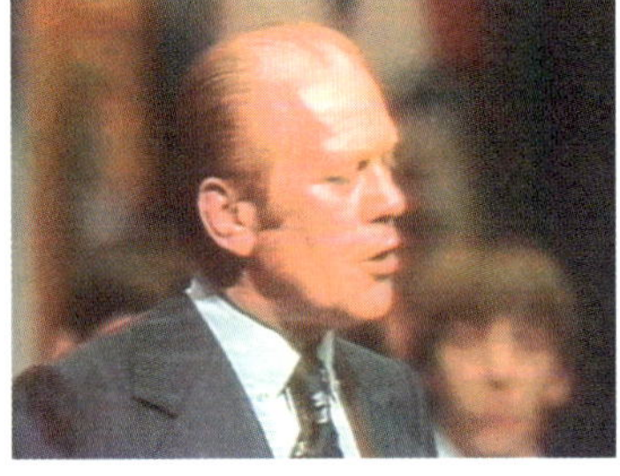

14:16

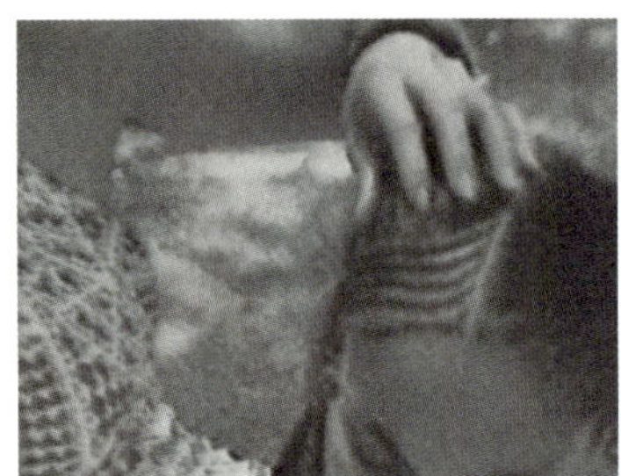

17:40

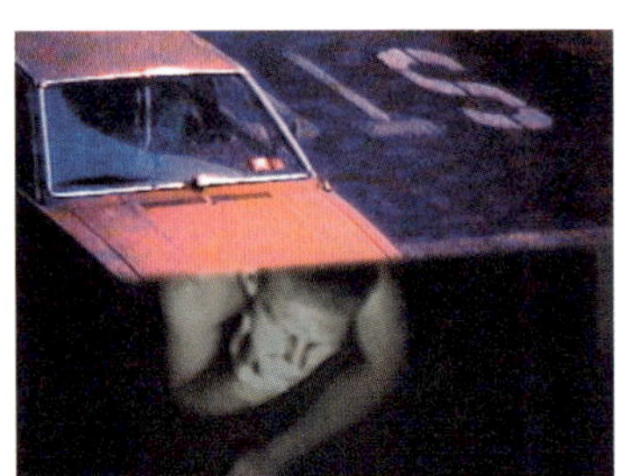

07:28

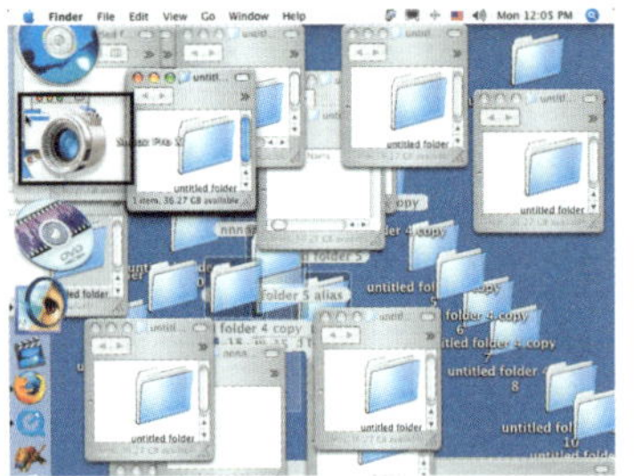

01:03

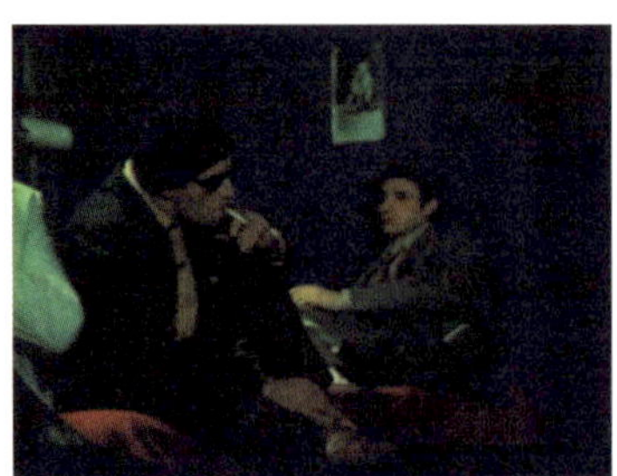

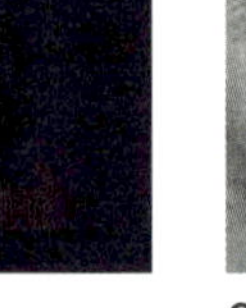

08:34

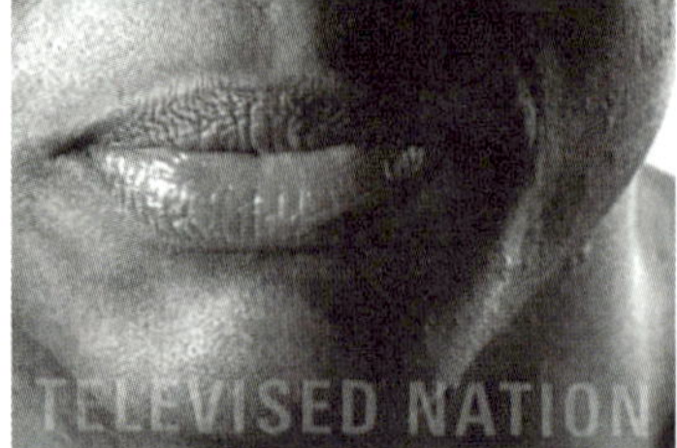

00:18

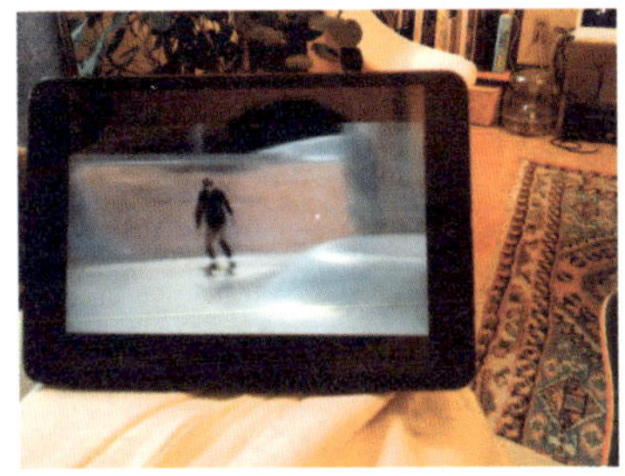

03:52

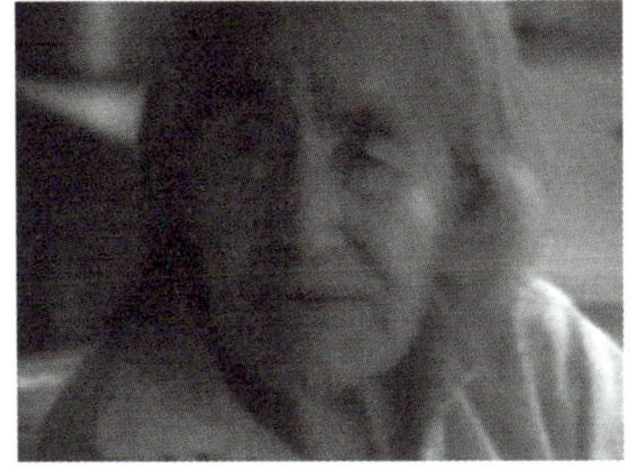

14:23

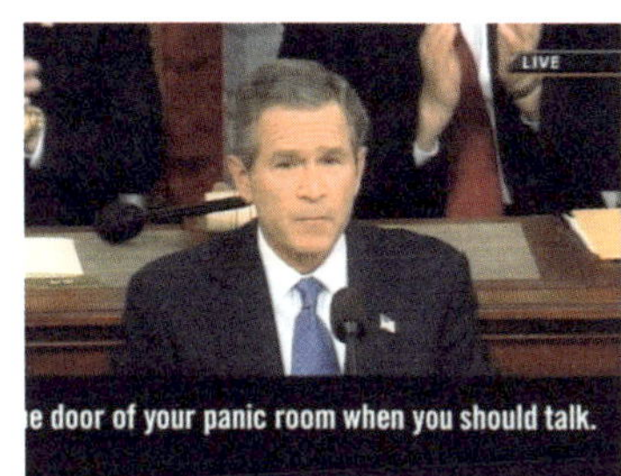

04:25

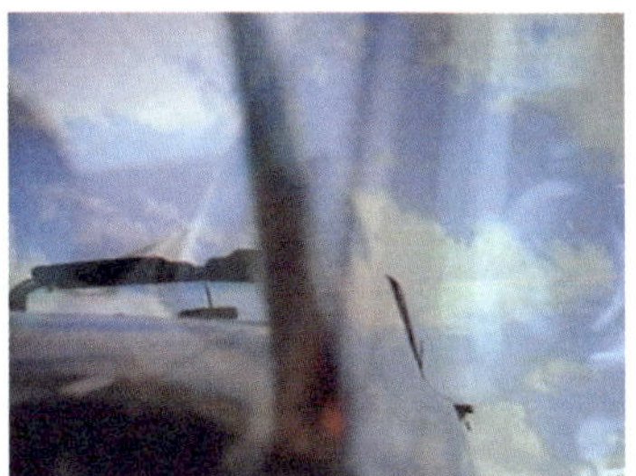

00:12

EAI ORAL HISTORY: LORI ZIPPAY, DIRECTOR EMERITA, EAI INTERVIEW WITH REBECCA CLEMAN & ALEX KLEIN

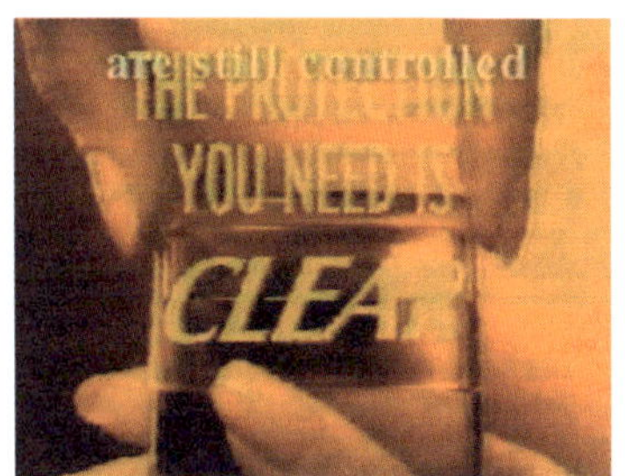

00:29

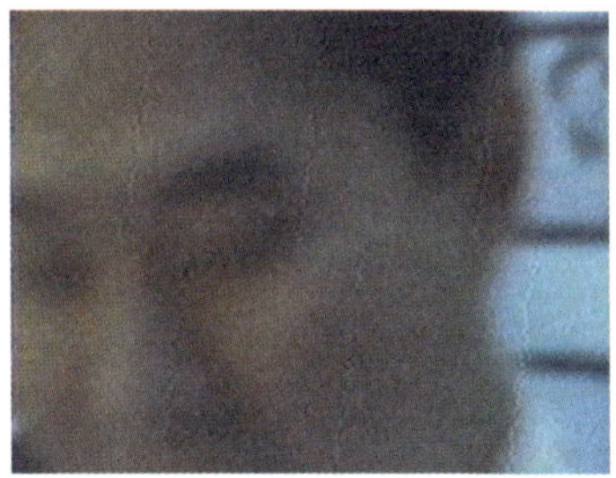

21:06

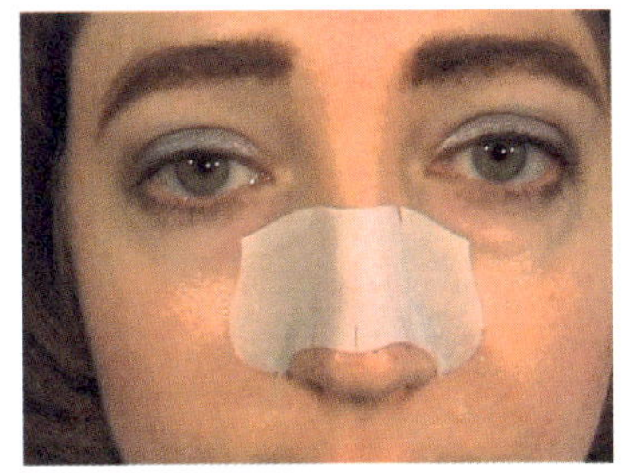

01:18

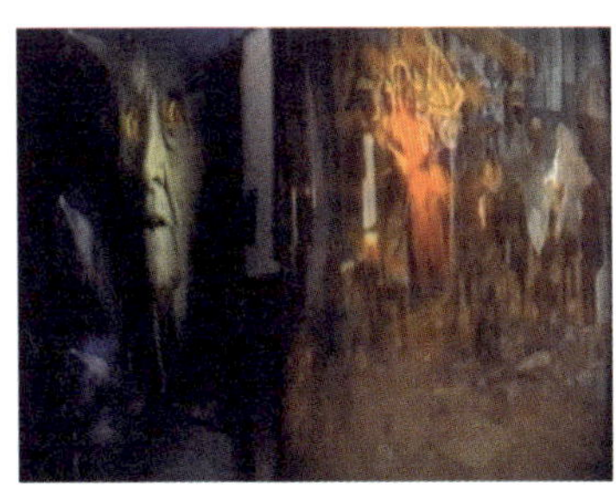

00:15

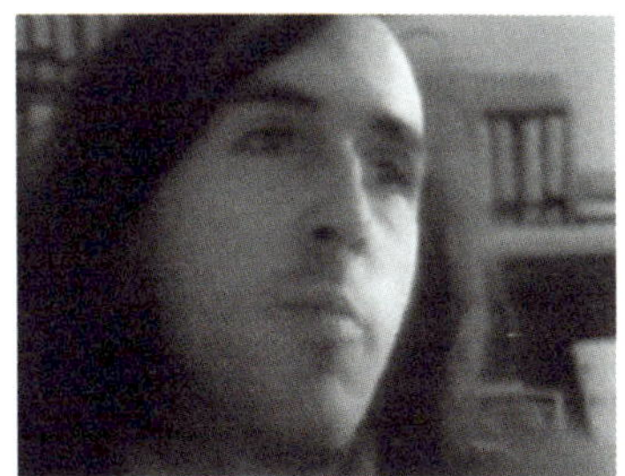

04:18

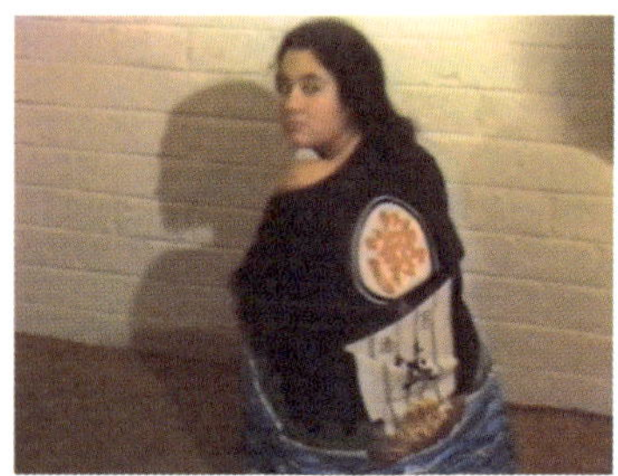

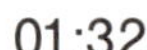
01:32

01:52

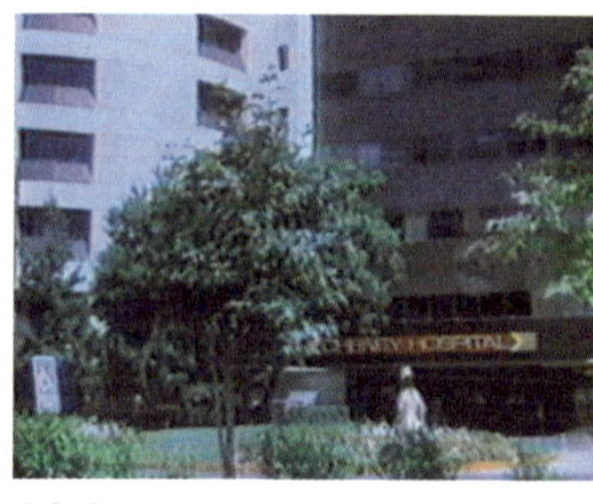
06:07

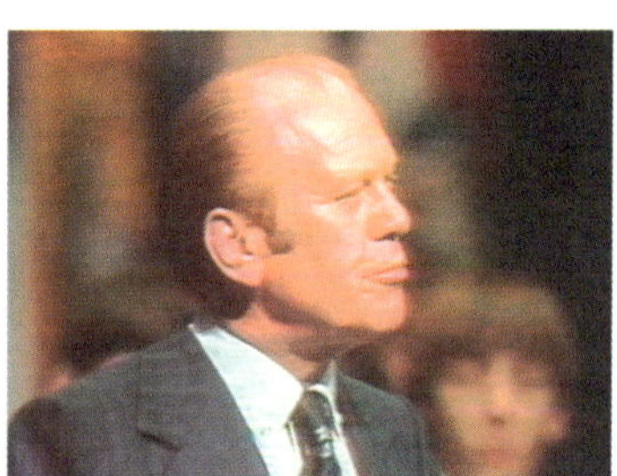
14:16

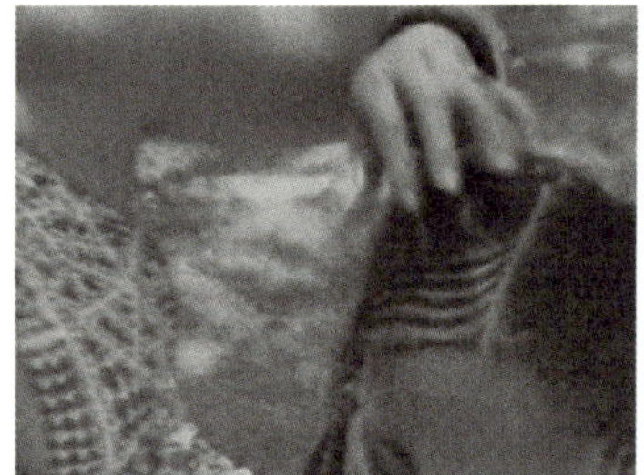
17:40

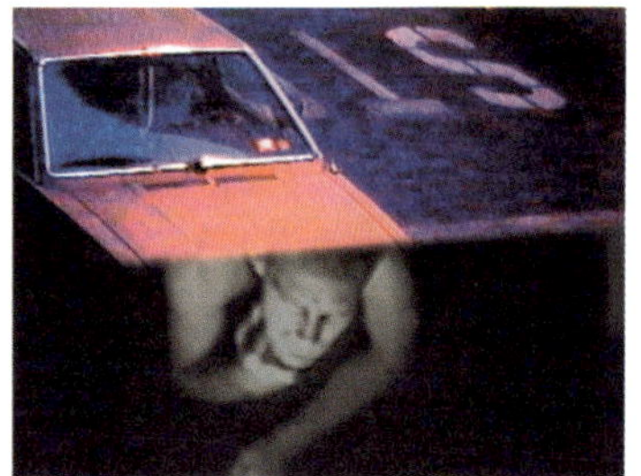
07:28

This interview was conducted over the course of two days in 2018. Lori Zippay served as EAI's Executive Director from 1985 until 2019, and is now Director Emerita.

Lori Zippay – Let's start with Howard Wise, EAI's founder. He had a gallery in Cleveland, the Howard Wise Gallery of Present Day Painting and Sculpture, before he moved to New York in 1960 and opened the Howard Wise Gallery on 57th Street. The gallery was dedicated to kinetic art and the art and technology movement, and Howard organized a number of groundbreaking shows, including *On the Move* (1964) and *Lights in Orbit* (1967).

For our purposes, the most important of these exhibitions is *TV as a Creative Medium* (1969). It was recognized as the first exhibition in the US dedicated to television and video as an art form. The show featured a really eclectic, diverse selection of works that presaged media art over the next decades, including media installation, performance art, closed-circuit video, video sculpture, etc. Among the works it included

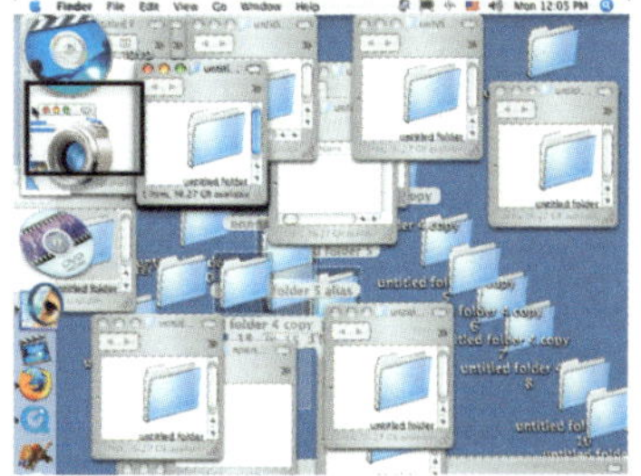
01:03

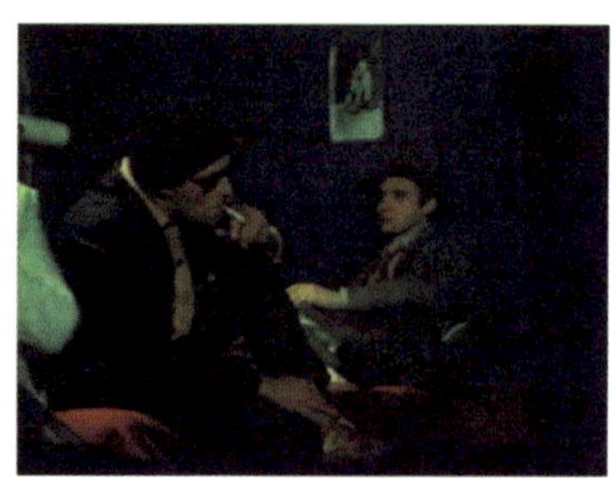
08:34

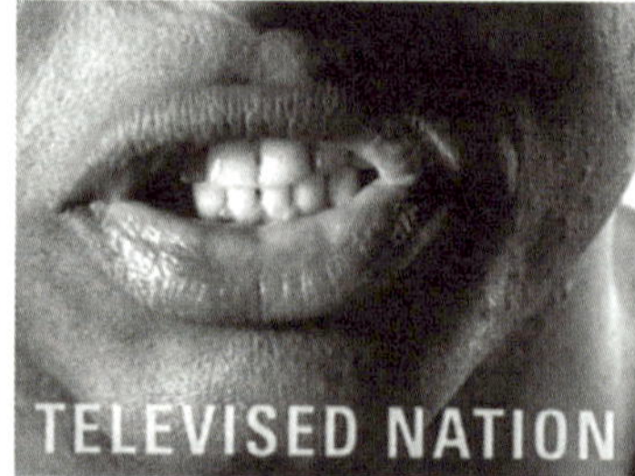

00:18

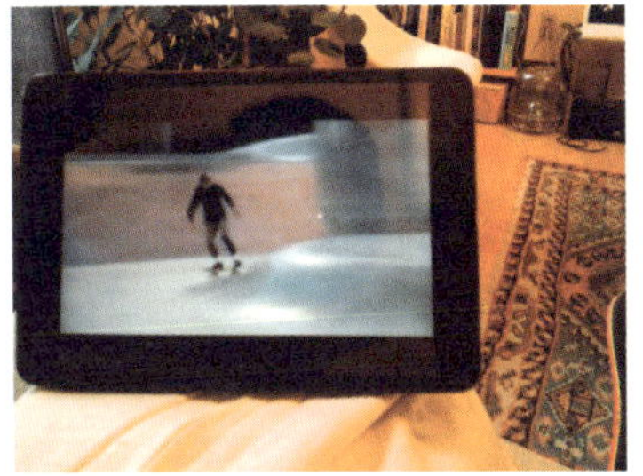
03:52

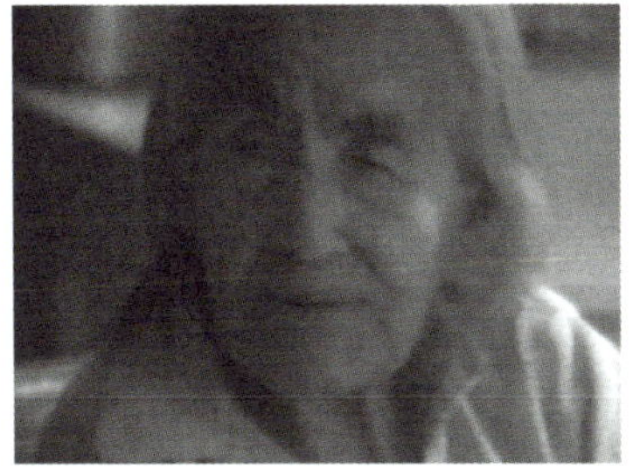
14:23

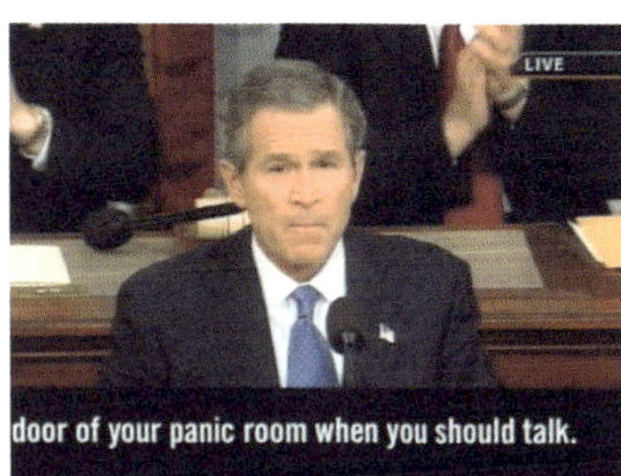

04:25

were the premiere of Nam June Paik's and Charlotte Moorman's *TV Bra for Living Sculpture*, Eric Siegel's *Psychedelevision in Color*, Paul Ryan's *Everyman's Moebius Strip*, and Ira Schneider and Frank Gillette's nine-channel, closed-circuit installation *Wipe Cycle*, which greeted visitors as they stepped off the elevator. It was a very prescient selection; it almost charts the subsequent decades of video art when you look at the diversity of approaches represented.

Alex Klein – When you think about it, 1969 is really early. This is only two years after the Sony Portapak was released on the market.

LZ – Yes, it was extremely early and the show was considered quite influential and provocative at the time.

I think it galvanized a set of artists who were already working in video and who saw this as heralding a new era. For Howard, it was a watershed and a catalyzing moment as well. Here was this gallery and gallerist who was championing what at this point was essentially an underground subcultural movement. We have to contextualize

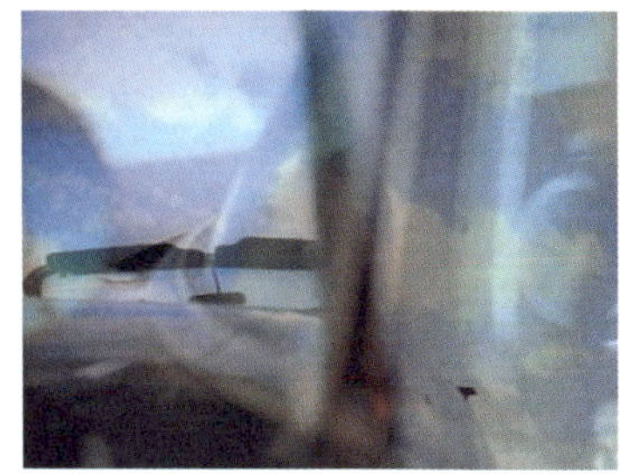
00:12

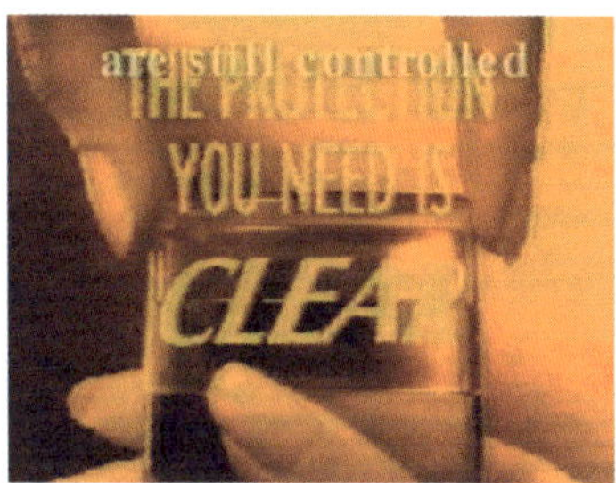

00:29

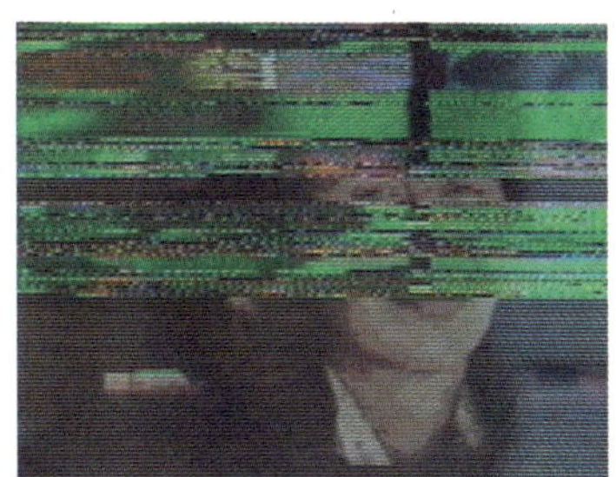
21:06

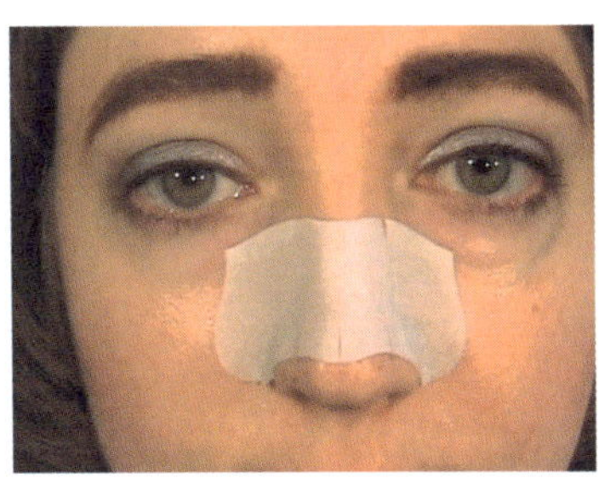
01:18

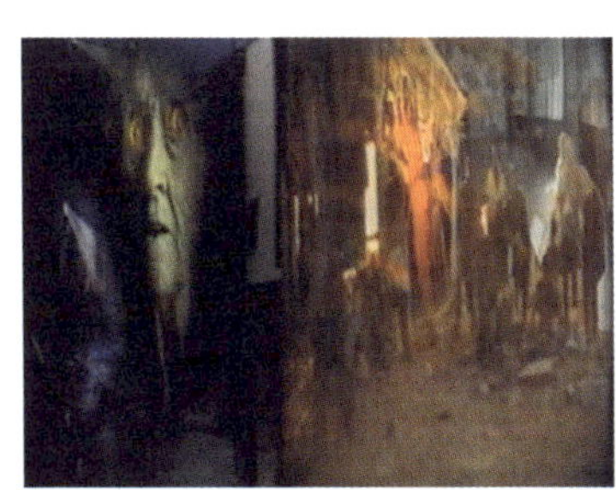
00:15

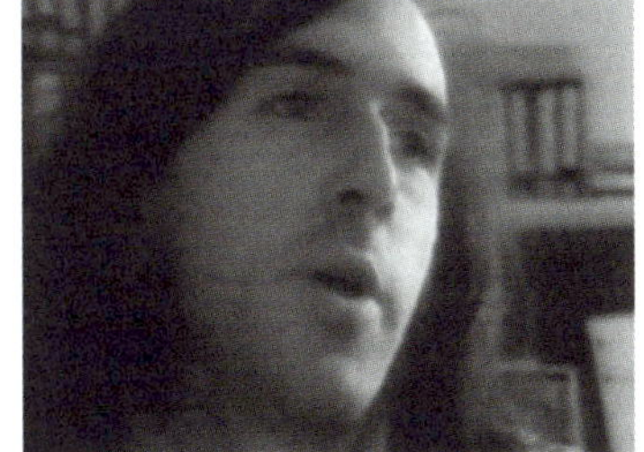
04:18

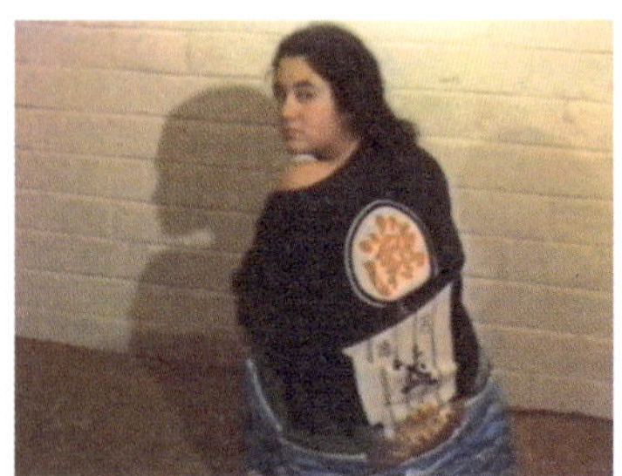

01:32

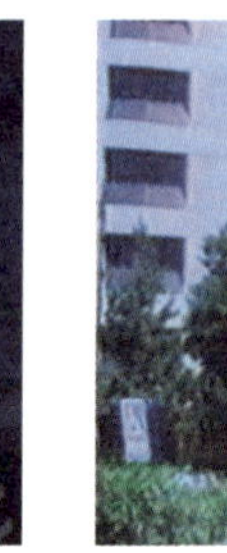

01:52

06:07

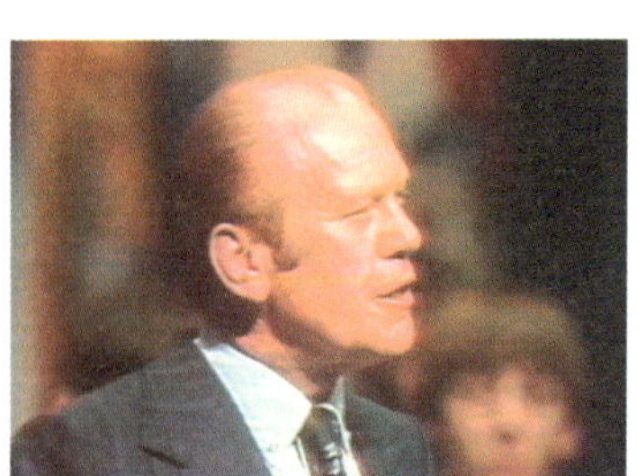

14:16

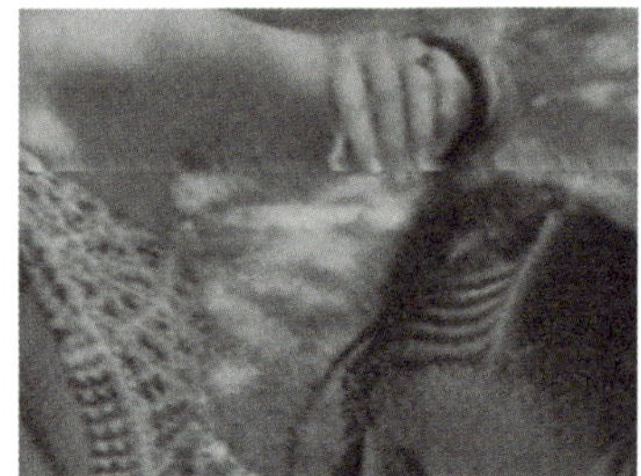

17:40

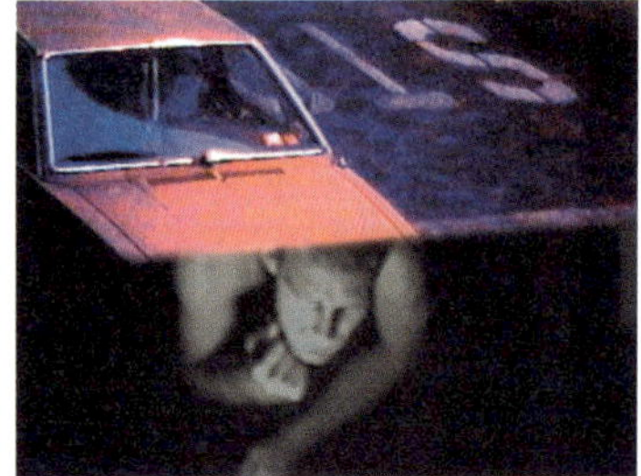

07:28

this in the historical moment, when video art occupied an "alternative" space. This was a time when artists were privileging process over product. This was obviously well before the internet, so television was the dominant mass cultural force. And this was also during the political and cultural climate of the late sixties and early seventies. All of these elements were working together intensely in that moment to create this alternative movement of video art and activism that Howard recognized early on and gave a platform to with his gallery.

EAI's online *Kinetic History* project is a great resource for materials about the organization's early history, the Howard Wise Gallery, and *TV as a Creative Medium*.[1] It provides access to contemporaneous reviews of the show, video clips, and related primary documents.

AK – What was his personal background?

LZ – He grew up in Cleveland, and he was educated at Le Rosey, a private school in Switzerland. His family business was Arco Industrial Coatings, which manufactured industrial paints.

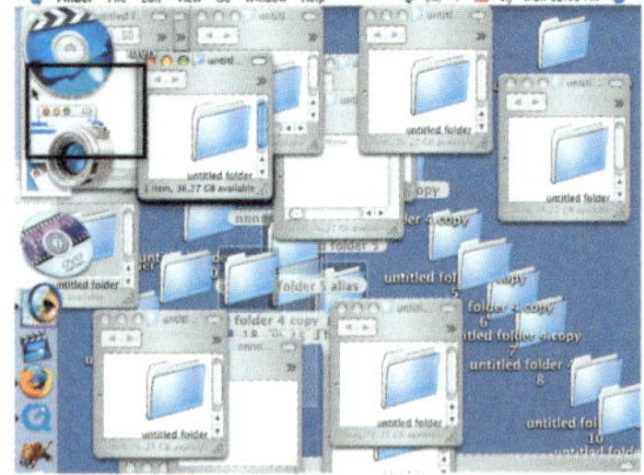

01:03

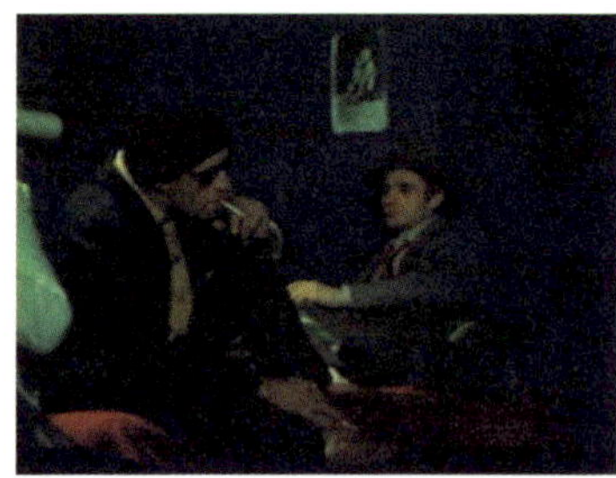

08:34

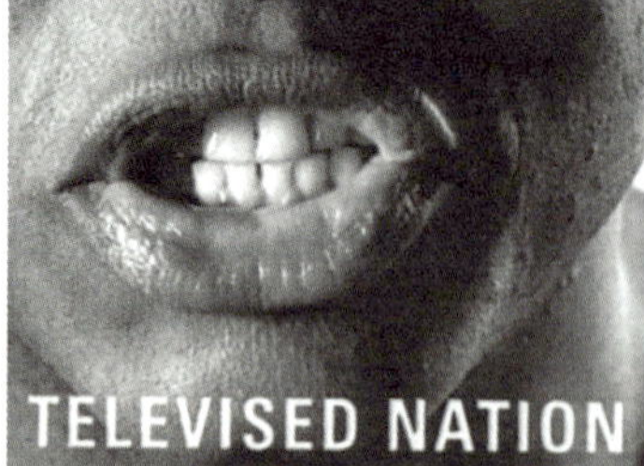

00:18

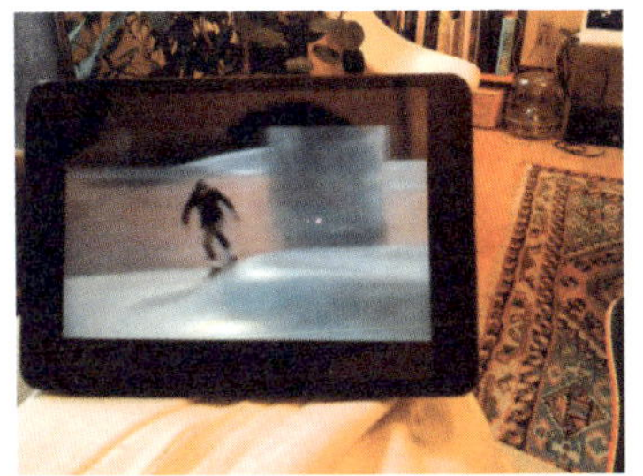
03:52

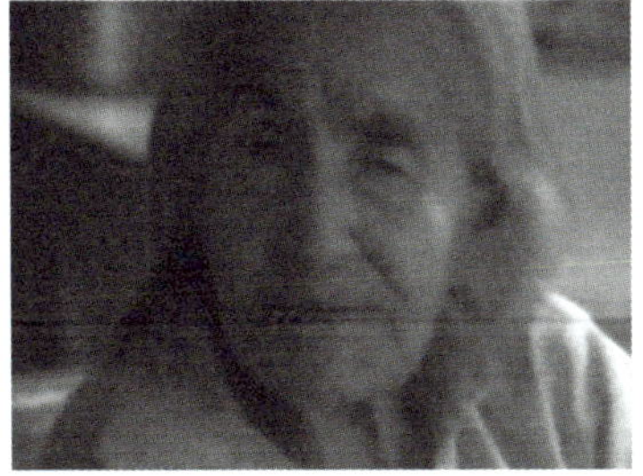
14:23

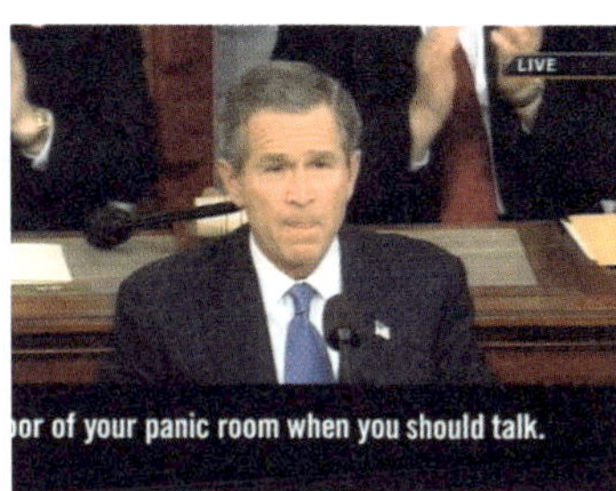

04:25

Rebecca Cleman – How old was he when he transitioned from the family business to his gallery?

LZ – He was already in his late fifties when he opened his gallery in New York, and in his late sixties when he founded EAI.

AK – So, he was a hip guy!

LZ – He really was. What is interesting is that in many ways he was actually an old-world, old-fashioned gentleman, you know. If you saw him, he was the last person you would imagine to be so prescient and such a hip avatar of this underground medium.

AK – Was he collecting art before?

LZ – He had a collection, primarily of kinetic art and Group Zero artists: Otto Piene, Takis, Heinz Mack, Len Lye.

AK – Perhaps that was a gateway to other media?

LZ – Exactly. So, in 1970 he closed the gallery to focus on these expanded media. I always like to quote from the letter Howard wrote to the artists saying that he was closing the gallery:

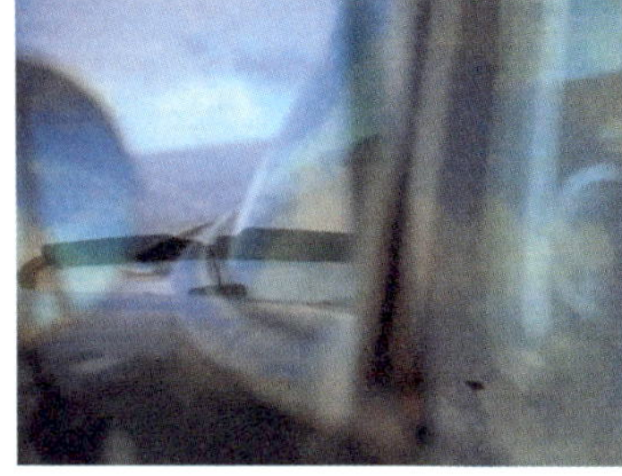
00:12

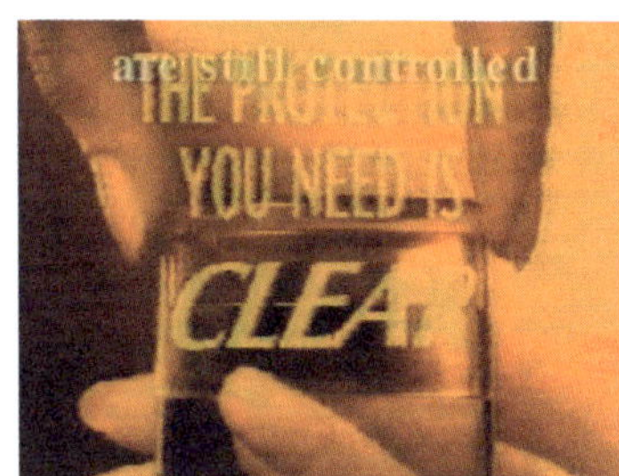

00:29

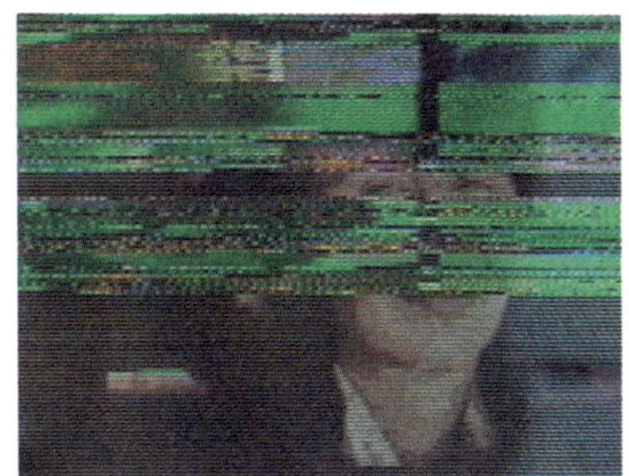
21:06

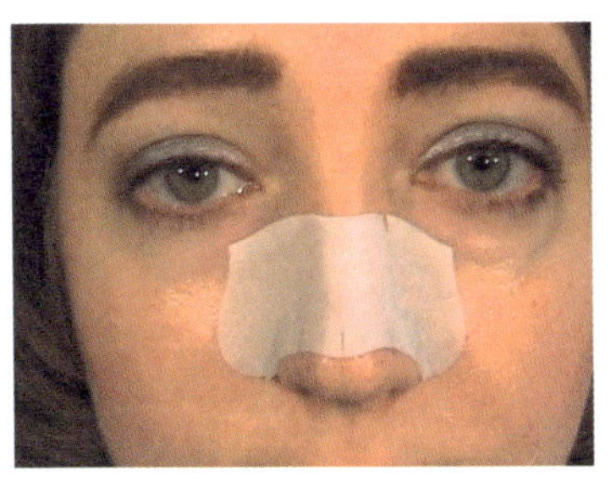
01:18

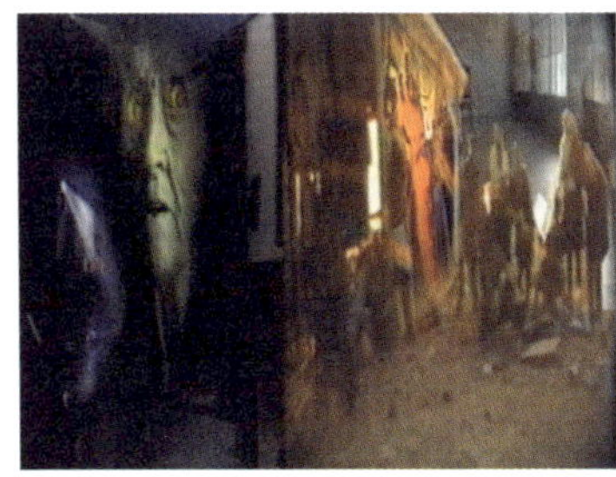
00:15

04:18

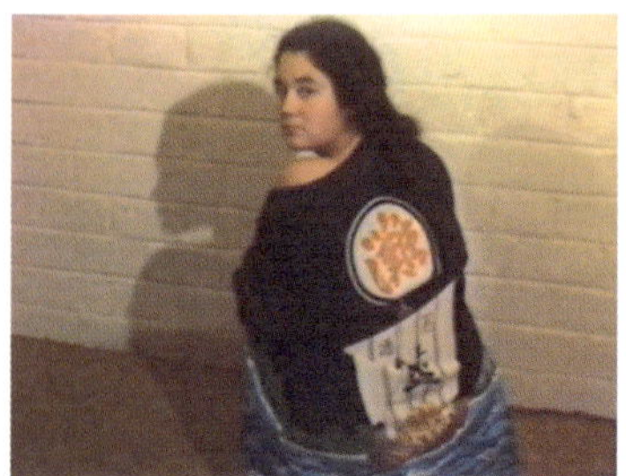

01:32

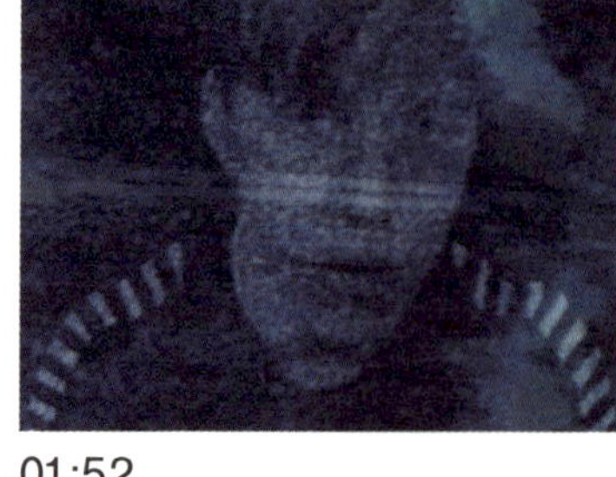

01:52

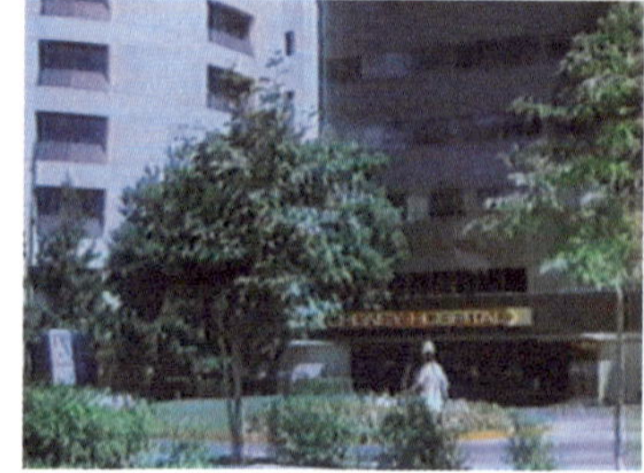

06:07

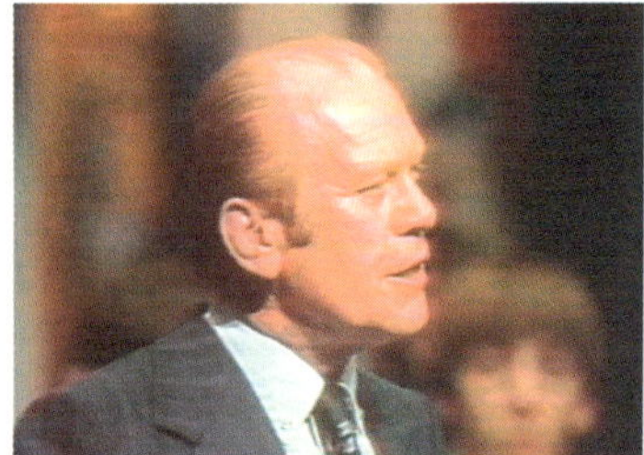

14:16

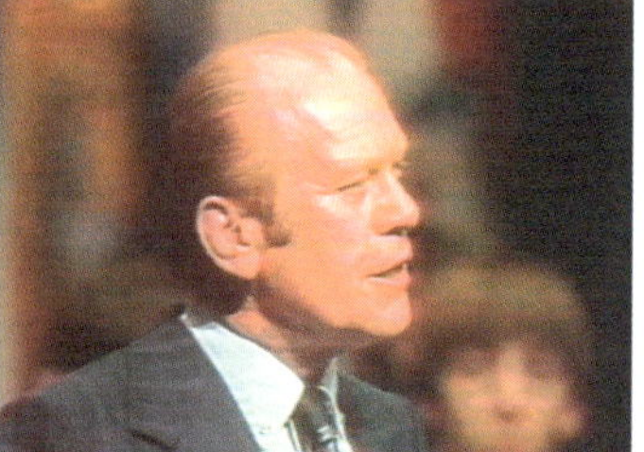

17:40

he wrote that he felt that video would allow artists to move out of the studio, out of the gallery, and into "the environment, the sky, the ocean, and even into outer space."

AK – That's very Group Zero.

LZ – That's very Group Zero, yes. It's wonderful. It's this utopian statement, but it's also prescient, because that's exactly what happened. Video allowed artists to move outside of the gallery and into outer space. It's such a Howard statement.

So, he closed the gallery and in 1971 founded EAI as a nonprofit organization. In its early years EAI was an umbrella organization to fiscally sponsor an extraordinary range of projects related to this nascent video movement. For example, for eight years EAI sponsored Charlotte Moorman's New York Avant-Garde Festivals.

AK – That's very interesting. So EAI's origins were rather expansive in its understanding of media?

LZ – Absolutely. The initial projects that were sponsored were very interdisciplinary, which speaks to this moment of creative fusion. For

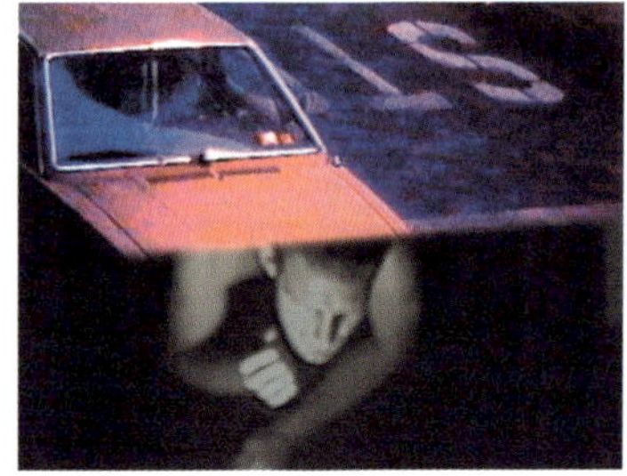

07:28

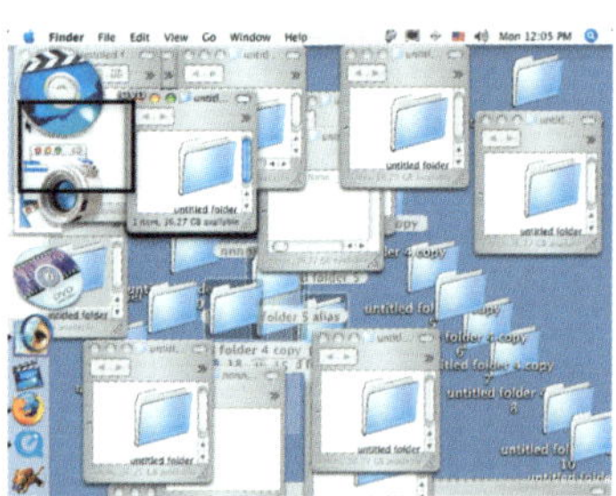

01:03

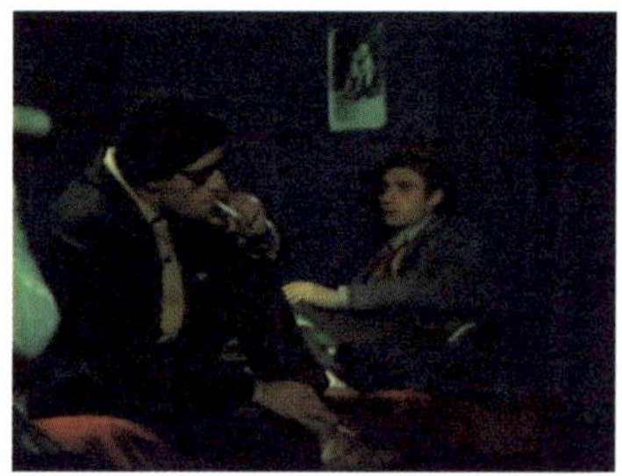

08:34

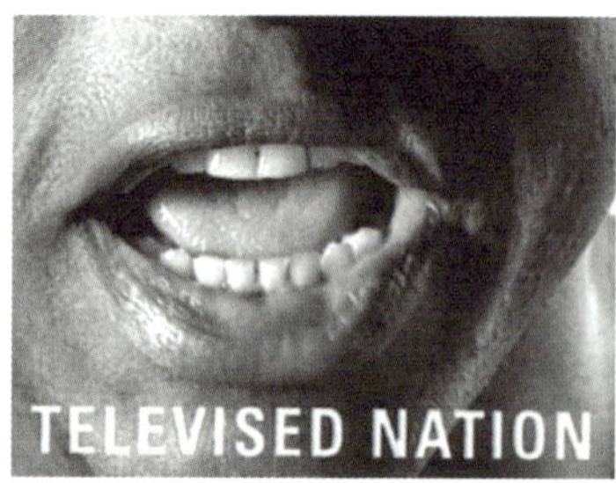

00:18

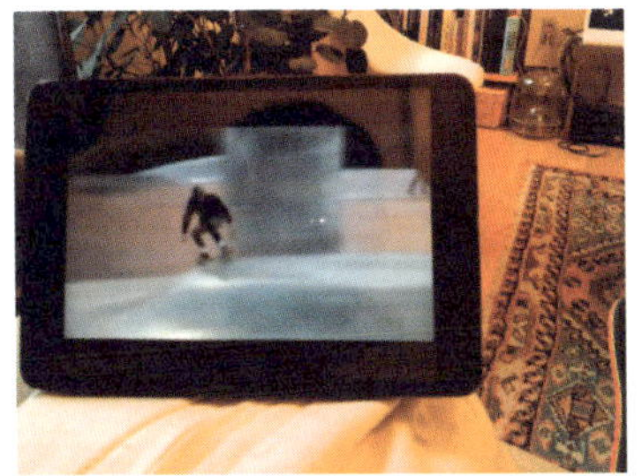
03:52

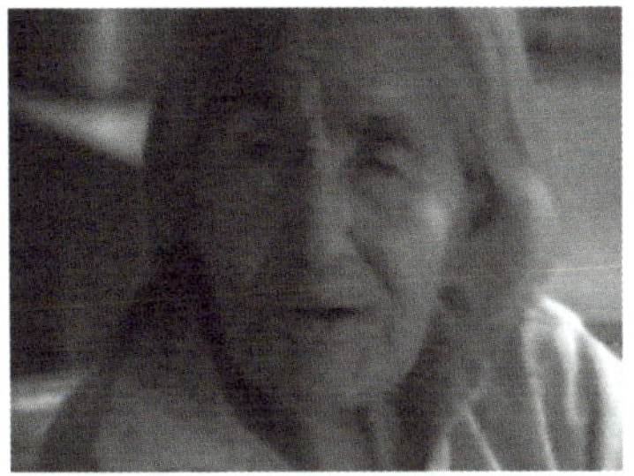
14:23

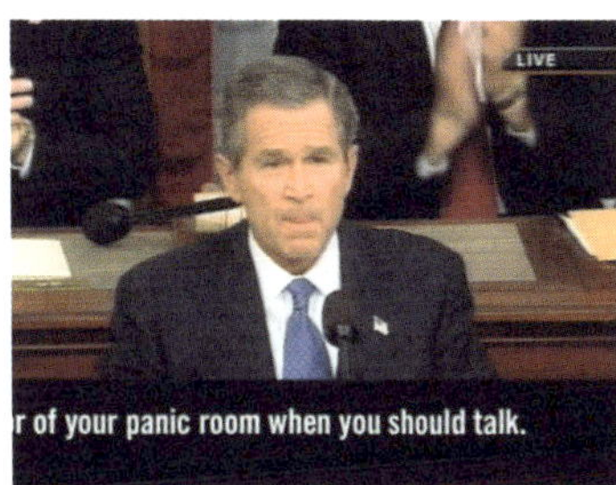

04:25

example, the development of Eric Siegel's video synthesizers and colorizers was sponsored by Howard and EAI. The first Computer Arts Festivals, from 1972 to 1974, were sponsored by EAI, as was the first Women's Video Festival at The Kitchen in 1972. Vasulka Video, which was the umbrella for the development of the Vasulkas' early image processing tools—the equipment was bought under EAI's auspices. The founding of The Kitchen was under the fiscal sponsorship of the EAI umbrella in 1971. EAI served as a kind of fiscal sponsor and administrative umbrella for all of these projects.

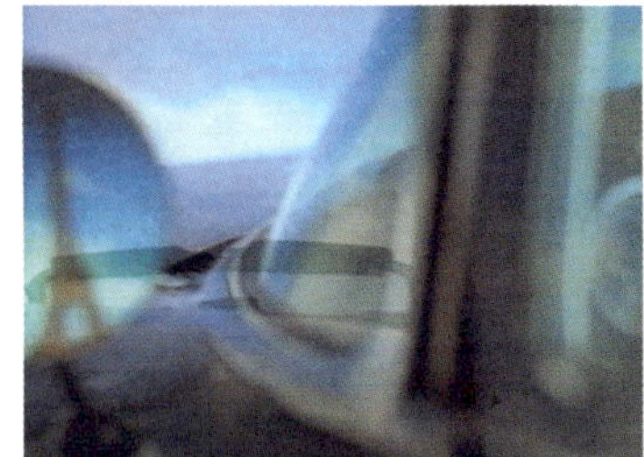
00:12

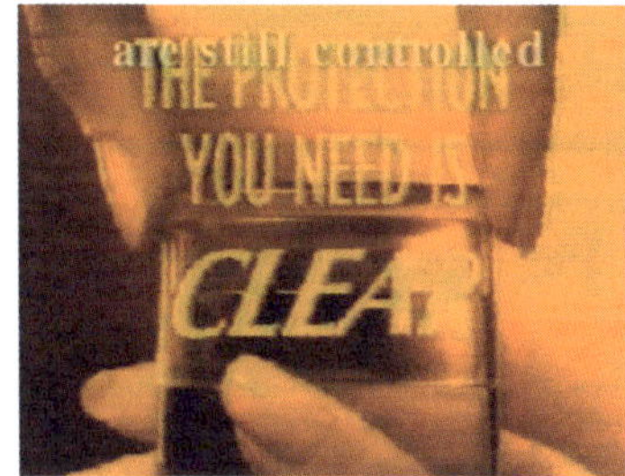

00:29

AK – Was EAI funded through Howard's personal money?

LZ – No, Howard would have contributed personal funds for some of these projects, but EAI was an umbrella for bringing in outside grants for these activities and for purchasing equipment. The first grants EAI received were from the New York State Council on the Arts [NYSCA], the Rockefeller Foundation and the National Endowment for the Arts [NEA].

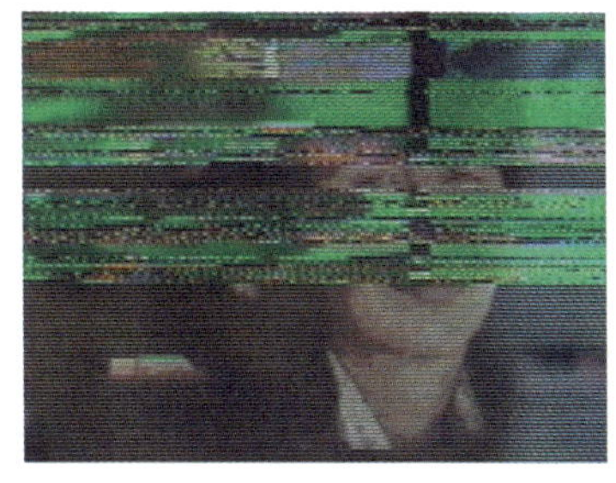
21:06

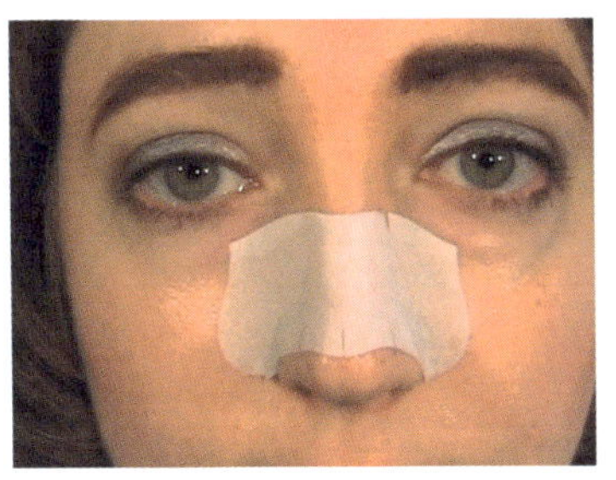
01:18

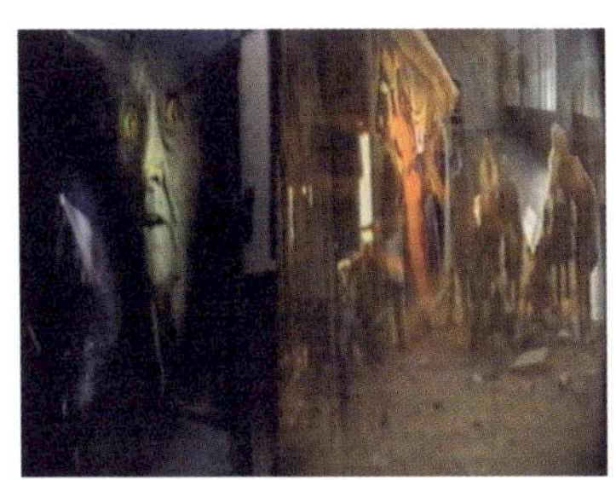
00:15

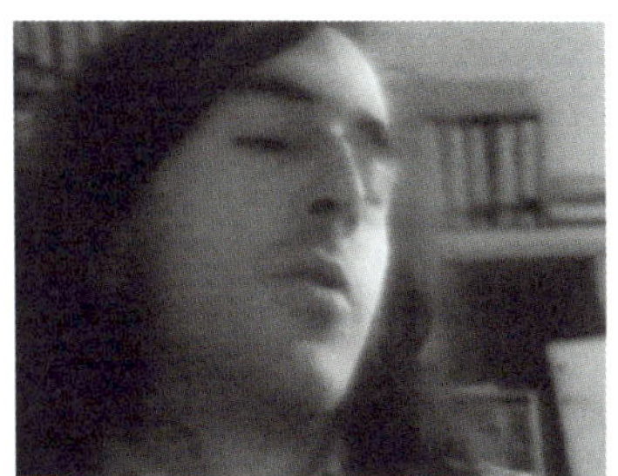
04:18

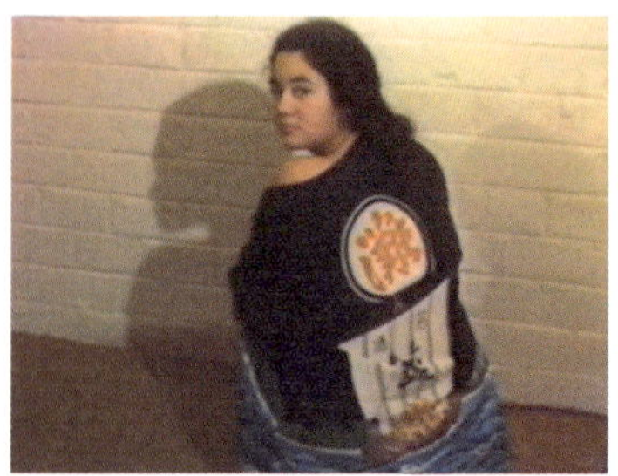
01:31

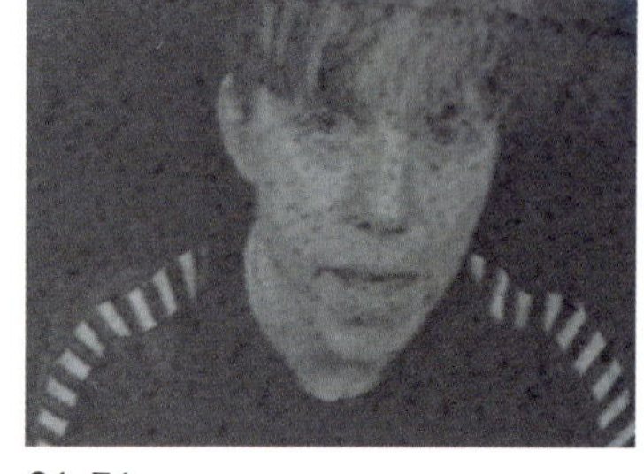
01:51

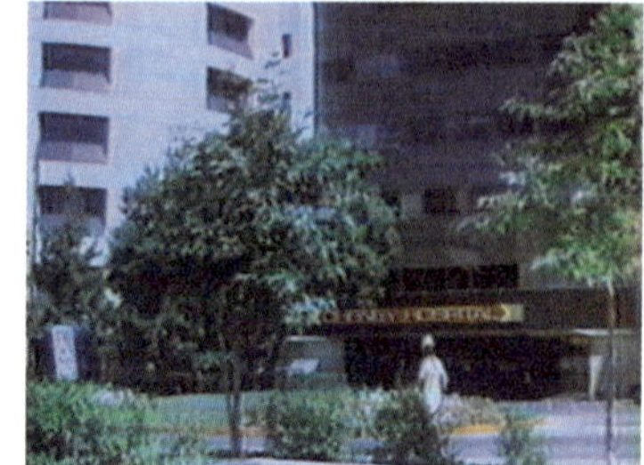
06:06

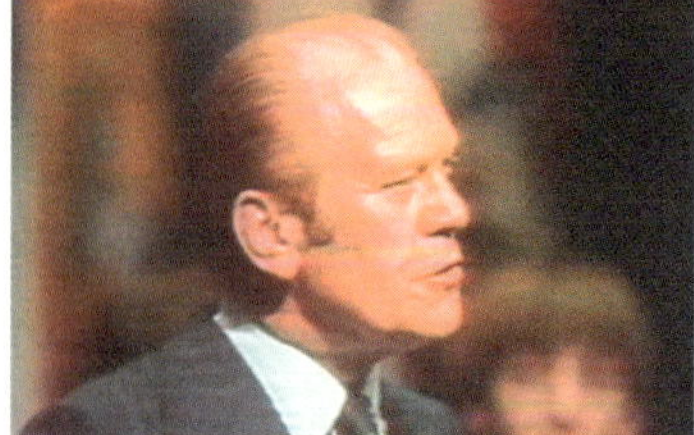
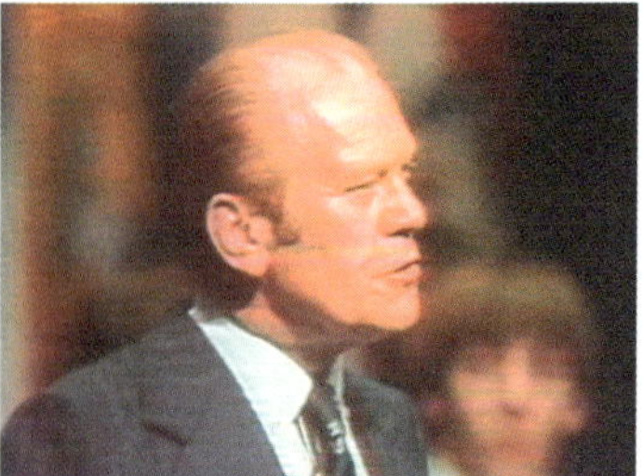
14:15

17:39

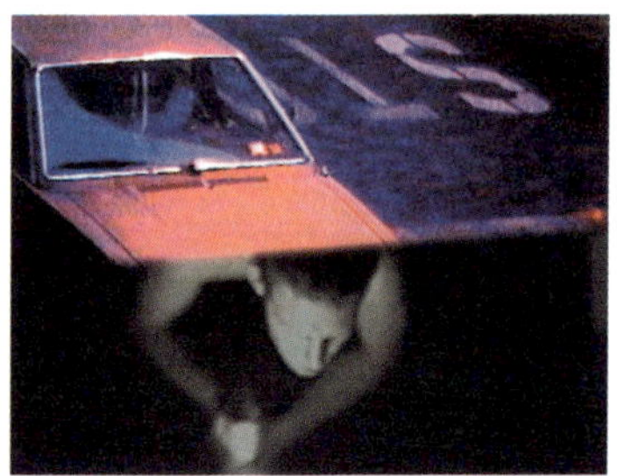
07:27

AK – Where was EAI originally located? Do you have a sense of what that space was like?

LZ – EAI was initially located at 2 West 13th Street, very briefly. I think it was just an office space. We have undated video footage of Eric Siegel playing a synthesizer in the middle of an office. It looks to be very small; it could have been Howard's personal office.

AK – So it wasn't set up with an editing suite?

LZ – Not yet. At that point, in 1971, EAI didn't have a technical facility. It was focused on providing administrative and fiscal support for artists and innovative projects in this new medium.

This is why I use the phrase "alternate paradigm" to describe EAI. It was during the moment of the alternative space movement: Artists Space was founded in 1972, and White Columns around the same time; Anthology Film Archives was founded in 1970. But they were primarily exhibiting and presenting spaces, whereas EAI was founded as a kind of alternative for providing financial and technical support. There were very few support structures for artists working

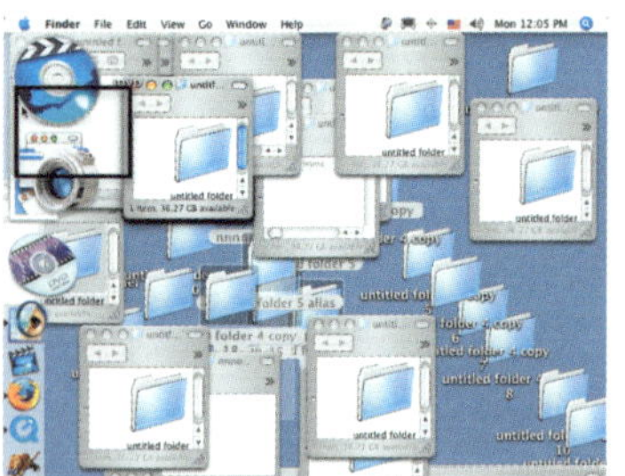
01:02

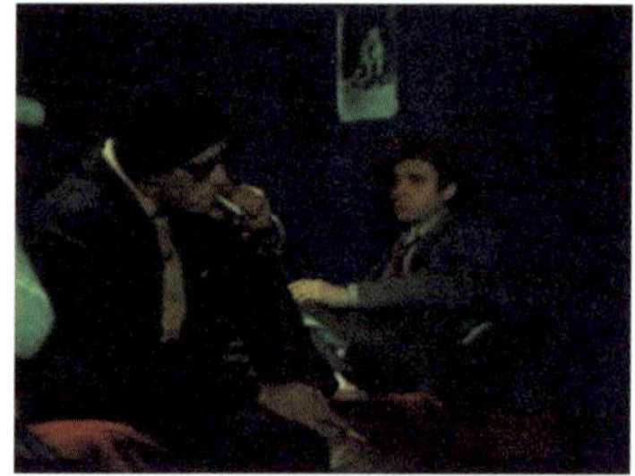
08:33

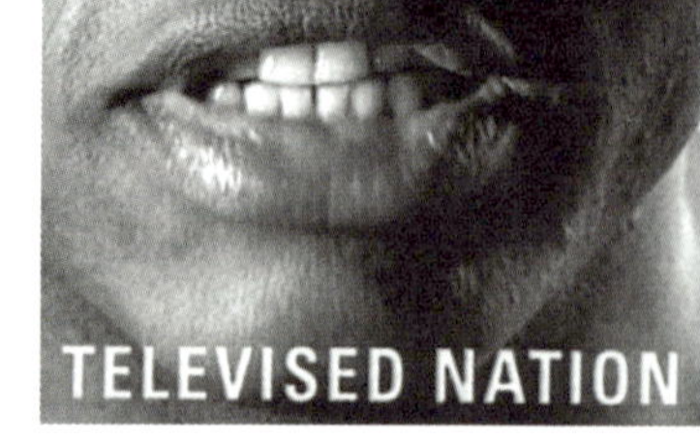

00:17

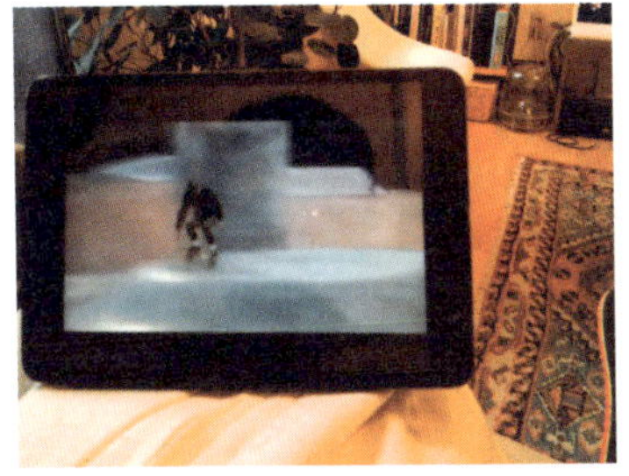
03:52

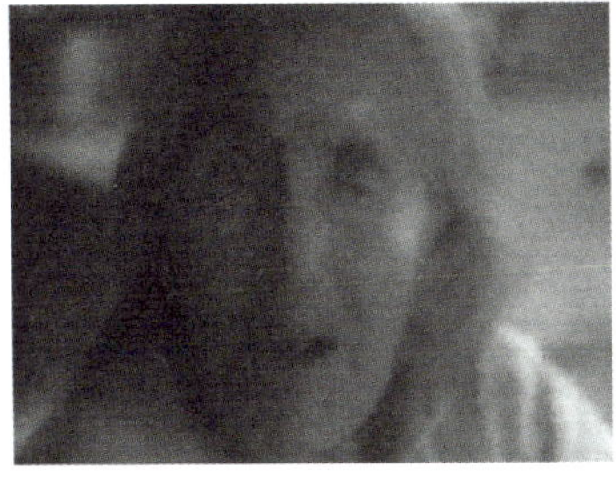
14:23

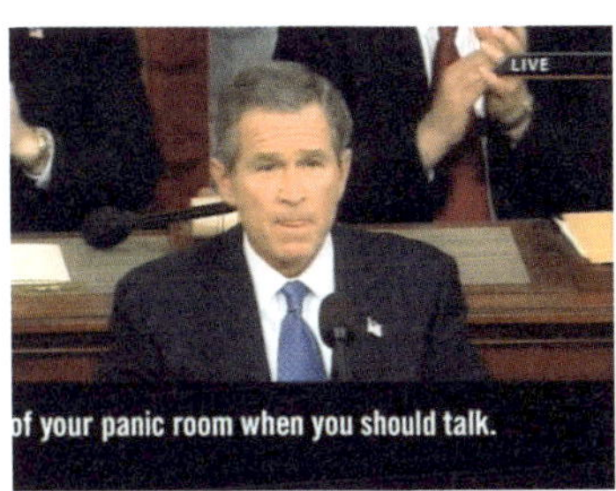

04:25

in non-object-based moving image and performance at that time. You know, if you look at this constellation of projects that EAI was supporting, it was a literal intermix of moving image, performance, site art, music, process art, activist art, etc. Much of it was time-based. I think Charlotte Moorman's festivals are a distillation of this idea. It was work that did not fit comfortably within the commercial gallery system, or within the commercial television system. It was work that existed outside of the mainstream art world.

AK – How did Wise come up with the name Electronic Arts Intermix? What did he intend with *intermix*?

LZ – The intermix of forms and ideas, I think, that defines that artistic and cultural moment.

AK – So interdisciplinary/intermixing?

LZ – Exactly. Because when you look at these projects, they are so interdisciplinary—it's really an eclectic creative mix. The term "video art" was hardly in use at that point. So, artists who were using video were also performance artists, activists, Fluxus artists, technicians, experimental

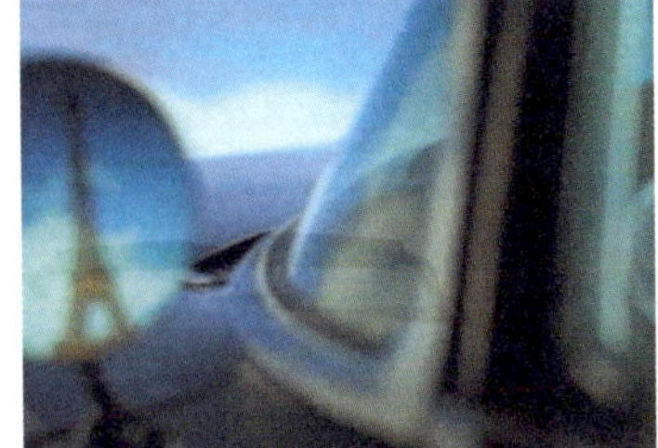
00:12

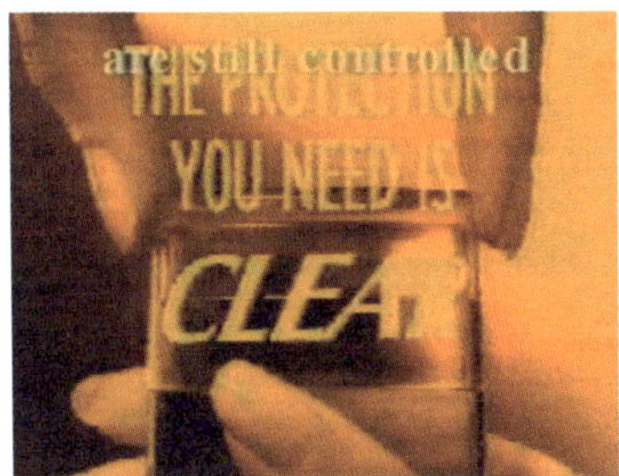

00:29

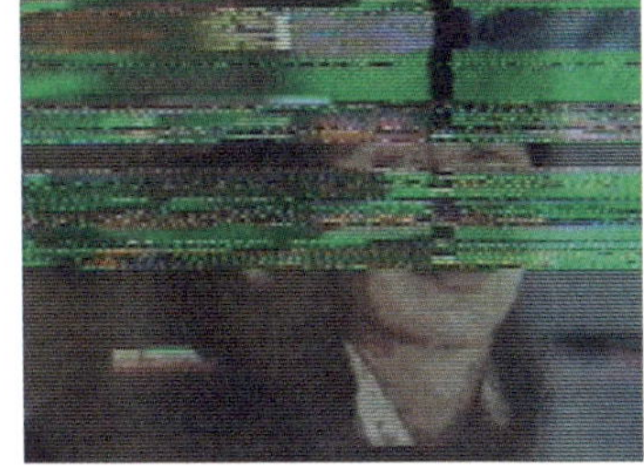
21:06

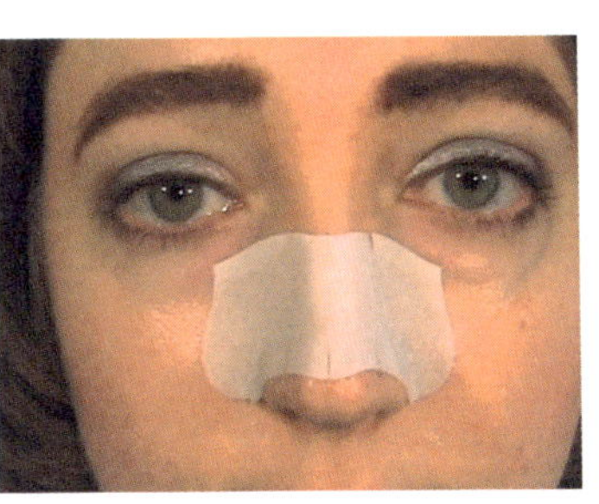
01:18

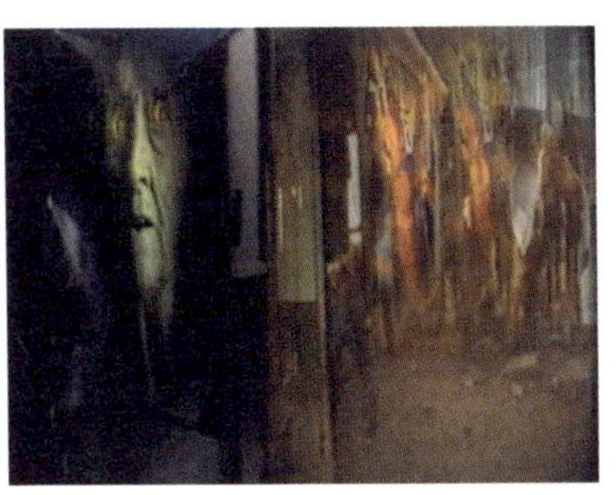
00:15

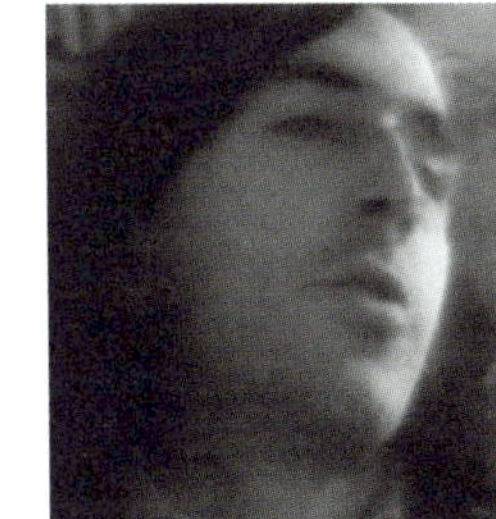
04:18

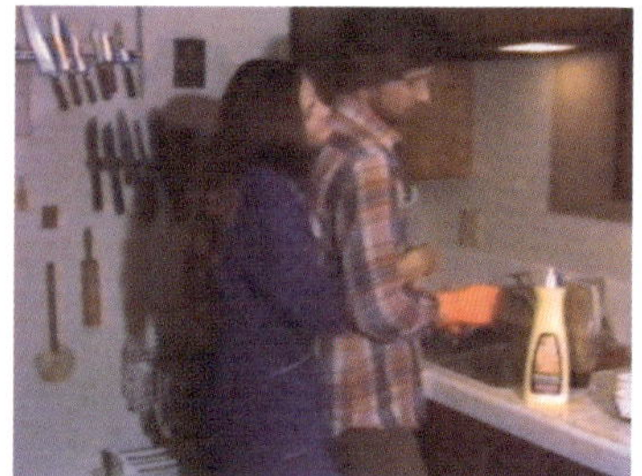
01:31

01:51

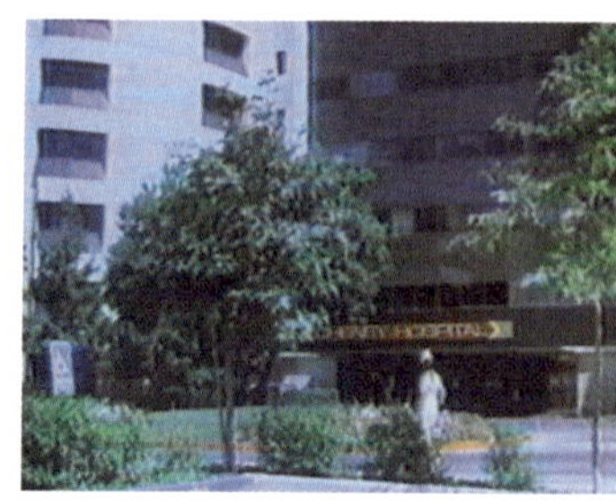
06:06

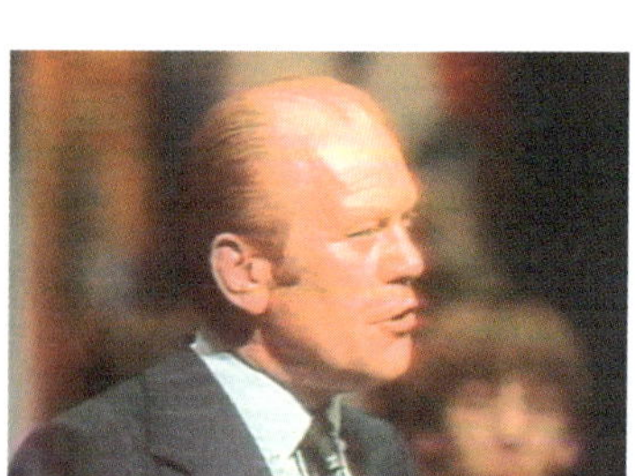
14:15

dancers—you know, it's really so diverse, and that's where the "intermix" comes from.

RC – In one of Howard's texts from this time, it might be in his manifesto for EAI, he quotes Marshall McLuhan, talking about the shift from the mechanical age to the electronic era. So, I'm guessing that "electronic art" comes from that.

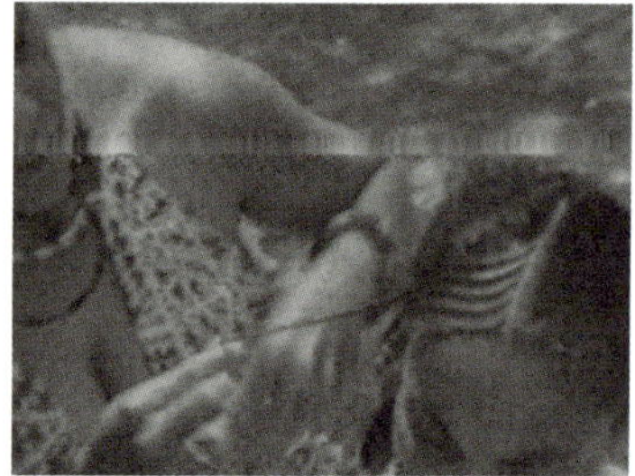
17:39

LZ – Right, exactly. And it wasn't only *video* art, because he was also interested in computer art—although I don't think many people really used the term "computer art" at that time.

AK – And later on you could point to projects like the book *The New Television: A Public/Private Art* (1977).

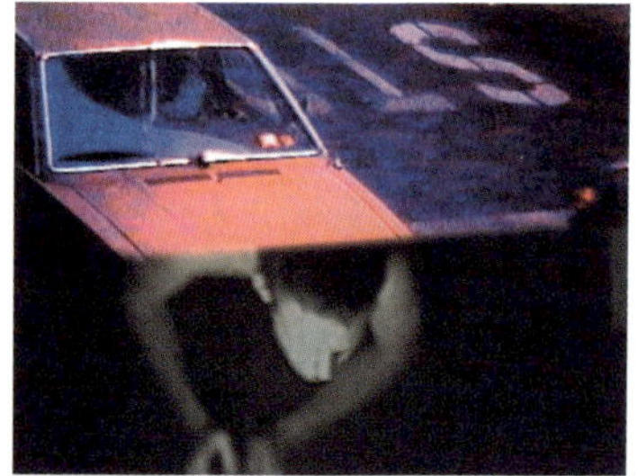
07:27

LZ – Oh! That's a hugely important project. That book was published on the occasion of the Open Circuits Conference at MoMA in 1974, which was partially supported with NYSCA funds through EAI. It was an extraordinary conference, which brought together the most remarkable array of artists, curators, thinkers, video artists, filmmakers, and theorists, such as Joan Jonas, Hollis Frampton, John Baldessari, Gregory Battcock,

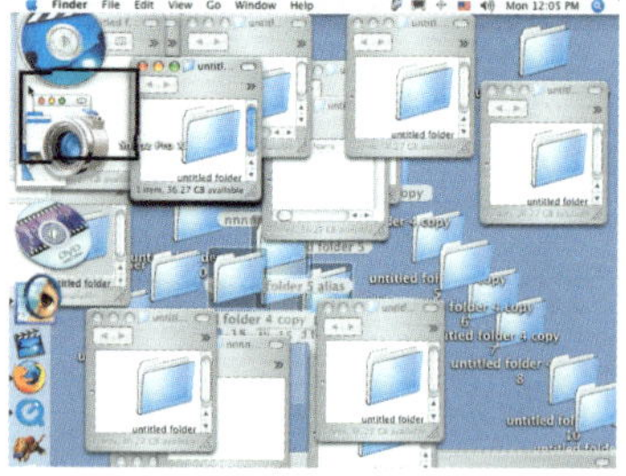
01:02

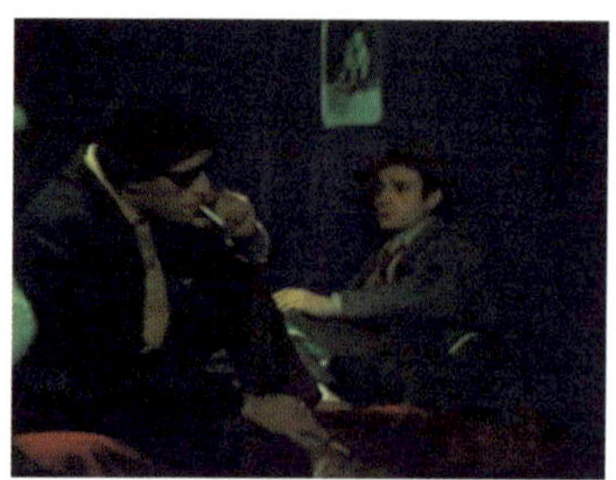
08:33

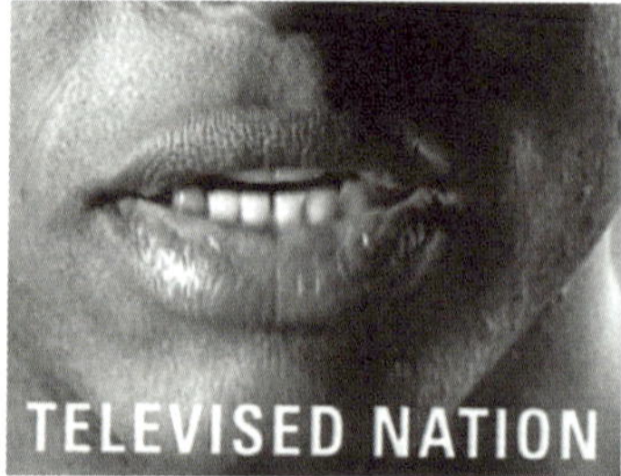

00:17

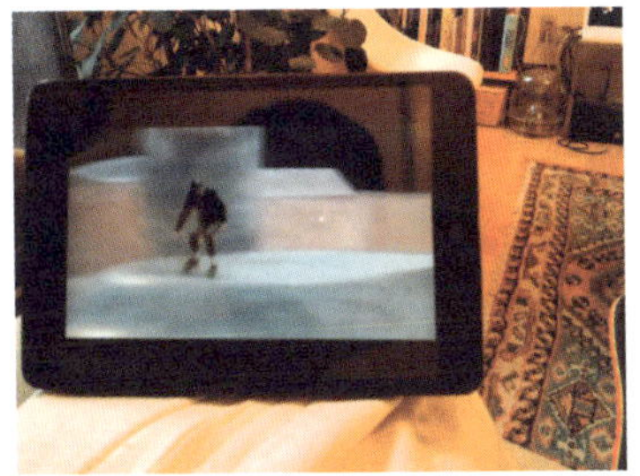
03:52

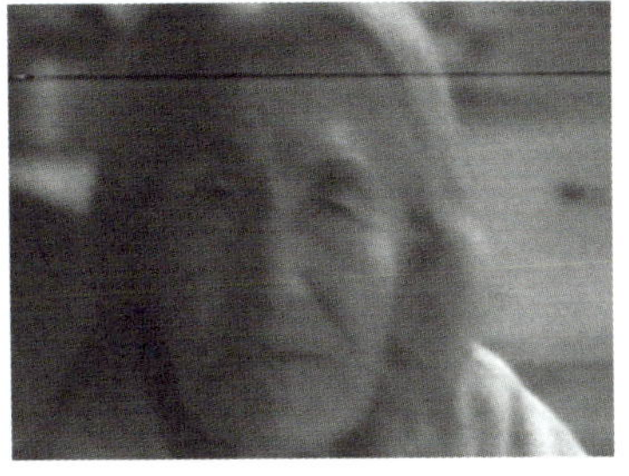
14:23

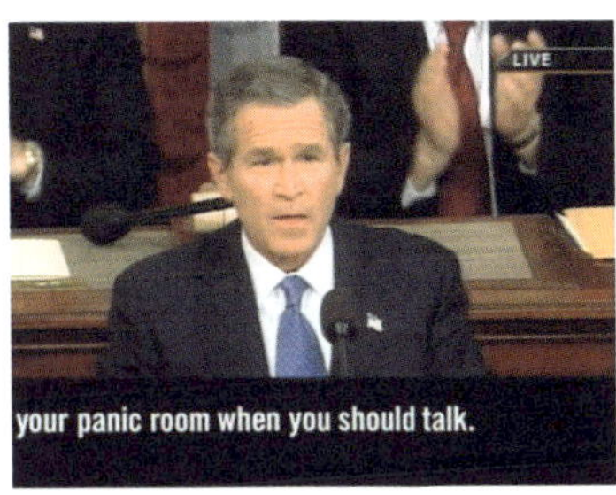

04:25

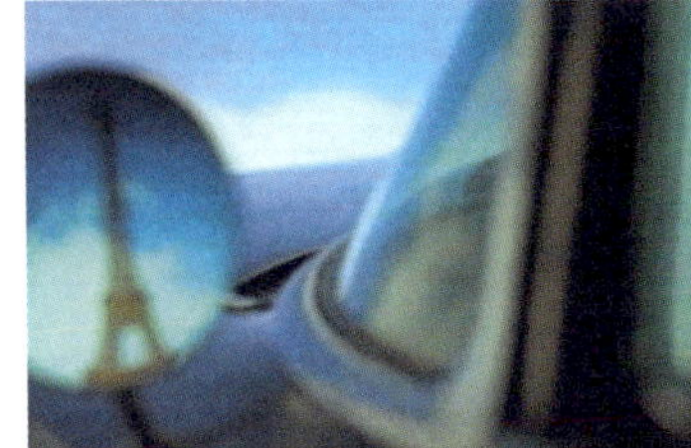
00:12

et al. The book, which includes transcripts and texts of the conference presentations, was published in 1977. The conference was organized at MoMA. The then-director of MoMA, John Hightower, formerly of NYSCA, originated the idea. The eventual three-day conference was organized by Douglas Davis, Fred Barzyk, and Gerald O'Grady, with Willard Van Dyke of the MoMA Film Department and Richard Oldenburg, who succeeded Hightower as MoMA director.

Like Charlotte's festivals, this conference was incredibly interdisciplinary in its approach. Whereas Charlotte's festivals were the articulation of an intermix of artists and art forms, the conference represented the articulation of that interdisciplinary mix in terms of thinkers, curators, and philosophers who were trying to grapple with this new medium and the ideas around it from the institutional or academic side. So, those two examples to me feel like the iconic sponsored projects of that era.

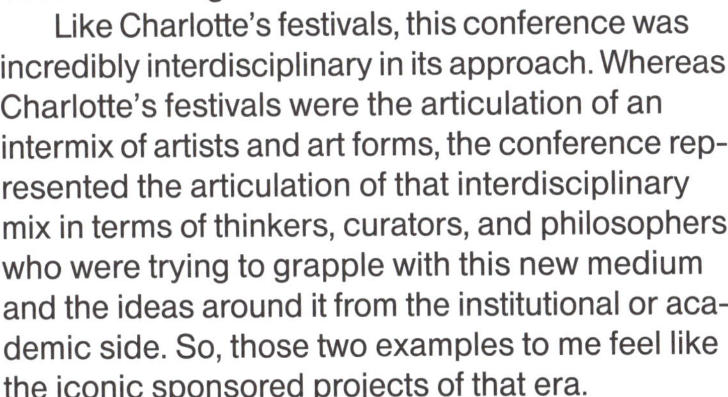

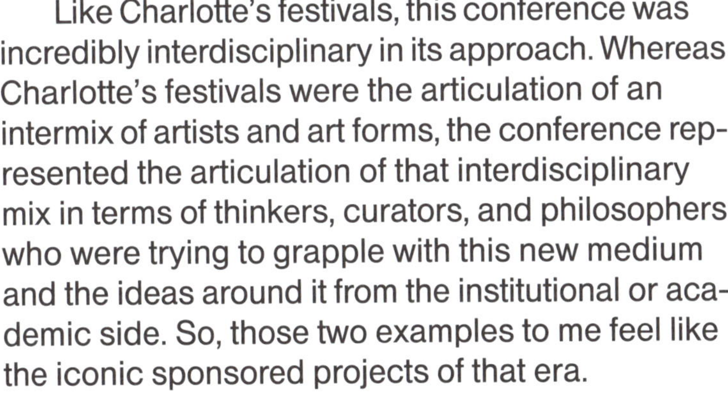

RC – Back in 1971, when EAI starts, was it just Howard by himself in an office, or were there other people with him?

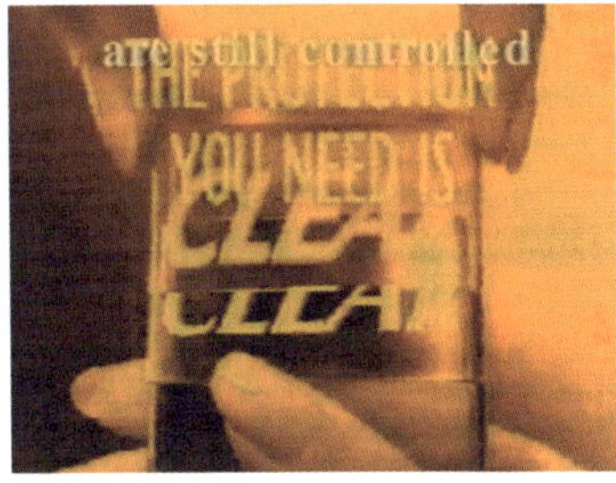

00:29

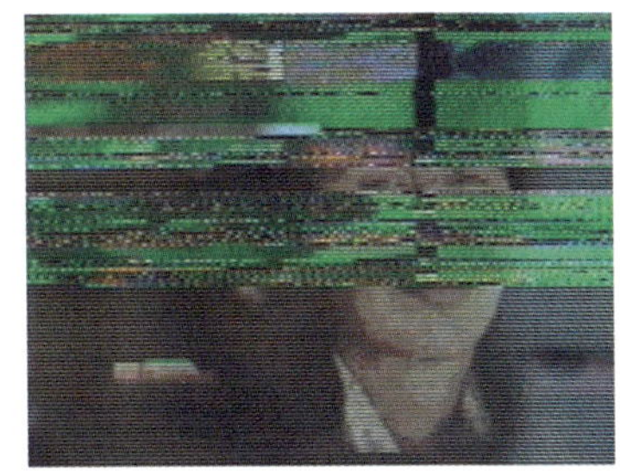
21:06

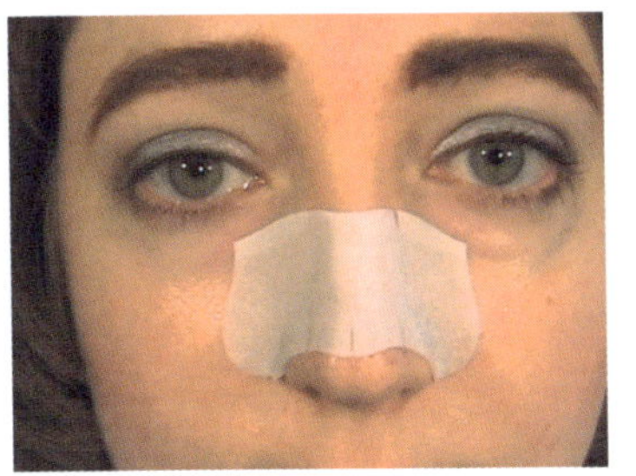
01:18

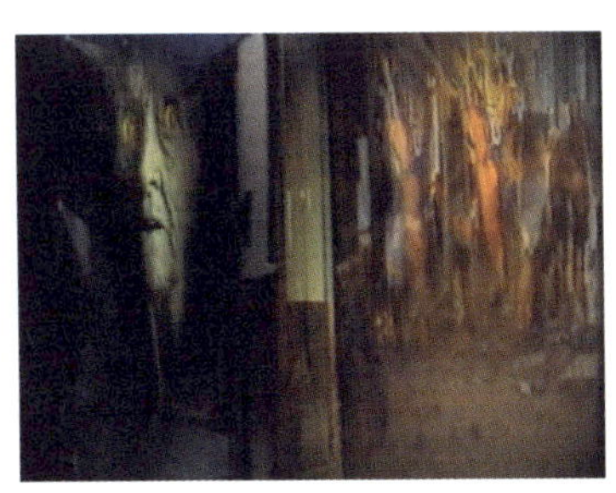
00:15

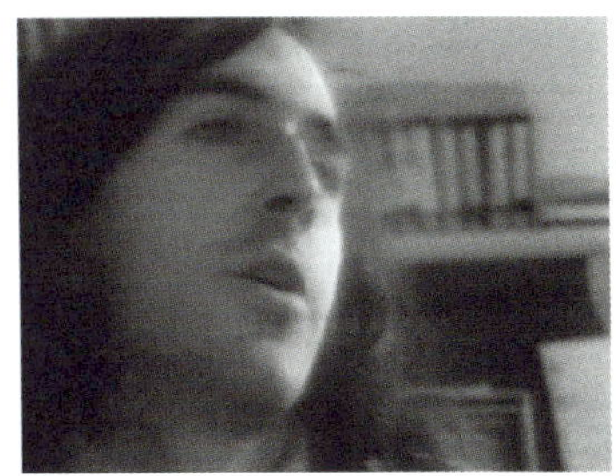
04:18

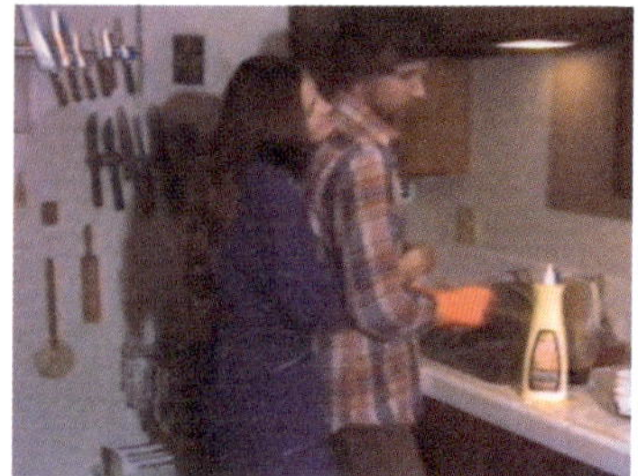
01:31

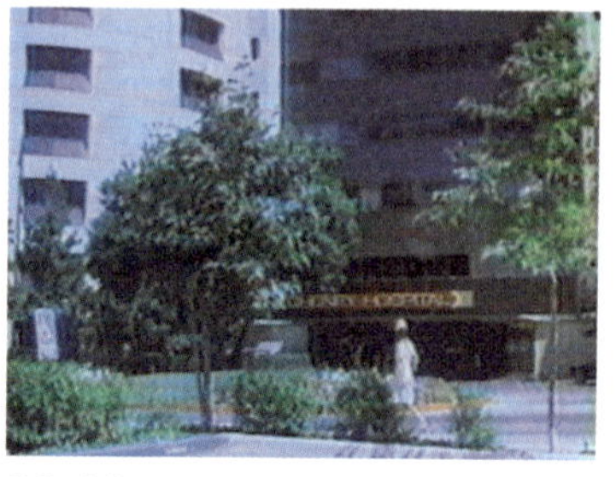
06:06

01:51

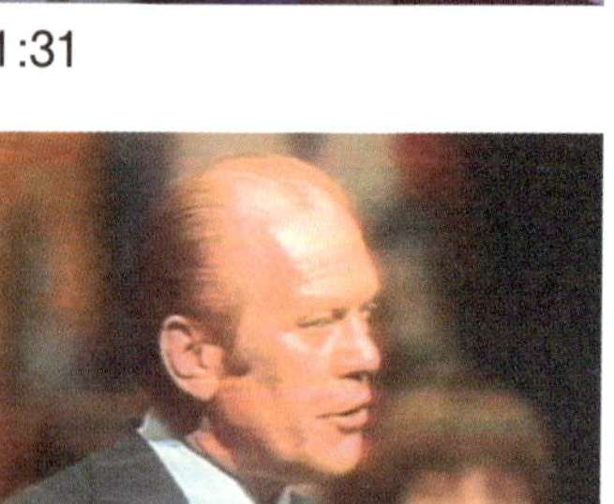
14:15

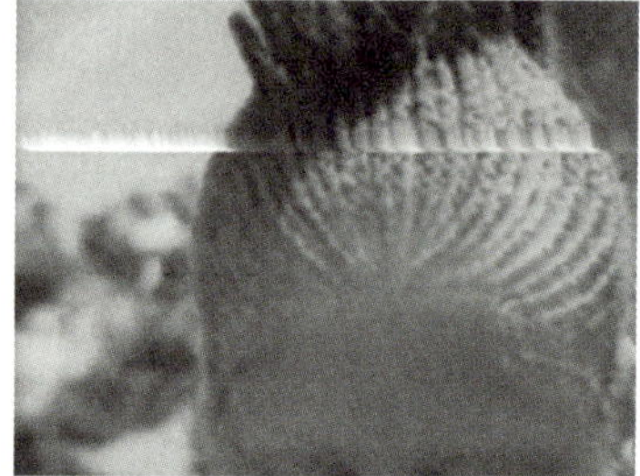
17:39

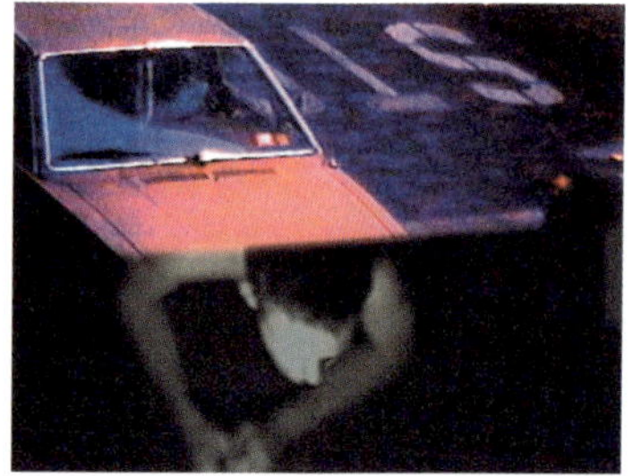
07:27

LZ – At the time EAI functioned as a support structure, there was a small administrative staff with Howard. In the early 1970s Ann Trayna worked with Howard as office manager.

Then in 1972, he founded the first free-standing project that was physically based at EAI, which was the editing facility. The original editing facility was at EAI's second space, at 84 5th Avenue.

AK – It seems like a radical shift from, "We're going to focus on creating administrative support for projects" to "Now we're going to have an in-house editing suite where artists are going to come and have access to resources." Do you have a sense of how that institutional shift came about?

LZ – There were several sponsored projects—Eric Siegel's synthesizers, Vasulka Video, the collective Perception—that were all equipment-based. Howard was very interested in equipment and technology and artist-made video tools. He fostered and supported kinetic art and technology-driven art.

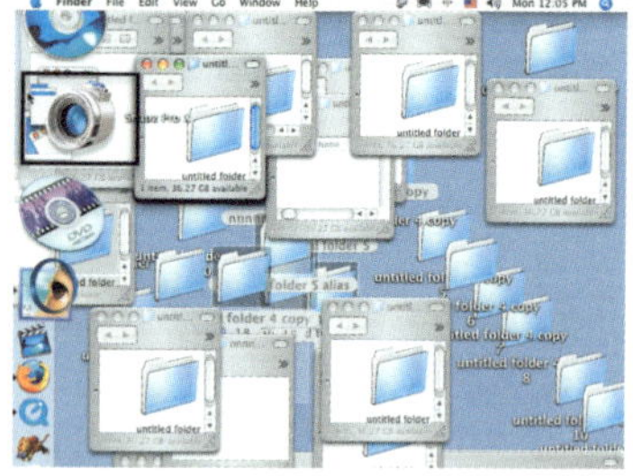
01:02

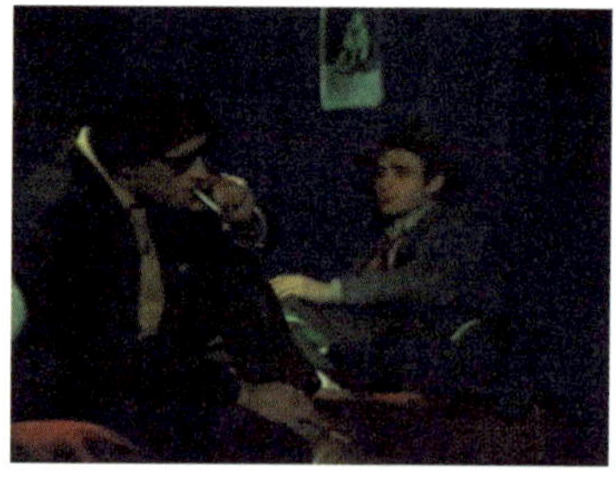
08:33

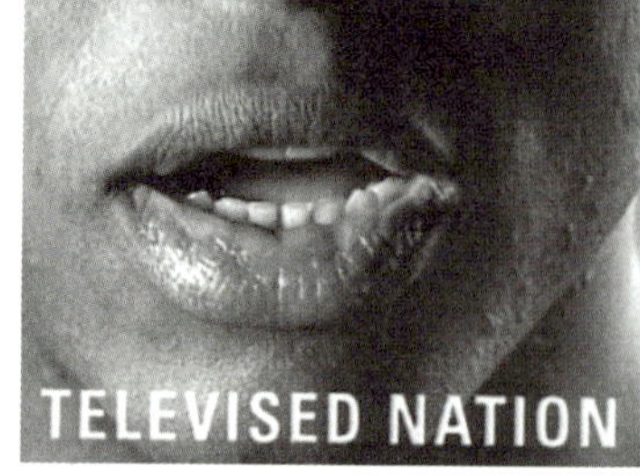

00:17

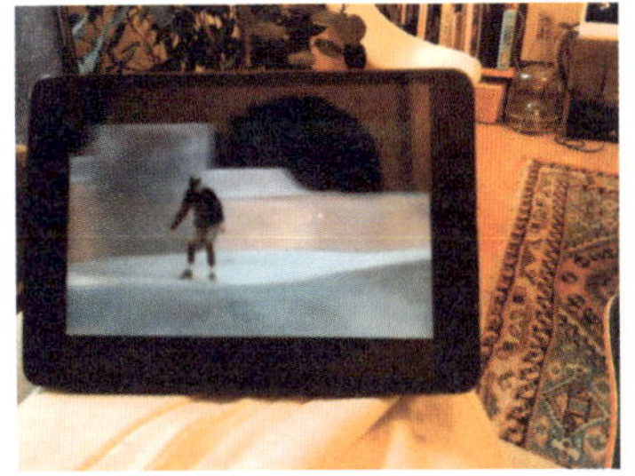
03:52

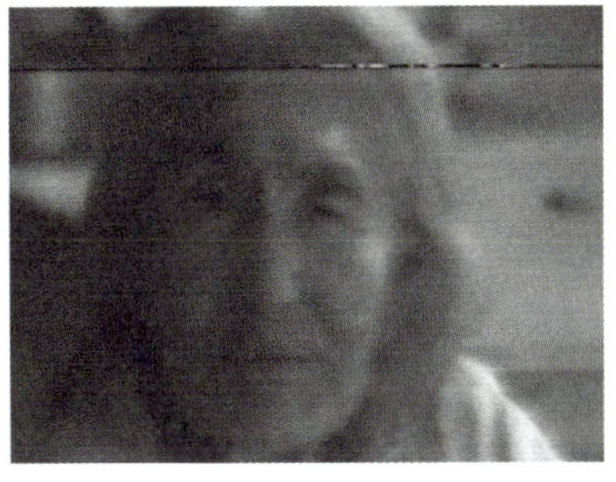
14:23

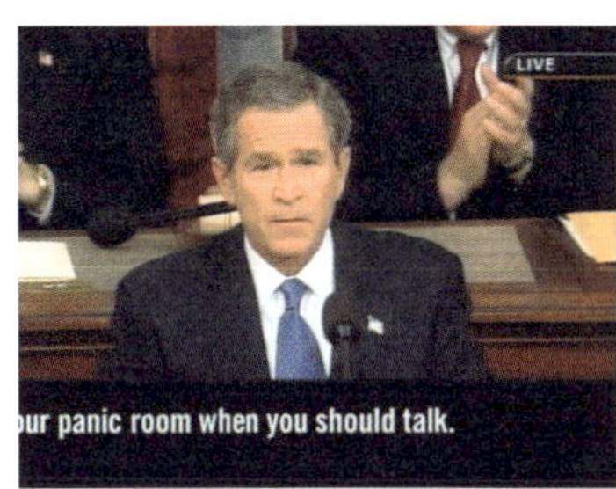

04:25

The use of these technological tools to create art and to foster social and political change interested him tremendously. It's not surprising to me that some of these early projects were really about tools for artists to be creating this new work. It spoke to a need of artists at the time. Artists had limited access to Portapaks, but other than editing in-camera—or at one of the "artists' laboratories" at public television stations in New York, Boston and San Francisco—there were very few studios, very few places to edit. So artists kind of rallied. We have correspondence in the files where artists were asking Howard about getting equipment.

AK – This is a good reminder of some of the technological challenges that artists faced. We are now in a moment where you can literally shoot and edit everything on your phone. I think that there's a real disconnect for a younger generation. They never went through the transition between analog and digital and don't have a sense of how difficult it was to actually make this stuff. Was the EAI facility free to use?

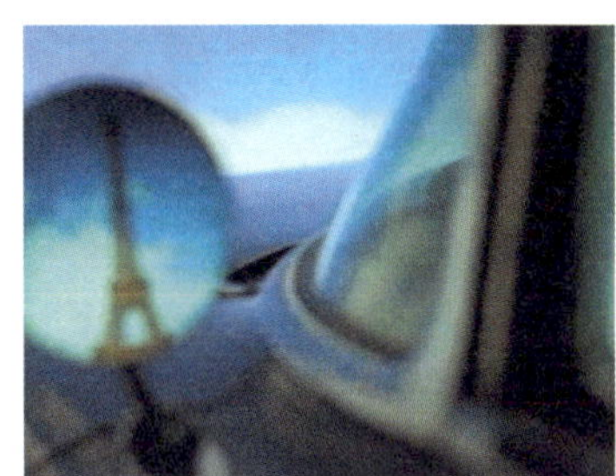
00:12

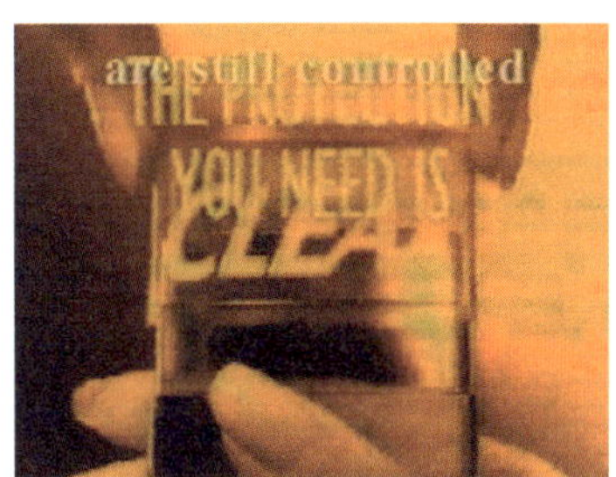

00:29

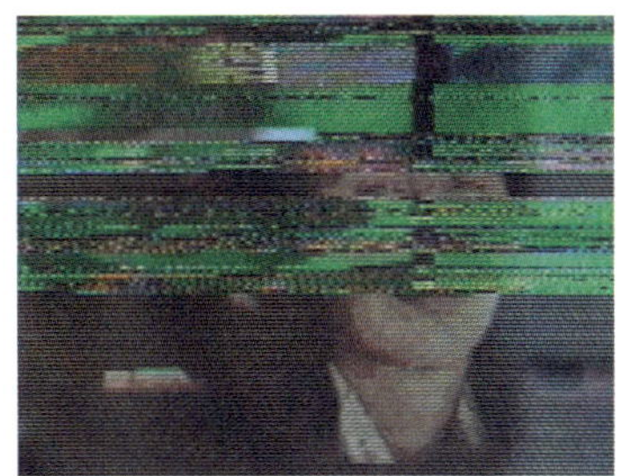
21:06

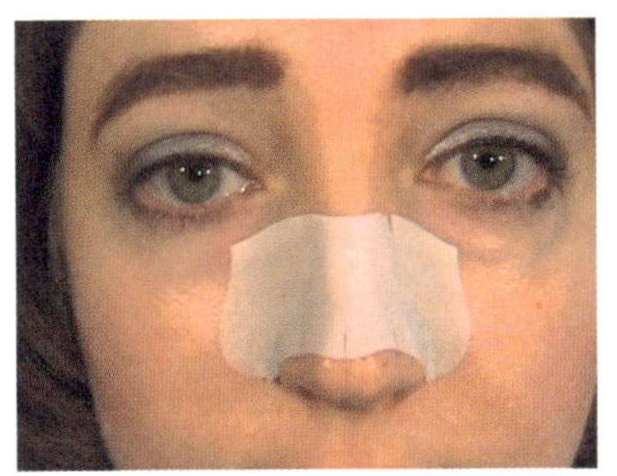
01:18

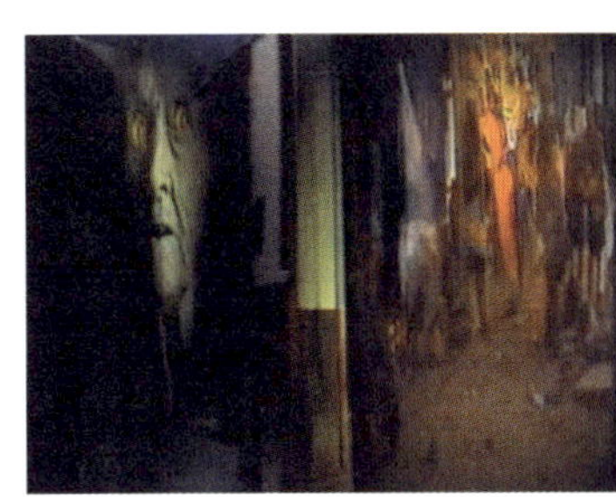
00:15

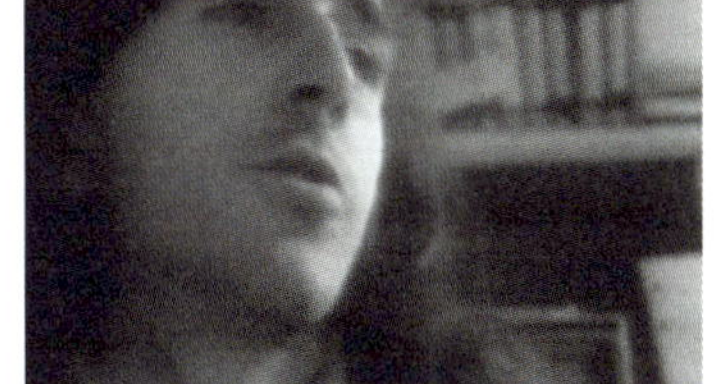
04:18

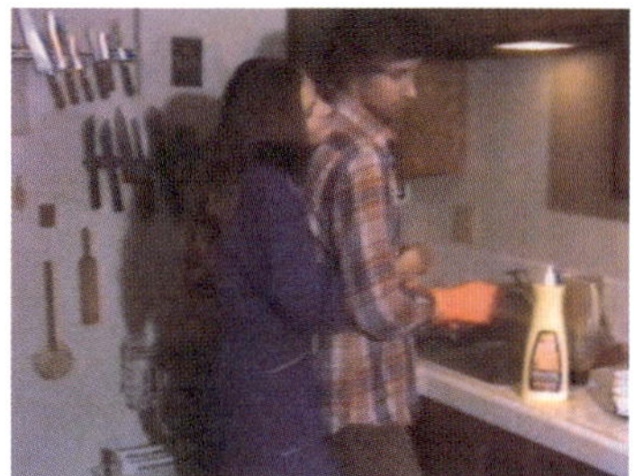
01:31

01:51

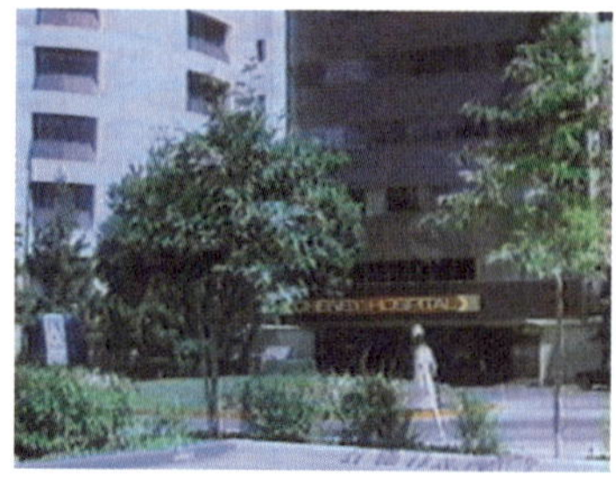
06:06

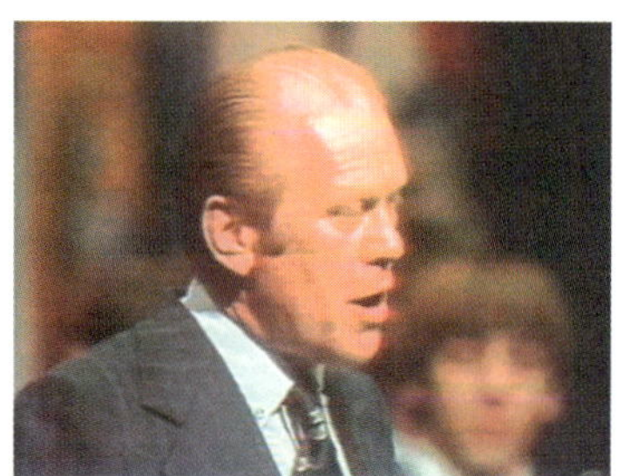
14:15

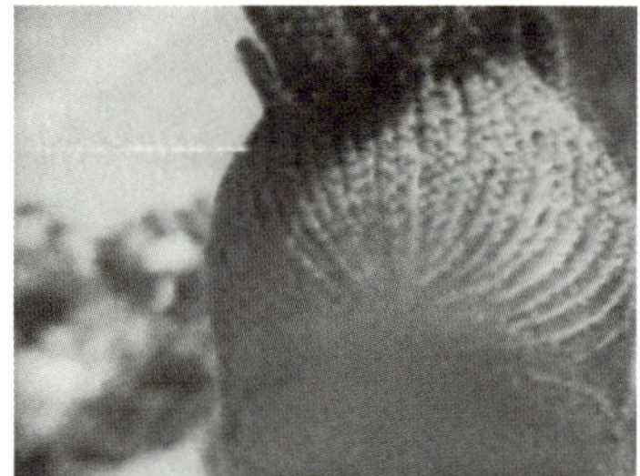
17:39

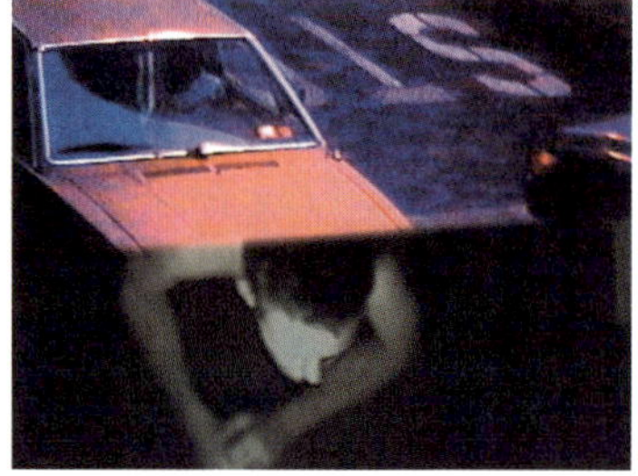
07:27

LZ – Yes, in the earliest years it was free. Artists had to submit applications, to make sure it was an artistic project and not a commercial one.

AK – Did they offer classes or provide technical assistance? I'm assuming that if this was new technology artists might not have had widespread access to these editing tools before?

LZ – John Trayna, a beloved and legendary figure, was the first chief editor/engineer, and he worked with countless artists as editor and collaborator. Doreen Hyman, Ann Volkes, David Pentecost, and Janice Putney were also key figures in the editing facility in the 1970s. We have records of classes and workshops in the late seventies.

AK – So, there were specialists on-site.

LZ – Exactly. The early editors were trained or hands on, because there was no existing network of nonprofit video editing spaces. This was the beginning of the ecosystem of nonprofit editing or artist-driven or artist-run editing facilities, which included Global Village in New York

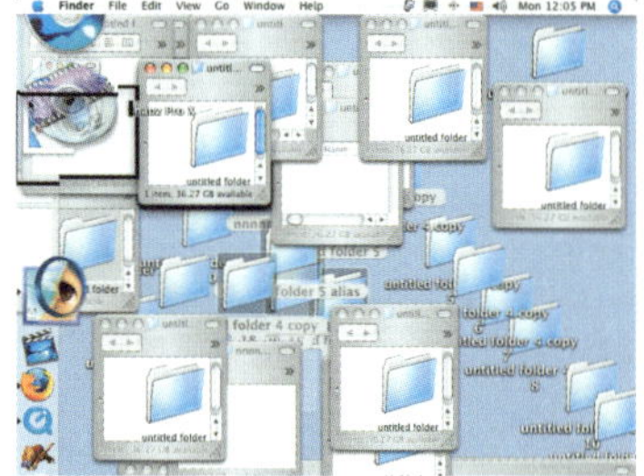
01:02

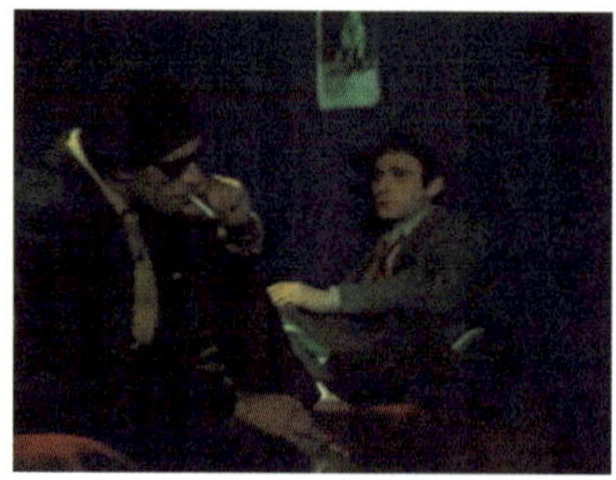
08:33

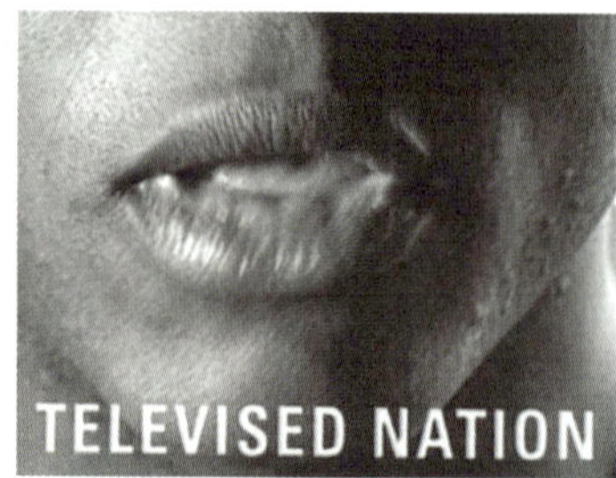

00:17

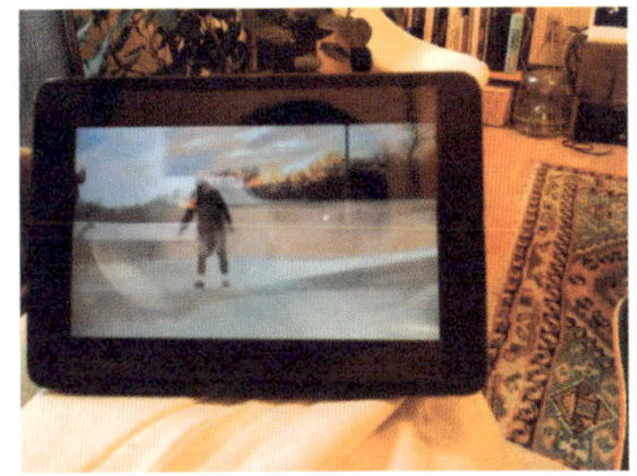
03:53

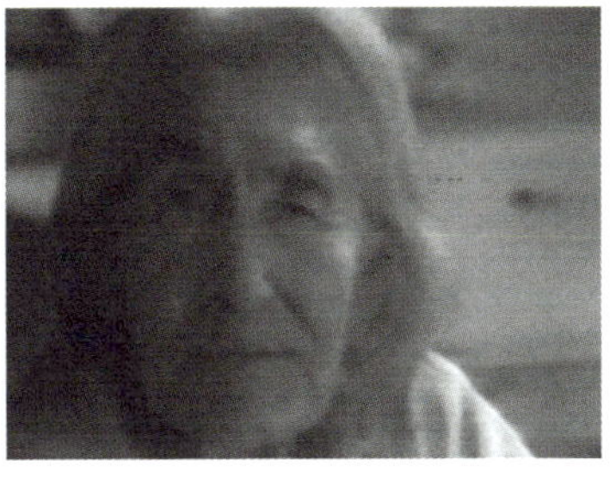
14:24

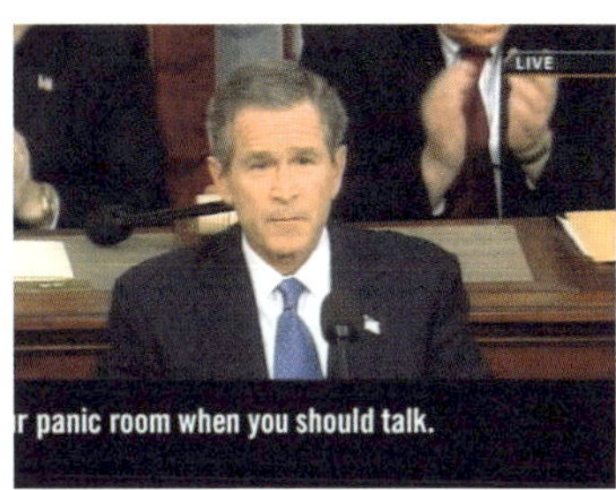

04:26

and the Experimental Television Center in Owego, to name a few notable places. It was a new paradigm in all ways.

AK – Would the editor help an artist who would come in with their footage?

LZ – Yes, exactly. Artists such as Mary Lucier, Shigeko Kubota, Juan Downey, Anthony Ramos, Willoughby Sharp, and Hannah Wilke, to name just a few, edited at EAI in the early seventies. The beginning of the editing facility really propelled EAI's direct interaction with artists—it's something that became extremely important over the next decades. It is something that, as you know, we maintain today. The editing facility was, particularly then, a key project of EAI. Hundreds of works have been produced in the editing facility over its history, some of them incredibly important. Over the years it's waxed and waned in significance for the organization, but we never lost this artist-driven ethos. Only recently have I come to realize how much it differentiates us from other organizations—even in terms of distribution—that we had this creative workspace

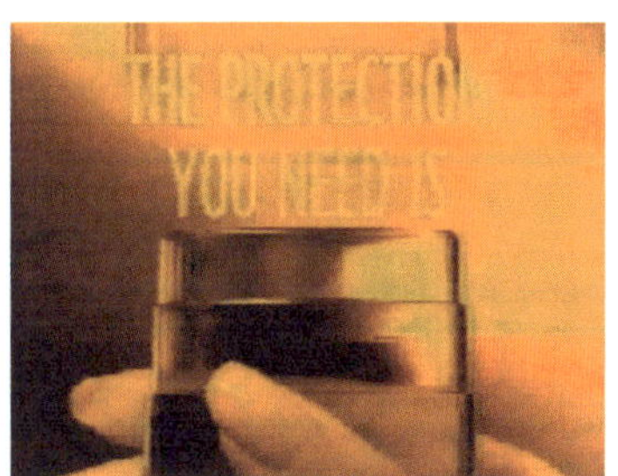
00:13

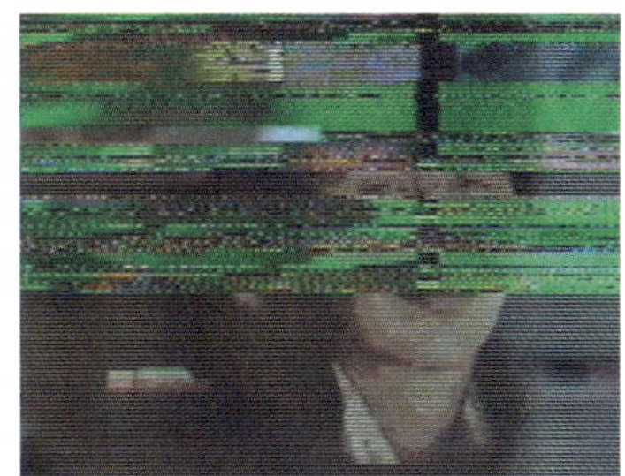

00:30

21:07

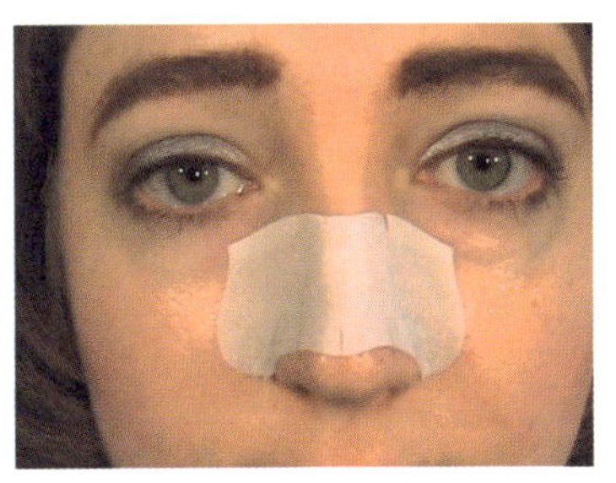
01:19

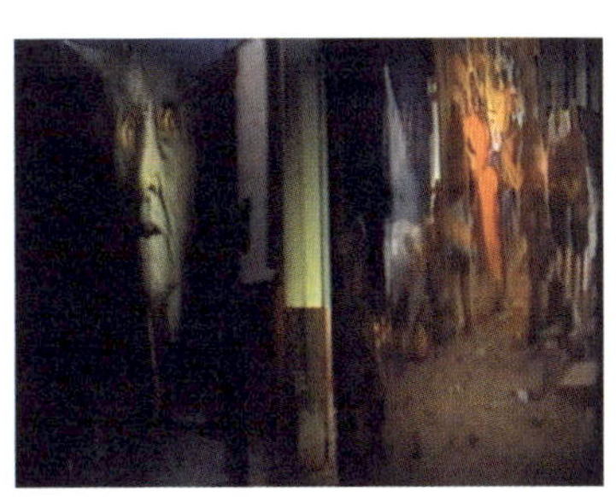
00:16

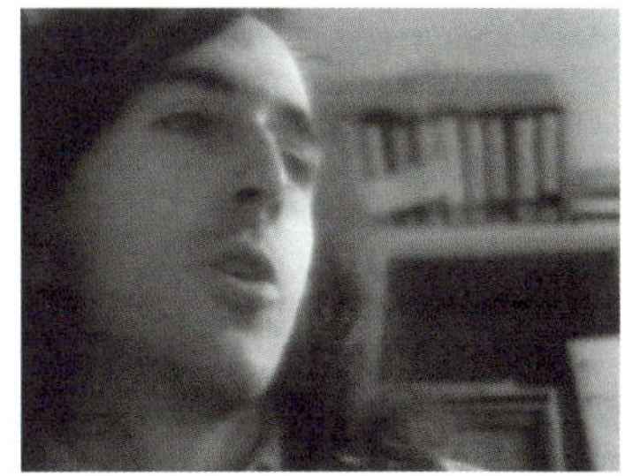
04:19

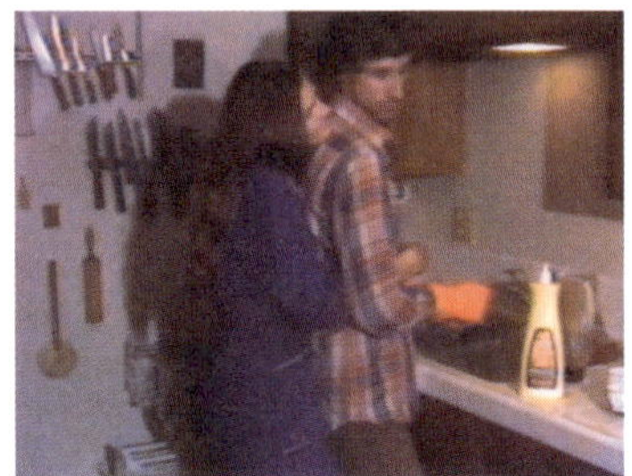
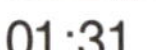
01:31

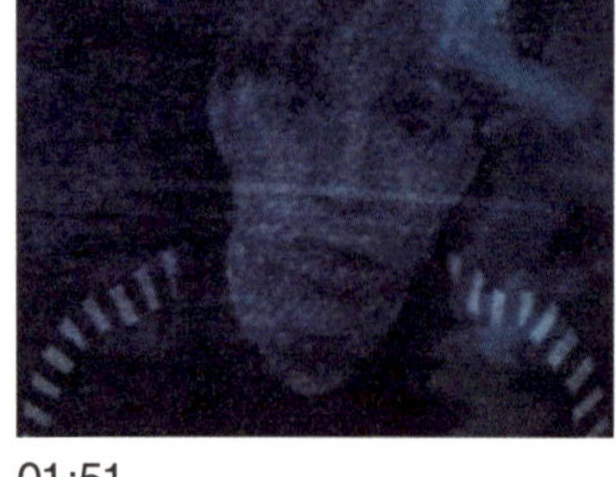
01:51

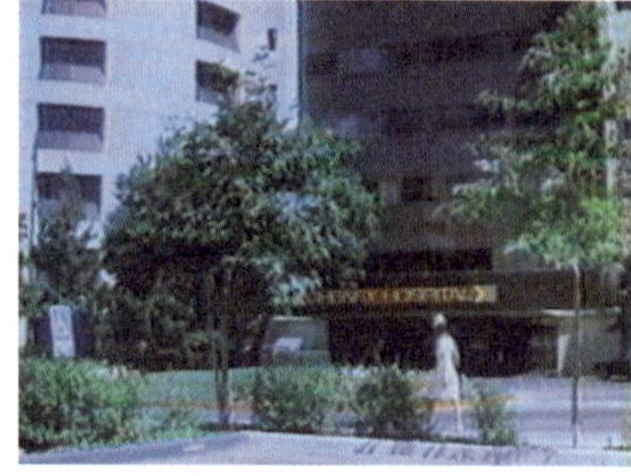
06:06

on-site, which allowed for ongoing relationships with artists over the years and maintaining a close relation to artists' production.

AK – I love seeing the credit "Edited at EAI" in many of the videos you distribute. At that point in time was there a distribution service or catalog? Or did the editing suite kind of lead to that decision to say "Hey, now we have artists producing work and we need to help distribute it and get people compensated?"

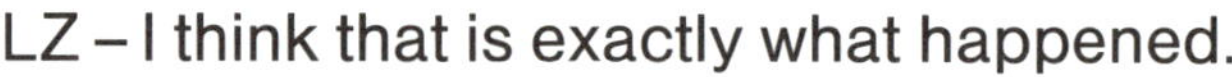
LZ – I think that is exactly what happened.

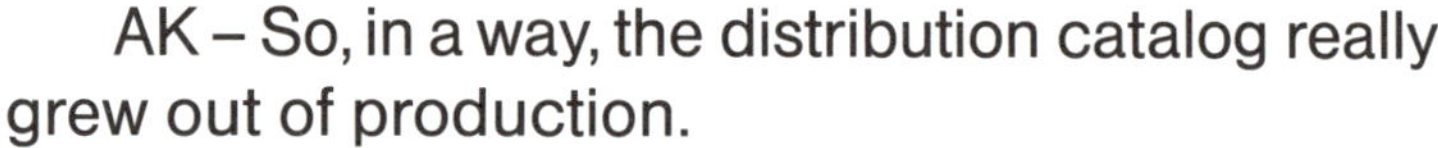
AK – So, in a way, the distribution catalog really grew out of production.

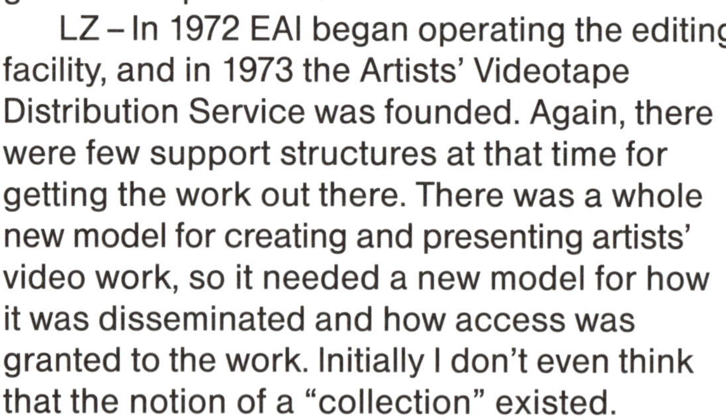
LZ – In 1972 EAI began operating the editing facility, and in 1973 the Artists' Videotape Distribution Service was founded. Again, there were few support structures at that time for getting the work out there. There was a whole new model for creating and presenting artists' video work, so it needed a new model for how it was disseminated and how access was granted to the work. Initially I don't even think that the notion of a "collection" existed.

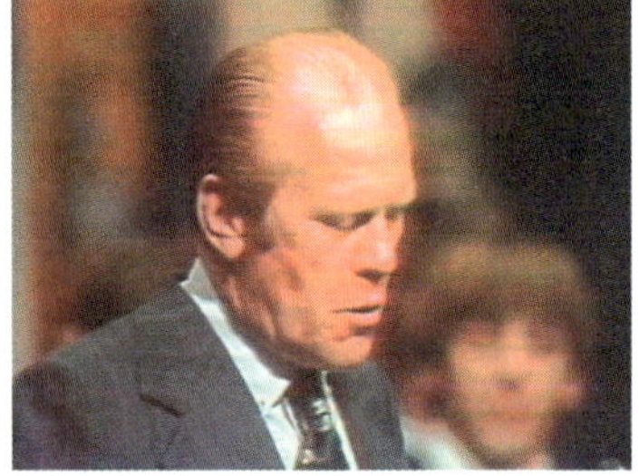
14:15

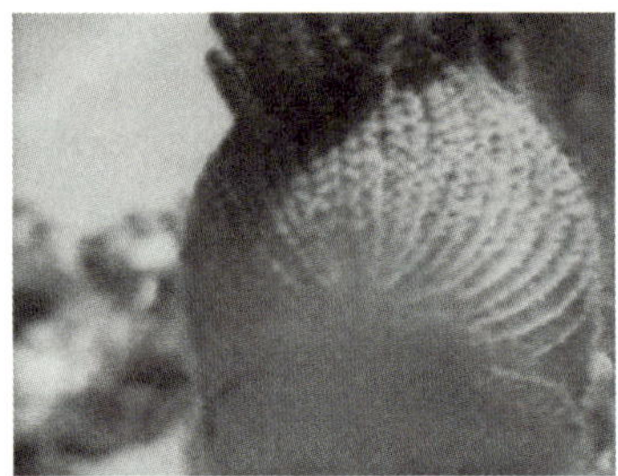
17:39

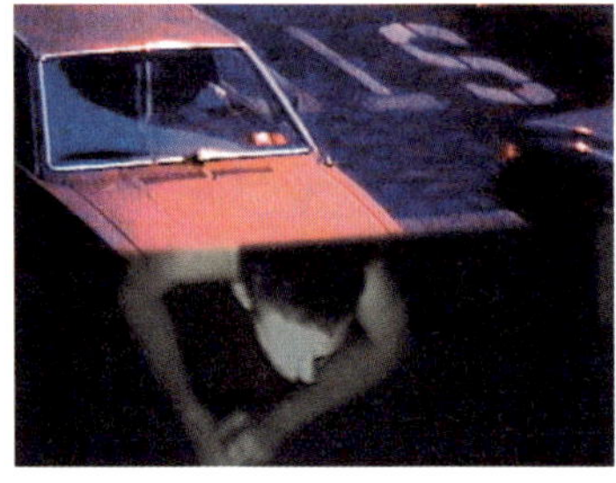
07:27

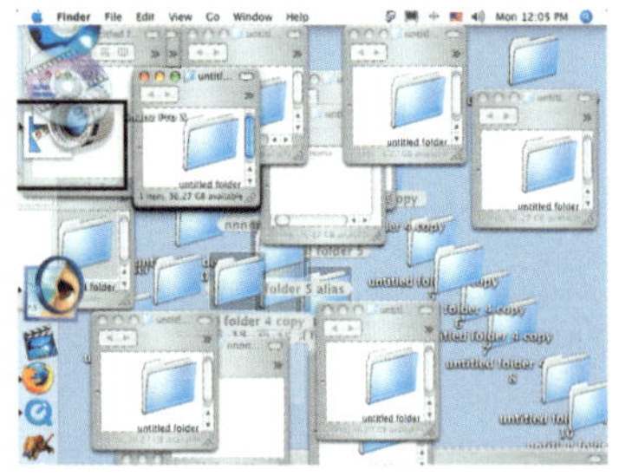
01:02

08:33

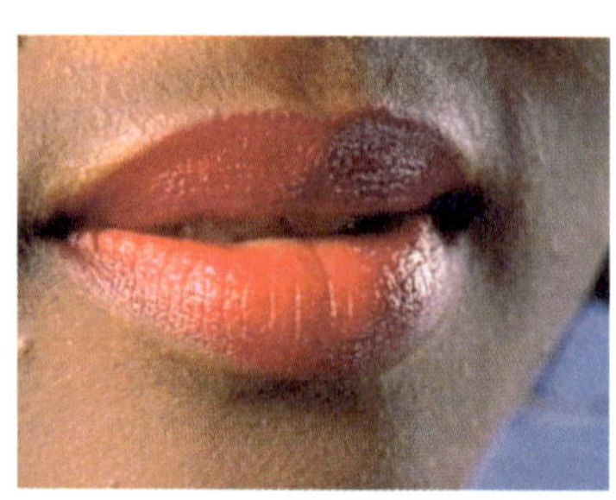
00:17

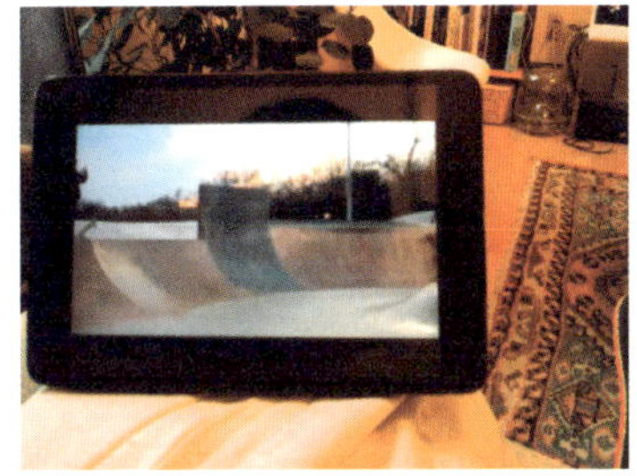

03:53

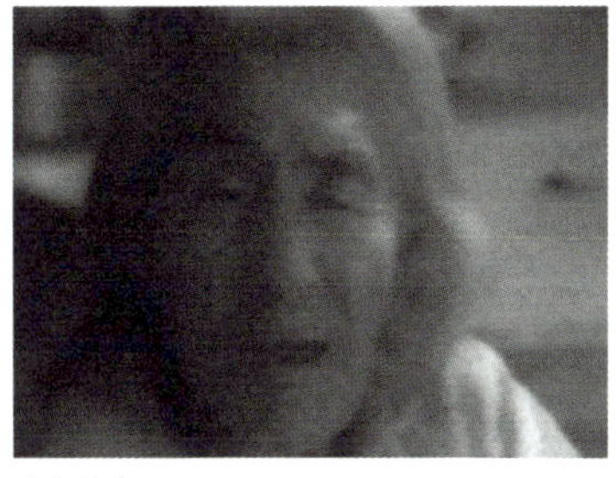

14:24

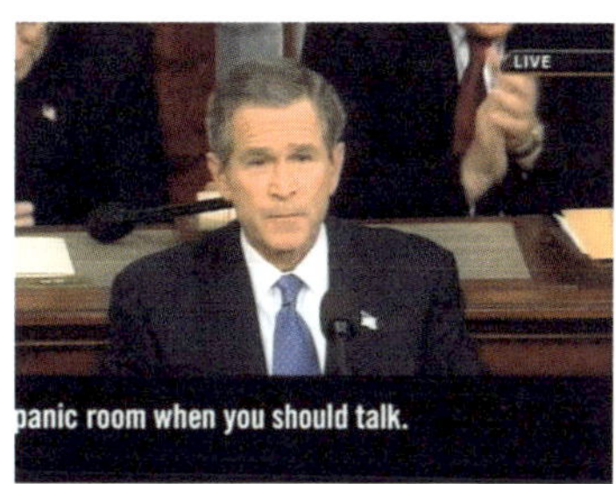

04:26

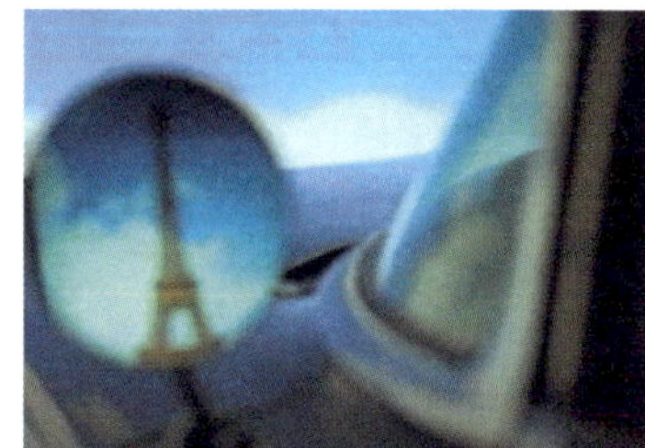

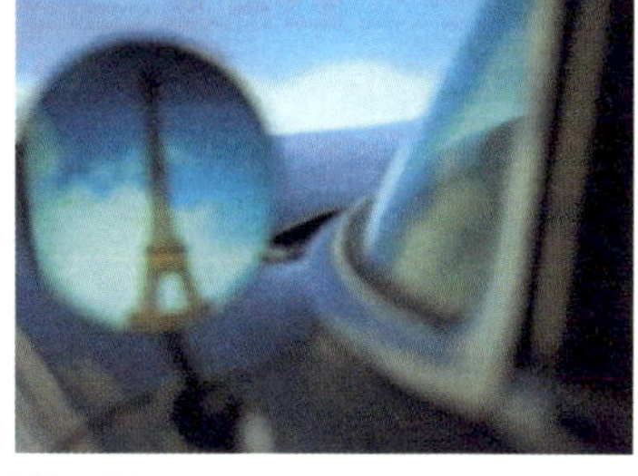

00:13

It certainly wasn't seen as an archive until much later. It was distribution. You can tell from the early catalogs that the structure was somewhat based on film distribution—some of the fee structures, the approach, and the attitude—but not fully. It was already starting to become a distinctive, hybrid model, something that was related to but not quite like film distribution and related to but not quite like gallery representation.

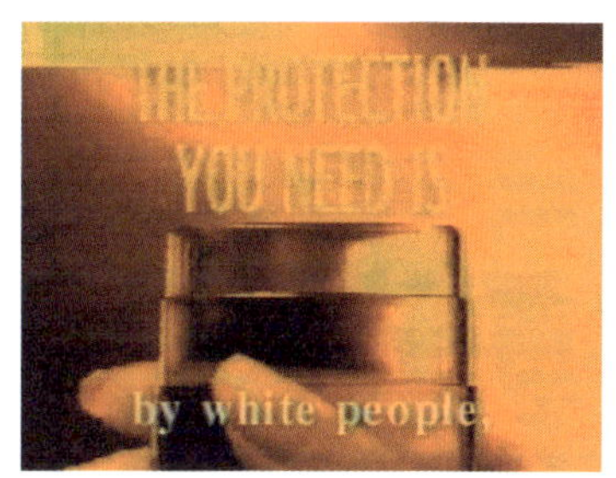

00:30

AK – How did EAI fit into the ecosystem of the New York art scene at that time? It was filling a need and wasn't doing what the galleries were doing, but was it in conversation with other art spaces? Along the lines of hybridity, it sounds like several other spaces kind of grew out of EAI. And likewise, other spaces were being founded around the same time like White Columns and Artists Space, or even Dia Art Foundation. And today you're located in Dia's Chelsea building.

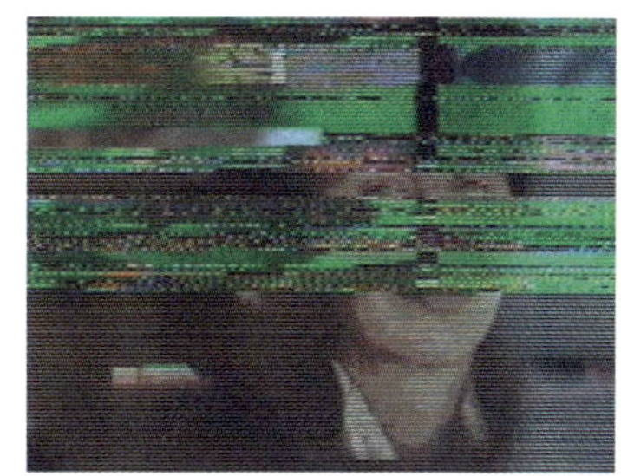

21:07

LZ – Not being there at the time, I can't say concretely, but EAI was very closely associated with all of the other video or time-based media organizations: Global Village, the Kitchen,

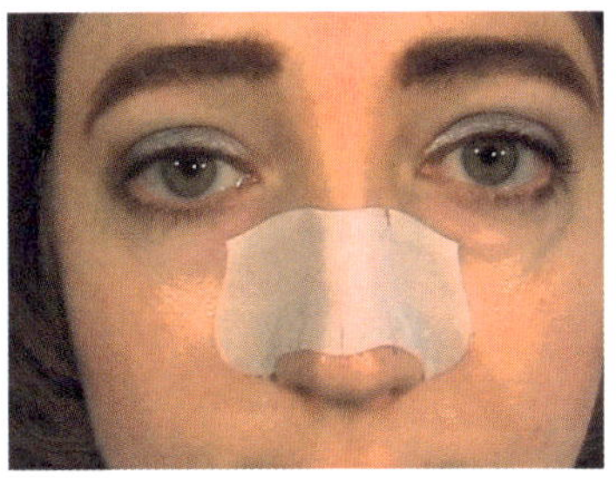

01:19

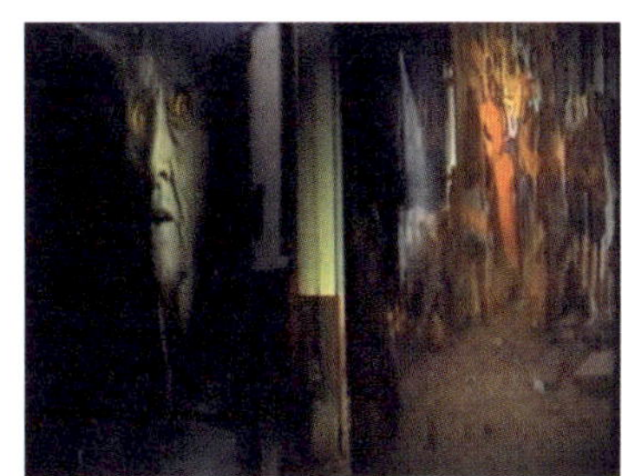

00:16

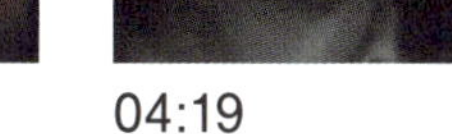

04:19

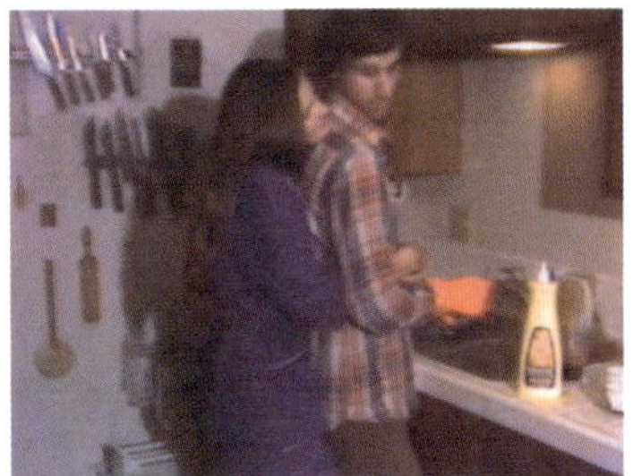
01:31

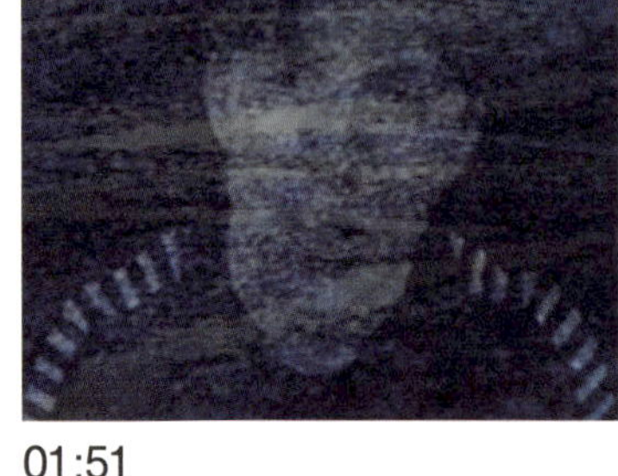
01:51

06:06

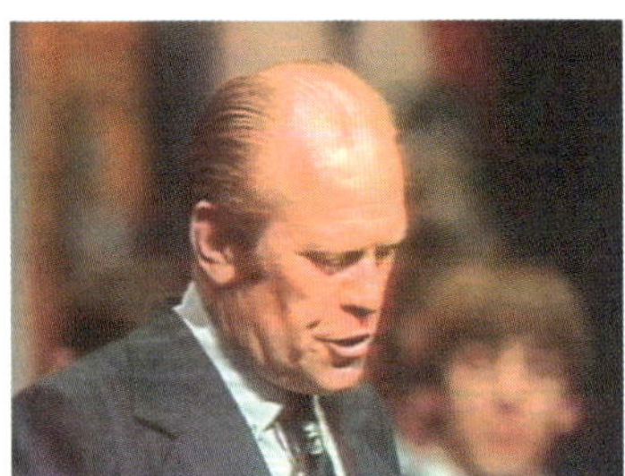
14:15

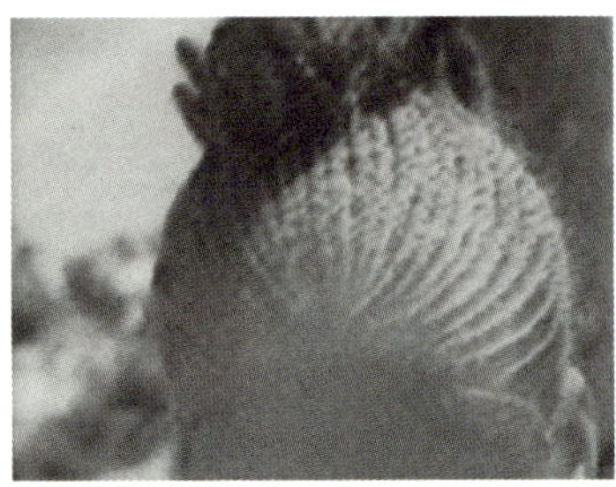
17:39

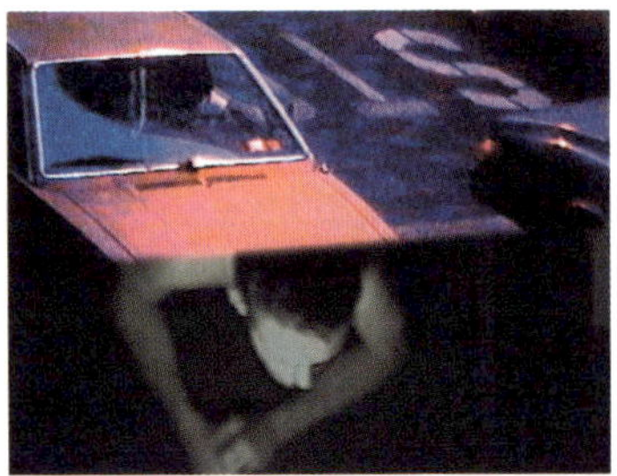
07:27

Anthology Film Archives, etc. Perhaps less so with Artists Space, White Columns, and other alternative exhibiting spaces. I don't see a lot of correspondence or evidence of interaction with those organizations in the 1970s.

AK – Perhaps because those organizations had a focus that was more object-based?

LZ – Yes, exactly. I feel like there were different but related alternative ecosystems. Clearly, there had to have been some interaction. Certainly there are artists that appear at all the different sites. Someone like Joan Jonas you see across multiple spaces and genres.

AK – You brought up this difference between film distribution and video distribution; there were these figures like Jonas Mekas. In New York there were film co-ops and a rigorous experimental cinema scene with its own support system. Can you talk a little more about the potential conversation between EAI and Anthology Film Archives? It's interesting to think how they could have been enmeshed, but distinguished themselves from each other in some ways.

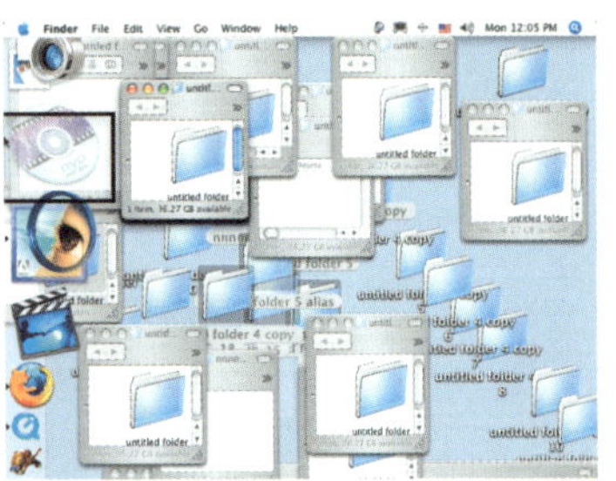
01:02

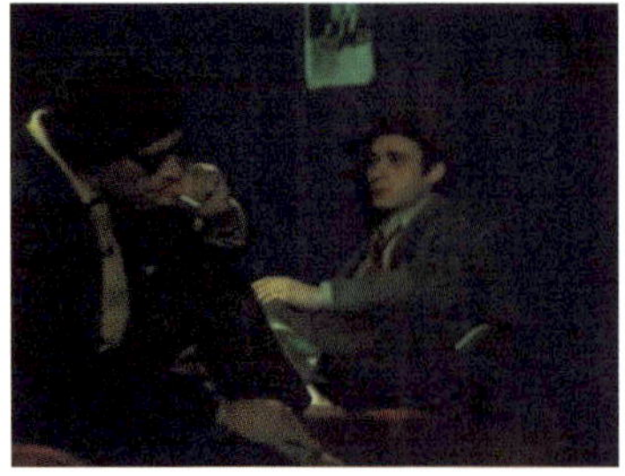
08:33

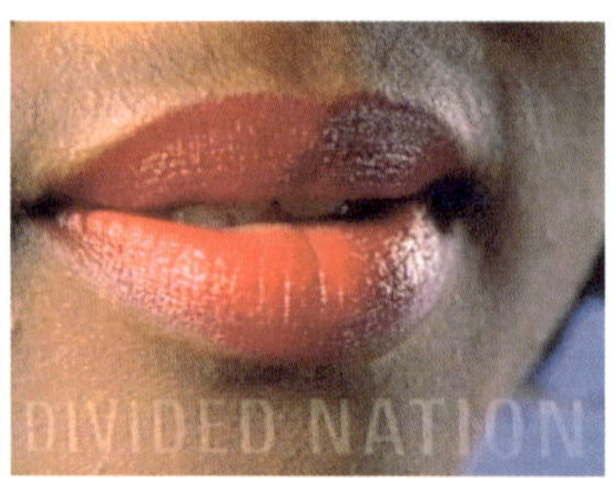

00:17

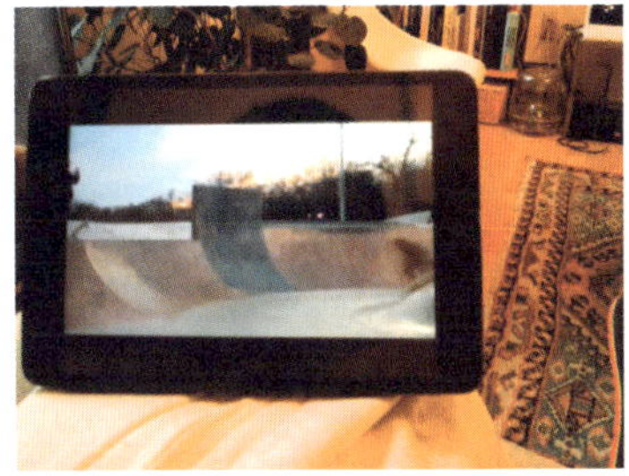

03:53

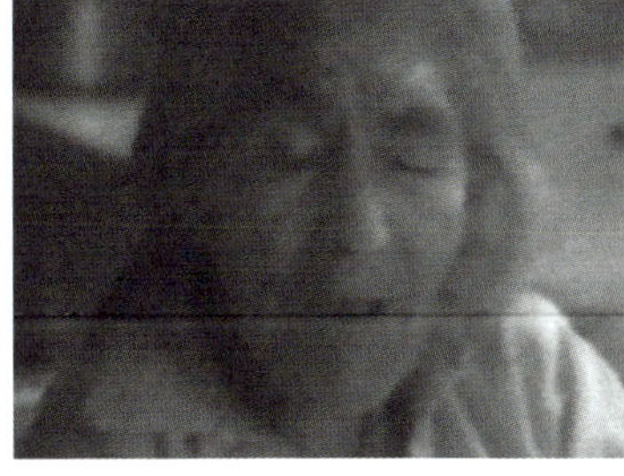

14:24

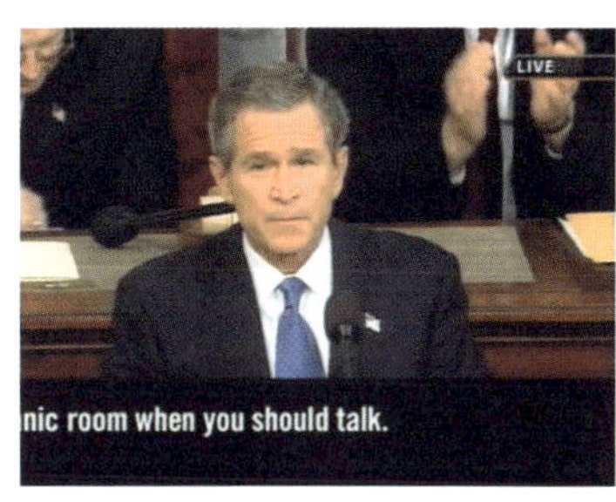

04:26

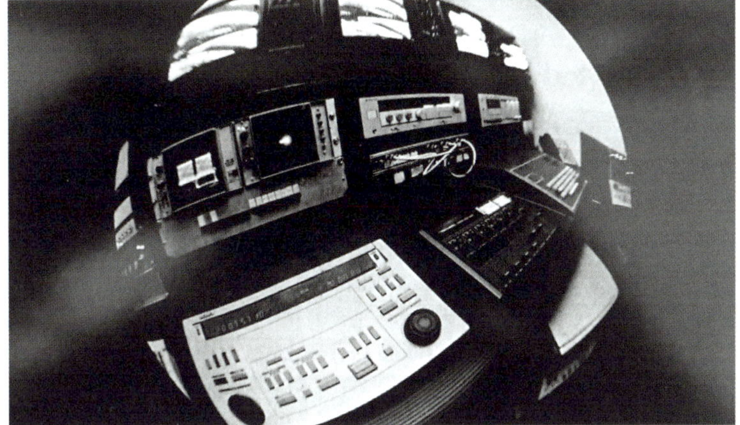

Postcard with fish-eye photograph of the EAI editing facility

00:13

00:30

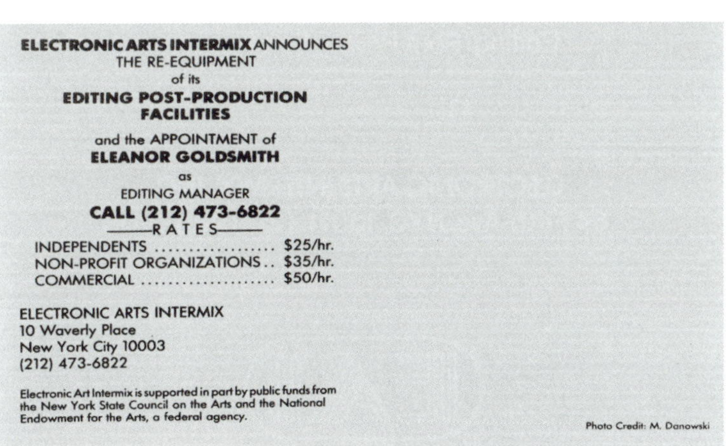

ELECTRONIC ARTS INTERMIX ANNOUNCES
THE RE-EQUIPMENT
of its
EDITING POST-PRODUCTION FACILITIES

and the APPOINTMENT of
ELEANOR GOLDSMITH
as
EDITING MANAGER
CALL (212) 473-6822

——RATES——

INDEPENDENTS .... $25/hr.
NON-PROFIT ORGANIZATIONS .. $35/hr.
COMMERCIAL .... $50/hr.

ELECTRONIC ARTS INTERMIX
10 Waverly Place
New York City 10003
(212) 473-6822

Electronic Art Intermix is supported in part by public funds from the New York State Council on the Arts and the National Endowment for the Arts, a federal agency.

Photo Credit: M. Danowski

Back of postcard advertising the EAI editing facility

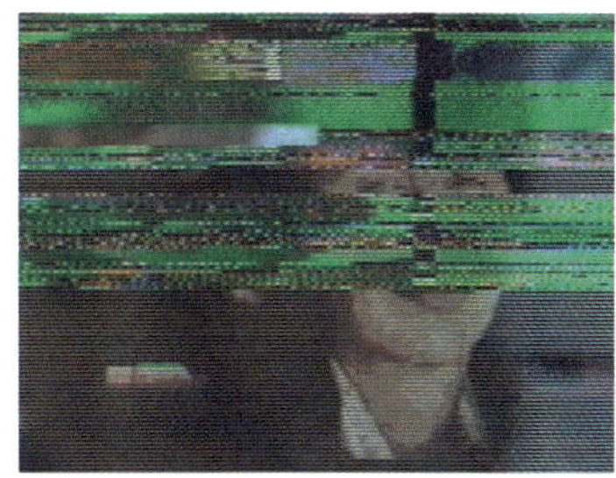

21:07

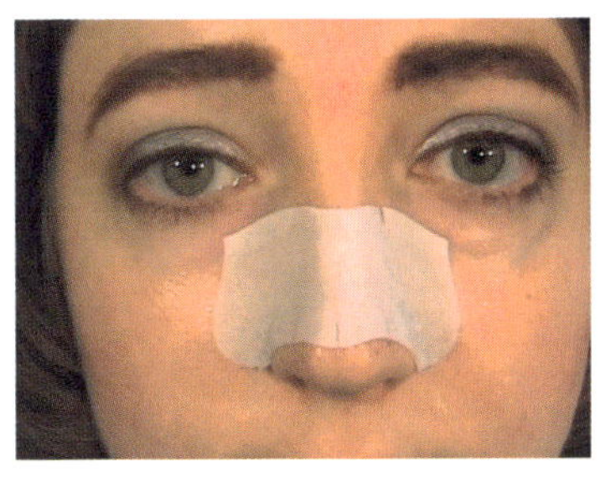

01:19

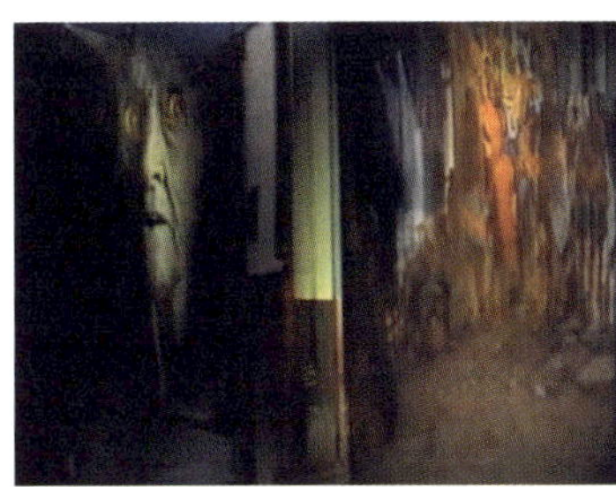

00:16

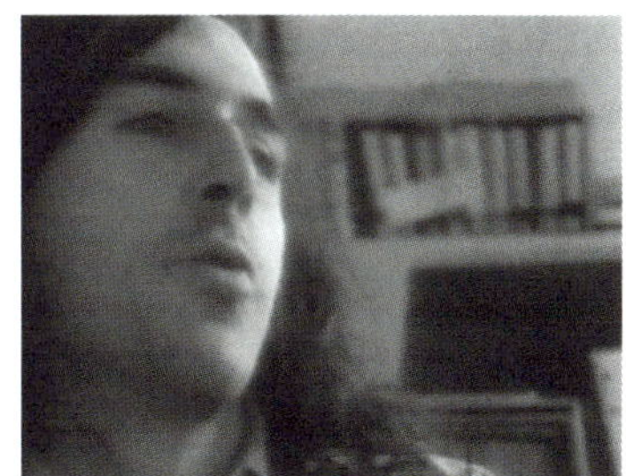

04:19

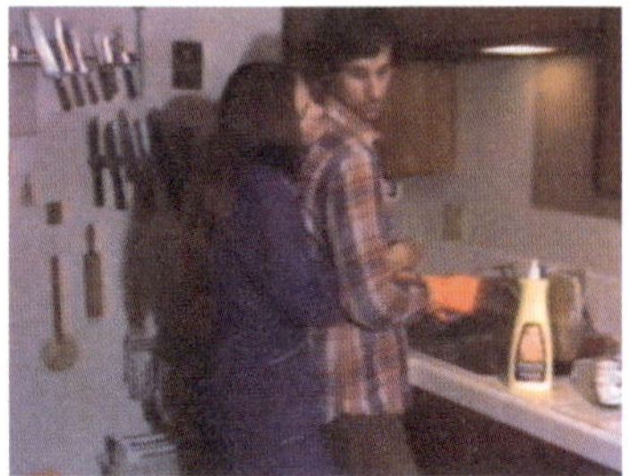

01:31

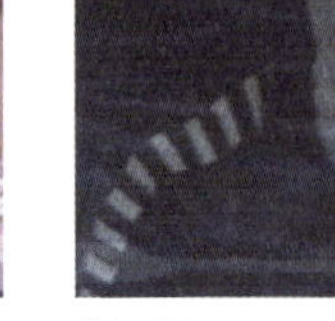

01:51

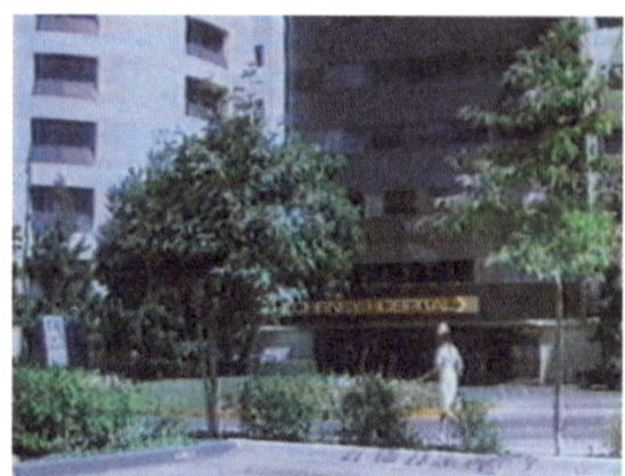

06:06

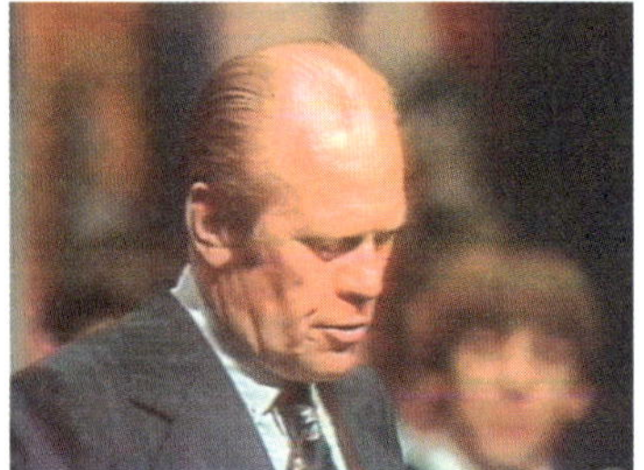

14:15

17:39

07:27

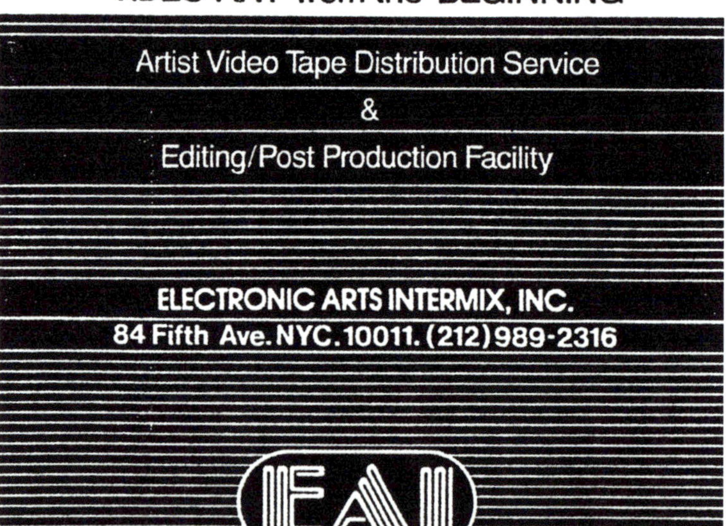

Ad for EAI's services, spring 1984

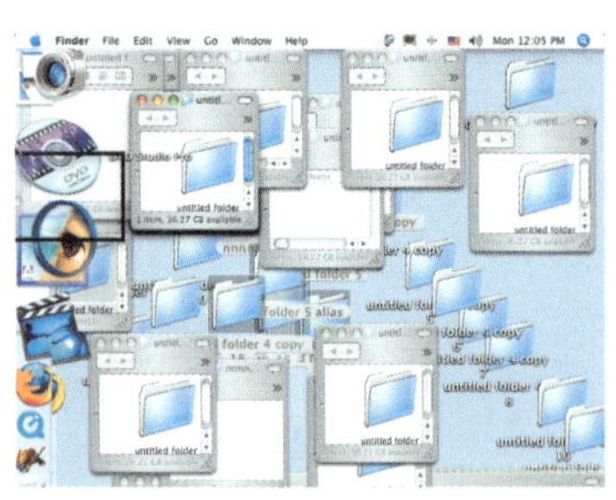

01:02

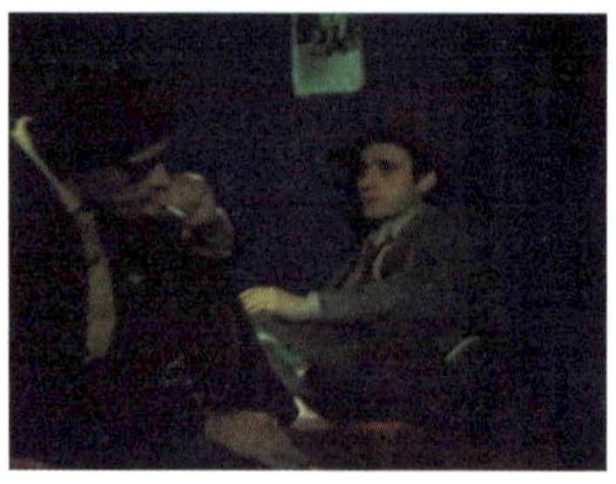

08:33

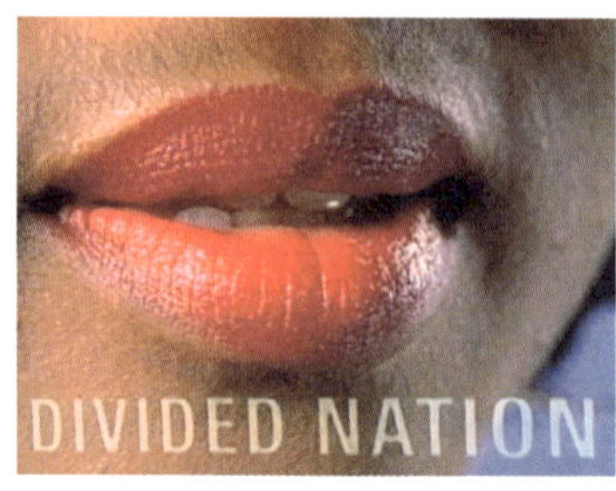

00:17

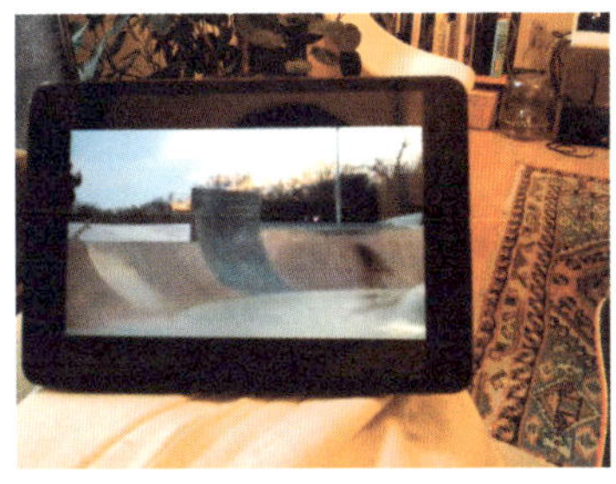

03:53

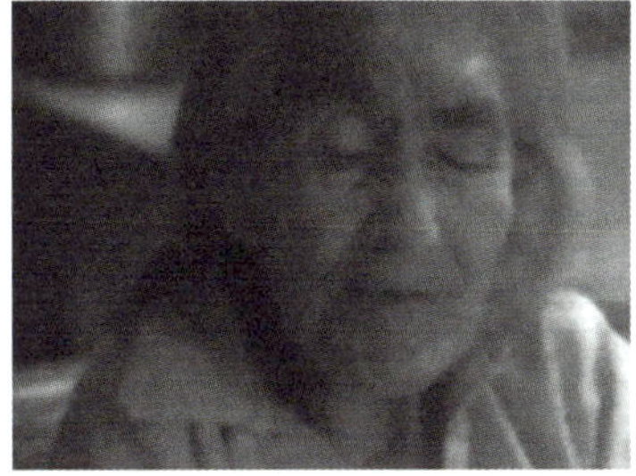

14:24

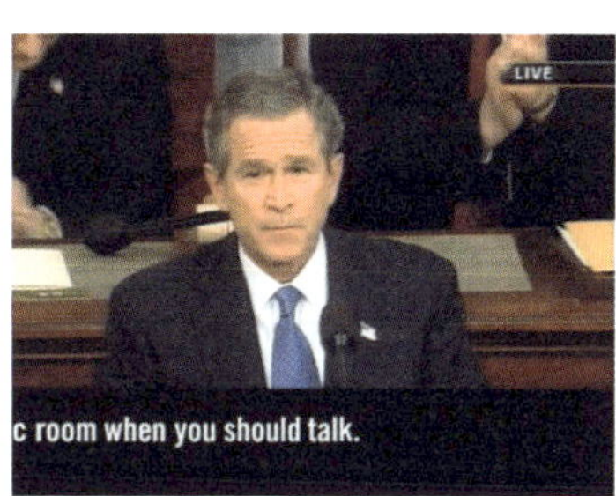

04:26

THE NEW TELEVISION:
ESSAYS, STATEMENTS, AND VIDEOTAPES BY VITO ACCONCI, JOHN BALDESSARI, GREGORY BATTCOCK, STEPHEN BECK, WOLFGANG BECKER, RENE BERGER, RUSSELL CONNOR, DOUGLAS DAVIS, ED EMSHWILLER, HANS MAGNUS ENZENSBERGER, VILEM FLUSSER, HOLLIS FRAMPTON, FRANK GILLETTE, JORGE GLUSBERG, WULF HERZOGENRATH, JOAN JONAS, ALLAN KAPROW,
A PUBLIC/PRIVATE ART
DAVID KATZIVE, HOWARD KLEIN, SHIGEKO KUBOTA, BRUCE KURTZ, JANE LIVINGSTON, BARBARA LONDON, EDWARD LUCIE-SMITH, TOSHIO MATSUMOTO, JOHN MCHALE, GERALD O'GRADY, NAM JUNE PAIK, ROBERT PINCUS-WITTEN, DAVID ROSS, PIERRE SCHAEFFER, RICHARD SERRA, ALLISON SIMMONS, GERD STERN, PAUL STITELMAN, HARALD SZEEMAN, STAN VANDERBEEK, EVELYN WEISS.

The New Television: A Public/Private Art, MIT Press, 1977

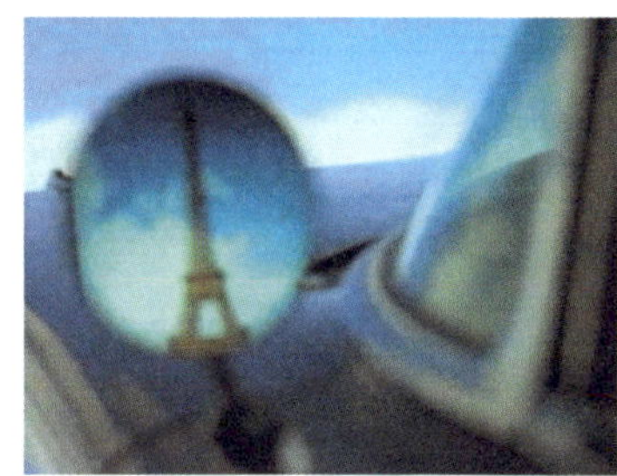

00:13

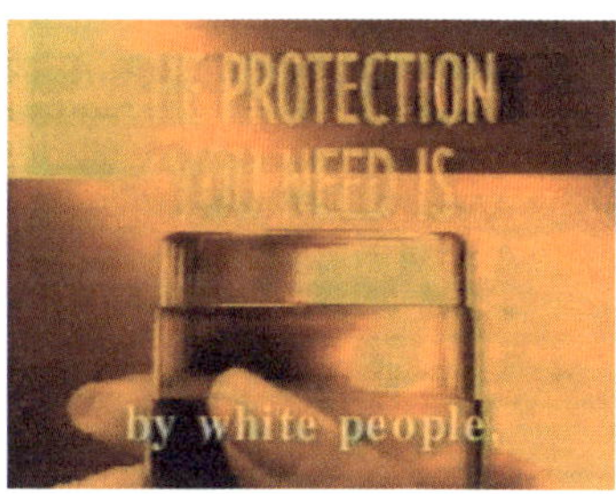

00:30

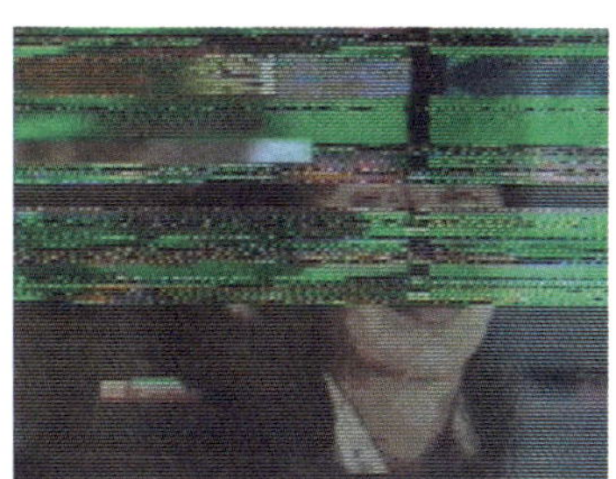

21:07

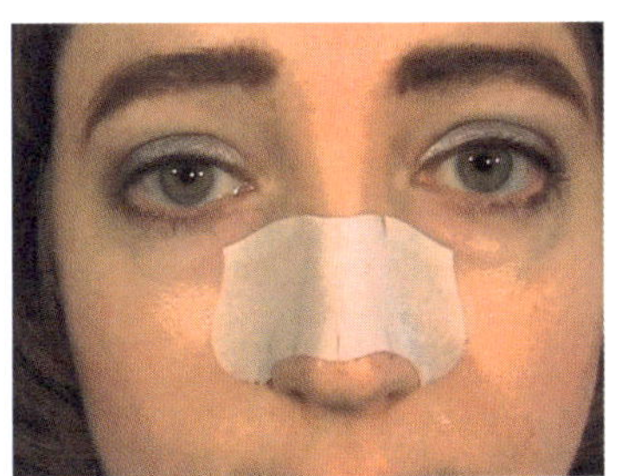

01:19

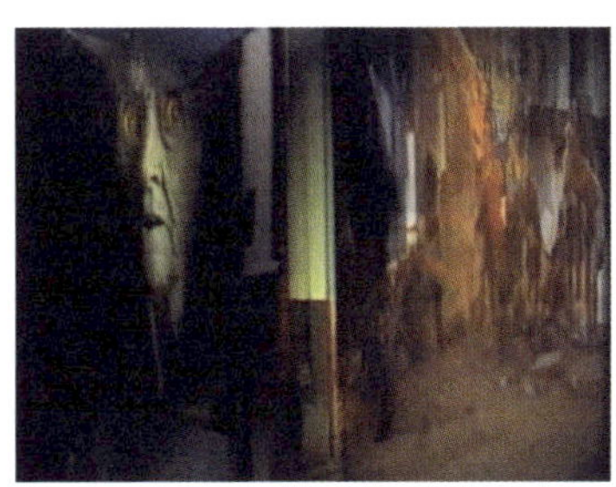

00:16

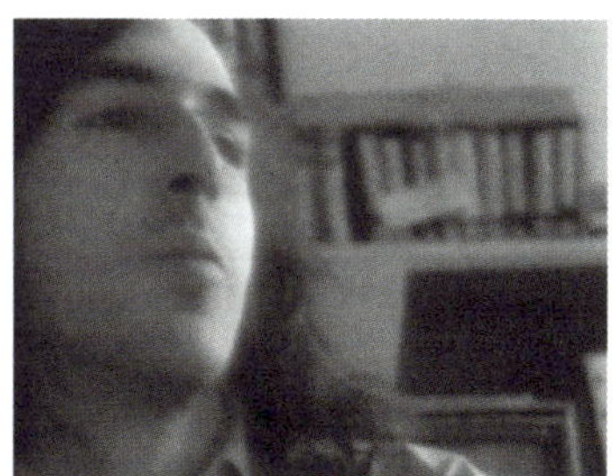

04:19

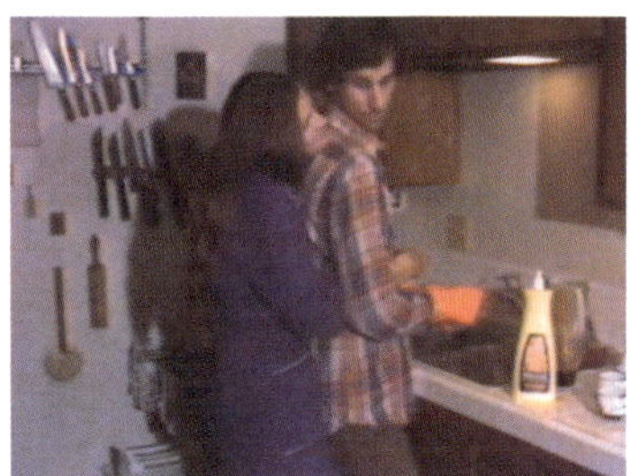

01:31

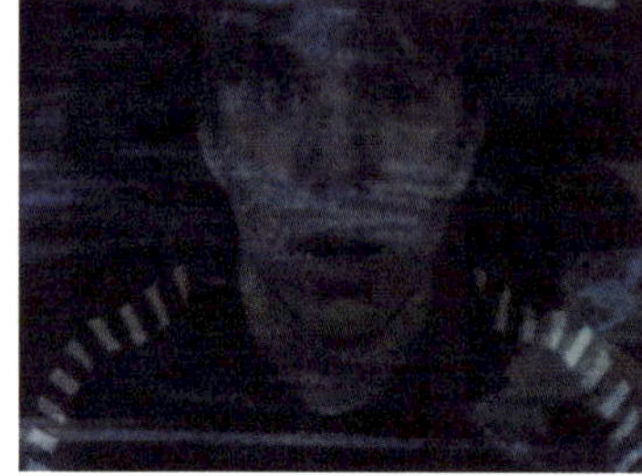

01:51

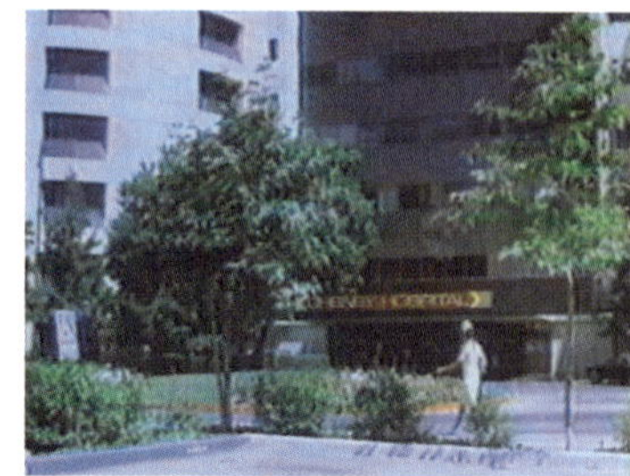

06:06

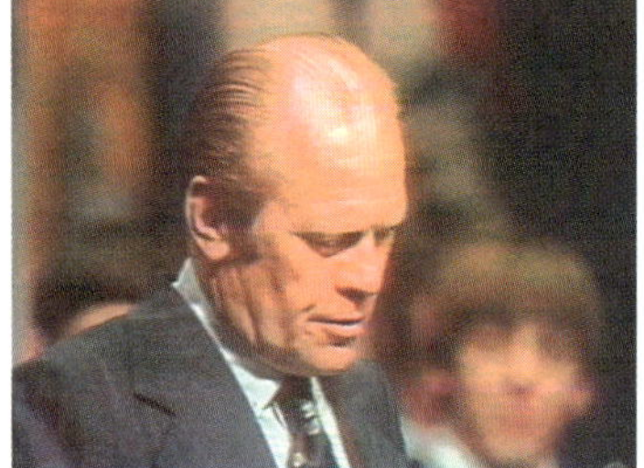

14:15

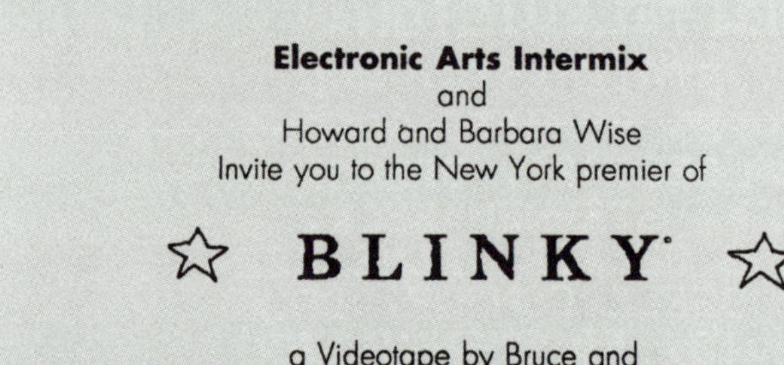

Invitation card for the premiere of Blinky, April 1989

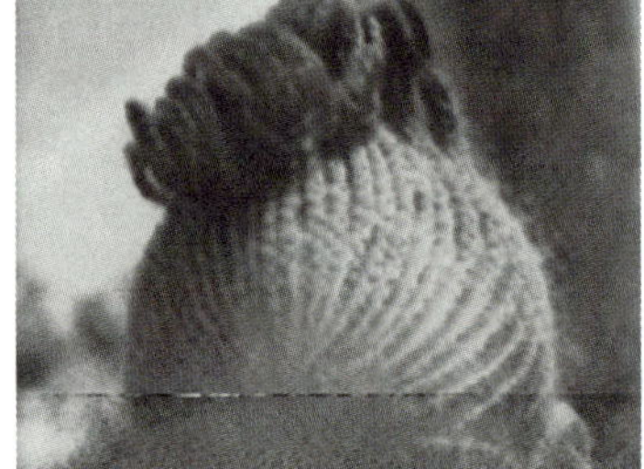

17:39

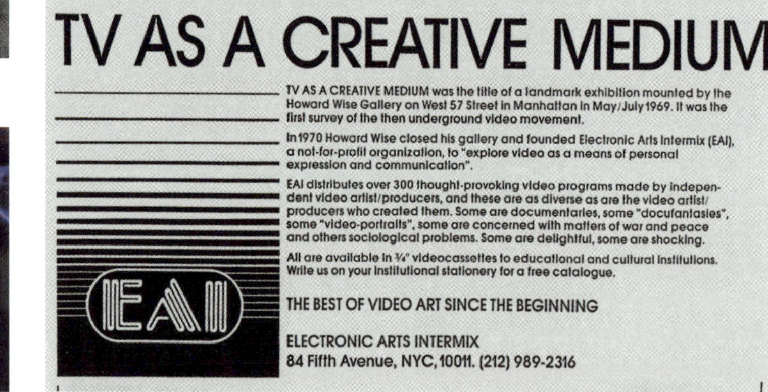

07:27

Ad for EAI, College Art Association program, 1984

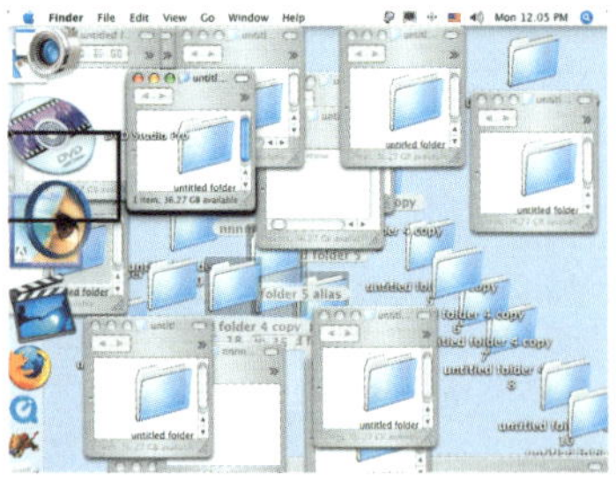

01:02

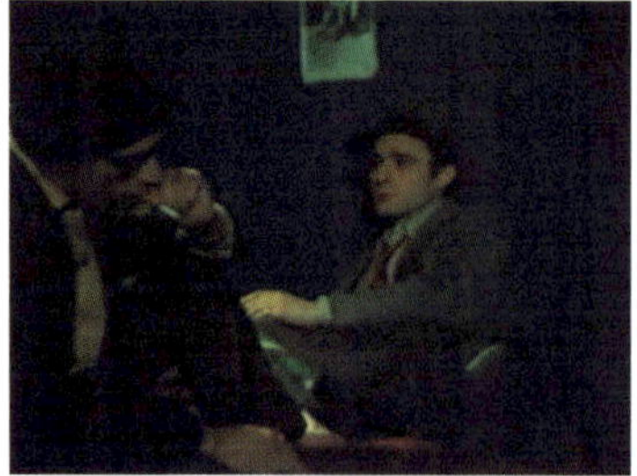

08:33

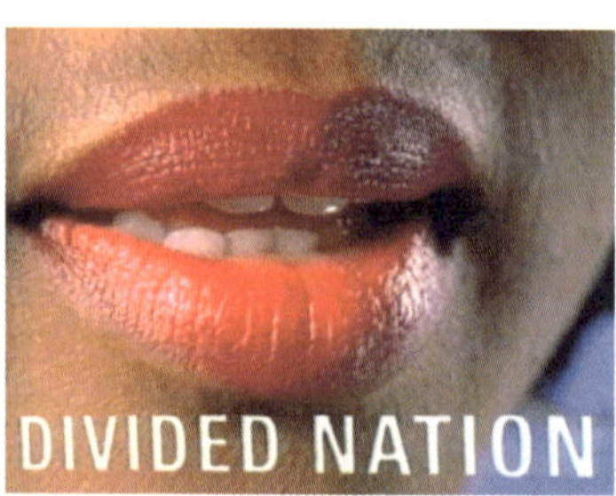

00:17

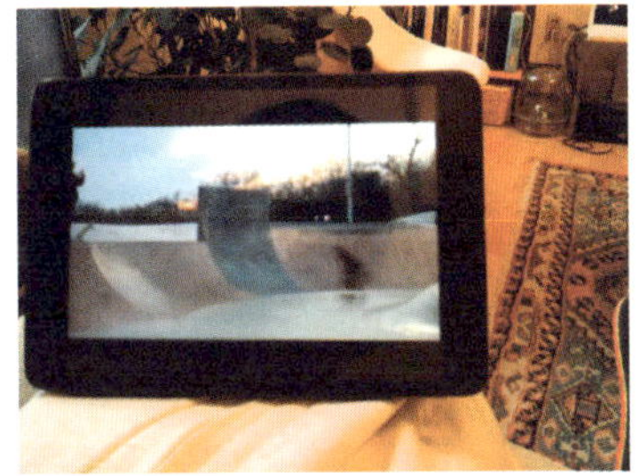

03:53

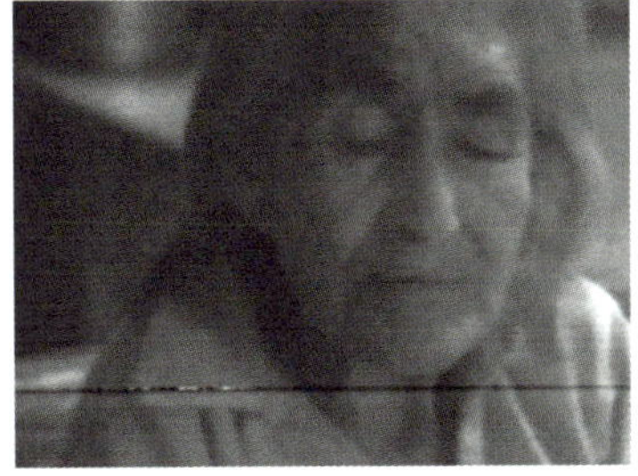

14:24

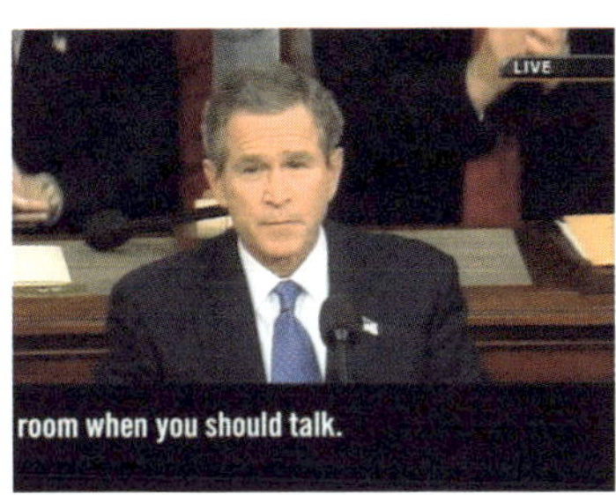

04:26

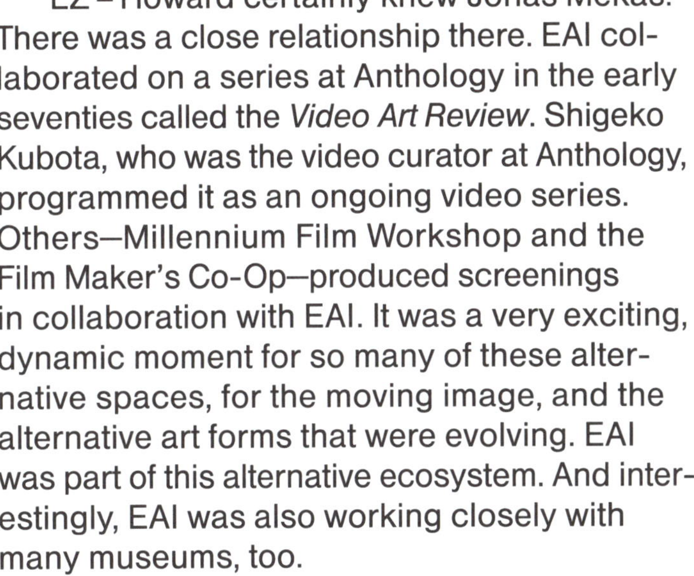

LZ – Howard certainly knew Jonas Mekas. There was a close relationship there. EAI collaborated on a series at Anthology in the early seventies called the *Video Art Review*. Shigeko Kubota, who was the video curator at Anthology, programmed it as an ongoing video series. Others—Millennium Film Workshop and the Film Maker's Co-Op—produced screenings in collaboration with EAI. It was a very exciting, dynamic moment for so many of these alternative spaces, for the moving image, and the alternative art forms that were evolving. EAI was part of this alternative ecosystem. And interestingly, EAI was also working closely with many museums, too.

Maybe because Howard already had a foothold in the art world through the gallery, EAI always had very strong ties to museums. And this was fostered through the distribution service, because it was one of the only places where you could go to get video art for exhibitions at that time. So, if a museum was doing a series of video screenings, they either came

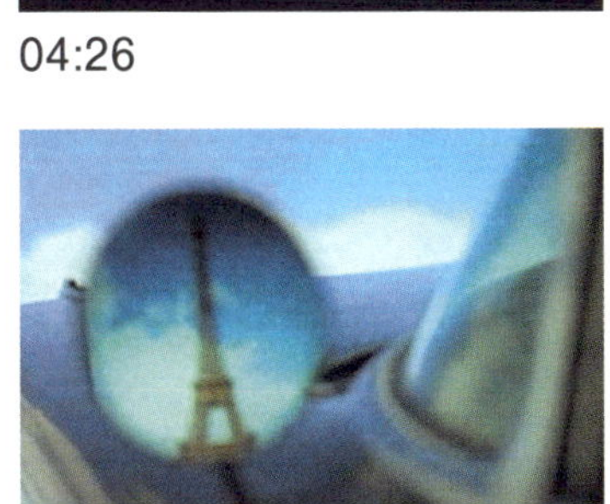

00:13

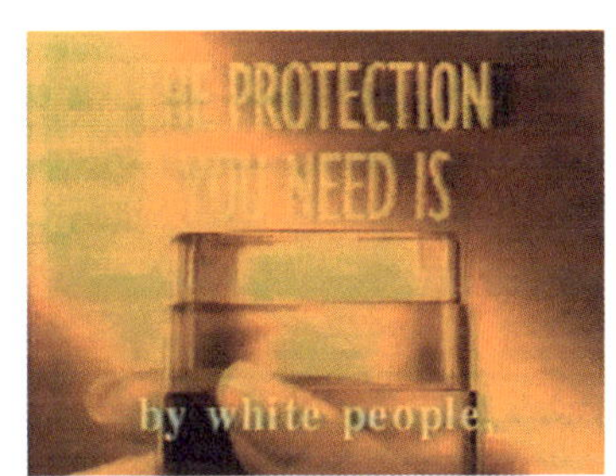

00:30

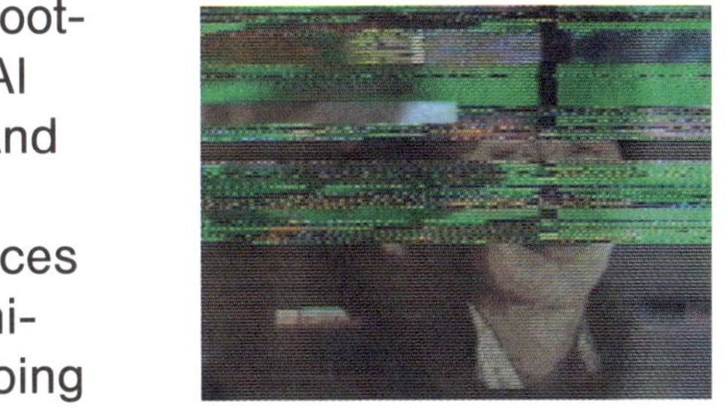

21:07

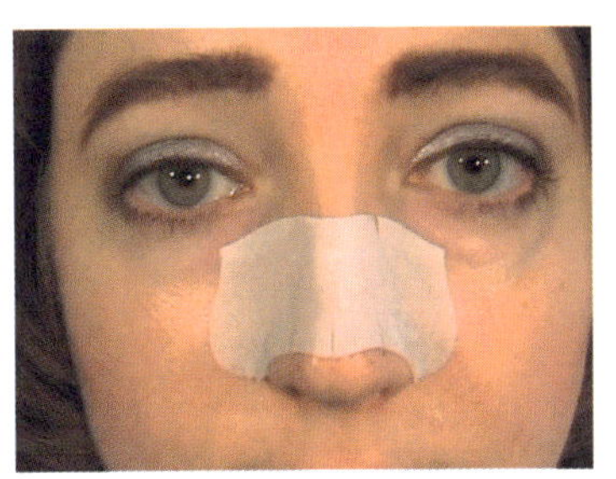

01:19

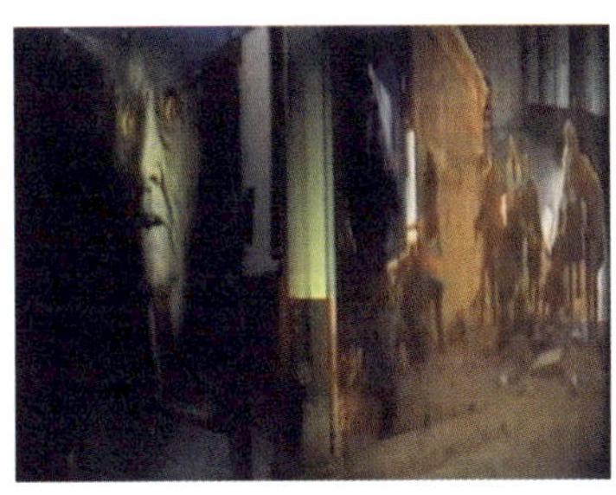

00:16

04:19

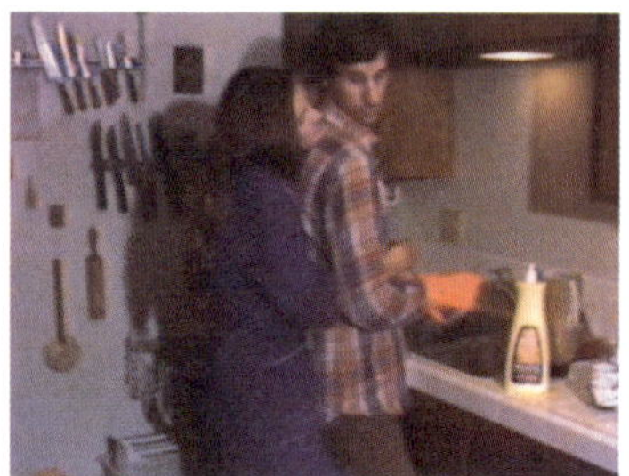
01:30

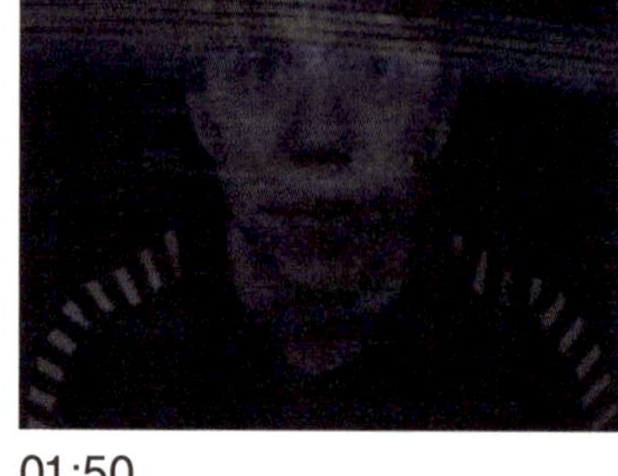
01:50

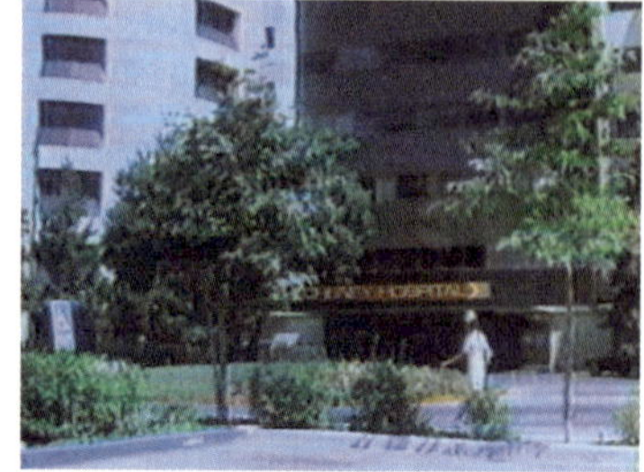
06:05

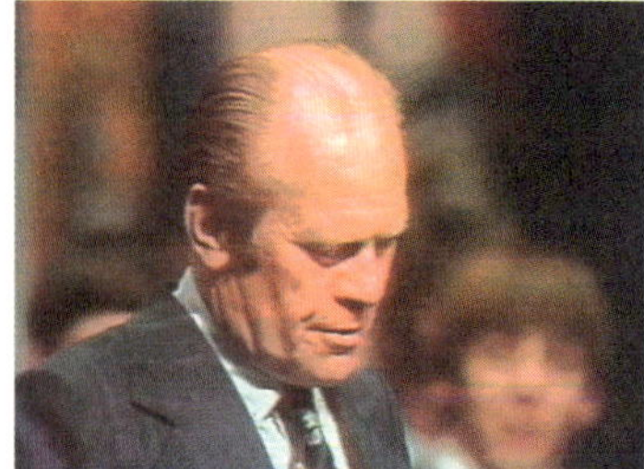
14:14

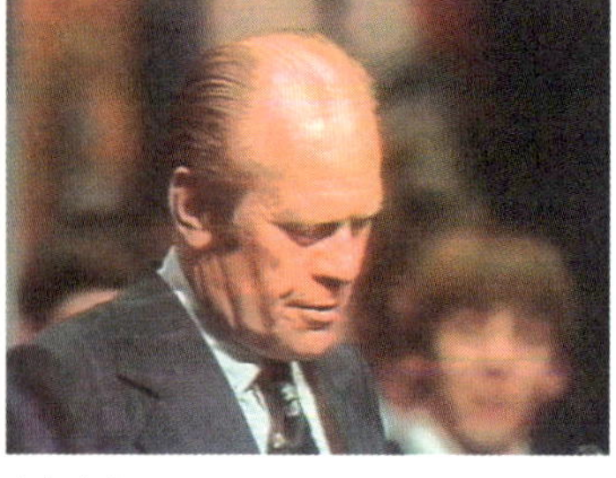
17:38

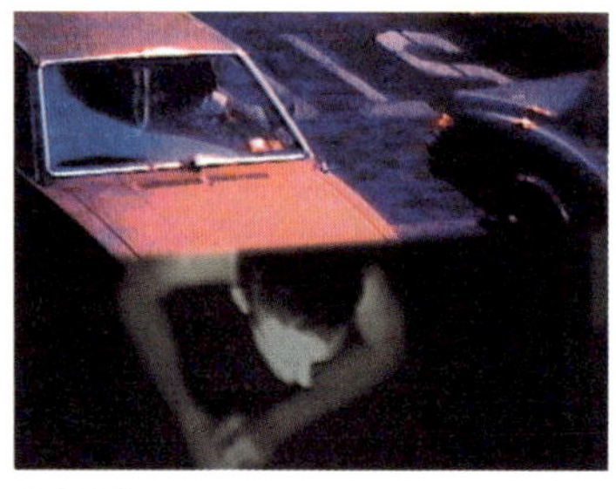
07:26

to EAI, or they went directly to the artist. Very early on there were strong ties to museums like MoMA and the Whitney Museum of American Art, going back to the early seventies. And very early on we worked with many European and international institutions. This is part of a little-known history: we had a European representative, Don Foresta, at the American Center on the Boulevard Raspail in Paris in the seventies. We had a small collection of EAI tapes at the center that he distributed to institutions throughout France. And Fujiko Nakaya—the great artist—was our Japanese representative at Scan Gallery/processart in Tokyo in the seventies. (Later, in the 1980s, we had a similar arrangement with Antoni Mercader at Videografia in Barcelona.) So that is something that speaks to the international presence of EAI very early on.

AK – So in 1973, the catalog starts, the distribution starts. At that point is EAI still on 13th Street, or has it moved?

LZ – By 1973, we're at 84 5th Avenue.

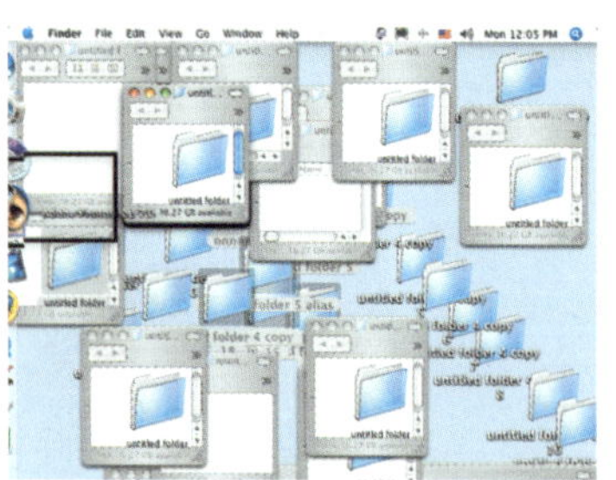
01:01

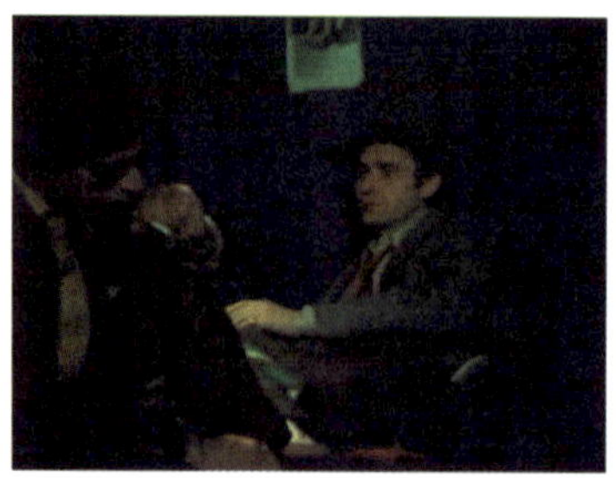
08:32

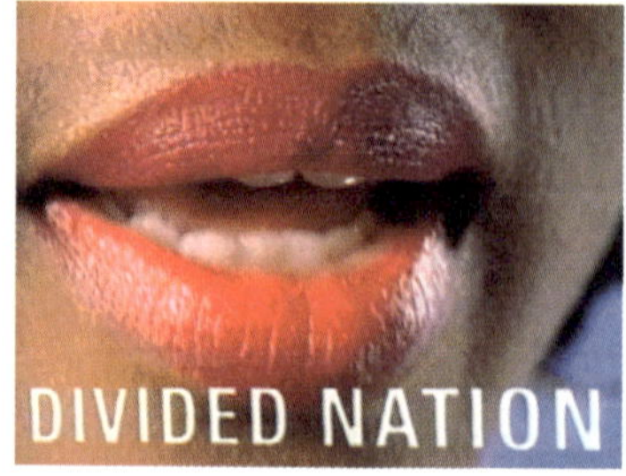

00:16

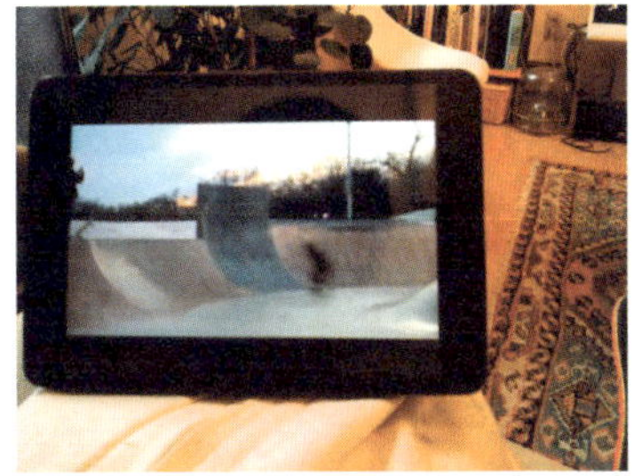

03:53

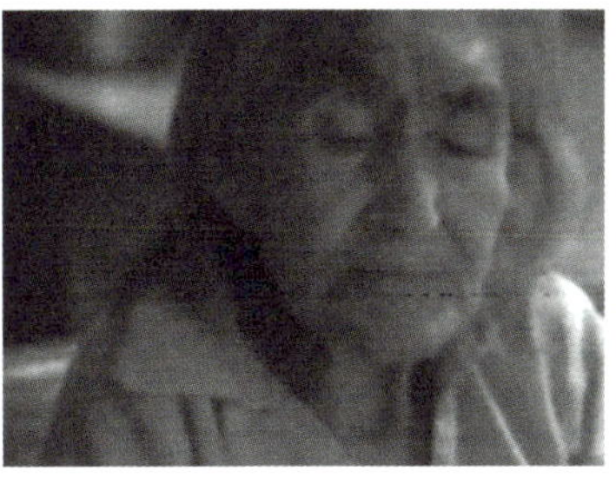

14:24

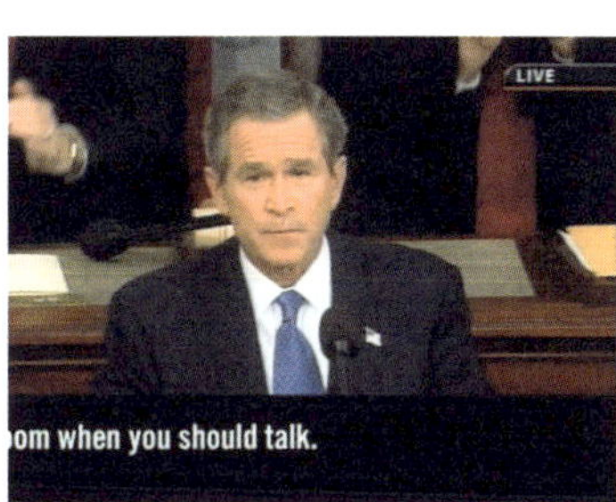

04:26

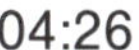

AK – So this became the hub that housed the now iconic editing suite. What was that space like? Was EAI set up to store tapes at that point?

LZ – It was primarily an office space. The tape storage was metal shelving from B&H, some of which we still use, almost fifty years later! There was already a small viewing room when I got there in 1981. At that point it was one of the only places for curators, educators, and other interested individuals to see artists' video works by request, outside of a screening or exhibition situation. It was a very popular service, because anyone who was coming through New York who wanted to see video art knew to come to EAI. We always had international visitors and those from across the country. There was also the editing room. At that point, by the time I got there, it was 3/4-inch editing—brand new 3/4-inch decks!

AK – And was it set up to work with one artist at a time?

LZ – Yes, exactly. And there was another dubbing station, for distribution—two more 3/4-inch

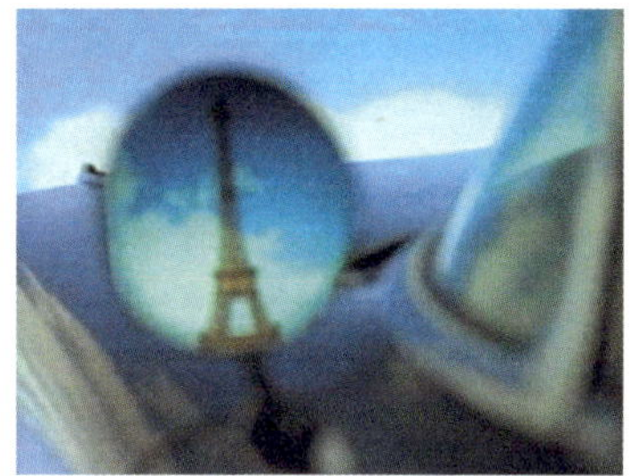

00:13

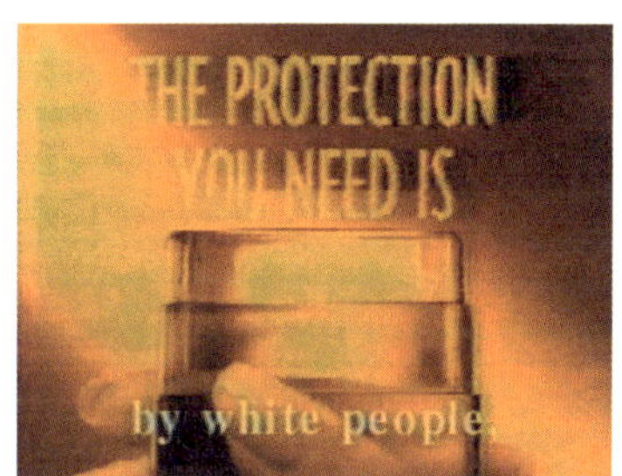

00:30

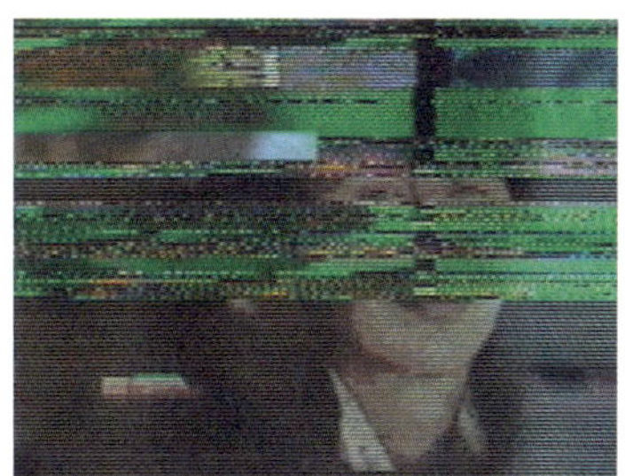

21:07

01:19

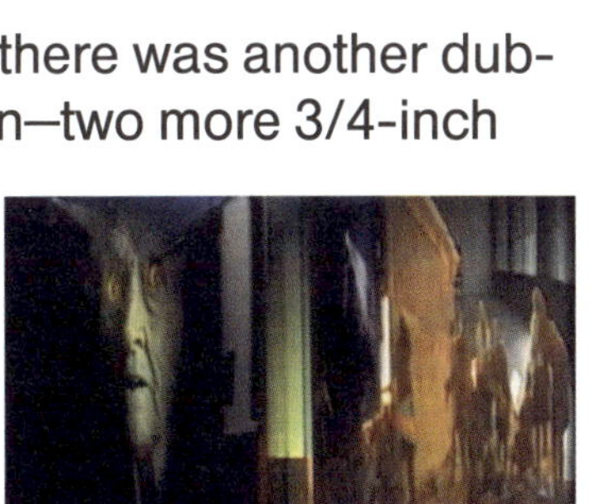

00:16

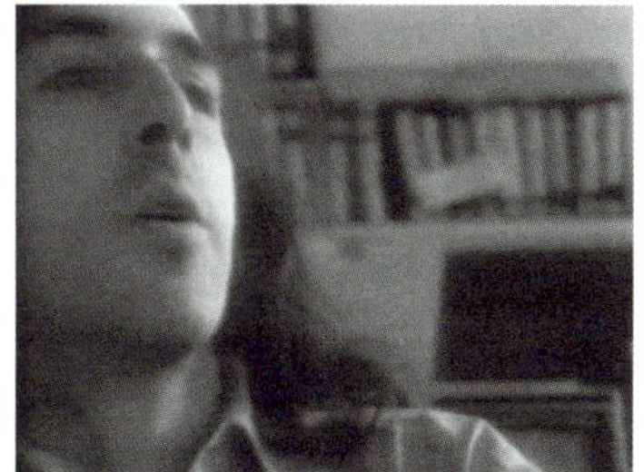

04:19

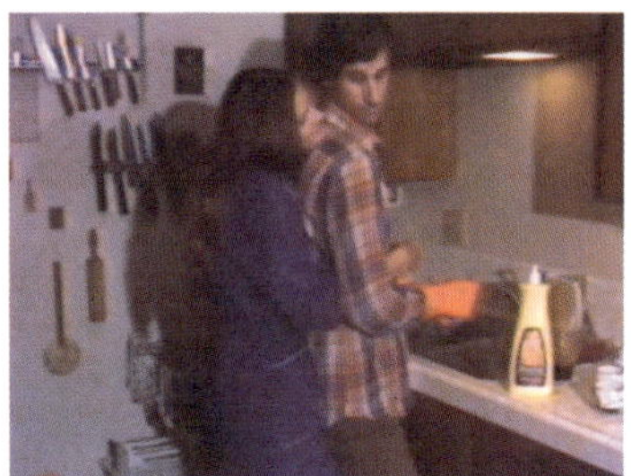

01:30

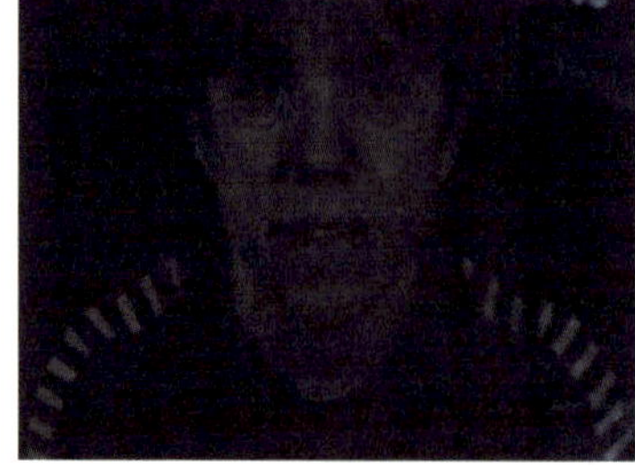

01:50

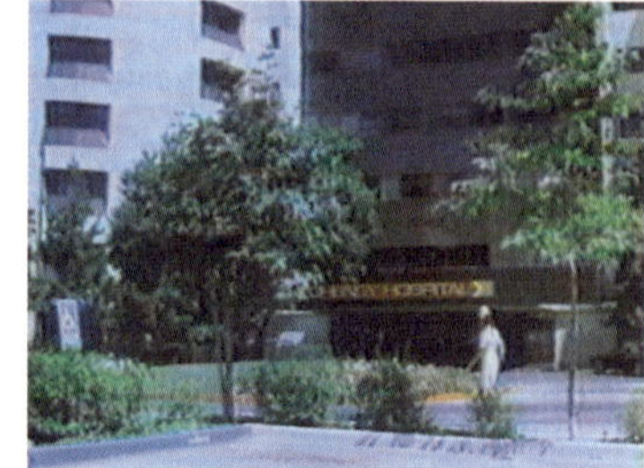

06:05

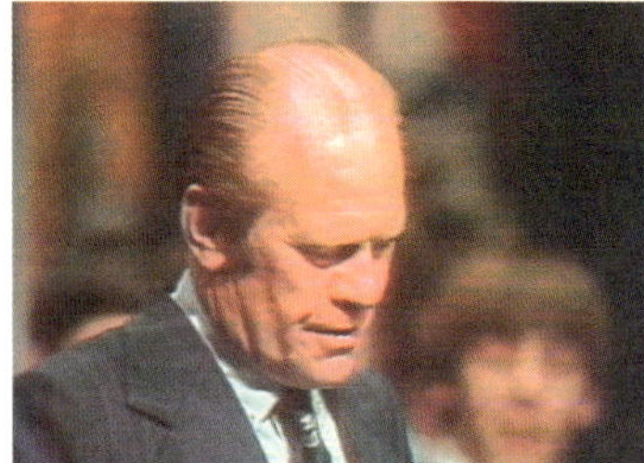

14:14

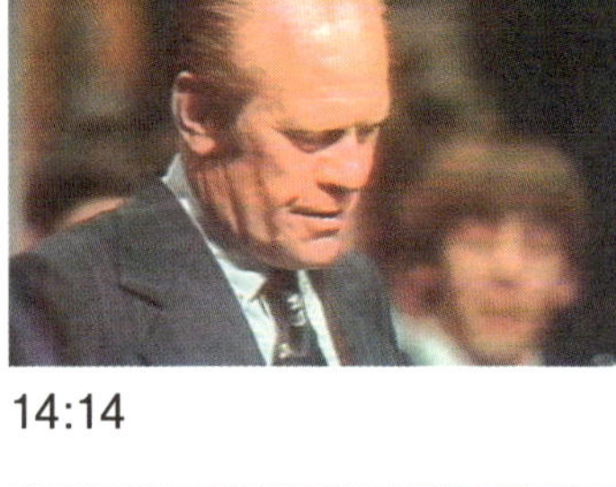

17:38

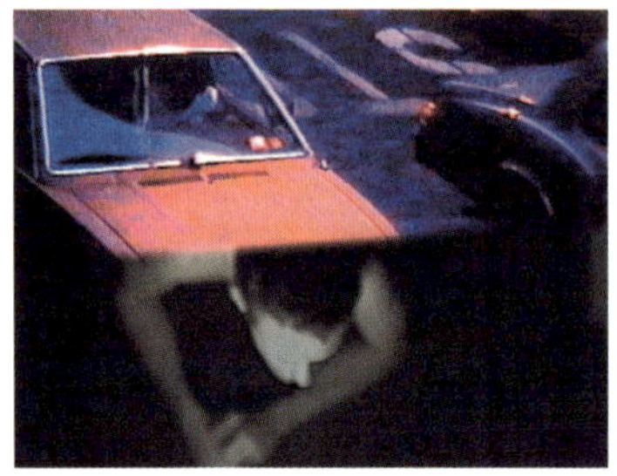

07:26

decks. And then offices, with a big Xerox machine. Howard still had an office at that point. But it was more office space than anything else. There was a tape library, which was the shelving with artists' master tapes, screening copies, and in-house copies. There was no sense at that time of archival storage. But there was a fairly sophisticated library system for identifying master tapes and tracking copies; it was an arcane system where every artist had a unique number, then the tape by that artist had a unique number, then the dubbed copy also had a unique number.

AK – Do you still have this system?

LZ – We kind of do, actually. It was an analog precursor to our archival database. We still have the original library cards that track the early tapes, which compose, in effect, the first database of the collection.

AK – Who were the early artists that EAI distributed?

LZ – *Ant Farm's Dirty Dishes* (1971) by the collective Ant Farm is Tape 001 in the collection.

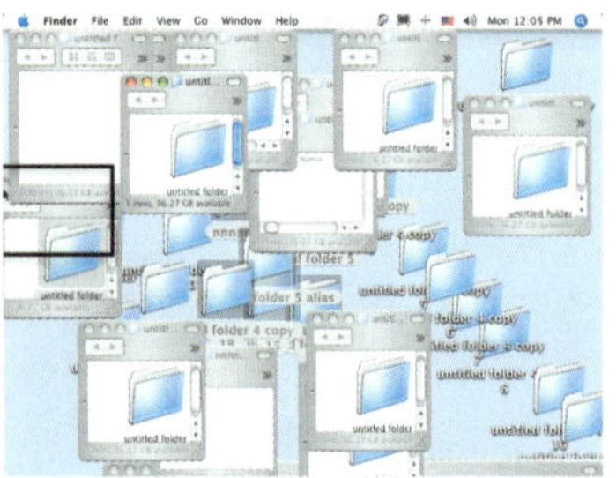

01:01

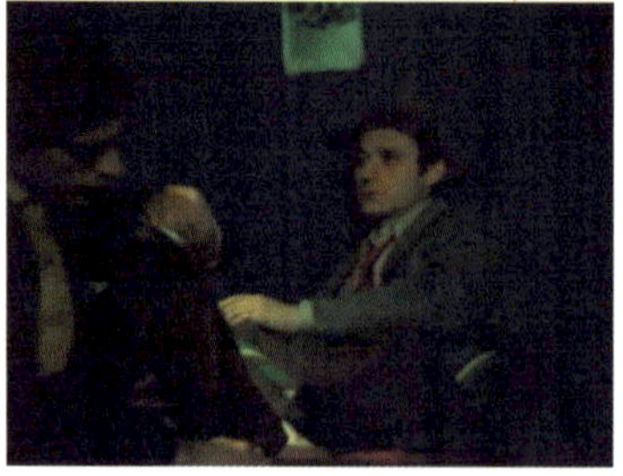

08:32

00:16

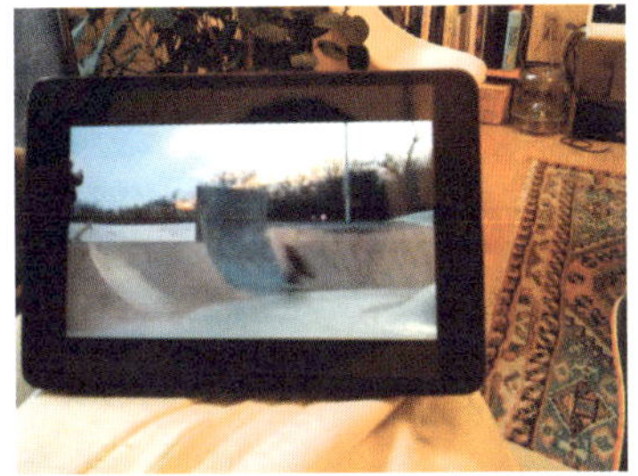
03:53

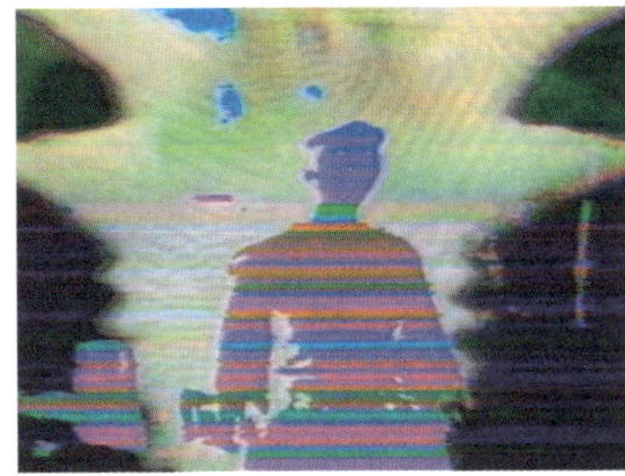
14:24

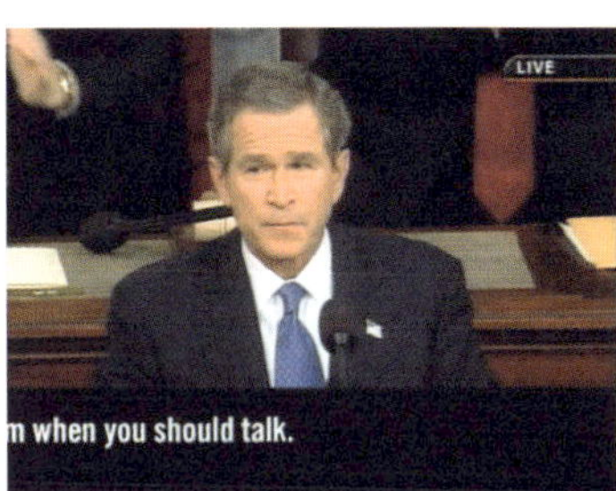

04:26

Nam June Paik, Peter Campus, Shigeko Kubota, the Vasulkas, and Juan Downey were among the first artists whose works were distributed.

AK – Do you have a sense of when every work came into the catalog? It's interesting to think what the landscape was at the time and to consider who your first fifty artists were. It points to social networks and communities, as well as what was in vogue.

LZ – There was a graduate student, Kara Malssen, from MIAP (New York University's Moving Image Archiving and Preservation Program) who did her thesis on the development of the early EAI distribution collection. Through research into that early card catalog and library numbering system, she was able to identify the first fifty artists and the first two hundred titles. As you suggest, it tells a fascinating narrative of the communities of artists and activists who were engaging with video in the early years. Now we're able to track those histories through our database of the collection, which in many ways grew out of that first card catalog.

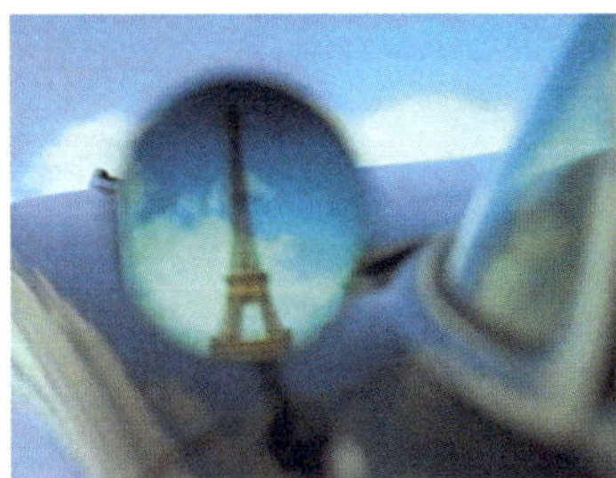
00:13

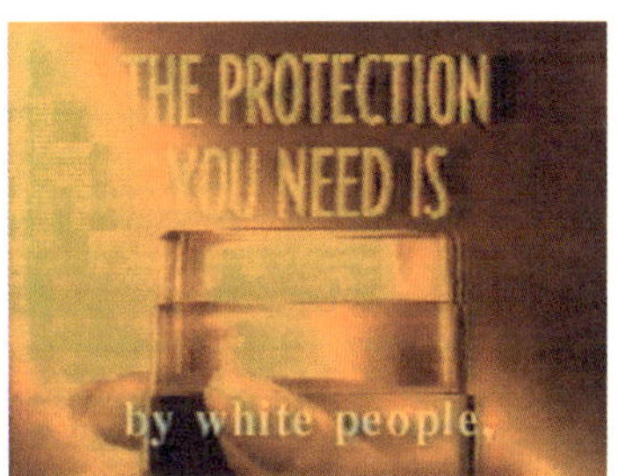

00:30

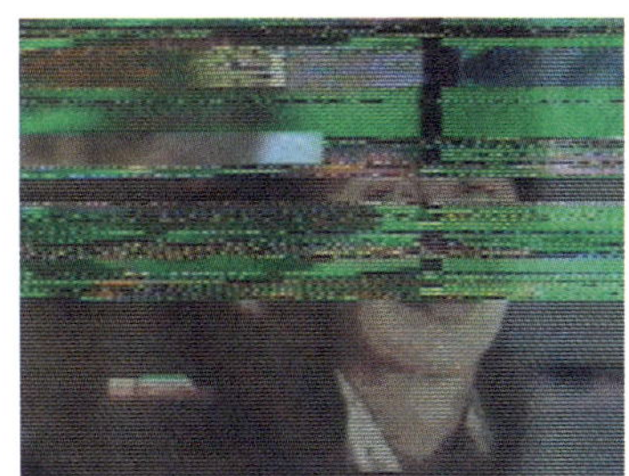
21:07

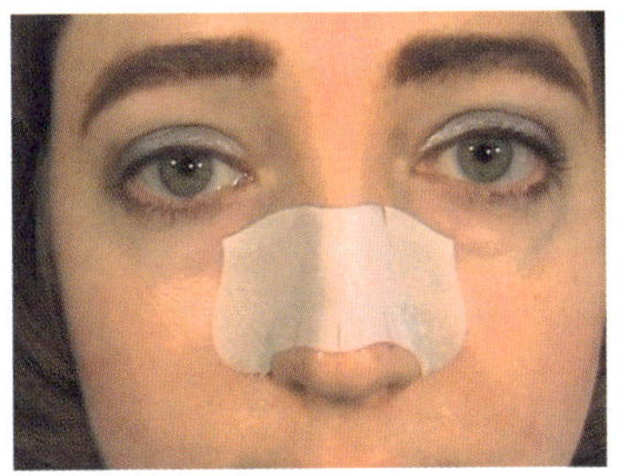
01:19

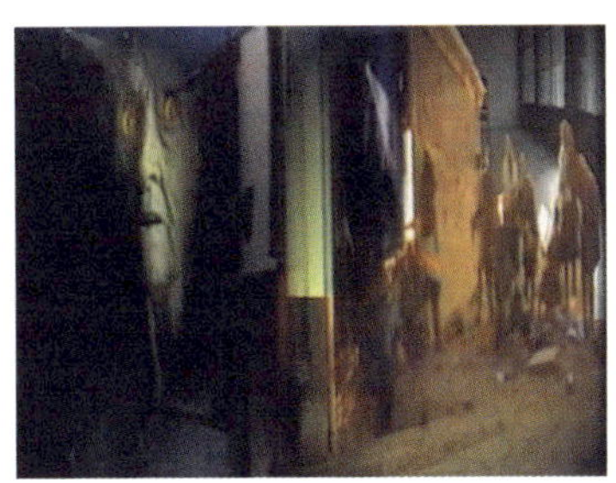
00:16

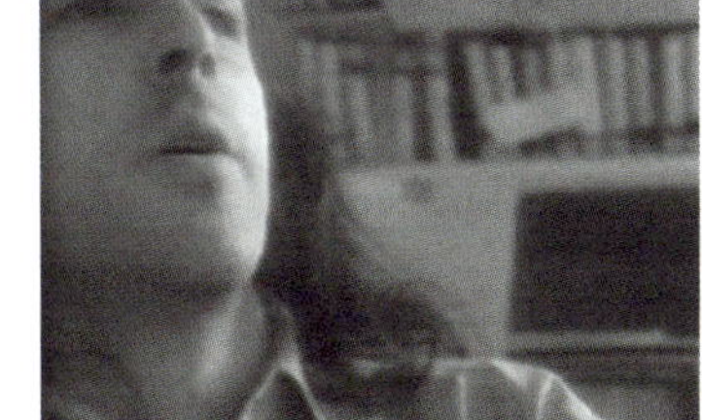
04:19

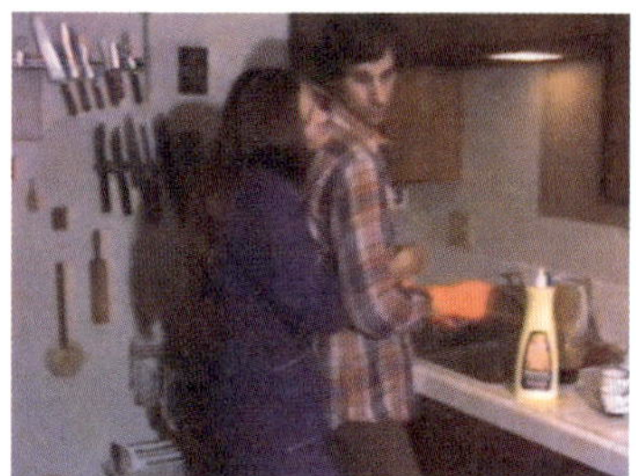

01:30

01:50

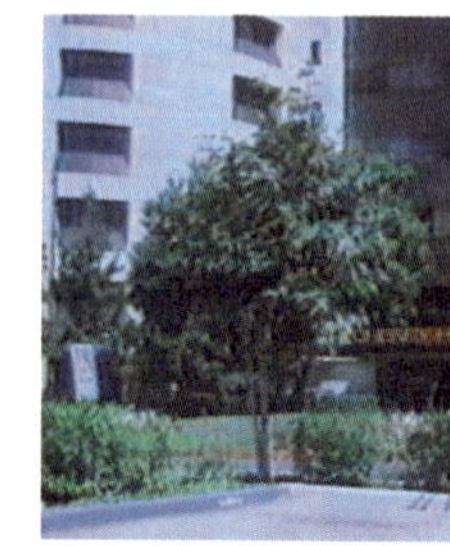

06:05

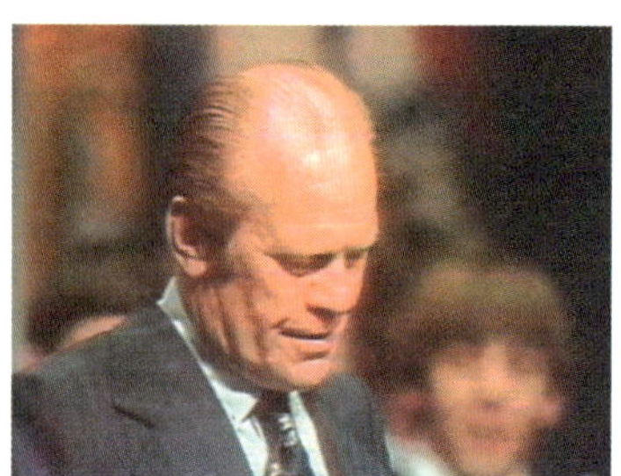

14:14

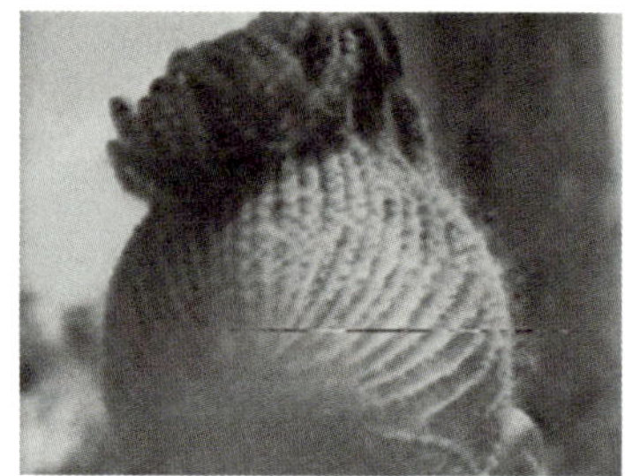

17:38

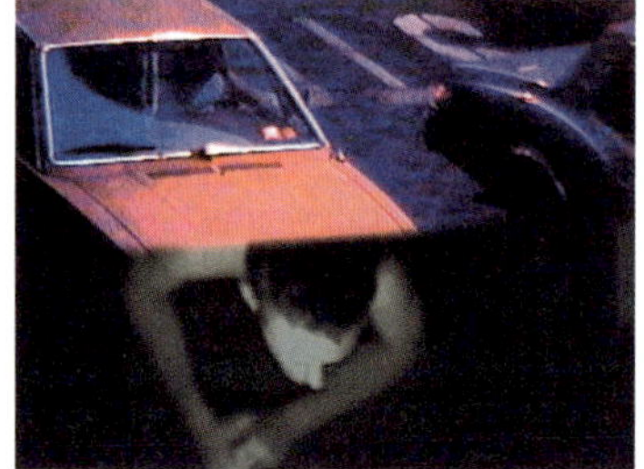

07:26

Our location at 84 5th Avenue was kind of odd. EAI was on the northwest corner of 14th Street. So, it was technically above 14th Street, but was still considered downtown. In the earliest years, when the facility offered 1/2-inch open reel editing, it was used by the first generation of pioneering video artists. By the time I got there in the early eighties, the scene had shifted. It was still a place to hang out, but it was a different group of artists, a different scene. There had been a shift in the late seventies where the artists' work had evolved with the technology, away from black-and-white Portapak performance, body art, guerrilla TV documentaries, and conceptual art. The shift to color cameras and to editing as an artistic and formal strategy—that changed everything. By the early eighties, the tide had turned away from durational or conceptual performance tapes.

When I started, in terms of editing, it was a different scene. I mean, the editing was still a primary focus of EAI in many ways. It was often around-the-clock editing. There were

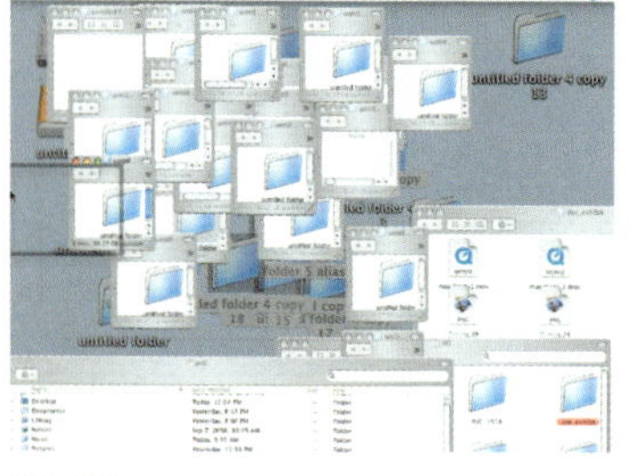

01:01

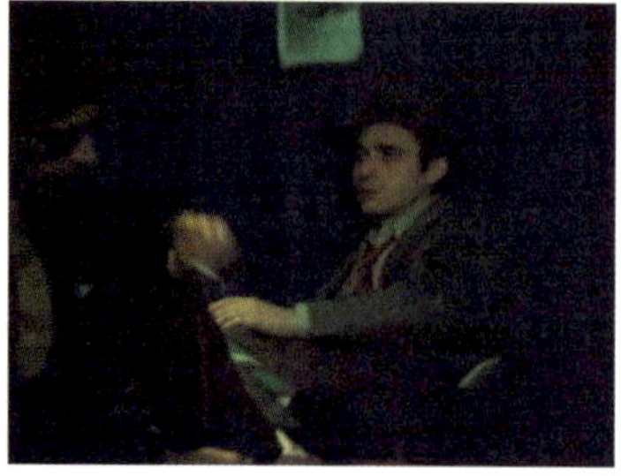

08:32

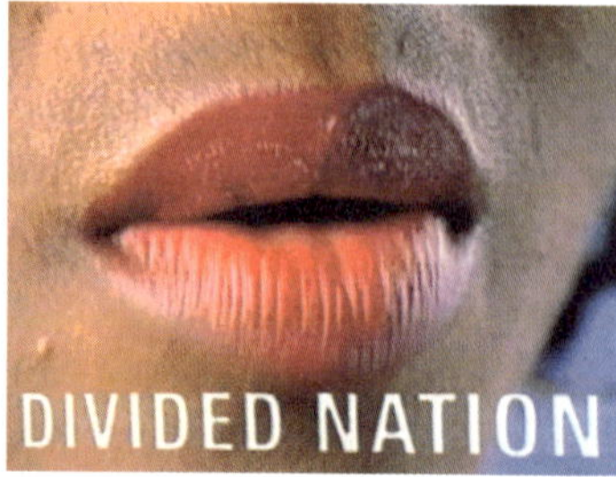

00:16

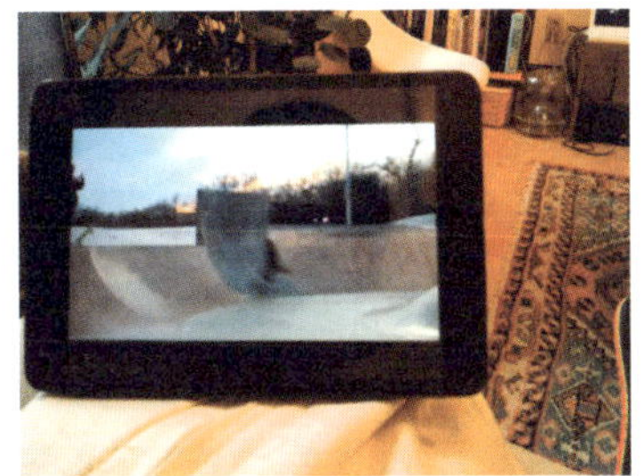
03:53

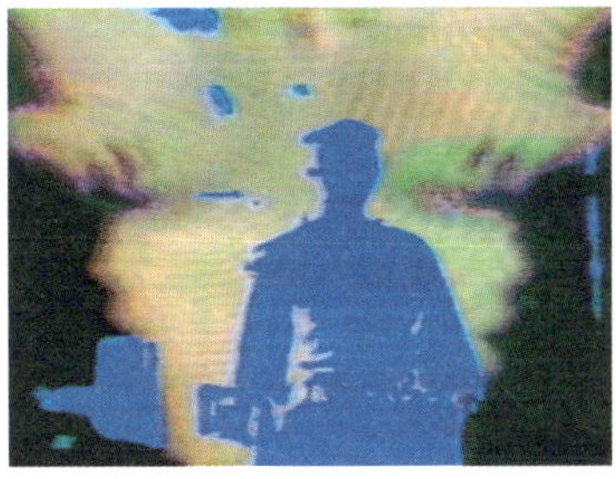
14:24

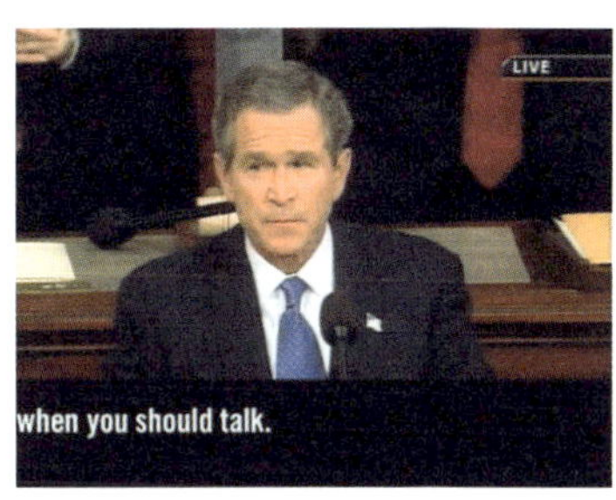

04:26

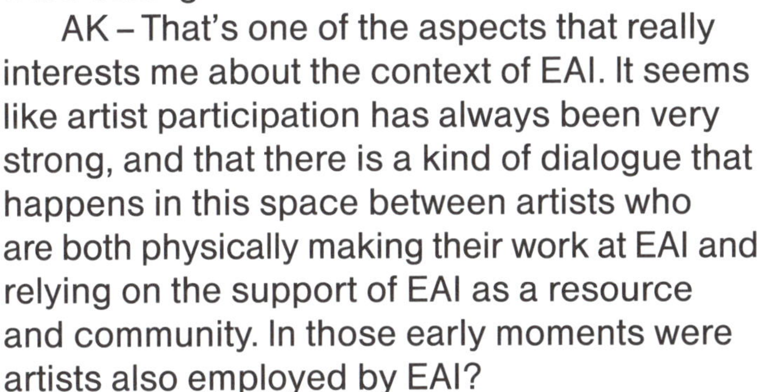

often waiting lists. There was a staff of five or so editors at any one time; it was amazing. It was club scene video, alternative music video, artists' public access cable TV projects. Artists like Tom Rubnitz, John Sex, TWINART, Mitchell Kriegman, Jaime Davidovich, Carole Ann Klonarides, Brian Eno, Nam June Paik, and Dara Birnbaum were editing.

AK – That's one of the aspects that really interests me about the context of EAI. It seems like artist participation has always been very strong, and that there is a kind of dialogue that happens in this space between artists who are both physically making their work at EAI and relying on the support of EAI as a resource and community. In those early moments were artists also employed by EAI?

LZ – Artists were always very involved and very present. Because of the intersection of editing and distribution, it's a place where artists' needs were—and still are—especially apparent. So, artists were just physically around from the very beginning, and that's something that

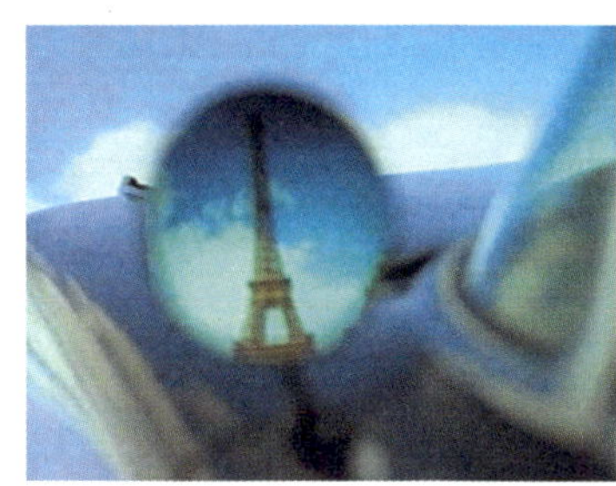
00:13

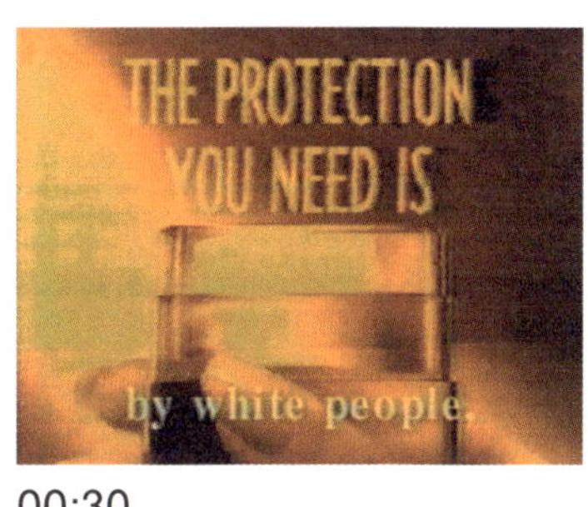

00:30

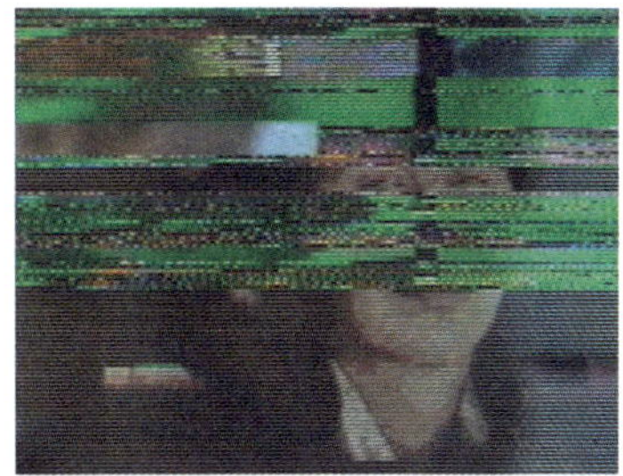
21:07

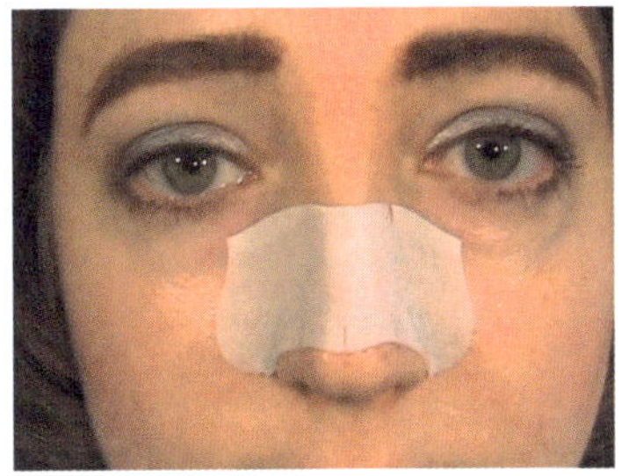
01:19

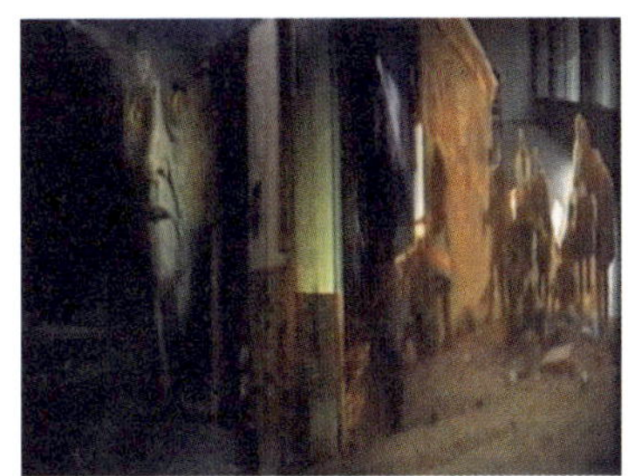
00:16

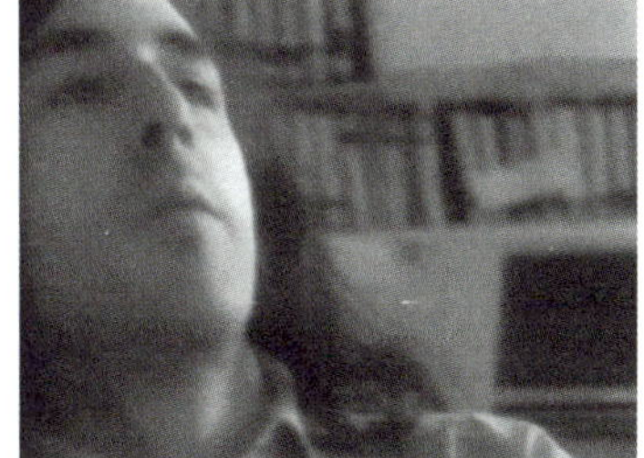
04:19

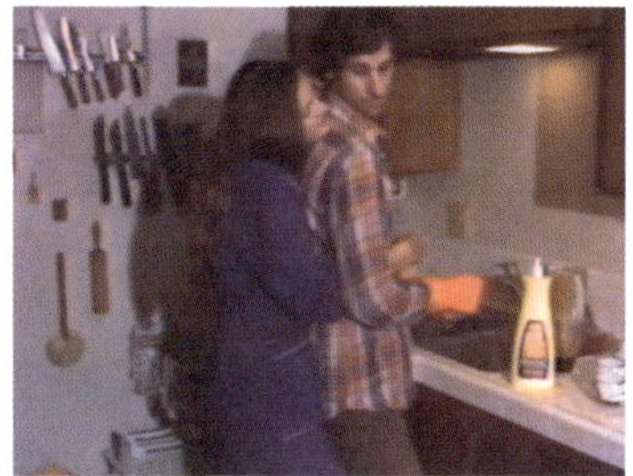
01:30

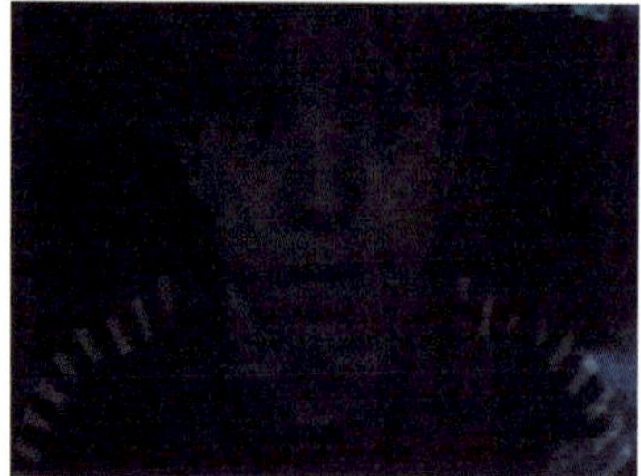
01:50

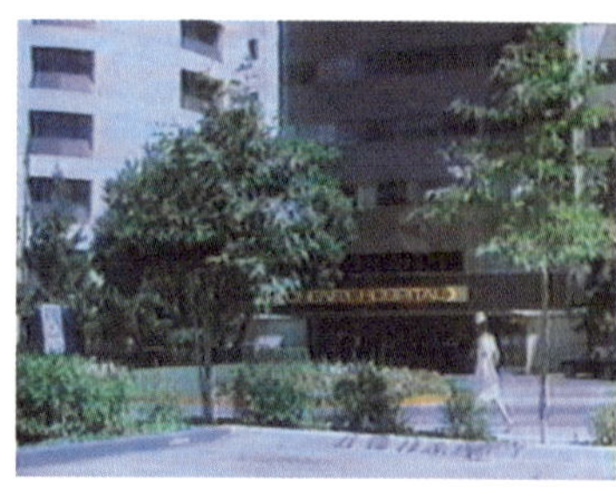
06:05

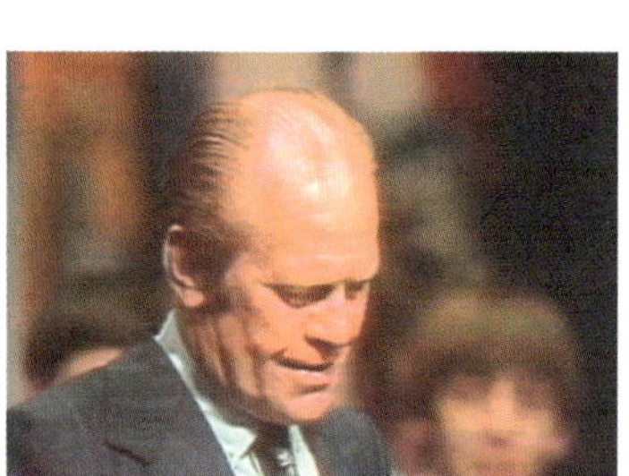
14:14

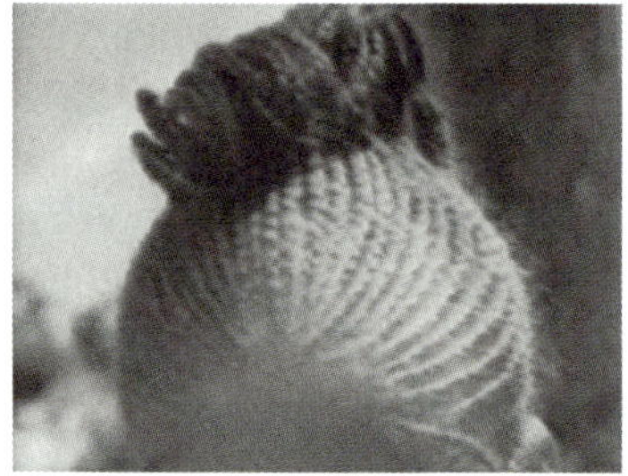
17:38

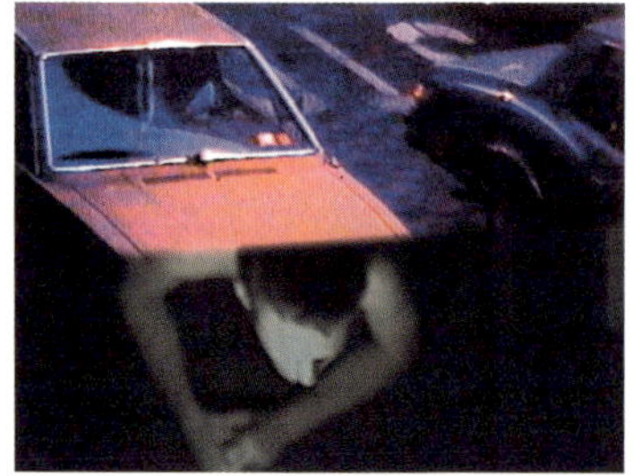
07:26

has carried forward. EAI has always been very hands-on with artists. Artists have been involved with the decisions that were made; artists have been involved in policy. We're constantly in touch with many artists; that's just the way it's always been. It may be because we're in New York, where there was a particularly active video art scene. There may be many other reasons why it has evolved that way, but we have always been very artist-driven. Artists always play a huge role in everything we do.

AK – I'd love to hear how you entered the picture. How did you first learn about EAI and what was your entry point?

LZ – My first job right after college was as an intern at MoMA with Barbara London in the Video Program, which was then under the Film Department—assisting with transcriptions, doing tasks around the office, etc. Already at that point it was impossible to be working with video and not be aware of EAI. What was amazing was that while working with Barbara I met so many artists who I still know and work with

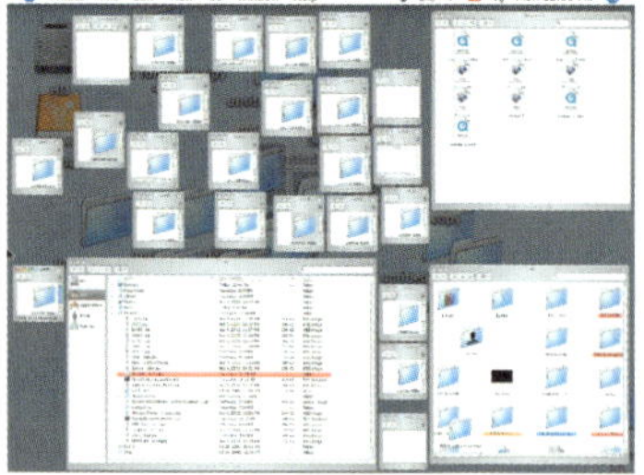
01:01

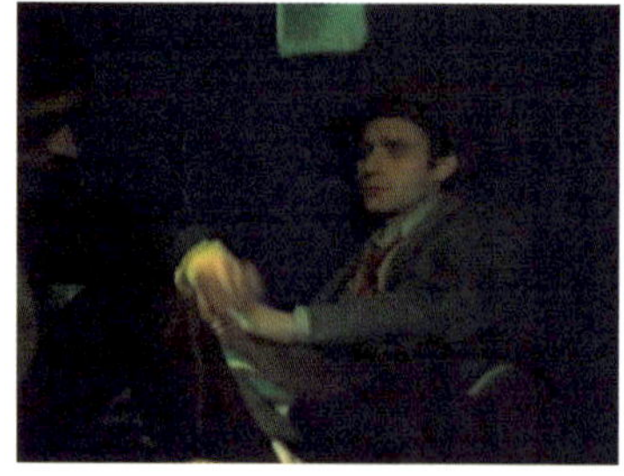
08:32

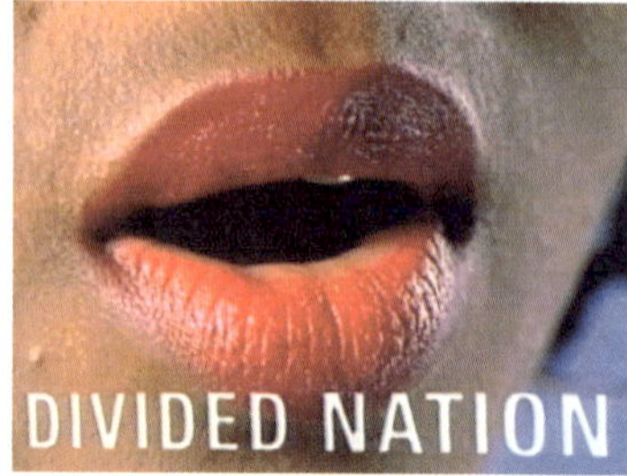

00:16

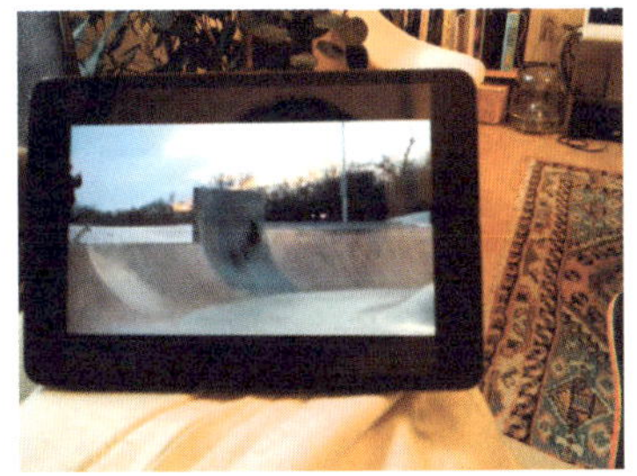
03:54

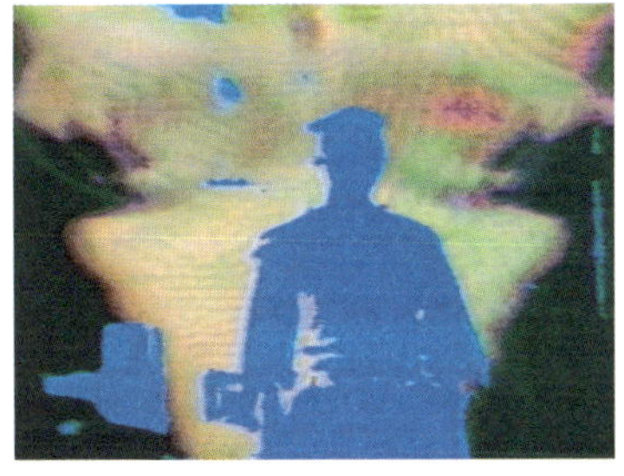
14:25

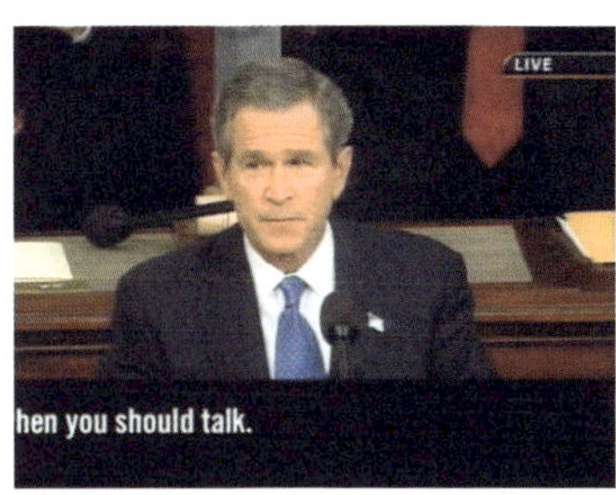

04:27

today at EAI. That's where I met Gary Hill, Tony Oursler, Judith Barry, Dan Graham, Bill Viola—Barbara was very generous in introducing me to artists and encouraging me to work with them.

AK – At MoMA you were working with EAI to borrow works for projects that you were doing with Barbara?

LZ – Yes, exactly, EAI was a known entity. Howard was a known figure at the time, too.

RC – Was Barbara friends with Howard?

LZ – She certainly knew him.

AK – Was it a very male-oriented scene and split along gender lines?

LZ – If you look at the roster of *TV as a Creative Medium*—it was all male, with the exception of Charlotte Moorman. But women were an important force in the video scene by the 1970s, particularly in comparison to more traditional art forms. This was during the second wave of feminism and the women's movement, and this was reflected in the political engagement of many women artists, as articulated through video. And by the time I entered the scene in the early

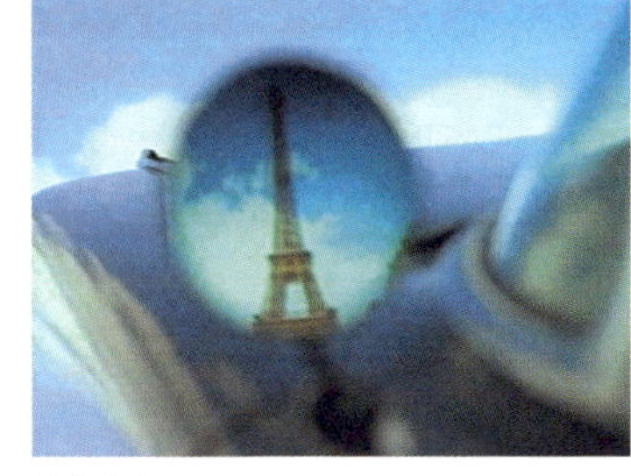
00:14

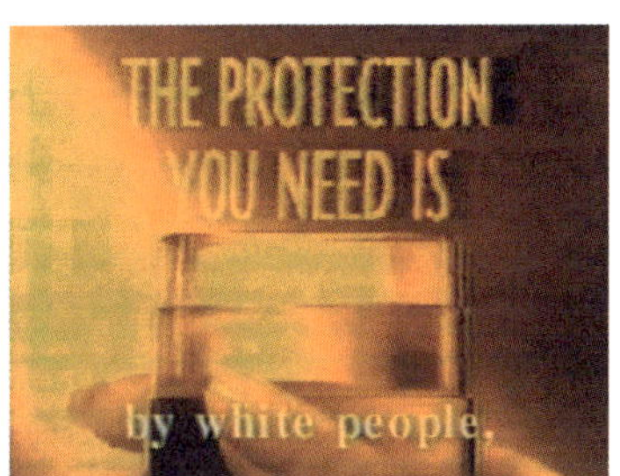

00:31

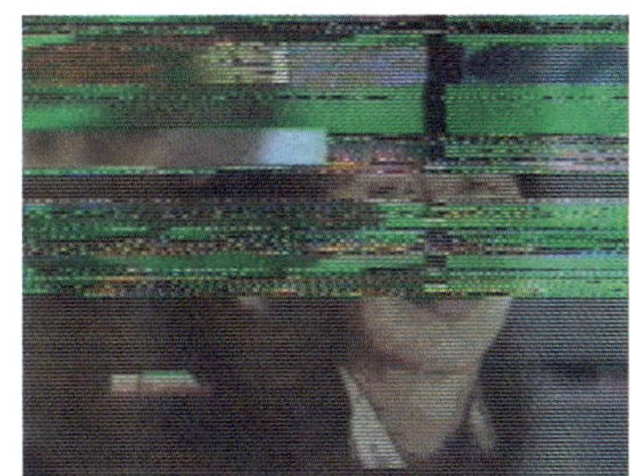
21:08

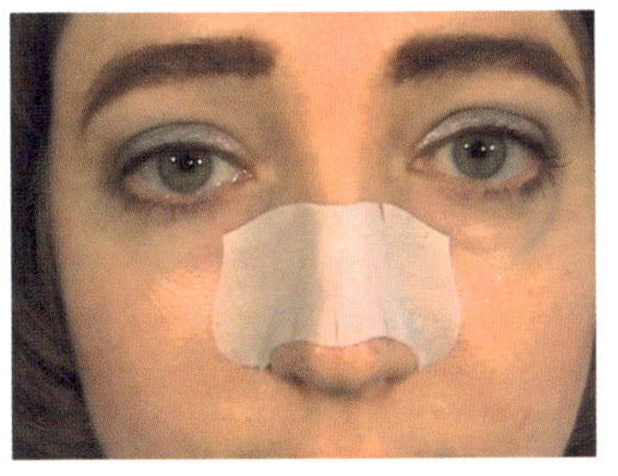
01:20

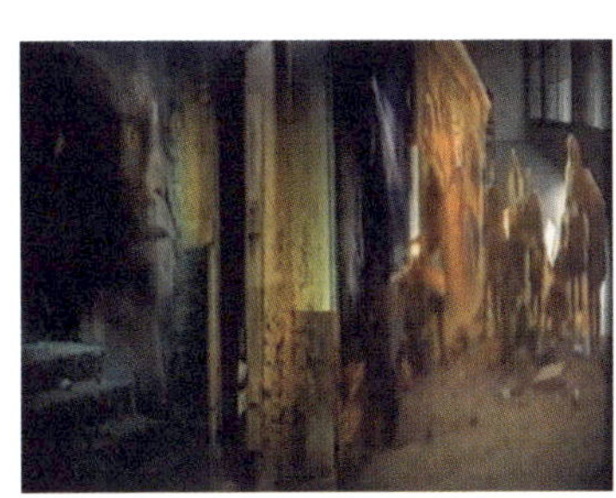
00:17

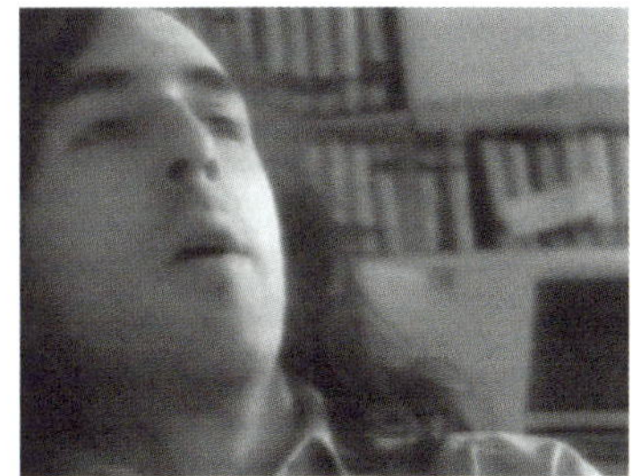
04:20

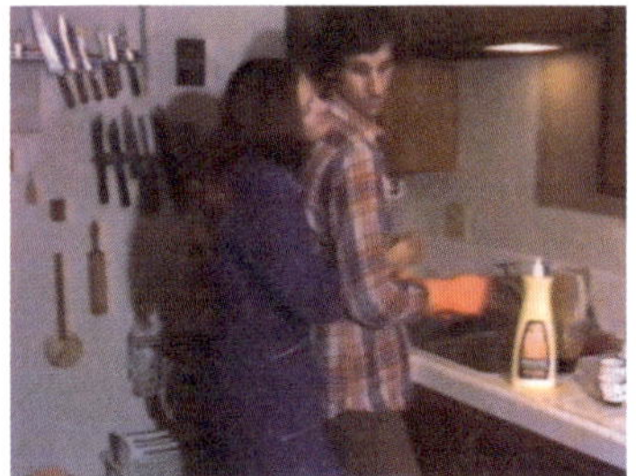
01:30

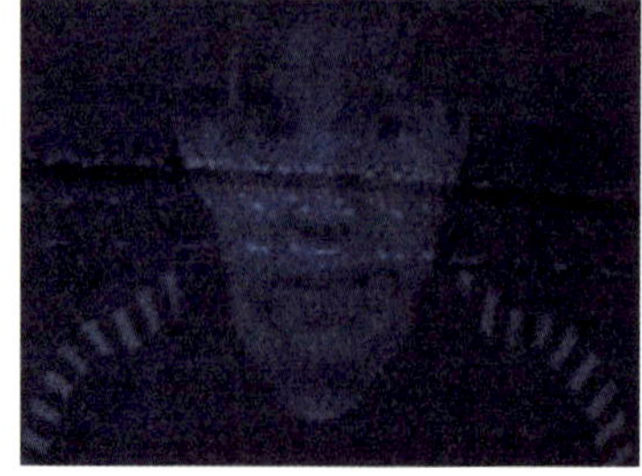
01:50

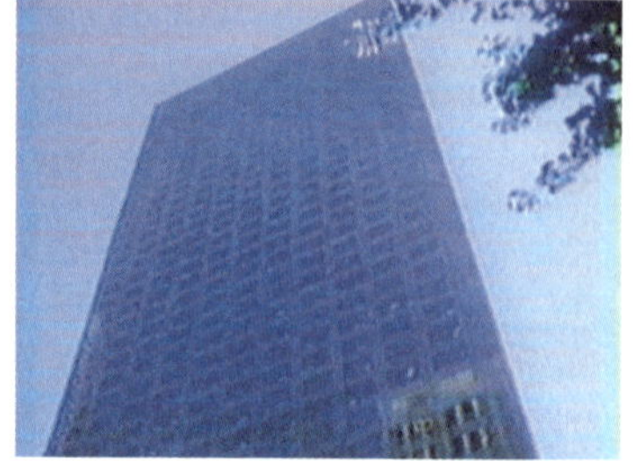
06:05

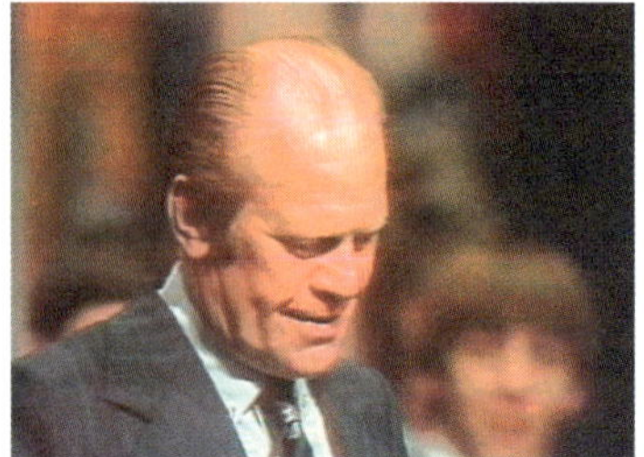
14:14

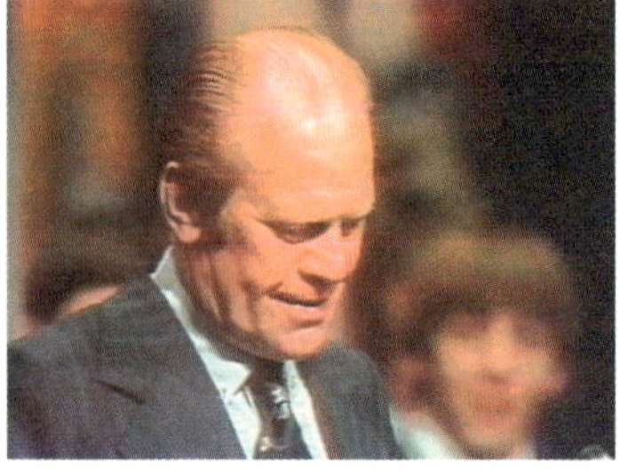
17:38

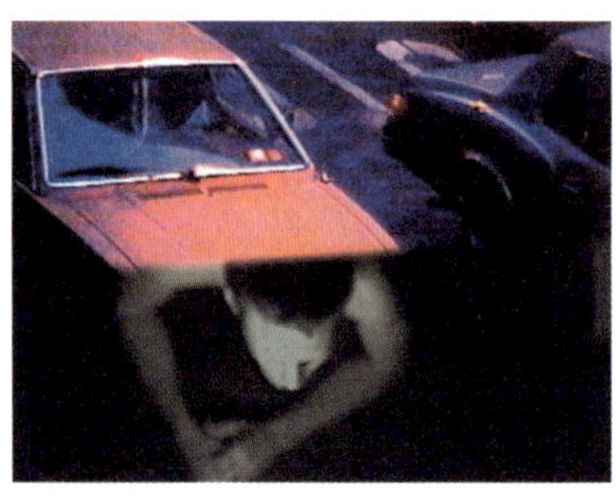
07:26

eighties, there were many more women involved and more women artists making and showing video. Women have always played key roles at EAI.

AK – I think this is really important to point out. These early histories that we inherit are often formed through the gender and racial divides, biases, and blind spots that existed thirty or forty years ago. These shape and still dominate our historical understanding. How did that transition from MoMA to EAI happen for you?

LZ – Barbara made the introduction. I went to Howard's house for the job interview. He took me around his living room to show me his art collection. He had seen that I had done my senior project at Bard College on Joseph Beuys and the Düsseldorf scene. So, he said, "Ah, you must know Group Zero." And I said, "Oh, I know of them, of course." He had me go around his house and he quizzed me on the pieces.

AK – He quizzed you? How stressful!

LZ – I was terrified. I went around the house with him, guessing. "Heinz Mack?" *Right*. "Otto Piene?" etc. And then he just thanked me,

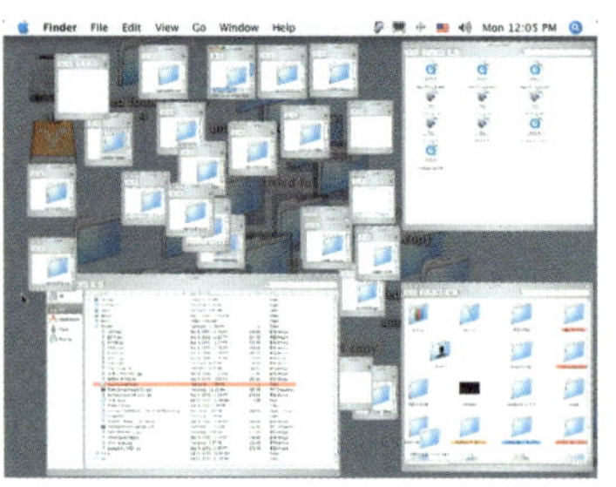

01:01

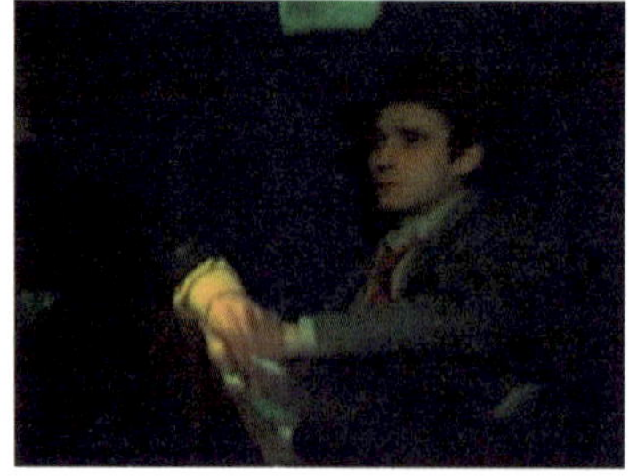
08:32

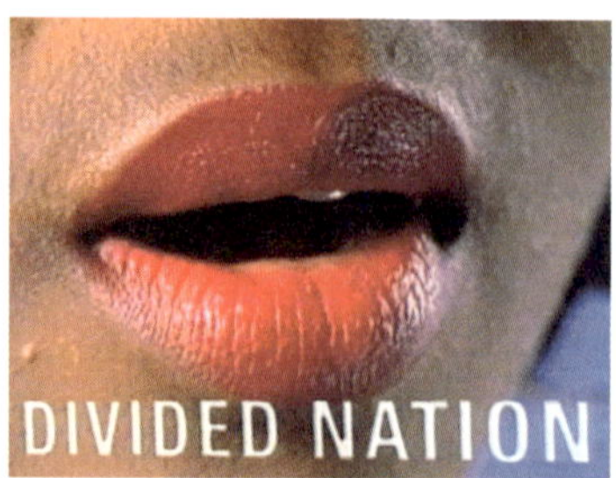

00:16

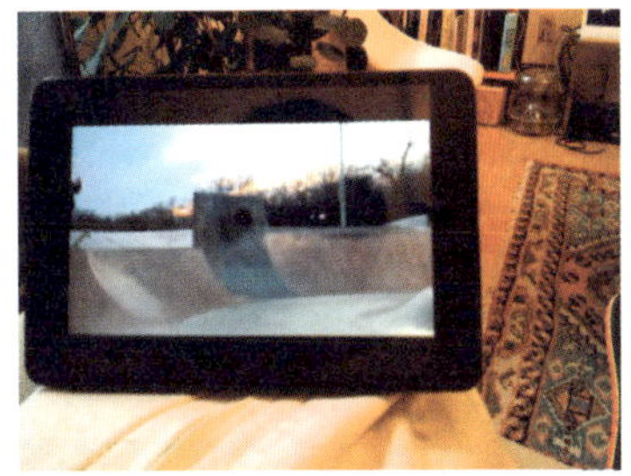

03:54

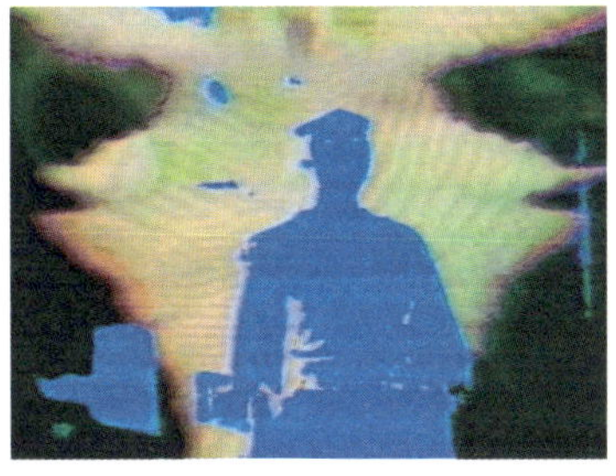

14:25

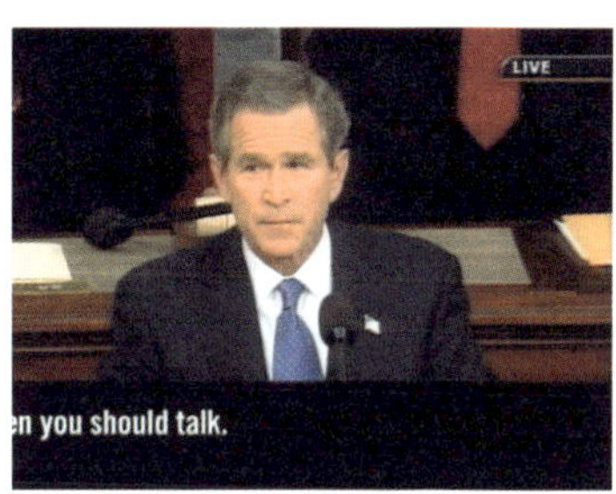

04:27

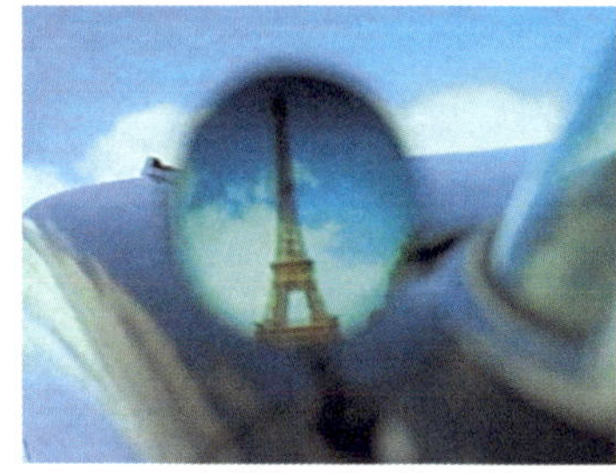

00:14

and I left, and I thought I would never hear from him again. And then the next day he called me. I think he needed some office equipment, and asked me if I would go with him to help him buy it. And I said, "Okay. Did I get the job?" And he said, "Of course, you've got the job! This is your first task."

AK – He must have been in his seventies at this point?

LZ – Yes, maybe even well into his seventies. So that was my transition to EAI.

AK – What was your first role at EAI?

LZ – I was an administrative assistant for Howard.

AK – What was he like to work with?

LZ – Howard was very kind, a bit idiosyncratic, and deeply engaged with the political causes of that time, particularly the anti-nuclear movement. When I got there, it was an important transitional moment, from the 1970s—from the pioneers and the early artistic and activist movements with Portapaks—to a changing downtown New York scene of the 1980s.

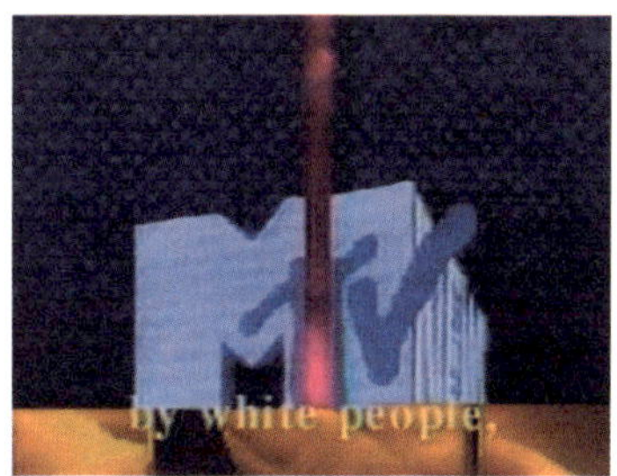

00:31

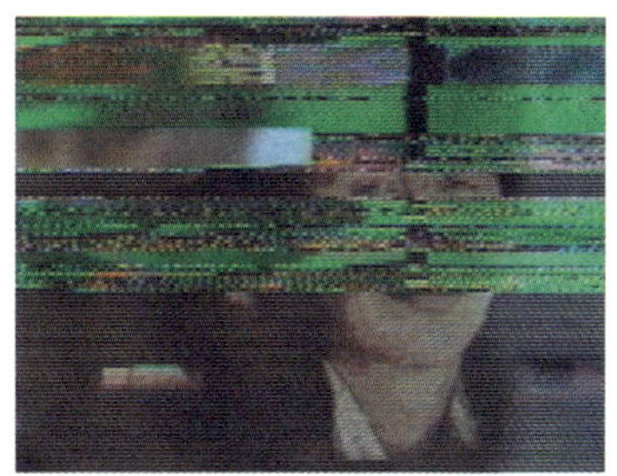

21:08

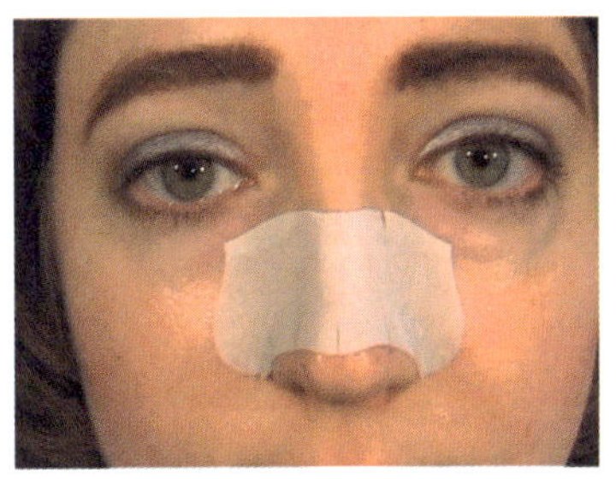

01:20

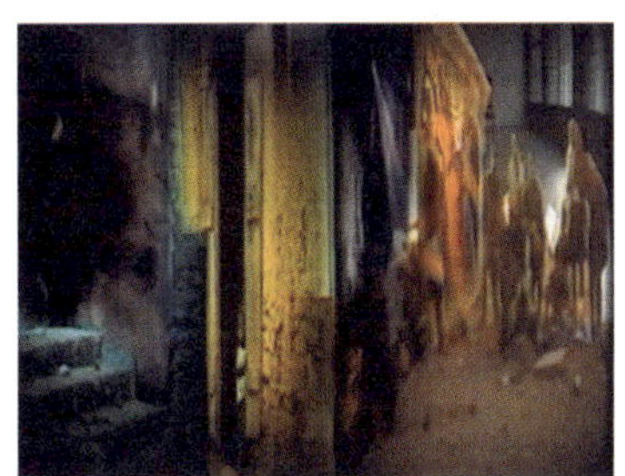

00:17

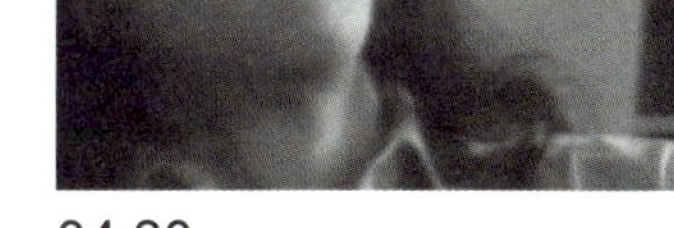

04:20

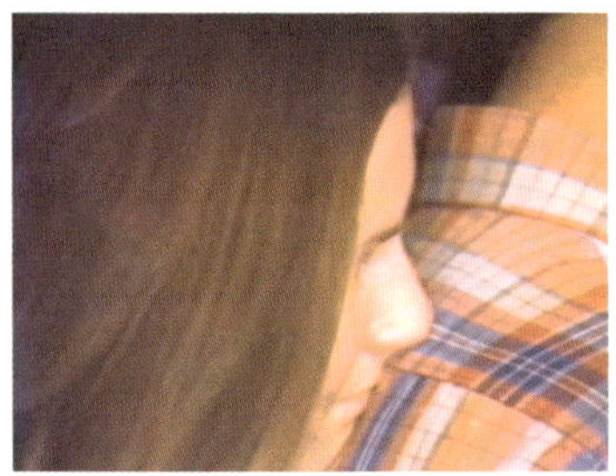
01:30

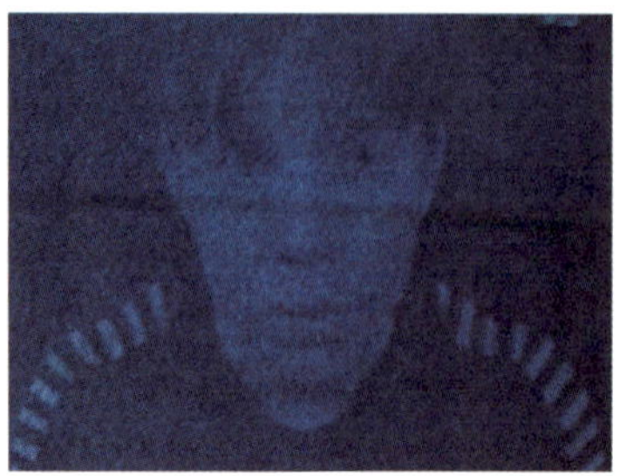
01:50

06:05

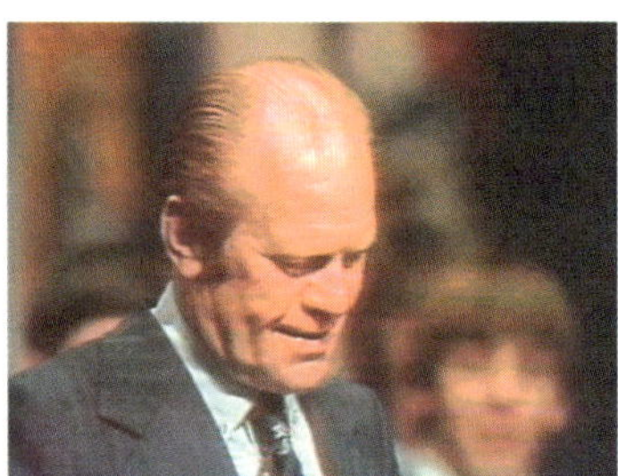
14:14

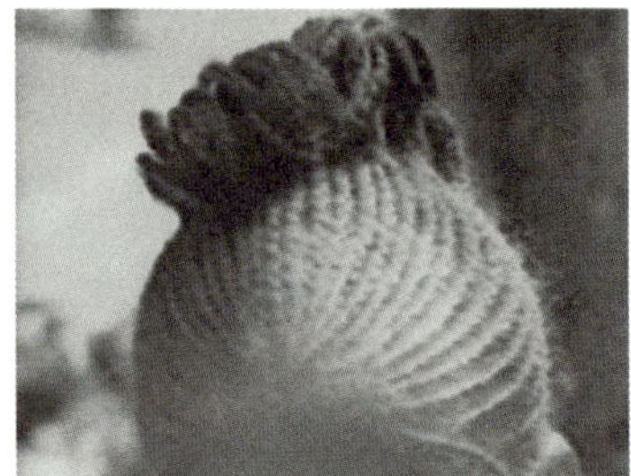
17:38

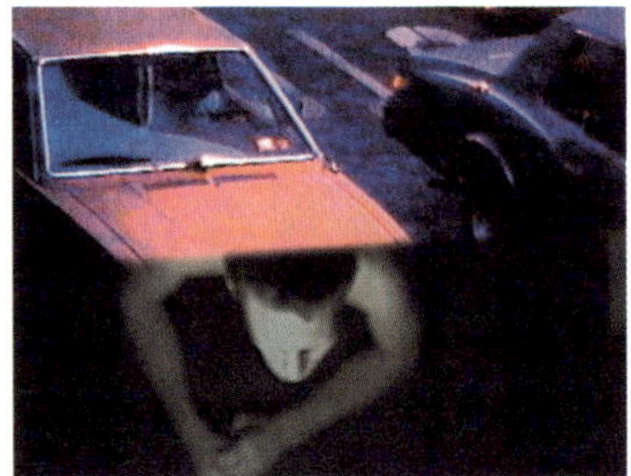
07:26

AK – I imagine that the Pictures scene introduced a very different set of critical questions around media.

LZ – Exactly, and then, as I mentioned earlier, in terms of the technology, in 1976/1977 there was a shift from black-and-white to color equipment. There were 3/4-inch editing systems and editing controllers available. Before, it was 1/2-inch open reel, with its laborious, manual editing processes, and suddenly you have the opportunity for relatively fast-paced editing. And then in 1981 MTV happens. So, artists' work had gone from 1/2-inch, open reel analog video to color, editing, narrative, music-based—it was about the cut. Artists were interested in the creative and conceptual potential of these technological changes, and the possibilities for showing work changed, and the conditions of how it was being made changed. In New York, these changes coincided with the downtown club scene—punk and new wave. There were so many different cultural shifts in New York at the time. And this is where I come into it.

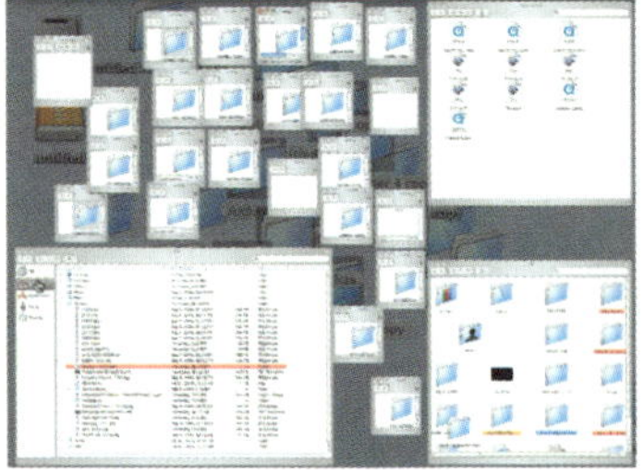
01:01

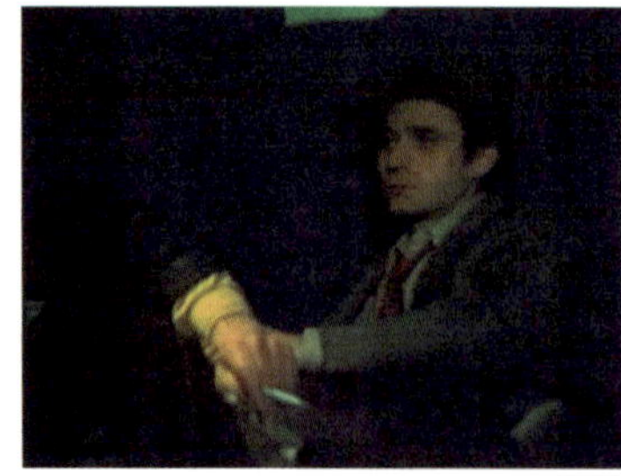
08:32

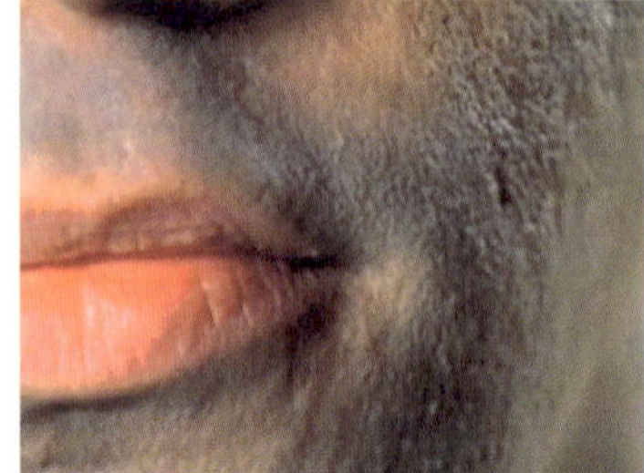
00:16

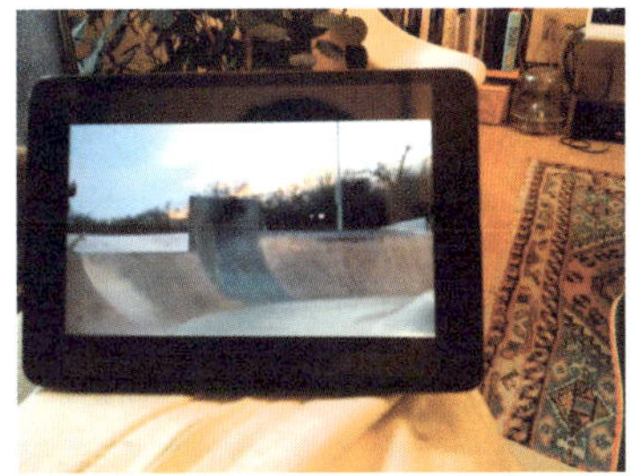
03:54

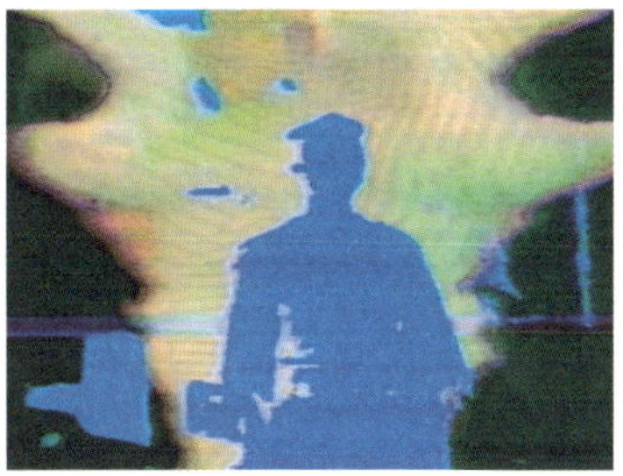
14:25

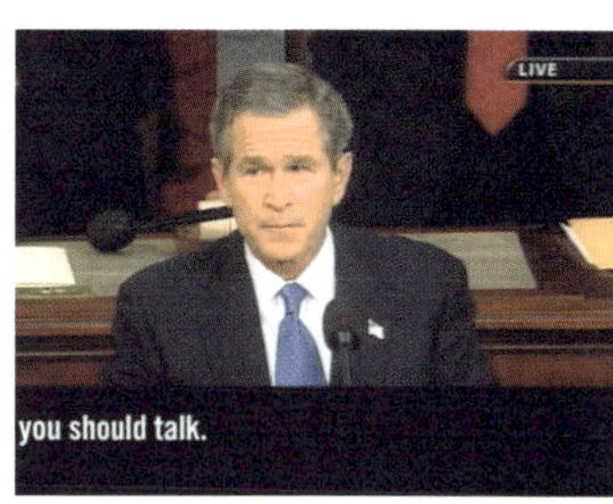

04:27

AK – Were you participating in that downtown scene, going to the Mudd Club and hanging out with those artists?

LZ – Yes, I was very young. I was in my early twenties. EAI artists Kit Fitzgerald and John Sanborn were running the video lounge at Danceteria. Clubs like the Mudd Club, Hurrah, Palladium, and the Peppermint Lounge had video screens and were showing music videos. This was the era of the VJs.

AK – Was material from EAI also creeping into these spaces?

LZ – Yes. Work that was being distributed and edited at EAI, certainly. Work by Tom Rubnitz and other East Village artists, works like Dara Birnbaum's *New Music Shorts* (1981). There were also video bars and video lounges in bars. It was a shift away from video being seen only in alternative art spaces and museums to a sudden burst of video being shown in public contexts, because of the new music club scene, and because of the new forms and technologies. So there was a different dialogue that marks a shift to artists

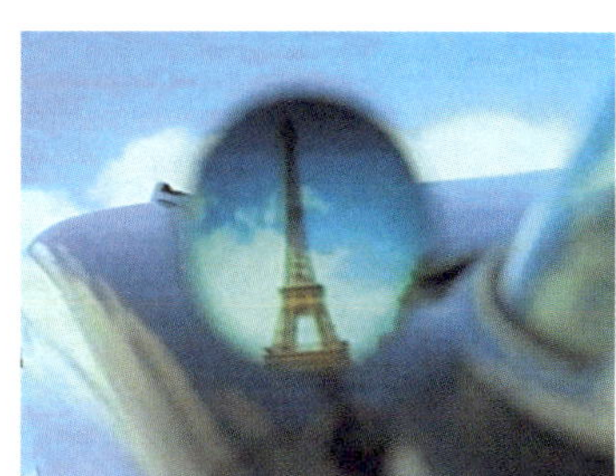
00:14

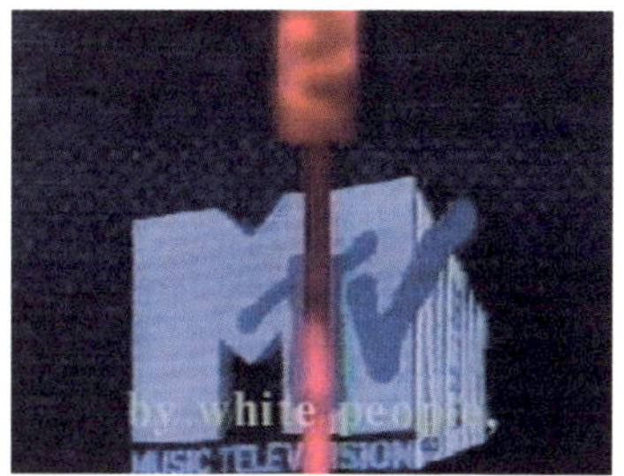

00:31

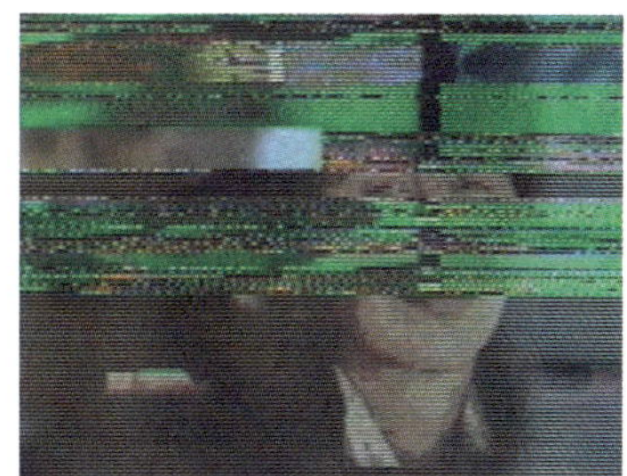
21:08

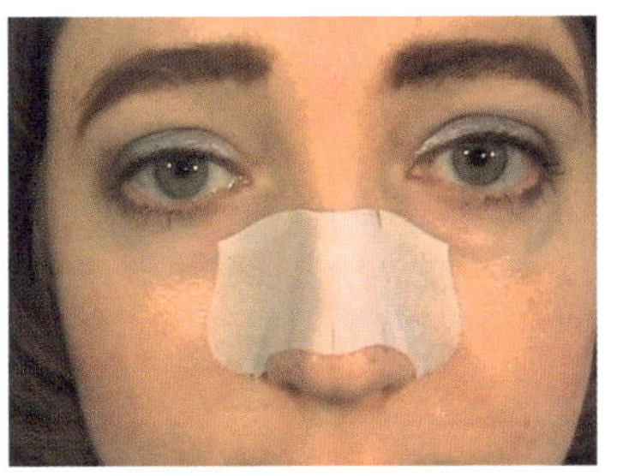
01:20

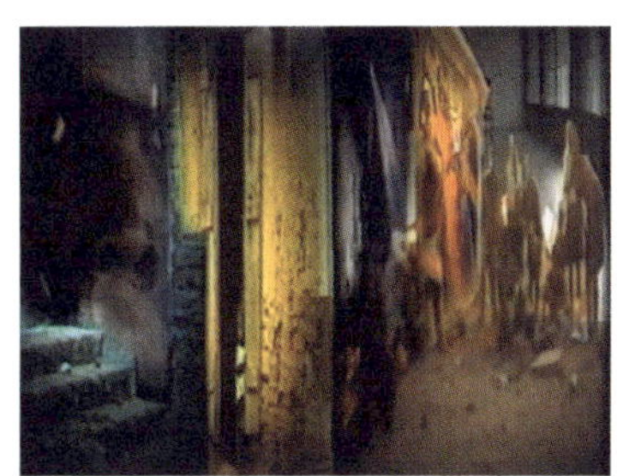
00:17

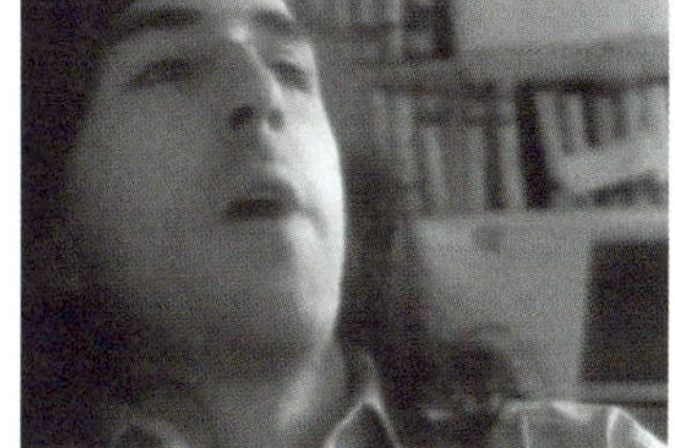
04:20

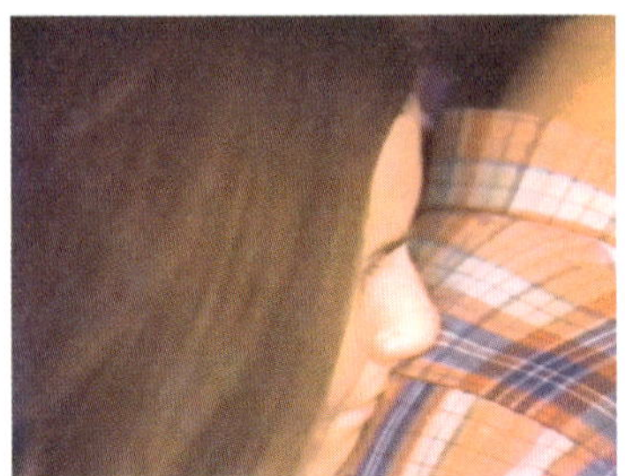
01:30

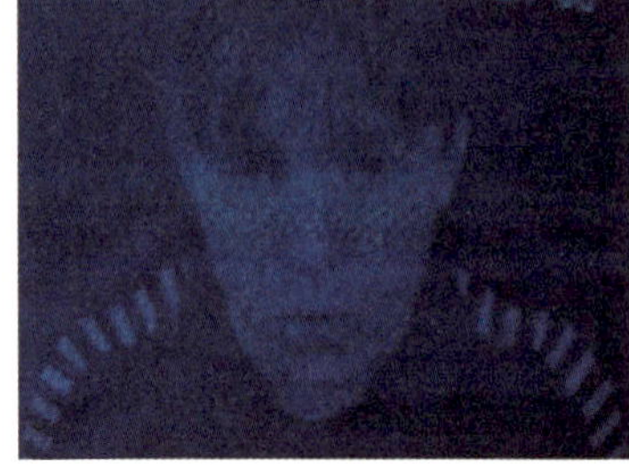
01:50

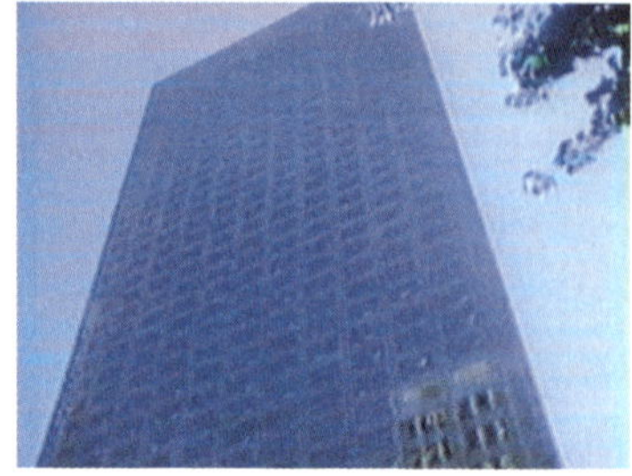
06:05

increasingly investigating the language of television and mass media. The early video scene was countercultural. It was a form that was driven by alternative impulses. By the 1980s that was complicated a bit, because on the one hand it was still oppositional in terms of art that's talking back to the media, but there was also a real interest in an exchange between video art and television in form and content. There was definitely an emphasis on media critique, but the dialogue was not so clear cut, no longer purely oppositional—or purely interventionist.

AK – And MTV was pretty radical when it started out.

LZ – As much as MTV stole from video art—and it did—some video artists were also interested in an exchange or dialogue with MTV.

AK – It's interesting to think of video in bars as a kind of populism of the medium. You didn't have to go to a rarified art-specific context. The club is still an alternative space of sorts, but a real cross-section of people would have been encountering these videos.

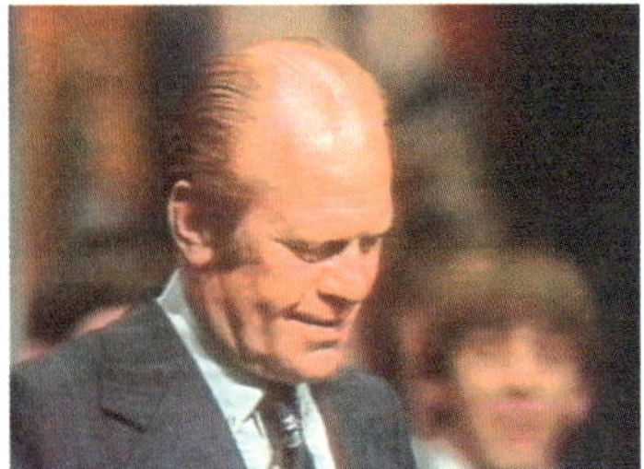
14:14

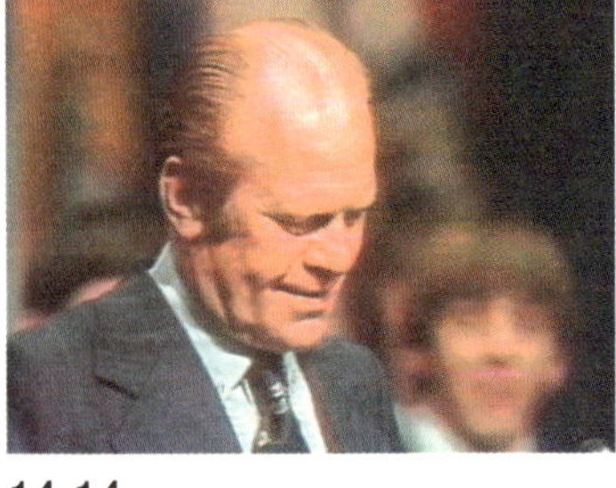
17:38

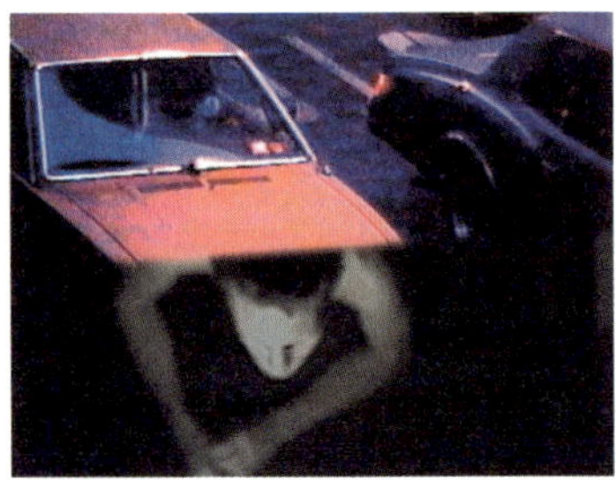
07:26

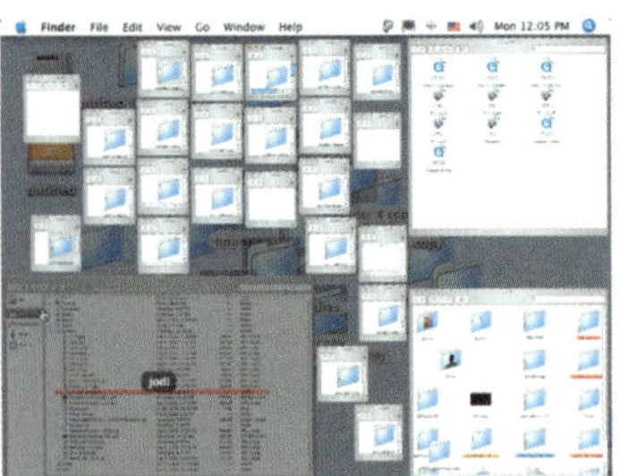
01:01

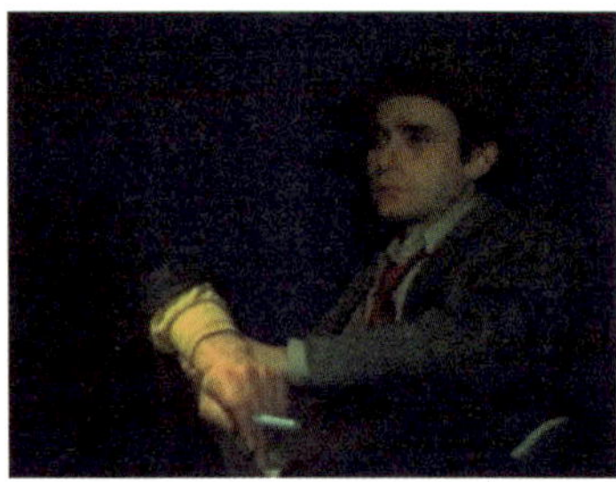
08:32

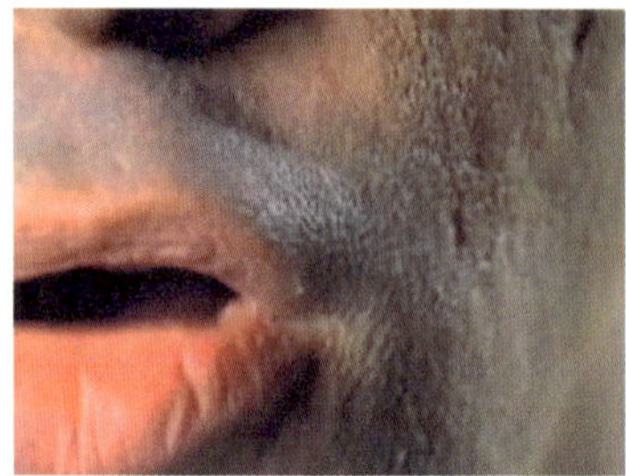
00:16

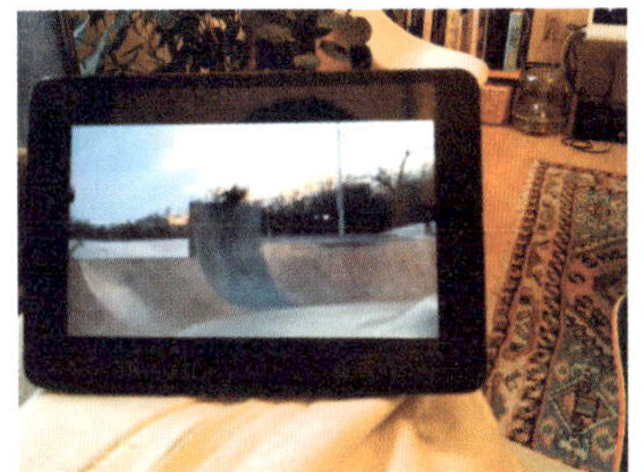
03:54

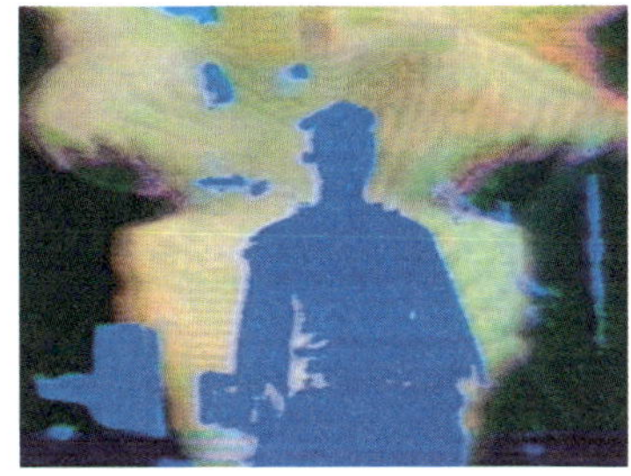
14:25

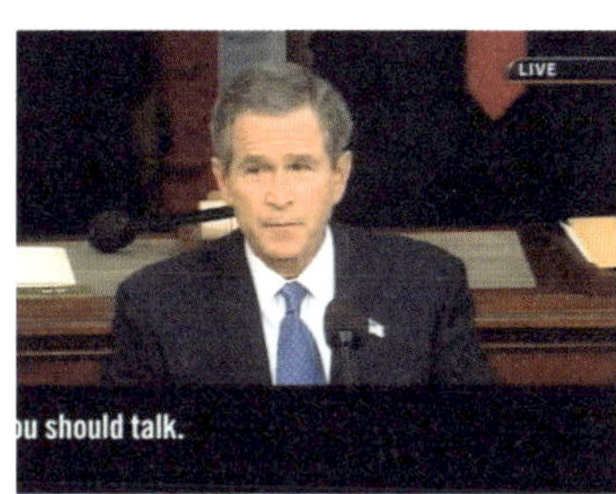

04:27

LZ – And also, there were several late-night TV shows, such as *Night Flight*, which was on USA Network on cable, that showed video art. EAI did several collaborations with them.

AK – So, EAI was collaborating with network television in order to get this work broadcast?

LZ – There were a number of commissioned projects for TV at that time, such as the Jimi Hendrix Videogram project, which was driven by Eric Trigg, who was at EAI until 1983. The Hendrix estate had discovered a series of tracks that had not been previously released and he worked with them to commission a series of artists to do music videos for these tracks, including Stephen Beck and Shalom Gorewitz.

RC – Dara Birnbaum did one.

LZ – Dara did one—*Fire!/Hendrix*, which was 1982. This was a moment when there were experiments with, as you say, the popularization of video and the changes in technology and artistic movements that led to work engaging with popular culture, rather than artists performing in black-and-white in front of the camera.

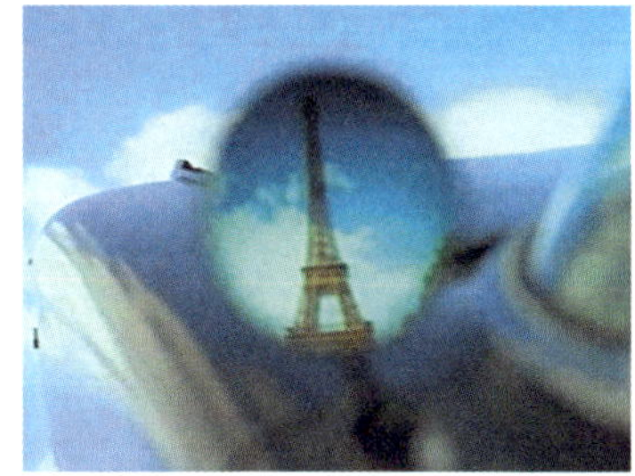
00:14

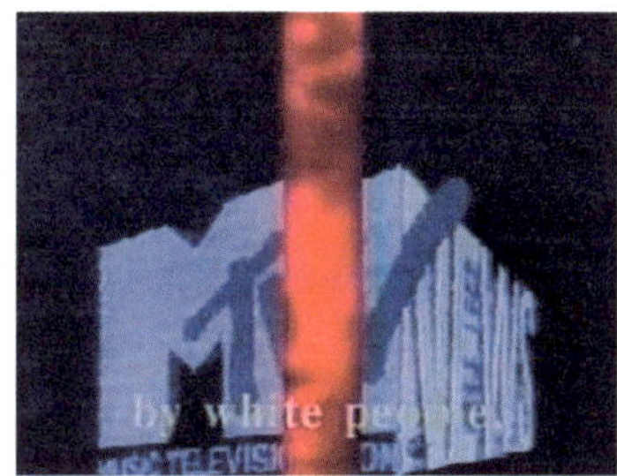
00:31

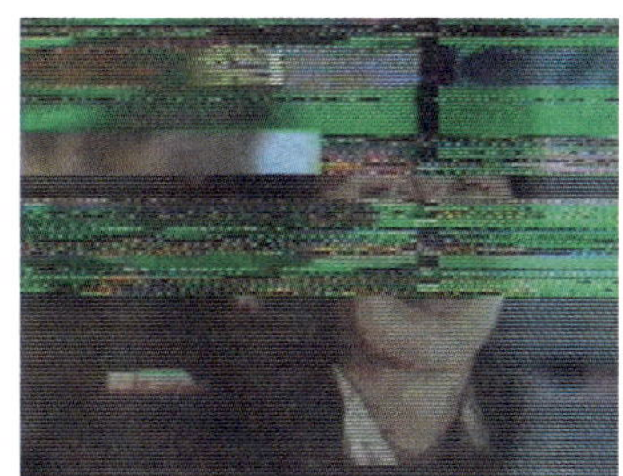
21:08

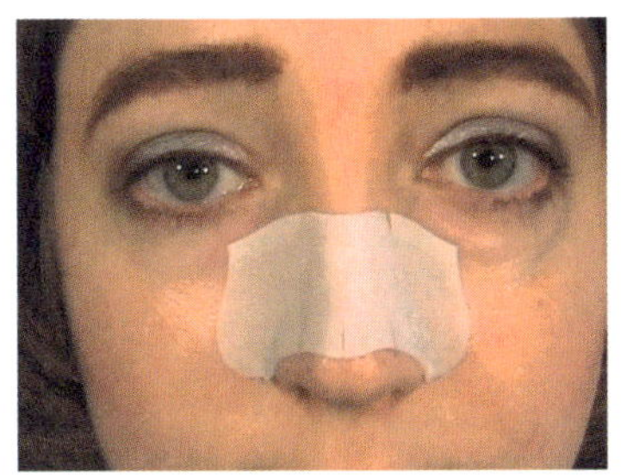
01:20

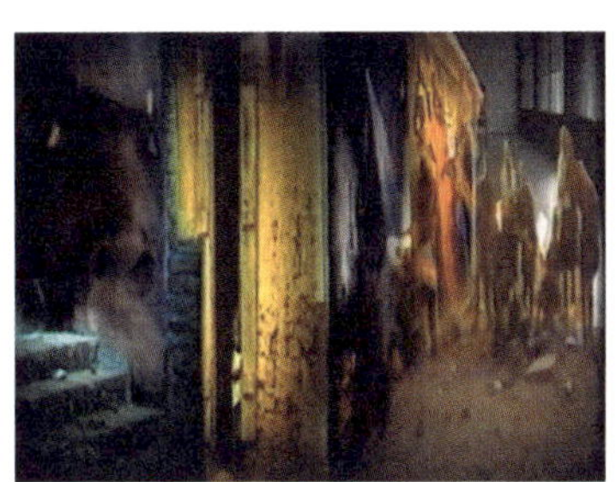
00:17

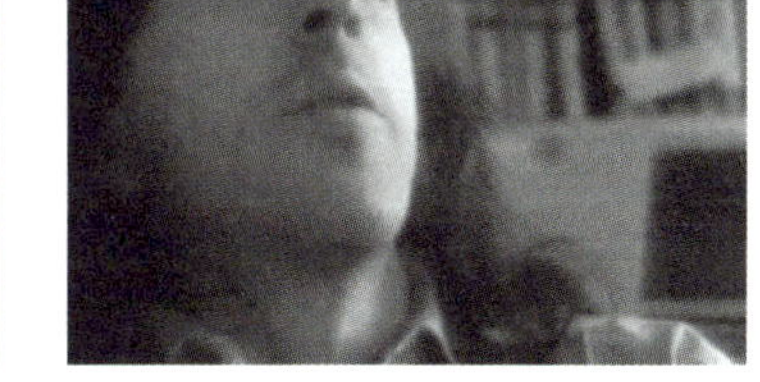
04:20

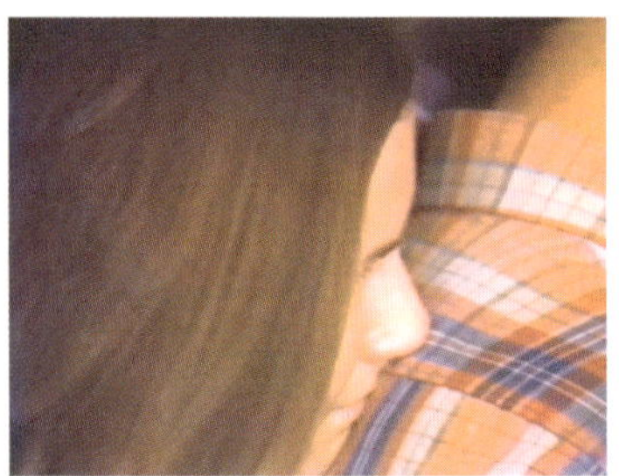
01:30

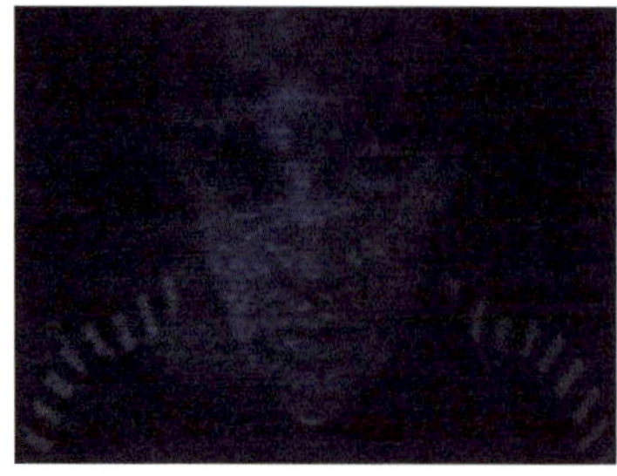
01:50

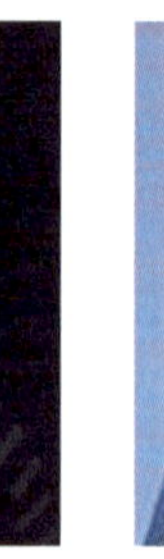
06:05

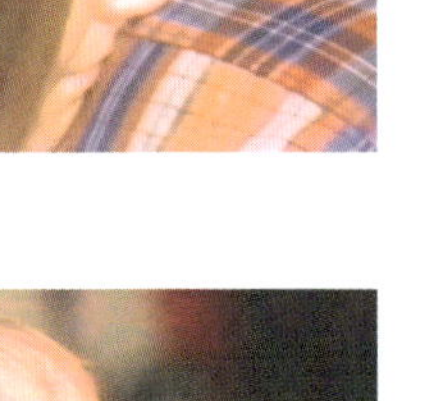
14:14

There was an engagement with rock music, fast editing, media culture.

AK – It was less about "video narcissism."[2]

LZ – Precisely. You could never have shown durational black-and-white video on commercial television or in bars or at a club in the early eighties. It was when the work switched to color and more fast-paced editing, with music, that it then migrated to these other public venues and contexts. So, it was a very important shift at that time.

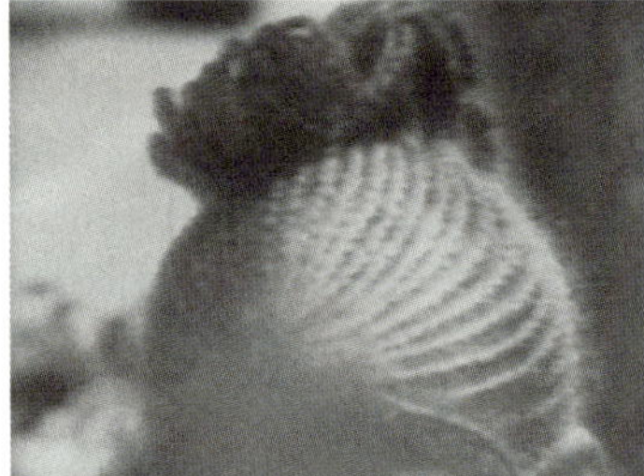
17:38

AK – Were the artists interested in having other avenues for their work?

LZ – Oh, absolutely. Although not all artists. Nam June Paik, of course, was always interested in seeing his work in public venues. And Dara Birnbaum, for example, was keen to have her work shown in different contexts. *Technology Transformation/Wonder Woman* (1978–1979) was famously first shown in a shop window in SoHo, at the H Hair Salon. She was very interested in having this work shown in a public context.

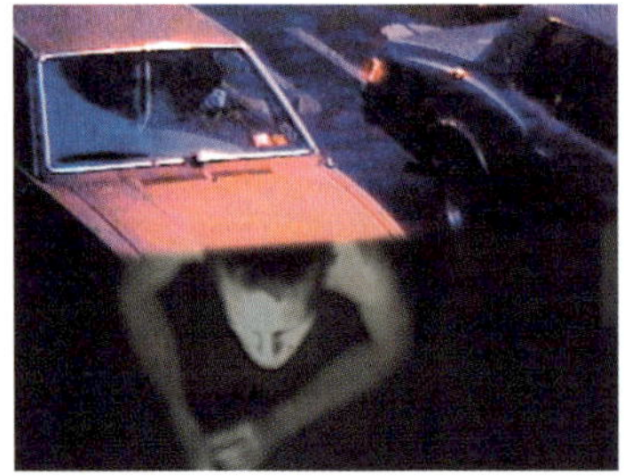
07:26

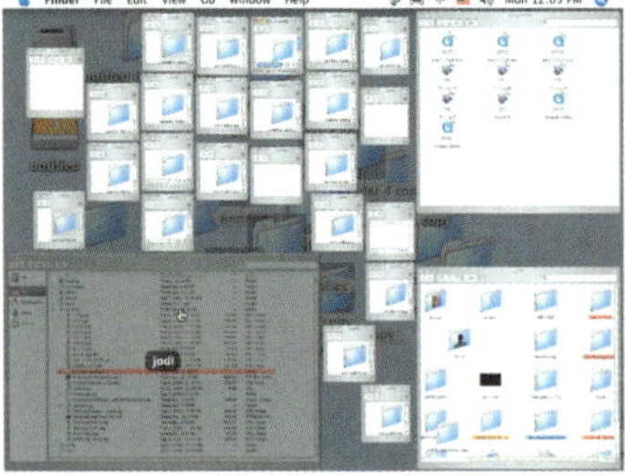
01:01

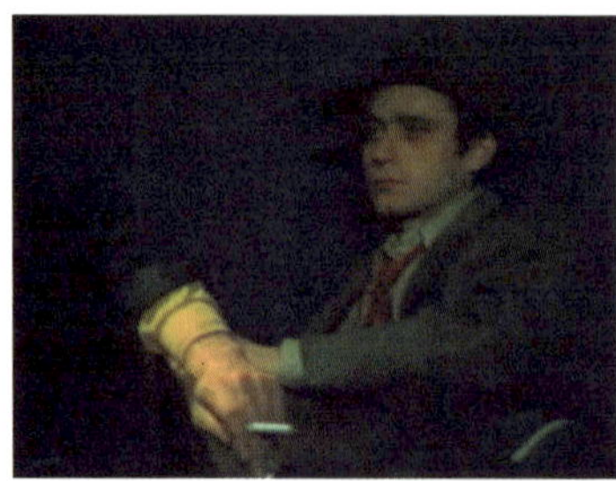
08:32

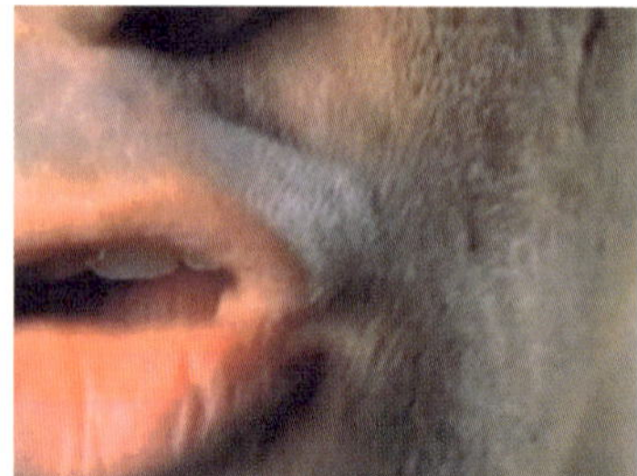
00:16

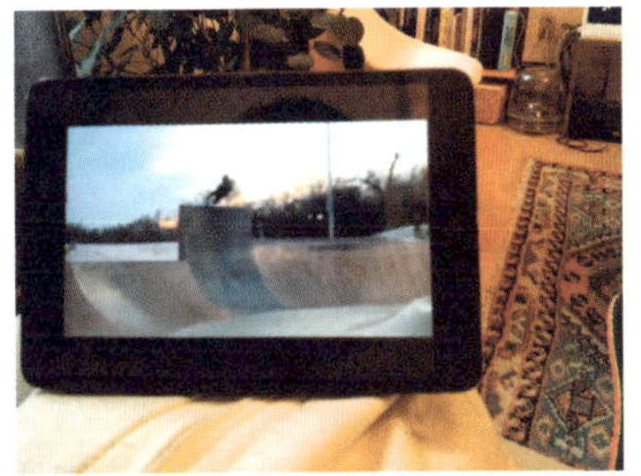
03:54

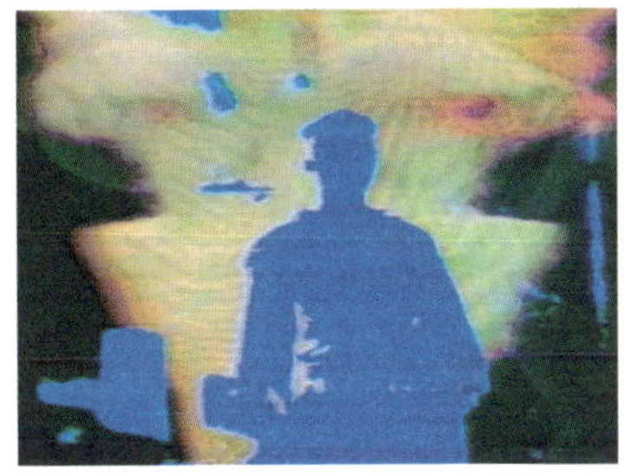
14:25

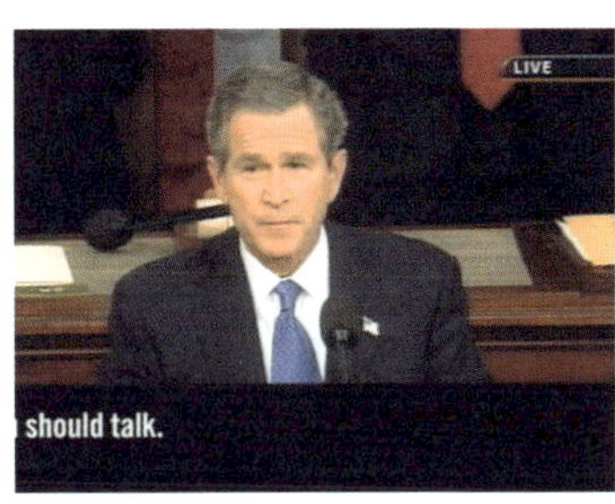

04:27

In 1986 we celebrated EAI's fifteenth anniversary with a party in the infamous Michael Todd Room at the Palladium, where we played artists' videos on a pyramid of monitors and on an enormous grid of giant screens that descended onto the packed dance floor. It was quite a spectacle, and thrilling at the time.

AK – In the early eighties, you're working for Howard. What was a typical day in the office for you?

LZ – I arrive probably at 9:00 am.

AK – 9:00 am! My goodness, when you've been out at Danceteria until 2:00 am the night before?

LZ – Exactly. [Laughs.] And the night editors—Pat Ivers, Jody O'Brien, Robin Schanzenbach—may just be leaving.

AK – Oh, they've been editing at night?

LZ – They've been editing at night with artists and with the club works. But that was how busy the editing facility was. And the world was different then. You went to clubs, you edited through the night because you were in your twenties and it was New York in the early 1980s.

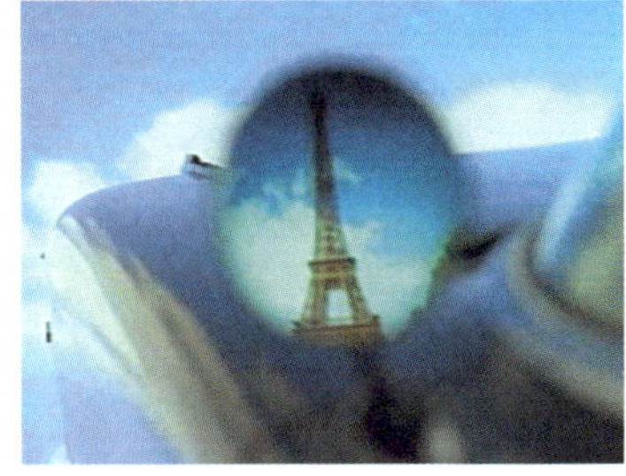
00:14

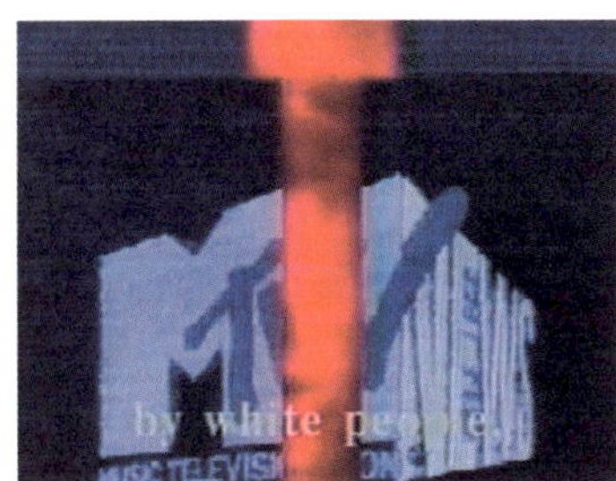
00:31

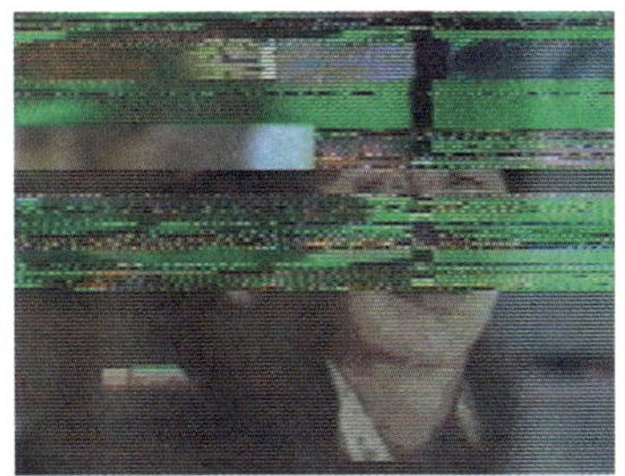
21:08

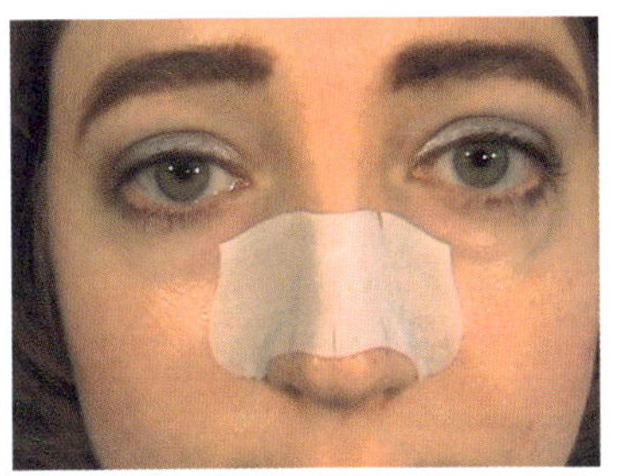
01:20

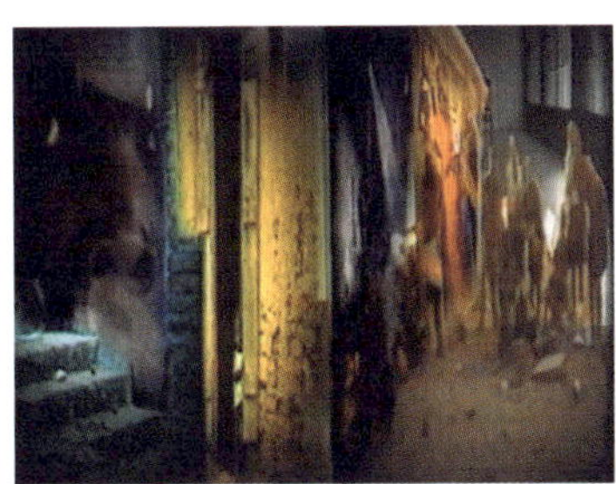
00:17

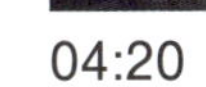
04:20

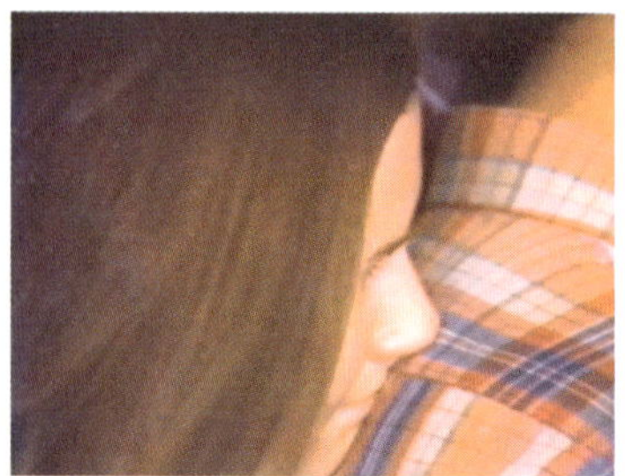
01:29

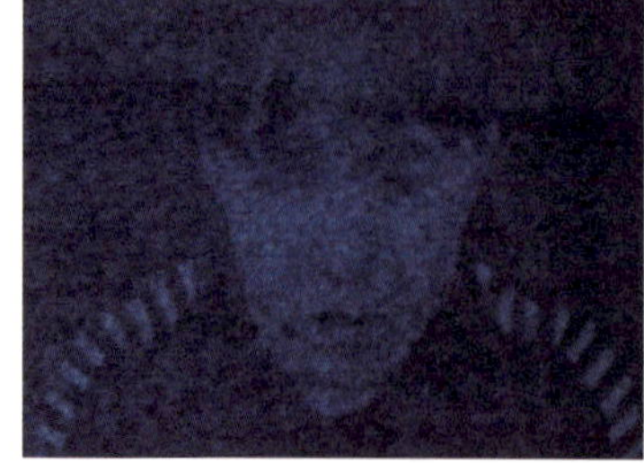
01:49

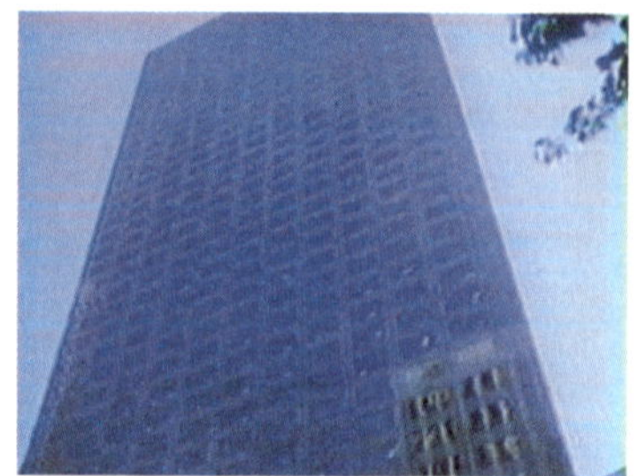
06:04

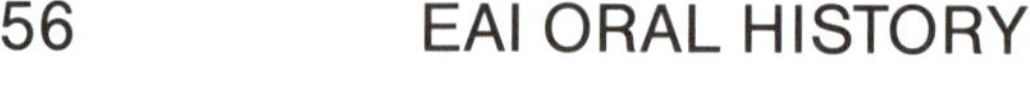

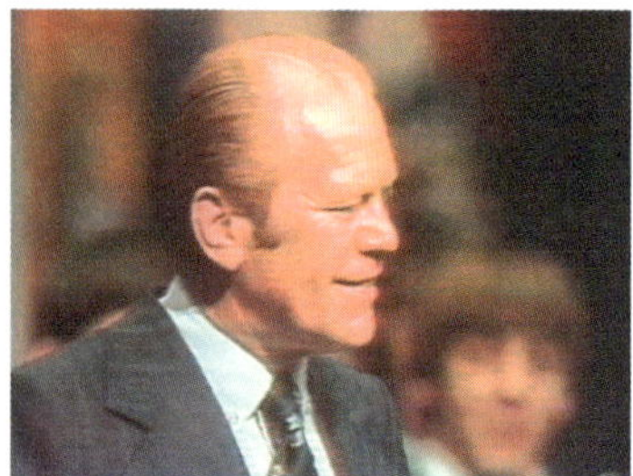
14:13

AK – How wonderful, you had energy and you were dancing and then you just went to EAI! It's a more professionalized world now.

LZ – You'd work all day, dance all night, and then keep working. [Laughs.] So, it was not unusual to come in and see one of the night editors leaving.

In the early eighties, Matt Danowski was the director of the editing facility and he would edit during the day. So the day editing would start and that's when artists and the cable access people would be editing.

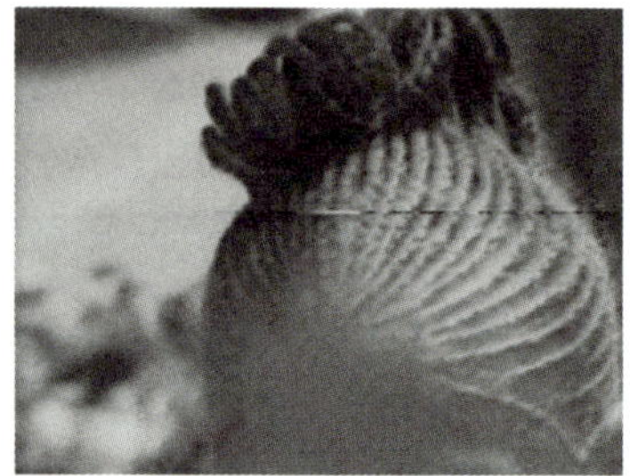
17:37

AK – Oh, that's another interesting connection. At this point, are you charging for editing services?

LZ – Yes. Editing fees were established in the early 1970s. The cable access editing generated earned income, so it was an important part of what was going on in the eighties. There was this wildly eclectic group of cable access people who were doing everything from renegade art projects to demonology to game show spoofs to—it was just crazy. At that point editing was of course analog and not digital, so if you

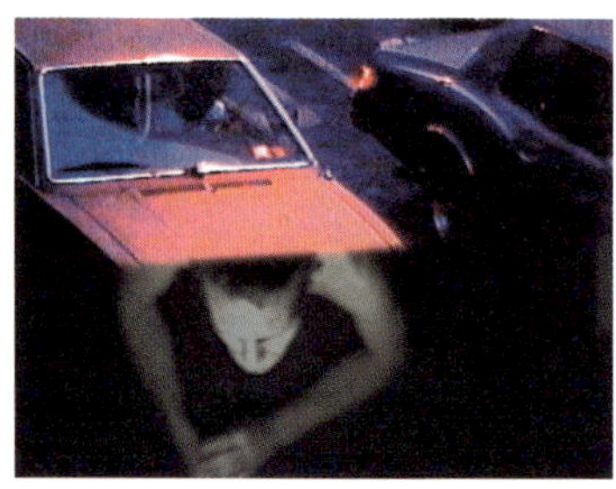
07:25

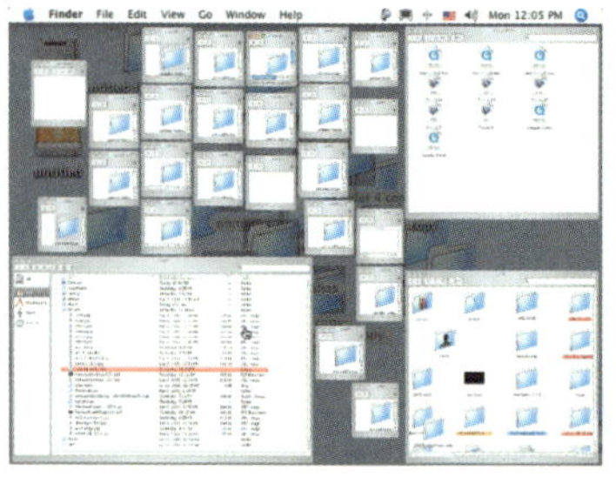

01:00

08:31

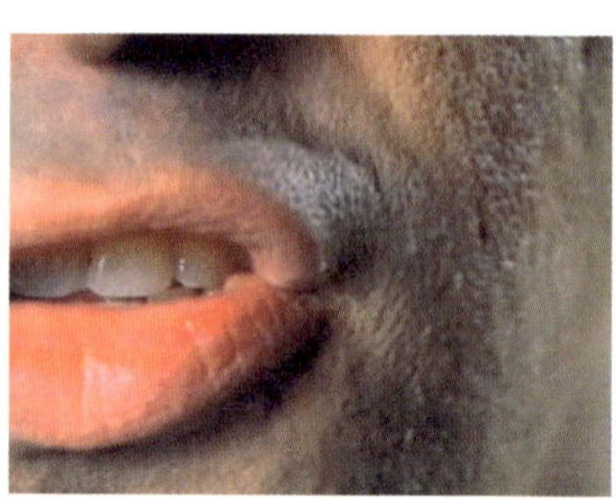
00:15

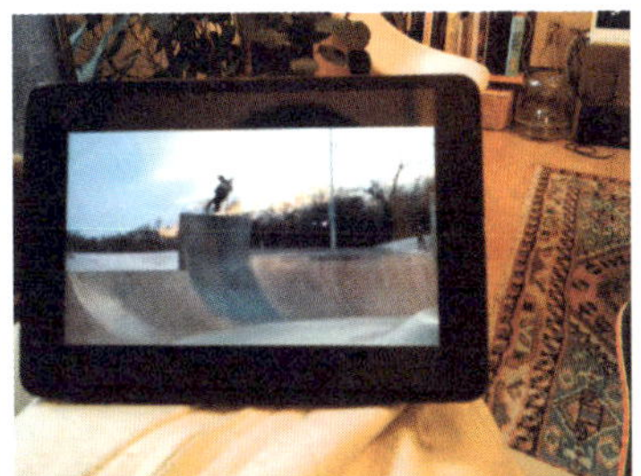
03:54

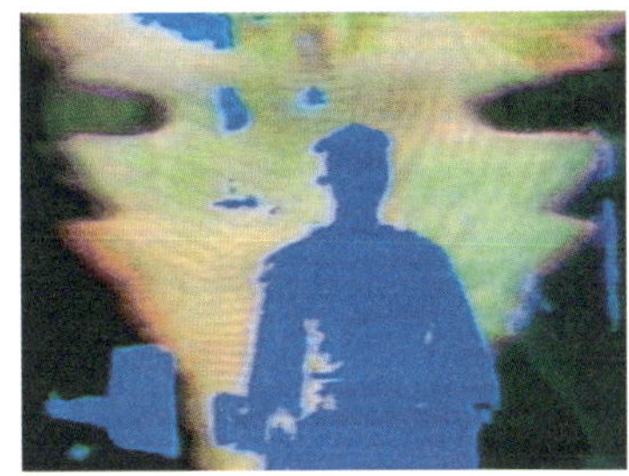
14:25

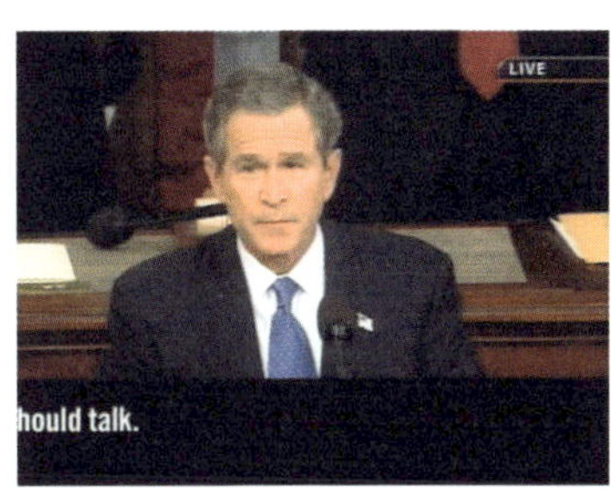

04:27

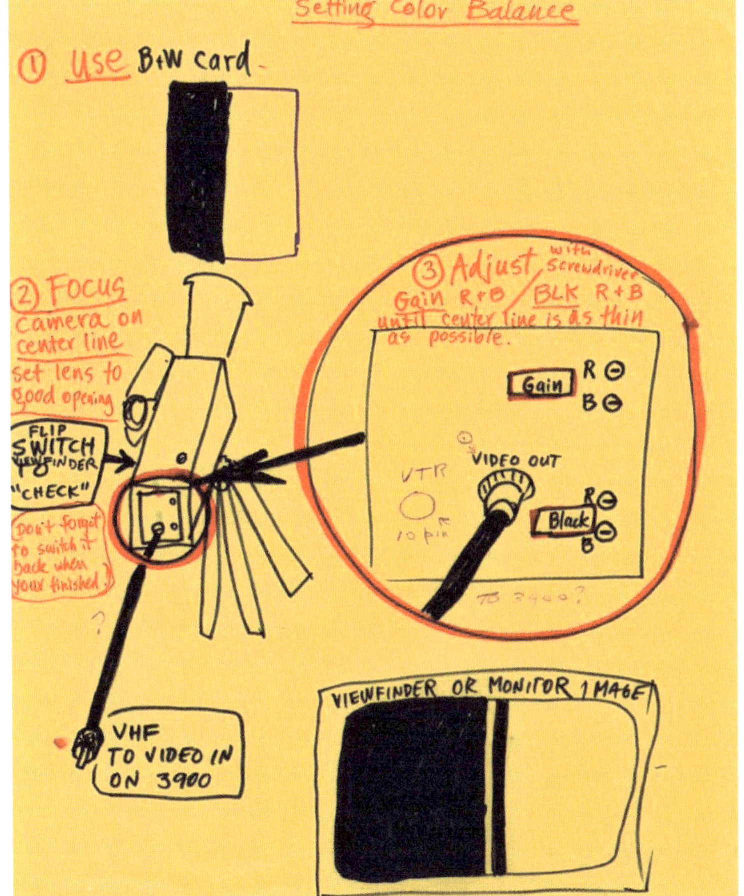

Drawing of equipment in the early EAI Editing Suite

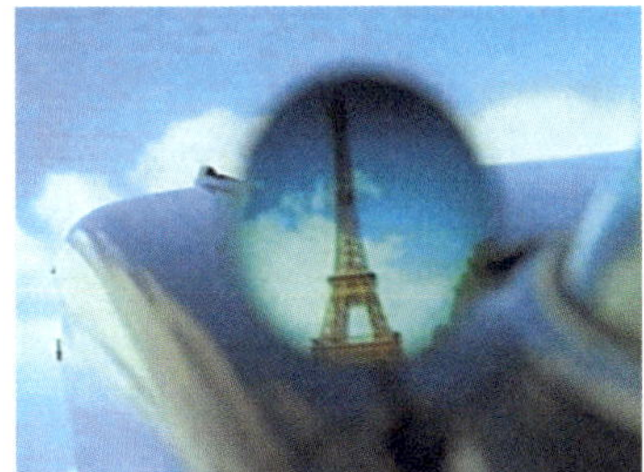
00:14

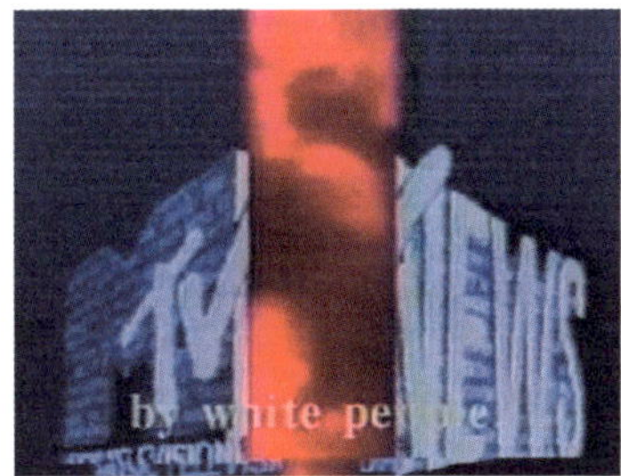
00:31

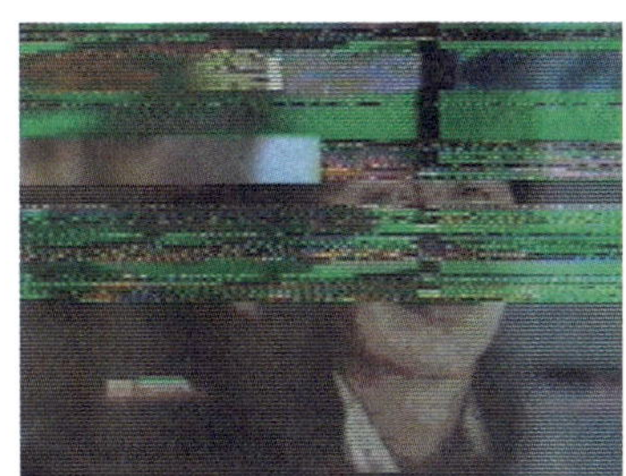
21:08

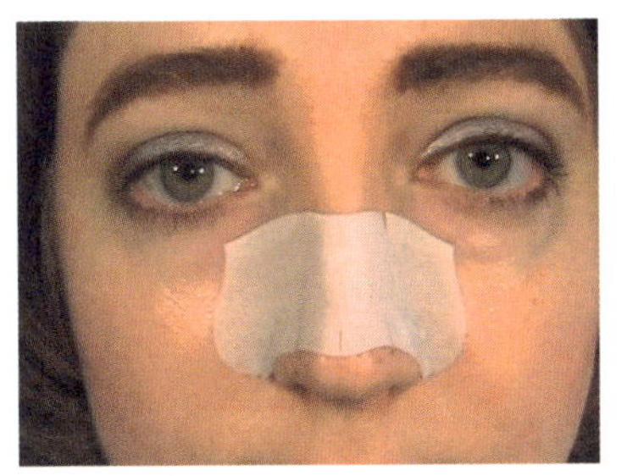
01:20

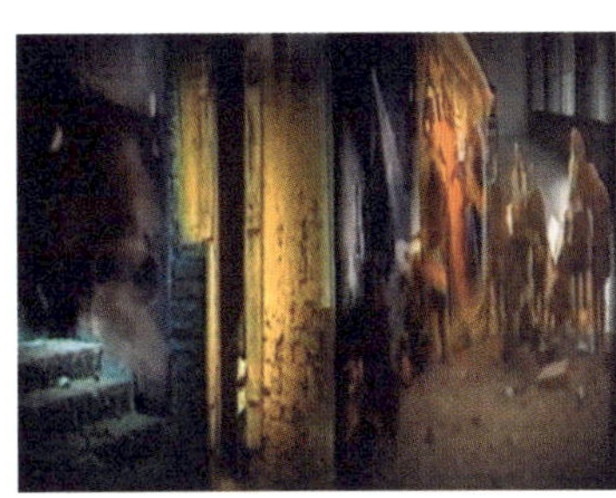
00:17

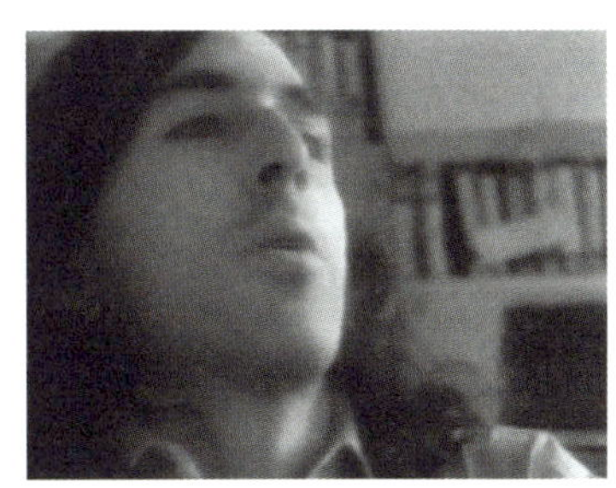
04:20

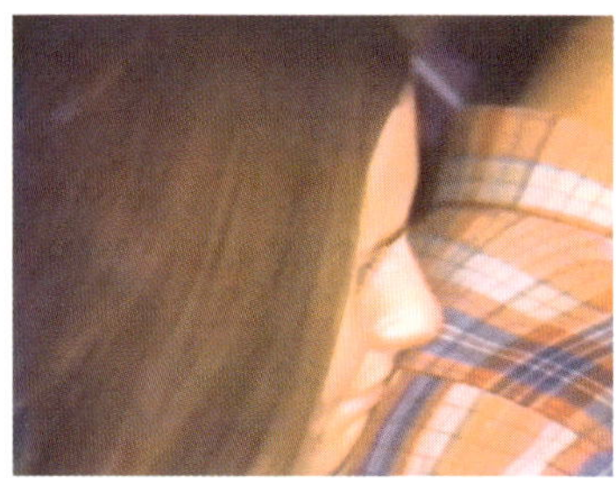

01:29

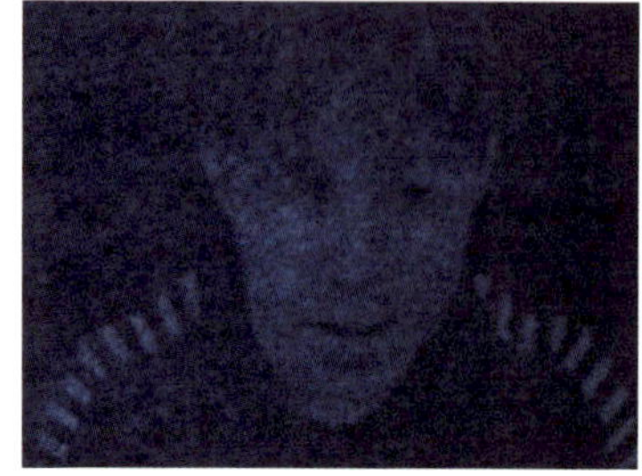

01:49

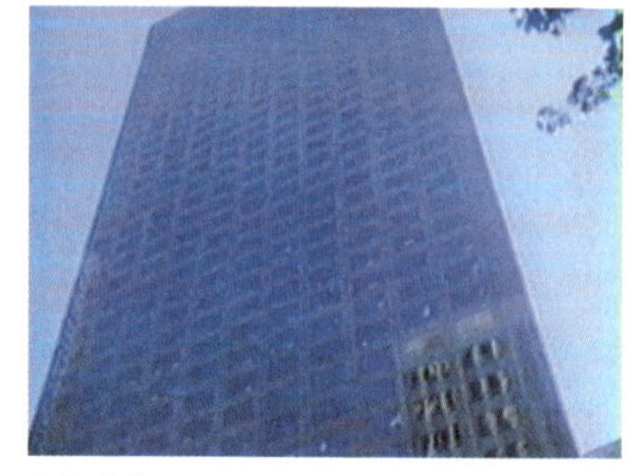

06:04

14:13

17:37

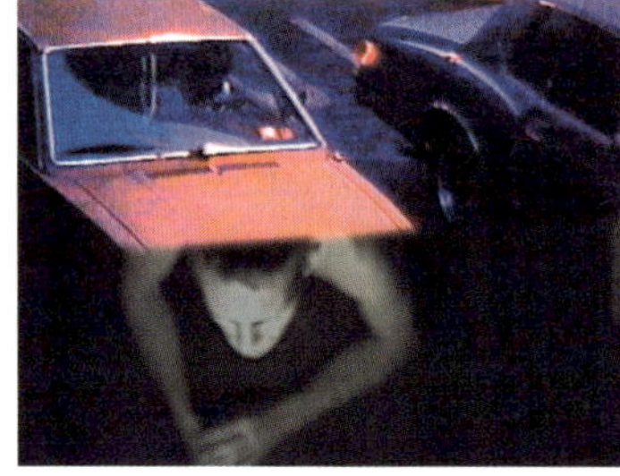

07:25

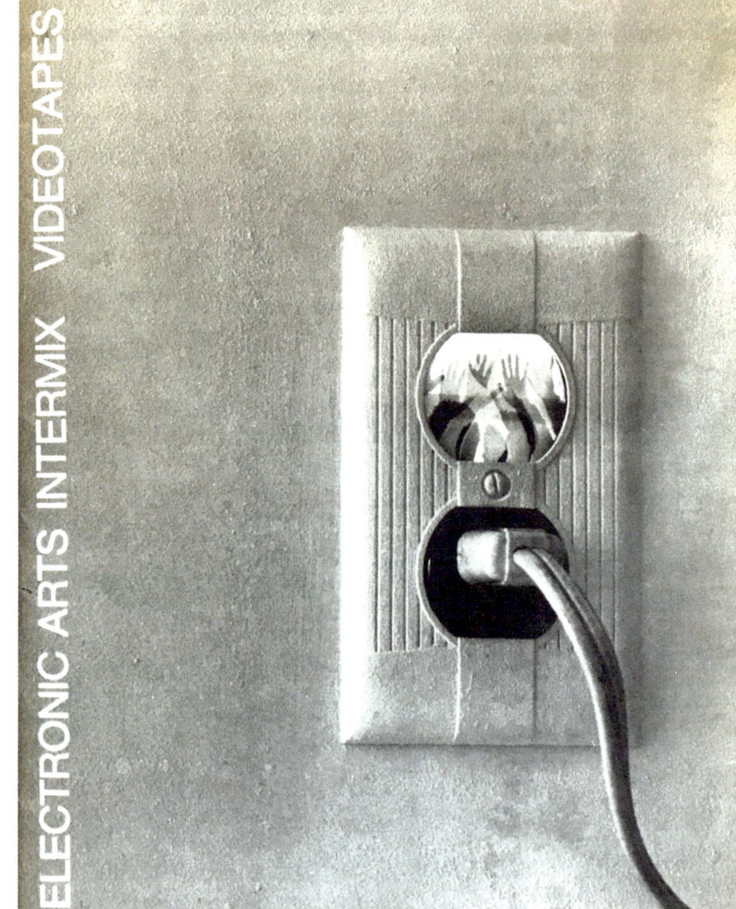

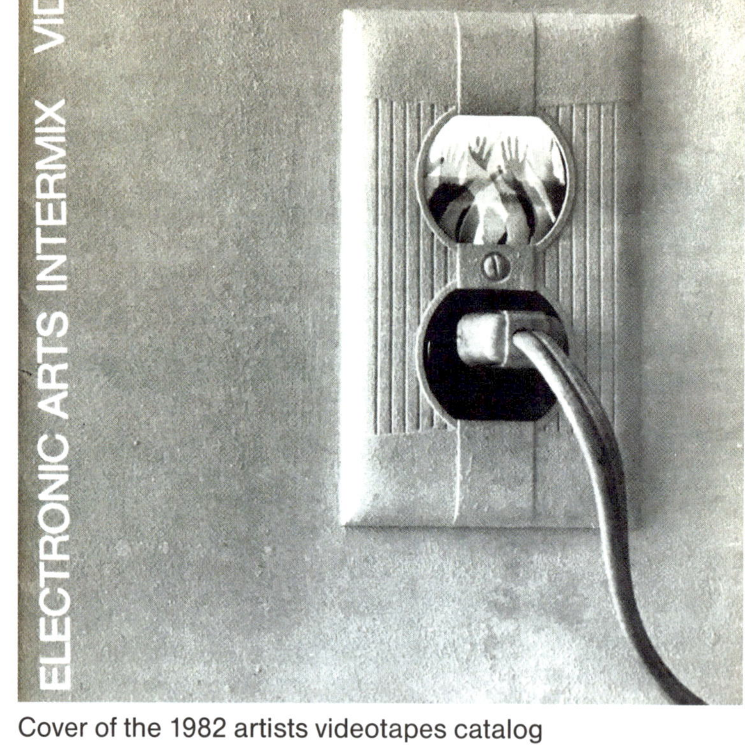

Cover of the 1982 artists videotapes catalog

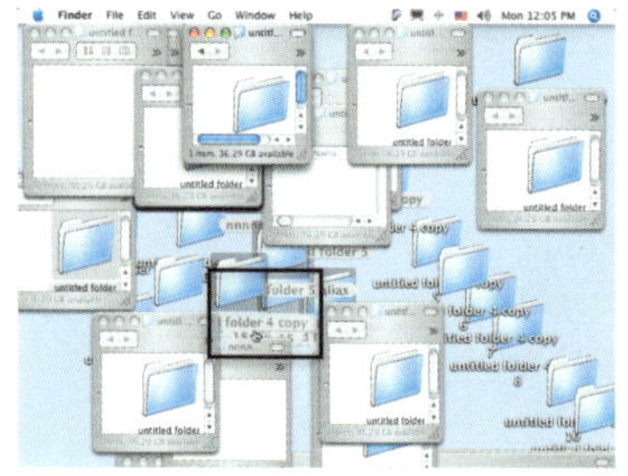

01:00

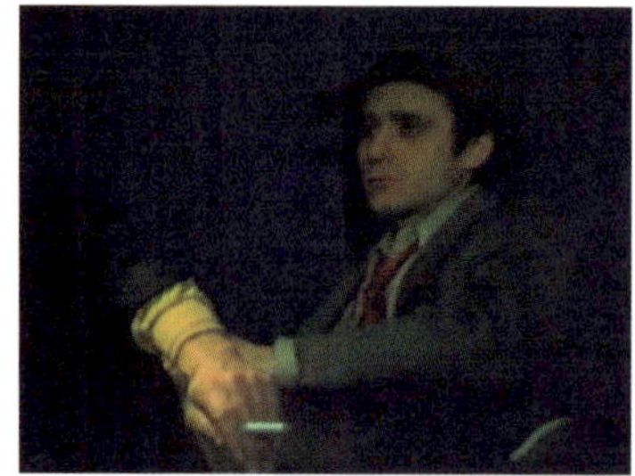

08:31

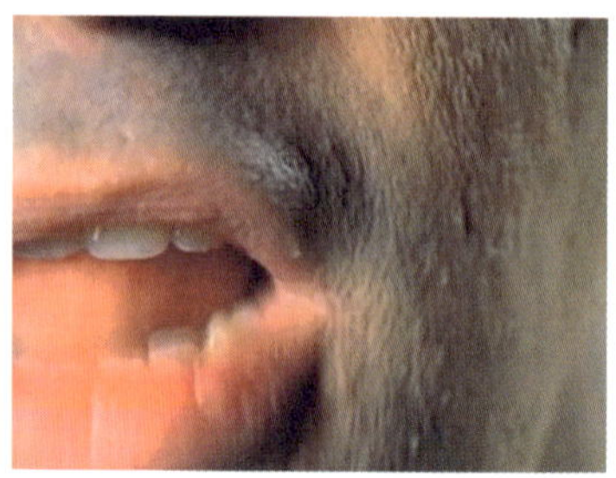

00:15

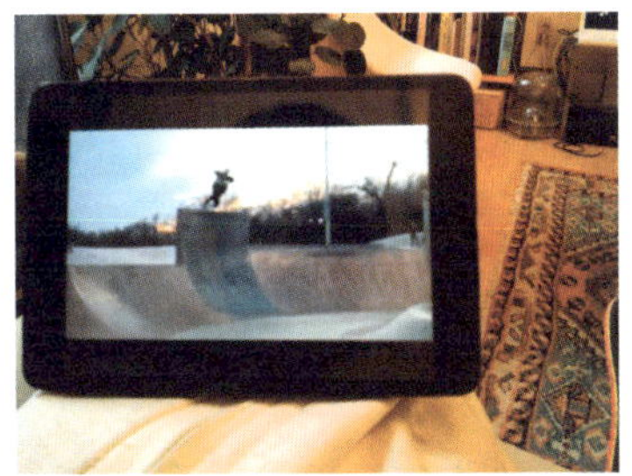
03:54

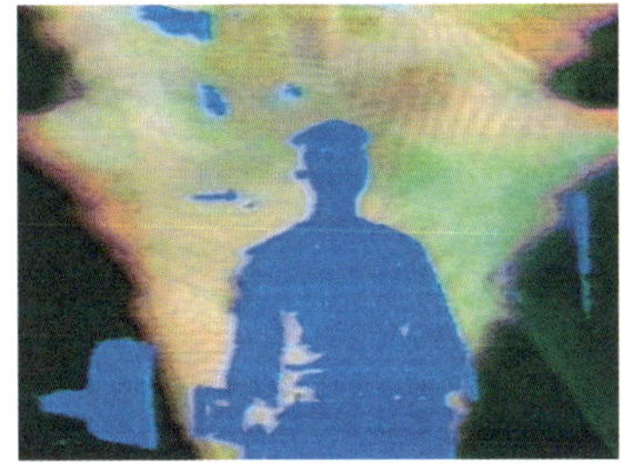
14:25

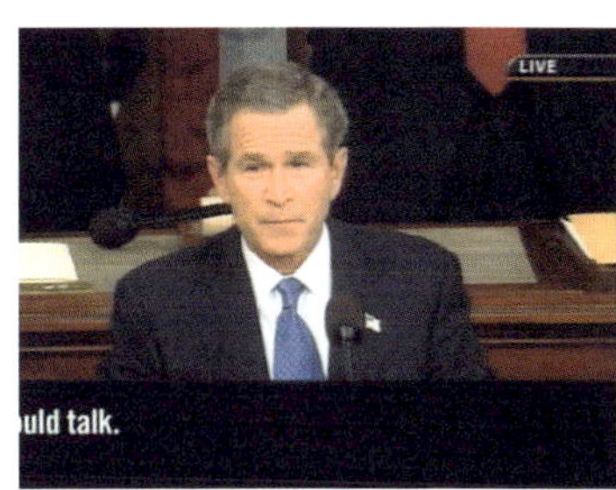

04:27

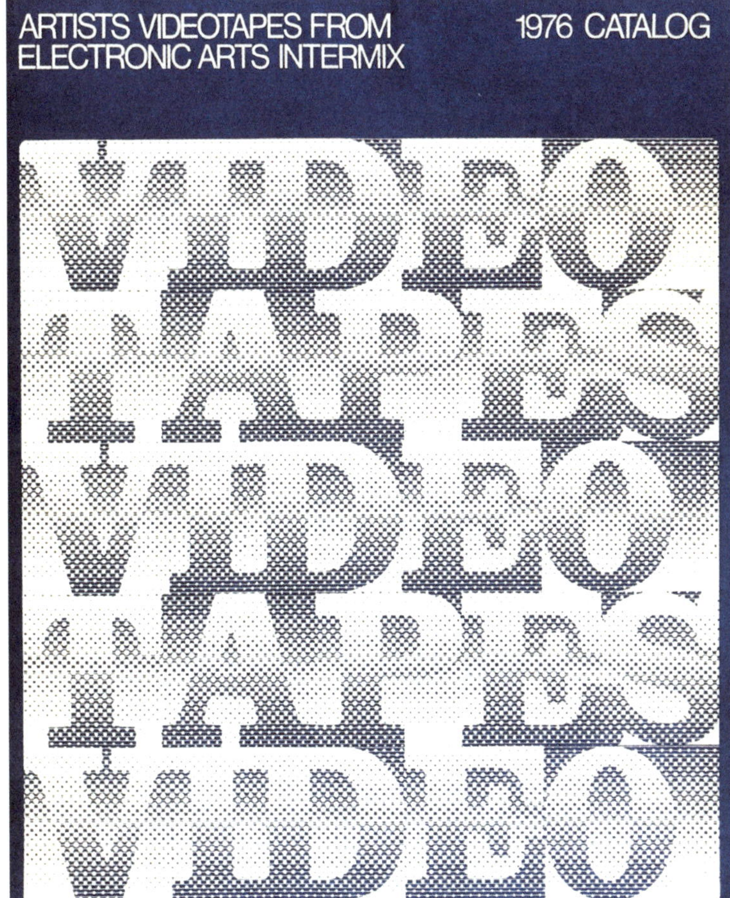

Cover of the 1976 artists videotapes catalog

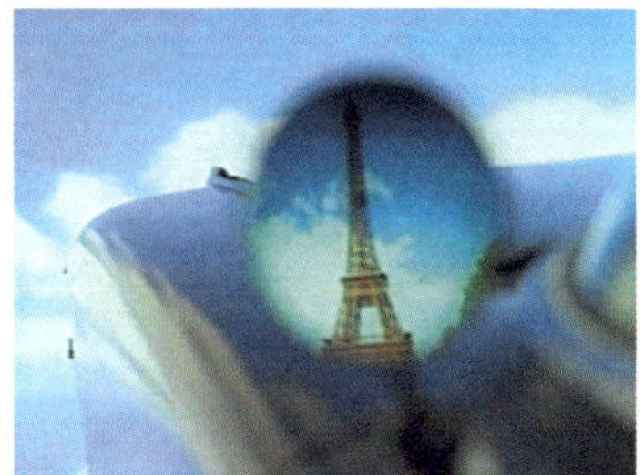
00:14

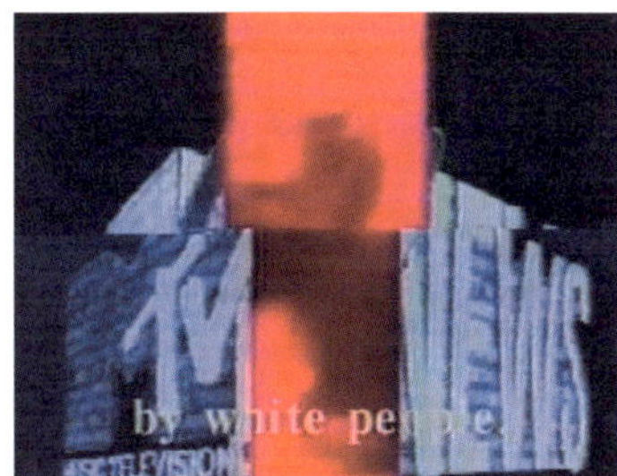
00:31

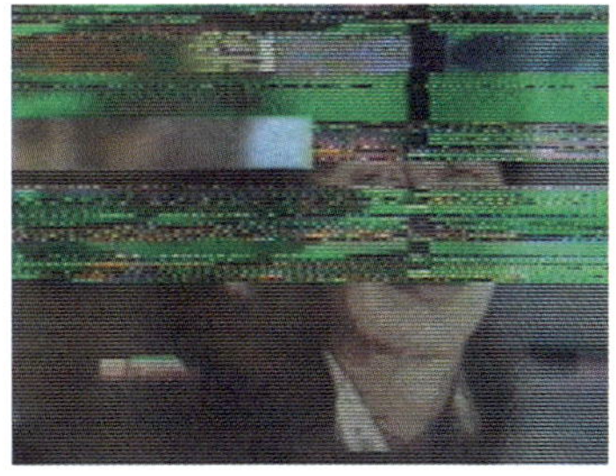
21:08

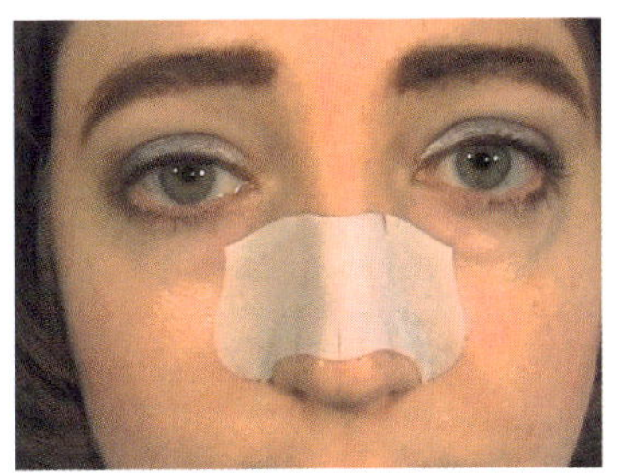
01:20

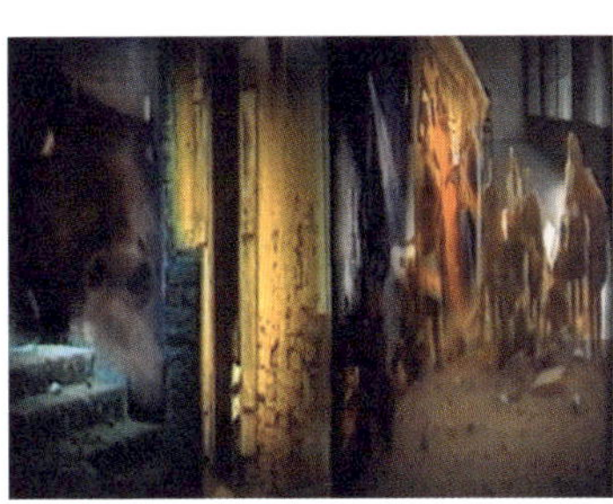
00:17

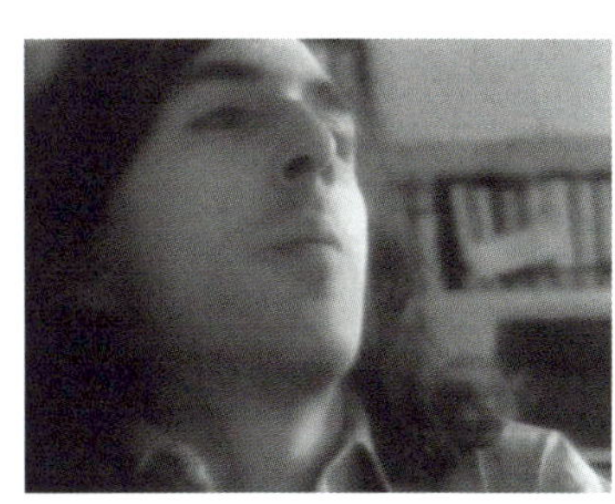
04:20

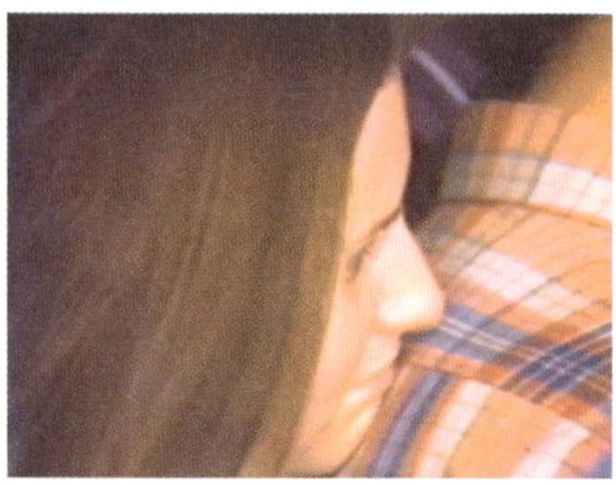

01:29

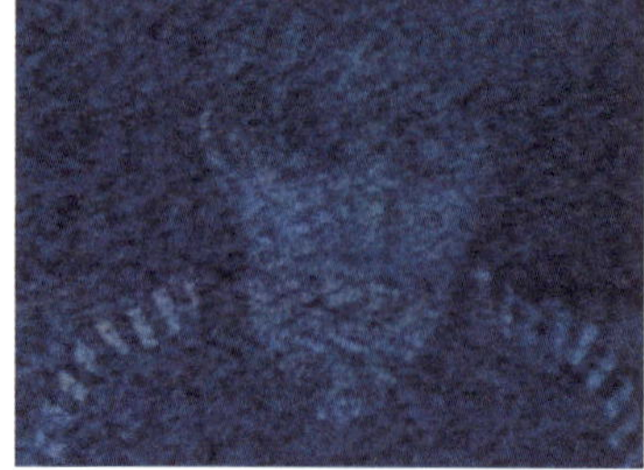

01:49

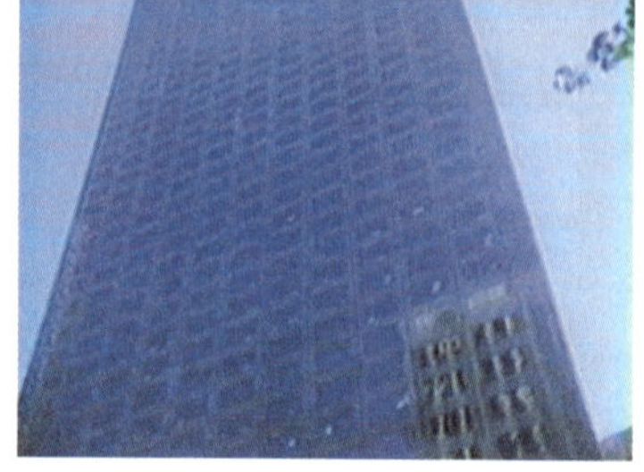

06:04

14:13

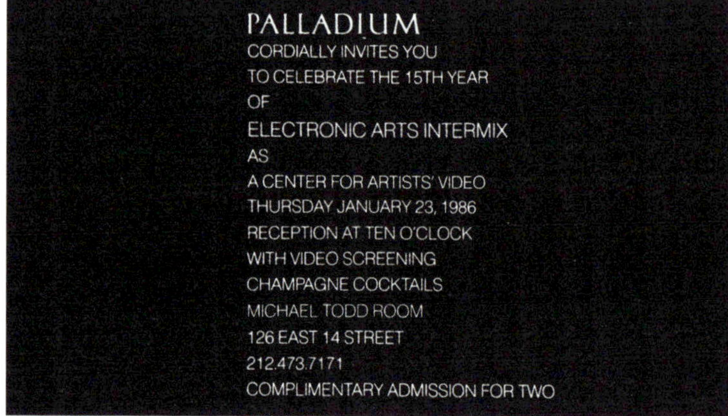

Postcard advertising EAI's 15th anniversary, 1986

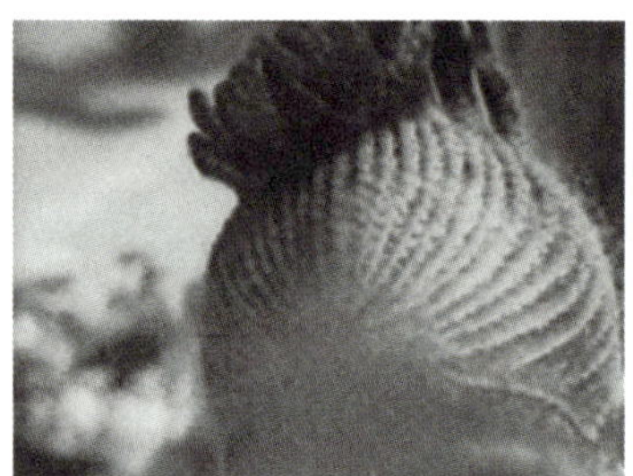

17:37

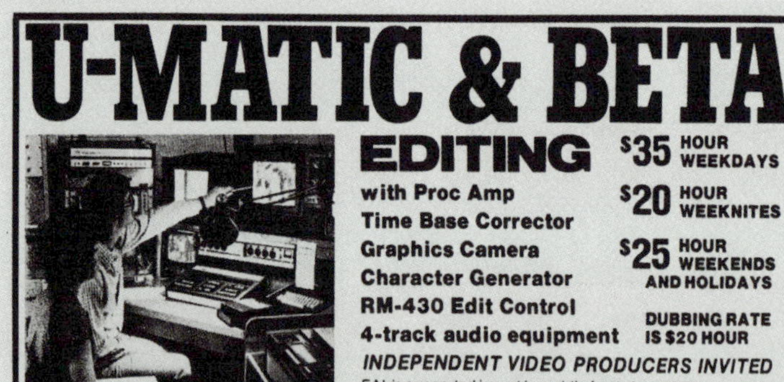

Flyer advertising U-Matic and Beta editing services

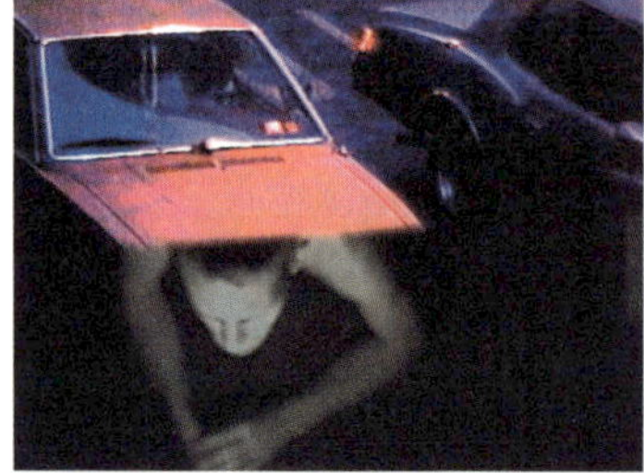

07:25

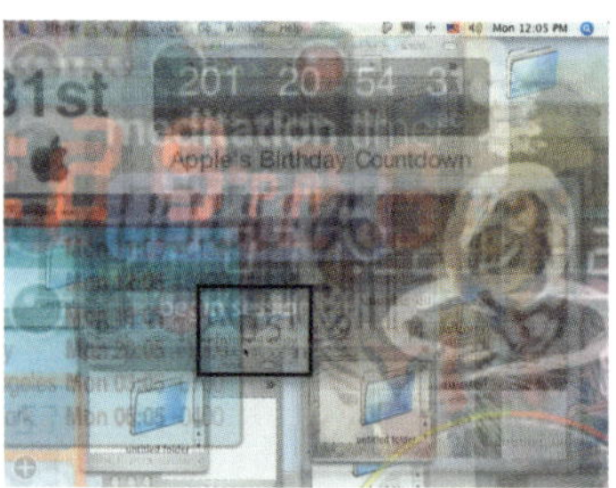

01:00

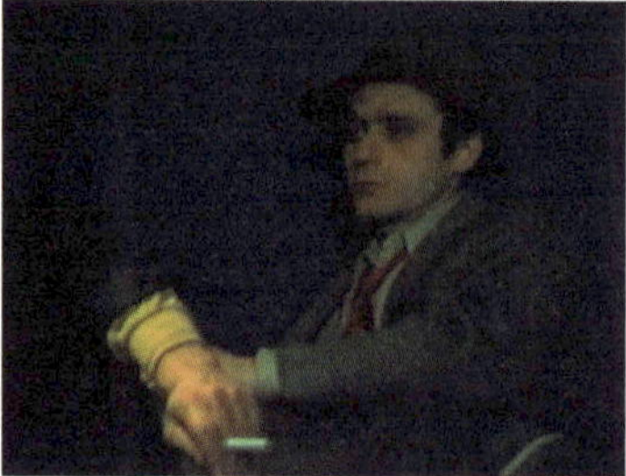

08:31

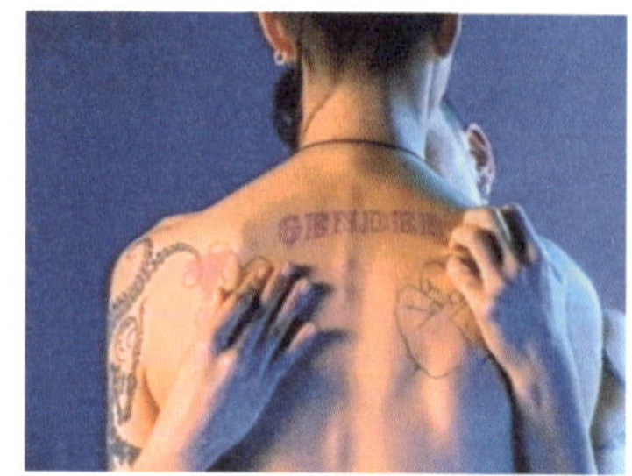

00:15

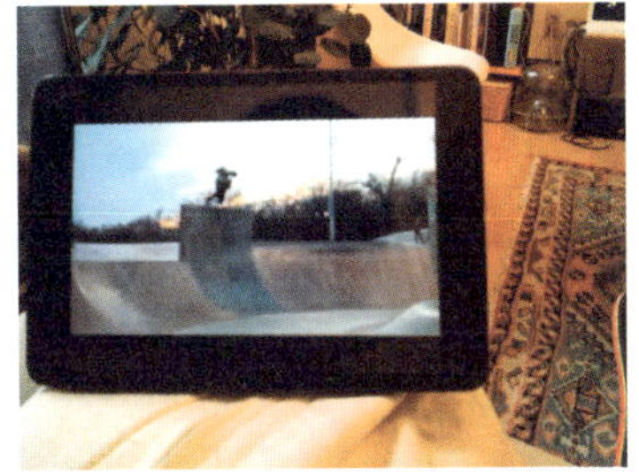

03:54

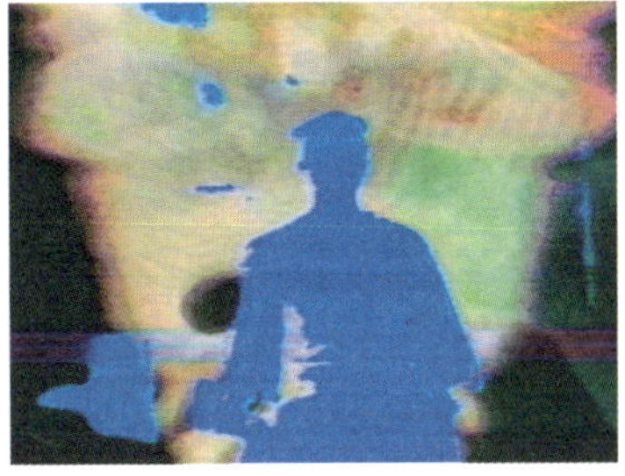

14:25

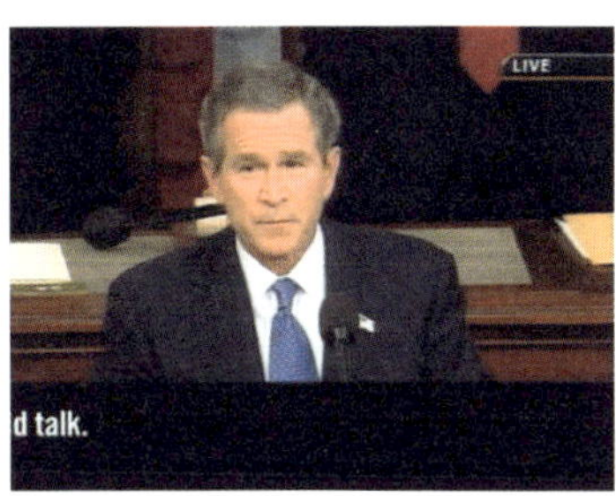

04:27

wanted to lay sound down you'd have to rewind the tape and rewind and rewind as you laid down edits. Whatever was being played in the editing room was the soundtrack to our days. Some days it would be Jimi Hendrix, other days it would be a demonologist. The physicality of the space was so different. Phones were ringing constantly because people talked on the telephone then.

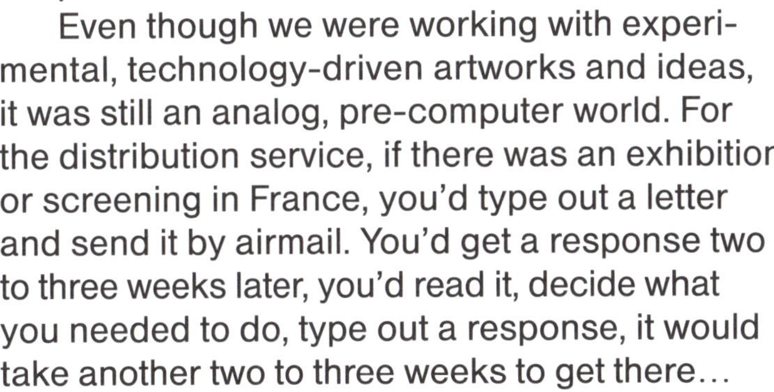

Even though we were working with experimental, technology-driven artworks and ideas, it was still an analog, pre-computer world. For the distribution service, if there was an exhibition or screening in France, you'd type out a letter and send it by airmail. You'd get a response two to three weeks later, you'd read it, decide what you needed to do, type out a response, it would take another two to three weeks to get there…

RC – —that's kind of nice!

LZ – The pace of everything—it was more—

AK – —humane—

LZ – —and analog. It was stressful for other reasons. But for distribution purposes, the

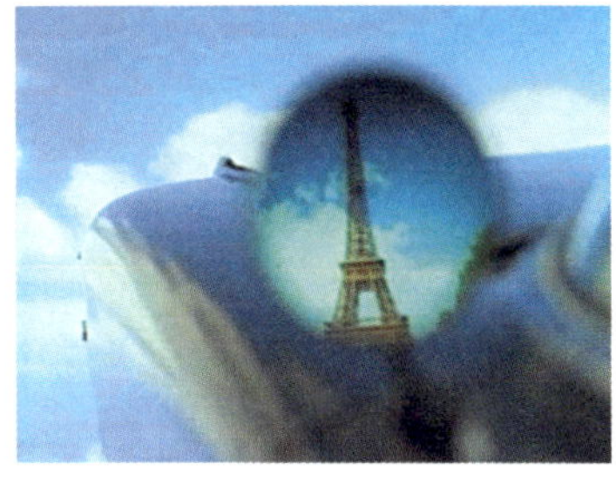

00:14

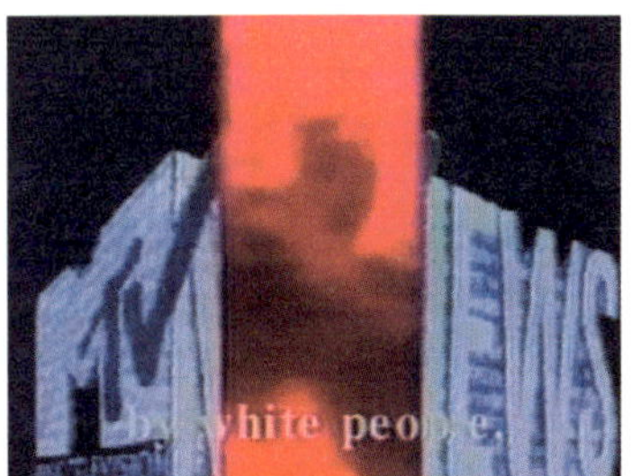

00:31

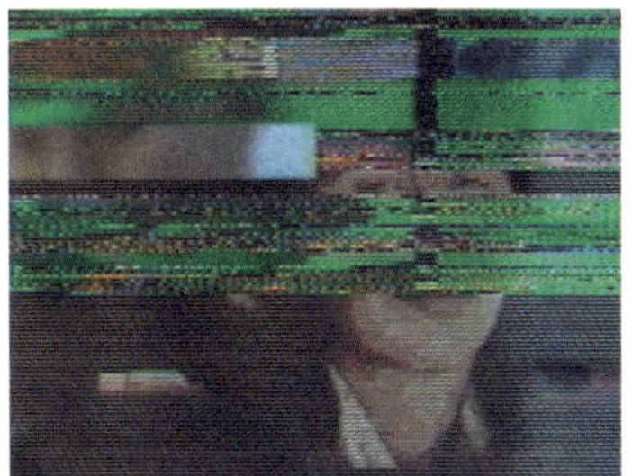

21:08

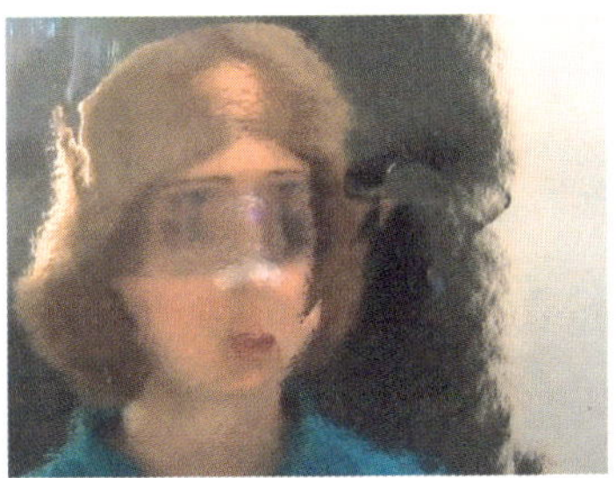

01:20

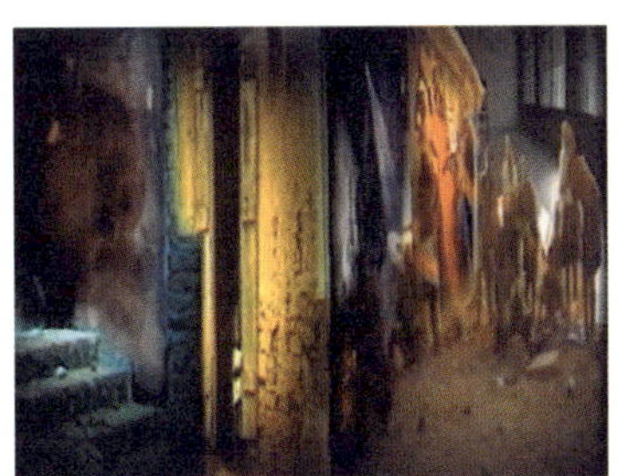

00:17

04:20

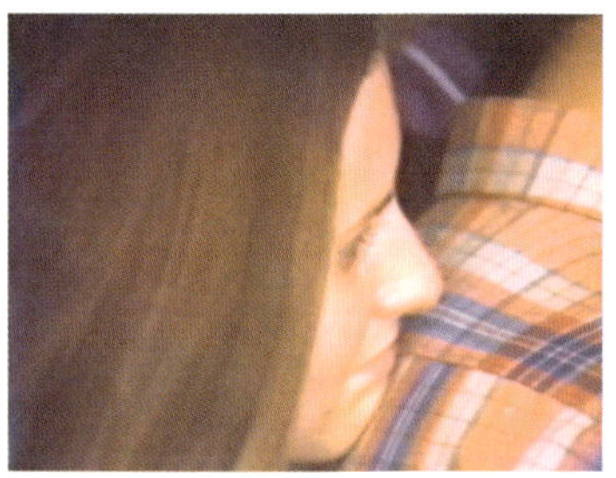

01:29

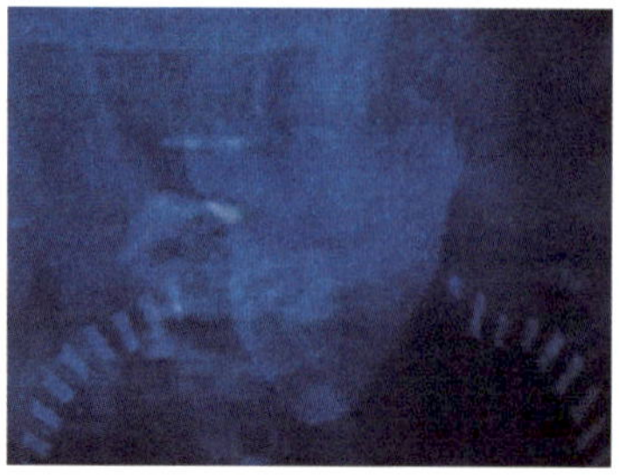

01:49

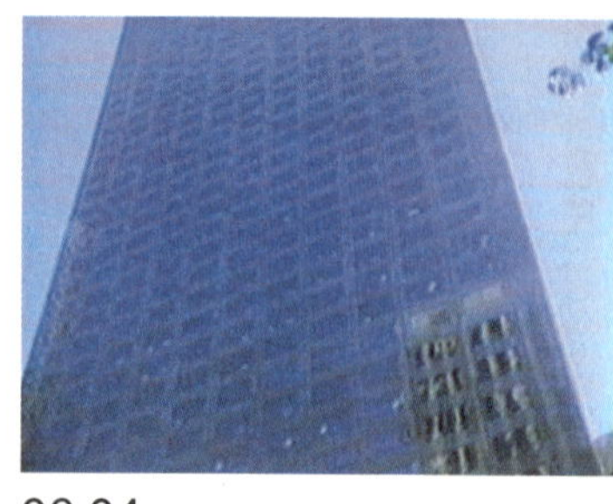

06:04

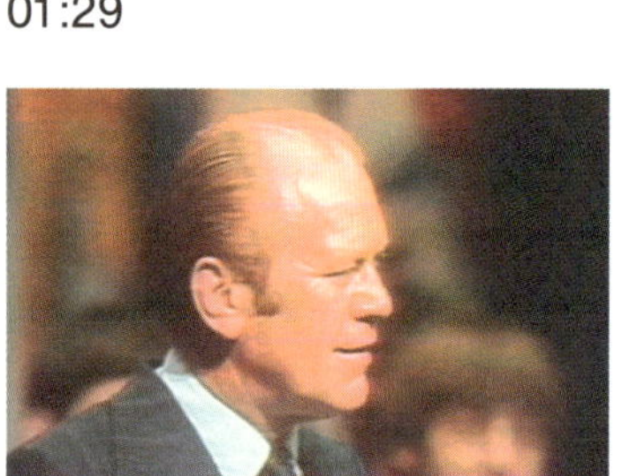

14:13

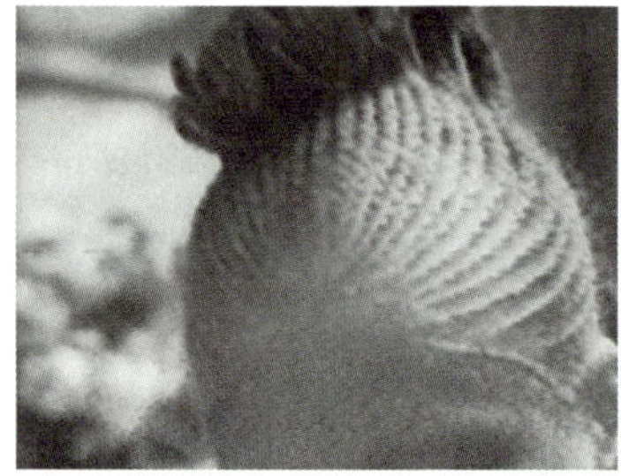

17:37

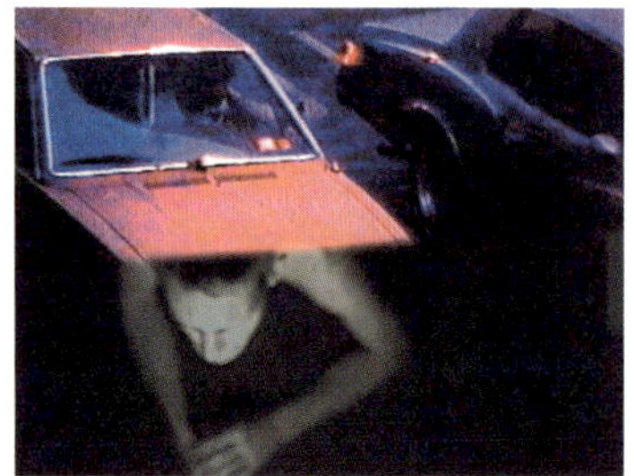

07:25

pace of communication was so different by phone or letter. It would take months to execute one transaction.

AK – You must have witnessed the genesis of a lot of really amazing work. It's incredible.

LZ – It's true. And just the joy of seeing certain artists—someone like Tony Oursler, for example, who we've worked with from the beginning, with his earliest video works. Just to be working with him as he was evolving as an artist, from the time he was a young artist—he's my age—to watch artists develop over the years is extraordinary.

I've noticed that we've referenced Dara Birnbaum repeatedly in our conversation. She's an artist who we've worked closely with across multiple facets of the organization—editing, distribution, preservation, exhibition—over the course of many decades. Carolee Schneemann would be another example.

AK – What was your trajectory within the organization?

LZ – I went from an administrative assistant to an administrator while Howard was active,

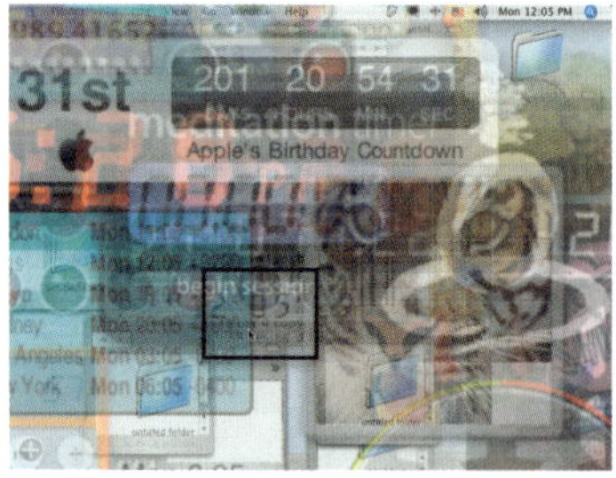

01:00

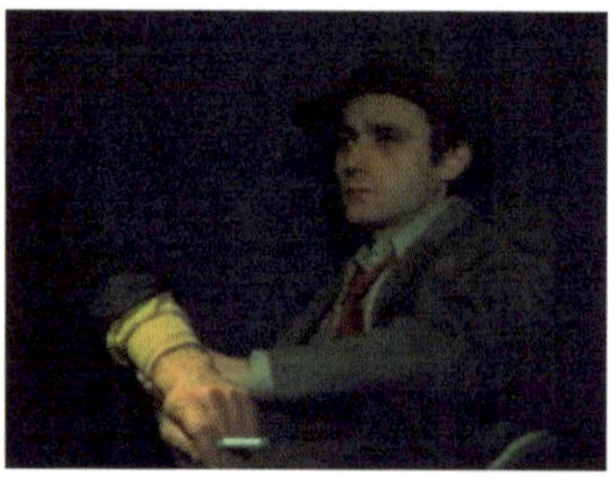

08:31

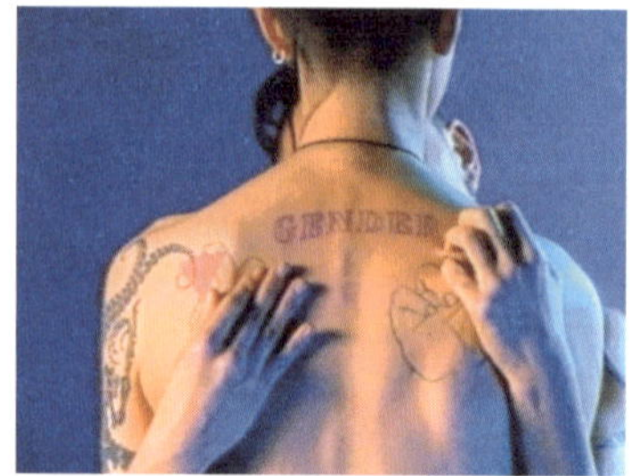

00:15

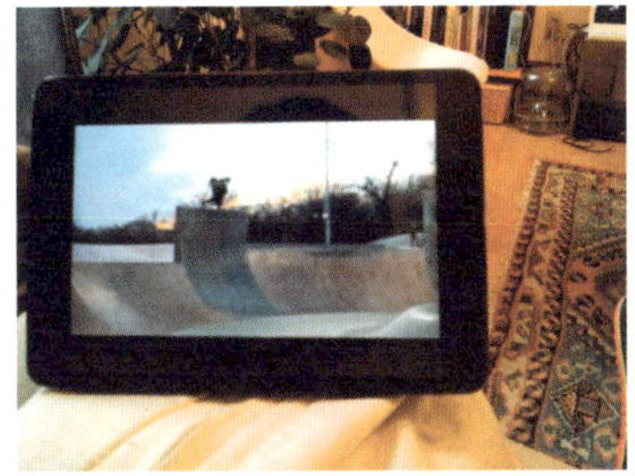

03:55

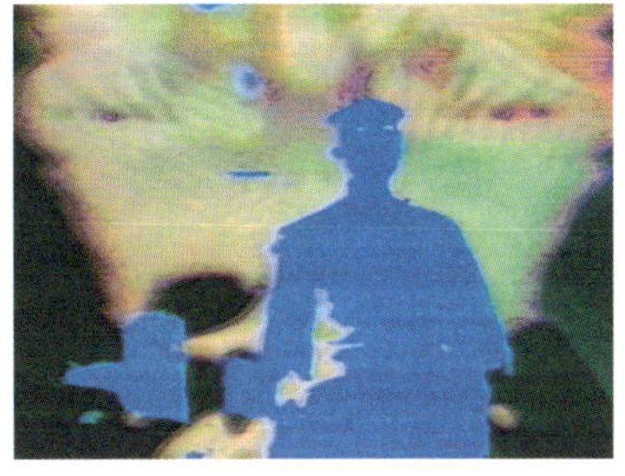

14:26

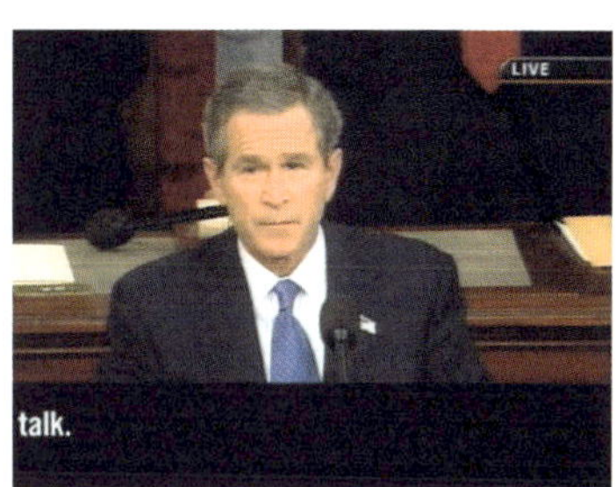

04:28

to distribution director, and then to executive director.

AK – How many people worked at EAI in the eighties?

LZ – Until 1985, it was Howard, about five full-time staff, and several part-timers, and then the rotating cast of editors. The editing staff was probably as big as the administrative and distribution staff.

RC – Wow.

AK – And how was EAI funded at that point? Was it surviving on the editing suite fees?

LZ – At that point EAI had NYSCA, NEA, and Rockefeller support, and earned income from fees from editing and distribution. Howard didn't take a salary.

AK – We talked a little bit about what the catalog looked like in 1973, but what was its texture like by the early eighties? Was it more formalized?

LZ – It was more formalized, but in some ways still evolving. There was a library system, but no preservation at that point. It was referred to as the "distribution collection."

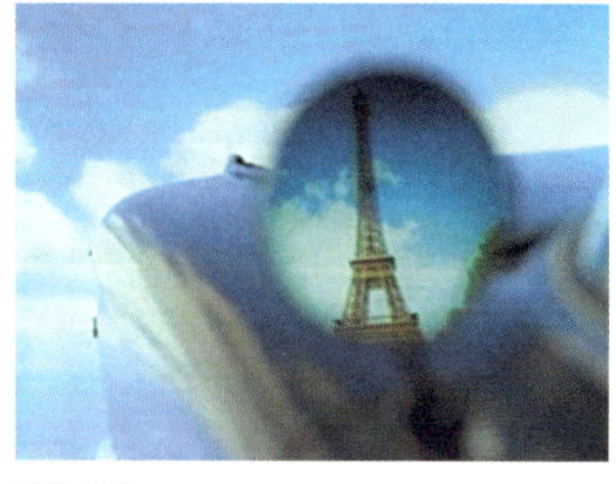

00:15

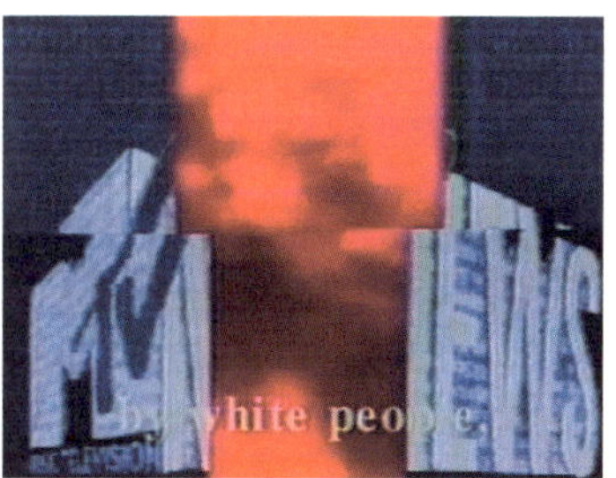

00:32

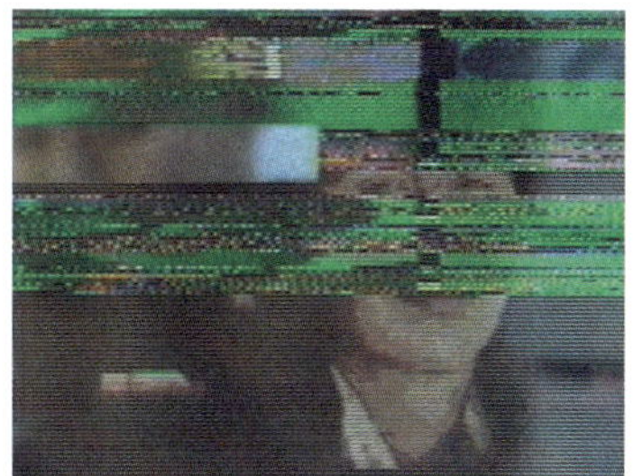

21:09

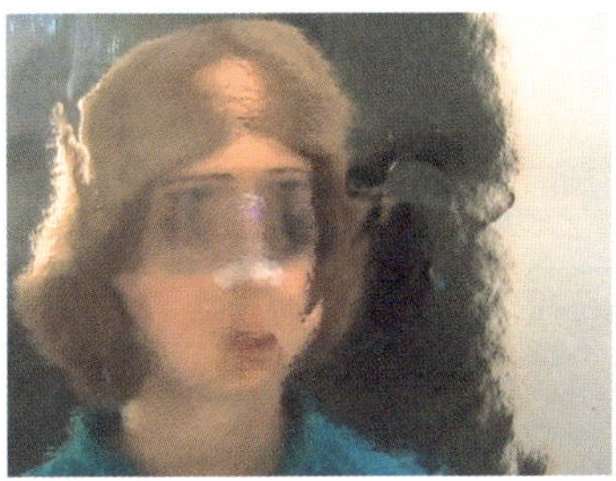

01:21

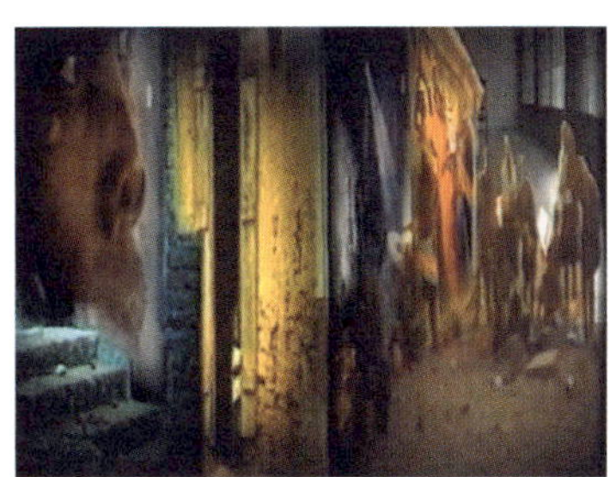

00:18

04:21

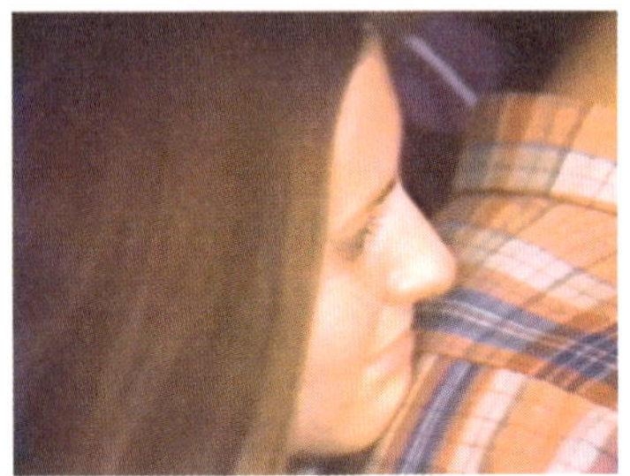
01:29

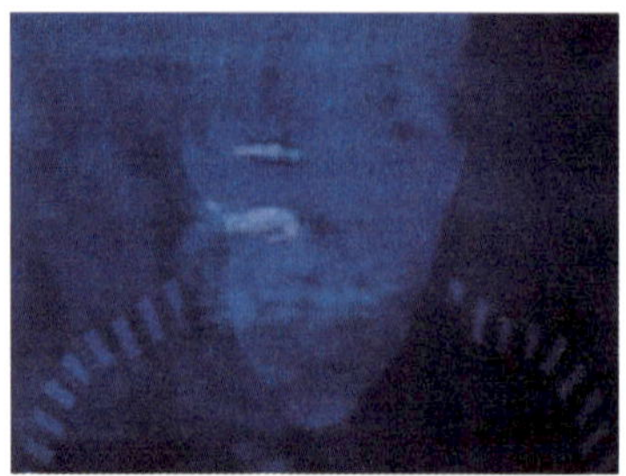
01:49

06:04

AK – That's interesting. So, that's ten years into the institution? I think that is often a moment when organizations tend to really come into their identities.

LZ – Yes, exactly. At that point we were still often distributing individual titles, whereas now we represent entire bodies of an artist's work, which was an important shift. So, if there was a specific work that we were interested in, we might say, "Okay, this seems like it would fit into a program at the Red Bar, so let's distribute this title." There wasn't a sense then of representing an artist's entire body of work.

AK – That's what I was going to ask, when does EAI start to say, "These are the artists that we're invested in, and this is an EAI artist."

LZ – At this point, there were still individual works coming and going and we'd sign a contract for a limited use, for example. So there's still a sense of ad hoc-ness, but not in a negative way.

AK – It sounds exciting!

LZ – It was, and the distribution collection was still much smaller then, just a few hundred

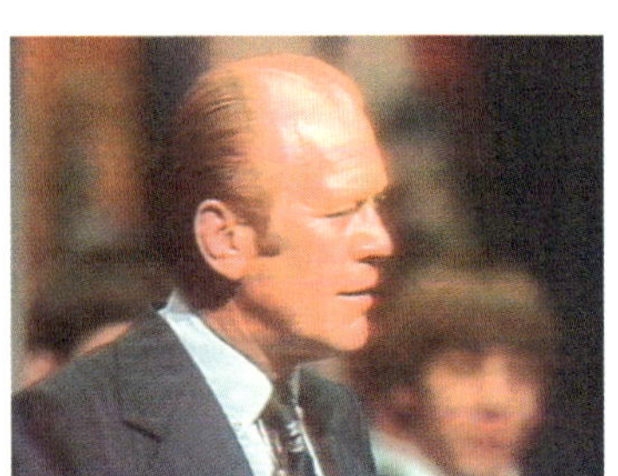
14:13

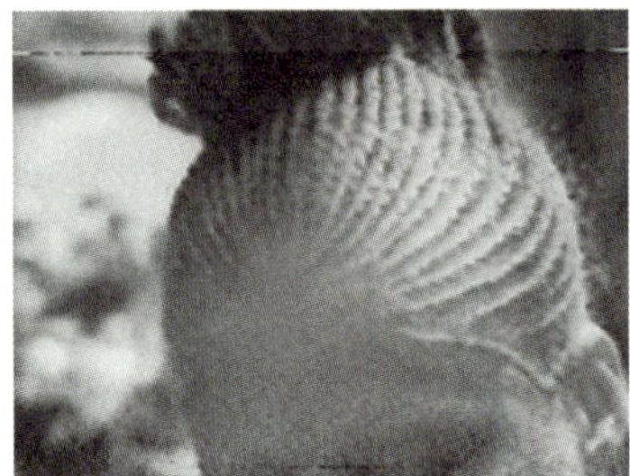
17:37

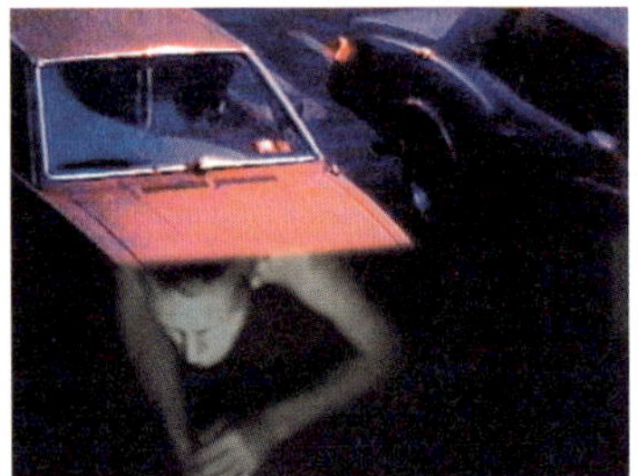
07:25

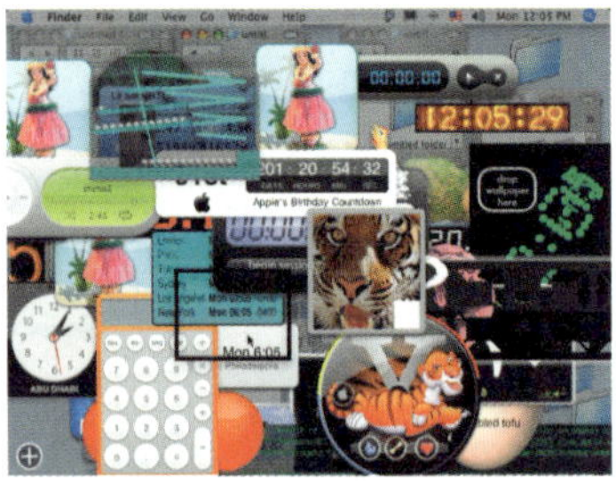
01:00

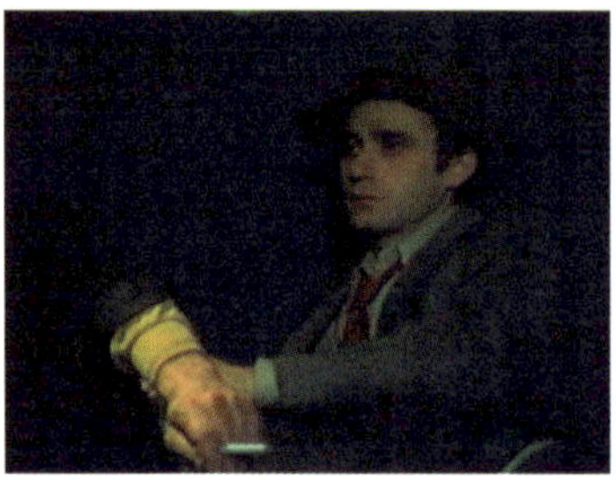
08:31

00:15

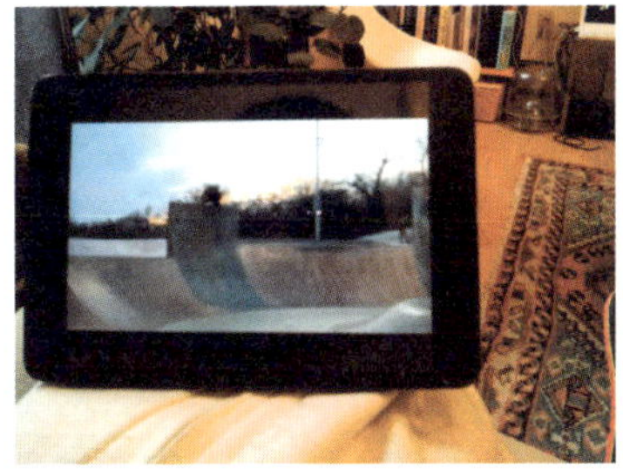

03:55

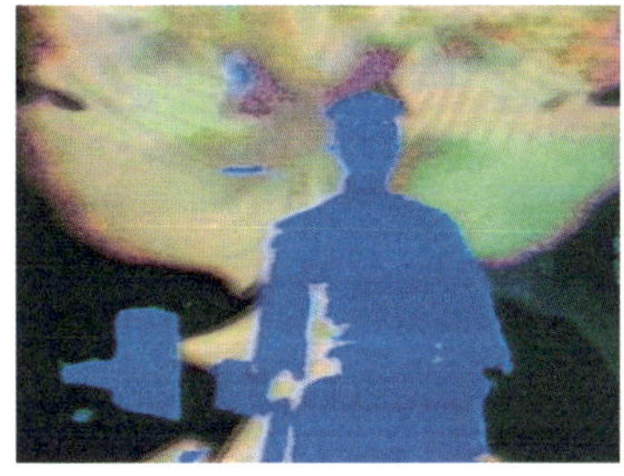

14:26

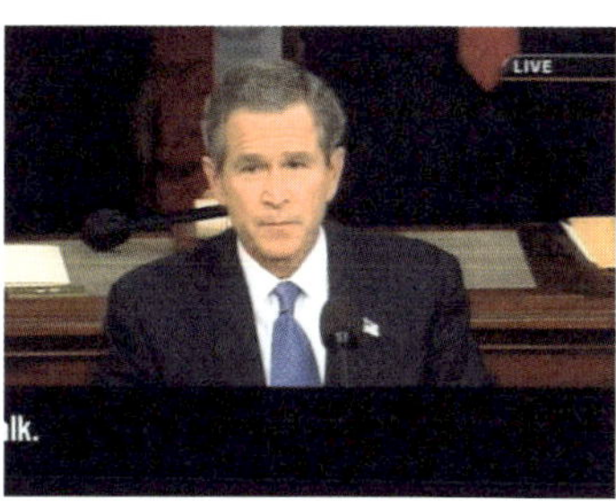

04:28

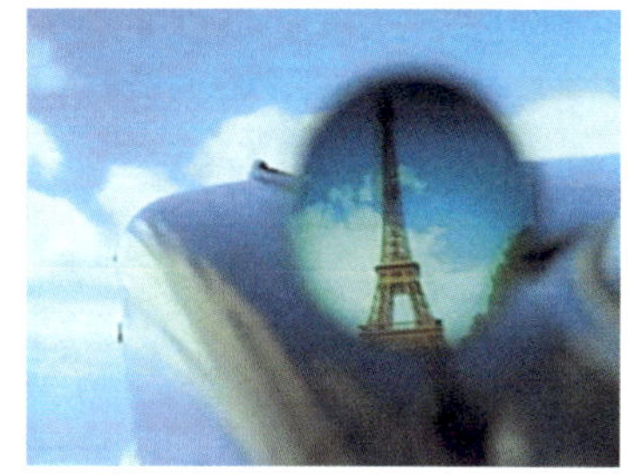

00:15

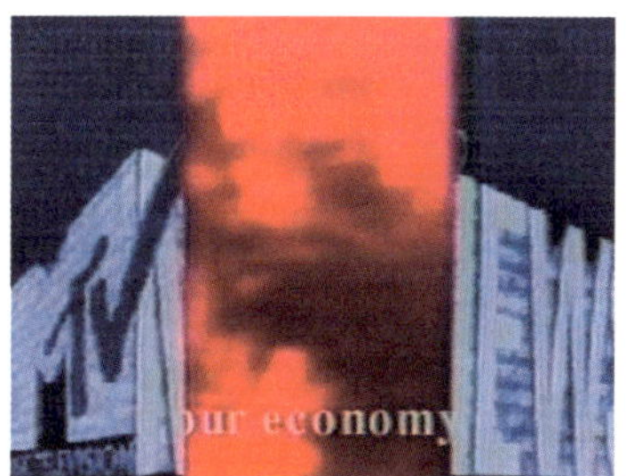

00:32

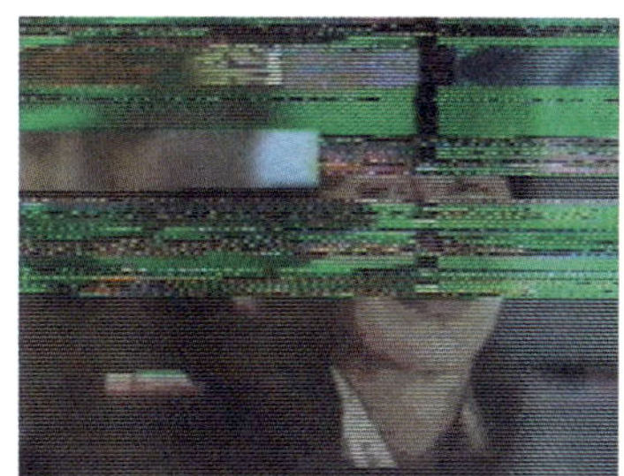

21:09

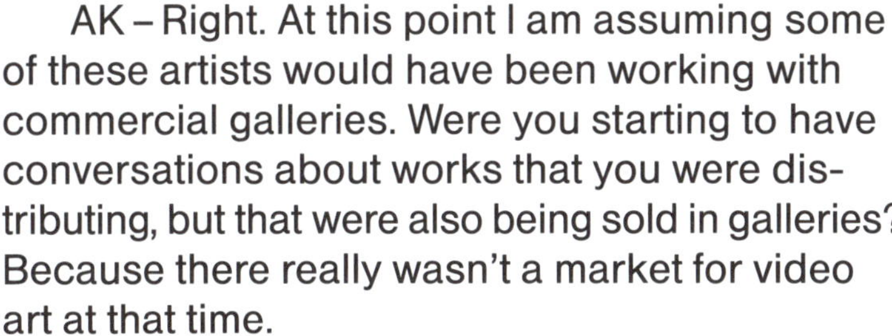

titles. (Today the collection has grown to nearly four thousand works.) There was much less of an investment in preservation. The physical process of distribution was entirely different back then. A tape would come into the distribution collection, you'd dub it, and send out the copy to a venue for a screening or exhibition. The technical process was much more spontaneous and fluid, because it was a different conception and context—we were only fifteen years into the medium.

AK – Right. At this point I am assuming some of these artists would have been working with commercial galleries. Were you starting to have conversations about works that you were distributing, but that were also being sold in galleries? Because there really wasn't a market for video art at that time.

LZ – Not really. What happened was that by the mid-1980s certain artists like Gary Hill, Mary Lucier, and Bill Viola started making video installations. These artists started to develop in a new direction that signaled a huge change. Artists

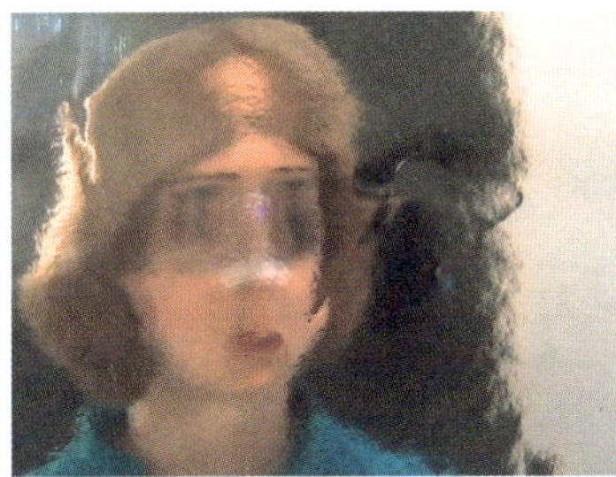

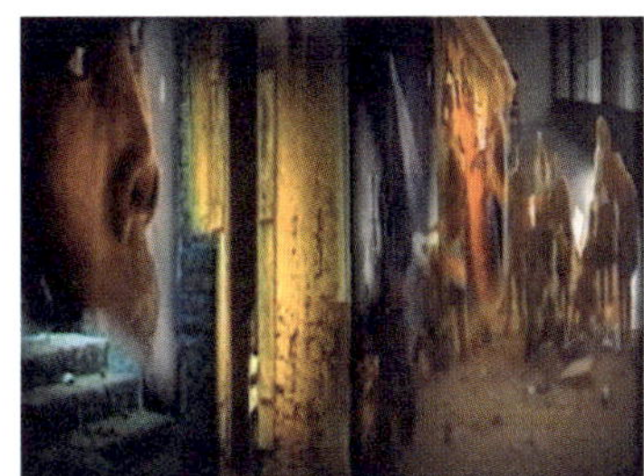

01:21

00:18

04:21

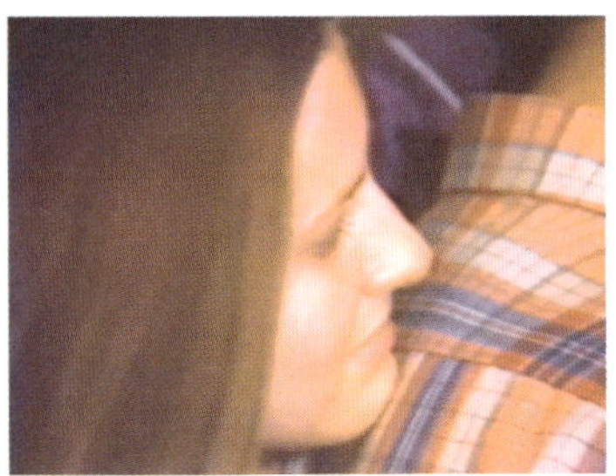
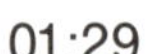
01:29

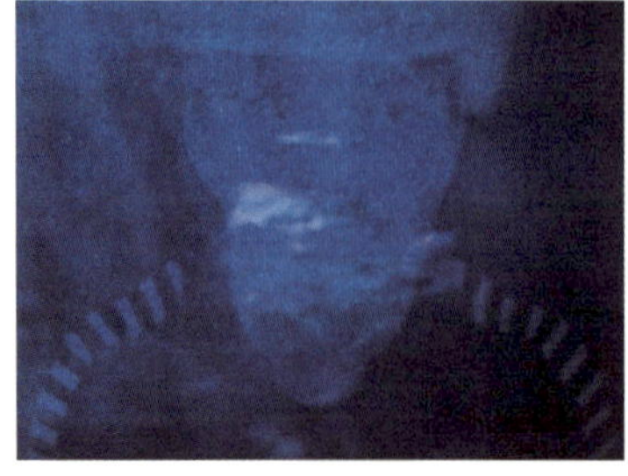
01:49

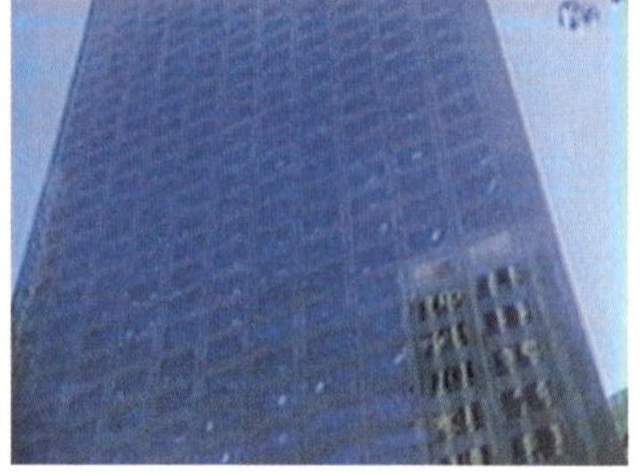
06:04

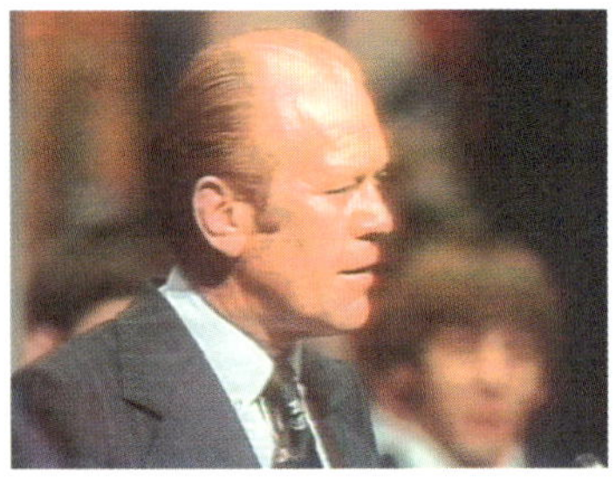
14:13

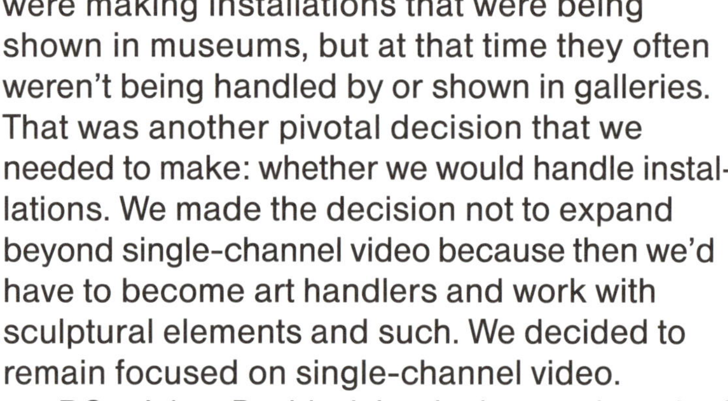
were making installations that were being shown in museums, but at that time they often weren't being handled by or shown in galleries. That was another pivotal decision that we needed to make: whether we would handle installations. We made the decision not to expand beyond single-channel video because then we'd have to become art handlers and work with sculptural elements and such. We decided to remain focused on single-channel video.

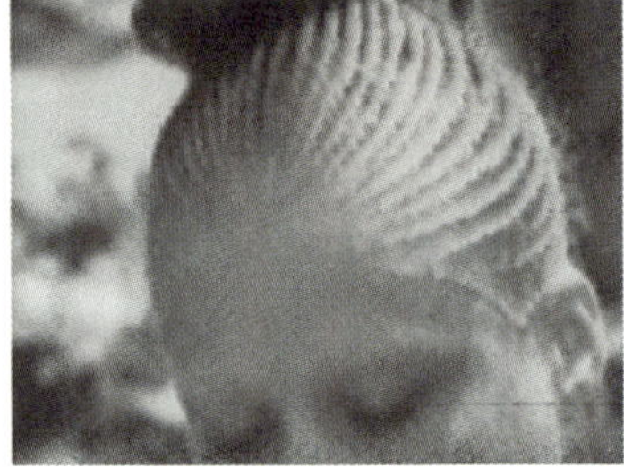
17:37

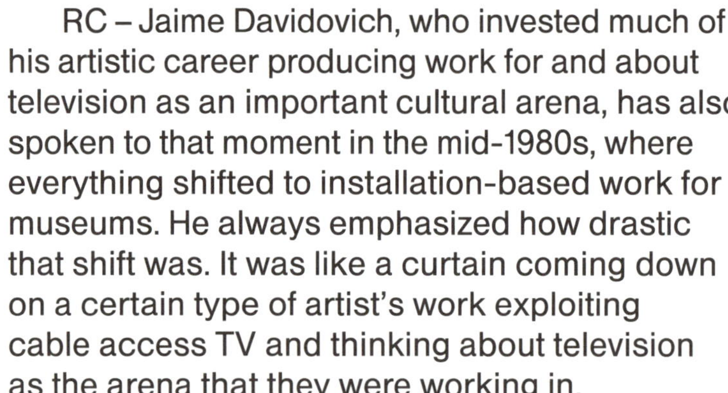
RC – Jaime Davidovich, who invested much of his artistic career producing work for and about television as an important cultural arena, has also spoken to that moment in the mid-1980s, where everything shifted to installation-based work for museums. He always emphasized how drastic that shift was. It was like a curtain coming down on a certain type of artist's work exploiting cable access TV and thinking about television as the arena that they were working in.

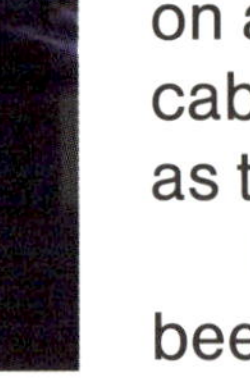
07:25

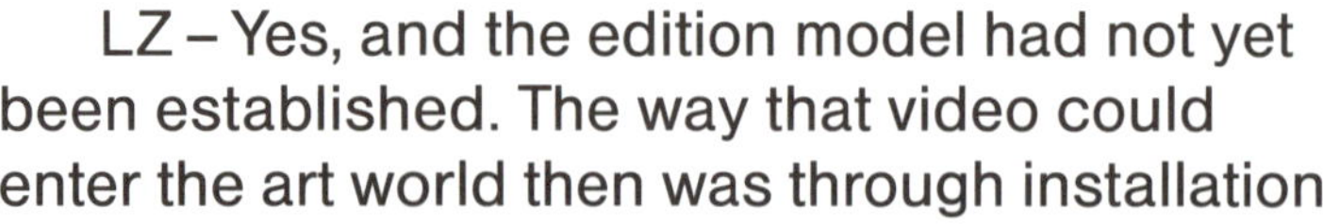
LZ – Yes, and the edition model had not yet been established. The way that video could enter the art world then was through installation.

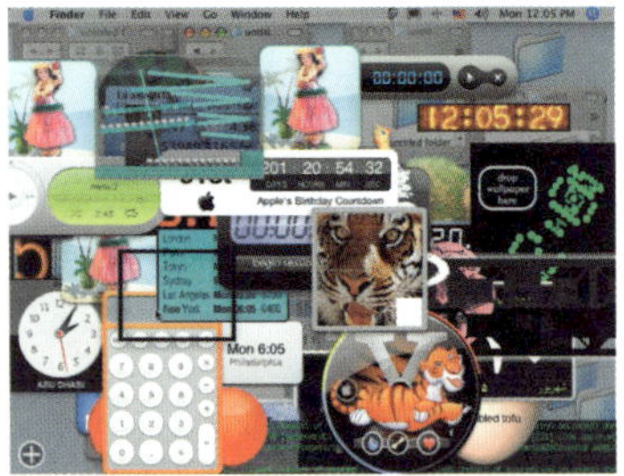
01:00

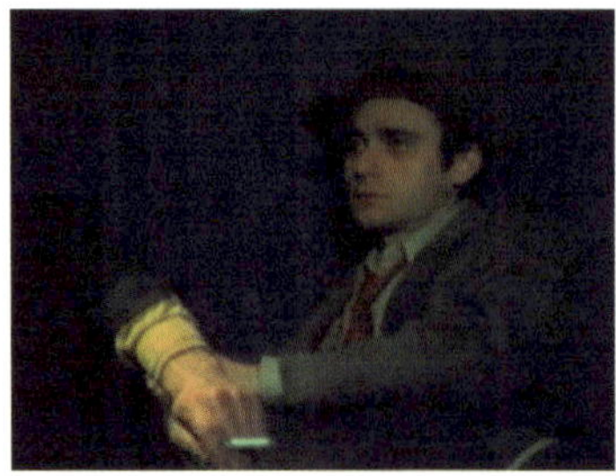
08:31

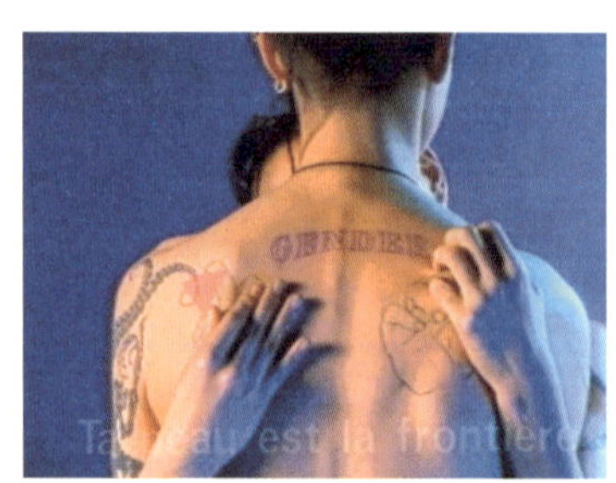
00:15

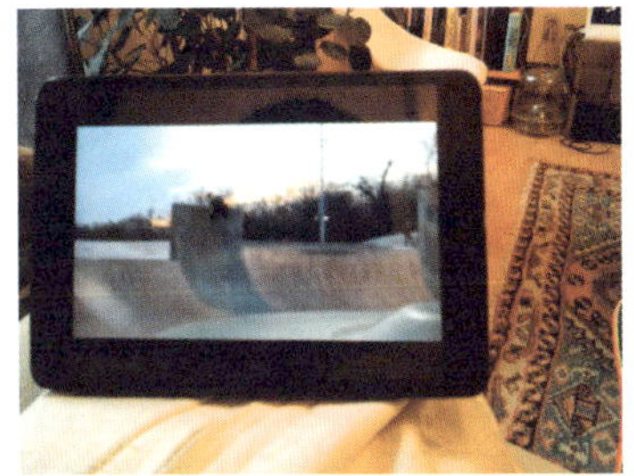
03:55

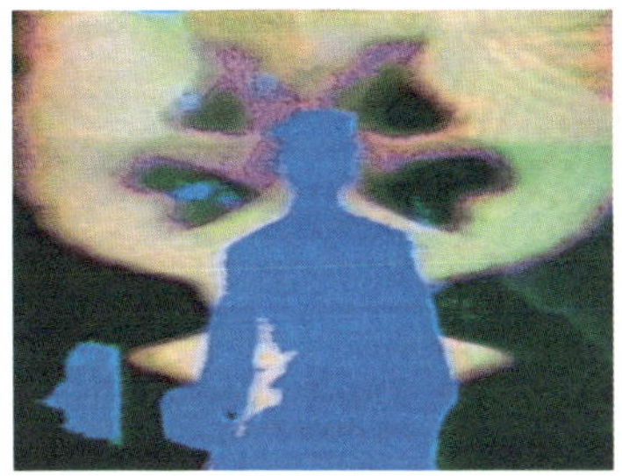
14:26

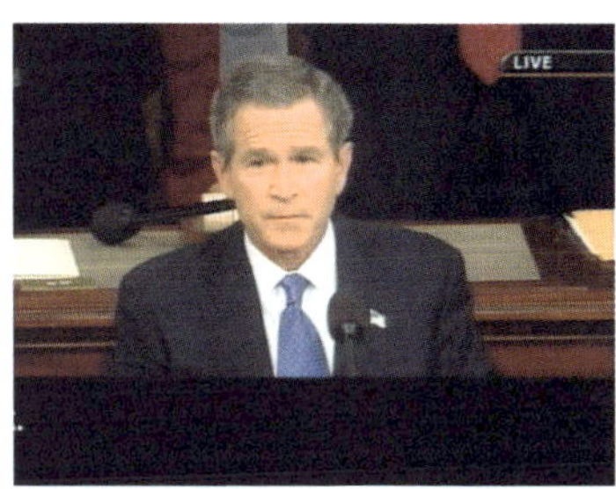

04:28

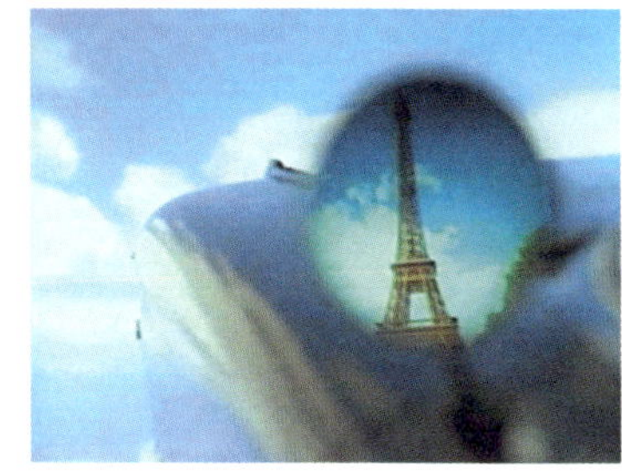
00:15

RC – A lot of arts funding was cut in President Reagan's second term, so artists had to start thinking about making money through selling their work via the art market.

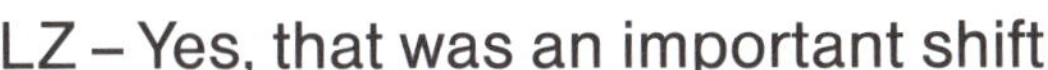

LZ – Yes, that was an important shift.

AK – What year did Howard leave EAI?

LZ – By the time we moved to 10 Waverly Place in 1985, he didn't have an office there. We'd have lovely lunches together and we'd talk about life and artists and we'd check in about EAI. But he wasn't very actively involved at that point.

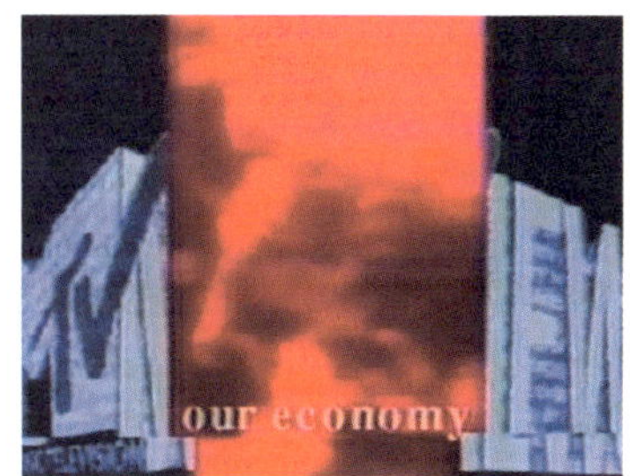

00:32

After Howard's death in 1989, his widow Barbara took on the role of board president. Barbi was a vivacious, larger-than-life figure who had performed in New York's experimental theater scene with the likes of Ethyl Eichelberger, Charles Ludlum and Stuart Sherman. Her parties were legendary—John and Yoko famously attended one in the seventies. When she entertained she would turn on all of the kinetic art pieces that filled her home, so that it came alive with a whirling, blinking, kaleidoscopic energy that mirrored her own. She was also a generous

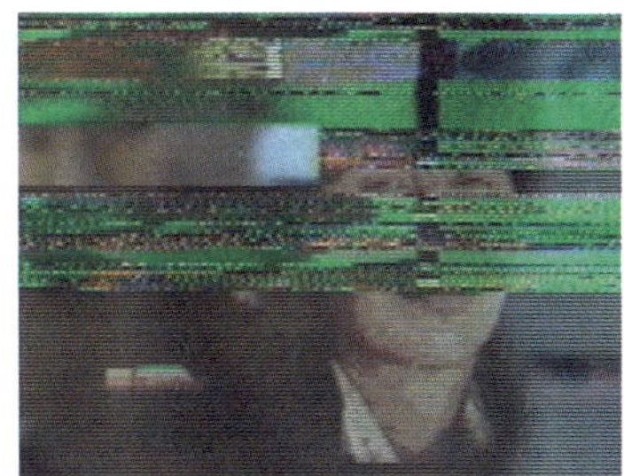
21:09

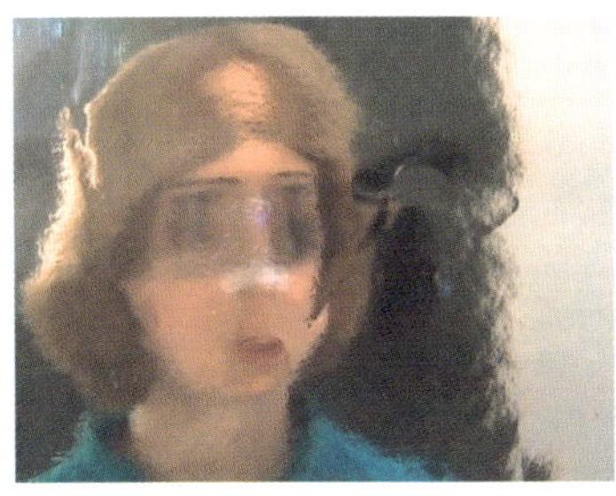
01:21

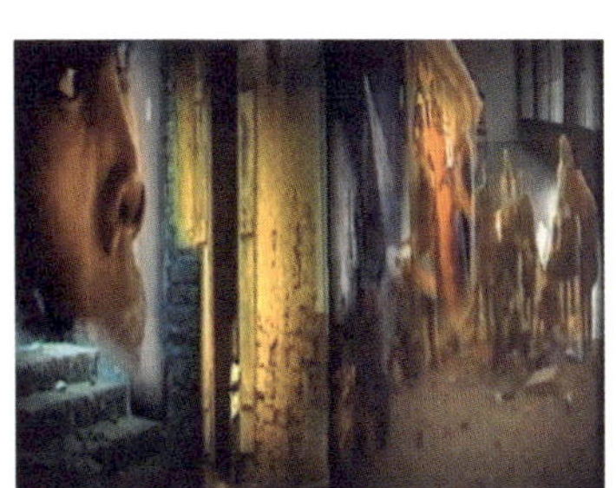
00:18

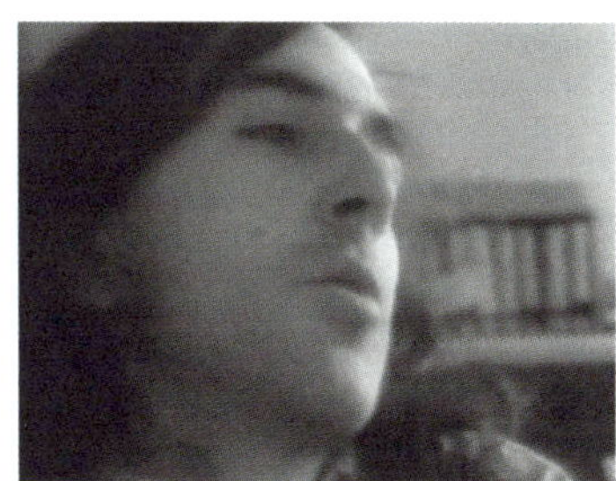
04:21

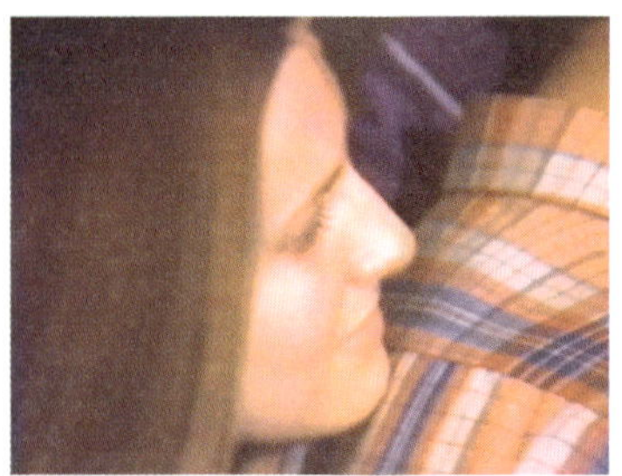
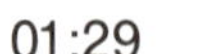

01:29

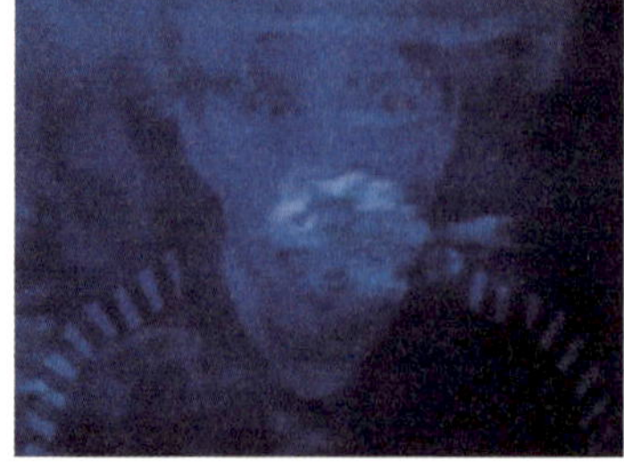

01:49

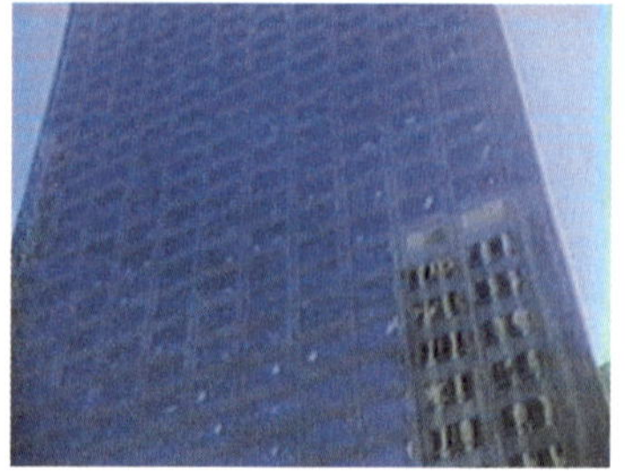

06:04

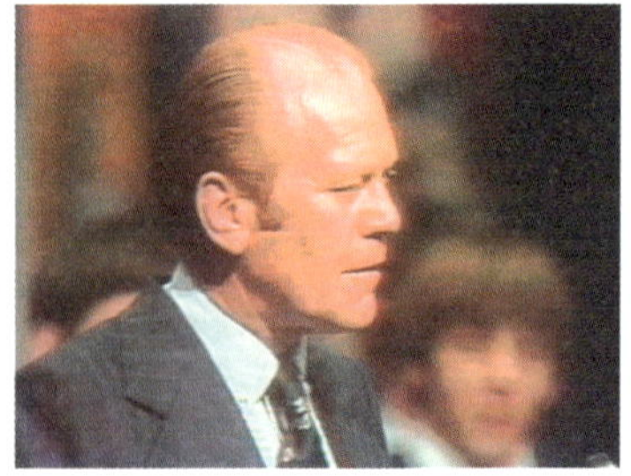

14:13

17:37

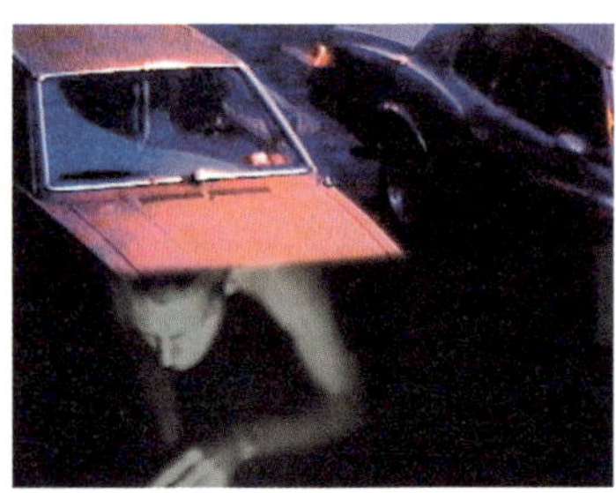

07:25

donor and passionate EAI champion until she passed away in 2011.

There are so many key individuals who played important roles in this history. John Hanhardt, who founded and for many years headed the Department of Film and Video at the Whitney Museum and later held similar positions at the Guggenheim Museum and the Smithsonian American Art Museum, was also a dedicated board member and long-time advocate for EAI's mission.

AK – Howard was in his eighties when you took over as director?

LZ – Yes.

AK – Wow, from starting in 1981 to steering the ship in 1985—that's a very quick succession.

LZ – Yes.

AK – So, you were still in your twenties at that point. And you moved to 10 Waverly Place—what prompted the move?

LZ – As in the histories of many nonprofits in New York, our lease was up and the rent was tripling and we just couldn't keep up. This is one

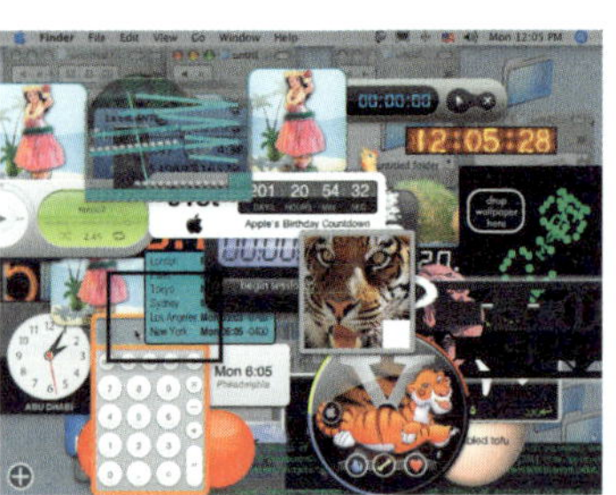

01:00

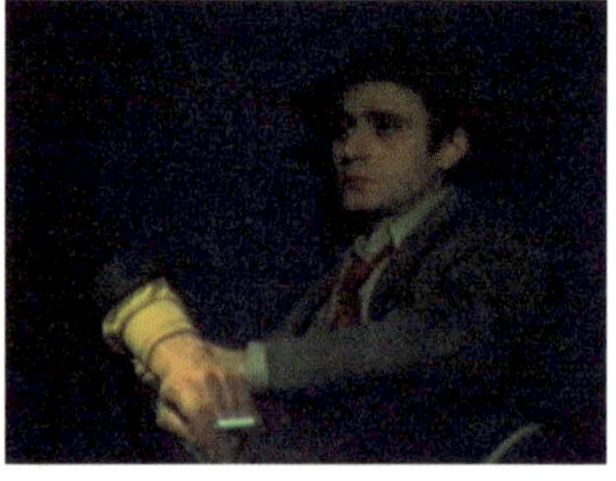

08:31

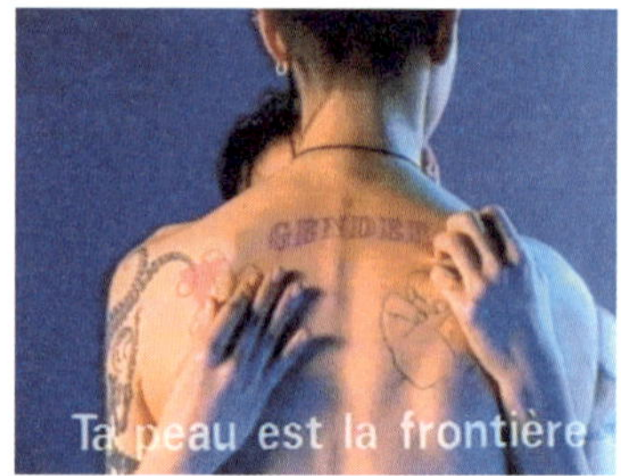

00:15

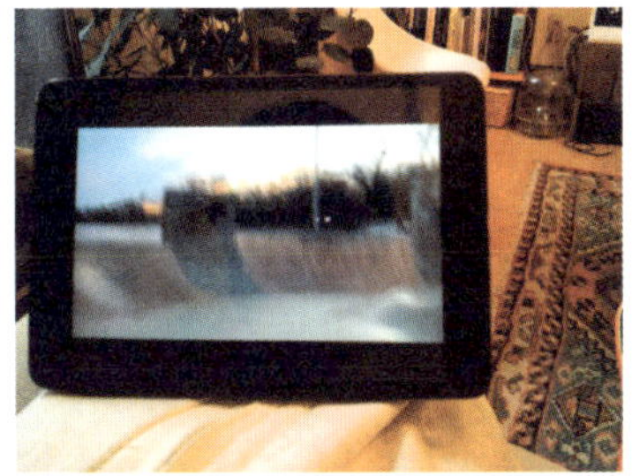

03:55

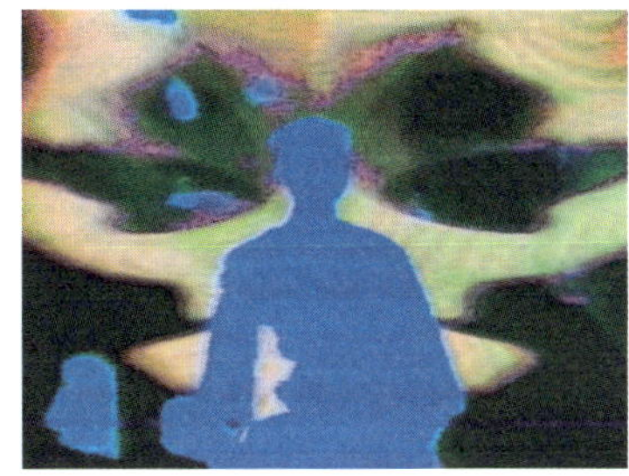

14:26

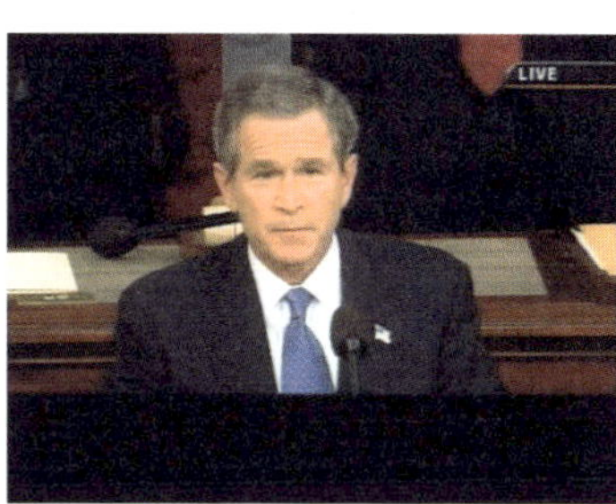

04:28

of the last things that Howard and I did together: we tried to make a partnership with NYU. For many reasons it didn't work out, but we got a space in an NYU-owned building, which was 10 Waverly Place. The story had a happy ending because the rent at the time was very inexpensive and it was a big open loft space, kind of like a bowling alley. It was unfinished and raw, a fabulous space above the Caffé Pane e Cioccolata, which is no longer there.

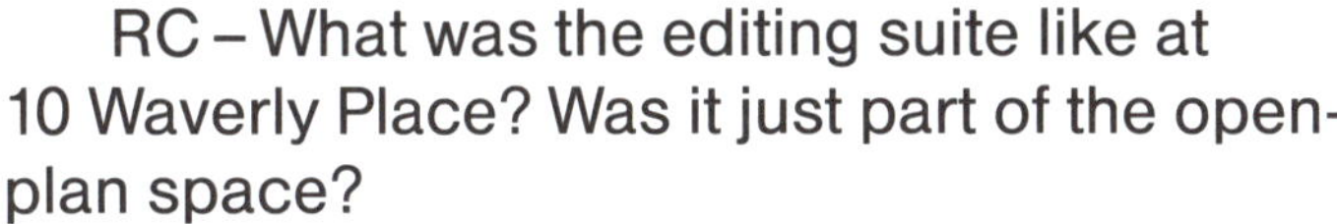

RC – What was the editing suite like at 10 Waverly Place? Was it just part of the open-plan space?

LZ – That and the viewing room were the only spaces that we built out.

AK – Was it still much of a scene?

LZ – Now, this is where the editing facility starts to become less of a scene. Another set of shifts start at this time as the technology keeps advancing. This is the advent of the Standby Program, which offered high-level commercial post-production facilities at low cost in off-hours to artists. Many artists were now

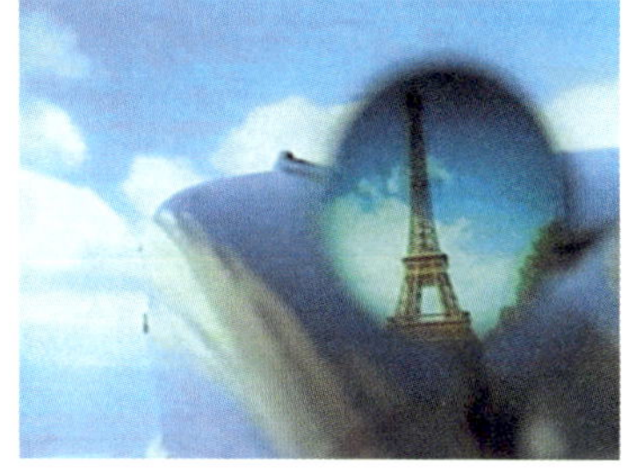

00:15

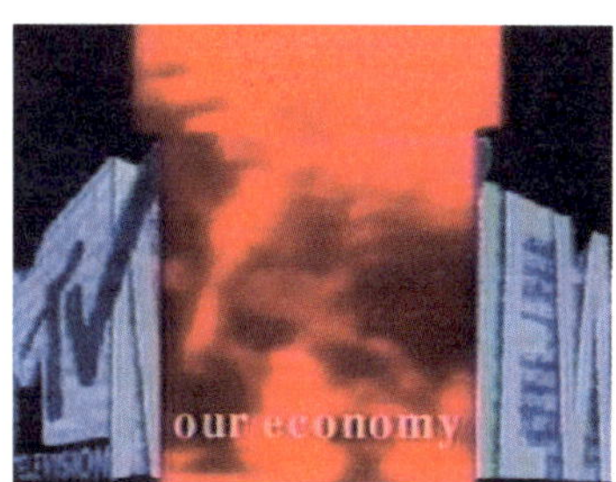

00:32

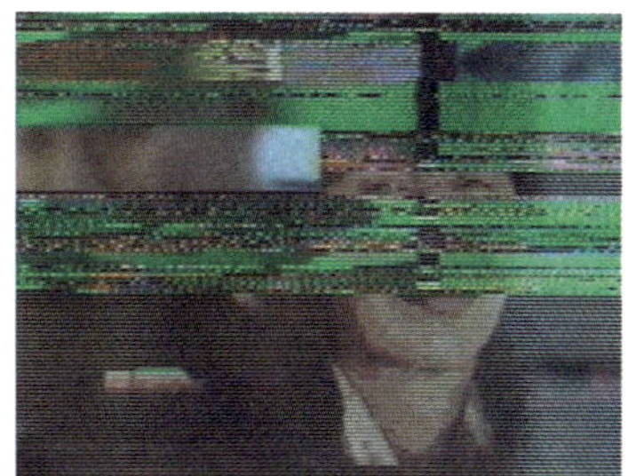

21:09

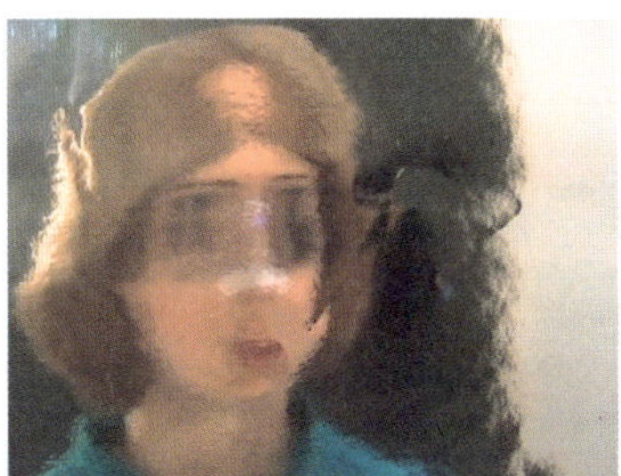

01:21

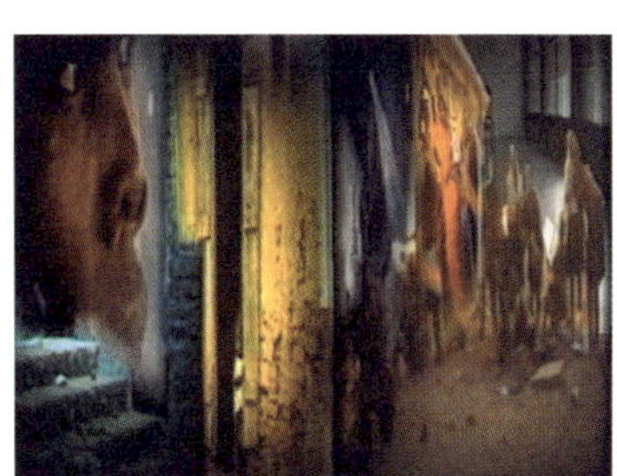

00:18

04:21

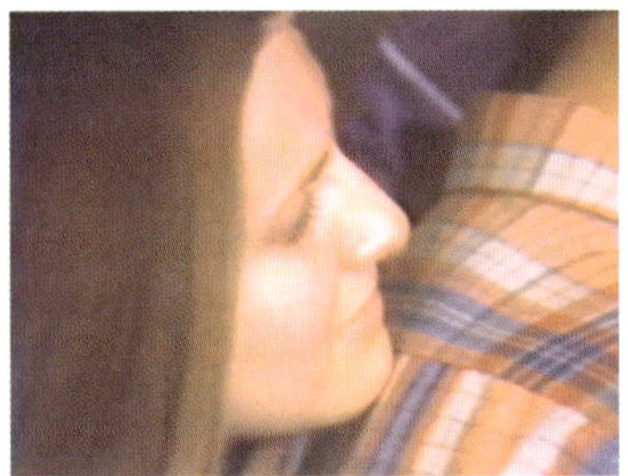

01:29

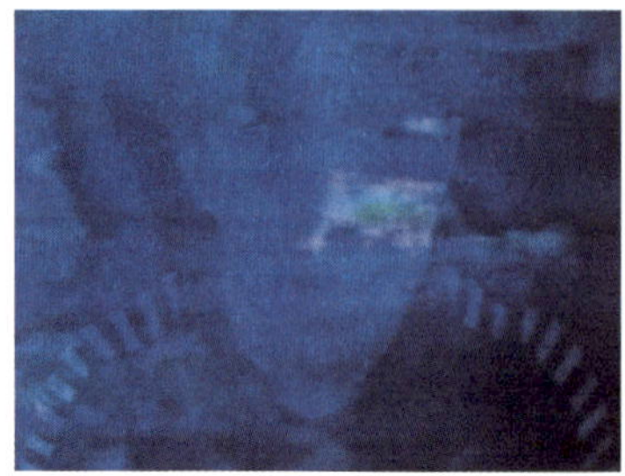

01:49

06:04

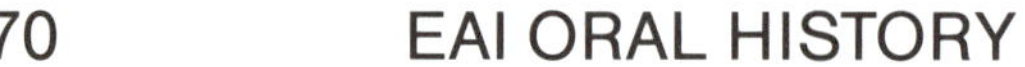

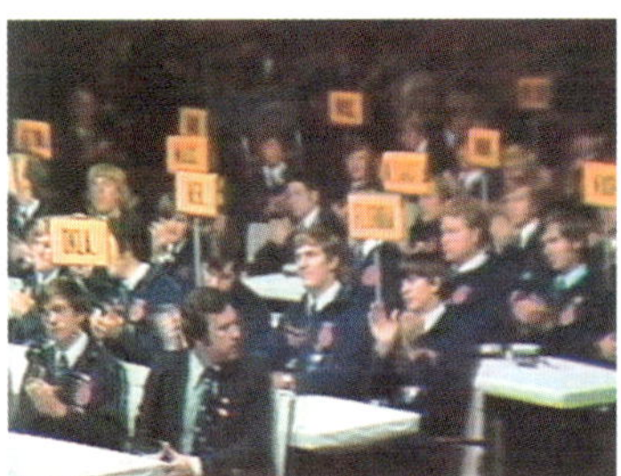

14:13

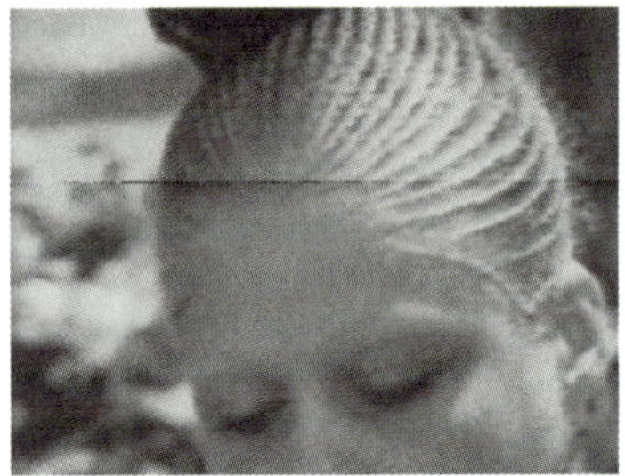

17:37

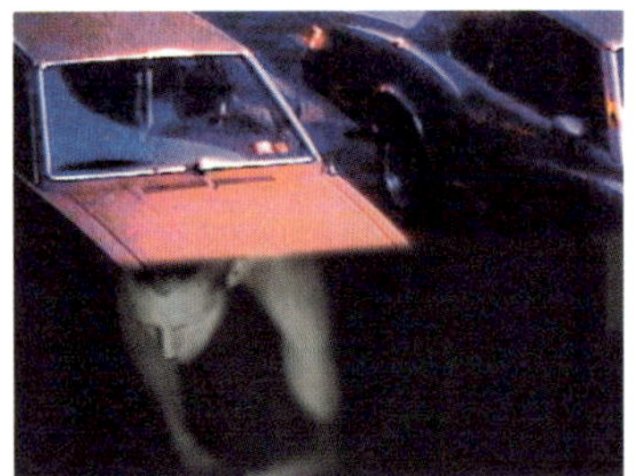

07:25

working with editing and post-production as a creative strategy, and many artists who previously worked at EAI were now working at other high-end facilities.

RC – Tony Cokes, for example, edited *The Bookof Love* (1992) both at EAI and Standby.

LZ – Many artists did that; they would do their offline editing at EAI and their online editing at Standby. (“Online” in those pre-internet days, of course, had a different meaning.)

LZ – Someone like Dara, by the late eighties, is no longer editing at EAI, she’s working with professional studios off-hours.

AK – Why is she doing that? Is it because they had better facilities?

LZ – Oh yes. That was another big decision that EAI had to make. At that point it would’ve cost many thousands of dollars to invest in high-end editing equipment. When we started editing 3/4-inch, it was just two decks and a controller. If you wanted to get up into high-end editing—a computer-based editing system, for example—the investment was so great. So, we had to

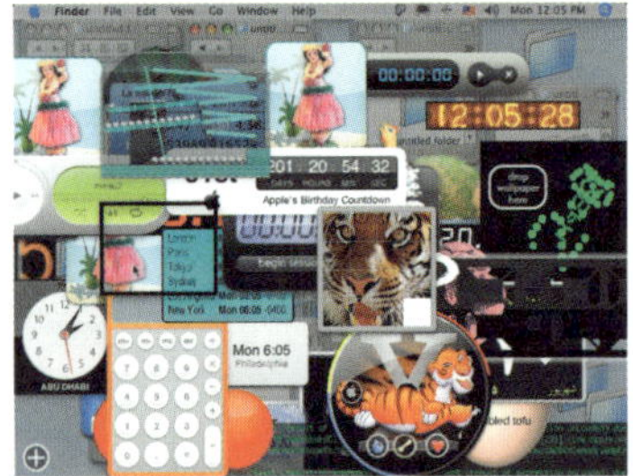

01:00

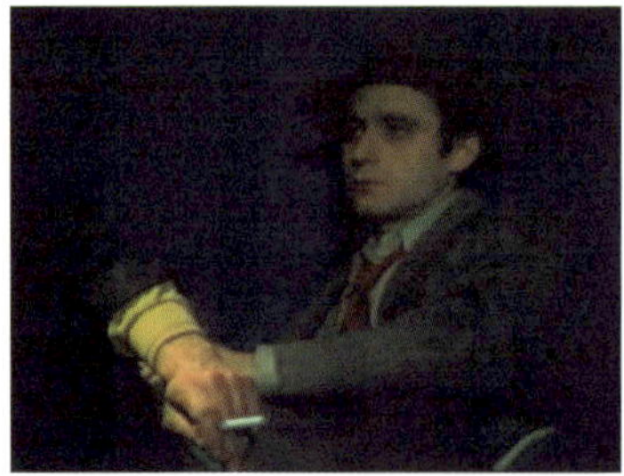

08:31

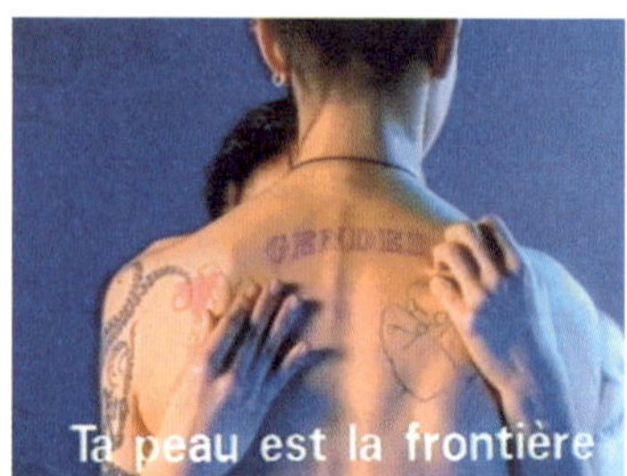

00:15

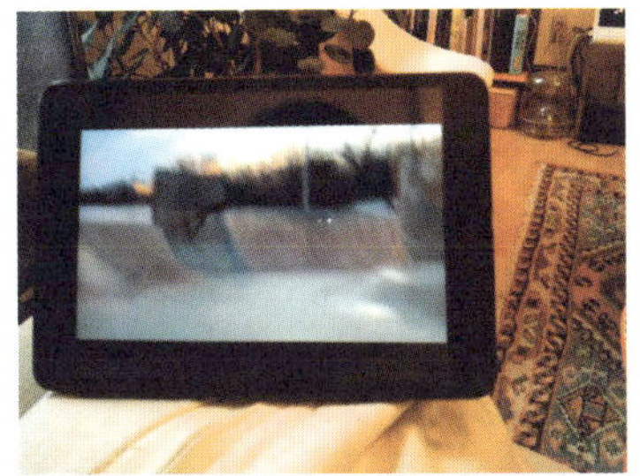
03:55

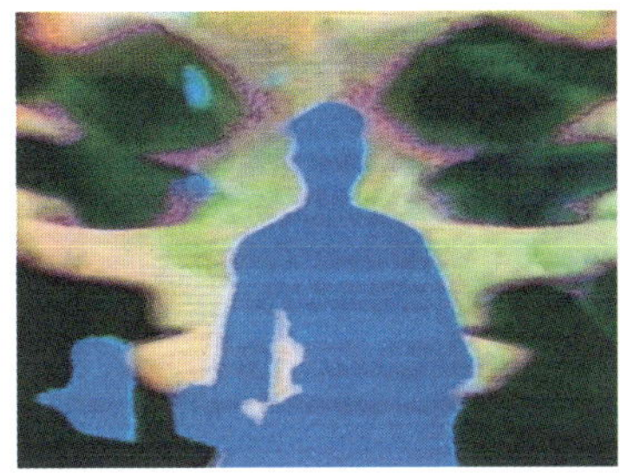
14:26

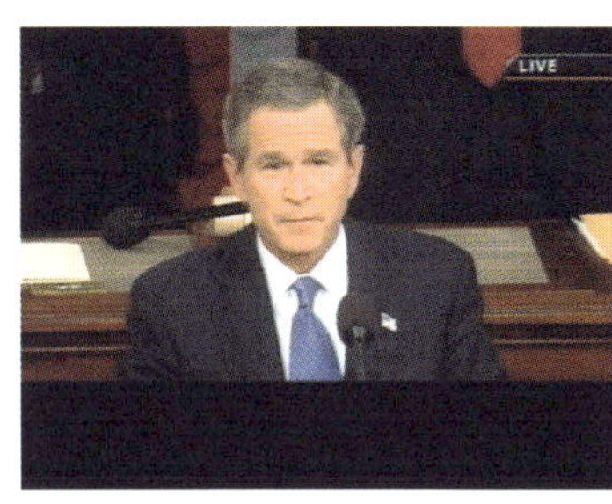

04:28

choose whether we wanted to do that kind of high-end editing in-house. What was great was that artists now had access to the commercial facilities' resources through nonprofit programs like Standby.

AK – Right, and the machines were getting increasingly specialized.

LZ – And that was not where we wanted to go. We wanted our technical facility to be adequate for distribution and to serve artists at a certain level. But we decided not to compete with commercial facilities that were also serving artists.

AK – It's interesting that this is all driven by artists' production. Is this the juncture when the emphasis shifted to the catalog and distribution of the collection?

LZ – By the mid-eighties the distribution service and the video collection had become the primary focus of the organization, which continues to be true today. A series of things happened in 1985 that changed everything for EAI, to be honest. Two things happened simultaneously and it's hard to untangle them to think of which one

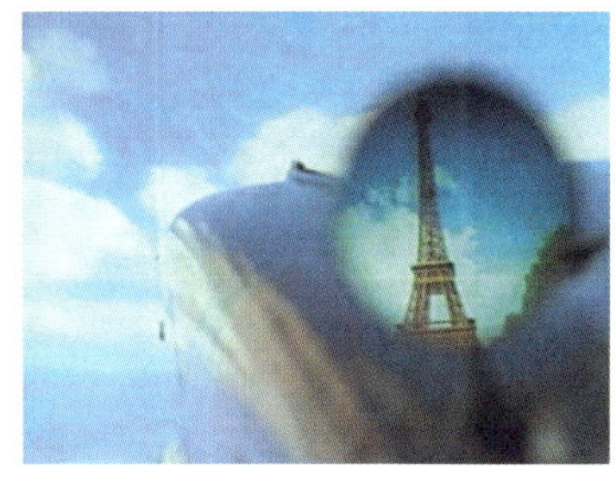
00:15

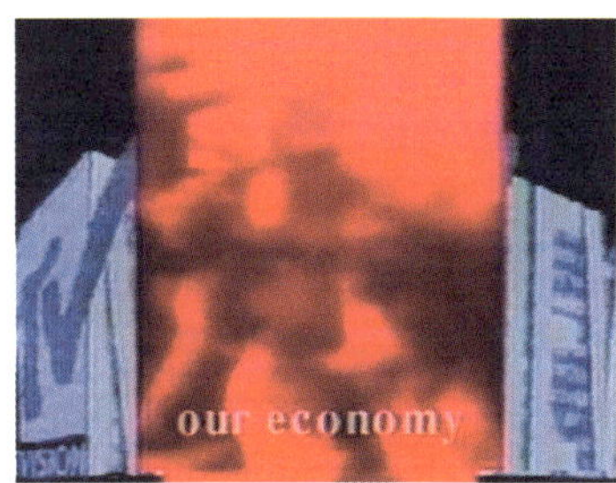

00:32

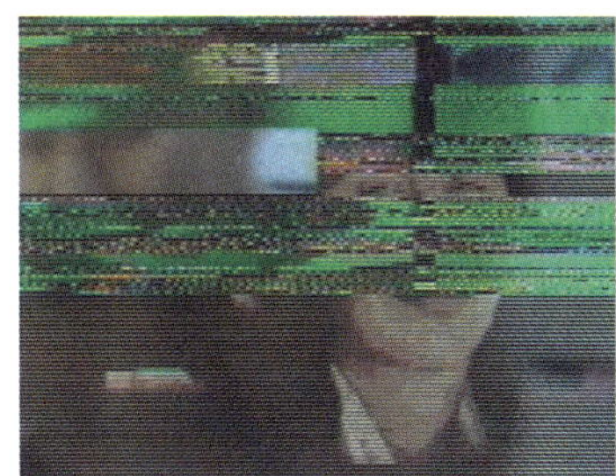
21:09

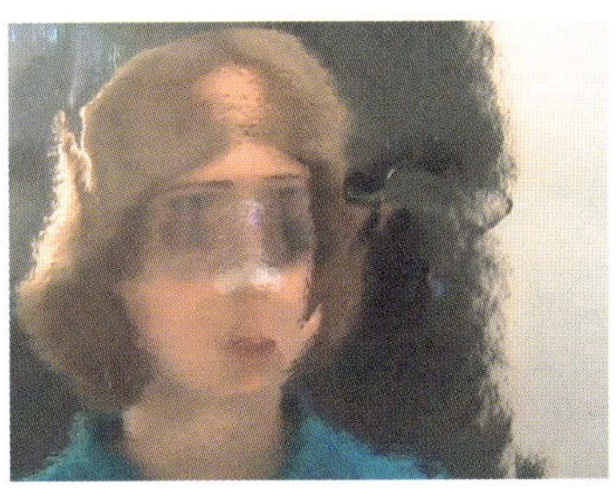
01:21

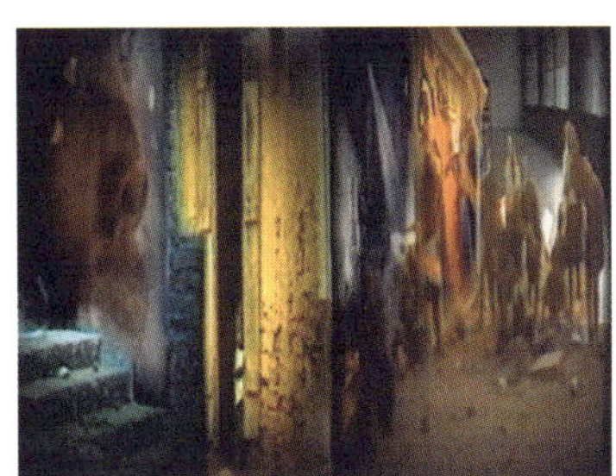
00:18

04:21

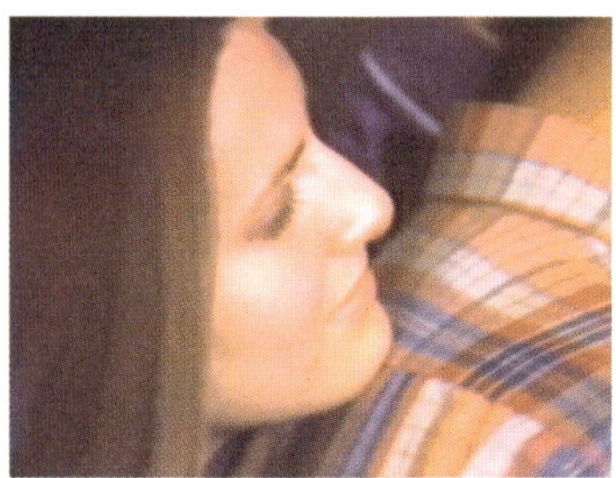

01:28

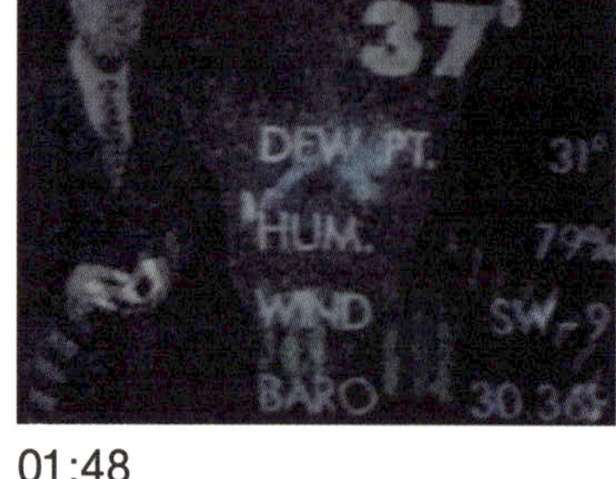

01:48

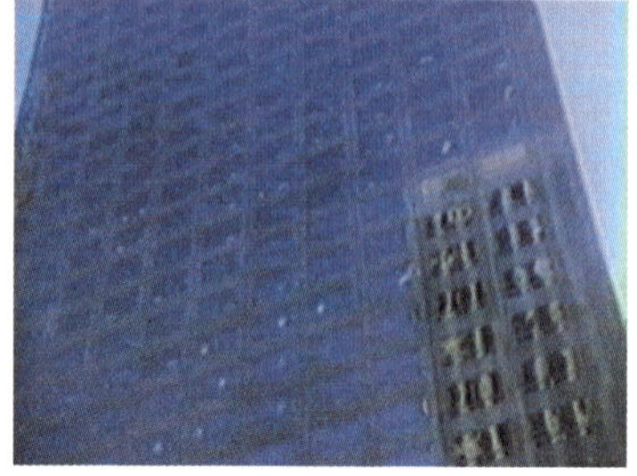

06:03

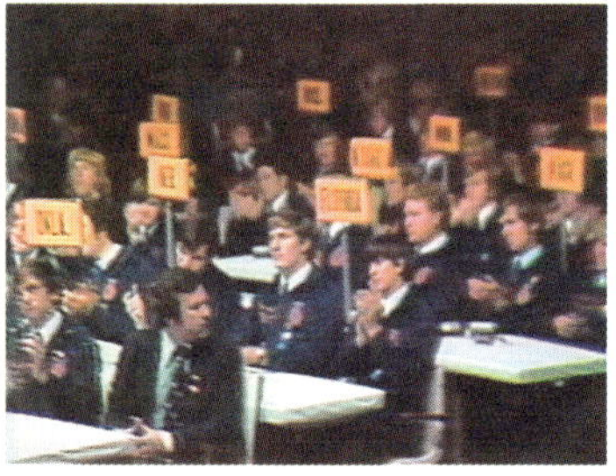

14:12

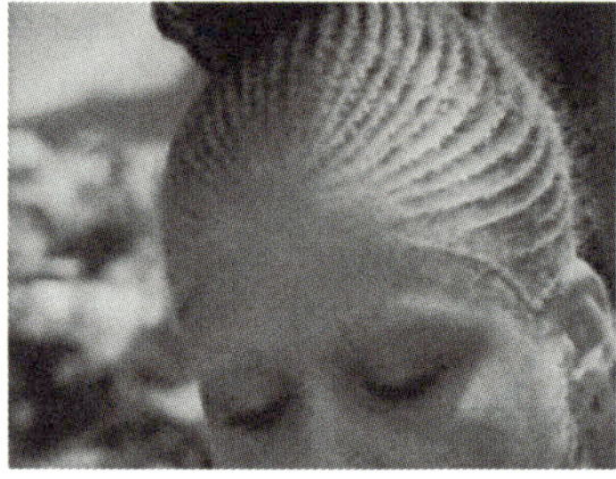

17:36

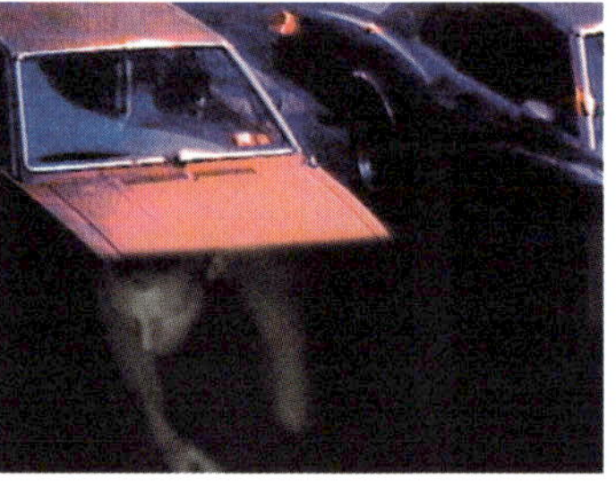

07:24

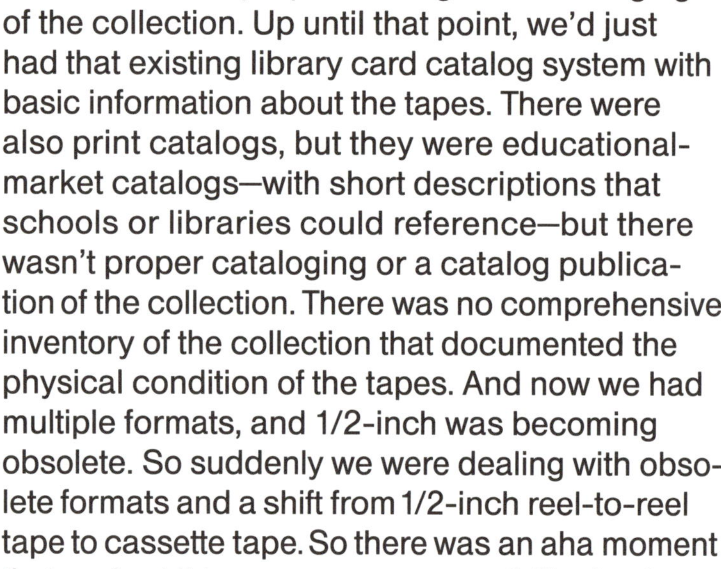

was first. But let's just say the first thing was my decision to do a proper catalog—and cataloging—of the collection. Up until that point, we'd just had that existing library card catalog system with basic information about the tapes. There were also print catalogs, but they were educational-market catalogs—with short descriptions that schools or libraries could reference—but there wasn't proper cataloging or a catalog publication of the collection. There was no comprehensive inventory of the collection that documented the physical condition of the tapes. And now we had multiple formats, and 1/2-inch was becoming obsolete. So suddenly we were dealing with obsolete formats and a shift from 1/2-inch reel-to-reel tape to cassette tape. So there was an aha moment that we had this enormous responsibility for the physical viability of the collection.

Video was still seen as being on the outside of mainstream artistic discourses at that time. Although video was actively being shown and collected by some major museums, it often wasn't being recognized properly within the

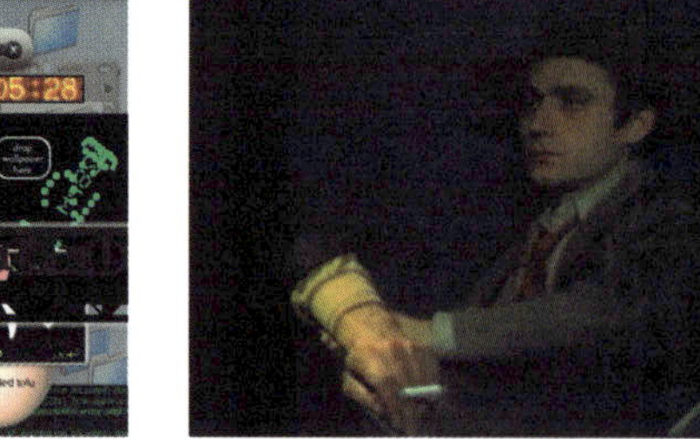

00:59

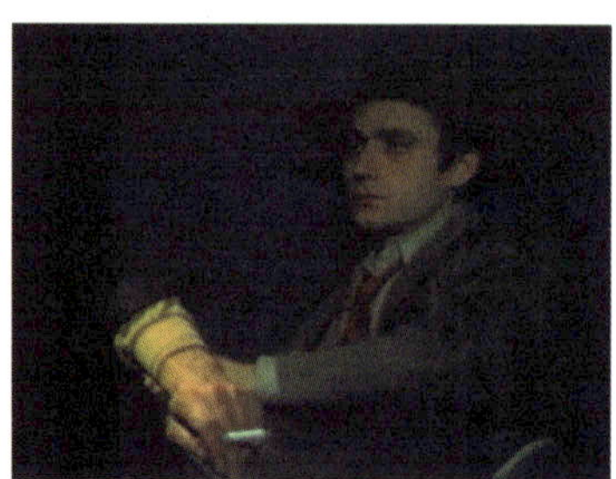

08:30

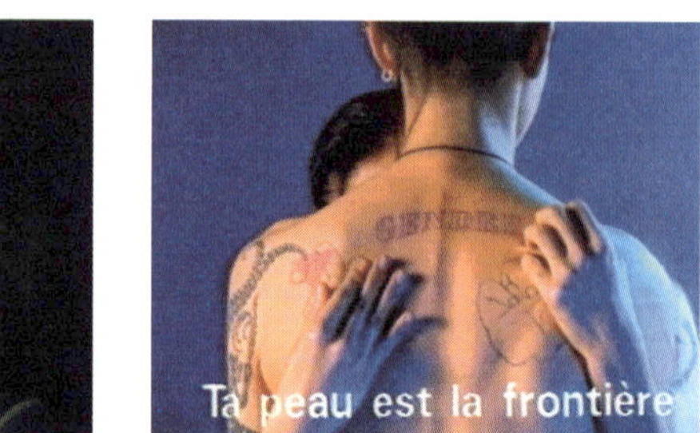

00:14

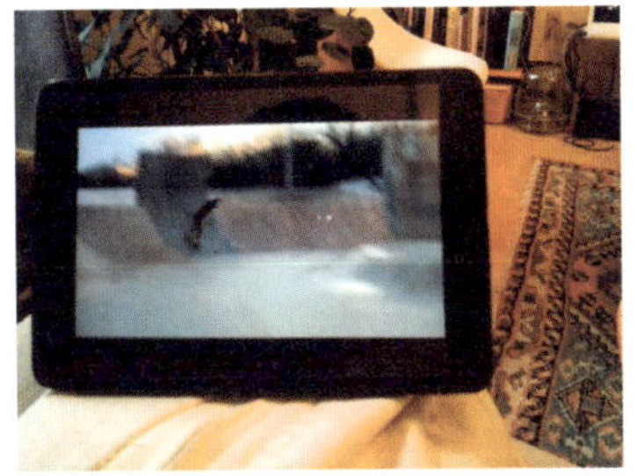
03:55

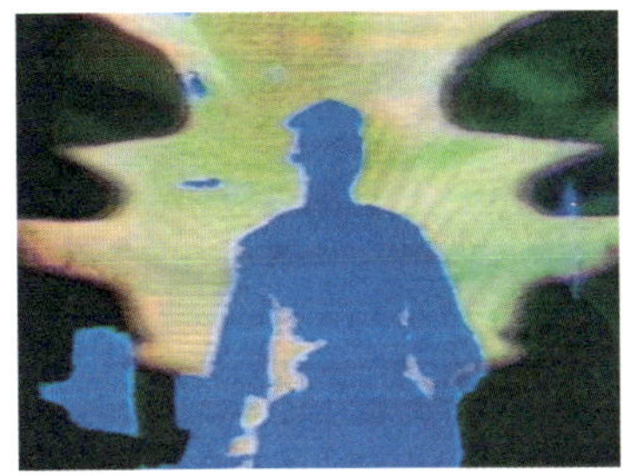
14:26

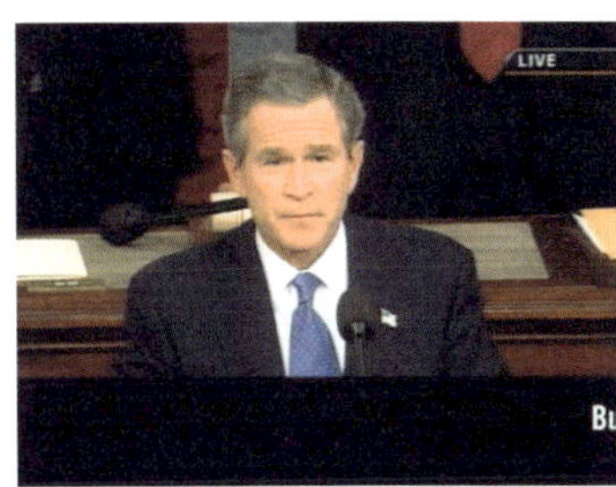

04:28

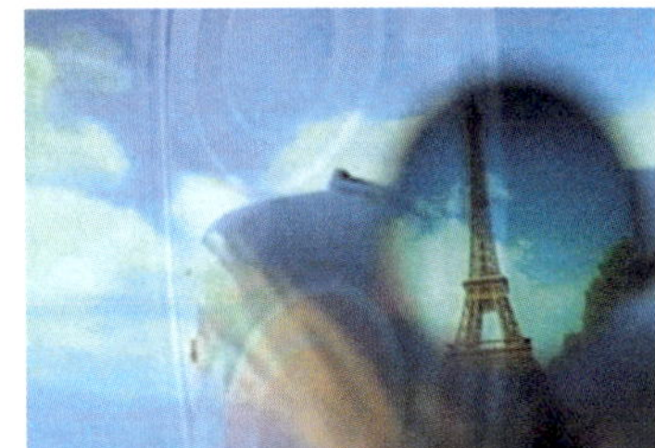
00:15

larger art world or in academia. Art historically it seemed set off to the side; it was seen as peripheral. We had artists who were in dialogue with the larger discourses in contemporary art, but their work wasn't getting the attention it deserved. It was marginalized. I felt very passionate about trying to help to correct that. And one of the things I felt that we should do was focus on a publication that described and inventoried the collection properly and placed it in an art historical context. And so that was a shift, when it became framed and thought of as a "collection." Because by that point it was fifteen years in and there was this need to really see it as art. That was when the idea to do a catalog publication and undertake these cataloging efforts first emerged. At the same time, we applied for and got the first grant that the NYSCA ever gave for video preservation. And, we got one of the first grants that the American Film Institute gave for cataloging a video art collection, through the NAMID (National Alliance of Moving Image Databases) project. So, those things happened

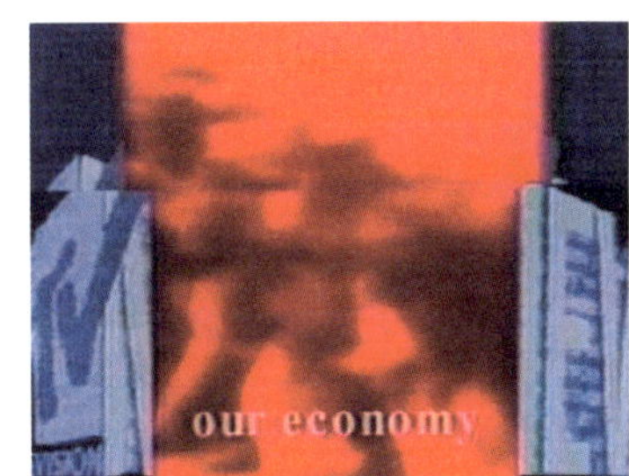

00:32

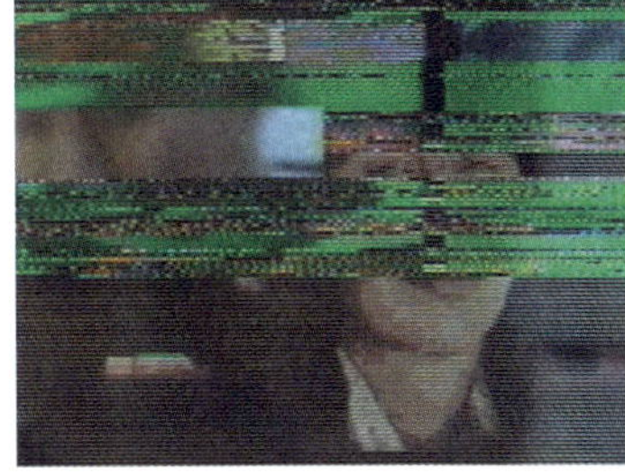
21:09

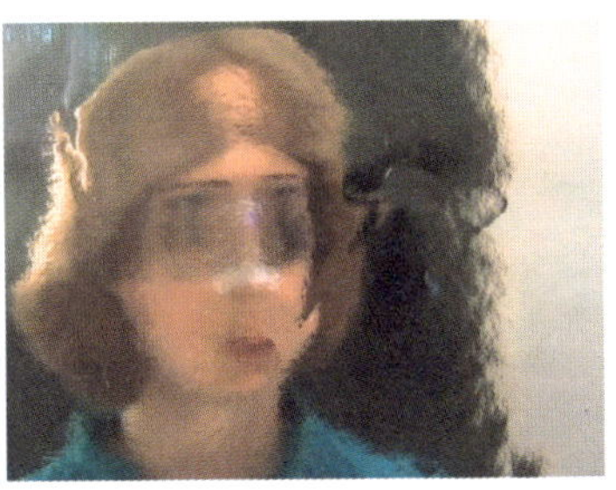
01:21

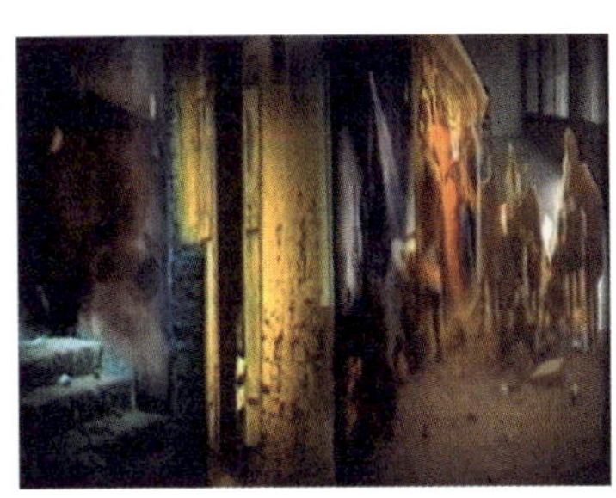
00:18

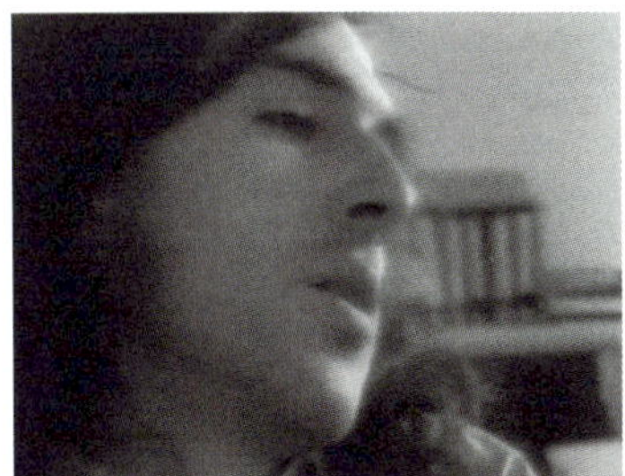
04:21

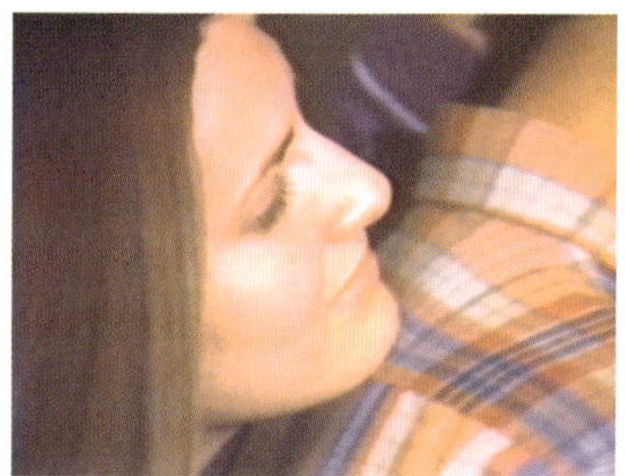
01:28

01:48

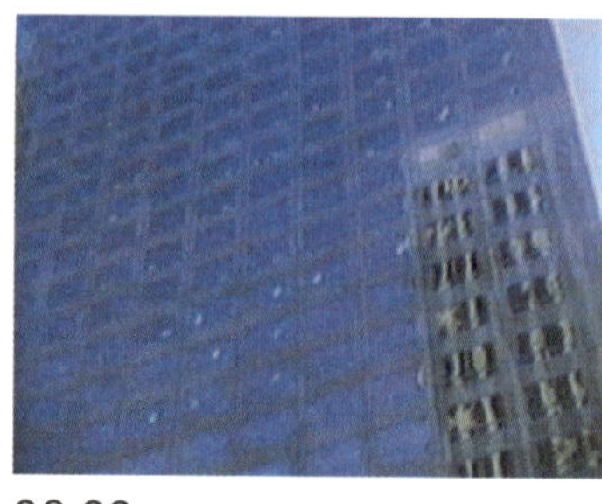
06:03

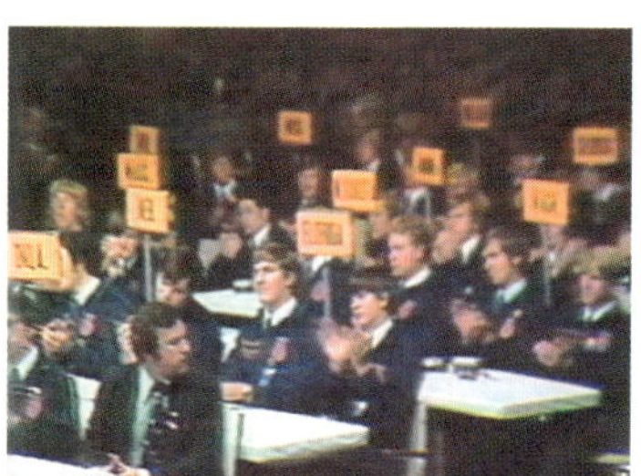
14:12

simultaneously, and they had a tremendous impact that is still being felt today.

Another important thing that happened at that same time was that Castelli/Sonnabend Videotapes and Films stopped distributing their video and film collection. When they disbanded, I started getting requests from individual artists to ask if EAI would like to handle their works—Vito Acconci, Eleanor Antin, John Baldessari, to name a few—that were not already in EAI's collection. This was how these artists entered into EAI. It was amazing because it brought in a whole stable of artists who had been in dialogue with what we had been doing but who were also more readily acknowledged and seen in the art world—it was another form of intermix. Once these artists came into our collection, there was a certain attention from the outside world since they were seen as representing the art world.

AK – And they weren't exclusively seen as video artists.

LZ – They were seen as the artists working in video. There was a shift in perception.

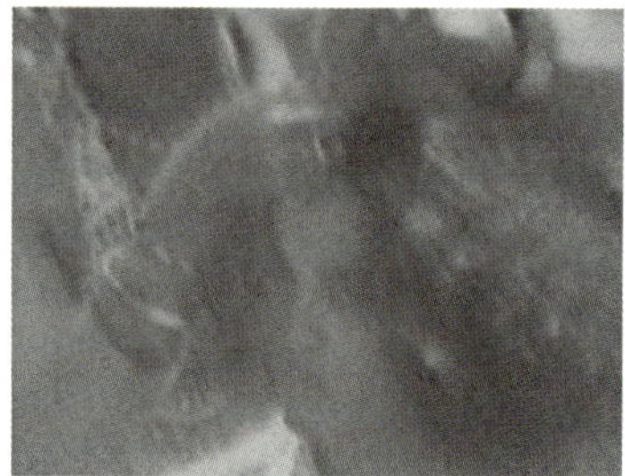
17:36

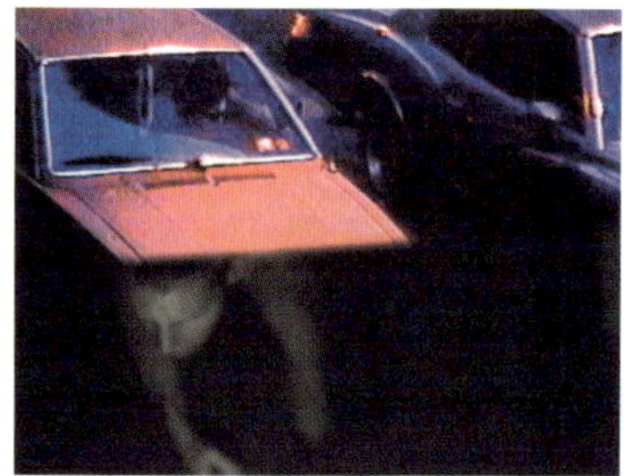
07:24

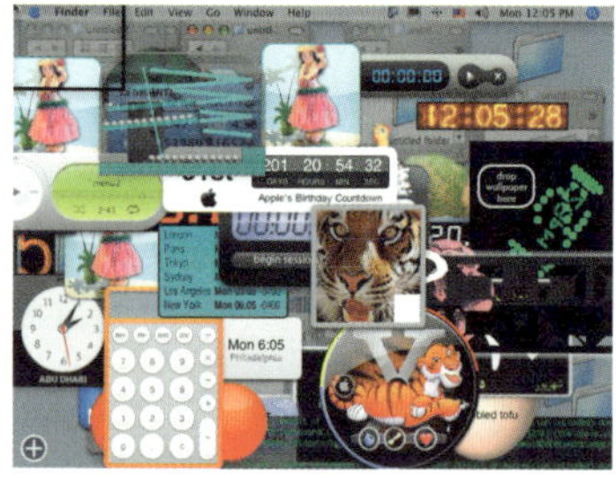

00:59

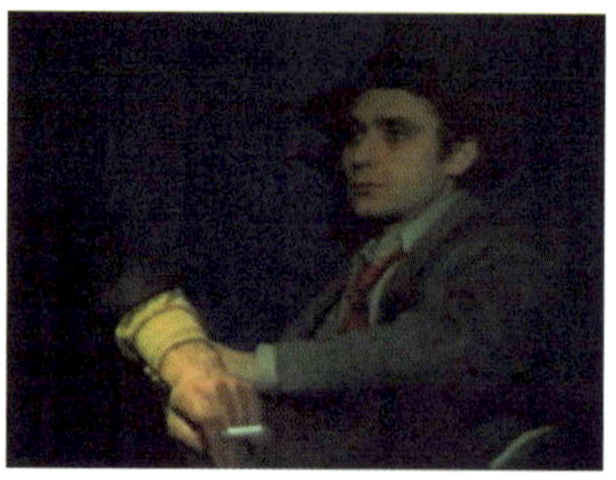
08:30

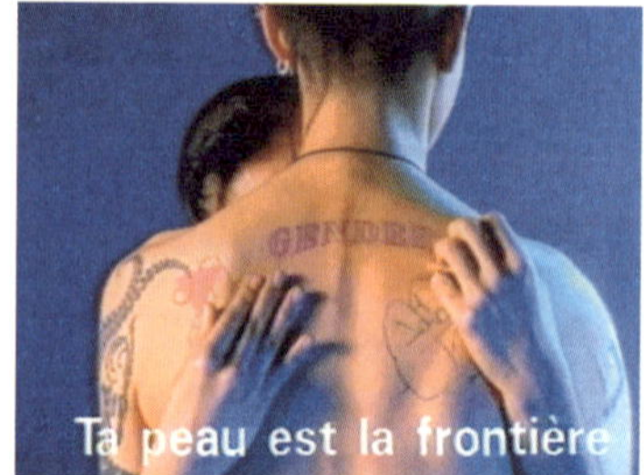

00:14

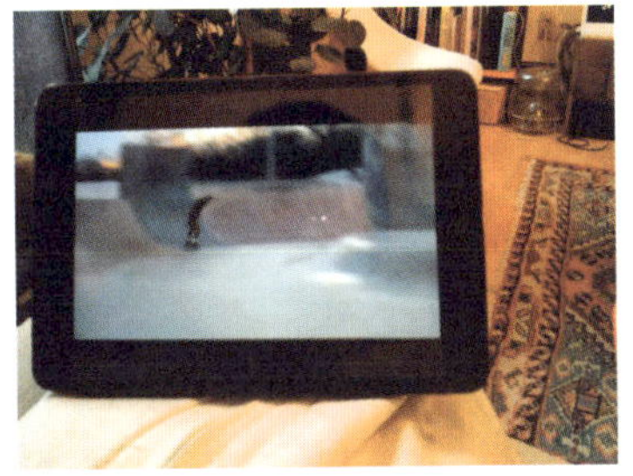
03:55

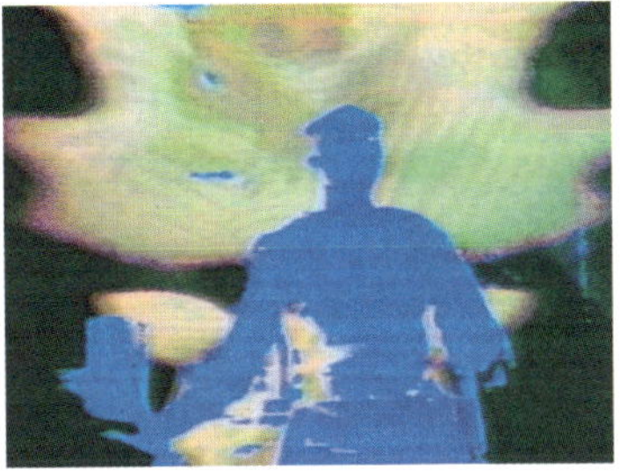
14:26

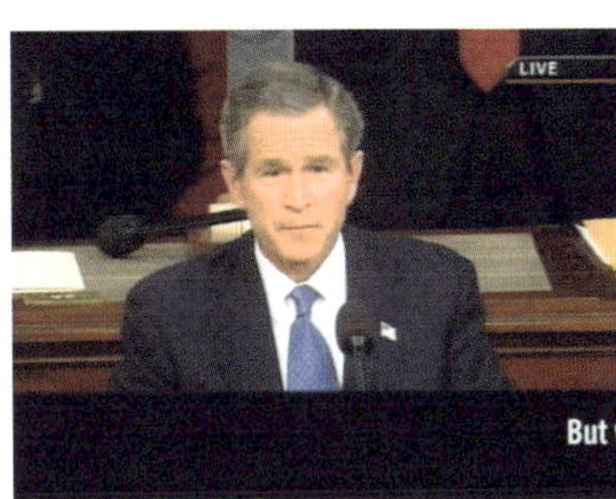

04:28

AK – It's the same thing in photography. There are photographers and then there are artists working with photography.

LZ – Exactly, and it was a different political and cultural landscape. So, all of these things happened simultaneously: the research into the catalog, the inventory of the collection, the grant for preservation, the grant for cataloging, and a new wave of artists coming into the collection. At the same time, we made the decision, for distribution purposes, that we could not list in the publication any work that was not technically viable. There were works that were not playable because they were on 1/2-inch reels and we didn't have workable 1/2-inch decks by then, so that's where the preservation efforts came in. There was this sudden realization that some of this work was unplayable and unviable and in order to provide access, we had to engage in preservation.

This all seems so obvious from our current perspective; of course access and preservation are totally and inextricably linked. This is one

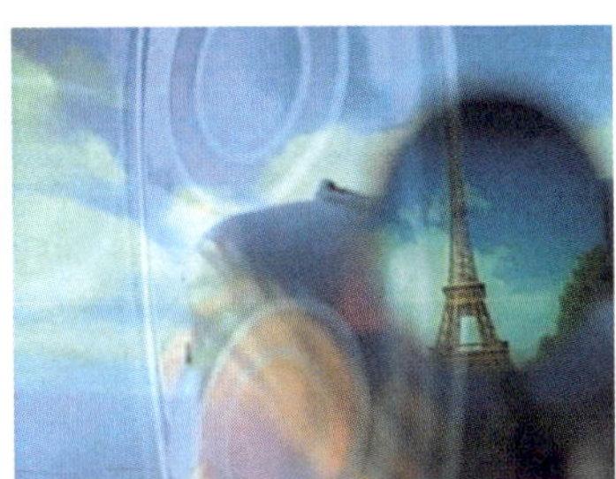
00:15

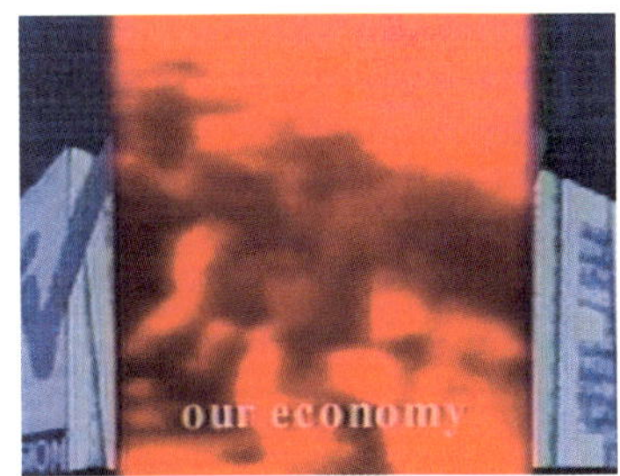

00:32

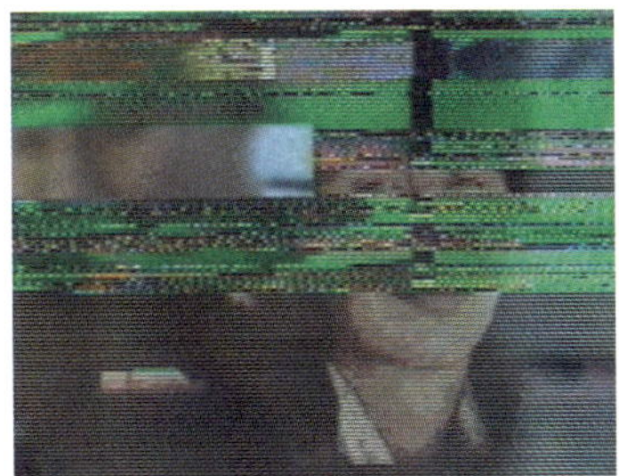
21:09

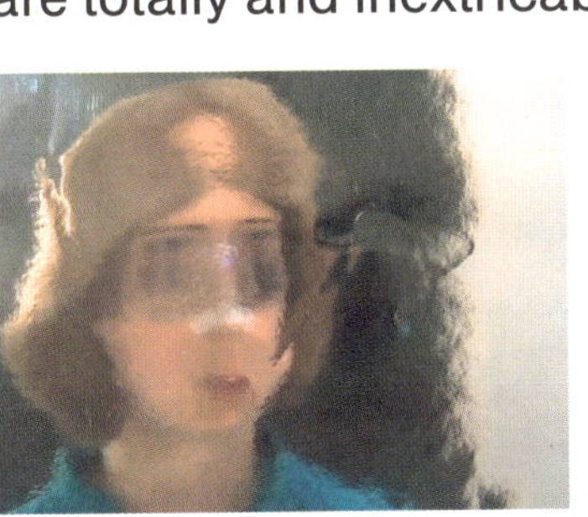
01:21

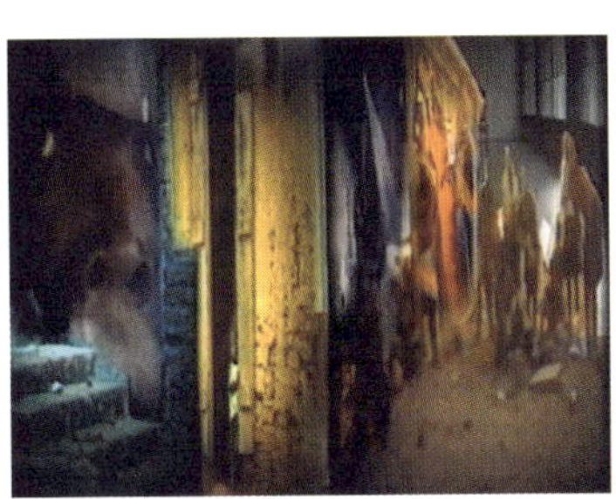
00:18

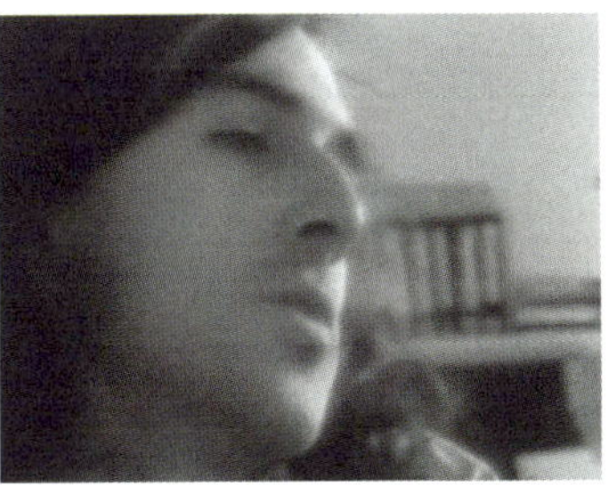
04:21

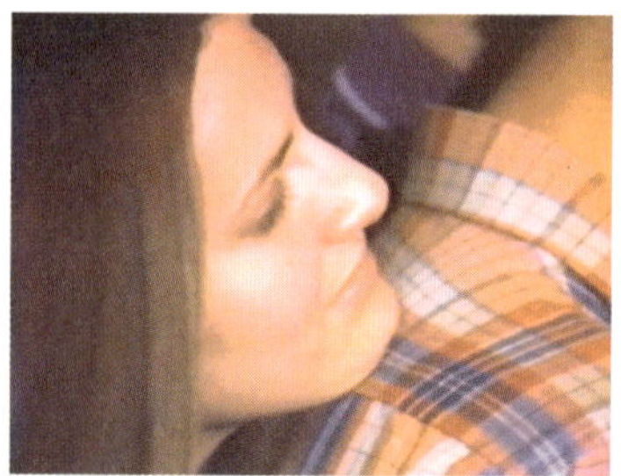

01:28

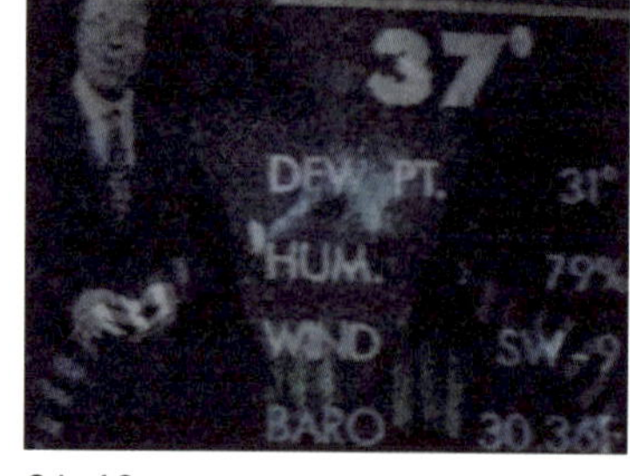

01:48

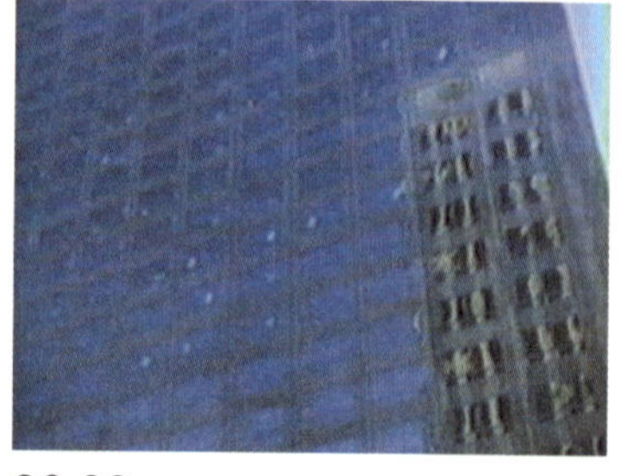

06:03

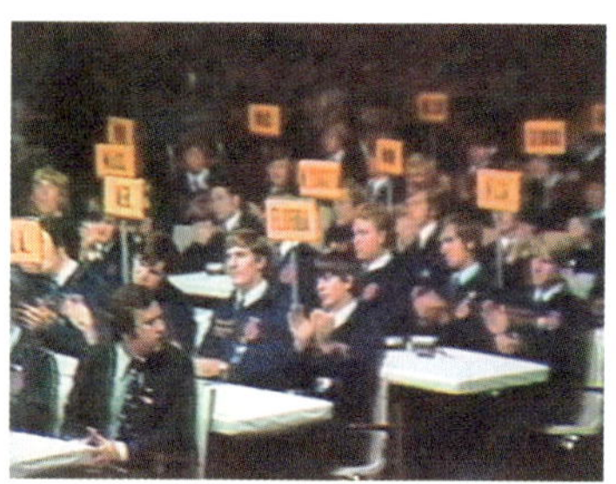

14:12

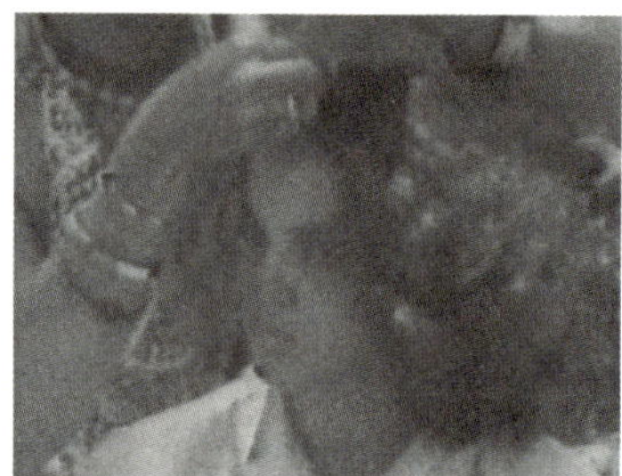

17:36

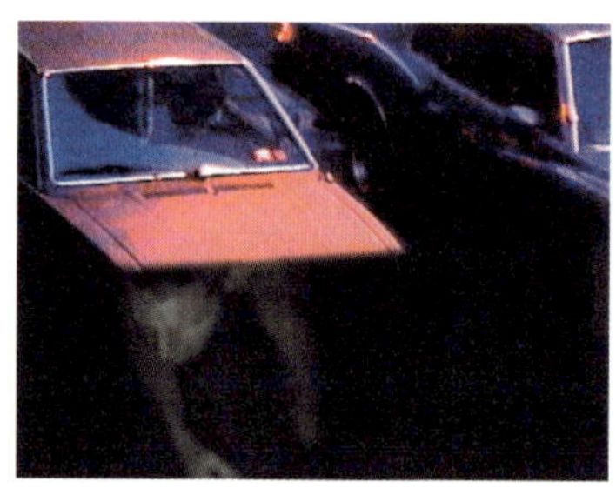

07:24

of our defining rallying cries at (EAI): preservation and distribution are integrally connected, and we have a dual mission in terms of the collection, which is preservation and access. But at that time it was somewhat controversial. It was not seen as something that was an obvious issue—the idea that there were preservation needs for this video art collection. There was a sense that this was an ephemeral medium, an impermanent medium, and why are you bringing museological ideas and practices to this collection.

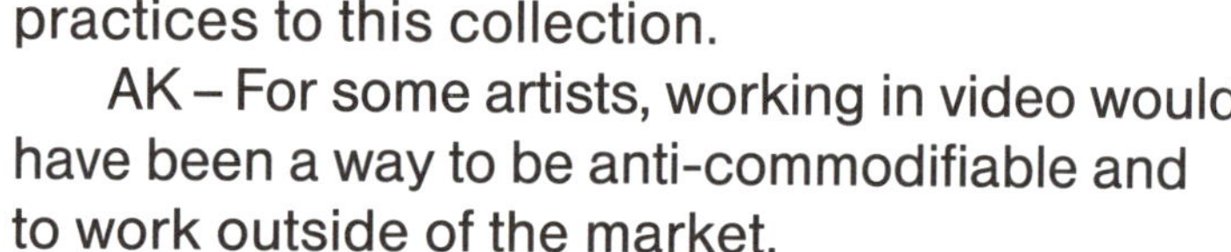

AK – For some artists, working in video would have been a way to be anti-commodifiable and to work outside of the market.

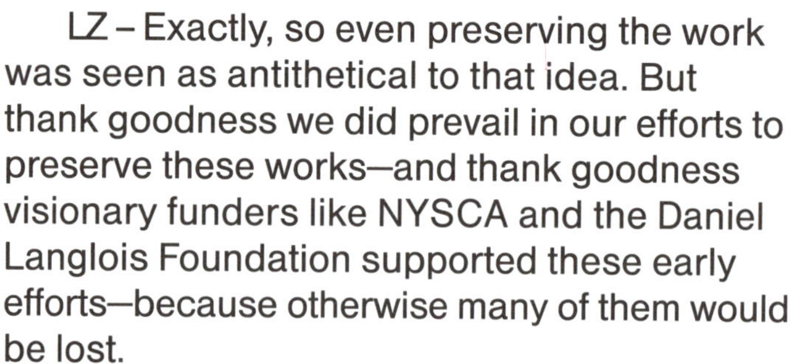

LZ – Exactly, so even preserving the work was seen as antithetical to that idea. But thank goodness we did prevail in our efforts to preserve these works—and thank goodness visionary funders like NYSCA and the Daniel Langlois Foundation supported these early efforts—because otherwise many of them would be lost.

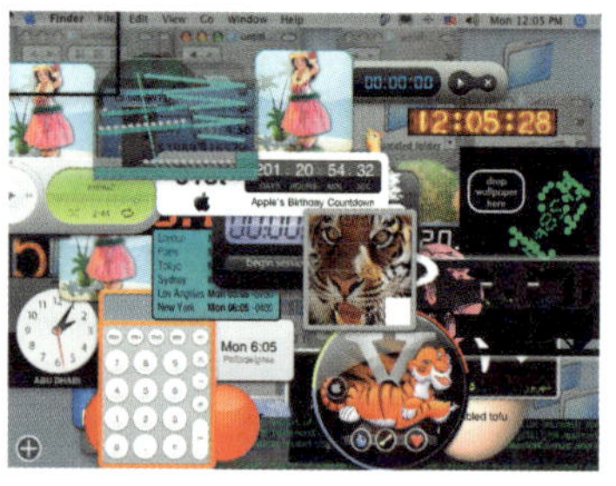

00:59

08:30

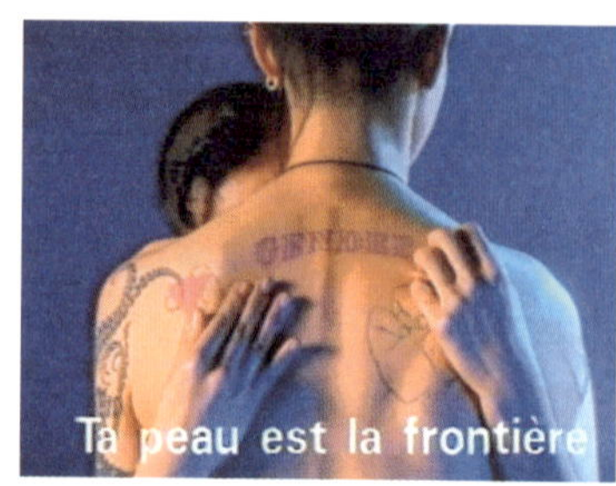

00:14

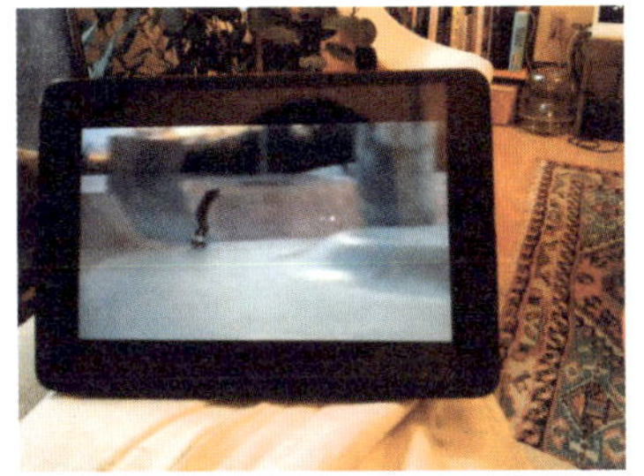

03:55

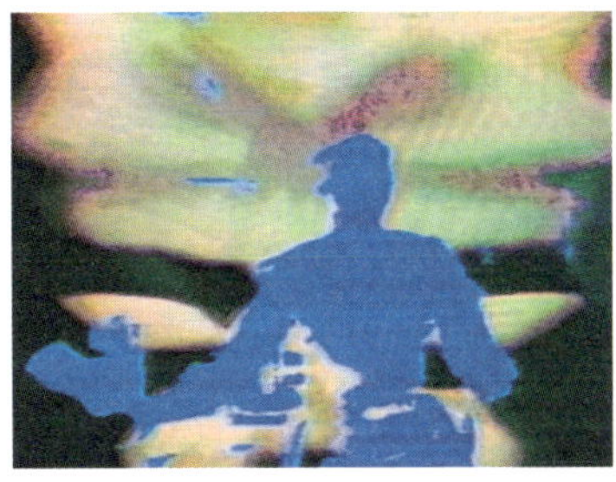

14:26

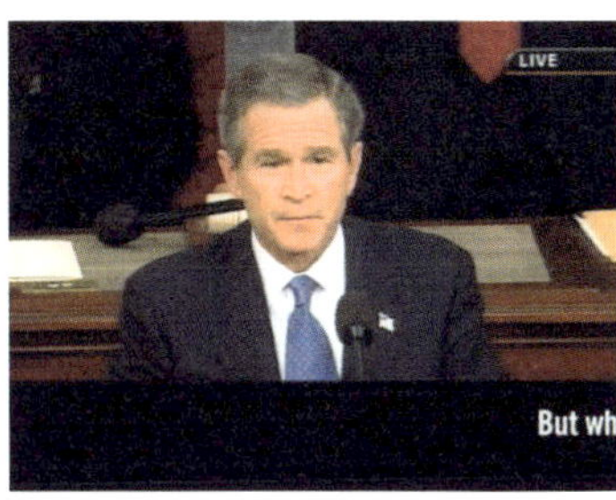

04:28

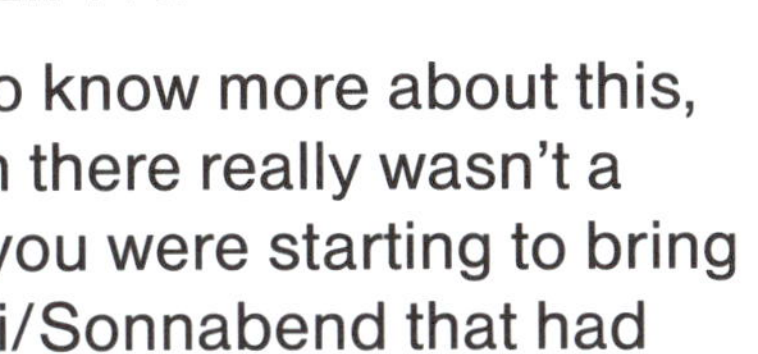

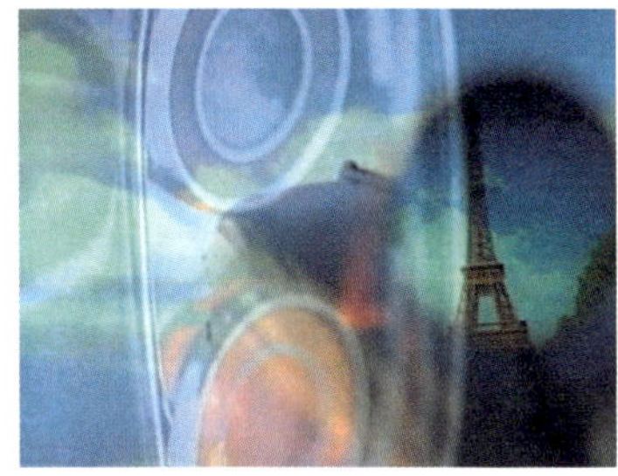

00:15

AK – I'm curious to know more about this, because even though there really wasn't a market for video art, you were starting to bring in artists from Castelli/Sonnabend that had commercial profiles.

LZ – Although remember at this time, in 1985, there was no commercial market for these black-and-white performance tapes, for example.

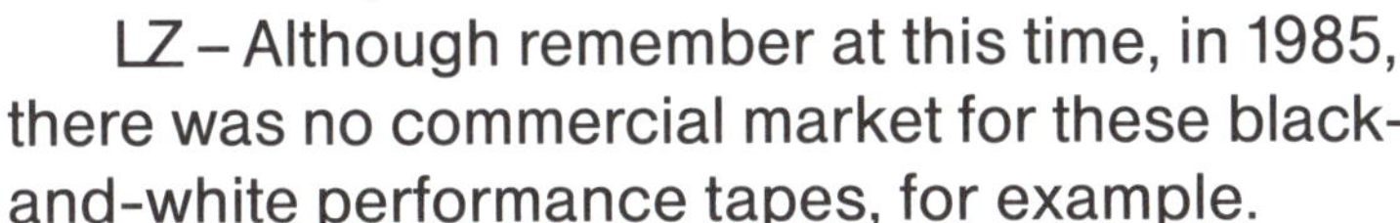

AK – Right. It wasn't fashionable at that point.

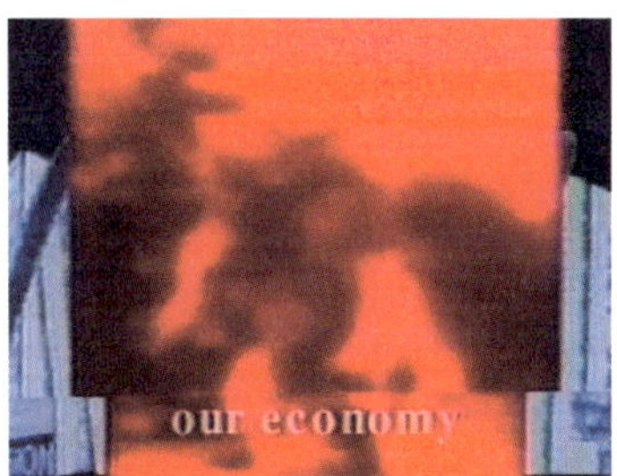

00:32

LZ – It only became fashionable—and widely recognized as important—again in the 1990s. Most contemporary artists were going in the exact opposite direction then. So, the prevailing mode of video art at this point was fast-paced, narrative, music-based, color, referencing pop culture and mass media. And I'm trying to preserve a video of someone picking hair off of their body in black-and-white for half an hour, or an hour-long "real time" document of an anti-war protest from the seventies.

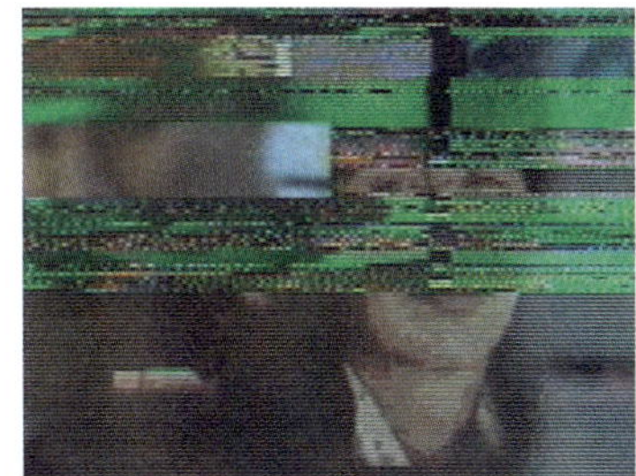

21:09

AK – How do you distinguish between the terms "archive," "collection," and "catalog?" It seems like there is a constant shift in how you are working with

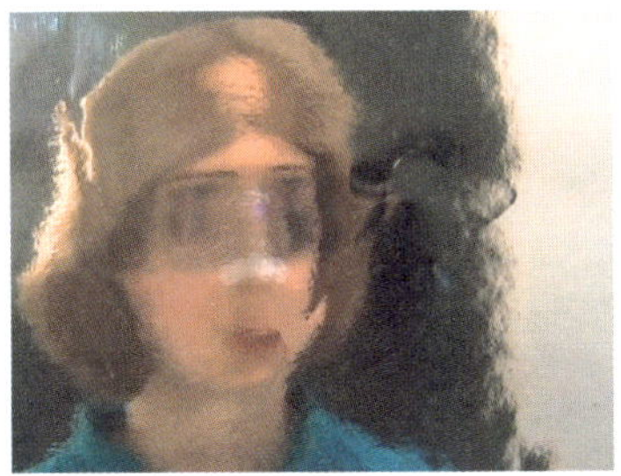

01:21

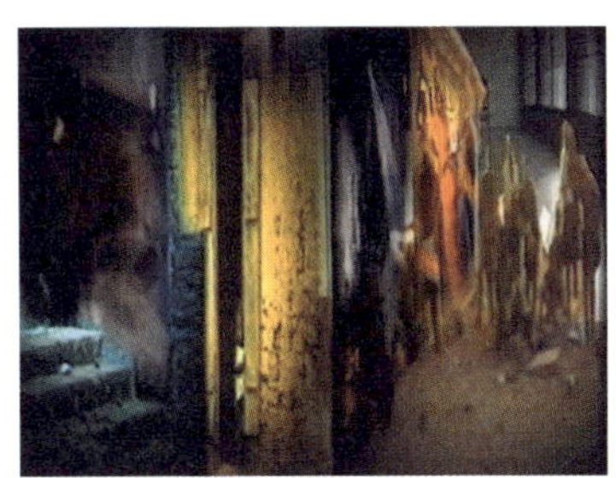

00:18

04:21

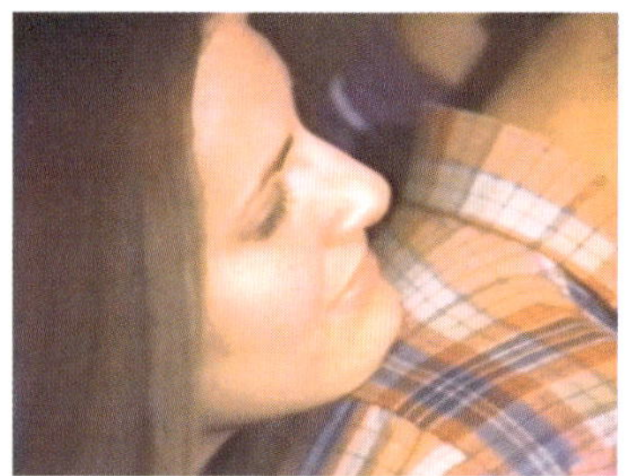
01:28

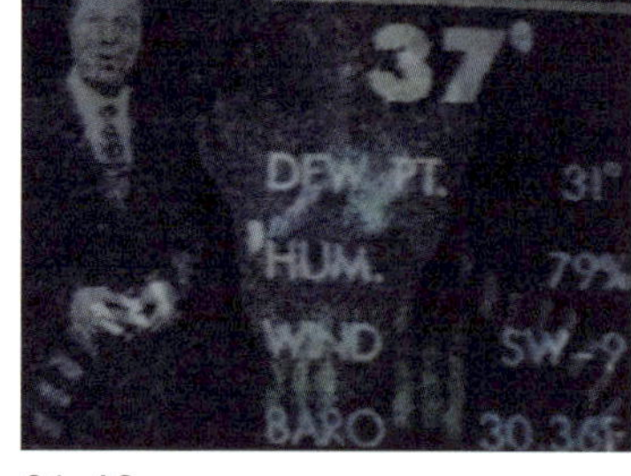

01:48

06:03

this material. I am sure there must be artists who you have worked closely with, but who have now passed away and left you in charge of advocating for their legacies and making sure that their work is accessible by migrating it to new formats.

LZ – Yes, exactly. Sadly, many of the artists of the first generation of video pioneers have passed away, and we have a tremendous responsibility to preserve their legacies and keep their work accessible. And the history of this collection is also the history of migration.

AK – I think that's immensely important. These questions of distribution, circulation, and as you mention, migration, are so integral to the conception of what EAI does and the medium itself. One could observe that these are the quintessential issues for any artist working in the twenty-first century.

LZ – It's so relevant. Some of the most important questions that we're asking as a culture and within art—issues around distribution, access and circulation—are the questions that these artists are asking and dealing with.

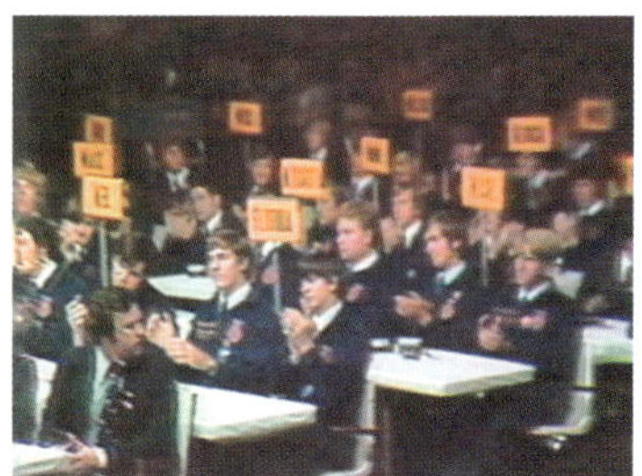
14:12

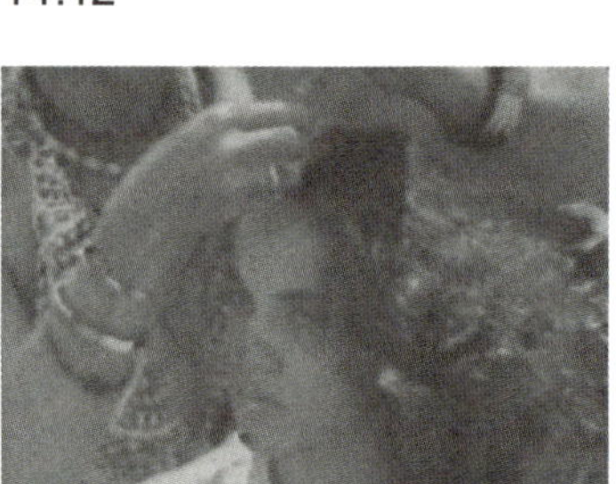
17:36

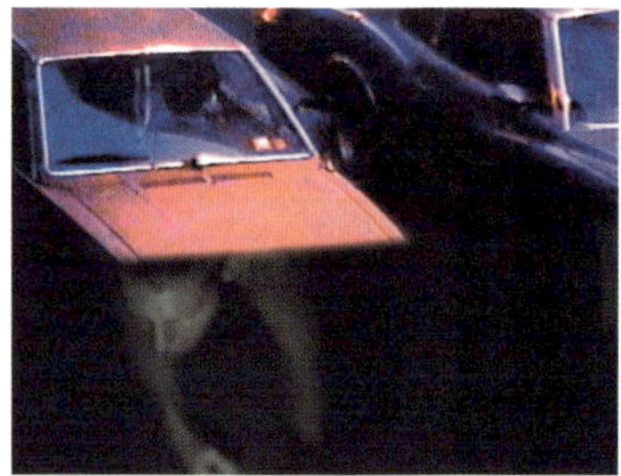
07:24

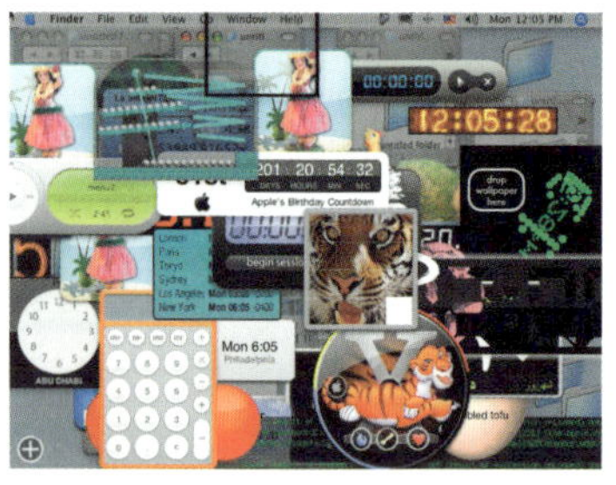

00:59

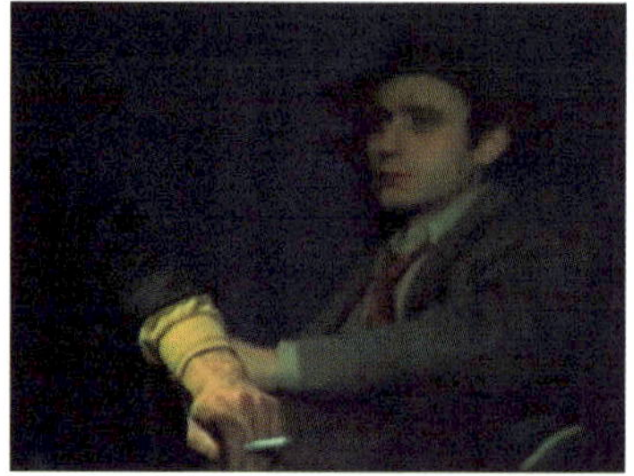
08:30

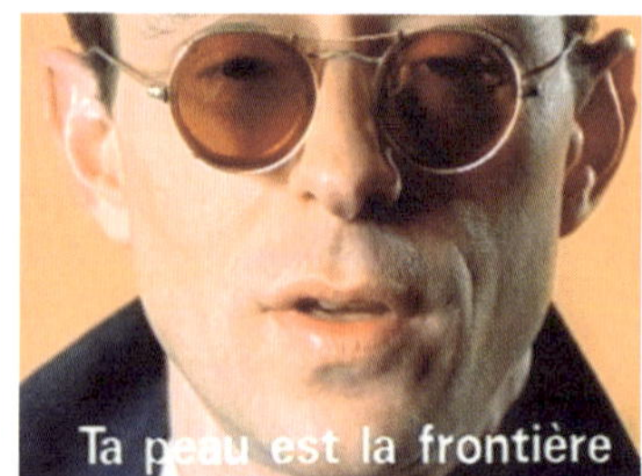

00:14

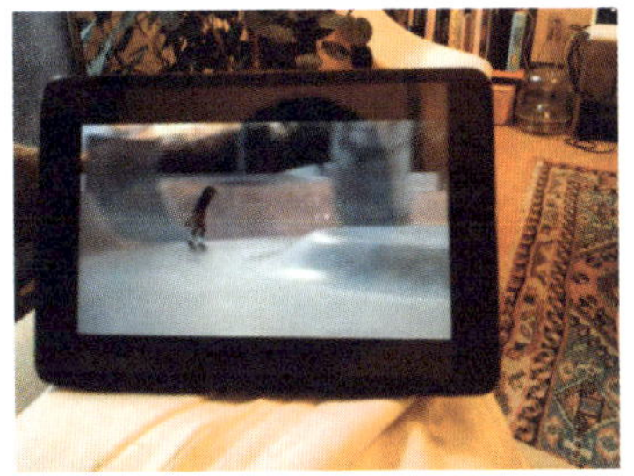

03:56

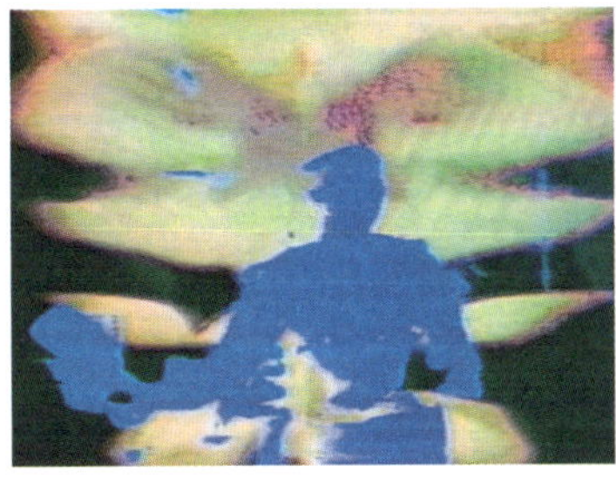

14:27

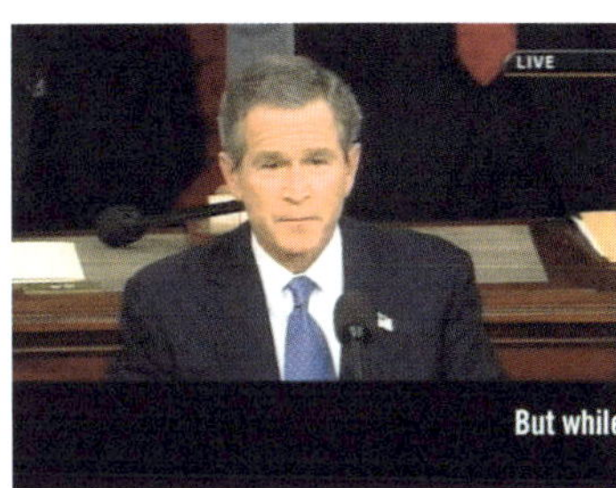

04:29

NEWS FROM ELECTRONIC ARTS INTERMIX

The New Automated Color Videotape Editing System

The biggest news around Electronic Arts Intermix, Inc. at the moment is the impending advent of the new automated half-inch color videotape editing system made possible by a grant from the Rockefeller Foundation. The equipment at this writing is in the Editing/Post Production Facility in the process of being set up, and should be in operation by the time this is in the mails.

We expect the new system to speed up time required for editing by a factor of from 4 to 10, thus enabling us to serve from four to ten times as many artists as we have been able to with our present one-inch B&W system. The new system will be hooked up with our present control and post-production equipment, including a Siegel Chrominance Processing Synthesizer (colorizor), a Special Effects Generator and a 3M Processing Amplifier. If you haven't heard about our Editing/PPF it's because it has been booked up for many weeks in advance, and therefore, we have not been able to publicize it until now. It is available for use by qualified video-artists under the supervision and instruction of John Trayna, EAI's Technical Director. There is no charge for these services. If interested, write for more detailed information and application blank. The Editing/PPF is supported by grants from the New York State Council on the Arts and the National Endowment for the Arts, a Federal Agency, as well as the Rockefeller Foundation.

EAI at the AAM Annual Meeting. Los Angeles June 23-27.

At Electronic Arts Intermix's booth at the American Association of Museums Meeting at the Biltmore Hotel, David Cort's VIDEO ART TRANSPOSER will be unveiled. Also shown will be a number of the videotape programs distributed by EAI. More on the TRANSPOSER on page 4.

New One-Time Showing Fee

EAI is instituting a one-time showing rate which will be half the one week rate, or $37.50 for "A" tapes and $50 for "B" tapes.

The Code

We have been asked the meaning of our code. "A" tapes are 30 minutes or less in length, "B" tapes are between 30 and 60 minutes in length. "C" rates are discontinued.

The first two digits indicate the artist. Thus, Paik's number is 63. The second two digits indicate the tape. Thus, A63 01 is Paik's half-hour program "Global Groove".

Revised Basic Fee Schedule

The revised basic fee schedule is:

Length of Program	Fee for Life of the Tape	Fee for One Month Rental	Fee for One Week Rental	Fee for One-Time Showing
A 0-30 minutes	$175	$125	$75	$37.50
B 30-60 minutes	$275	$200	$100	$50

Add $4.00 shipping and handling charge for each shipment.

ELECTRONIC ARTS, INTERMIX, INC.
84 FIFTH AVENUE
NEW YORK, N.Y. 10011
(212) 989-2316

Organizational press release, circa 1977

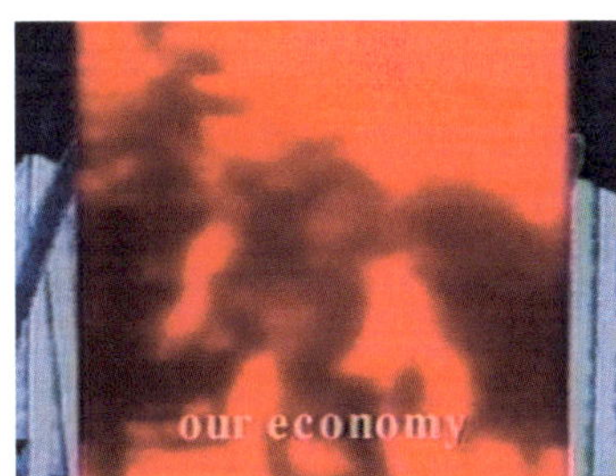

00:16

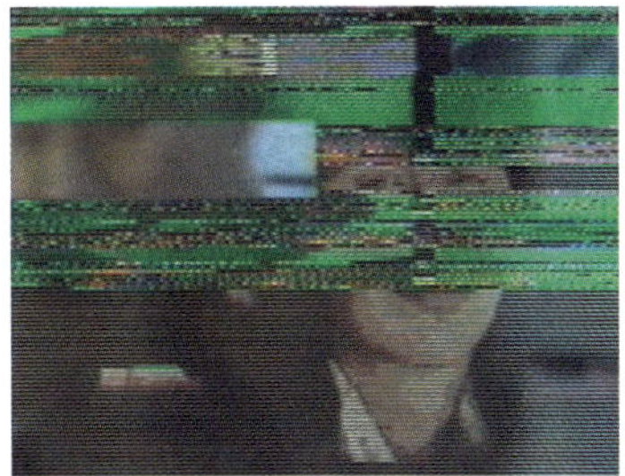

00:33

21:10

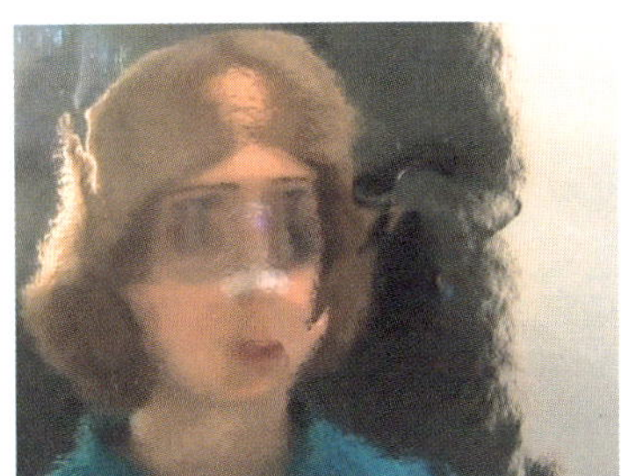

01:22

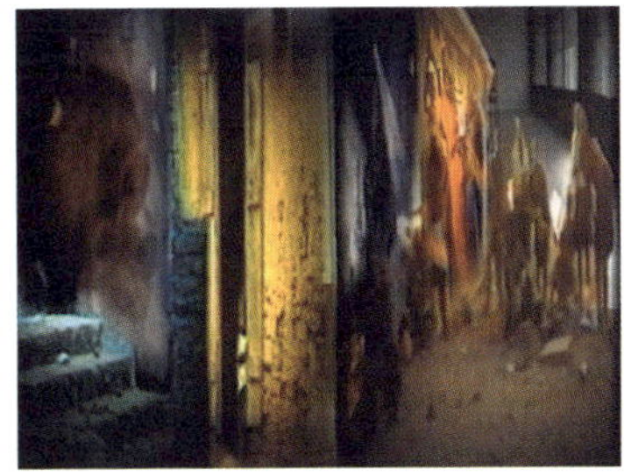

00:19

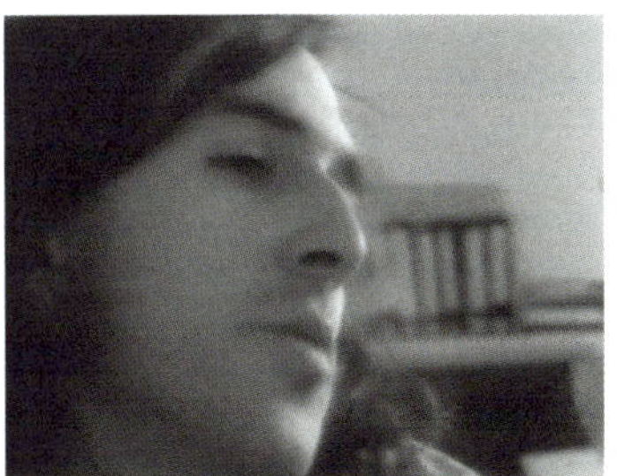

04:22

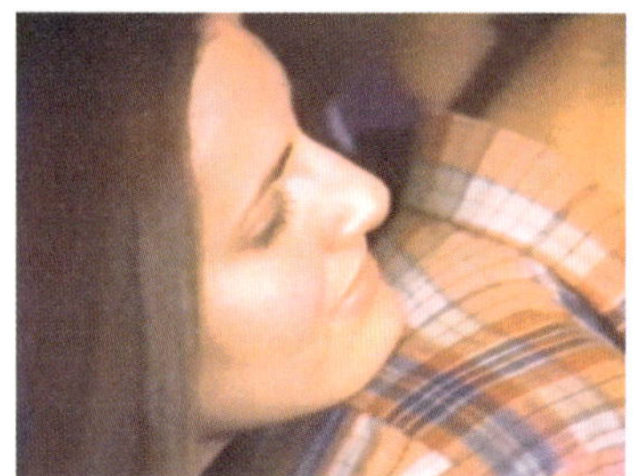
01:28

01:48

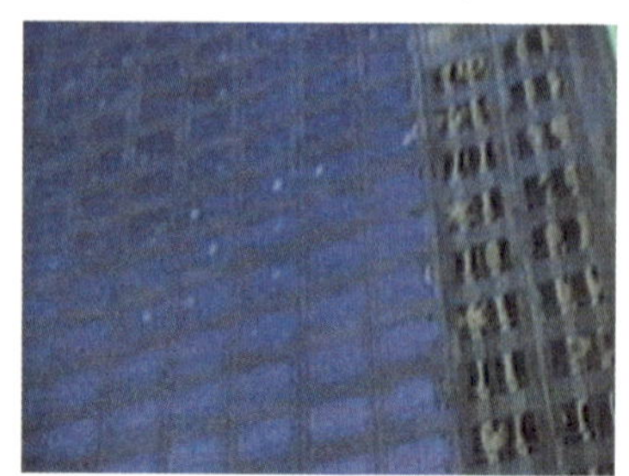
06:03

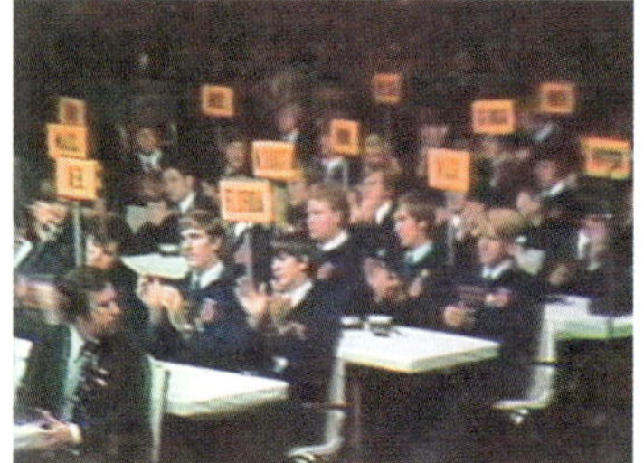
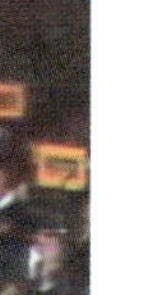
14:12

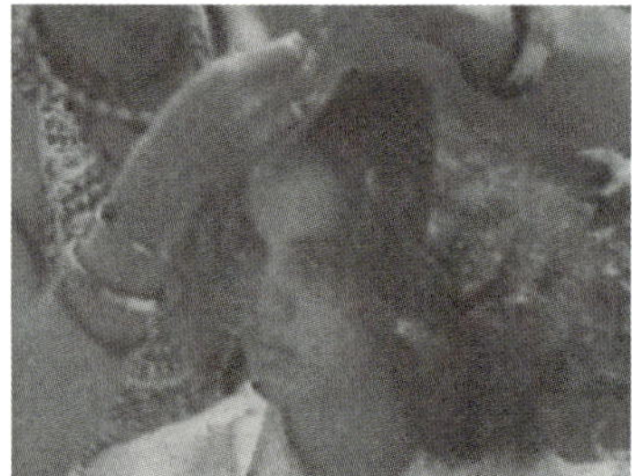
17:36

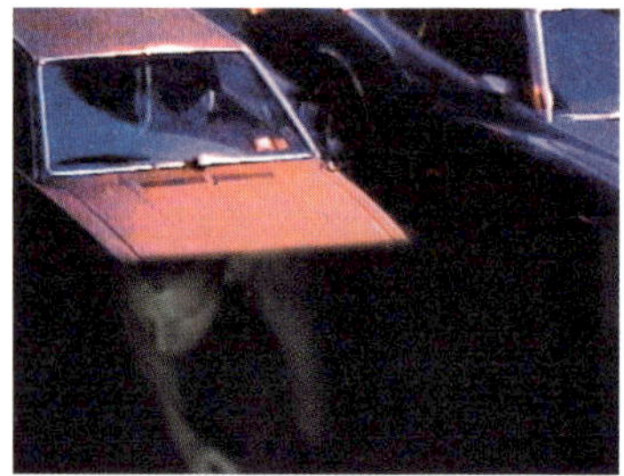
07:24

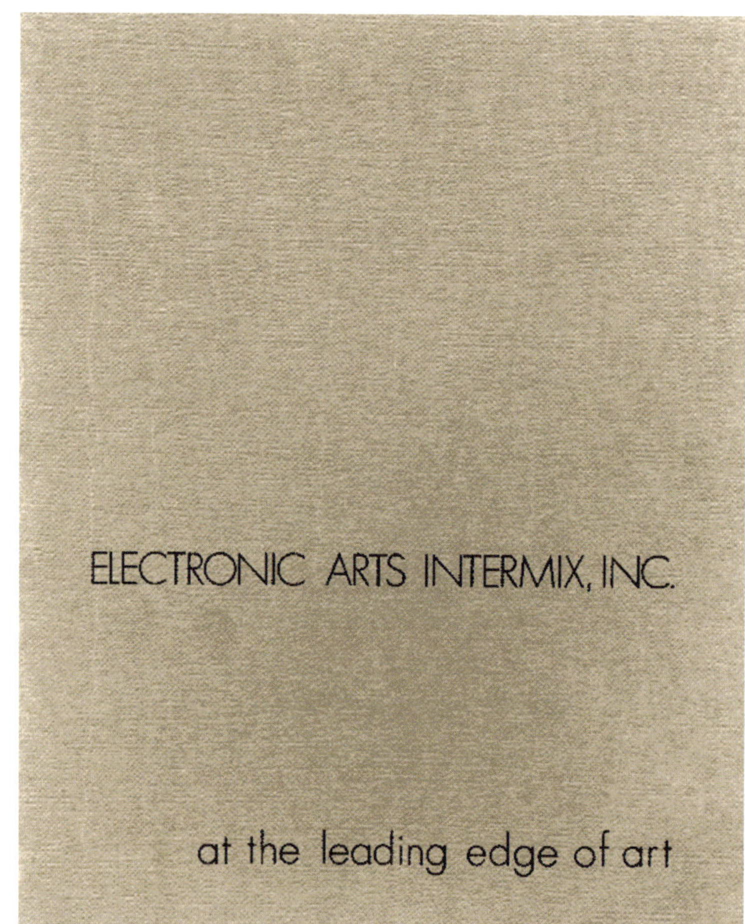

At the Leading Edge, a “manifesto” written by Howard Wise

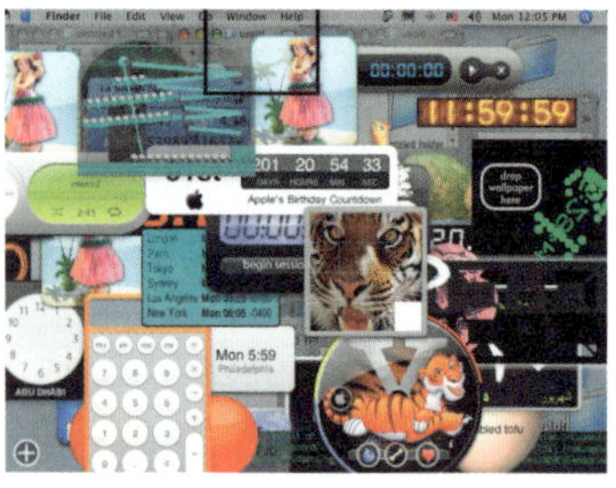

00:59

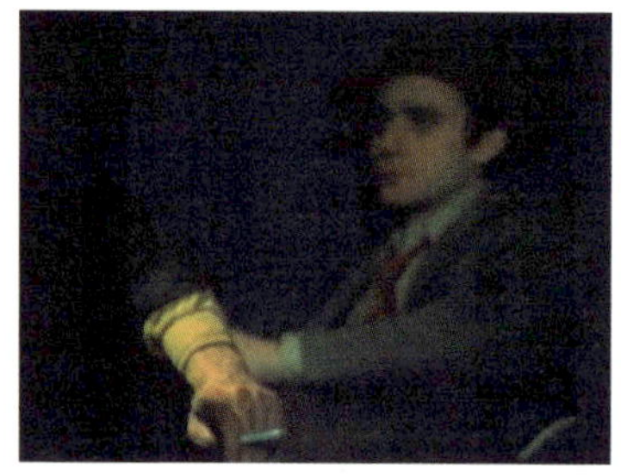
08:30

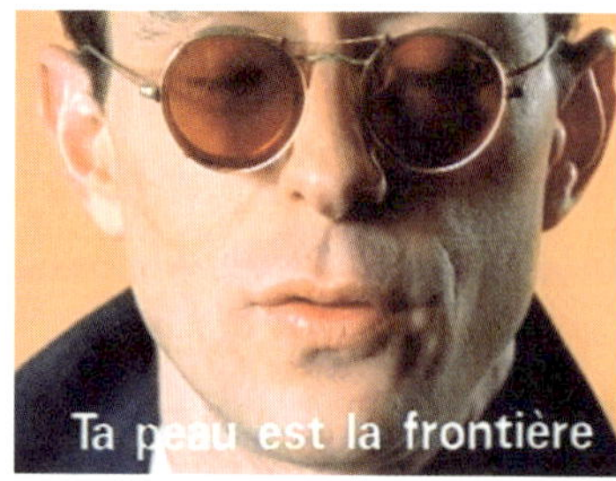

00:14

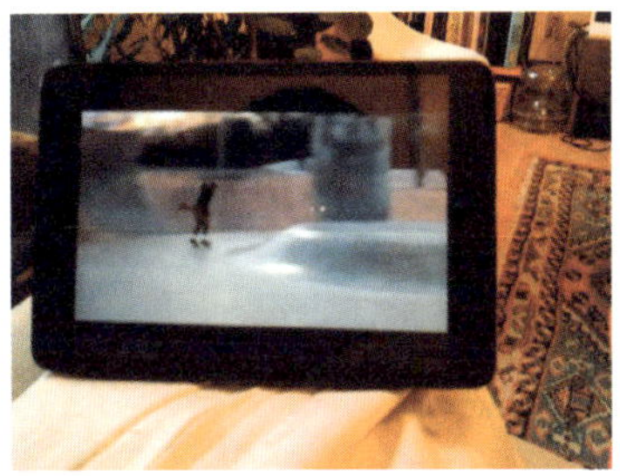
03:56

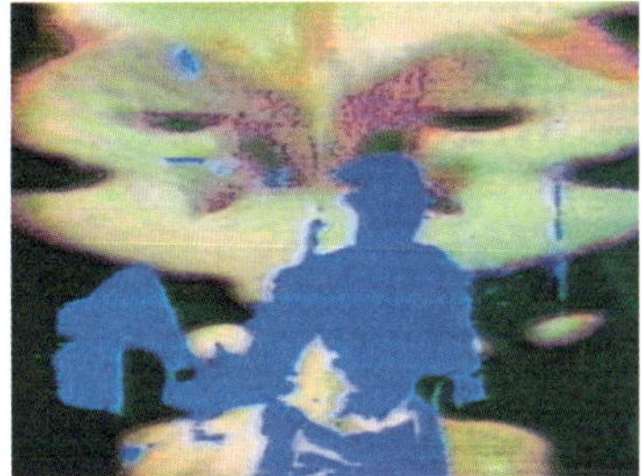
14:27

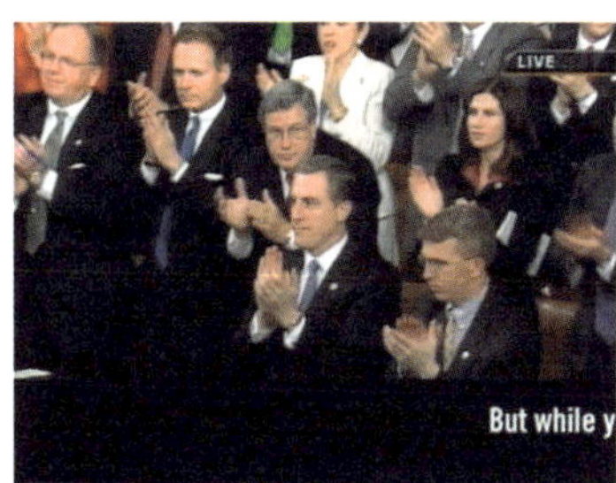

04:29

ELECTRONIC ARTS INTERMIX, INC. 84 FIFTH AVENUE NEW YORK, N.Y. 10011 (212) 989-2316

RULES FOR THE USE OF THE EDITING ROOM

We hope that your work in this facility goes smoothly, with a minimum of delays and problems. We spend a portion of our time every day repairing and maintaining the equipment to insure that you and other artists find it in proper work order.

You can assist us in this effort by observing the following rules:

1. The door to the corridor must be locked at all times.
2. Do not permit any person not specifically authorized by EAI to enter the premises.
3. All persons present at an editing session must sign in and out, including time and date.
4. All personal belongings, other than tapes, must be left in the viewing room.
5. Do not remove, or permit anyone accompanying you to remove anythings that is in the E/PPF at the time that you enter.
6. No eating, drinking or smoking is allowed in the editing room.
7. Do not use, or permit others to use the telephone for long-distance calls or toll calls or for any lengthy personal calls or otherwise abuse the privilege of using the telephones.
8. Any problems with the equipment should be entered into the notebook which is kept on the right hand wall above the decks. This is especially important in enabling us to diagnose and correct a problem before it becomes a crisis.
8. When not using the graphics camera, treat it as you would any video camera:
   Turn the camera off;
   Stop down the lens;
   Replace the lens cap.
9. When you are ready to leave the E/PPF, please remember this procedure:
   Turn off: Lights
   Main Power Switch
   Camera
   Audio Amplifier

   Do <u>not</u> turn off: Time Base Corrector
   Test Signal/Sync Generator

   Please: Coil cables and return to pegboard
   Replace dust covers on decks
   Clean up all trash and put it in the wastebaskets

   SIGN OUT

   Lock both locks and, if it is your final night, put keys through the mail slot.
   This closing procedure is essential for our work the following day and for the safety of the equipment.

Your cooperation with these few rules is necessary to our continuing operation and your working relationship with us.

2/24/78

THE ARTISTS VIDEOTAPE RESOURCE

Rules for the Editing and Post Production Facilities, 1978

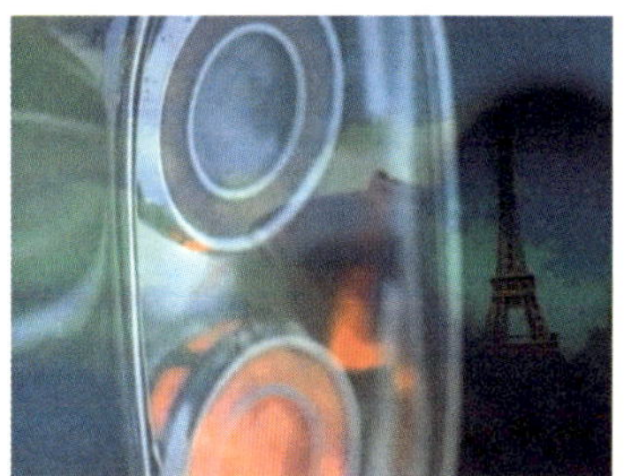
00:16

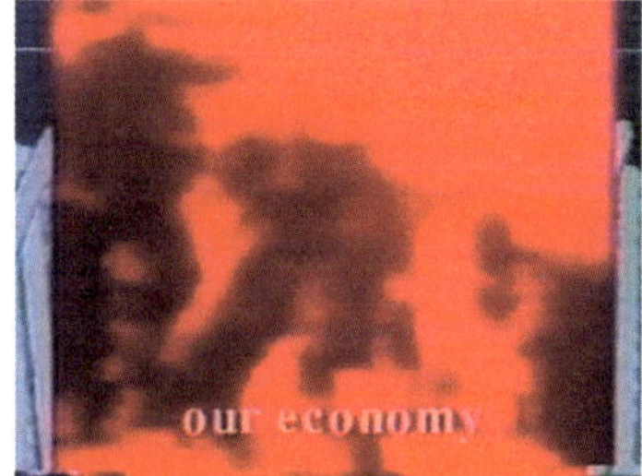

00:33

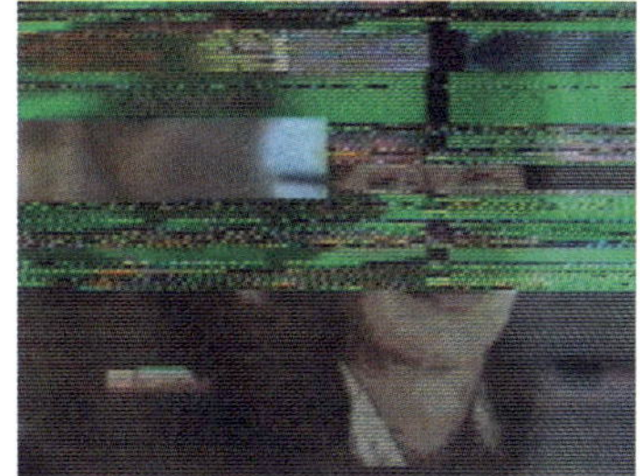
21:10

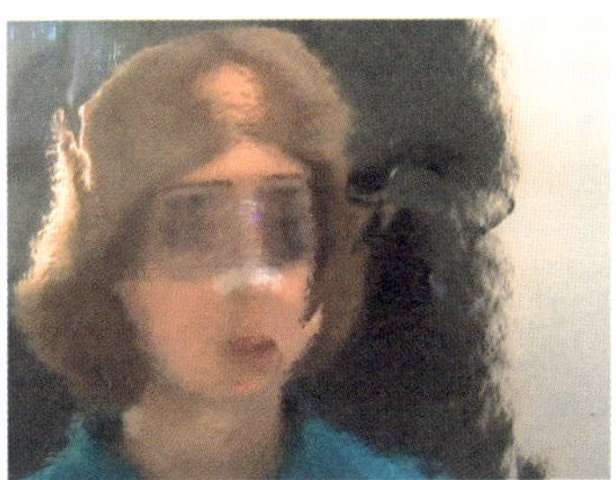
01:22

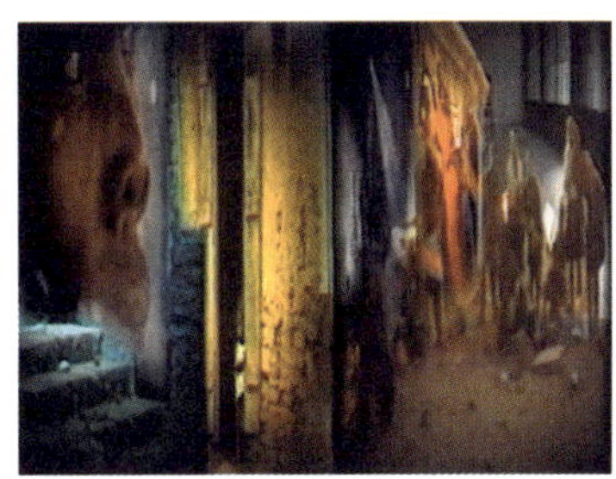
00:19

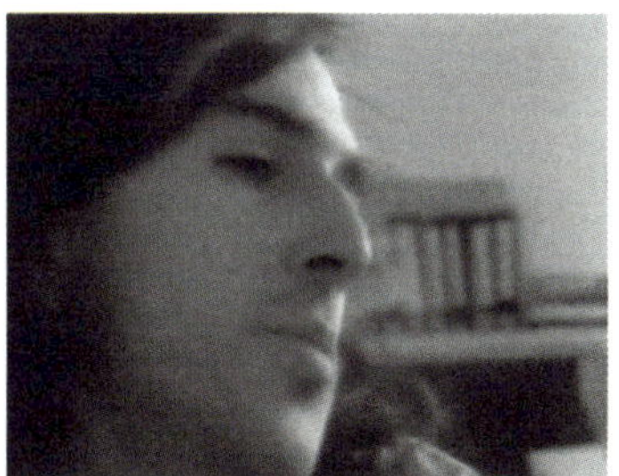
04:22

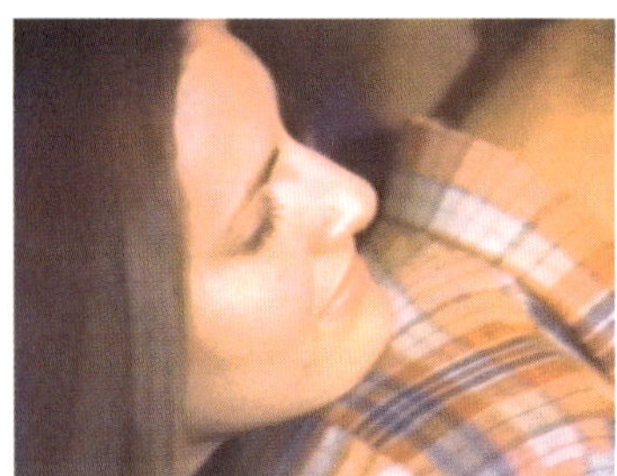

01:28

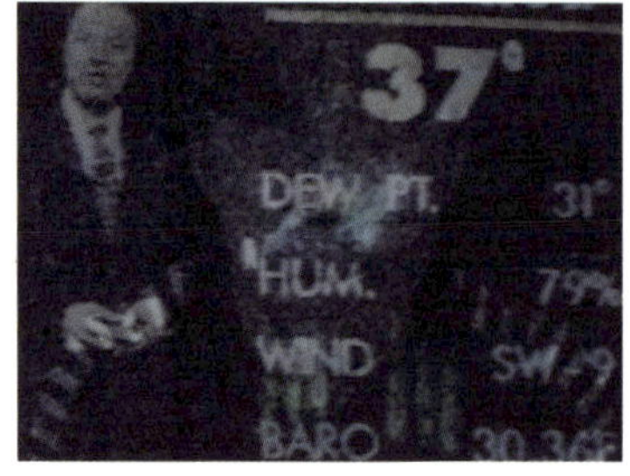

01:48

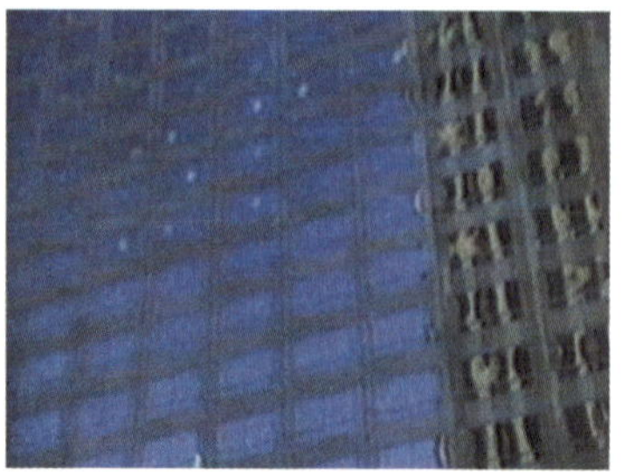

06:03

14:12

17:36

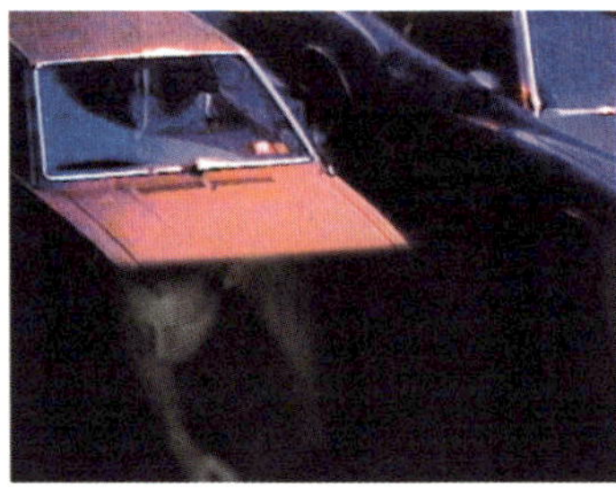

07:24

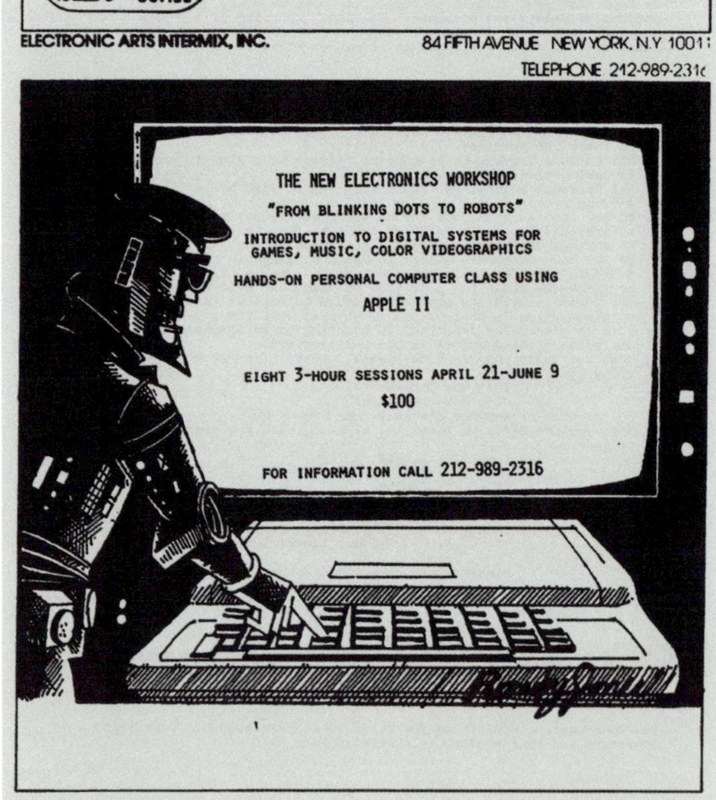

Ad for EAI workshop teaching editing on the Apple II

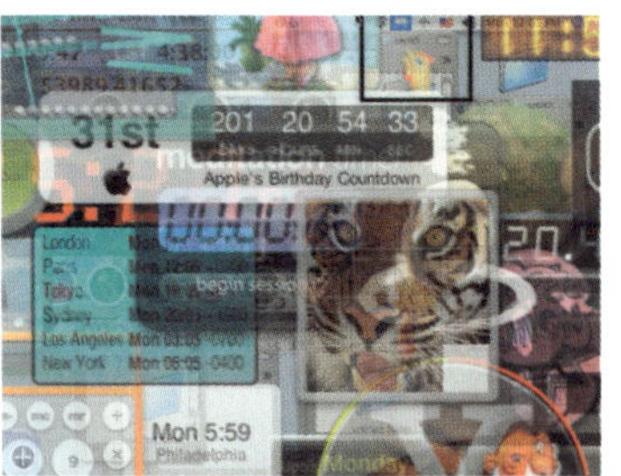

00:59

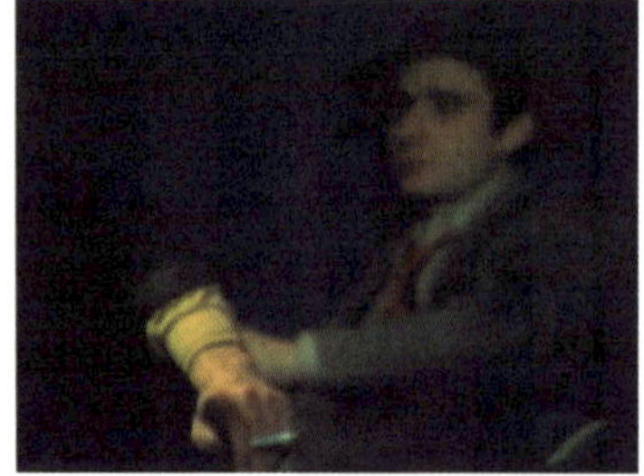

08:30

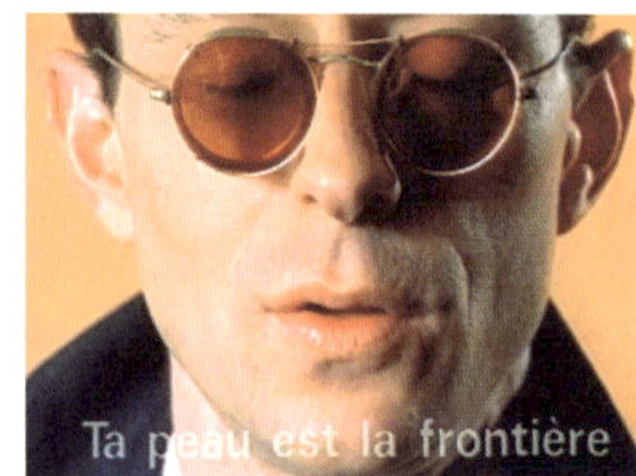

00:14

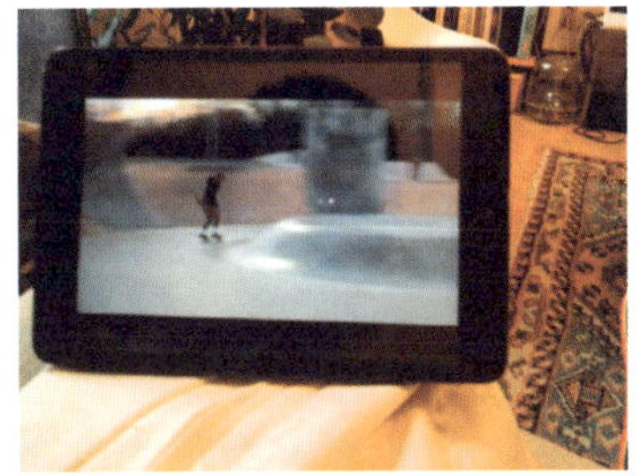
03:56

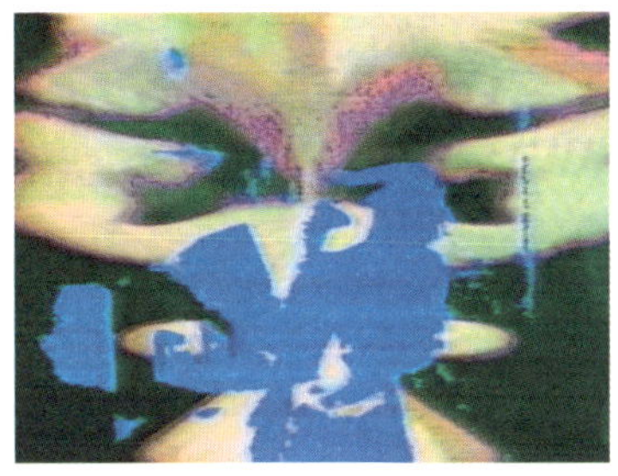
14:27

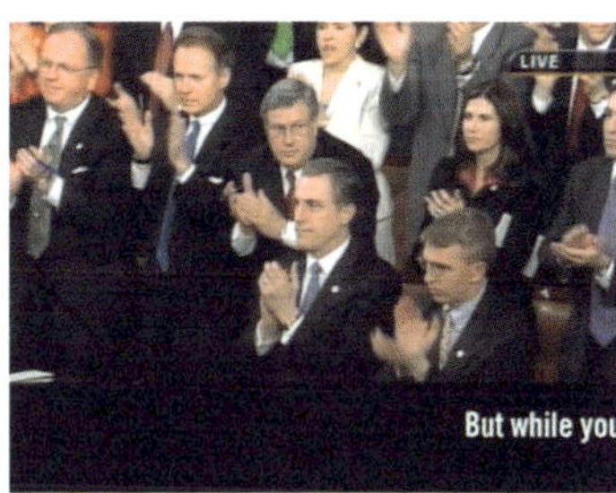

04:29

AK – How did you develop a fee structure that advocated for artists to be compensated? That's something in particular that I have so much respect for.

LZ – That was something that was in place from the beginning. That was part of the DNA of the organization and was always part of the economic model: every time the work gets shown, the artist gets paid a royalty.

AK – Was there another group of EAI artists that were coming into the fold at that point?

LZ – I'm trying to think of the major shifts and acquisitions in the late eighties. That's when the decision was made that we'd invest in an artist's body of work and not just individual titles. I think once we started doing preservation and cataloging, and began compiling thorough bibliographies and biographies of the artists, the work we were doing around each artist suddenly became immense. We also invested in an off-site archival media storage facility to house artists' originals, rare materials, and preservation masters in a temperature- and humidity-controlled environment.

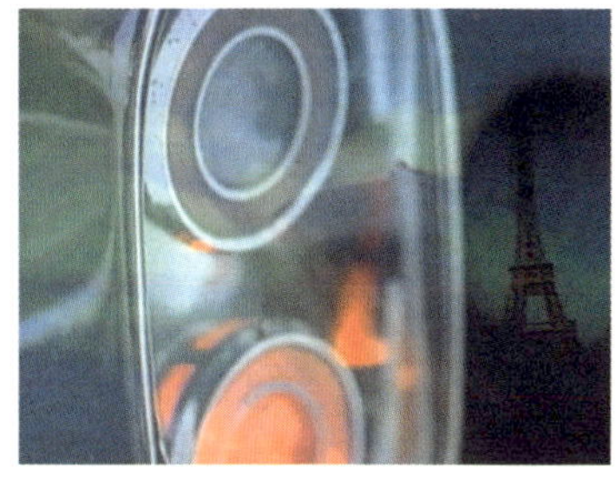
00:16

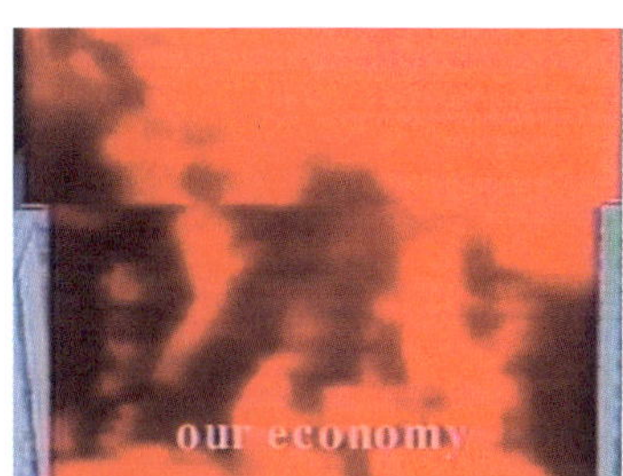

00:33

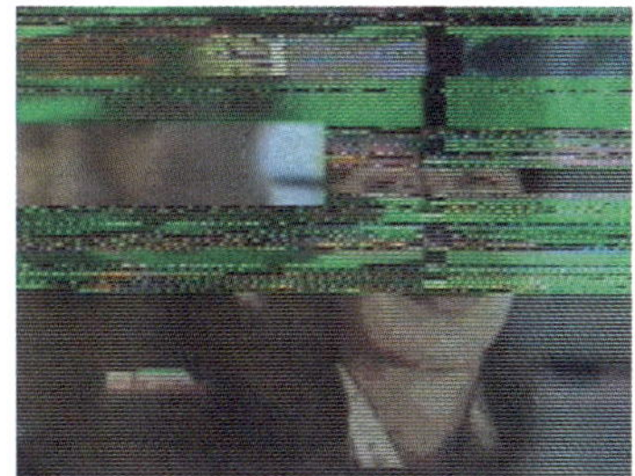
21:10

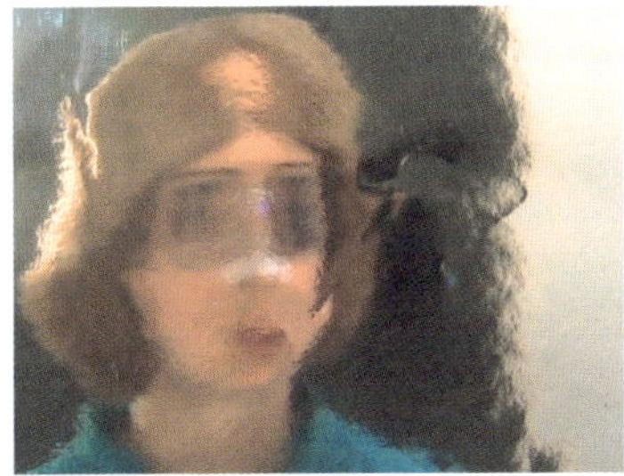
01:22

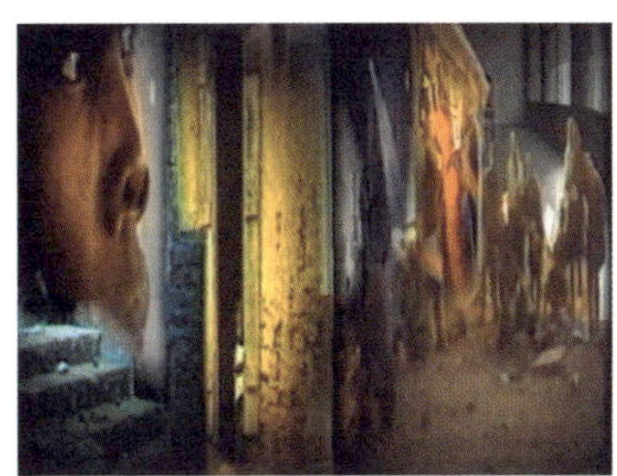
00:19

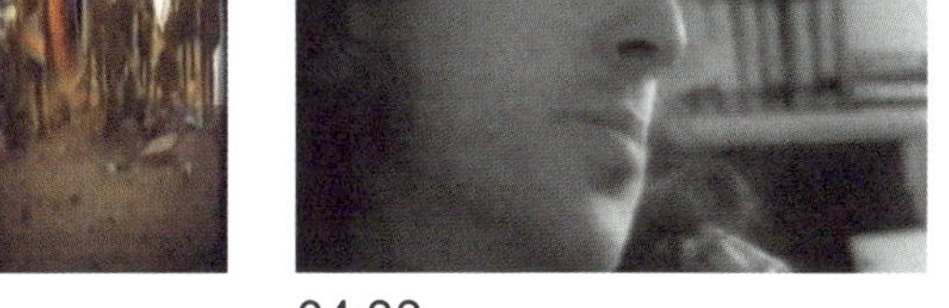
04:22

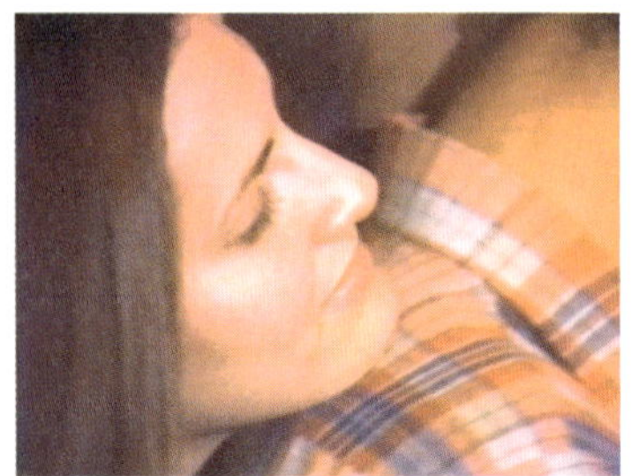

01:28

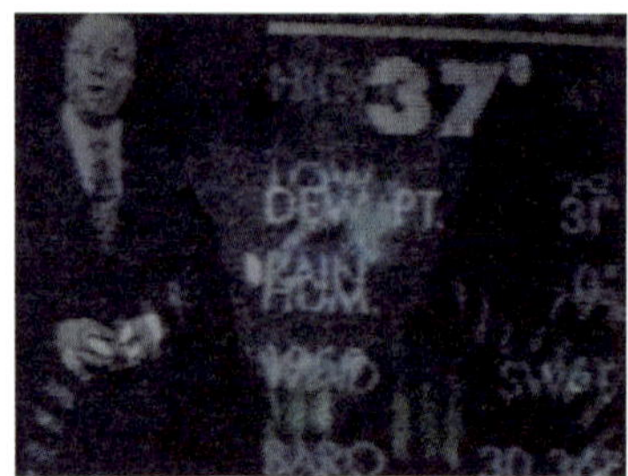

01:48

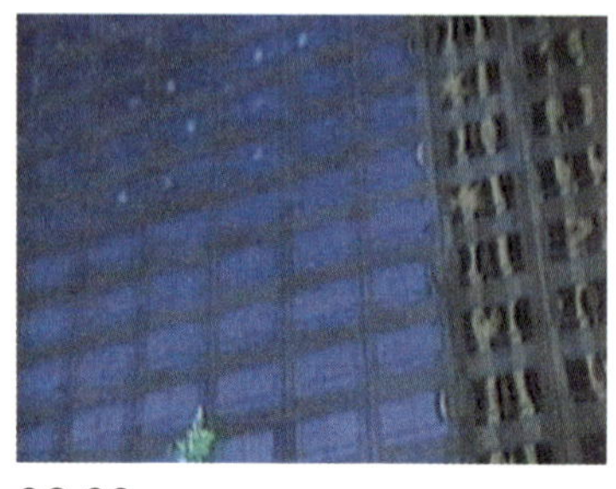

06:03

RC – It was a more art historical relationship to the work.

LZ – Exactly. Suddenly taking on an individual title became less realistic and less interesting. And this reflected the shift in approach to how we were collecting, cataloging, and preserving the works.

We worked on the catalog publication for at least five years, or longer than that. It was published in 1991, in both a softcover edition and as a hardcover book published by Abbeville Press. It took that long for the publication to come out. I had a portable computer that was the size of a toaster oven that I rented every month. It was so heavy, it was like a suitcase and I took it home every weekend to write. We got a grant from the American Film Institute in 1986. That was the grant that allowed me to rent that computer—not even buy it—just to rent it. And I would carry it with me everywhere. Even thinking that one would try and write a several hundred page text on a word processor and edit it manually—it was incredible. But that's a different story.

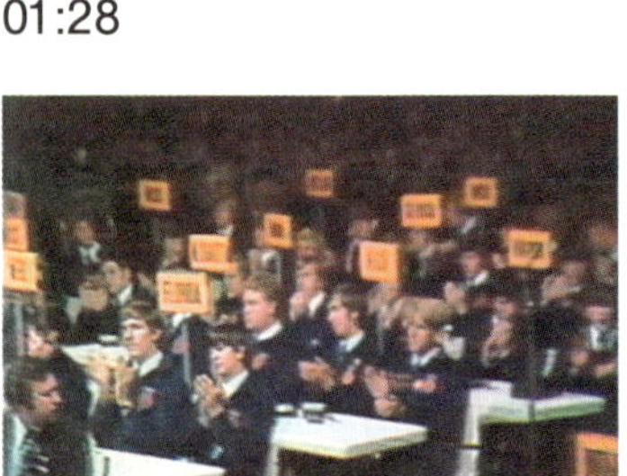

14:12

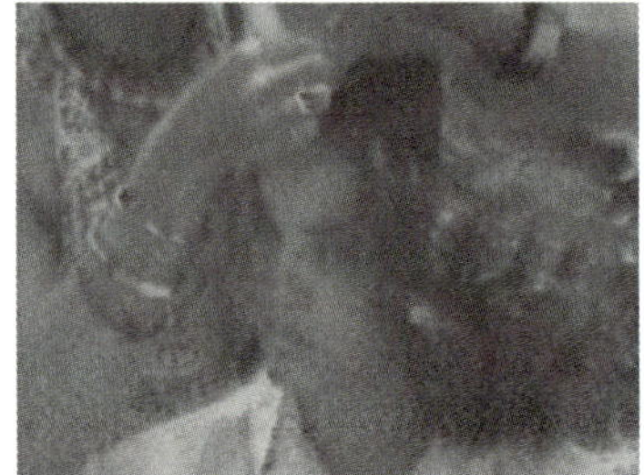

17:36

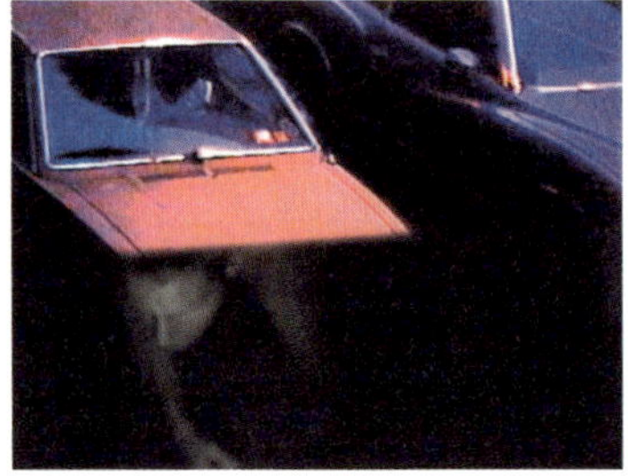

07:24

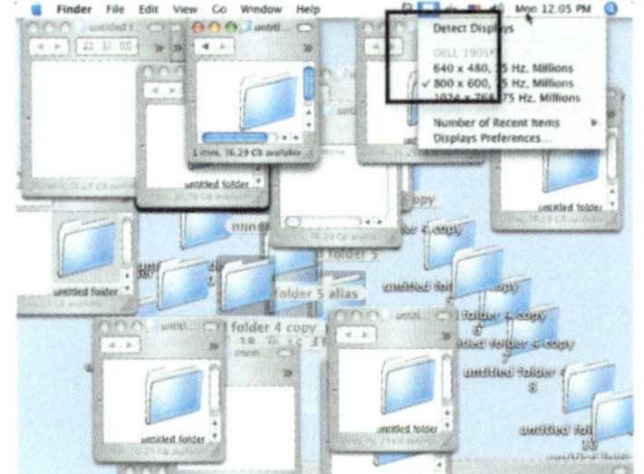

00:59

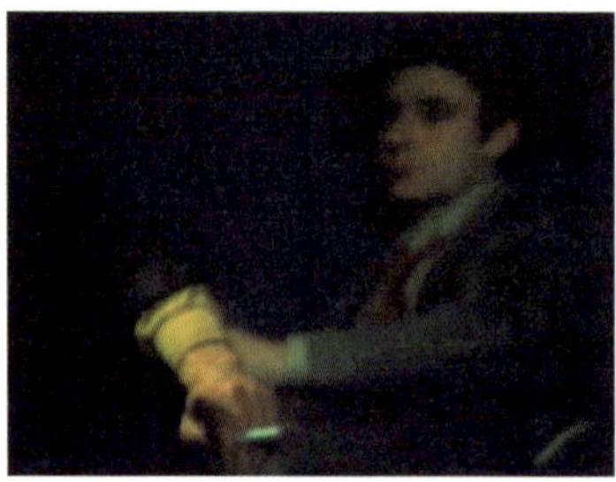

08:30

00:14

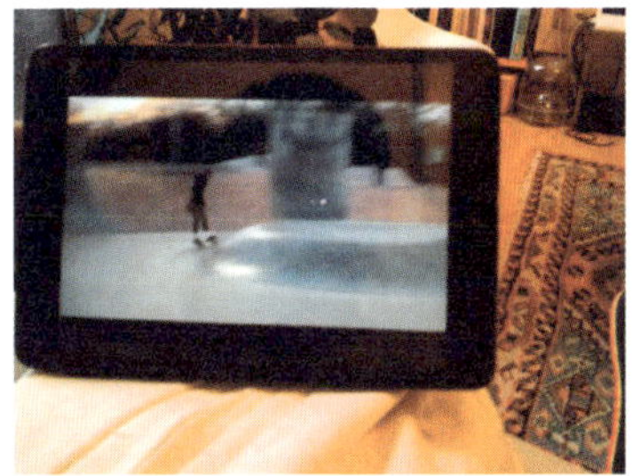
03:56

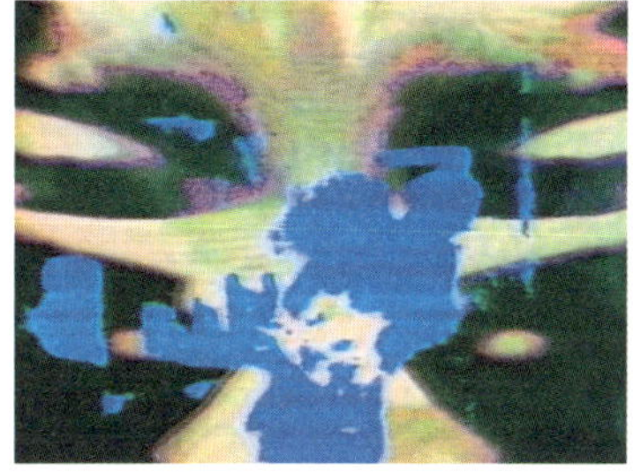
14:27

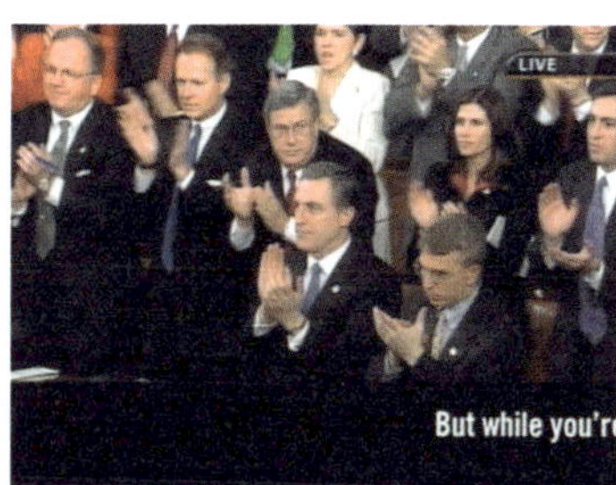

04:29

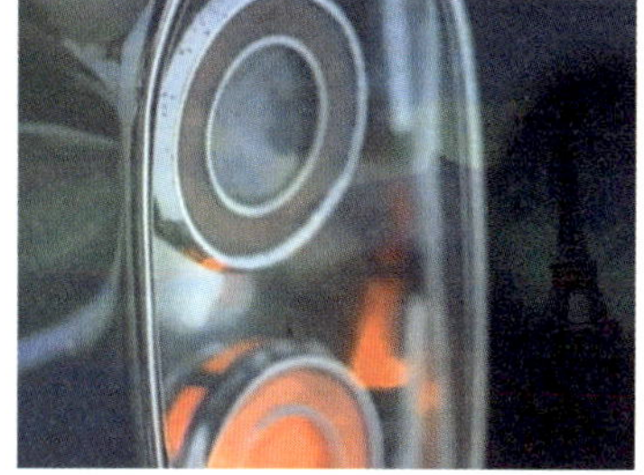
00:16

AK – What was the criteria for artists to become part of EAI's collection at this point?

LZ – Strong work that is video-specific, that speaks to the times, the technology, and the artistic discourses, and that works within this distribution model and allows itself to be circulated in this way, if that makes sense?

AK – And remains single-channel.

LZ – Exactly.

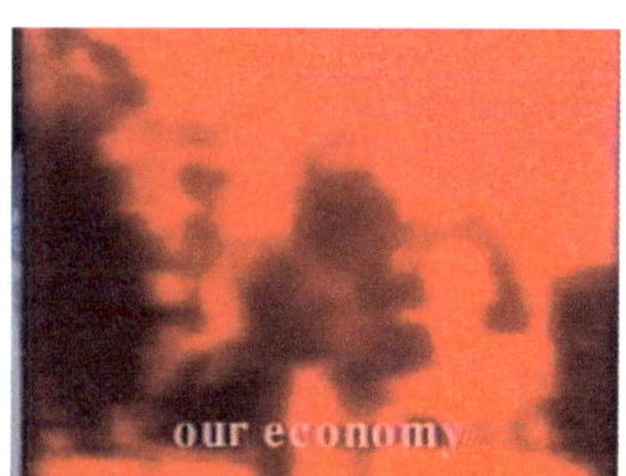

00:33

AK – So, at this point you were interested in working with artists who already had several videos under their belts?

LZ – There was still a lot of young work coming into the collection, but we wanted to see a sense of commitment to the medium, rather than someone who would ever only do one video. We were interested in artists who were invested in video as a *creative medium* and as an artistic tool.

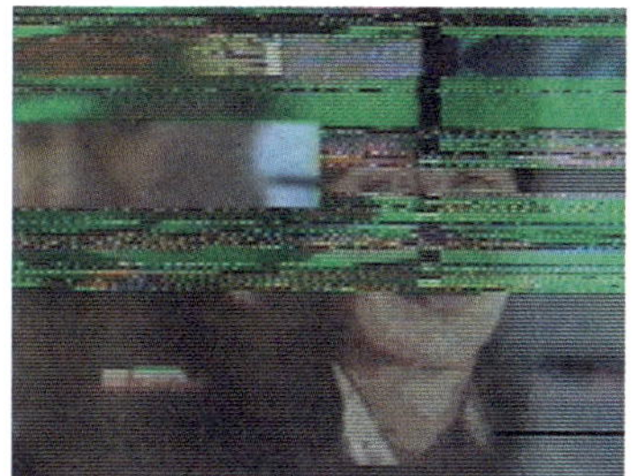
21:10

RC – And that would fit within a history, because EAI is tracking an alternative art history for media art, so it's thinking about how that work speaks to EAI's founding and reflects the

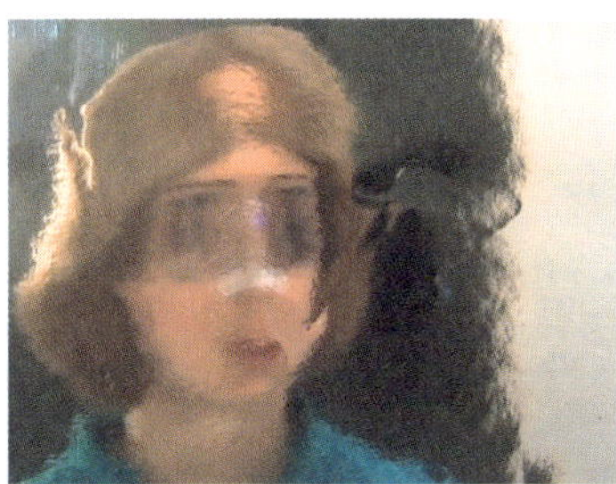
01:22

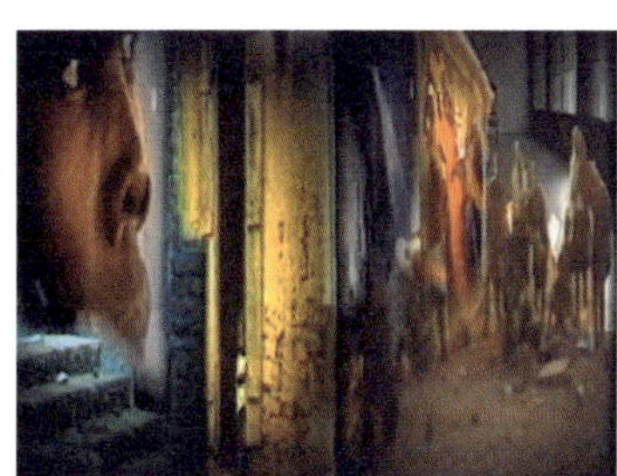
00:19

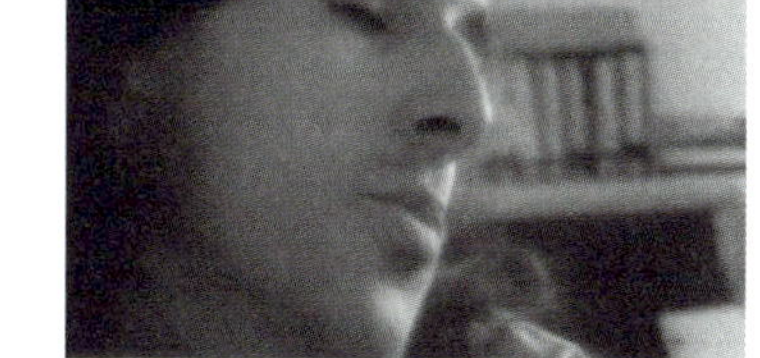
04:22

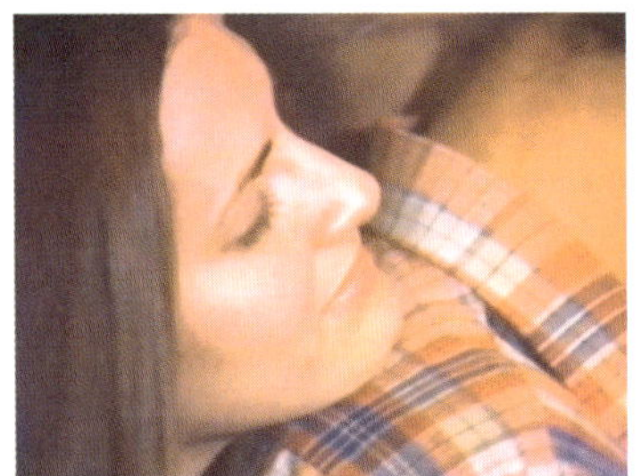
01:28

01:48

06:03

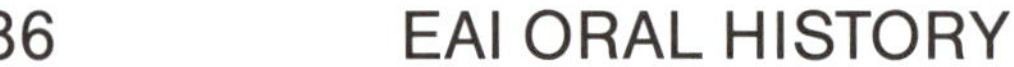

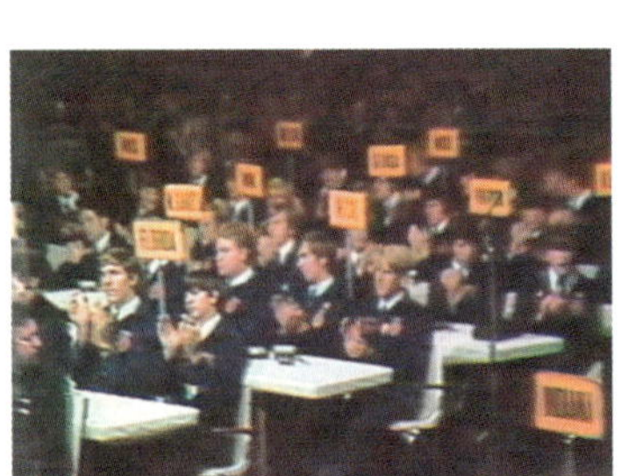
14:12

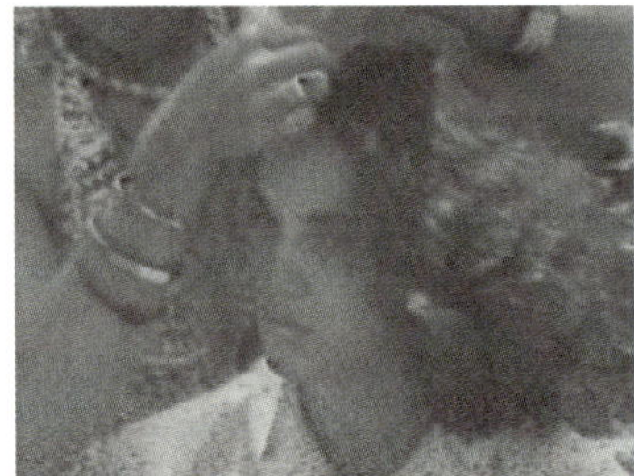
17:36

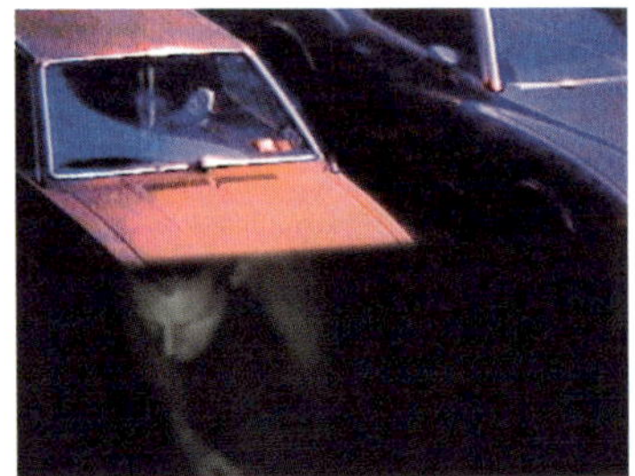
07:24

entire trajectory of the organization. We still talk about that.

AK – That's interesting because that's when it becomes a more self-reflexive process, whereas before it was a little more heat of the moment. And subsequently it became "how are we advocating for and situating these artists?"

RC – And how are we going to define it moving forward?

LZ – Exactly.

AK – So, by the late 1980s, what is the staff size at EAI?

LZ – It's probably about seven people.

AK – Is that counting editing people?

LZ – At this point, there's one primary editor or technical director, and one or two backup editors. Kirk Von Heflin and Eleanor Goldsmith succeeded Matt Danowski as editors after he left in 1987.

AK – So editing really is starting to recede.

LZ – Well, editing had been receding since the mid-eighties. In 1988 we moved from 10 Waverly Place to 536 Broadway, in the heart

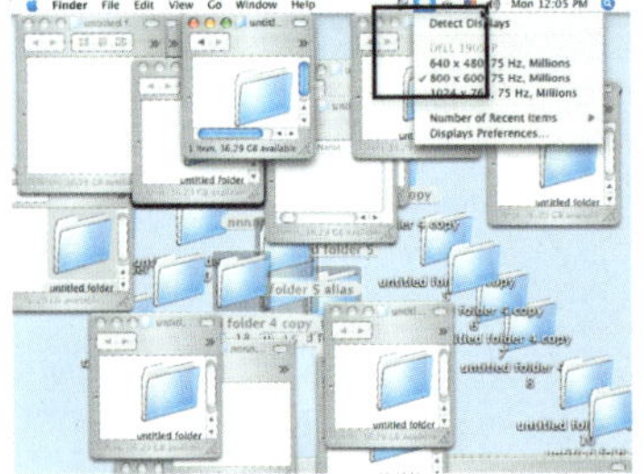
00:59

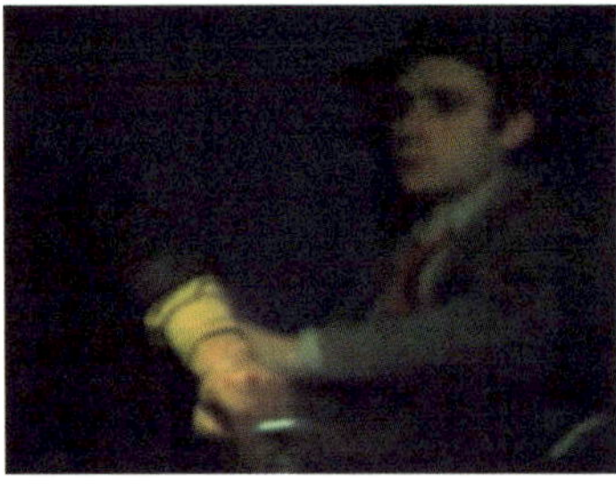
08:30

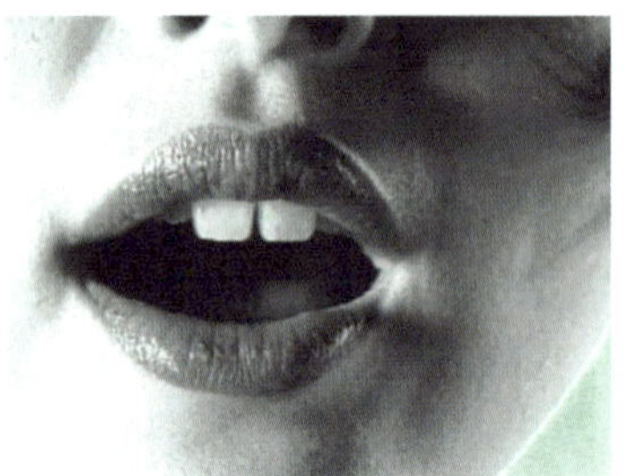
00:14

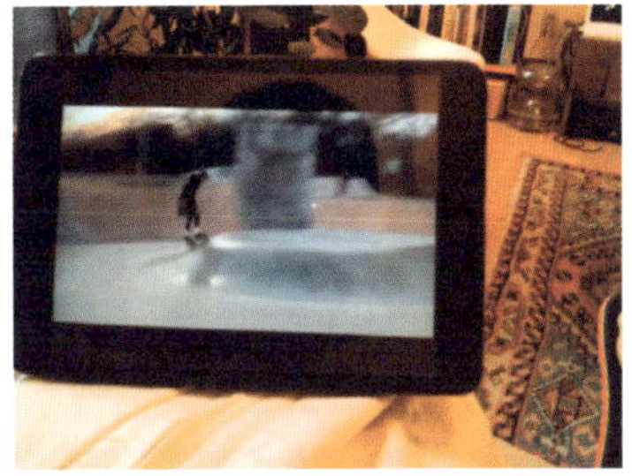
03:56

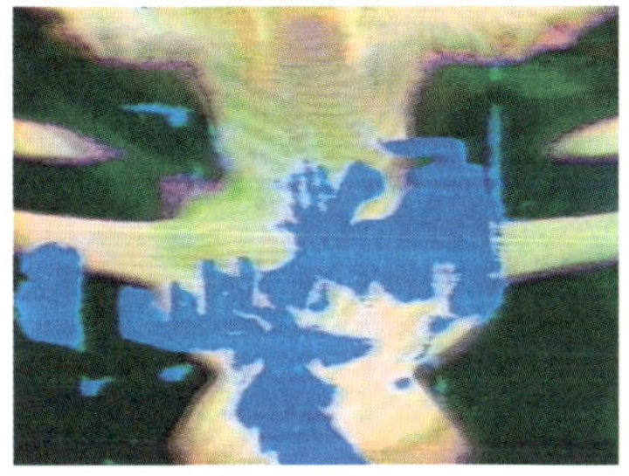
14:27

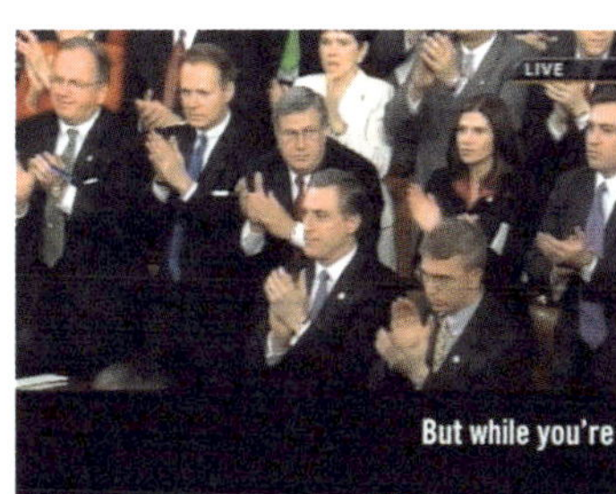

04:29

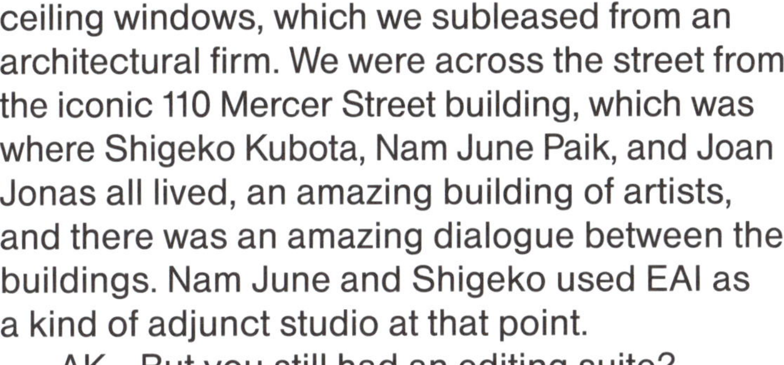
of SoHo. That was a beautiful space with floor-to-ceiling windows, which we subleased from an architectural firm. We were across the street from the iconic 110 Mercer Street building, which was where Shigeko Kubota, Nam June Paik, and Joan Jonas all lived, an amazing building of artists, and there was an amazing dialogue between the buildings. Nam June and Shigeko used EAI as a kind of adjunct studio at that point.

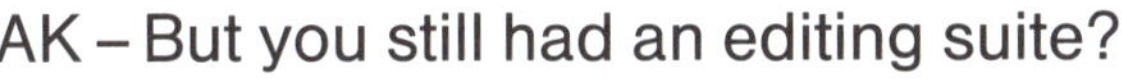
AK – But you still had an editing suite?

LZ – We still had an editing suite. After waning in importance in the mid-eighties, at the end of the eighties into the 1990s there was a resurgence of editing and it became more important again—there was a return of the art world to video, in terms of artists making video, and a parallel return to activism, a return to low-end video. An aesthetic and a production mode that had been unfashionable in the eighties was suddenly back in vogue in the nineties, with the advent of camcorders.

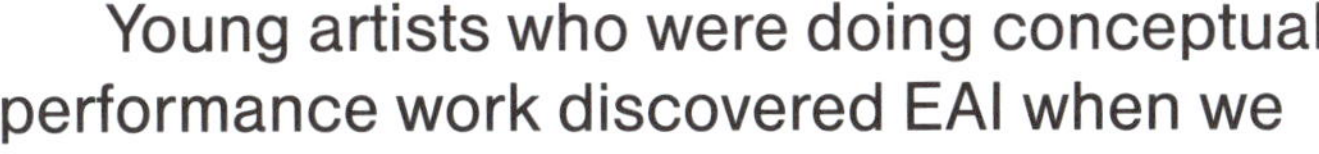
Young artists who were doing conceptual performance work discovered EAI when we

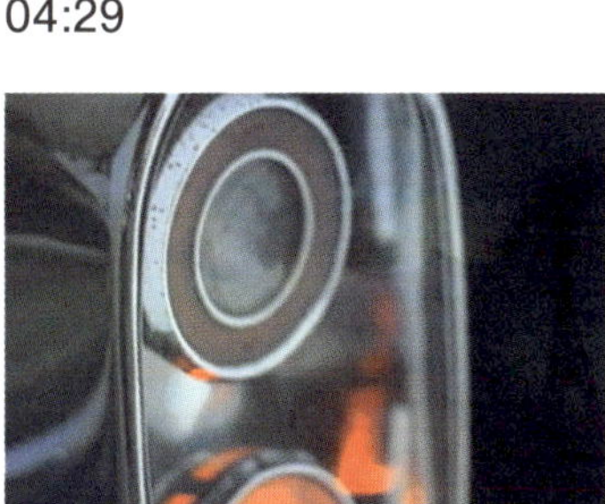
00:16

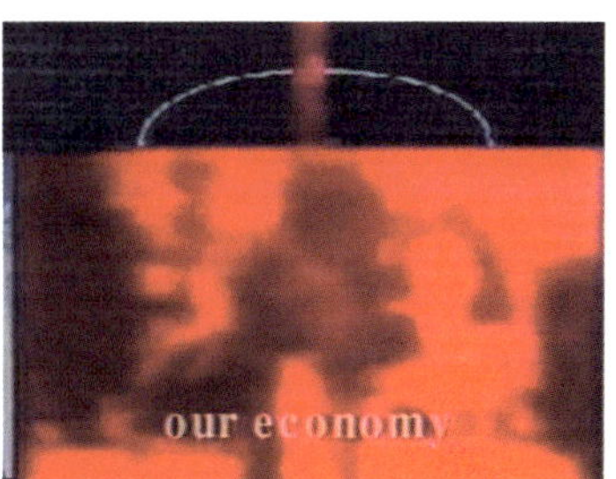

00:33

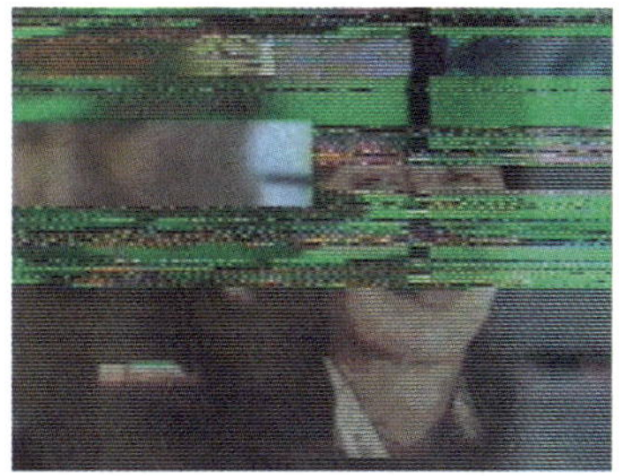
21:10

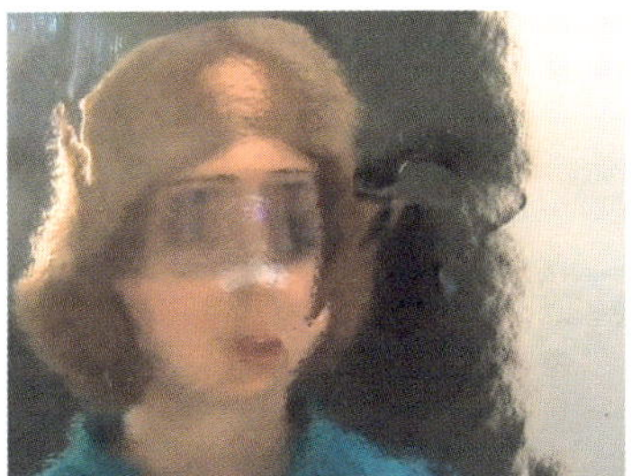
01:22

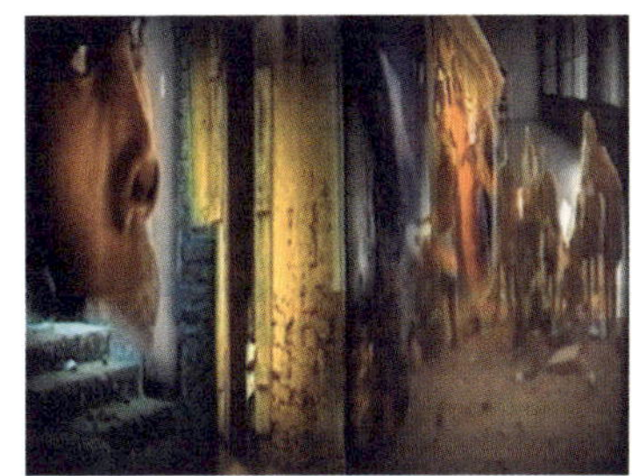
00:19

04:22

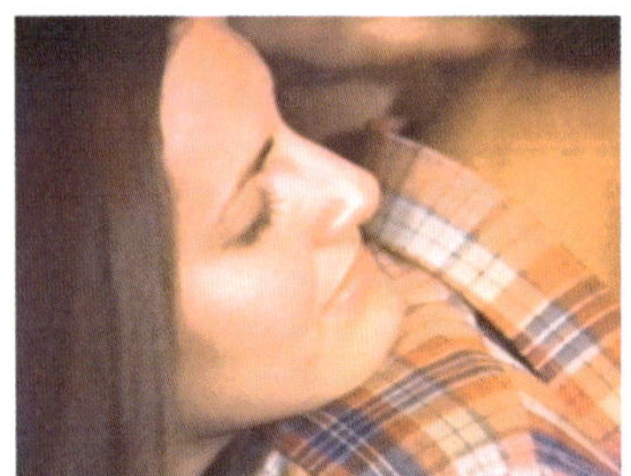
01:27

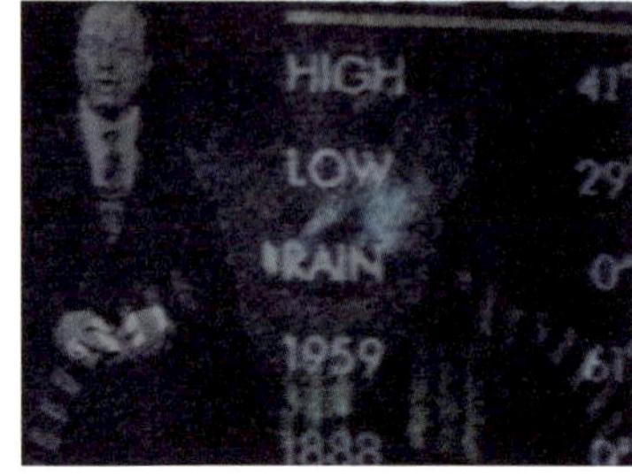

01:47

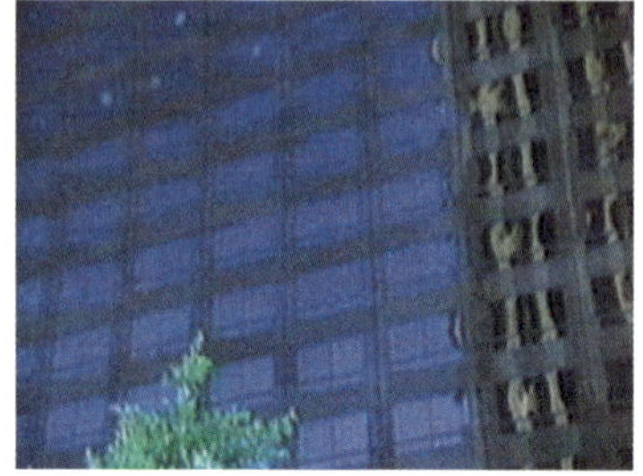
06:02

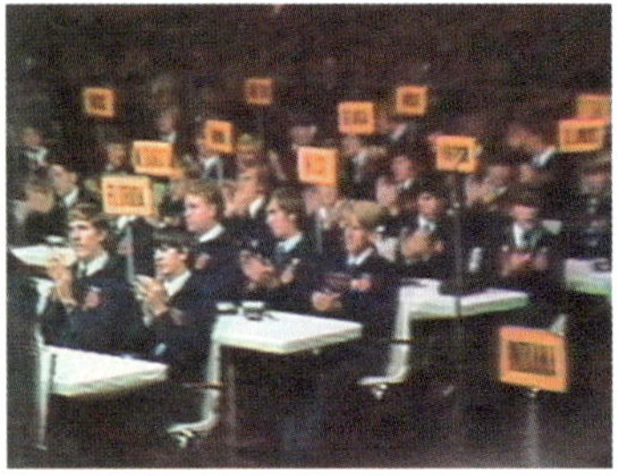
14:11

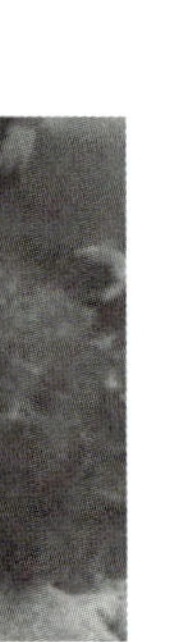
17:35

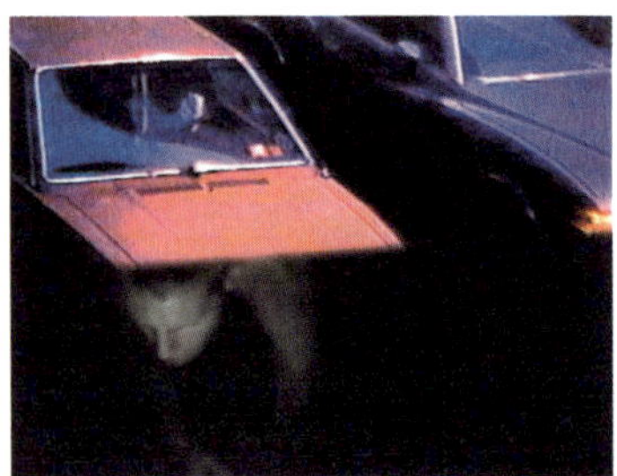
07:23

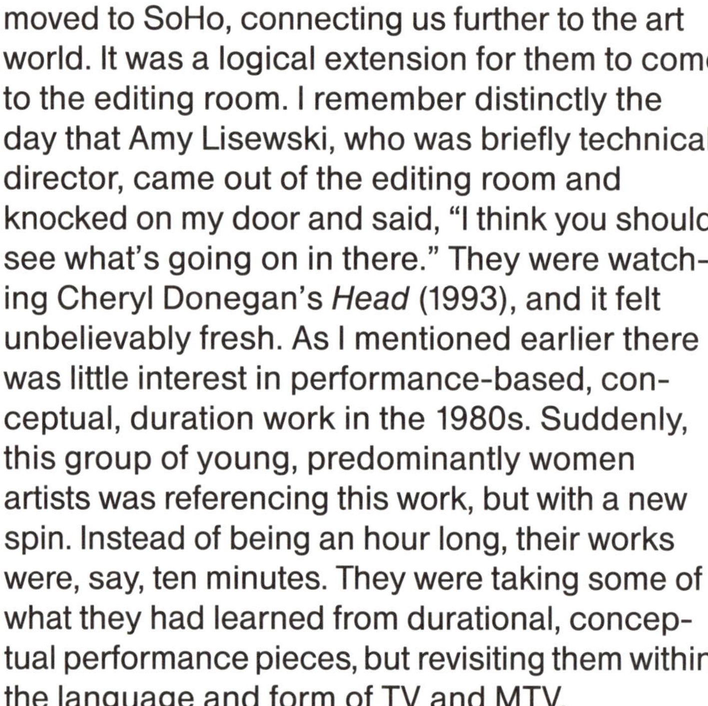
moved to SoHo, connecting us further to the art world. It was a logical extension for them to come to the editing room. I remember distinctly the day that Amy Lisewski, who was briefly technical director, came out of the editing room and knocked on my door and said, “I think you should see what’s going on in there.” They were watching Cheryl Donegan’s *Head* (1993), and it felt unbelievably fresh. As I mentioned earlier there was little interest in performance-based, conceptual, duration work in the 1980s. Suddenly, this group of young, predominantly women artists was referencing this work, but with a new spin. Instead of being an hour long, their works were, say, ten minutes. They were taking some of what they had learned from durational, conceptual performance pieces, but revisiting them within the language and form of TV and MTV.

Also during this same time period when the facility saw this resurgence of neo-conceptual performance artists, a number of activist media collectives, such as ACT UP, DIVA TV, House of Color, and I Object, were also doing work at

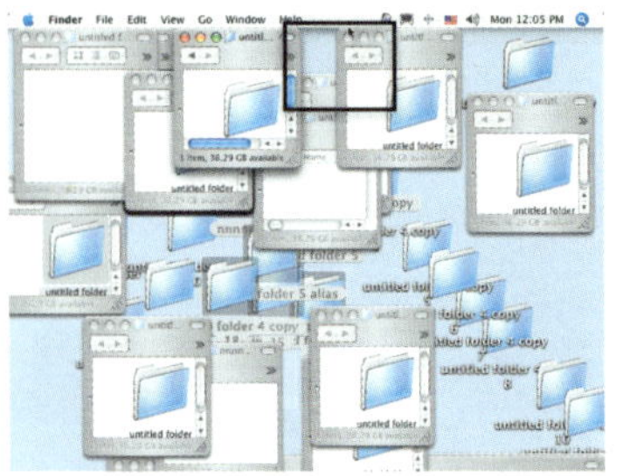
00:58

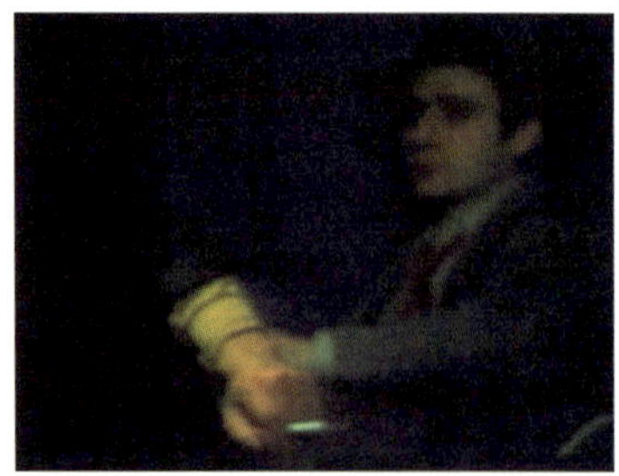
08:29

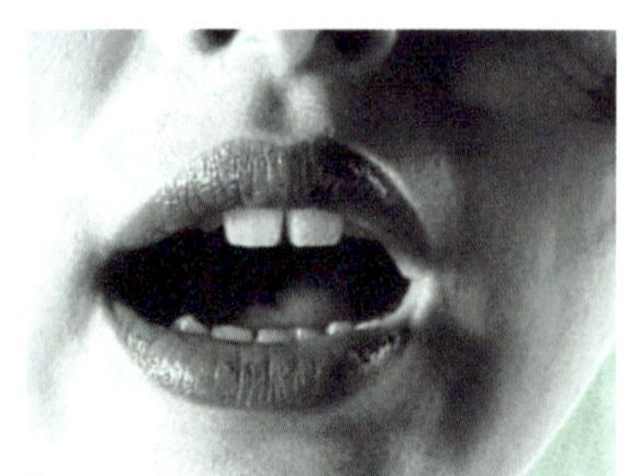
00:13

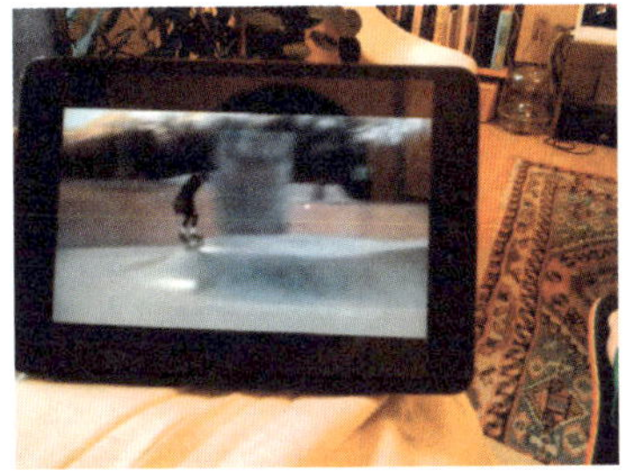
03:56

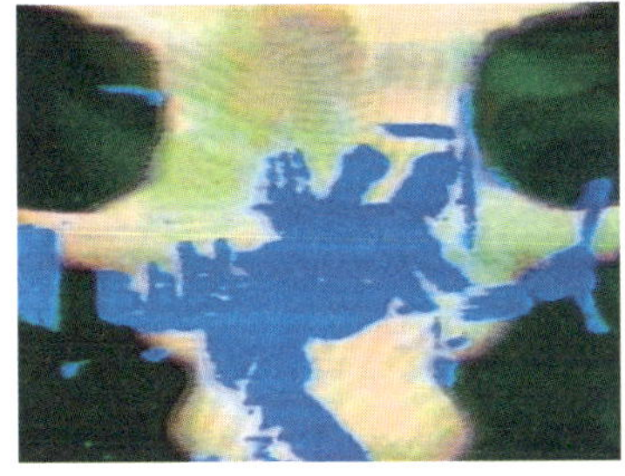
14:27

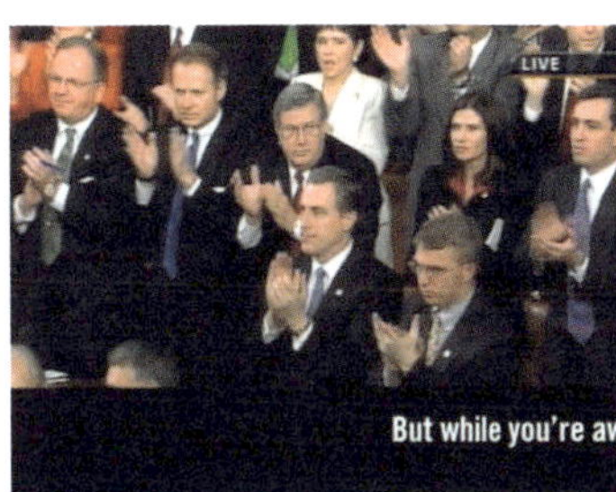

04:29

EAI. They were making low-end, politically motivated activist work around the AIDS crisis and issues of racial and gender identity, and editing at EAI—mostly we just gave them the time for free. That was a hugely important and exciting wave of activity, alongside the new performance artists. There was also a sense of a relation between the conceptual body-based work, which often engaged political ideas, and the activist work, which often included elements of performance. So there were two related threads in this resurgence of low-end video at EAI in the 1990s that also resulted in an influx of more diverse and politically engaged works coming into the collection.

RC – The early 1990s was also a key moment for Robert Beck/Buck, who at that point was the technical director following his time in the Whitney Independent Study Program. (Beck changed his given name to Buck as a work of art in 2008.)

LZ – Yes, exactly. Ivar Smedstad was the technical director in the SoHo space in the late

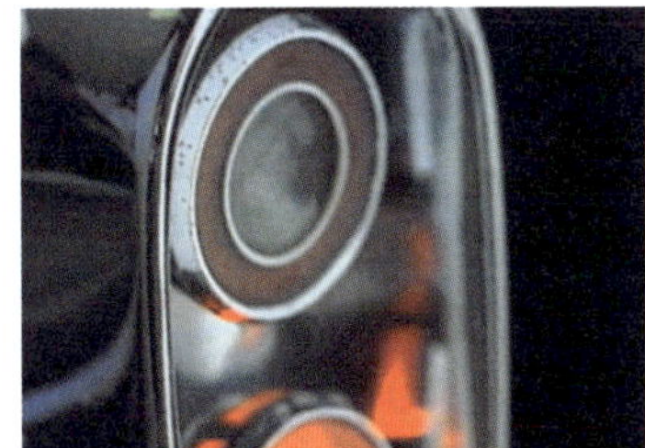
00:16

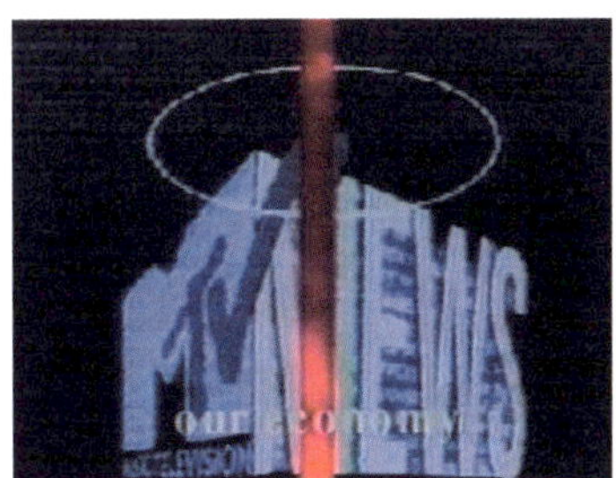
00:33

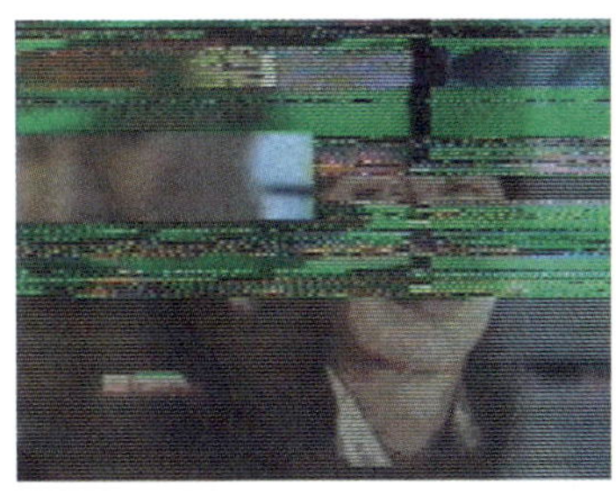
21:10

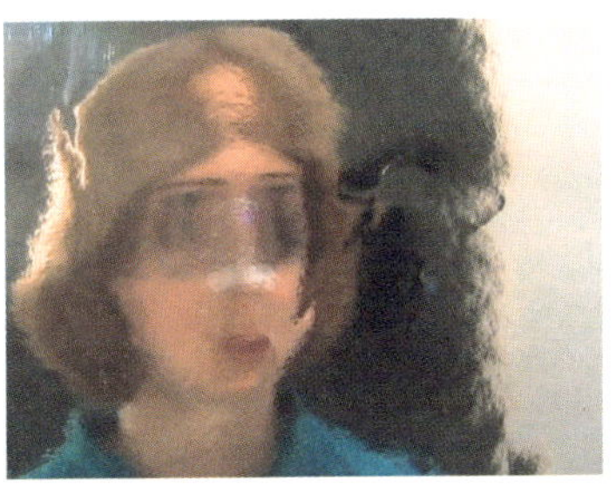
01:22

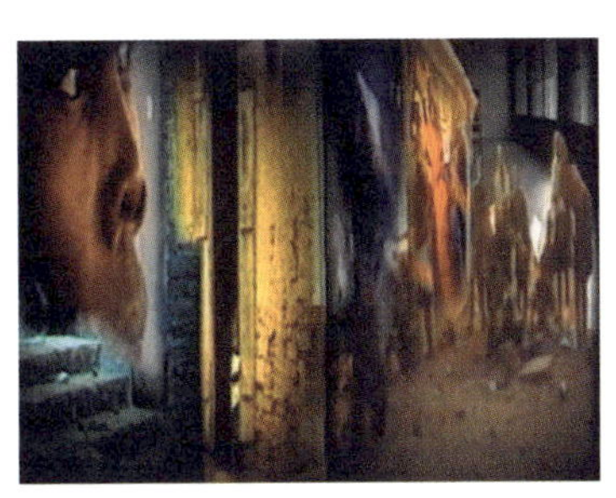
00:19

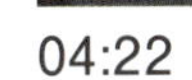
04:22

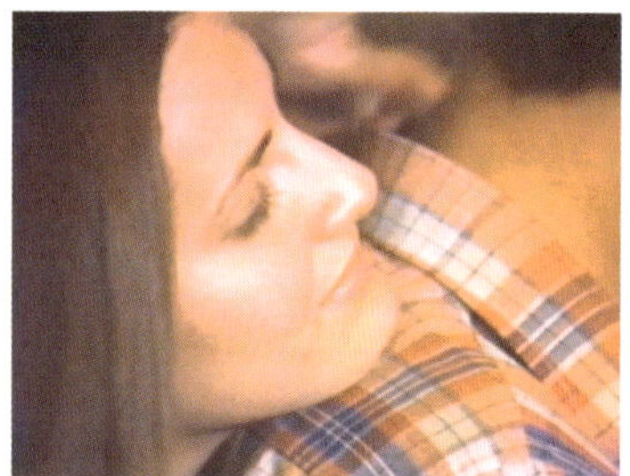

01:27

01:47

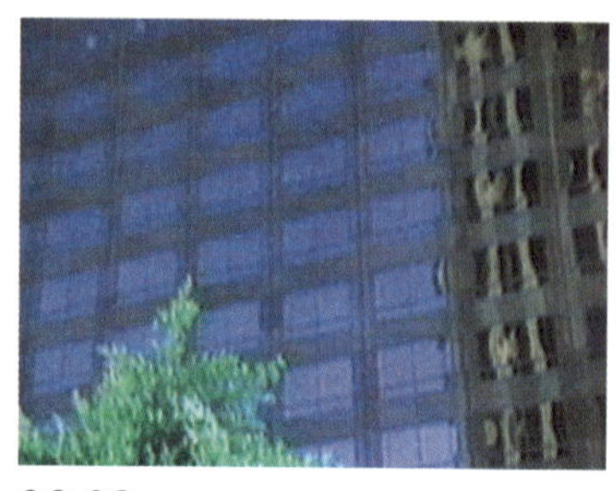

06:02

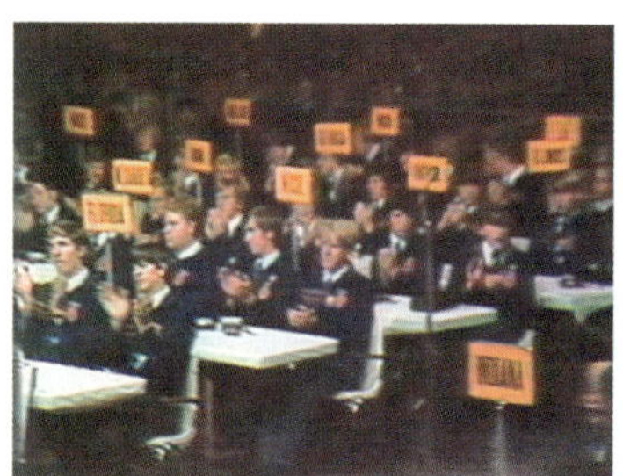

14:11

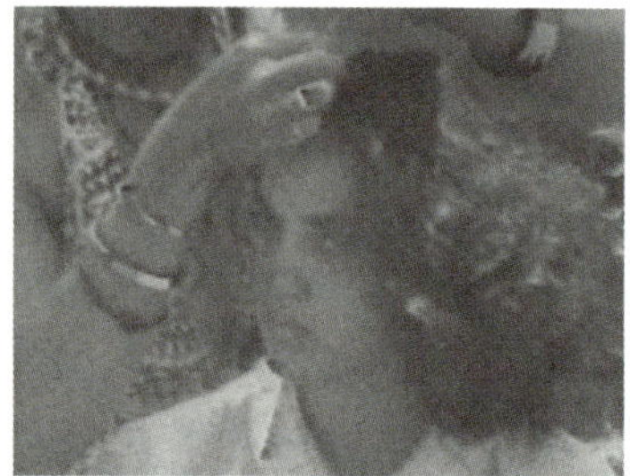

17:35

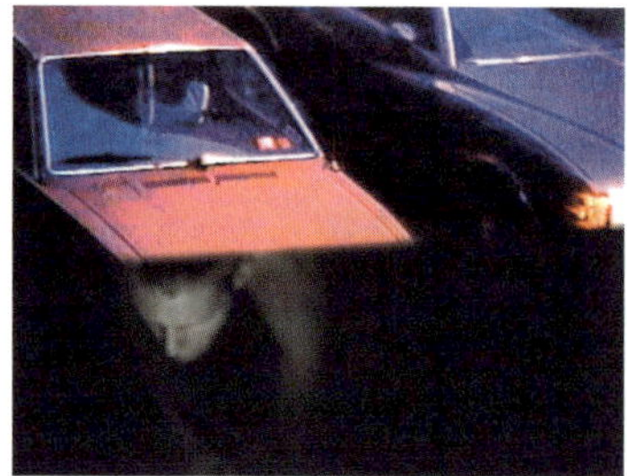

07:23

1980s and Bob took over as editor from Ivar. Bob had been there for many years and in many different guises. He was the director of distribution, special projects director, technical director, assistant director, designer. He was key to so many major projects and brought so much creative energy to EAI for many years.

AK – In the early 1990s there was another kind of interaction with television, such as Alex Bag's cable access show, *Unicorns and Rainbows*.

LZ – Exactly. Many of those performance-based works by women, including Cheryl Donegan, Kristin Lucas, Ursula Hodel, Alix Pearlstein, and Alex Bag were exhibited at MoMA in the program *Young and Restless*, which was organized by Stephen Vitiello, EAI's director of distribution at the time. Stephen played several important roles at EAI, including preservation and special projects director, from 1988 until 2000. EAI toured that program to venues around the world.

In terms of the distribution of the collection, it was an interesting moment, when it seemed

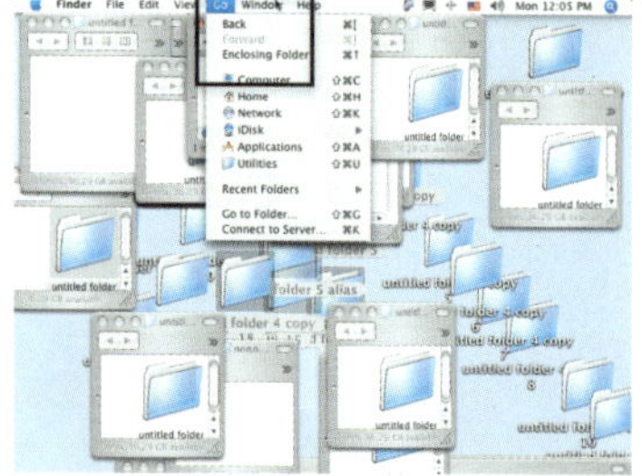

00:58

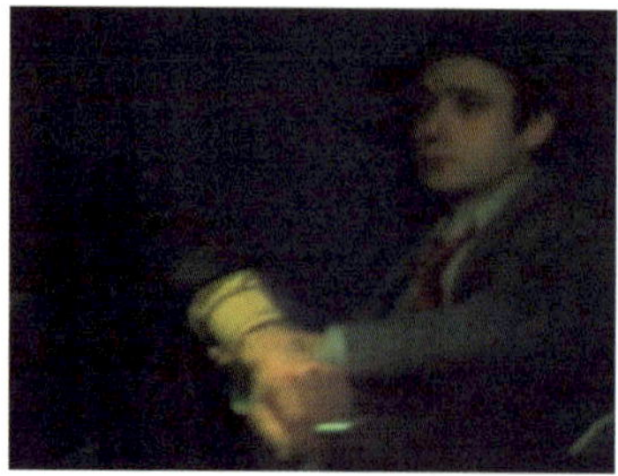

08:29

00:13

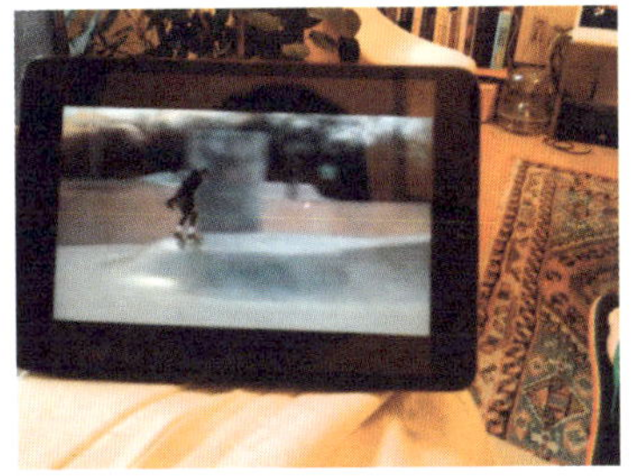
03:56

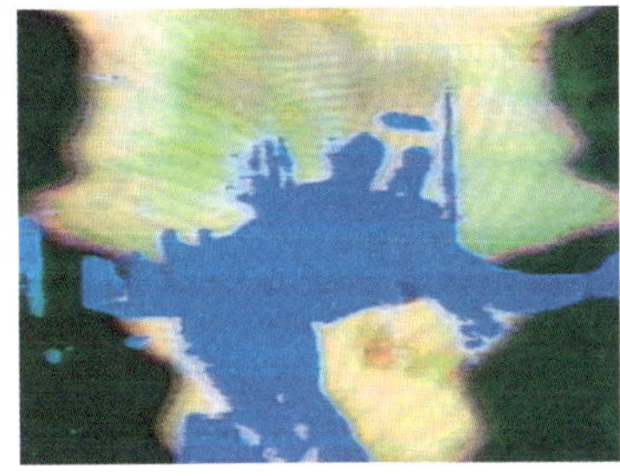
14:27

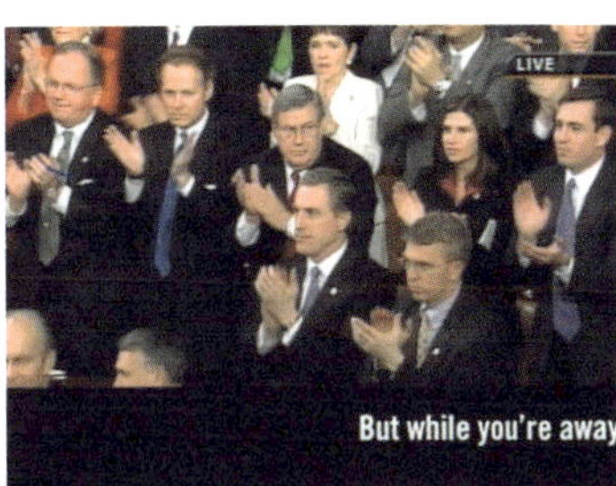

04:29

that EAI's collection was really recognized by the larger art world. So, artists like Mike Kelley were coming to us with their video works, and Gordon Matta-Clark's estate came to us with his films, for example. And that was wonderful. That was a moment when it felt that EAI was recognized as being an important resource and collection.

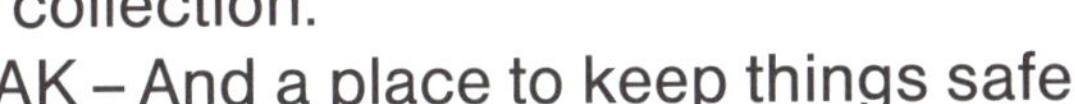

AK – And a place to keep things safe.

LZ – Yes, the preservation program was fully realized at that point. I think by then we had already started working with our off-site storage facility in New Jersey. So, there was a shift as we became more professionalized in terms of our preservation and distribution practices, and were further connected to the larger art world via the artists and the collection. And there was a concurrent shift in terms of the space. It was less scrappy. And this was reflected in a shift to the professionalization of the non-profit world. The alternative moment was then in the past, and we were perceived to be more of an institution.

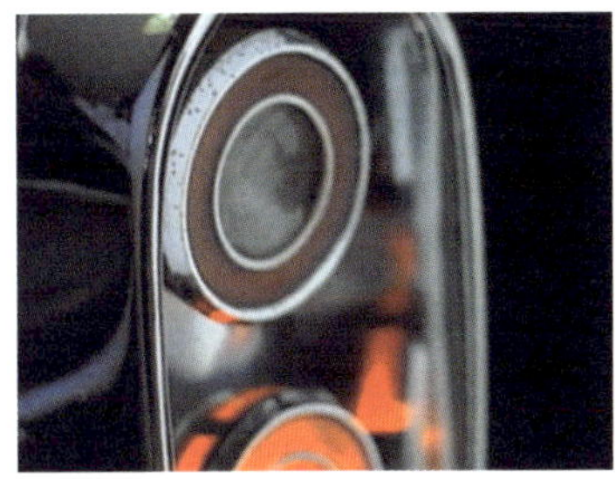
00:16

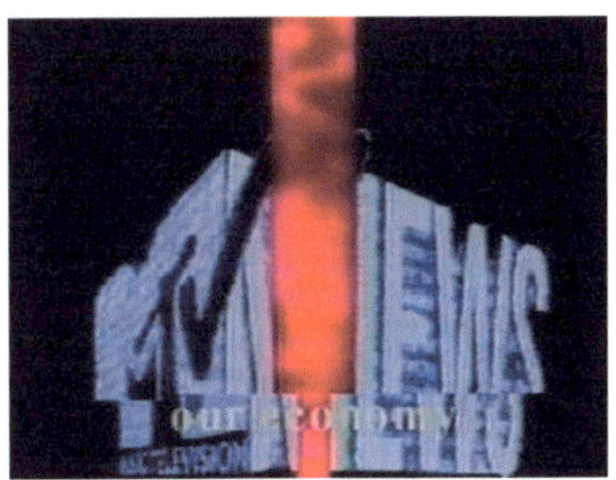
00:33

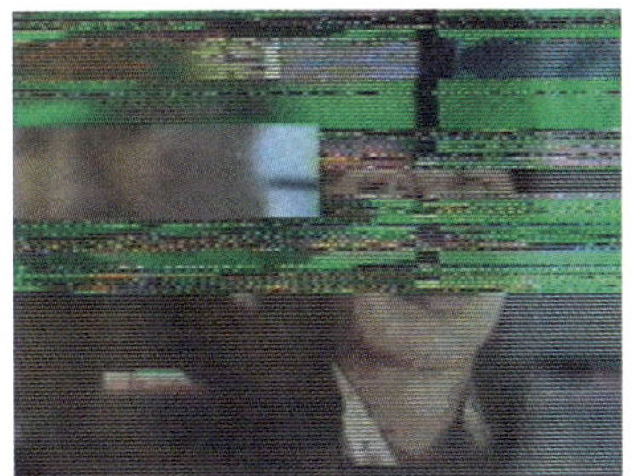
21:10

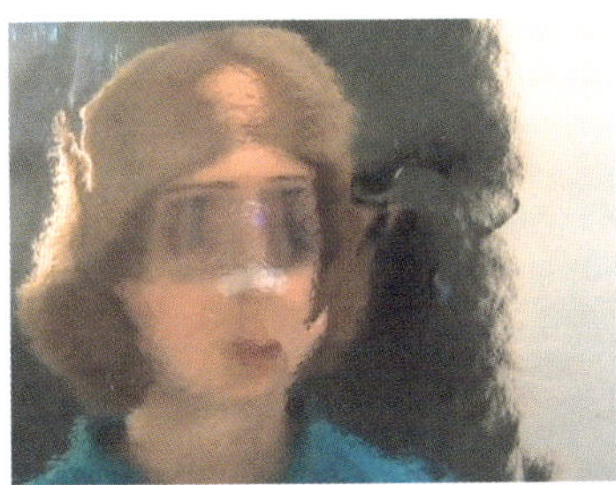
01:22

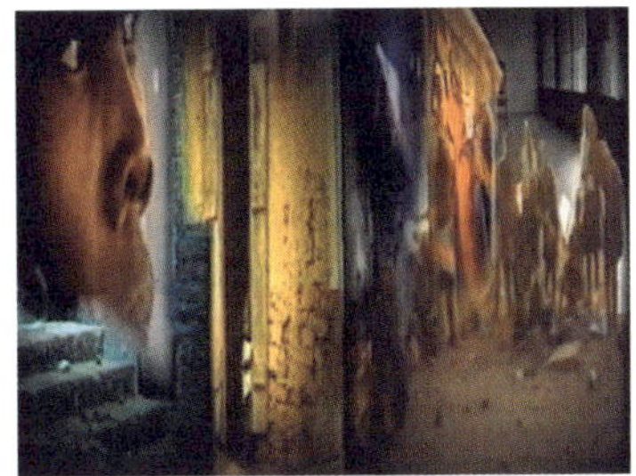
00:19

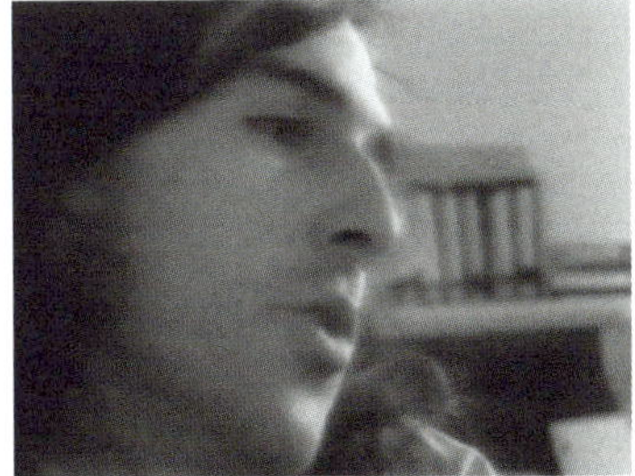
04:22

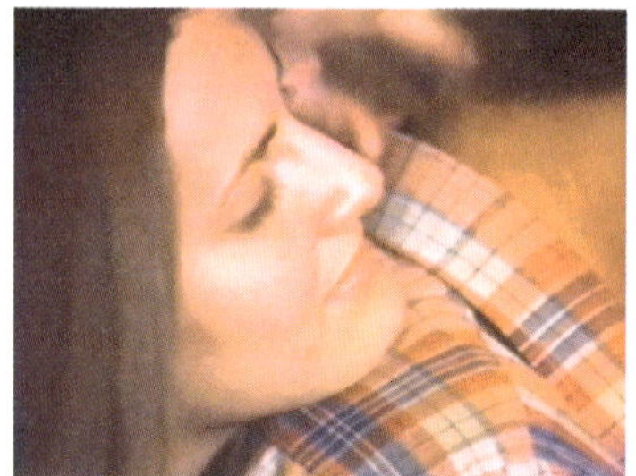
01:27

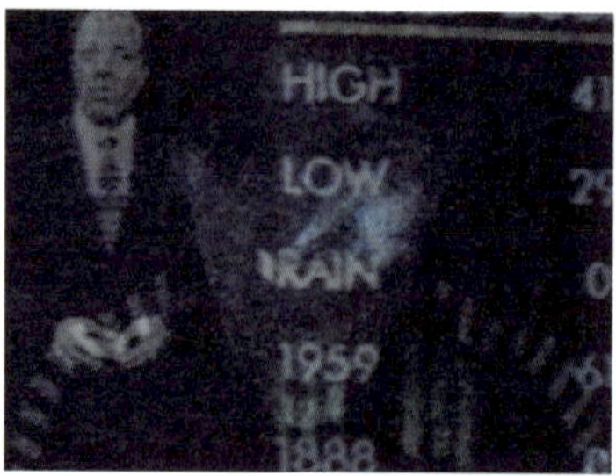

01:47

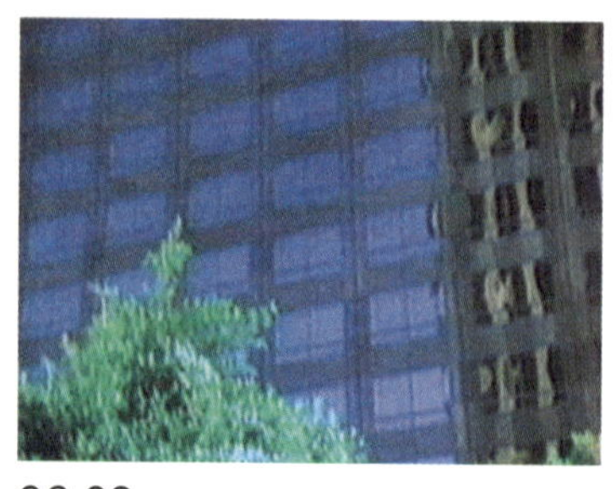
06:02

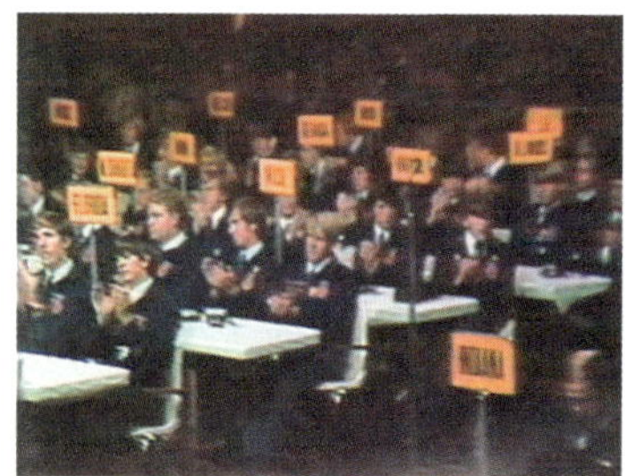
14:11

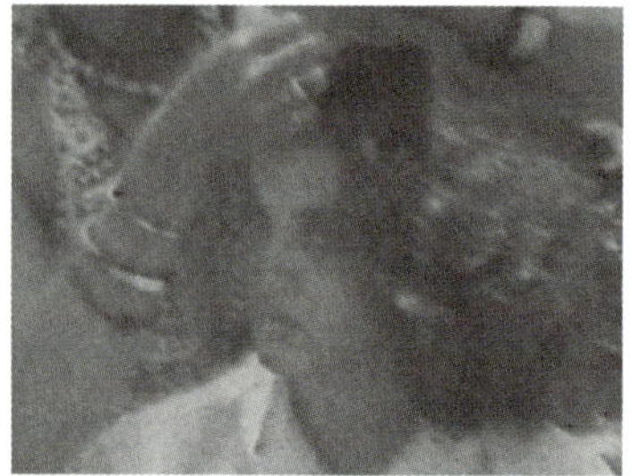
17:35

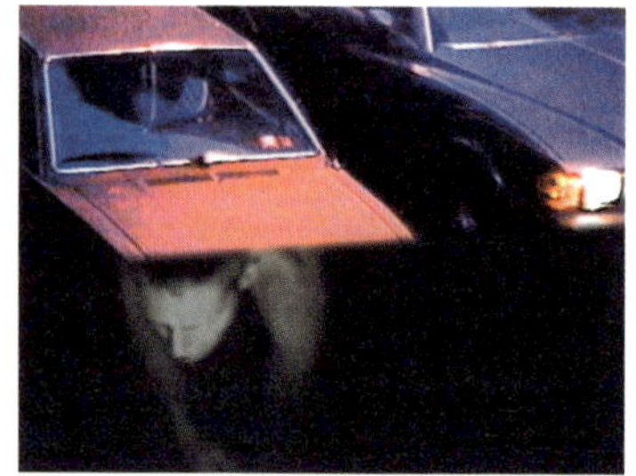
07:23

So the EAI collection really started to be recognized as a major institutional resource in the 1990s, and we take very seriously our responsibility for the stewardship of the collection and the advancement of professional standards for preservation and distribution. At the same time, I feel that we have to maintain our alternative spirit, which is part of our organizational DNA and our history. Because we didn't emerge fully formed in the 1990s—we came out of this alternative context. Presenting current work in dialogue with that historical framework is also important.

Another enormous change that once again shifted everything, and which continues to have ramifications today, was when major galleries started to actively show and sell limited-edition video. It effectively began in the 1990s with Matthew Barney, who was among the first artists to successfully create limited editions of single-channel videos. Ivar Smedstad was friends with Peter Strietmann, who started editing with Barney. Peter brought him to EAI, where they

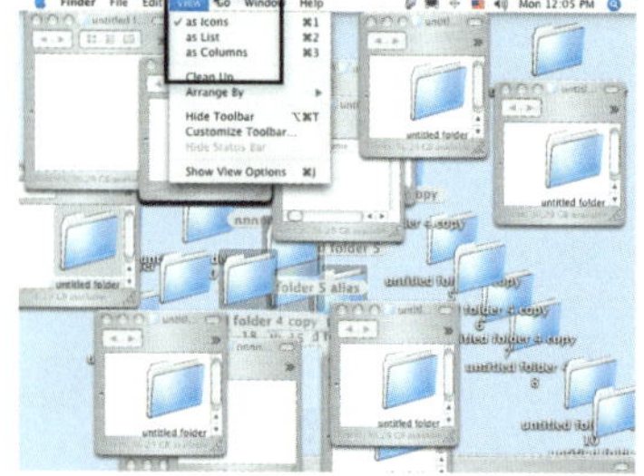
00:58

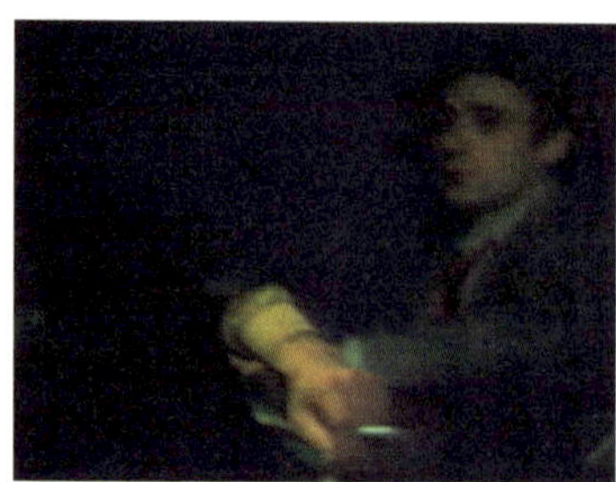
08:29

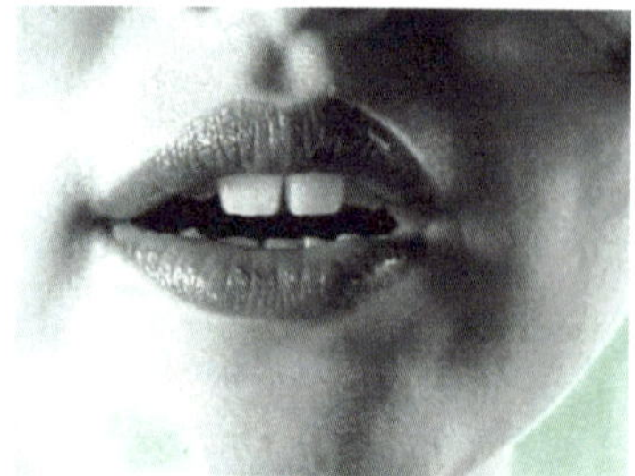
00:13

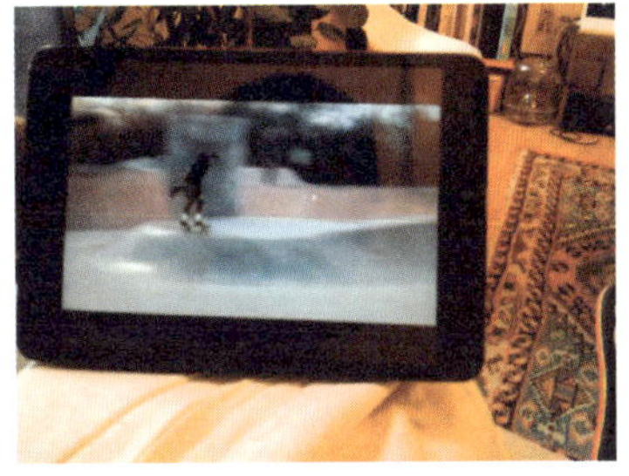
03:56

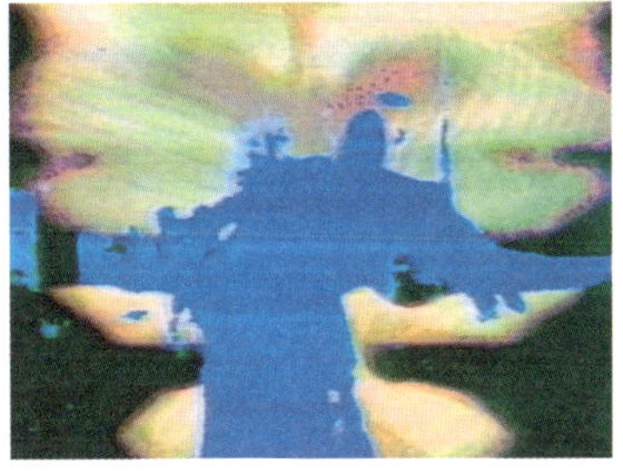
14:27

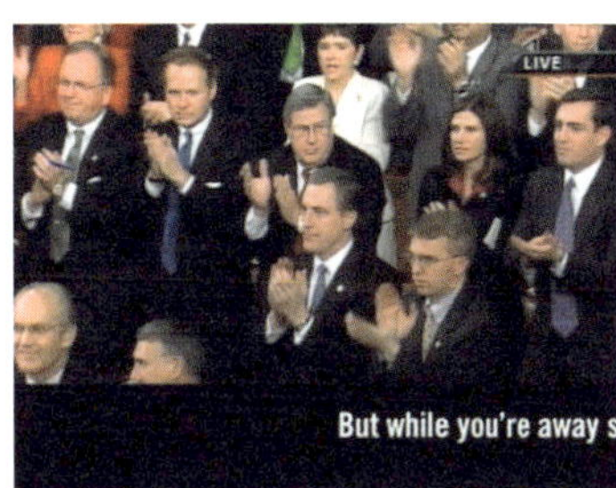

04:29

edited the early “OTTO” piece, *OTTOshaft* (1992). (Peter Strietmann went on to become the director of photography and editor of the *Cremaster Cycle* and continues to work with Barney today.)

There were so many things happening with video in the larger art world that were impacting us at that moment.

AK – Right, and a few years later in 1998 the Bill Viola show at the Whitney. These were big things.

LZ – That was very high profile. Going further back there was Documenta IX in 1992 when Gary Hill’s *Tall Ships* was the talk of the town—it was a major sixteen-channel installation. It was one of the many installations that was recognized as ushering in a new era of large-scale installation, in terms of the art world. It was the beginning of the era of the projected image entering the gallery. That moment where the video monitor in the museum or gallery transitioned to the projected image was a huge shift.

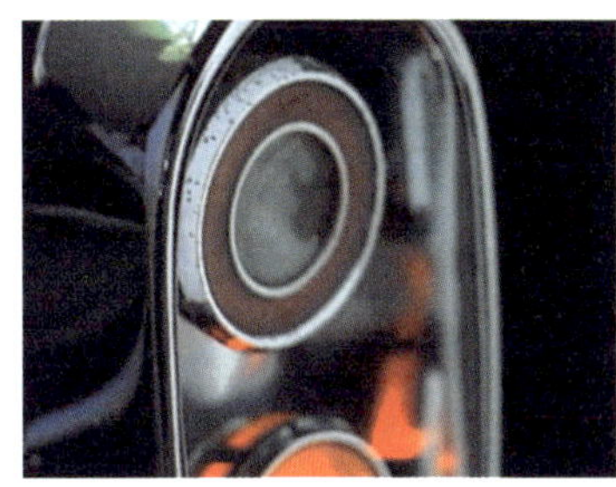
00:16

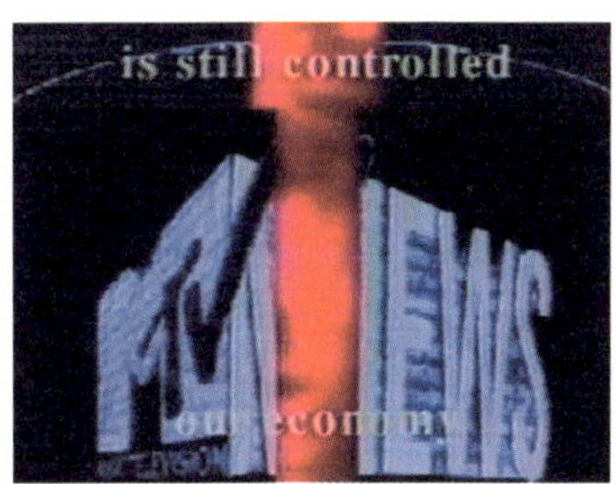

00:33

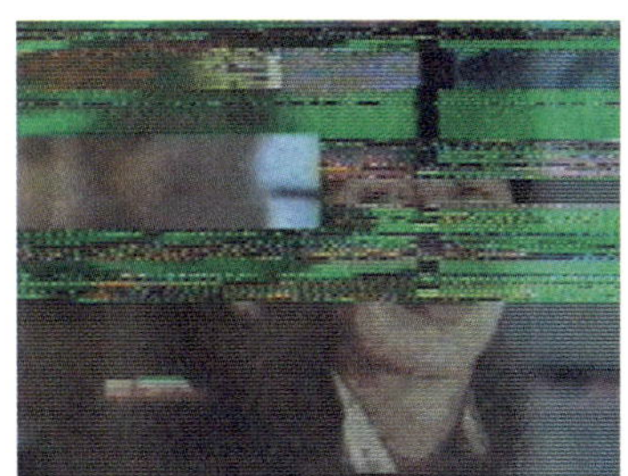
21:10

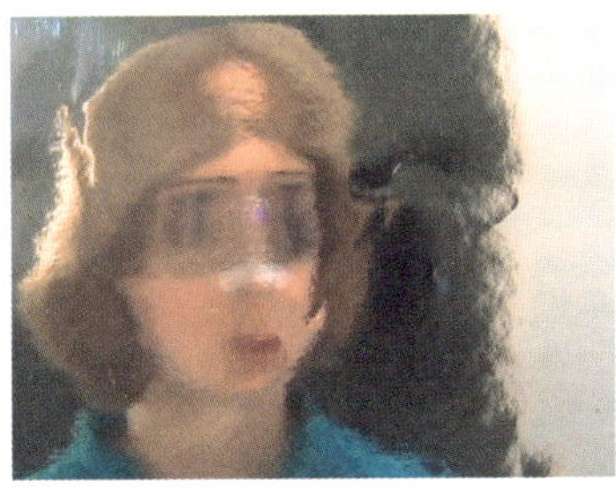
01:22

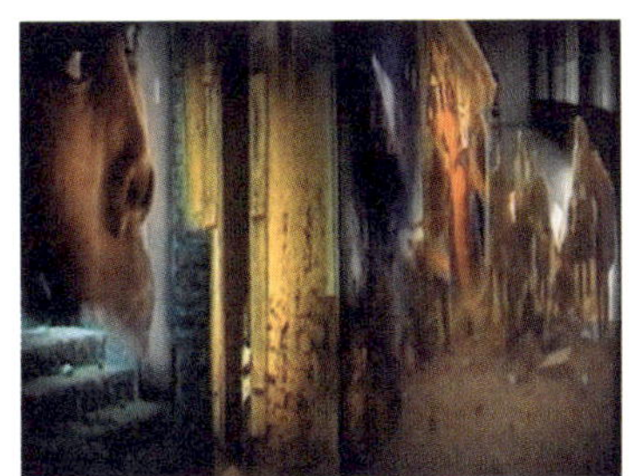
00:19

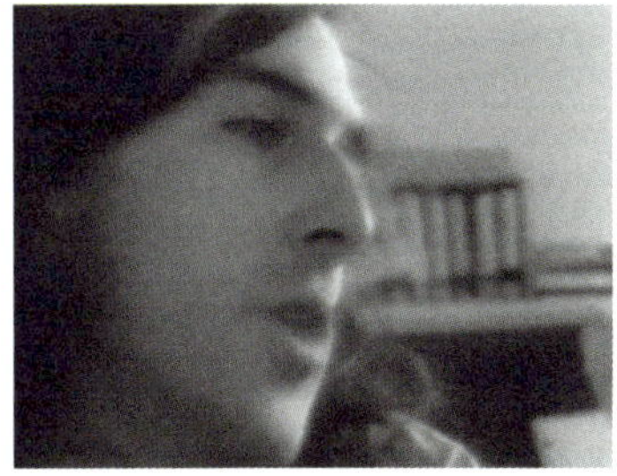
04:22

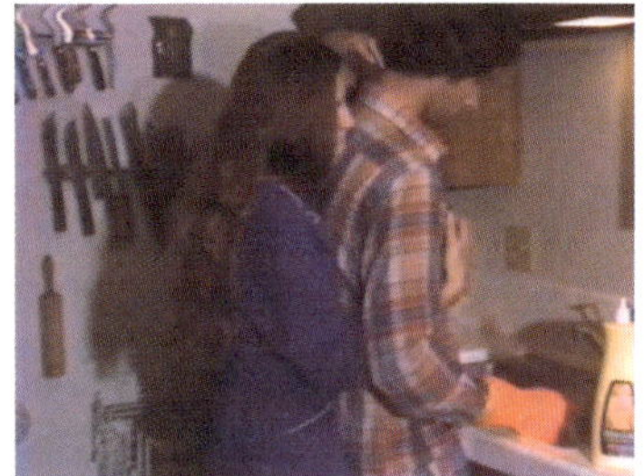

01:27

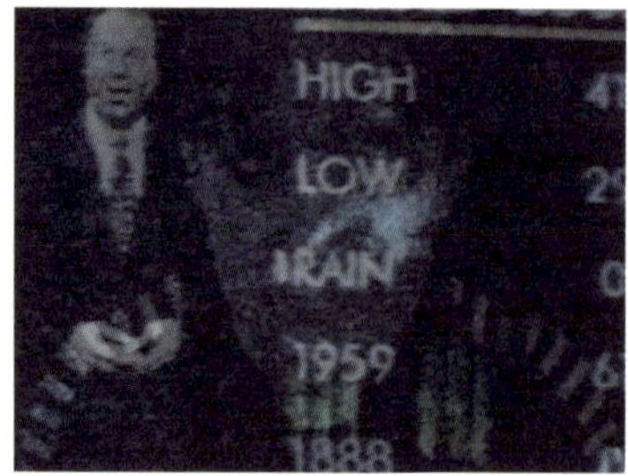

01:47

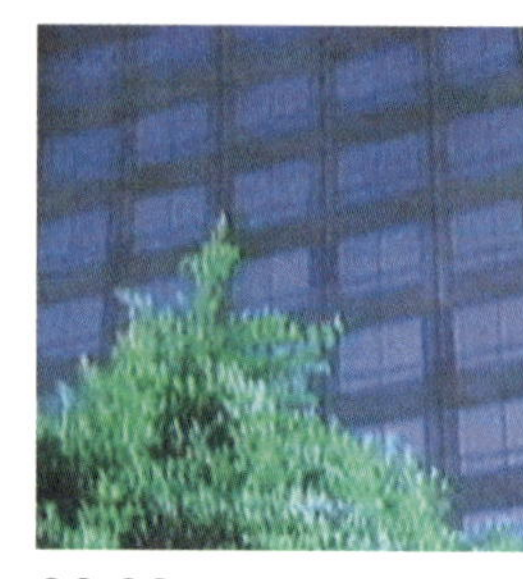

06:02

AK – Which then, in the 1990s, led to the reconsideration of projected film with Chrissie Iles's *Into the Light* exhibition at the Whitney in 2001.

LZ – Exactly, that was a pivotal show. At the same time, there were huge changes in the art market and distribution with the editioning of video works. First there was the era of the signed, limited-edition VHS tape in the 1990s and then in the 2000s DVDs suddenly became the art market solution, so signed DVDs were being sold as editions. It's hard to overstate how important that change was for the field—the final, complicated adoption of the edition system for artist's video. The art world finally, successfully found a way to speak to the notion of artificial scarcity, which seemed antithetical to the original idea of video as a democratic, reproducible, accessible medium.

AK – How did you negotiate those conversations with galleries on behalf of artists also in EAI's collection?

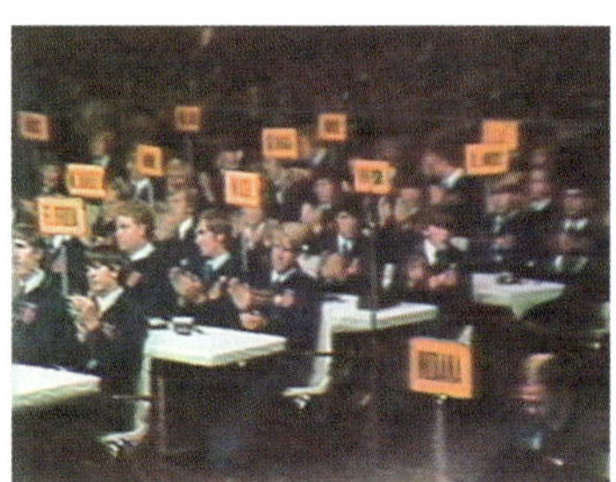

14:11

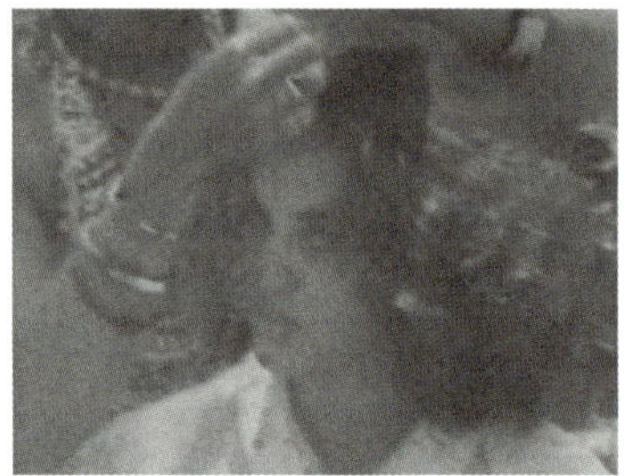

17:35

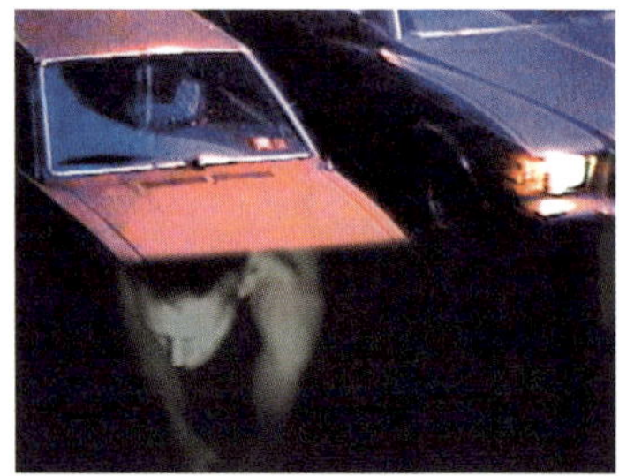

07:23

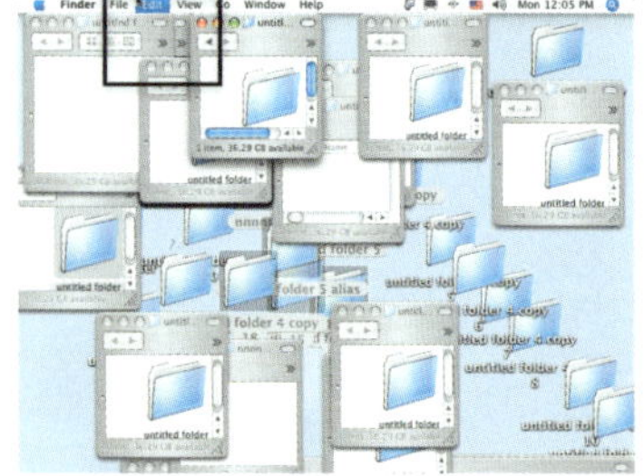

00:58

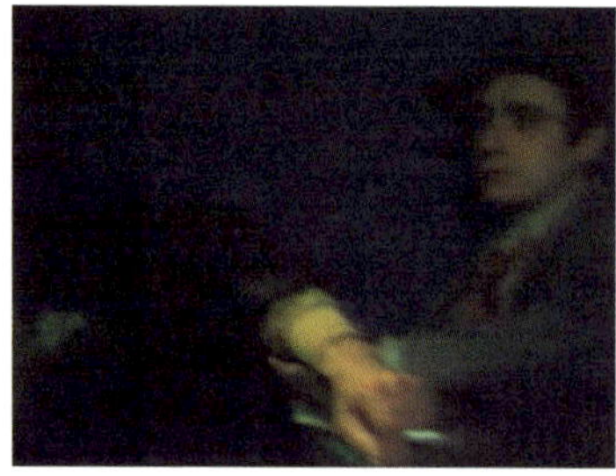

08:29

00:13

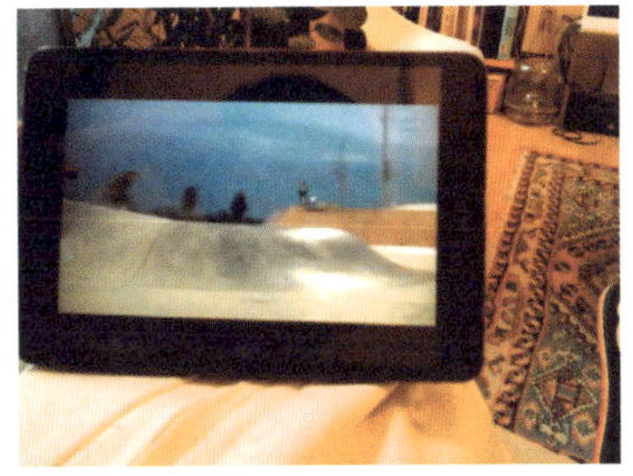
03:57

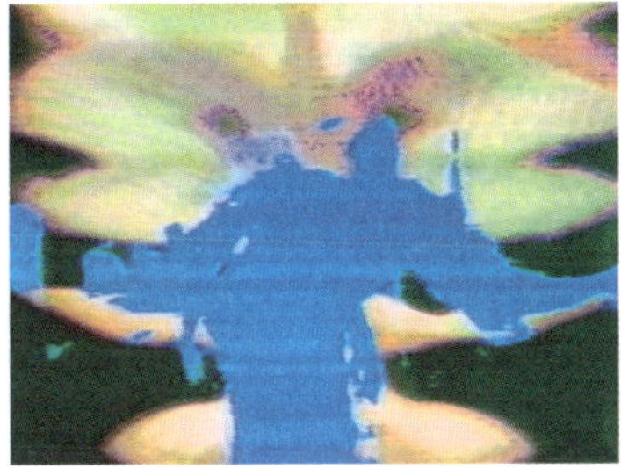
14:28

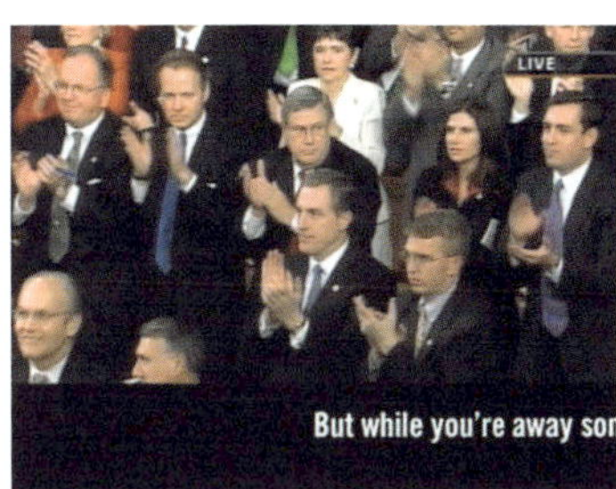

04:30

LZ – It was complicated for a long time. Today, of course, we work closely alongside many wonderful galleries and gallerists to more fully represent the artists' works.

AK – What prompted the transition from the SoHo location to Chelsea?

LZ – So much of the life of nonprofits in New York is about real estate and neighborhoods—the cultural and economic changes. At the Broadway space in SoHo, we were the subtenants of an architectural firm. It was a 12,000- or 15,000-square-foot loft, most of which was held by the architects. They were young and very "pow-pow-pow." And one day we came in and their door was wide open, and there was nothing in the space. They had gone bankrupt and disappeared overnight. They had abandoned the space. They must've moved during the night because they just left piles of junk.

We were left with an enormous loft on Broadway. I negotiated terms with the landlord, so we could stay temporarily. But it wasn't sustainable. I started looking for strategic partnerships

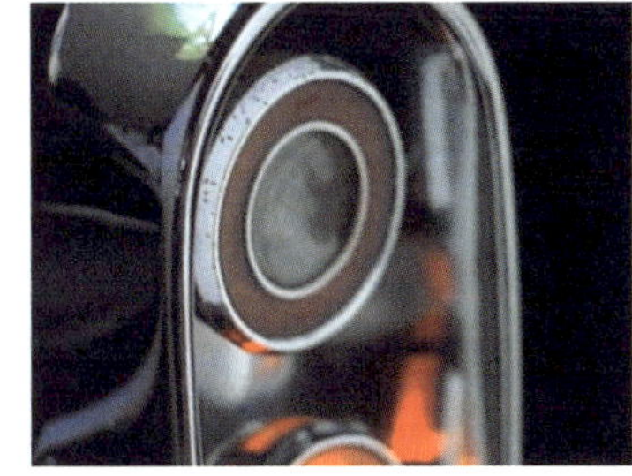
00:17

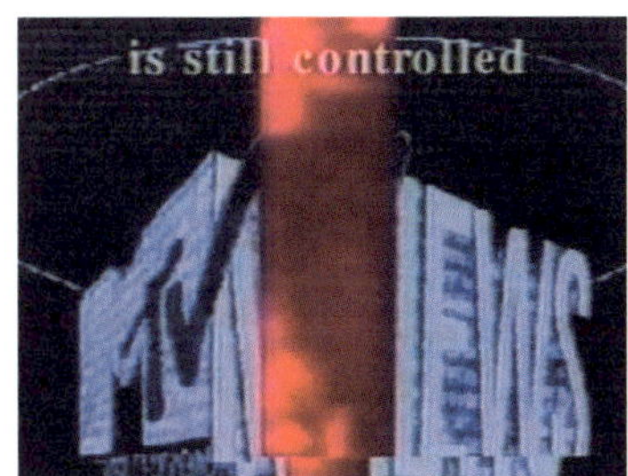

00:34

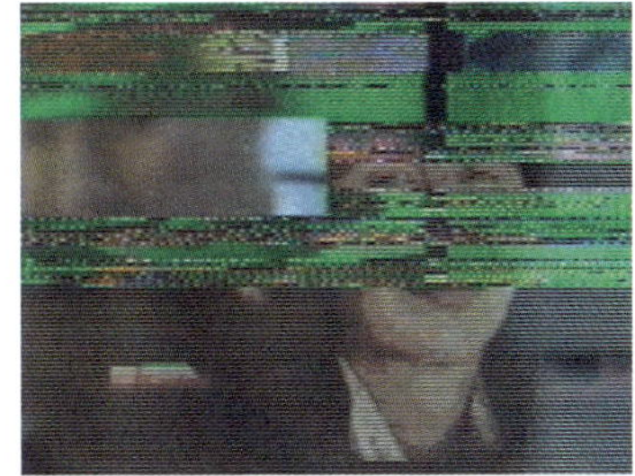
21:11

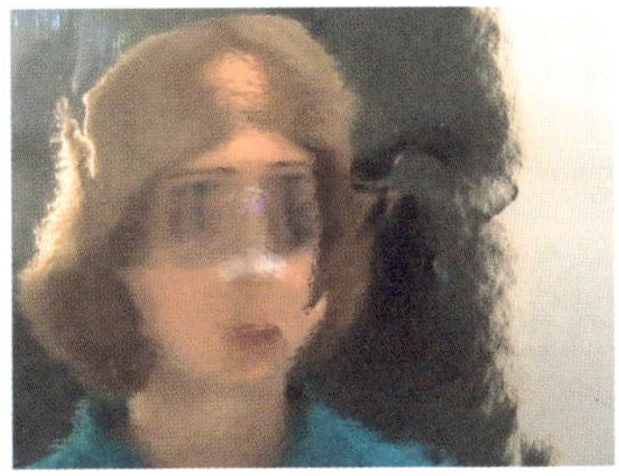
01:23

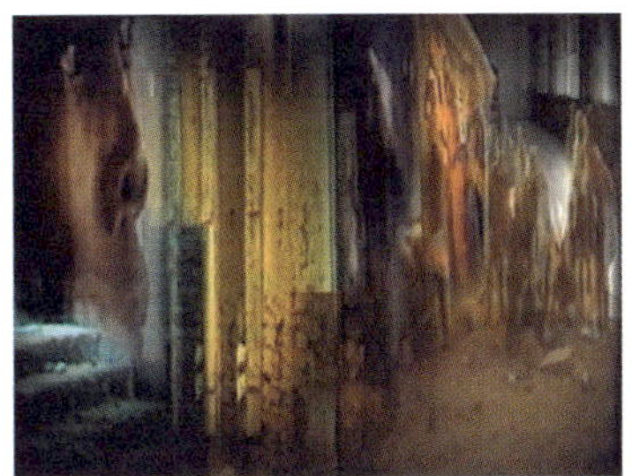
00:20

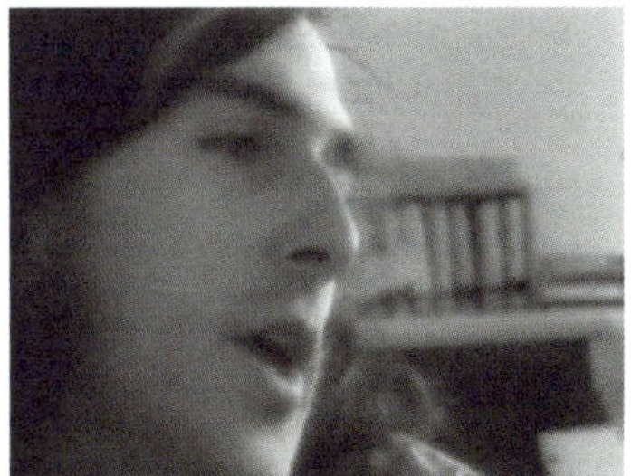
04:23

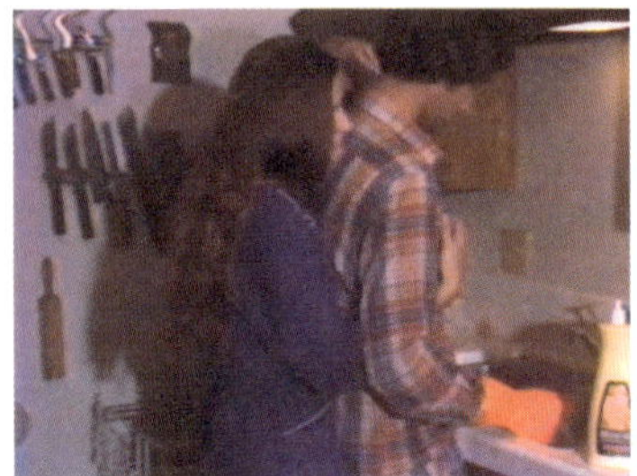

01:27

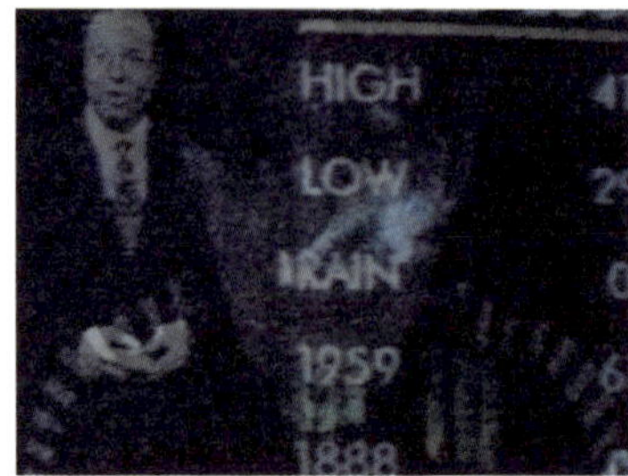

01:47

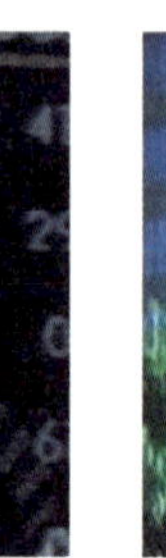

06:02

with other institutions, particularly museums, to give us a secure space, for sustainability for the future.

In the early eighties, as I mentioned, we had looked into strategic partnerships with educational institutions, with universities, which was interesting as a model. The museum model was perhaps more interesting for us, but also had benefits and drawbacks in finding the right institutional fit. We were hoping to retain our autonomy and identity while securing a viable long-term home.

AK – It would have been interesting if EAI had successfully become part of a museum to see if it would have changed the way that video and media would have been approached in institutions. I mean, I wonder if it would have had an effect from the inside.

LZ – I think within a large museum context, the EAI distribution model might have been difficult to sustain.

AK – Right. It's hard to compromise. It would've become part of the museum's collection.

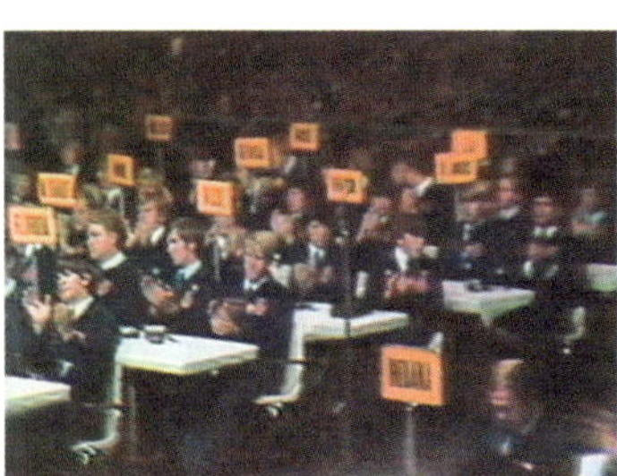

14:11

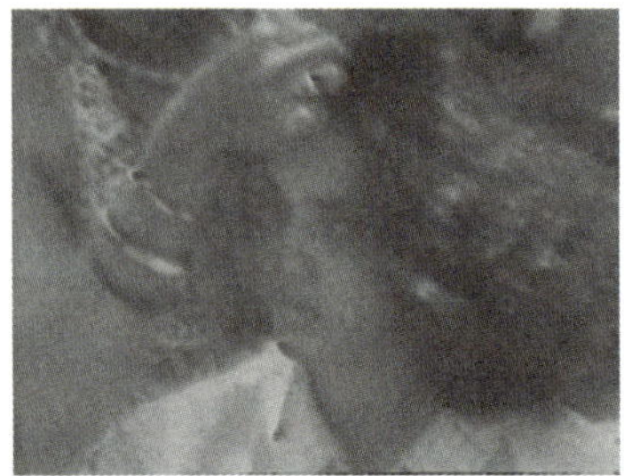

17:35

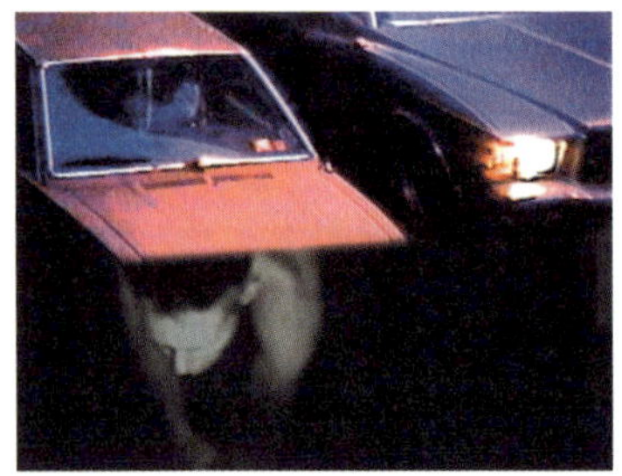

07:23

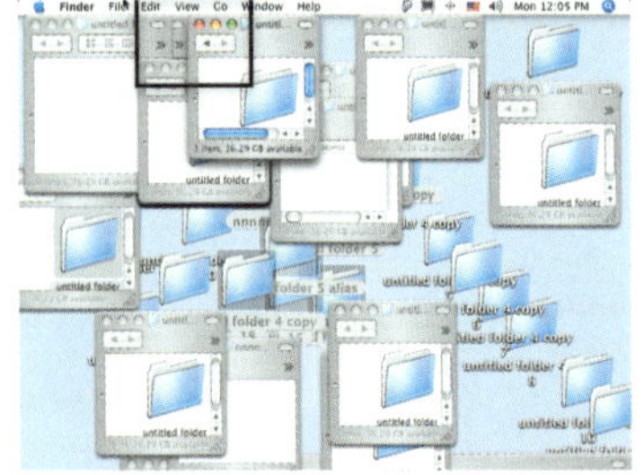

00:58

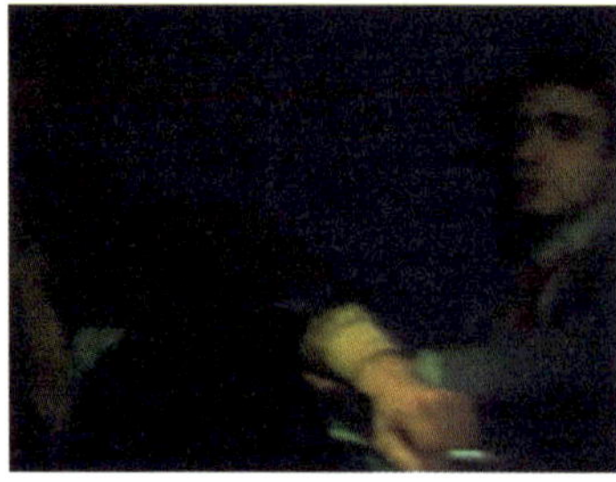

08:29

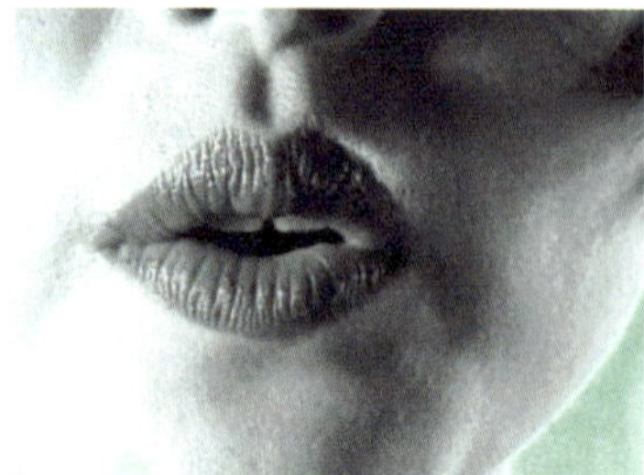

00:13

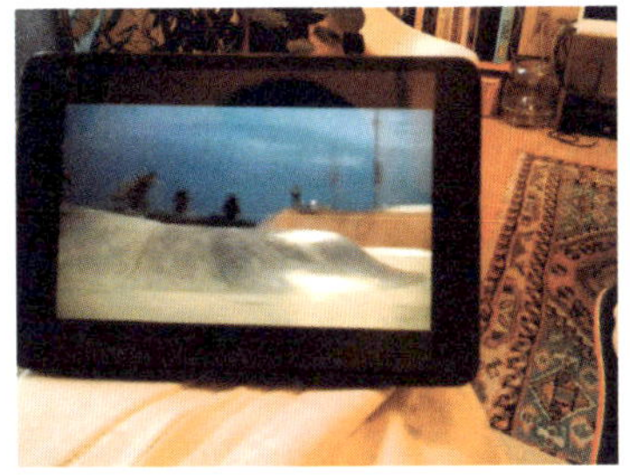
03:57

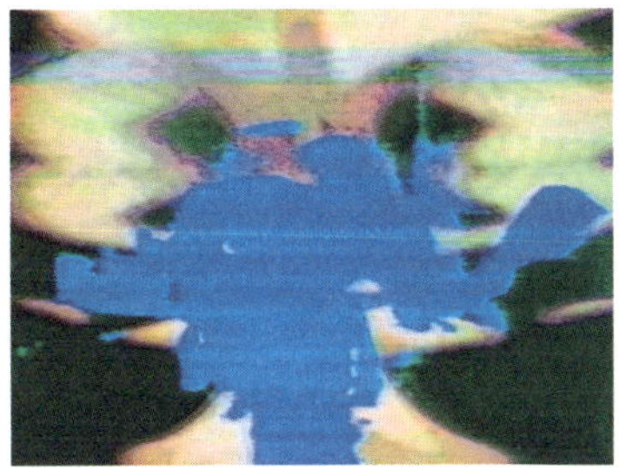
14:28

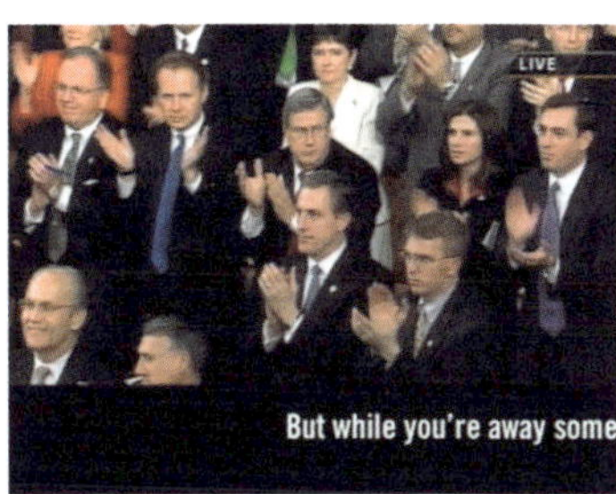

04:30

LZ – The priority was securing a space for us and securing a space for the collection.

AK – I think, it also gets back to the heart of what EAI does, and that taps into the conversation about editioning and the way that institutions and galleries think about video versus the way we're talking about it.

LZ – Yes, exactly. And what happened was, I was approached by Michael Govan, who was the director of Dia Art Foundation at the time, to form a strategic alliance with Dia that would allow us to occupy a secure space in a Dia building and collaborate on programming with them.

AK – What year was that?

LZ – That was 1997. So that was yet another moment that changed everything and propelled us forward. As we've seen, there are certain pivotal years in which major developments seem to cause seismic shifts forward, and the Dia partnership, friendship, and strategic alliance opened up a world of new opportunities and possibilities.

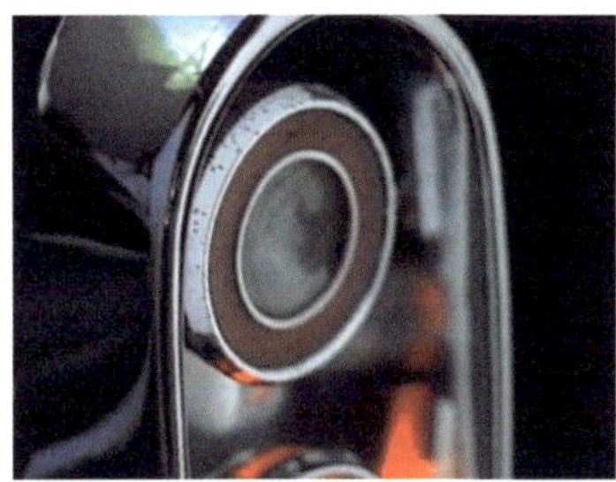
00:17

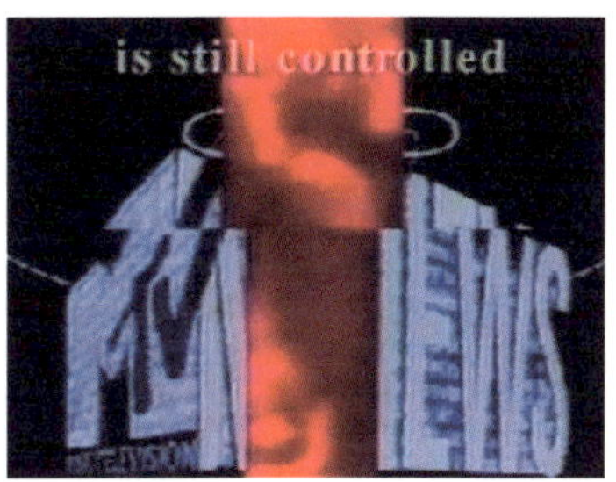

00:34

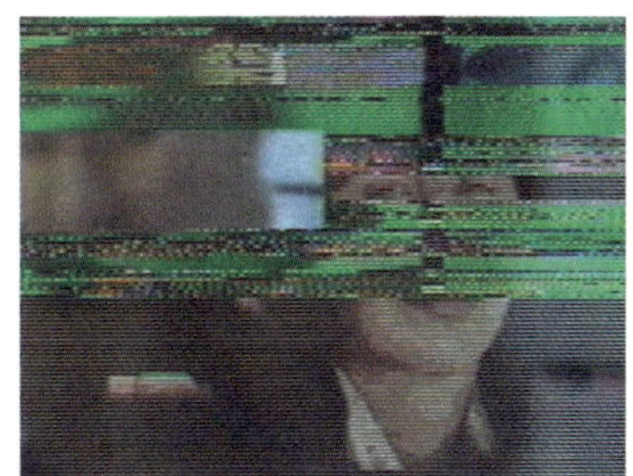
21:11

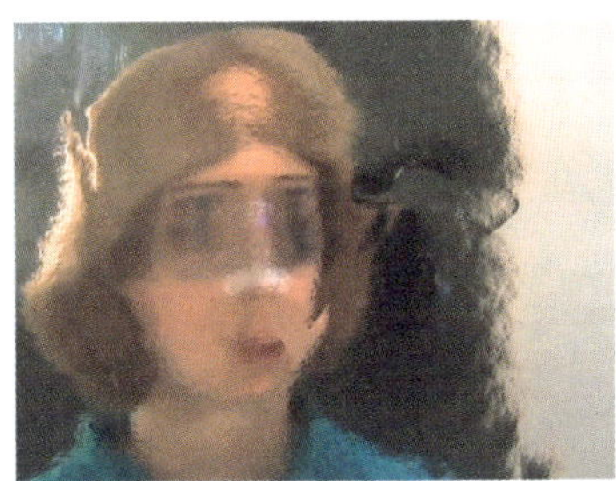
01:23

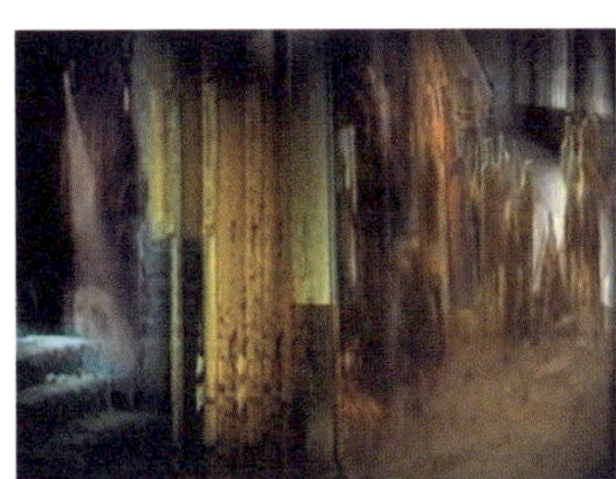
00:20

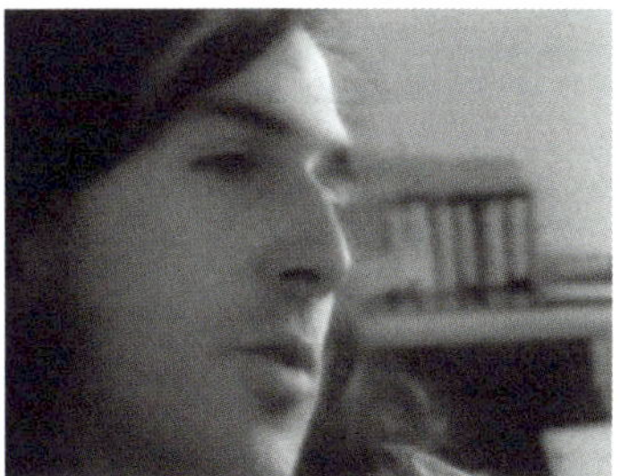
04:23

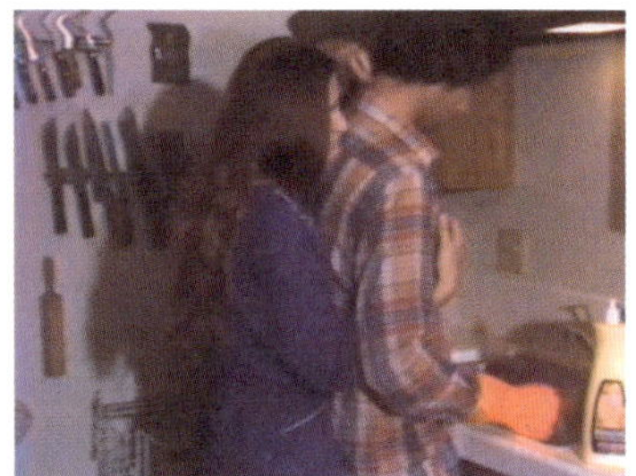

01:27

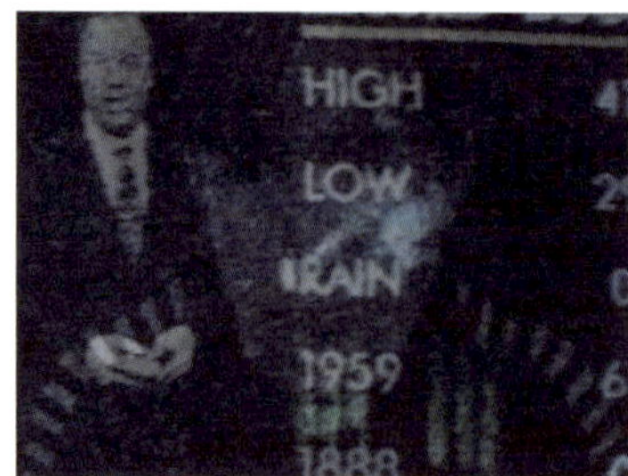

01:47

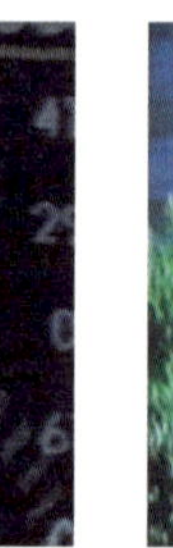

06:02

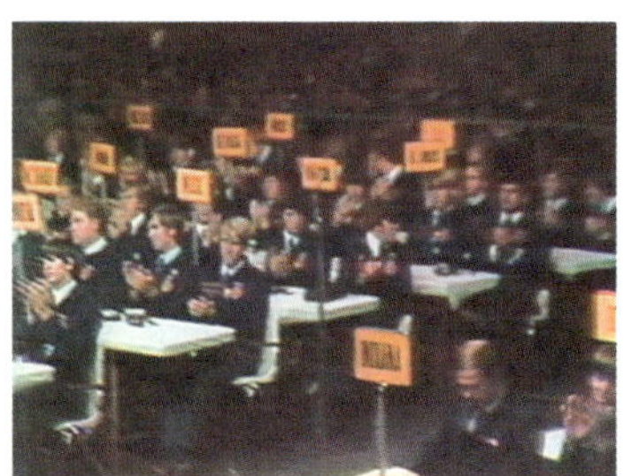

14:11

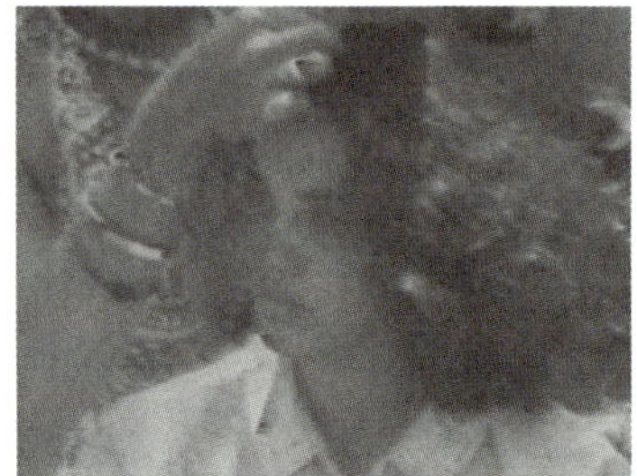

17:35

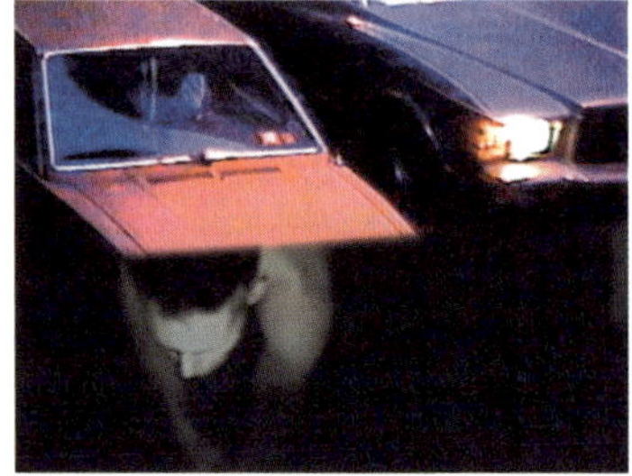

07:23

The same day we moved into the Dia space at 542 West 22nd Street, across the street from our current space, Richard Serra's *Torqued Ellipses* were arriving to be installed in Dia's exhibition space in Chelsea. (They are now permanently installed at Dia:Beacon.) The enormous steel sculptures were coming down the West Side Highway on flatbed trucks and they turned onto 22nd Street at the same time that EAI's moving trucks arrived there. That image is indelible.

At that point in West Chelsea, there were tumbleweeds rolling down the street after 5:00 pm. Dia felt like a real outpost. The building that we were in had a tool and die company on the ground floor. Dia basically carved out space for us in their offices and we moved in. The tape library was back by the freight elevators and we put the editing room in a repurposed janitor's closet. Everything was just jerry-rigged but fit in somehow. It was extraordinary. We had a separate entrance, but because of the way the space was configured, we could also go through Dia's

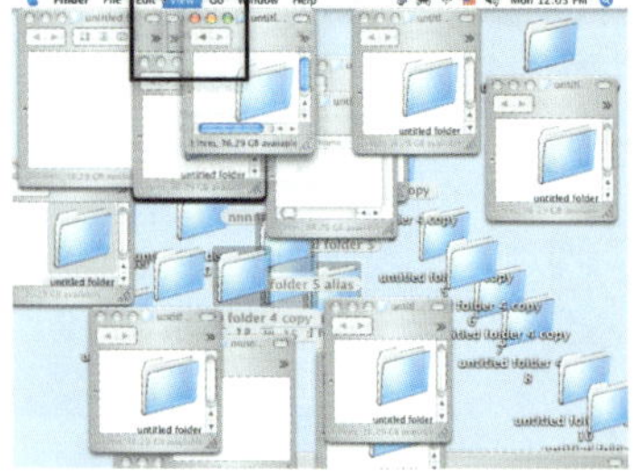

00:58

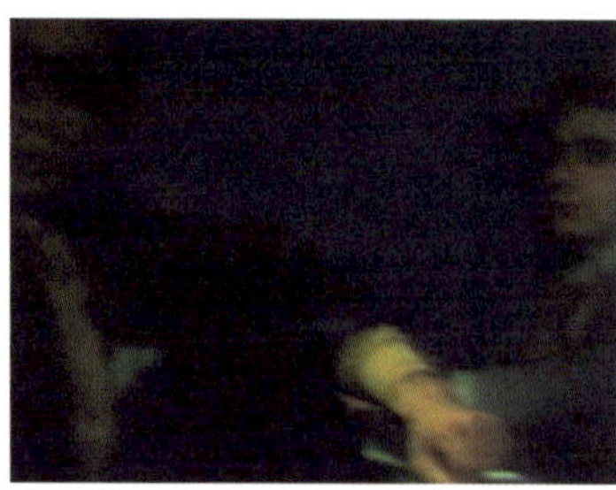

08:29

00:13

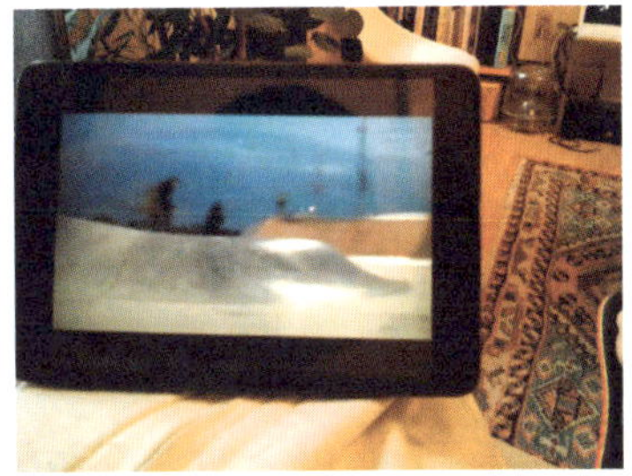
03:57

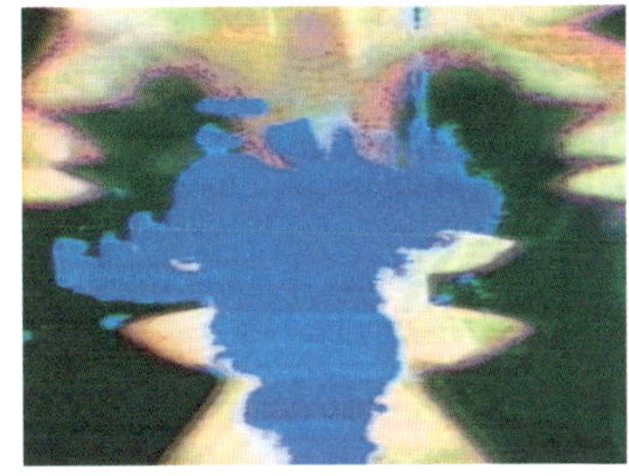
14:28

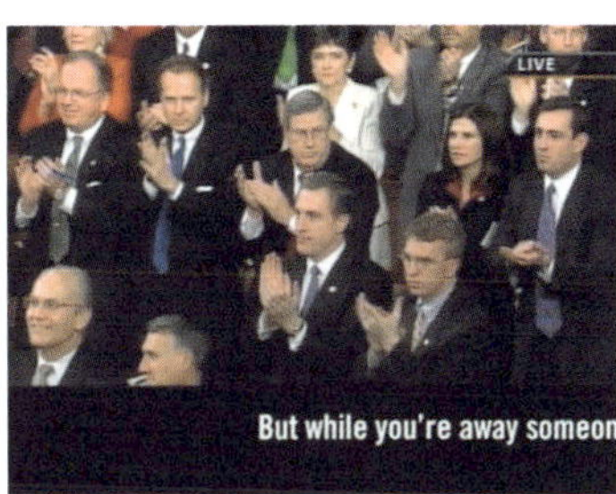

04:30

offices to get to EAI, so it was very convivial and collegial, a kind of comingling of staffs and office space.

AK – Did that lead to organic collaborations?

LZ – Yes. That was the era when Dan Graham had his Rooftop Urban Park Project with the *Two-Way Mirror Cylinder and a Video Salon* on the rooftop of Dia's building, and we did a number of collaborative programs for that space.

AK – I remember going to see the Joan Jonas event.

LZ – The Joan Jonas program in 1997 was magical. We had just done preservation and transfers of a number of her early film and video projects that are now iconic, canonical works. No one had seen *Song Delay* (1973) for over a decade, and we showed it on the rooftop, among other restored pieces, including beautiful color footage of *Glass Puzzle*. Joan performed inside Dan's sculptural pavilion on the rooftop, responding live to her own projected pieces, and it was just extraordinary. We did an evening of Dan and Dara's music-related video pieces

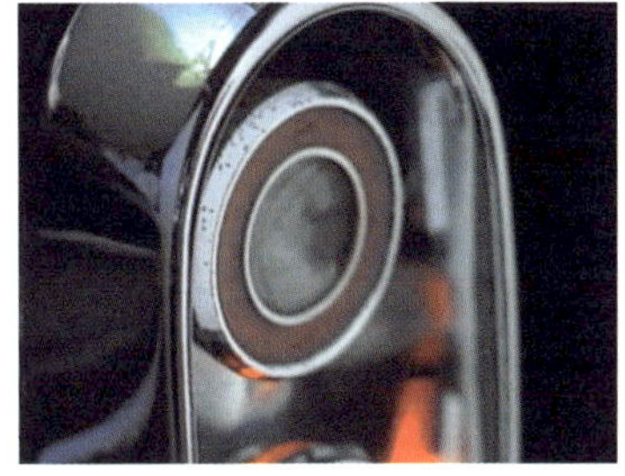
00:17

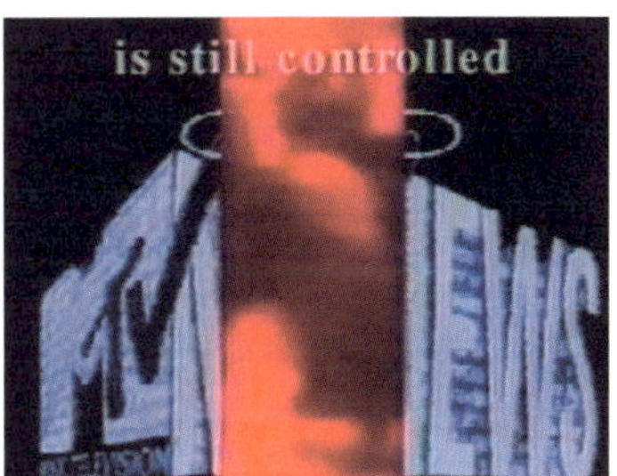

00:34

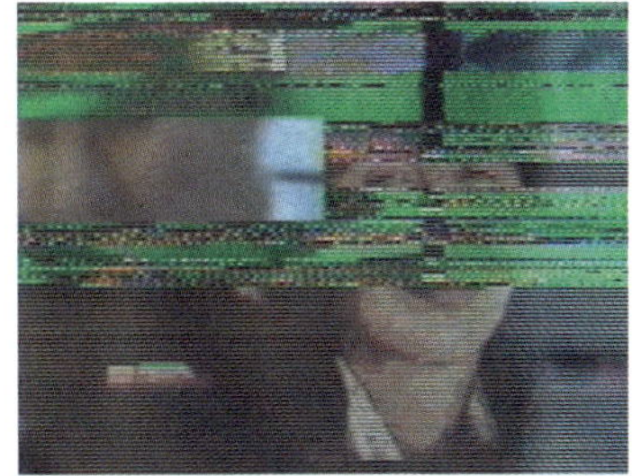
21:11

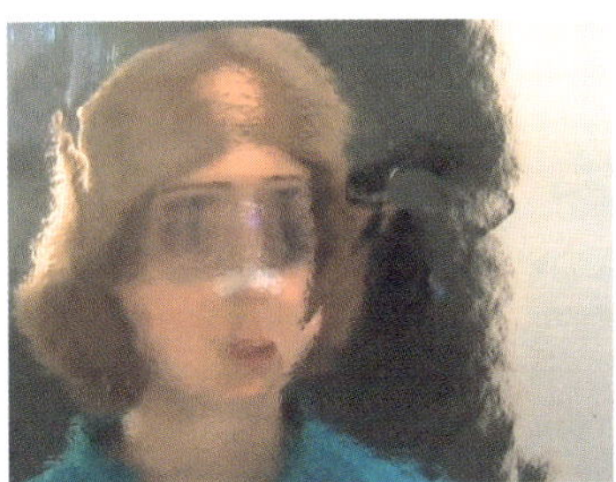
01:23

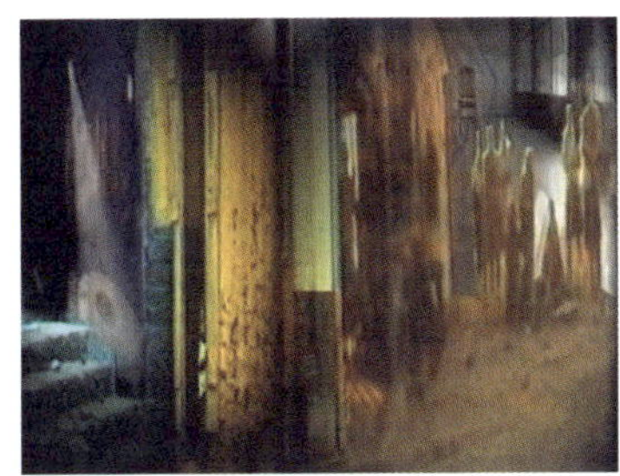
00:20

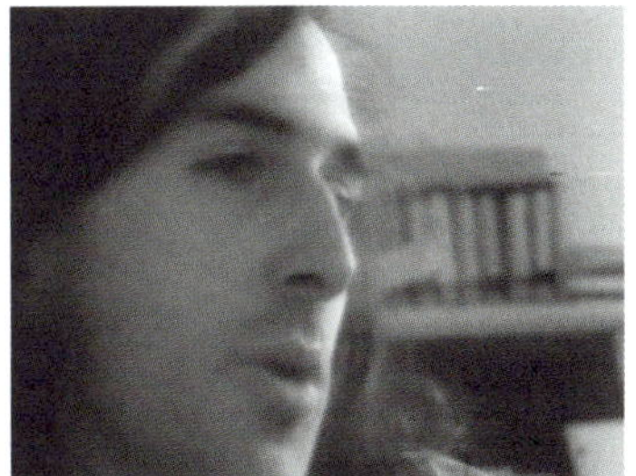
04:23

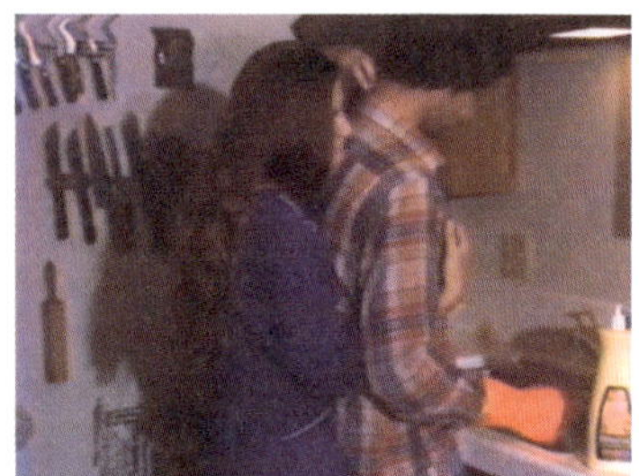
01:27

01:47

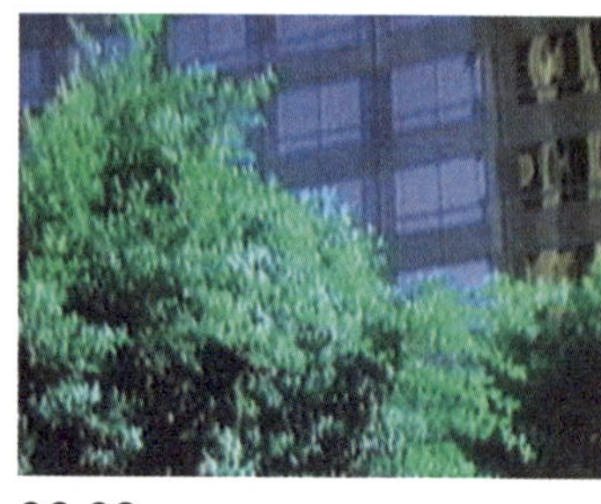
06:02

in 2002, which was fantastic. And we were also programming video programs for Dan's rooftop café. Every month we would change the program in the café. And then we did a series of artist talks in the ground-floor Dia Bookshop with artists such as Marina Abramović, Vito Acconci, and Karen Finley.

AK – I also have a vivid memory of attending the Abramović talk in the Dia Bookshop. What year did you launch your website?

LZ – It was 1997.

AK – Which is still early.

LZ – Oh, it was very early. It was considered ahead of its time.

AK – That was a good seven or eight years before YouTube.

LZ – In addition to collaborating on programming with Dia, we collaborated on several significant grants, including a Lila Wallace-Reader's Digest Fund grant, which allowed us to create our dynamically driven database and online catalog. We had already created a website in which we literally took the print catalog

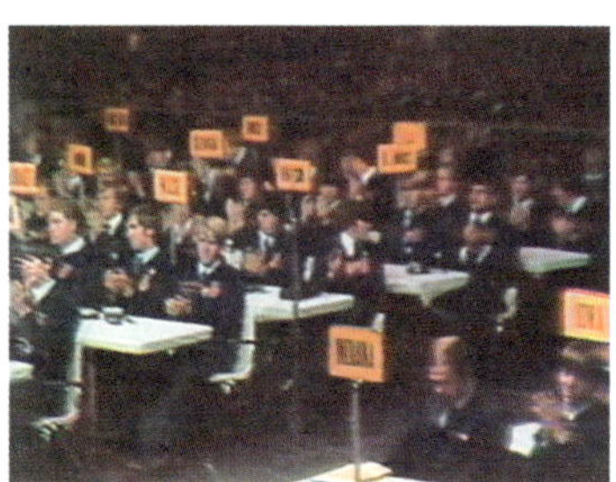
14:11

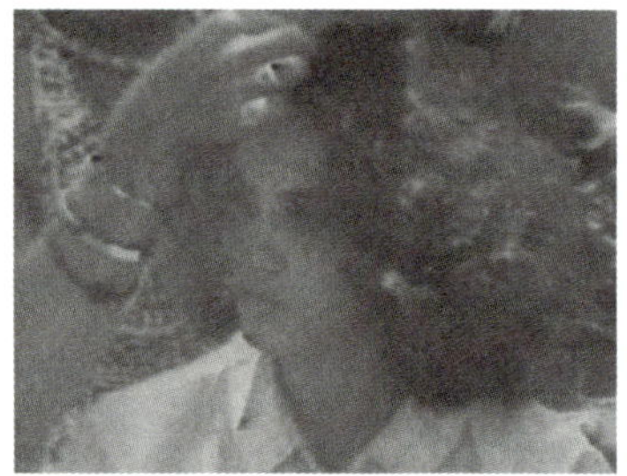
17:35

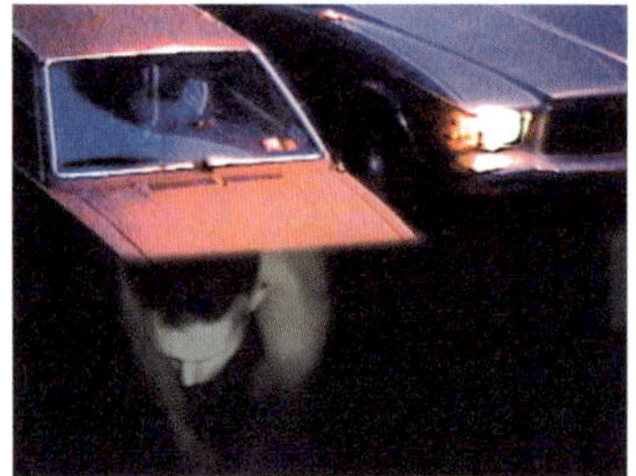
07:23

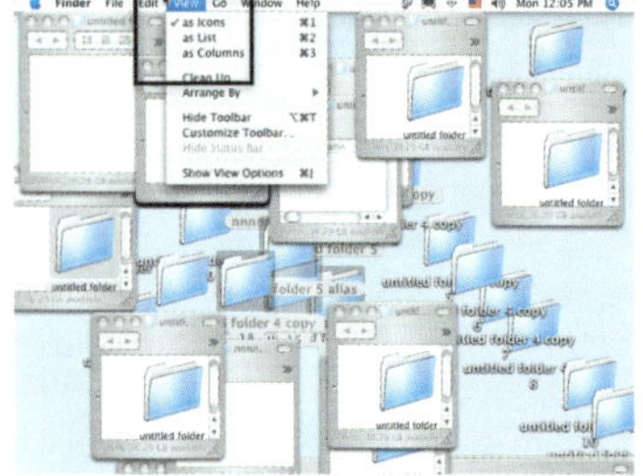
00:58

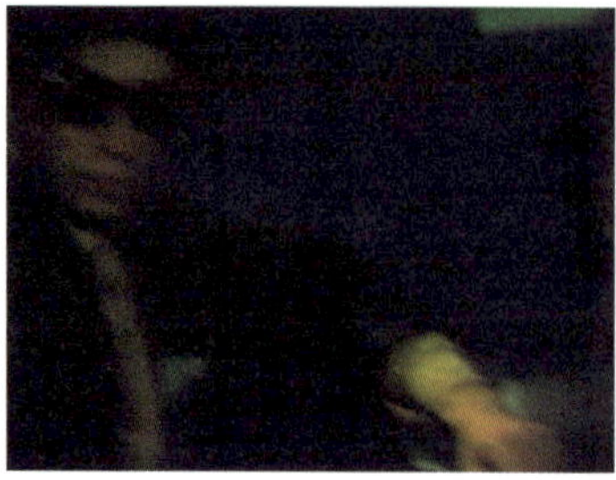
08:29

00:13

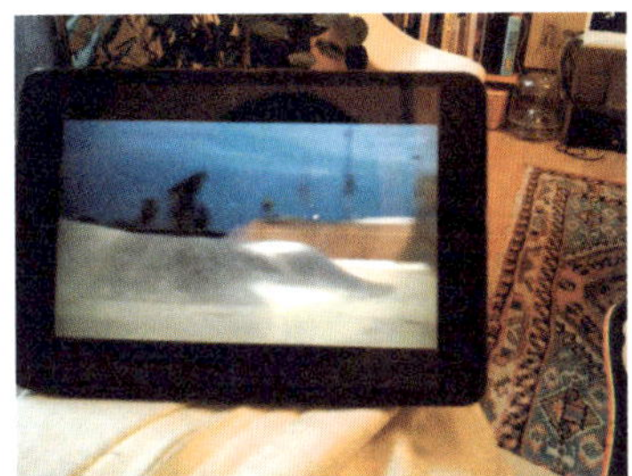

03:57

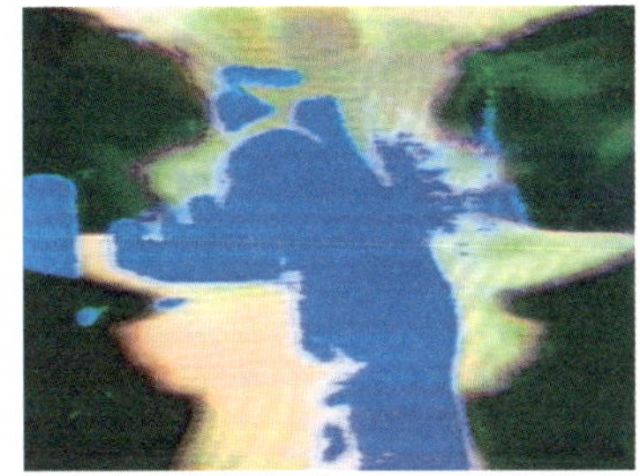

14:28

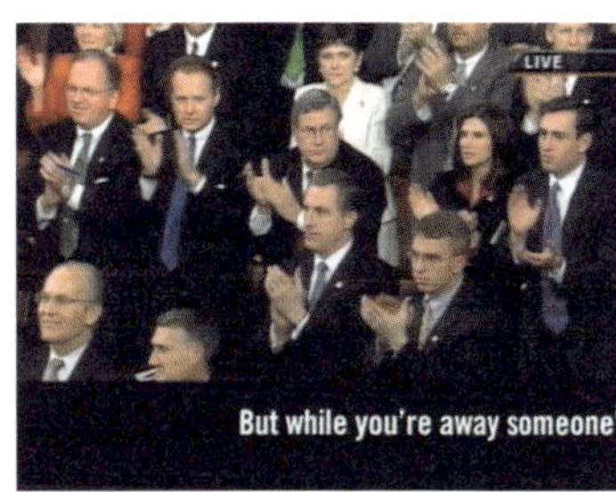

04:30

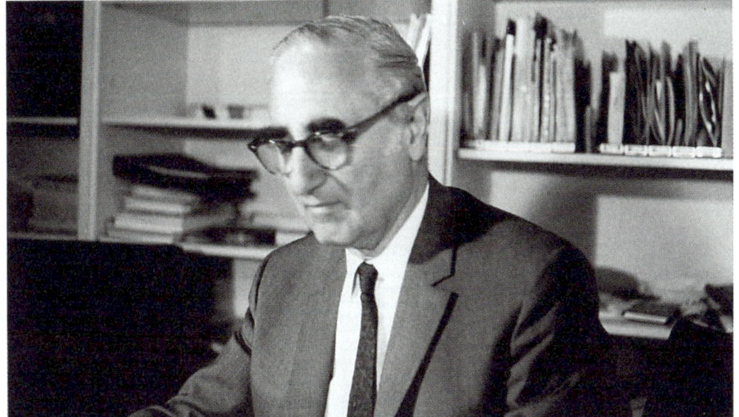

Howard Wise at 50 West 57th Street, June 1969

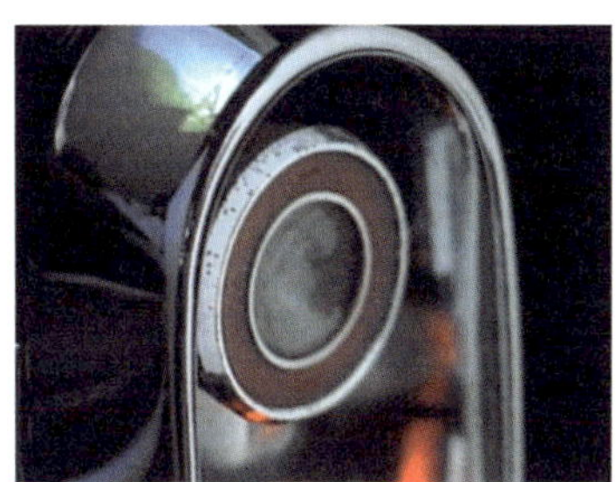

00:17

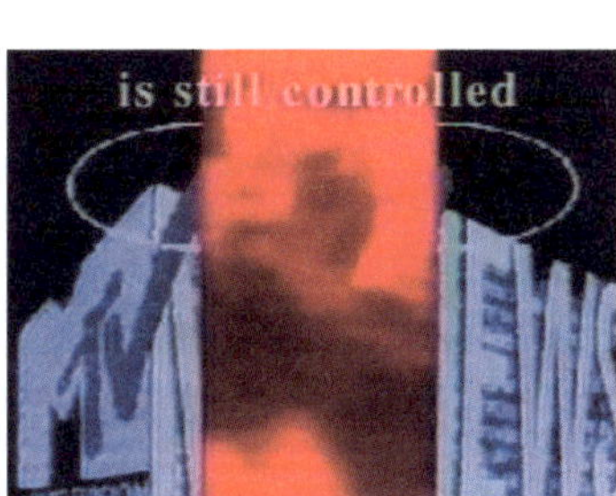

00:34

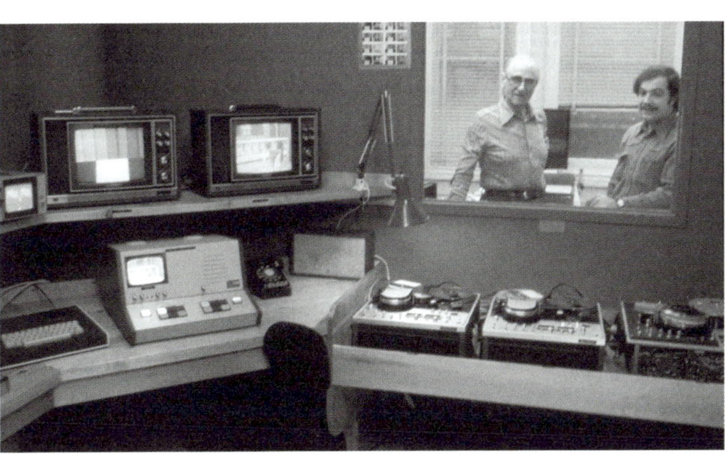

Howard Wise and John Trayna at the EAI Video Editing Facility

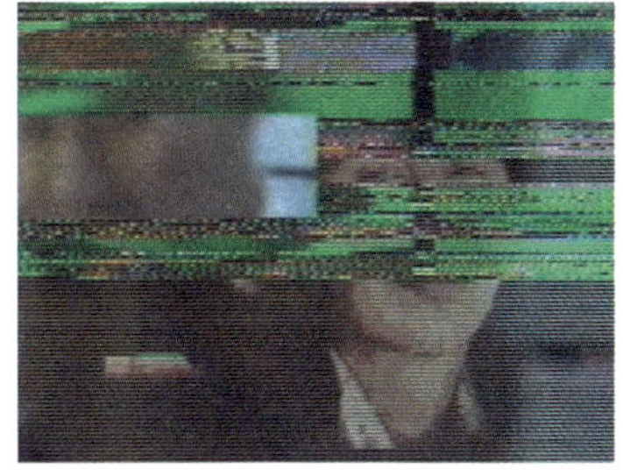

21:11

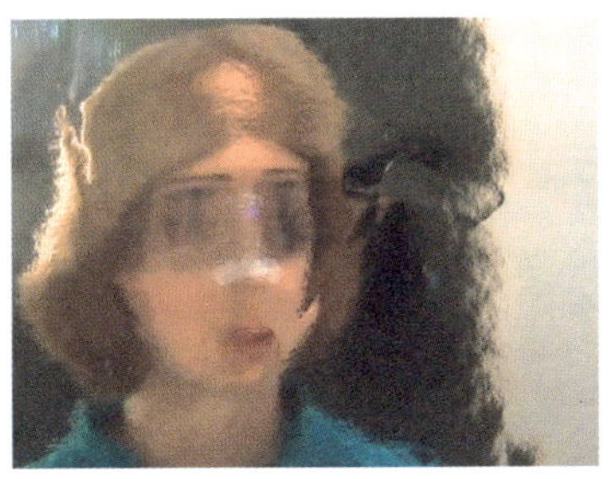

01:23

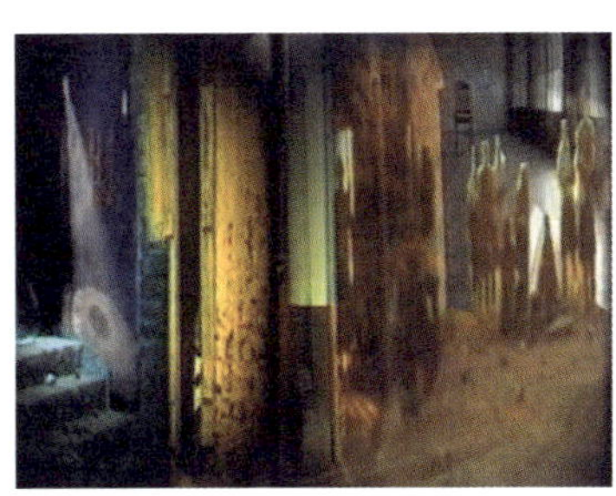

00:20

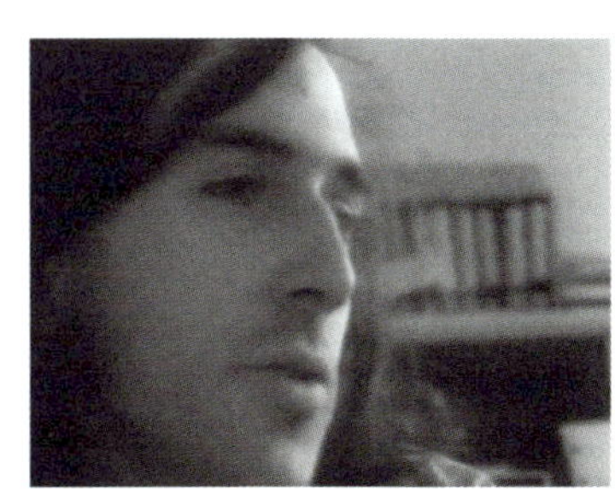

04:23

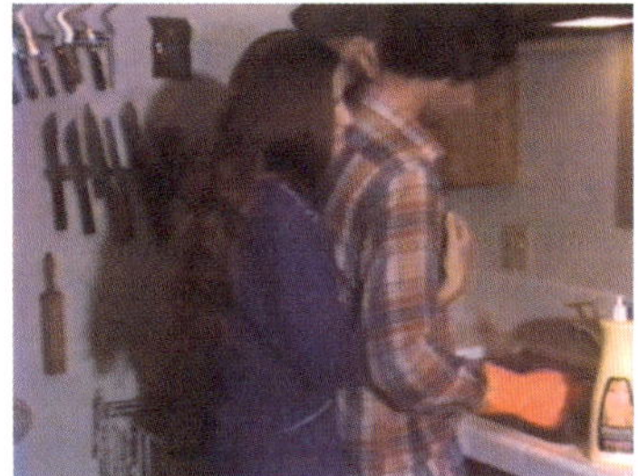

01:27

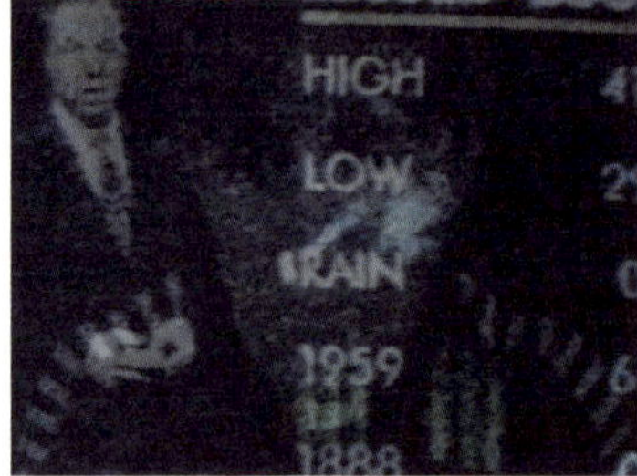

01:47

06:02

14:11

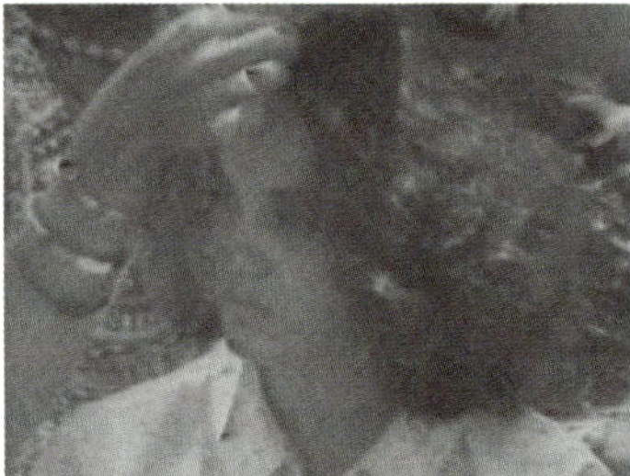

17:35

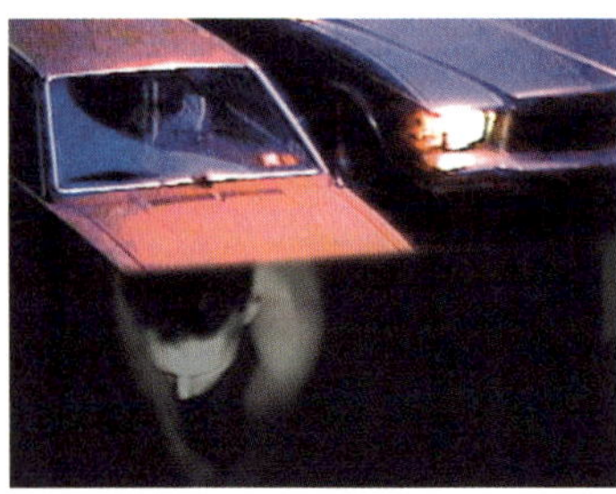

07:23

HOWARD WISE GALLERY 50 WEST 57TH STREET NEW YORK NY 10019 – 265-0465

December 15, 1970

To the friends of the Gallery:

It is with mixed emotions that I inform you that the current show, "Three Sounds" by Howard Jones, which closes December 19, will be the last exhibition at my Gallery.

It may seem paradoxical to you that at the height of the Gallery's success I am withdrawing from the exhibition scene.

The most important considerations which have impelled me to make this decision are that many artists, among them some of the most adventuresome, are focusing their energies on works of such scope that these can only be hinted at in the Gallery, and cannot be shown or realized here. These artists are going out of the Gallery into the environment, the sky, the ocean, even into outer space. Others are seeking imaginative ways of utilizing modern technology to humanize people instead of for commercial or destructive purposes, which de-humanize us all.

Furthermore, as modern technology becomes more sophisticated, artists who use its products as their medium are producing works of increasing complexity, with result that it becomes increasingly demanding of the Gallery's resources to mount exhibitions of those who are exploring in depth the potentials of scientific developments.

Although many of these visionary projects are "impractical" and are not readily realizable at this time, they nevertheless are of great importance, for they may stimulate the imagination of those who control our destinies, and suggest what might be done if only they were able to apply their intelligence to making this a better world for people to live in.

I hope to contribute to the realization of some of these projects, particularly to those which are susceptible of diffusion over television.

Most important of all, I feel that I must try to put to maximum social use whatever I possess in the way of training, ability and experience (and I have gained much in the eleven years I have operated my Gallery here).

I cannot stand idly by when the existence of our society and ourselves as individuals is so darkly threatened. I sense and feel deeply the problems that menace us, but this does not mean that I am a pessimist. On the contrary, I believe that these problems are soluble, if only we will use our heads and our hearts with determination and apply our vital energies towards their resolution. After all, our brains have gotten us into this mess, and our brains can get us out of it, if only we use them. I intend to do whatever I can to this end.

I wish to express my deep gratitude to all those who, by their interest and support, have contributed to the success of the Gallery.

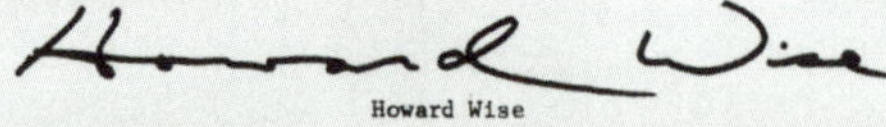

Howard Wise

Letter by Howard Wise announcing the closure of his gallery

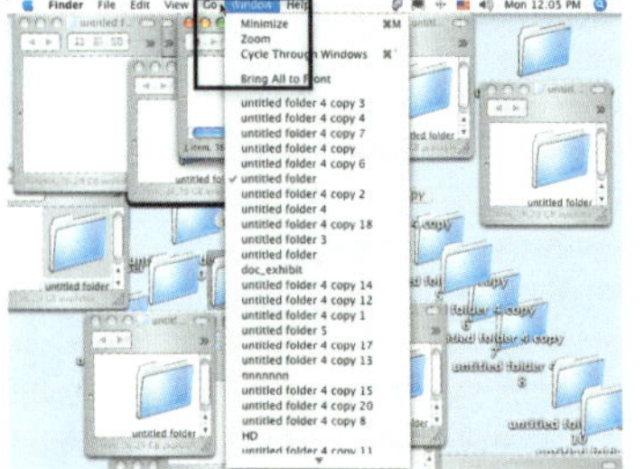

00:58

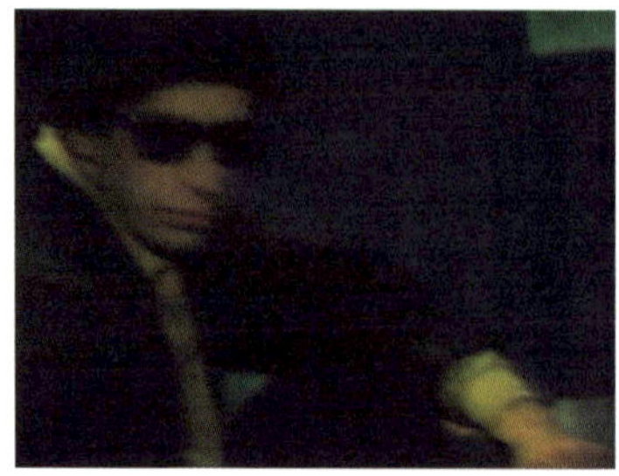

08:29

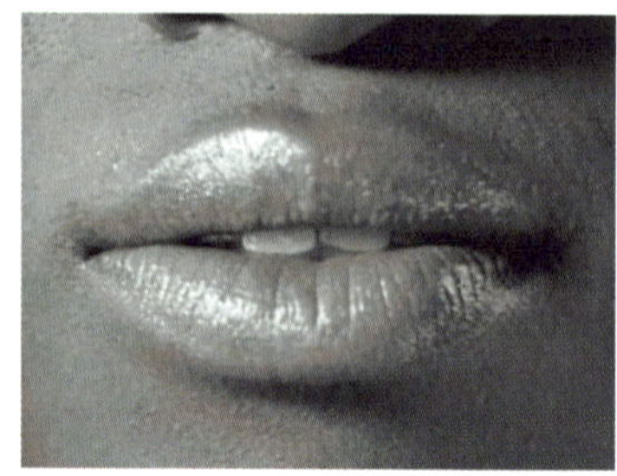

00:13

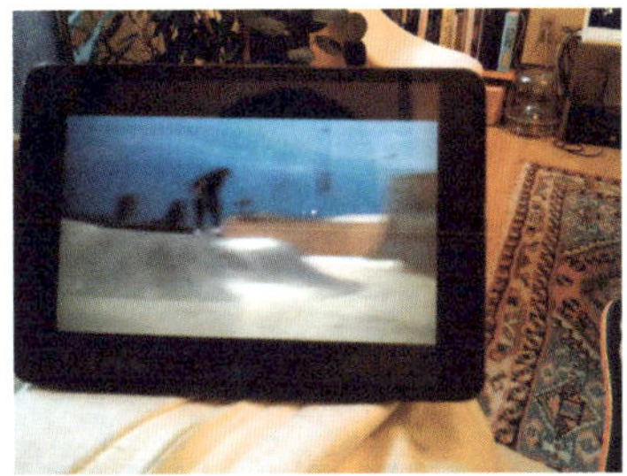

03:57

14:28

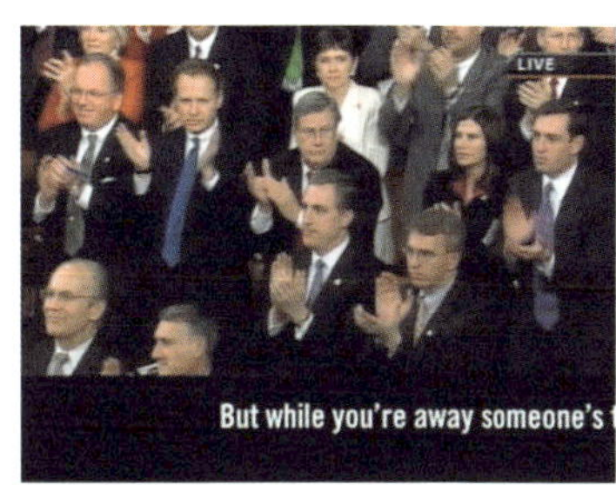

04:30

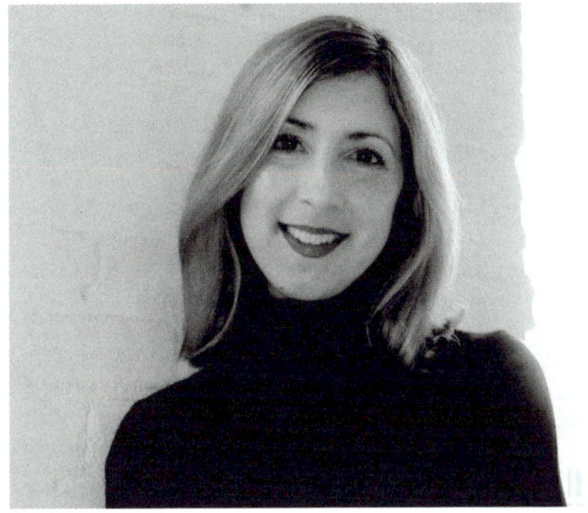

Lori Zippay, Executive Director of EAI (1981-2019)

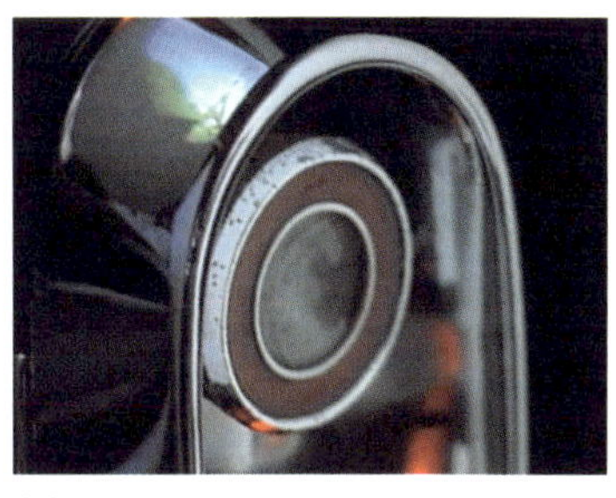

00:17

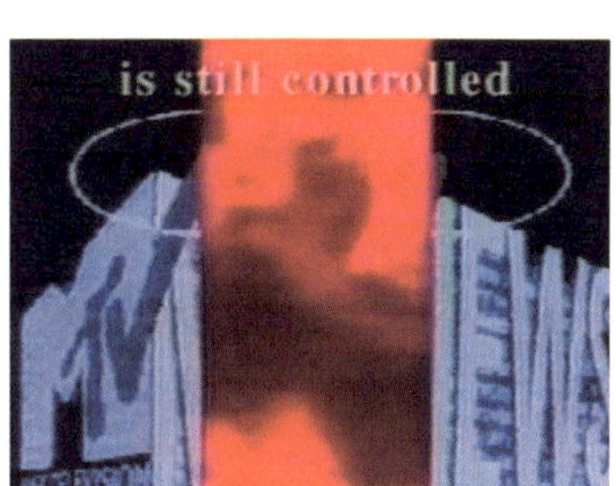

00:34

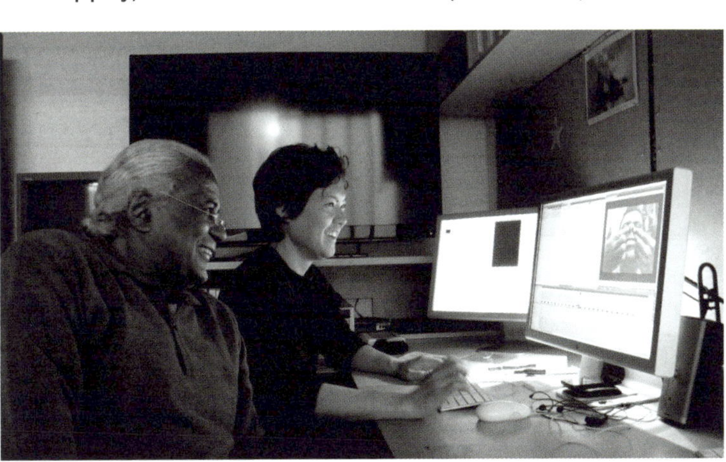

Anthony Ramos and Trevor Shimizu in the EAI editing facility

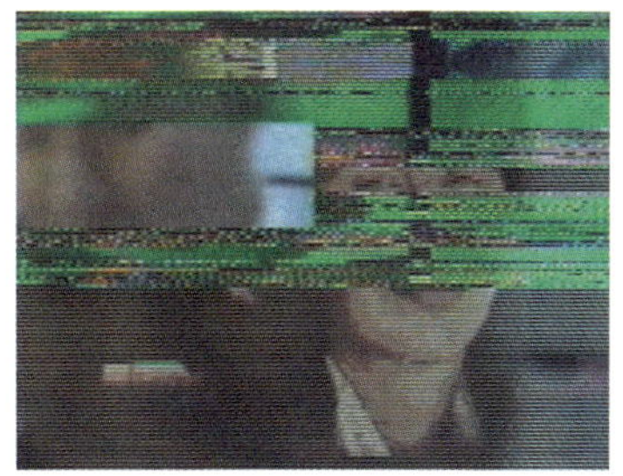

21:11

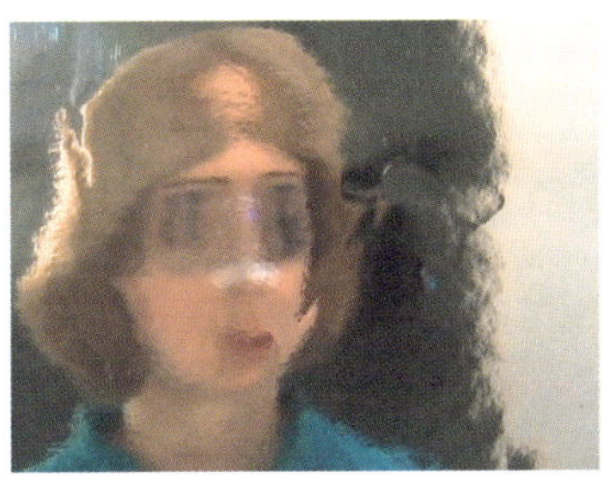

01:23

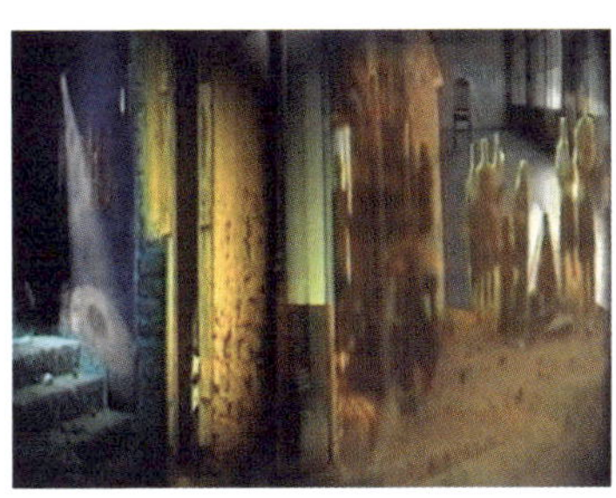

00:20

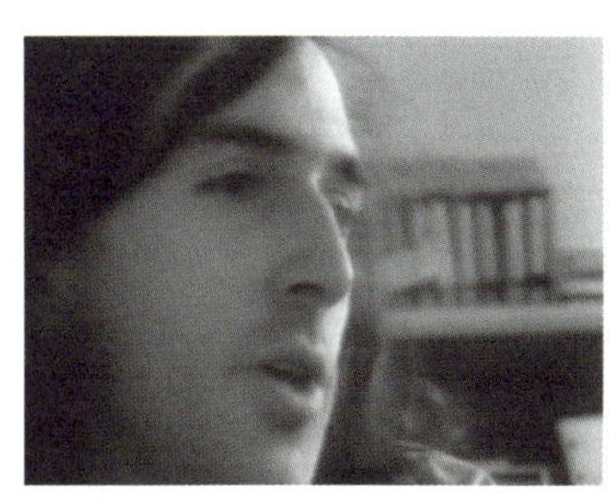

04:23

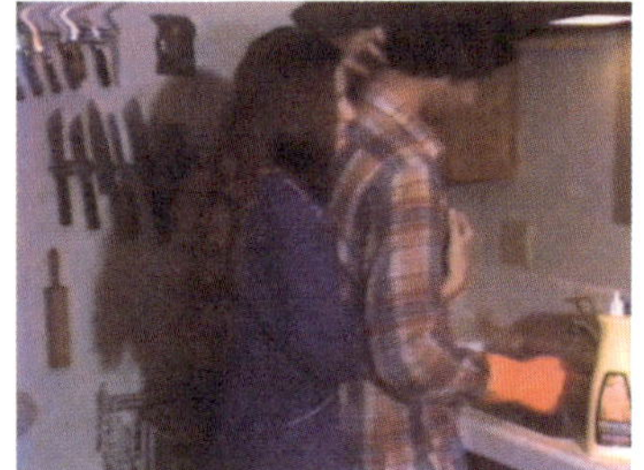

01:26

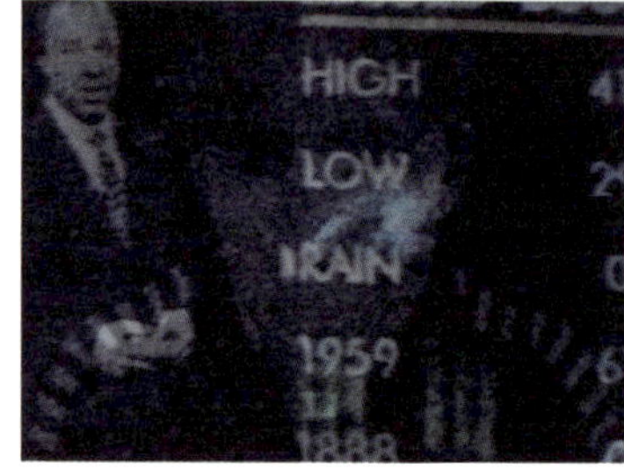

01:46

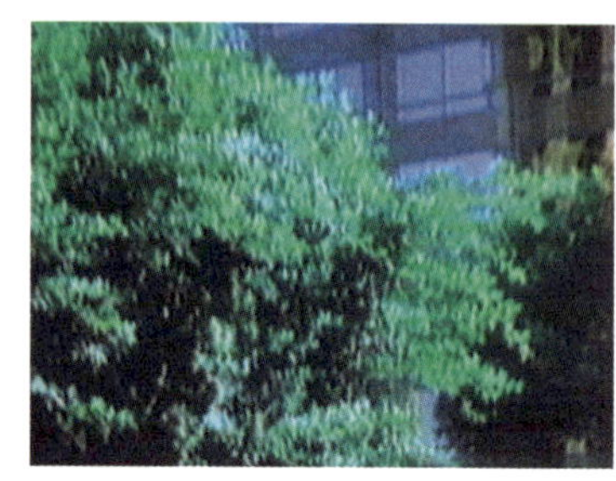

06:01

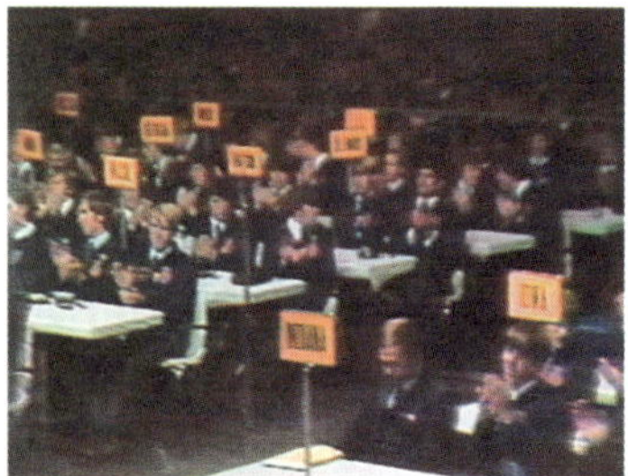

14:10

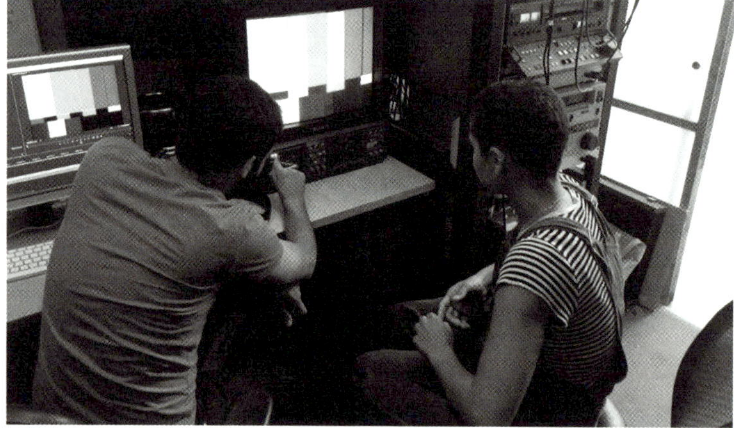

Technical director Jon Dieringer and Emir West, 2017

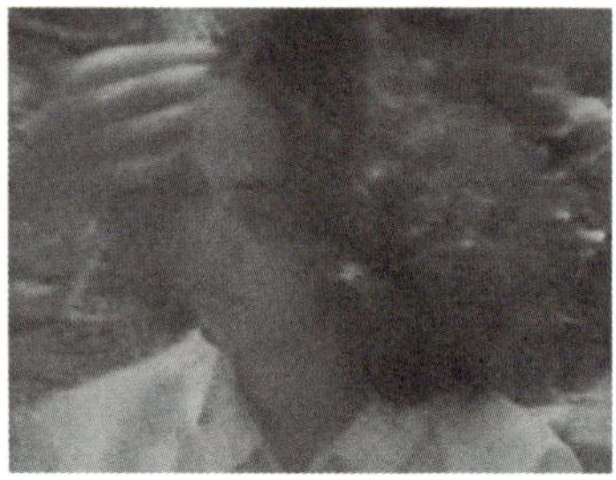

17:34

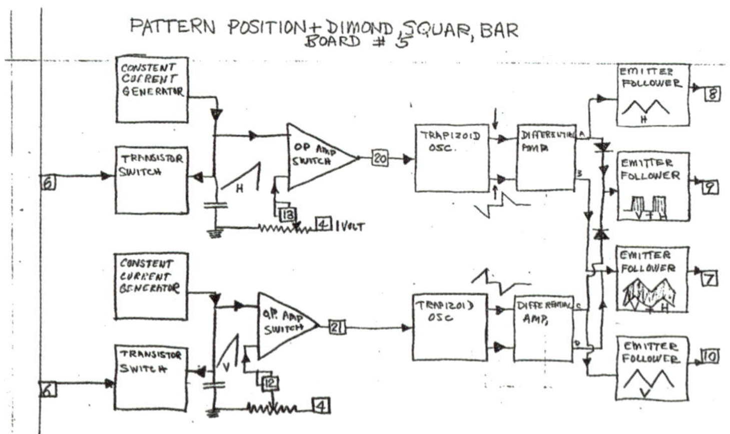

Drawing demonstrating an electronic video synthesizer

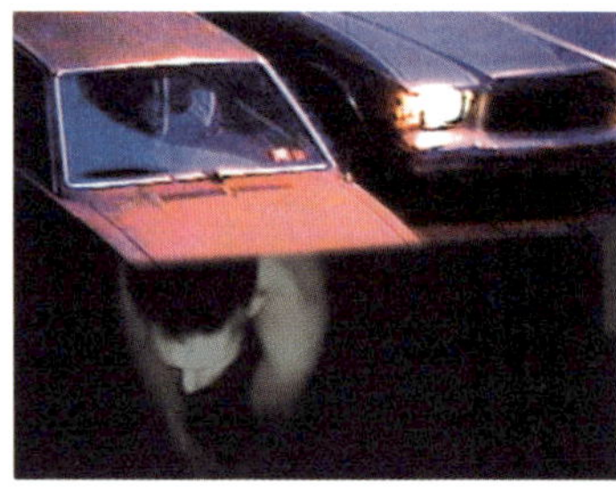

07:22

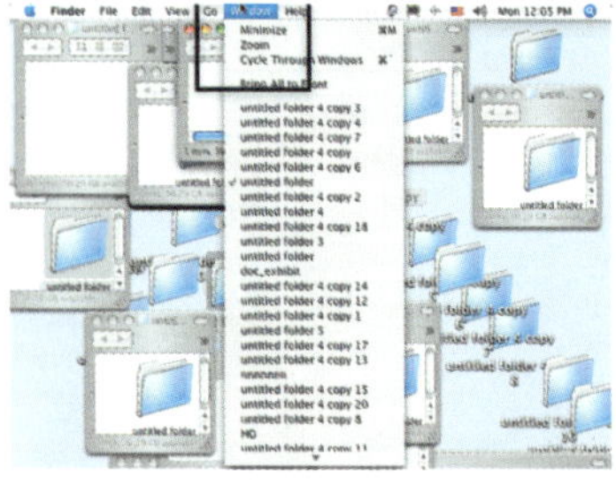

00:57

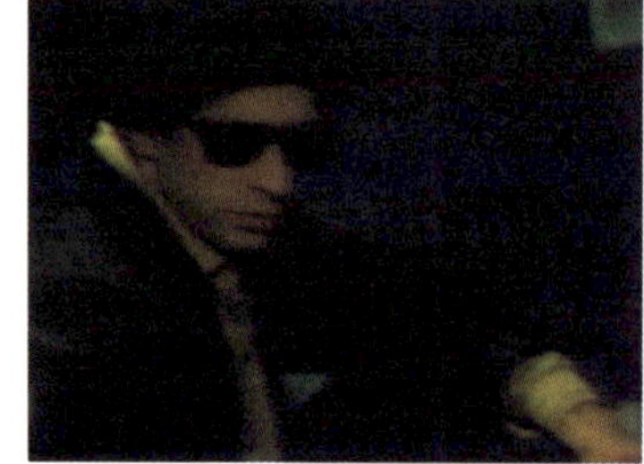

08:28

00:12

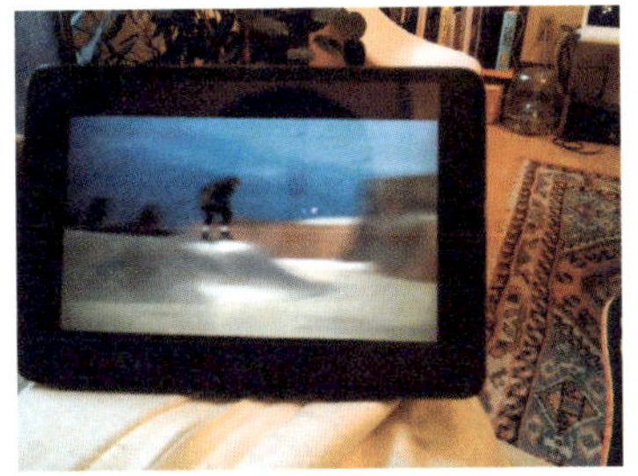

03:57

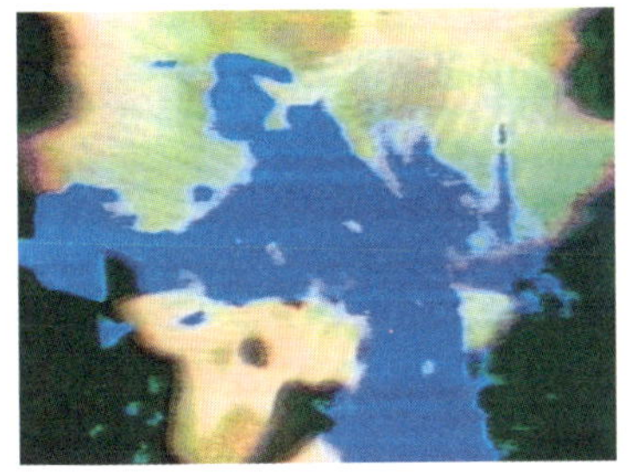

14:28

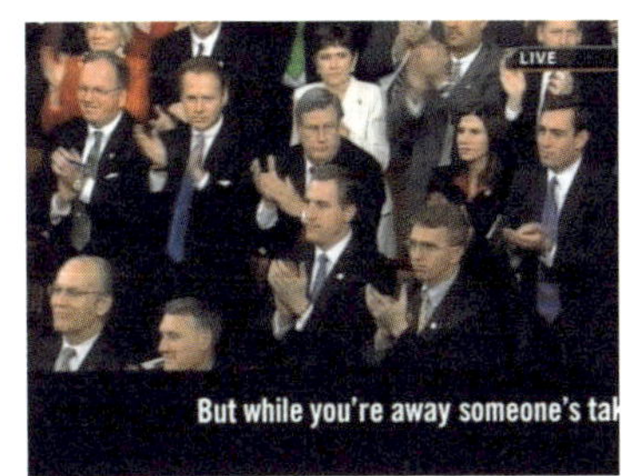

04:30

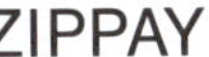

publication and put it online. Through the Lila Wallace grant we were able to work with Peter Berry and John Sharp of Supercosm to make the database-driven online catalog, which was an enormous advancement. Galen Joseph-Hunter, who was a key EAI staff member in many administrative and programmatic roles—including associate director—from 1997 through the late 2000s, was also pivotal to that project.

In the same year I won a $50,000 Absolut Angel Award to further develop EAI's online catalog. Absolut Vodka sponsored these awards to individuals for only two years, to support entrepreneurial projects that merged art and technology for the advancement of nonprofits. This came about through Sara Tucker, Dia's IT director and the force behind Dia's pioneering artists' web projects, because she told me about the award and urged me to apply.

In 1997 we also partnered with Dia on a grant to the New Art Trust to transfer Bruce Nauman's

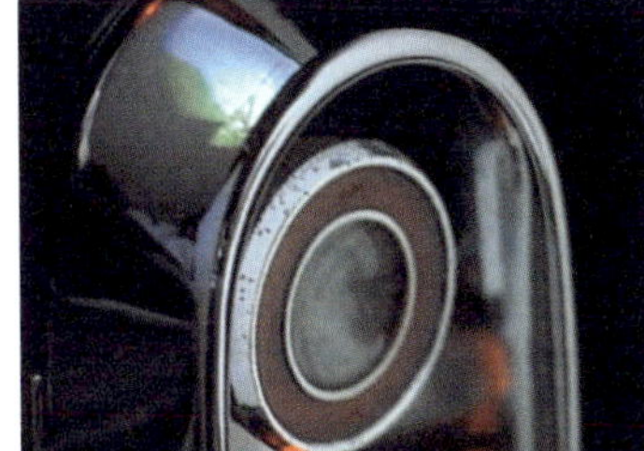

00:17

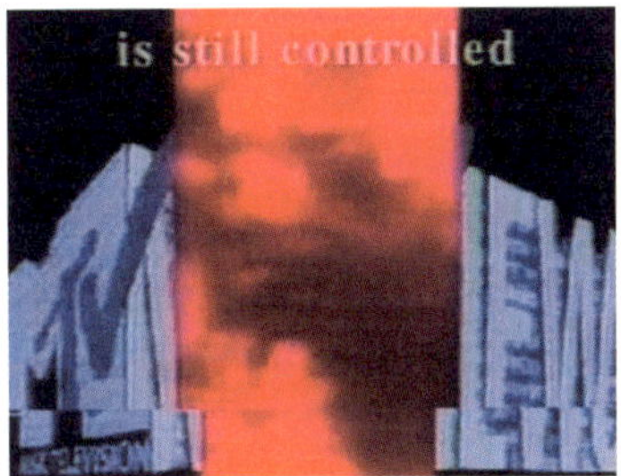

00:34

21:11

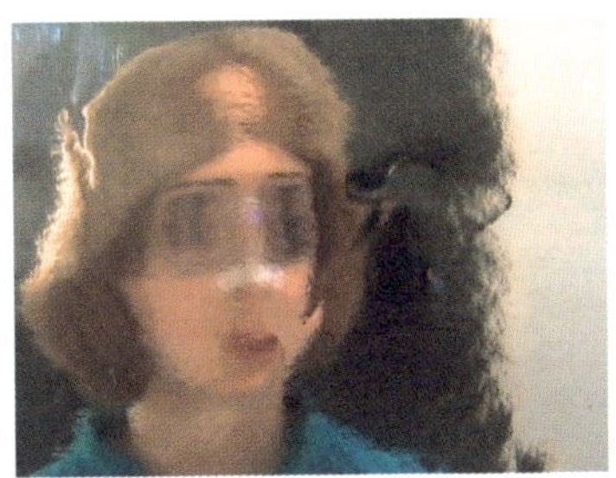

01:23

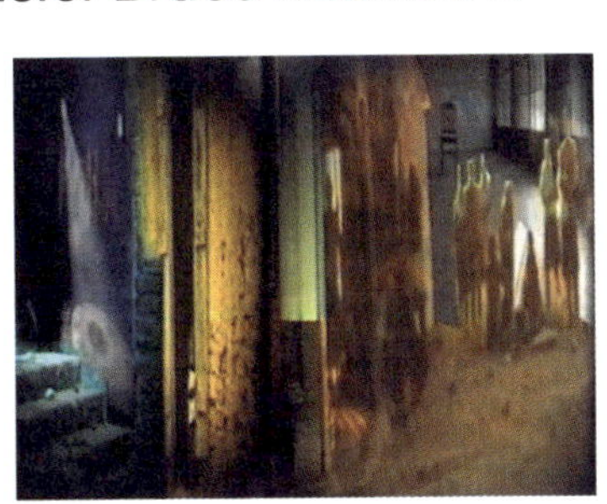

00:20

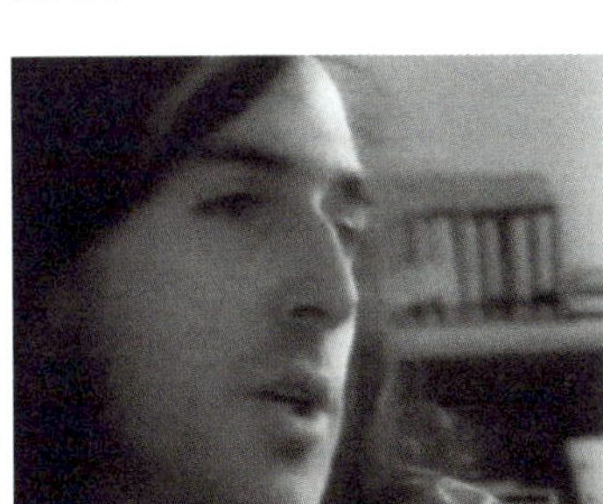

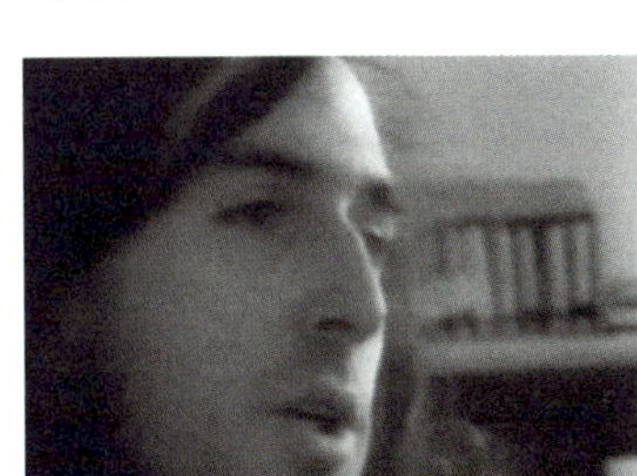

04:23

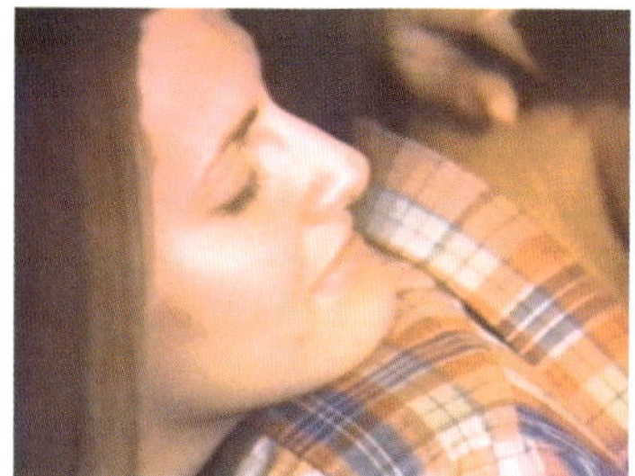

01:26

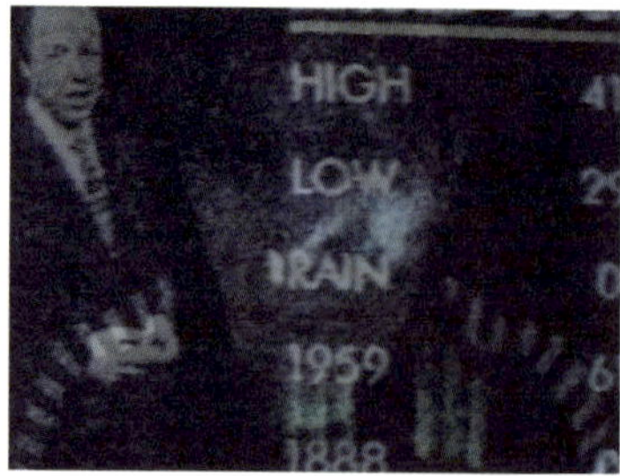

01:46

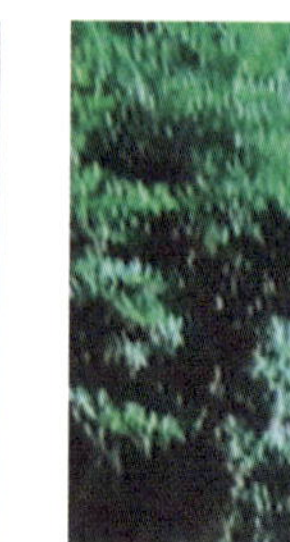

06:01

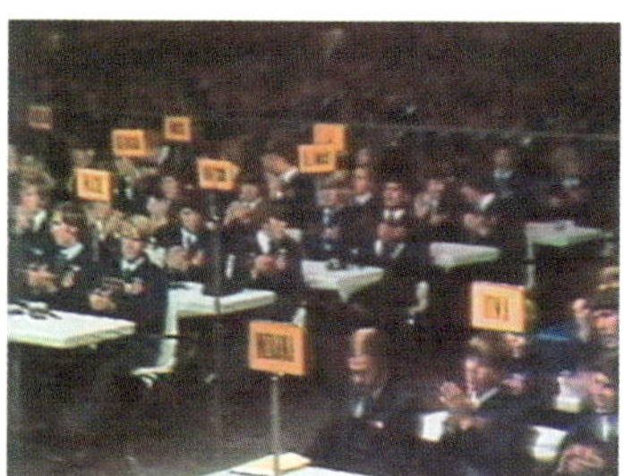

14:10

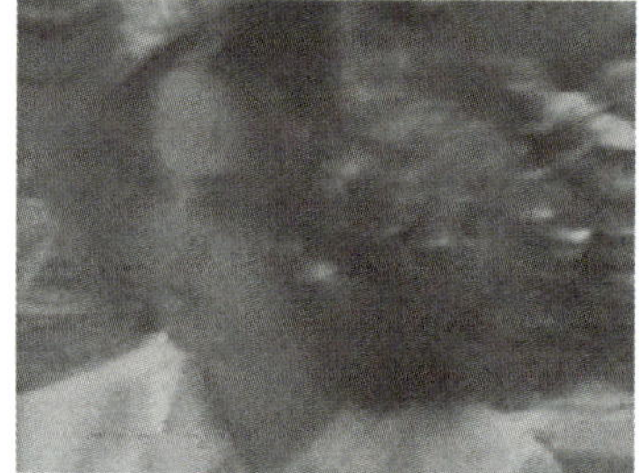

17:34

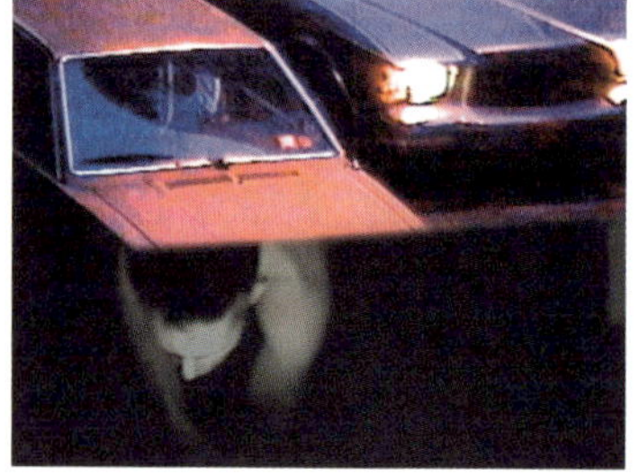

07:22

early 16 mm films, which had been out of circulation, to video for distribution. That's when Nauman's video and film works from the 1960s and 1970s first came into distribution at EAI. Up until that time, Nauman was not in EAI's collection. It was the beginning of an incredibly important relationship.

That year we also made a significant technical upgrade. With a contribution from Barbara Wise, we were able to acquire a Beta SP editing system, which was considered very high-end at the time; it was the archival standard format in the late 1990s. To go from 3/4-inch to Beta SP equipment was a major leap.

This all happened within a short time span. As I said, the late 1990s was another moment—like the one in the 1980s when our catalog publication and preservation program pushed us forward—where a number of major advancements occurred simultaneously. There was a critical mass of exciting developments—structurally, financially, technically, creatively—happening all at one time.

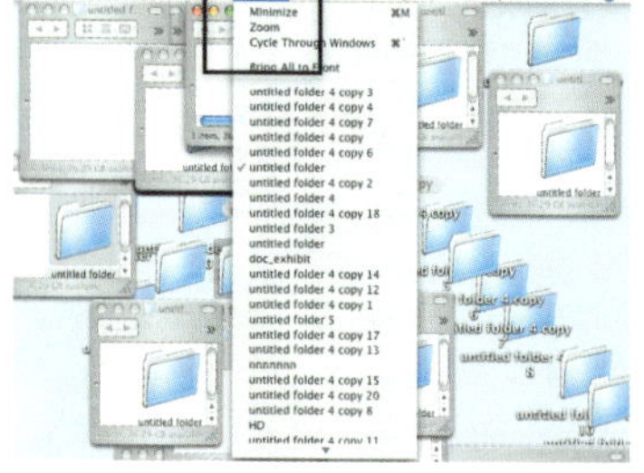

00:57

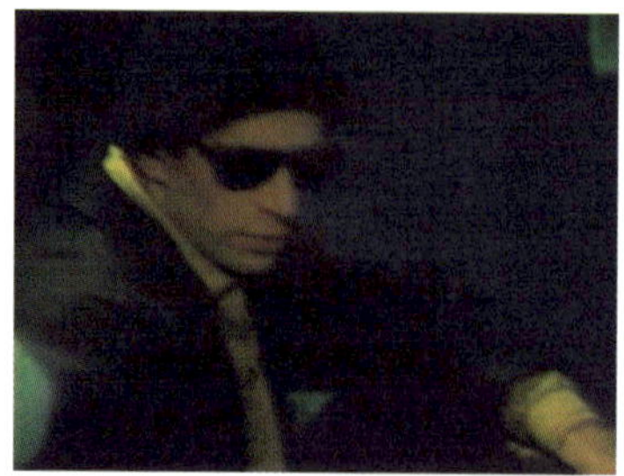

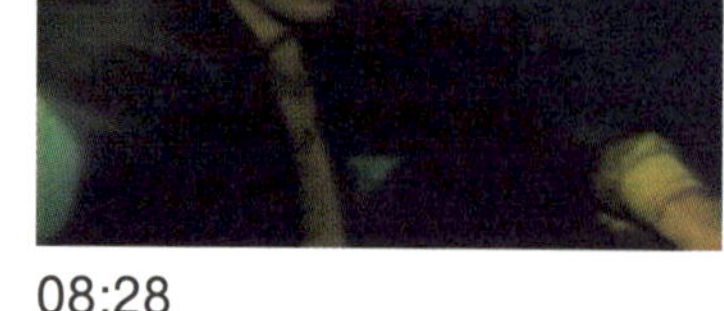

08:28

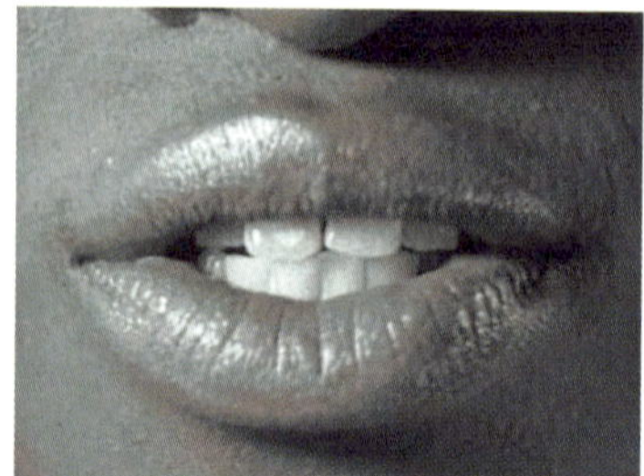

00:12

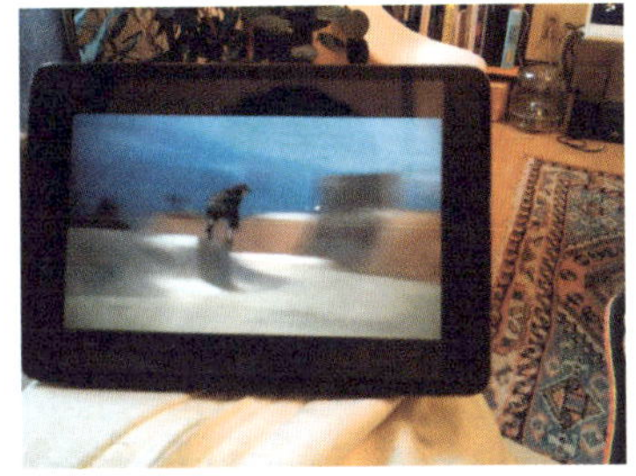
03:57

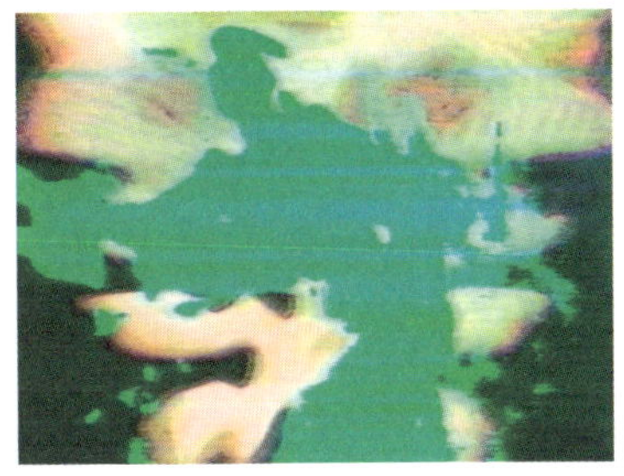
14:28

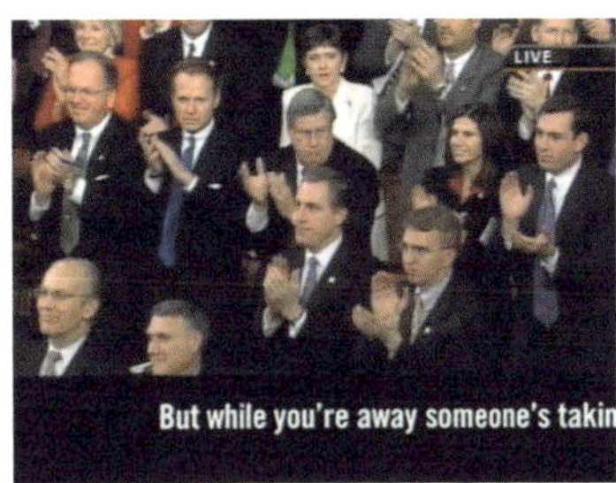

04:30

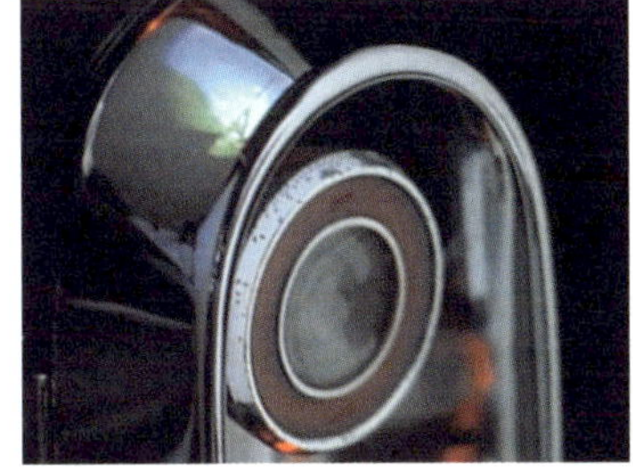
00:17

AK – We take it for granted now with the internet, but it wasn't that long ago that a lot of these artworks weren't accessible.

LZ – Exactly. They had never been transferred or seen since the 1960s or 1970s in some cases.

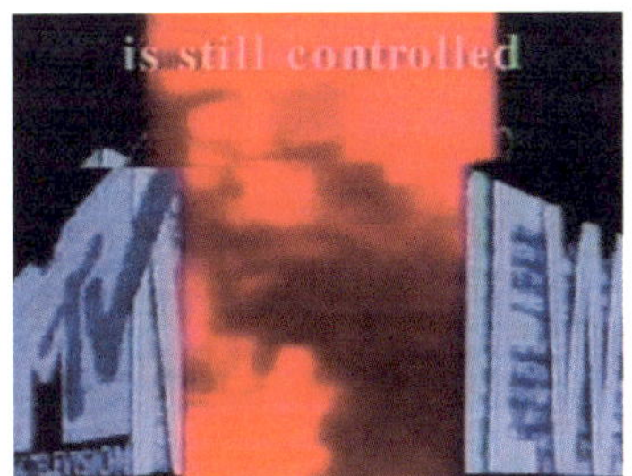

00:34

AK – I think that it is really important to acknowledge how EAI has brought a lot of these artworks and artists back into visibility. It was certainly important to my own education in New York in the nineties. Can you talk a little bit more about the role of preservation?

LZ – Preservation has been key not only in maintaining the collection, but also in bringing important "lost" historical works to light. There were many cases of this in the nineties. For example, Nam June Paik and Jud Yalkut's collaborations that are now considered iconic works, such as *Video-Film Concert* (1966–72), which includes *Beatles Electroniques* and *Waiting for Commercials*, were only transferred from film and put into distribution in the nineties. And now they're recognized as pivotal works

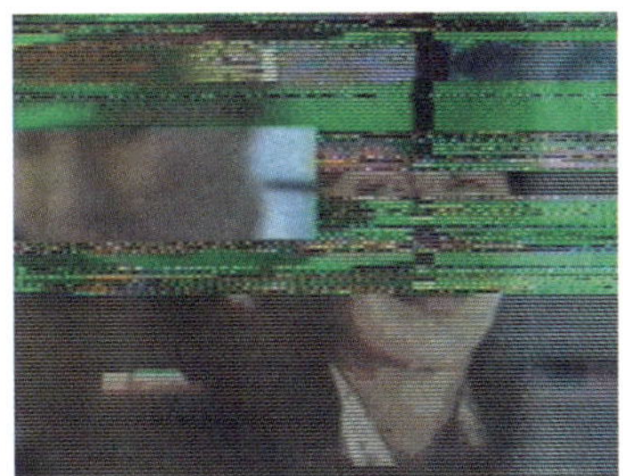
21:11

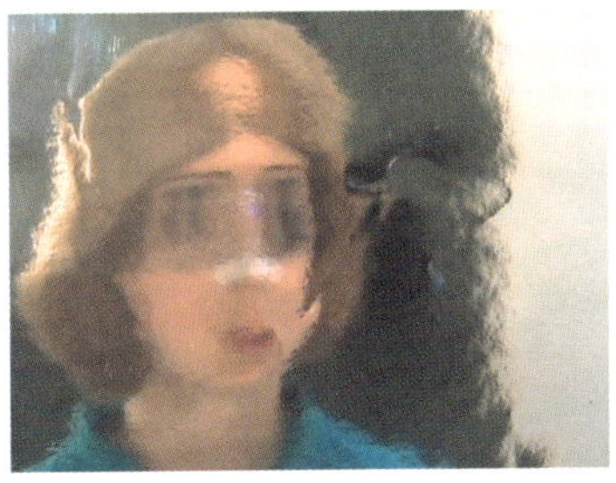
01:23

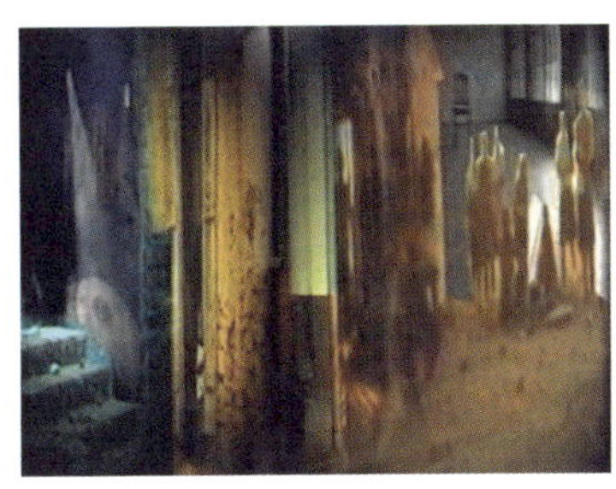
00:20

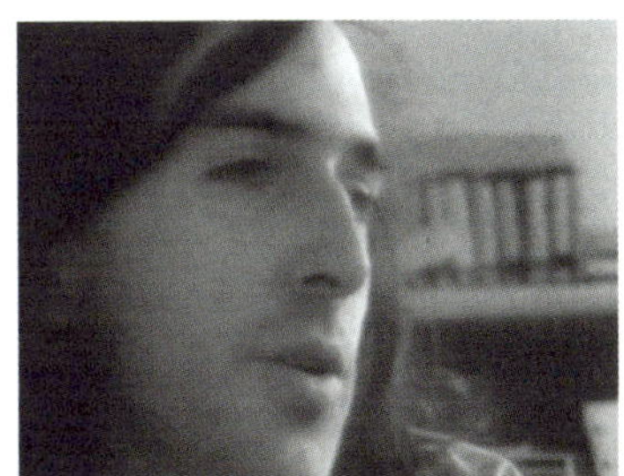
04:23

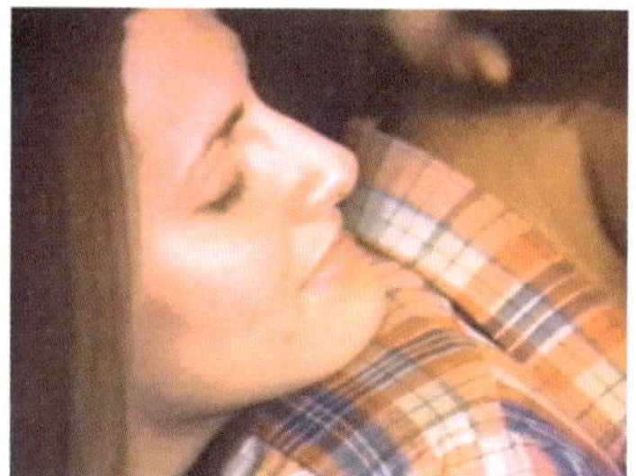

01:26

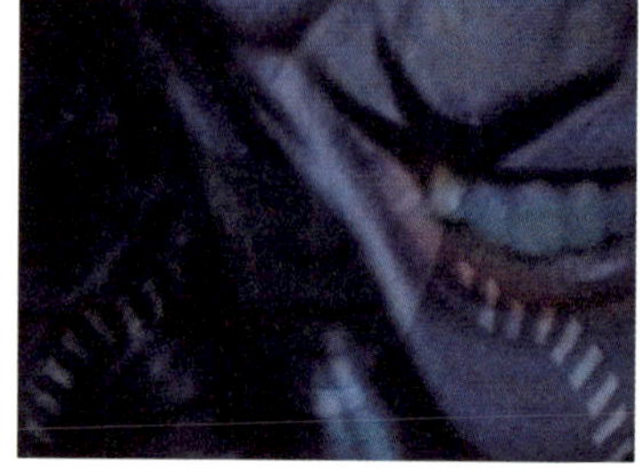

01:46

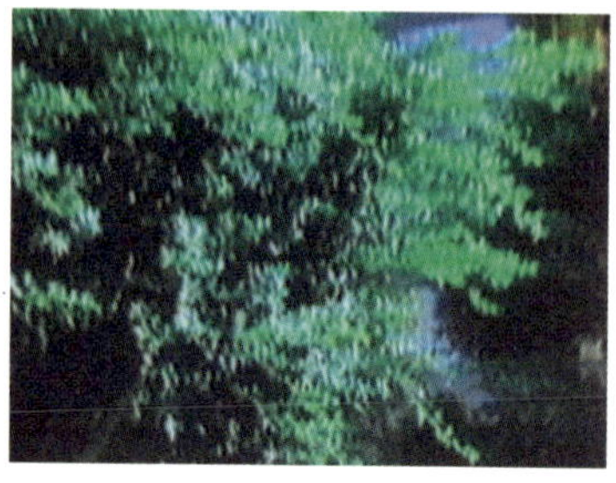

06:01

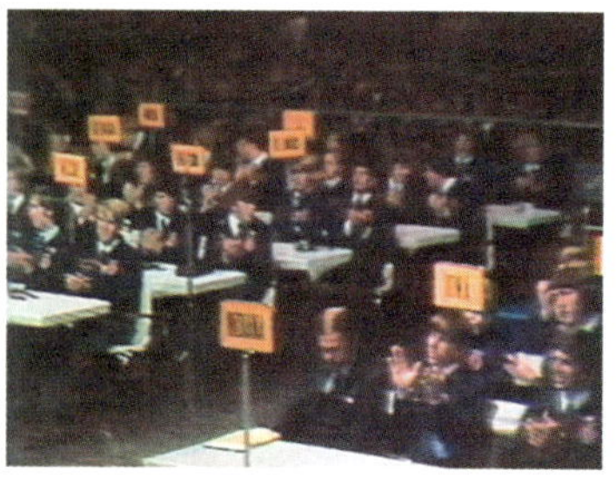

14:10

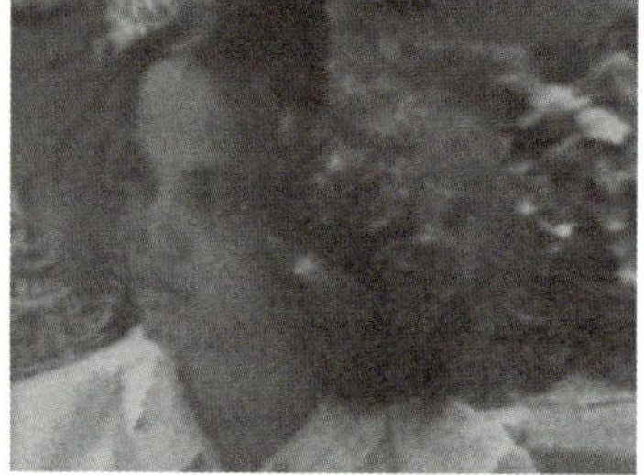

17:34

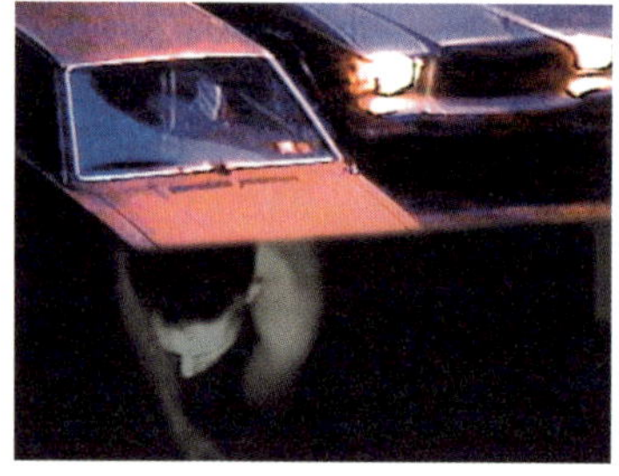

07:22

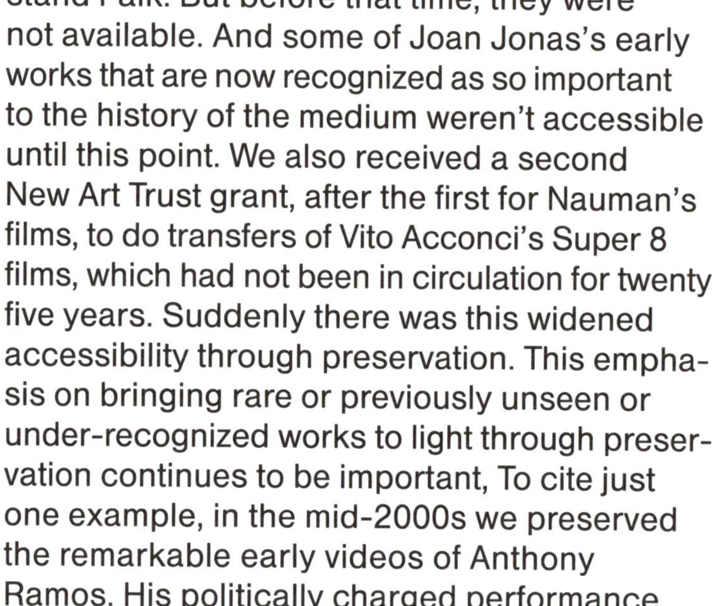

that everyone should know and study to understand Paik. But before that time, they were not available. And some of Joan Jonas's early works that are now recognized as so important to the history of the medium weren't accessible until this point. We also received a second New Art Trust grant, after the first for Nauman's films, to do transfers of Vito Acconci's Super 8 films, which had not been in circulation for twenty-five years. Suddenly there was this widened accessibility through preservation. This emphasis on bringing rare or previously unseen or under-recognized works to light through preservation continues to be important, To cite just one example, in the mid-2000s we preserved the remarkable early videos of Anthony Ramos. His politically charged performance works were revelatory.

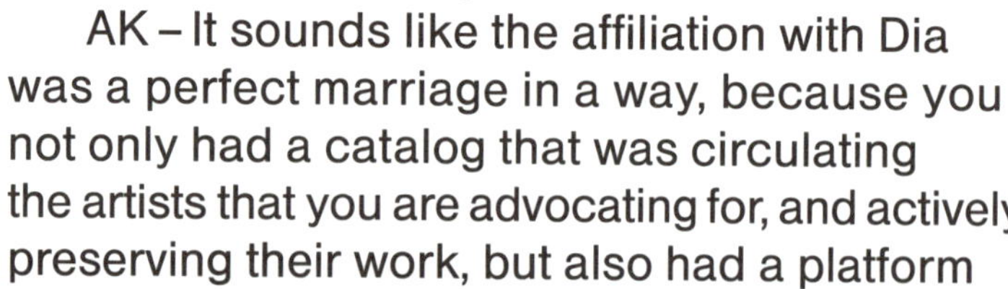

AK – It sounds like the affiliation with Dia was a perfect marriage in a way, because you not only had a catalog that was circulating the artists that you are advocating for, and actively preserving their work, but also had a platform

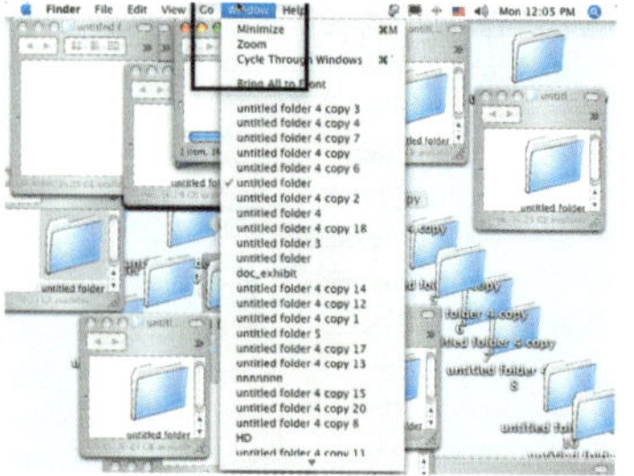

00:57

08:28

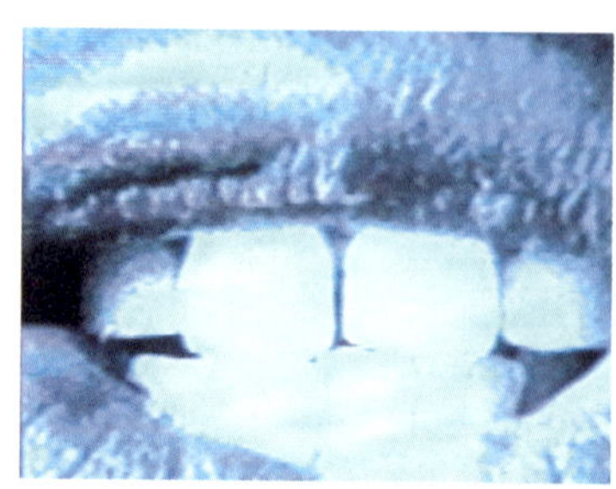

00:12

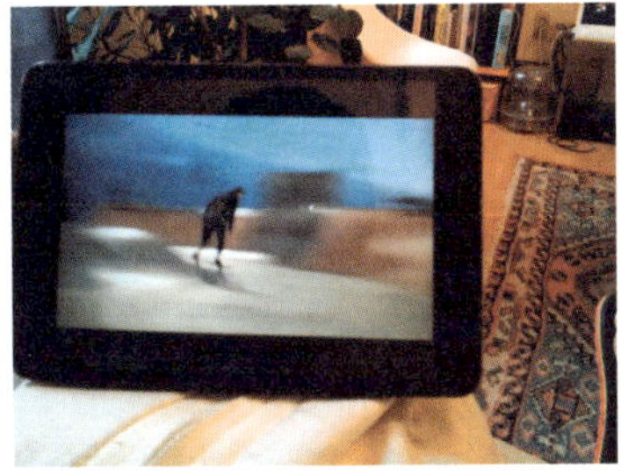

03:57

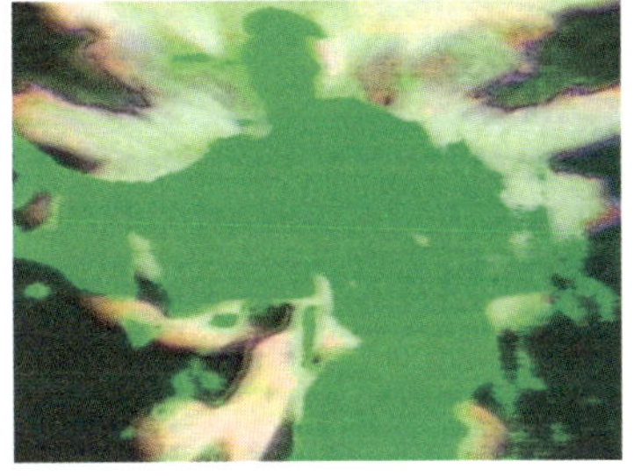

14:28

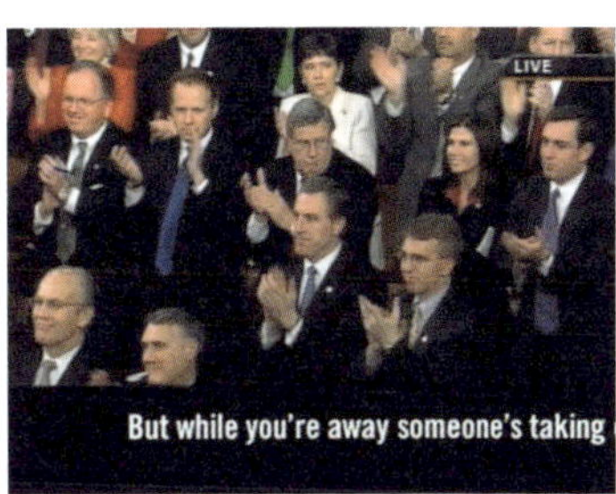

04:30

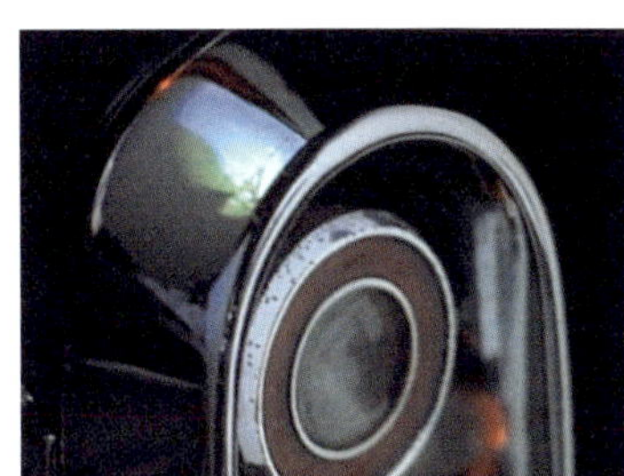

00:17

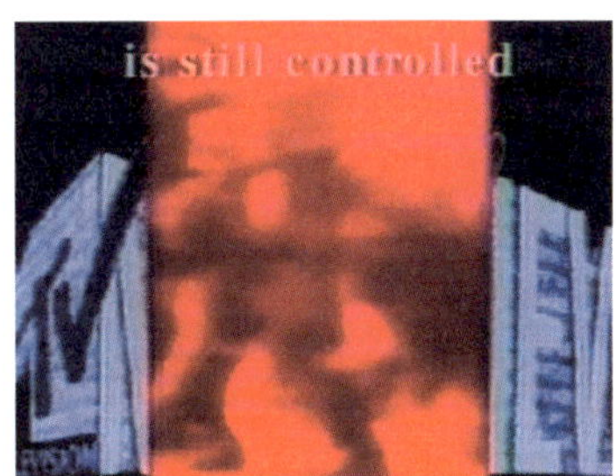

00:34

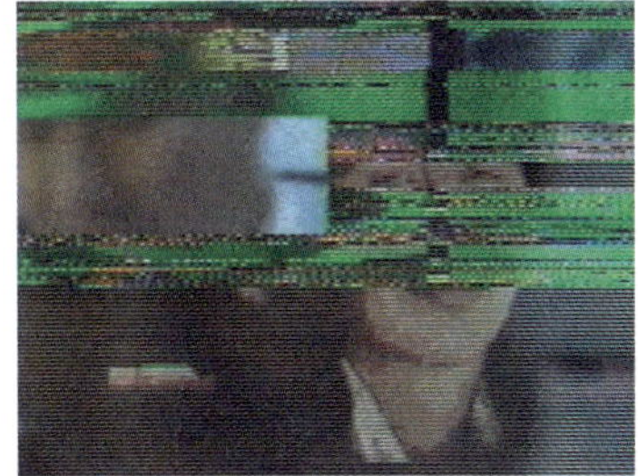

21:11

to present the work in a way in which you previously couldn't.

LZ – Exactly. There was something that I'd always wanted—to have some kind of an exhibition space or a public programs space for EAI. Just before the Dia partnership began, we started doing collaborations around the city with institutions to do public programs—like at the Museum of Art and Design, to name one example. We started doing more of those kinds of events around the city, but we were eager to do our own public programs. At this time we were preserving and introducing works into distribution that were historically important but had never been seen, and I was eager for EAI to present these works, to call attention to our preservation efforts. It was so exciting to be uncovering these works; it was revelatory and adding to scholarship. So, Dia was key in giving us that platform to actually present the works. For example, we premiered Dara Birnbaum's newly preserved two-channel *Attack Piece* (1975) in a program at Dia. Then, of course,

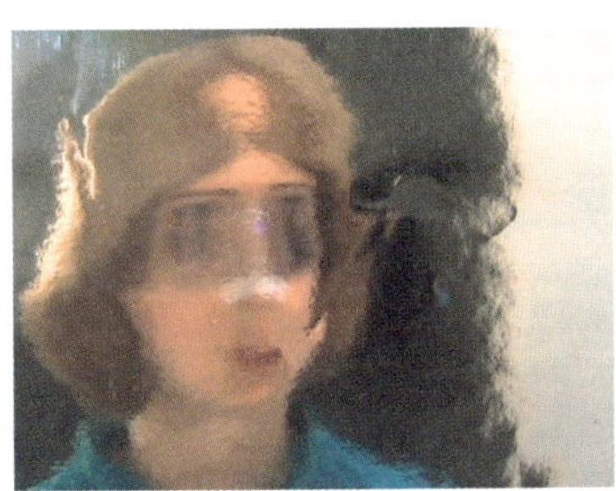

01:23

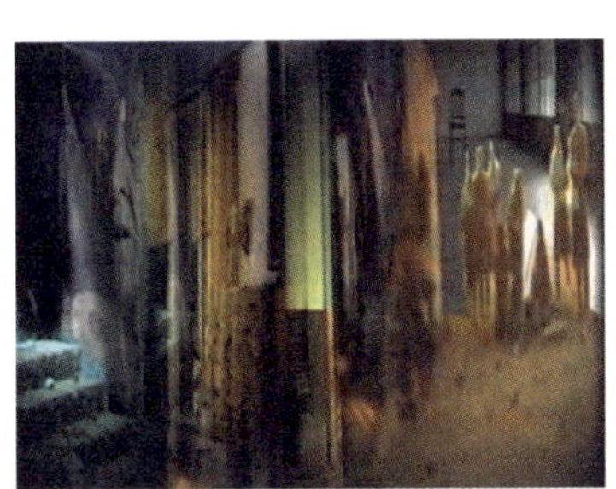

00:20

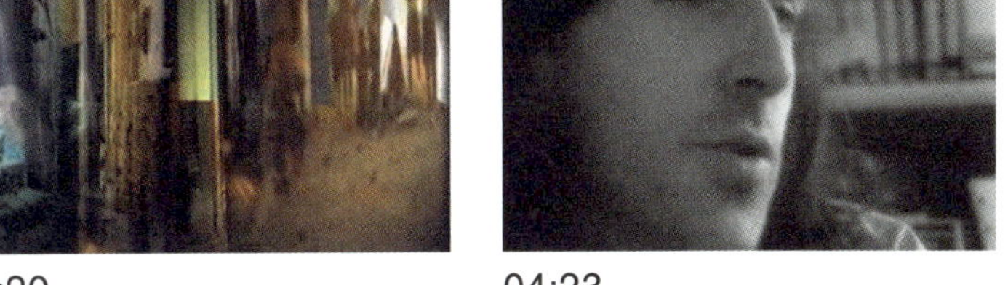

04:23

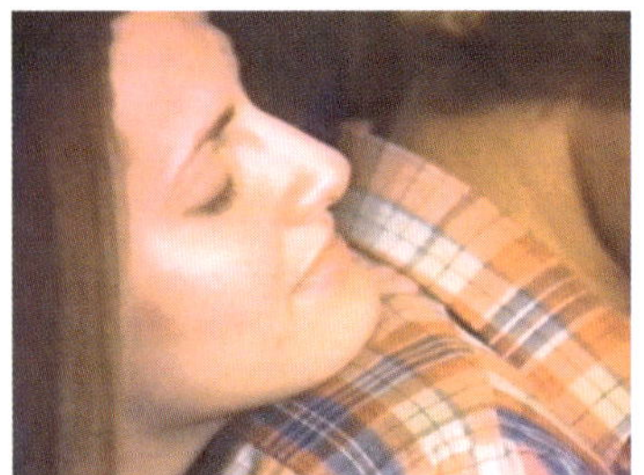
01:26

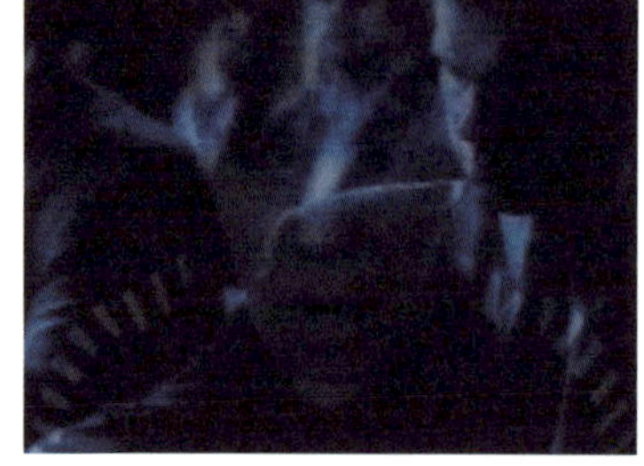
01:46

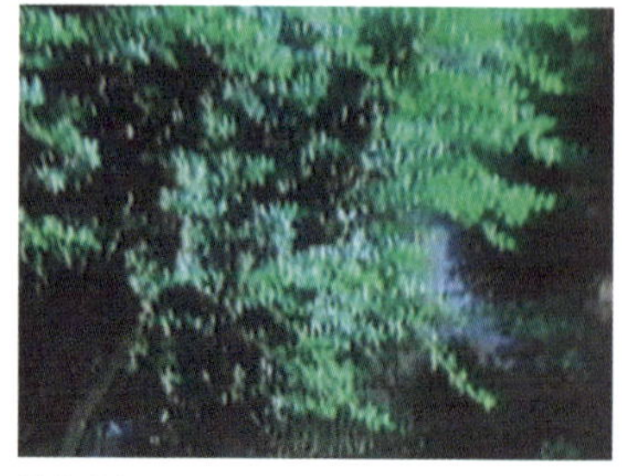
06:01

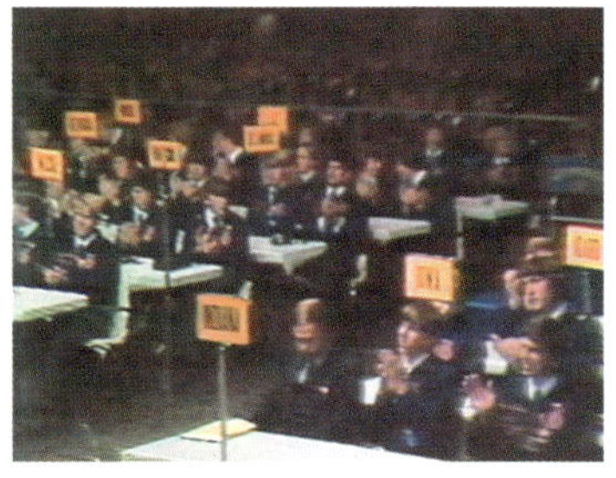
14:10

we presented those Joan Jonas works that had just been restored and transferred. So the Dia exhibition and screening collaborations absolutely gave us a way to highlight works that we were dealing with in other realms—distribution, preservation. The establishment of a regular public program series also led to crucial funding from the New York City Department of Cultural Affairs.

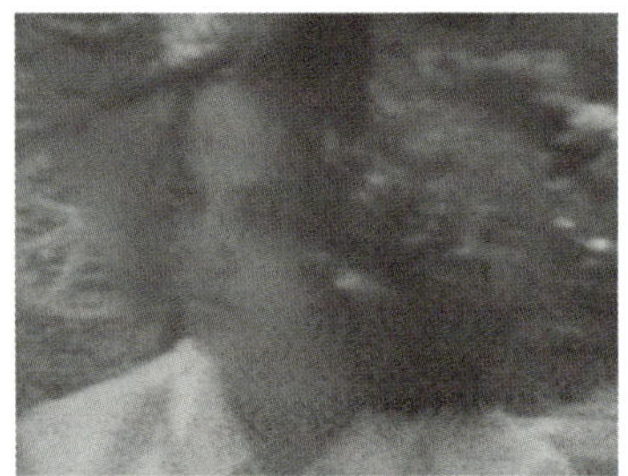
17:34

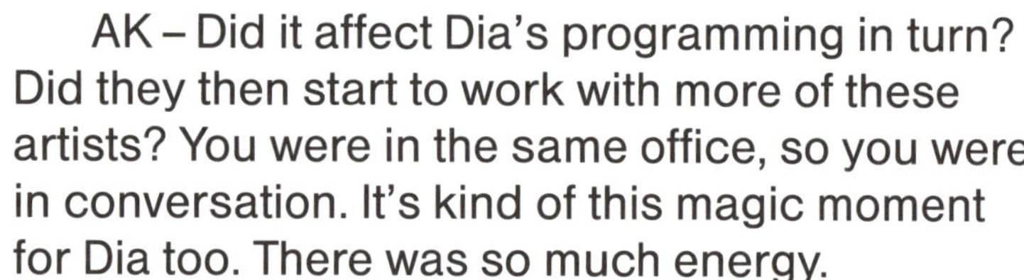

AK – Did it affect Dia's programming in turn? Did they then start to work with more of these artists? You were in the same office, so you were in conversation. It's kind of this magic moment for Dia too. There was so much energy.

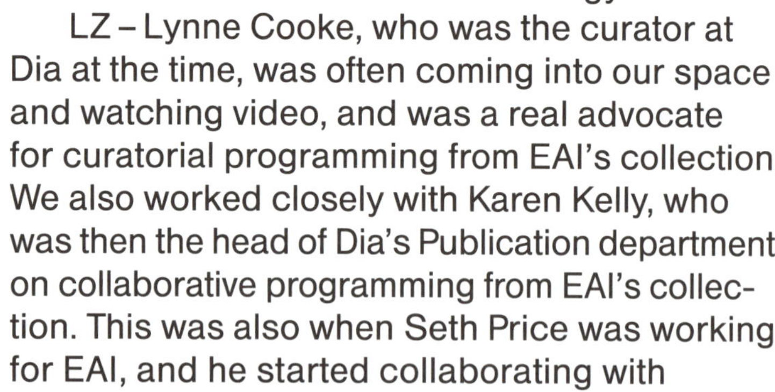

LZ – Lynne Cooke, who was the curator at Dia at the time, was often coming into our space and watching video, and was a real advocate for curatorial programming from EAI's collection. We also worked closely with Karen Kelly, who was then the head of Dia's Publication department, on collaborative programming from EAI's collection. This was also when Seth Price was working for EAI, and he started collaborating with

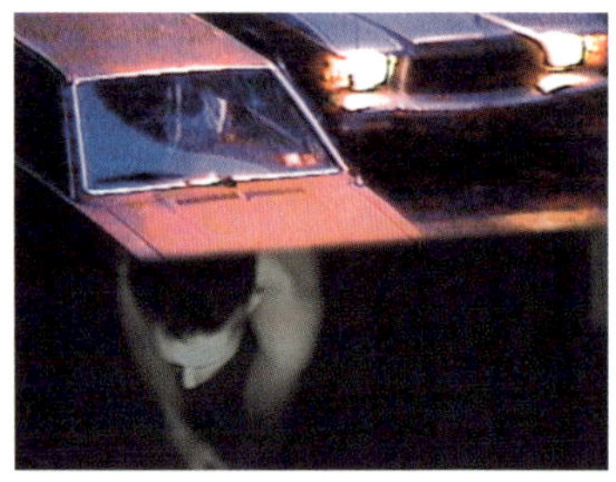
07:22

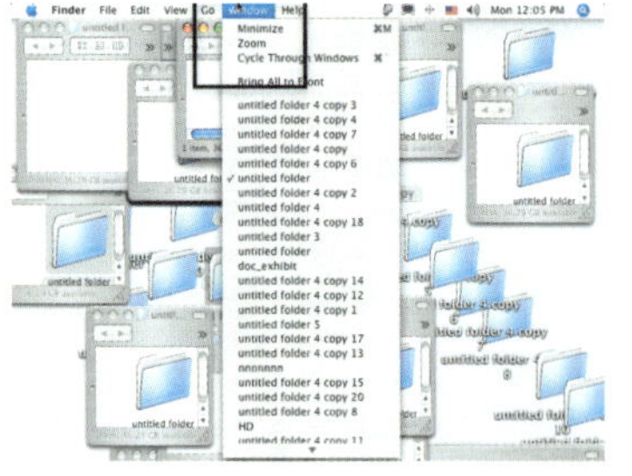
00:57

08:28

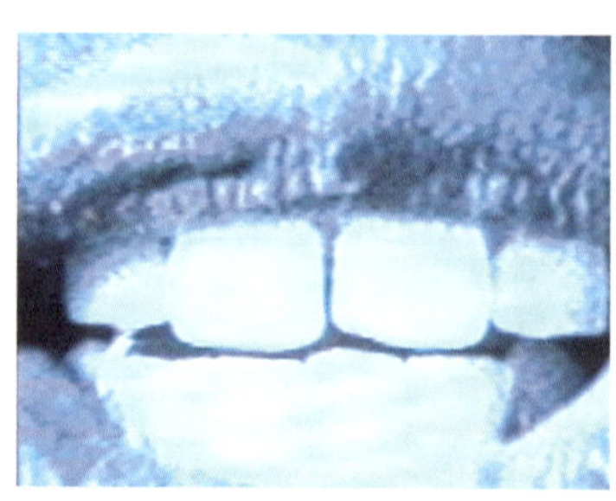
00:12

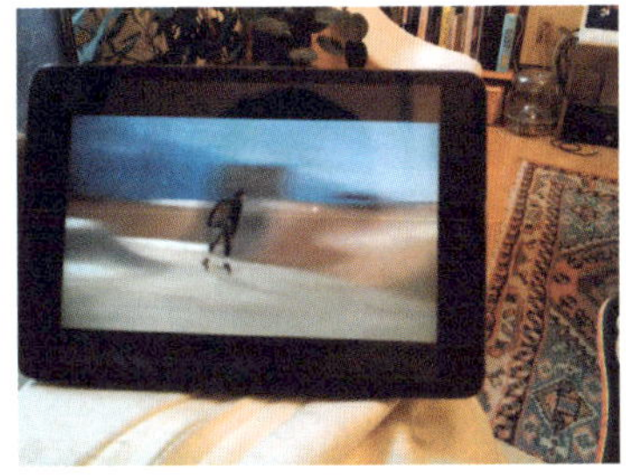
03:58

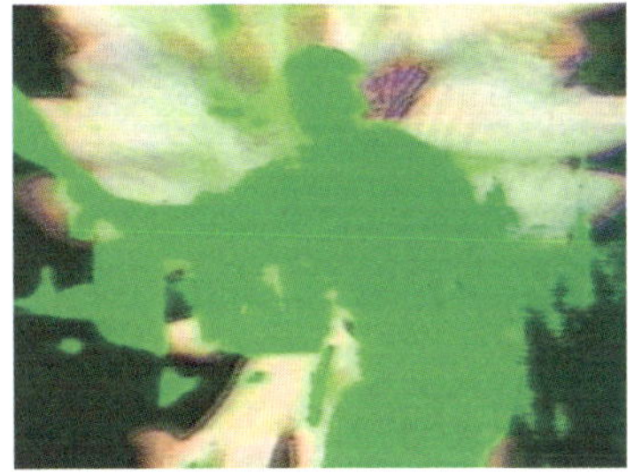
14:29

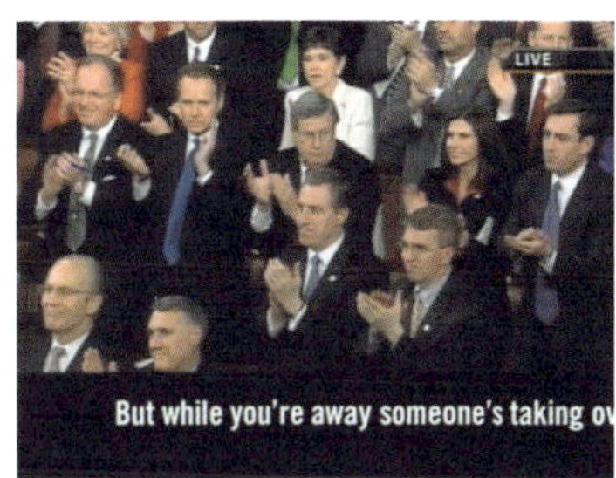

04:31

Bettina Funcke and Wade Guyton, who were both working for Dia.

AK – Had he just graduated from school?

LZ – Yes, he had, from Brown University. Tony Cokes, who had been one of Seth's professors, recommended him for the job. They ended up collaborating later. Seth was a technical coordinator for a short time, then Bob [Beck/Buck] left, and he became technical director.

AK – That's another instance of a nice connection taking place between artists in the context of EAI. It's important to incorporate those kinds of moments in institutional histories—it demonstrates that these things are not discrete or accidental, and that everything's relational.

LZ – Everything's connected.

RC – So, we're talking about the late nineties, Seth is taking over as technical director. I remember when I started in August 2000, Bob's primary role was as image coordinator and designer.

LZ – Oh, of course. He was EAI's designer then.

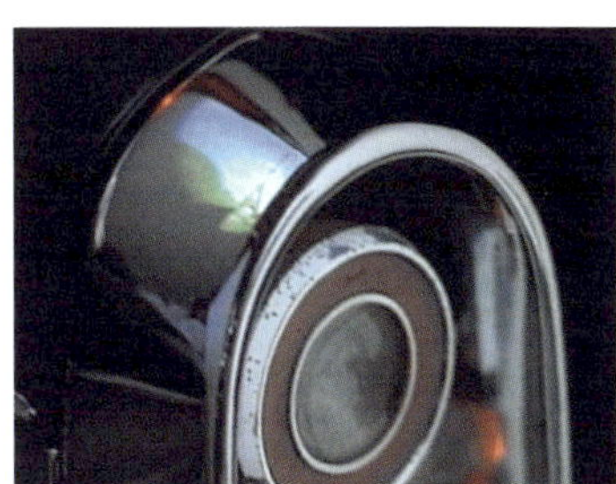
00:18

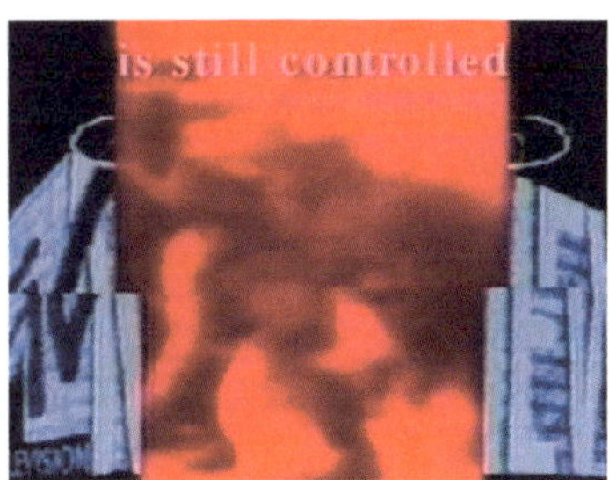

00:35

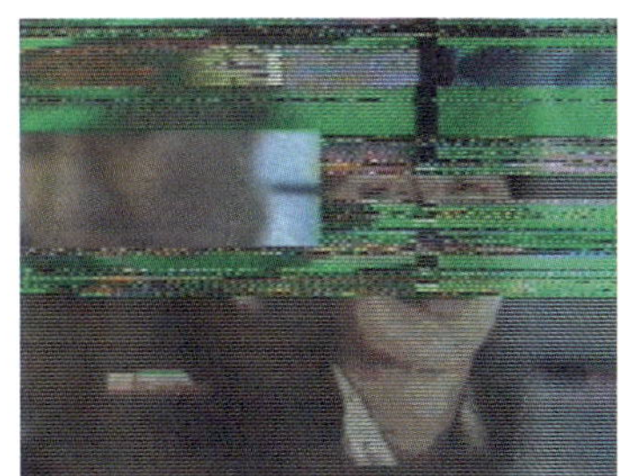
21:12

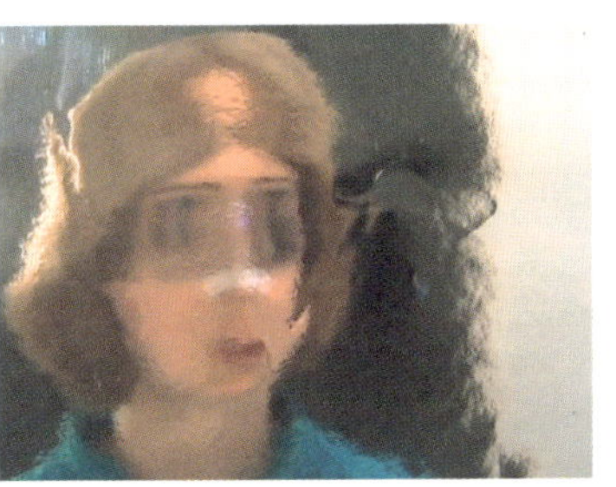
01:24

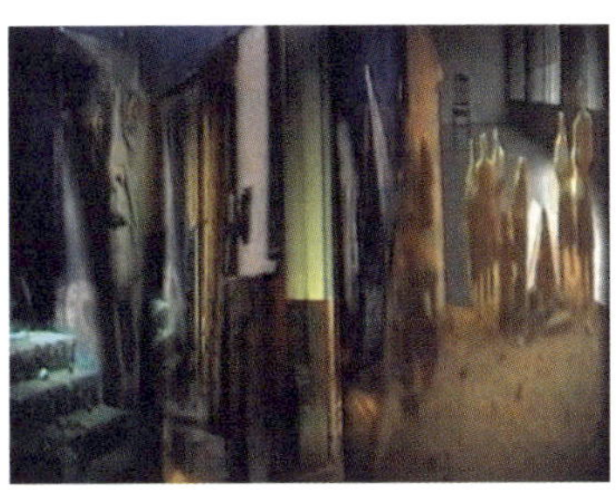
00:21

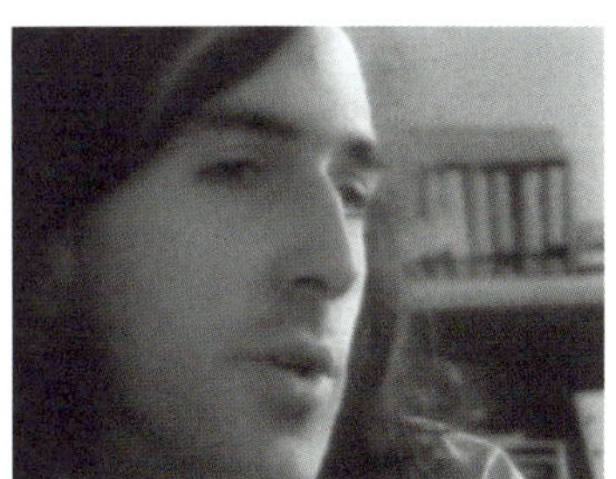
04:24

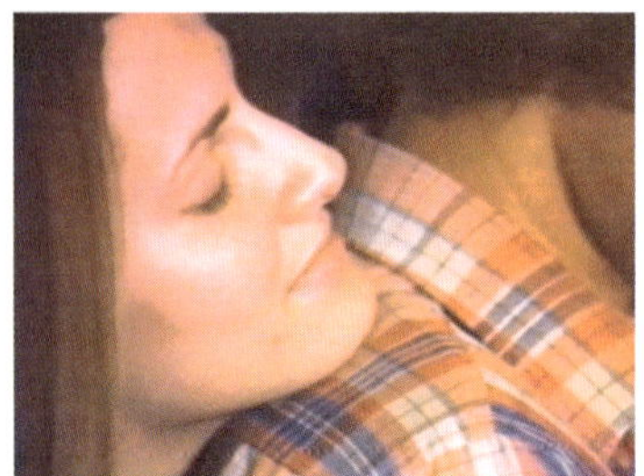
01:26

01:46

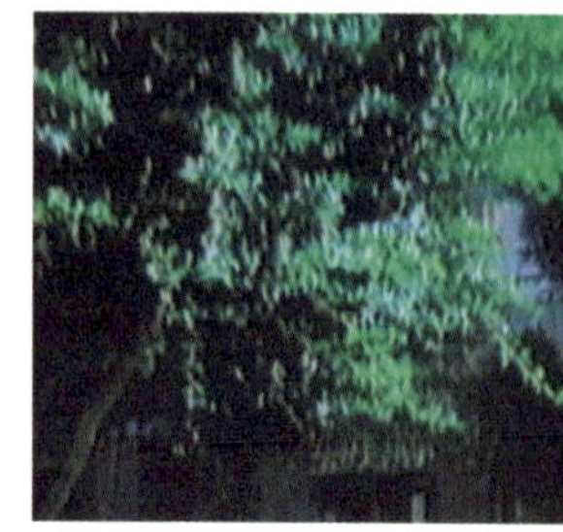
06:01

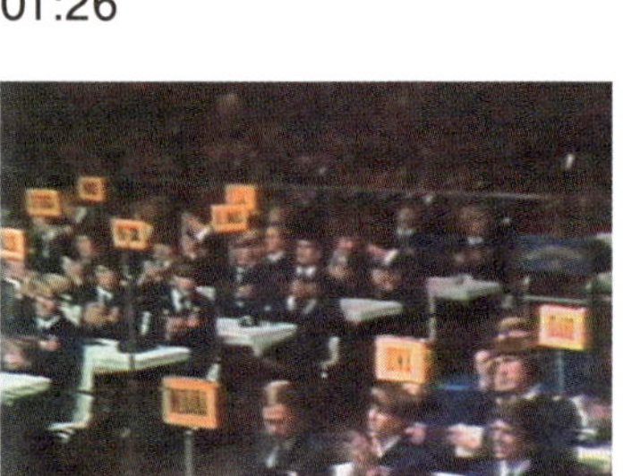
14:10

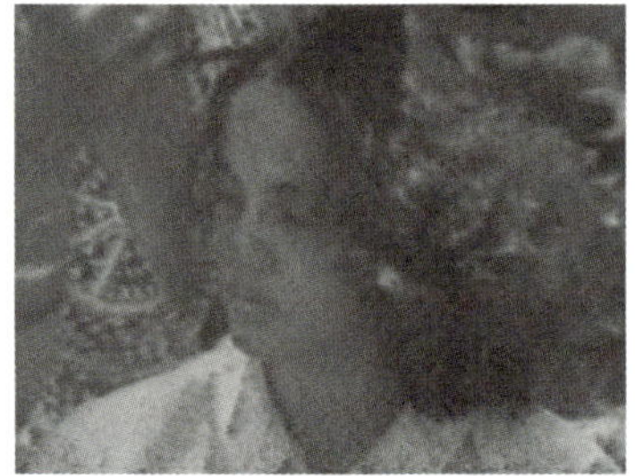
17:34

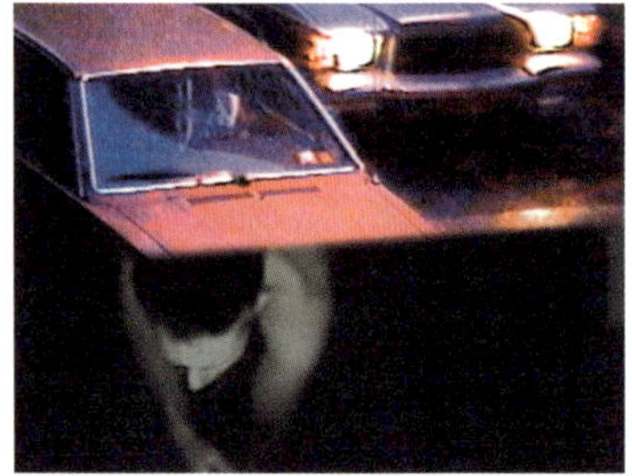
07:22

RC – Because of his brilliant photographic eye and attention to detail. I remember those office spaces very well—they were very intimate. There was this closet-like space that was converted into a viewing room that had a gigantic wall-sized poster of Howard Wise. And I remember Karen Kelly and Barbara Schroeder, now Dancing Foxes Press, sat across the way from the editing facility. Bettina was there too. The editing facility, tape library, and packing area was where all the cool kids hung out.

LZ – Because it was apart from the offices—it was in a separate space down the hall near the freight elevator.

AK – Oh interesting. And you were in that space until what year?

LZ – 2002. Then Dia undertook a major renovation project on the building across the street, at 535 West 22nd Street, and we went with them. They built out the space we occupy now.

AK – Did you consult with them about what you needed?

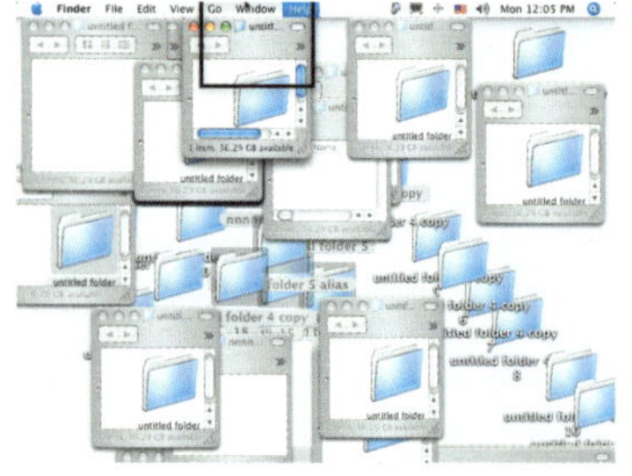
00:57

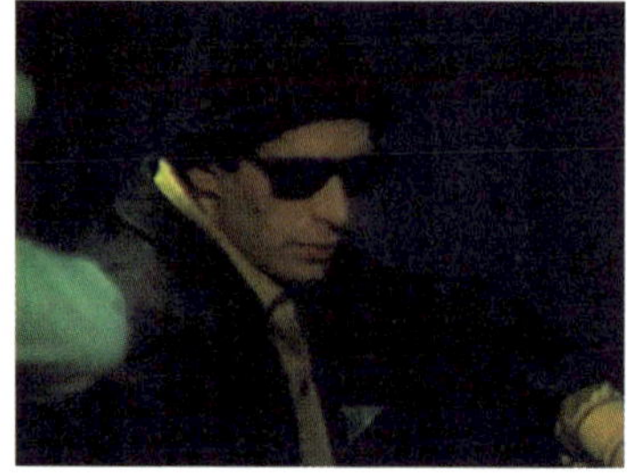
08:28

00:12

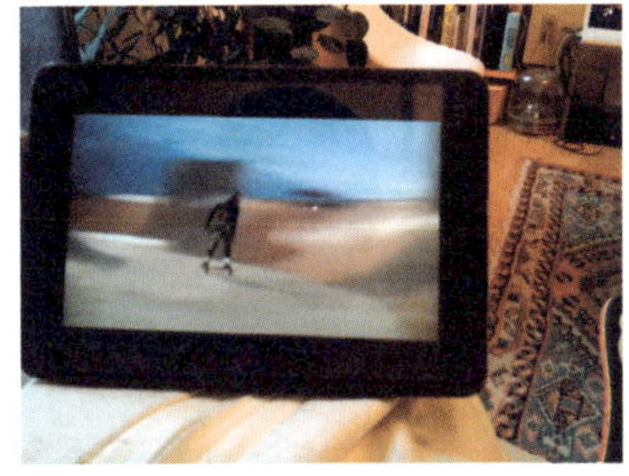

03:58

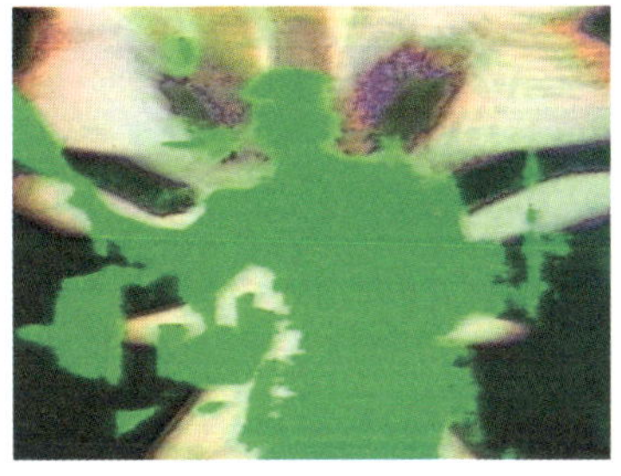

14:29

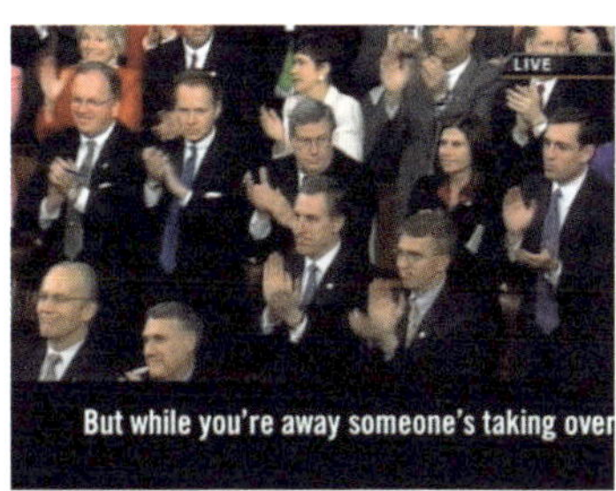

04:31

LZ – Absolutely. The interior architect designed the spaces with our input.

AK – Do you still lease from Dia?

LZ – Yes, and it has been and remains an incredibly significant and positive relationship for EAI. We're still doing collaborative programming. One of the highlights of our collaborations with Dia was the survey exhibition *Circa 1971: Film and Video from the EAI Archive*, which was installed at Dia:Beacon on the occasion of EAI's fortieth anniversary in 2011–2012. The show featured nineteen artists' video works created in and around the year of EAI's founding. It was thrilling to see activist works by collectives like Videofreex, conceptual works by artists like Lynda Benglis and Nancy Holt, technical experiments by the Vasulkas, and the politically engaged performances of Anthony Ramos—which had been newly preserved—in dialogue not only with one another, but also with works from the same period in Dia's collection.

AK – Rebecca, what was your pathway within EAI?

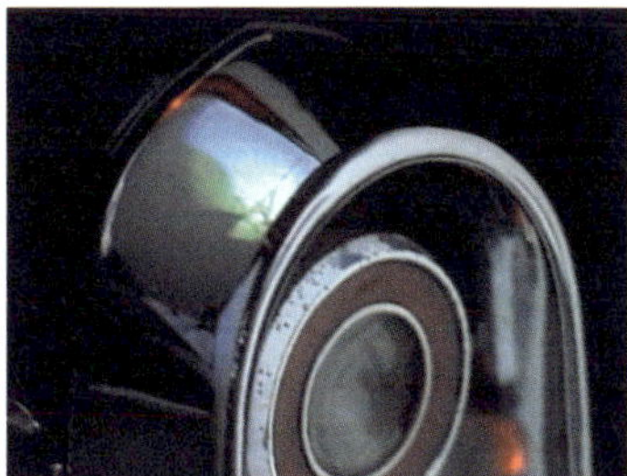

00:18

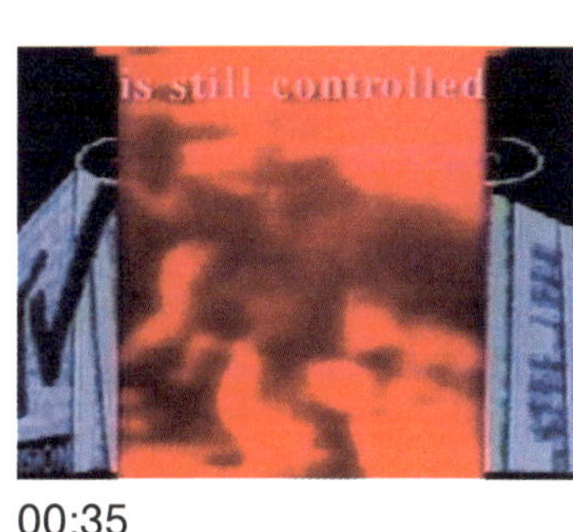

00:35

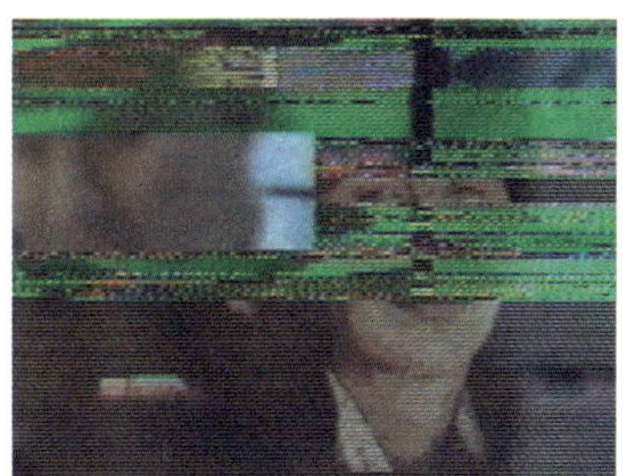

21:12

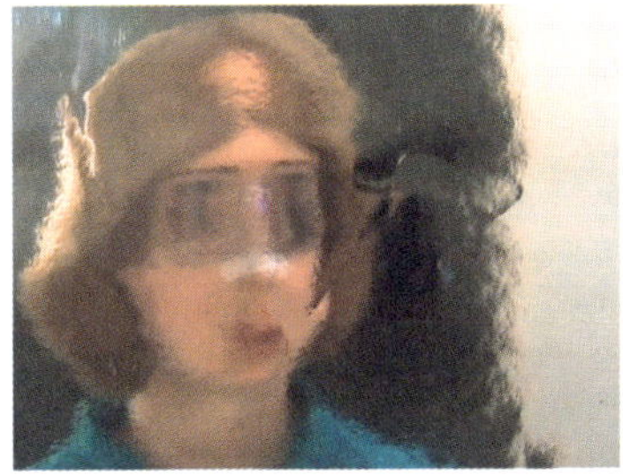

01:24

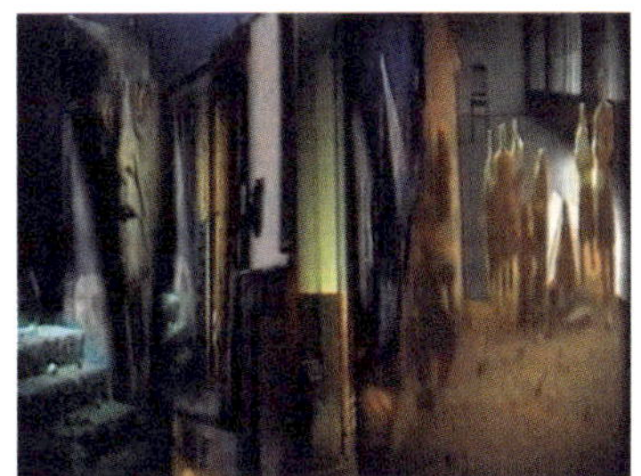

00:21

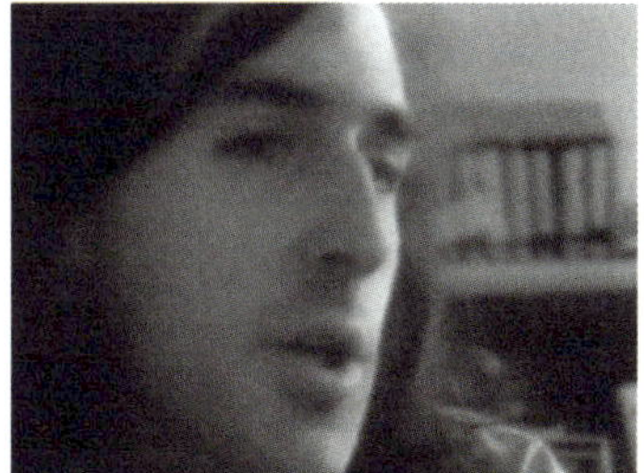

04:24

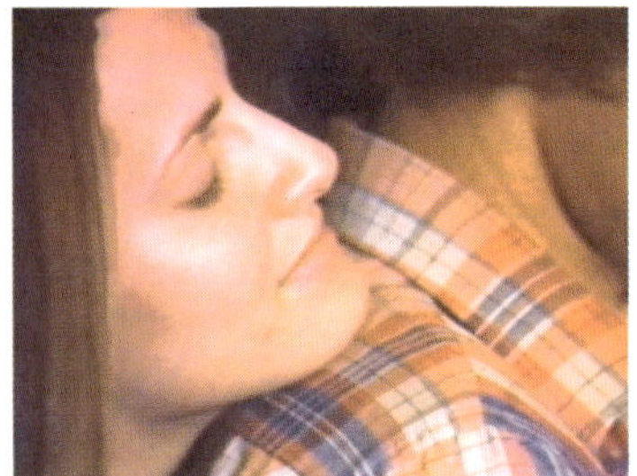
01:26

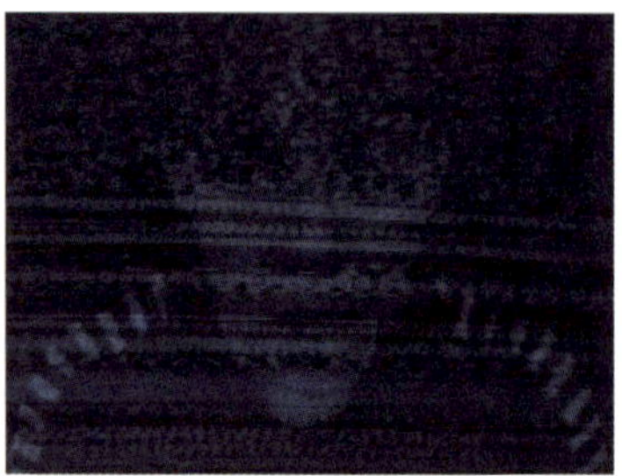
01:46

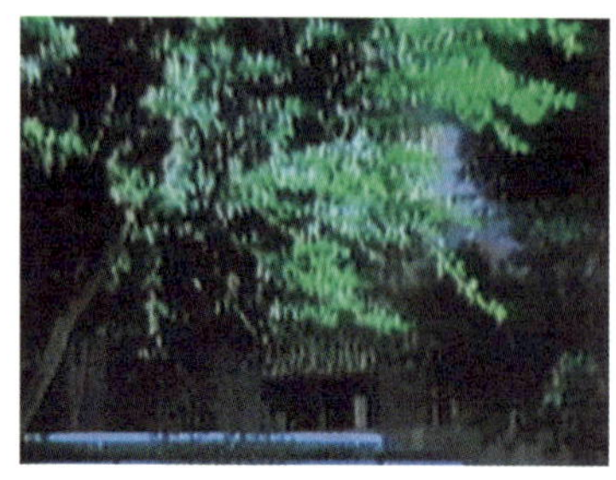
06:01

RC – All through distribution—distribution assistant, distribution coordinator, and then distribution director and now, with Lori's departure this year, executive director. I guess I climbed up the distribution tree.

AK – Has that changed a lot over the years? I'm assuming that your entry point mirrors that time when the internet was becoming more of a presence and I would imagine that has really affected the way that people understand what the catalog is and the way that work is distributed. Not to mention the bootlegs that started appearing online, UbuWeb, etc.

LZ – All of that developed since the time you've been here. You started in the early internet days. You arrived around the same time as John Thomson, who was the director of distribution through the 2000s and now runs the New York gallery Foxy Production.

RC – When I started we were still receiving orders via fax. We were just starting to use email heavily, but computer access felt like a luxury. There were still a lot of phone calls

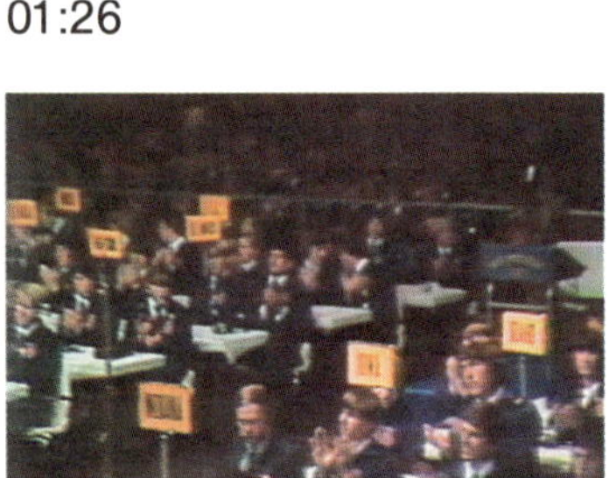
14:10

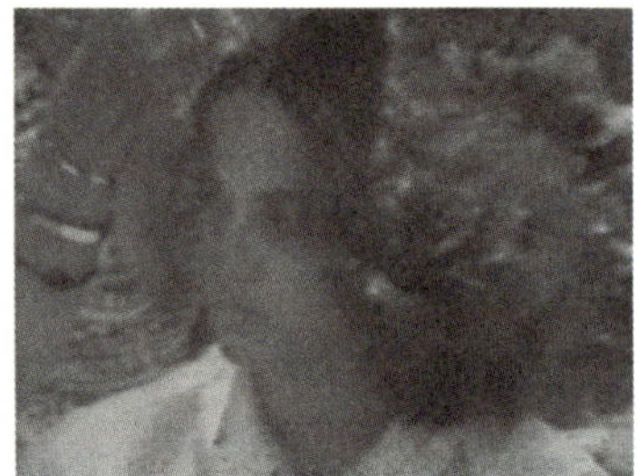
17:34

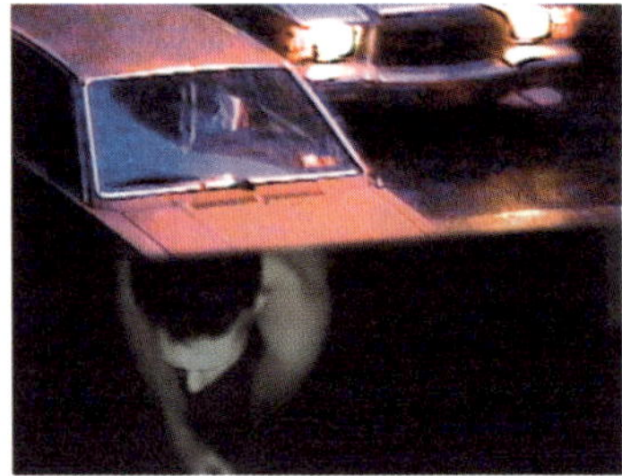
07:22

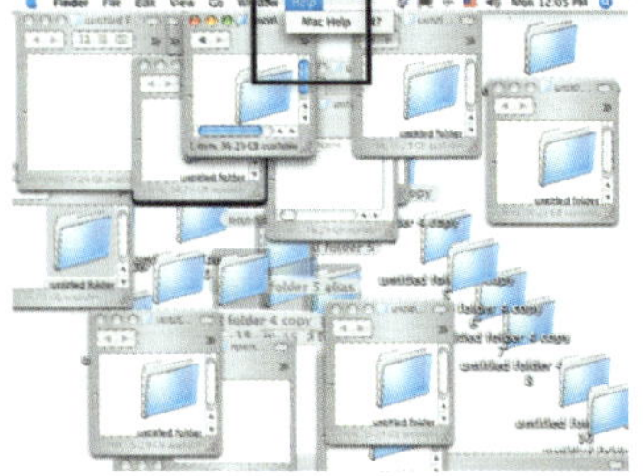
00:57

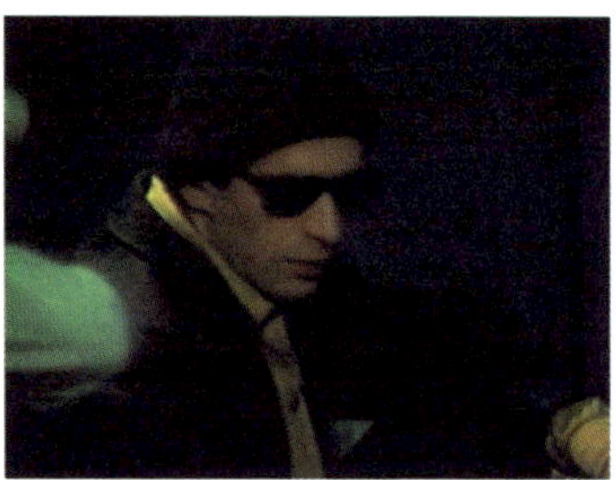
08:28

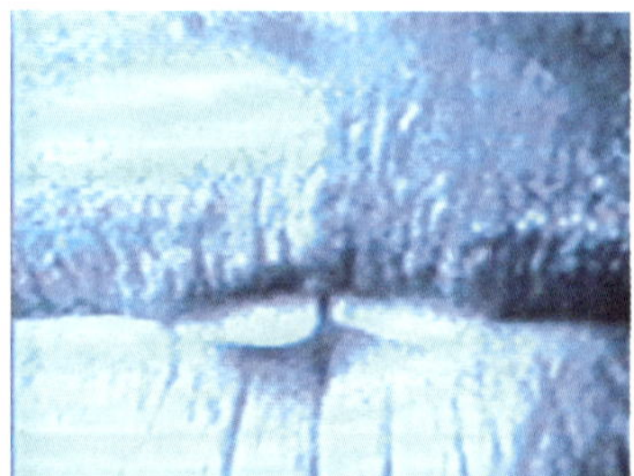
00:12

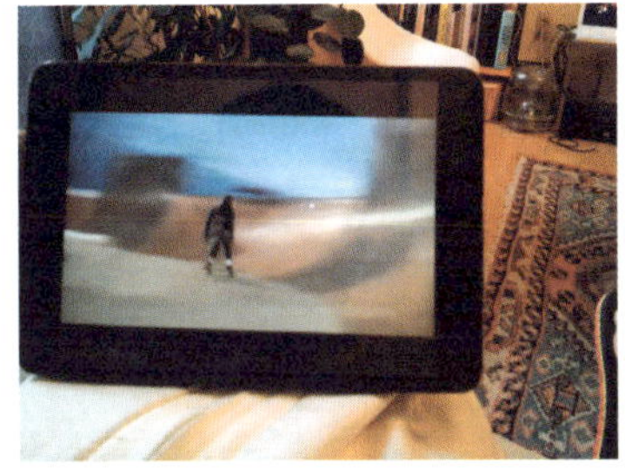
03:58

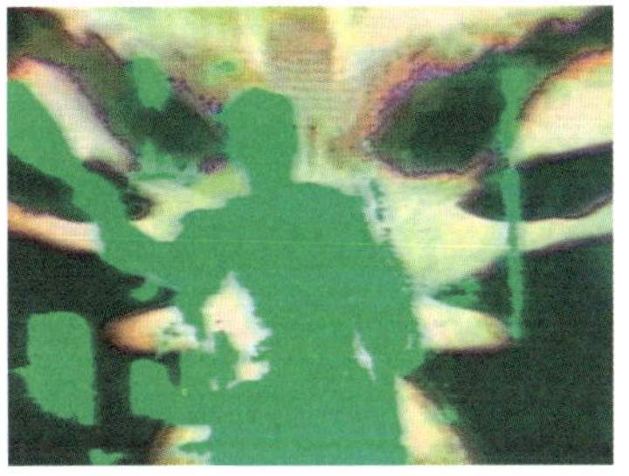
14:29

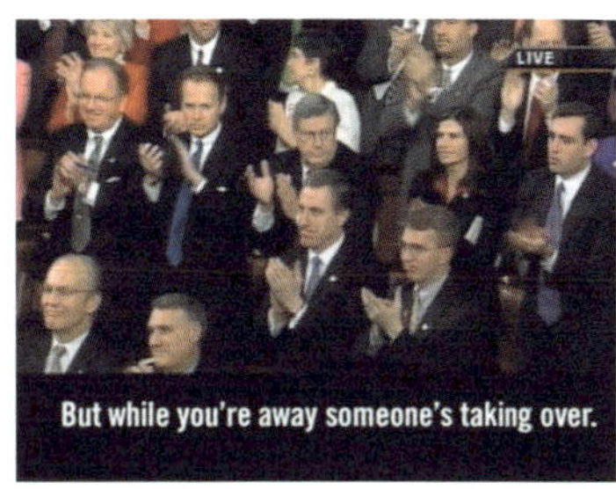

04:31

and mailed correspondence. A typewriter was prominently featured in our work area. We had heavy traffic coming in to use our on-site viewing room, and of course the closet with the giant poster of Howard.

AK – I assume there aren't as many people coming through now because everyone can just go online? It really changes the relationship—in 2001 there was a major shift in technology as well as a shift in New York. There was a pre-9/11 New York and a post-9/11 New York, and that also affected real estate.

LZ – Yes.

RC – I think zoning laws changed in the aftermath of September 11. Mayor Michael Bloomberg wanted to open this area up to development, and that's why we're seeing all of the luxury high-rises springing up now.

LZ – And there's the High Line.

RC – And the High Line!

AK – Is there a moment in your day-to-day work that you remember thinking about the complications of the internet where all of a sudden

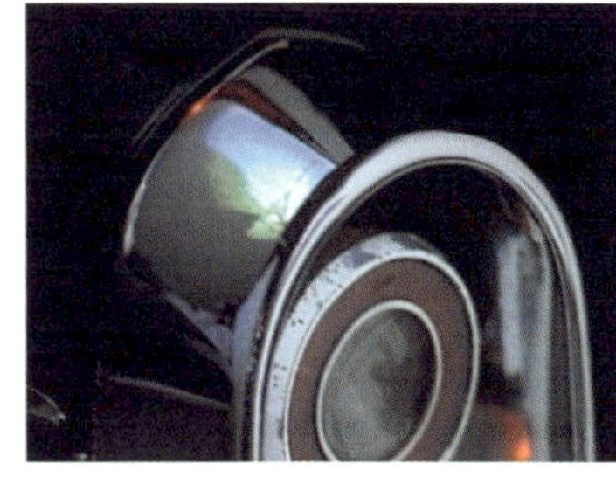
00:18

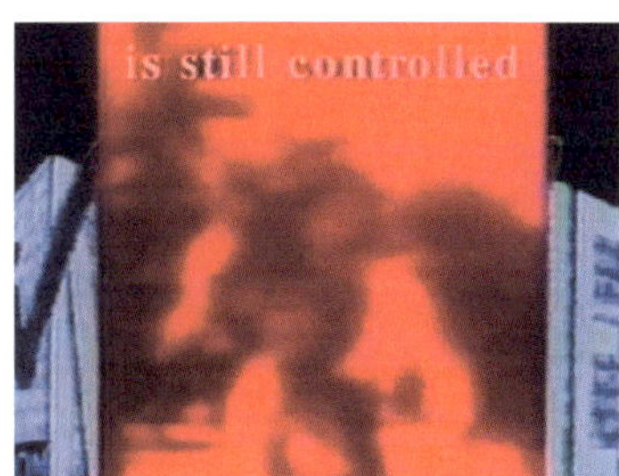

00:35

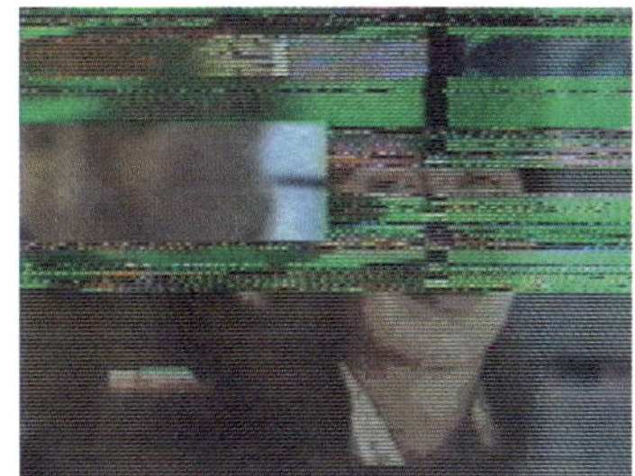
21:12

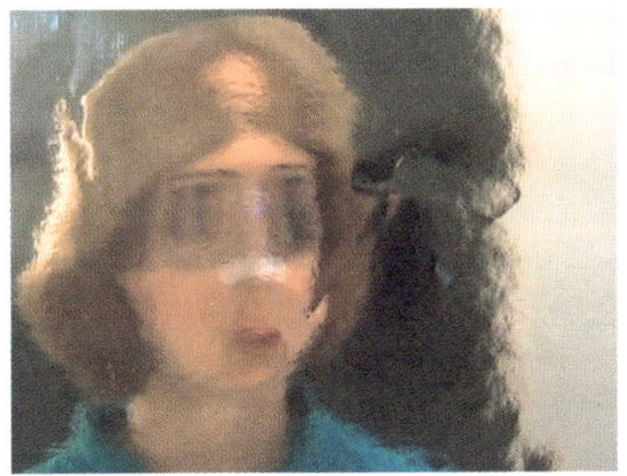
01:24

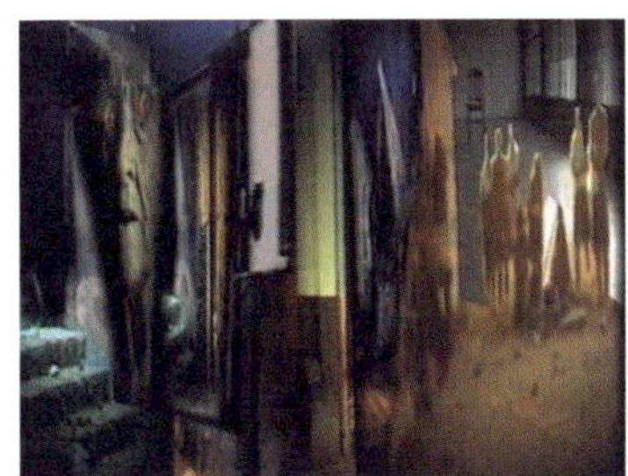
00:21

04:24

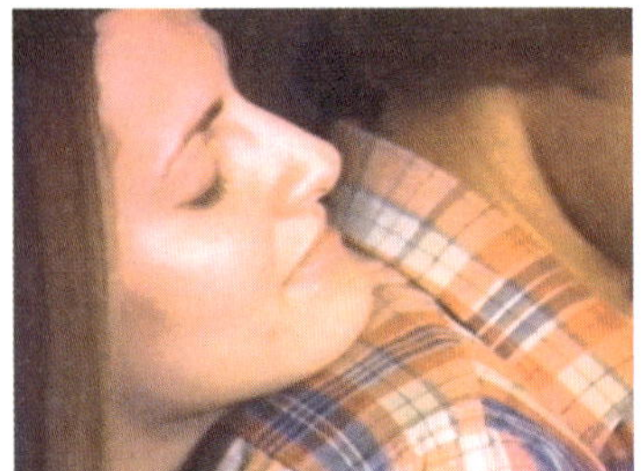
01:26

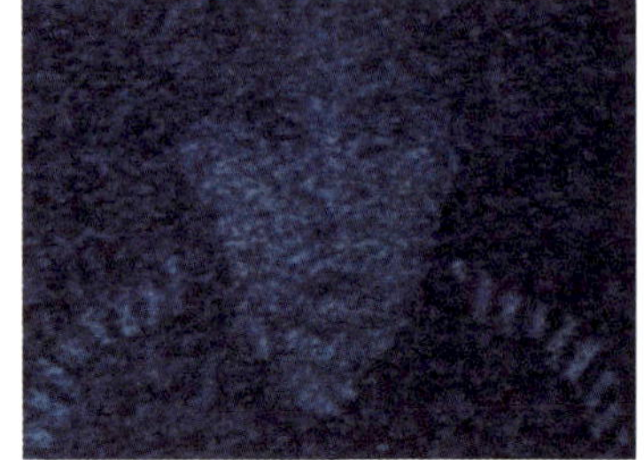
01:46

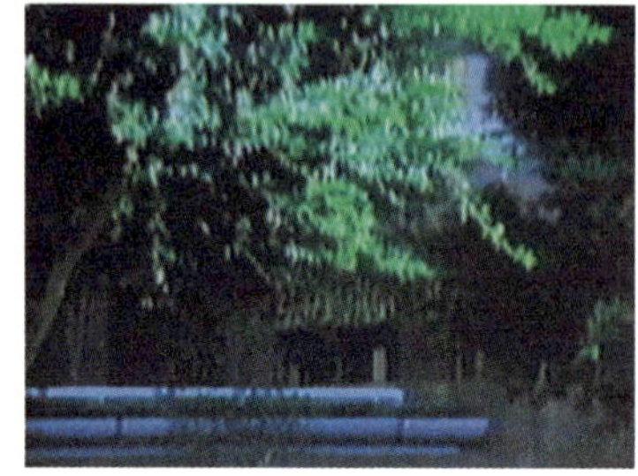
06:01

something changed, like, “Hey, we have to contend with this,” or the first time one of your works ended up bootlegged online and you thought, “Wait a second, I have to think about what this means because we want people to have access, but it’s not going through our channels?” Because it’s different from say a bootleg VHS that someone has in their personal collection. We all have our little stashes off the record, but it’s different when it goes online and it’s actively circulating and with varying degrees of quality.

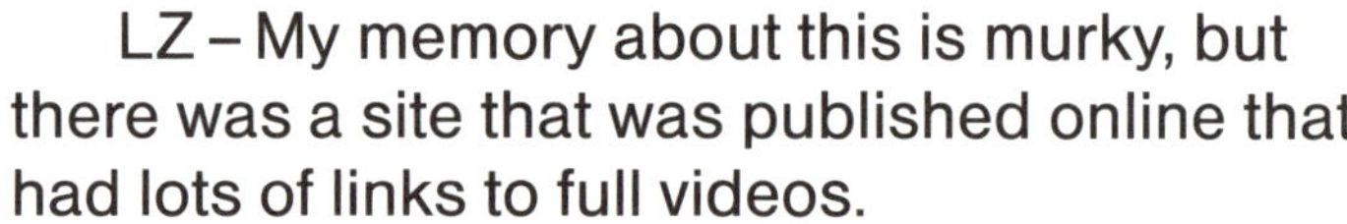
LZ – My memory about this is murky, but there was a site that was published online that had lots of links to full videos.

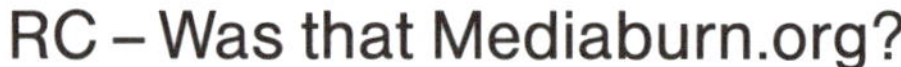
RC – Was that Mediaburn.org?

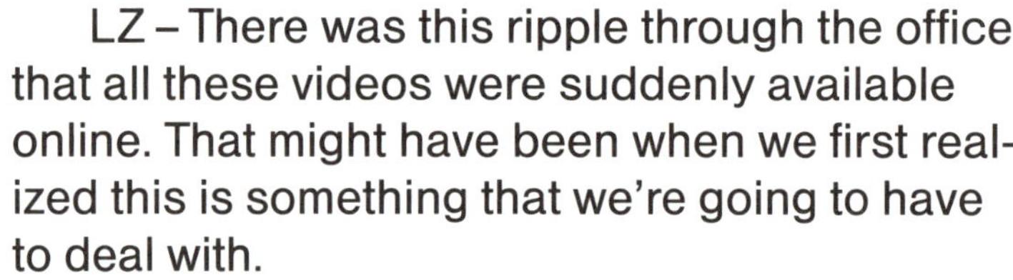
LZ – There was this ripple through the office that all these videos were suddenly available online. That might have been when we first realized this is something that we’re going to have to deal with.

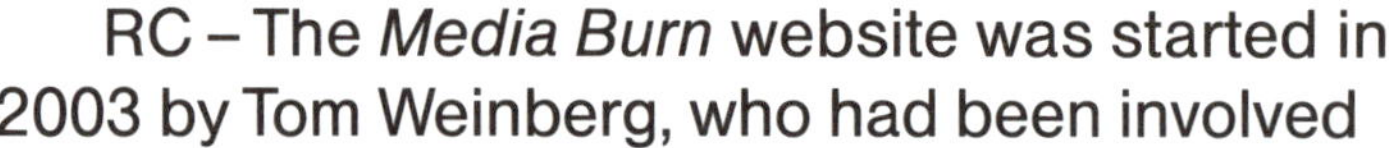
RC – The *Media Burn* website was started in 2003 by Tom Weinberg, who had been involved

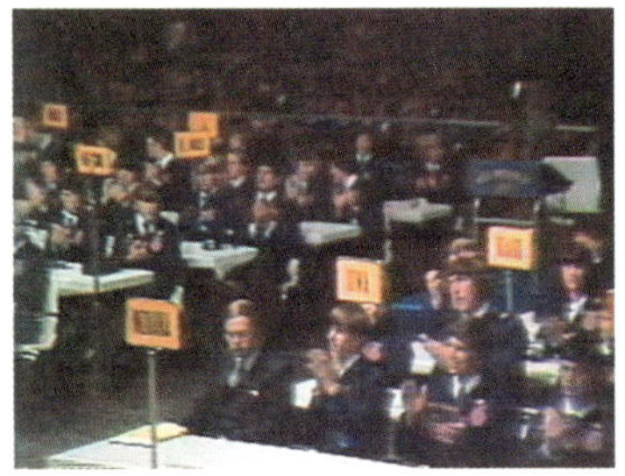
14:10

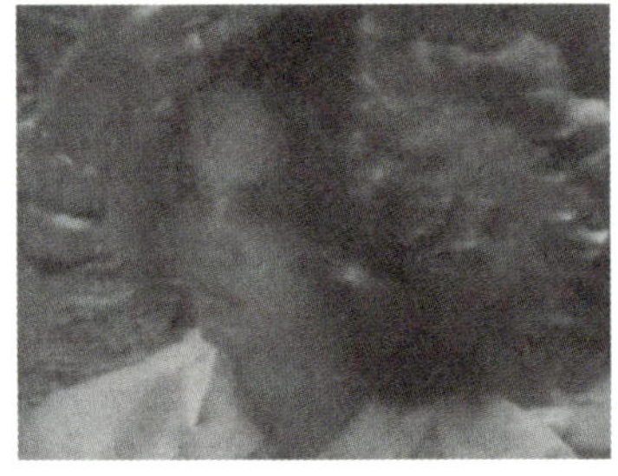
17:34

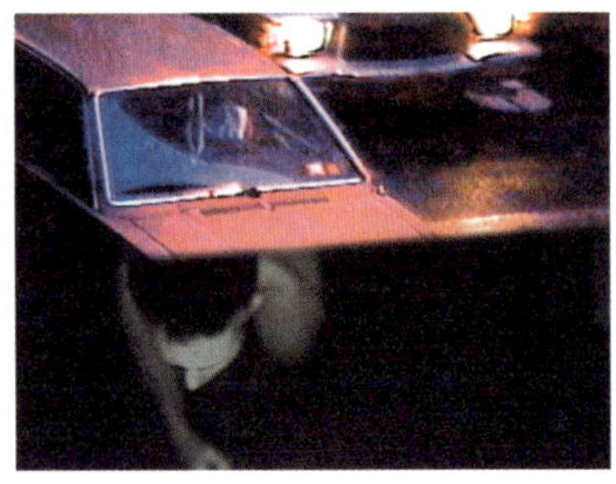
07:22

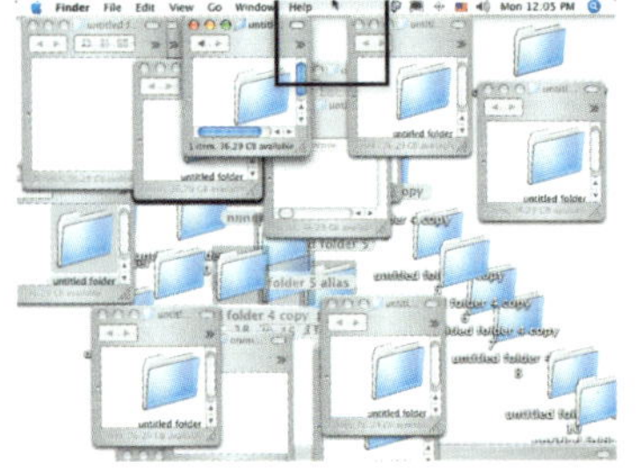
00:57

08:28

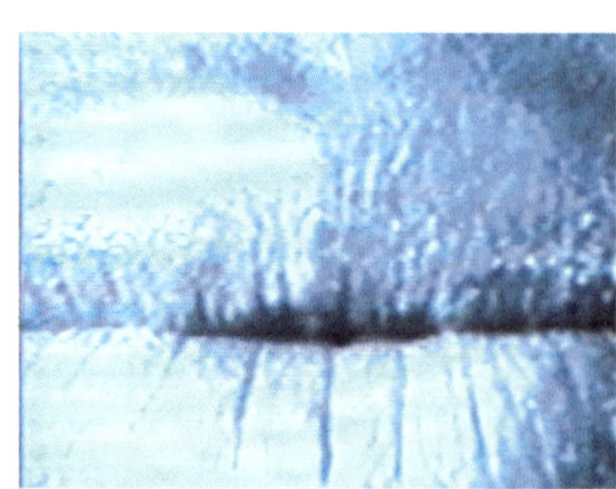
00:12

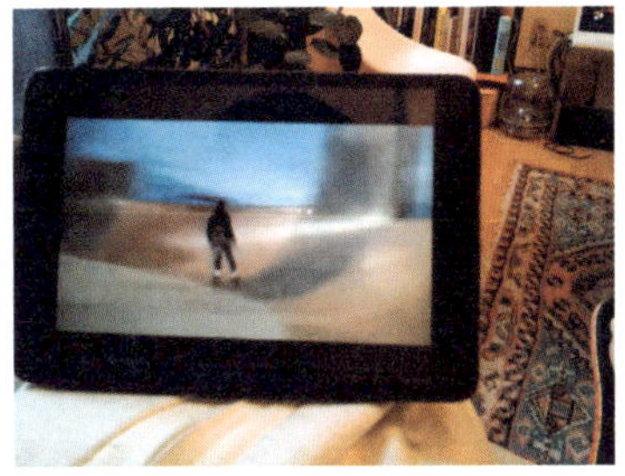
03:58

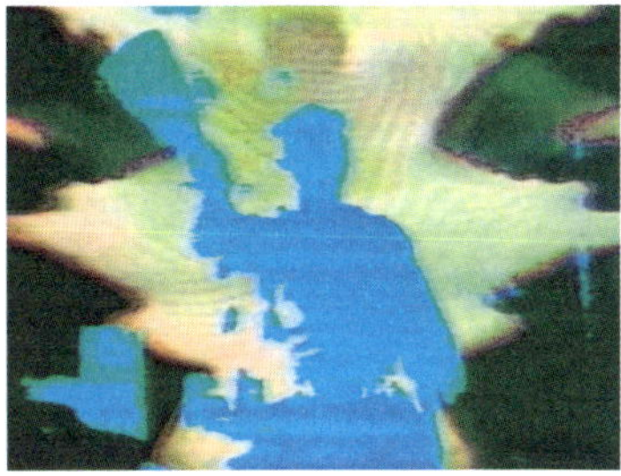
14:29

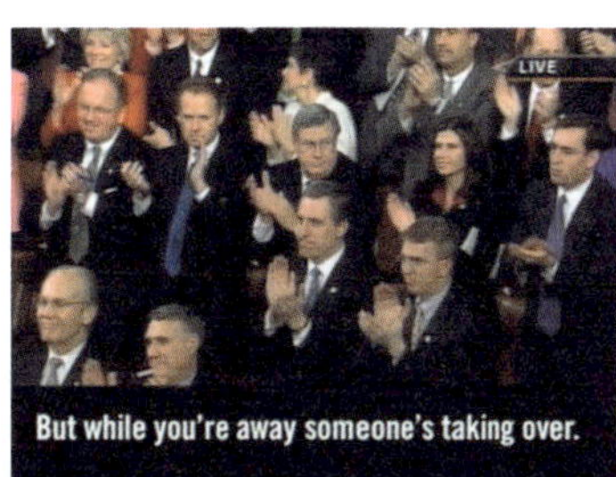

04:31

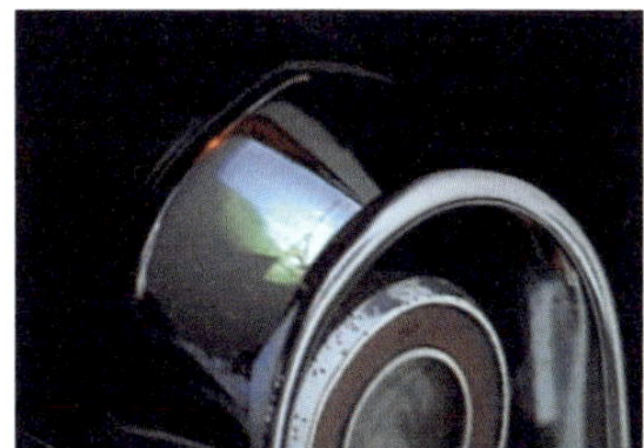
00:18

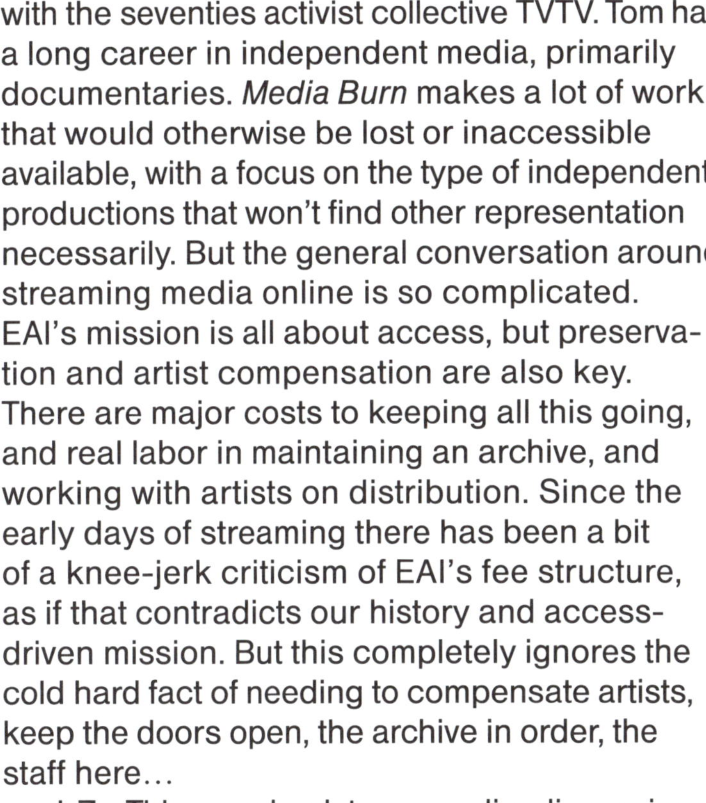
with the seventies activist collective TVTV. Tom has a long career in independent media, primarily documentaries. *Media Burn* makes a lot of work that would otherwise be lost or inaccessible available, with a focus on the type of independent productions that won't find other representation necessarily. But the general conversation around streaming media online is so complicated. EAI's mission is all about access, but preservation and artist compensation are also key. There are major costs to keeping all this going, and real labor in maintaining an archive, and working with artists on distribution. Since the early days of streaming there has been a bit of a knee-jerk criticism of EAI's fee structure, as if that contradicts our history and access-driven mission. But this completely ignores the cold hard fact of needing to compensate artists, keep the doors open, the archive in order, the staff here…

LZ – This goes back to our earlier discussion about some of these major shifts that were happening, when the art market embraced the

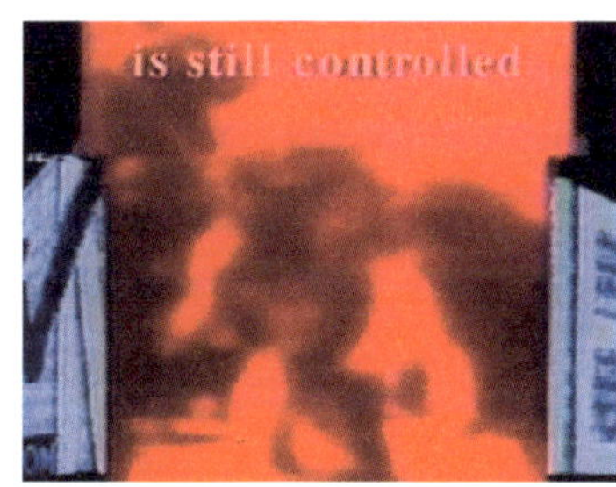

00:35

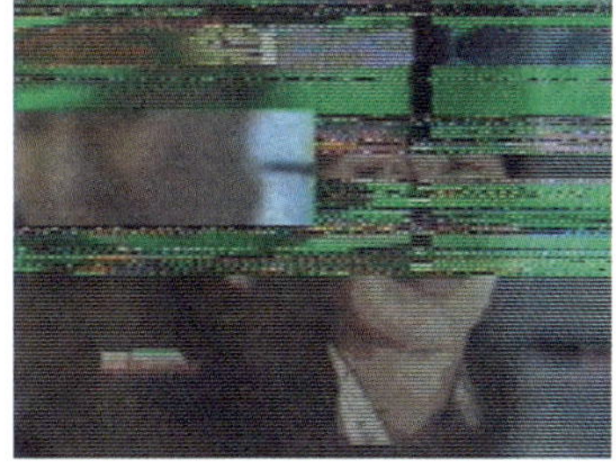
21:12

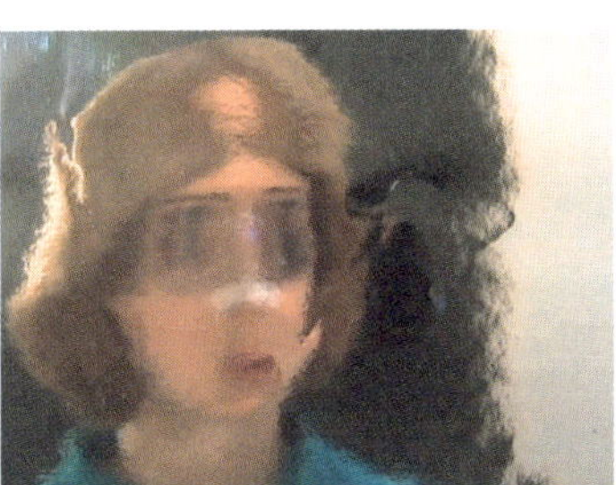
01:24

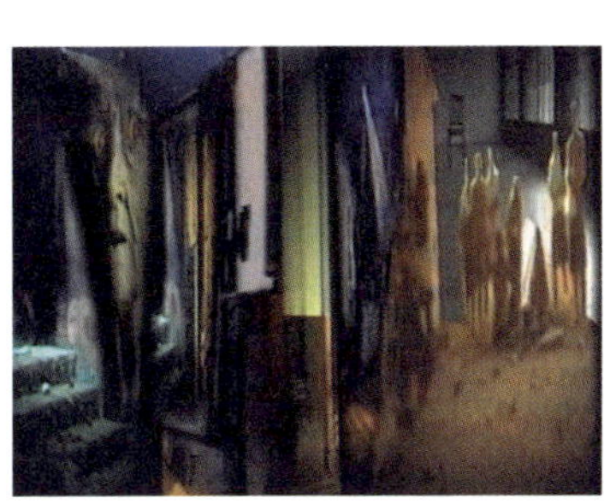
00:21

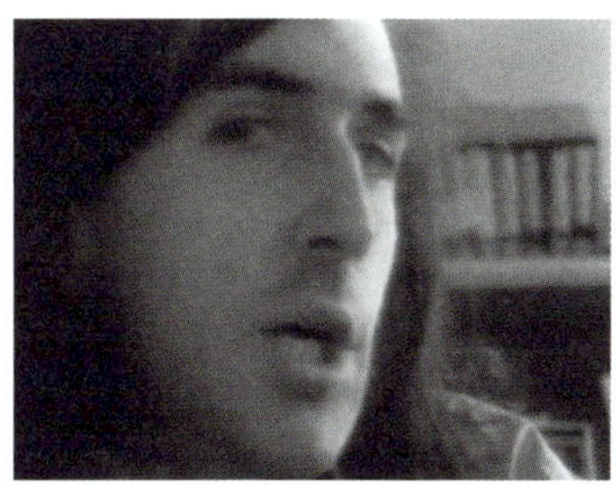
04:24

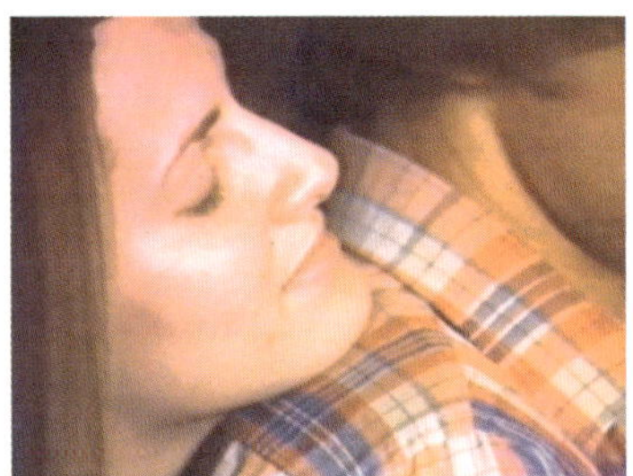
01:26

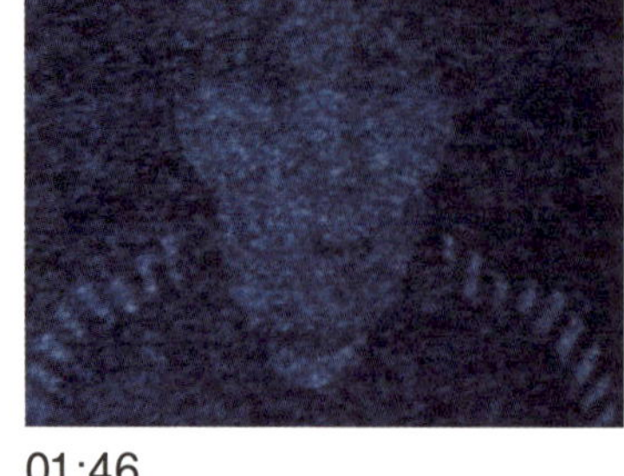
01:46

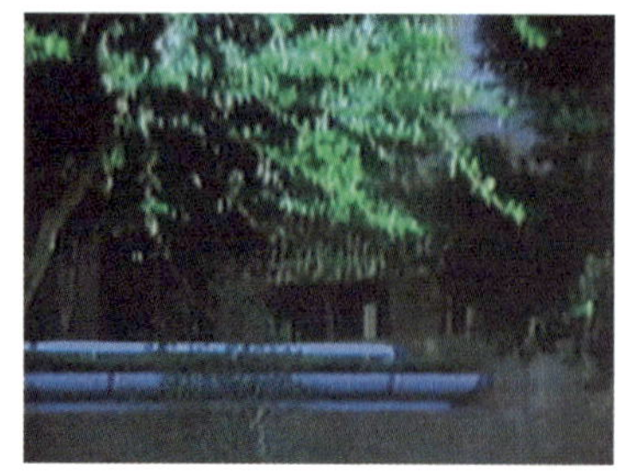
06:01

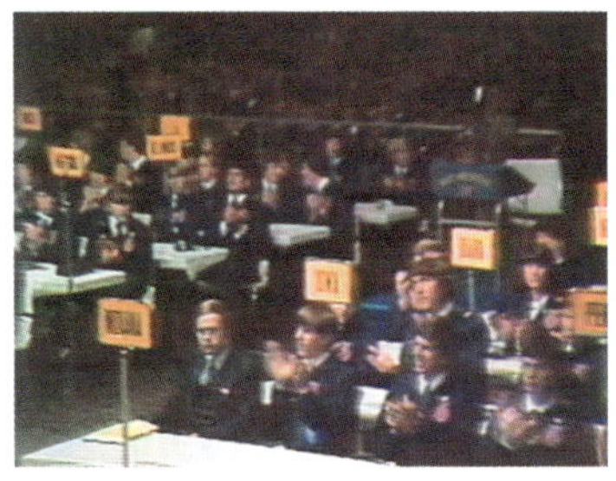
14:10

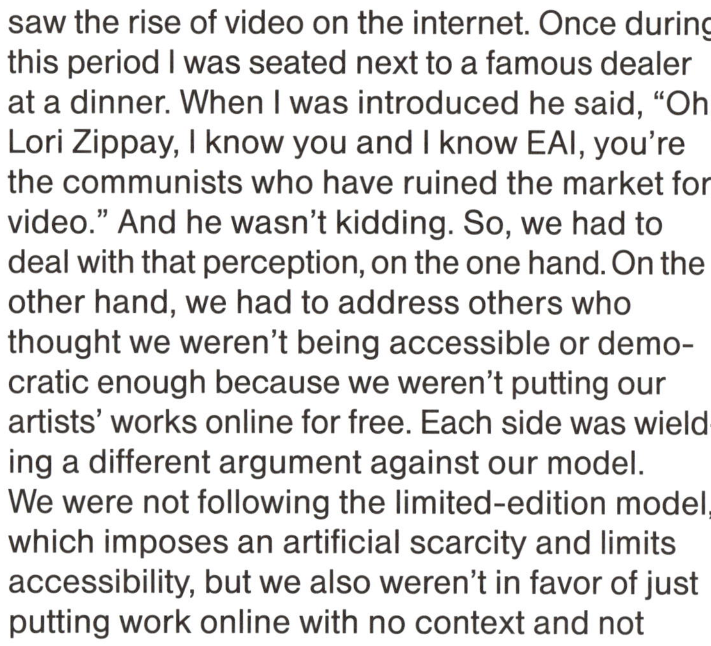
limited-edition model at the same time that we saw the rise of video on the internet. Once during this period I was seated next to a famous dealer at a dinner. When I was introduced he said, “Oh, Lori Zippay, I know you and I know EAI, you’re the communists who have ruined the market for video.” And he wasn’t kidding. So, we had to deal with that perception, on the one hand. On the other hand, we had to address others who thought we weren’t being accessible or democratic enough because we weren’t putting our artists’ works online for free. Each side was wielding a different argument against our model. We were not following the limited-edition model, which imposes an artificial scarcity and limits accessibility, but we also weren’t in favor of just putting work online with no context and not paying the artists.

Now the reality is that all of these models—the limited edition, online streaming, and nonprofit distribution—are co-existing and we have found our place in it. And I think the gallerists now understand what we do to support

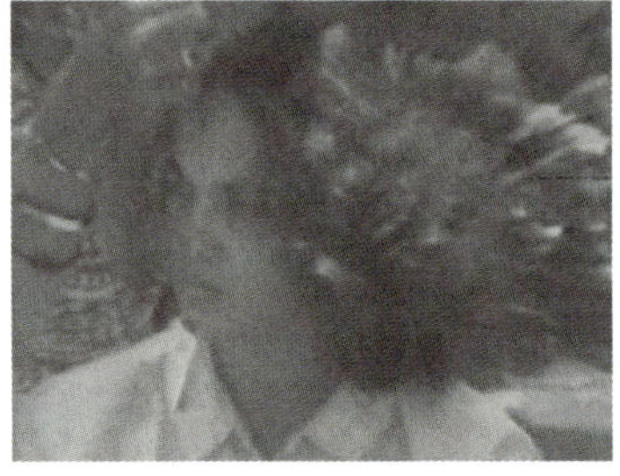
17:34

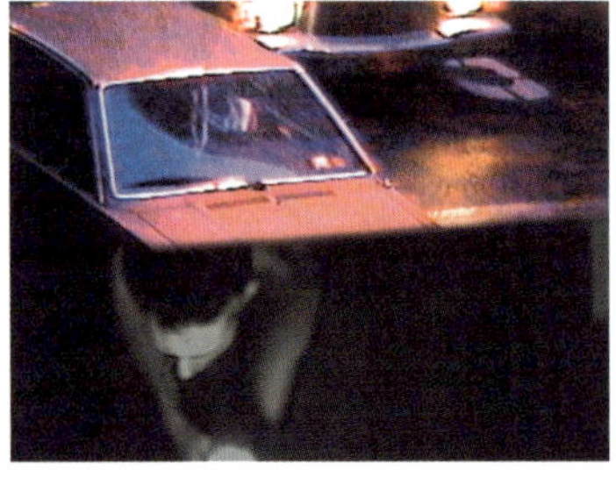
07:22

00:57

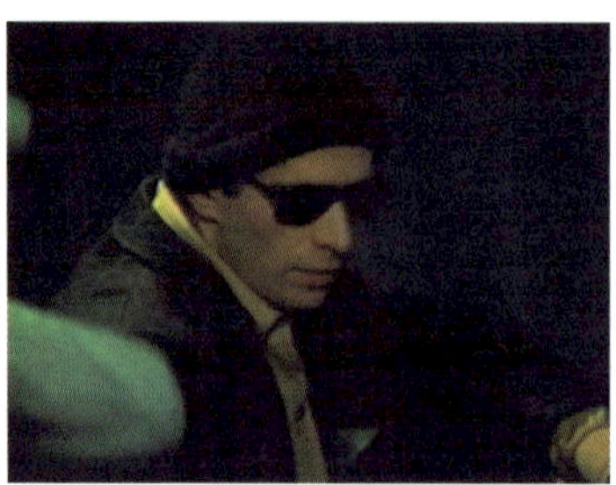
08:28

00:12

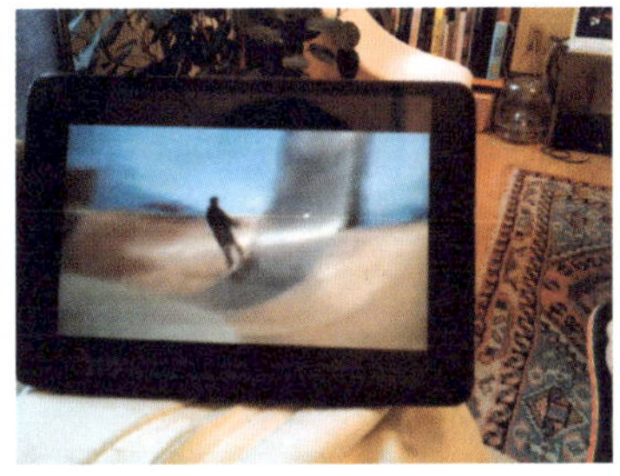
03:58

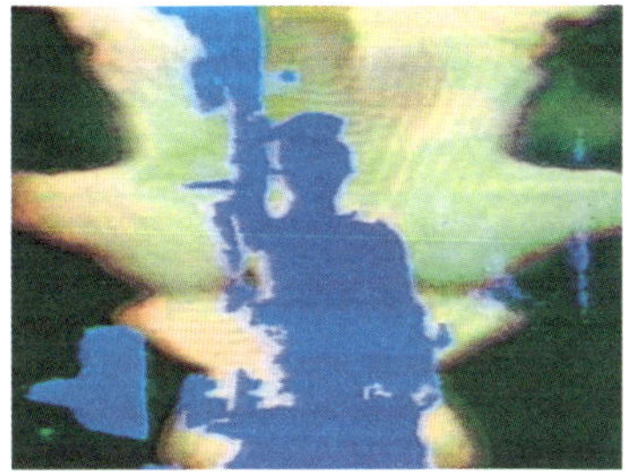
14:29

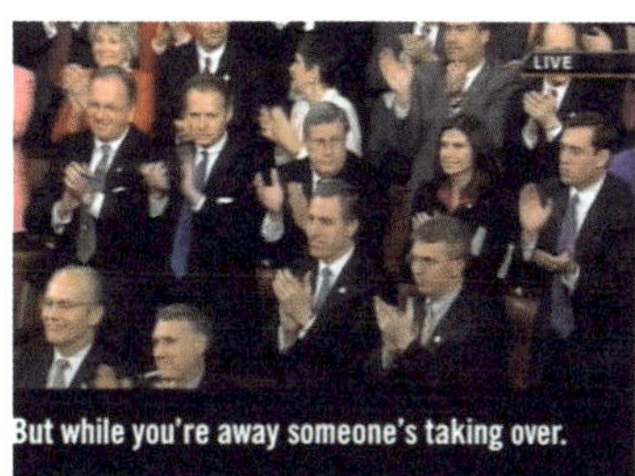

04:31

the artists and preserve their works, which also supports the galleries' efforts. And we've developed a successful model for streaming artists' works that gives it an art historical context and allows the artists to be paid. But there was definitely a volatile moment around these issues.

AK – It still feels volatile to me.

RC – I think it is volatile in a different way.

AK – When did you start streaming work online? Was this in the early 2000s?

LZ – No, that was later. There was yet another pivotal moment. You know, we've mentioned how real estate defines so many of the transitions at a nonprofit organization like EAI, but the pivotal grants do as well. In 2007–2008 NYSCA gave us a major grant—they had a one-time call for a digitization grant, for digital conversion. And we put in for a grant for the digitization of the collection for access and preservation that had three tiers to it with the idea of three goals for access. One, was an internal, on demand video site, so our viewing room would be controlled by a digital interface. We would no longer

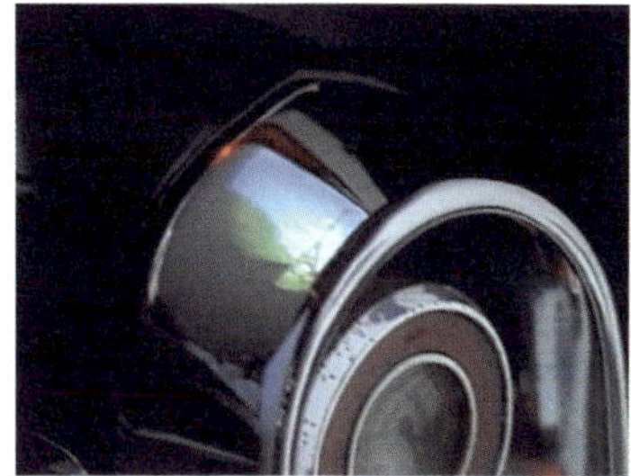
00:18

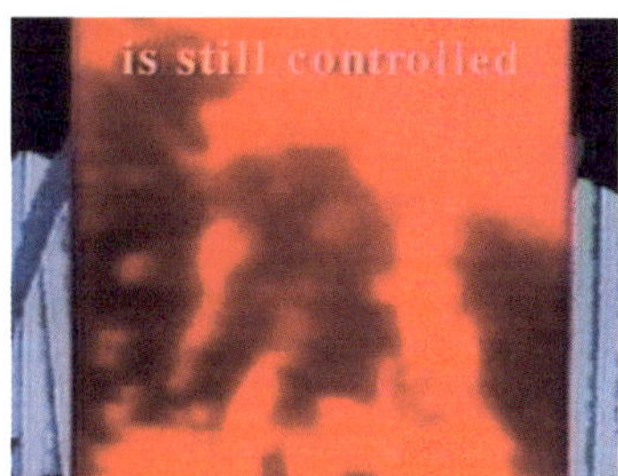

00:35

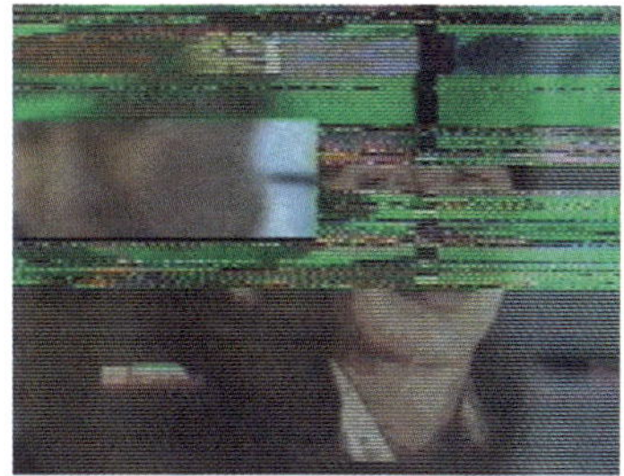
21:12

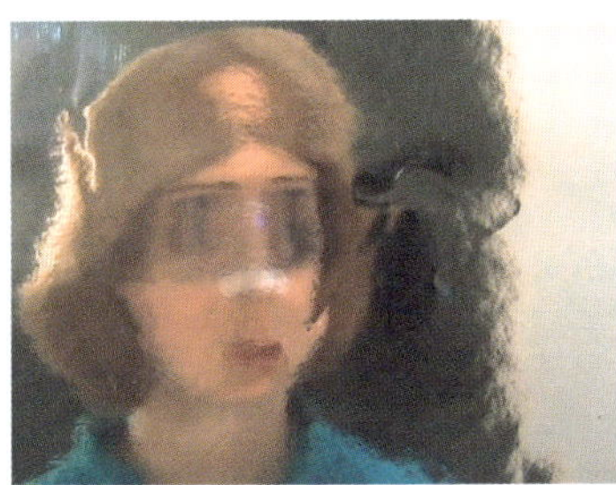
01:24

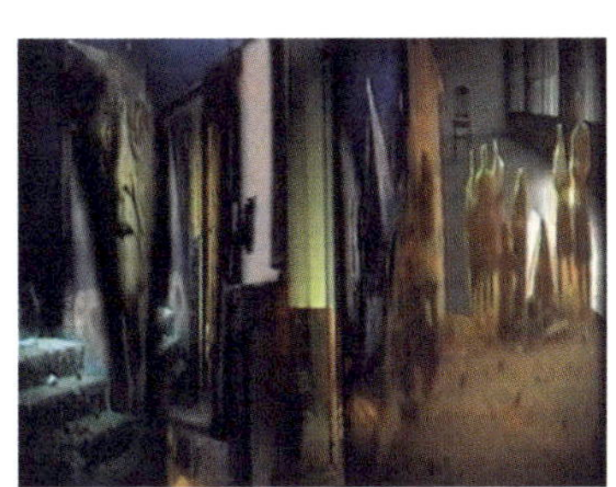
00:21

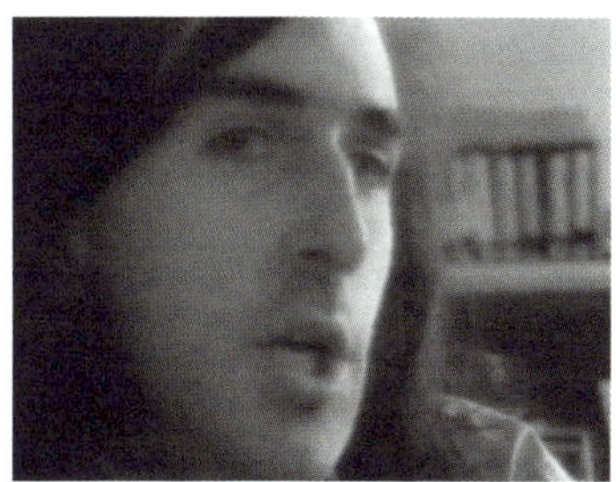
04:24

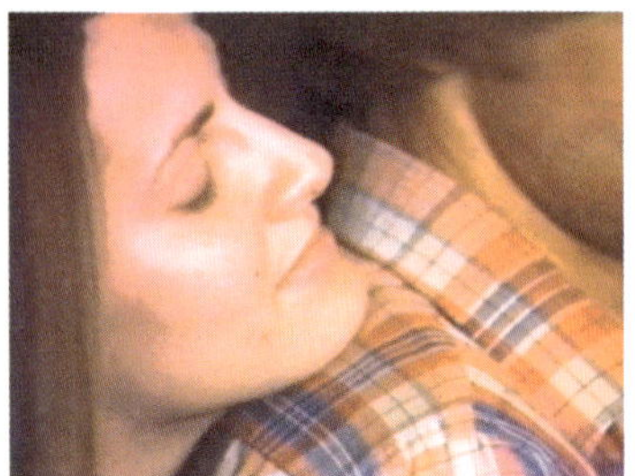

01:25

01:45

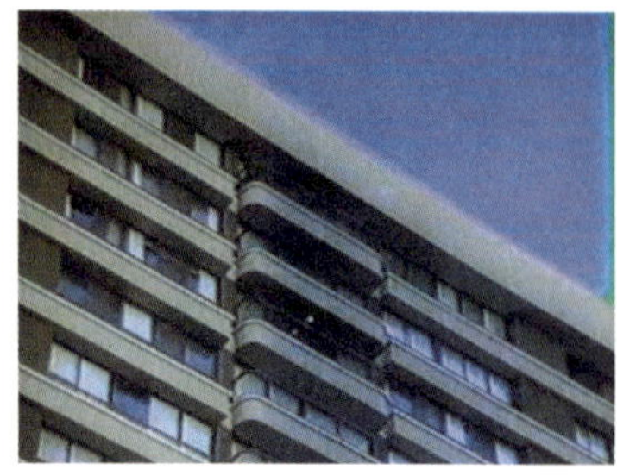

06:00

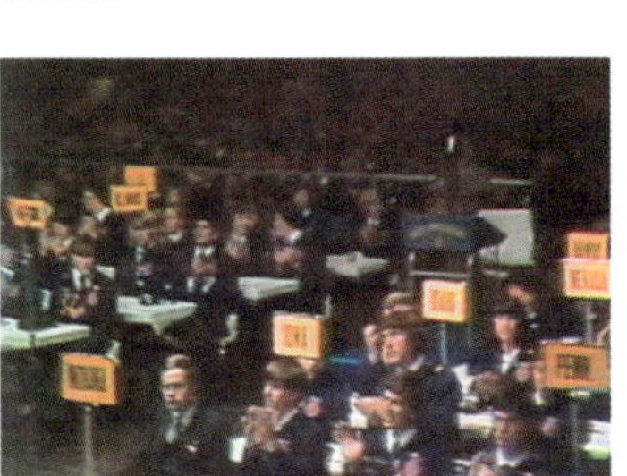

14:09

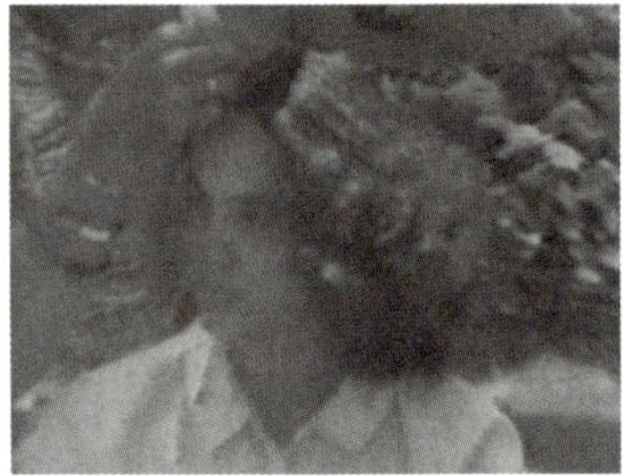

17:33

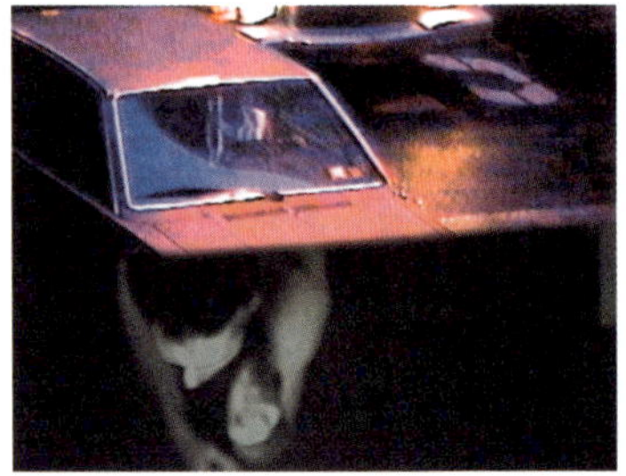

07:21

have to physically carry tapes in and put them into a deck and push Play. The second was an online video viewing site, so people off-site could remotely view works in the collection for research and study. Then the third goal was—down the line—to do an educational streaming platform. So, that one grant essentially started all of our major digitization and streaming initiatives. It was so important for us. Many of the pivotal transitions in our history have been driven by pivotal grants.

AK – And technological changes.

LZ – Exactly…

AK – We briefly touched on this earlier, but it's a challenge with moving image work to keep up with the technology and to continue to migrate it between platforms.

LZ – I always say that the history of the collection is the history of migration. The collection is just migration upon migration upon migration. And it's always changing.

AK – Do you keep the original formats, like the Beta tapes and things like that?

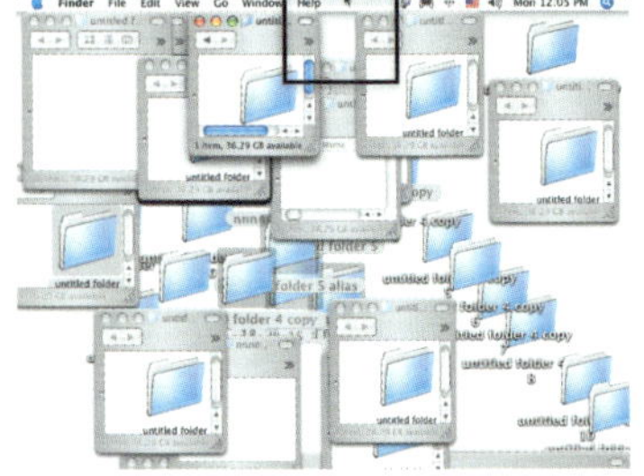

00:56

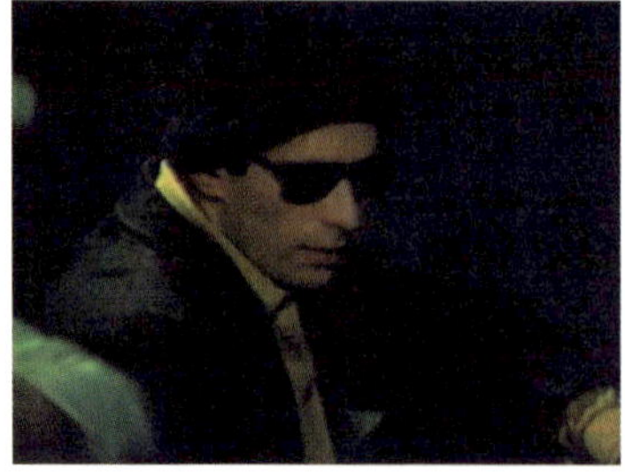

08:27

00:11

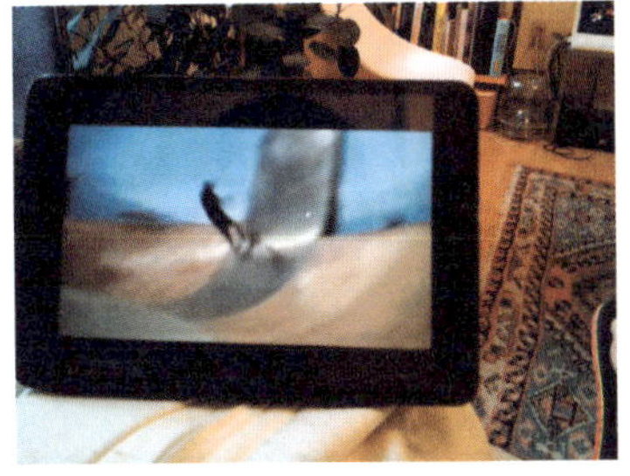
03:58

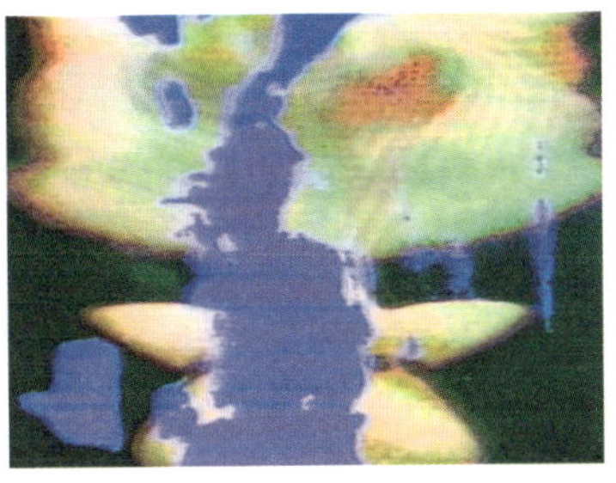
14:29

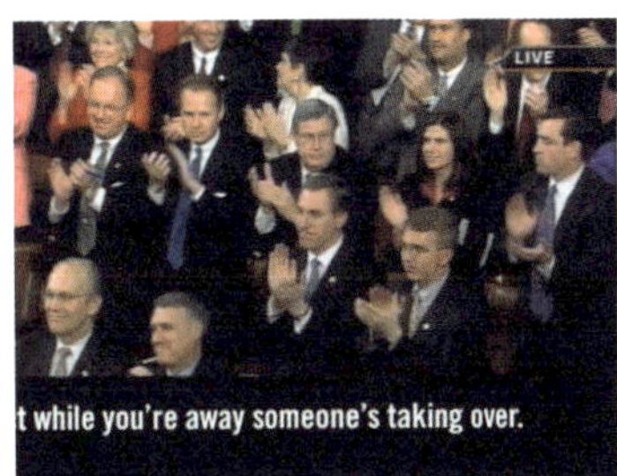

04:31

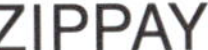

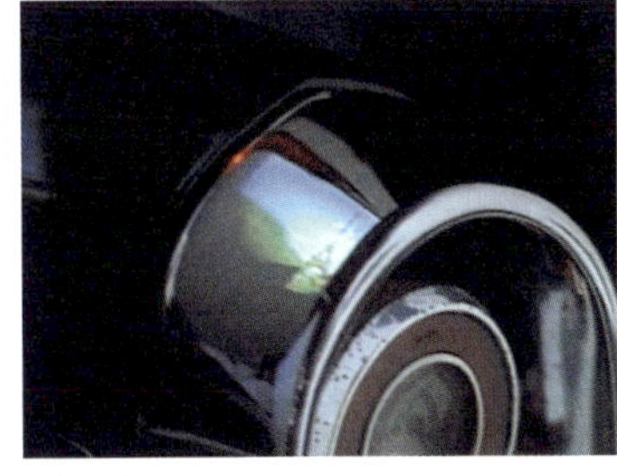
00:18

LZ – Yes, we keep the original formats.

RC – I remember you saying at one point that when somebody asked you how many video formats there were you said you stopped counting at 100.

LZ – I think it was really fifty-six or something.

AK – Really, it's that many?

RC – It's more than anyone would imagine.

LZ – It was like open reels and cassettes in the seventies, then all of the "D's": D1, D2, D3, D4, D5–

RC – Laser discs…

LZ – Laser discs, every kind of 1/2-inch, 1-inch open reel, analog broadcast standards, cartridges–

RC – Remember how S-VHS was really big when I started?

LZ – Oh yeah, it was the archival standard for a moment.

AK – So, you must have a mega server or something to back things up?

LZ – It's a never-ending process. We have redundant physical backups. We have a

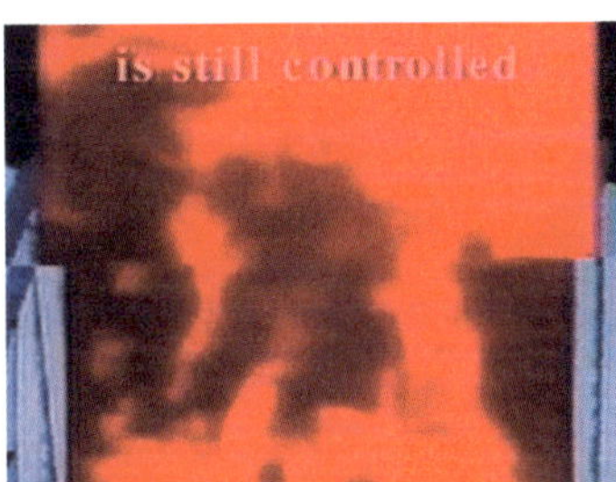

00:35

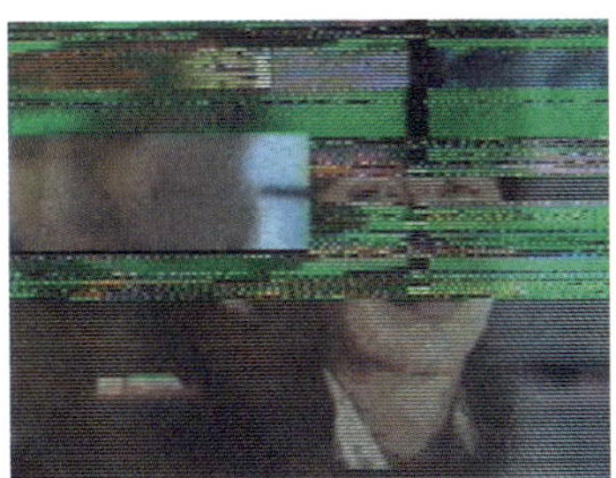
21:12

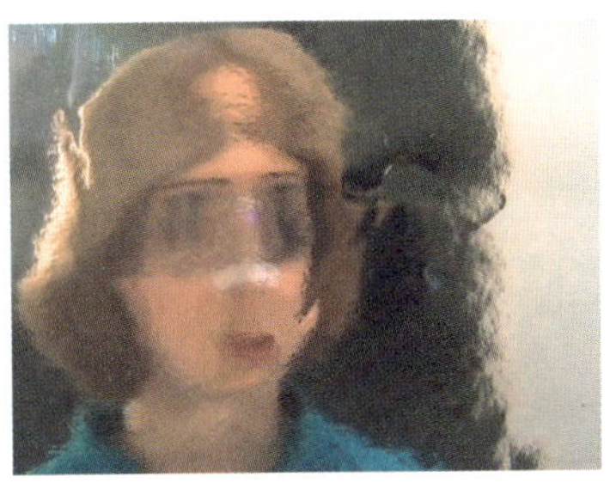
01:24

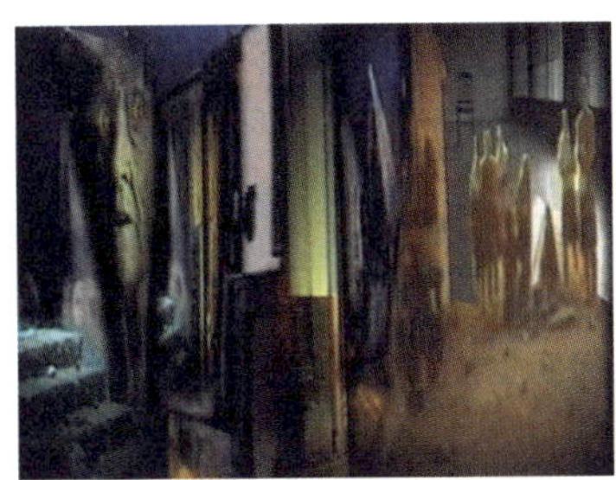
00:21

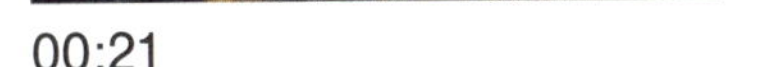

04:24

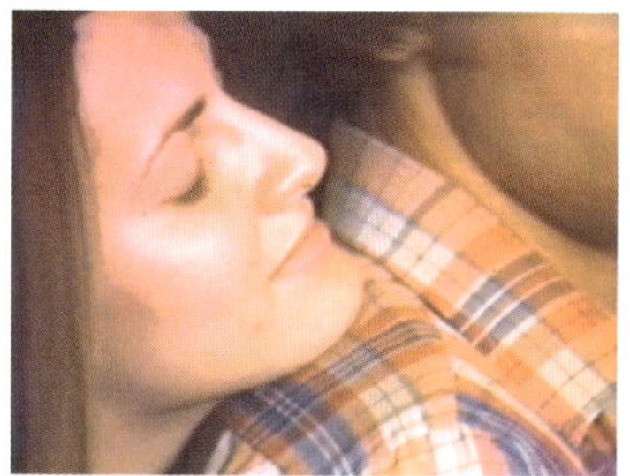
01:25

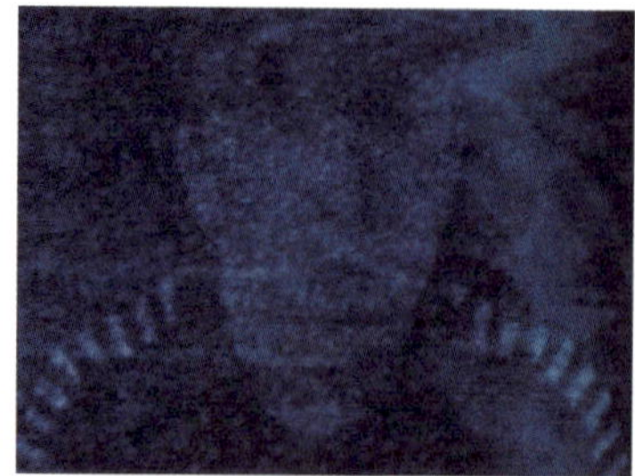
01:45

06:00

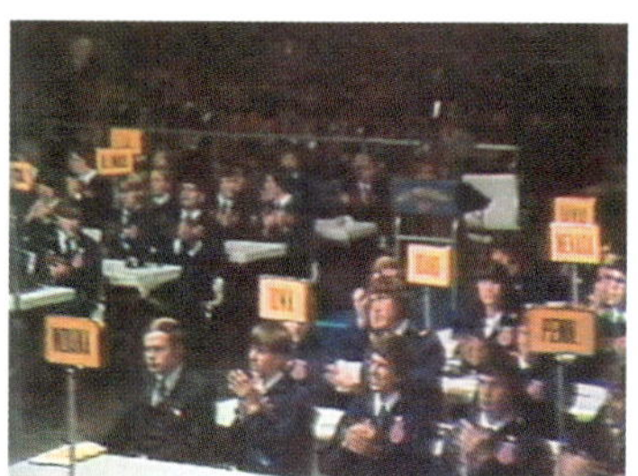
14:09

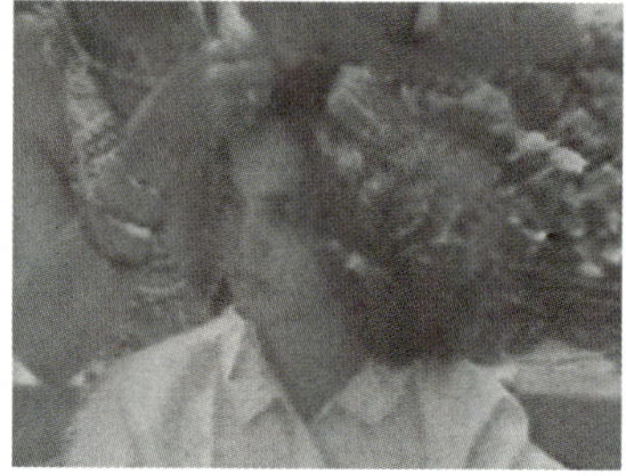
17:33

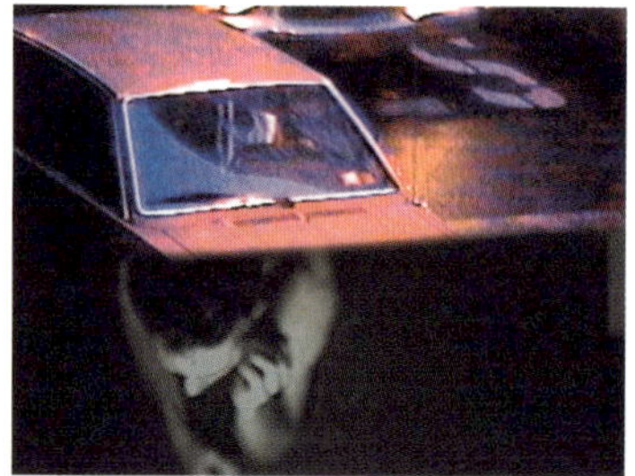
07:21

mega-server, and the off-site storage facility in New Jersey. We've been spending the summer preparing for the next big development: cloud storage. In 2019 we received a significant grant from the Ostrovsky Family Fund for an advanced digital storage system for the long-term preservation and accessibility of the EAI collection. It's truly one of the most significant and far-reaching advancements in the history of the organization. Knowing that the collection is being digitally stored and maintained at the highest level—I'll finally be able to sleep at night.

RC – This is another point to make because we're an international distributor, working with a wide range of institutions and collections. It's impossible for us to do anything monolithically or to make any absolute change because we have to consider organizations all over the world with different resources and budgets. So, there are actually some institutions that can't work with digital files yet. There are schools that still need DVDs as opposed to digital files.

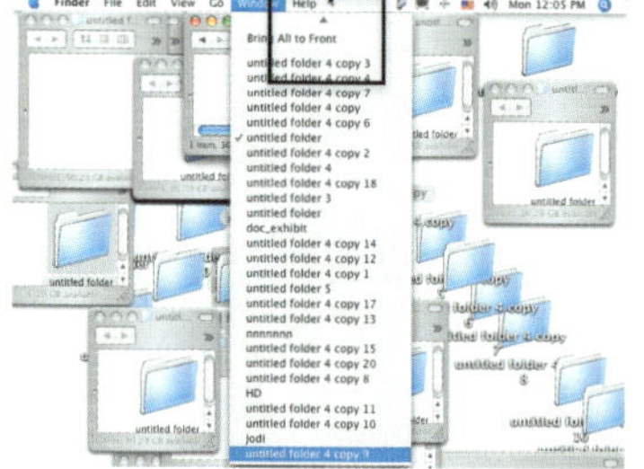
00:56

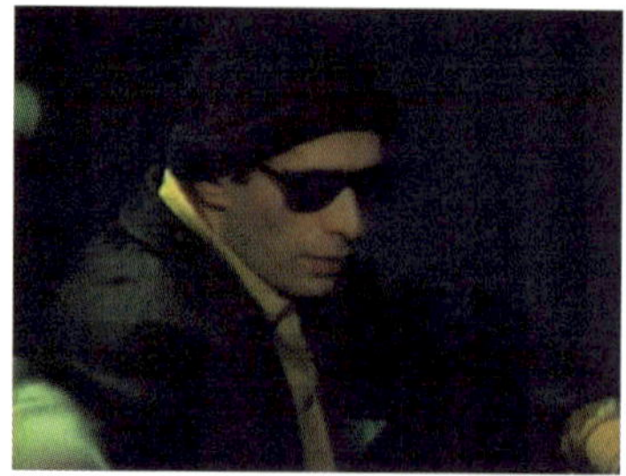
08:27

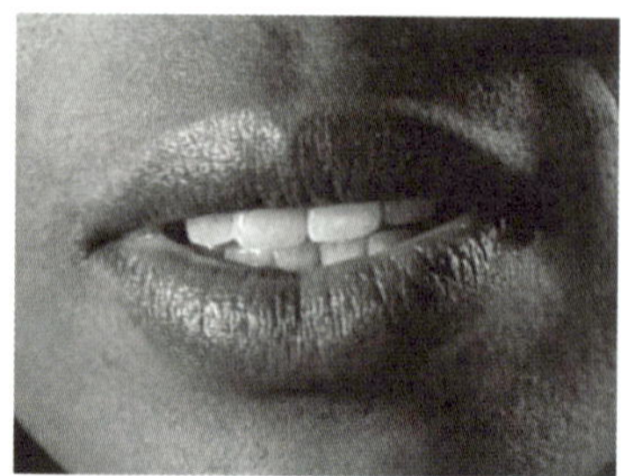
00:11

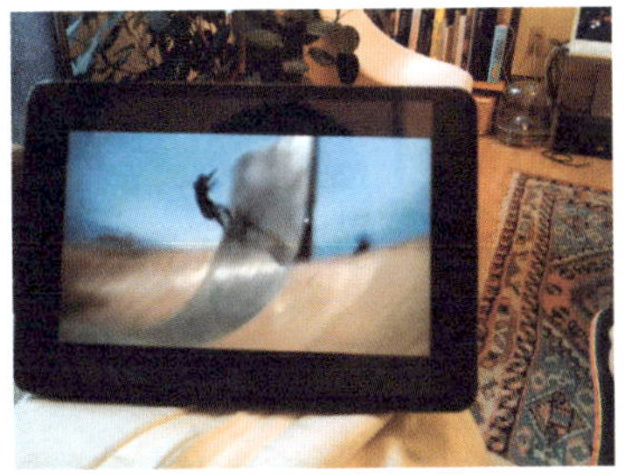
03:58

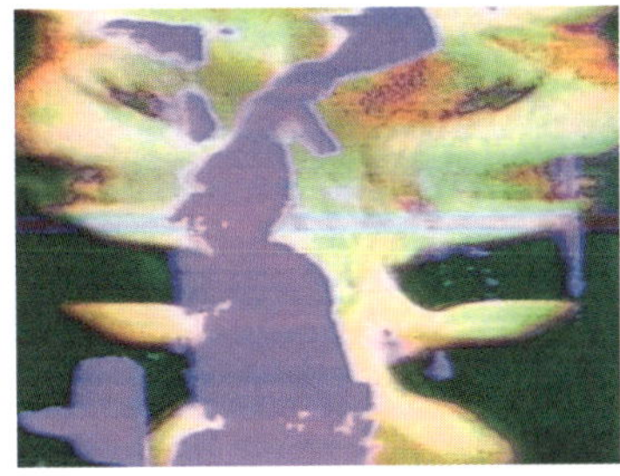
14:29

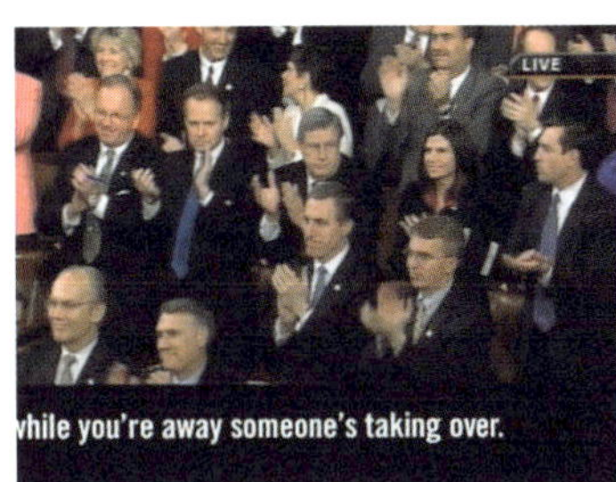

04:31

LZ – This is something that you can speak to at great length, Rebecca, but distribution was once something that was quite monolithic and straightforward: you'd press Play, Record to make a copy of a tape and put it in a bubble bag and send it out, and that was basically distribution. Obviously, it's gotten so much more complicated, which is ironic and counterintuitive in the age of streaming, when you click and everything comes to you on your computer. What we're doing now at EAI with distribution is like an artisanal, bespoke, custom-made process. Every order is distinctive, from beginning to end. It's like a Venn diagram, with two overlapping circles: one represents the artists and one represents the exhibitors, and where the circles overlap is EAI. We work with both the artists and institutions on issues such as exhibition conditions, display formats, quality control, and digital delivery modes, all of which is highly specific to each artist, each work, each institution, each context. It's ironic to me that in the age of streaming and getting content online, what goes on behind the scenes here is so much more

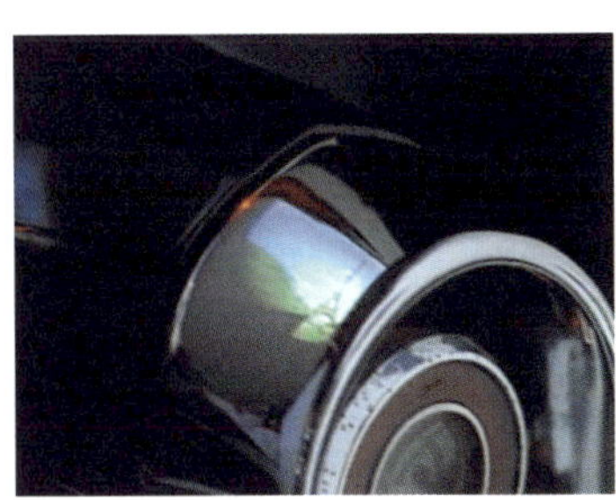
00:18

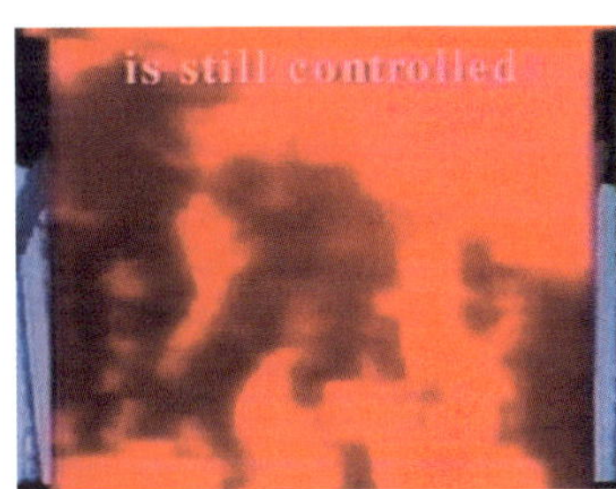

00:35

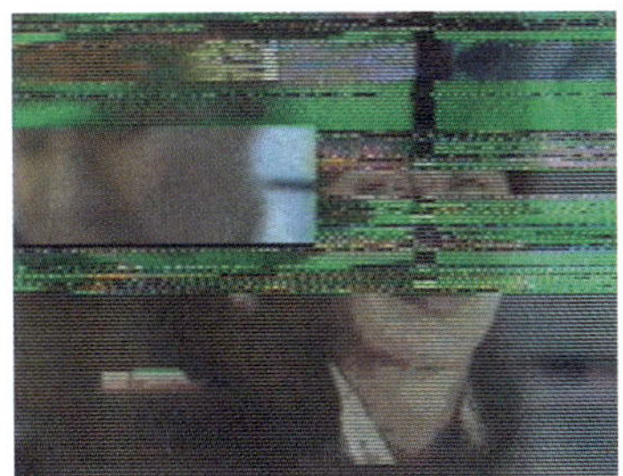
21:12

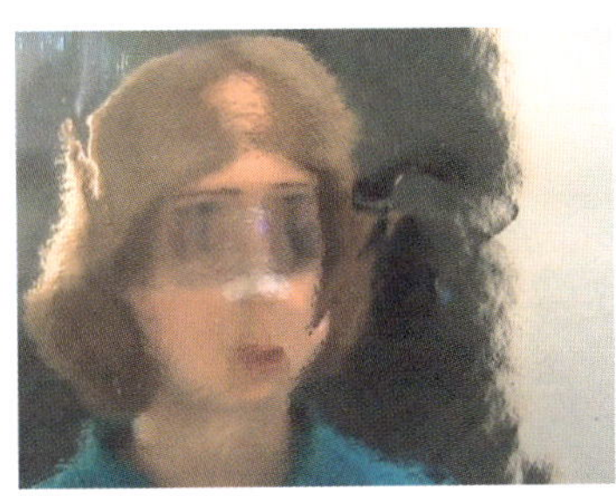
01:24

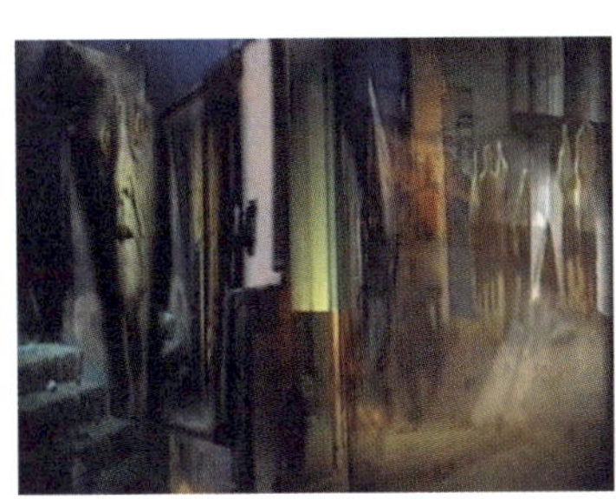
00:21

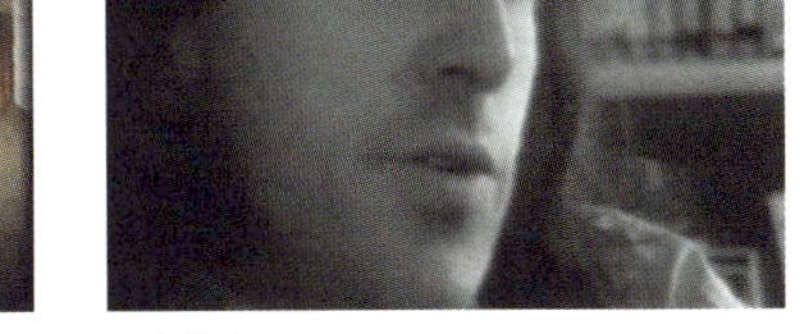
04:24

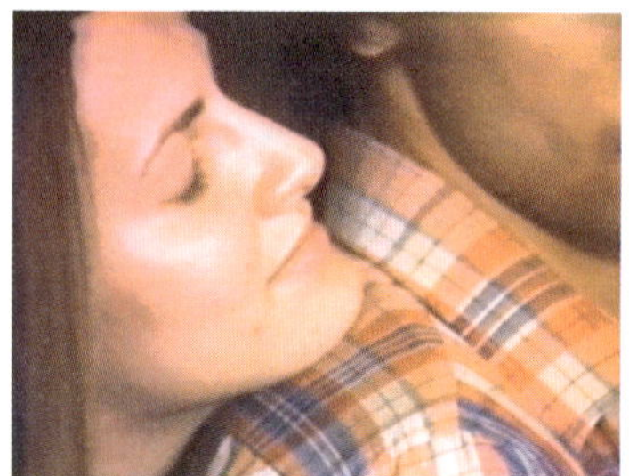
01:25

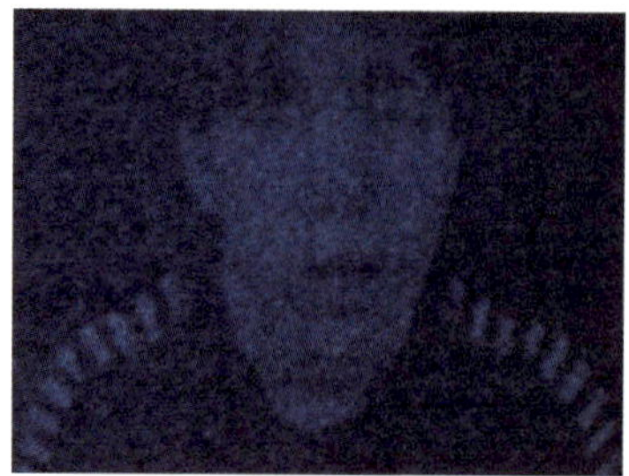
01:45

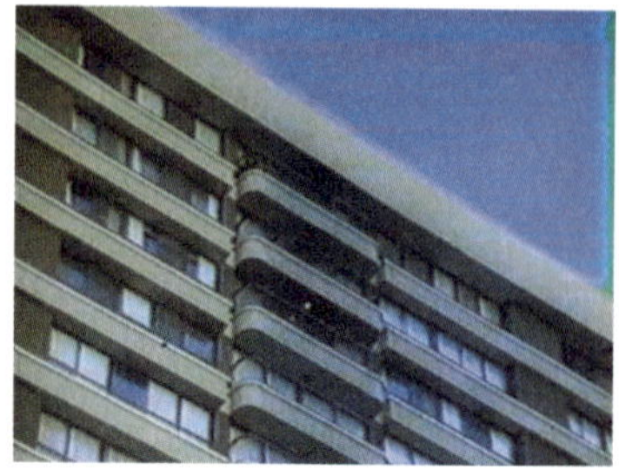
06:00

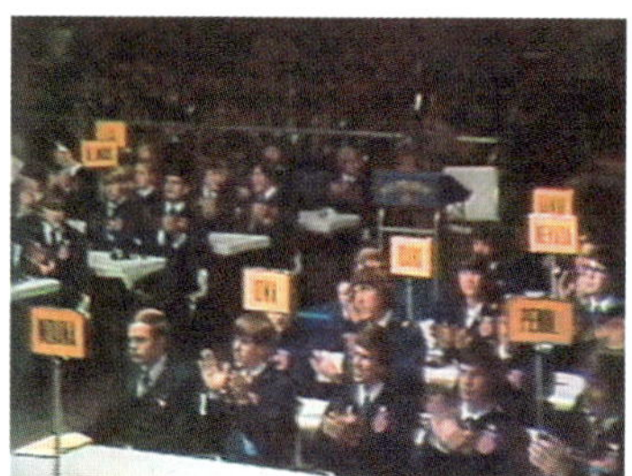
14:09

labor-intensive and time-intensive and complex than it was in the past.

RC – That's a pivotal moment as well, that transition from analog to digital, considering that the vast majority of our catalog is analog-based video, much of which is best displayed on CRT monitors, which are getting increasingly more difficult to find, as we learned from our *Broadcasting* exhibition, Alex. Most of our collection requires increasingly obsolete technology to remain true to its origin. Of course, we're also working with artists like Sondra Perry, making some of the most sought-after digital work. So, that's also a challenge: carrying the history forward while keeping up with the new. And in general, the exhibition of media has gotten much more complicated and involving.

AK – When you work with an institution and you're sending out a video, do you have stipulations about display from the artist? How do you have those conversations so that they don't end up getting projected somewhere random on a wall at the wrong aspect ratio?

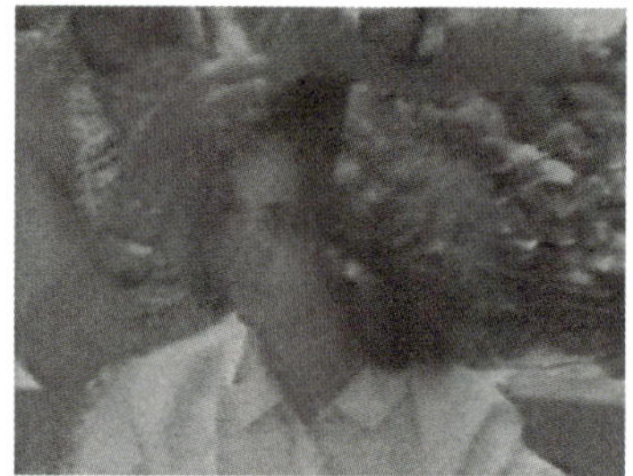
17:33

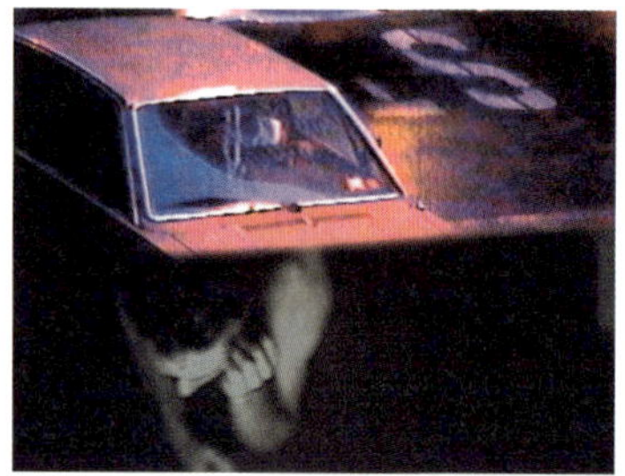
07:21

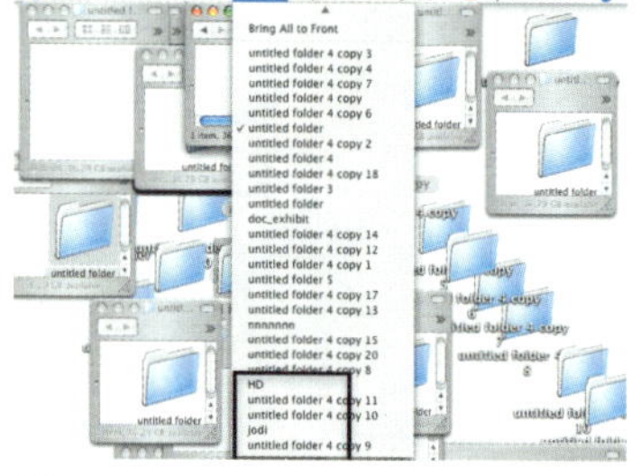
00:56

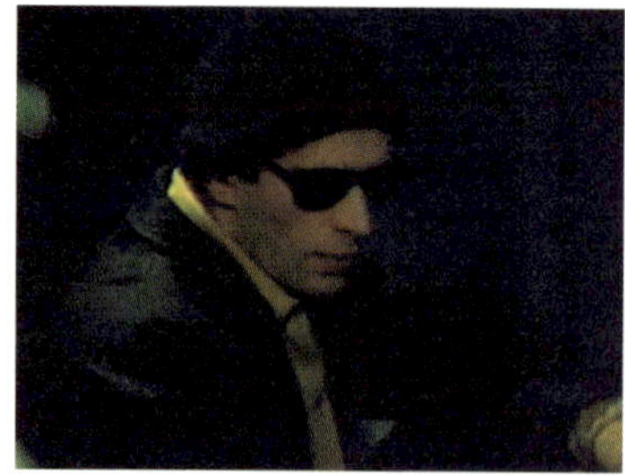
08:27

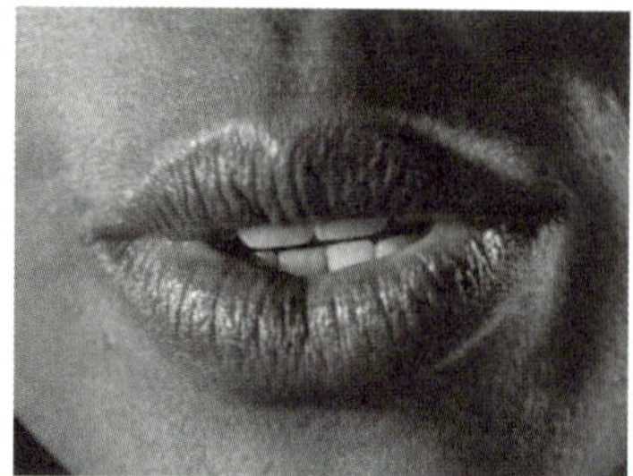
00:11

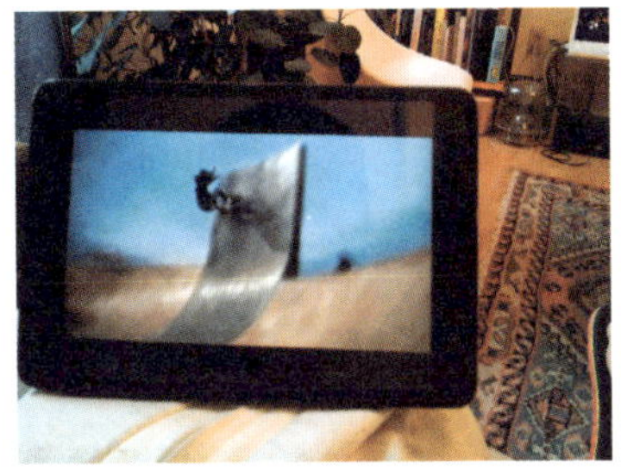

03:58

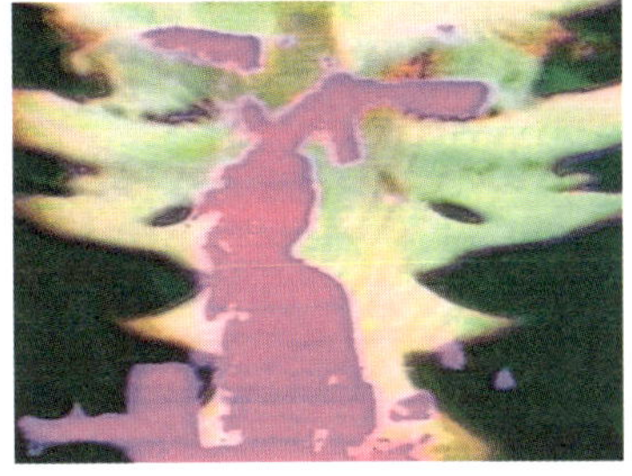

14:29

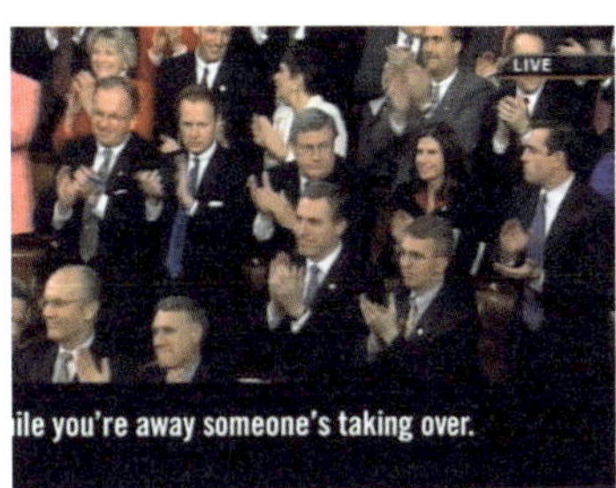

04:31

RC – It's all over the map, really. We're positioned in the middle of the conversation between the institution and the artist and it really depends on the artist, or the estate, or the representative that we're working with, as well as the institution and its resources. Some of our artists feel very strongly about how works are presented and have stipulations, such as wanting a longer work to be seen as a durational work in a cinematic setting. Other artists don't want to stipulate things like that because the work has a different relationship to the public and exhibition, like Nauman's video-native works. Since we are so artist-driven, the artist has final say on all of this. It can get a little complicated when we're dealing with an estate or gallery representatives rather than the artist directly, but we have good relationships there as well. We see one of our primary roles as being that conduit between the artist and the exhibiting institution.

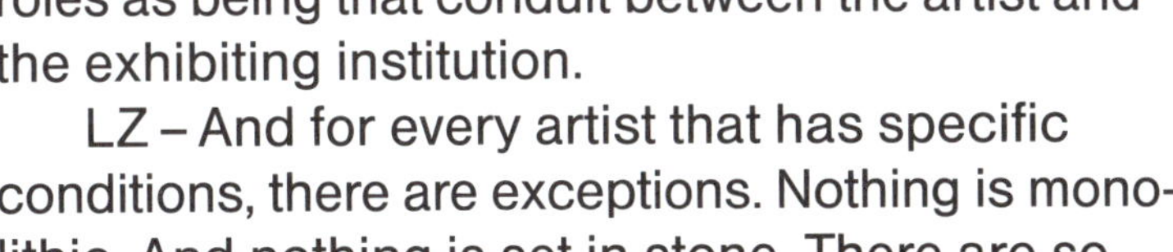

LZ – And for every artist that has specific conditions, there are exceptions. Nothing is monolithic. And nothing is set in stone. There are so

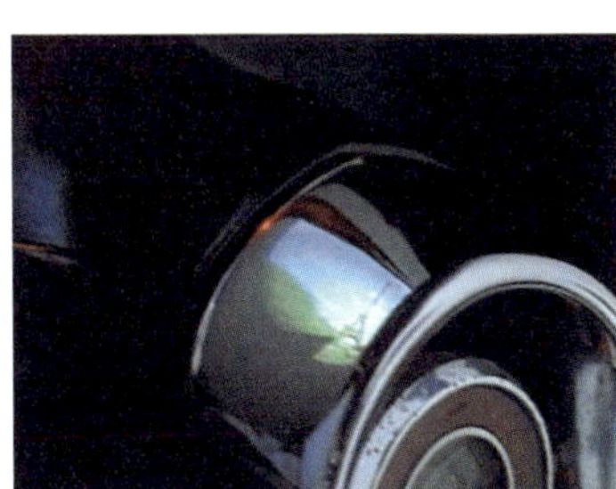

00:18

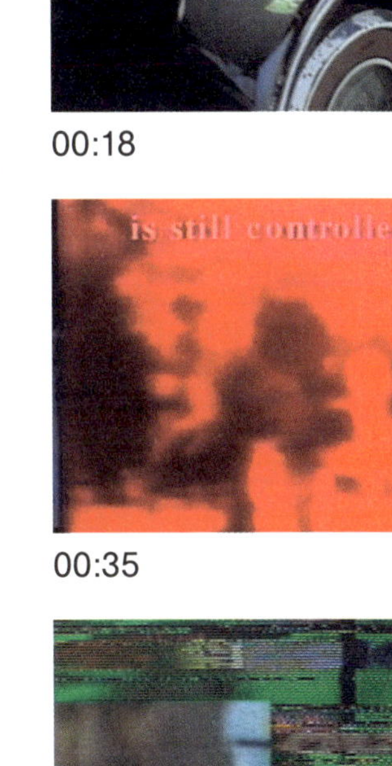

00:35

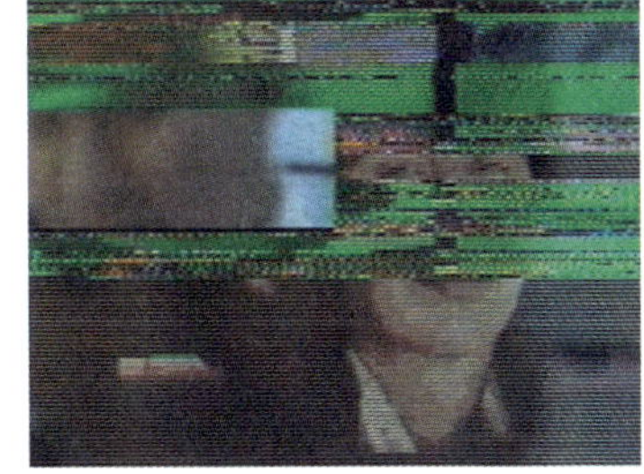

21:12

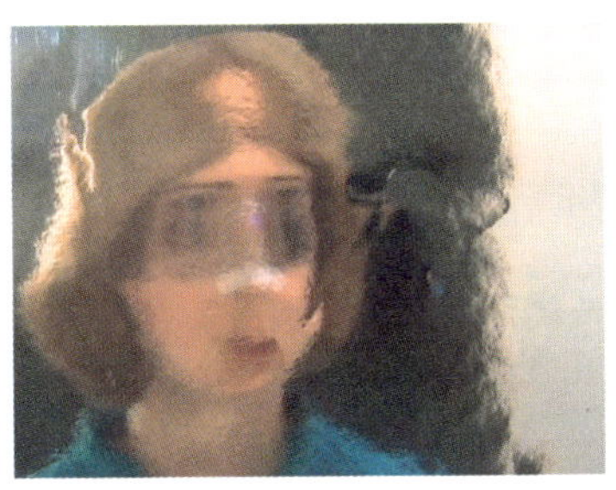

01:24

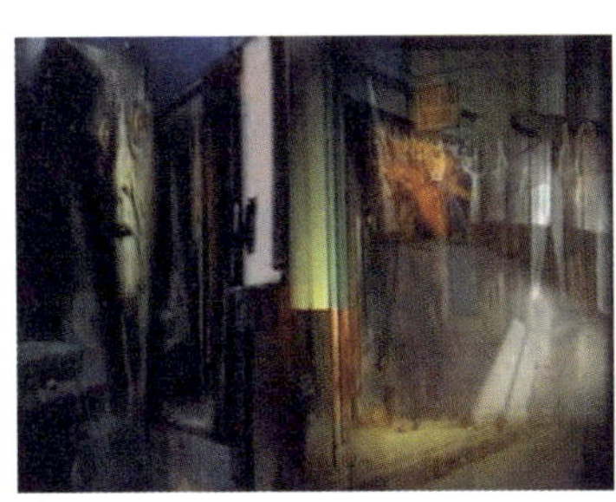

00:21

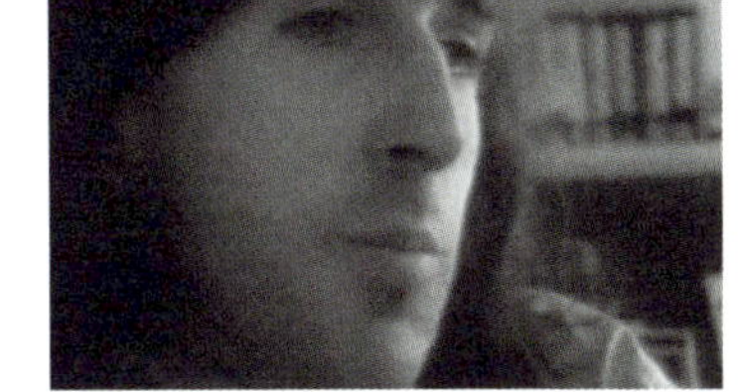

04:24

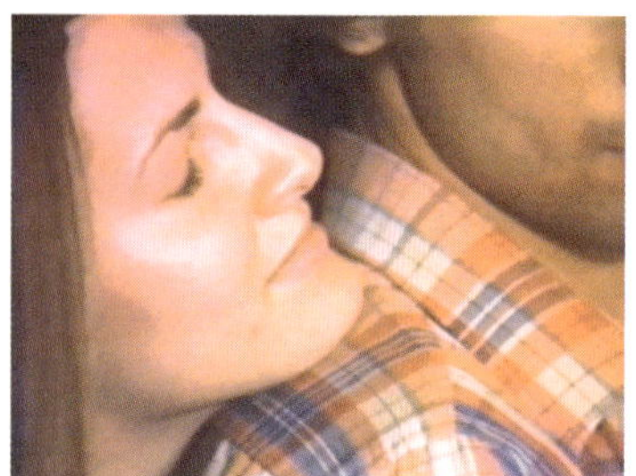
01:25

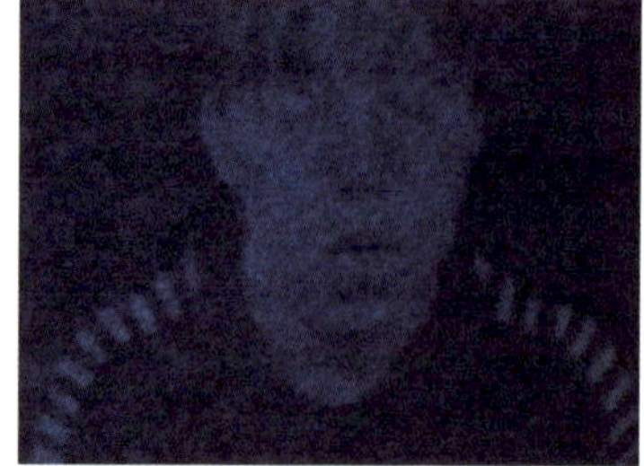
01:45

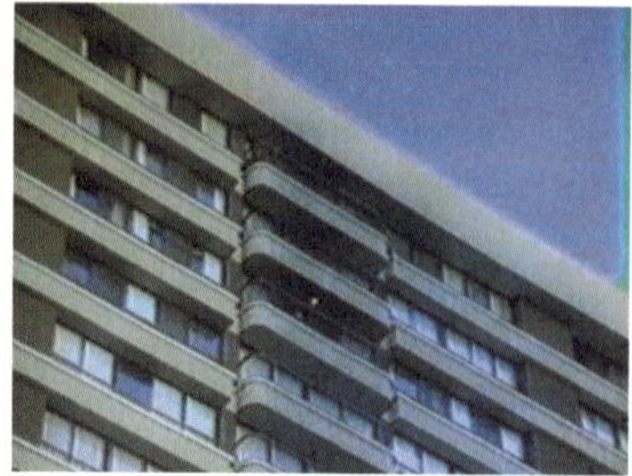
06:00

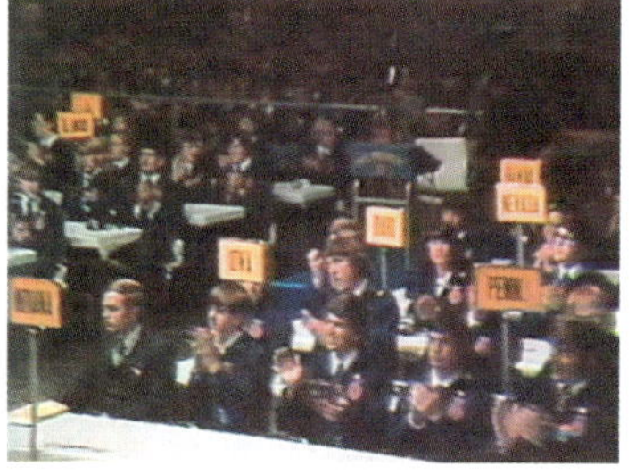
14:09

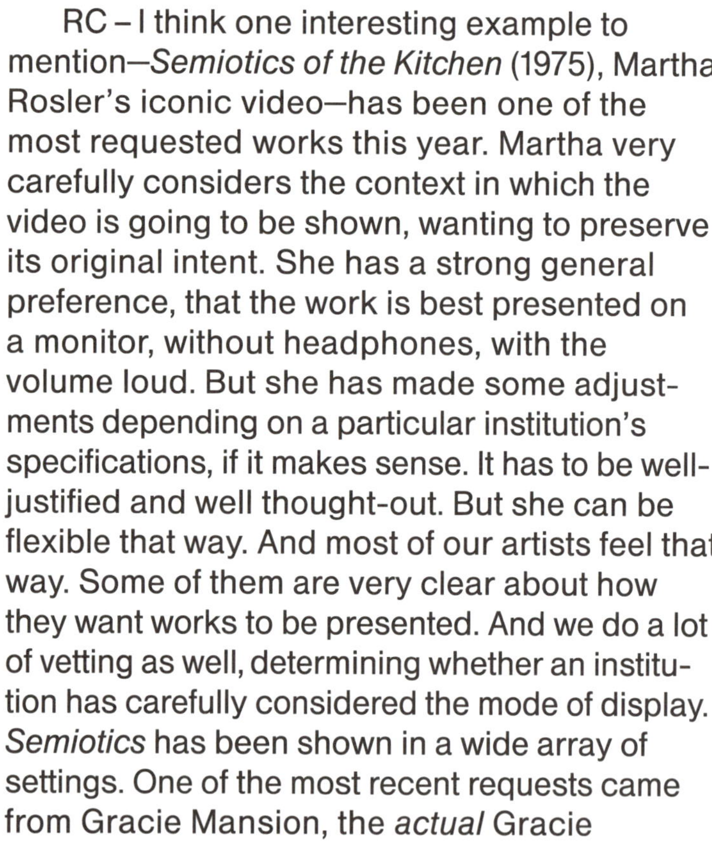

many variables. This idea of variability is the only constant with video.

RC – I think one interesting example to mention—*Semiotics of the Kitchen* (1975), Martha Rosler's iconic video—has been one of the most requested works this year. Martha very carefully considers the context in which the video is going to be shown, wanting to preserve its original intent. She has a strong general preference, that the work is best presented on a monitor, without headphones, with the volume loud. But she has made some adjustments depending on a particular institution's specifications, if it makes sense. It has to be well-justified and well thought-out. But she can be flexible that way. And most of our artists feel that way. Some of them are very clear about how they want works to be presented. And we do a lot of vetting as well, determining whether an institution has carefully considered the mode of display. *Semiotics* has been shown in a wide array of settings. One of the most recent requests came from Gracie Mansion, the *actual* Gracie

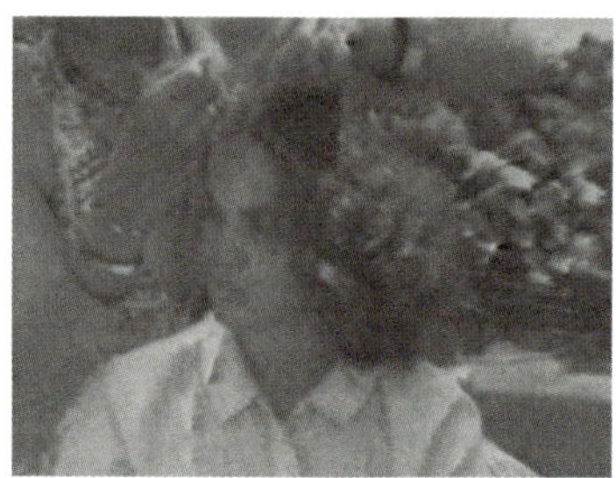
17:33

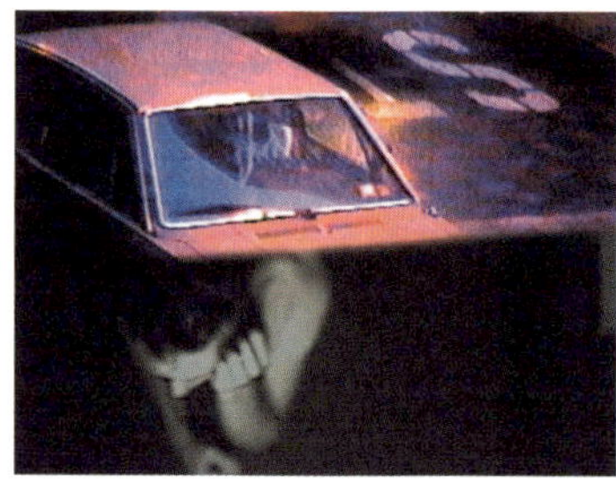
07:21

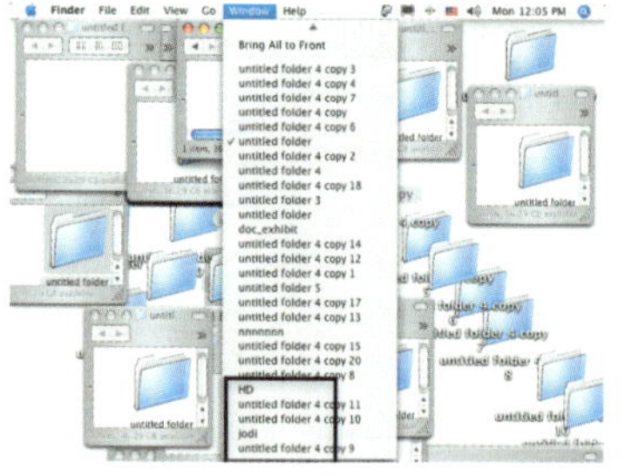
00:56

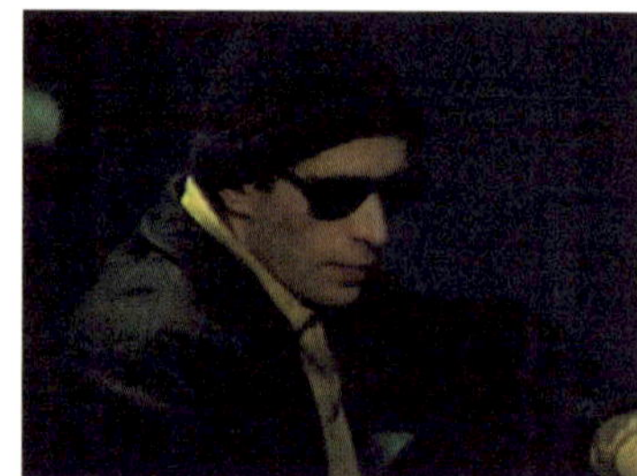
08:27

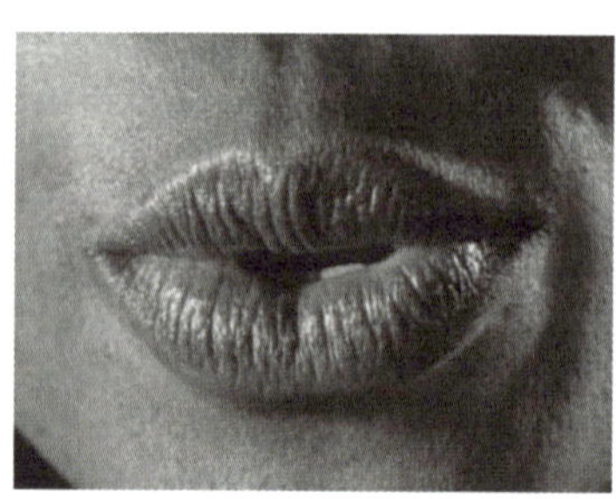
00:11

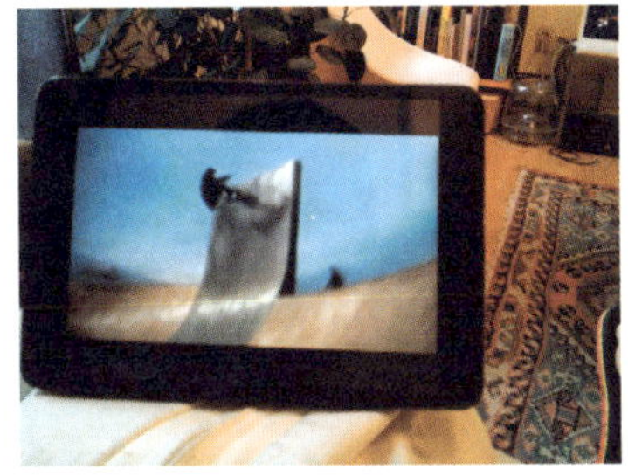

03:59

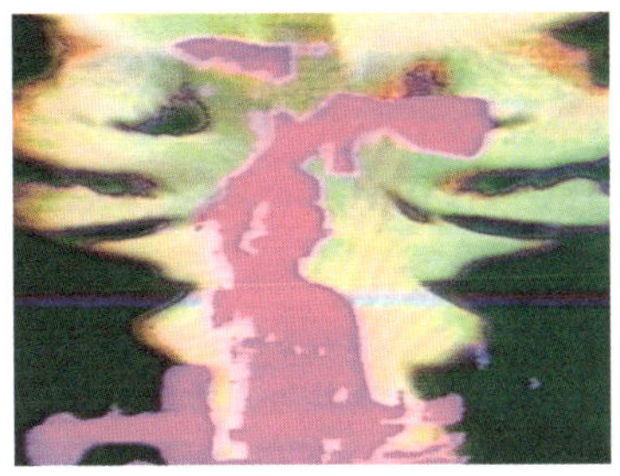

14:30

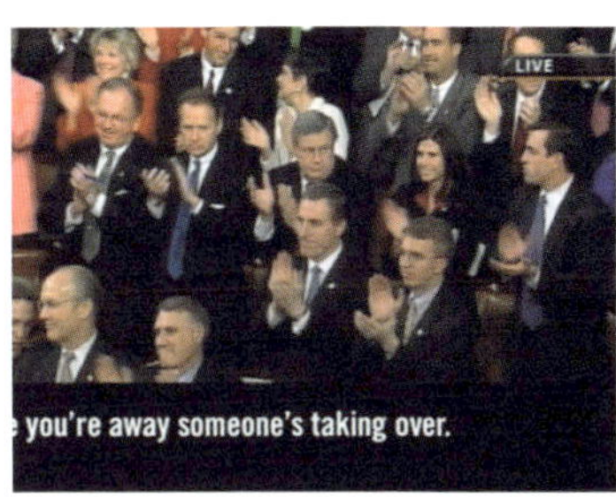

04:32

Mansion—the mayor's residence. They plan to show it on a vintage 1940s monitor.

AK – Can you talk about the educational service you offer? What year did it start?

RC – I want to say 2012, or 2013.

LZ – We got the NEA grant in 2013 that went toward the first pilot phase. The NEA has been wonderfully supportive of our Educational Streaming Service over several years.

RC – There were a number of things leading up to it. It wasn't as if we hadn't considered this possibility before, but I remember having a conversation with a librarian from Rochester. She asked if we were getting into streaming "because I work at the reserves shelf and I sit here and look out at a sea of students with their MacBooks and you've heard of Mac the Ripper, right?" She knew that all of those students were ripping the files off the DVDs.

She ended up inviting me to a retreat that had been organized by a group of librarians who asked distributors and some filmmakers to come together to discuss how to move forward with

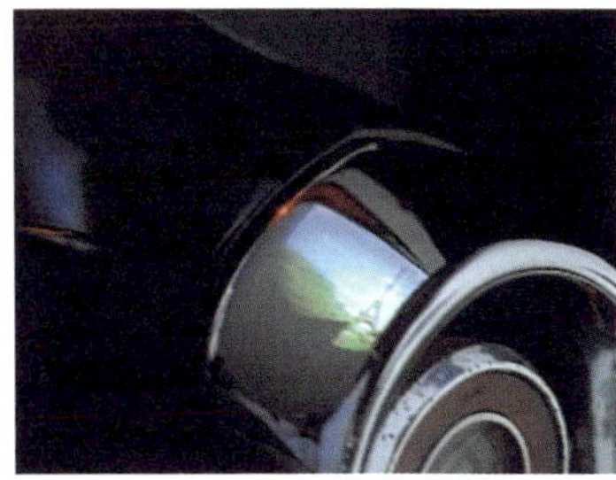

00:19

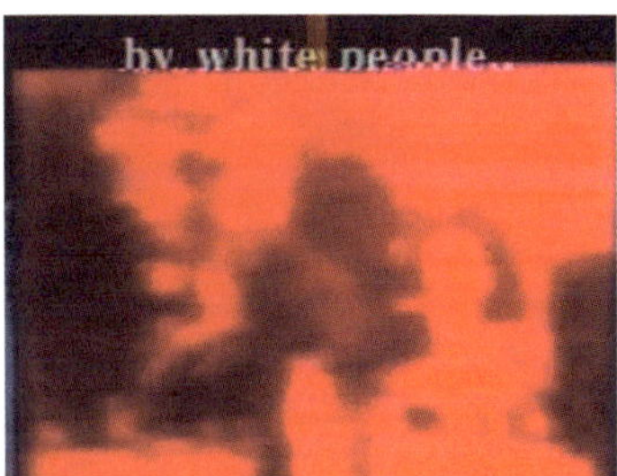

00:36

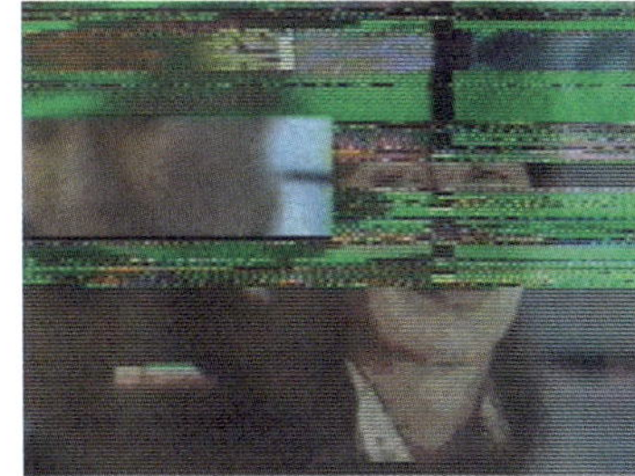

21:13

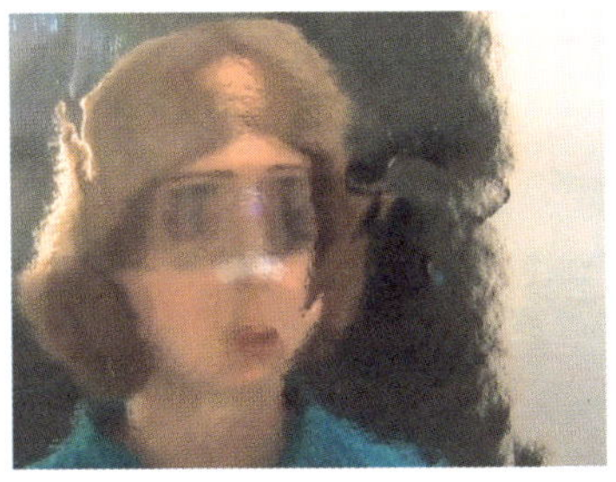

01:25

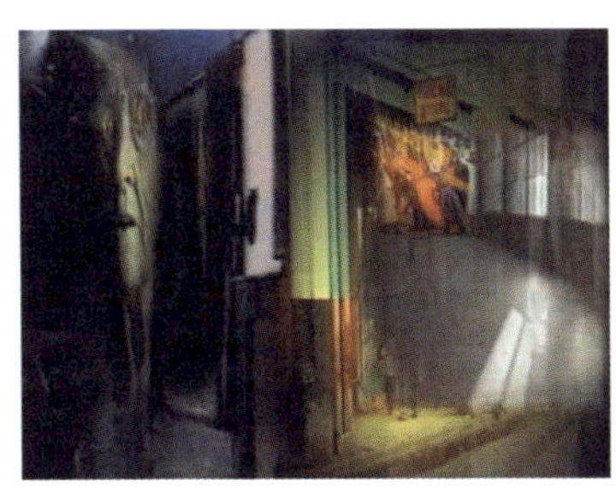

00:22

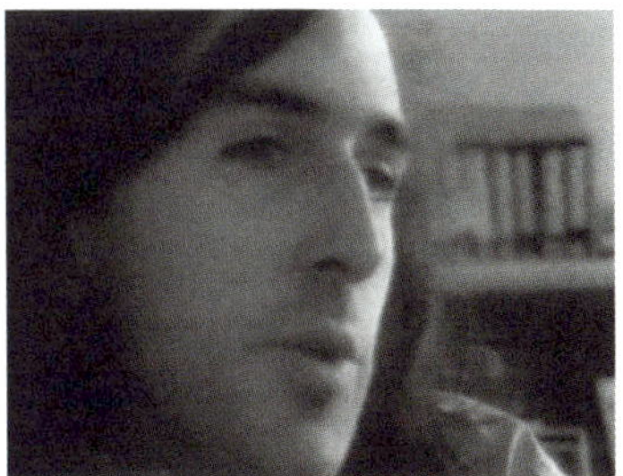

04:25

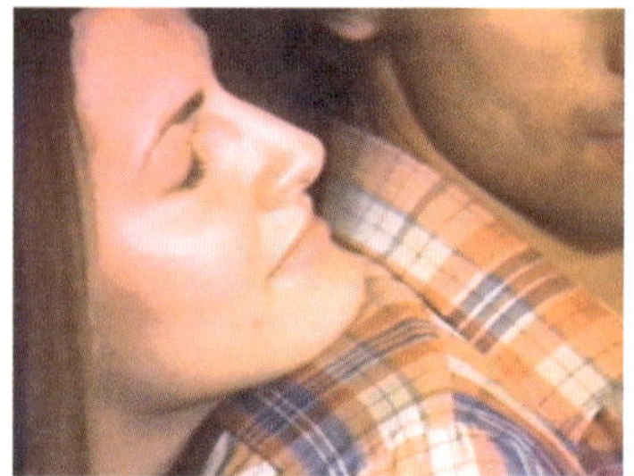

01:25

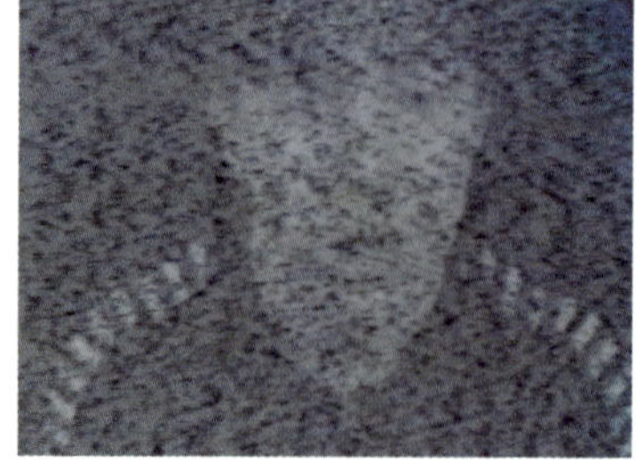

01:45

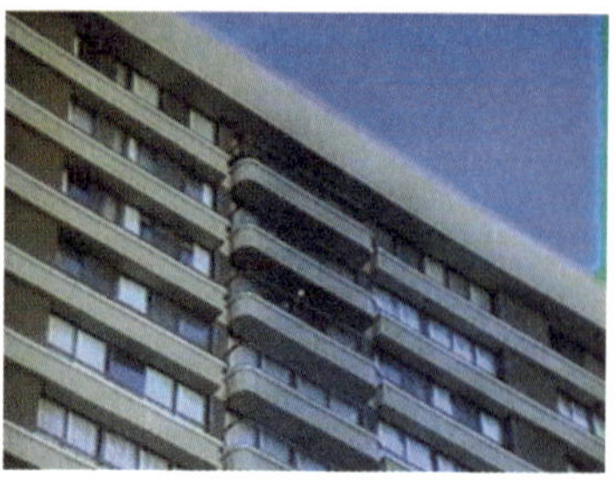

06:00

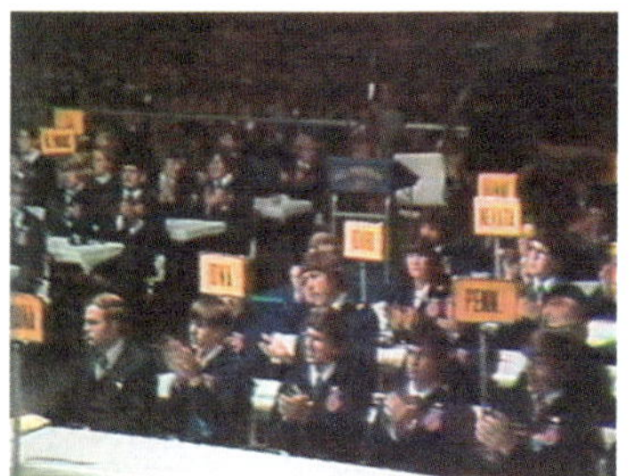

14:09

streaming video for libraries. This was at the time of the Google Books copyright case, and other changes in copyright law that favored fair use in educational settings. I thought it was great that this group of librarians was outreaching to distributors, recognizing the impact it might have on our business models. At the time, they made it sound like they were all going to get rid of their DVDs and VHS tapes and switch over to digital subscriptions. But we've found out that it hasn't been quite so immediate…

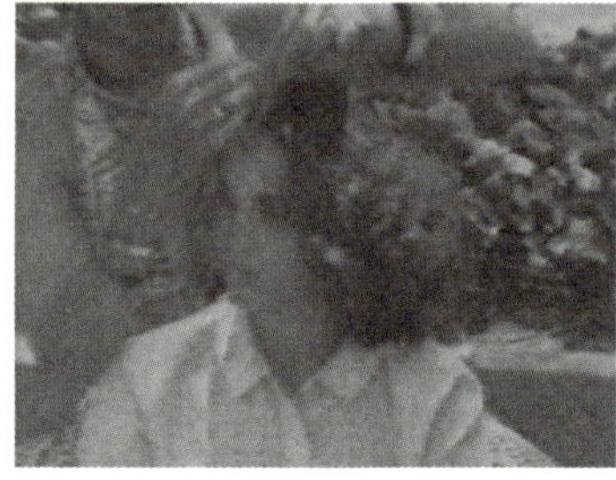

17:33

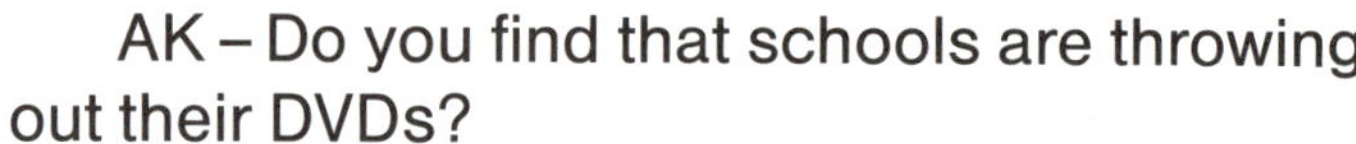

AK – Do you find that schools are throwing out their DVDs?

RC – Some are. Some have completely transitioned to streaming subscriptions.

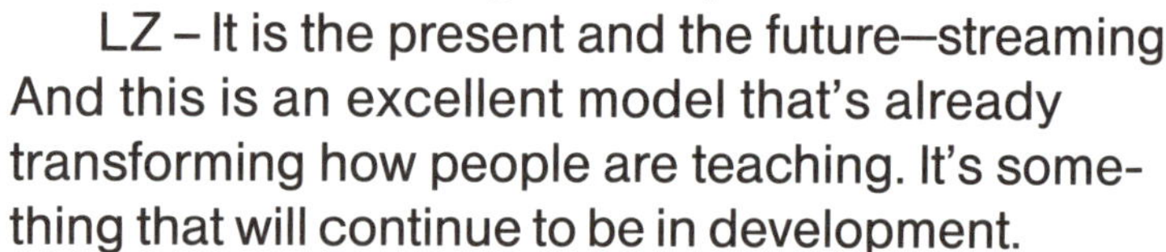

LZ – It is the present and the future—streaming. And this is an excellent model that's already transforming how people are teaching. It's something that will continue to be in development.

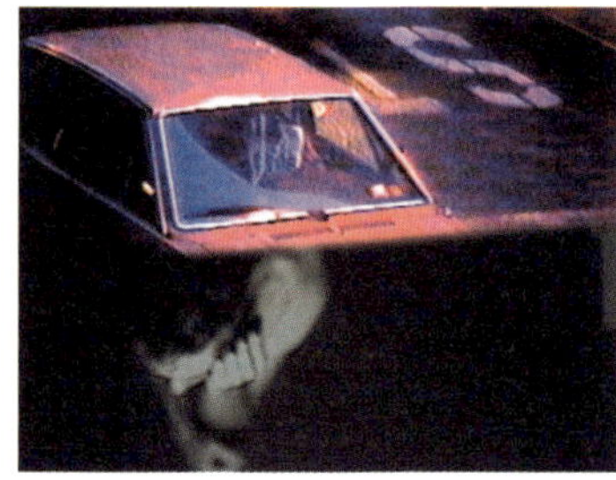

07:21

AK – Every art professor needs access to videos.

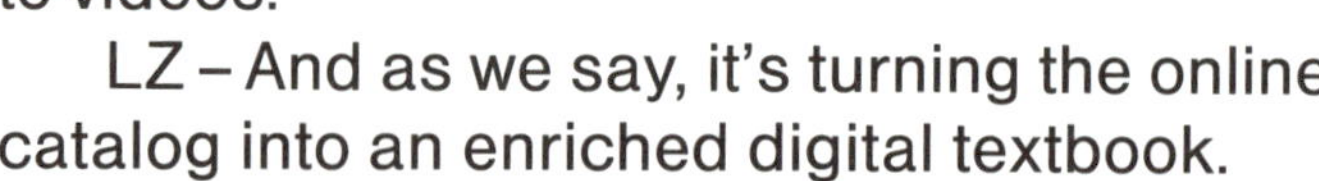

LZ – And as we say, it's turning the online catalog into an enriched digital textbook.

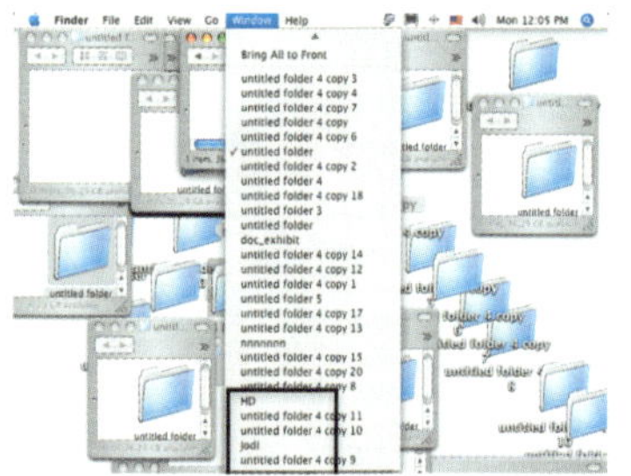

00:56

08:27

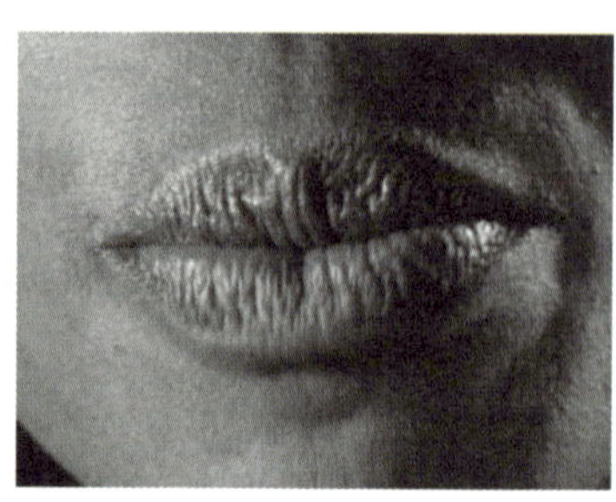

00:11

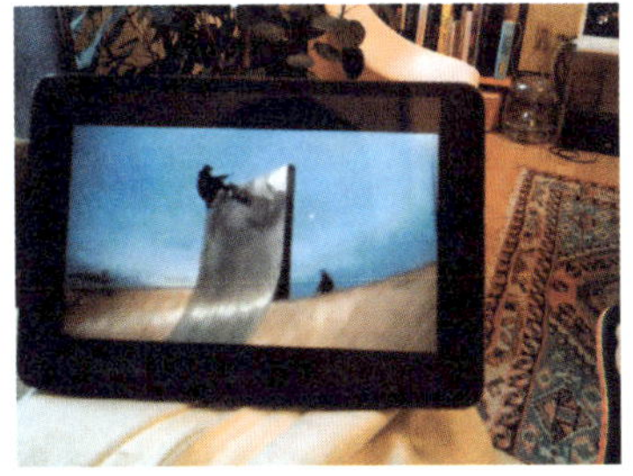
03:59

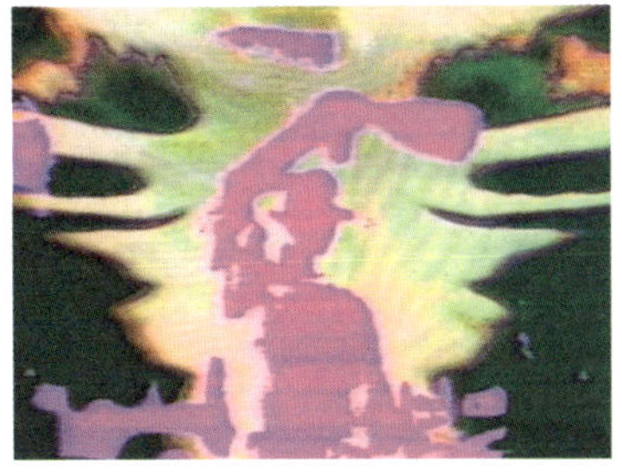
14:30

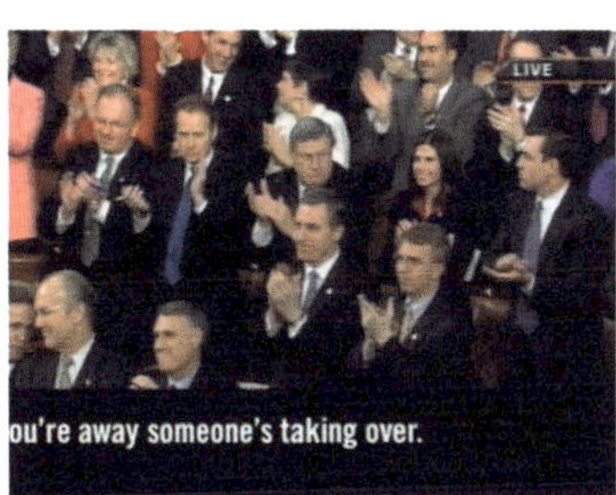

04:32

In some ways, our current distribution activities address issues relating to the two main coexisting but opposite models for disseminating video art—streaming and limited editions—while forging a third path. With the EAI model, we're working with streaming for our educational distribution, wherein you can access thousands of titles for educational use. At the same time, we're also working with the "life of work" license, an archival acquisition model for museums and collections that is much more preservation-based. So, we're working at two different extremes that define how video is circulating today, both of which are important and speak to different needs, different audiences, and different contexts.

RC – I think it gets back to the internet and to that transition from analog to digital. And just as the libraries were saying that they were thinking about getting rid of their DVD stock, we started to hear from museums that they were no longer going to accept DigiBeta tape as an acquisition format anymore. One prominent

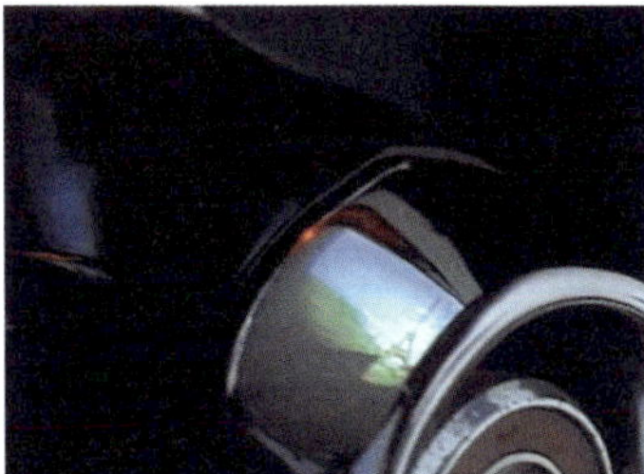
00:19

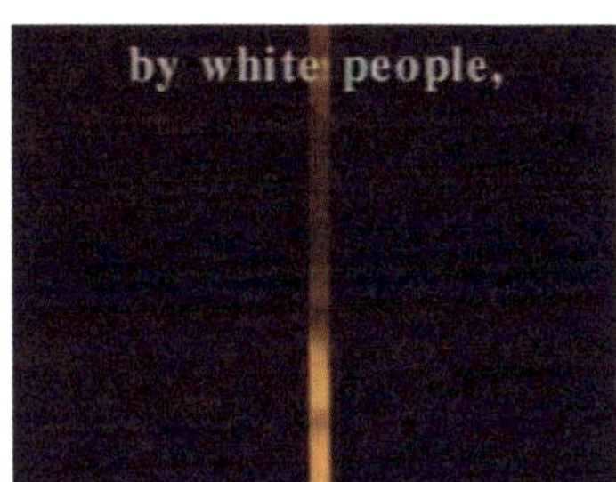

00:36

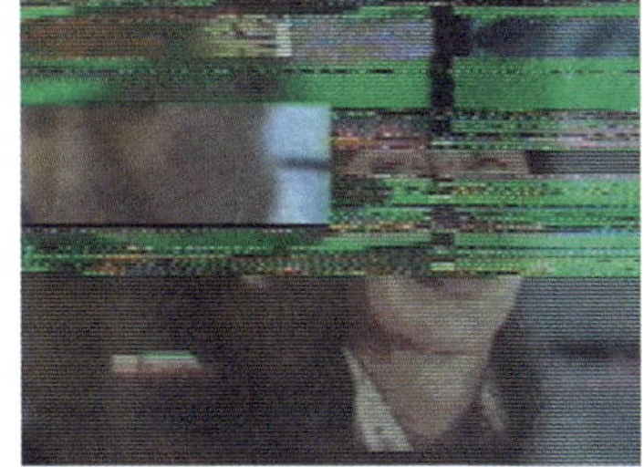
21:13

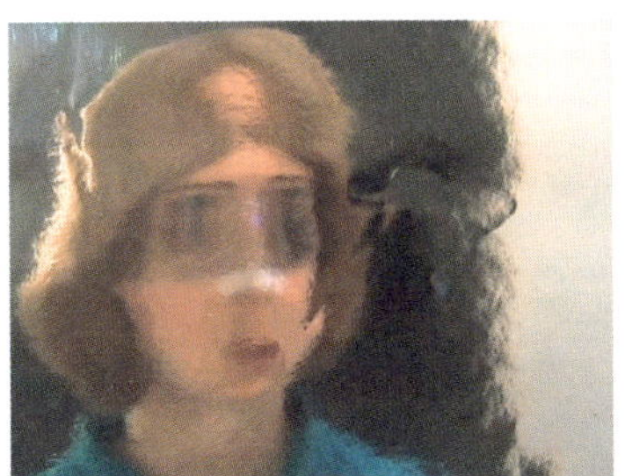
01:25

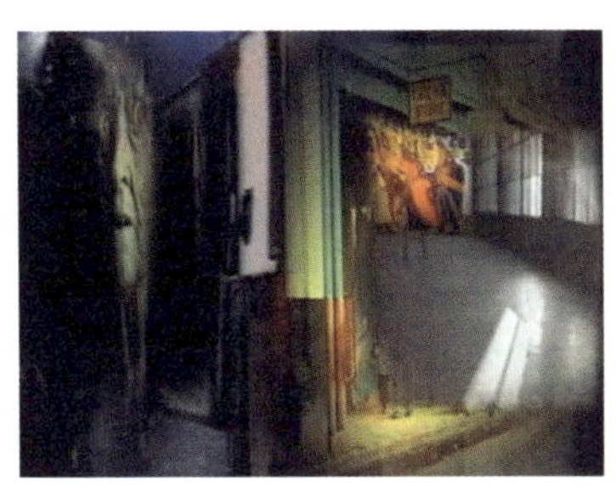
00:22

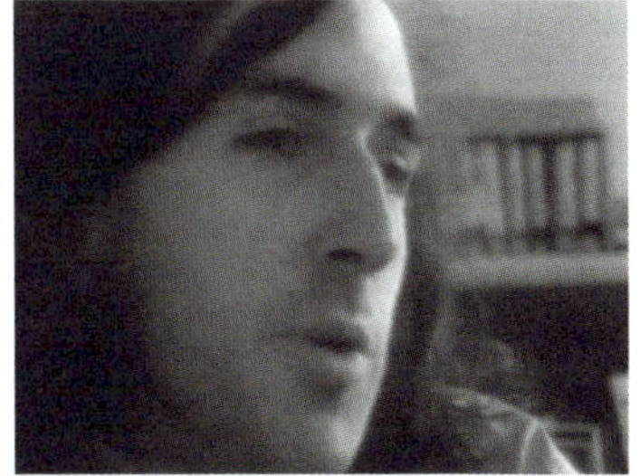
04:25

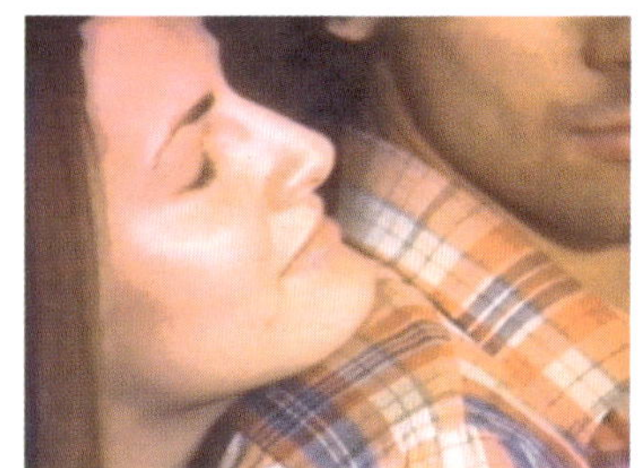
01:25

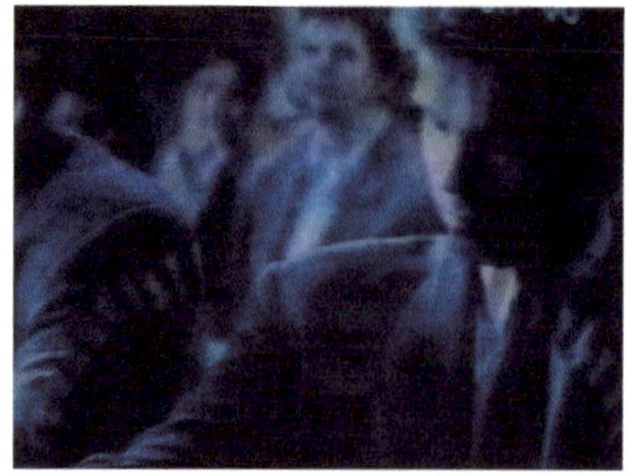
01:45

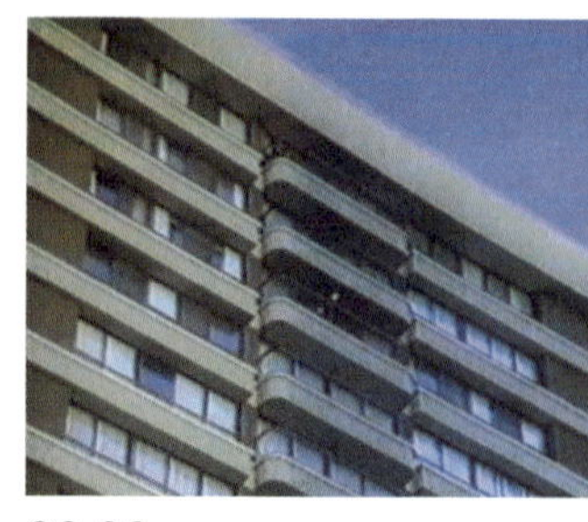
06:00

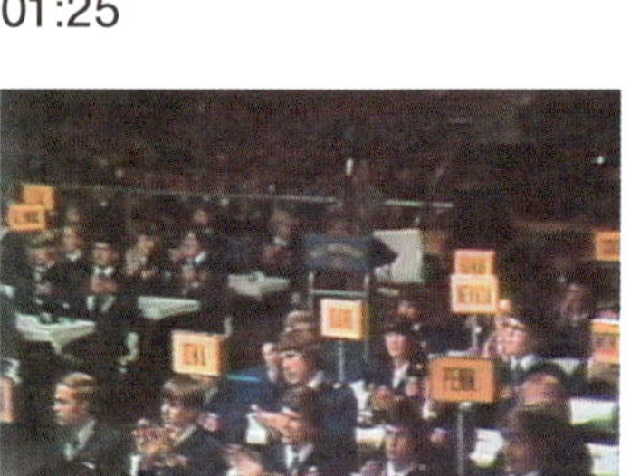
14:09

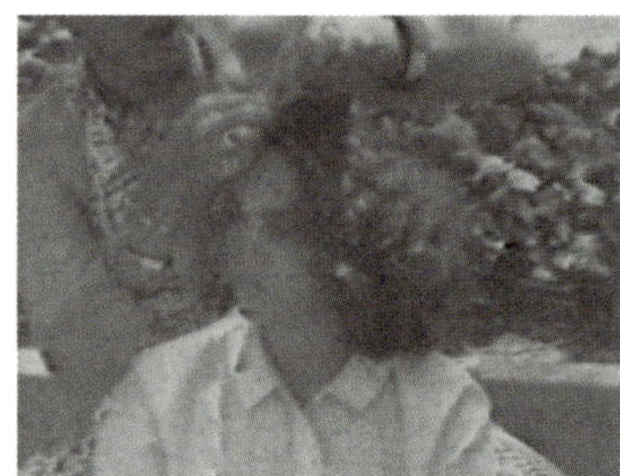
17:33

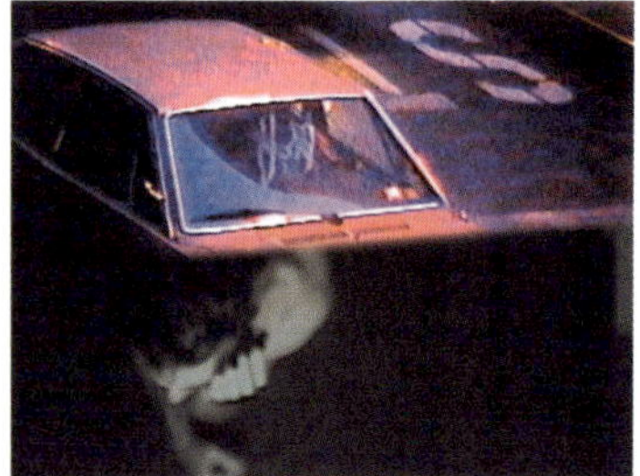
07:21

museum made that very clear to us. So, we had to sit down and come up with a different licensing model for file formats, which we did.

AK – Earlier we talked a lot about the editing suites. Do you still have editing suites that people come and use?

LZ – Yes.

AK – I get the sense that it is still a hub for artists and a space where artists continue to transfer knowledge and skills. That's something that I'm very interested in within EAI's history—the artists who have passed through here and have come into contact with an older generation of artists and then vice-versa have gone on and continued those conversations. It's exciting to think about EAI as a connection between an earlier generation of video pioneers and another generation of artists more closely associated with the internet era such as Seth Price, Josh Kline (who was also the director of EAI's public programs in the 2000s), Antoine Catala, Trevor Shimizu, or Sondra Perry.

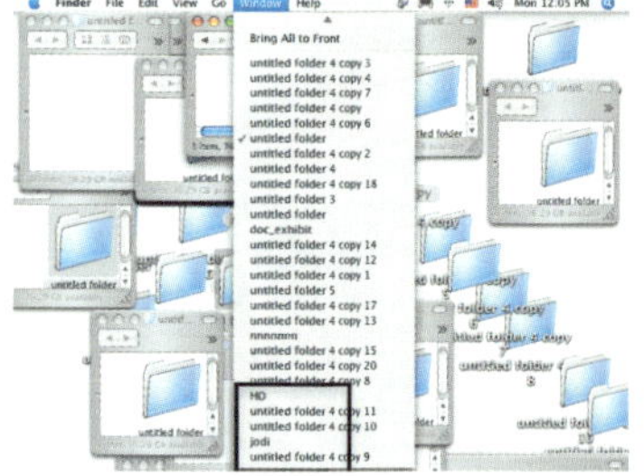

00:56

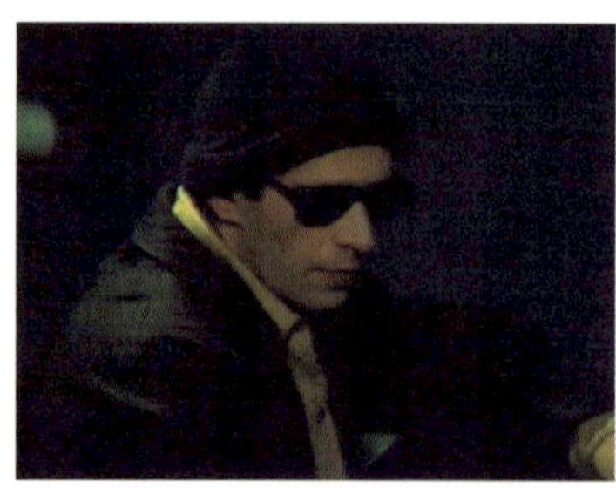
08:27

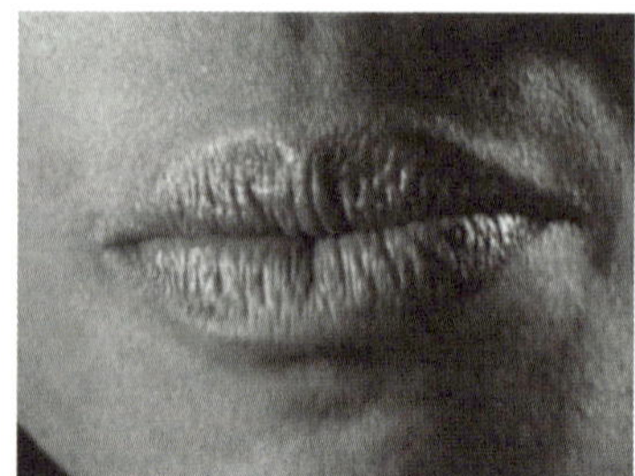
00:11

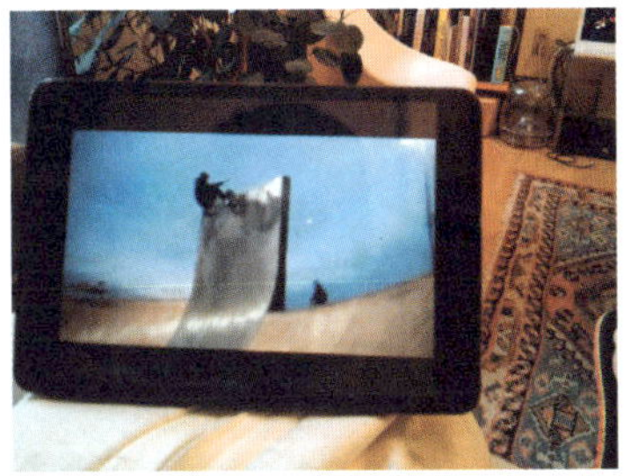
03:59

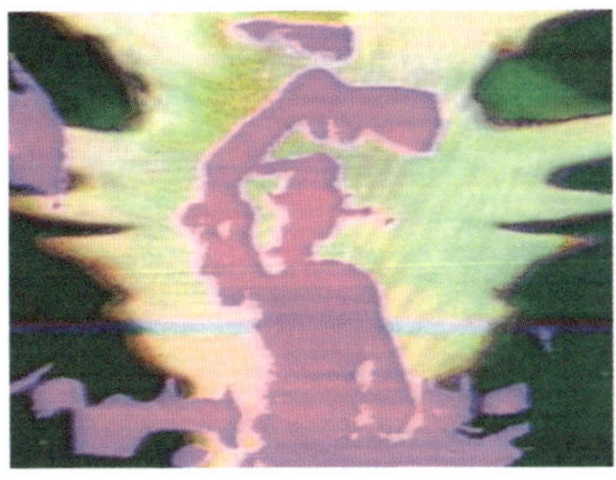
14:30

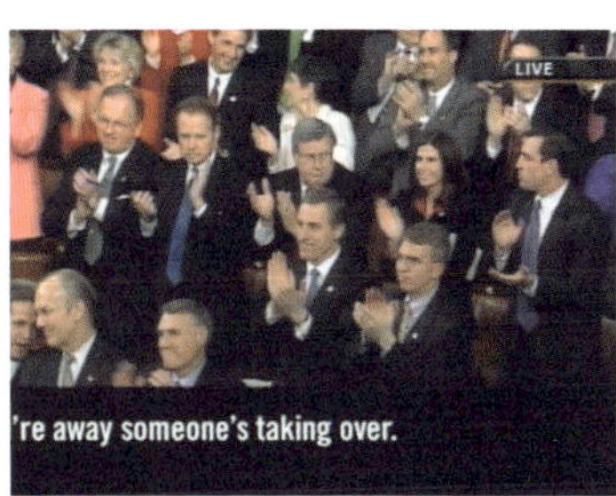

04:32

LZ – Exactly. There was a big shift in editing technologies in the 2000s, where you went from artists working with an editor as a mediator or, in some cases a collaborator, at a technical facility. This was also key to some of the editors in EAI's workspace, who worked closely with the artists and who were themselves artists, like Robert Beck/Buck, Seth Price, and Trevor Shimizu, who was the technical director in the mid-2000s. The big shift came at the point when the artist's laptop became a primary editing facility. Now, for some artists there's no need to go to a facility because they are their own editor. But there are artists who still want the process of working with an editor. For example, Carolee Schneemann was at EAI every Thursday for a long time; she worked closely with Trevor. Artists like Dan Graham, Dara Birnbaum, Cheryl Donegan, and Shigeko Kubota really forged relationships with editors based on collaborations. But then there's the younger generation, the post-internet, digital-world artists, who have never been without a computer.

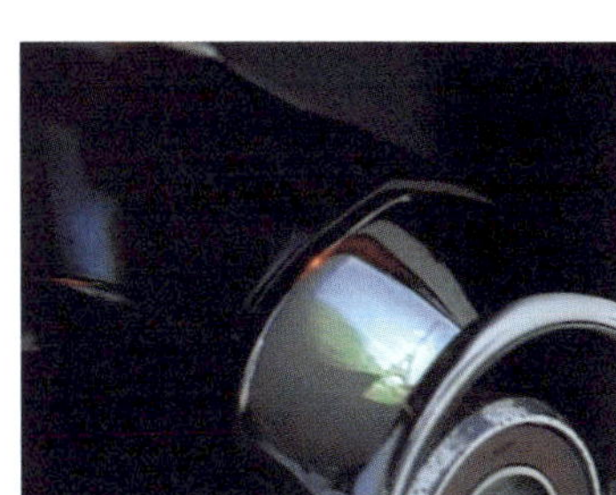
00:19

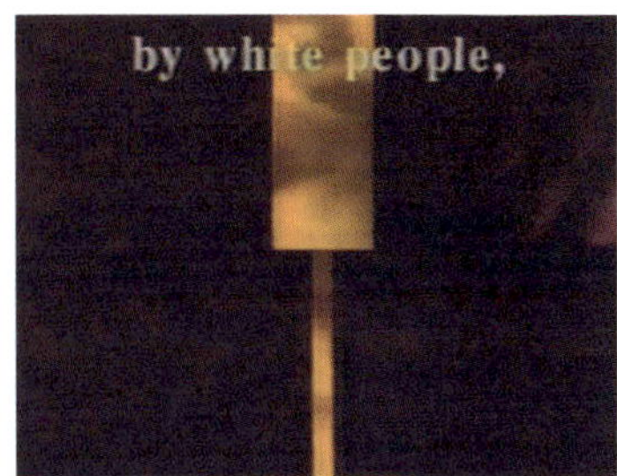

00:36

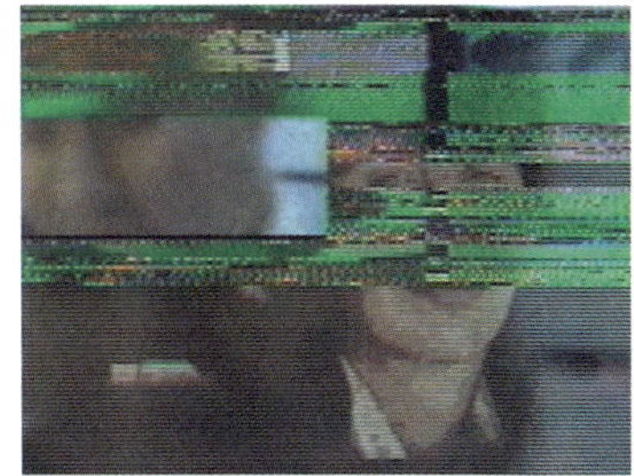
21:13

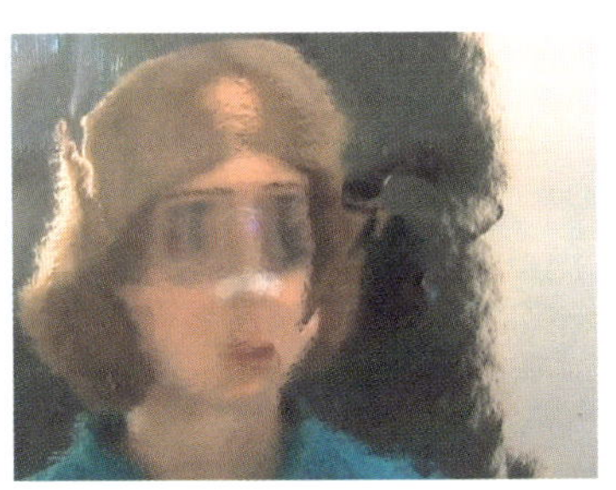
01:25

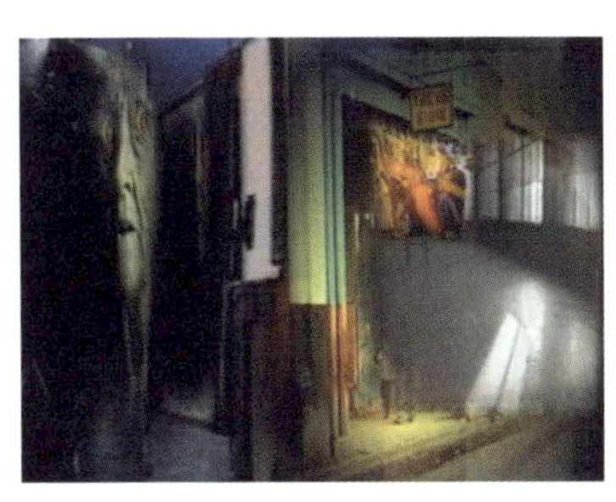
00:22

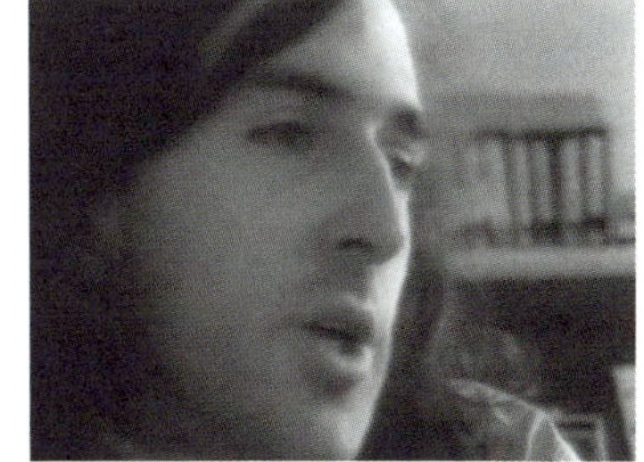
04:25

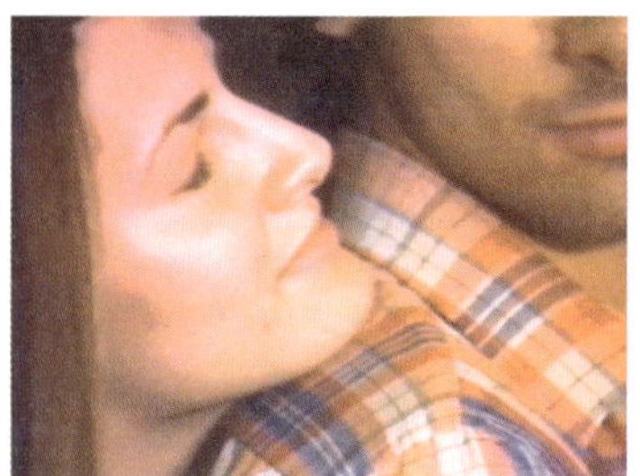

01:25

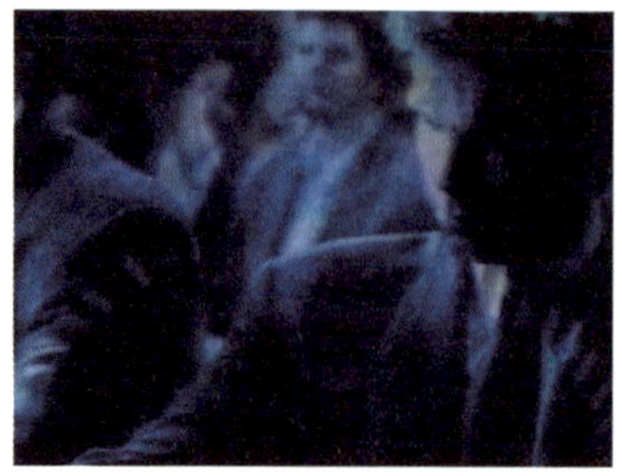

01:45

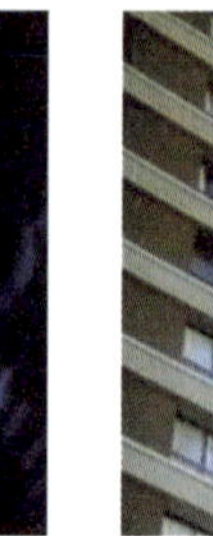

06:00

RC – And yet, just as the editing facility came back in the early nineties, you never know. I remember Sondra used our editing facility heavily to render her multiplex-sized "wall of skin" for the *Resident Evil* installation at The Kitchen in 2016. She couldn't have done that rendering on her own computer. Sondra was also self-sufficient in our tech suite though, because she'd interned previously and we'd employed her for a number of tech jobs that came up, because she was so great. It went on for a few days. We'd come into the office and almost forget she was in there, quietly rendering her wall of skin, for hours and hours and hours. Of course, it was incredible to see the end result.

LZ – As we speak about Sondra and this new generation of artists, I wanted to note that EAI will celebrate its fiftieth anniversary in 2021. What I find remarkable—and gratifying—is that this "alternative paradigm" that was founded in 1971 is still relevant to artists and their art almost fifty years later. Throughout all of these changes and shifts—in the art, the economic and cultural

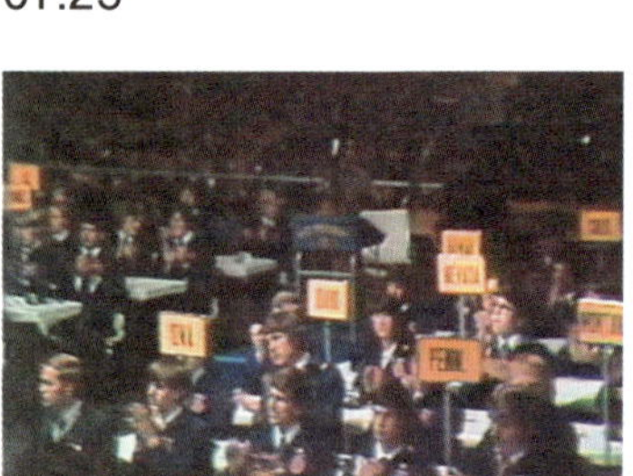

14:09

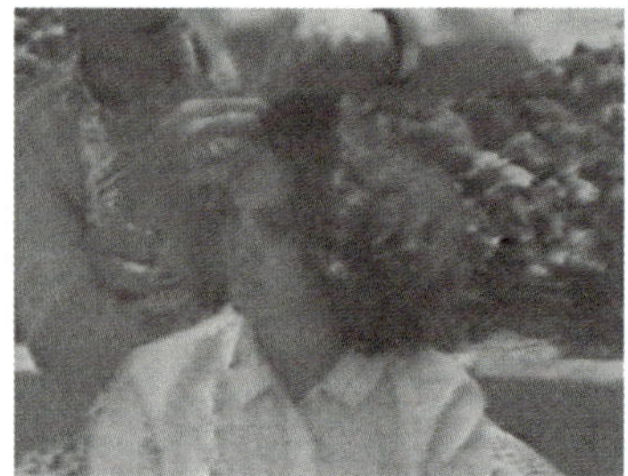

17:33

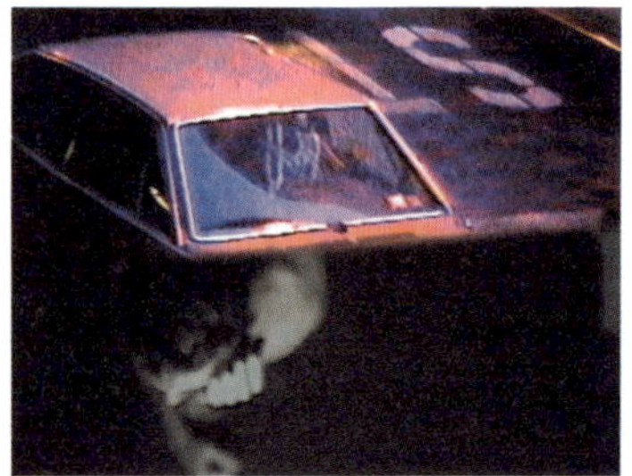

07:21

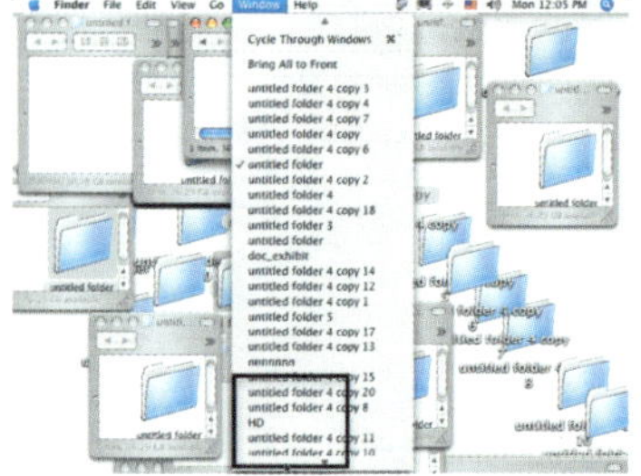

00:56

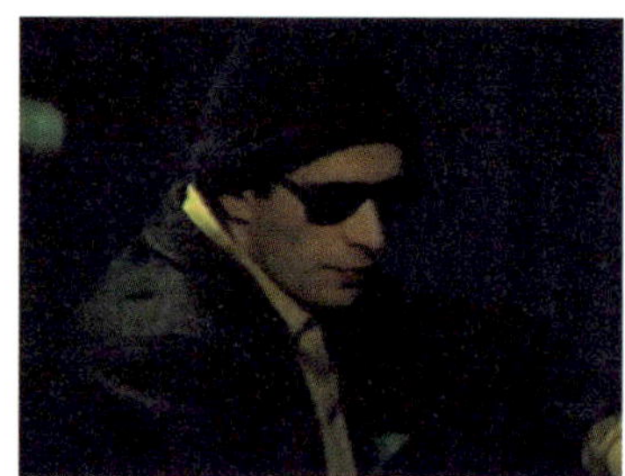

08:27

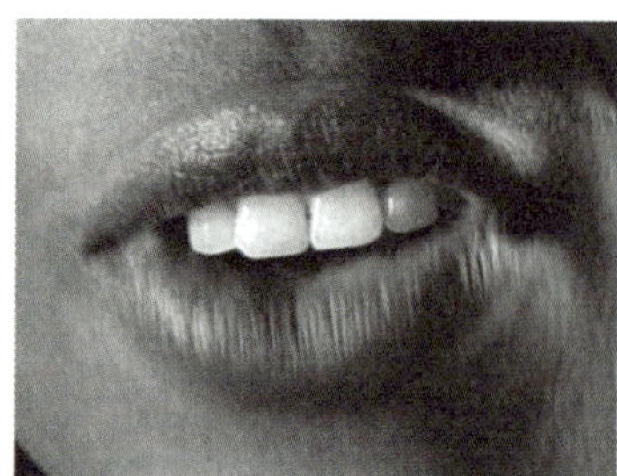

00:11

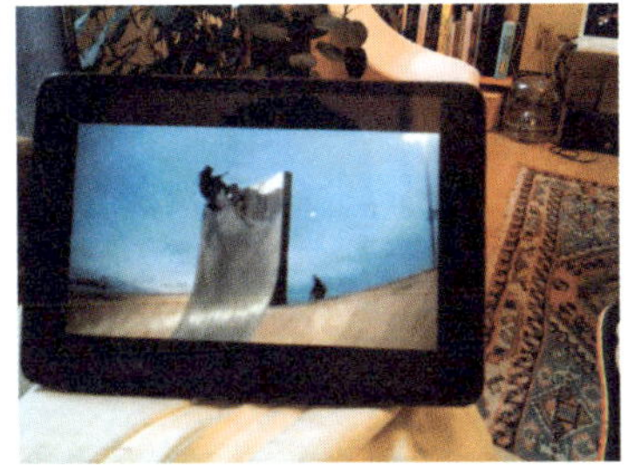

03:59

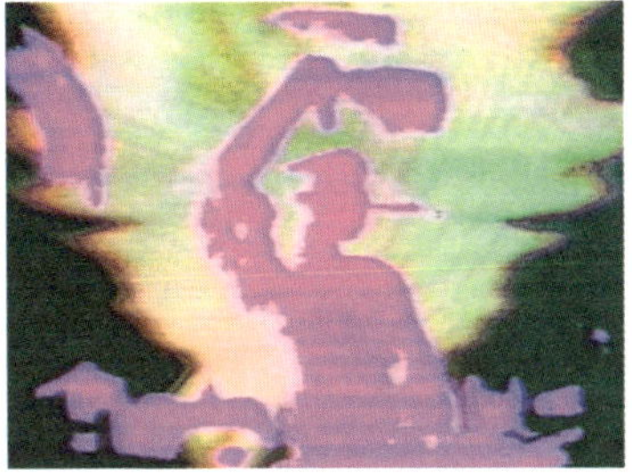

14:30

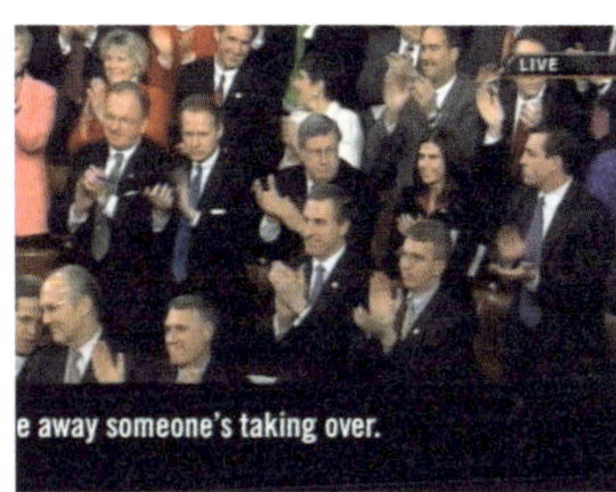

04:32

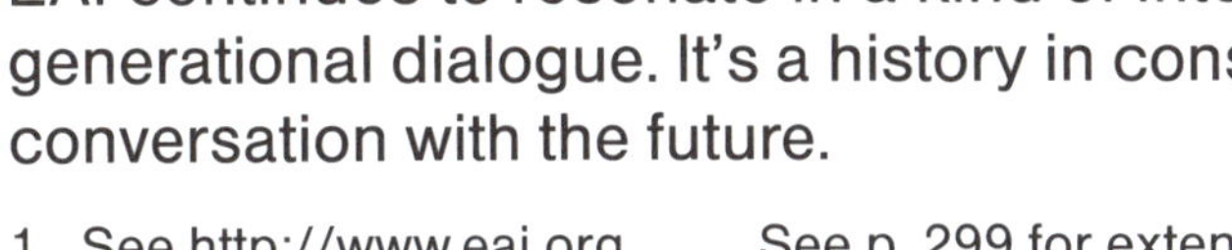

conditions, the technologies—the foundational philosophy and distinctive ecosystem that define EAI continues to resonate in a kind of intergenerational dialogue. It's a history in constant conversation with the future.

1 See http://www.eai.org/kinetic
2 Rosalind Krauss, "Video: The Aesthetics of Narcissism," *October* Vol.1 (Spring 1976), 50–64.

See p. 299 for extended image captions.

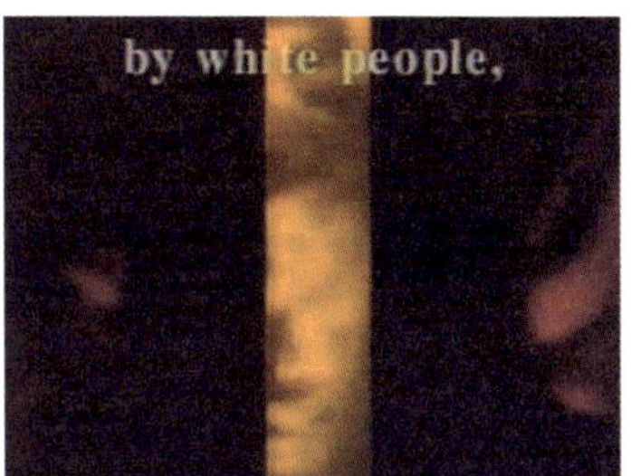

00:19

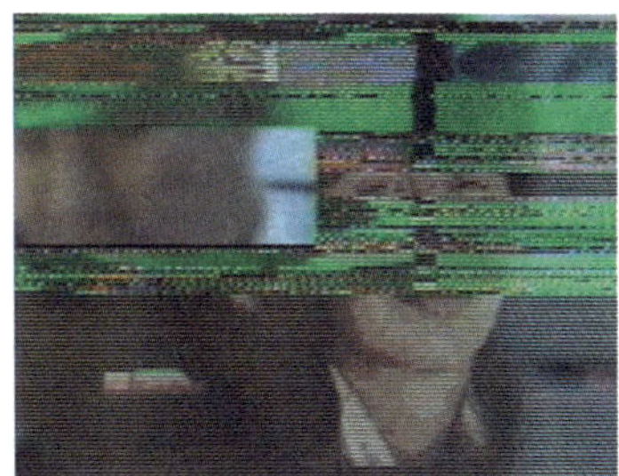

00:36

21:13

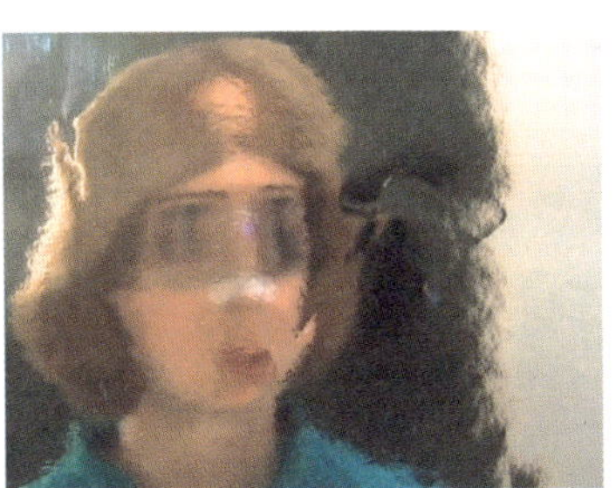

01:25

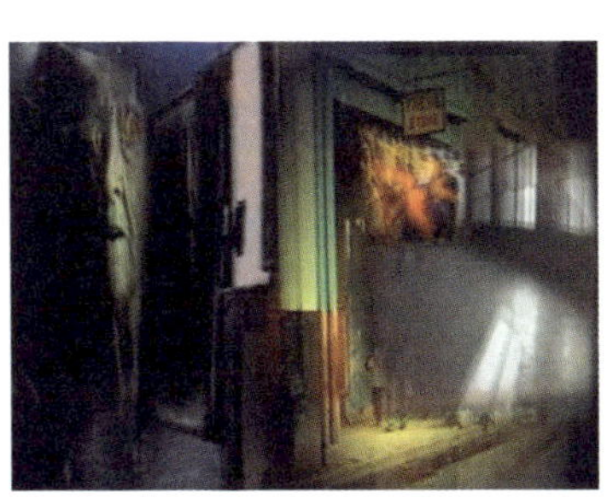

00:22

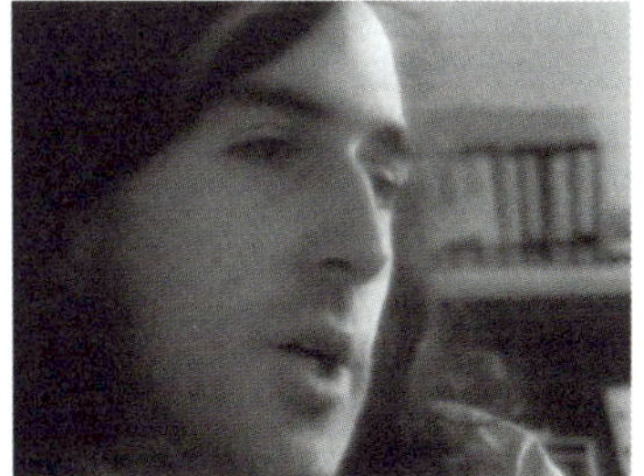

04:25

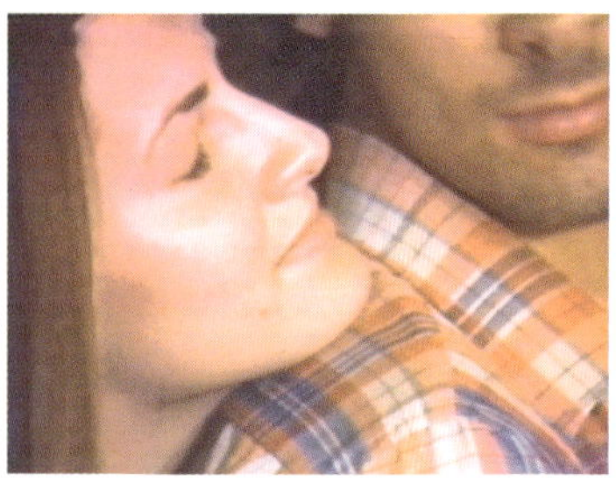
01:25

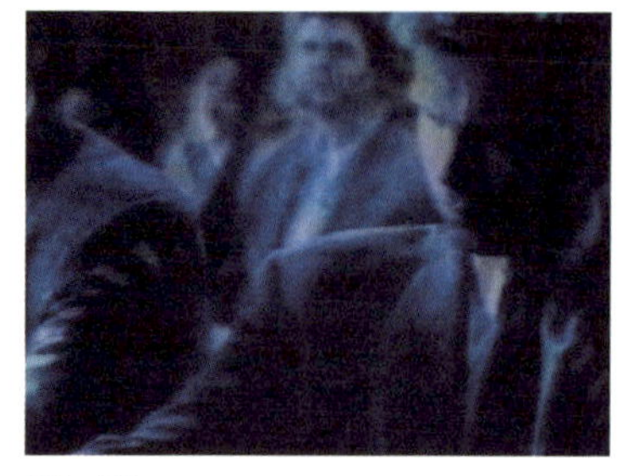
01:45

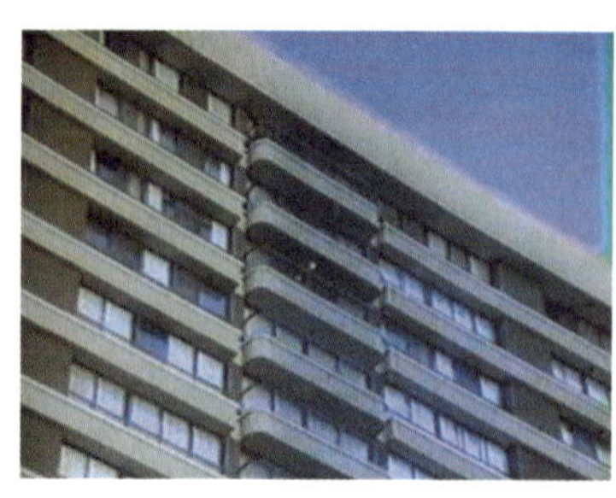
06:00

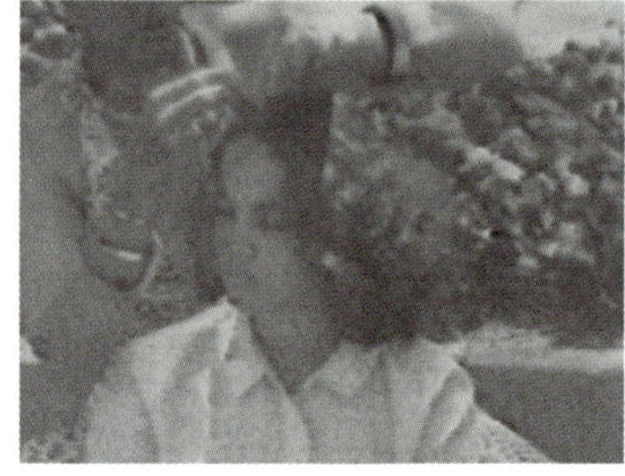
14:09

AT THE LEADING EDGE
REBECCA CLEMAN

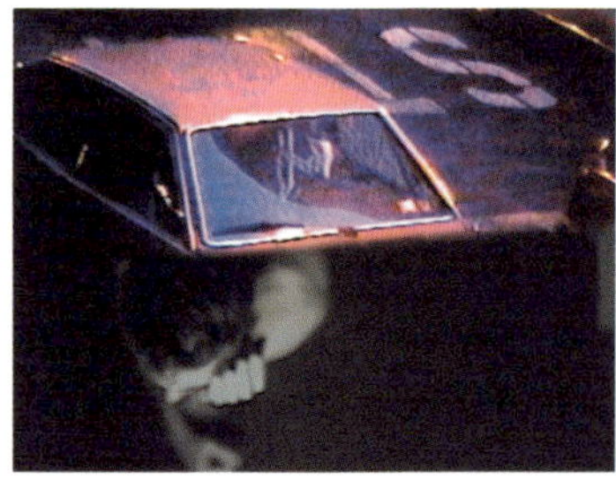
17:33

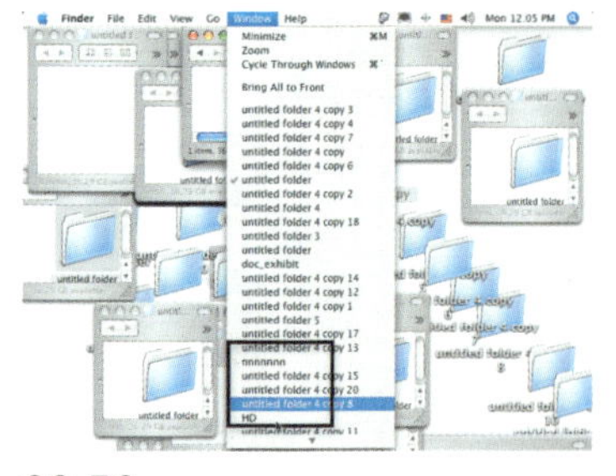
07:21

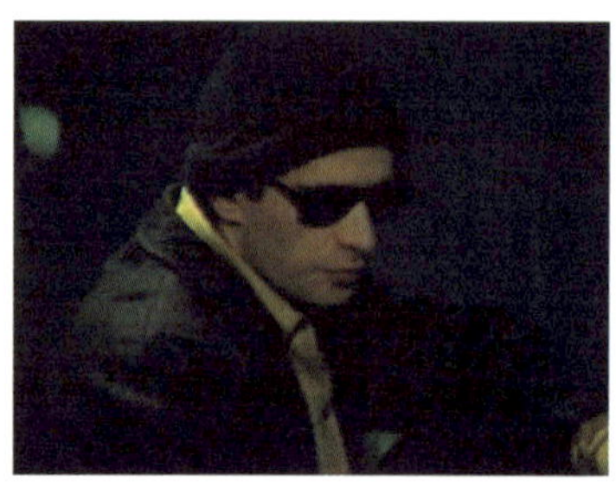
00:56

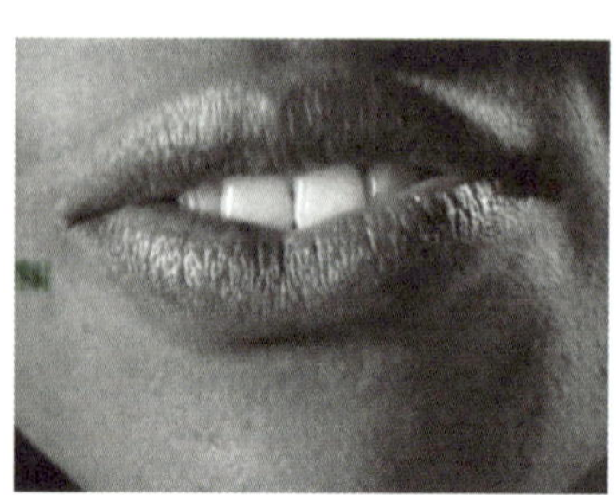
08:27

00:11

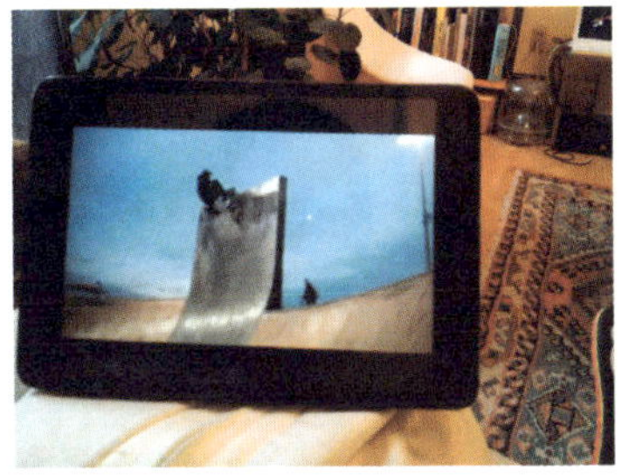
03:59

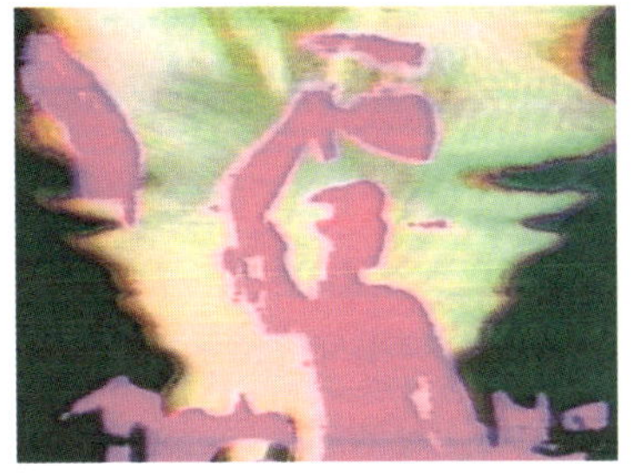
14:30

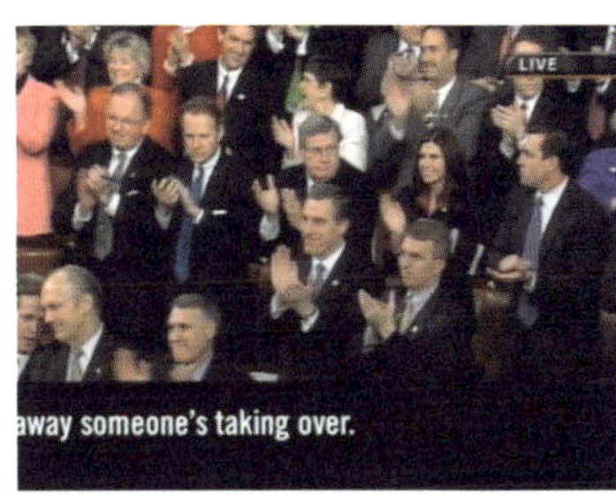

04:32

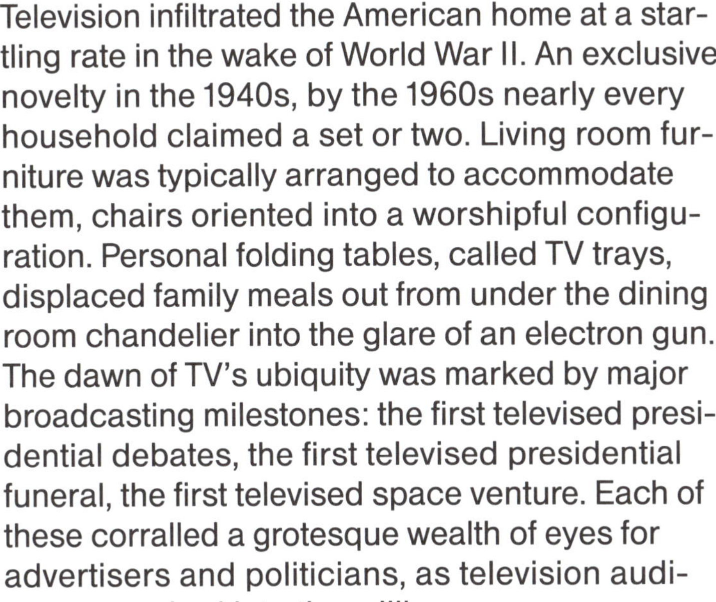

Television infiltrated the American home at a startling rate in the wake of World War II. An exclusive novelty in the 1940s, by the 1960s nearly every household claimed a set or two. Living room furniture was typically arranged to accommodate them, chairs oriented into a worshipful configuration. Personal folding tables, called TV trays, displaced family meals out from under the dining room chandelier into the glare of an electron gun. The dawn of TV's ubiquity was marked by major broadcasting milestones: the first televised presidential debates, the first televised presidential funeral, the first televised space venture. Each of these corralled a grotesque wealth of eyes for advertisers and politicians, as television audiences reached into the millions.

At the close of the decade, in May 1969, the Howard Wise Gallery opened the first exhibition in the US focused on television. *TV as a Creative Medium* featured eleven projects that dismantled or creatively altered the TV sets that occupied so many homes, demonstrating how this opaque technology could be playfully retooled. This fit

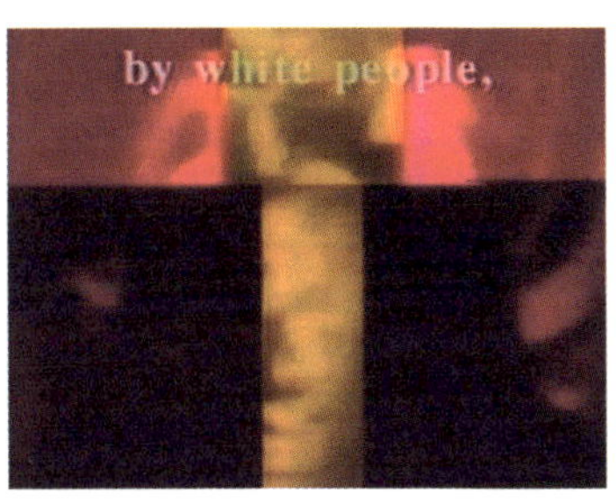
00:19

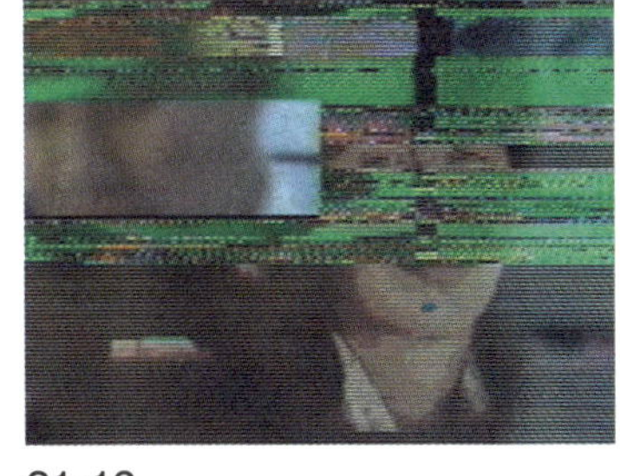

00:36

21:13

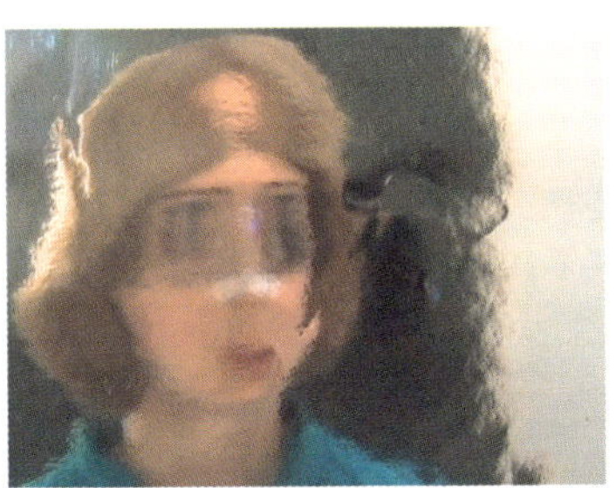
01:25

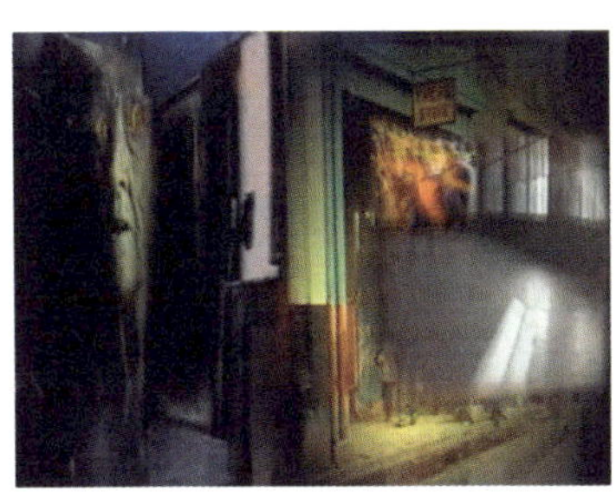
00:22

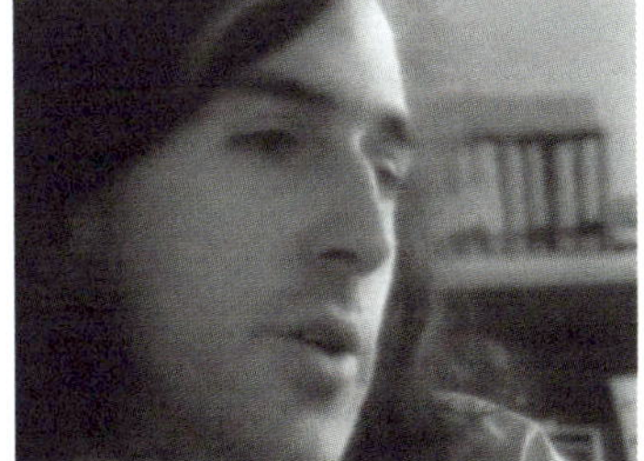
04:25

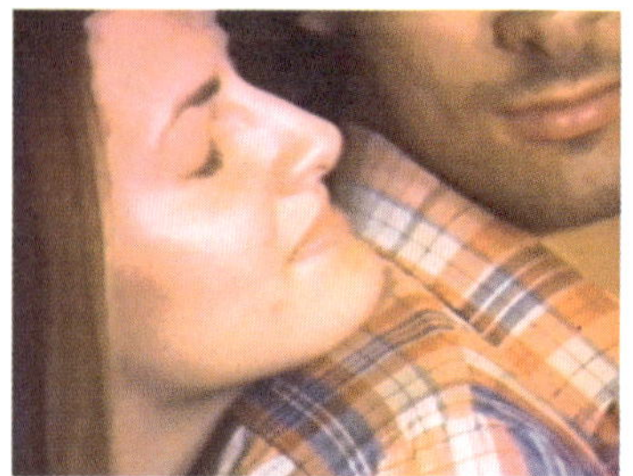
01:24

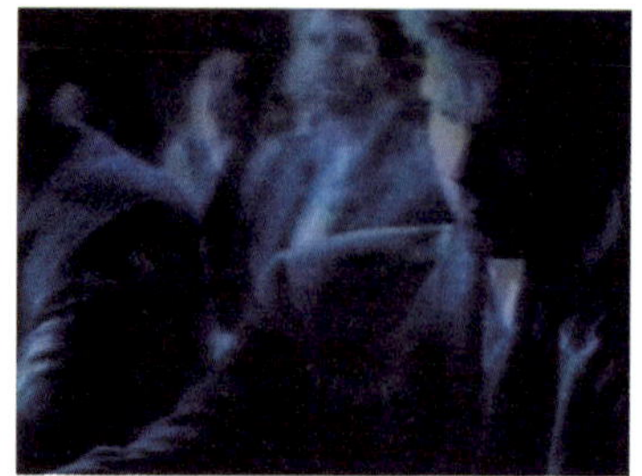
01:44

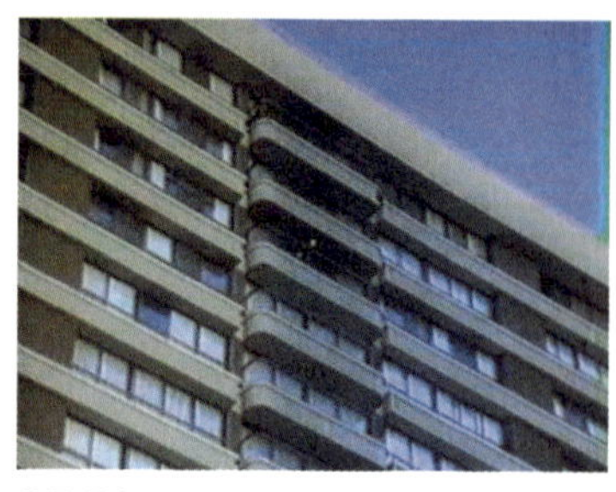
05:59

in with Wise's established reputation as a patron of artists working with technology, including such noteworthy figures as Tony Martin, Marta Minujin, Hans Haacke, Otto Piene, Nam June Paik, and Bruno Munari. The shows Wise hosted at his gallery engaged visitors with art that was involving and participatory, defying the one-way, sitting-ducks consumer dynamic that television engendered.

Right off the elevators, visitors to *TV as a Creative Medium* encountered a bank of TV sets arranged in a grid, a configuration they were more likely to find in an electronics store. Nine monitors cycled content across their screens, switching ceaselessly between network broadcasts, raw video footage of protests and street situations, and a live closed-circuit feed of the gallery. Cameras captured each viewer's image and ingested it into the feed: there you were, cycling within a display of ever-flowing information, embodying the present tense of live video against the edited past of broadcast programming and pre-recorded tapes. What an

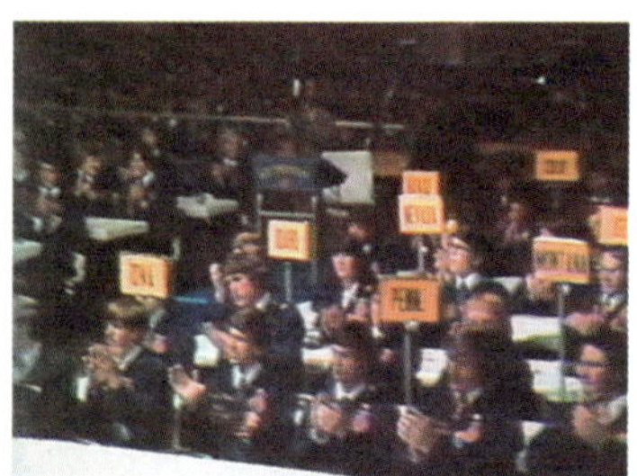
14:08

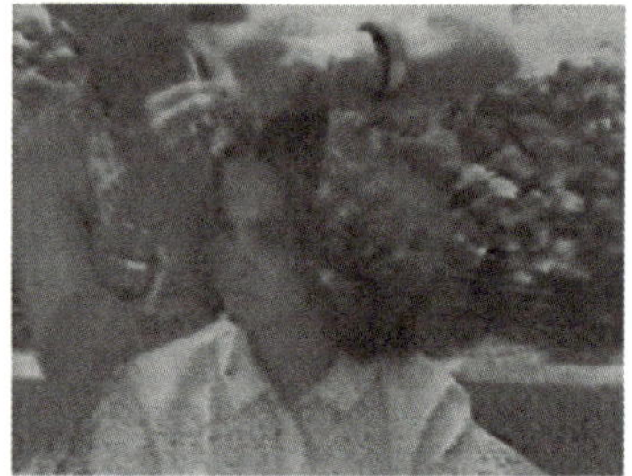
17:32

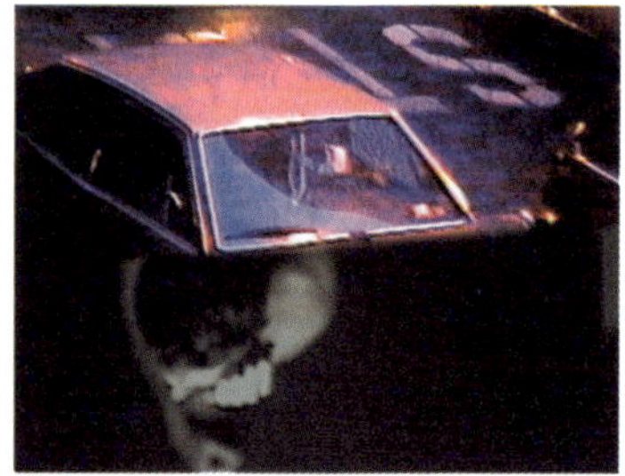
07:20

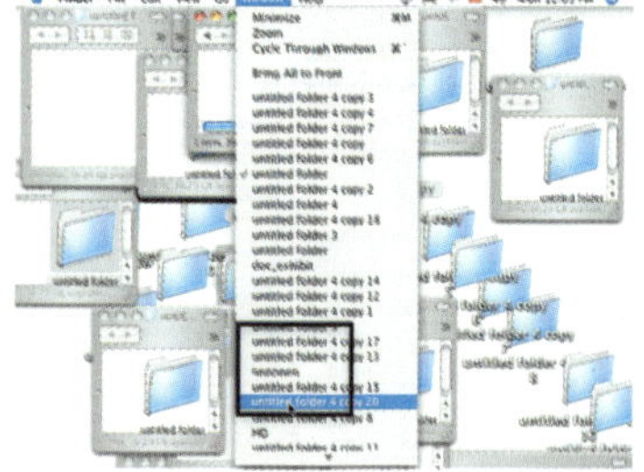
00:55

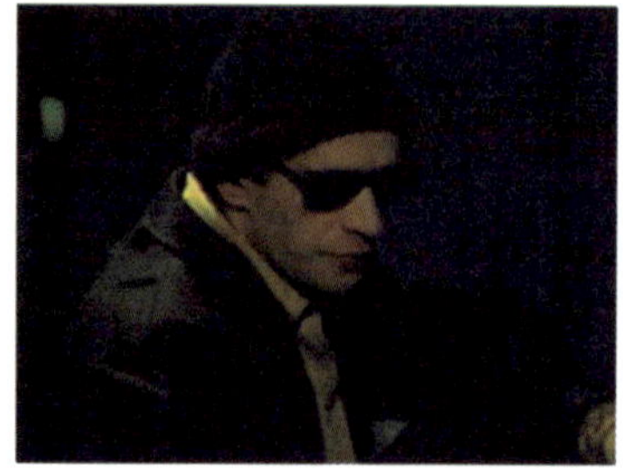
08:26

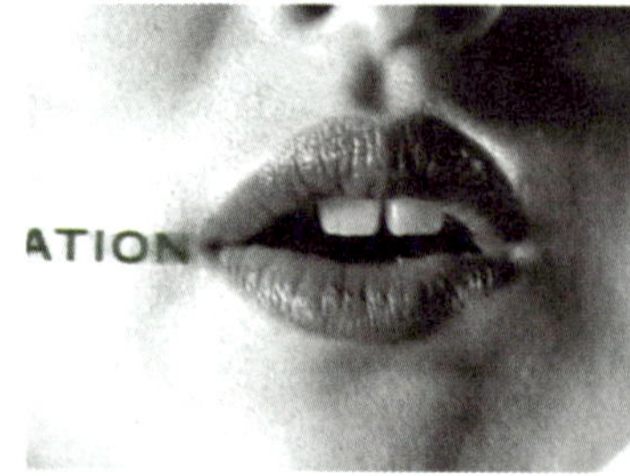

00:10

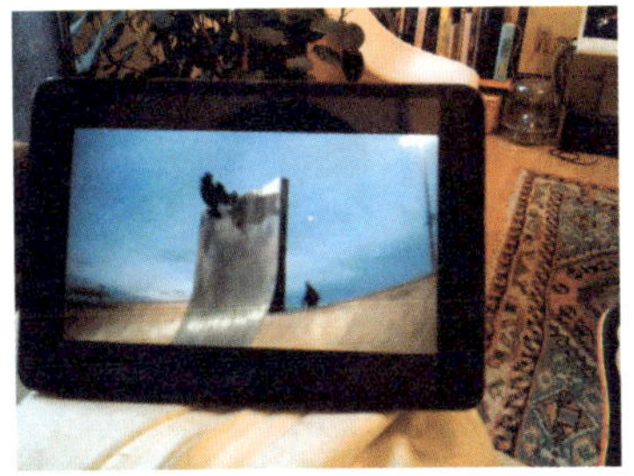
03:59

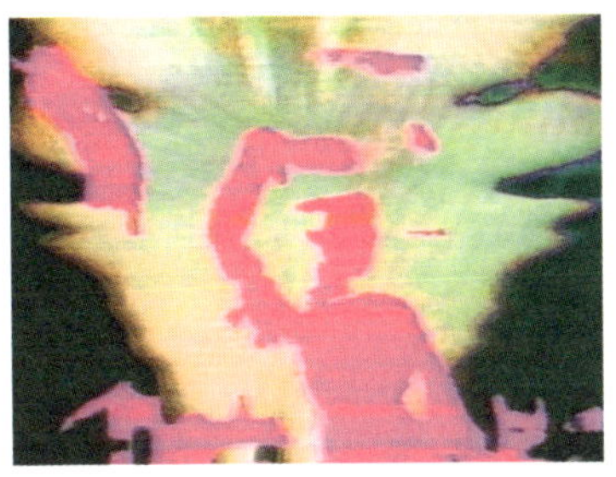
14:30

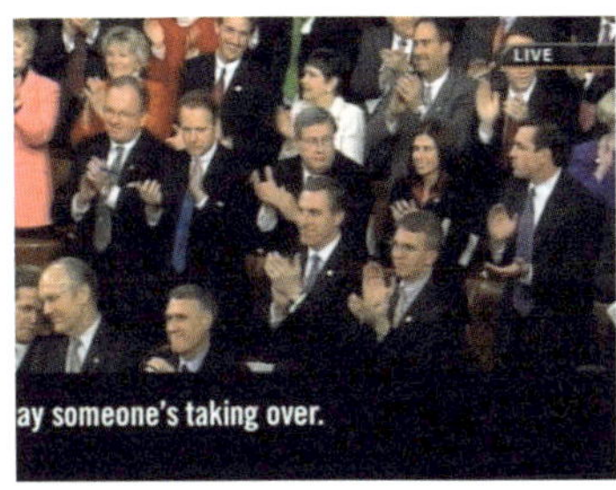

04:32

unexpected jolt it would have been at that time, to find one's own body suddenly made content.

Ira Schneider and Frank Gillette's *Wipe Cycle*, constructed with funds from Wise's personal account, announced the exhibition's radical intentions. Television was demystified and wrested from network control, while also being used as a new medium for artistic expression. In the exhibition brochure, Wise wrote:

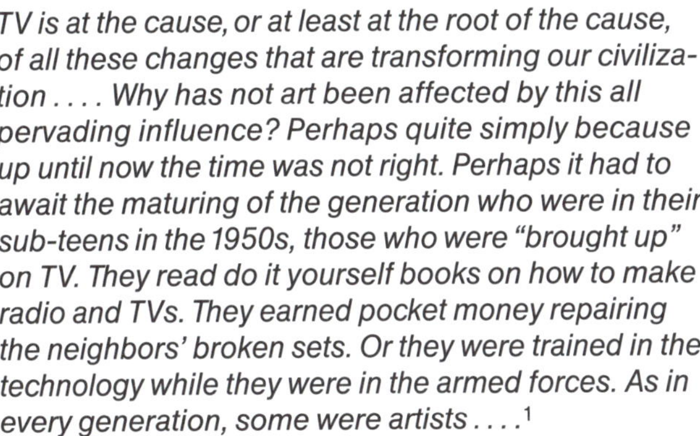

> *TV is at the cause, or at least at the root of the cause, of all these changes that are transforming our civilization . . . . Why has not art been affected by this all pervading influence? Perhaps quite simply because up until now the time was not right. Perhaps it had to await the maturing of the generation who were in their sub-teens in the 1950s, those who were "brought up" on TV. They read do it yourself books on how to make radio and TVs. They earned pocket money repairing the neighbors' broken sets. Or they were trained in the technology while they were in the armed forces. As in every generation, some were artists . . . .*[1]

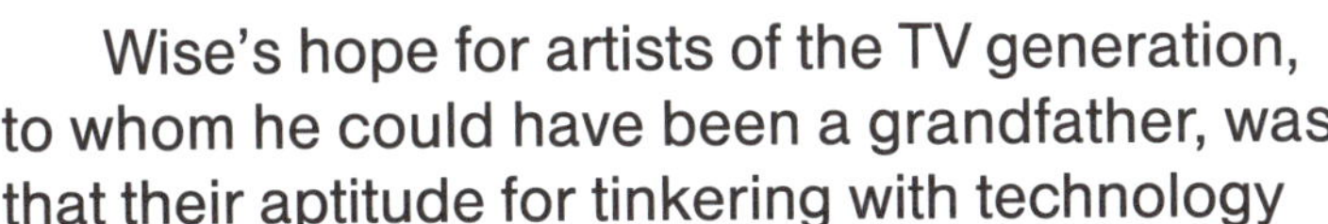

Wise's hope for artists of the TV generation, to whom he could have been a grandfather, was that their aptitude for tinkering with technology

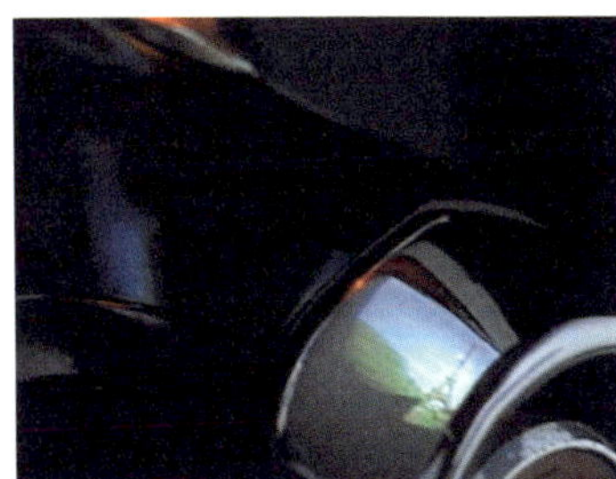
00:19

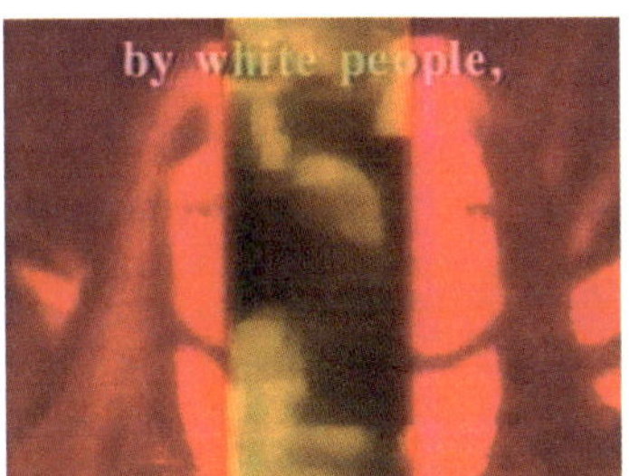

00:36

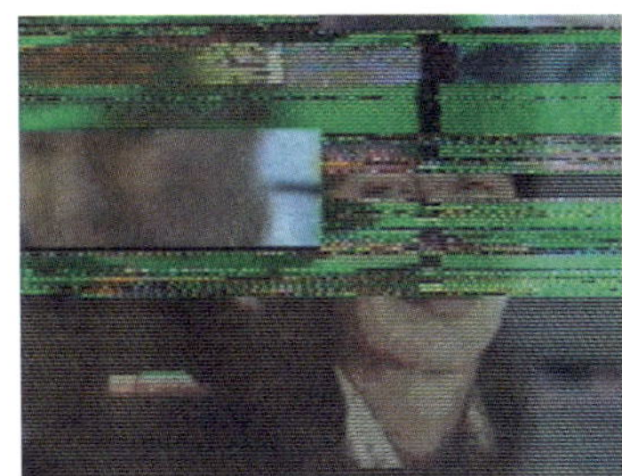
21:13

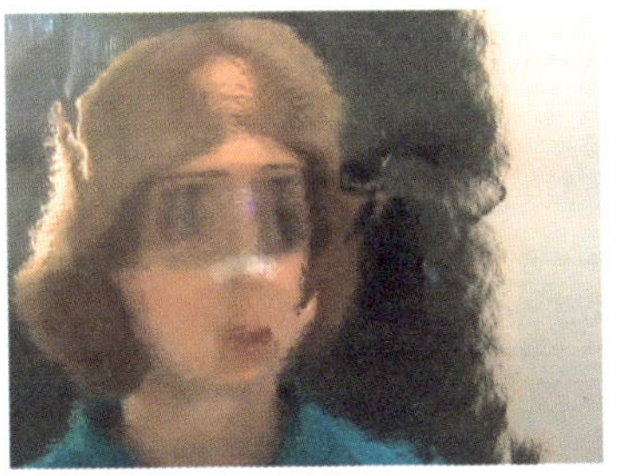
01:25

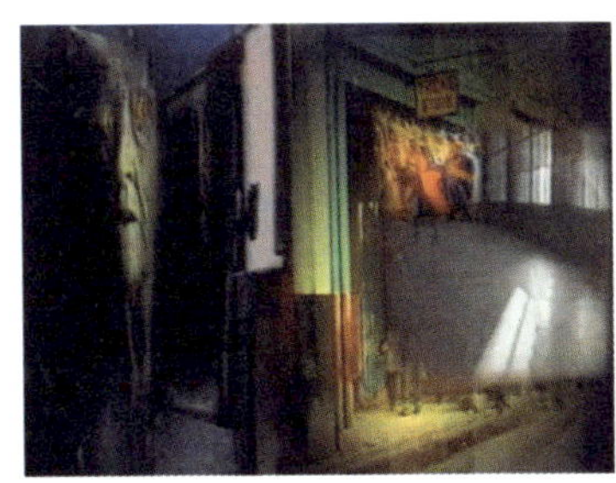
00:22

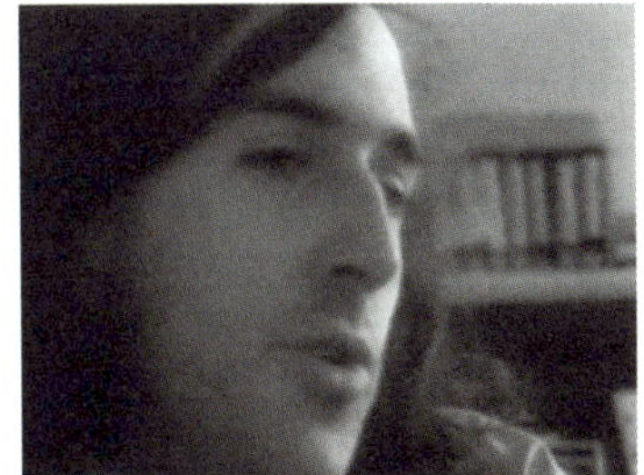
04:25

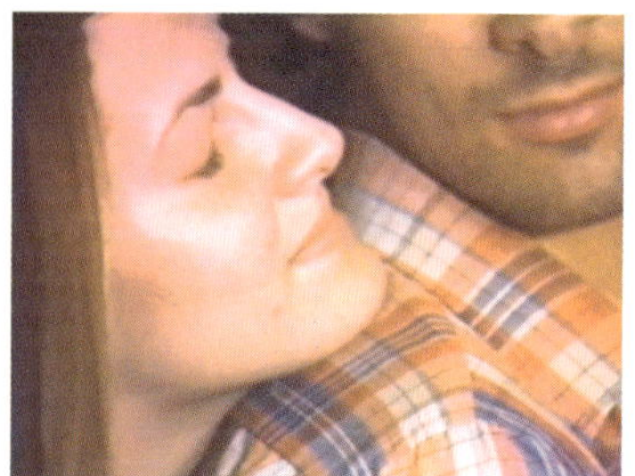
01:24

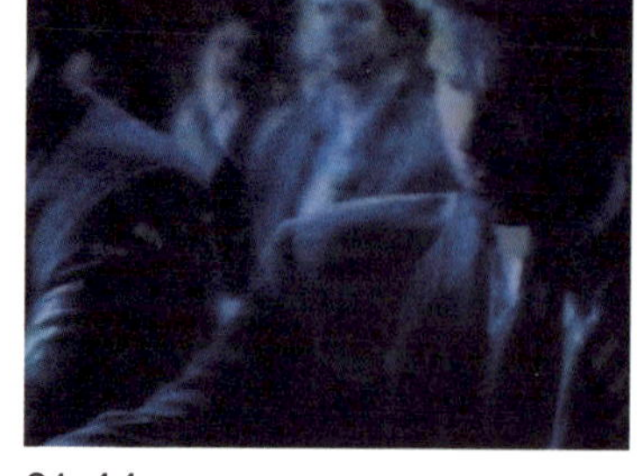
01:44

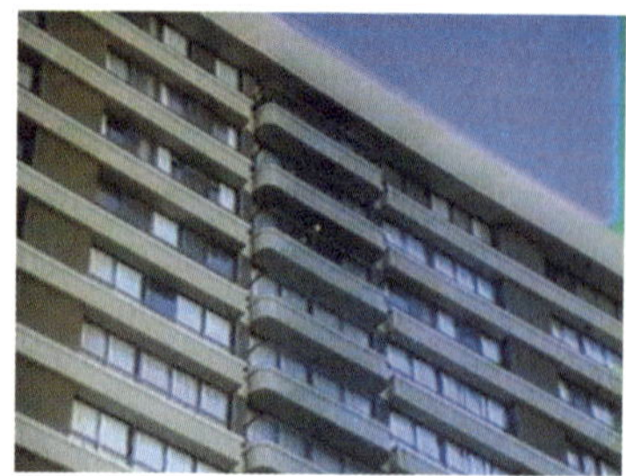
05:59

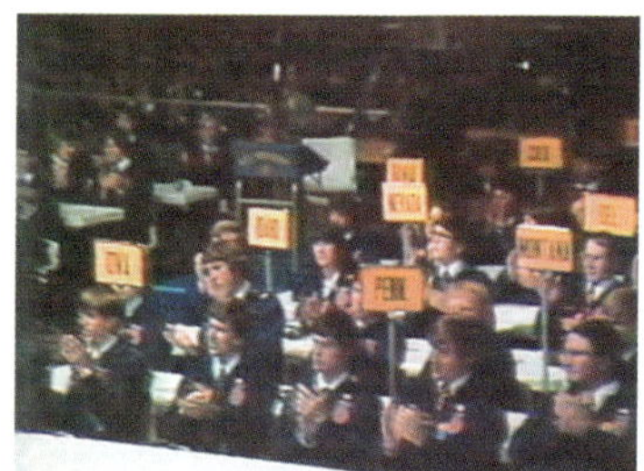
14:08

17:32

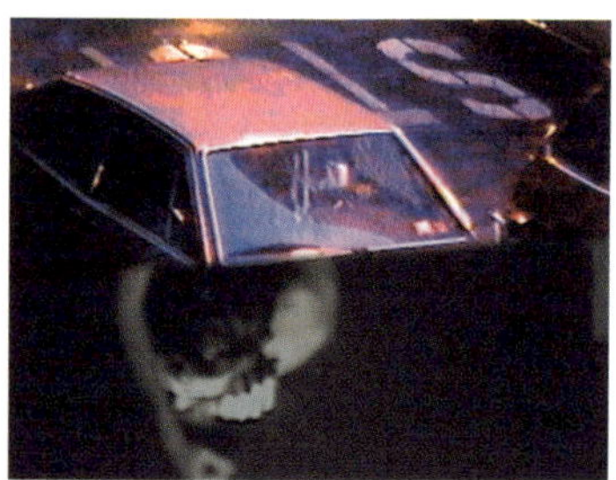
07:20

would be put to good use. This also represented a new kind of artistic identity, a departure from the famous 1949 *Life* magazine profile of Jackson Pollock that styled the artist as a postwar American hero, complete with dangling cigarette and paint-spattered jeans—the embodiment of art as a rarified, individualistic pursuit. Clement Greenberg, Abstract Expressionism's most decisive proponent, felt strongly that the gallery should be reserved for this kind of art, specifically painting and sculpture, and not the intermedia art he derided as invading the visual arts scene.[2] Greenberg's negative view ironically mirrored Wise's anticipation that the next generation would flee the gallery altogether "into the environment, the sky, the ocean, even into outer space."[3]

TV as a Creative Medium simultaneously upended conventions of the television and art industries by intermixing art and science, technology and human expression. TV sets hummed and glowed and beckoned viewers to engage with them, encouraging participation over the

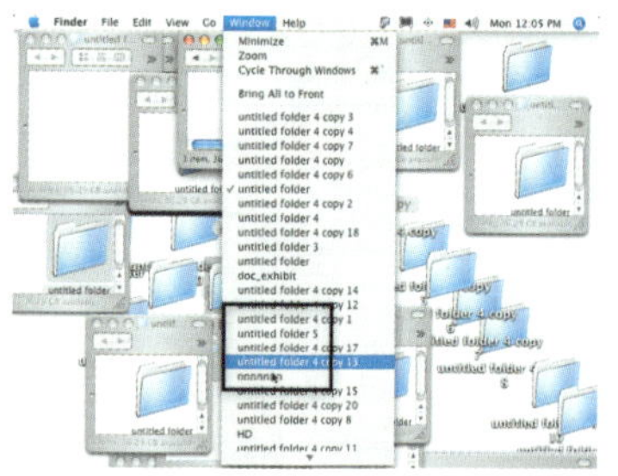
00:55

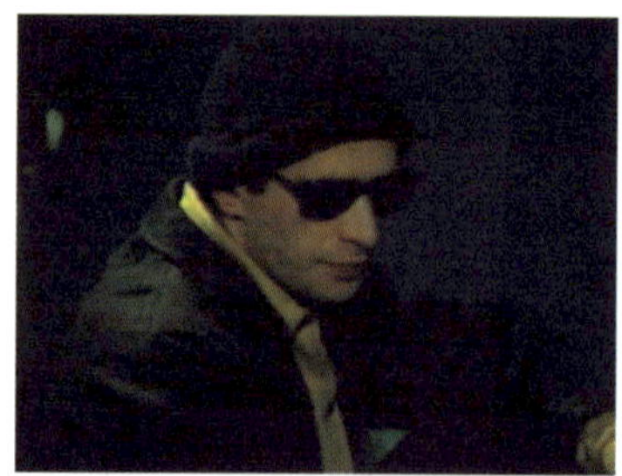
08:26

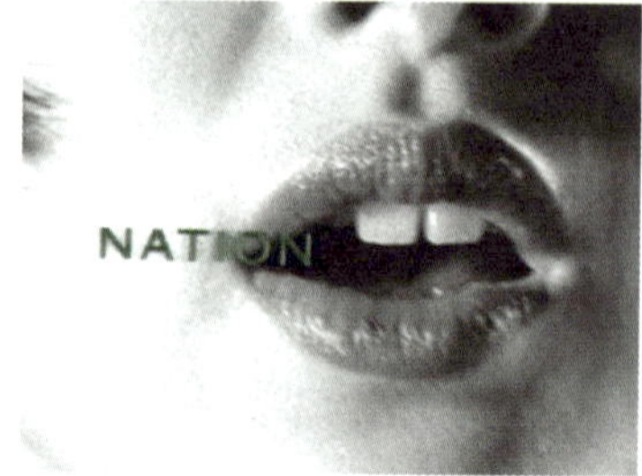
00:10

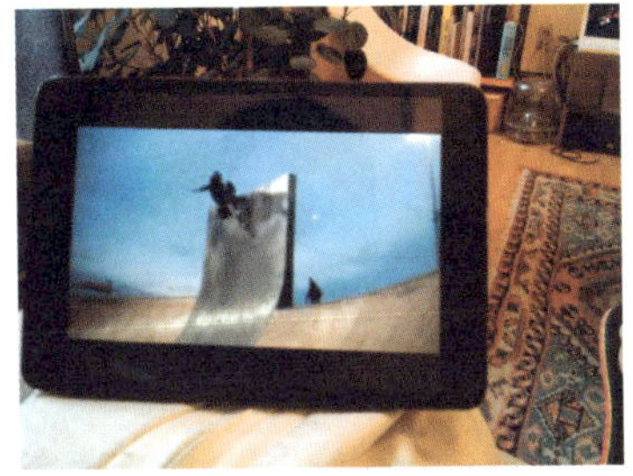
03:59

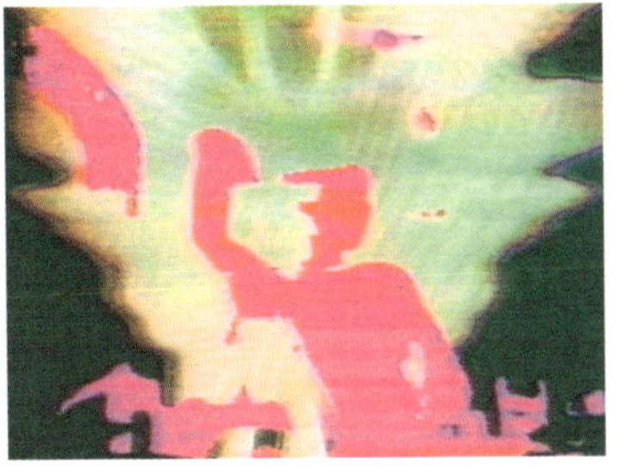
14:30

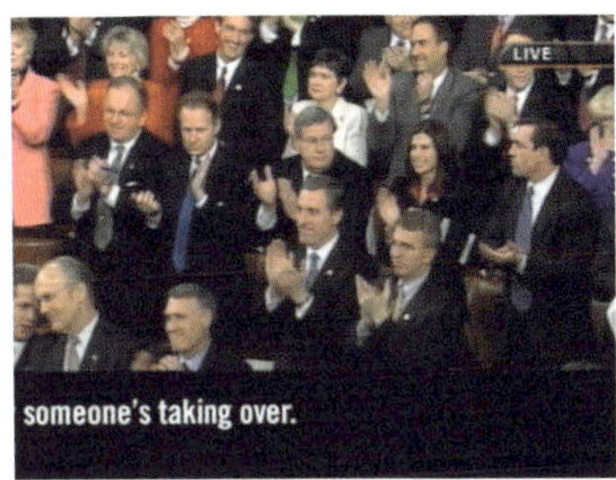

04:32

mute reverence Greenberg or network talking heads expected. Earl Reiback, a nuclear physicist and artist with patents related to sound, light, and nuclear radiation, presented three monitors with their inner mechanisms exposed, painted with color phosphors and filled with neon gas, the flow of electrons creating dazzling abstract effects. Nam June Paik and Charlotte Moorman's *TV Bra for Living Sculpture* fitted tiny TVs in place of Moorman's brassiere, humanizing and humbling the technology by foregrounding her live performance as she played the cello. Aldo Tambellini, a poet, painter, sculptor, and filmmaker, altered a television so that it distorted the broadcast signal into a glistening white spiral that he likened to a celestial pattern.

Paul Ryan's *Everyman's Moebius Strip* was more of a therapeutic aide than an artwork. Ryan had studied with communications theorist Marshall McLuhan, and was most interested in using television to nurture a particular social dynamic. In his CCTV feed project, visitors were invited into a television "confessional," where they

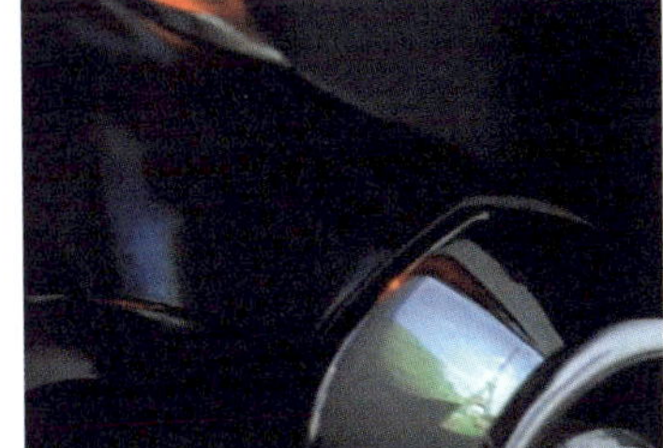
00:19

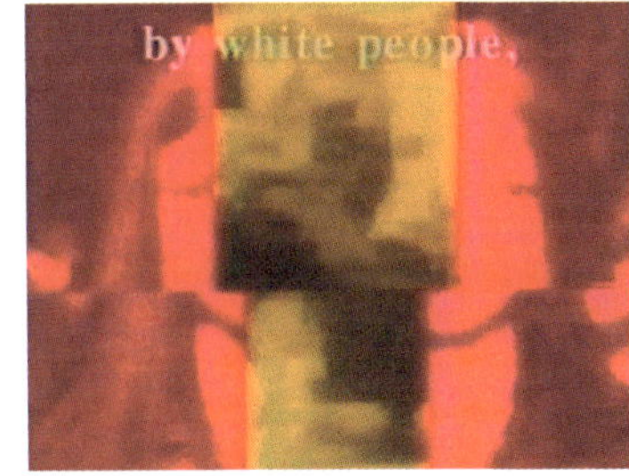

00:36

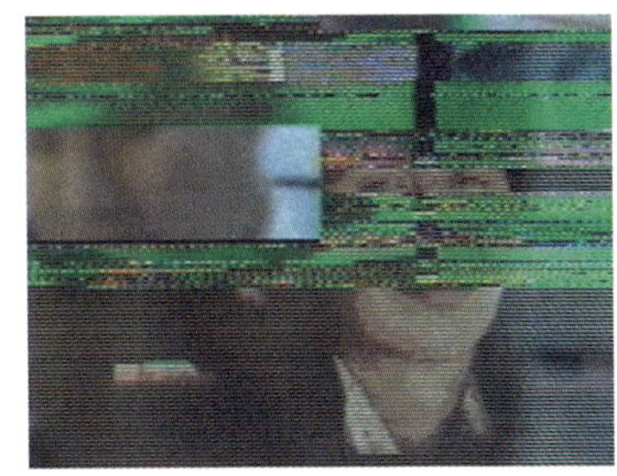
21:13

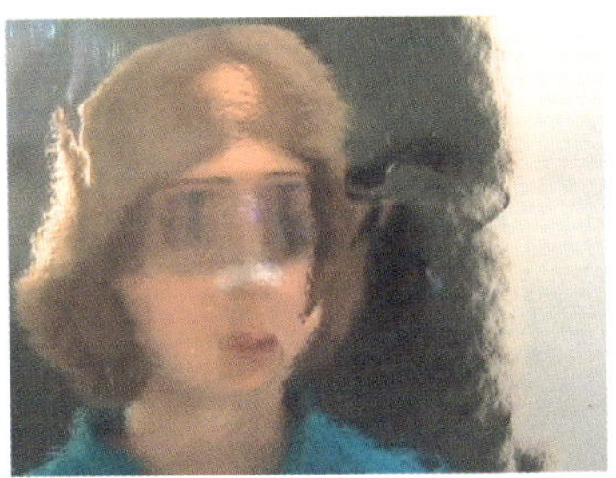
01:25

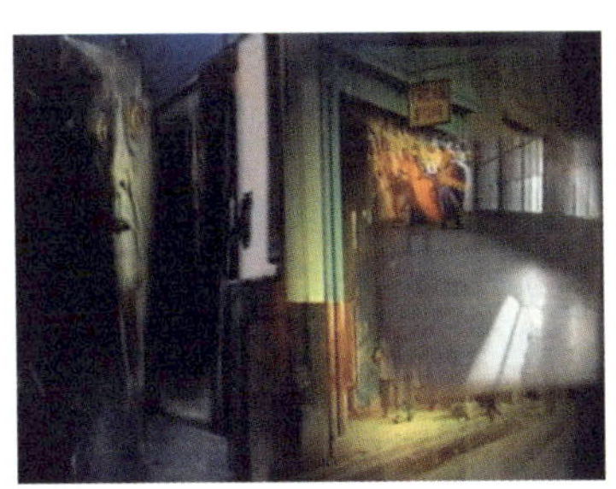
00:22

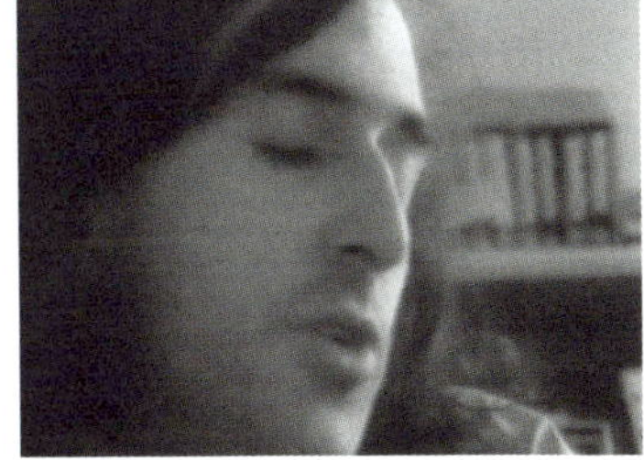
04:25

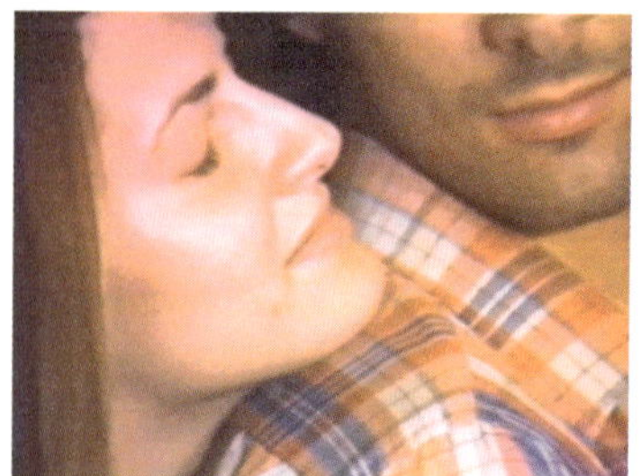
01:24

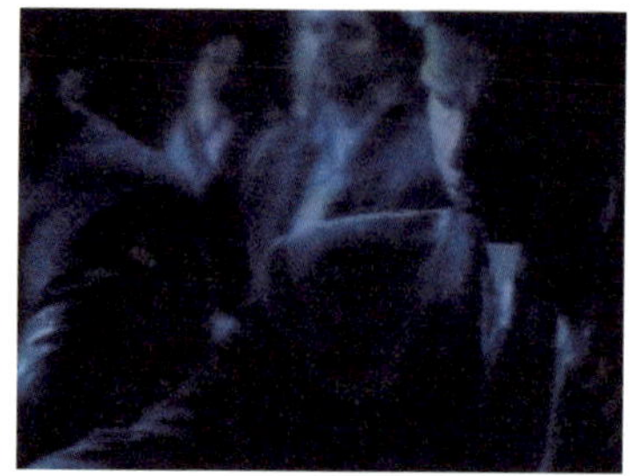
01:44

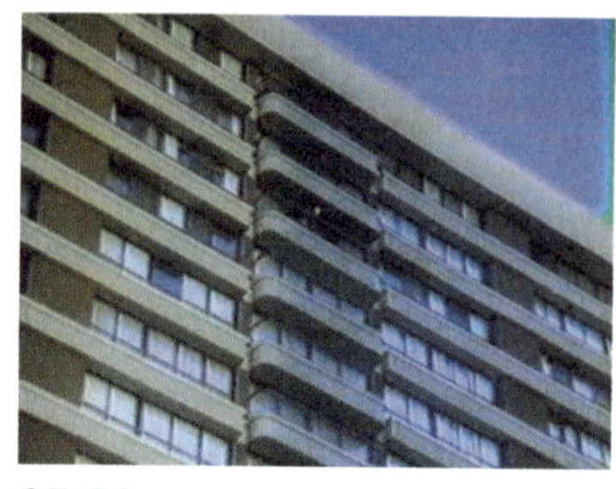
05:59

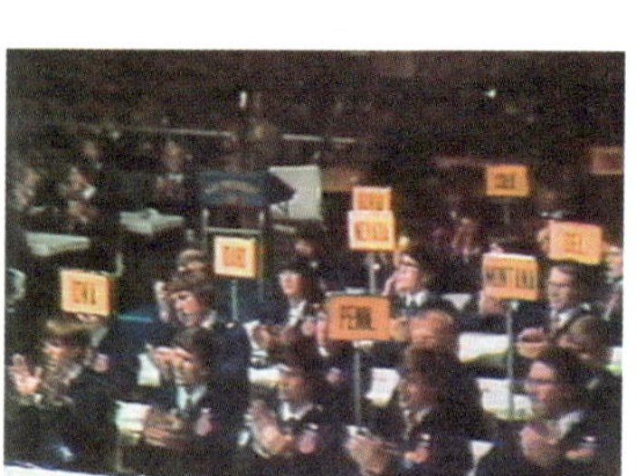
14:08

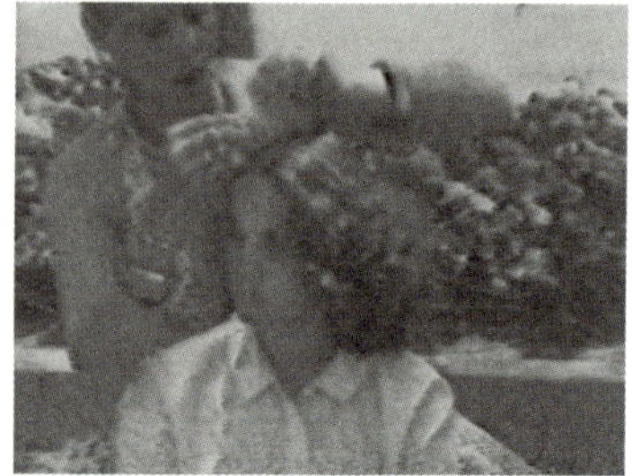
17:32

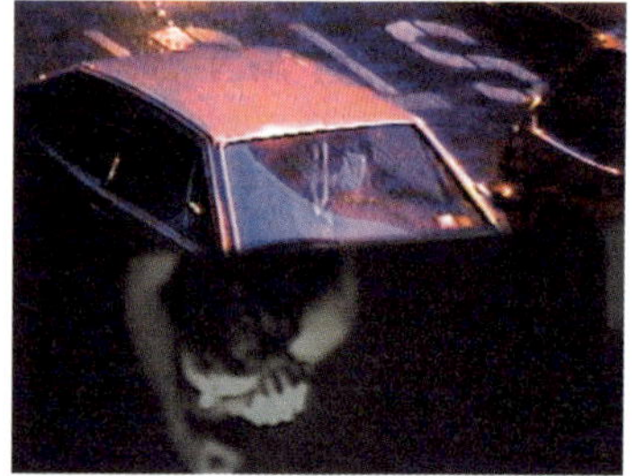
07:20

were encouraged to freely express themselves to an objective camera. The recording of their admissions was instantly erased, maintaining the privacy of their public exposure, though the process of participating so intimately with a television system would have a considerable psychological, and sociological, effect.

Consumer recording and publishing devices are so commonplace today that it might be hard to appreciate how incredible this engagement with TV would have been back then. The bulky sets in living rooms were not only mysterious in their operations, but also connected to spectacular events that extended into the realms of the unknown and otherworldly (underscored by then popular programs like *The Twilight Zone* and *The Outer Limits*). Via television, earthlings were granted a view of their vulnerable planet for the first time. Photographs of Earth taken by a weather satellite were televised in 1960, at one end of a space race that would culminate in the 1969 moon landing. On that historic occasion, television showed remarkable live video of the

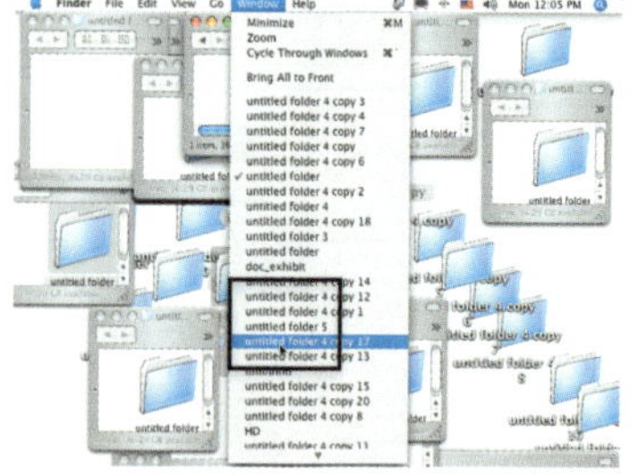
00:55

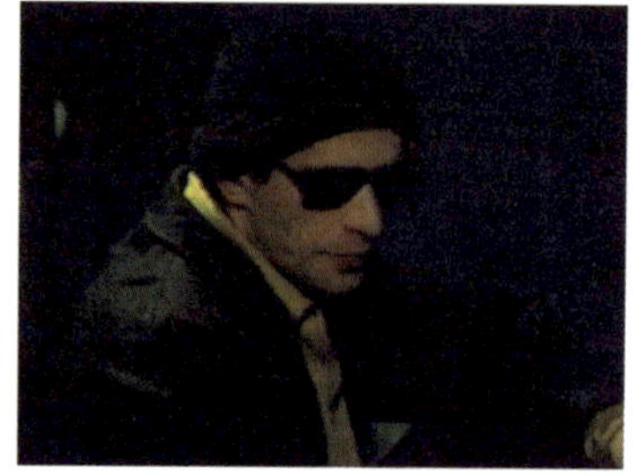
08:26

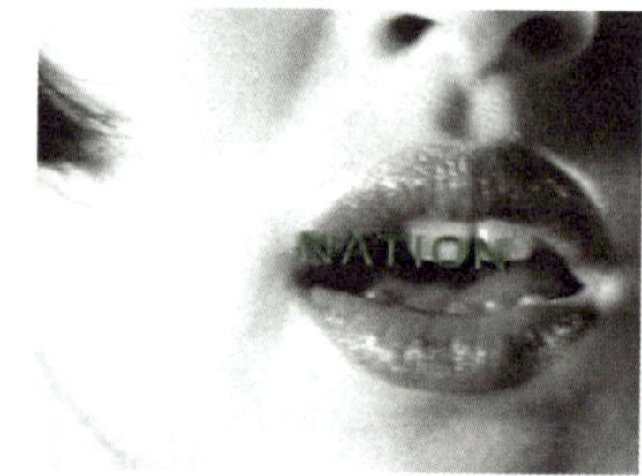

00:10

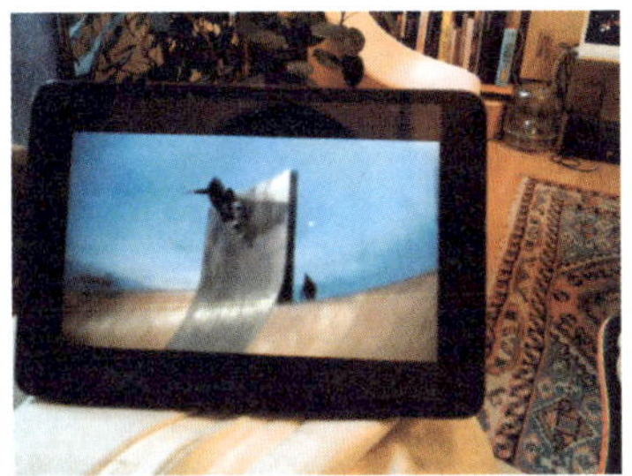
03:59

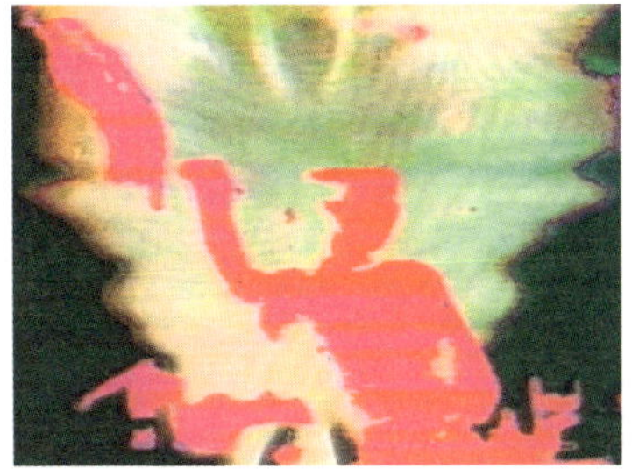
14:30

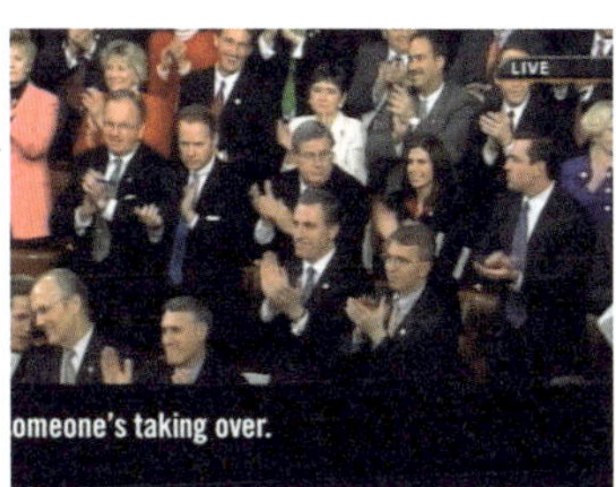

04:32

NASA Apollo 11 astronauts stepping into the spacecraft, calmly flipping dials in their ship as it hurtled them to their unfathomable destiny on the lunar surface.

CBS and anchorman Walter Cronkite led the ratings, broadcasting from a windowless studio in Manhattan with only occasional breaks for deli sandwiches and soda. The stuff of science fiction was domesticated, filtered into the quotidian routines of American life. The proximity of Cronkite's legendary broadcast to Wise's gallery, just a few blocks down 57th Street in Manhattan from the CBS studio, physically represented how psychologically intertwined these events were. The excitement of space exploration was adjacent to a countercultural movement that took up the images of Earth in space as a symbol of unity and of our collective role in maintaining what Buckminster Fuller fancifully called "Spaceship Earth."[4]

The images of our planet hanging like a marble in space became an emblem for Stewart Brand's *Whole Earth Catalog* (1968–1971), a key

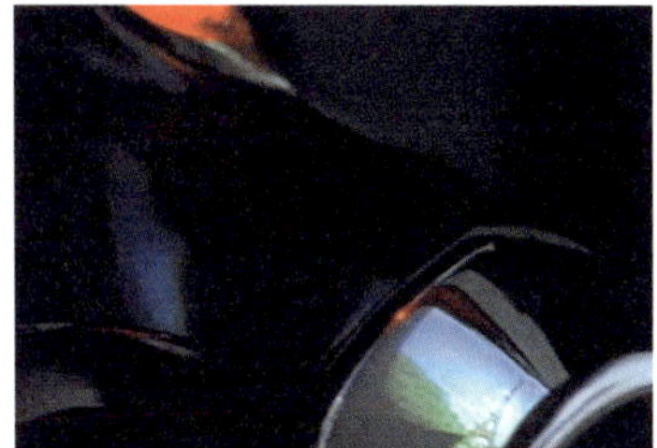
00:19

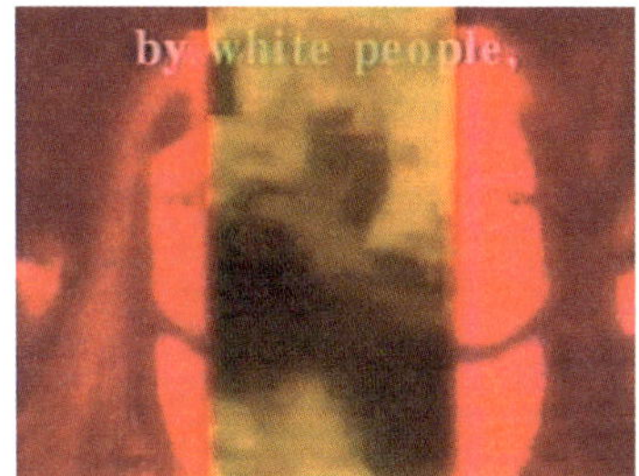

00:36

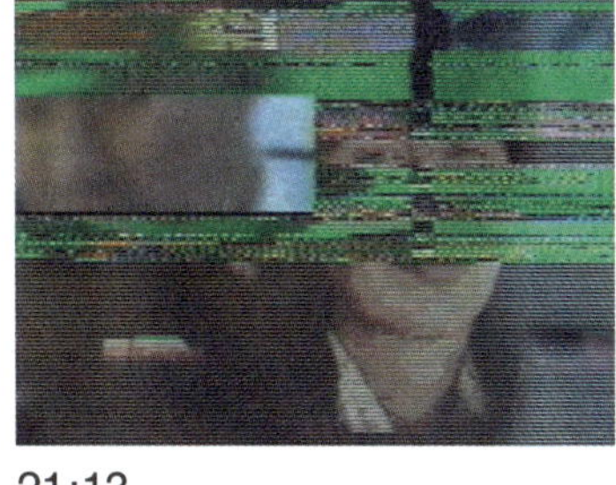
21:13

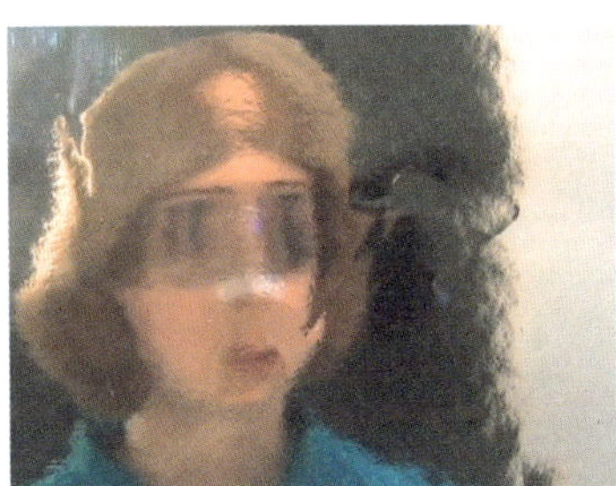
01:25

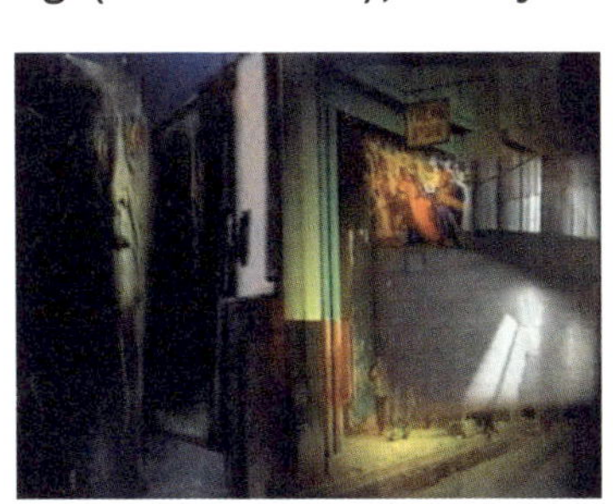
00:22

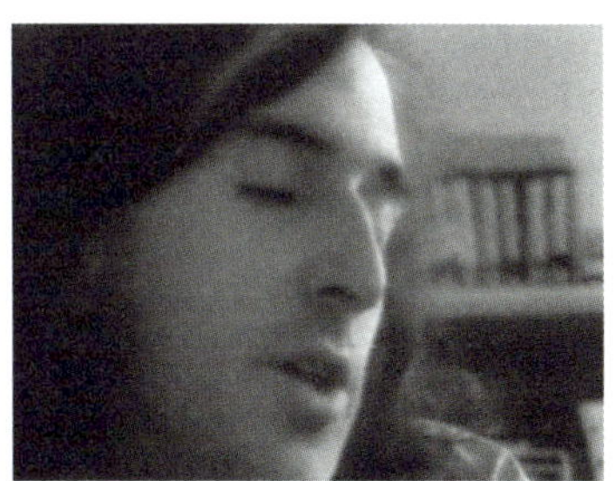
04:25

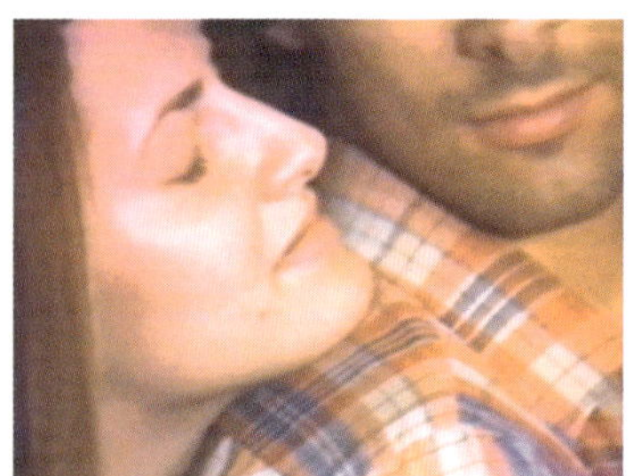

01:24

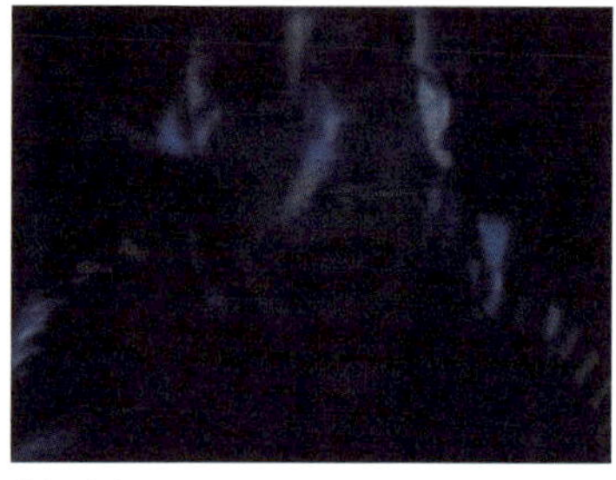

01:44

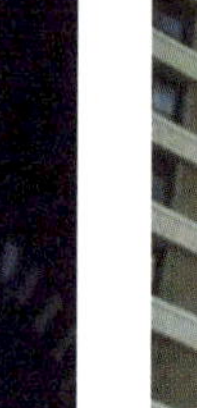

05:59

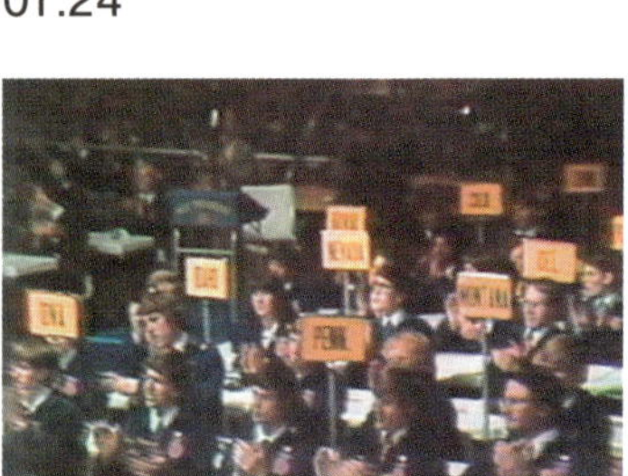

14:08

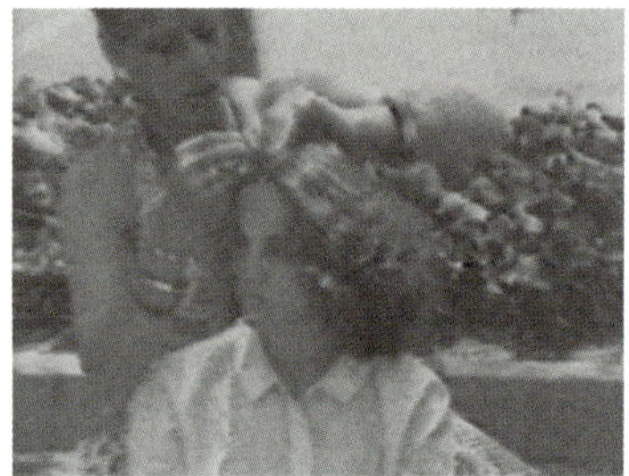

17:32

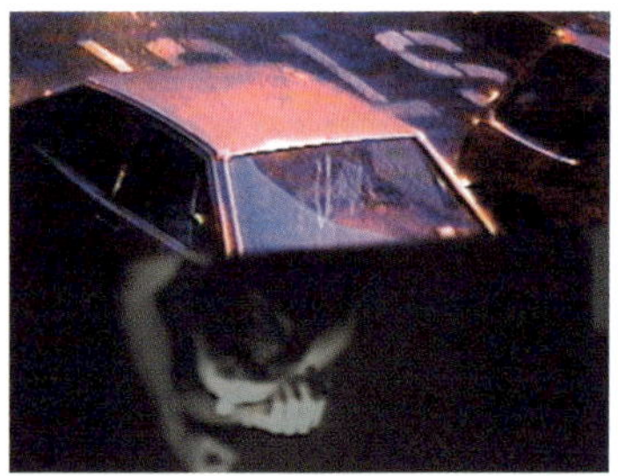

07:20

publication of the counterculture. Part of a thriving underground publishing scene, the periodical departed from conventional product magazines and catalogs through its editorial focus, emphasizing self-sufficiency, resource exchange, ecology, and alternative lifestyles. The Earth's physical wholeness and oneness, confirmed by NASA photographs that Brand was instrumental in making public, inspired an ethos of planetary harmony and collectivity. The postwar consumerist push, and especially the focus on innovation, whether in the domestic or military realm, was reconceived to empower individuals by giving them access to tools and information that they could use to improve their lives and their communities. In the spring of 1969, a group involved with the *Whole Earth Catalog* convened Alloy, a gathering in a geodesic dome in the New Mexico desert. An intentional alternative to Cold War research and development summits, Alloy brought together individuals from diverse areas of expertise to discuss appropriate technology and sustainable development.[5]

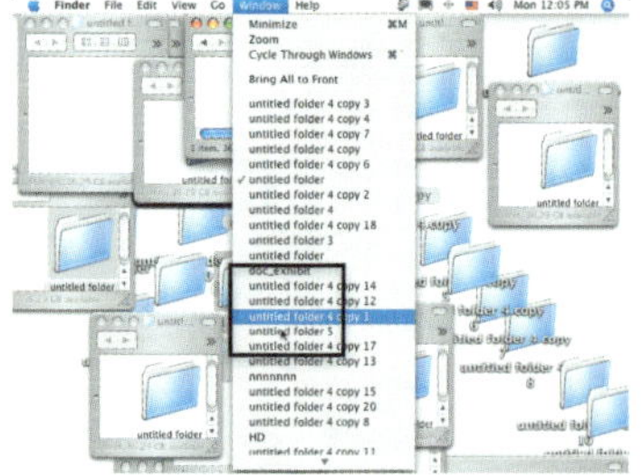

00:55

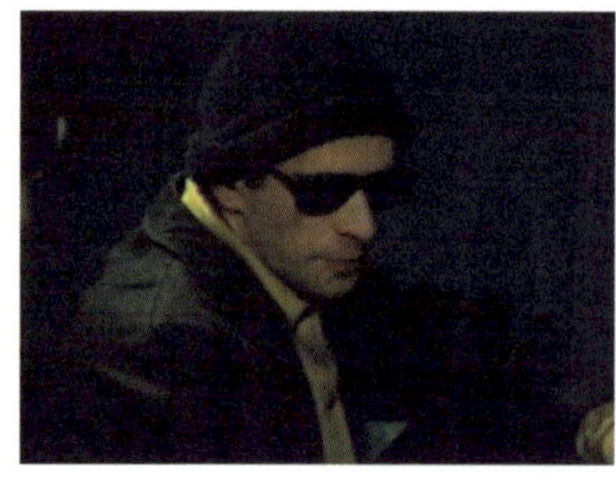

08:26

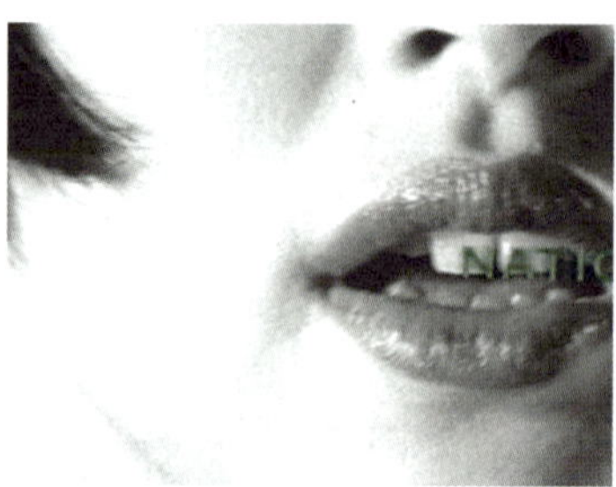

00:10

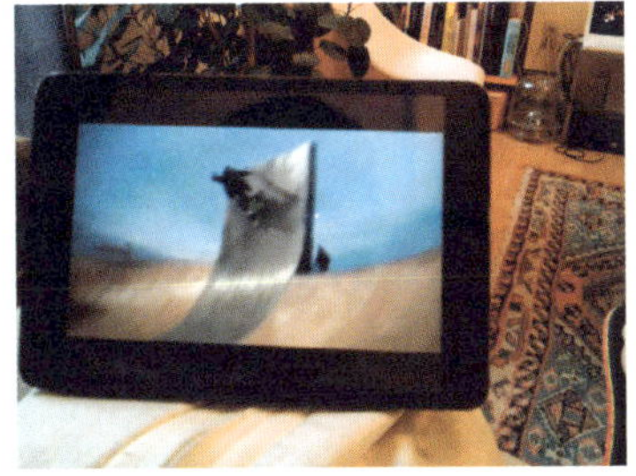
04:00

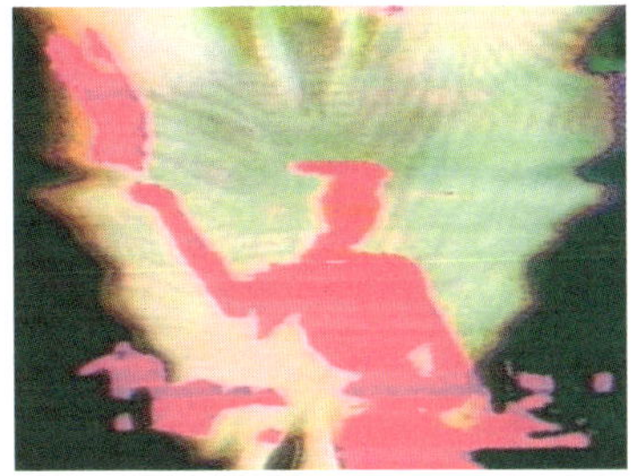
14:31

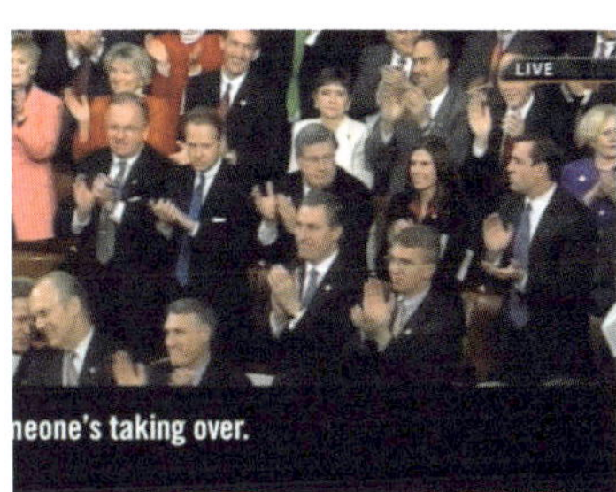

04:33

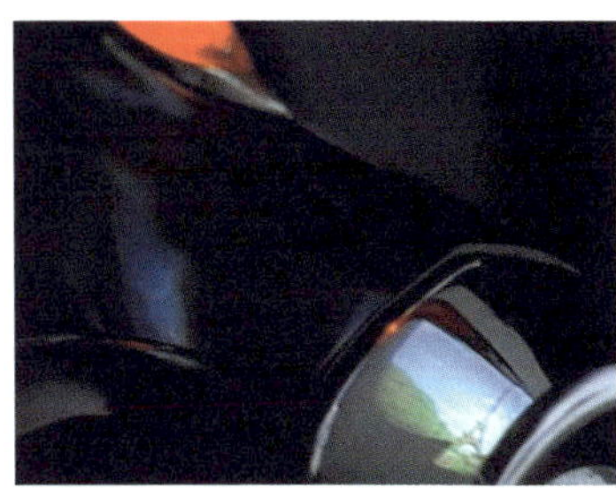
00:20

Alloy's merging of the counterculture with a technology-focused subculture also characterized the spirit of *TV as a Creative Medium*, which in some ways was less exhibition than catalytic event that galvanized the activities of a video subculture.

One important outgrowth of the show, for instance, was the formation of the Raindance collective, initially comprising *TV* contributors Schneider, Gillette, and Ryan, along with Louis Jaffe, Marco Vassi, and Michael Shamberg, a journalist who reviewed the show for *Time* magazine. Raindance's name and structure were conceived as a progressive alternative to the RAND Corporation, a postwar think tank providing research and analysis to the US military and government. Raindance aspired to a wide range of functions, including funding subversive video projects through a "Center for the Decentralization of Television." Though this did not come to fruition, the collective published some of the most important texts about video and television at the time.

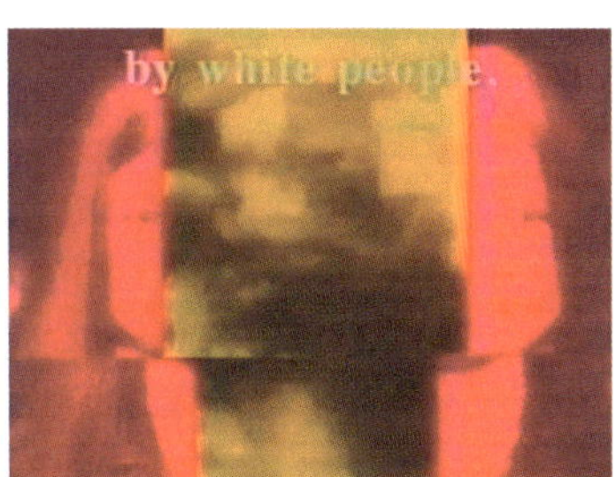

00:37

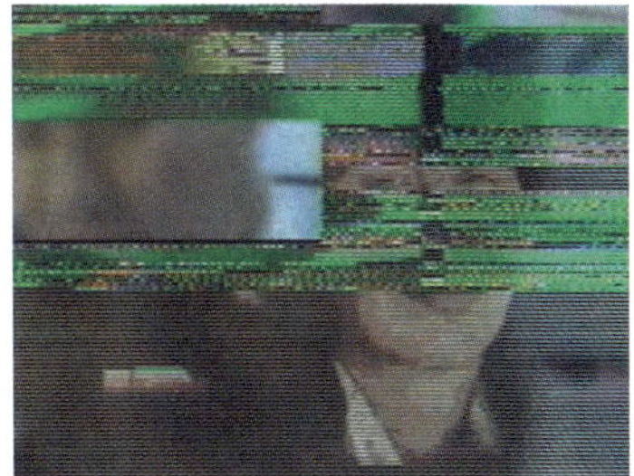
21:14

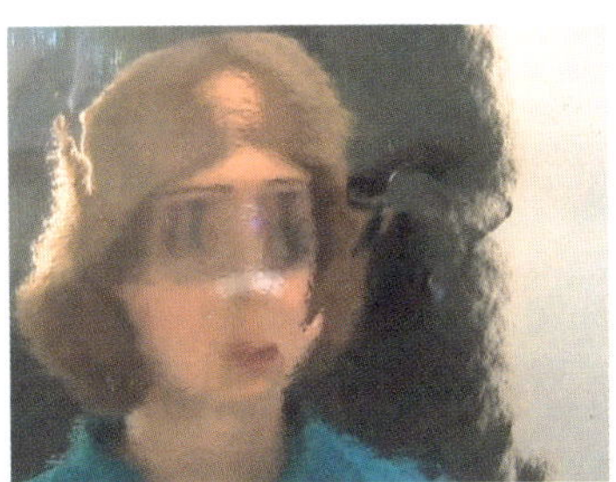
01:26

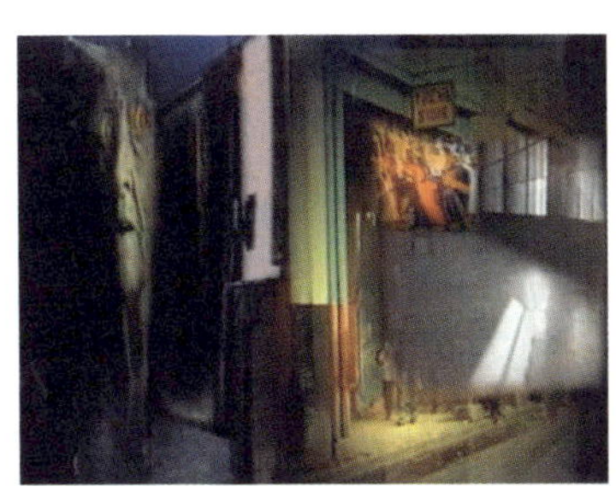
00:23

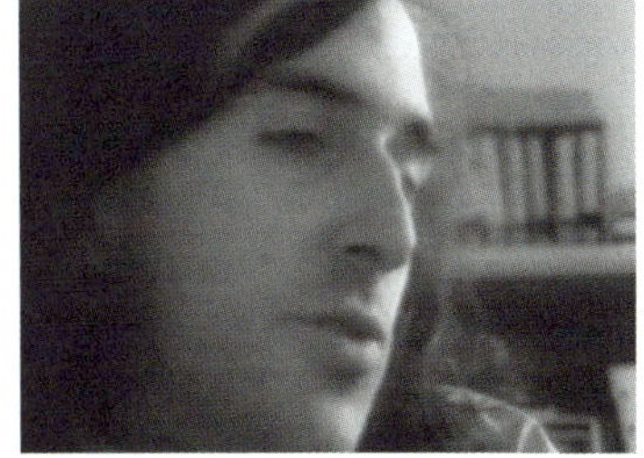
04:26

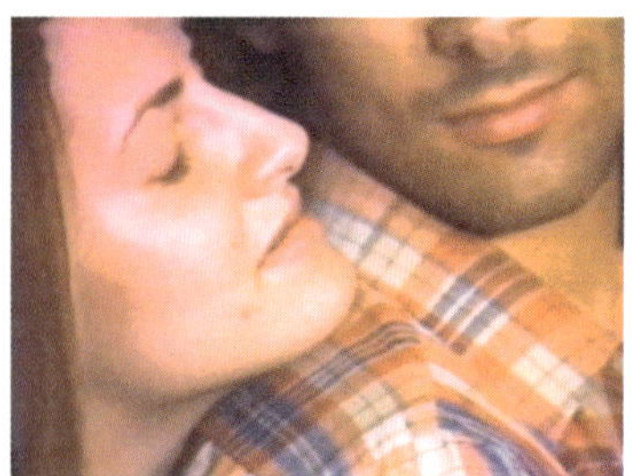

01:24

01:44

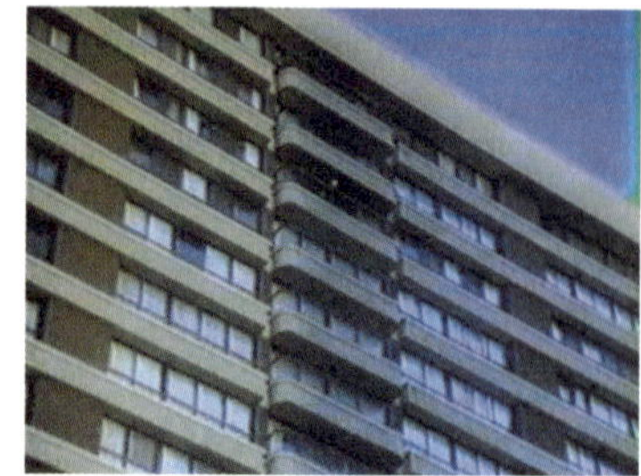

05:59

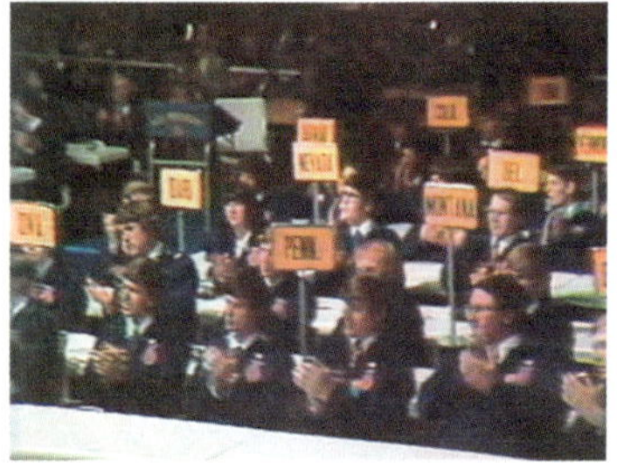

14:08

From 1970 to 1974, Raindance circulated *Radical Software*, a periodical focused on the liberating potential of video, television, and computer technologies. In their first "Address to Readers," the editors declared:

> *Power is no longer measured in land, labor, or capital, but by access to information and the means to disseminate it. As long as the most powerful tools (not weapons) are in the hands of those who would hoard them, no alternative cultural vision can succeed. Unless we design and implement alternative information structures which transcend and reconfigure the existing ones, other alternate systems and lifestyles will be no more than products of the existing process.*[6]

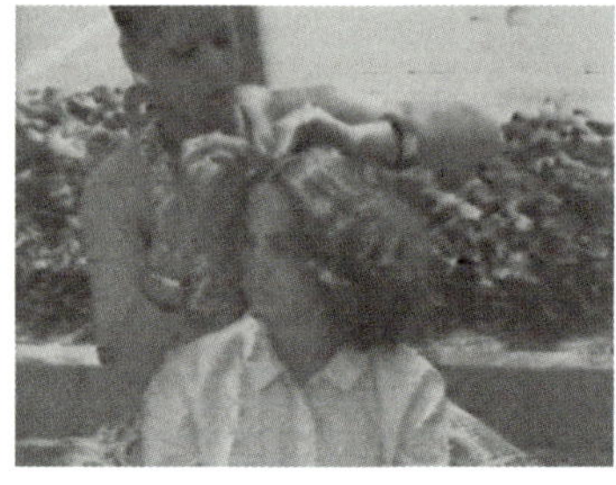

17:32

The prioritizing of information and communication over quantifiable commodities was a guiding principle for the counterculture, for the video subculture, for artists influenced by the Fluxus embrace of impermanence and spontaneity, and for the unclassifiable activities of the interdisciplinary postwar art scene. All of this provided an antidote to the dehumanizing institutions of commerce and state, and the merciless pull

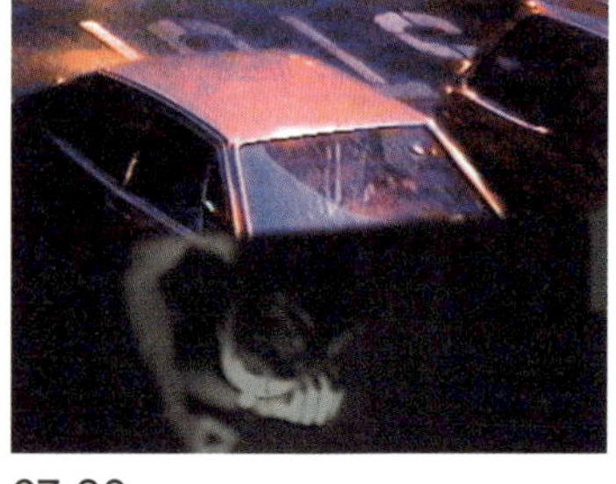

07:20

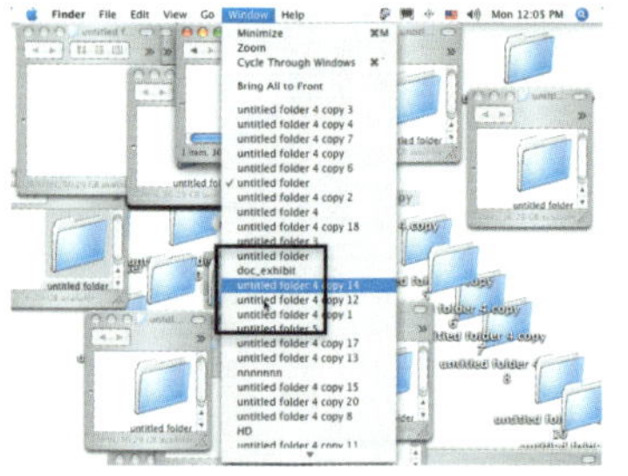

00:55

08:26

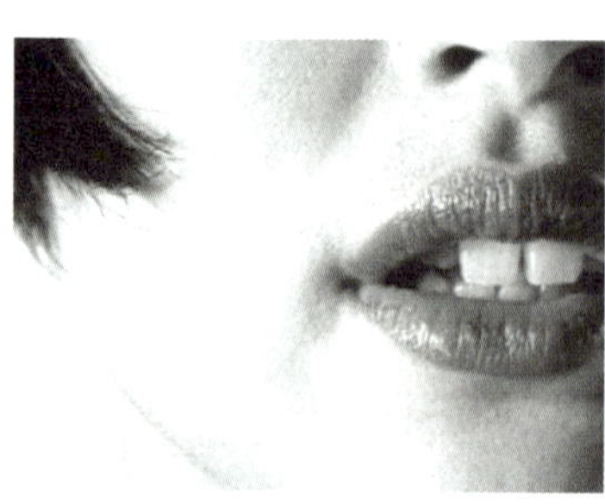

00:10

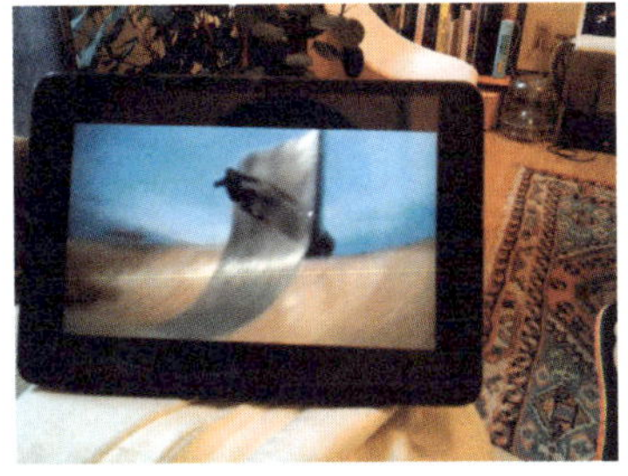
04:00

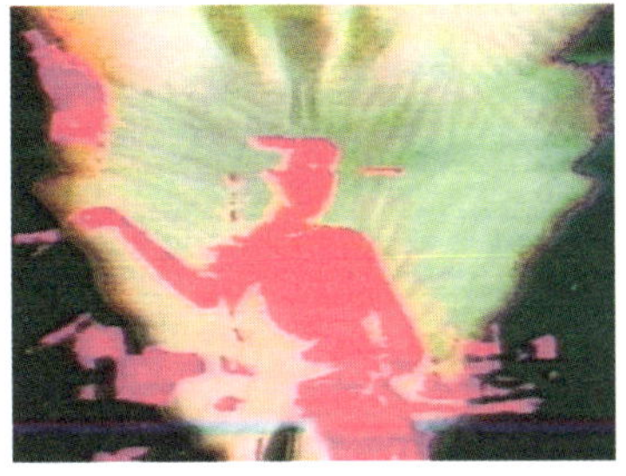
14:31

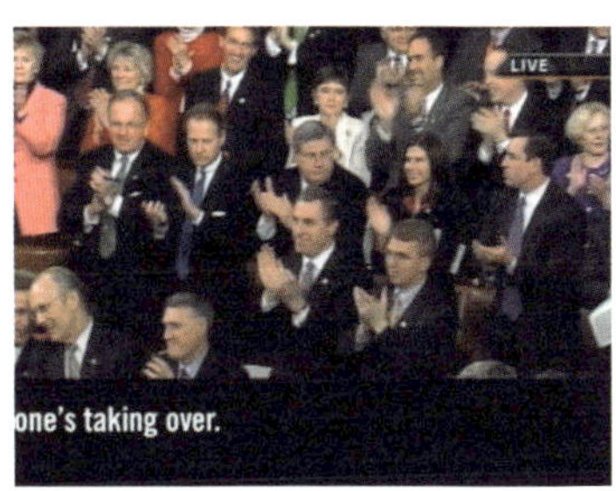

04:33

of capitalism. A collaborative and supportive environment sustained a rebellion that thrived in the 1960s and 1970s.

Sony's Portapak video camera and recorder, the first consumer-grade video equipment to come on the market in the late sixties, was critical to this. For the new equipment, Raindance published *Guerrilla Television* (1971), a self-described "meta-manual" authored by Shamberg. If the *Whole Earth Catalog* was not merely a catalog of products, *Guerrilla Television* was not just a user manual for the Portapak. Practical, how-to information was prefaced by a vivid account of the unbalanced power dynamics of corporate media, showing how individuals had been robbed of their agency and autonomy, and made the subjugated inhabitants of "Media-America."

The Portapak was one tool within a broader media ecology that fostered an oppositional dynamic, providing access to information and the means to distribute it broadly and freely. Unlike the handheld smartphone, which can record, edit, and disseminate video content with ease, the

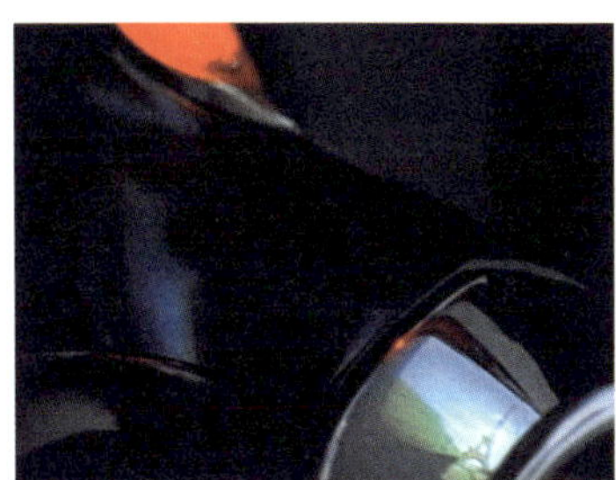
00:20

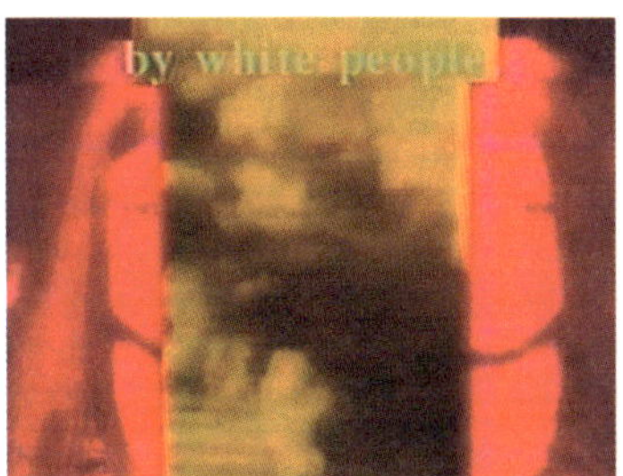

00:37

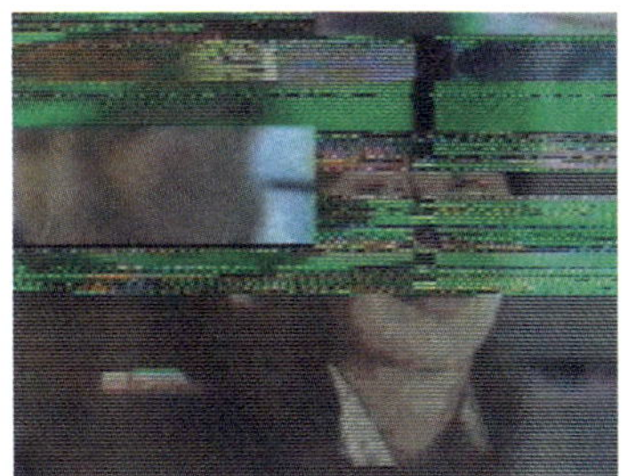
21:14

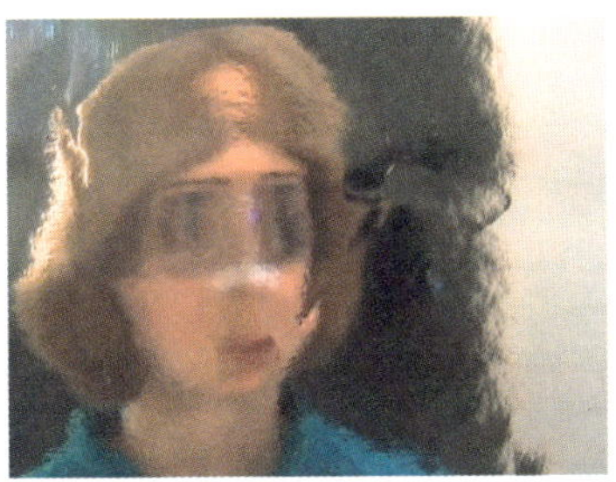
01:26

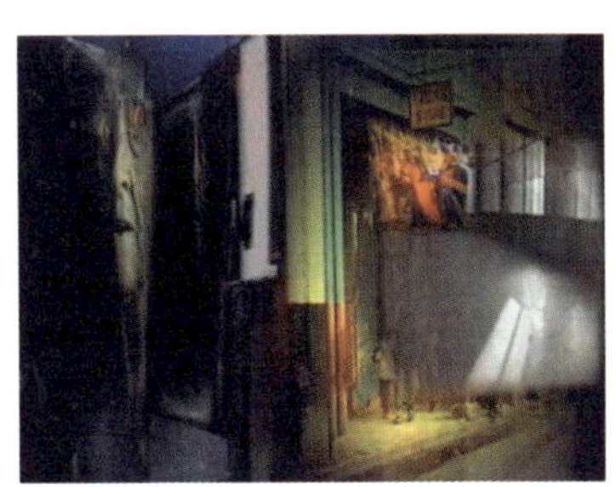
00:23

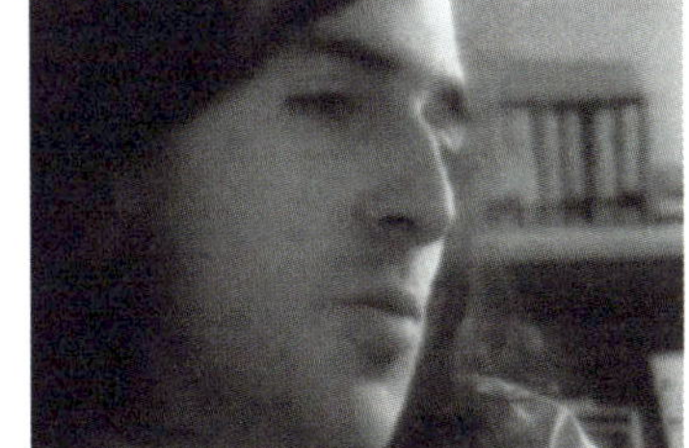
04:26

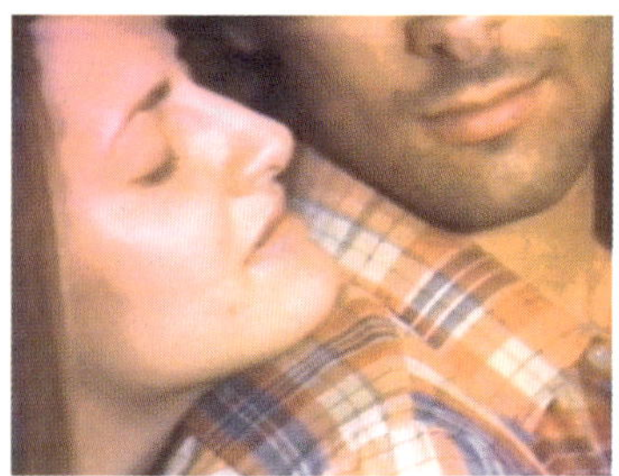
01:24

01:44

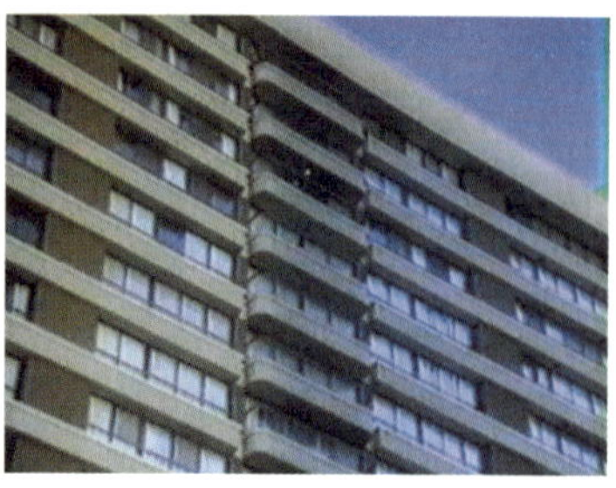
05:59

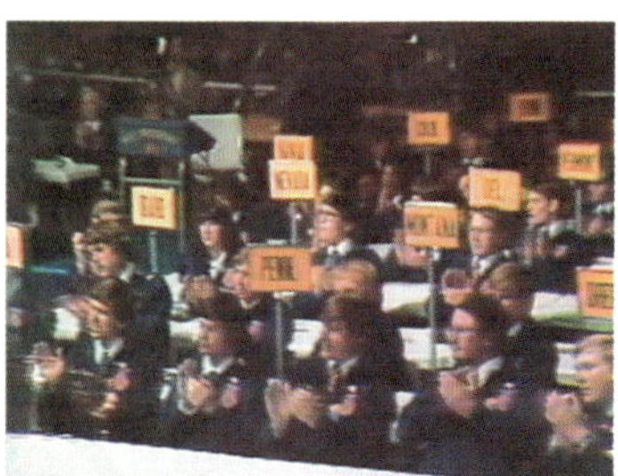
14:08

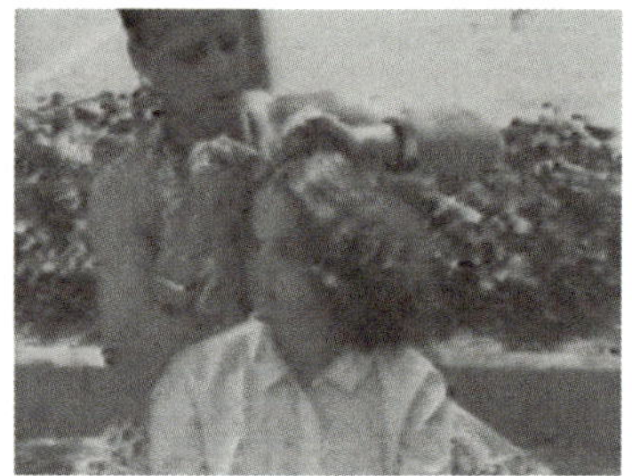
17:32

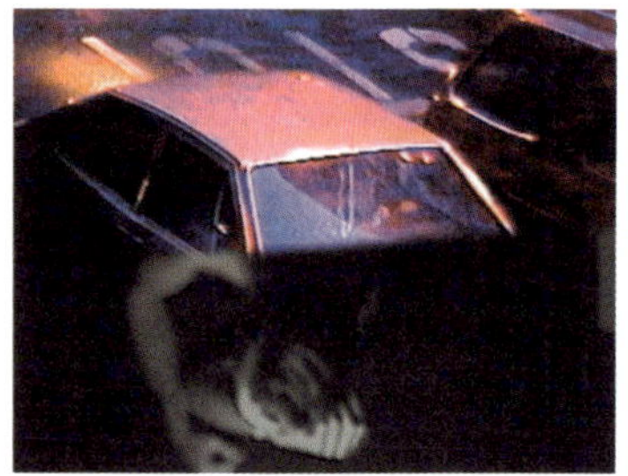
07:20

Portapak was cumbersome and required facilities for editing and distribution. This need conjured a supportive network that included artist residences at public broadcasting stations, generous grants from foundations and government agencies, and artist-friendly editing facilities. Howard Wise became an important part of this constellation.

Wise had spent most of his life at the helm of Arco Industrial Coatings in Cleveland, a supplier of paints, varnishes, and enamels that included coatings for tanks, hand grenades, air-dropped bombs, and the like. Arco's involvement in the war effort might have heightened Wise's awareness of the threat of the military-industrial complex and its horrifying escalations. In the wake of the success of *TV as a Creative Medium*, he sent a letter to his mailing list announcing that he was closing his gallery. He did not mince words: "I cannot stand idly by when the existence of our society and ourselves as individuals is so darkly threatened."[7]

In 1971, Wise founded Electronic Arts Intermix (EAI), a nonprofit center for video and television

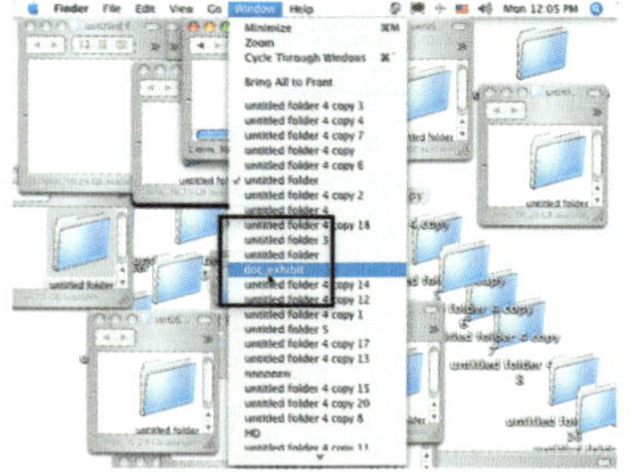

00:55

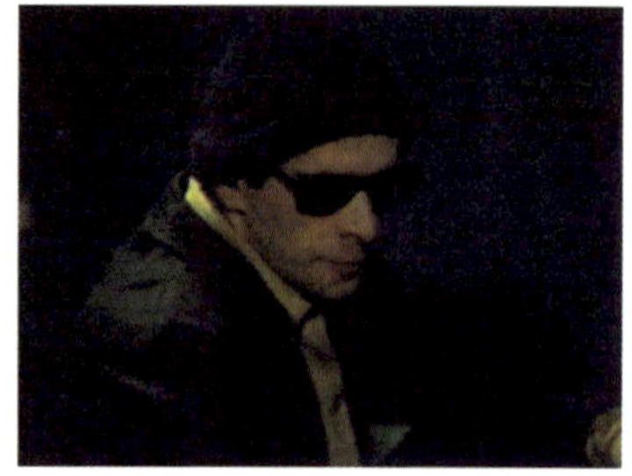
08:26

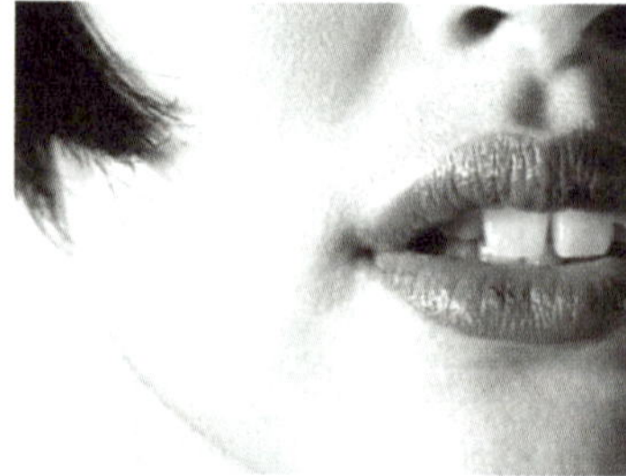
00:10

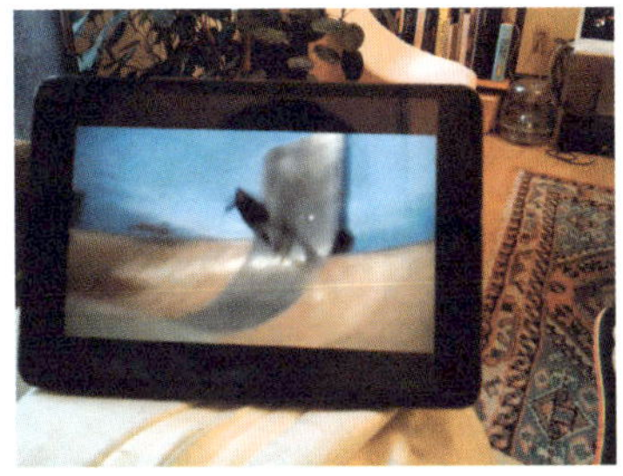
04:00

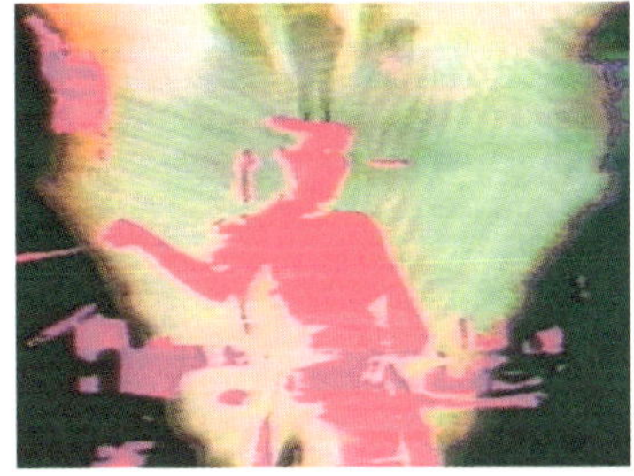
14:31

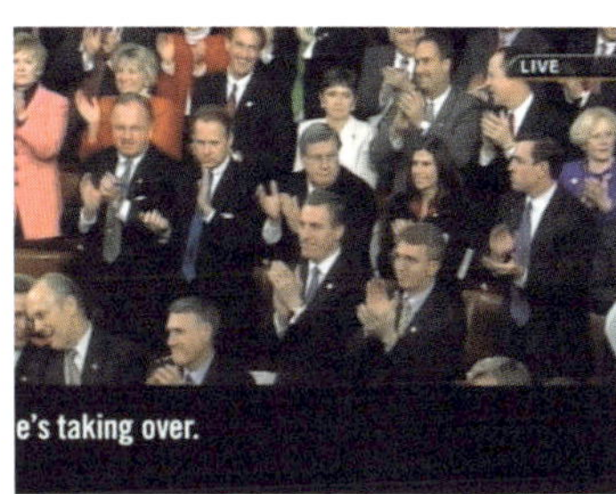

04:33

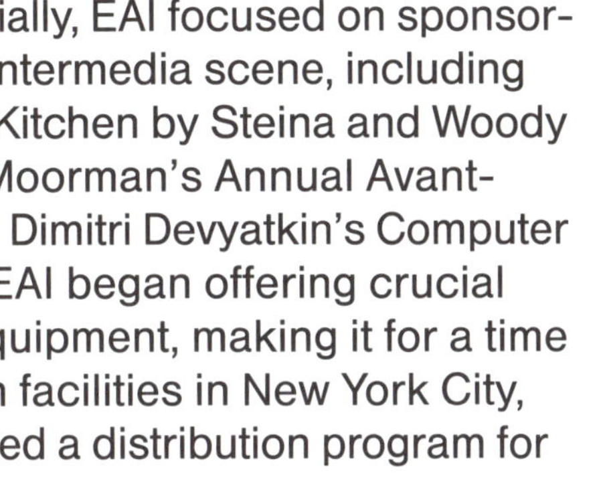

experimentation. Initially, EAI focused on sponsoring initiatives in the intermedia scene, including the founding of The Kitchen by Steina and Woody Vasulka, Charlotte Moorman's Annual Avant-Garde Festivals, and Dimitri Devyatkin's Computer Art Festivals. Soon EAI began offering crucial access to editing equipment, making it for a time one of the only such facilities in New York City, and in 1973 EAI started a distribution program for artists' video works.

Wise's manifesto, *Electronic Arts Intermix: At the Leading Edge of Art*, outlined the advantages of video and television in reaching outside the traditional art channels:

> *"Science and technology have provided this pretested electronic medium for use by the artist as a means of his expression, and at the same time have provided the mechanics for the dissemination of his work—most homes are electronically equipped, ready to receive the artist's message: they have TV sets already installed."*[8]

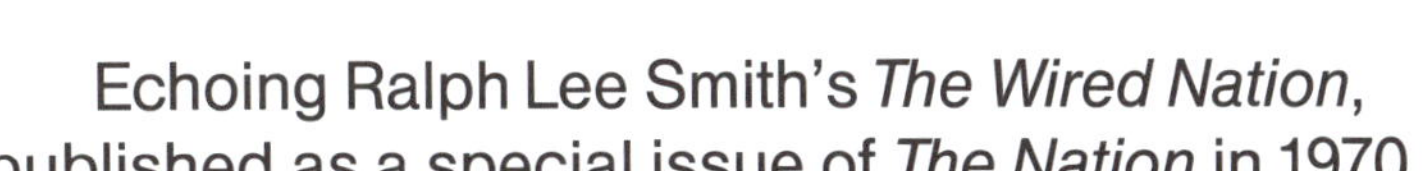

Echoing Ralph Lee Smith's *The Wired Nation*, published as a special issue of *The Nation* in 1970,

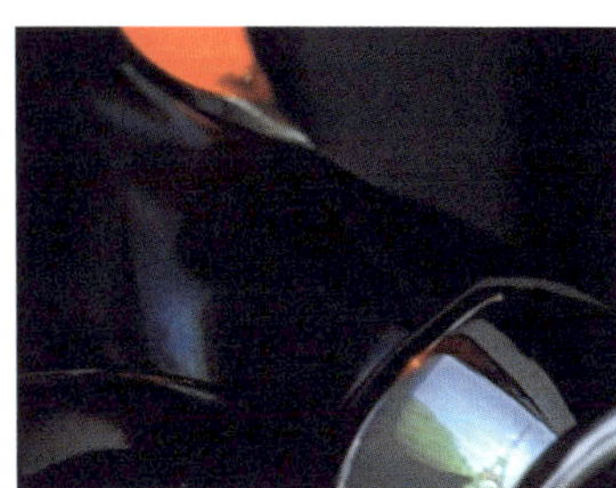
00:20

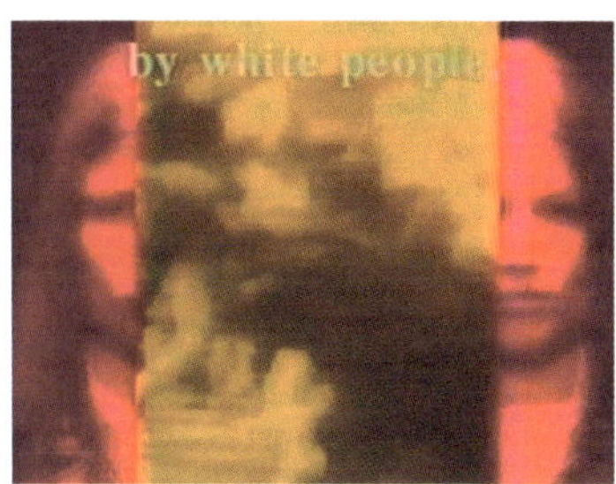

00:37

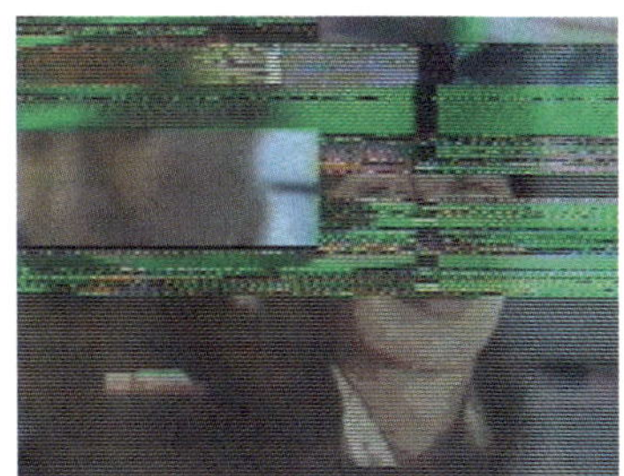
21:14

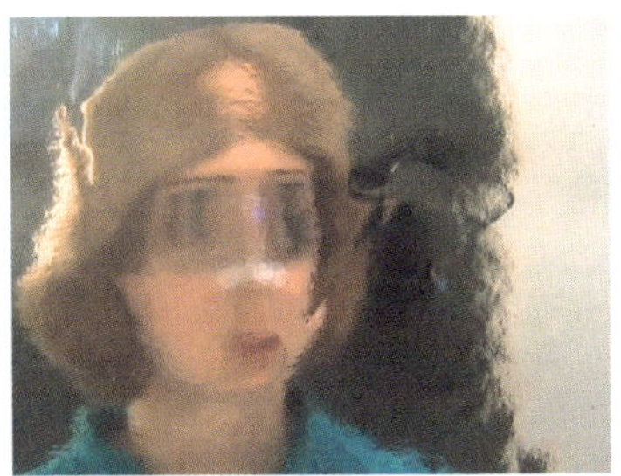
01:26

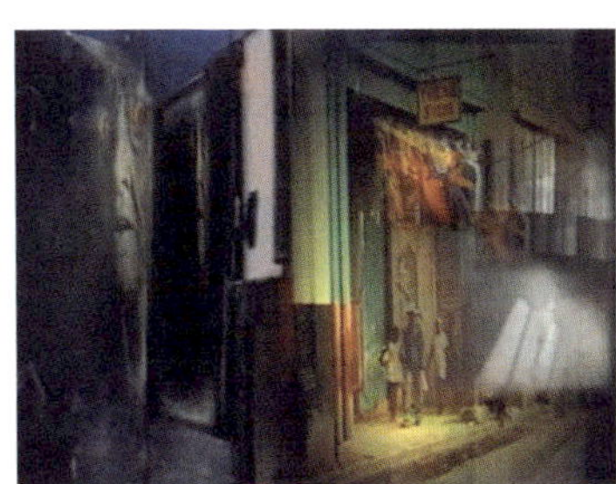
00:23

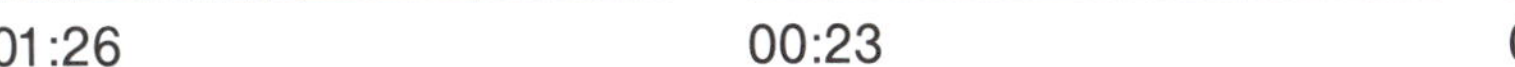
04:26

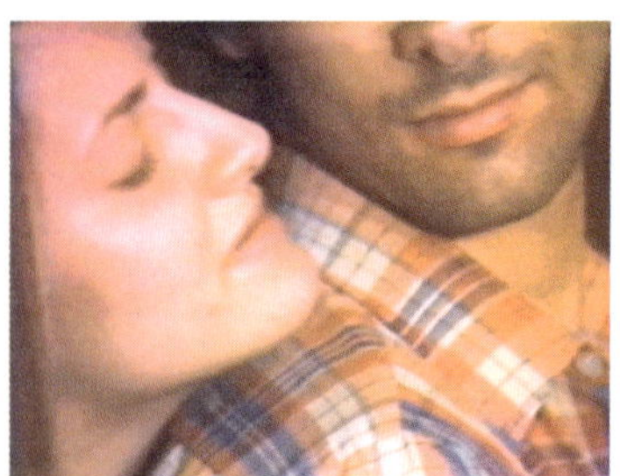

01:24

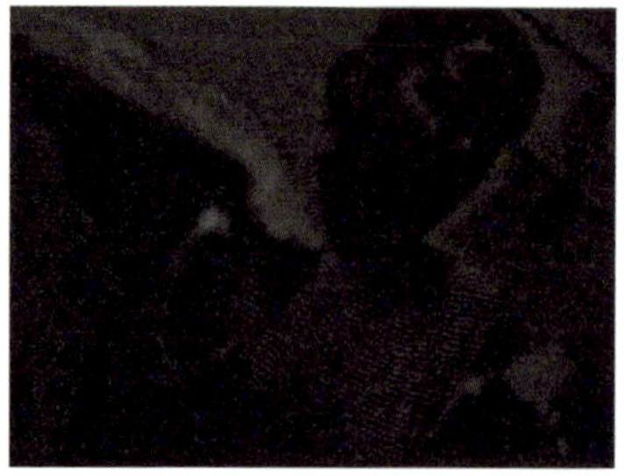

01:44

05:59

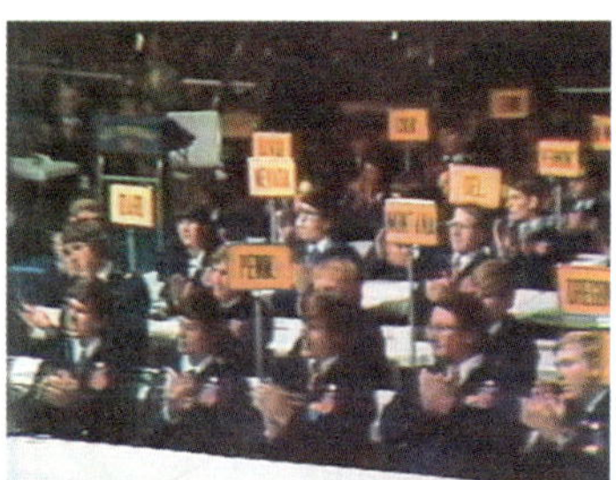

14:08

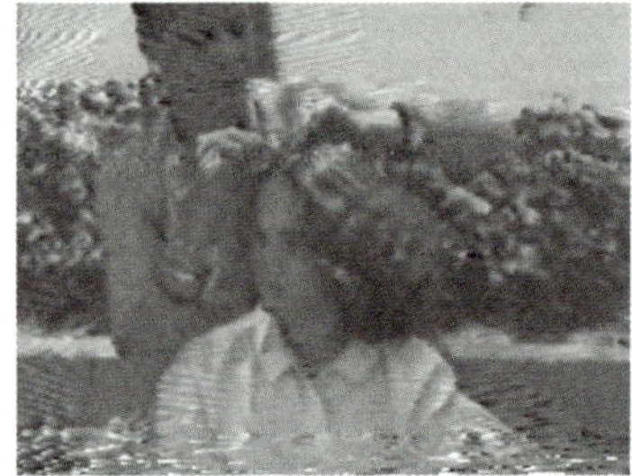

17:32

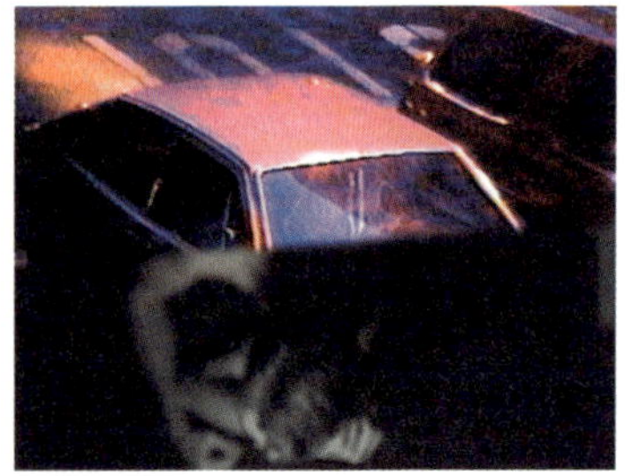

07:20

Wise looked to cable television as the major new creative arena. Smith's report described the potential virtues of cable as an alternative to over-the-air transmissions and the stranglehold of broadcast networks. Coaxial cables enabled the rapid transfer of vast amounts of information, for potentially less overhead, and could open up the narrow network-dominated roadway to a wide, multichannel "electronic superhighway," providing content that would appeal to diverse audiences and not to just one homogenous mass of consumer eyes.

Histories of video art tend to give the Sony Portapak outsized attention; advances in cable television and the arrival of public access were at least equally important, especially as new channels complemented the counterculture's proposition that a new means of circulating information was necessary for a successful communication revolution. In his manifesto, Wise identified the unique formal and structural advantages of video, always in connection to television. Another important development, the

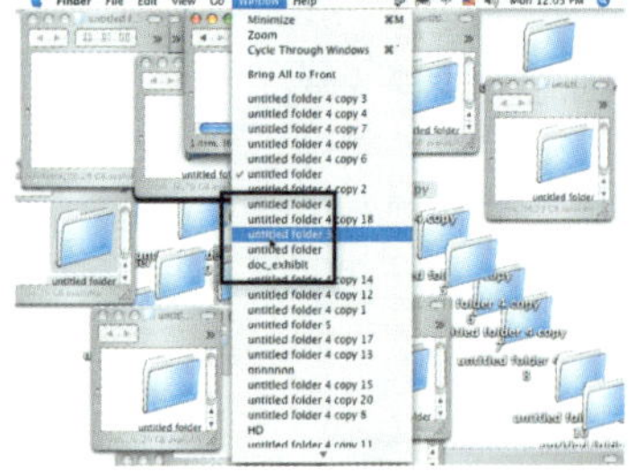

00:55

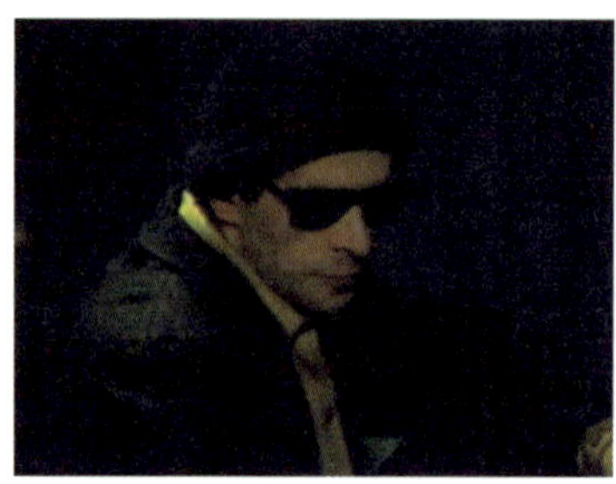

08:26

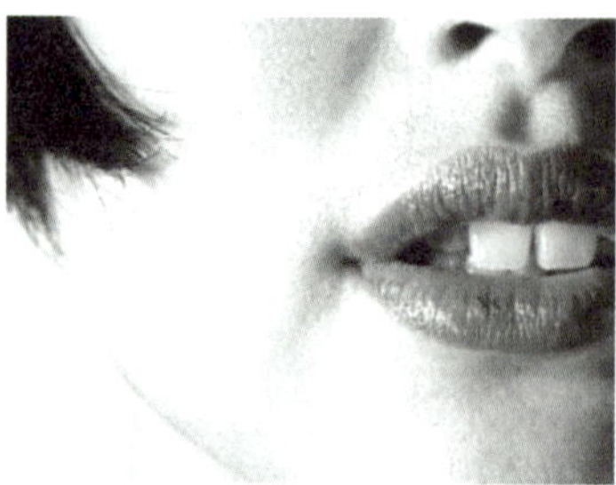

00:10

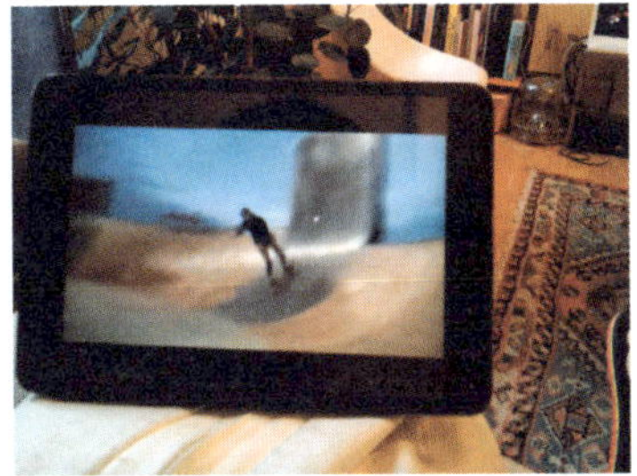

04:00

14:31

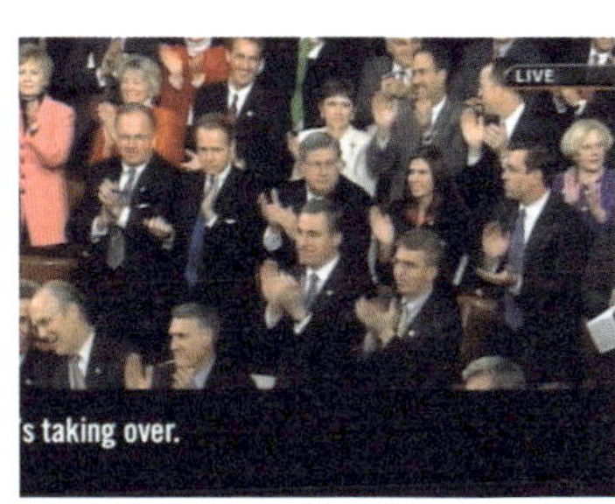

04:33

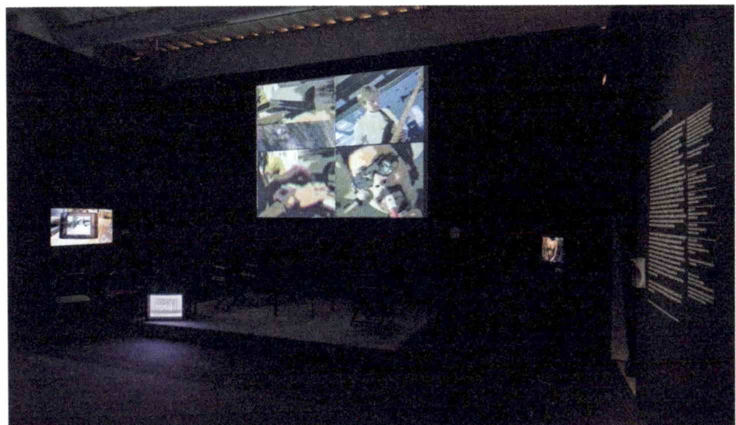

Broadcasting: EAI at ICA, installation view, ICA

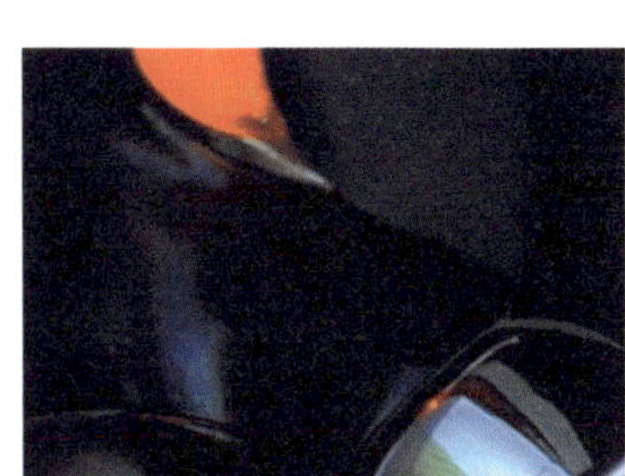

00:20

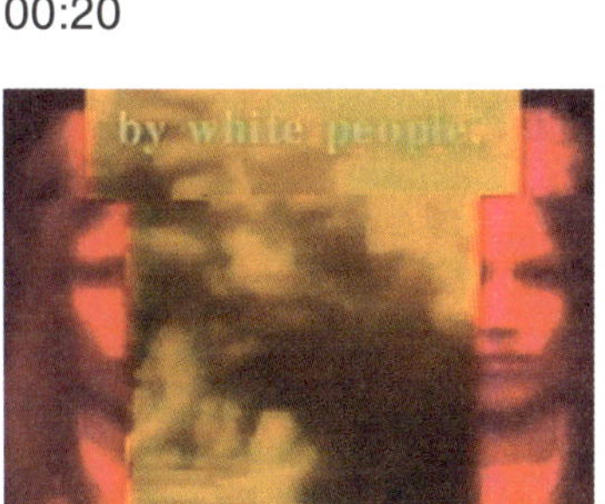

00:37

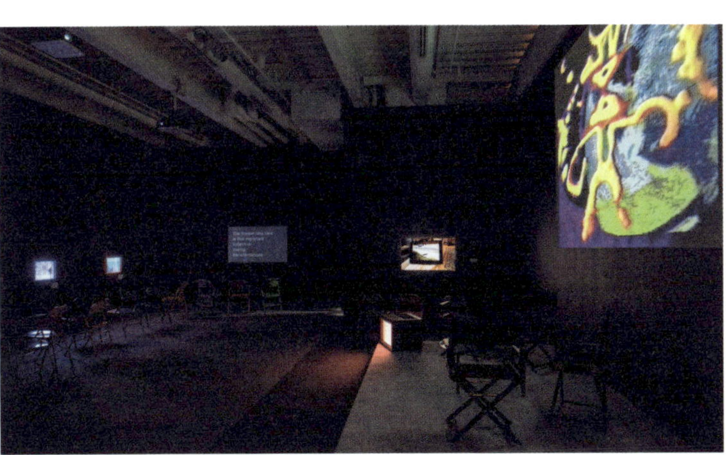

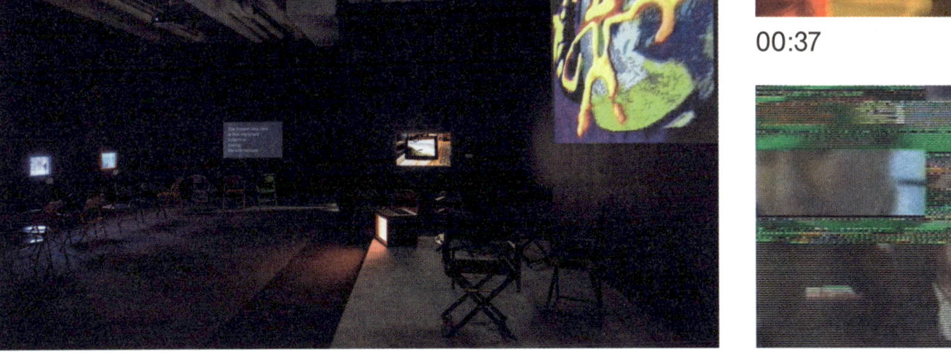

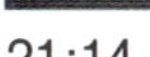

Broadcasting: EAI at ICA, installation view, ICA

21:14

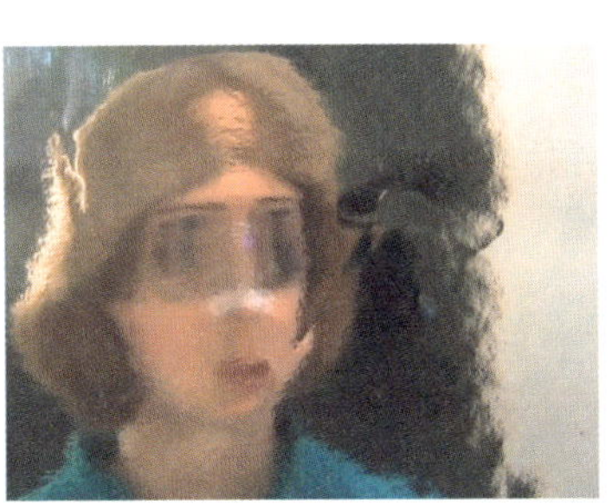

01:26

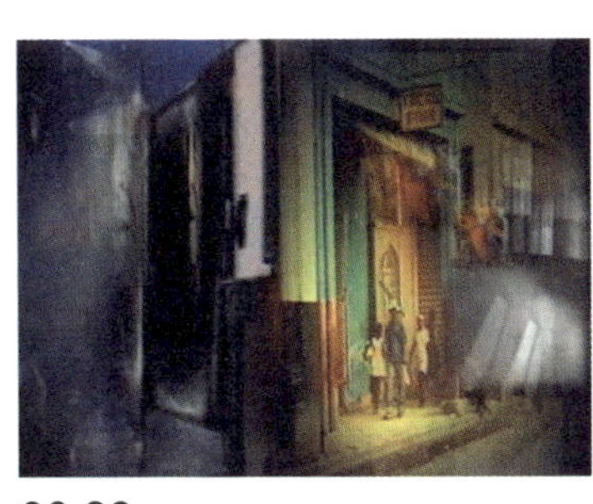

00:23

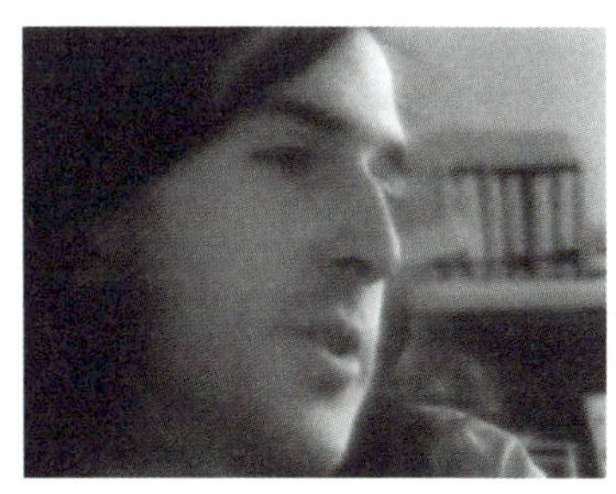

04:26

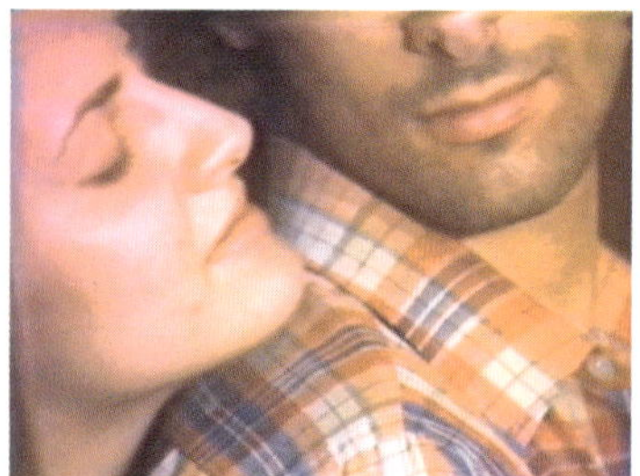
01:24

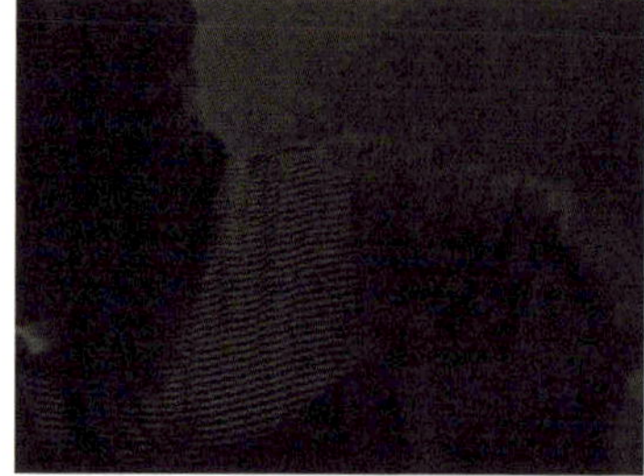
01:44

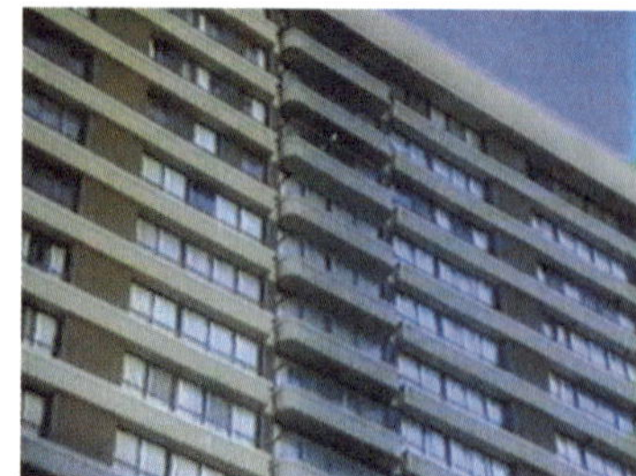
05:59

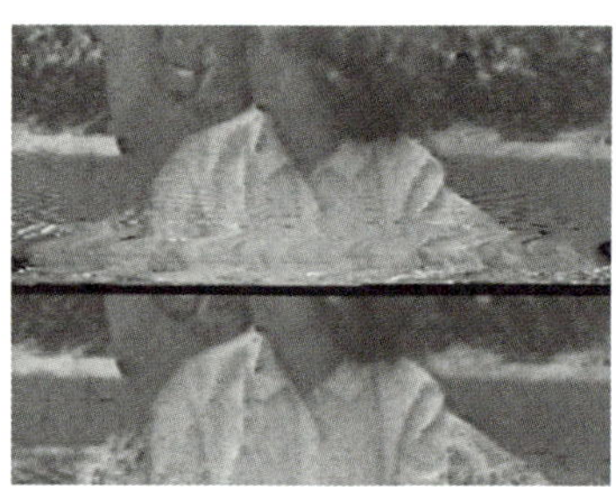
14:08

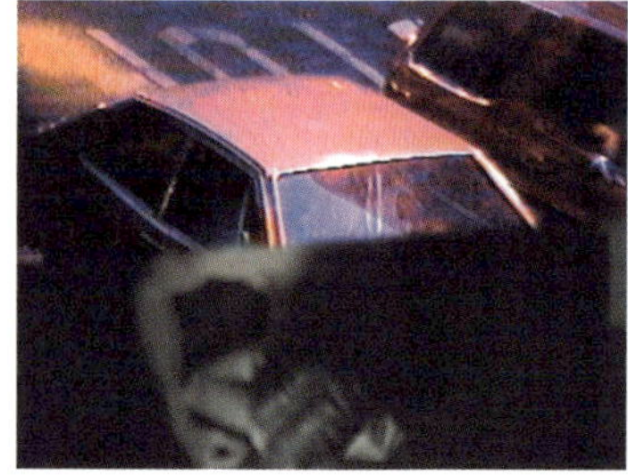
17:32

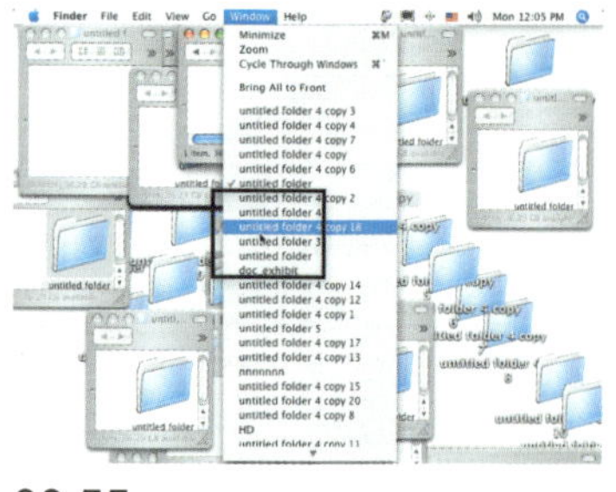
07:20

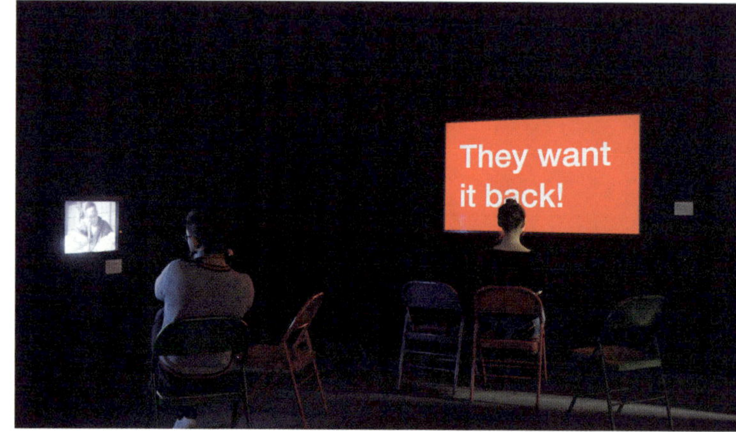

Broadcasting: EAI at ICA, installation view, ICA

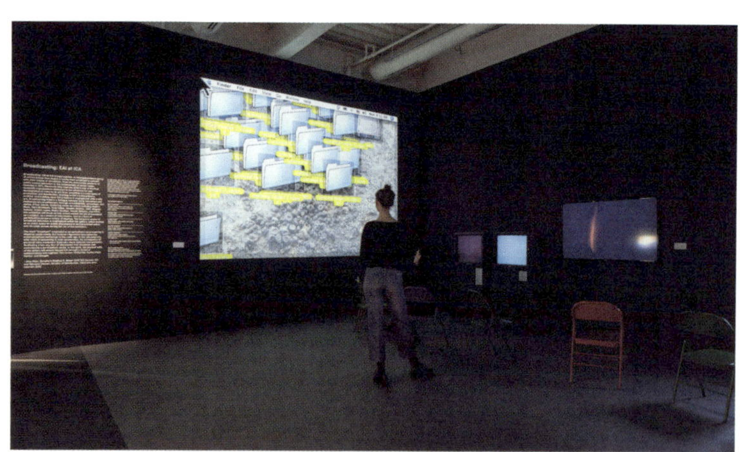
Broadcasting: EAI at ICA, installation view, ICA

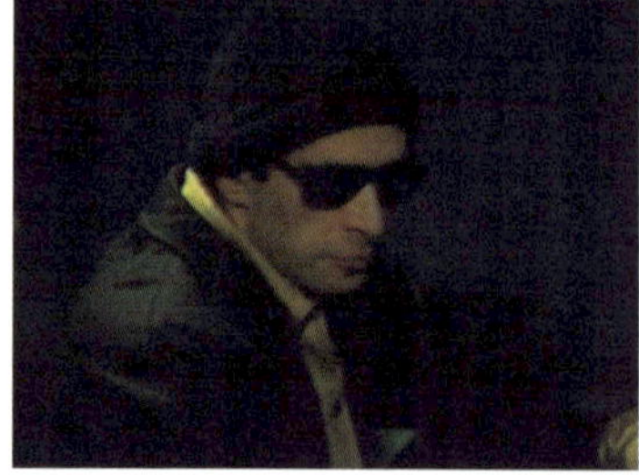
00:55

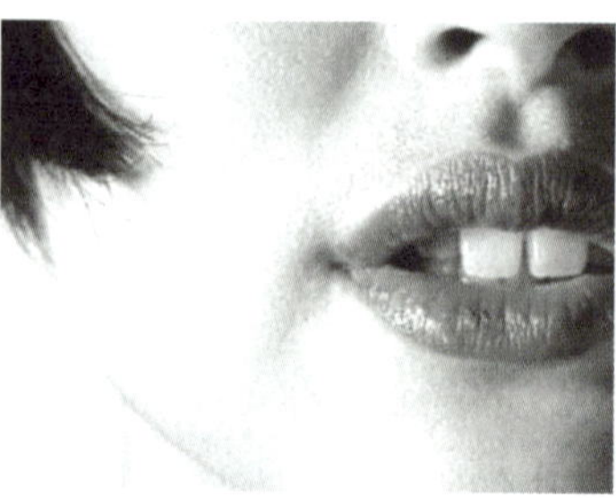
08:26

00:10

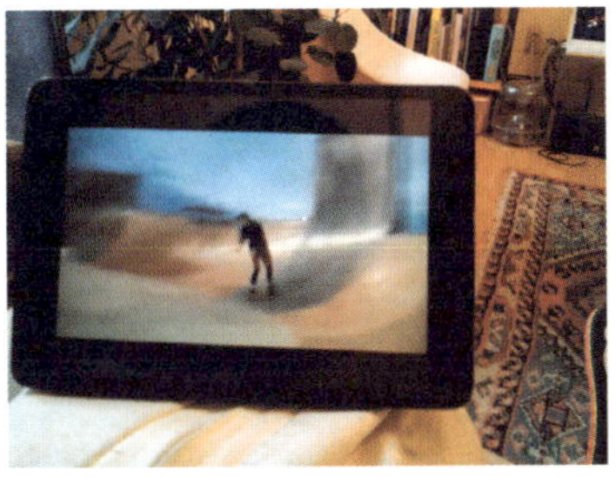
04:00

14:31

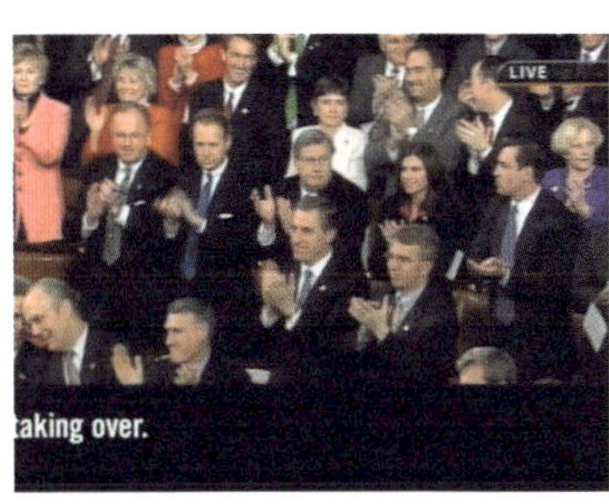

04:33

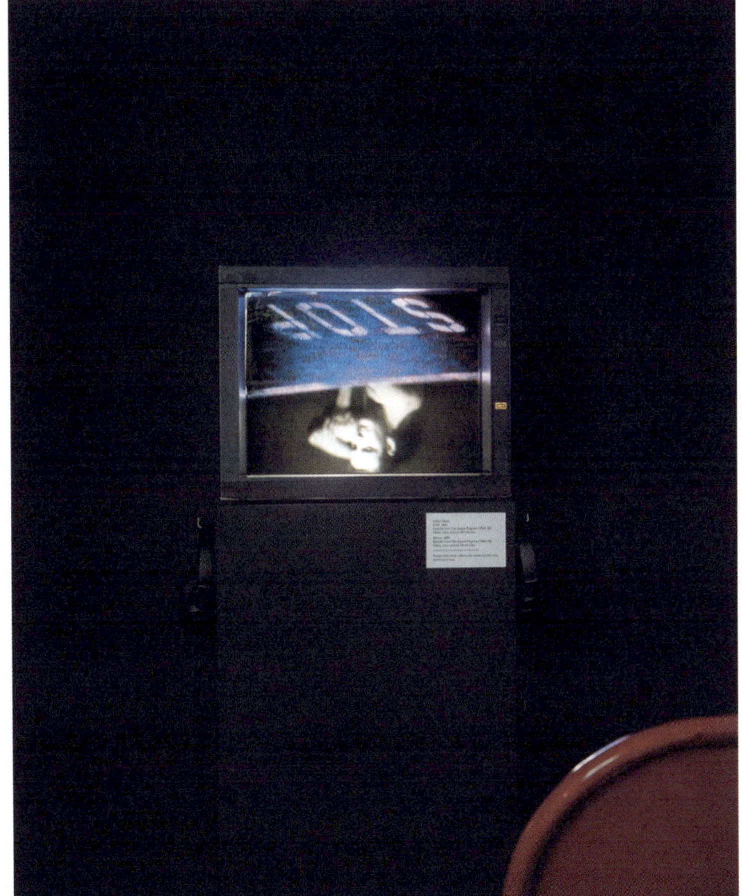
Broadcasting: EAI at ICA, installation view, ICA

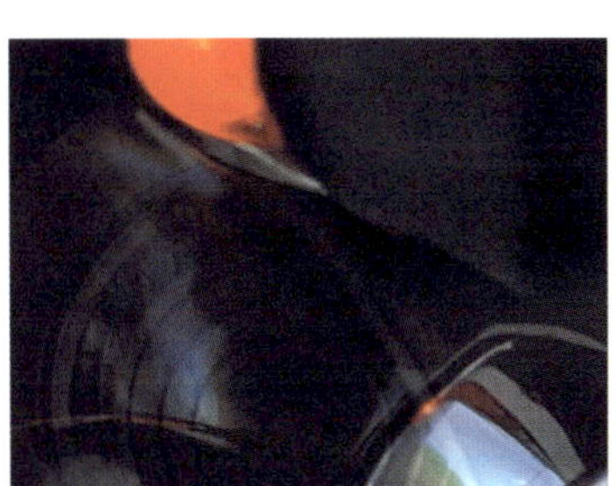
00:20

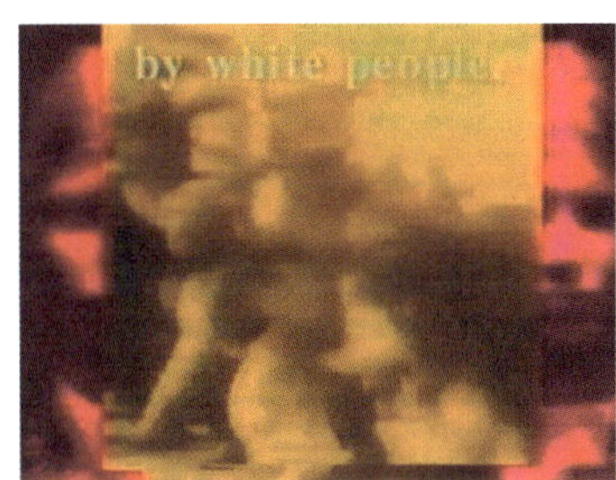

00:37

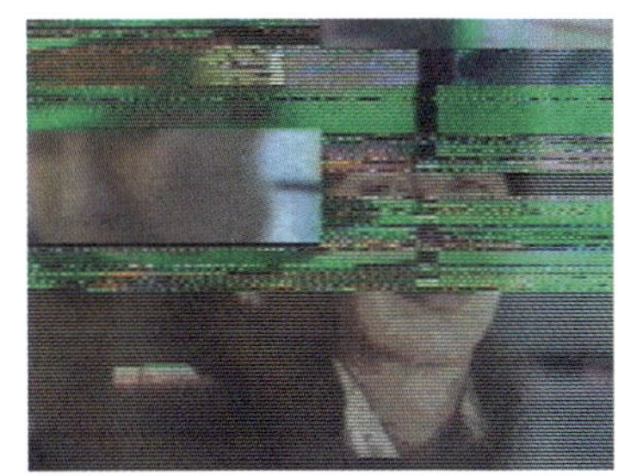
21:14

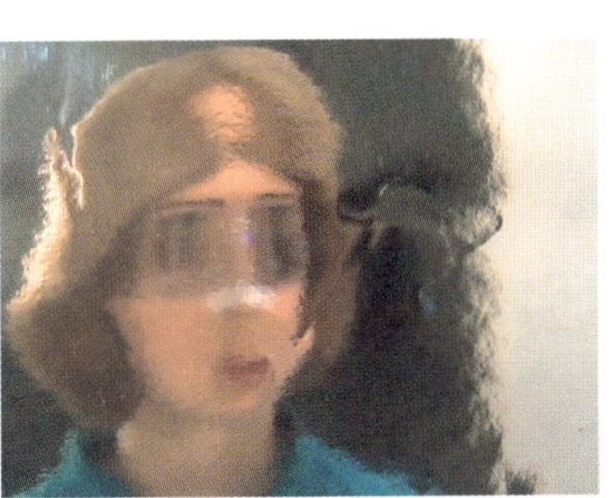
01:26

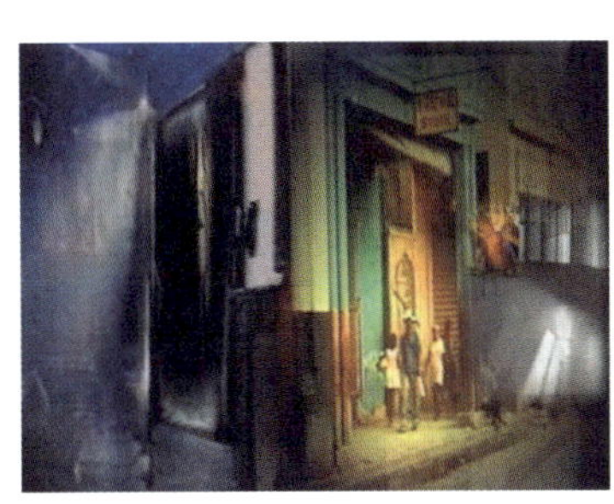
00:23

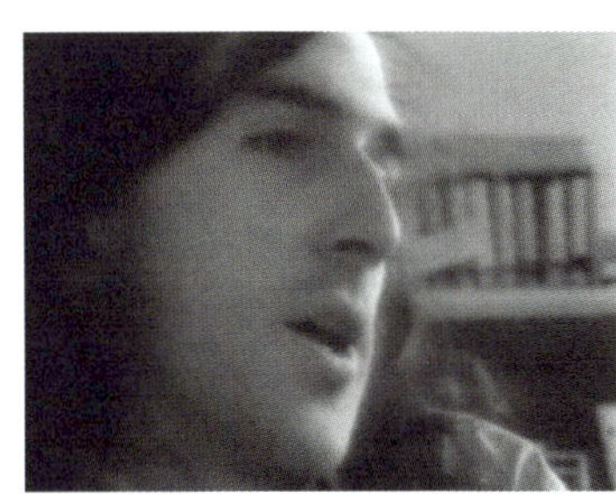
04:26

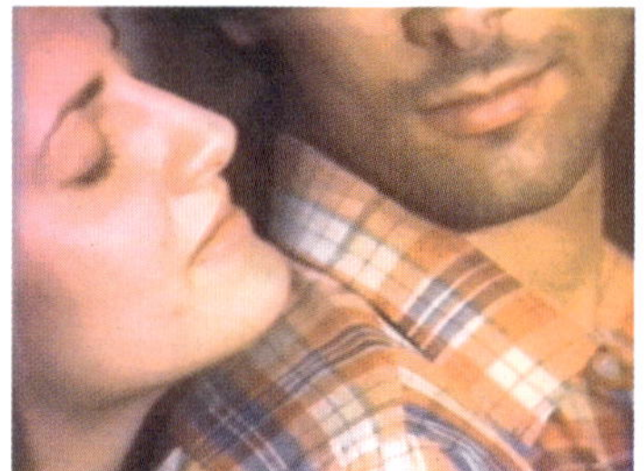

01:23

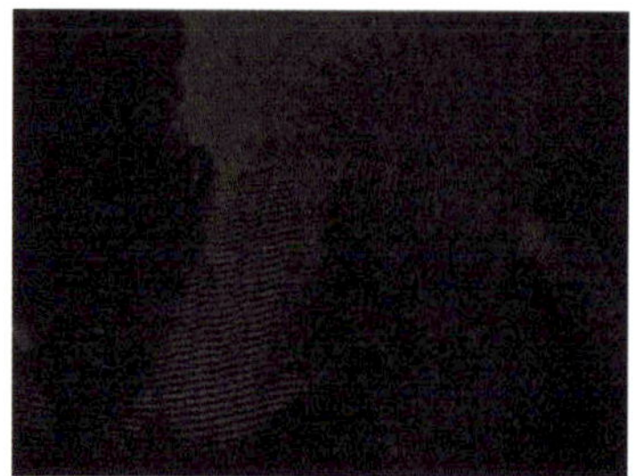

01:43

05:58

14:07

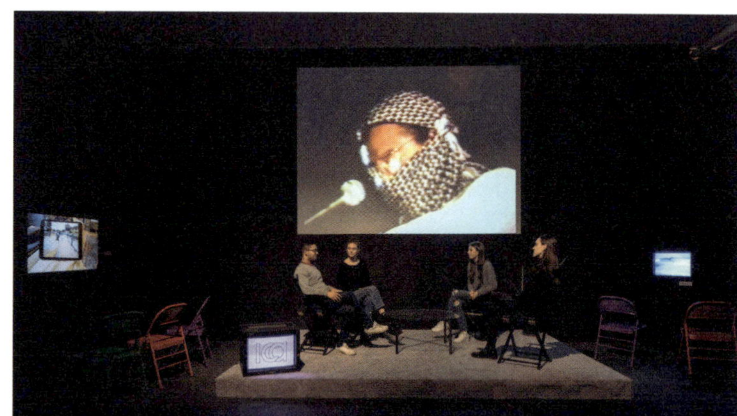

Broadcasting: EAI at ICA, installation view, ICA

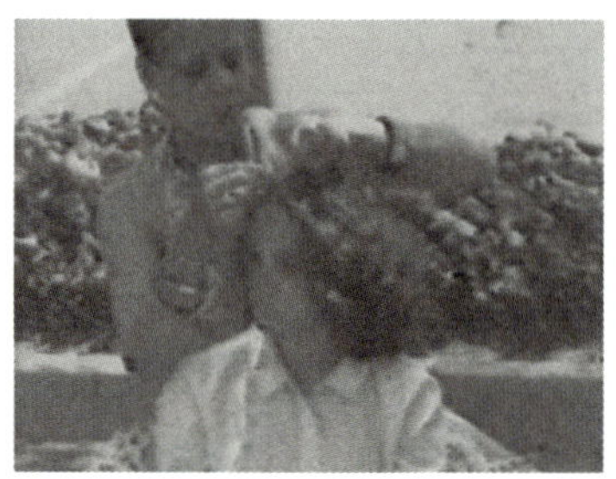

17:31

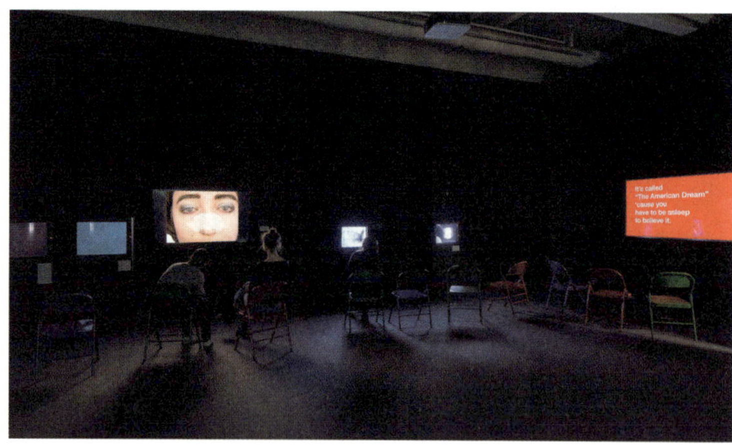

Broadcasting: EAI at ICA, installation view, ICA

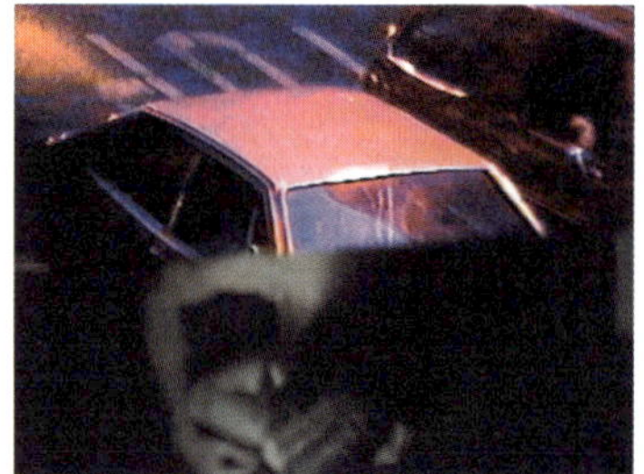

07:19

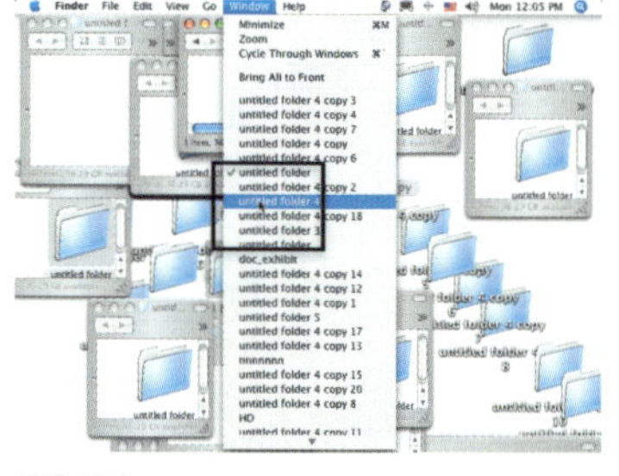

00:54

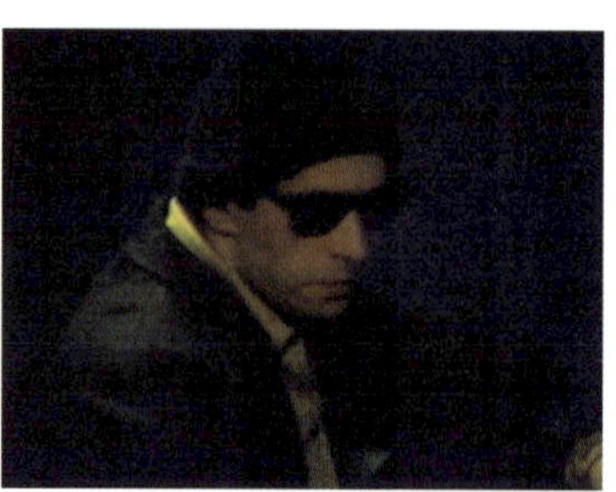
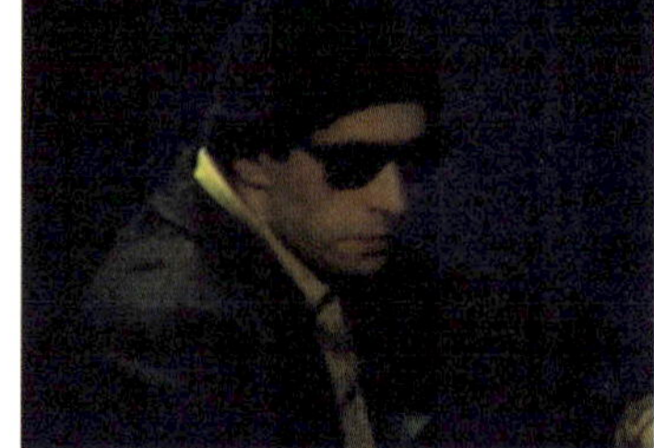

08:25

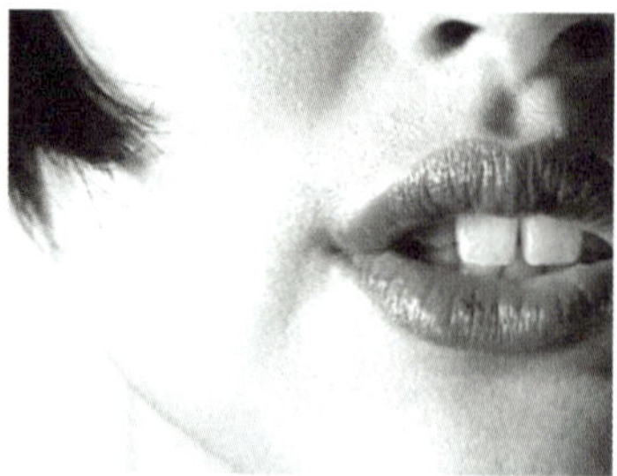

00:09

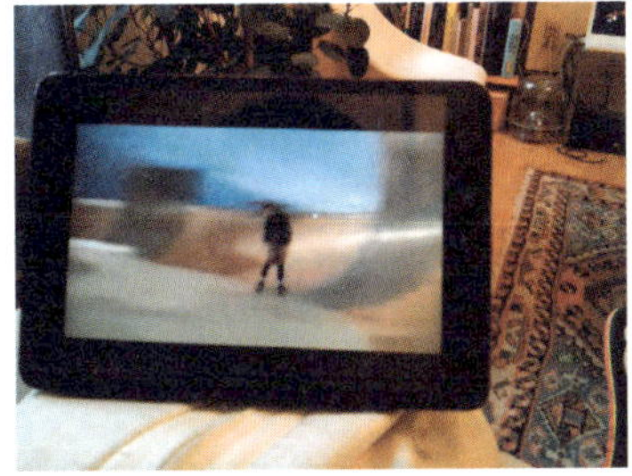

04:00

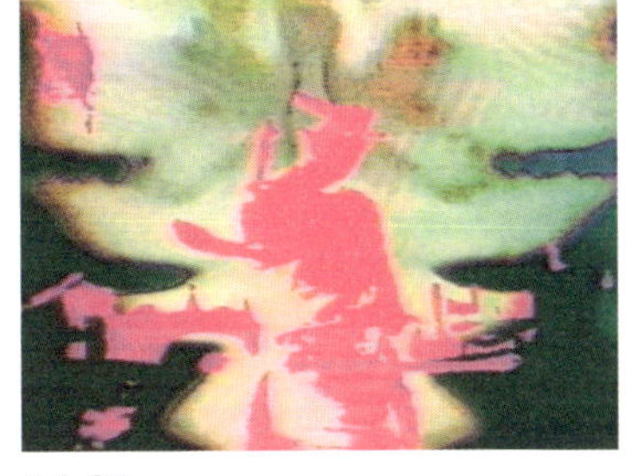

14:31

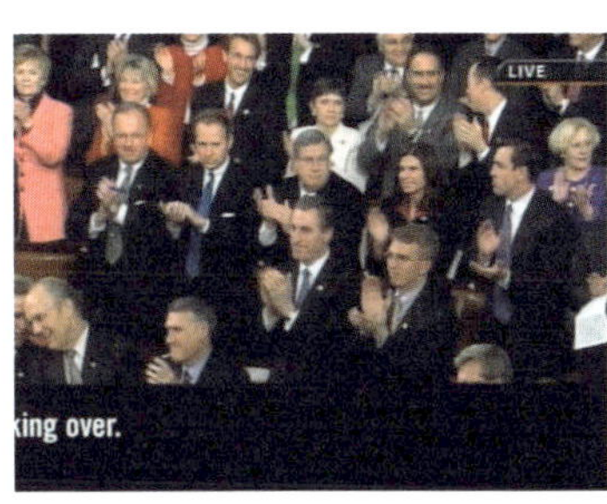

04:33

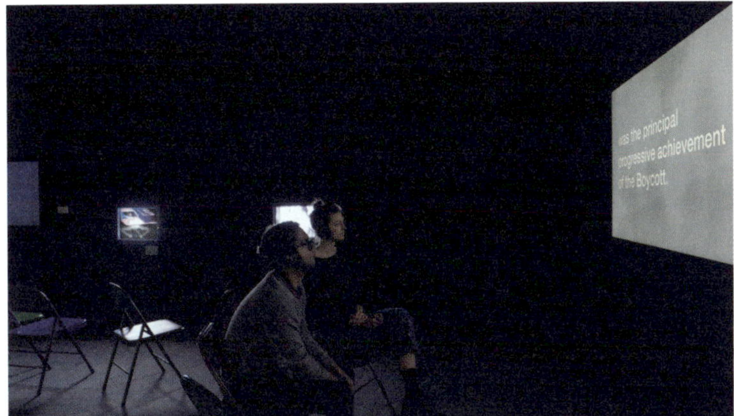

Broadcasting: EAI at ICA, installation view, ICA

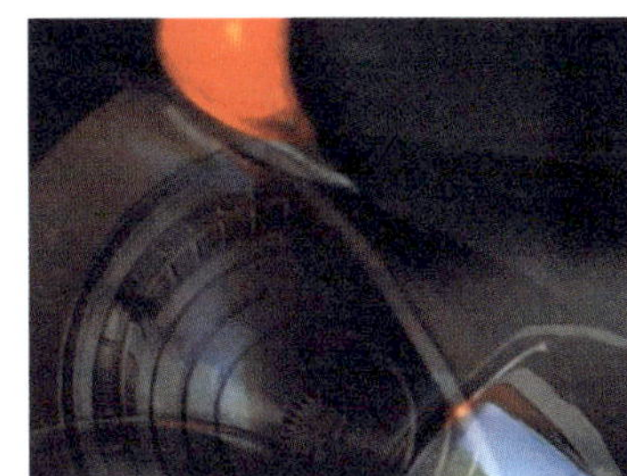

00:20

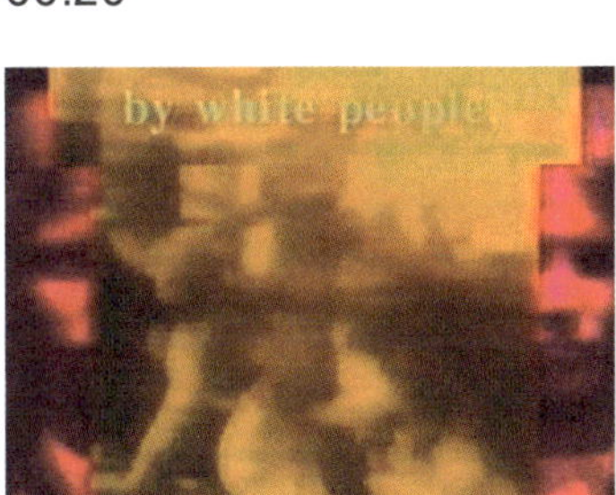

00:37

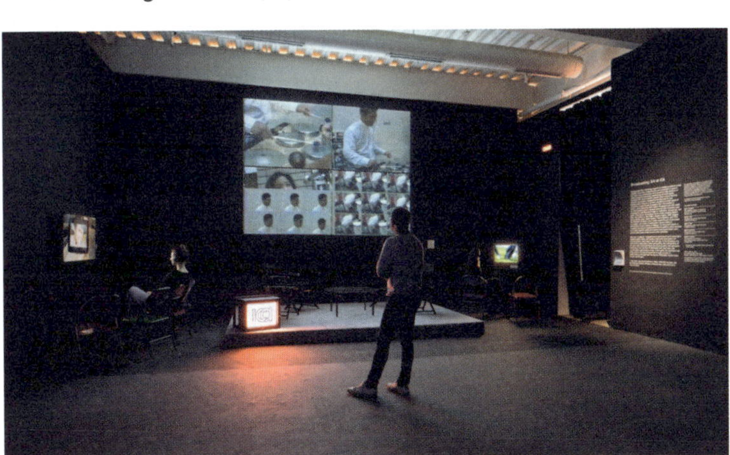

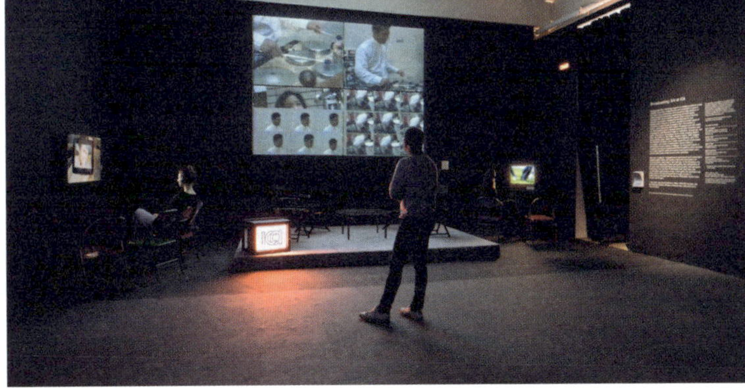

Broadcasting: EAI at ICA, installation view, ICA

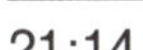

21:14

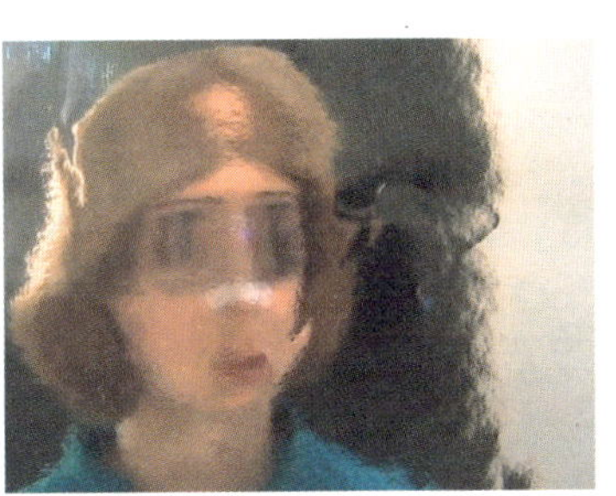

01:26

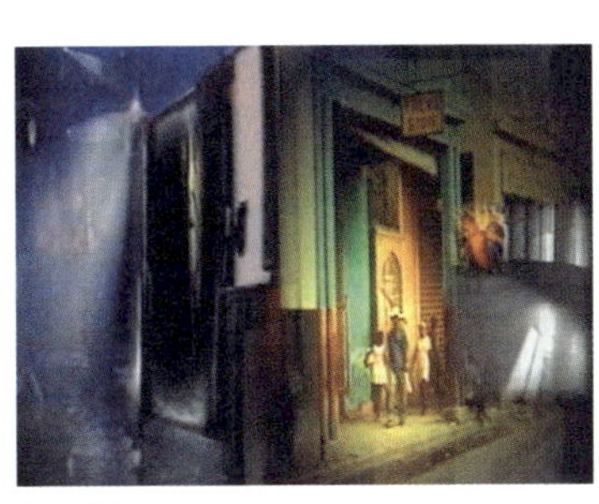

00:23

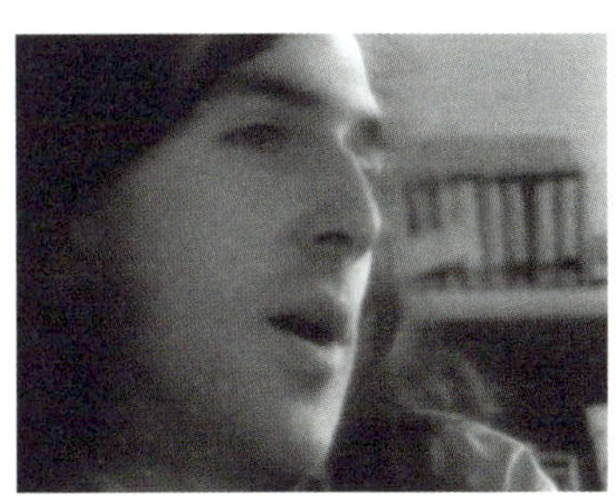

04:26

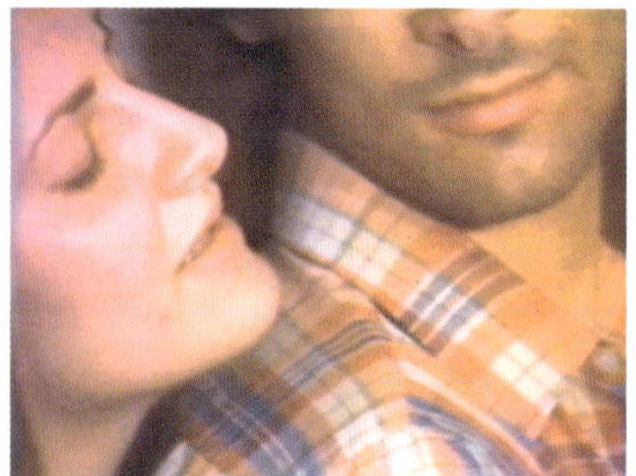

01:23

01:43

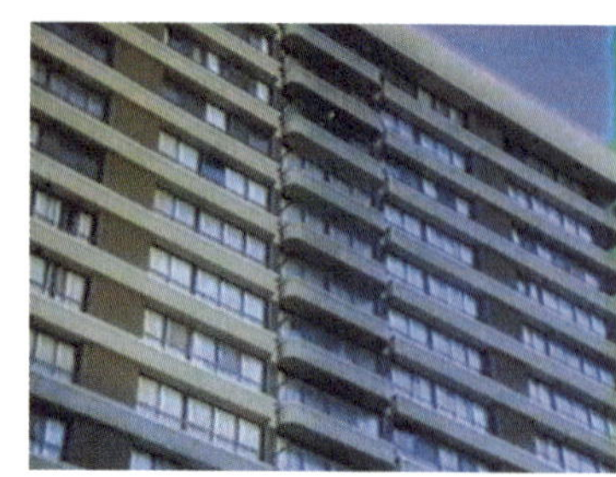

05:58

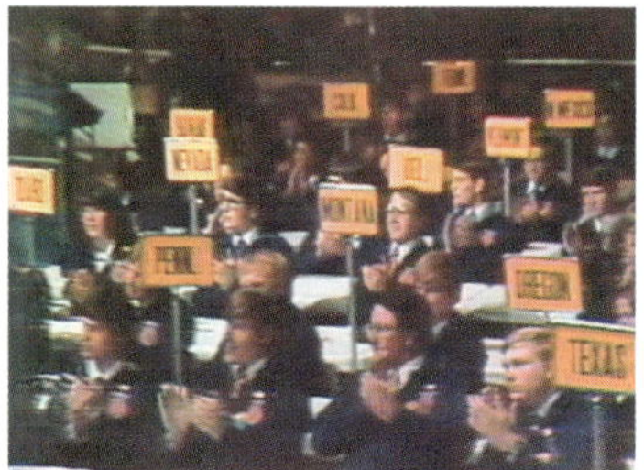

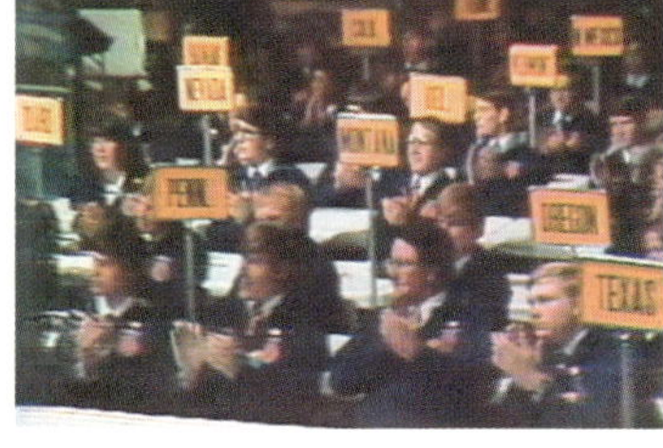

14:07

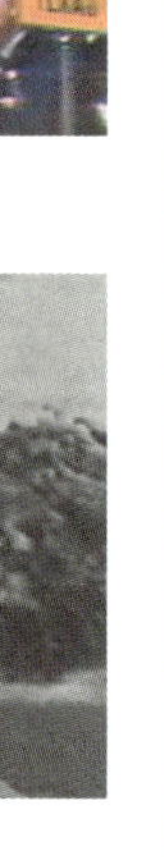

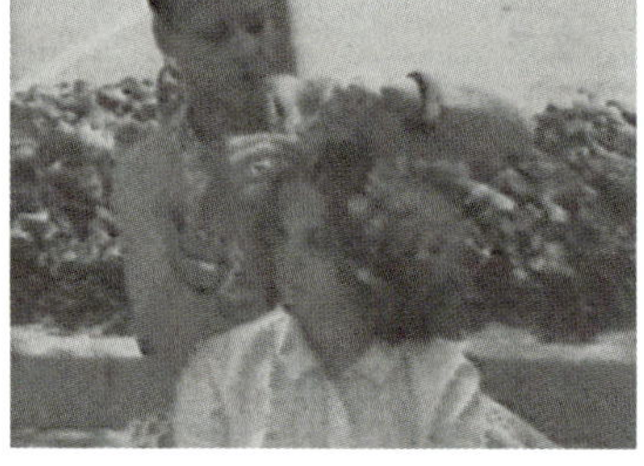

17:31

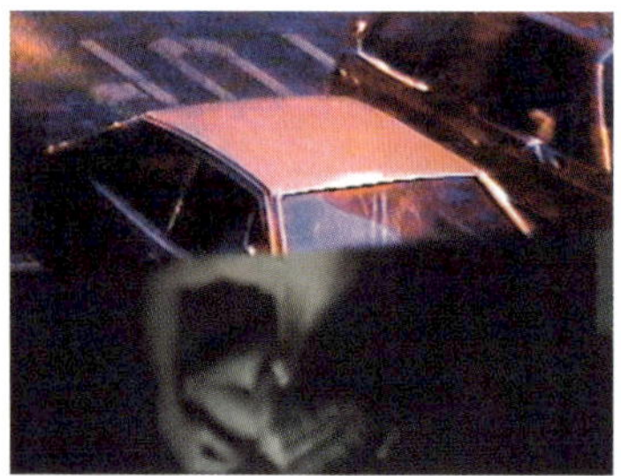

07:19

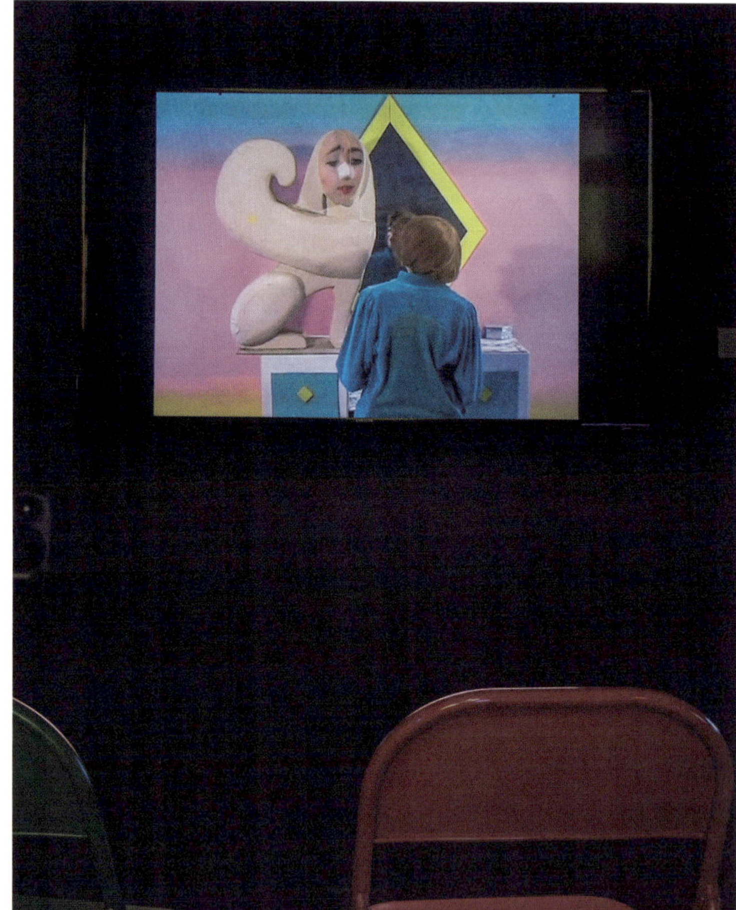

Broadcasting: EAI at ICA, installation view, ICA

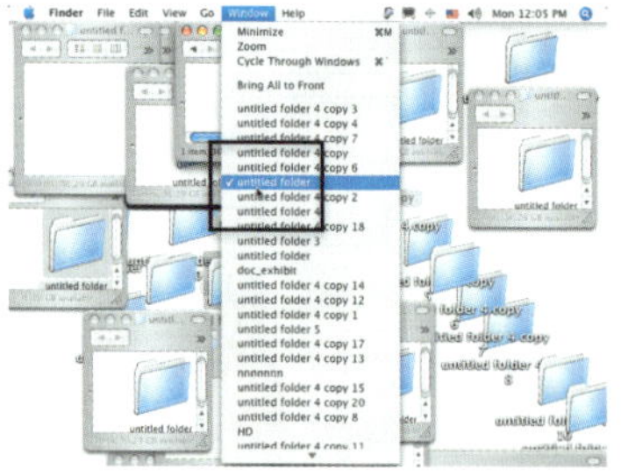

00:54

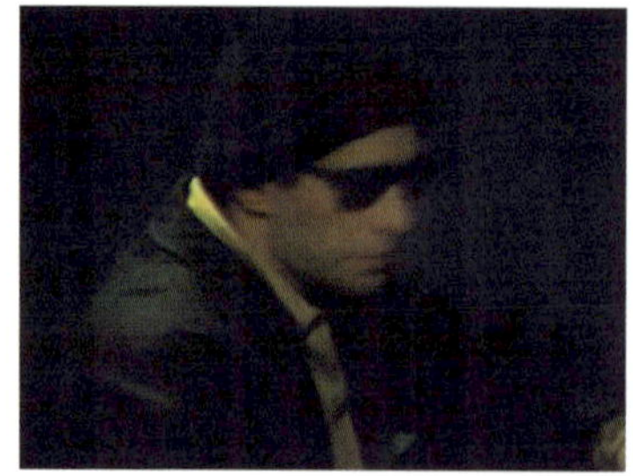

08:25

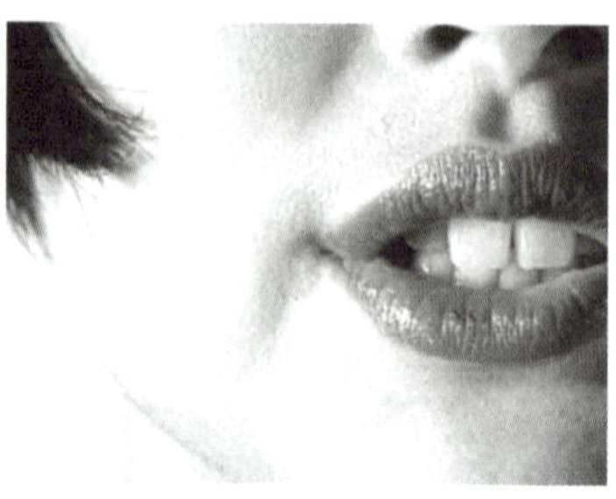

00:09

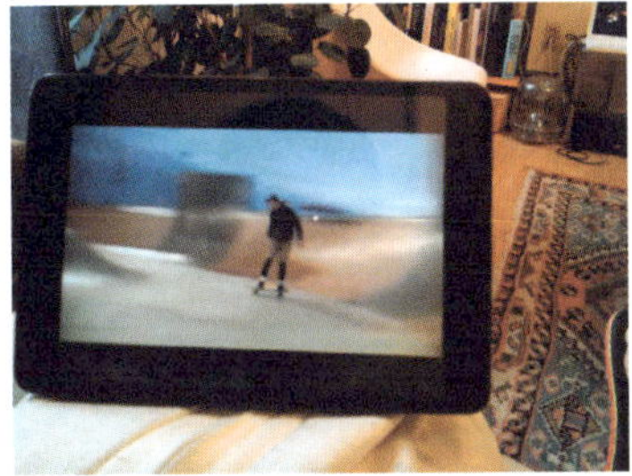

04:00

14:31

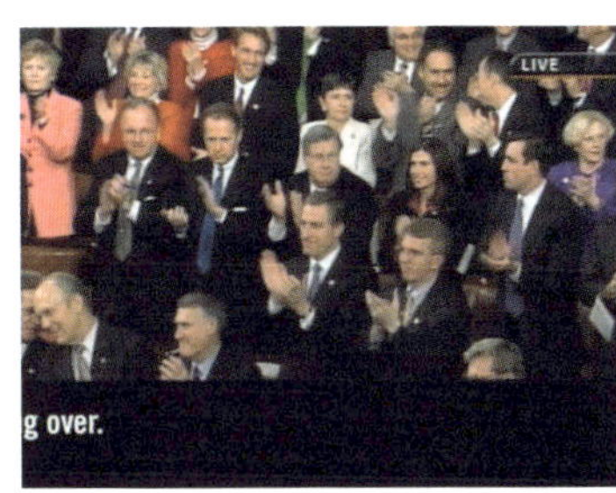

04:33

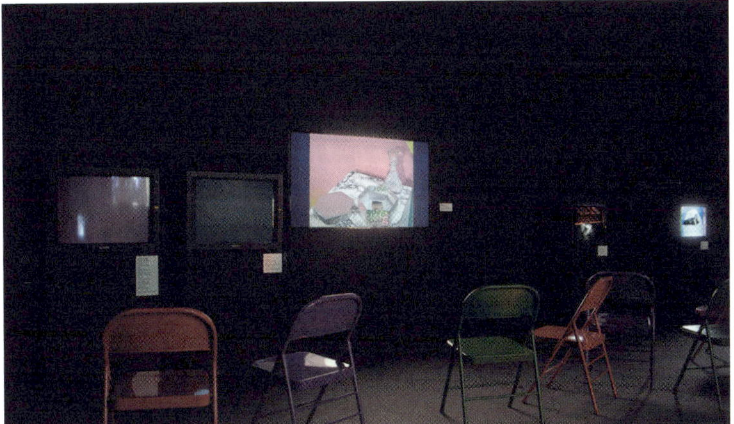

Broadcasting: EAI at ICA, installation view, ICA

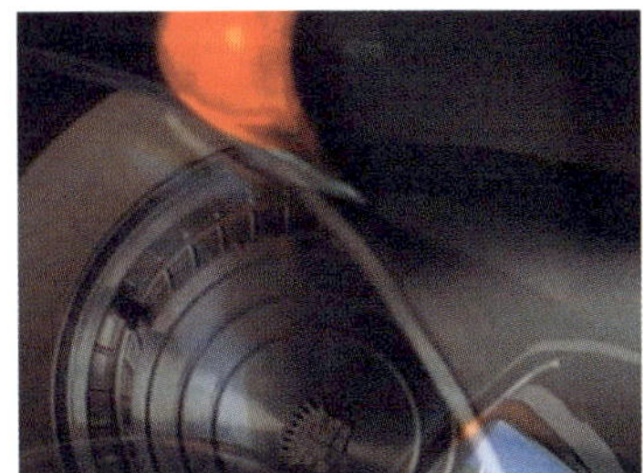

00:20

00:37

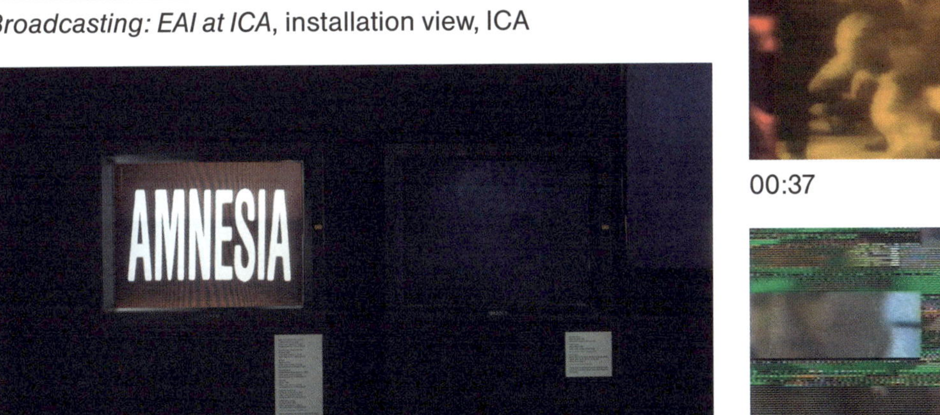

Broadcasting: EAI at ICA, installation view, ICA

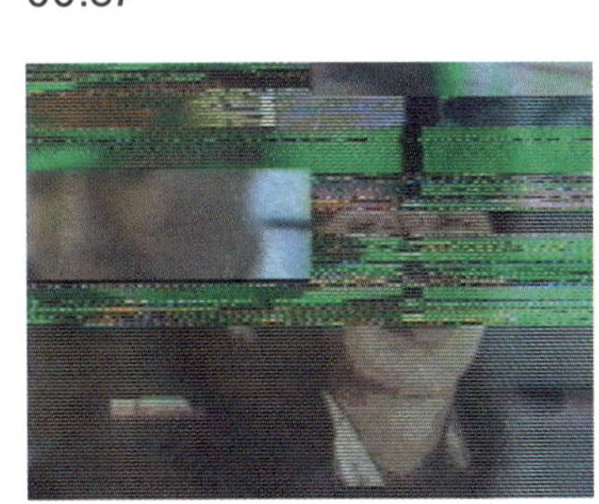

21:14

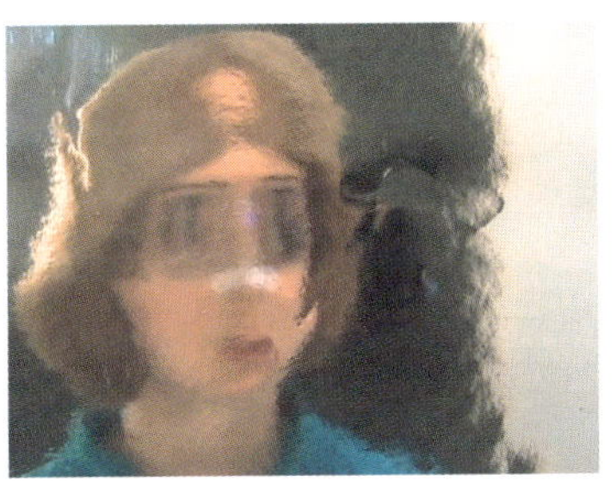

01:26

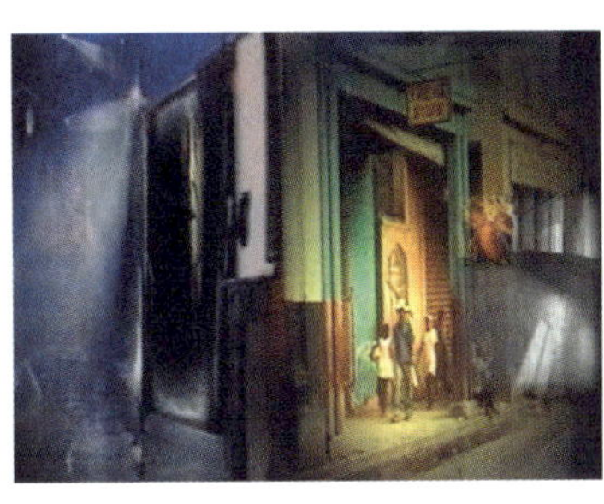

00:23

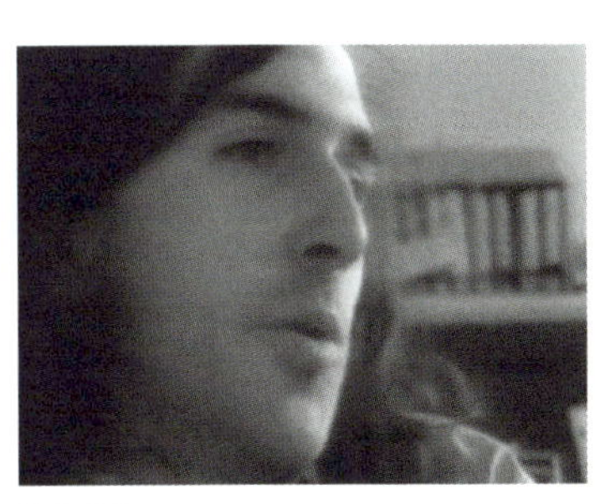

04:26

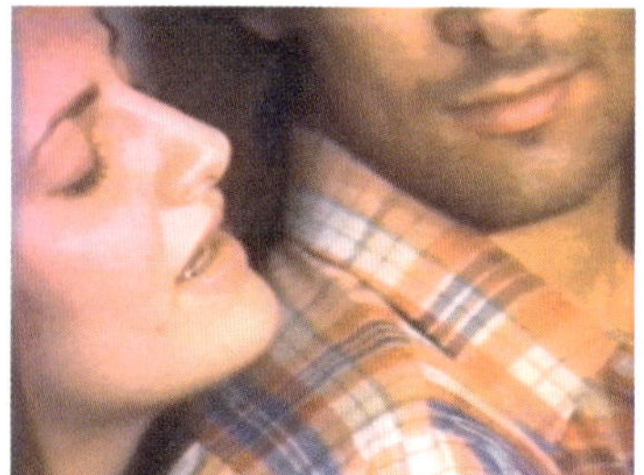

01:23

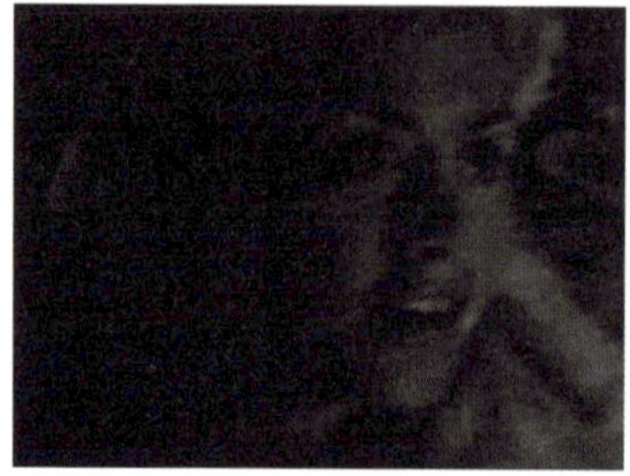

01:43

05:58

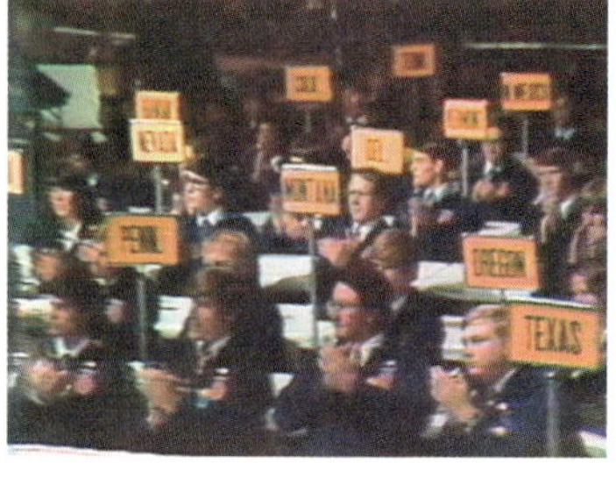

14:07

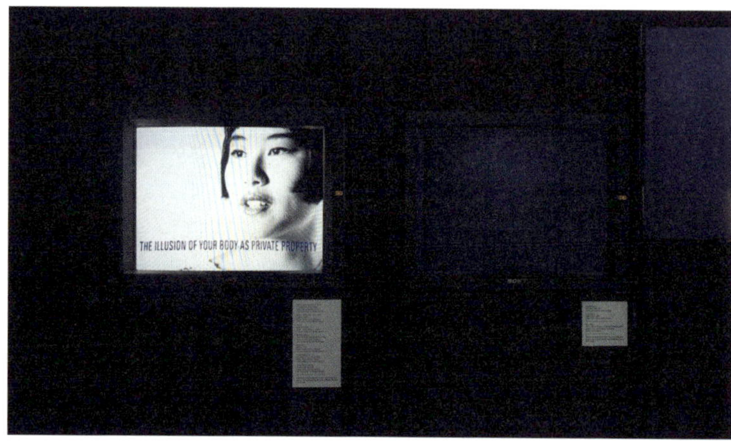

Broadcasting: EAI at ICA, installation view, ICA

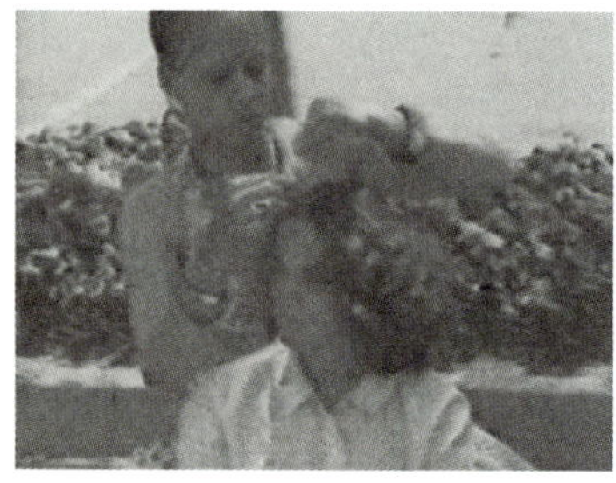

17:31

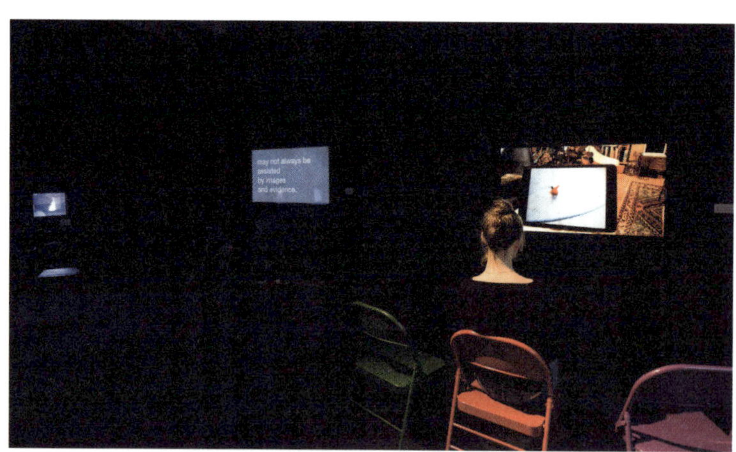

Broadcasting: EAI at ICA, installation view, ICA

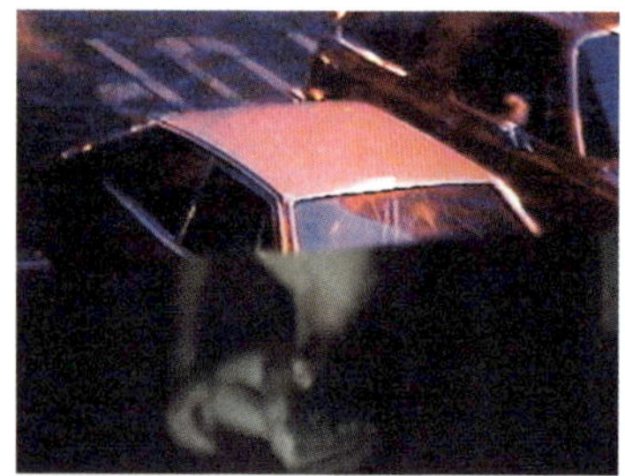

07:19

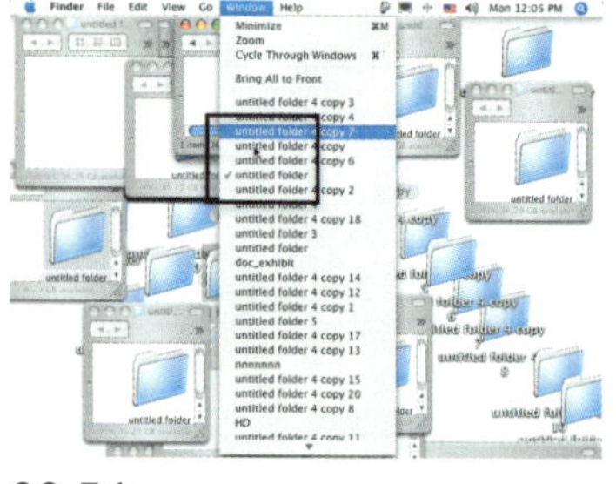

00:54

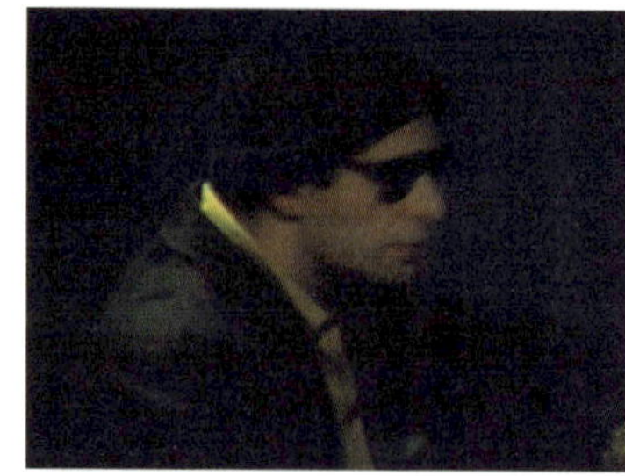

08:25

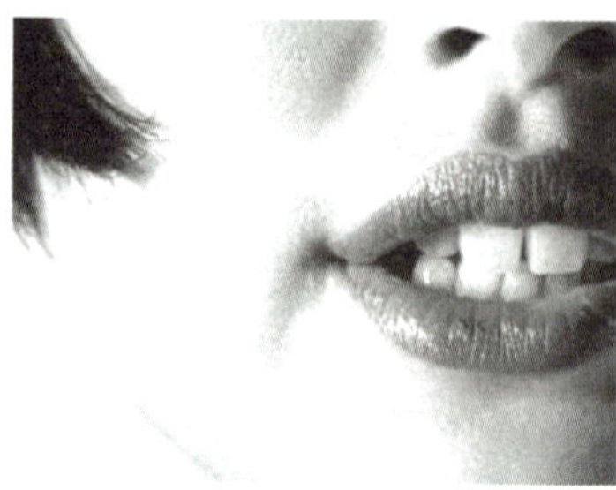

00:09

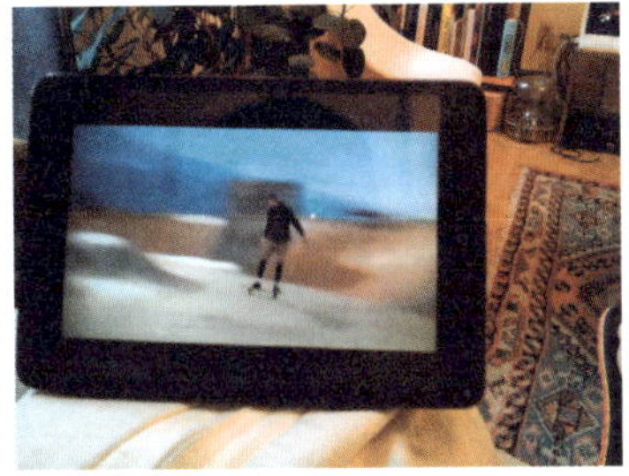

04:00

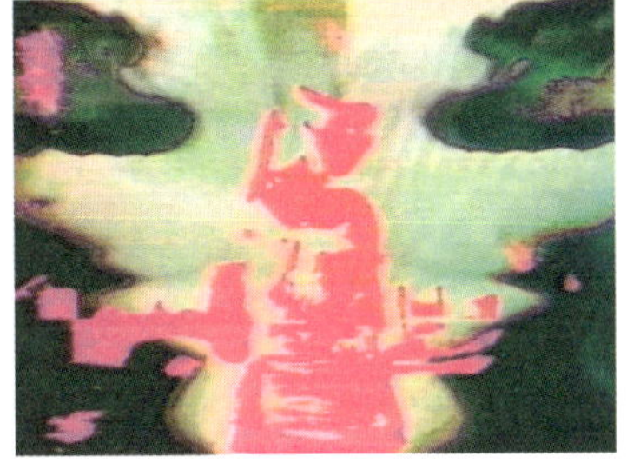

14:31

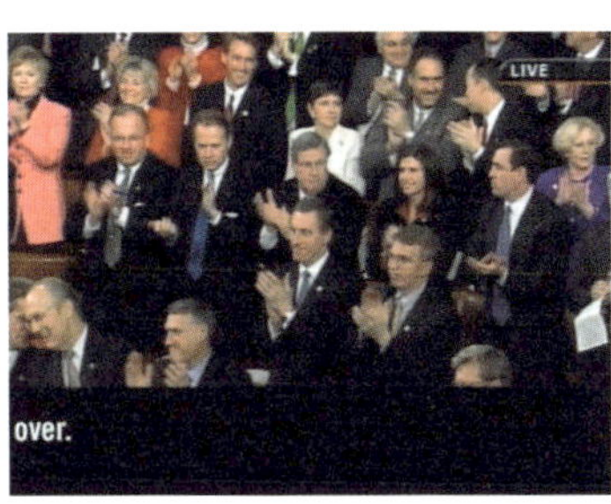

04:33

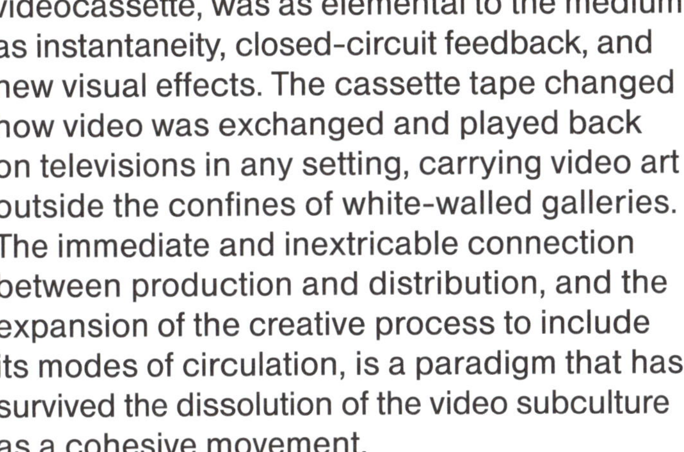

videocassette, was as elemental to the medium as instantaneity, closed-circuit feedback, and new visual effects. The cassette tape changed how video was exchanged and played back on televisions in any setting, carrying video art outside the confines of white-walled galleries. The immediate and inextricable connection between production and distribution, and the expansion of the creative process to include its modes of circulation, is a paradigm that has survived the dissolution of the video subculture as a cohesive movement.

By the mid-1970s, cable television disappointed Smith's vision, as he had warned that it likely would. New legislation favored the commercial conglomerates that would turn cable into what it is today: a lucrative expansion of television into the realm of niche, branded content that more effectively commodifies audiences, and, as the Sinclair Broadcast Group has so sinisterly demonstrated, radicalizes them. The shift from video art's initial ambition to infiltrate and transform television to its institutionalization within

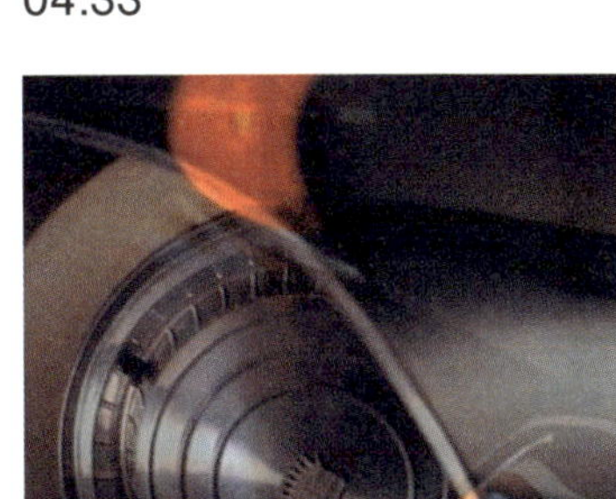

00:20

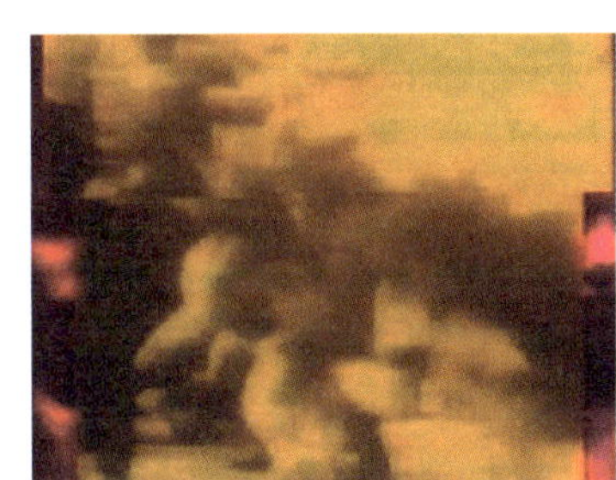

00:37

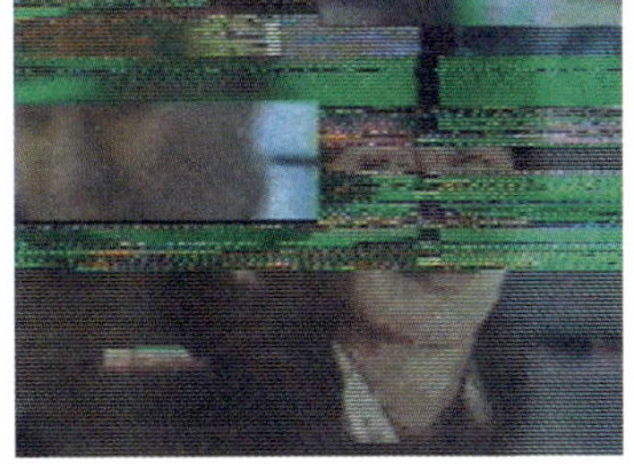

21:14

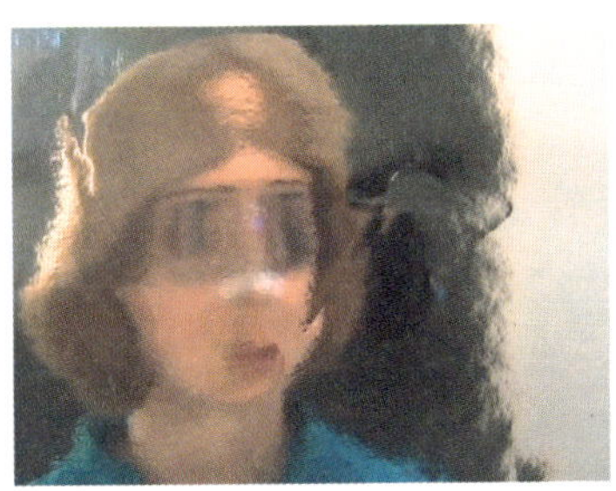

01:26

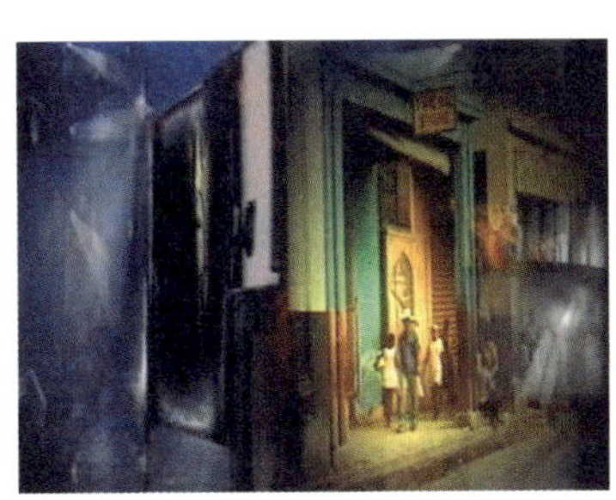

00:23

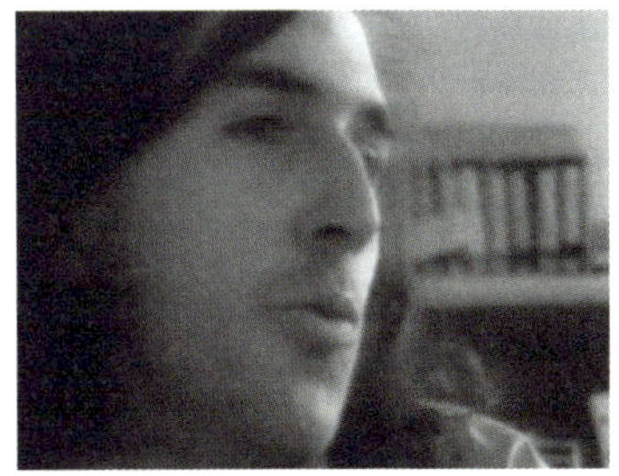

04:26

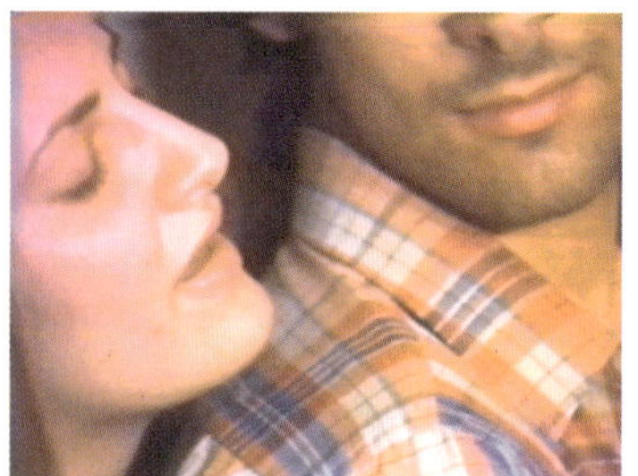

01:23

01:43

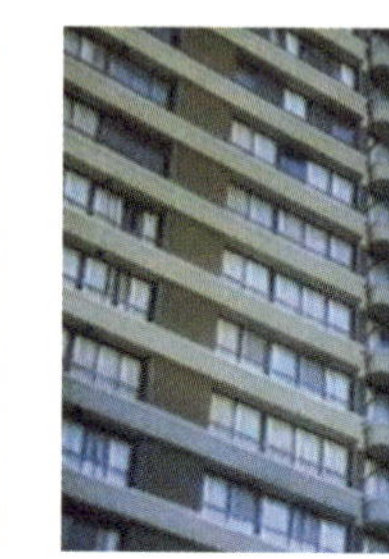

05:58

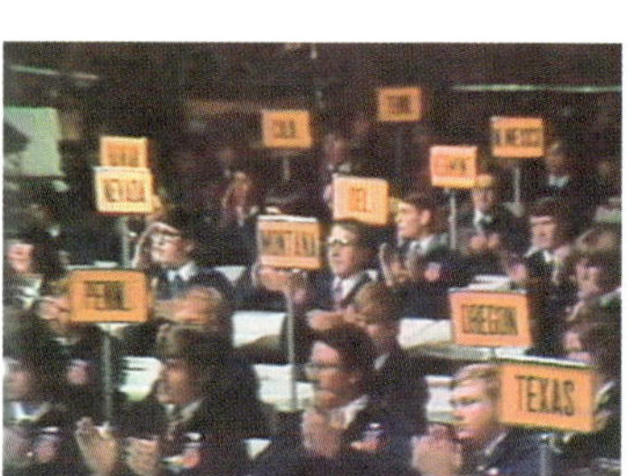

14:07

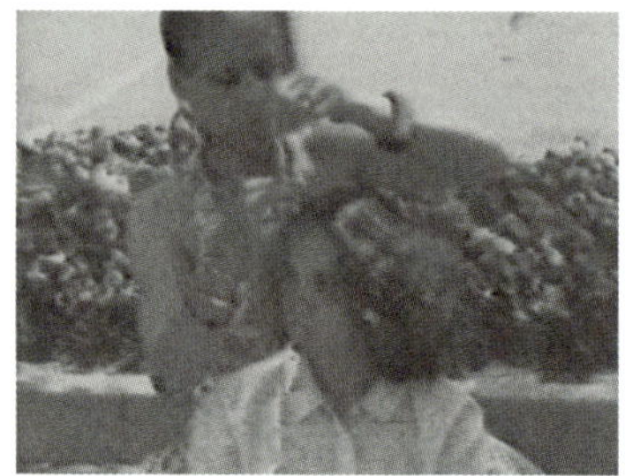

17:31

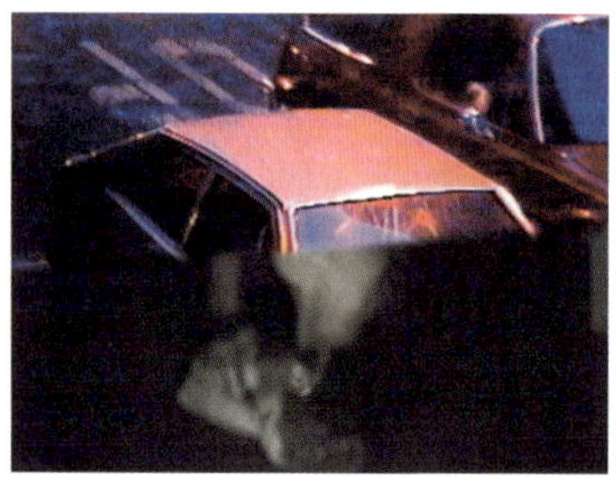

07:19

the arts was the focus of a symposium Wise helped sponsor at MoMA in 1974. *Open Circuits: An International Conference on the Future of Television* considered the position of video art as it was becoming increasingly clear that the arts context, and not cable television, was its future.

Ronald Reagan's reelection in 1984 marked a terminus for the wellspring of funding nurturing video artists (and all artists). Drastic cuts in government support for the arts signaled a sea change in the resources available to artists, and forced many of them to consider other ways of sustaining themselves, including the art market. That same year, Martha Rosler published an influential essay, "Shedding the Utopian Moment," which considered how once-subversive video art was becoming commodified and museologized to the point of being divorced from television, and its social concerns, altogether.[9] This has only become more apparent as the dominant model for video art is now the limited edition, an artificial imposition of scarcity on an infinitely reproduceable form.

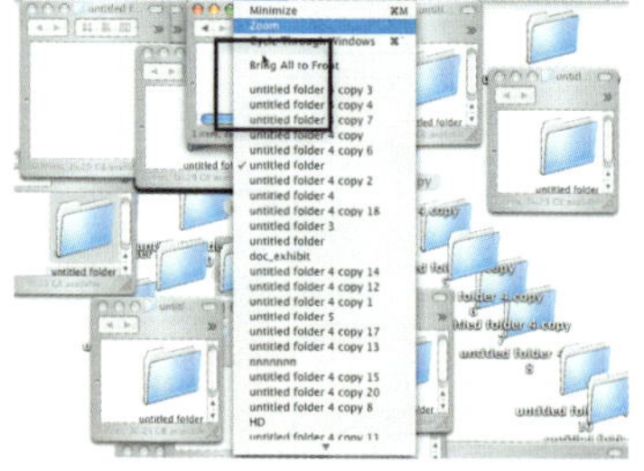

00:54

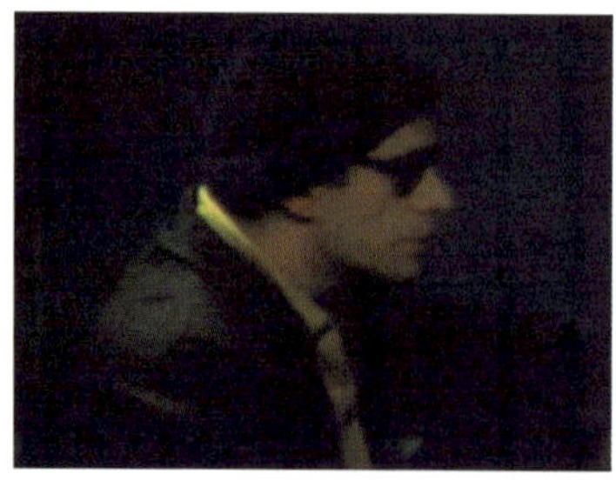

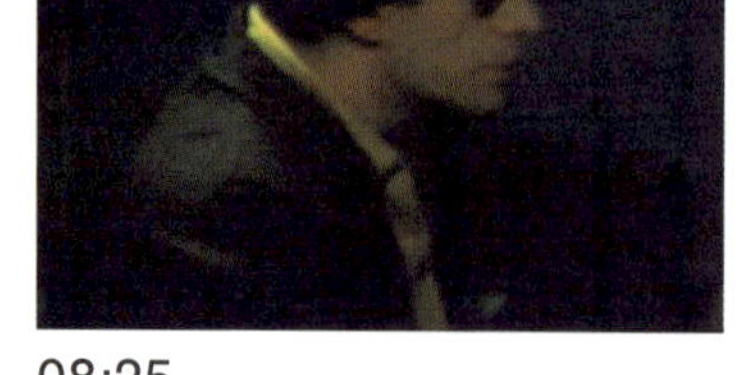

08:25

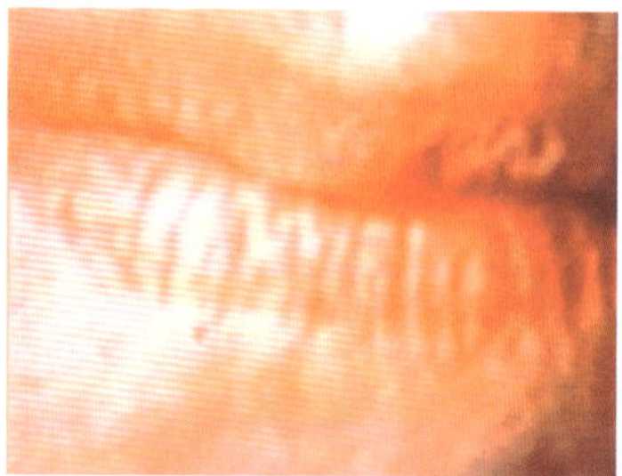

00:09

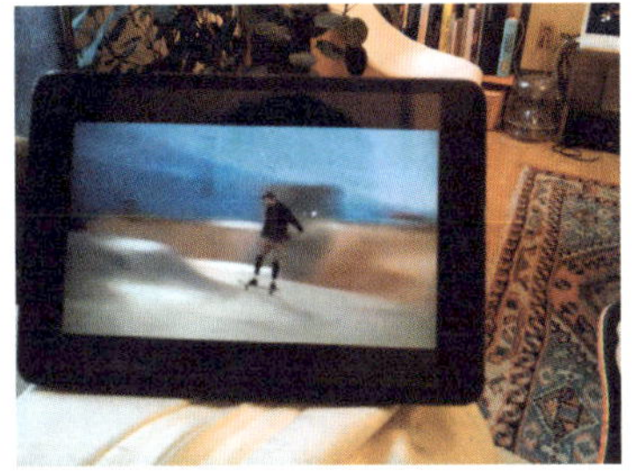

04:01

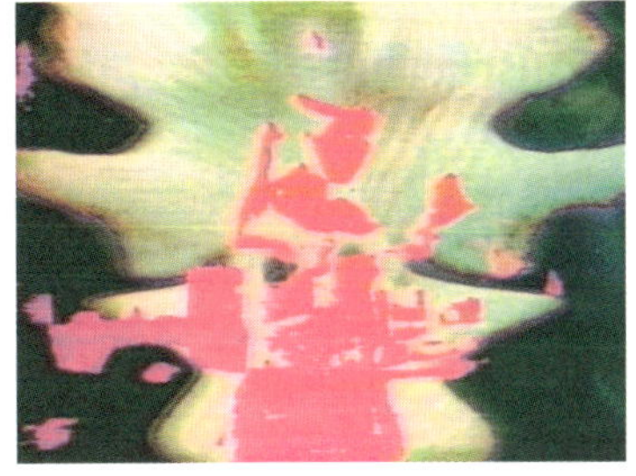

14:32

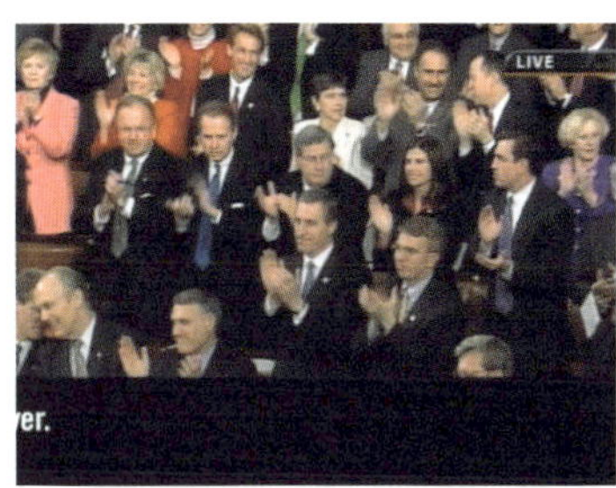

04:34

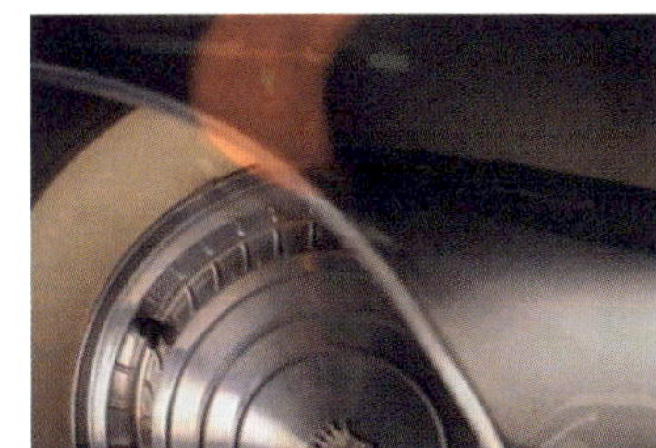

00:21

It would seem that all this would bring Wise's hope for extraterrestrial diffusion crashing down to earth. And yet, EAI has remained an important hub for artists working with video and media through the decades. In the late 1970s, a new generation began producing videos influenced by, and departing from, those of their forebearers. MTV had a profound effect, as did advances in editing equipment. The counterculture's aspiration to change the social role of television shifted to an artistic critique of the medium through appropriation and mimicry. Transitioning into the 1990s, in response to the oppressive politics of the Reagan years and the staggering toll of the AIDS crisis, another generation returned to the collectivist, activist-oriented video of the guerrilla television era. During this period EAI's editing facility hosted ACT UP, DIVA-TV, House of Color, and X-PRZ, among many other groups, and fostered a noticeable trend of low-fi, performance-based videos that explored the politics of representation and resisted the slickness of mainstream media.

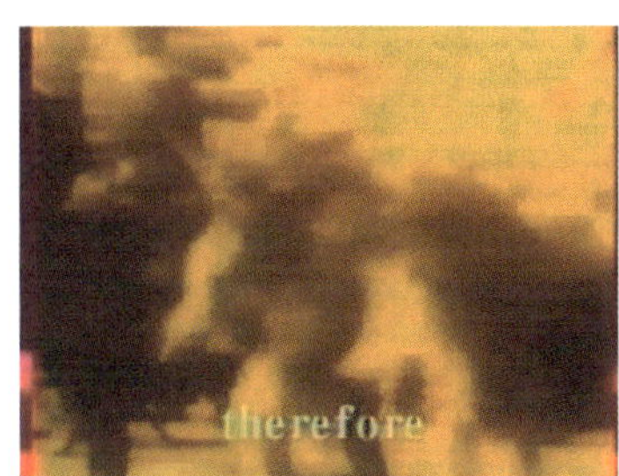

00:38

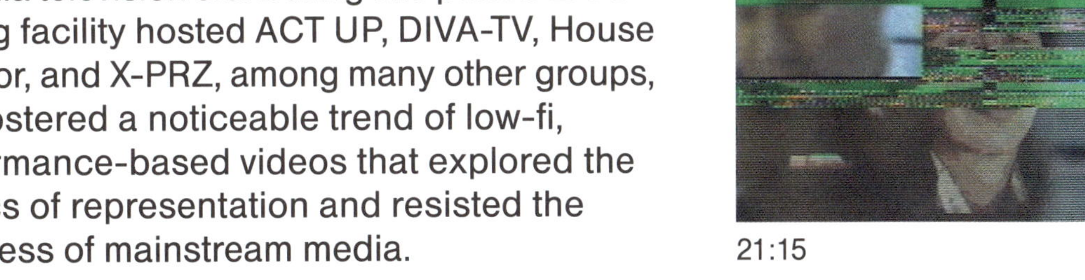

21:15

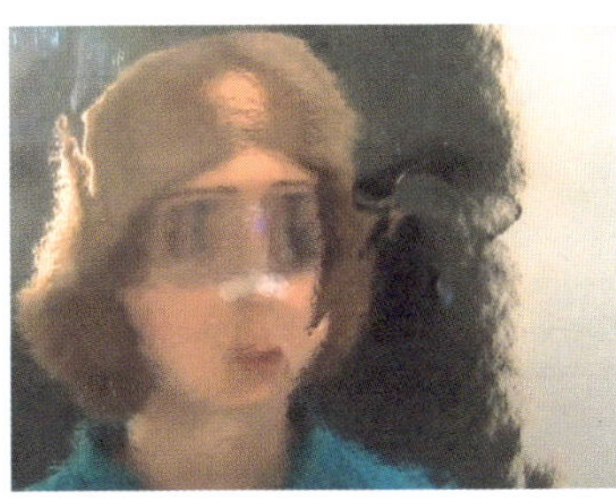

01:27

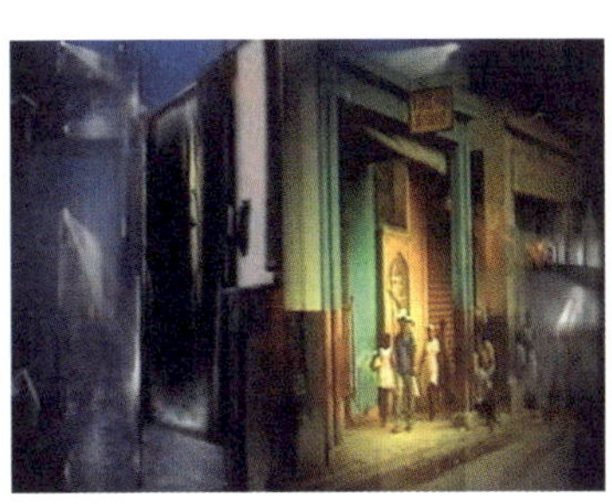

00:24

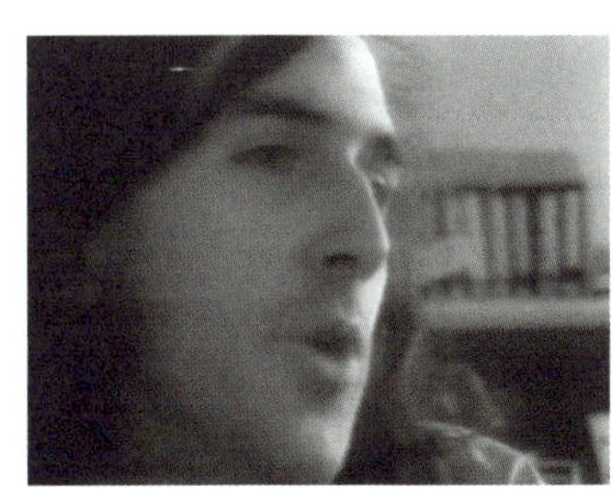

04:27

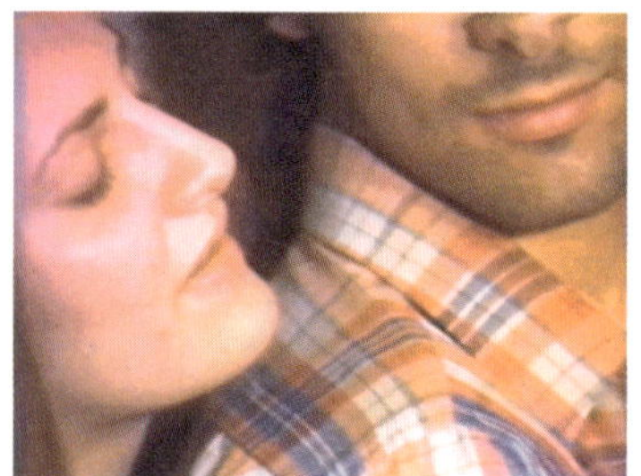

01:23

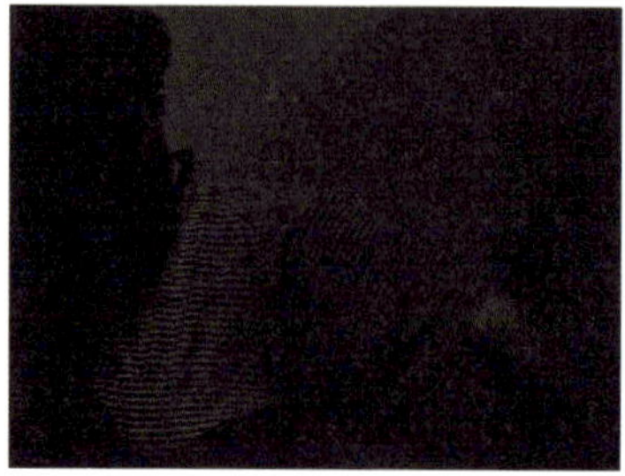

01:43

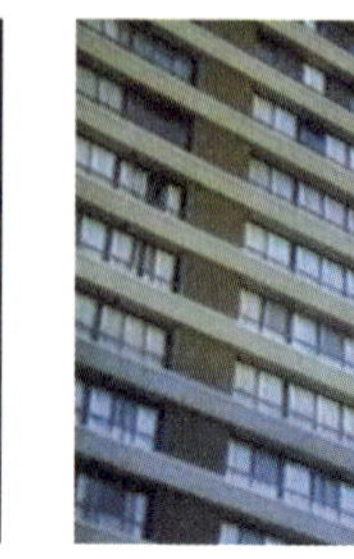

05:58

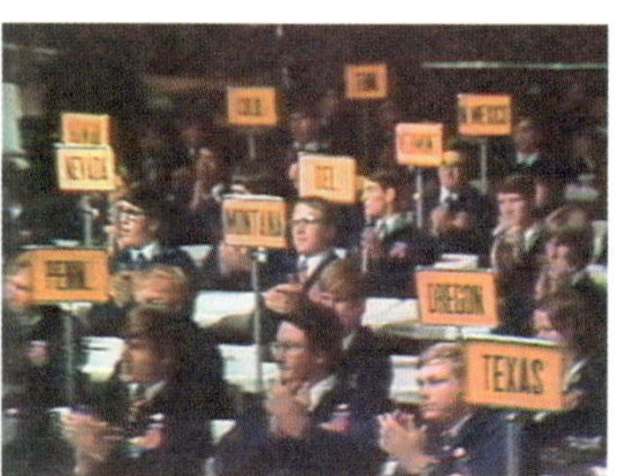

14:07

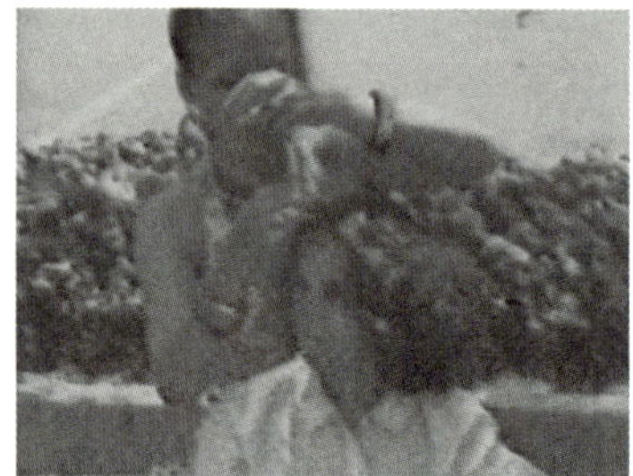

17:31

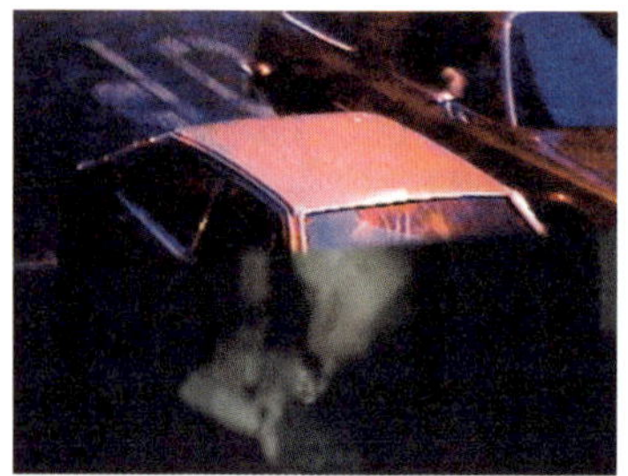

07:19

The blooming of the internet in the late 1990s introduced yet another new platform for creative expression that echoed many of the hopes for cable television in the 1970s. At first, early internet users emphasized the importance of sharing resources and information, and of keeping technology free from commercial control, pointing to the *Whole Earth Catalog* as a precursor. And then, with the emergence of YouTube and social media in the 2000s, there arose new online subcultures devoted to access and open global communication. Each of these communications revolutions are eventually subsumed by the commercial models that undergird them, but they relay forward ideas that have long proved to be transformative.

All the while, EAI expanded its representation of artists' video, and pivoted to stewardship and distribution as its main programs. Wise's successor, Lori Zippay, who joined EAI in 1981, strongly advocated for the significance of the collection by formalizing a preservation program and developing an expansive catalog that has

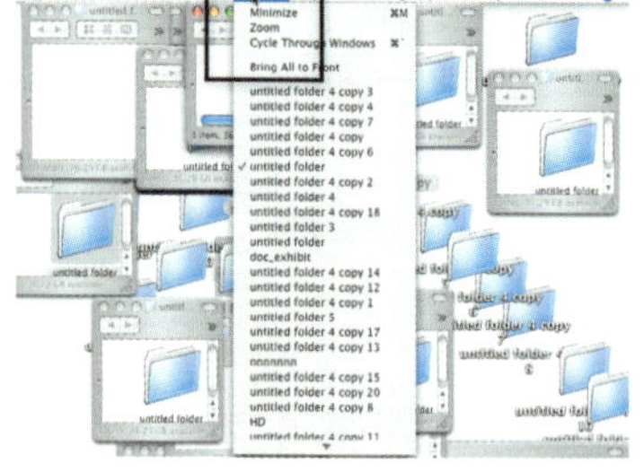

00:54

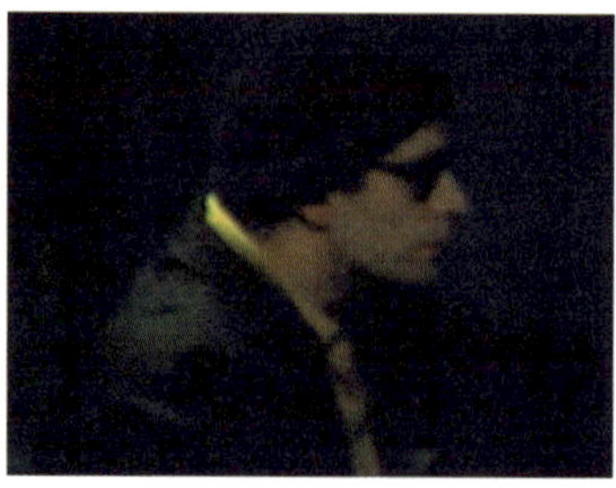

08:25

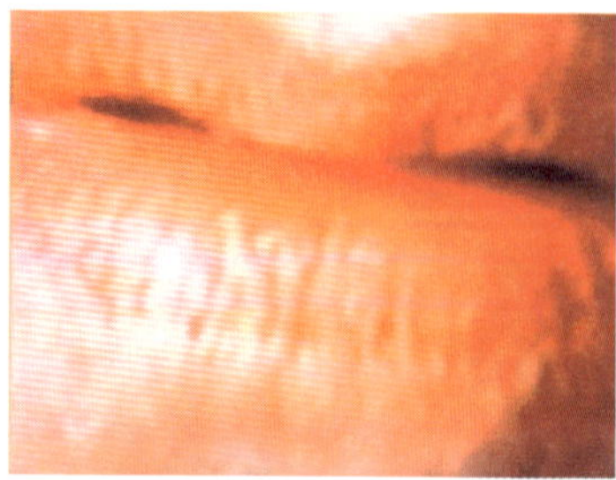

00:09

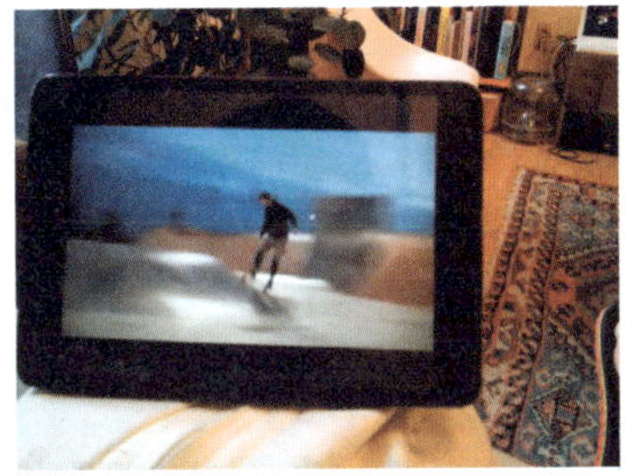

04:01

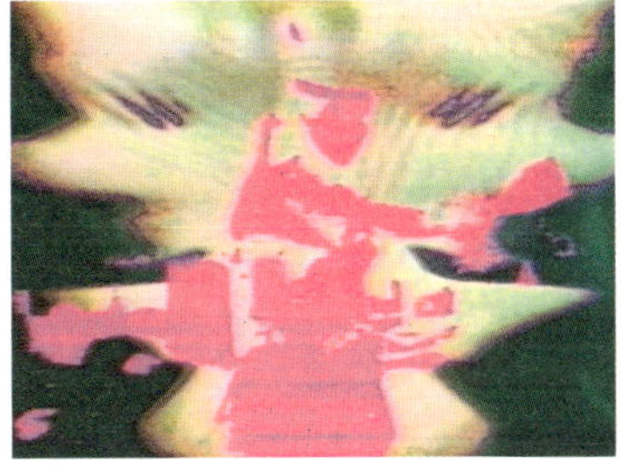

14:32

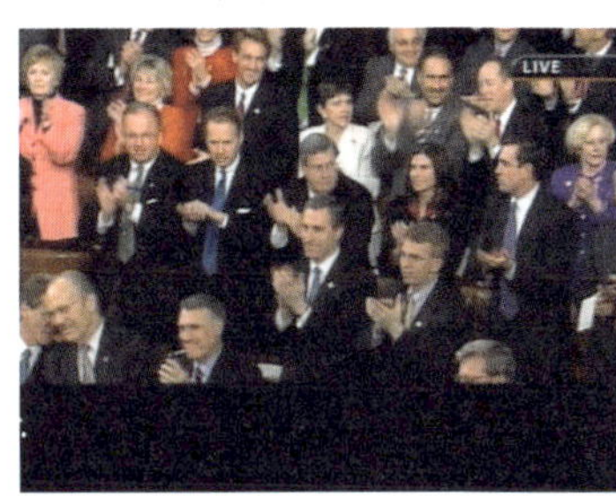

04:34

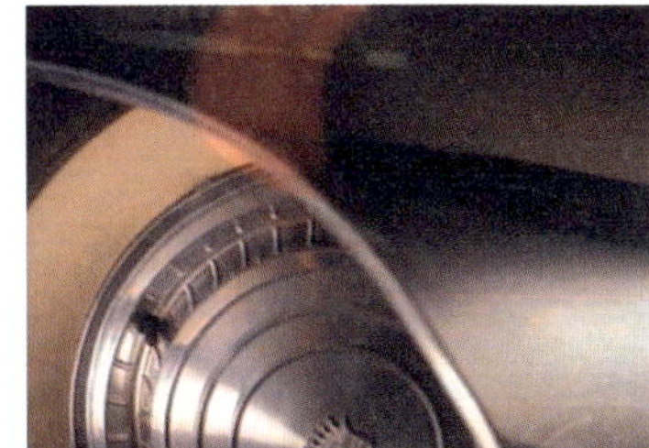

00:21

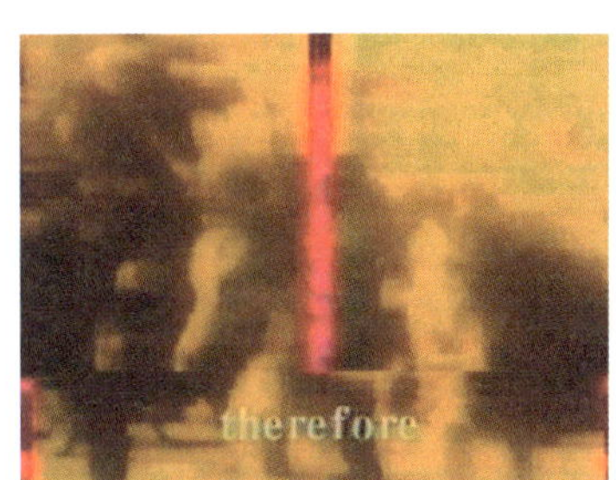

00:38

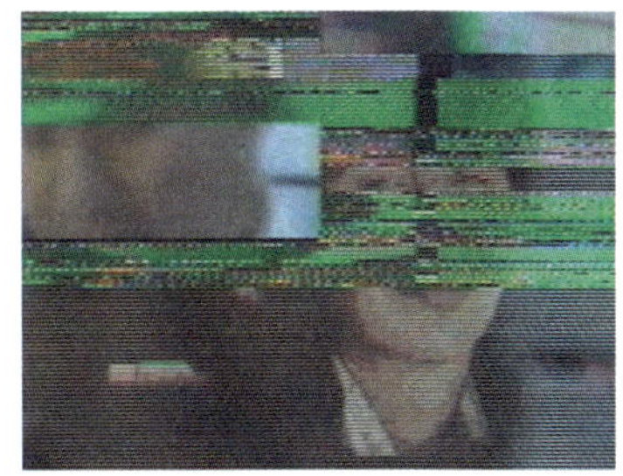

21:15

become a major scholarly resource. In the early 2000s, shortly after EAI went online with its catalog, then technical director Seth Price published an influential essay that extended the tenets of the avant-garde movements of the twentieth century into the internet era. *Dispersion* considered how artmaking could and would be influenced by the new production and dissemination strategies of internet consumer culture, and raised provocative questions about art's place when removed from its traditional institutions and markets. In seeking to reach the public, art must contend with new sites for this interaction, suggesting again how distribution might be taken up as a radical artistic strategy.[10]

Marcel Duchamp looms large for Price, as he does in any consideration of art's shifting relationship with the public in the age of mass media and consumerism, but he is not a lone beacon. It is with the advent of photography and electronic communication in the nineteenth century that the foundation for this shift can truly be found. Frederick Douglass's writings about the

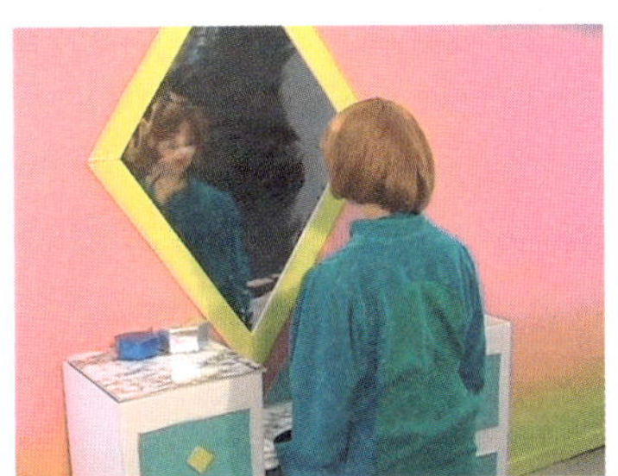

01:27

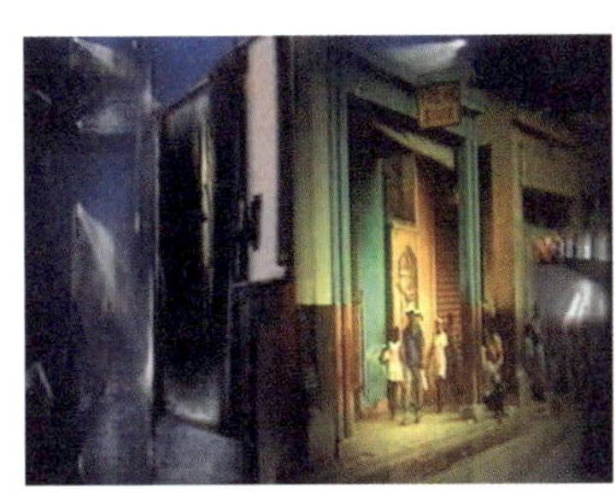

00:24

04:27

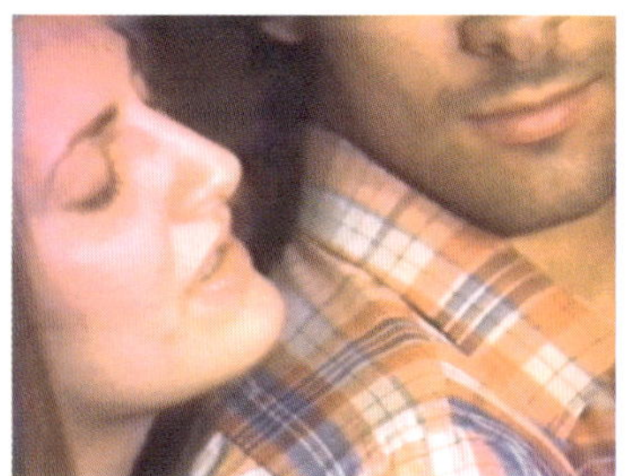
01:23

01:43

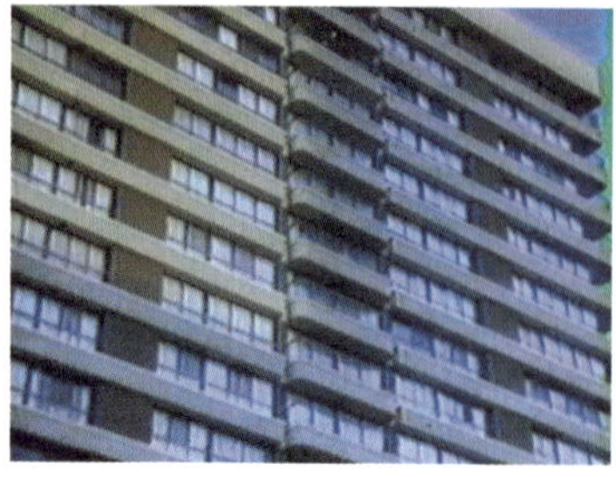
05:58

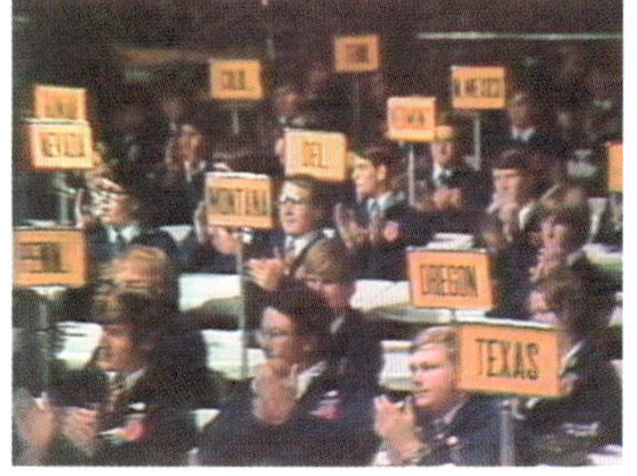

14:07

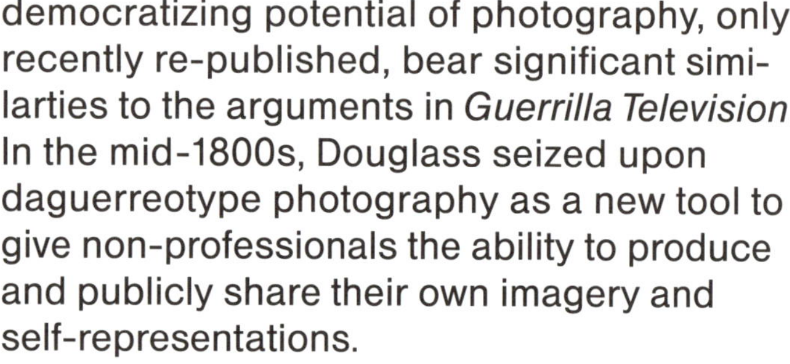
democratizing potential of photography, only recently re-published, bear significant similarties to the arguments in *Guerrilla Television*. In the mid-1800s, Douglass seized upon daguerreotype photography as a new tool to give non-professionals the ability to produce and publicly share their own imagery and self-representations.

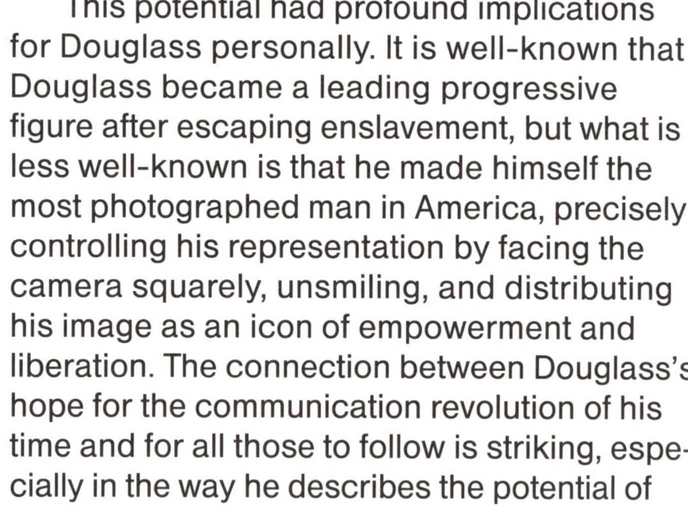
This potential had profound implications for Douglass personally. It is well-known that Douglass became a leading progressive figure after escaping enslavement, but what is less well-known is that he made himself the most photographed man in America, precisely controlling his representation by facing the camera squarely, unsmiling, and distributing his image as an icon of empowerment and liberation. The connection between Douglass's hope for the communication revolution of his time and for all those to follow is striking, especially in the way he describes the potential of the information age well before the existence of computers, let alone the internet:

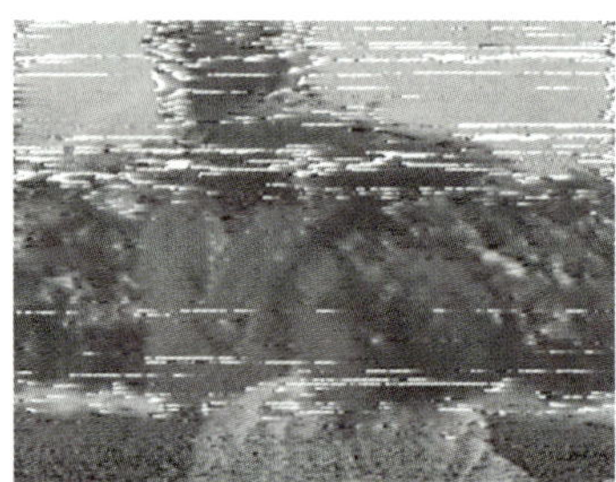
17:31

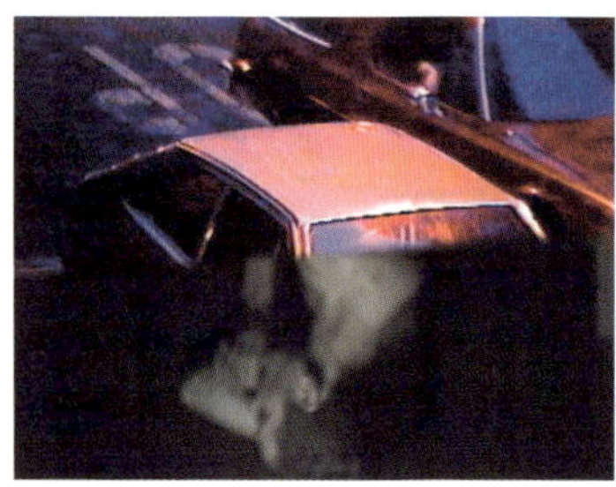
07:19

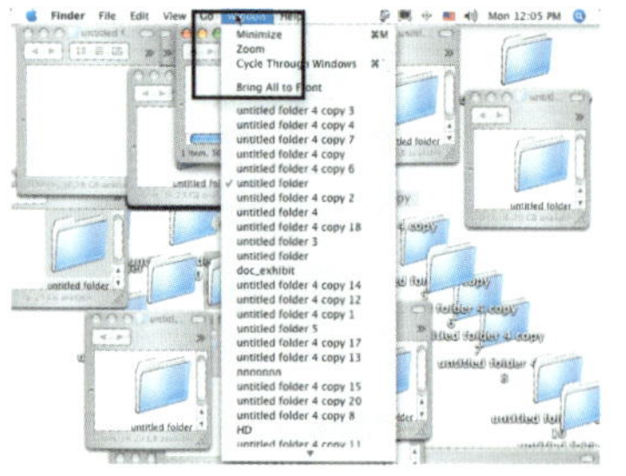

00:54

08:25

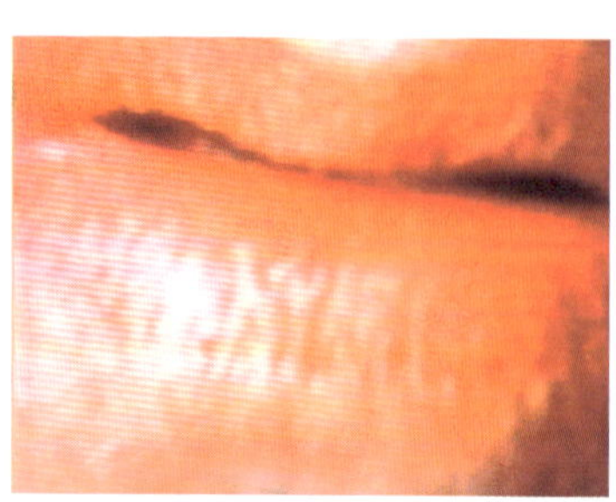
00:09

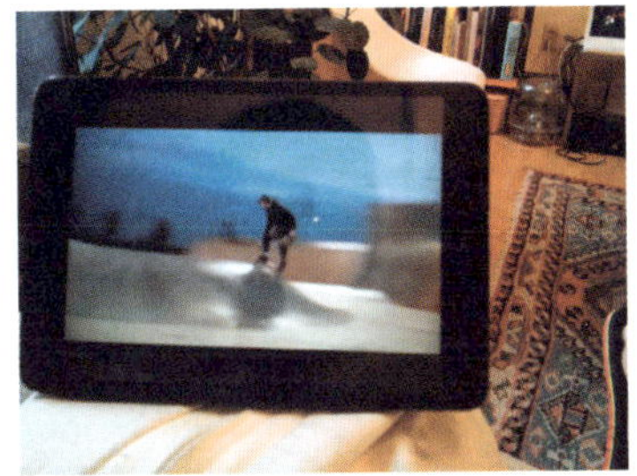

04:01

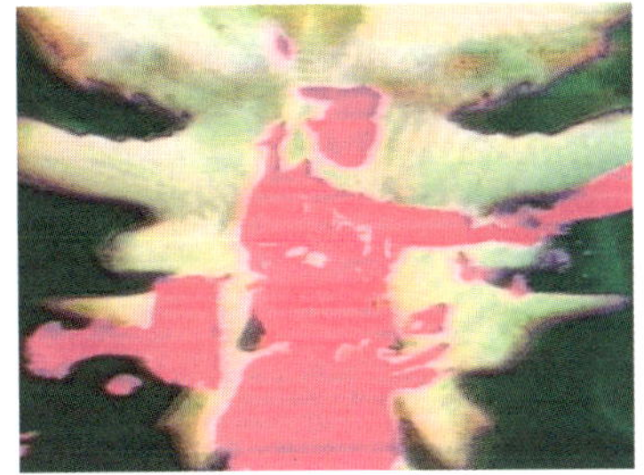

14:32

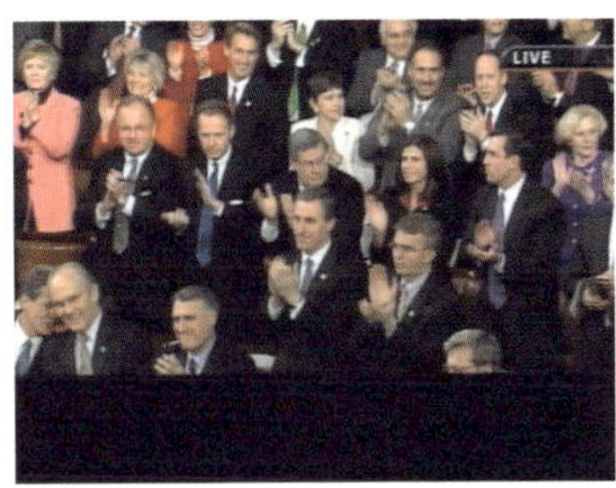

04:34

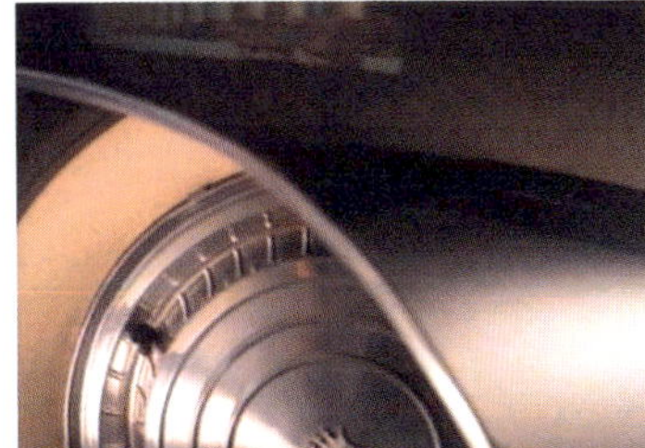

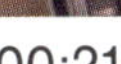

00:21

The increased facilities of locomotion, the growing inter-communication of distant nations, the rapid transmission of intelligence over the globe—the world-wide ramifications of commerce—bringing together the knowledge, the skill, and the mental power of the world, cannot but dispel prejudice, dissolve the granite barriers of arbitrary power, bring the world into peace and unity, and at last crown the world with justice, liberty, and brotherly kindness.[11]

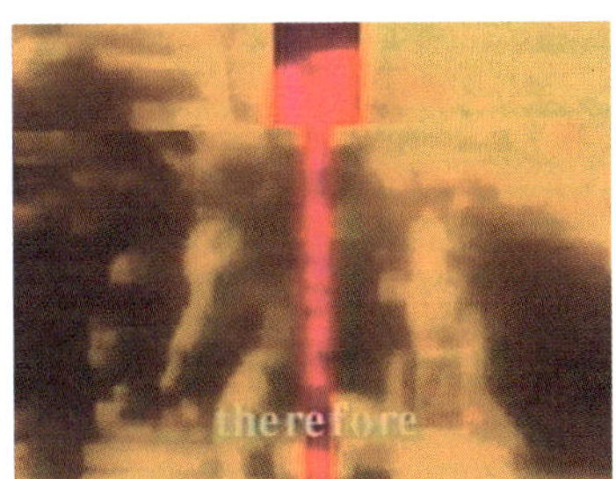

00:38

From the perspective of the twenty-first century, which has seen the concentration of power aided by monolithic corporations with names that affirm the scale of their control (Amazon, Alphabet, SpaceX), this declaration is called into question. The beleaguered year 2020 once again vividly demonstrated how vulnerable our planet is, threatened by a global pandemic, violent political extremism, and escalating climate change. Television, though no longer the dominant cultural mediator, has made new incursions into our lives. In concert with social media, which caters to self-selected tribes of bitterly divided political and cultural affiliations, TV has achieved a perverted version of participatory media.

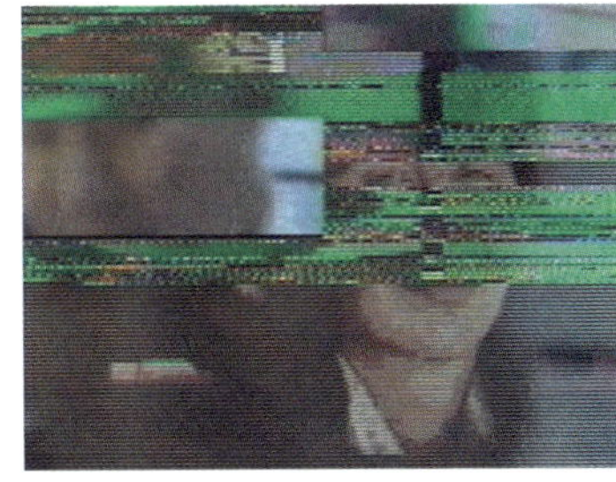

21:15

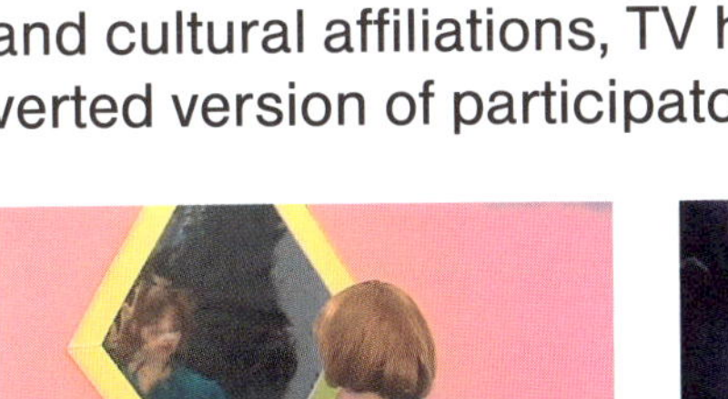

01:27

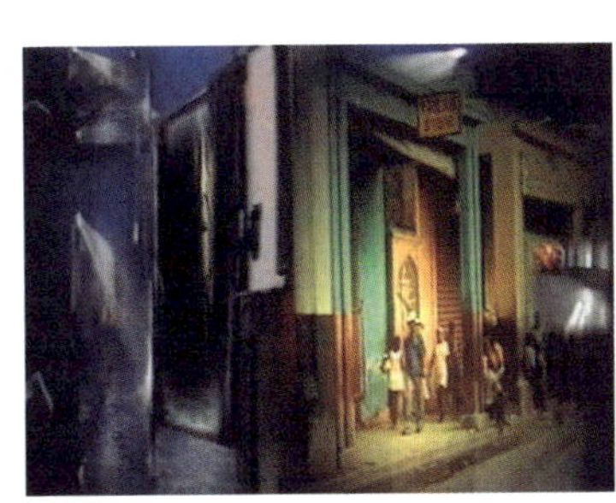

00:24

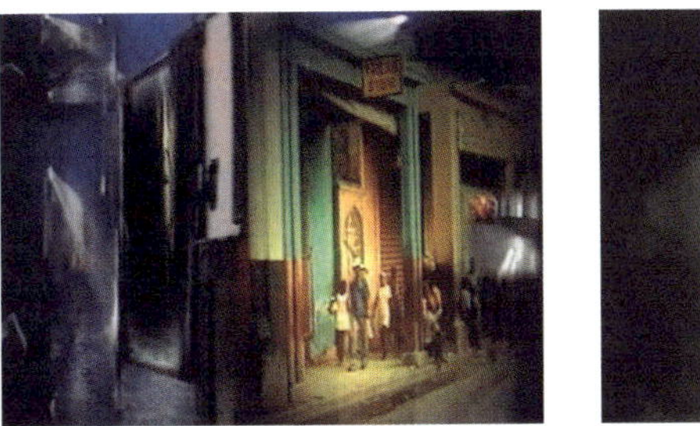

04:27

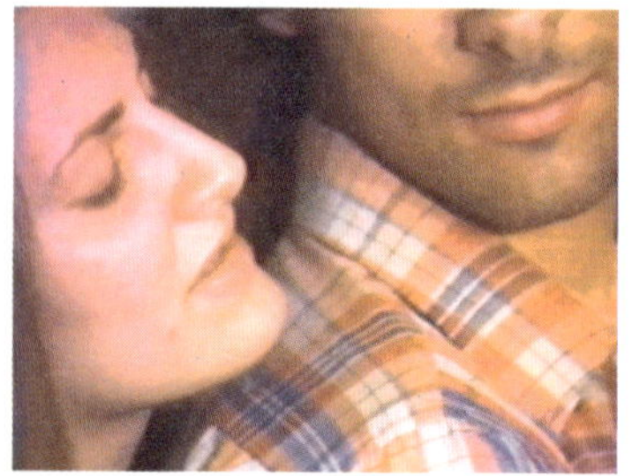
01:23

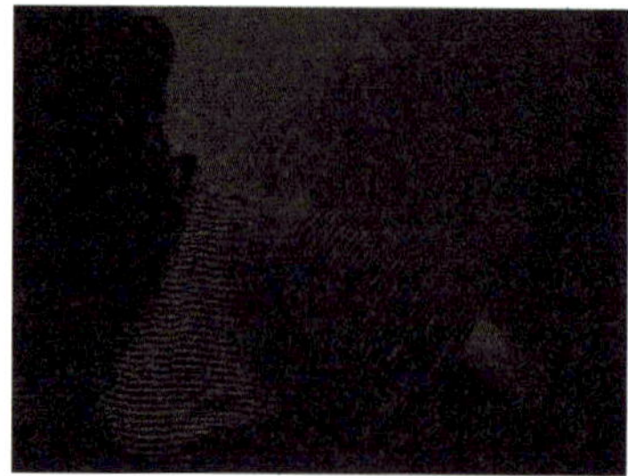
01:43

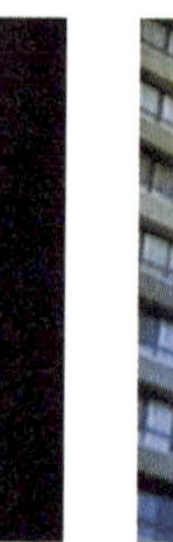
05:58

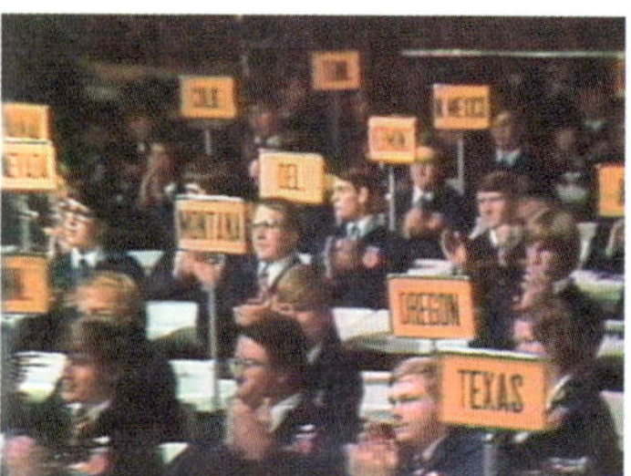

14:07

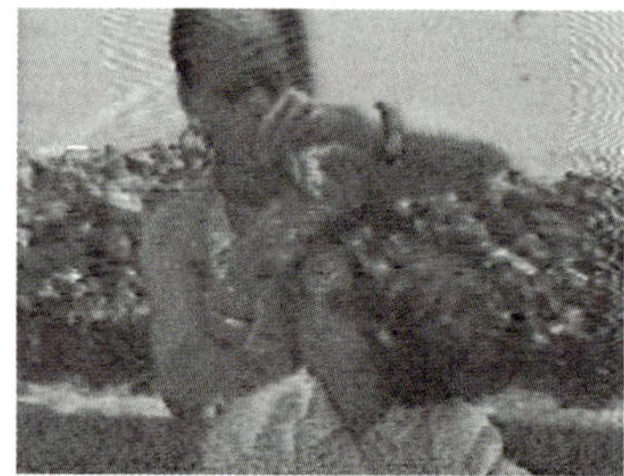
17:31

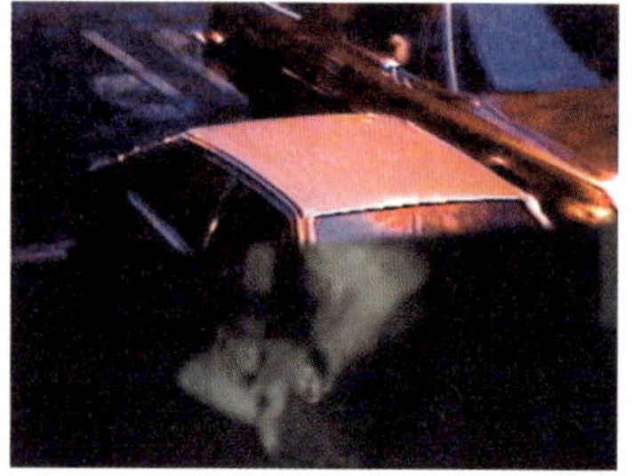
07:19

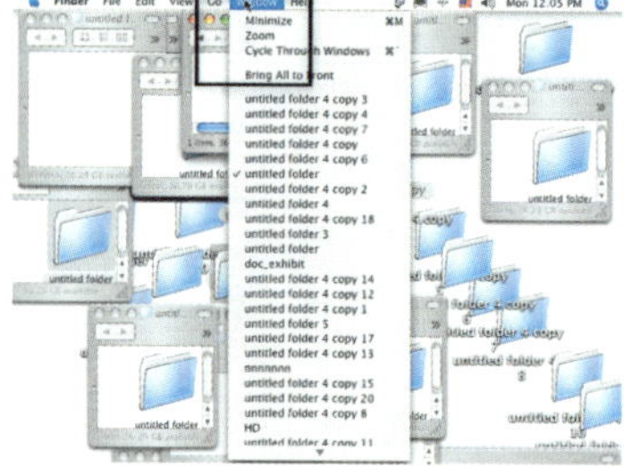

00:54

The COVID-19 pandemic has forced people to spend most of their time isolated at home, experiencing the world mediated by screens. Big broadcast events have defined the year, echoing those from television's apotheosis: a space launch, presidential debates, and sports tournaments. The SpaceX launch on May 30, 2020 the first to test the collaboration of a private company and NASA, occurred in tandem with growing media coverage of George Floyd's murder by a police officer. Once the video of this horrific incident was made public, it ignited the accumulated tinder of centuries of such visual evidence, luring record numbers of protesters from their quarantines to demonstrate in the streets. The Black Lives Matter outcry was so urgent and widespread that seemingly untouchable institutions, including major corporations, sports leagues, and art museums, were directly challenged and impacted. Ultimately, Douglass was correct about the capacity of mass media to dispel prejudice by inciting a powerful resistance to the top-down structures harboring inequity and racial injustice.

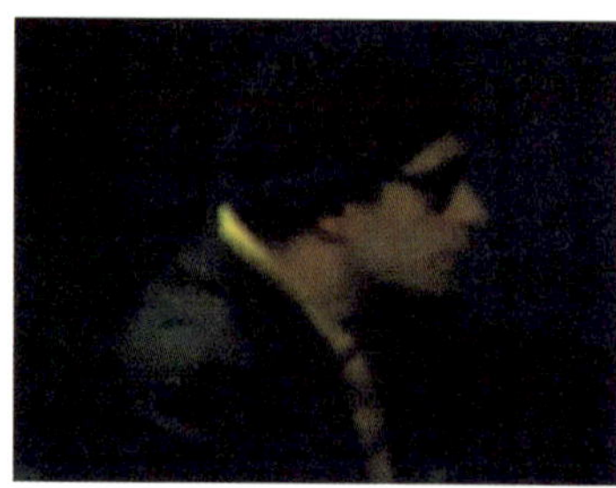
08:25

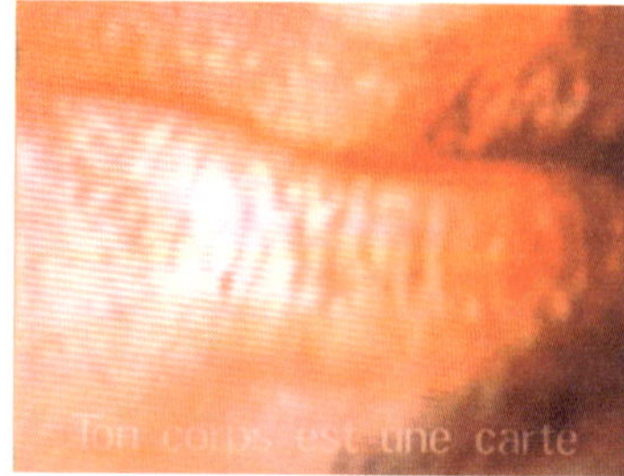

00:09

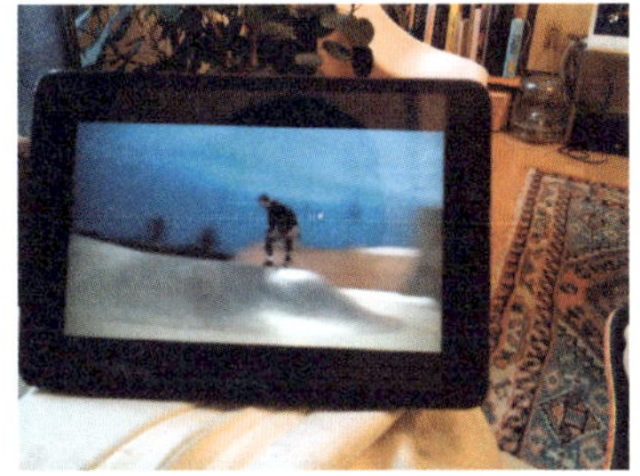
04:01

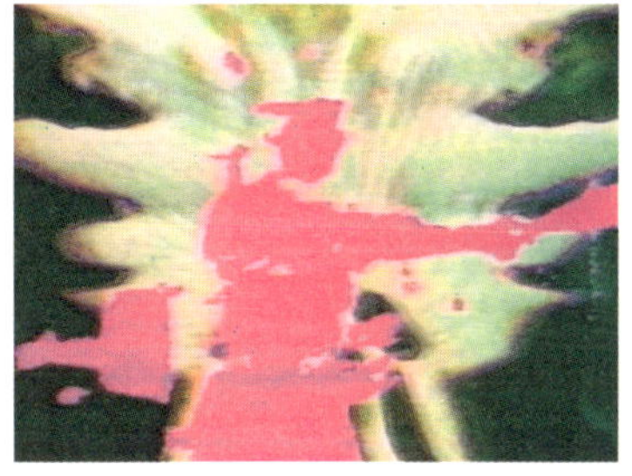
14:32

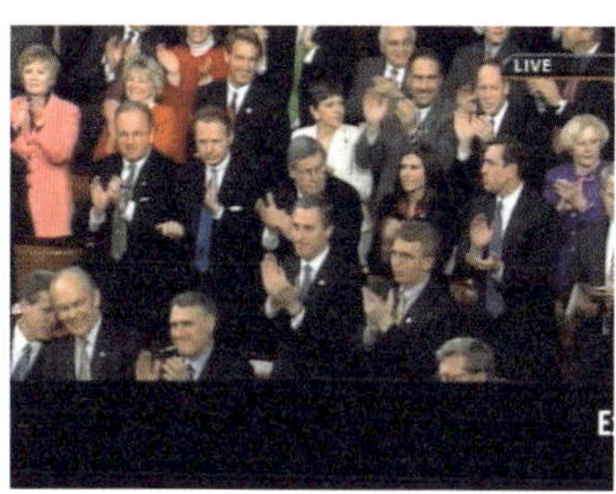

04:34

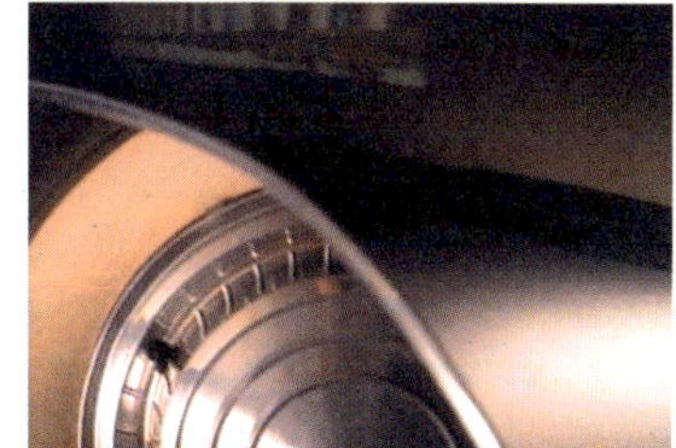
00:21

The year 2021 marks the fiftieth anniversary of an earlier rebellion that is, sadly, as relevant now as it was then. In 1971, EAI was incorporated, *Guerrilla Television* was published, public-access television arrived in New York, and David Cort made *Mayday Realtime*, a now "classic" guerrilla television tape that documented May Day street protests in D.C., including scenes of police violently confronting antiwar demonstrators. This milestone year, launched with an insurrection attempt by white supremacist groups, captured on video and broadcast to the public, has already explicitly reaffirmed that the struggle against oppressive forces is ongoing.

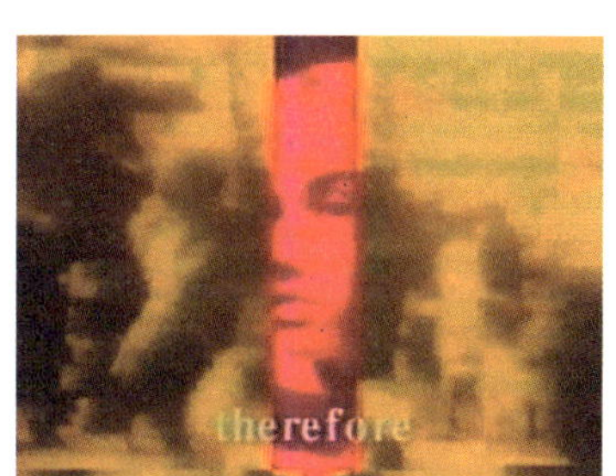

00:38

When Wise wrote his *Leading Edge* manifesto, technological innovation was infused with political potential. This potential is worn away by the pressures of commodification, including those of the art market. At the fifty-year mark, EAI can no longer claim—and has no interest in claiming—to be at the leading edge of technology art. Though it still offers editing equipment

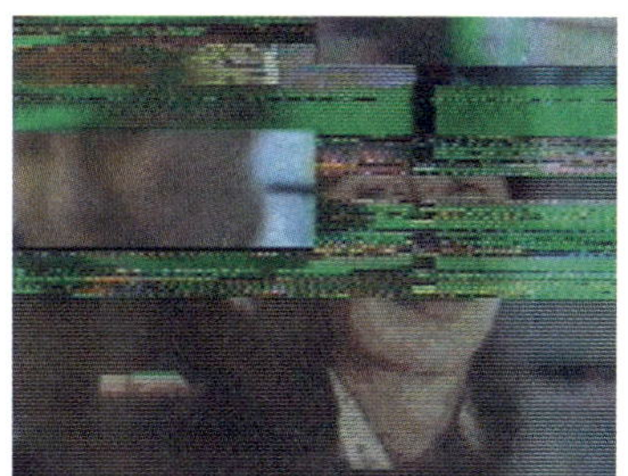
21:15

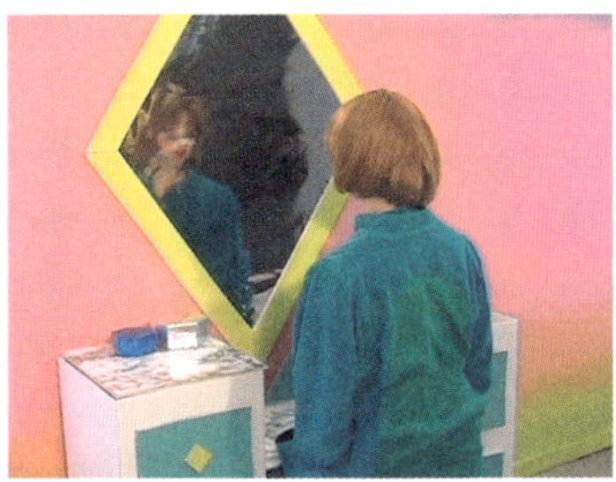
01:27

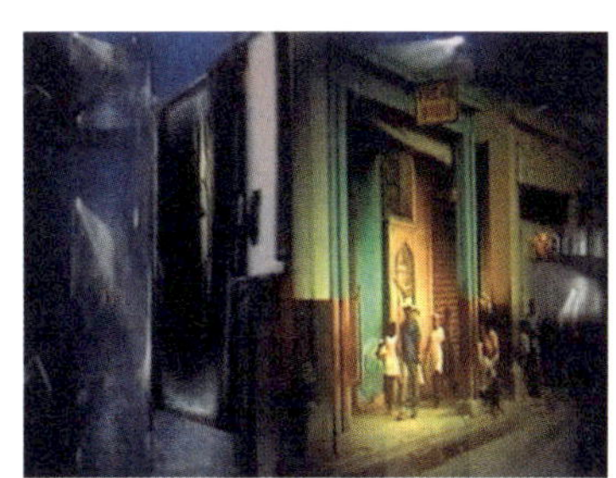
00:24

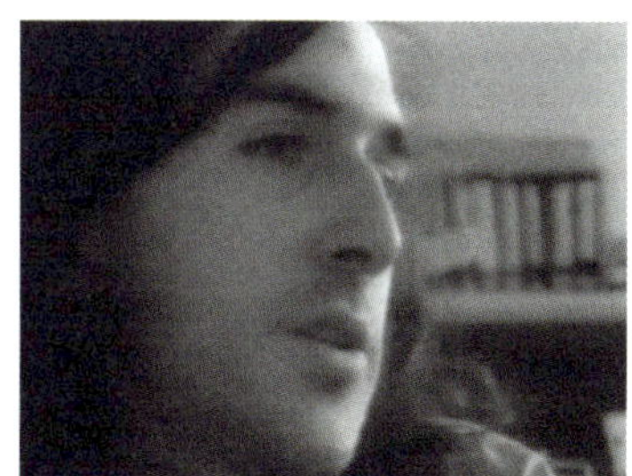
04:27

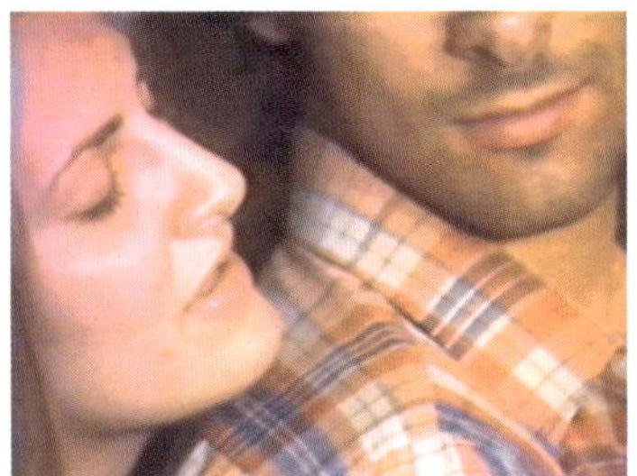
01:23

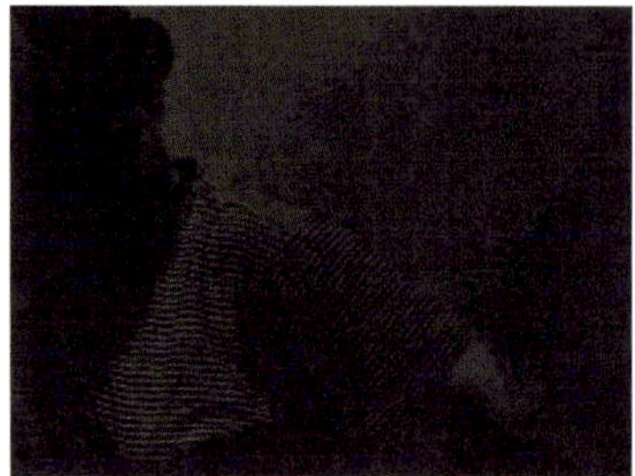
01:43

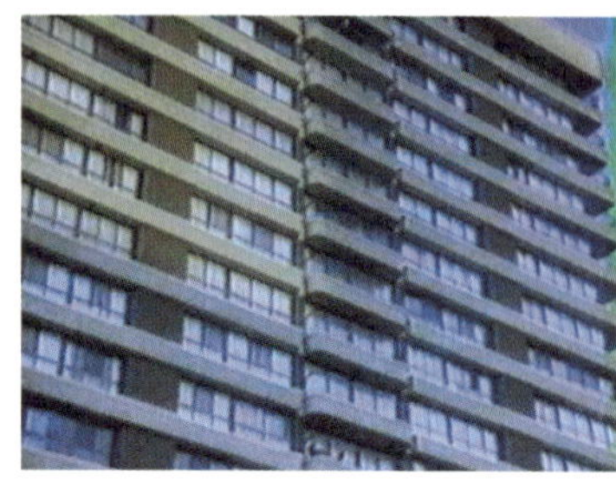
05:58

to those who need access, most artists are now able to edit their videos on their personal computers or phones. The art and technology nexus has been taken up by commercial galleries as a generator of public spectacle, fitting them into the zone of the mainstream entertainment industry.

These developments have not diminished EAI's important role, in fact they have emboldened the organization. Over five decades, its collection has grown to nearly four thousand titles by over two hundred artists, and the distribution program has a global reach. Generations of scholars, curators, artists, and activists have turned to EAI as an important resource. Artists continue to lead the way to new forms and new aesthetics, and especially to new ways of reaching the public. Video in particular is an inherently uncontainable medium, one that is migratory, readily duplicated, and easy to disperse. Those who choose to embrace its qualities are a self-selected group. It is incredible to see how organically EAI sustains an intergenerational

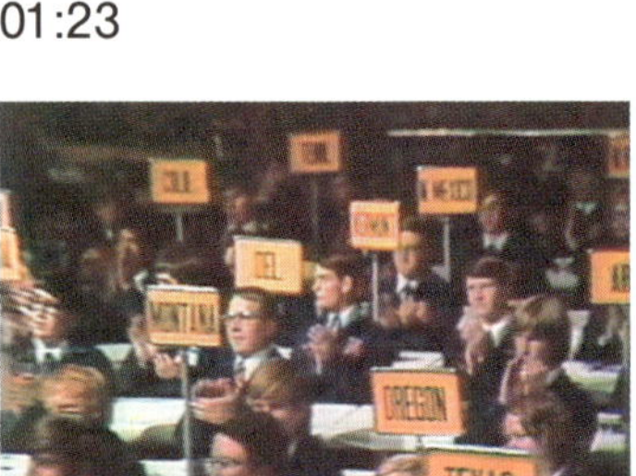

14:07

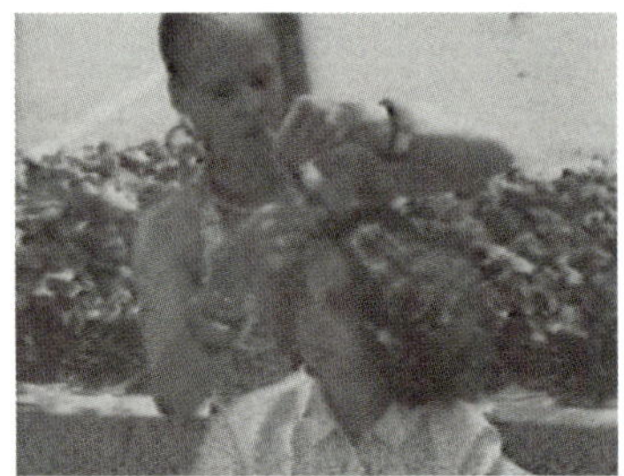
17:31

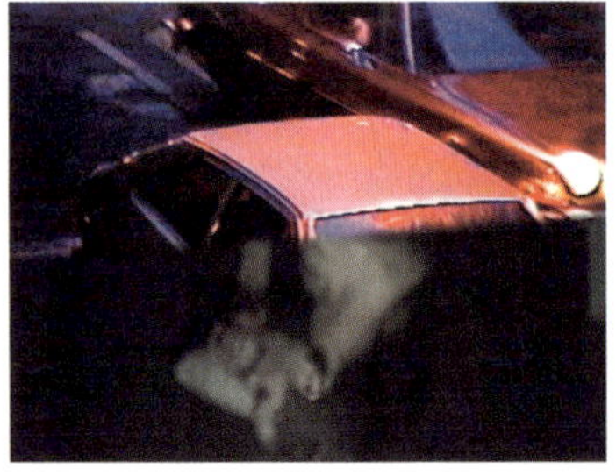
07:19

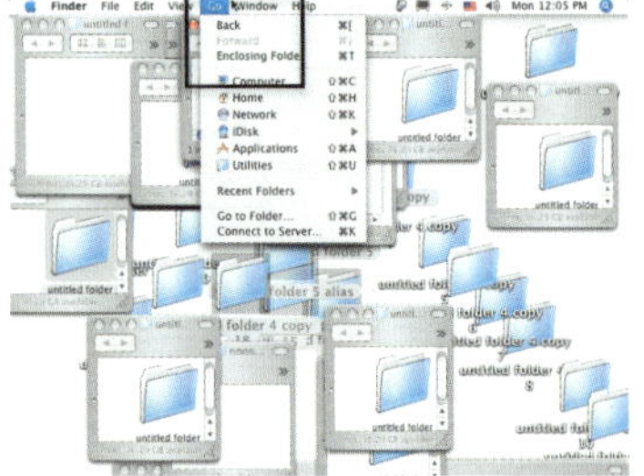
00:54

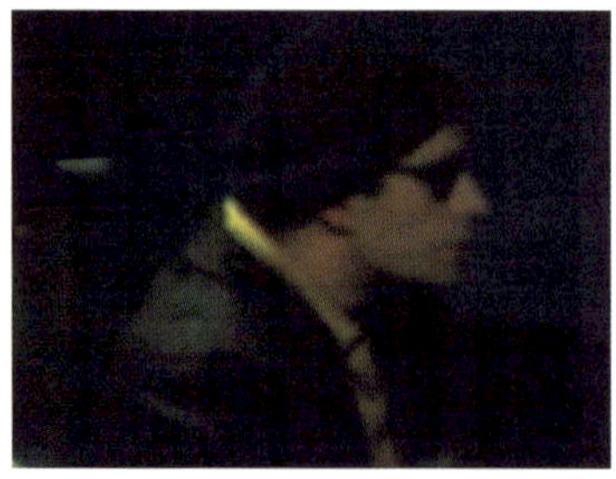
08:25

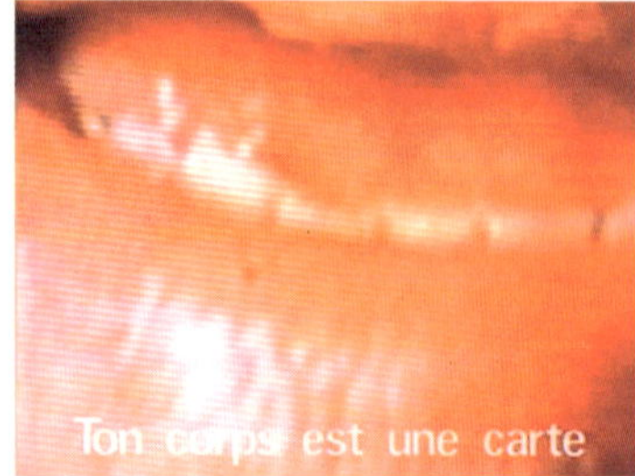

00:09

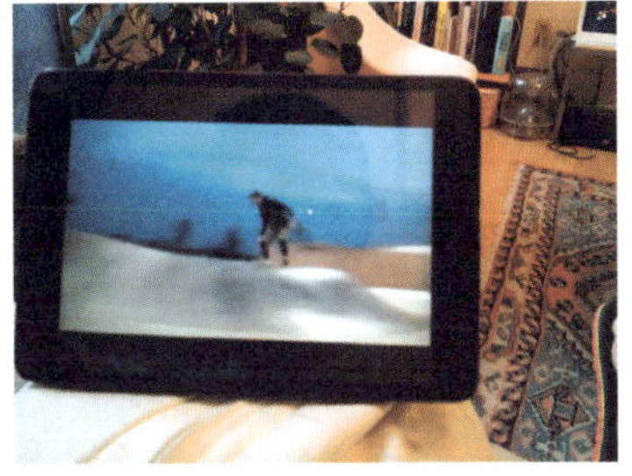
04:01

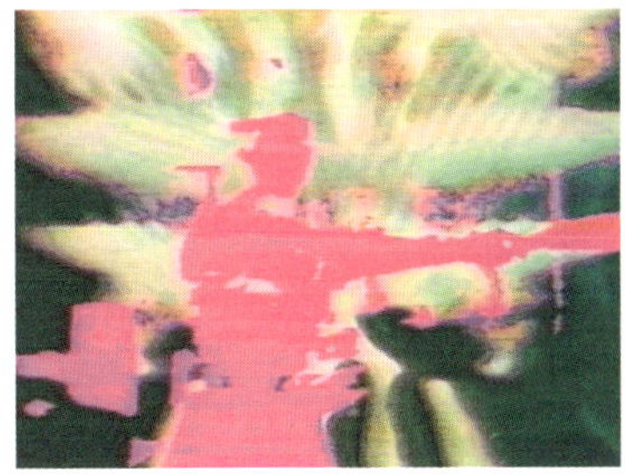
14:32

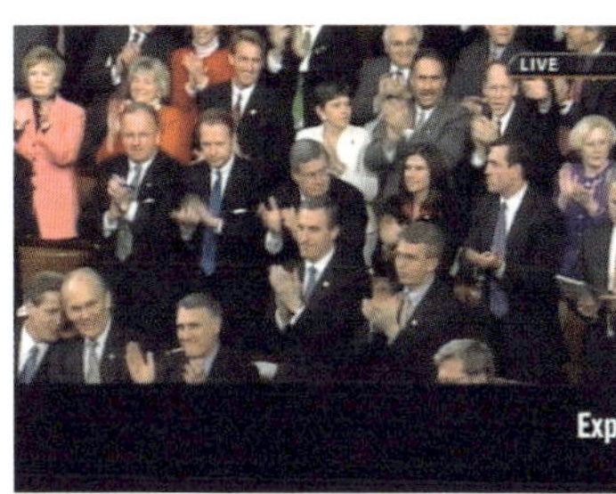

04:34

dialog that unites its canon of artists, engaged with media not for its commercial potential, but for its accessibility and cultural potency.

1 Howard Wise, *TV as a Creative Medium* exhibition brochure (New York, May 17–June 14, 1969).
2 Clement Greenberg, "Intermedia," in *Clement Greenberg: Late Writings*, ed. Robert C. Morgan (Minneapolis: University of Minnesota Press, 2003), 93.
3 From Wise's letter announcing the closure of his gallery, December 16, 1970.
4 Buckminster Fuller published his influential book *Operating Manual for Spaceship Earth* in 1969.
5 Discussed in Fred Turner's *From Counterculture to Cyberculture: Stewart Brand, the Whole Earth Network, and the Rise of Digital Utopianism* (Chicago: University of Chicago Press, 2006), 96–97.
6 Beryl Korot, Phyllis Gershuny, eds., "Address to Readers," *Radical Software I*, no. 1 (Spring 1970).
7 Letter from Howard Wise, December 16, 1970. See pg. 102
8 Wise, *Electronic Arts Intermix, Inc: At the Leading Edge of Art* (New York, 1973).
9 Martha Rosler, "Shedding the Utopian Moment," in *Decoys and Disruptions: Selected Writings, 1975–2001* (London: MIT Press, 2004), 53–85.
10 Seth Price, *Dispersion*, 2002.

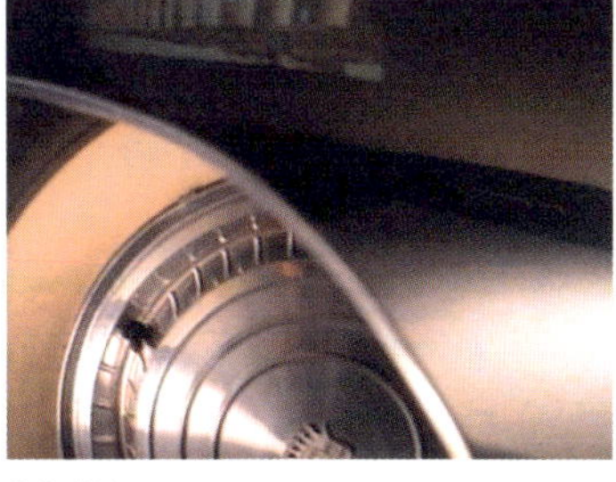
00:21

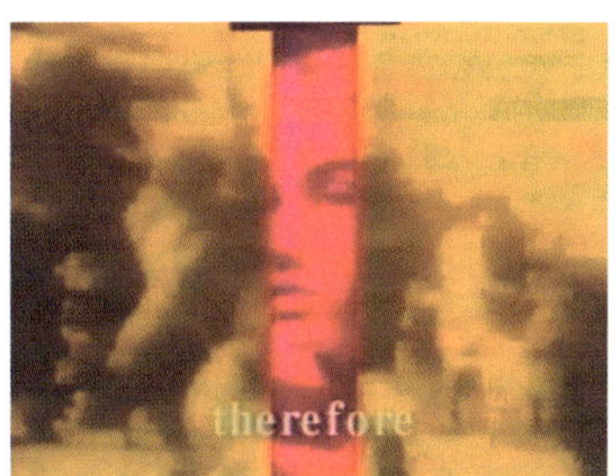

00:38

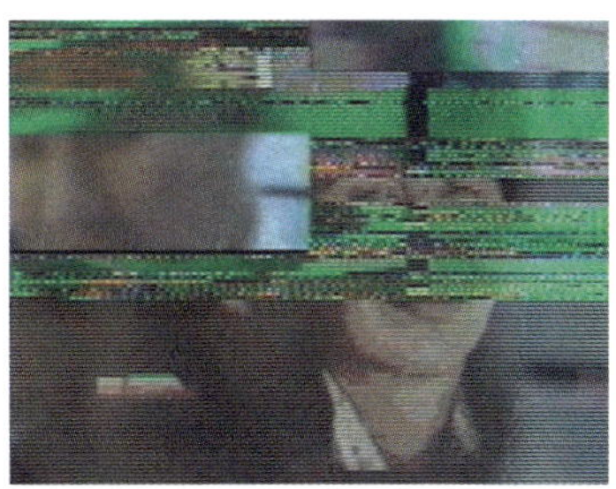
21:15

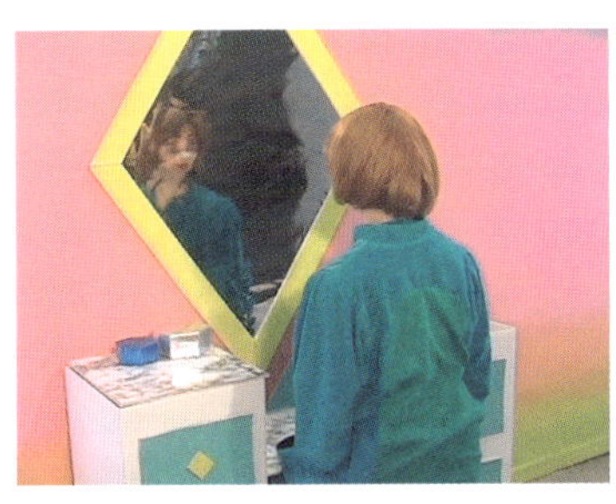
01:27

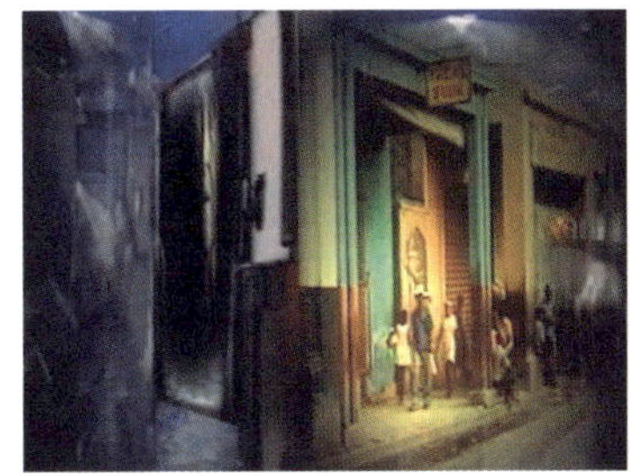
00:24

04:27

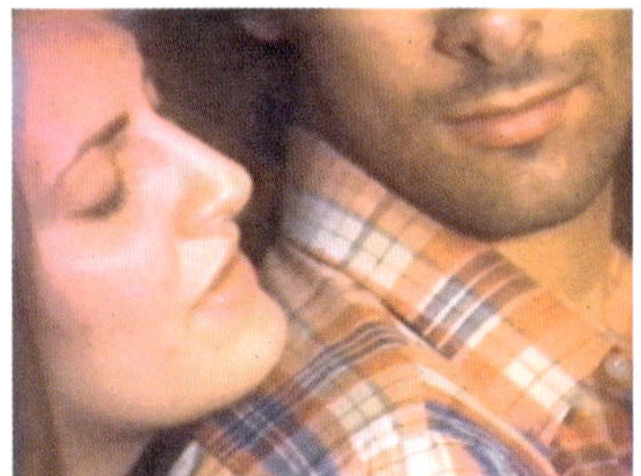

01:22

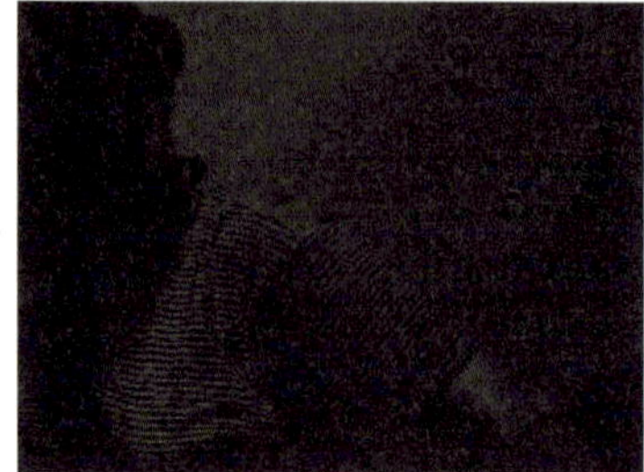

01:42

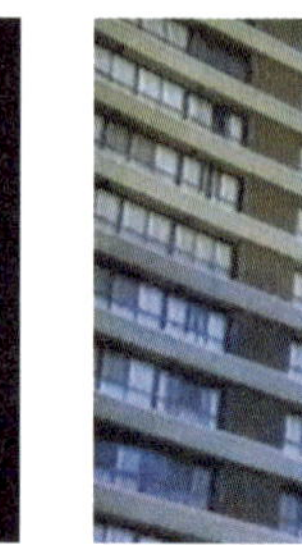

05:57

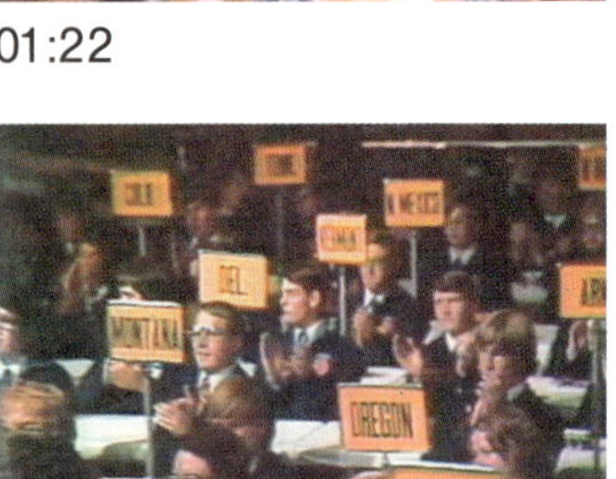

14:06

11 Frederick Douglass, “Lecture on Pictures,” in *Picturing Frederick Douglass: An Illustrated Biography of the Nineteenth Century’s Most Photographed American*, eds. John Stauffer, Zoe Trodd, Celeste-Marie Bernier (New York: Liveright Publishing, 2015), 131.

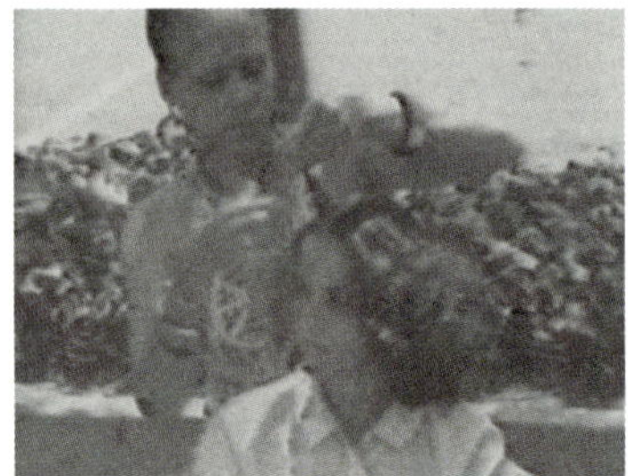

17:30

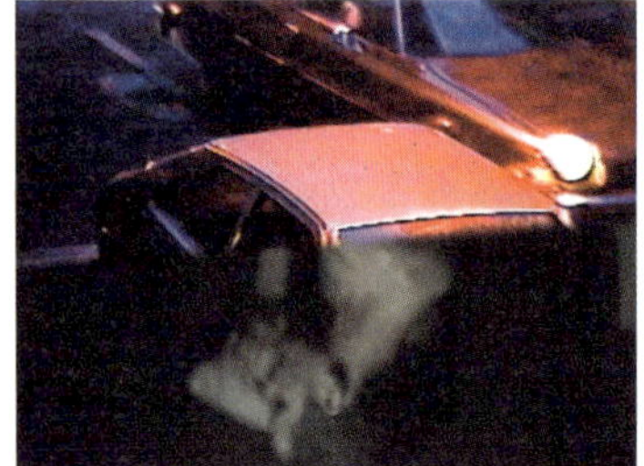

07:18

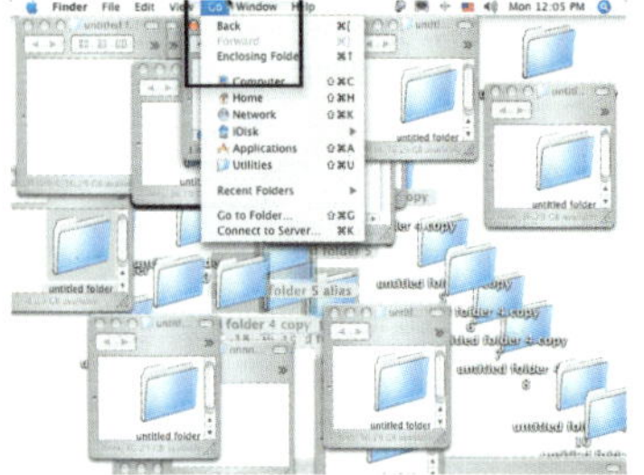

00:53

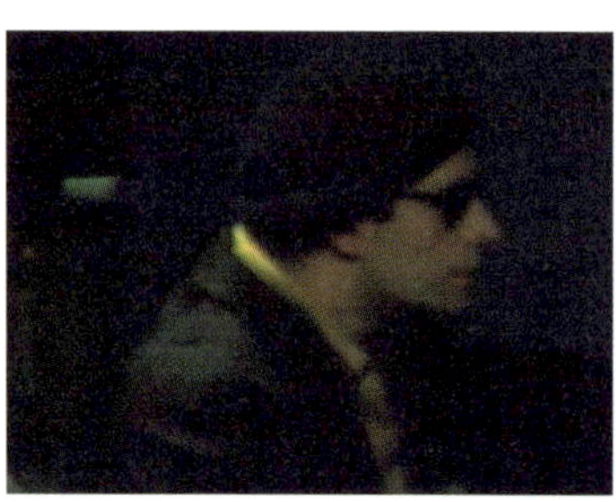

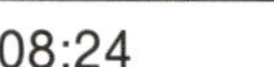

08:24

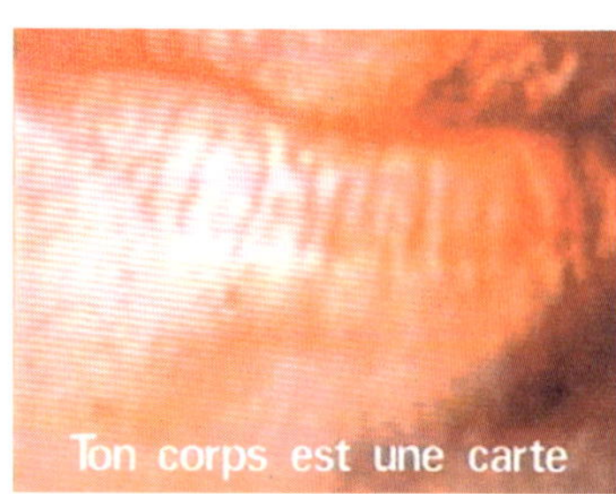

00:08

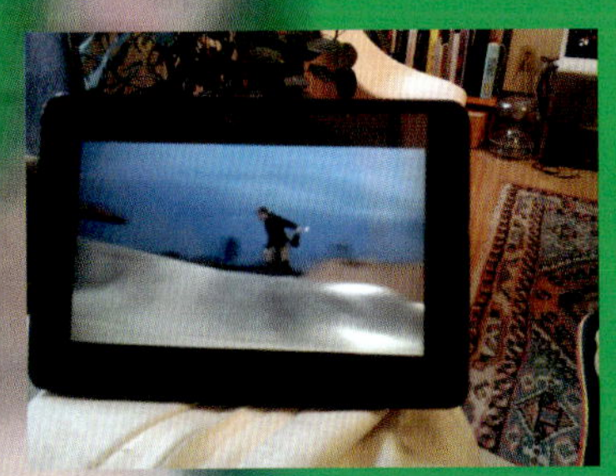
04:01

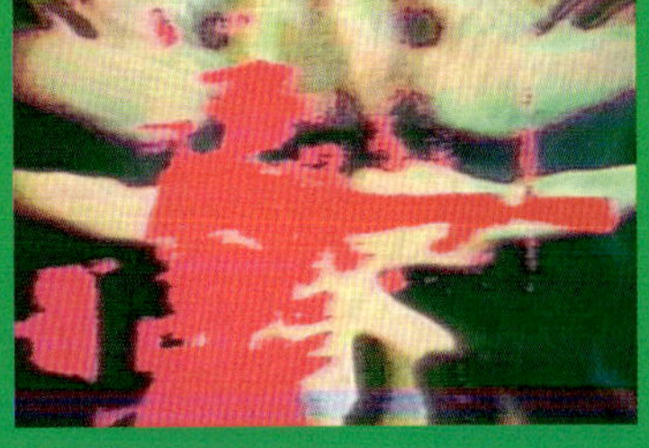
14:32

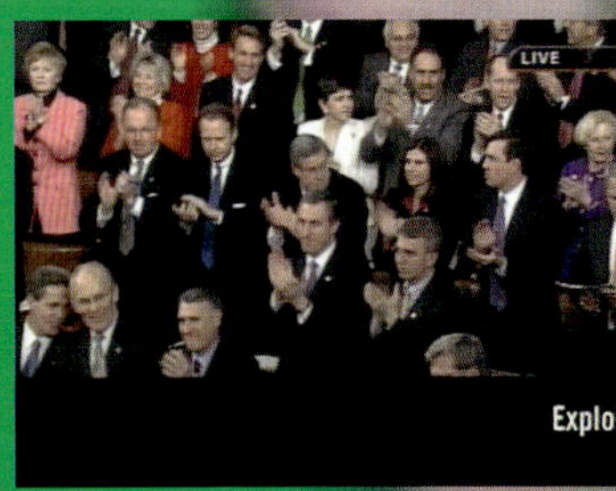

04:34

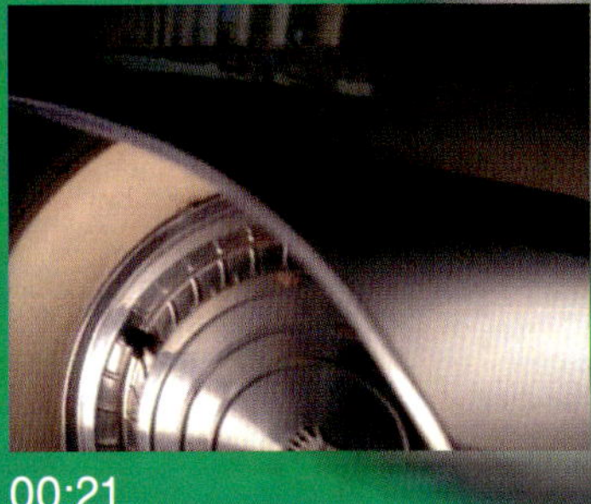
00:21

BROADCASTING: EAI AT ICA
WORKS IN THE EXHIBITION

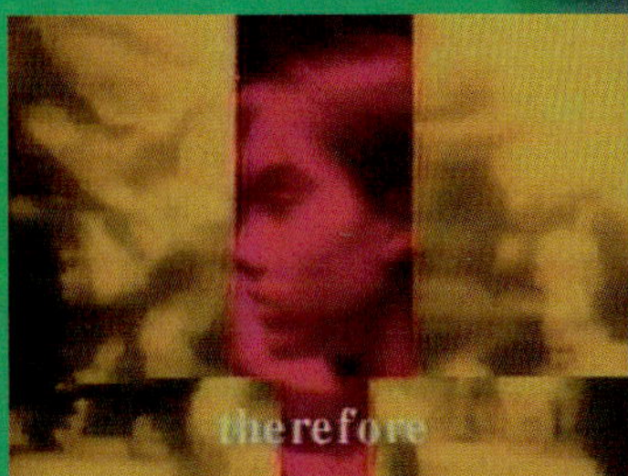

00:38

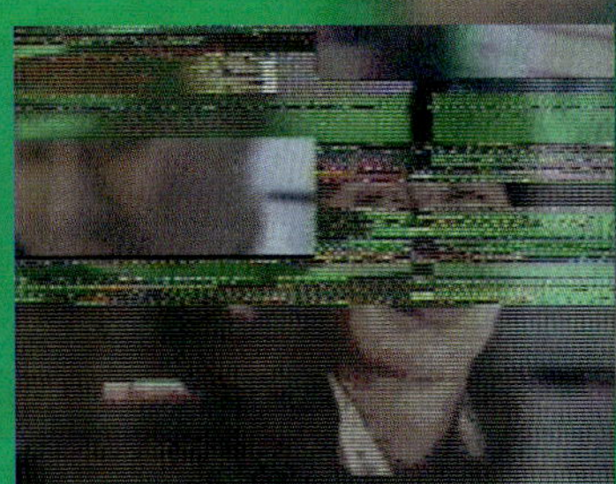
21:15

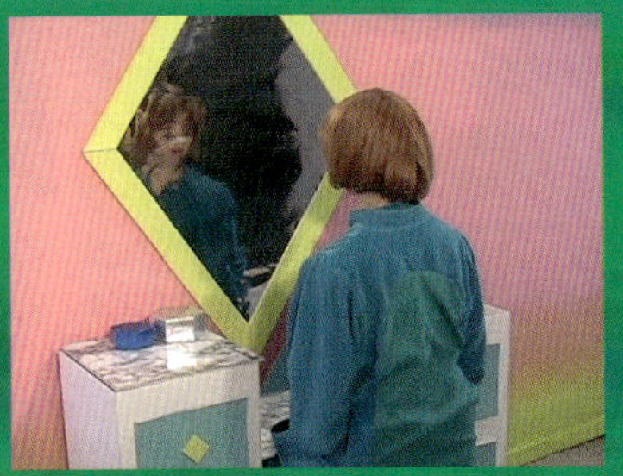
01:27

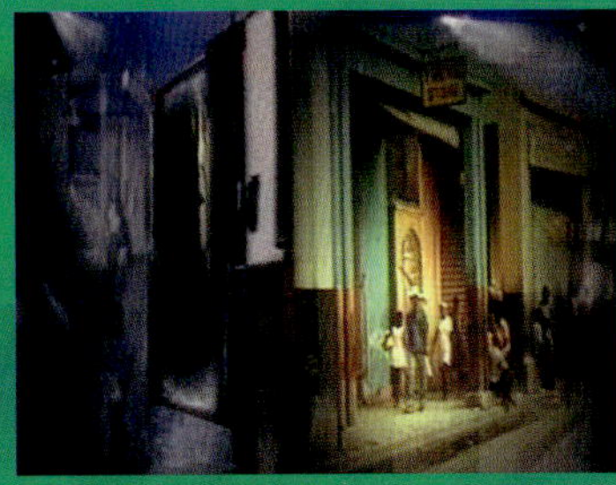
00:24

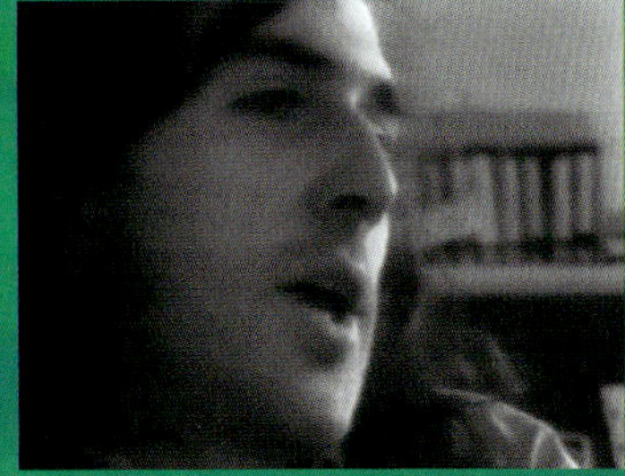
04:27

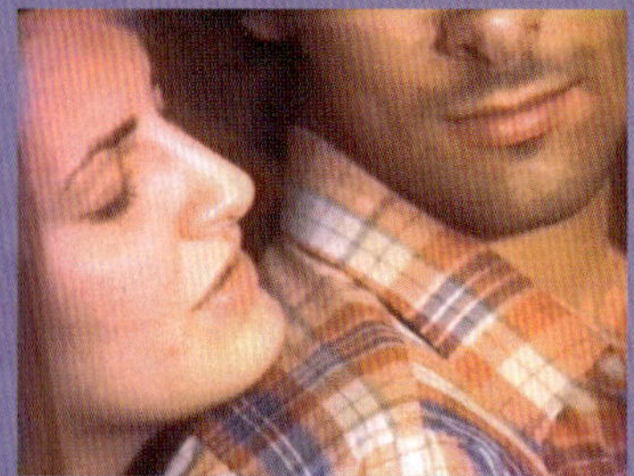
01:22

01:42

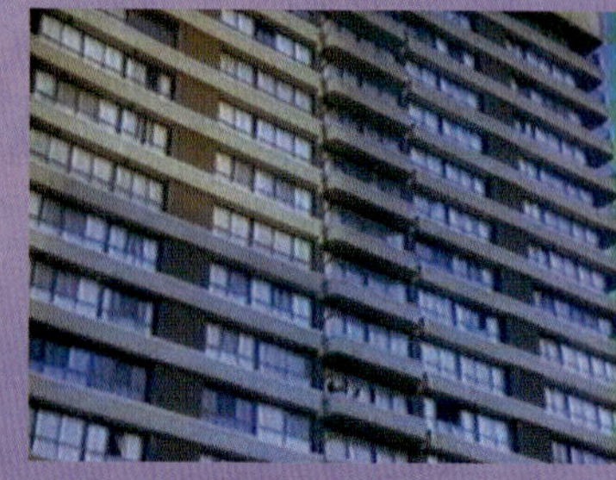
05:57

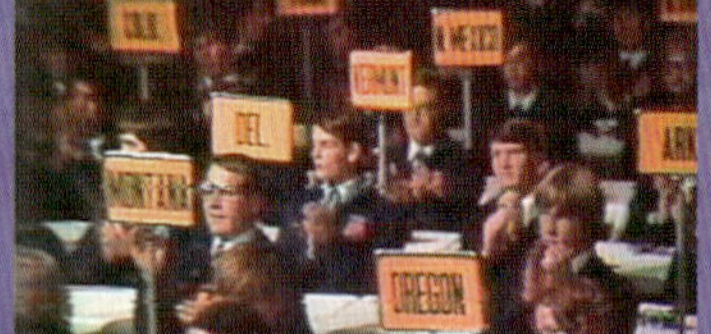

14:06

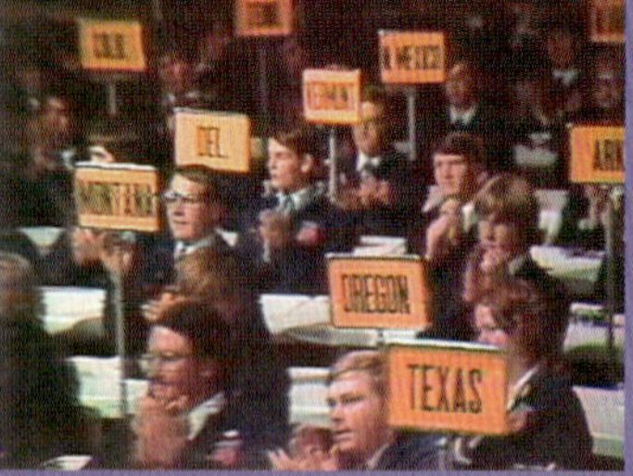
17:30

ROBERT BECK/BUCK
(Born 1959, Towson, MD; lives New York)
Episodes from the series *The Space Program* (1985–1986)
STOP, 1985, video, color, sound, 28 minutes
Mirror, 1985, video, color, sound, 28 minutes
TV Architecture, 1985, color, sound, 28 minutes (This video was displayed on the exterior of the ICA building on Sansom Street.)

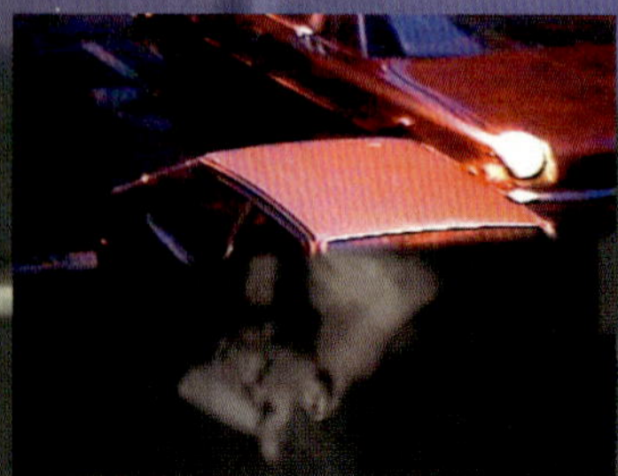
07:18

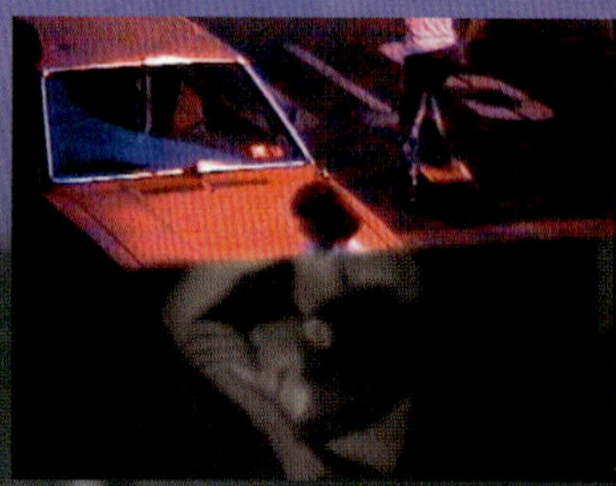

Robert Beck, who changed his father's name by a single vowel as an act of art currently works under the name Robert Buck. Beck/Buck is most known for his paintings, drawings, sculptures, and installations, and for his precise use of materials, yet film and television have profoundly influenced his career and self-representation. For decades, Beck/Buck held different administrative positions at EAI, including technical director and chief editor. In the context of EAI, his artistic career can be seen to parallel, by chance, the rise of home video and the increasing popularity of reality television and the found-footage genre.

At the start of this career is Beck's/Buck's conceptual cable-access series, *The Space Program*. Broadcast regularly on Manhattan Cable Television for the better part of a year, Beck/Buck undertook each half-hour

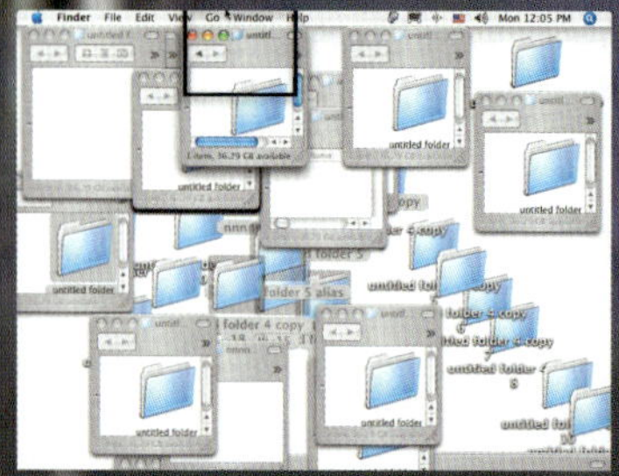
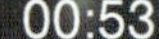
00:53

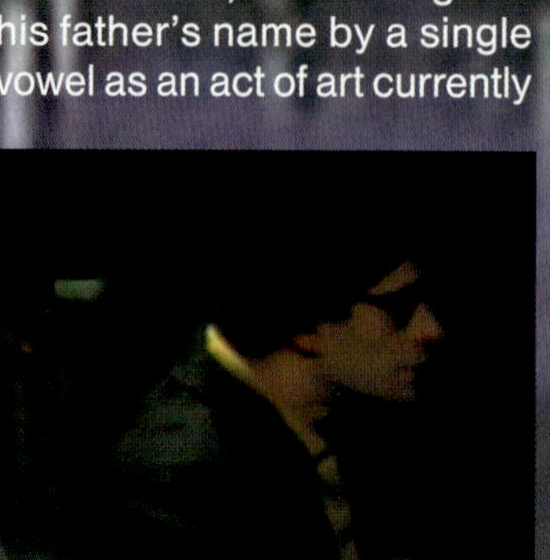
08:24

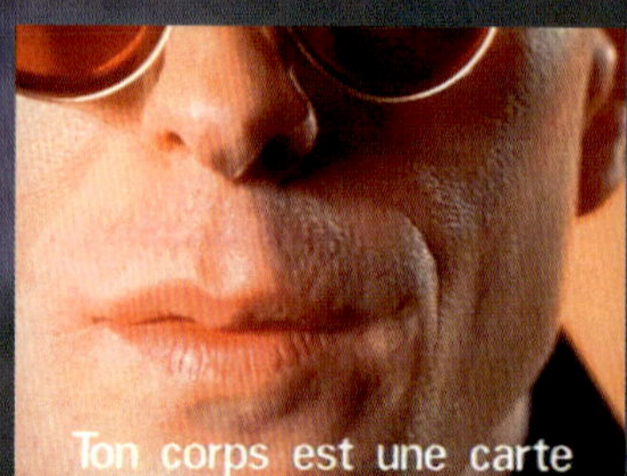

00:08

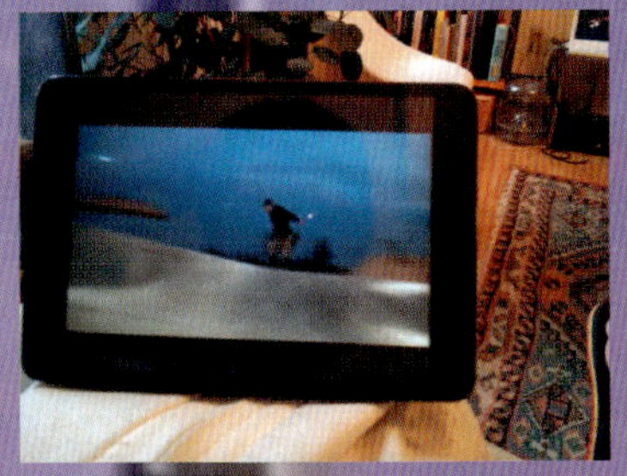

04:01

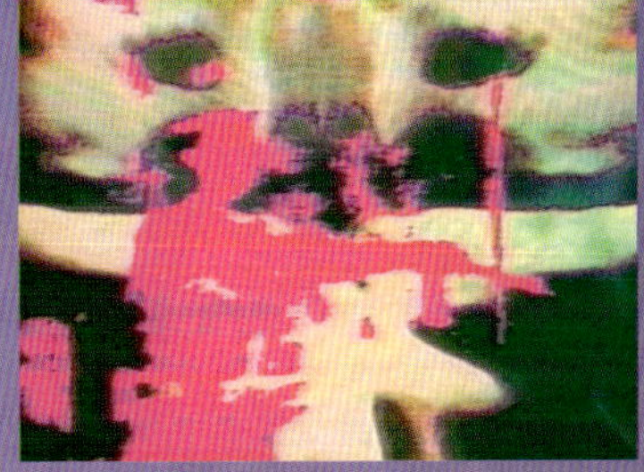

14:32

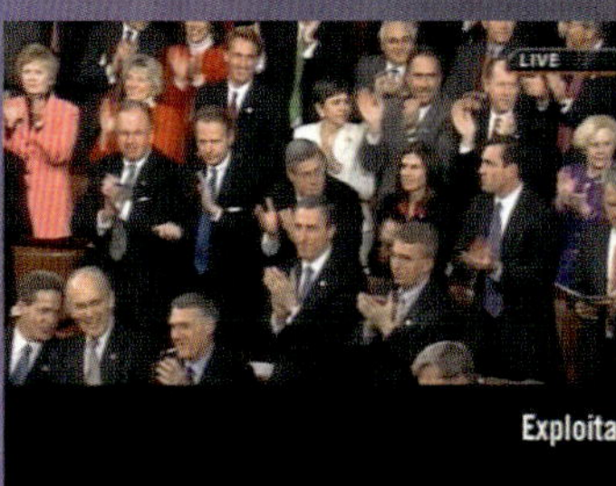

04:34

episode as a conceptual performance, using duration, the context of television, and video technology as expressive tools. The abrupt juxtaposition of private and public space, and of personal and impersonal video footage, is starkly conveyed in the *STOP* episode. The artist, bare-chested, is seen in a black-and-white closed-circuit feed, gazing at a street scene that the viewer watches via a live, color video feed. The dislocation of time, self, and physical space is represented in a minimal composition, combining the two video feeds in a single scene.

In the *Mirror* episode, the grainy static of a lost broadcast signal appears to be slowly scratched away by the artist to reveal a fragmented view of his face, mirrored in a closed-circuit feed. At the conclusion of this graphic intervention, Beck/Buck taps on the screen, calling attention to the physical and conceptual membrane between himself and his viewers. *TV Architecture* collects establishing-shots of buildings and structures from TV shows, isolated from their narrative function. *The Space Program* series was likely encountered by accident, with no context other than the haphazard surrounding television programs, emphasizing art's capacity to unsettle the known and open a path into the unknown.

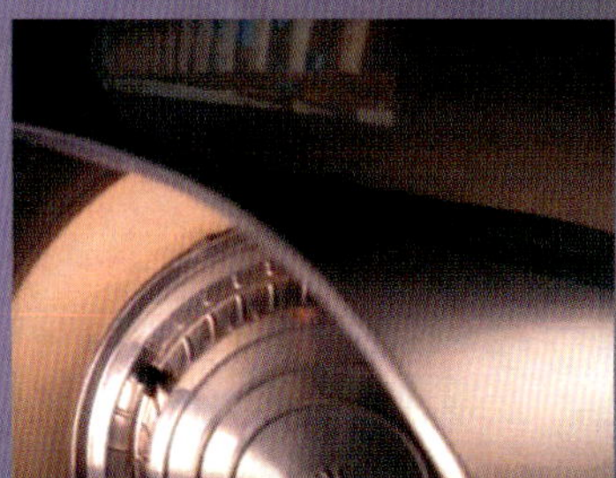

00:21

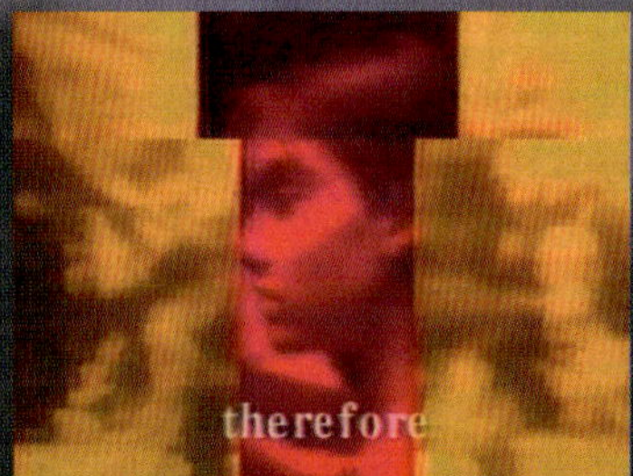

00:38

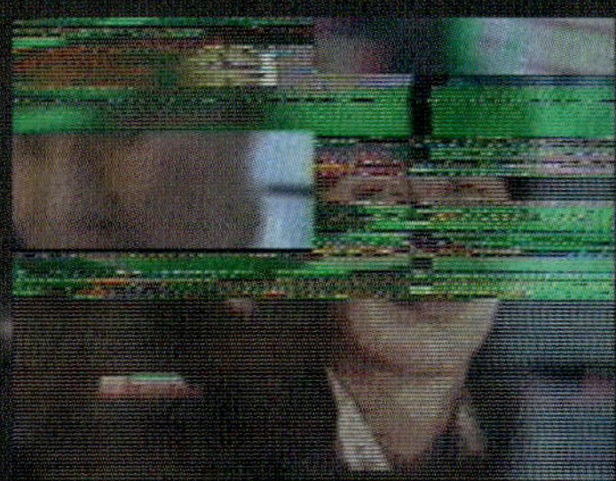

21:15

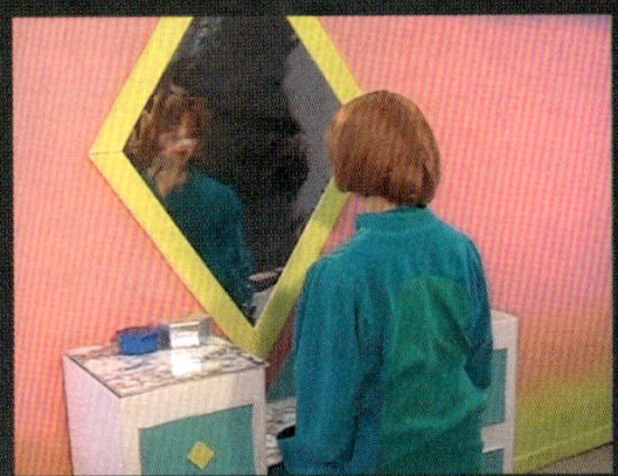

01:27

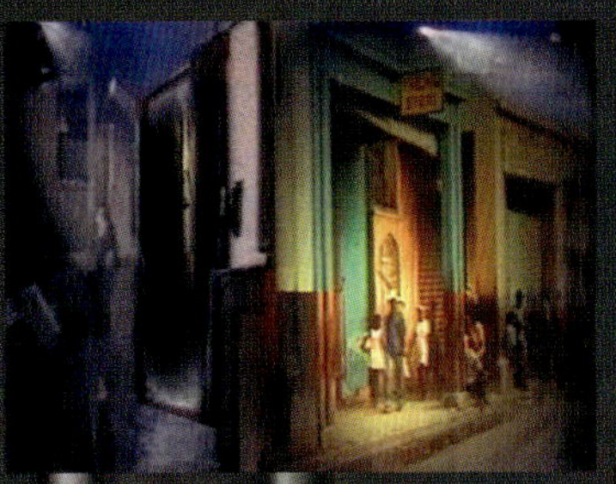

00:24

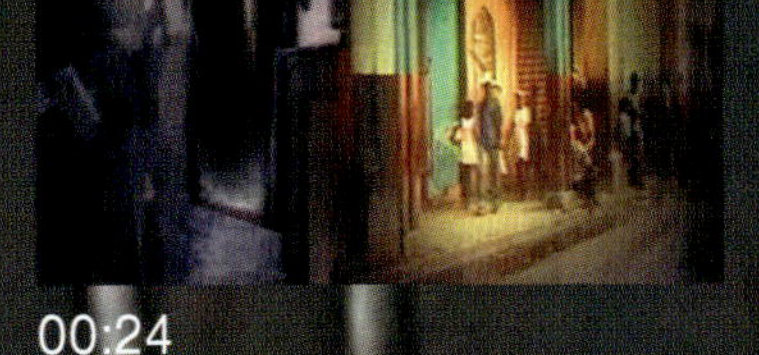

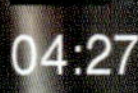

04:27

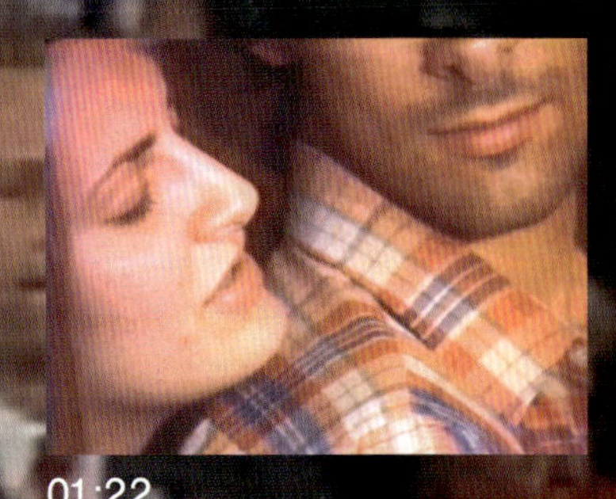

01:22

01:42

05:57

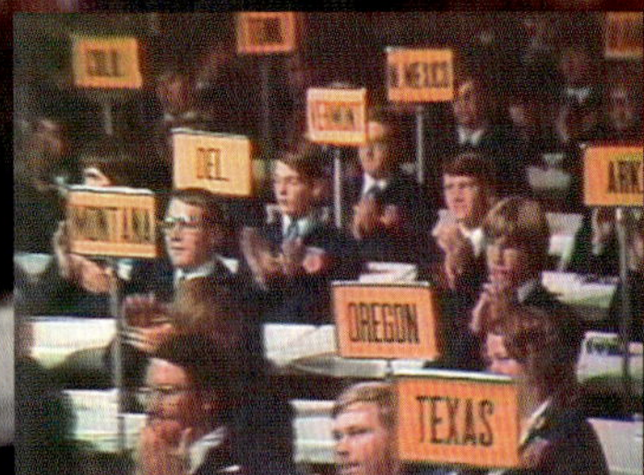

14:06

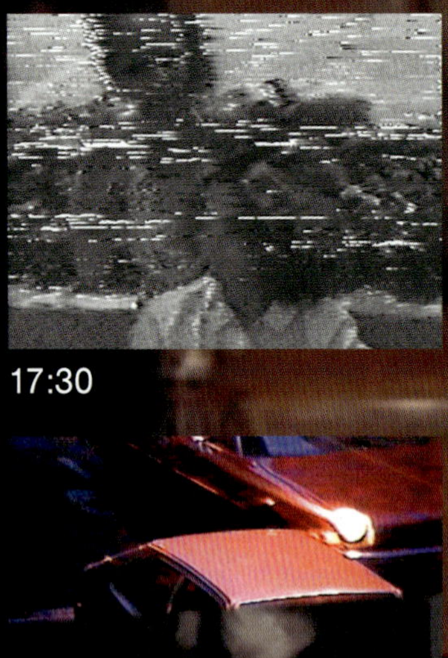

17:30

07:18

DARA BIRNBAUM
(Born 1946, New York; lives New York)
MTV: Artbreak, 1987, video, color, sound, 0:30 minutes

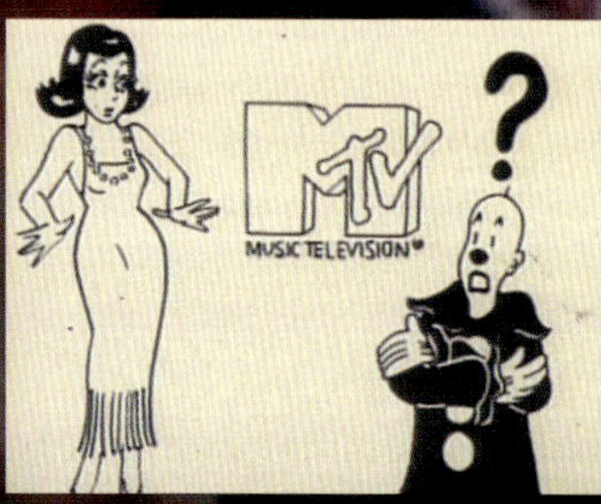

Dara Birnbaum's provocative video works are among the most influential and innovative contributions to the contemporary discourse on art and television. In her videotapes and multimedia installations, Birnbaum uses low-end and high-end video technology to subvert, critique, or deconstruct the power of mass media images and gestures to define mythologies of culture, history and memory. Through a dynamic televisual language of images, music, and text, she exposes the media's embedded ideological meanings and posits video as a means of giving voice to the individual. Birnbaum has stated that she wanted to "define the language of video art in relation to the institution of television." In her radical media critiques of the late 1970s, including the seminal *Technology/Transformation: Wonder Woman* (1978–1979), she used rigorous tactics of deconstruction and appropriation to dismantle television's codes of representation. Among the first artists to apply these strategies to subvert the language of television texts, she turned its vocabulary back on itself in a powerful critique.

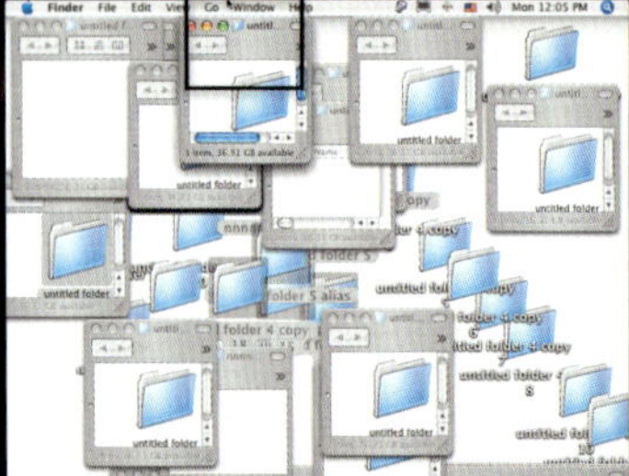

00:53

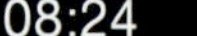

08:24

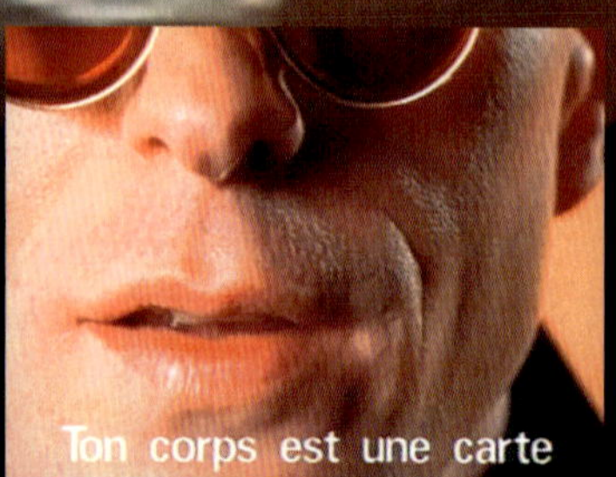

00:08

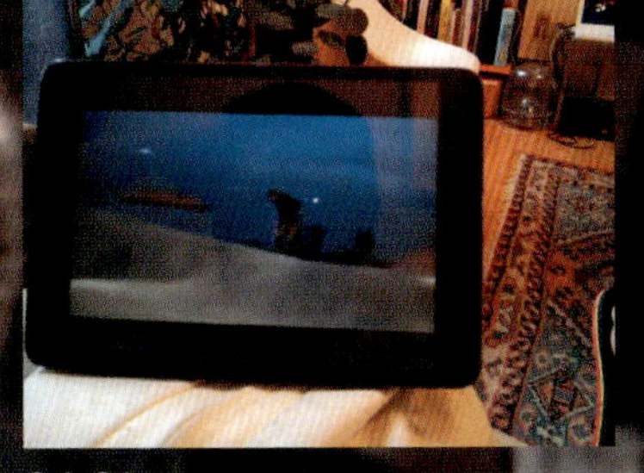
04:01

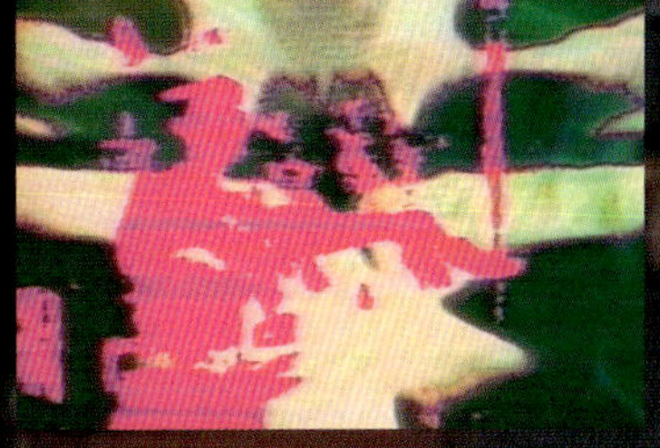
14:32

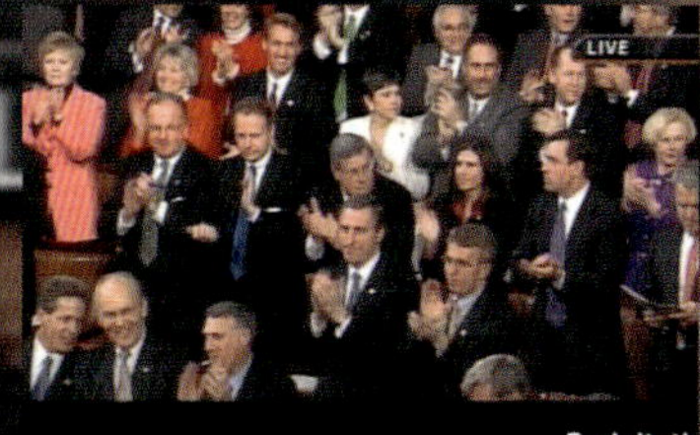

04:34

MTV: Artbreak, commissioned by MTV Networks, aired as a dynamic thirty-second spot that provided a condensed history of animation highlighting the representation of women, from the cell imagery of Max Fleischer's *Out of the Inkwell* series to the contemporary digital effects of television. In Birnbaum's vision, Fleischer's spilled inkwell releases cartoon bubbles containing images of women from MTV music videos. Birnbaum reverses the traditional gender roles of producer and product of commercial imagery: the final image is that of a female artist on whose video "palette" we see a glimpse of Fleischer.

TONY COKES
(Born 1956, Richmond, VA; lives Providence, RI)
Evil.6: Making the Case/ Faking the Books, 2006, digital video, color, sound, 10 minutes
Evil.27: Selma, 2011 / 2017 refix, digital video, color, sound, 9 minutes
Evil.35: Carlin / Owners (George Carlin Speaks), 2012 / 2017 refix, digital video, color, sound, 8 minutes

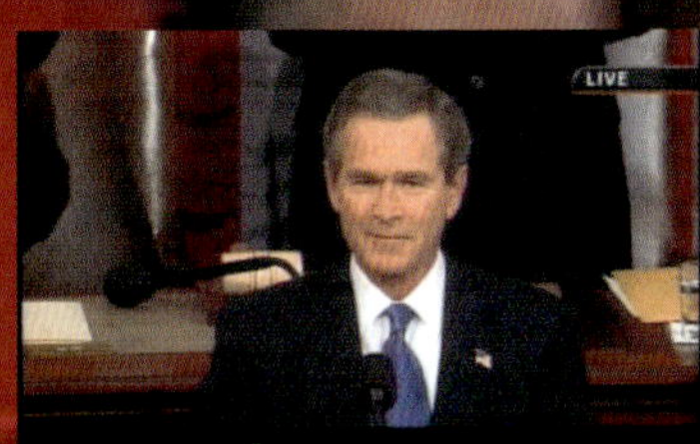

In his videos and installations produced since the mid-1980s and his work with the collective X-PRZ, Tony

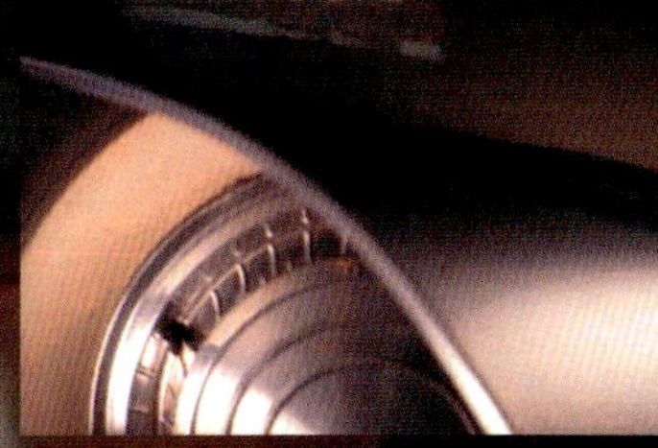
00:21

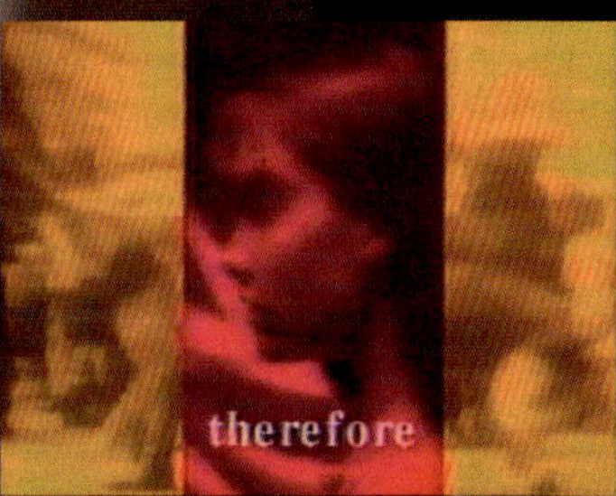

00:38

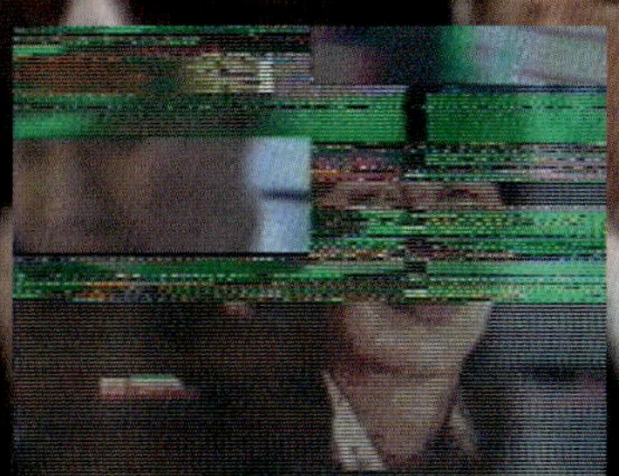
21:15

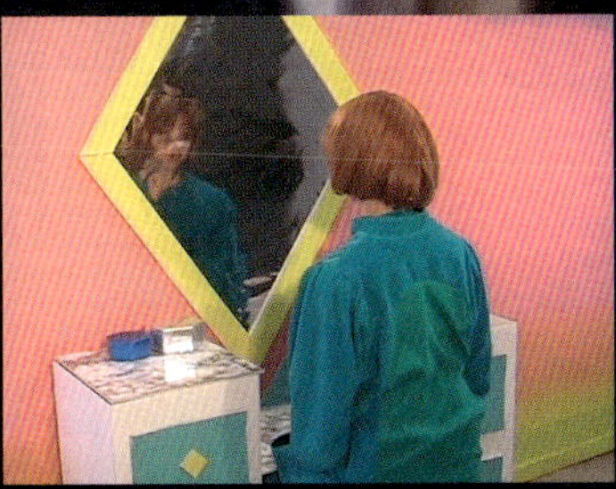
01:27

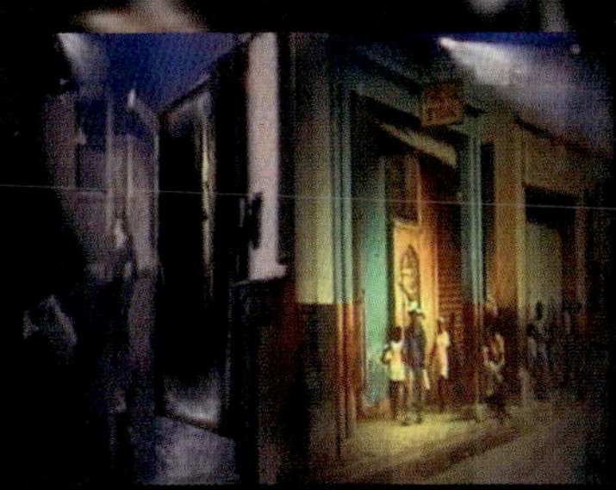
00:24

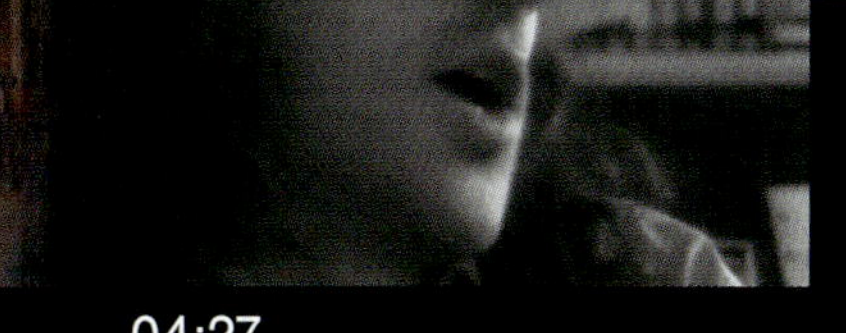
04:27

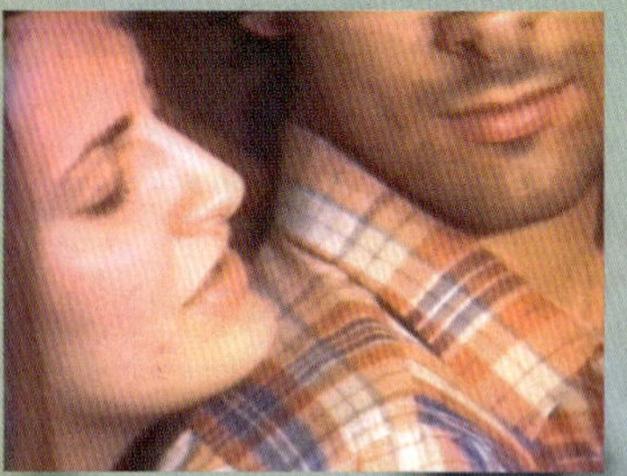
01:22

01:42

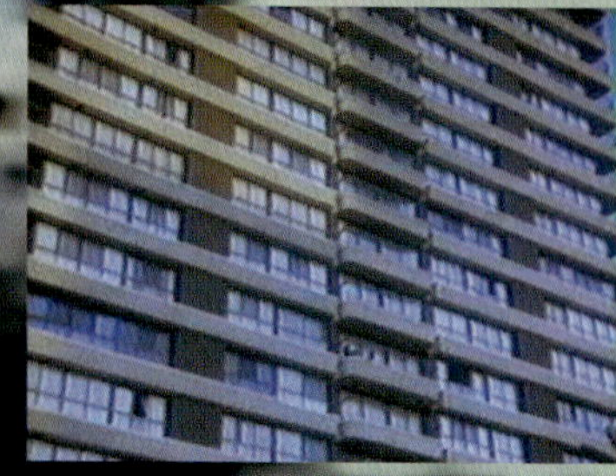
05:57

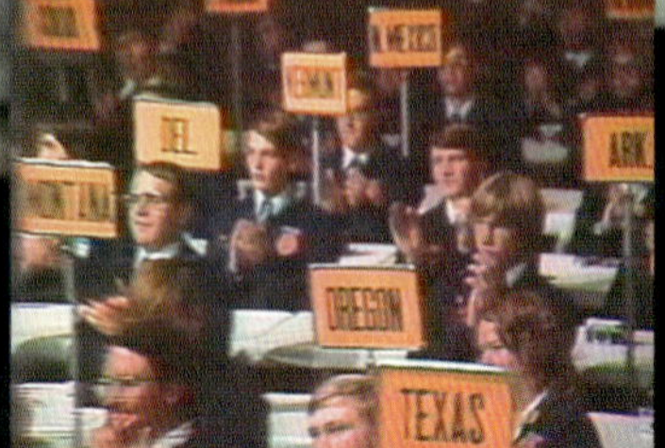

14:06

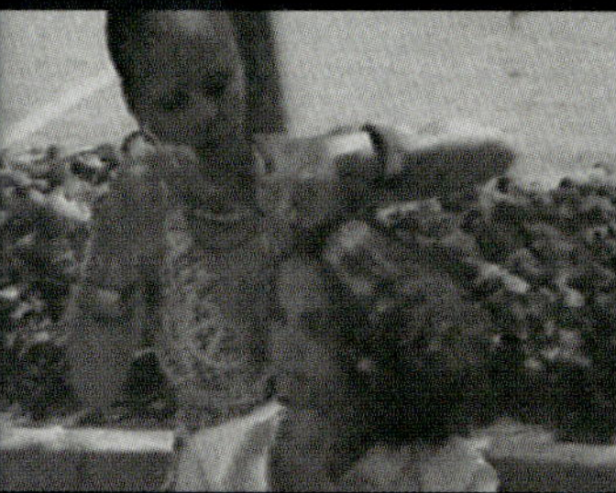
17:30

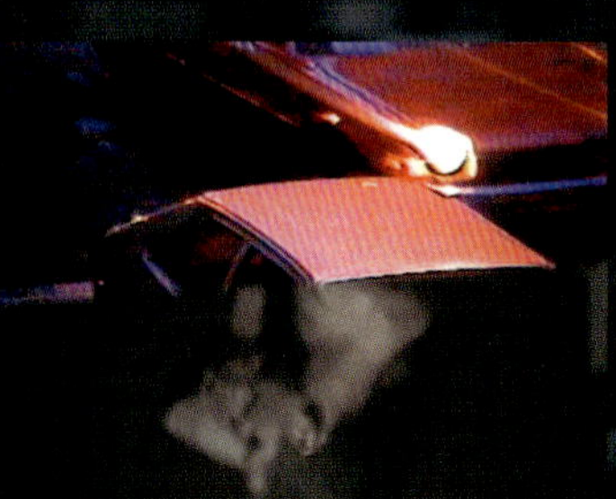
07:18

Cokes has engaged in cogent investigations of identity and opposition. His works question the construction of subjectivities (personal, cultural and historical), and how race, gender and class are perceived through what he terms the "representational regimes of image and sound," as perpetuated by Hollywood, the media, and popular culture. By reframing and repositioning appropriated text, archival footage, and audio, Cokes brings renewed attention to often forgotten information and its relevance for our contemporary moment.

His ongoing *Evil* series, begun in 2003, focuses on a critique of the ideological forces driving American politics and the corrosive inner workings of capitalism. In *Evil.6: Making the Case/ Faking the Books*, an edited transcript from George W. Bush's 2003 televised State of the Union address, in which he outlined the case for the invasion of Iraq, scrolls along the screen like a news ticker. The footage, edited by artist Benj Gerdes to isolate the pauses between Bush's sentences, is juxtaposed with the enthusiastic clapping of Congress and a soundtrack by Munich electropop band Lali Puna.

The tension between how we privilege visibility versus audibility is further explored in *Evil.27: Selma*, where a text by collective Our Literal Speed about the audio documentation of the civil rights movement is set to songs by The Smiths. Cokes writes, "I wanted to embrace the text's call to rethink social movements in tandem with shifts in media forms (the movement from

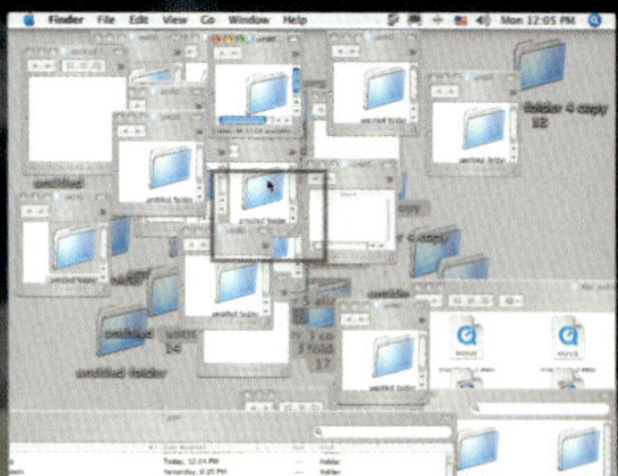
00:53

08:24

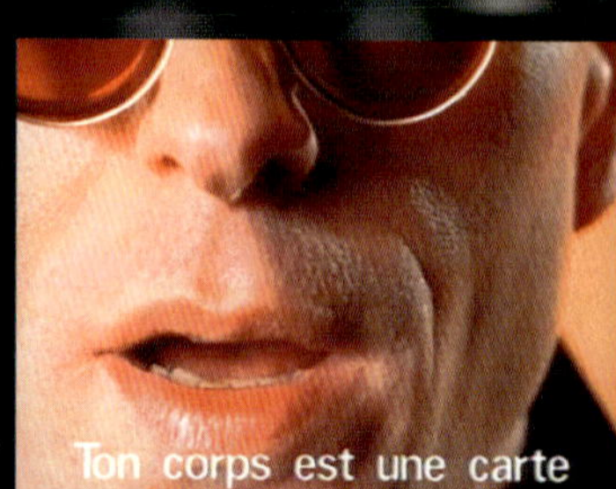

00:08

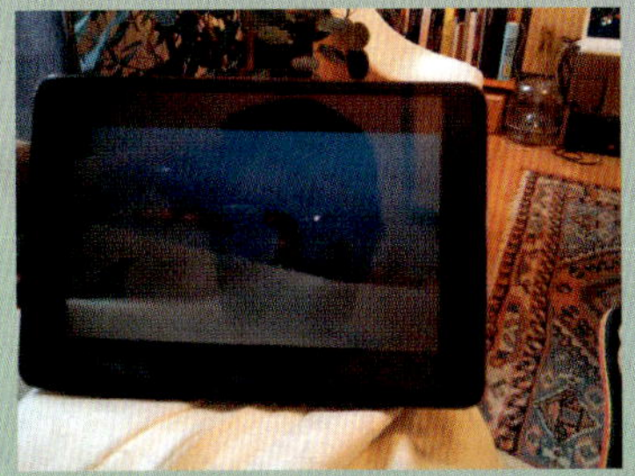
04:02

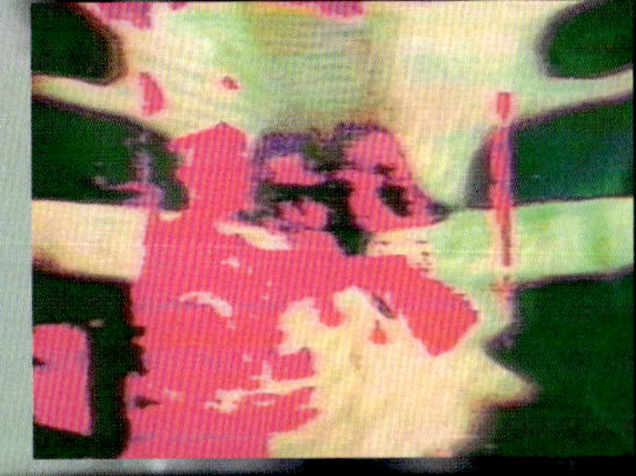
14:33

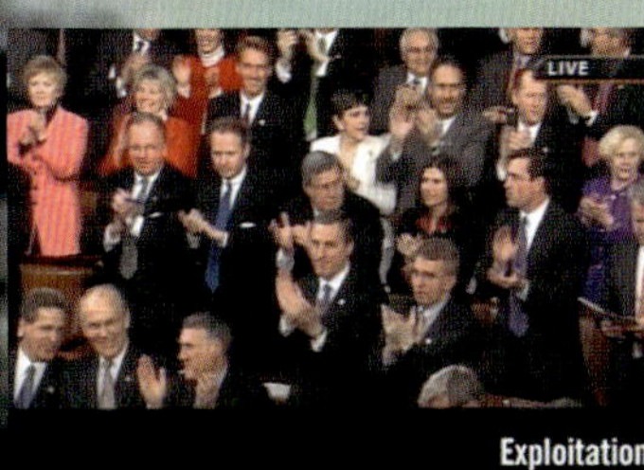

04:35

radio to television) as potentially reflecting a change in conditions of possibility or imaginative horizons for political action." Similarly, *Evil.35: Carlin/Owners (George Carlin Speaks)*, juxtaposes music by postpunk band Gang of Four with a monologue found on YouTube by comedian and social critic George Carlin. Set against the band's staccato rhythms, Carlin's sharp critique eludes nostalgic reference and highlights unresolved aspects of technology and syntax.

ULYSSES JENKINS
(Born 1945, Los Angeles; lives Los Angeles)
Inconsequential Doggereal, 1981, video, color, sound, 15:21 minutes
Bay Windows, 1991, video, color, sound, 84:45 minutes

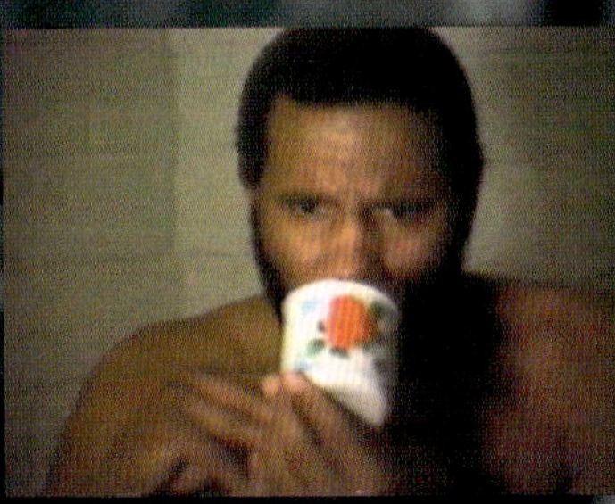

Throughout his career, Ulysses Jenkins has interrogated questions of race and gender as they relate to ritual, history, and the power of the state. From his work with Video Venice News, a Los Angeles media collective he founded in the early 1970s, to his

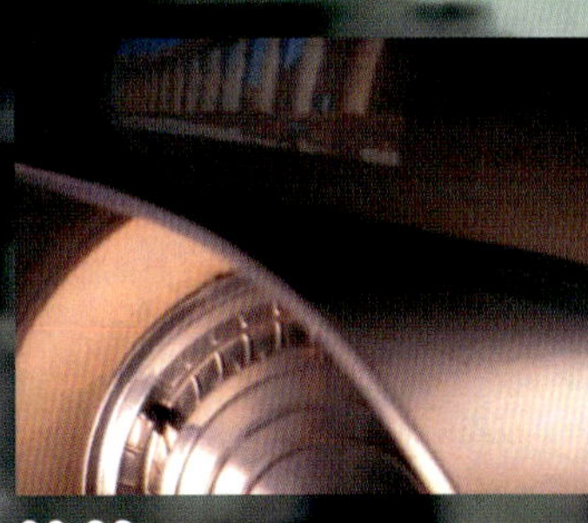
00:22

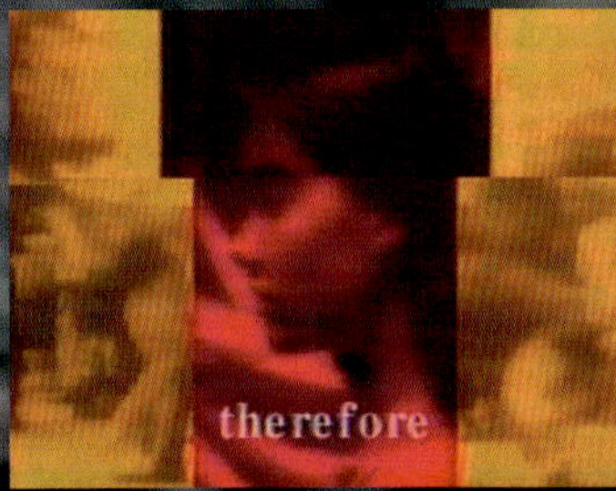

00:39

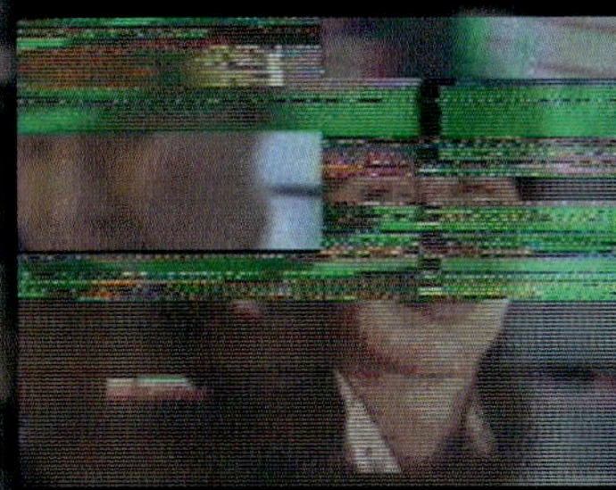
21:16

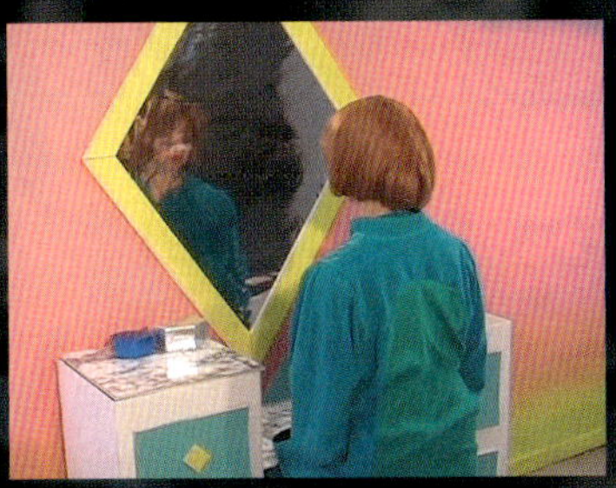
01:28

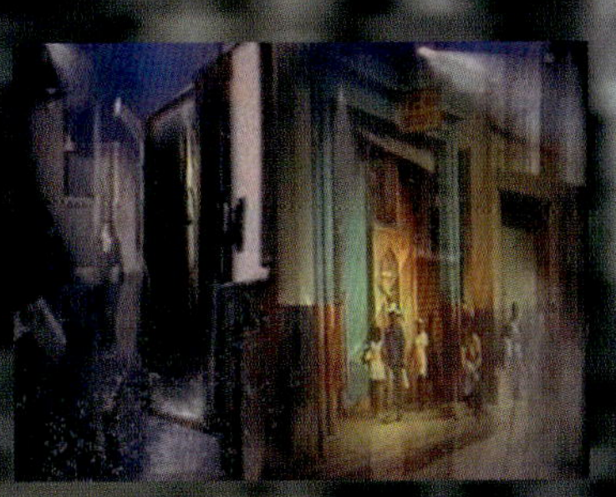
00:25

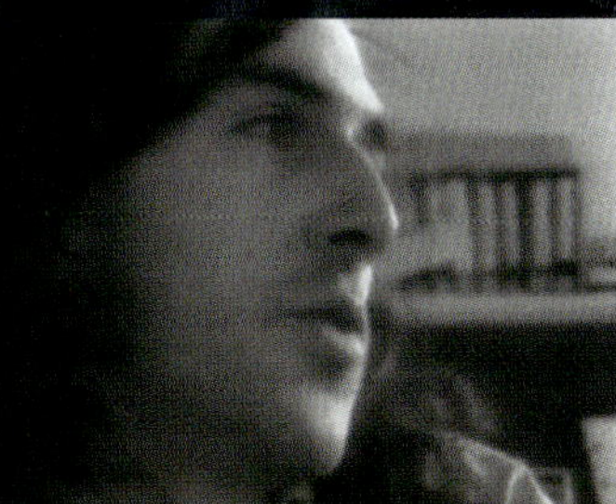
04:28

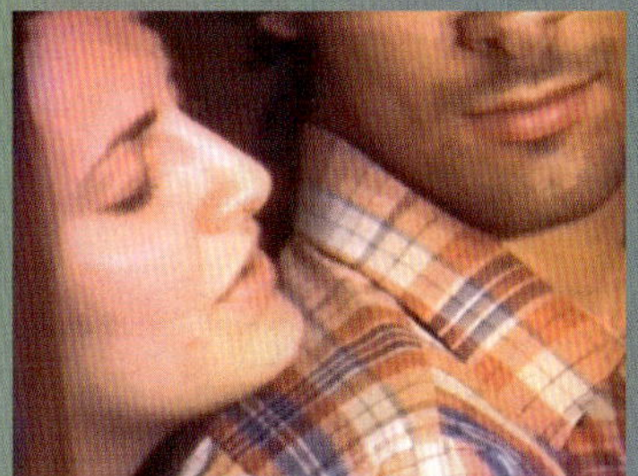

01:22

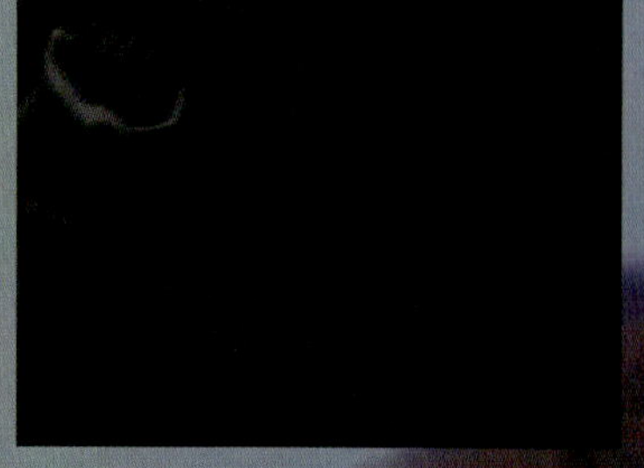

01:42

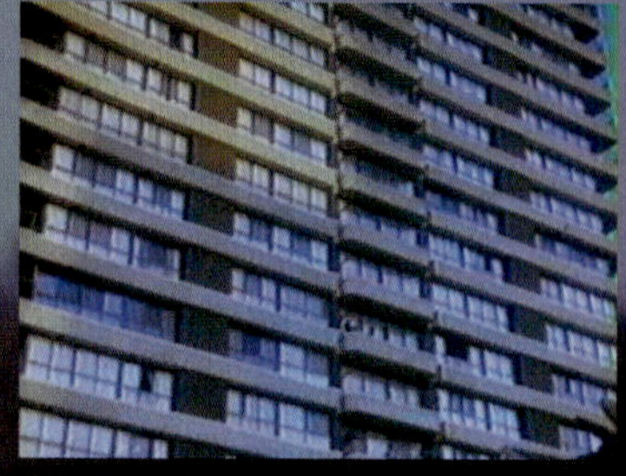

05:57

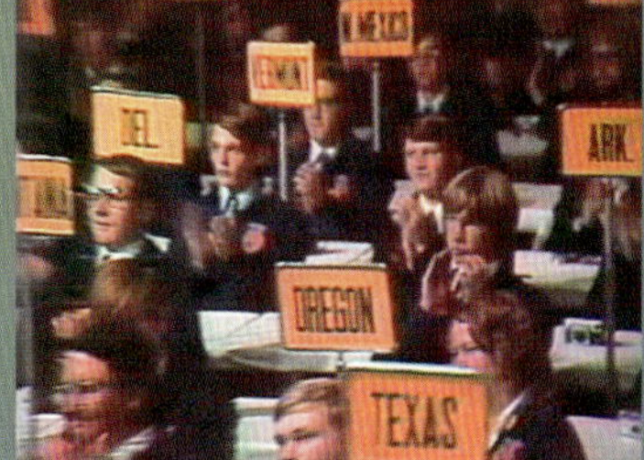

14:06

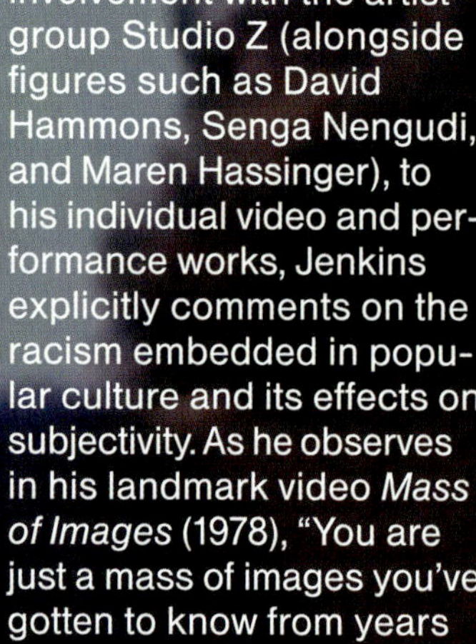

involvement with the artist group Studio Z (alongside figures such as David Hammons, Senga Nengudi, and Maren Hassinger), to his individual video and performance works, Jenkins explicitly comments on the racism embedded in popular culture and its effects on subjectivity. As he observes in his landmark video *Mass of Images* (1978), “You are just a mass of images you’ve gotten to know from years and years of TV shows.”

This challenge to mainstream media takes a more expressive and performative turn in *Inconsequential Doggereal*. A play on the word *doggerel*, Jenkins’s “doggereal” suggests that time and reality is more disjunctive and absurd than we like to believe. In the video we see the artist naked and vulnerable interspersed with characters who perform gendered stereotypes. With its fast cuts and appropriated footage, it takes inspiration from Surrealist and Dada filmmaking and the then-nascent music video culture of MTV.

Influenced by Kit Galloway and Sherrie Rabinowitz’s *Hole-in-Space* (1980) and his involvement with their Electronic Café, Jenkins became increasingly interested in the communicative potential of video technology. As a result, while he was living in Northern California in the early 1990s he embarked on a series of video phone performances and workshops. Notable among them is his ambitious *Bay Windows*, which broadcast the ecological infractions and societal oppressions faced by indigenous communities, often in remote locations. Staged in 1990 at the Exploratorium in

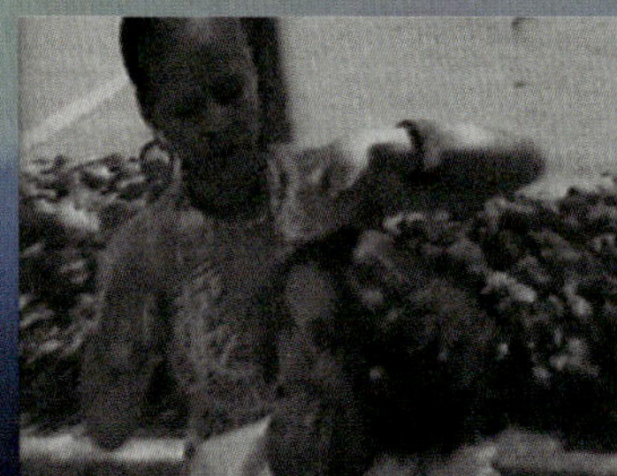

17:30

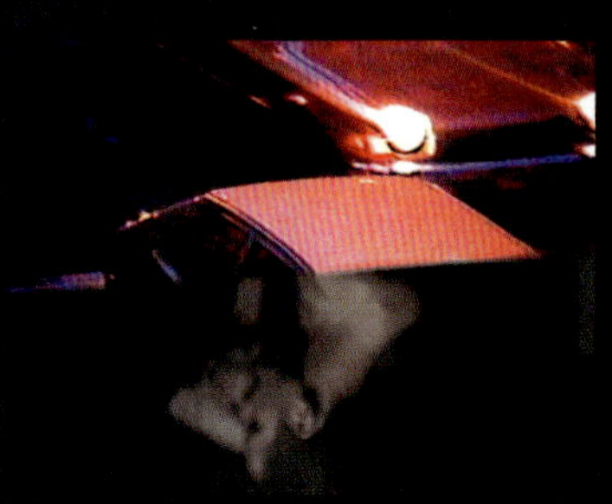

07:18

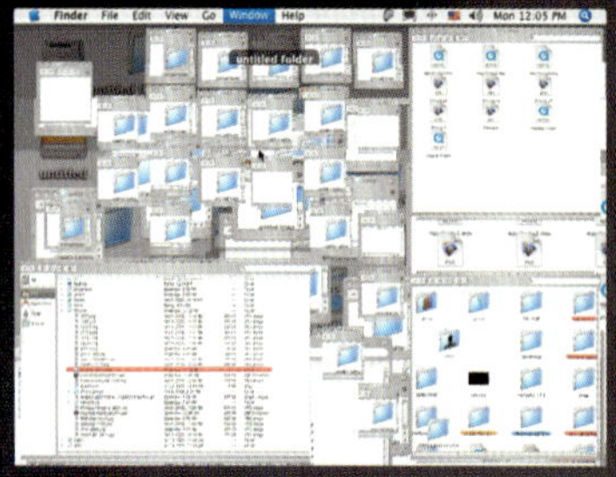

00:53

08:24

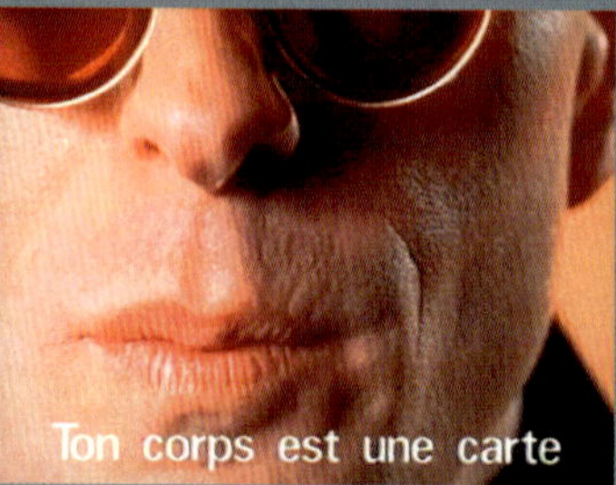

00:08

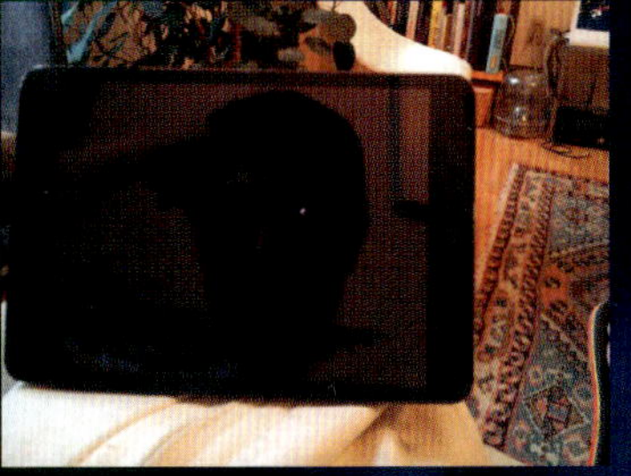
04:02

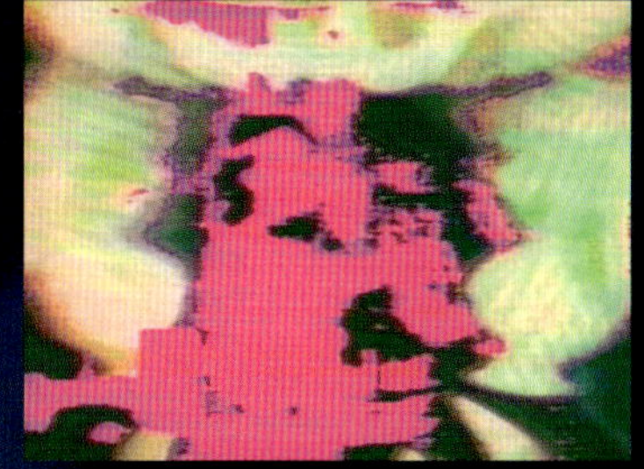
14:33

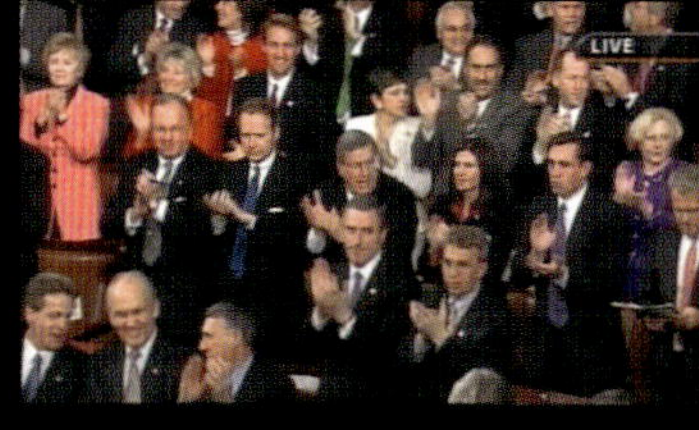

04:35

corporate and alternative communities. Lucas disrupts the insinuation of technology into daily life, and demystifies technology tools with the aim of encouraging individuals to recognize their own agency. Anticipating the rise of domestic stars on YouTube and social media, Lucas transforms herself into a public figure capable of instigating action in her audience.

As Lucas describes in the EAI Online Catalogue, *Cable Xcess* as "a public service announcement/infomercial which informs viewers about the consequences of long-term exposure to electromagnetic fields. I perform as both spokesperson and case study, transmitting a pirate broadcast through my body (body as satellite), educating viewers about early signs of exposure, and sharing alternative methods for coping with contamination. At a midpoint in the video my perspective on the situation changes and I speak instead as an advocate in the form of a testimonial about how exposure to these fields has led me to become super-powered."

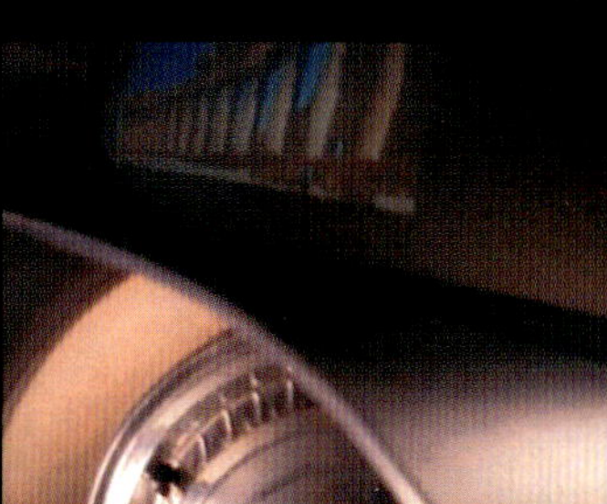
00:22

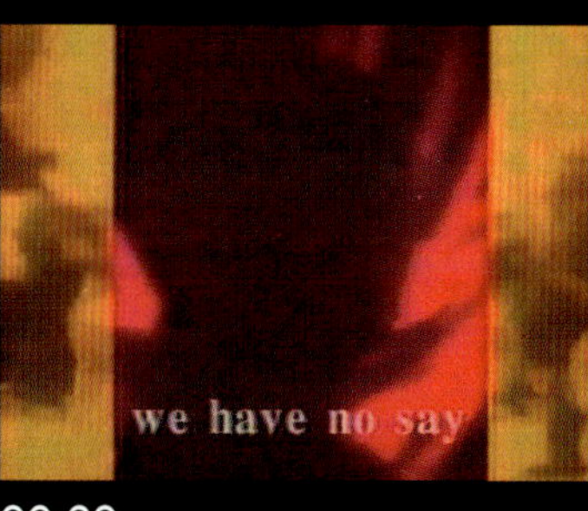

00:39

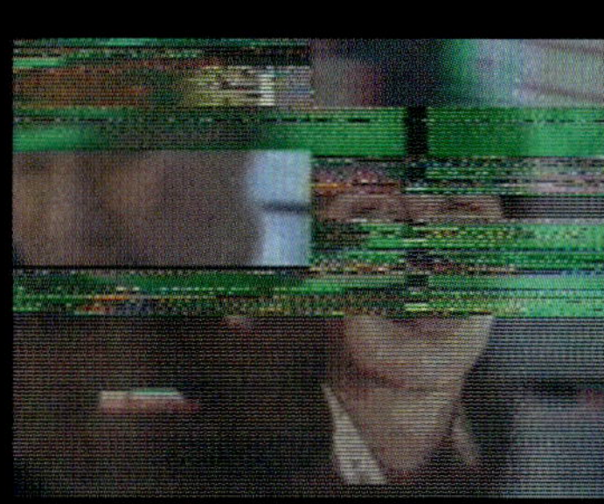
21:16

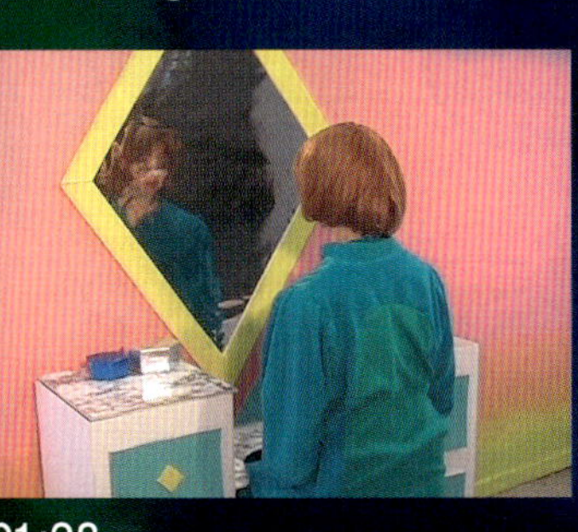
01:28

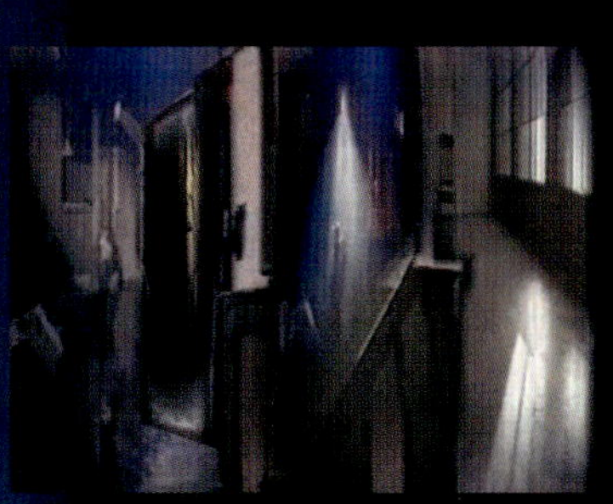
00:25

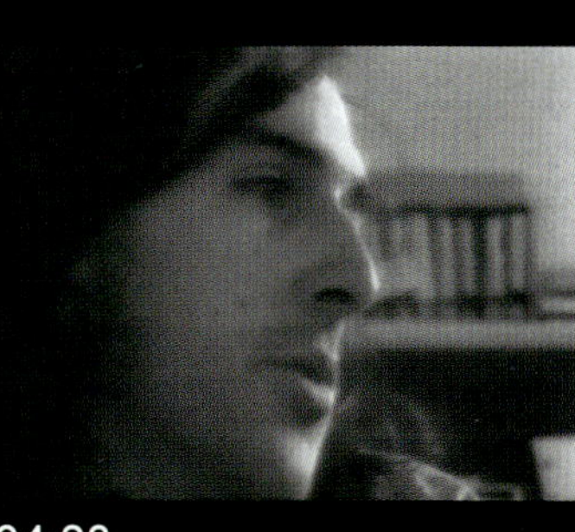
04:28

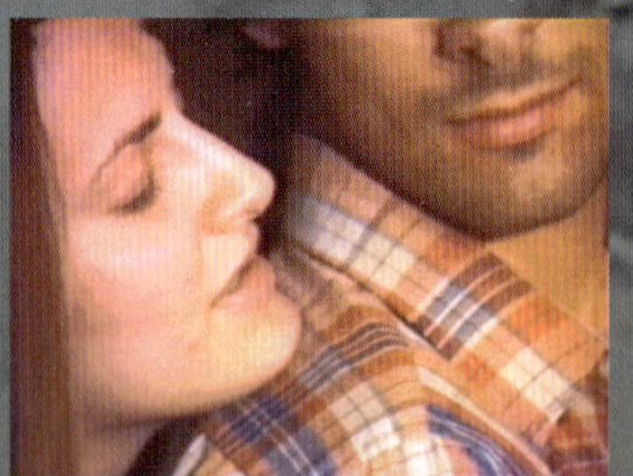

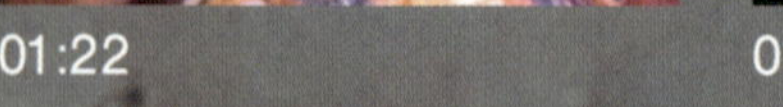

01:22

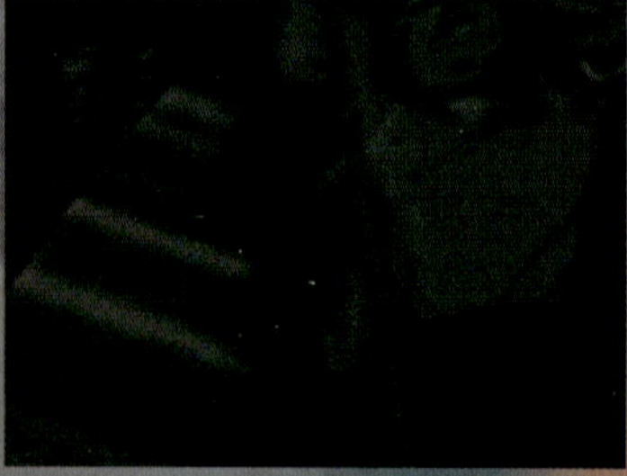

01:42

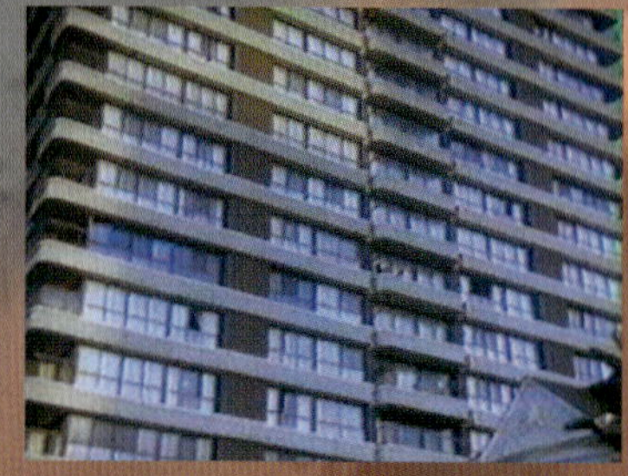

05:57

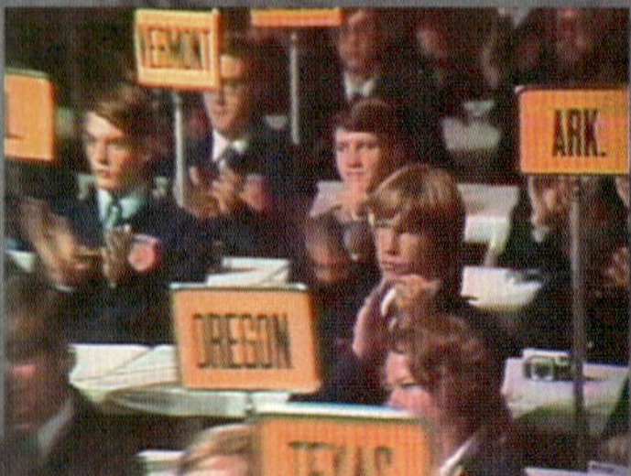

14:06

SHANA MOULTON
(Born 1976, Oakhurst, CA; lives Oakhurst, CA)
Whispering Pines 7, 2006, video, color, sound, 4:43 minutes

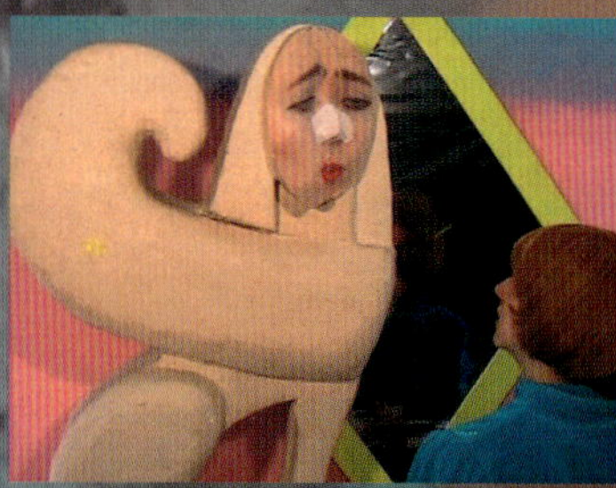

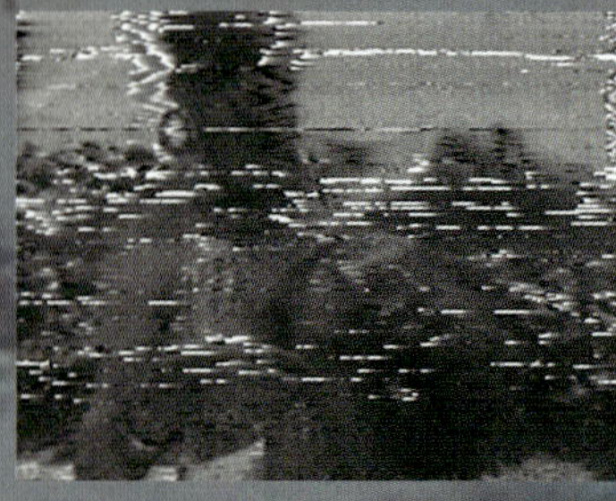

17:30

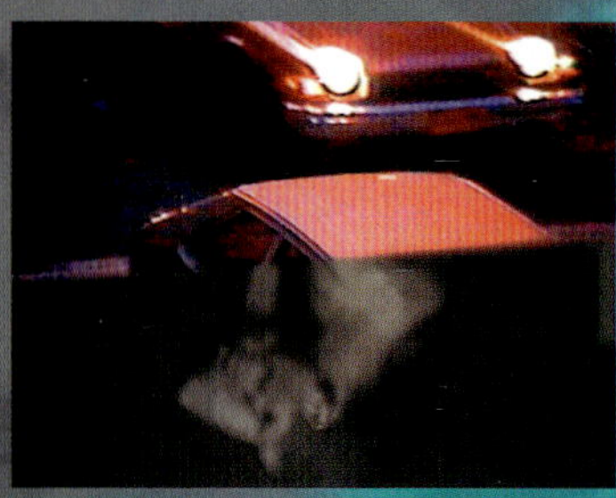

07:18

Shana Moulton creates evocatively oblique narratives in her video and performance works. Combining an unsettling, wry humor with a low-tech, Pop sensibility, Moulton often plays a character whose interactions with the everyday world are both mundane and surreal, in a domestic sphere just slightly askew. As her protagonist navigates the enigmatic and possibly magical properties of her home decor, Moulton initiates relationships with objects and consumer products that are at once banal and uncanny.

The *Whispering Pines* series takes inspiration from the Surrealist images of René Magritte, the uncanny world of David Lynch's *Twin Peaks*, and the grotesqueries of commodity culture as it relates to gender. In *Whispering Pines 7*, Moulton's character Cynthia is confronted with a distorted mirror image that renders the familiar extremely strange. While Cynthia performs her nose-pore cleaning routine in front of the mirror, a sphinx appears and sings a song from the animated movie *The Last Unicorn*, which laments becoming a woman.

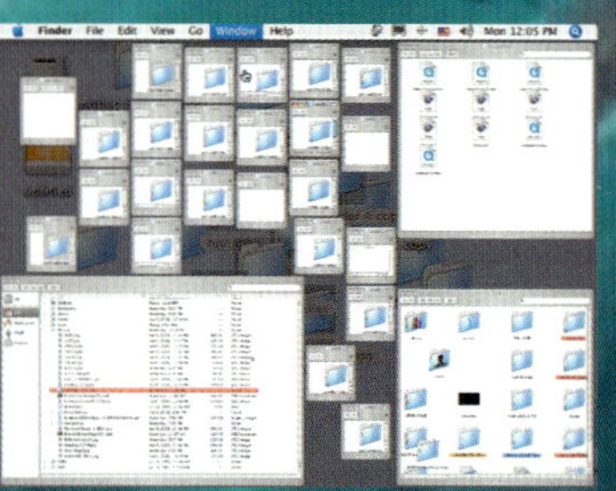

00:53

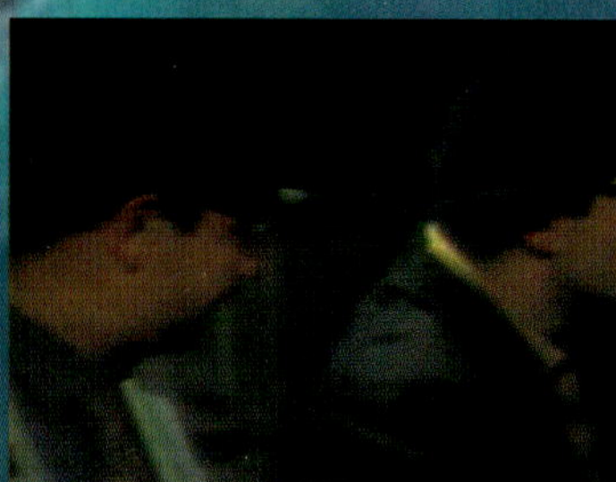

08:24

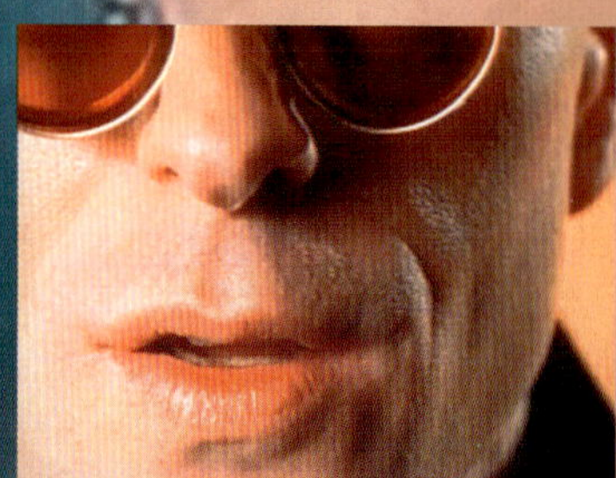

00:08

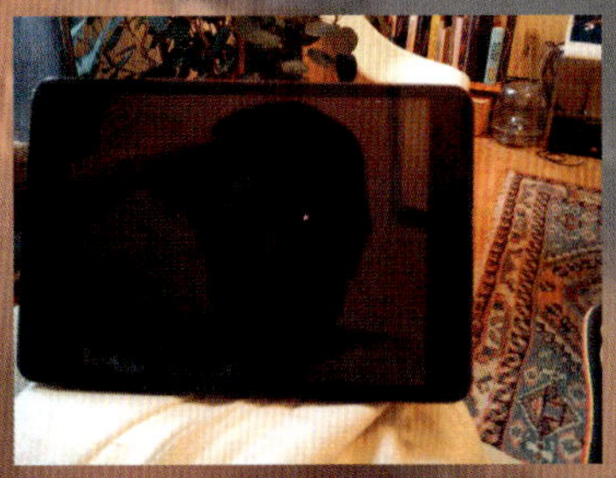

04:02

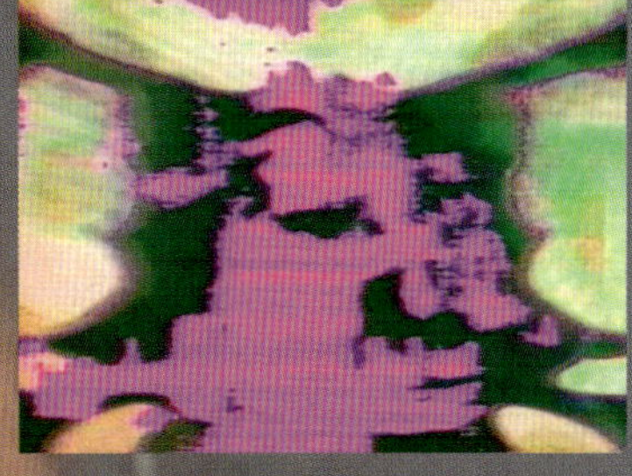

14:33

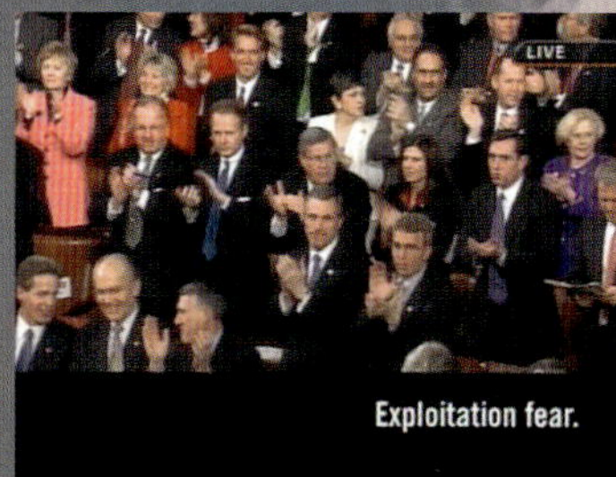

04:35

TREVOR SHIMIZU
(Born 1978, Santa Rosa, CA; lives New York)
The Lonely Loser Trilogy: Skate Videos, 2013, single-channel video, color, sound, 14:02 minutes

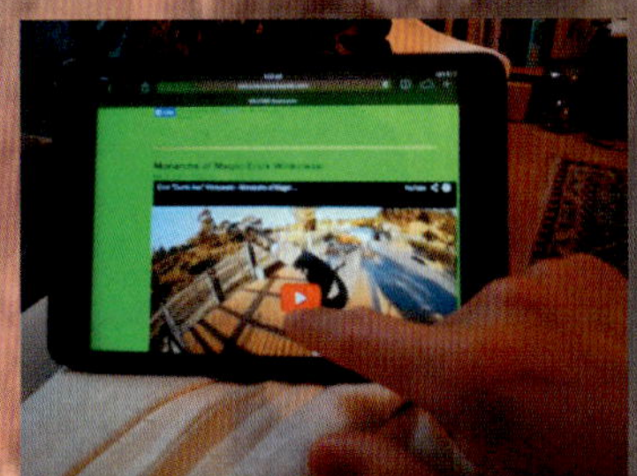

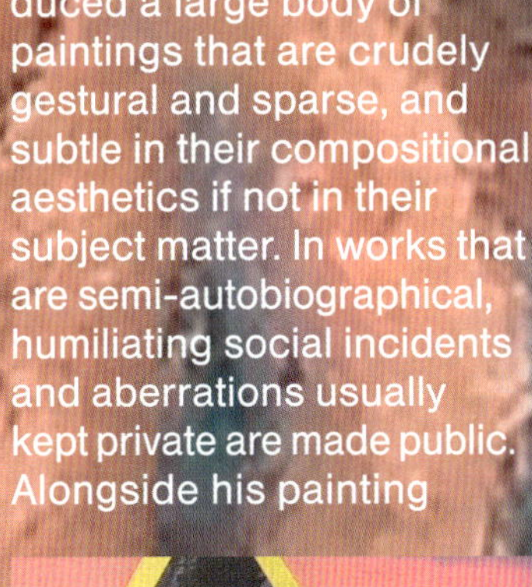

Trevor Shimizu has produced a large body of paintings that are crudely gestural and sparse, and subtle in their compositional aesthetics if not in their subject matter. In works that are semi-autobiographical, humiliating social incidents and aberrations usually kept private are made public. Alongside his painting practice, Shimizu has produced video art that emphasizes how his personal and public identity has been shaped by home video and the banality of television and media consumerism. As a former technical director of Electronic Arts Intermix, he developed close friendships and collaborations with artists including Dan Graham, Carolee Schneemann, Shigeko Kubota, and Dara Birnbaum. The influence of other EAI artists, especially the droll, self-deprecating humor of Michael Smith, and Mike Kelley's unflinching portrayals of American culture, are also clearly evident.

Self-representation is a theme across Shimizu's work, which often incorporates the artist as a surrogate who is elusively aligned with Shimizu. In the three videos that comprise his *Lonely Loser Trilogy*, the artist records

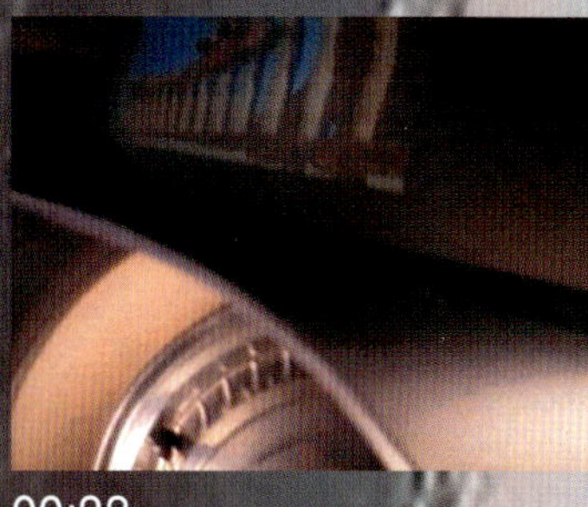

00:22

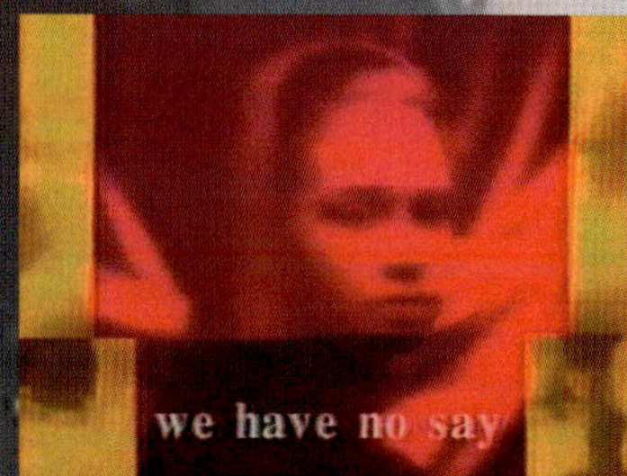

00:39

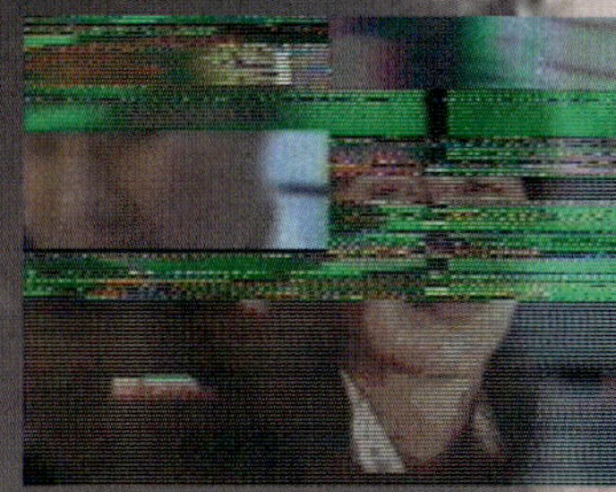

21:16

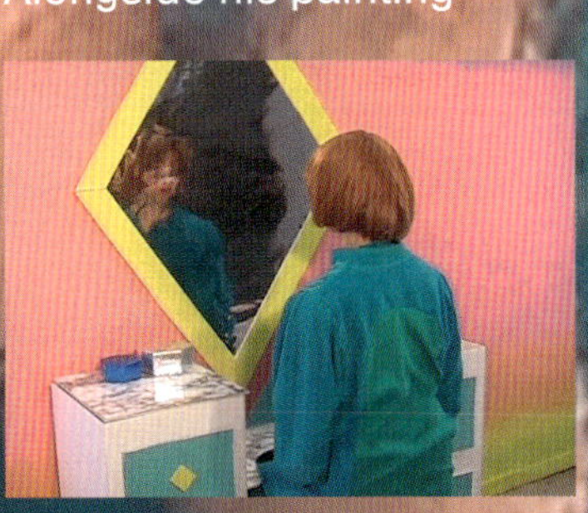

01:28

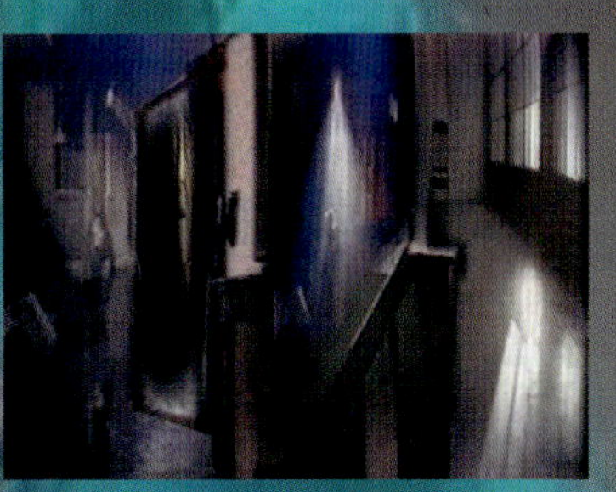

00:25

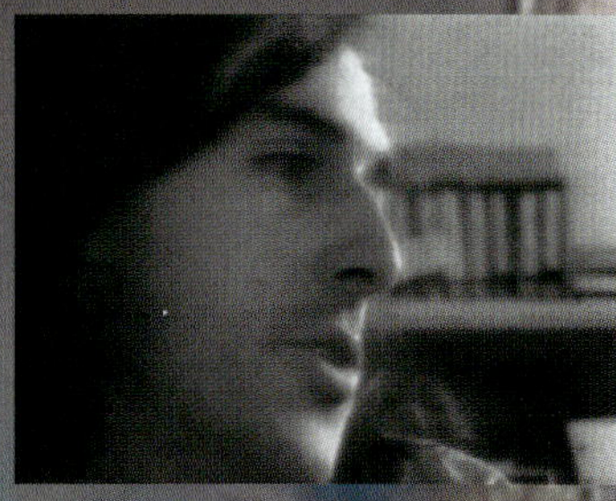

04:28

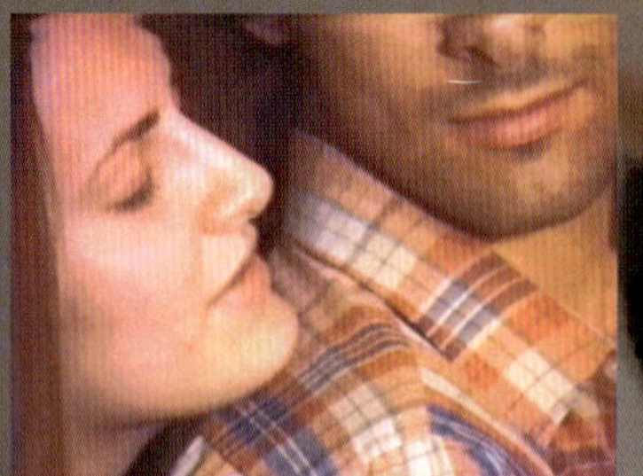
01:21

01:41

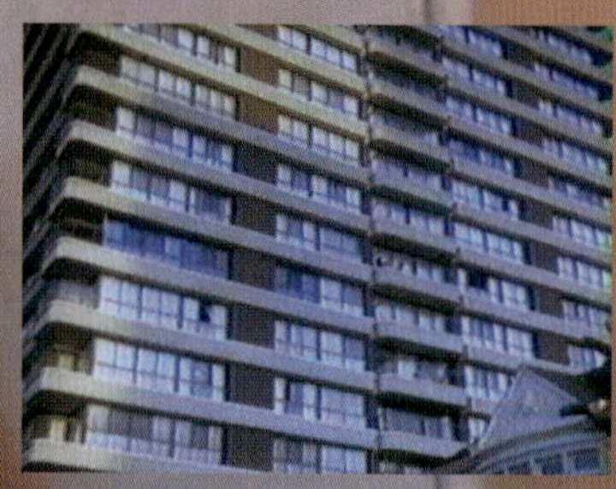
05:56

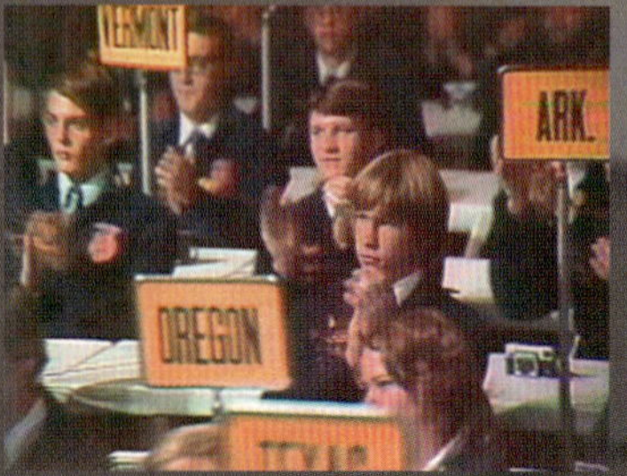

14:05

extended browsing sessions online, each one featuring a high-energy, macho sport that underscores Shimizu's pathetic living room spectatorship. *Skate Videos* was recorded with a pair of Google Glasses, further emphasizing the housebound loser's dependency on gear to compensate for inaction. The domestication of skate videos that in youth might have represented teenage rebellion conjures a poignant portrait of the artist as an adult.

TRANS-VOICES, 1992
This selection of 60-second shorts was produced in 1992 as part of *TRANS-VOICES*, a collaboration between the American Center, Paris, with the Whitney Museum of American Art and the Public Art Fund. Conceived as a multimedia public art project for the conclusion of the twenty-first century, *TRANS-VOICES* invited over fifty artists to make works for radio, television, and subway platforms in Paris and New York. A quarter century later these politically charged interventions—which address issues ranging from xenophobia and consumerism to identity and postcolonial geographies—are still relevant in our contemporary moment.

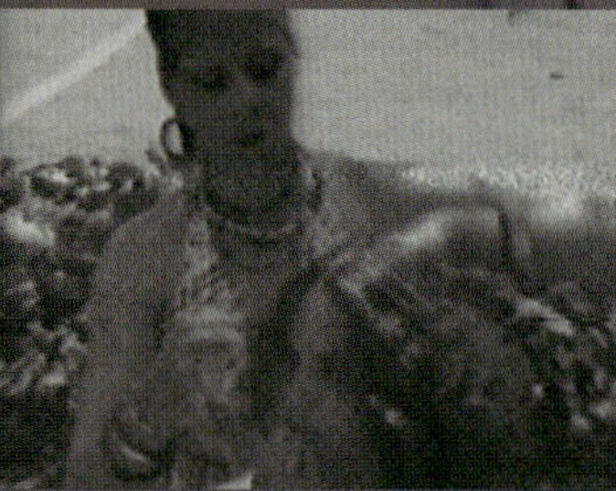
17:29

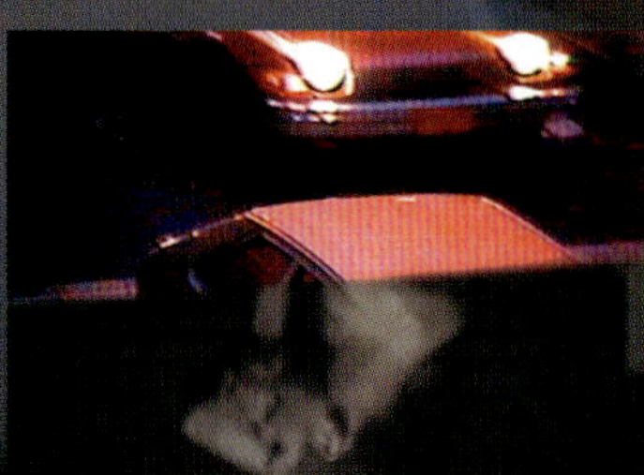
07:17

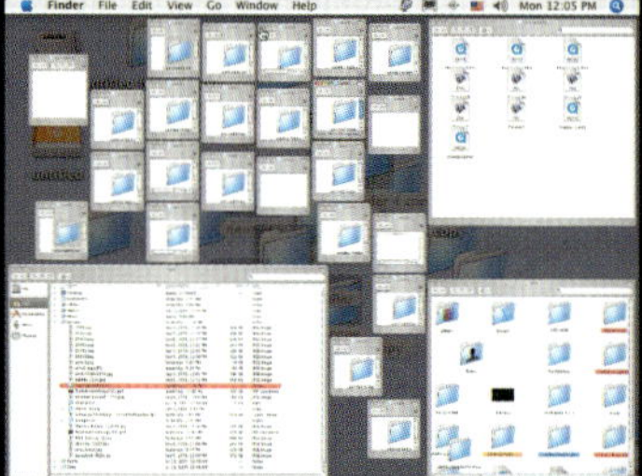
00:52

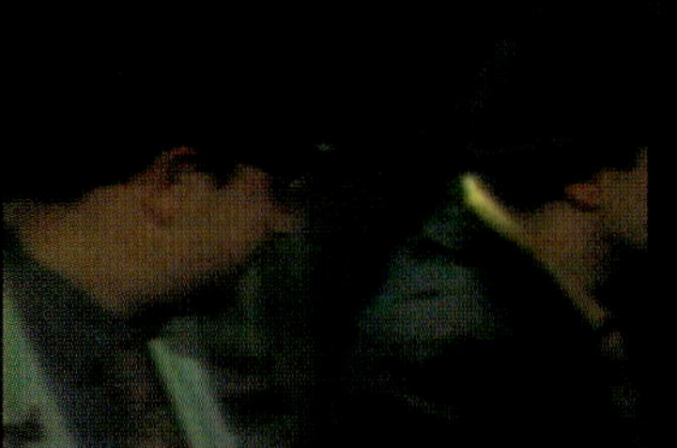
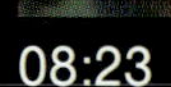
08:23

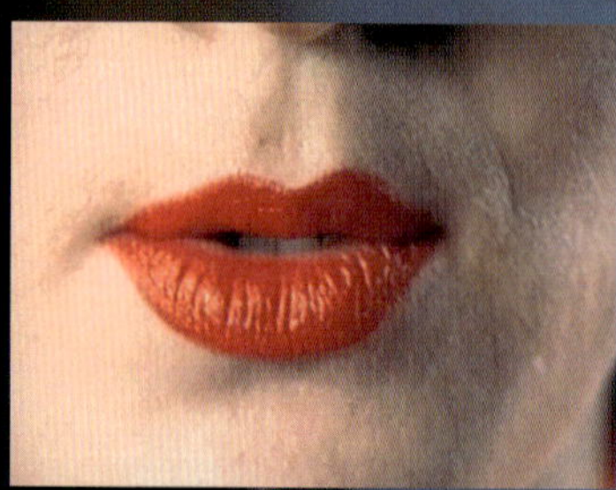
00:07

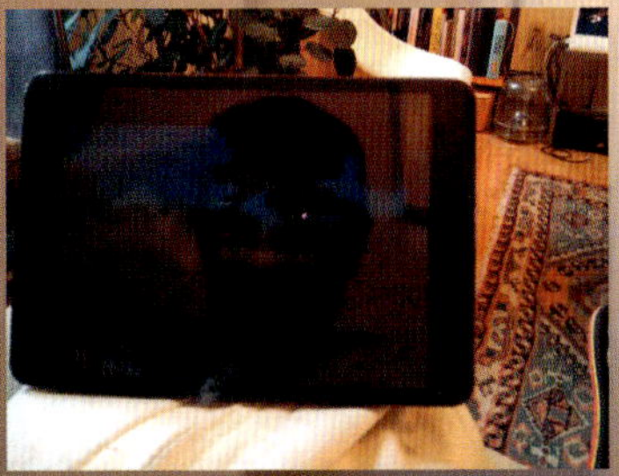

04:02

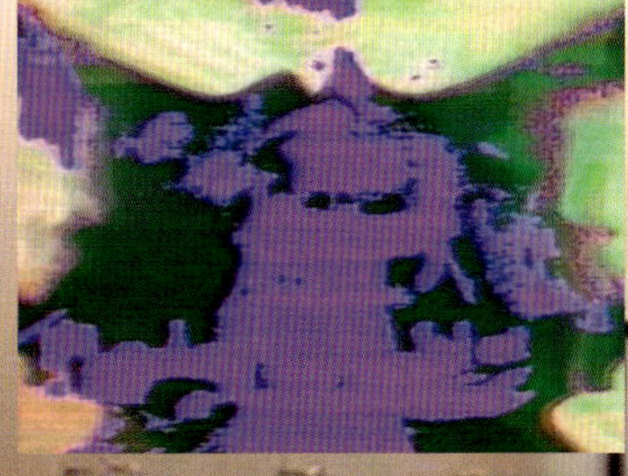

14:33

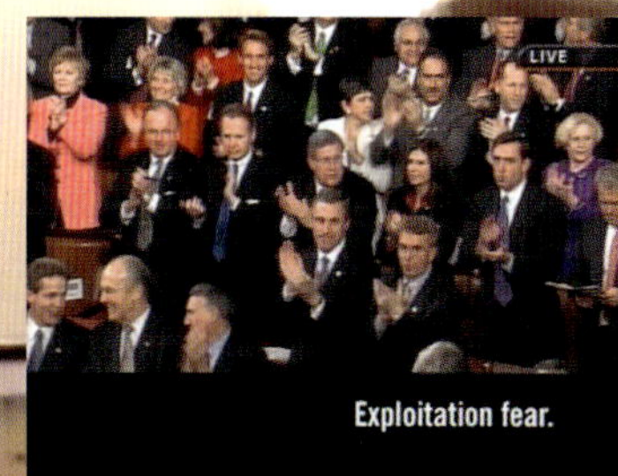

04:35

BETH B
(Born 1955, New York; lives New York)
TRANS-VOICES: Amnesia

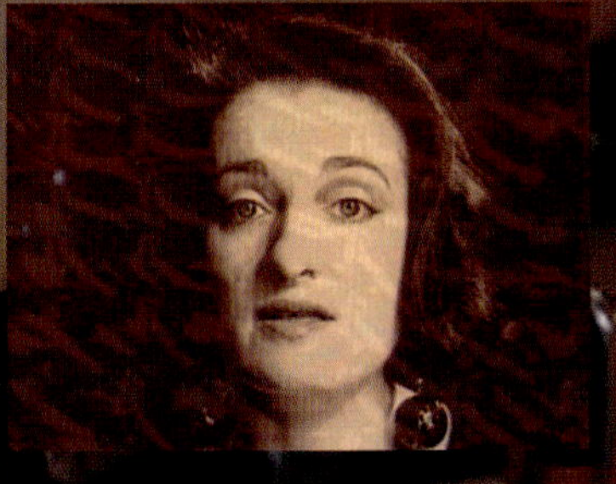

Among her accomplishments, Beth B was a co-founder of the artist's group Colab (Collaborative Projects Inc.), and organizer of the video program of the landmark Times Square Show in 1980. In *Amnesia* she offers a chilling cautionary tale and a stark, uncompromising portrayal of the escalation of xenophobic sentiment in the neo-conservative climate of both France and the United States.

DARA BIRNBAUM
(Born 1946, New York; lives New York)
TRANS-VOICES: Transgressions

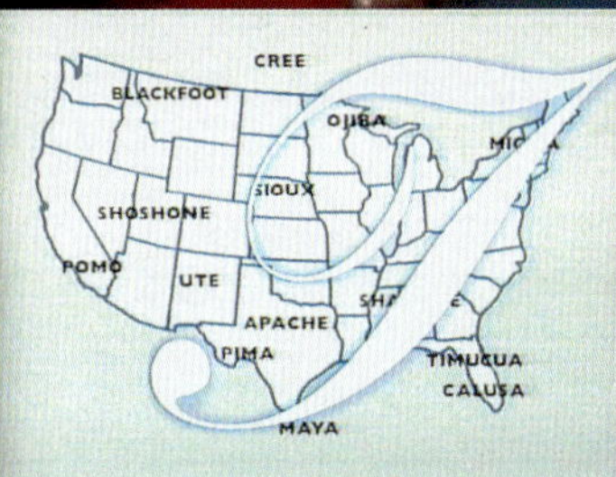

Birnbaum swiftly traces the geopolitical history of the United States and then France, charting their constant reconfigurations across maps rendered malleable through special effects. A densely layered soundtrack guides the viewer through this "anti-terrain," in which boundaries are arbitrary and national identities unstable.

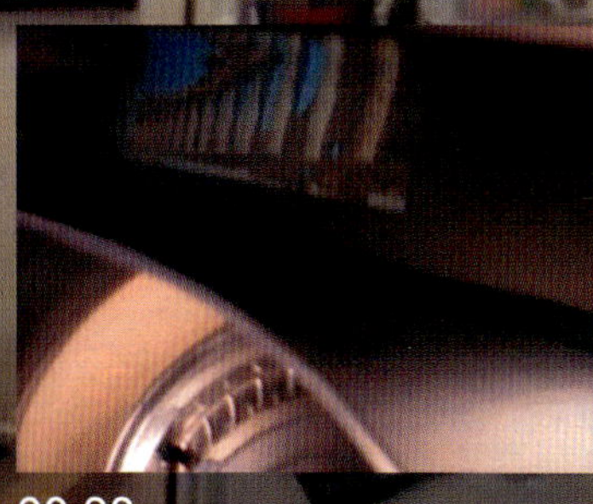

00:22

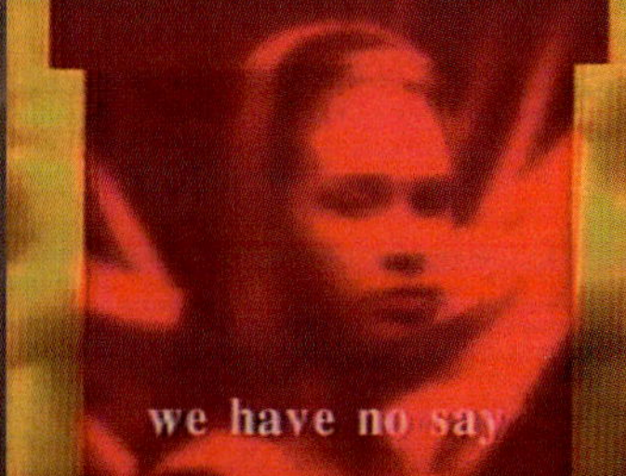

00:39

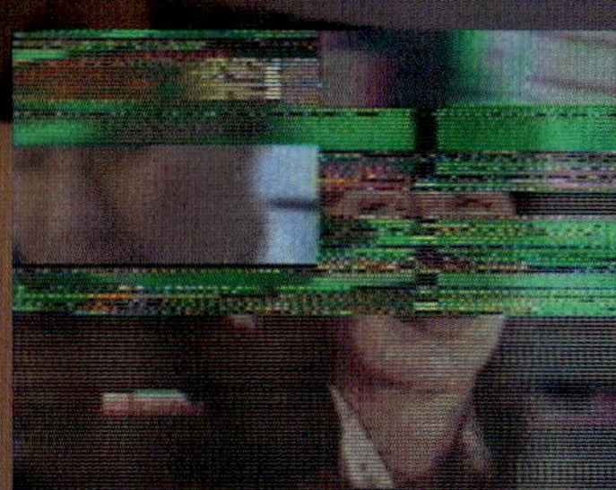

21:16

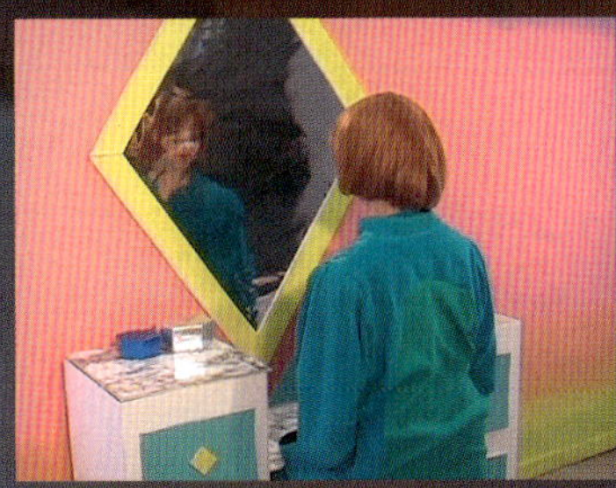

01:28

00:25

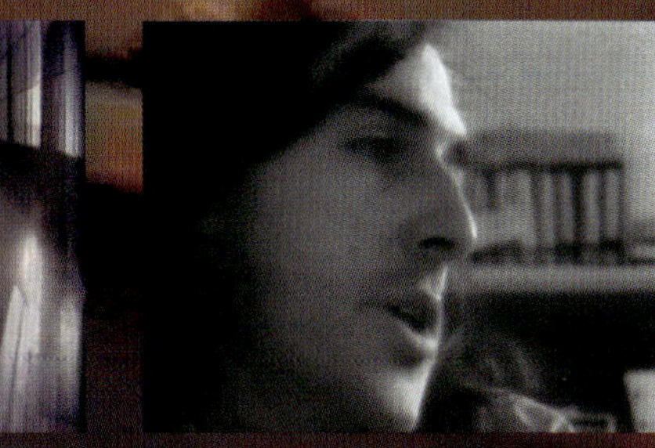

04:28

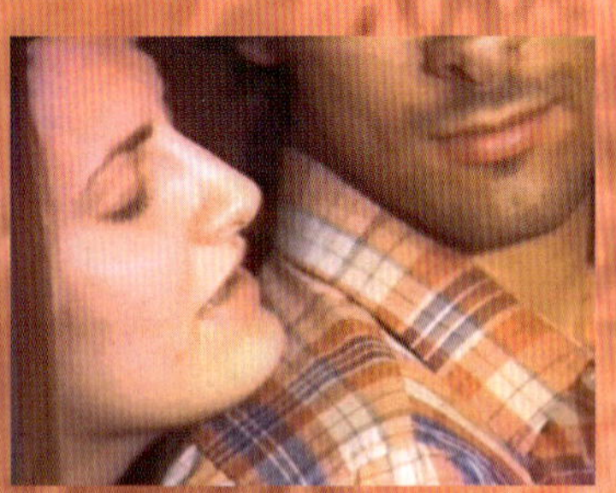

01:21

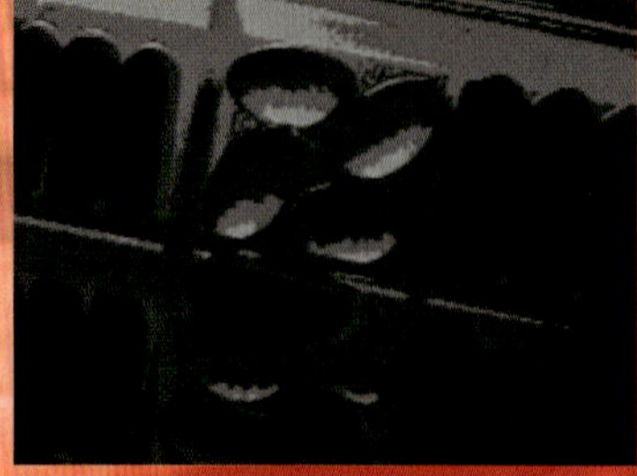

01:41

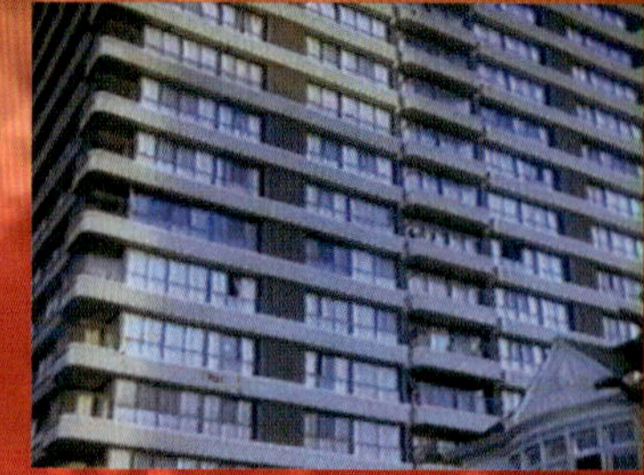

05:56

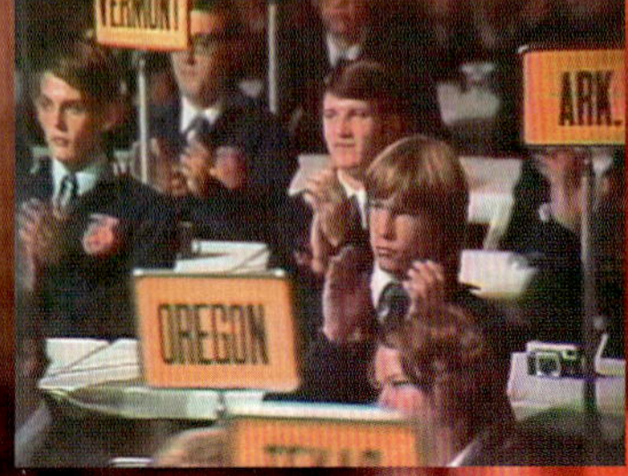

14:05

PHILIP MALLORY JONES
(Born 1947, Chicago; lives Atlanta)
TRANS-VOICES: Paradigm Shift

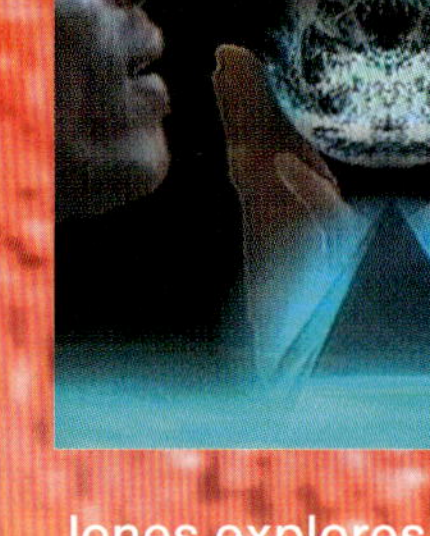

17:29

Jones explores the emerging global African diaspora culture and consciousness through nonverbal storytelling and an evocative, transcultural language of sound and image construction. *Paradigm Shift* presents a poetic meditation on the cultures of the African diaspora in a richly visualized collage of sounds and images derived from African cosmology, tracing the long historical struggle to define a transcultural African race.

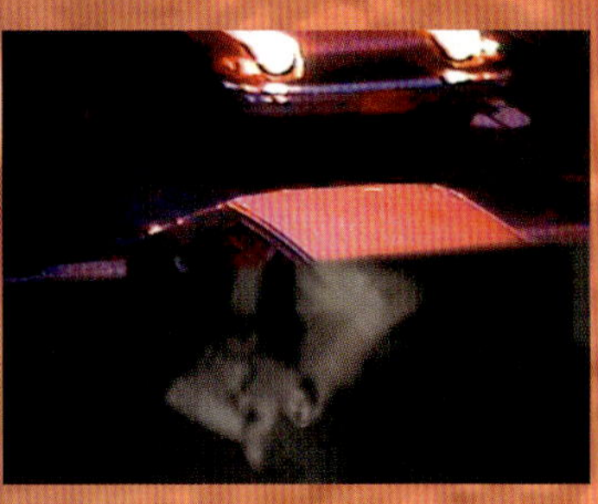

07:17

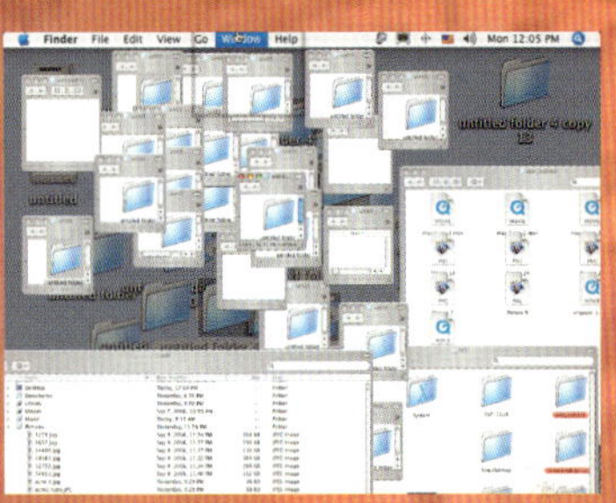

00:52

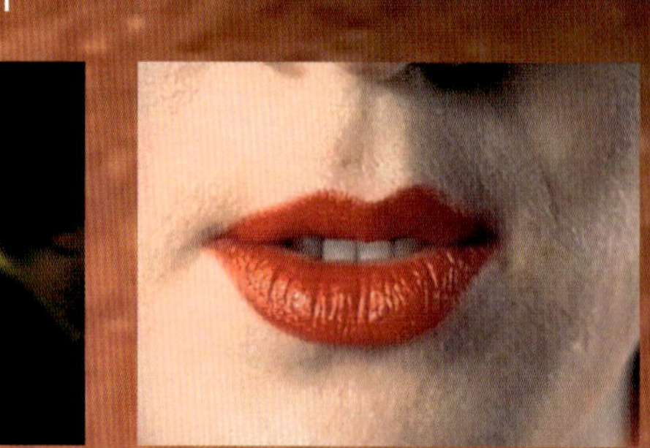

08:23

00:07

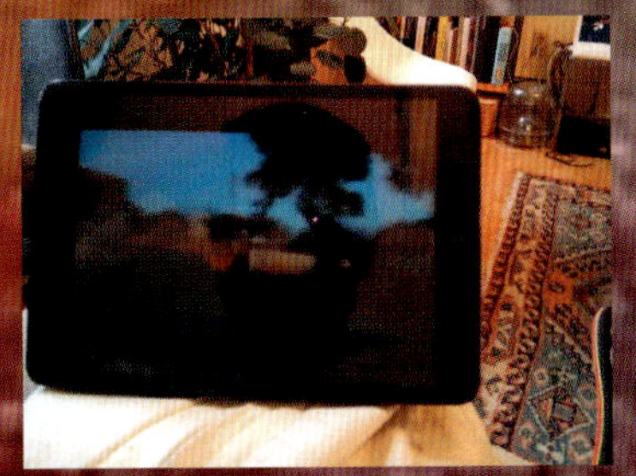
04:02

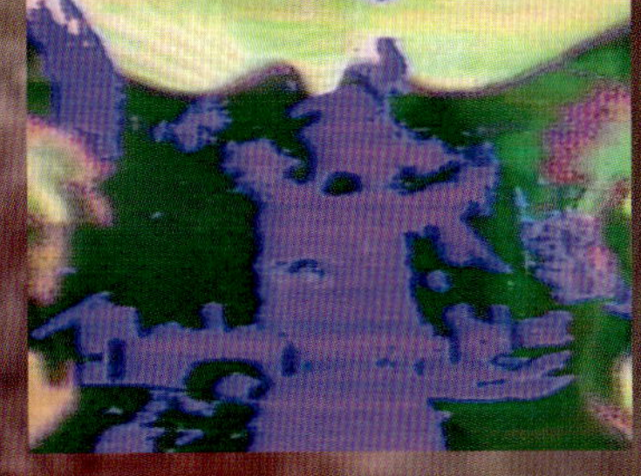
14:33

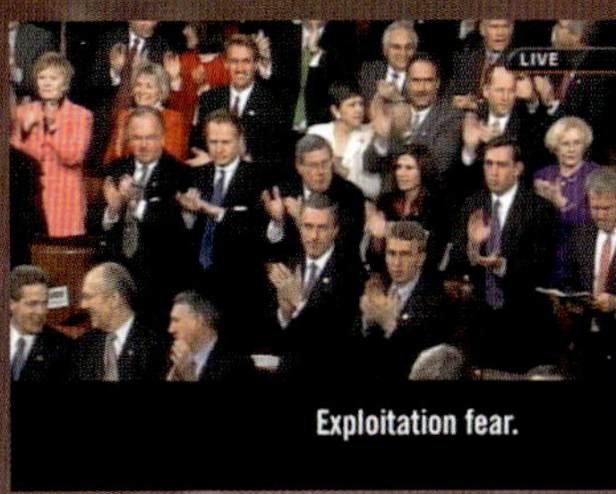

04:35

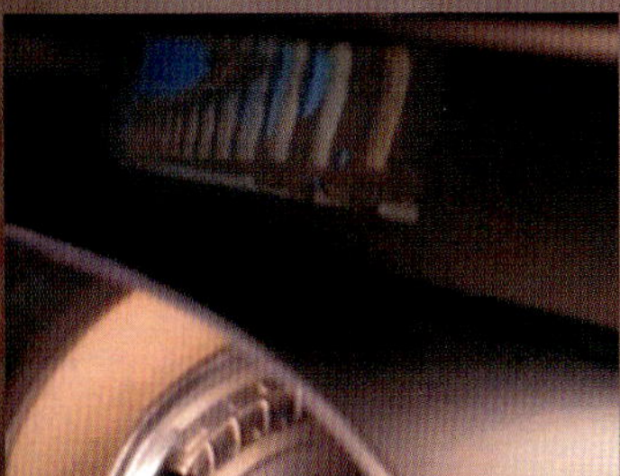
00:22

TOM KALIN
(Born 1962, Chicago; lives New York)
TRANS-VOICES: Nation

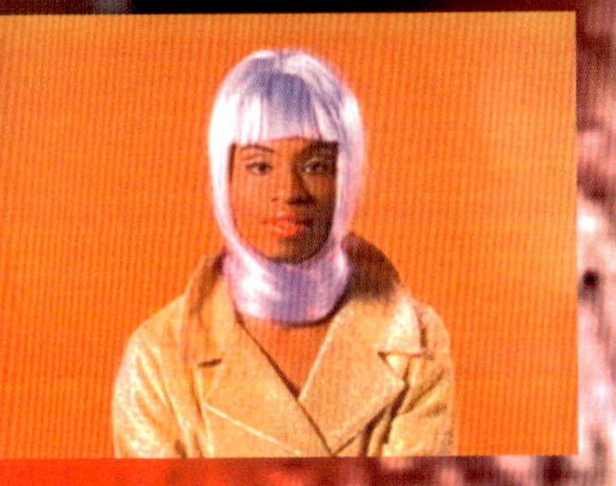

Tom Kalin began his career as a founding member of the AIDS activist collective Gran Fury. In this highly stylized and deftly edited provocation a cast of performers, diverse in national origin, recite statements meant to challenge viewers' secure notions of national identity. Kalin asserts that bodies are very real battlegrounds, territories that are contested and controlled by the same political forces that determine borders or set national policies.

VICTOR MASAYESVA, JR.
(Born 1951, Hotevilla, AZ; lives Hotevilla, AZ)
TRANS-VOICES: Two Faces of One Room

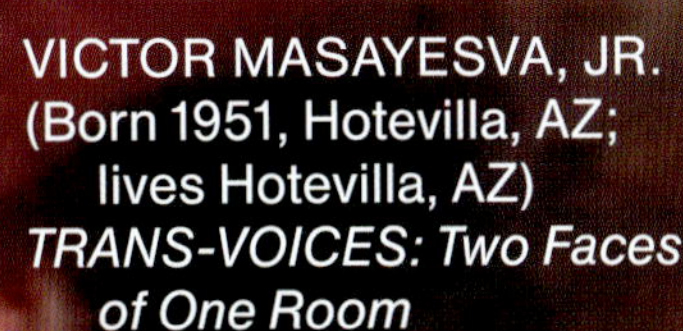

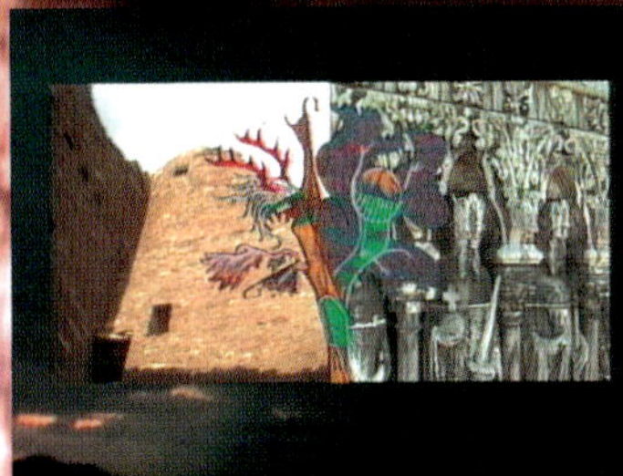

Victor Masayesva, Jr. has created a rich body of video and photographic work that represents the culture and traditions of Native Americans—particularly the Hopi of Southwest Arizona—through poetic visualizations. He employs computer animation and graphics in lyrical translations of myths, rituals, and history as a way to articulate the richness of his heritage in his own

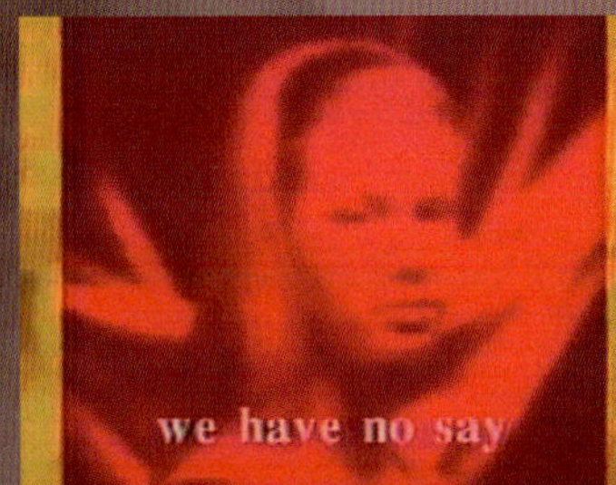

00:39

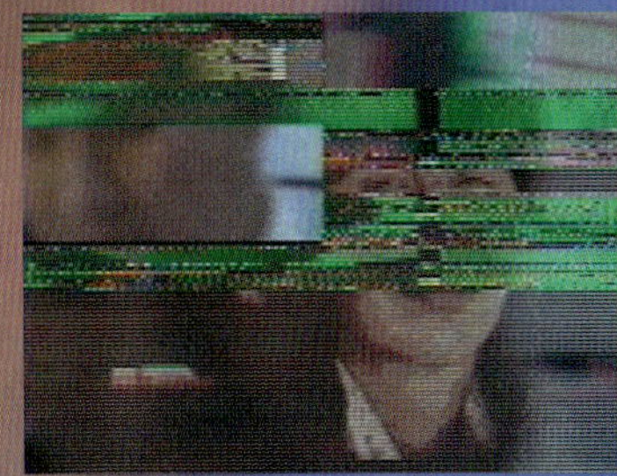
21:16

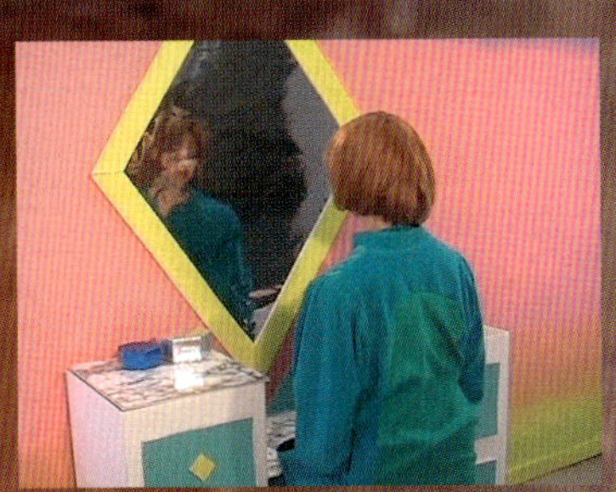
01:28

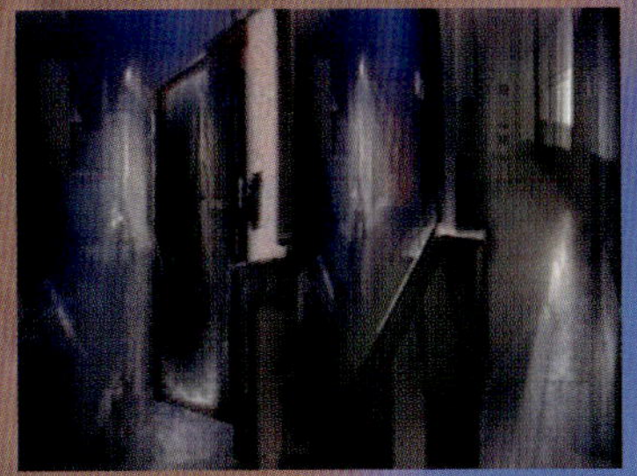
00:25

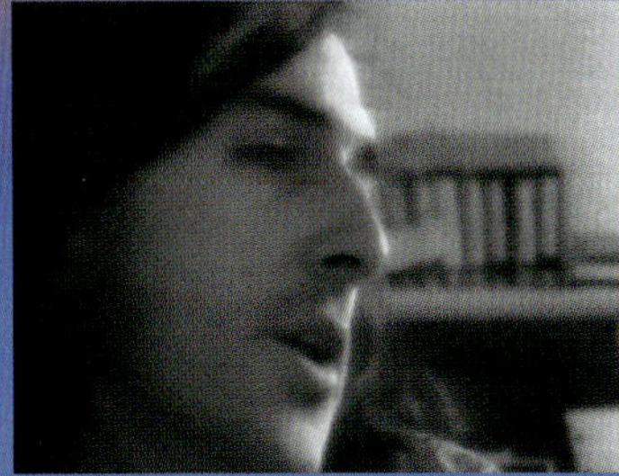
04:28

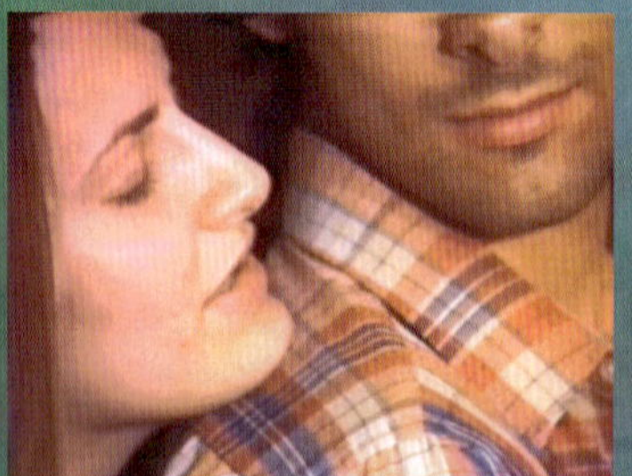
01:21

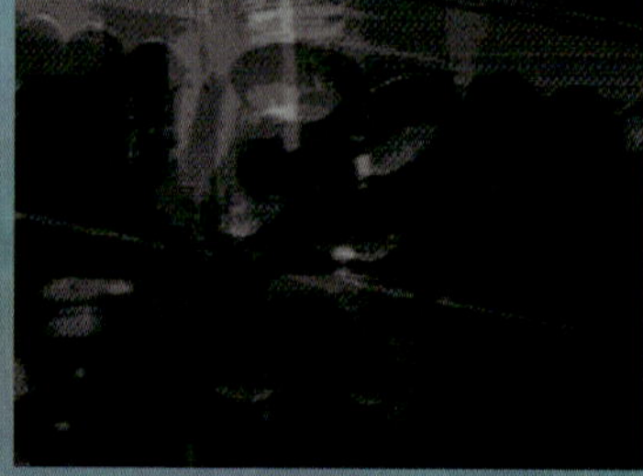
01:41

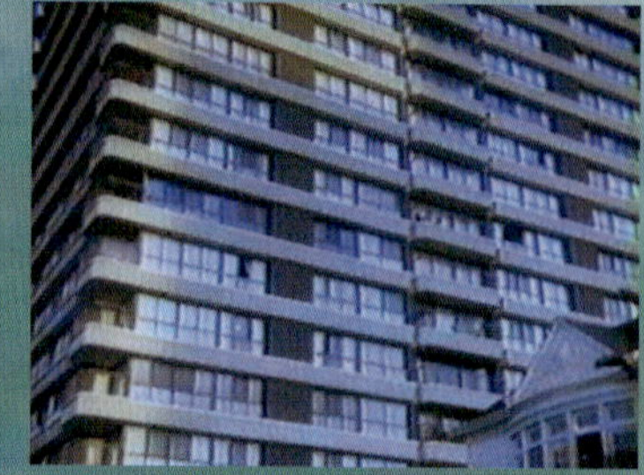
05:56

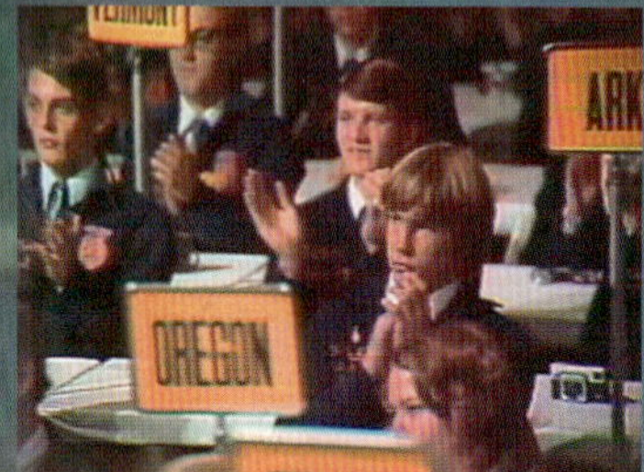

14:05

language. In *Two Faces of One Room*, he juxtaposes two sacred architectural structures of two dissimilar cultures—the kiva of the Native American and the cathedral of Western Europe—to contemplate their cultural and spiritual differences.

NAM JUNE PAIK
(Born 1932, Seoul; died 2006, Miami)
PAUL GARRIN
(Born 1957, Philadelphia; lives New York)
TRANS-VOICES: A Tale of Two Cities

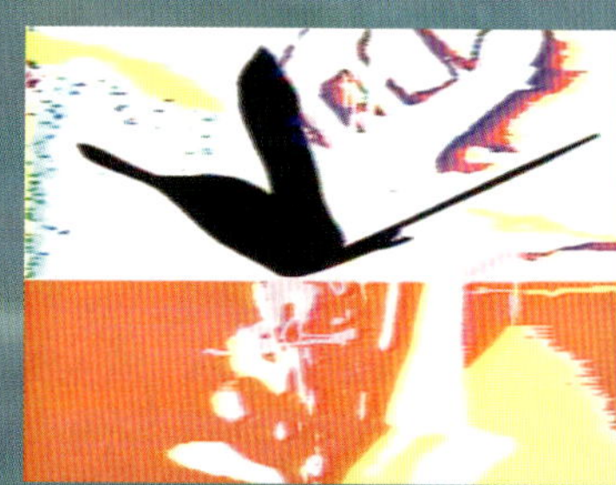

Television on speed, Nam June Paik's *A Tale of Two Cities* is a potpourri of pop personalities, avant-garde antics, and international cultural kitsch, where past, present and future collide in the kaleidoscopic, hyperkinetic, televisually "now."

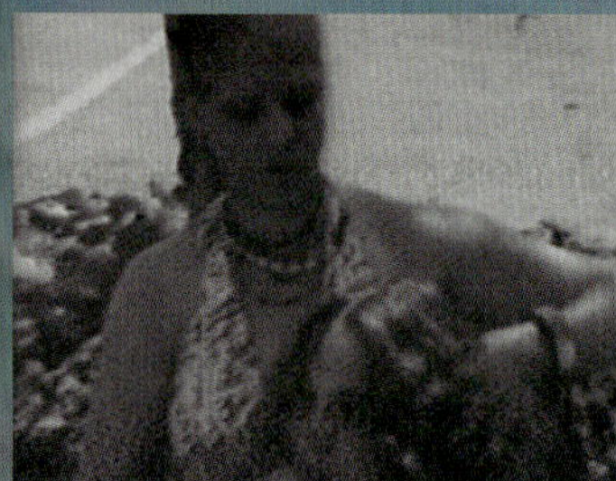
17:29

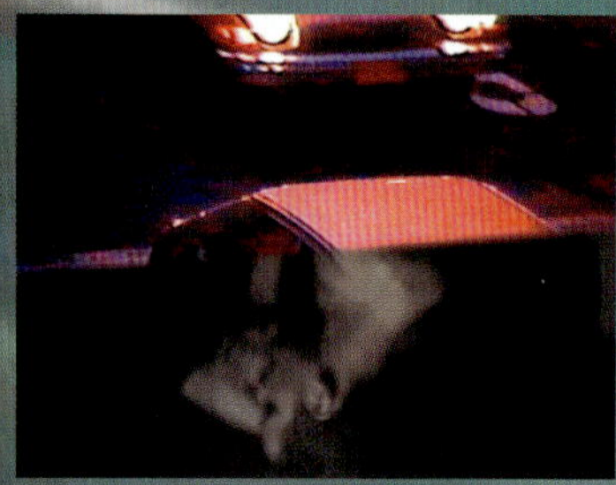
07:17

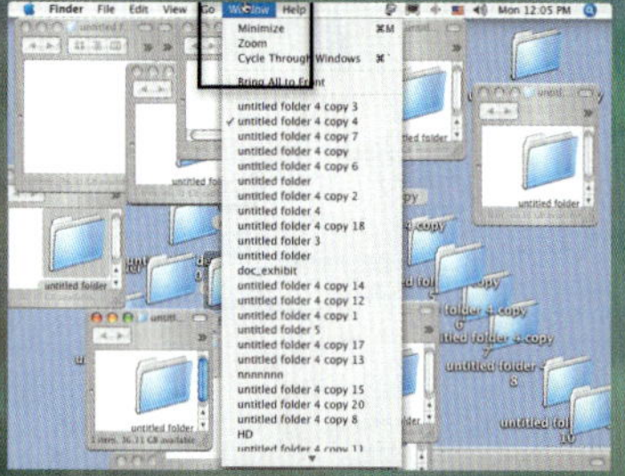
00:52

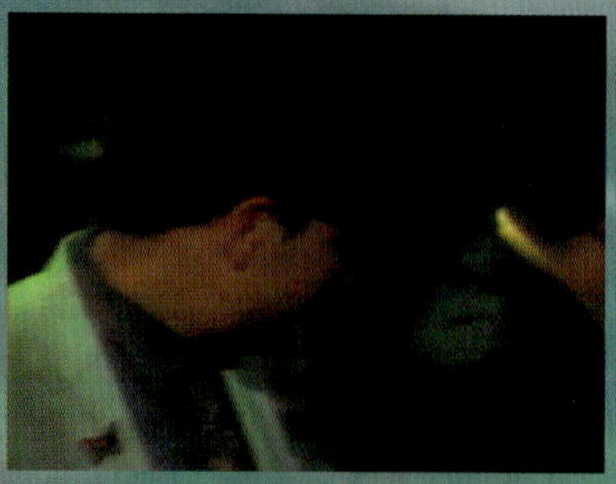
08:23

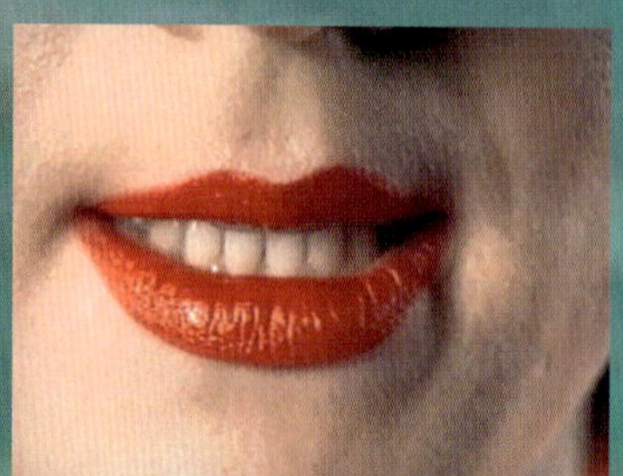
00:07

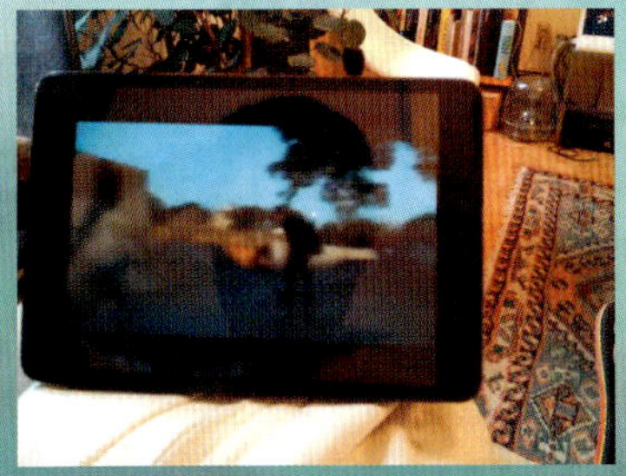
04:02

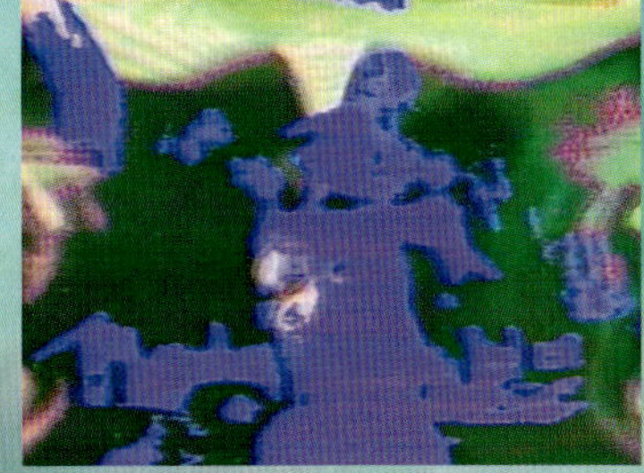
14:33

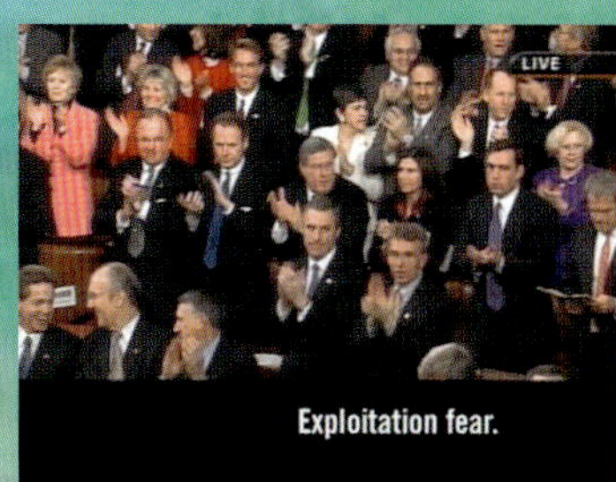

04:35

BRUCE YONEMOTO
(Born 1949, San Jose, CA; lives Los Angeles)
NORMAN YONEMOTO
(Born 1946, Chicago; died 2014, Los Angeles)
TRANS-VOICES: ahistory

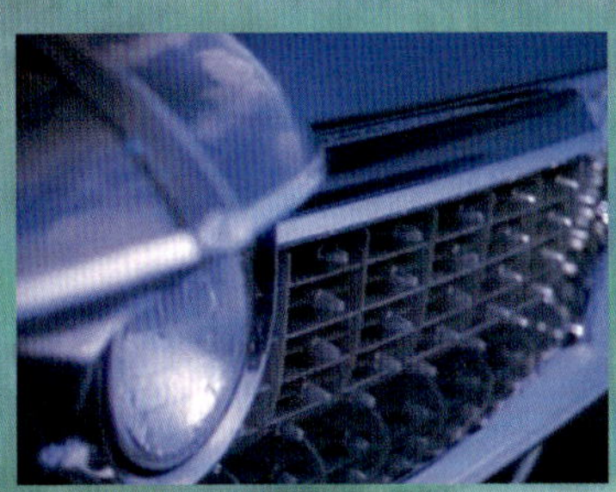

Since the mid-1970s California-based artists and brothers Bruce and Norman Yonemoto have produced a body of collaborative videos that deconstruct and rewrite the cultural mythologies embedded in mass media. In *ahistory* they depict Europe's enchantment with American consumer culture, as well-known European architectural landmarks– the Eiffel Tower, the Acropolis, London Bridge—are reflected in the glossy surface of a 1960s Cadillac convertible, the ultimate symbol of the "golden age" of American consumerism.

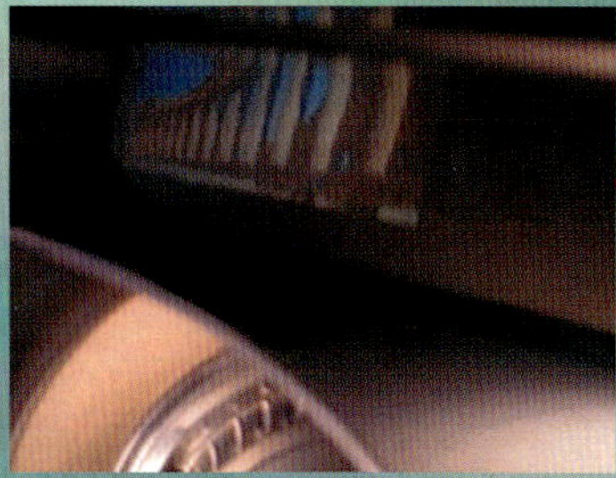
00:22

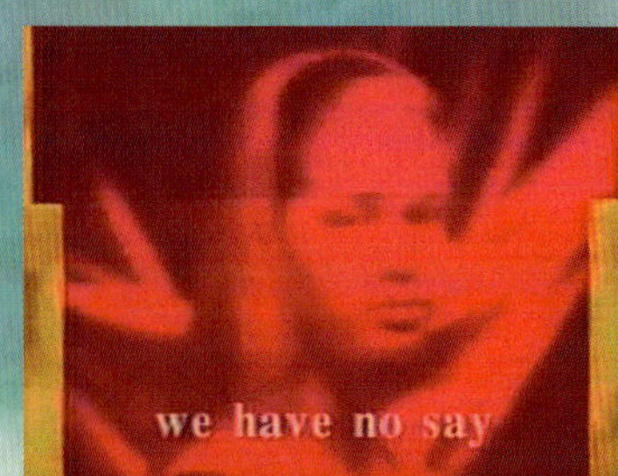

00:39

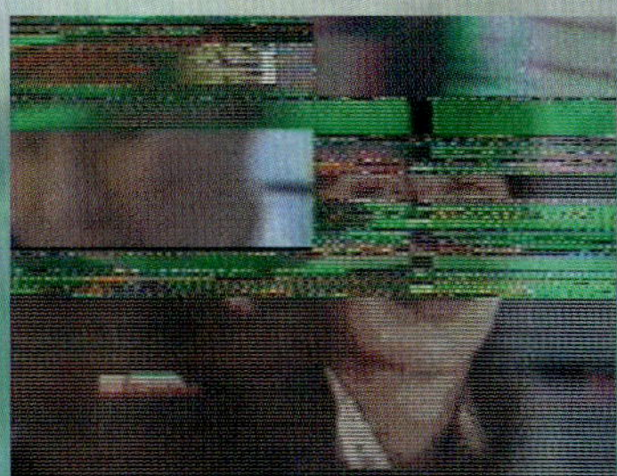
21:16

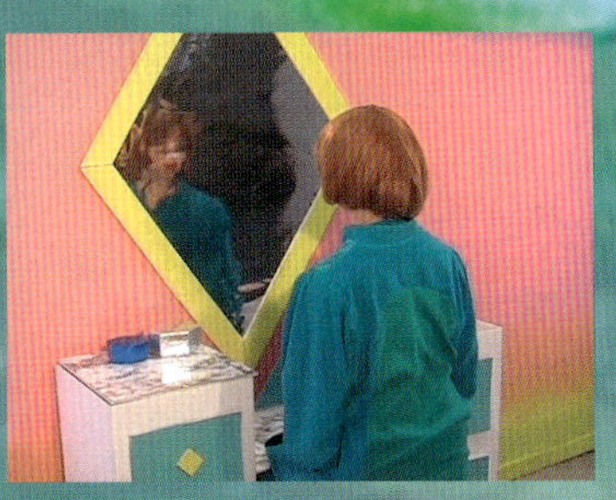
01:28

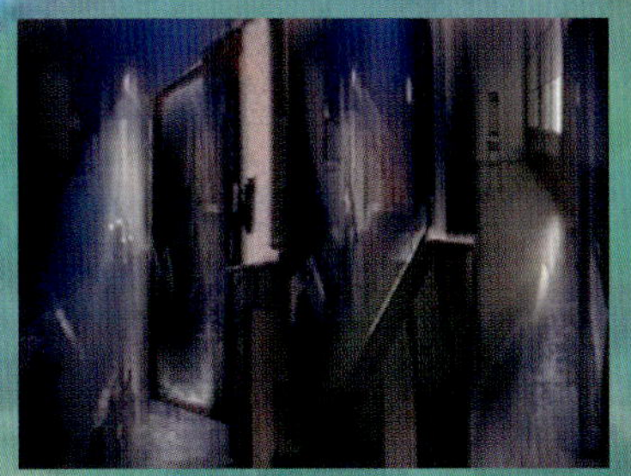
00:25

04:28

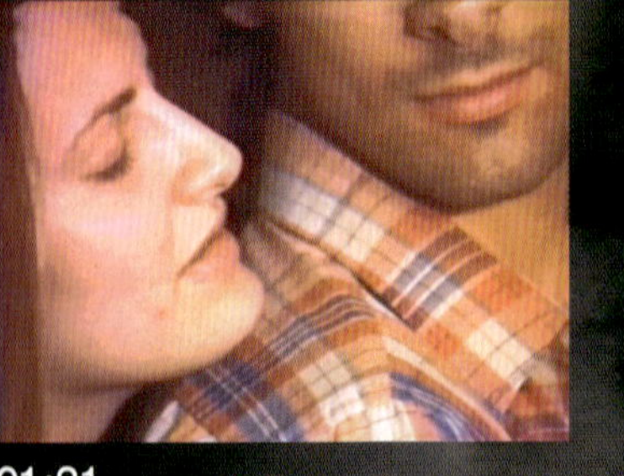

01:21

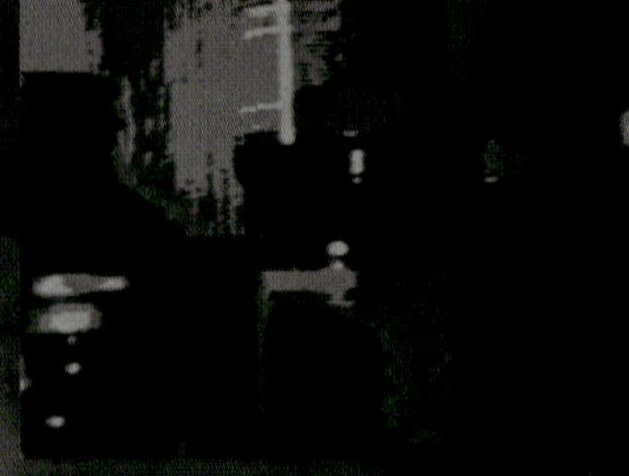

01:41

05:56

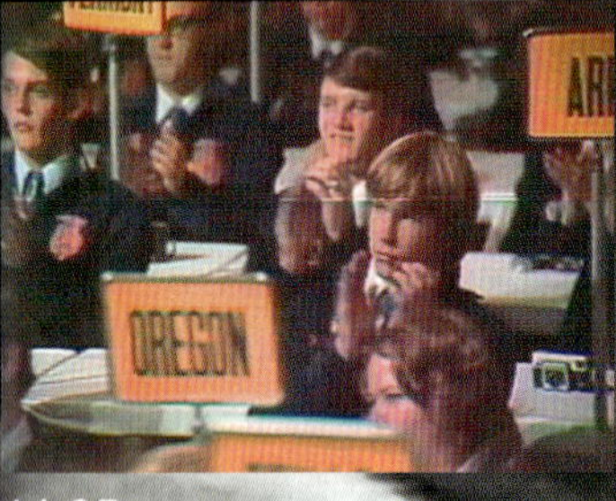

14:05

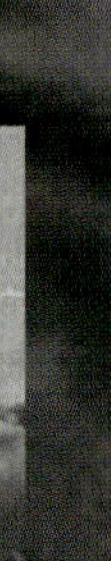

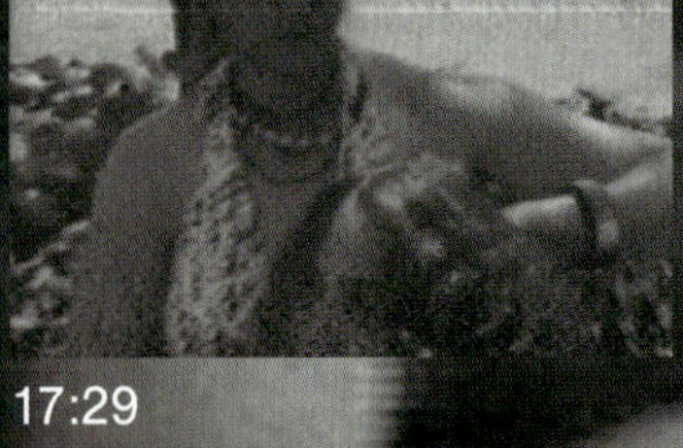

17:29

BROADCASTING: GUERRILLA MEDIA WORKS IN THE EXHIBITION SLOUGHT

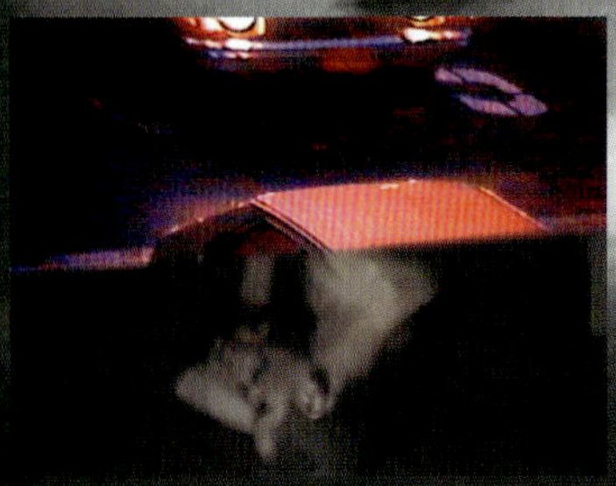

07:17

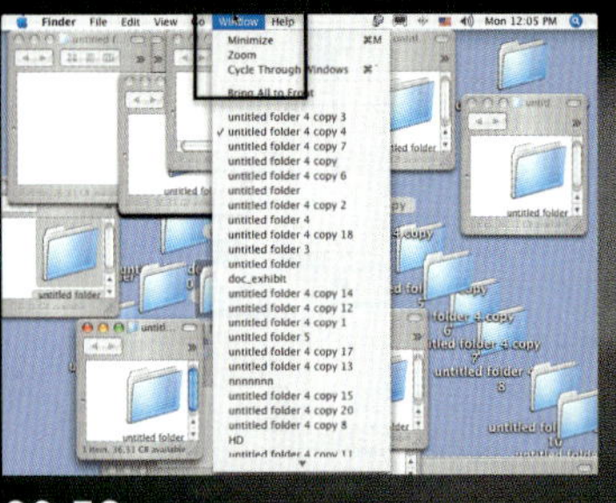

00:52

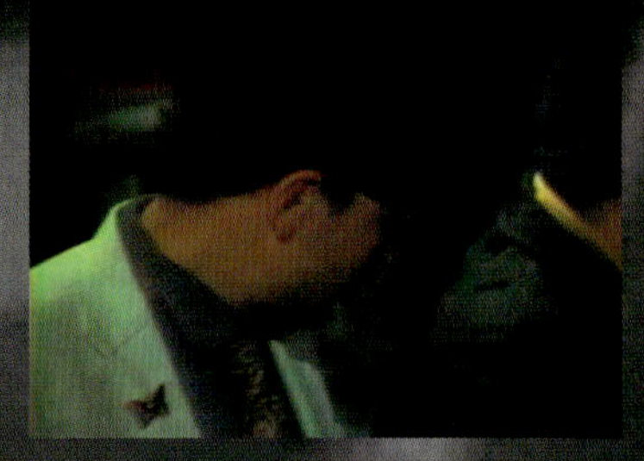

08:23

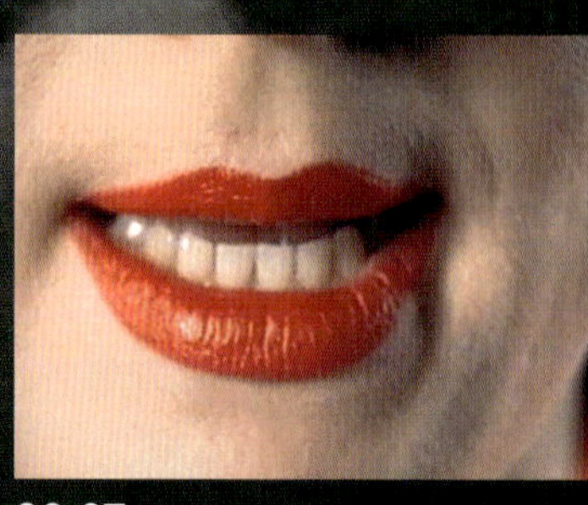

00:07

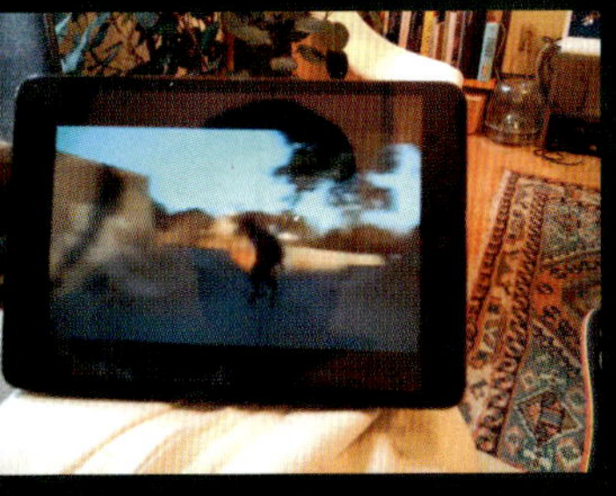
04:03

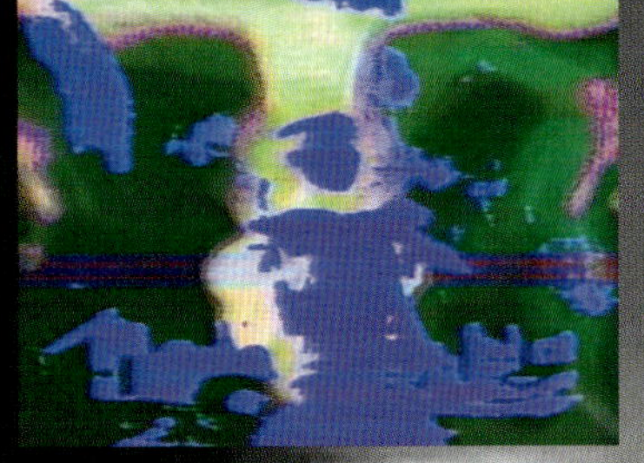
14:34

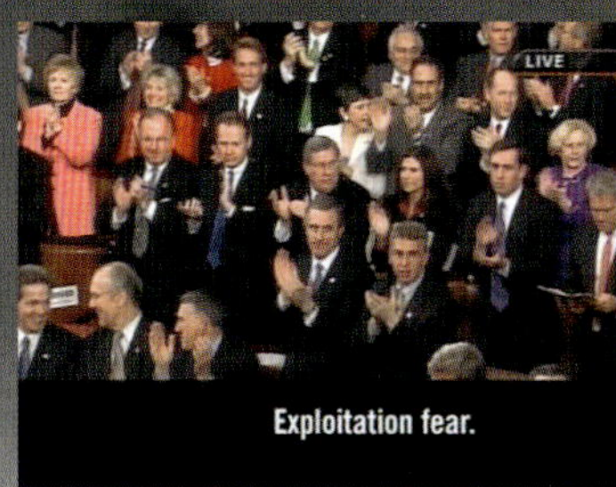

04:36

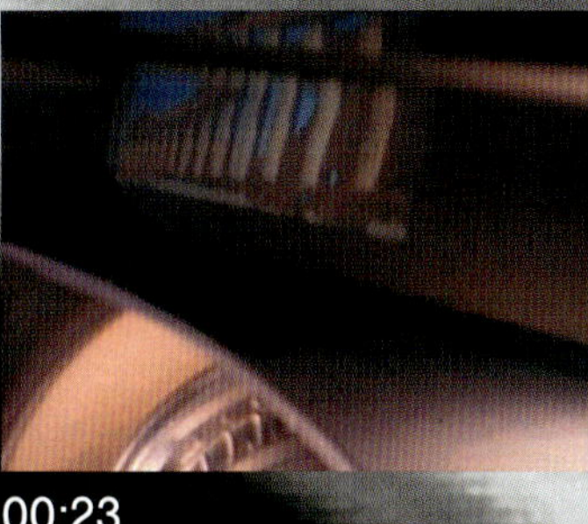
00:23

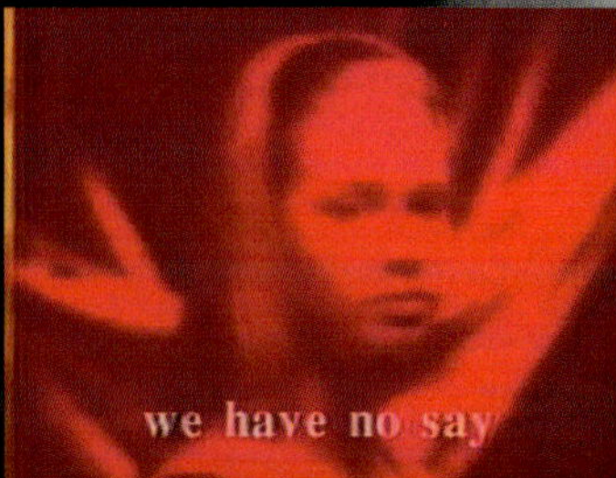

00:40

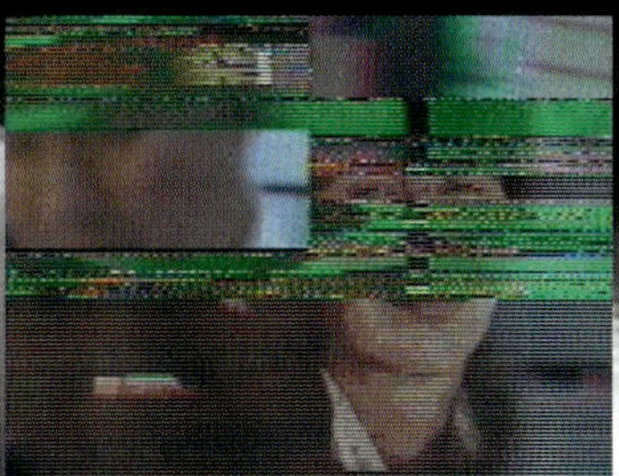
21:17

DCTV
Since its inception in 1972, DCTV has been at the forefront of the independent social-issue documentary movement, and has contributed to several landmarks of that genre. Founded by Jon Alpert and Keiko Tsuno in New York's Chinatown as a community-based organization, DCTV offers video training, equipment, and social-issue programming. DCTV's forceful investigative reporting, presented in Emmy Award–winning documentaries, represents compelling advocacy journalism.

In 1974 DCTV made history as the first American television crew to be invited to Cuba since the 1959 revolution. The resulting *Cuba: The People* (1974) was the first 1/2-inch color videotape to be shown nationally on public television, and one of the first independent video documentaries to be broadcast. As the first American journalists allowed into Vietnam after the US withdrawal, DCTV continued to break new ground with *Vietnam: Picking Up the Pieces* (1978), which examined the aftermath of American involvement in the war.

Employing a direct interview approach and a signature up-close reporting strategy that focuses on the voices of ordinary people, DCTV has produced an extensive body of work that addresses inequality and injustice in the United States. Alpert has also produced numerous programs as a correspondent for NBC *Nightly News* and the *Today* show. DCTV's initial success in broadcasting its work

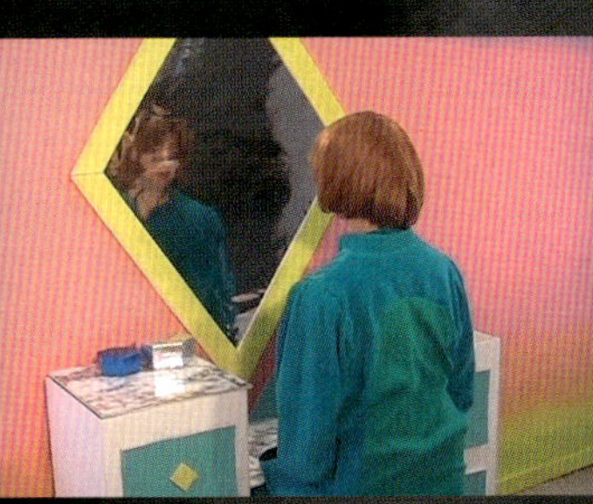
01:29

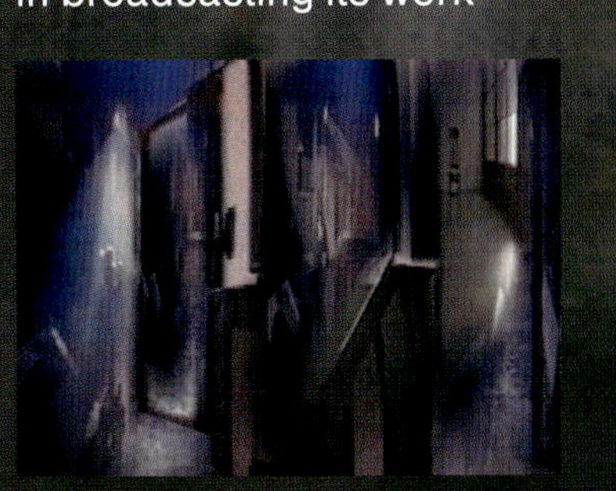
00:26

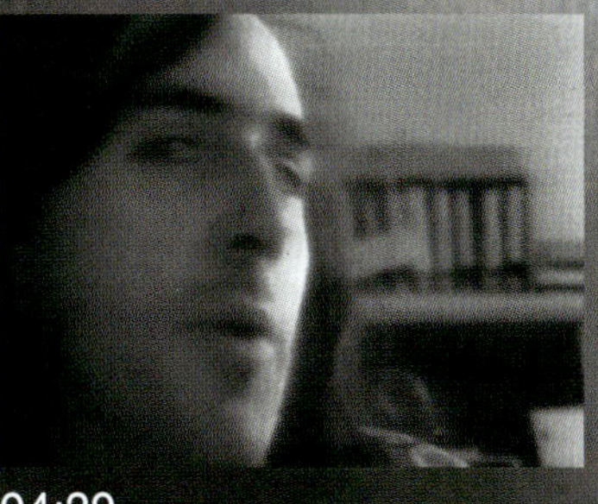
04:29

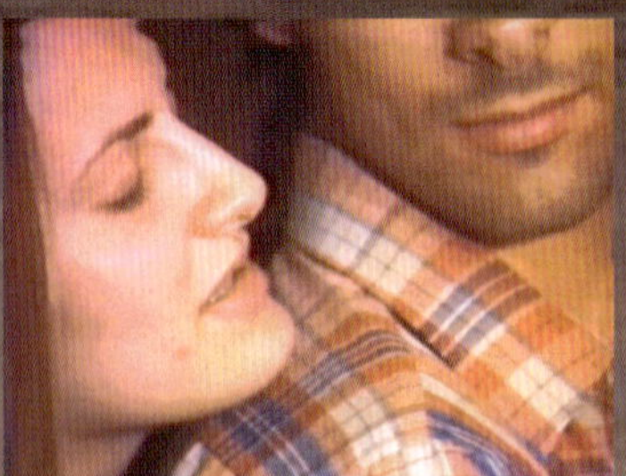
01:21

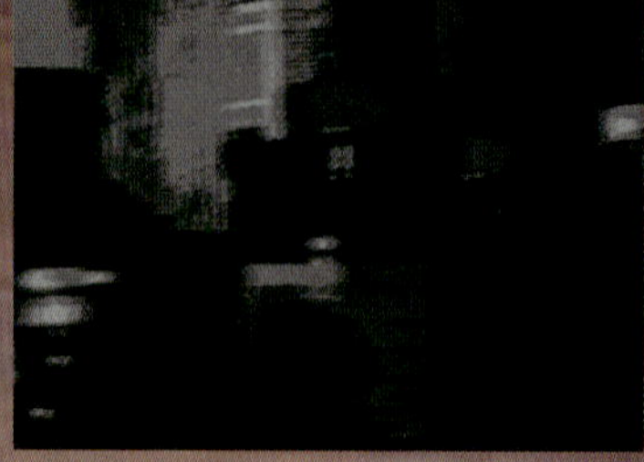
01:41

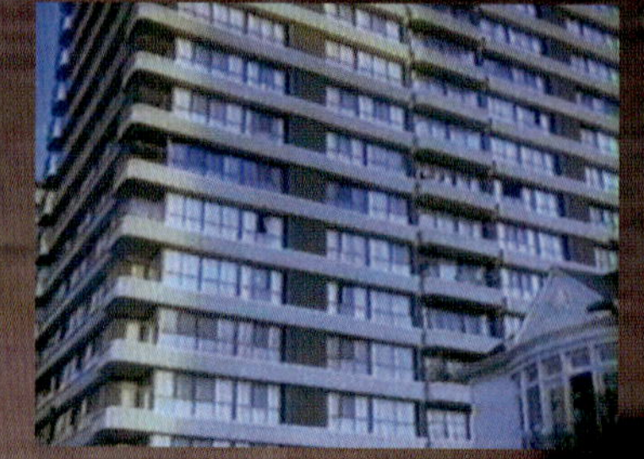
05:56

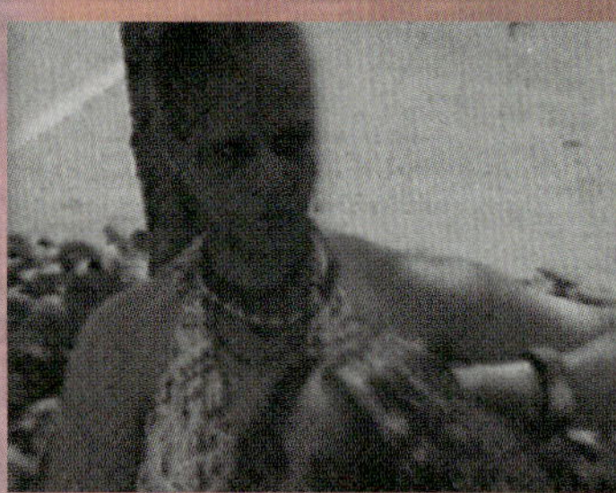
14:05

helped open television to other independent documentarians. DCTV is recognized as among the foremost producers of social-issue documentaries and advocacy journalism.

DCTV
VTR: Downtown Community Television Center, 1975, video, black-and-white and color, sound, 29:08 minutes

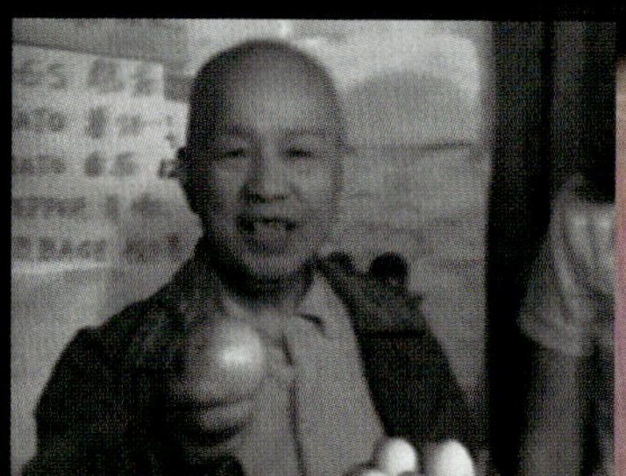

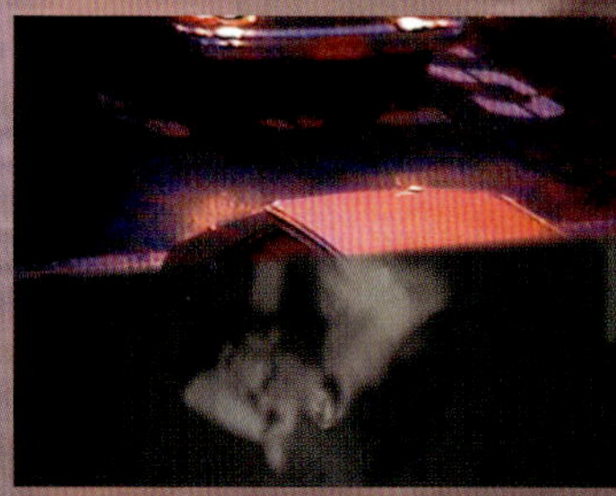
17:29

In this informational documentary, produced as part of the *Video Tape Review* series of New York public television station WNET/Thirteen, interviews with Jon Alpert and Keiko Tsuno are interspersed with excerpts from their extensive body of work.

07:17

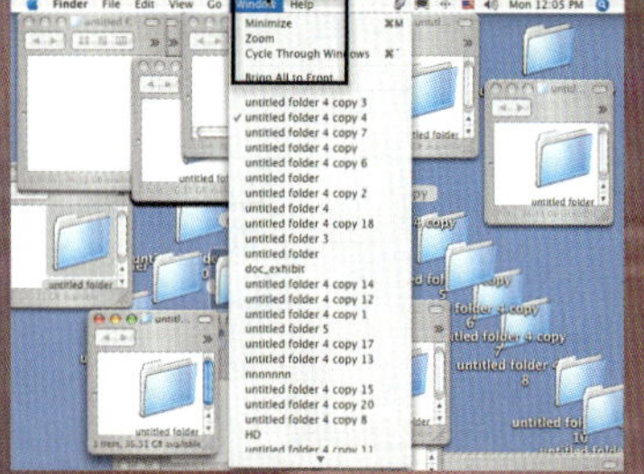

00:52

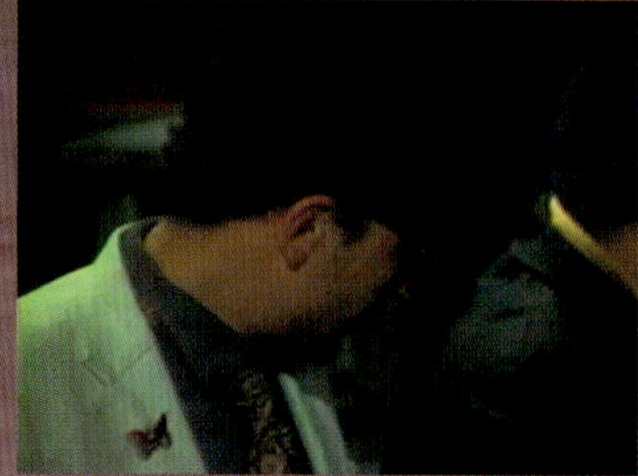
08:23

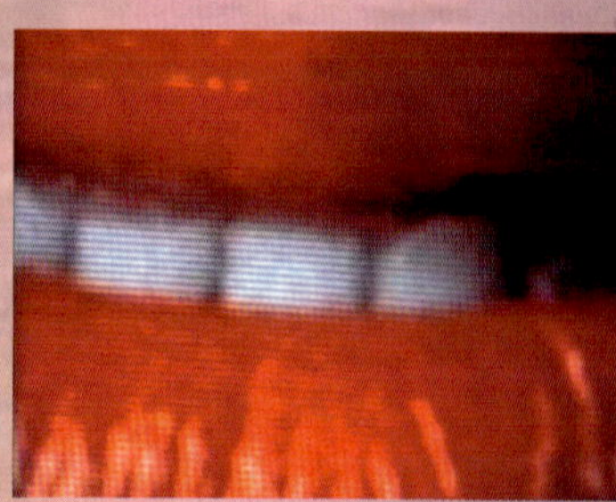
00:07

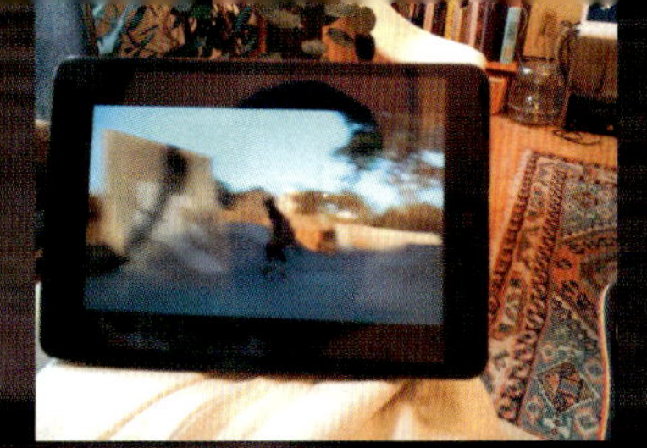
04:03

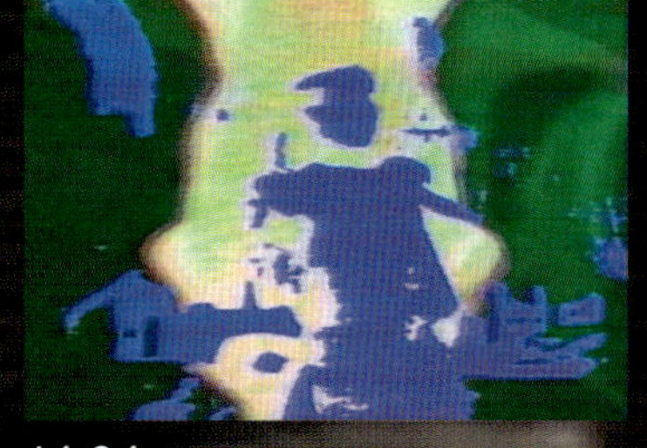
14:34

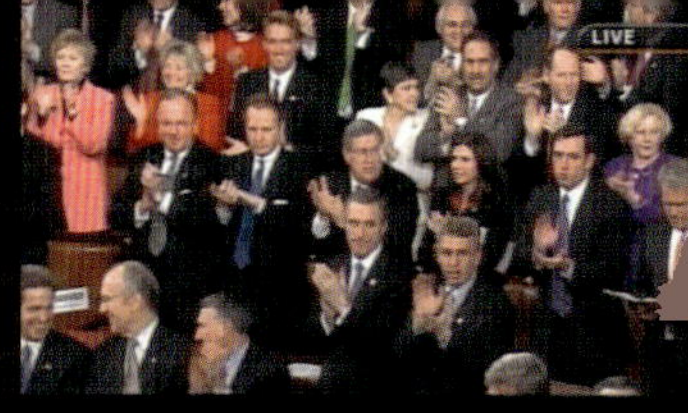

04:36

MARTHA ROSLER AND PAPER TIGER TELEVISION
In her work in video, phototext, performance, critical writing, and installation, Martha Rosler constructs incisive social and political analyses of the myths and realities of contemporary culture. Articulated with deadpan wit, Rosler's video works investigate how socioeconomic realities and political ideologies dominate ordinary life. Presenting astute critical analyses in accessible forms, Rosler's inquiries range from questions of public space to issues of war, women's experiences, and media information.

Paper Tiger Television (PTTV) is an open, nonprofit, volunteer video collective that began in 1981. Through the production and distribution of public access series, media literacy/video production workshops, community screenings, and grassroots advocacy, PTTV works to challenge and expose the corporate control of mainstream media. PTTV believes that increasing public awareness of the negative influence of mass media and involving people in the process of making media is mandatory for the long-term goal of information equity.

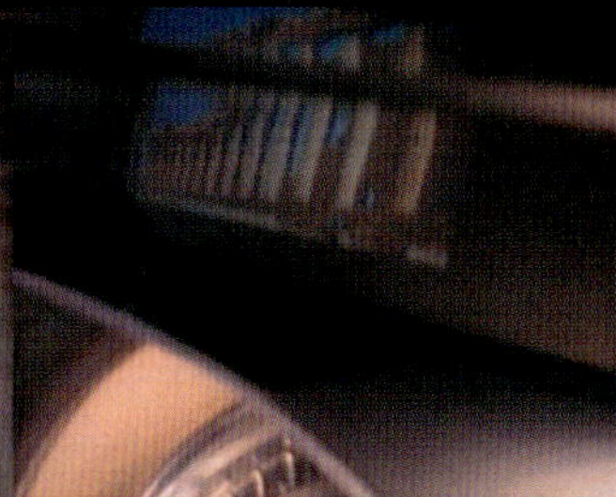
00:23

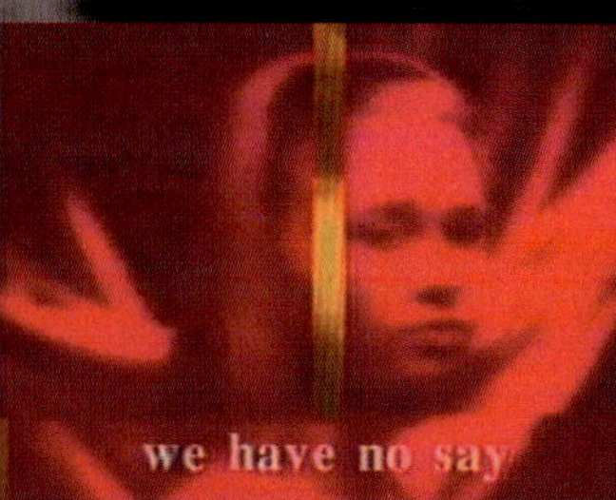

00:40

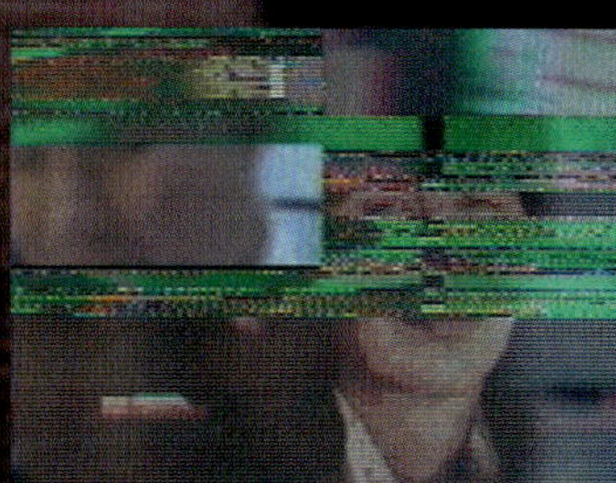
21:17

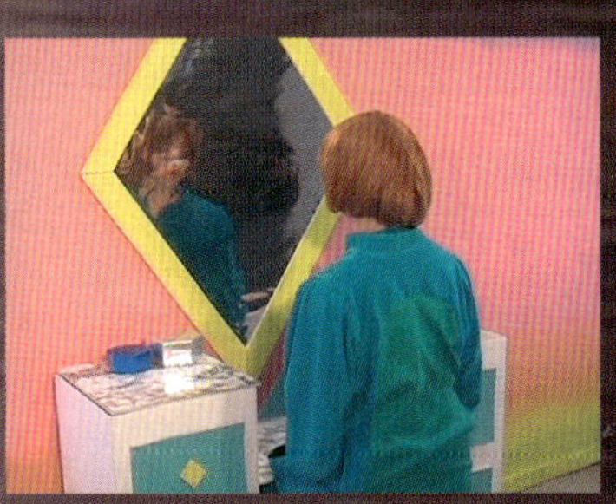
01:29

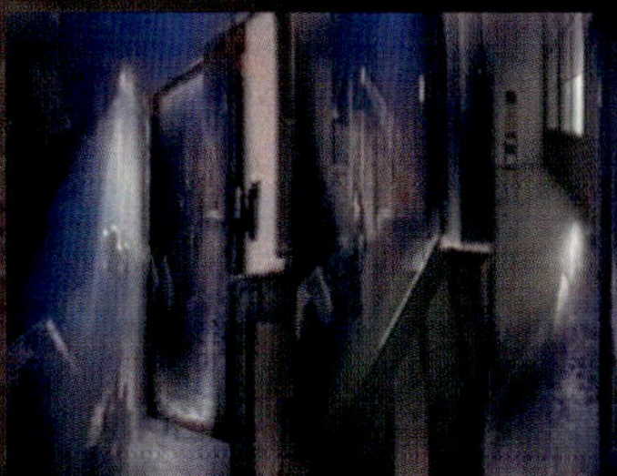
00:26

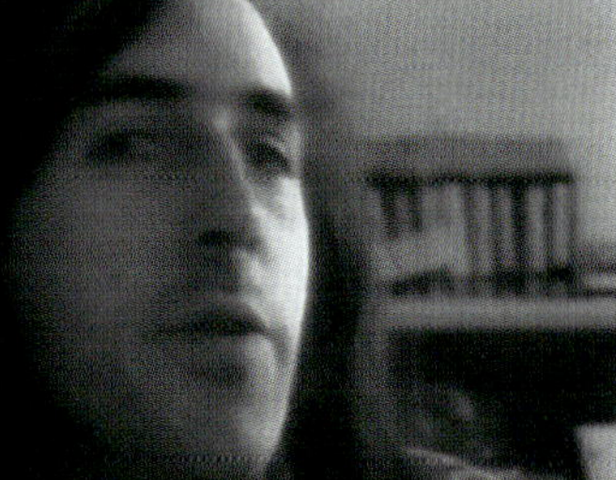
04:29

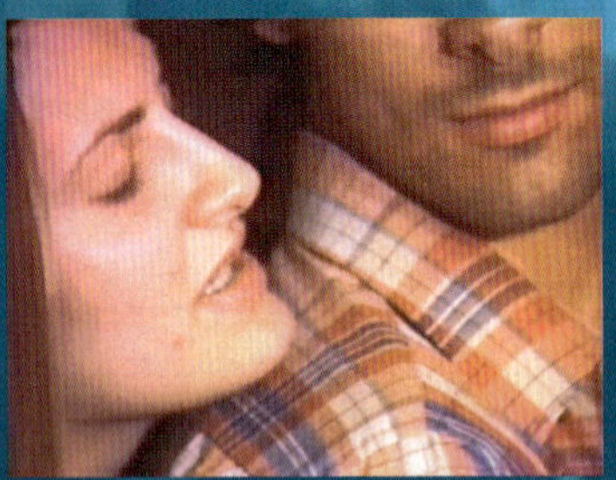
01:21

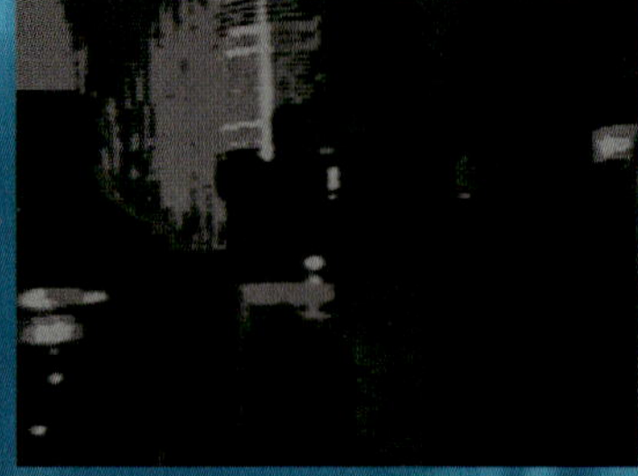
01:41

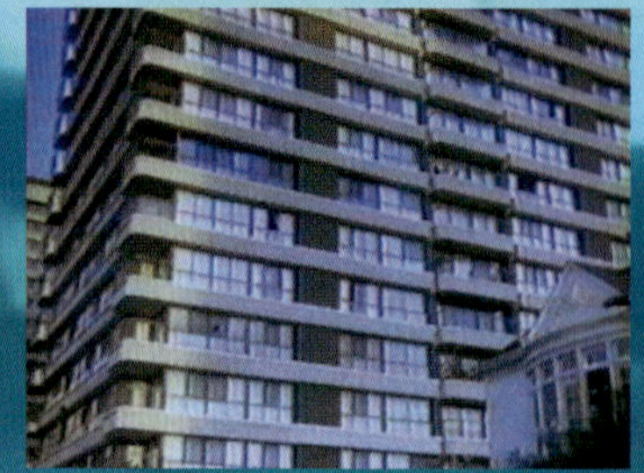
05:56

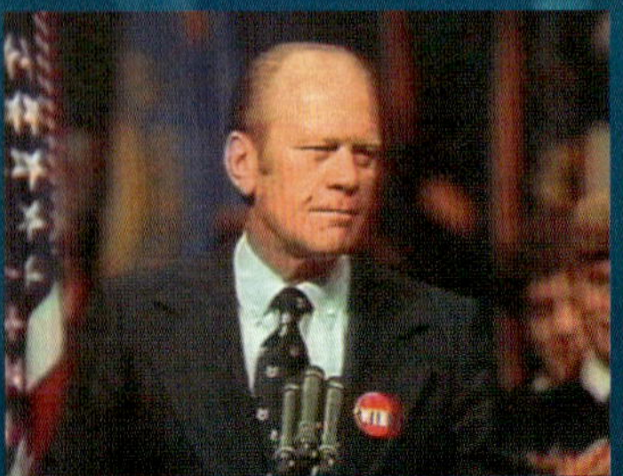
14:05

194 BROADCASTING: GUERRILLA MEDIA

MARTHA ROSLER AND PAPER TIGER TELEVISION
Born to Be Sold: Martha Rosler Reads the Strange Case of Baby $/M, 1988, video, color, sound, 35:18 minutes

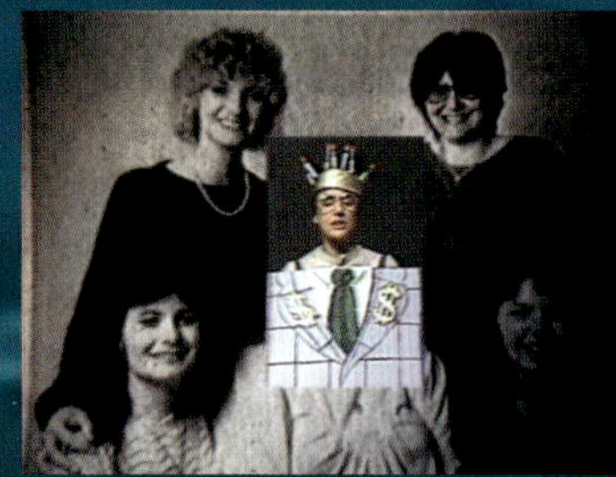

Born to be Sold is PTTV and Rosler's acerbic and witty interpretation of the notorious "Baby M" case, in which a natural—"surrogate"—mother and father of a baby fought each other for custody of the child. Rosler assumes various roles in the controversy: baby, sperm, lawyer, judge, and the two women in the case. Reconstructing the story from its trial by media and court transcripts, Rosler views surrogate mother Mary Beth Whitehead's actions as an attempt to defy the identity assigned by her class and gender, and sees the verdict favoring the Sterns as an endorsement of the father's phallic right, his jurisprudential entitlement. Her analysis demonstrates how political, class, and ideological systems are played out on the body of the woman.

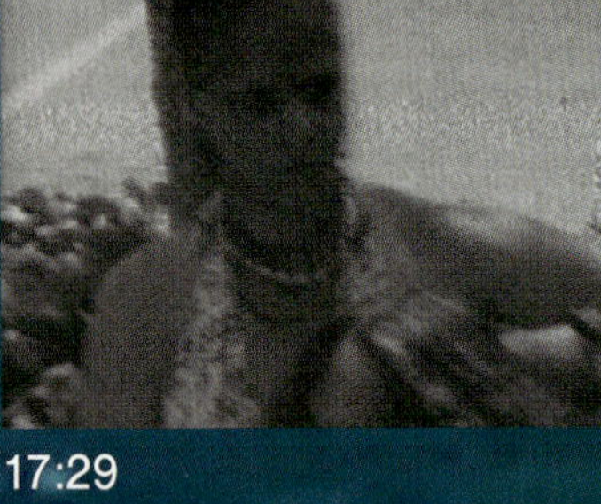
17:29

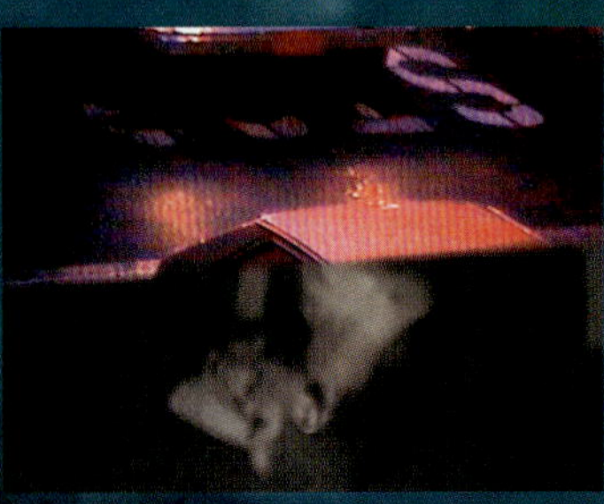
07:17

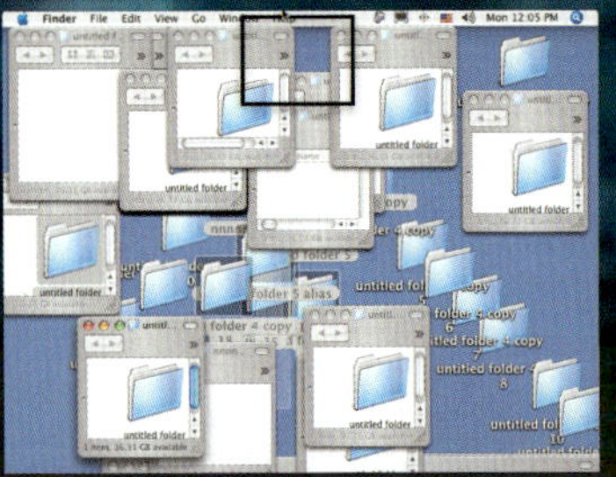
00:52

08:23

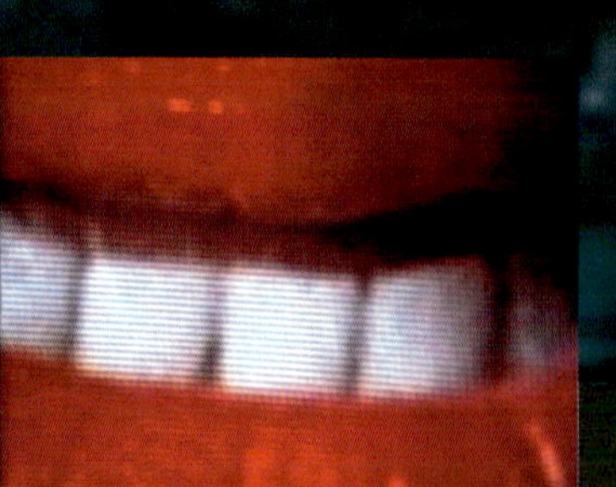
00:07

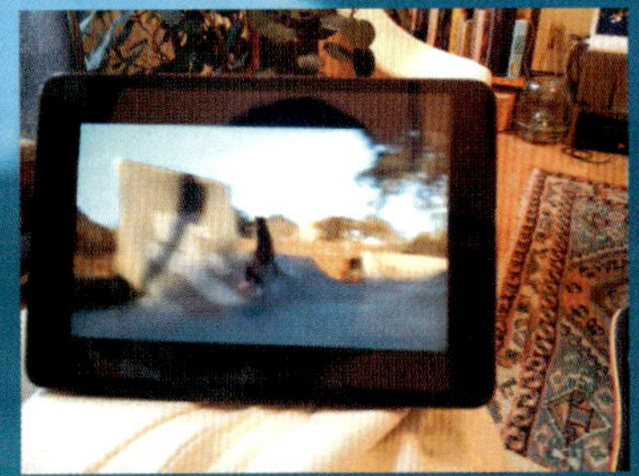

04:03

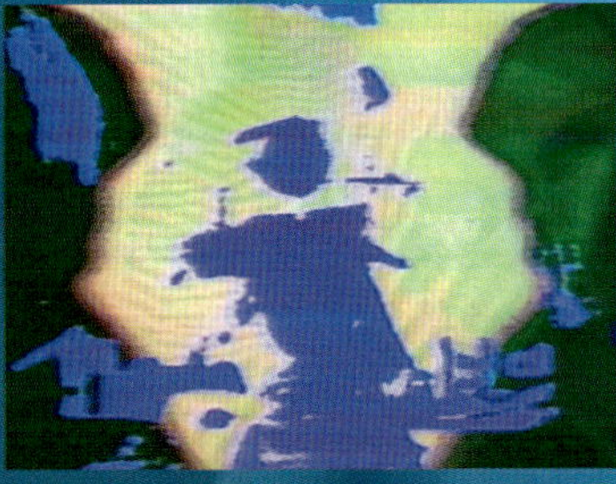

14:34

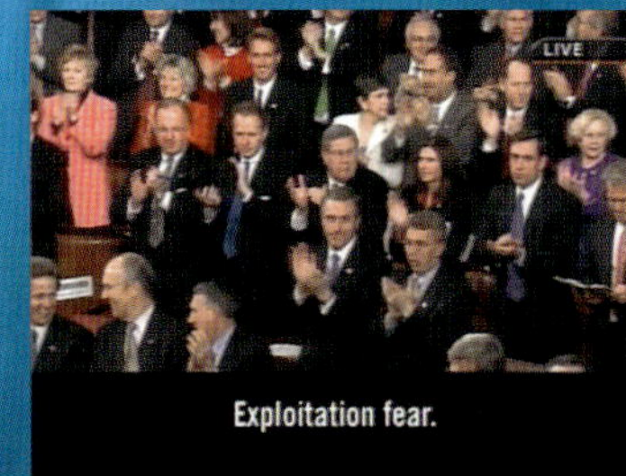

04:36

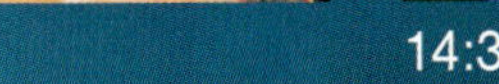

RADICAL SOFTWARE GROUP (RSG)
Radical Software Group is a loosely defined ensemble of artists and programmers, working collaboratively in digital media. The group was named in honor of *Radical Software*, the short-lived but seminal 1970s magazine that investigated nascent video technology with much the same irreverent spirit that RSG now brings to digital culture. The group, whose membership shift(ed) according to the project, has focused largely on network environments and interface design, including the award-winning software tool Carnivore.

RADICAL SOFTWARE GROUP (RSG)
RSG-BLACK-1, 2005, video, color, sound, 22:04 minutes

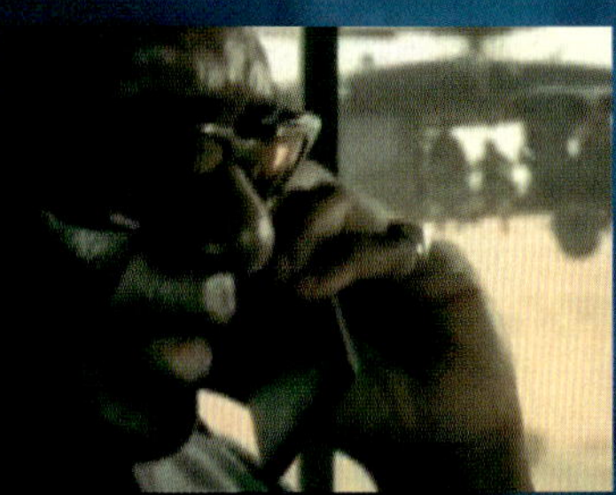

RSG-BLACK-1 is a new cut of a Hollywood blockbuster portrayal of a 1993 US raid in Somalia. In the RSG version, all the white characters have been programmatically edited out. The result is a 22-minute conceptual investigation of representation and ideology. A timely and chilling critique, the narrative highlights the entertainment industry's images of those it sees as "other."

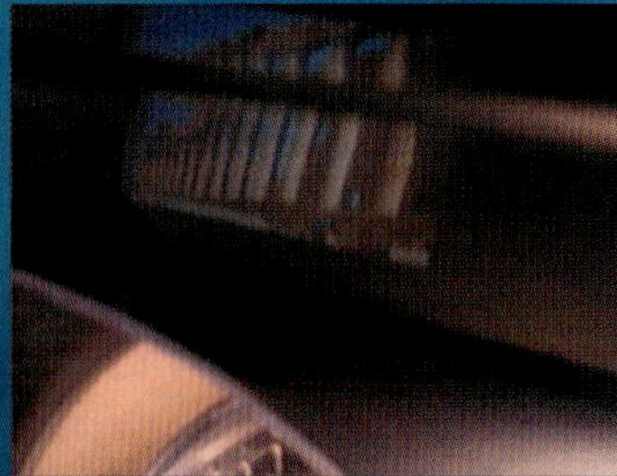

00:23

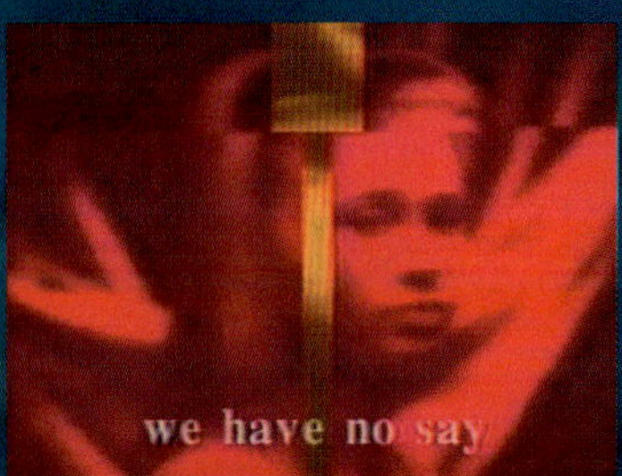

00:40

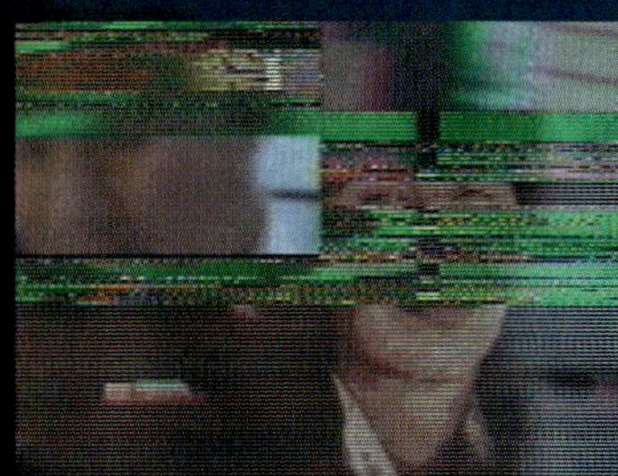

21:17

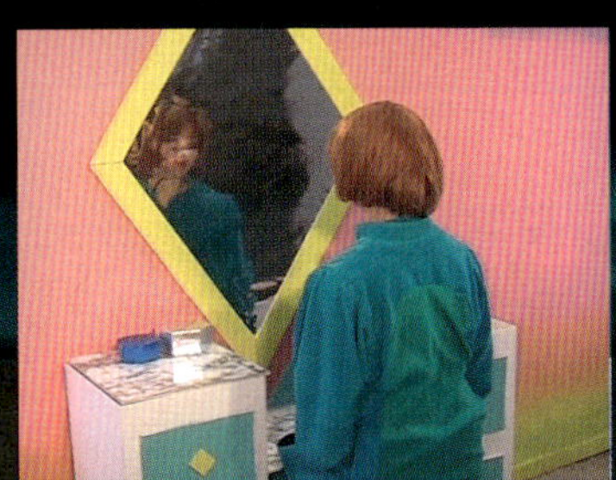

01:29

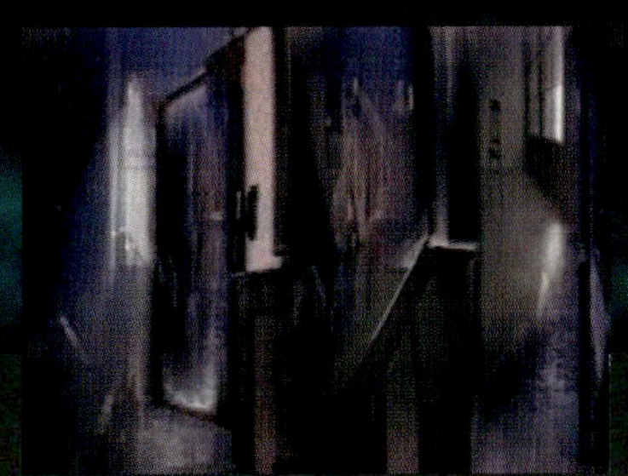

00:26

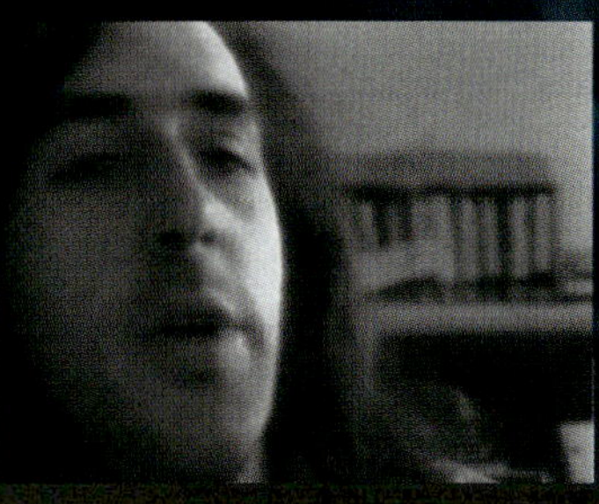

04:29

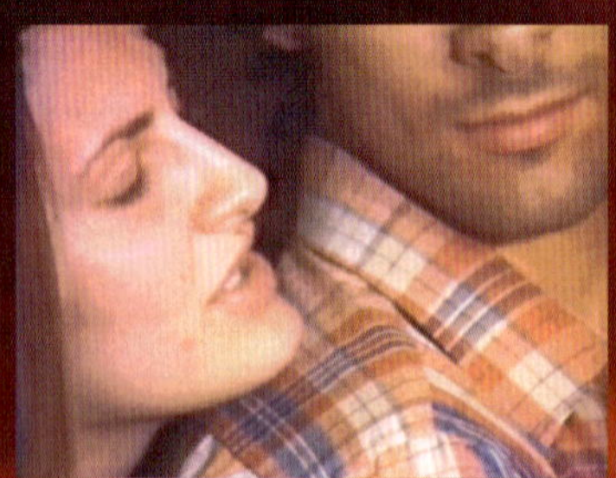

01:21

01:41

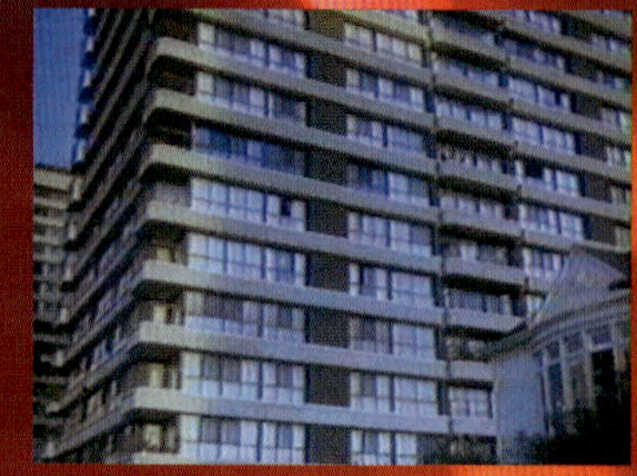

05:56

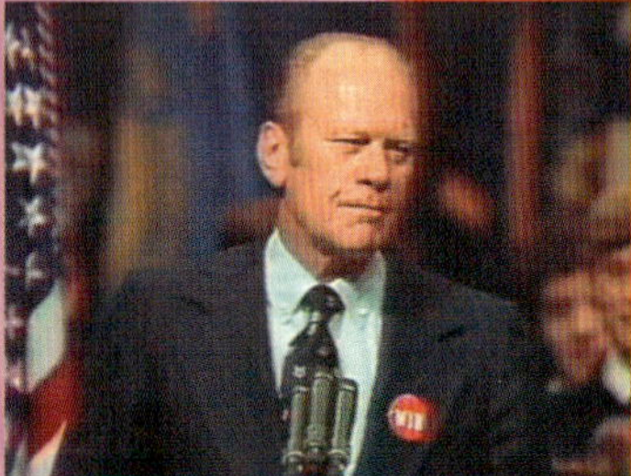

14:05

196 BROADCASTING: GUERRILLA MEDIA

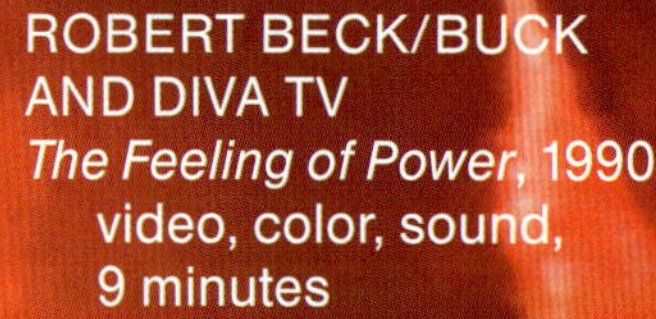

ROBERT BECK/BUCK AND DIVA TV
The Feeling of Power, 1990, video, color, sound, 9 minutes

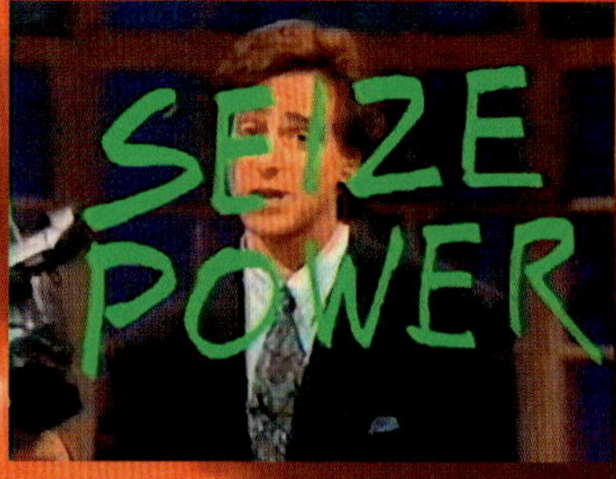

The urgency of the AIDS crisis and issues around the politics of identity and representation were catalysts for a new wave of activist movements in the late 1980s and early 1990s. With the increasing availability of relatively inexpensive video equipment, artists and activists (in an echo of the late 1960s and 1970s) again took up video as a political tool, turning to editing facilities like EAI to produce works that challenged the images and narratives of mainstream media with empowered self-representations. One such group was DIVA TV, or Damned Interfering Video Activist Television, an affinity group of ACT UP that formed in 1989. In *The Feeling of Power*, artist, EAI editor, and DIVA TV member Robert Beck/Buck documents a 1989 ACT UP protest at Trump Tower and offers a self-reflexive manifesto of this new video activism.

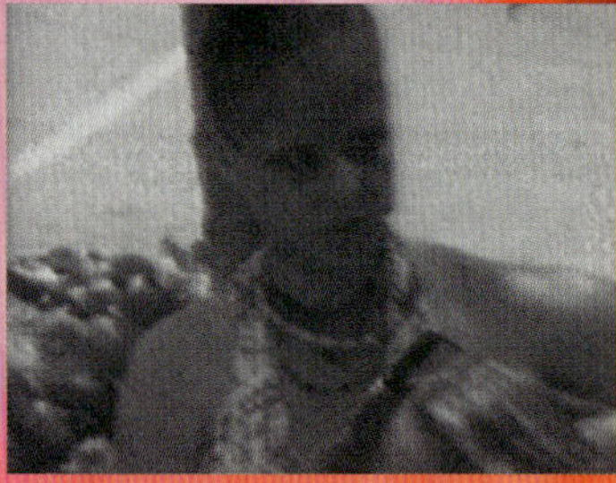

17:29

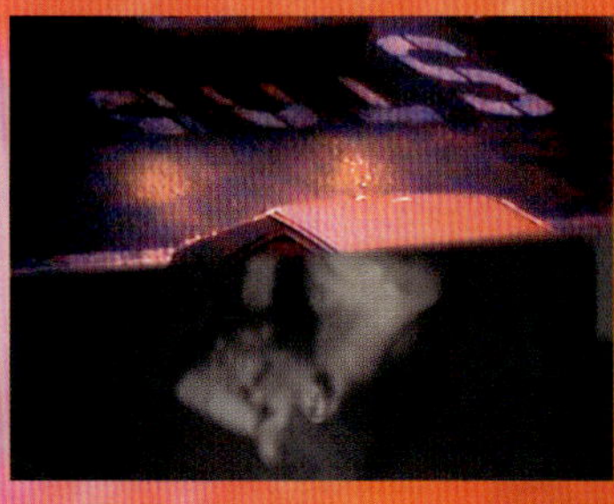

07:17

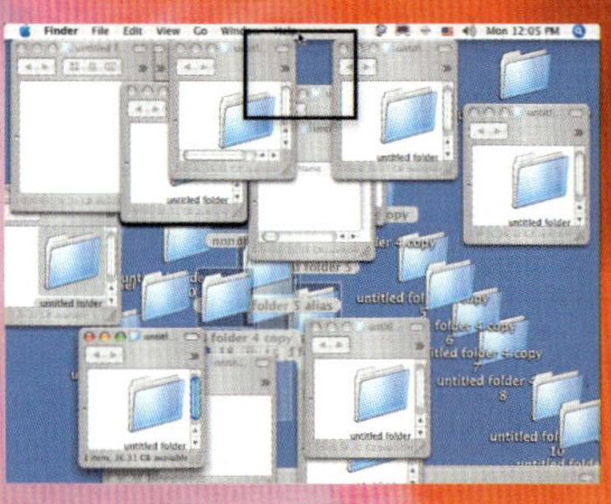

00:52

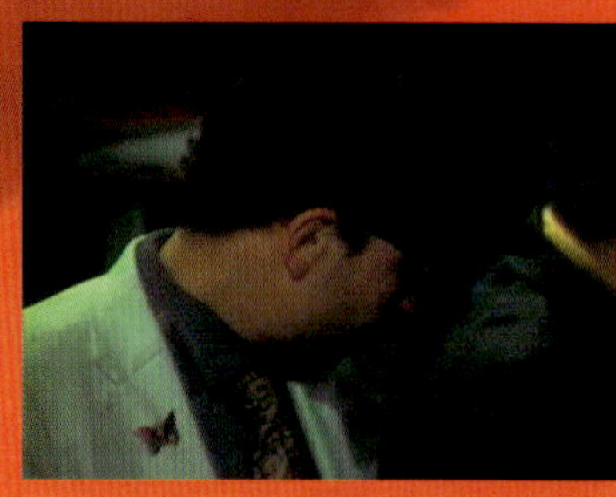

08:23

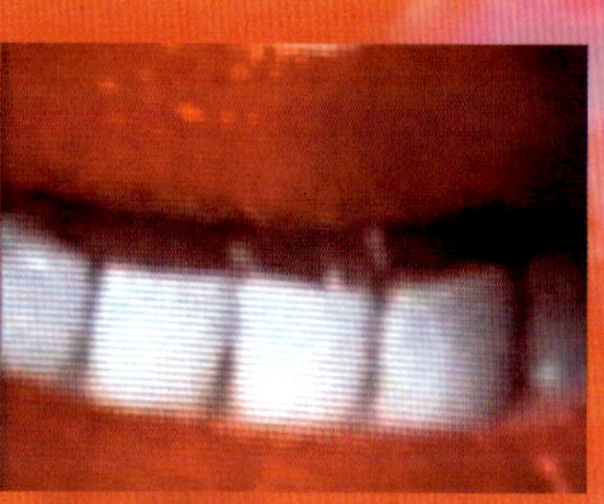

00:07

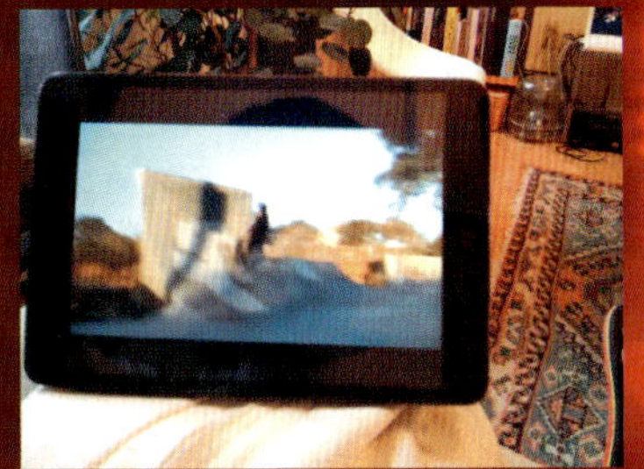

04:03

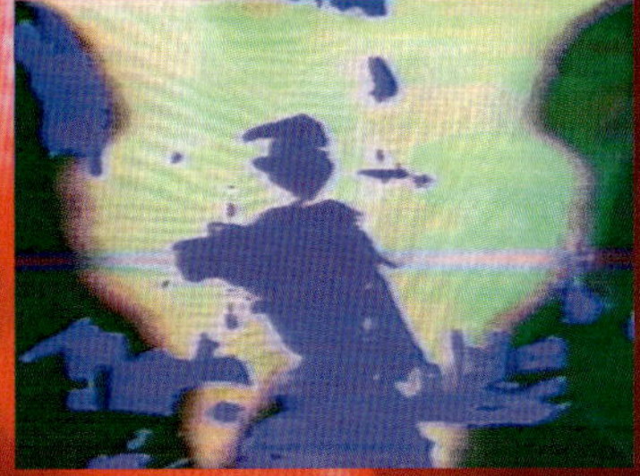

14:34

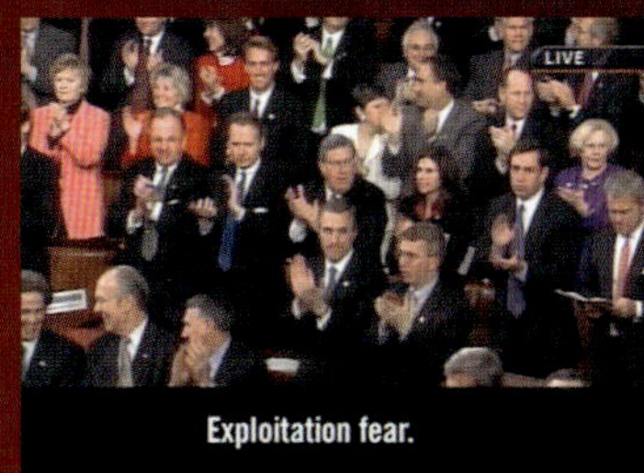

04:36

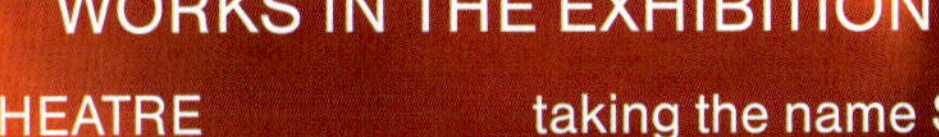

SQUAT THEATRE

Squat Theatre—whose core members included Stephan Balint, Peter Berg, Eva Buchmuller, Peter Halasz, and Anna Koos—was a major presence in New York's downtown art and theater scene from 1977 until 1985. The collective formed in Budapest, Hungary, as an independent theater company in 1970, during the Cold War. After their performances were banned by the Hungarian government, they resorted to performing in members' apartments—a solution they embraced. In 1976 the authorities gave them the "choice" to either cease doing theater or leave the country and never return. Squat emigrated, first to Paris and then to New York. In 1977, the company presented its first storefront play, a commission by the Rotterdam Arts Council in The Netherlands, taking the name Squat Theatre. Partially inspired by the squatter movement in the West, the company's new name also grew out of their determination to occupy blank spots on the map of artistic and intellectual terrain.

After emigrating to New York, Squat Theatre rented a four-story building on West 23rd Street, which they would occupy until 1985. The ground-floor storefront became a performance space, and the collective lived on the floors above. Seated on risers in the back of the store, spectators faced a stage in front of a window that looked out onto the street, providing a permanent, live, and often highly theatrical background to the performances. The action of an unscripted play would unfold in the space between

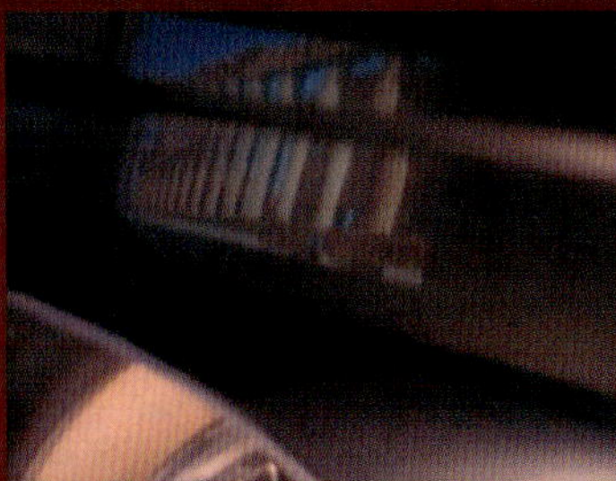

00:23

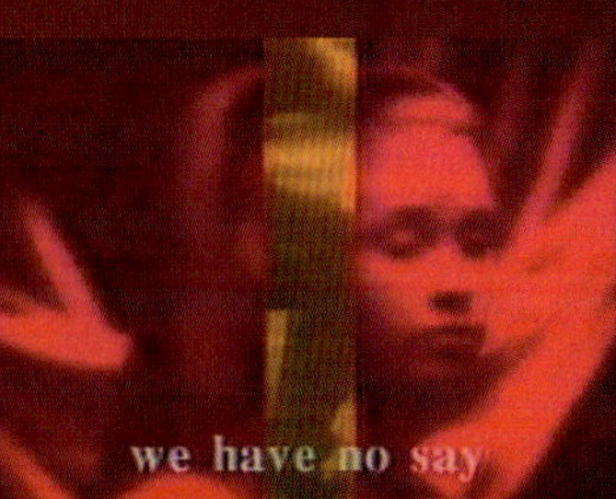

00:40

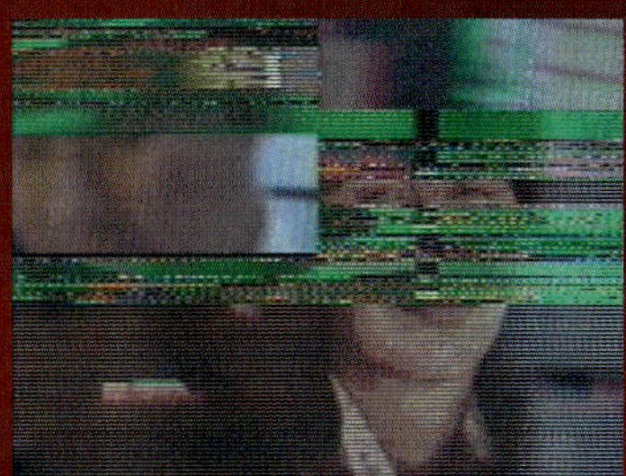

21:17

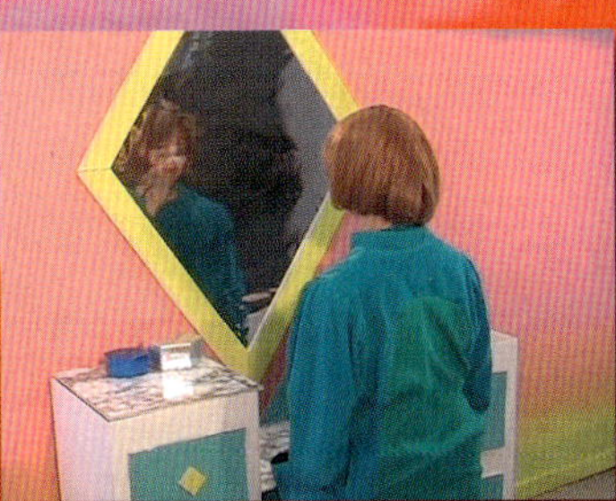

01:29

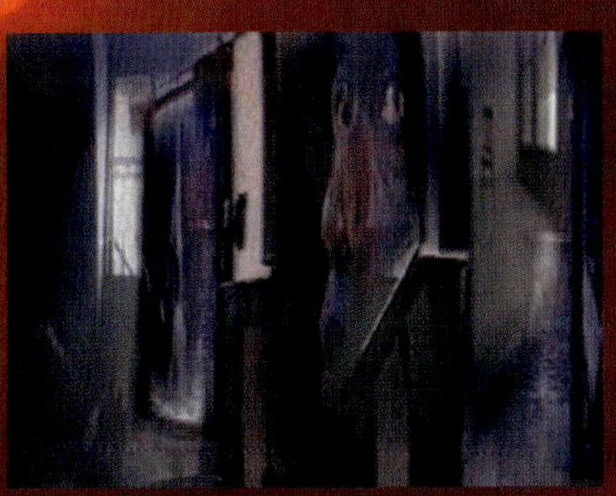

00:26

04:29

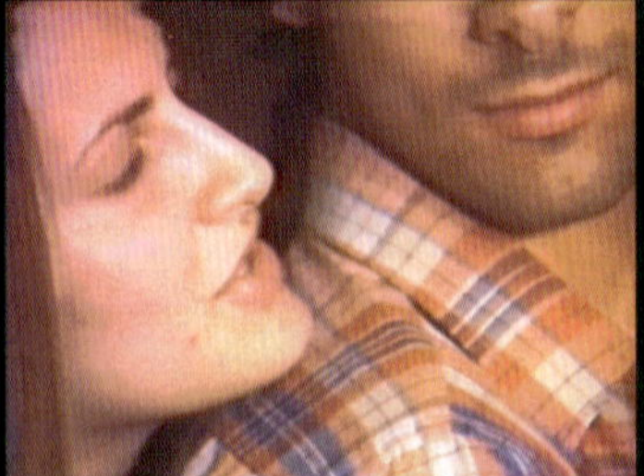

01:21

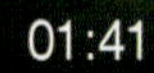

01:41

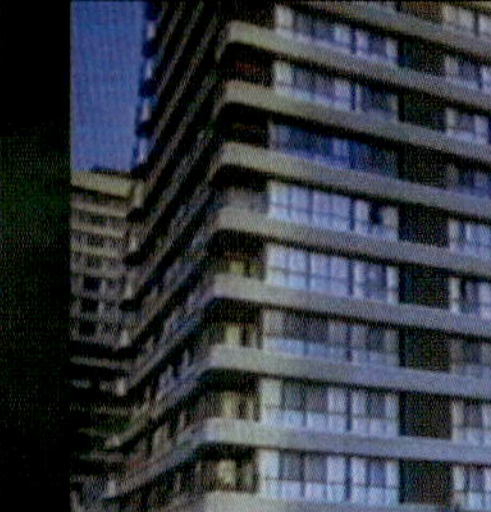

05:56

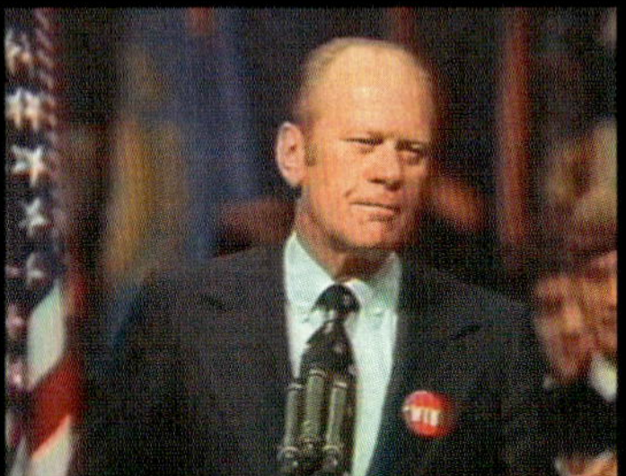

14:05

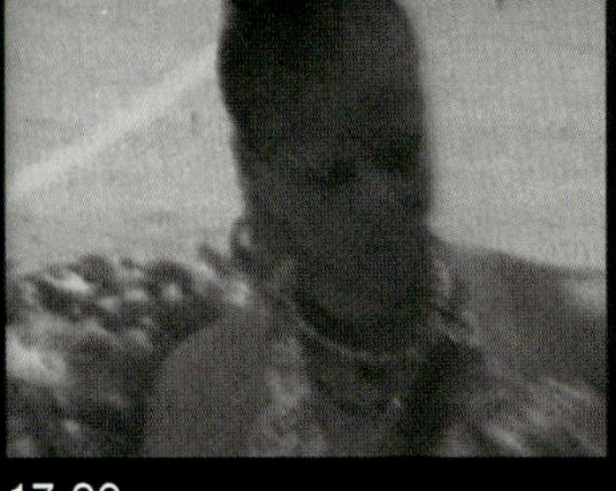

17:29

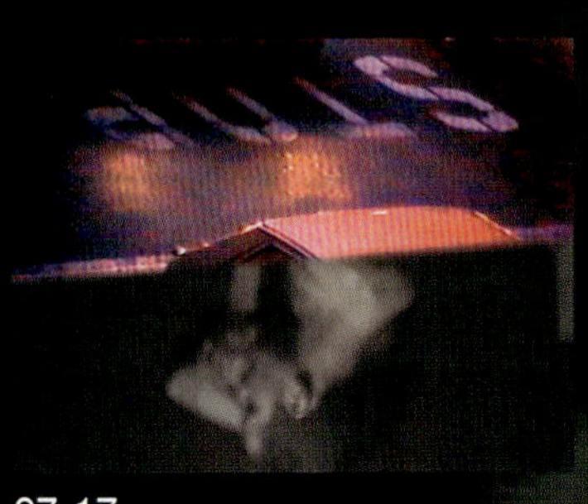

07:17

the audience and the window, often inviting unwitting participation by the outside world. The space also functioned as a venue for jazz, no-wave, and funk music, featuring performers such as John Lurie's Lounge Lizards, Sun Ra, and Defunkt.

With its radical notions of theater, Squat questioned role playing, the act of spectatorship, and the boundaries between art and life, the fictive and the real. In an essay in the catalog for the 1996 Squat Theatre exhibition at Artists Space, Alisa Solomon wrote: "Squat made spectators regard themselves in the act of spectating, and contemplate the complicity of their imagination in the construction of fictive events. Luring us back and forth over the boundary between art and life, they didn't seek to make that boundary vanish . . . . The result was a series of cognitive double-takes, each startling and instantaneous, and complicating the one that had come before.

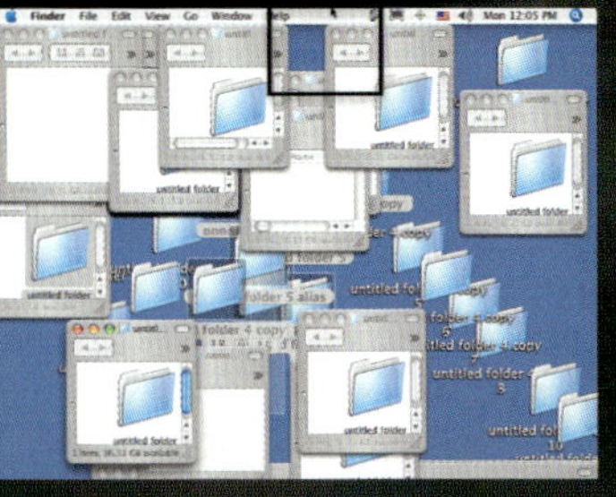

00:52

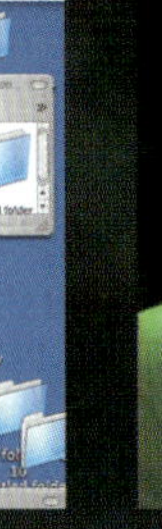

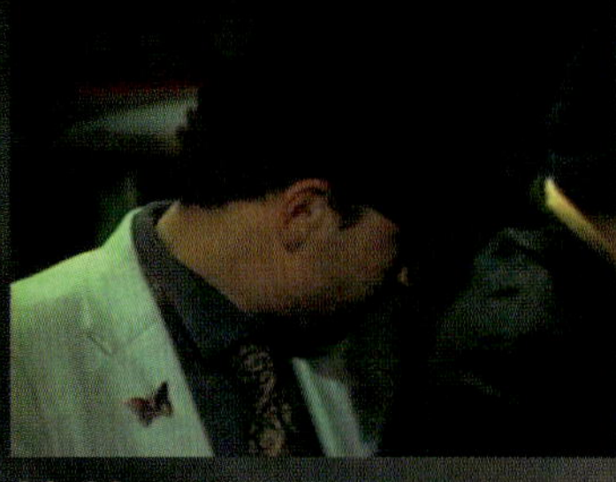

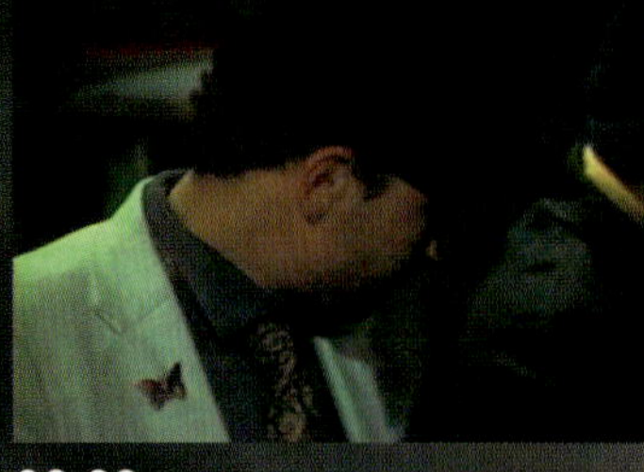

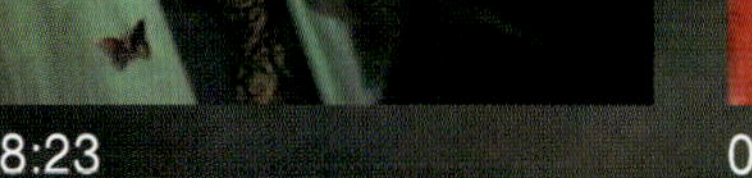

08:23

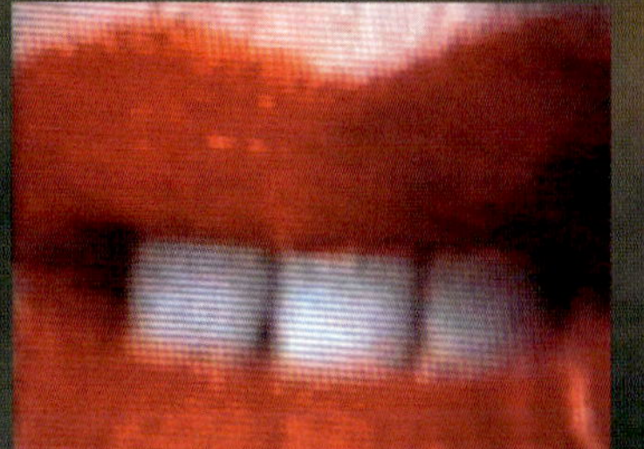

00:07

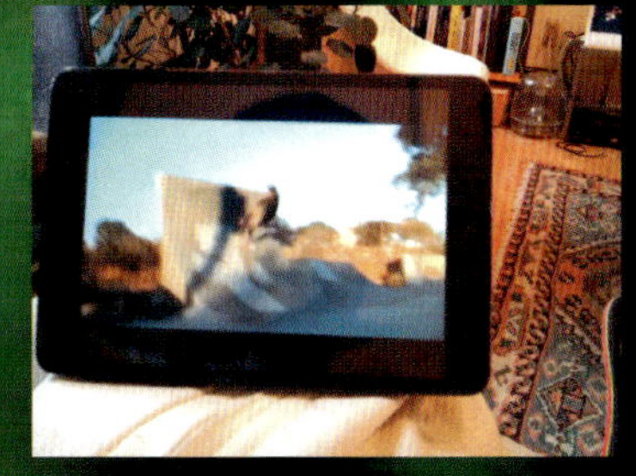

04:03

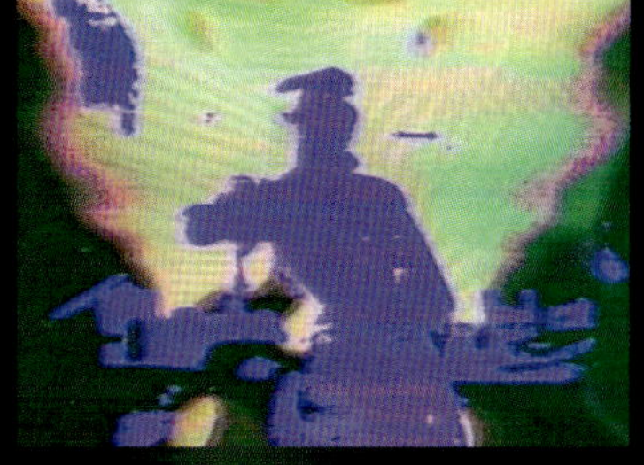

14:34

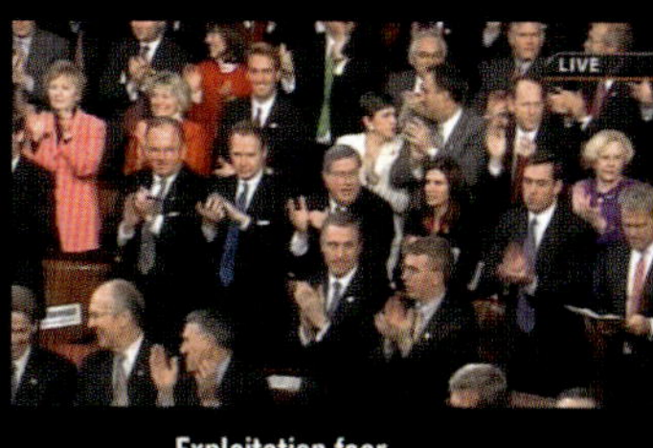

04:36

SQUAT THEATRE
Andy Warhol's Last Love, 1978–1981, video, black-and-white and color, sound, 60 minutes

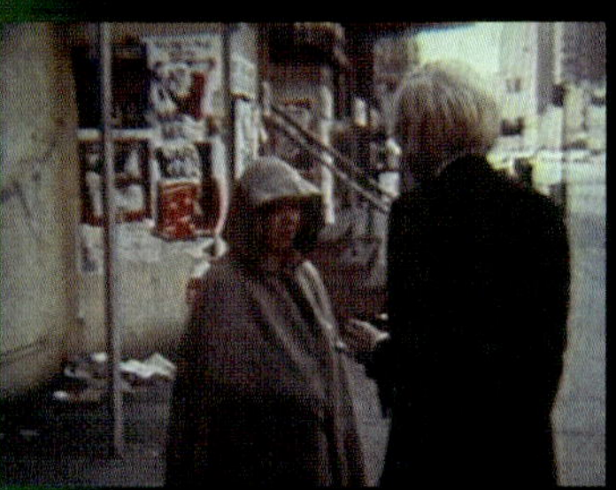

Performance Camera: Larry Solomon.
An Imperial Message camera: Michel Auder.
Editor: Roughcut Studio.
Music: Blondie, Kraftwerk
Appearance by Kathleen Kendel as the White Witch.

How did Andy Warhol meet Ulrike Meinhof? By chance. Meinhof is one of the legends of our age, her personality as tragically failing as Warhol's. Completely his opposite, she turned politics into tragic poetry; she had to meet Warhol, who turned exhausted art into daily food. The artist who gained freedom in complete unity with the existing world and the revolutionary who did not find freedom until death—they had things to say to each other. Documentation of this live performance includes the film piece, *An Imperial Message*, the text of which is taken from a parable by Franz Kafka; it depicts the bizarre encounter between the character of Warhol, who rides horseback through the city streets, and Meinhof, played by child actor Eszter Balint, known later for her performance in Jim Jarmusch's *Stranger Than Paradise*.

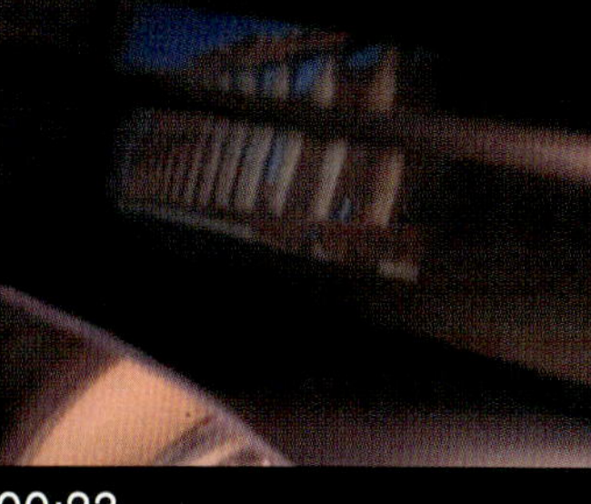

00:23

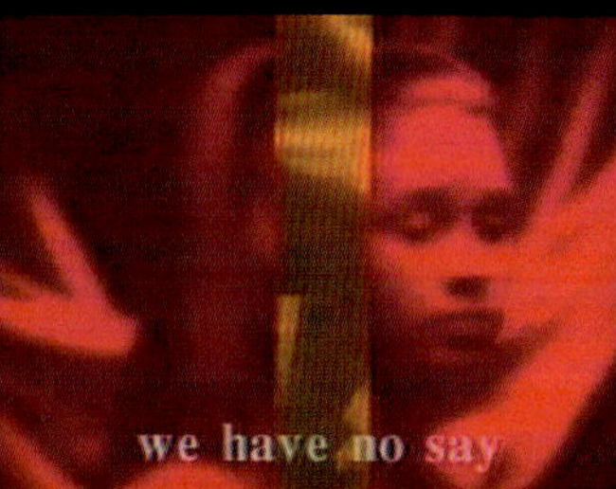

00:40

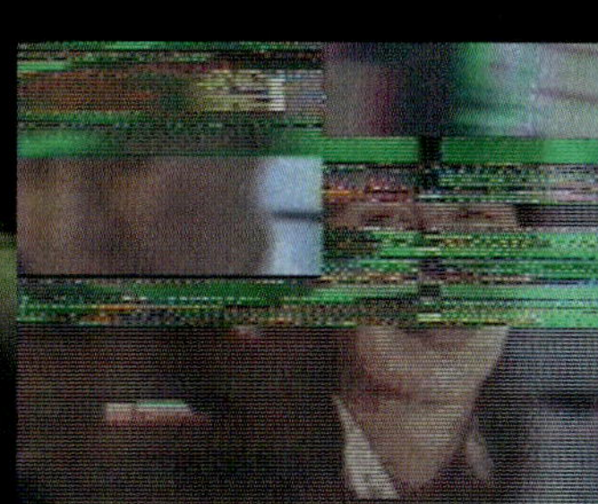

21:17

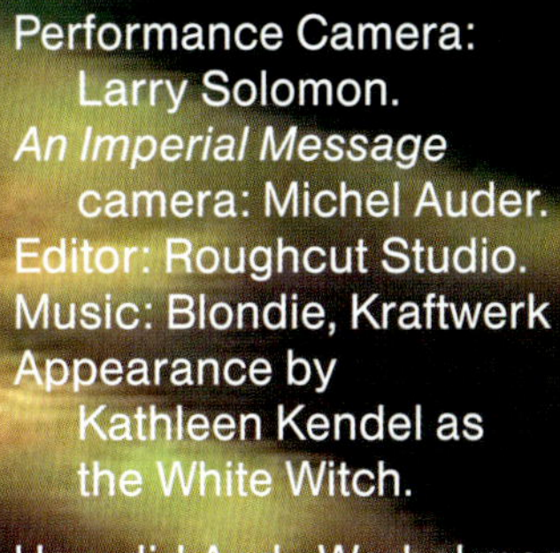

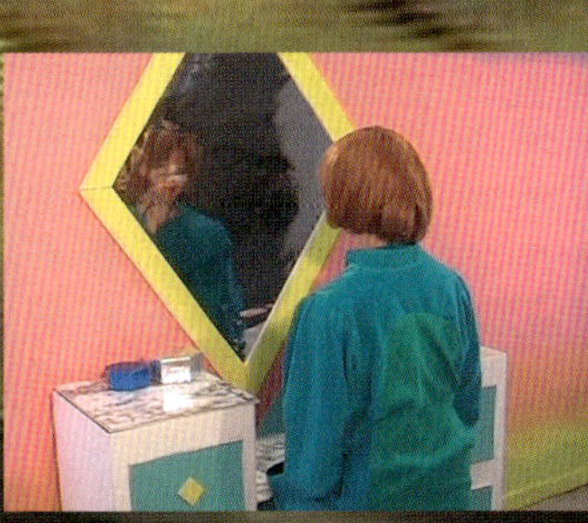

01:29

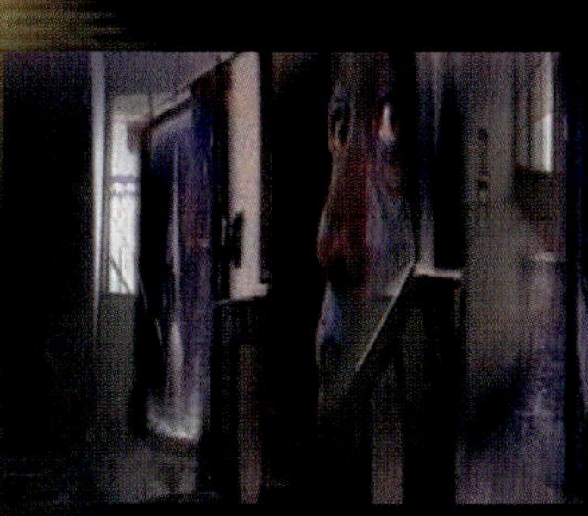

00:26

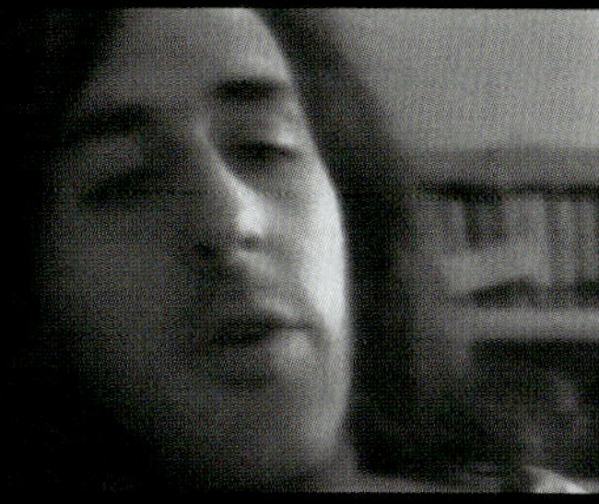

04:29

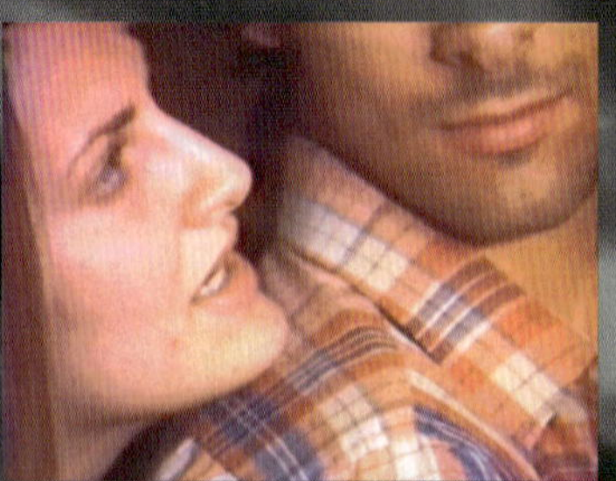

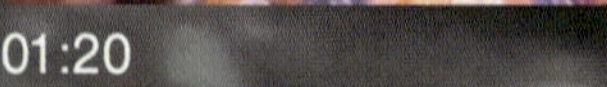

01:20

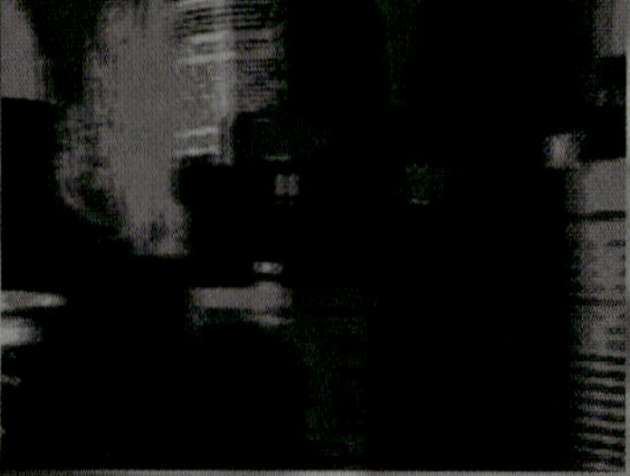

01:40

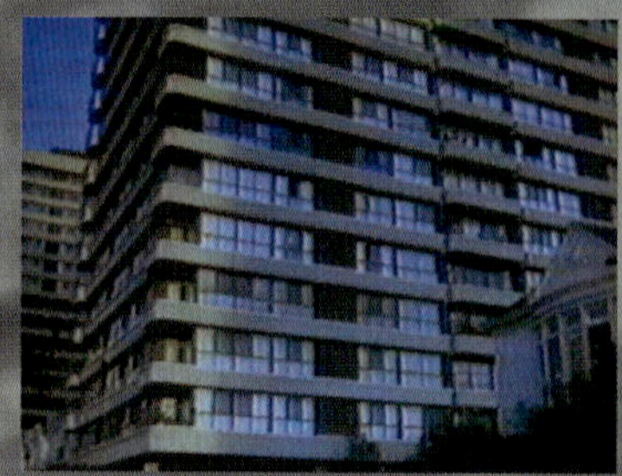

05:55

200 BROADCASTING: GUERRILLA MEDIA

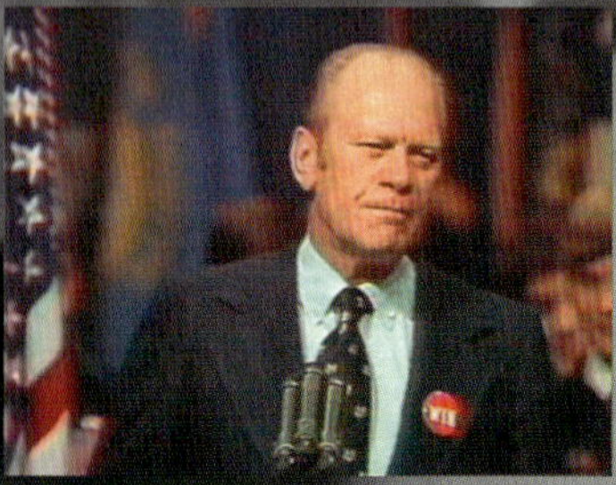

14:04

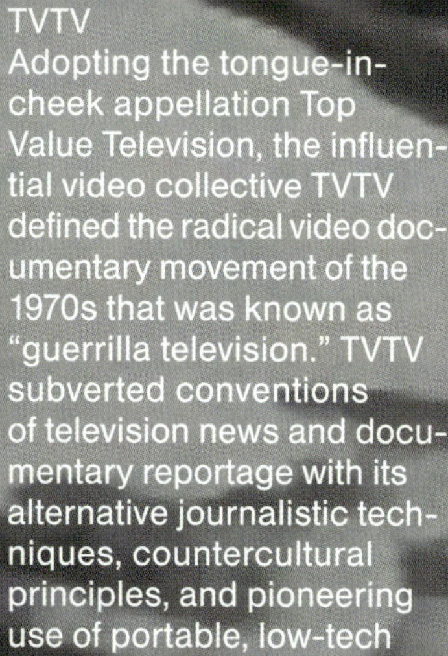

TVTV

Adopting the tongue-in-cheek appellation Top Value Television, the influential video collective TVTV defined the radical video documentary movement of the 1970s that was known as "guerrilla television." TVTV subverted conventions of television news and documentary reportage with its alternative journalistic techniques, countercultural principles, and pioneering use of portable, low-tech video equipment.

With its roots in the Vietnam-era climate of political revolt, TVTV's philosophy was articulated in founding member Michael Shamberg's 1971 manifesto *Guerrilla Television*, a treatise that advocated video and public-access cable systems as tools of opposition and activism. Guerrilla television was envisioned as a radical break from the ideology and technocratic control of broadcast television, a means to "demonstrate the potential of decentralized video technology."

Originally organized to provide alternative news coverage of the 1972 Republican and Democratic presidential conventions in Miami, TVTV was an ad hoc collective that at times included such videomakers as Shamberg, Skip Blumberg, Nancy Cain, Allen Rucker, Hudson Marquez, and Megan Williams. The group's groundbreaking coverage of the 1972 conventions, which pioneered the use of portable, lightweight Portapak equipment for news-gathering, resulted in the award-winning programs *The World's Largest TV Studio* and *Four More Years*.

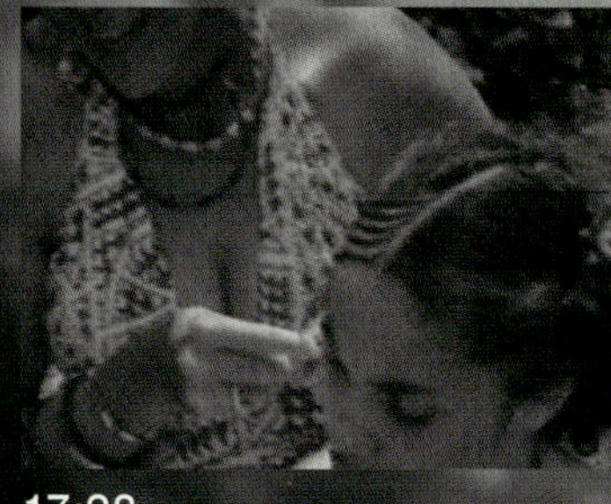

17:28

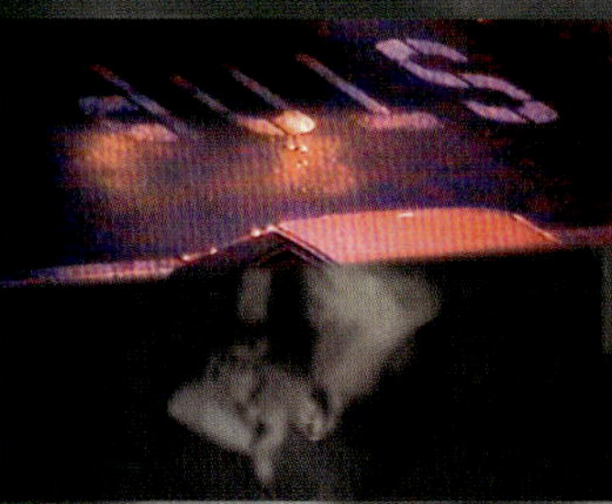

07:16

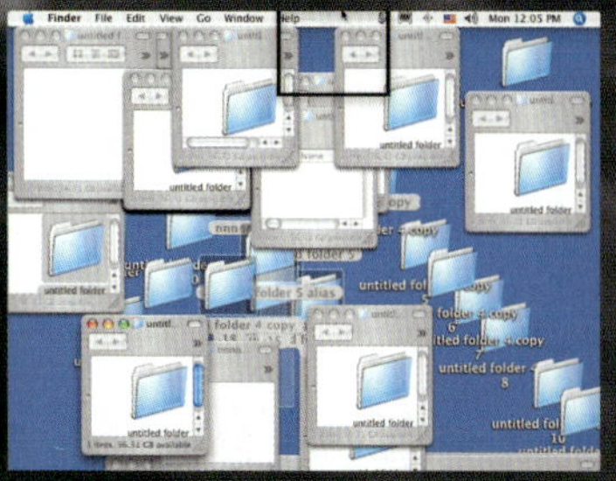

00:51

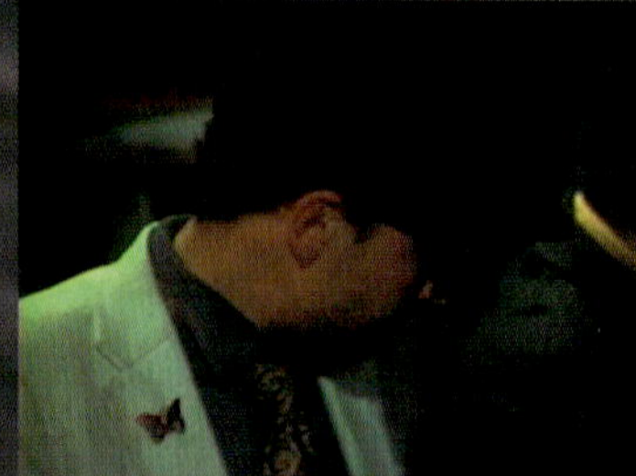

08:22

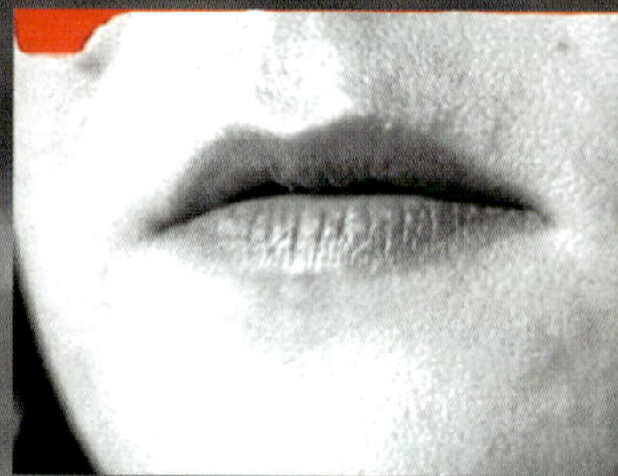

00:06

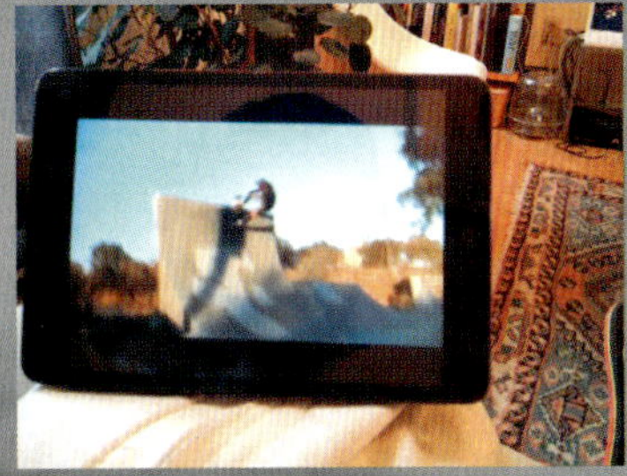

04:03

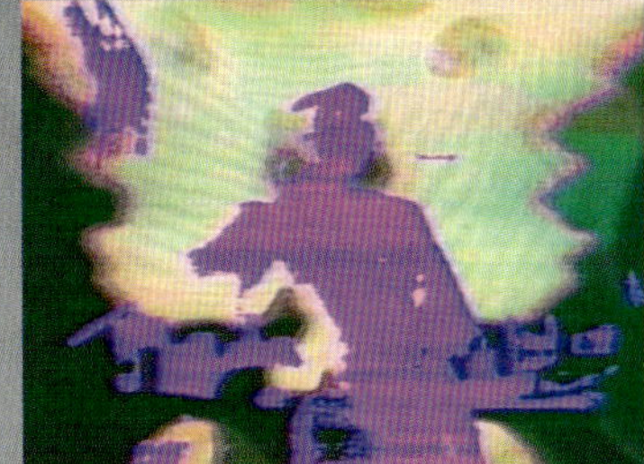

14:34

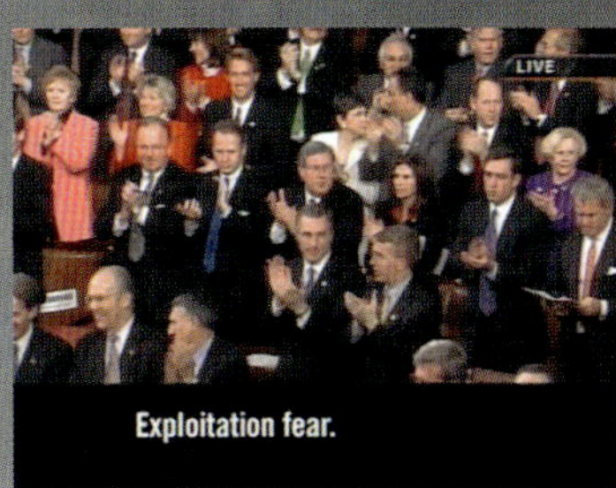

04:36

These landmark documentaries, which introduced an innovative, behind-the-scenes approach to broadcast journalism, are also vivid time capsules of an era. "Instead of stand-up reportage or sit-down analysis we wanted to see if TV could cover politics by letting people and events speak for themselves," wrote a TVTV member. Their irreverent skepticism toward the political establishment, and the access afforded by their low-tech equipment, resulted in an irreverence and spontaneity that was unique in broadcast journalism. Their use of portable video systems influenced commercial television's now-standard use of mobile ENG (electronic news gathering) reporting.

While TVTV's freewheeling, subjective reportage and their debunking of the sacred cows of the political and media establishments were influenced by the New Journalism of the late 1960s and 1970s, the use of video as a vehicle for alternative communication was central to their project. TVTV production and editing crews included members of such video collectives as Raindance, Ant Farm, and Videofreex. In their coverage of political spectacles and media events, TVTV's signature techniques included deadpan, candid interviews, the use of such devices as fish-eye lenses and rudimentary graphics, and the absence of authoritative voiceover commentary.

TVTV produced an award-winning expose on the Guru Maharaj Ji and his followers, *The Lord of the Universe* (1974), the first Portapak video documentary produced for national

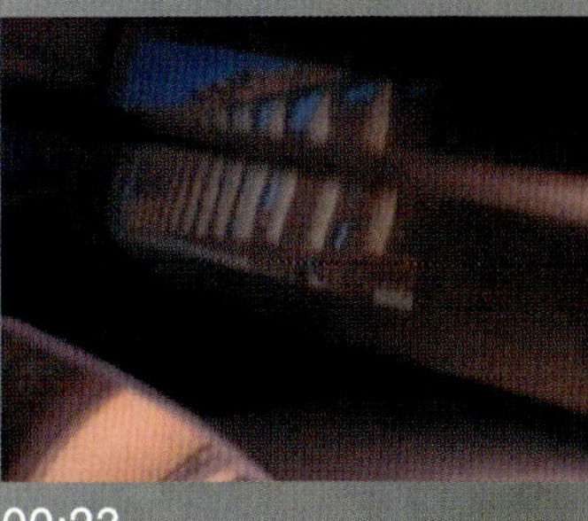

00:23

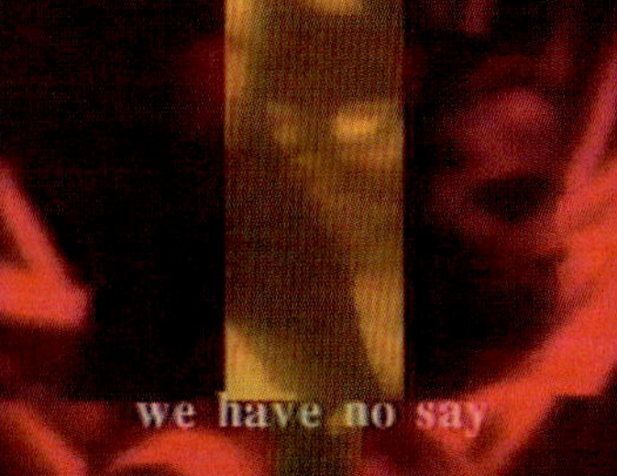

00:40

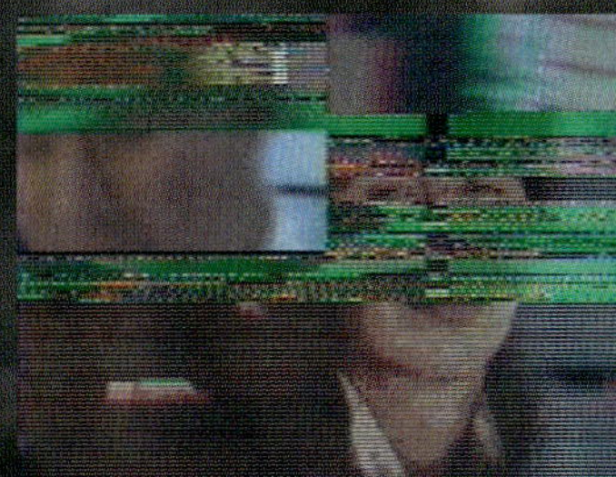

21:17

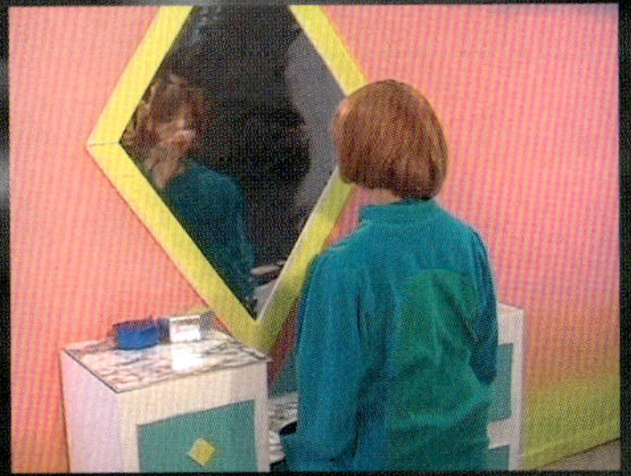

01:29

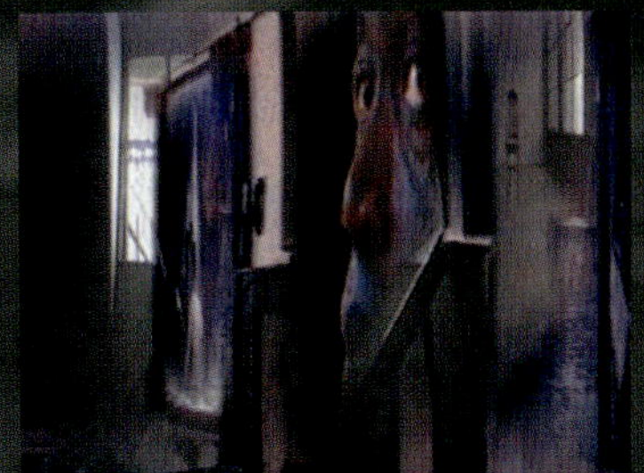

00:26

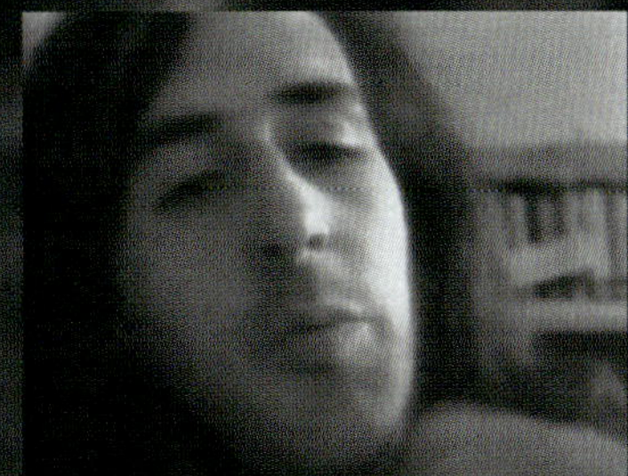

04:29

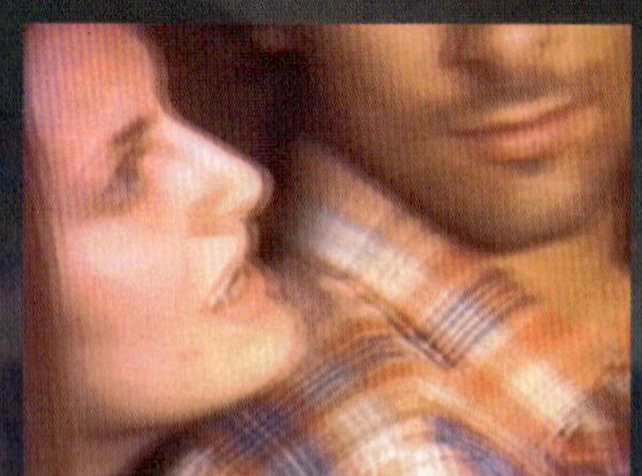

01:20

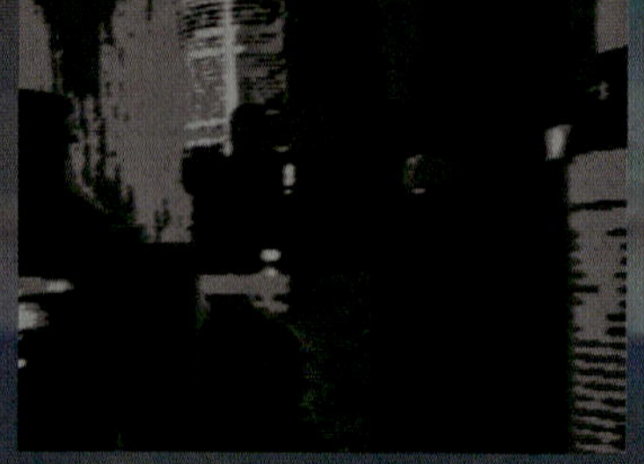

01:40

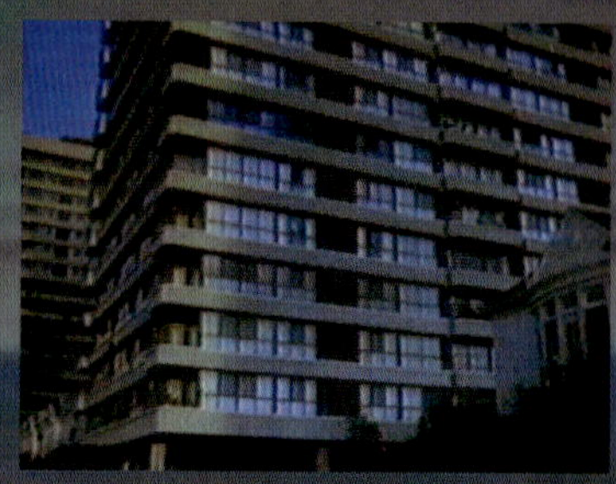

05:55

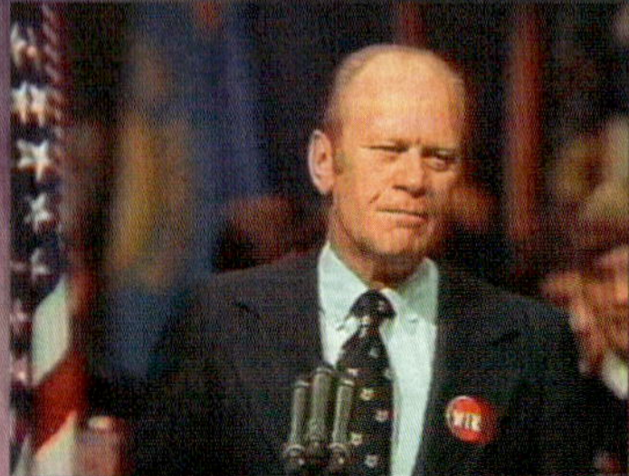

14:04

17:28

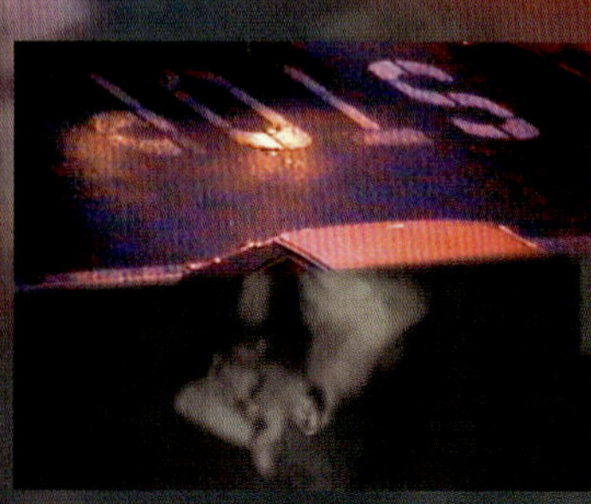

07:16

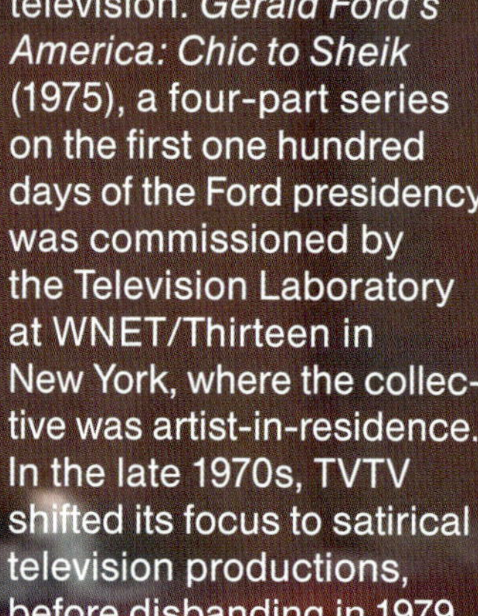

television. *Gerald Ford's America: Chic to Sheik* (1975), a four-part series on the first one hundred days of the Ford presidency, was commissioned by the Television Laboratory at WNET/Thirteen in New York, where the collective was artist-in-residence. In the late 1970s, TVTV shifted its focus to satirical television productions, before disbanding in 1979.

TVTV
Gerald Ford's America: Chic to Sheik, 1975, video, black-and-white and color, sound, 28 minutes

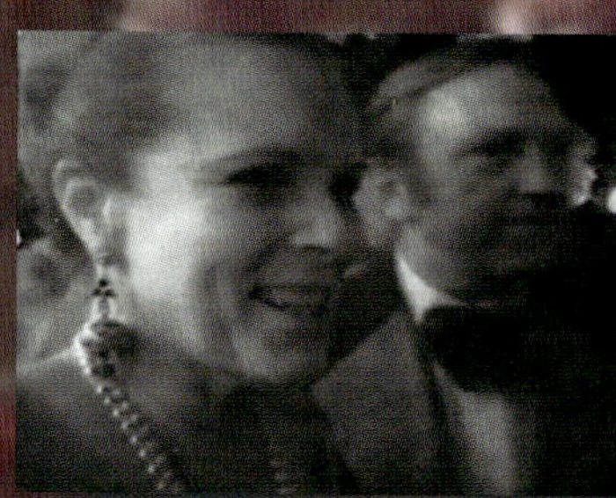

In *Chic To Sheik*, TVTV take's on the Washington Establishment and its social scene. Examining the assertion that political deal-making occurs at the social level, they take careful note of the high cost of entertaining: $10,000 for one diplomatic function. As an ironic footnote to history, the tape culminates in a party for the Shah of Iran at the Iranian Embassy,

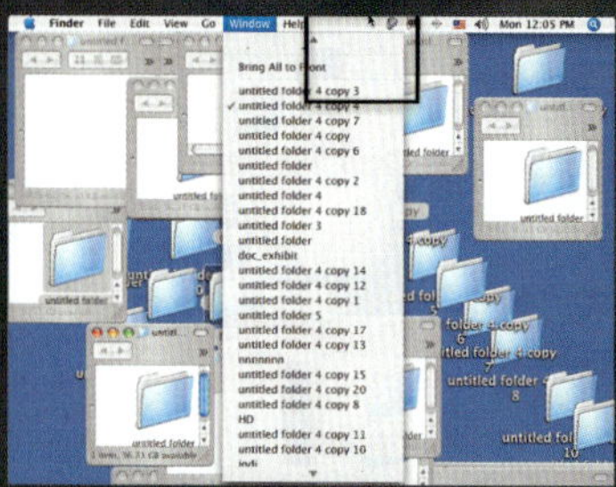

00:51

08:22

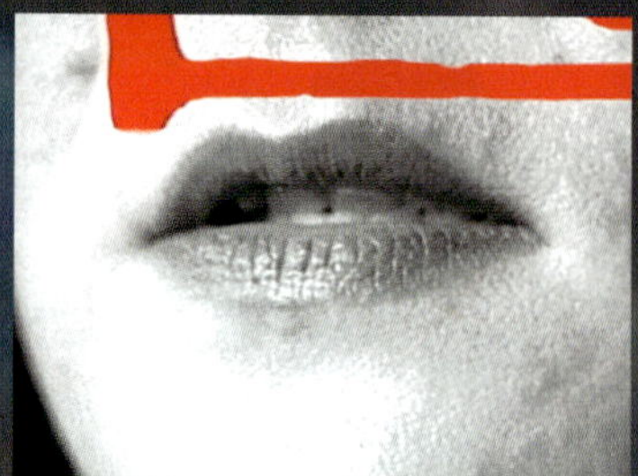

00:06

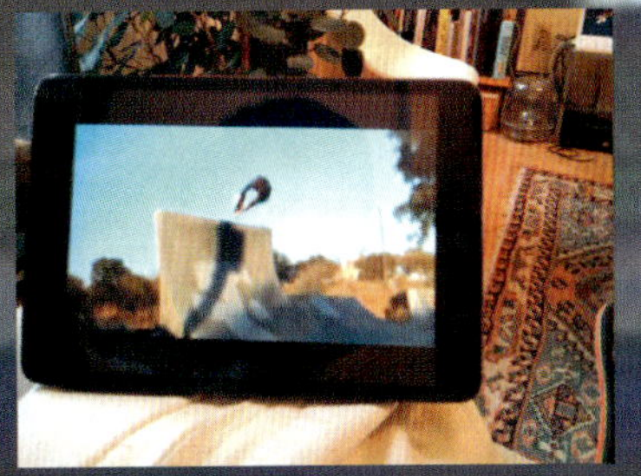
04:03

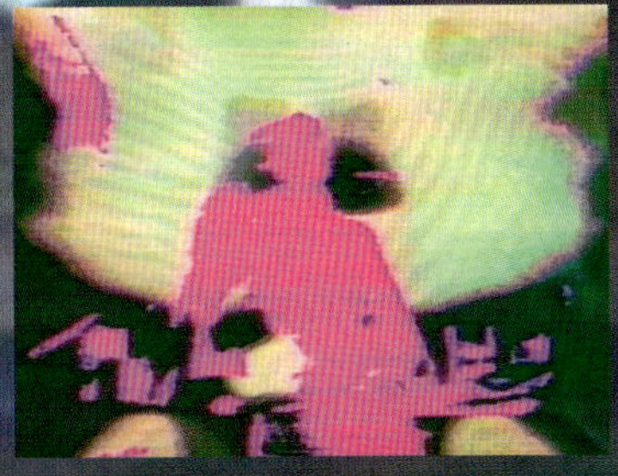
14:34

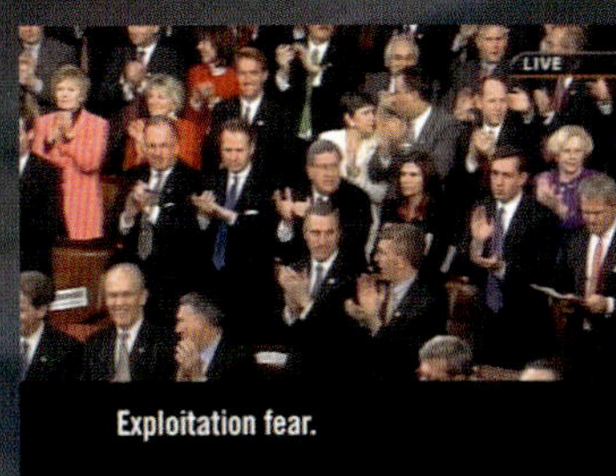

04:36

complete with birthday toasts to the soon-to-be-ousted ruler.

TVTV
Gerald Ford's America: WIN, 1975 Video, color, sound, 28 minutes

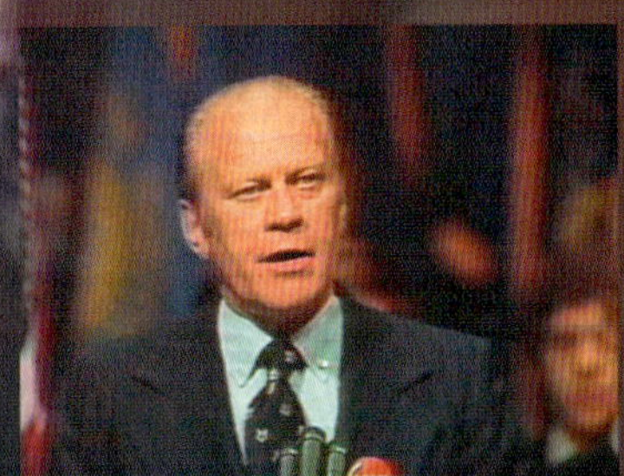

Production: Wendy Appel, Skip Blumberg, Bill Bradbury, Nancy Cain, Frank Cavestany, Wilson Chao, Steve Christiansen, Steve Conant, Michael Couzens, Mary DeOreo, Bart Friedman, Paul Goldsmith, Anda Korsts, Andy Mann, Hudson Marquez, Allen Rucker, Paul Ryan, Michael Shamberg, Jodi Sibert, Elon Soltes, Megan Williams.

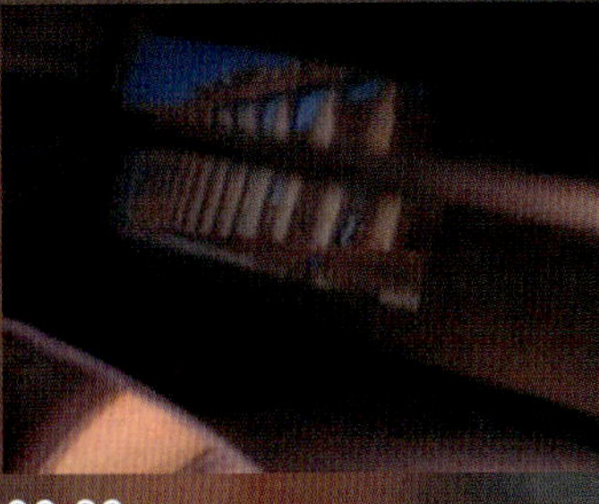
00:23

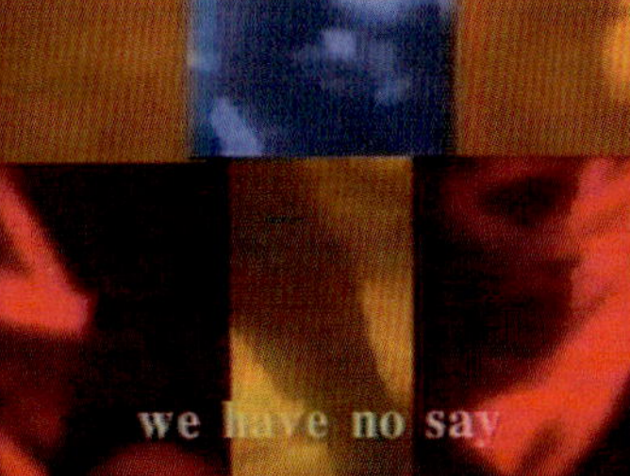
00:40

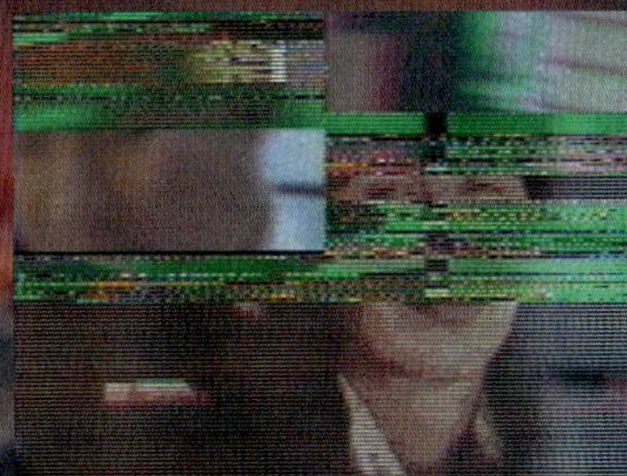
21:17

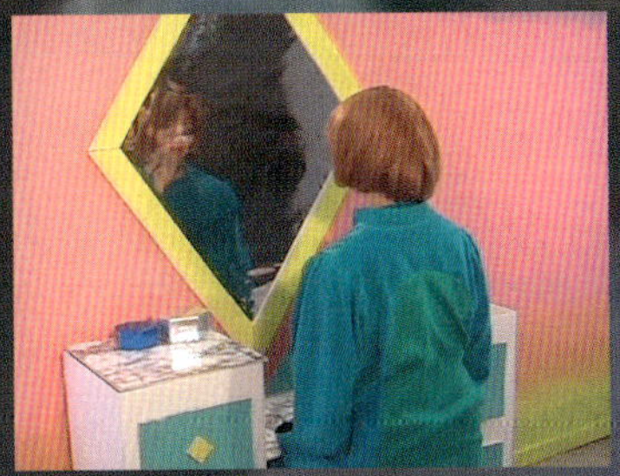
01:29

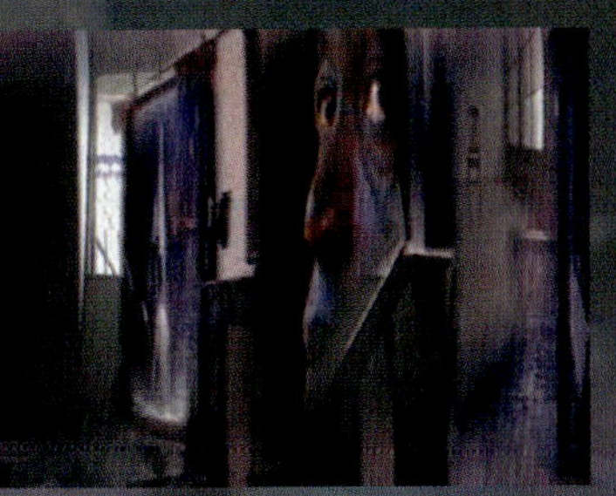
00:26

04:29

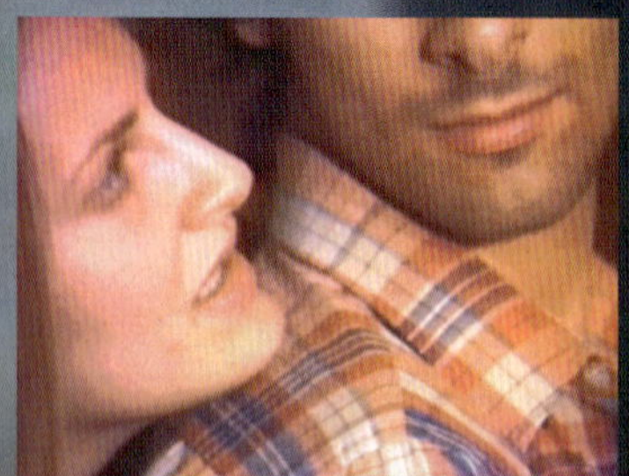

01:20

01:40

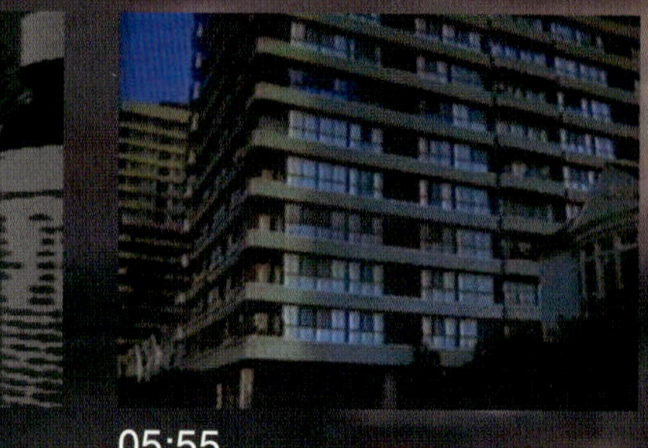

05:55

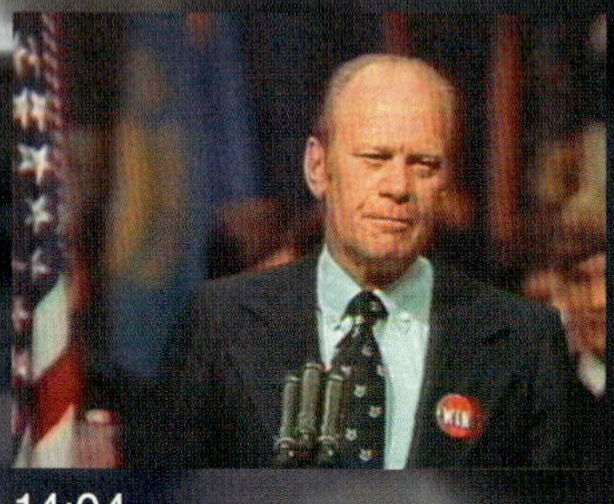

14:04

17:28

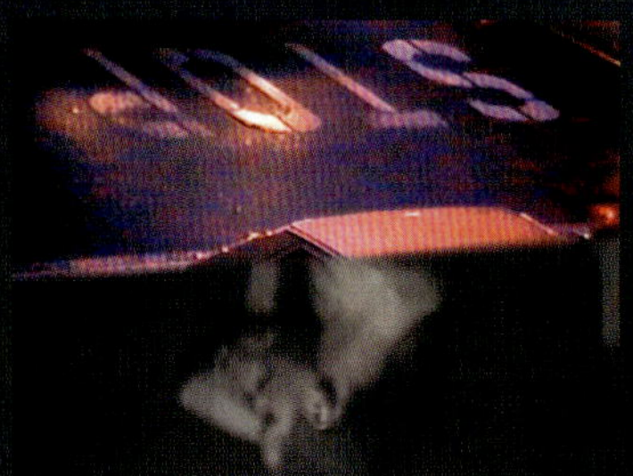

07:16

204 BROADCASTING: GUERRILLA MEDIA

Editors: Wendy Appel, Frank Cavestany, Anda Korsts, Megan Williams.
Produced by TVTV and the TV Lab at WNET/Thirteen.
Producer: David Loxton. Videotape Editor: Philip F. Falcone, Jr.

The four-part series *Gerald Ford's America* scrutinizes the first one hundred days of the Ford presidency. In WIN (the title refers to the slogan "Whip Inflation Now"), the TVTV crew follows Ford on a goodwill tour of his old constituency in Ann Arbor, Michigan. Having promised to end the "national nightmare" of Vietnam and Watergate, Ford took office only to face inflation and a looming recession. Ironically contrasting political rhetoric with the reality of working and middle-class America, TVTV juxtaposes a main point of Ford's platform—that Americans should curb their spending habits—with a GOP fundraiser in which wealthy patrons bid extravagantly for a football once held by Ford.

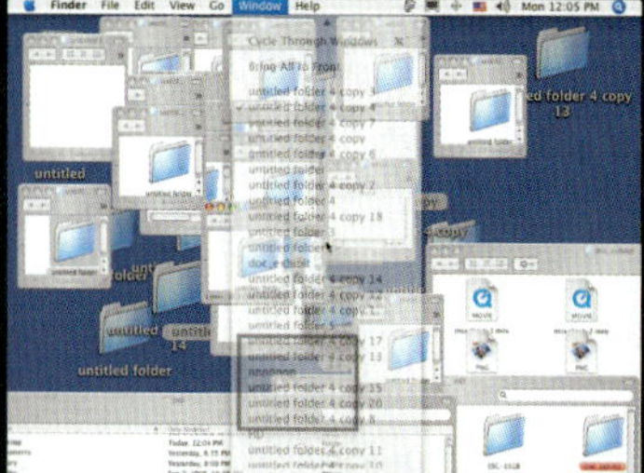

00:51

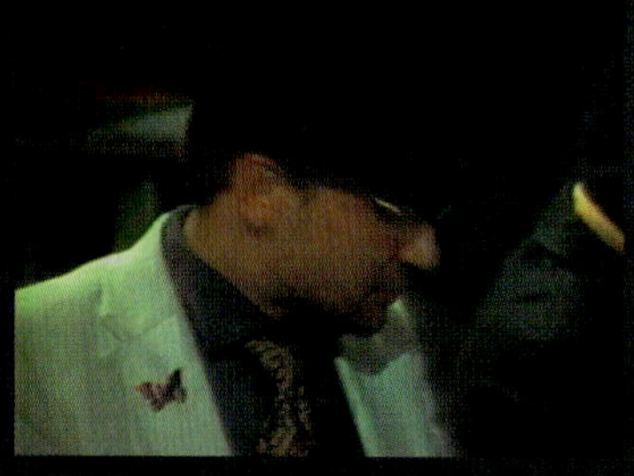

08:22

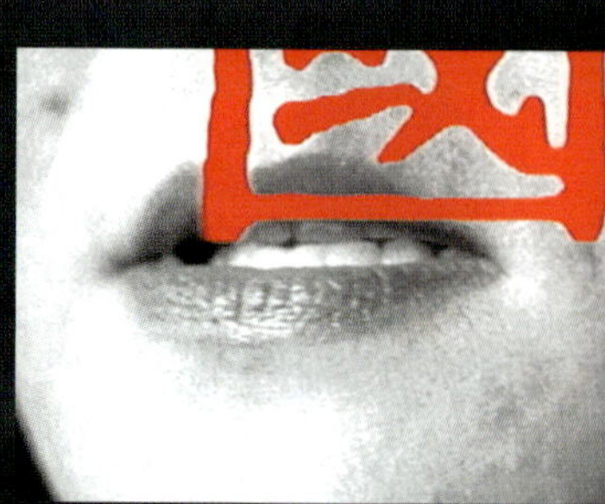

00:06

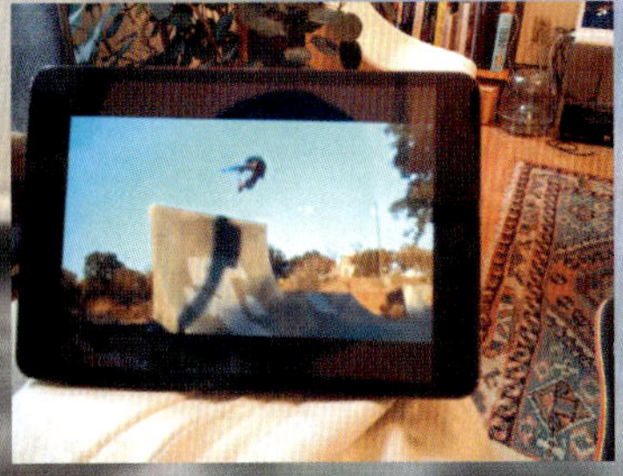

04:03

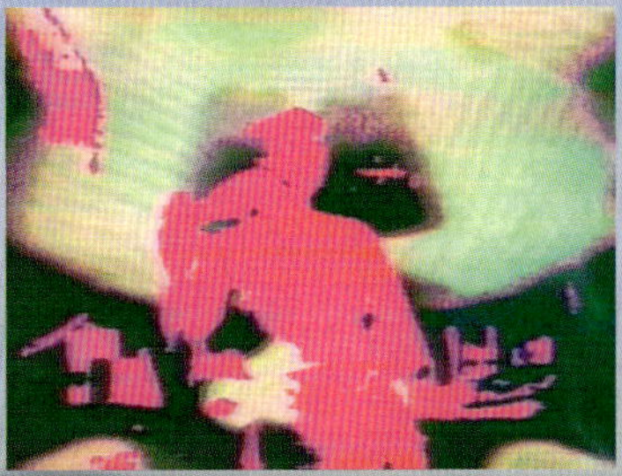

14:34

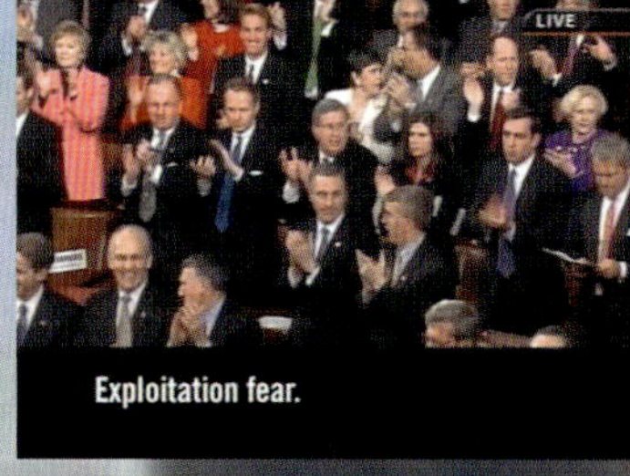

04:36

TVTV
VTR: TVTV, 1975, video, black-and-white and color, sound, 28:30 minutes

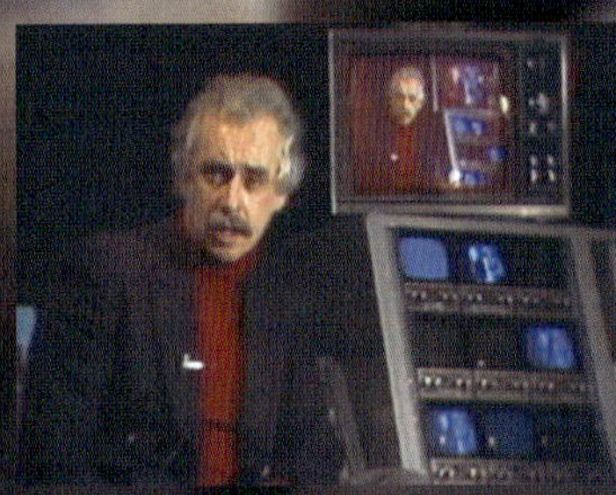

With: Russell Connor.
Producers: Candida Harper, David Silver.
Videotaped by Andy Mann.
A production of the TV Lab at WNET/Thirteen.
Executive Producer: David Loxton.
Engineering Supervisor/ Editor: John J. Godfrey.

A documentary about TVTV shot by one of its own members, this first segment of WNET/Thirteen's VTR series was produced while the collective was in Washington, D.C. working on *Gerald Ford's America*. Videotaped by Andy Mann, *VTR: TVTV* includes equipment demonstrations by Alan Rucker, Megan Williams and Skip Blumberg, among others; TVTV members elaborating on the collective's working methods and philosophy; and excerpts from *Four More Years, The Lord of the Universe*, and *Gerald Ford's America*. The result is a revealing, behind-the-scenes look at the energy, humor, and intelligence that informed TVTV's unique video journalism.

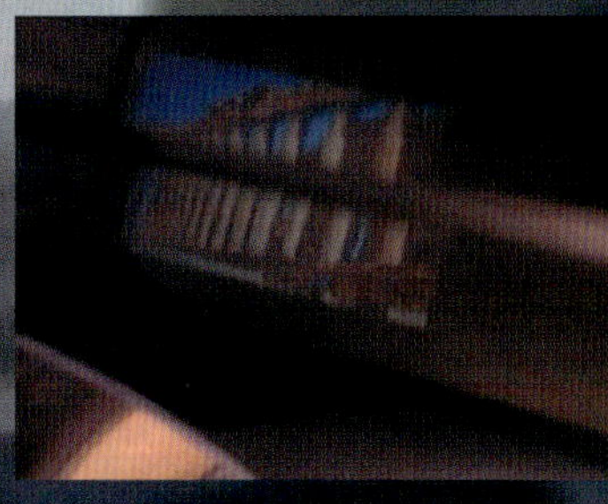

00:23

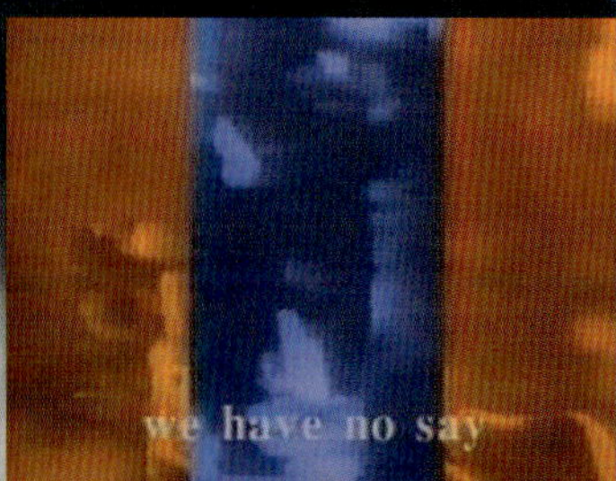

00:40

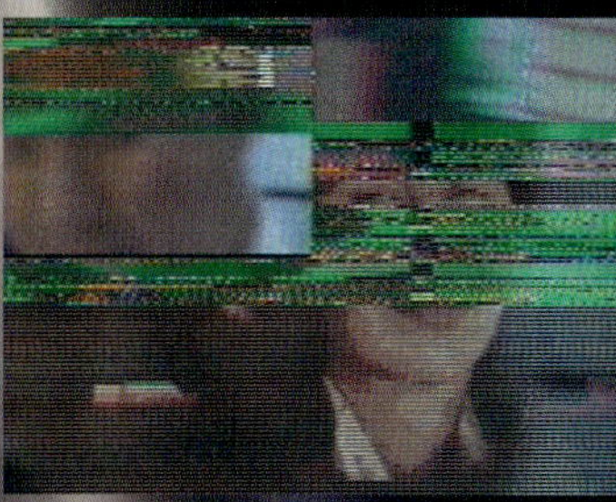

21:17

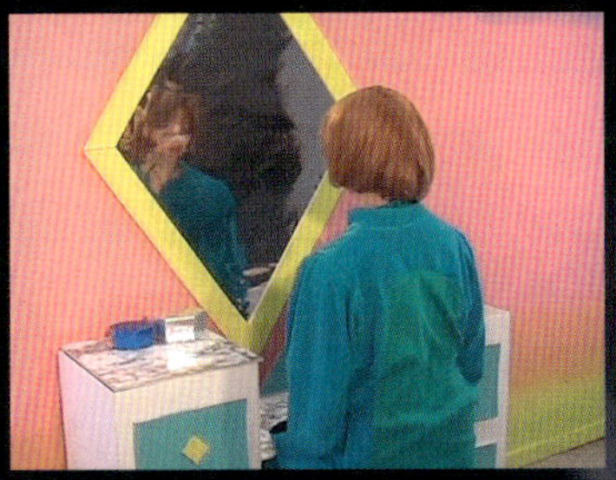

01:29

00:26

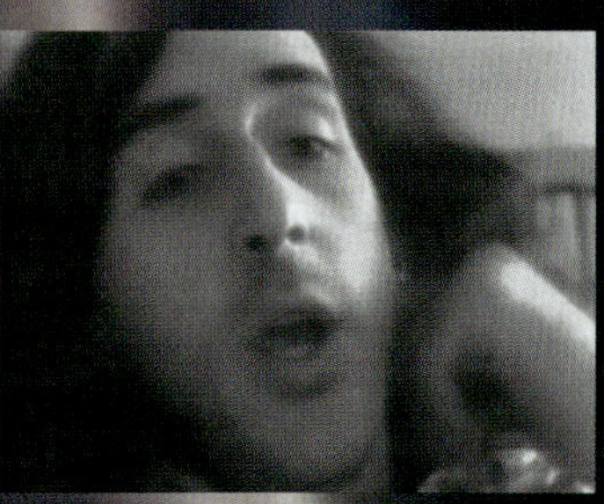

04:29

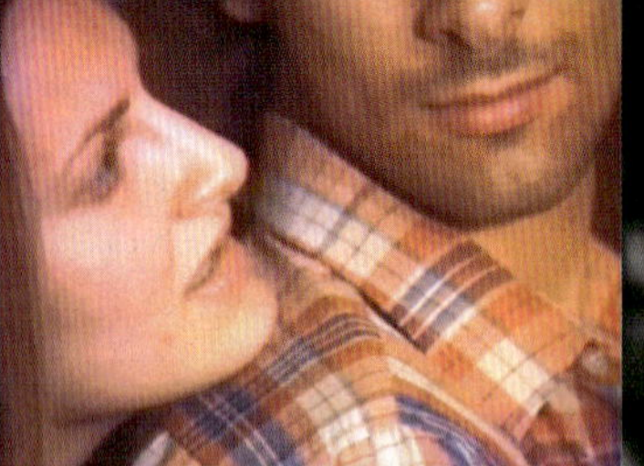

01:20

01:40

05:55

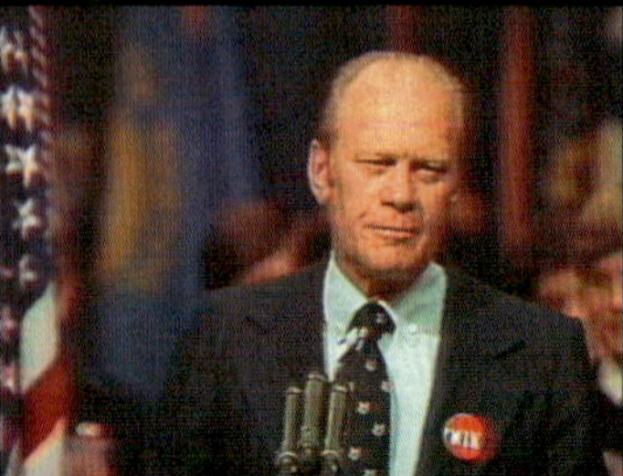

14:04

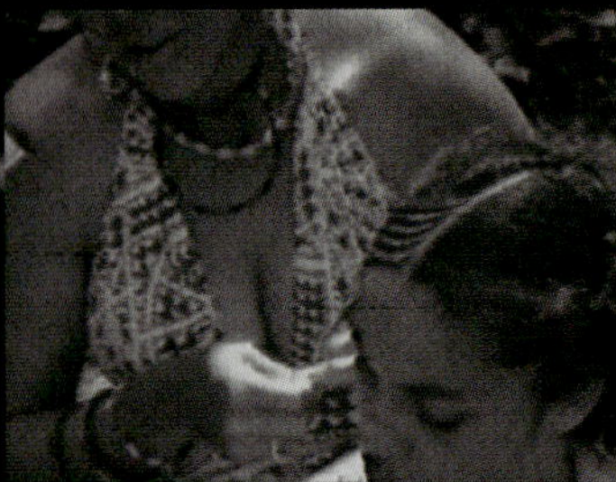

17:28

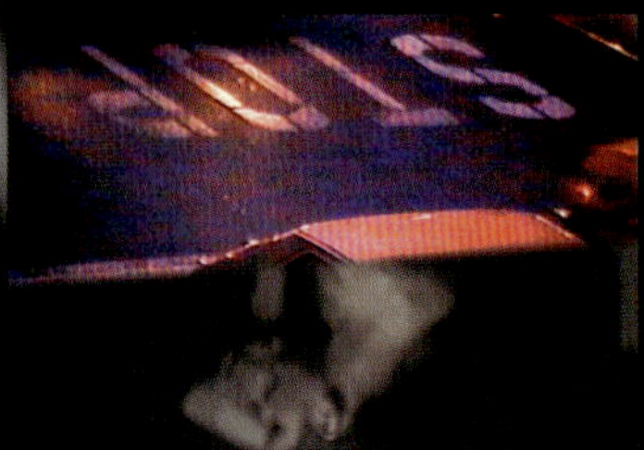

07:16

206 BROADCASTING: GUERRILLA MEDIA

VIDEO VENICE NEWS
Remnants of the Watts Festival, 1972–1973, compiled 1980, video, black-and-white and color, sound, 60 minutes

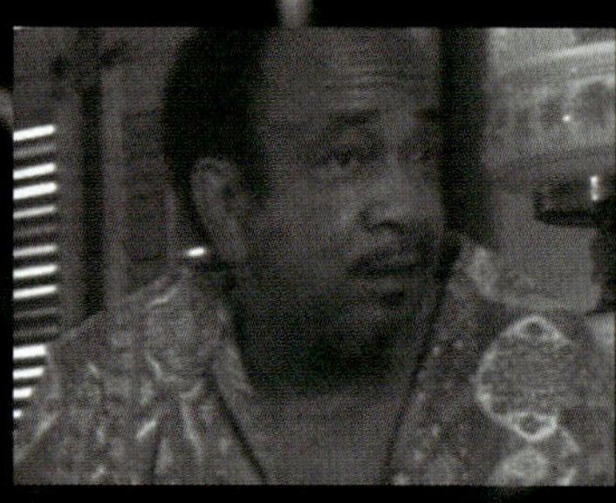

The collective from Venice, California, known as Video Venice News documented the Watts Festival in 1972 and 1973. Writes member Ulysses Jenkins: "This videotape program presents an overview of what was a historical event in the black and brown community of Southeast Los Angeles . . . more notably recognized as Watts, CA… [it] is a documentary of a time and place, which was a major outlet for a community . . . I hope that what this presentation divulges and provides is an understanding of the issues that are facing the African American communities in this country." This historically important tape examines the issue of covert surveillance that has defined the relationship between the state and the African American community in the United States.

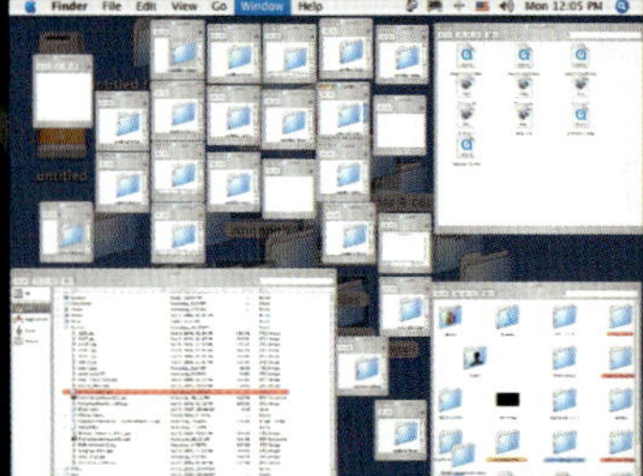

00:51

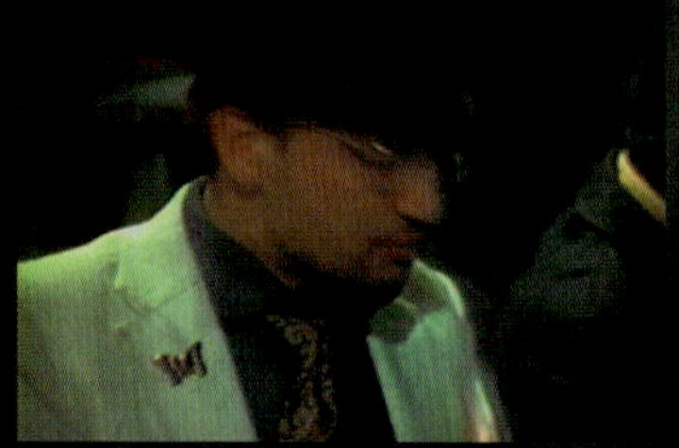

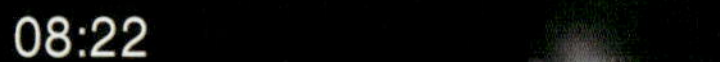

08:22

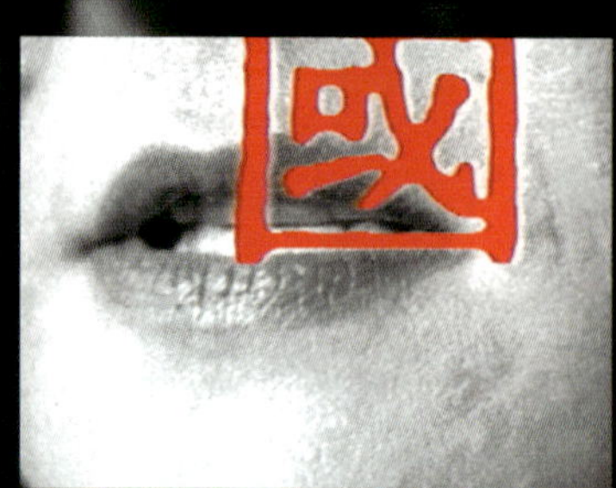

00:06

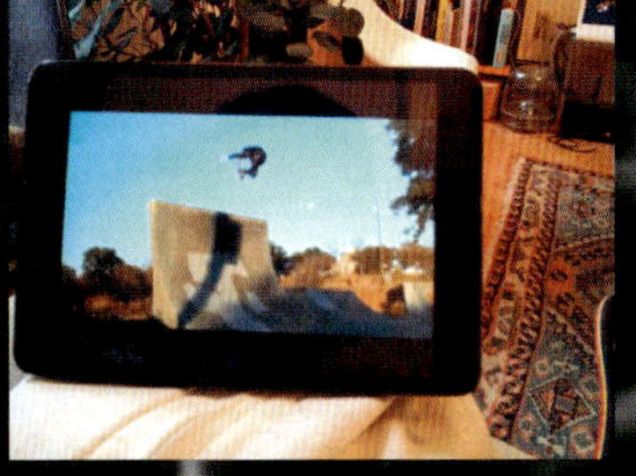

04:04

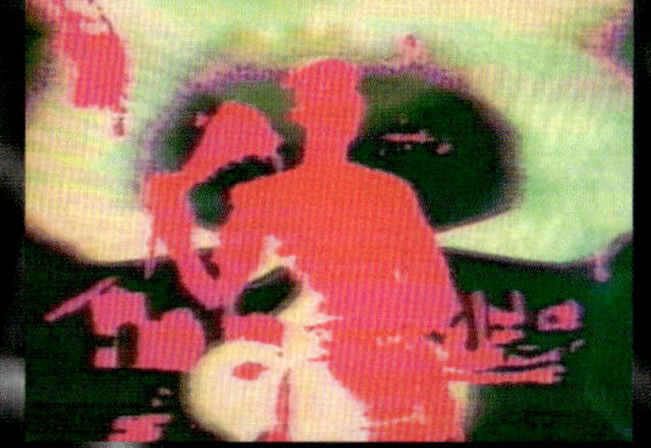

14:35

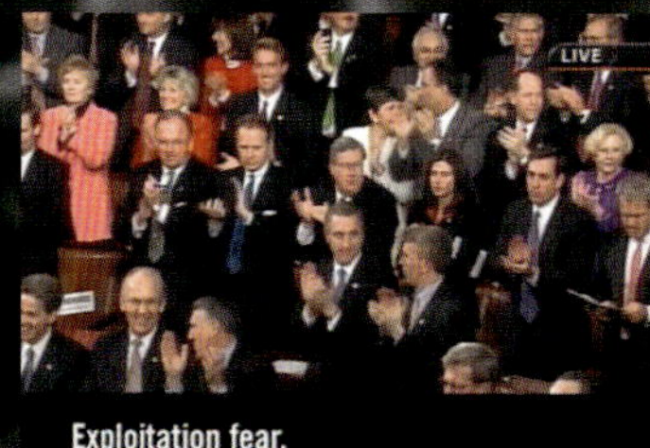

04:37

X-PRZ
X-PRZ was an "art band" of four artists—Tony Cokes, Doug Anderson, Kenseth Armstead, and Mark Pierson—working in installation, photography, painting, sculpture, and video. In existence from 1991 to 2000, the group was dedicated to the production of engaging, hybridized, and humorous cultural actions.

X-PRZ
No Sell Out . . . or i wnt 2 b th ultimate commodity/ machine (Malcolm X Pt. 2), 1995, video, color, sound, 5:37 minutes

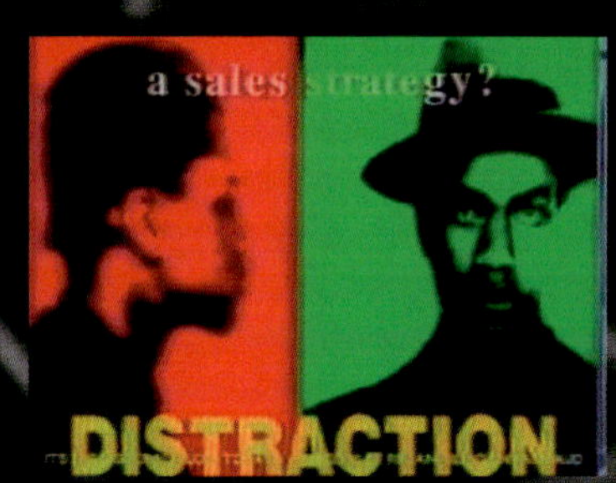

Music: R.E.M, "King of Comedy;" NIN, "Happiness Is Slavery."
Production facilities: The Devil's Workshop, Power Macintosh 7100/66 with Adobe Premiere 4.0, Scholarly Technology group, Brown University, Quadra 800 with Adobe Premiere 4.0.
Post-production facility:

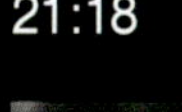

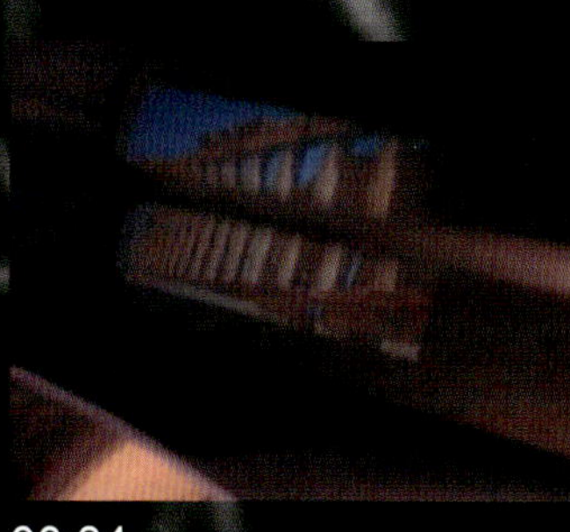

00:24

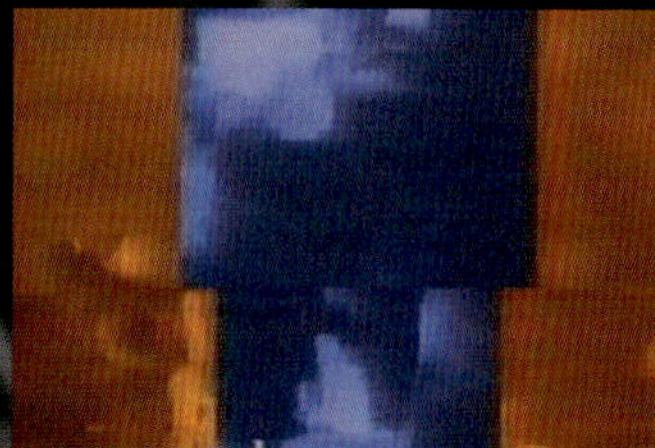

00:41

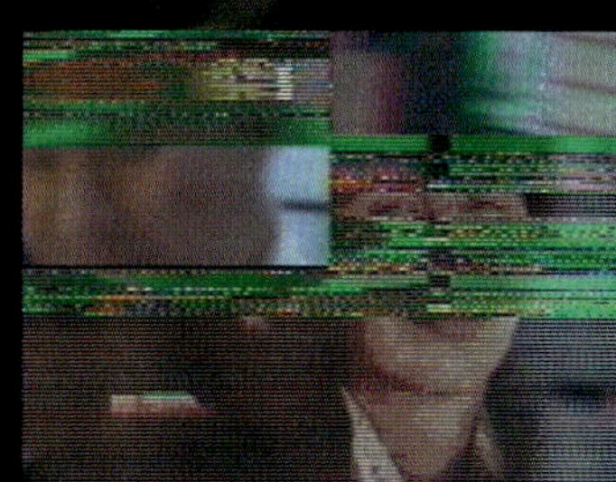

21:18

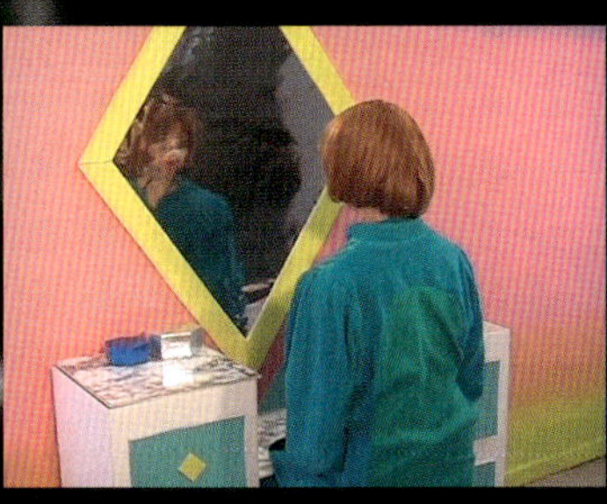

01:30

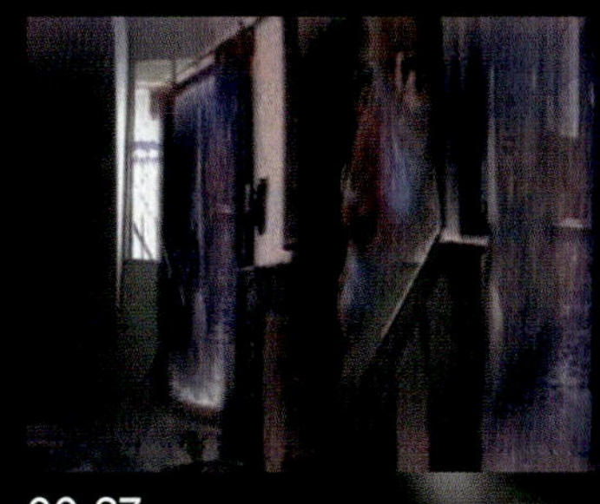

00:27

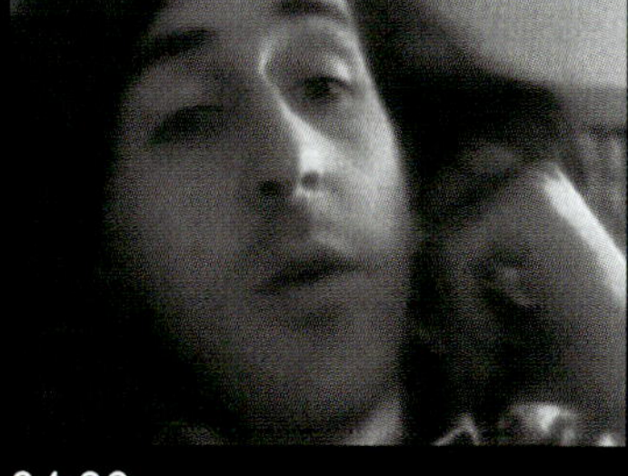

04:30

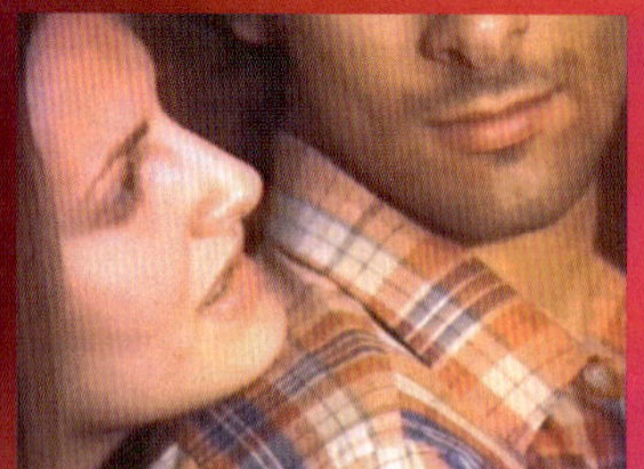
01:20

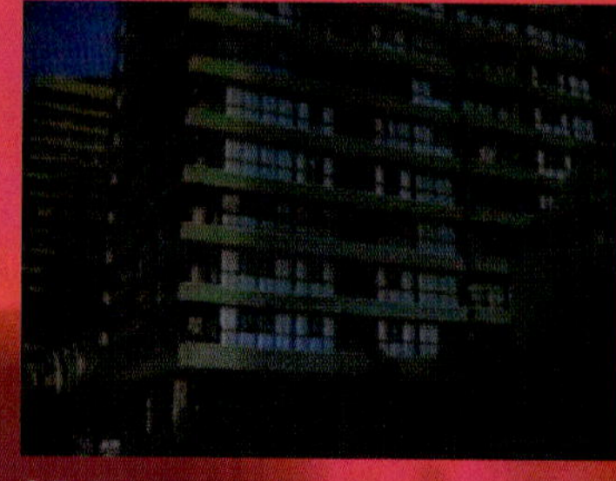
05:55

01:40

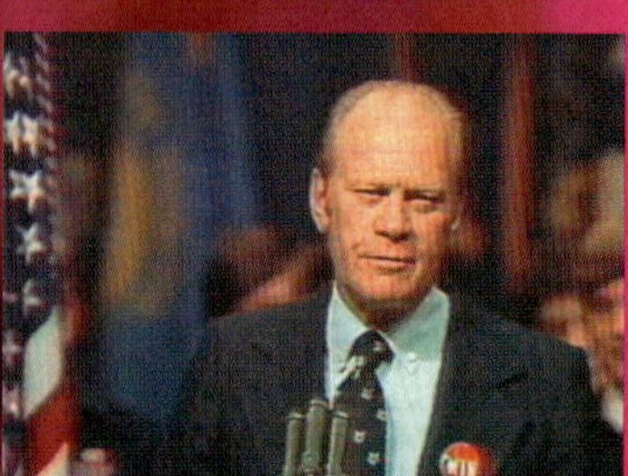
14:04

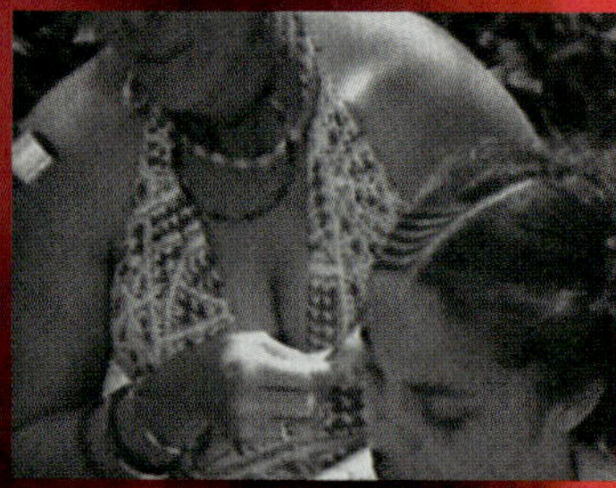
17:28

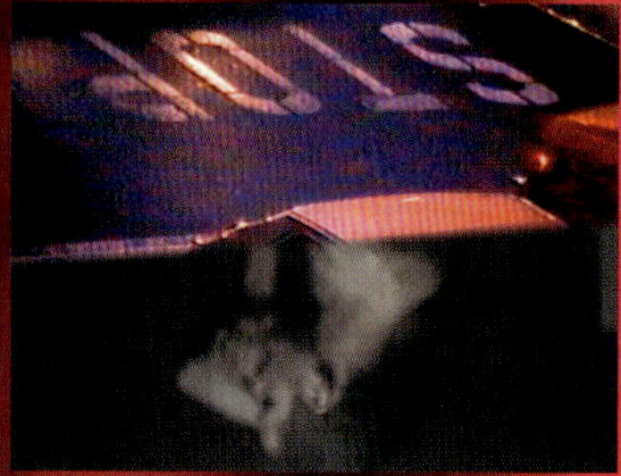
07:16

208 BROADCASTING: GUERRILLA MEDIA

Robert Beck, Electronic Arts Intermix.

States Tony Cokes: "*No Sell Out* employs desktop video (Adobe Premiere) to position images of Malcolm X in tension with commercial culture. It is a result of a series of loaded questions we ask ourselves, and now wish to impose on viewers . . . Mr. X is the serialized signifier that sparks problematic readings and profits in rap music, 'political art' and fashionable sportswear . . . Is X the sign of a meaningful difference, or just another hip style thang?" Appropriating an MTV-like format to critique and question the capitalist commodification of the activist's subversive politics, X-PRZ sets computer-manipulated imagery of the man against advertising logos, archival footage, TV imagery, and a propulsive soundtrack of music by REM and Nine Inch Nails.

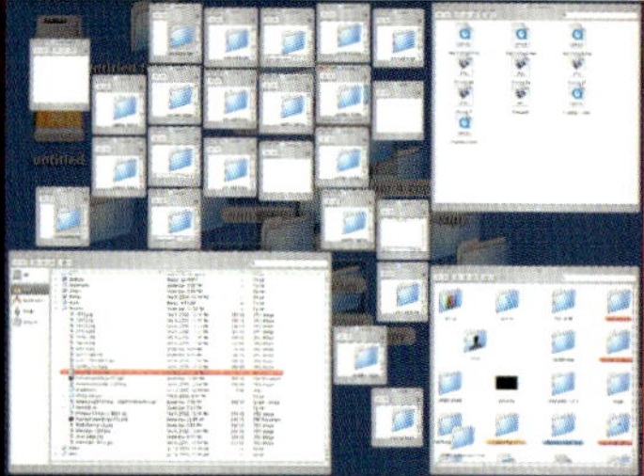
00:51

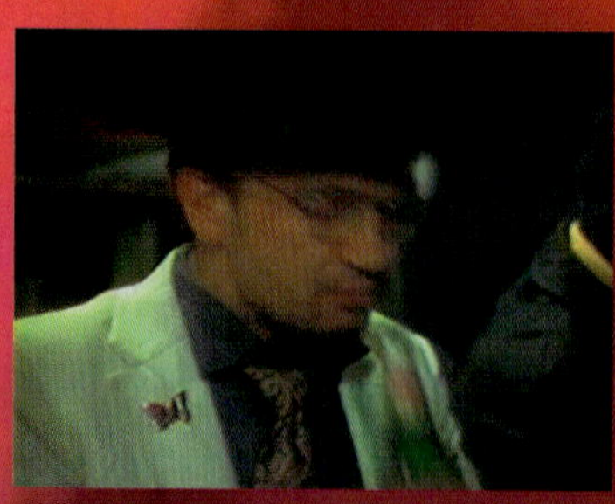
08:22

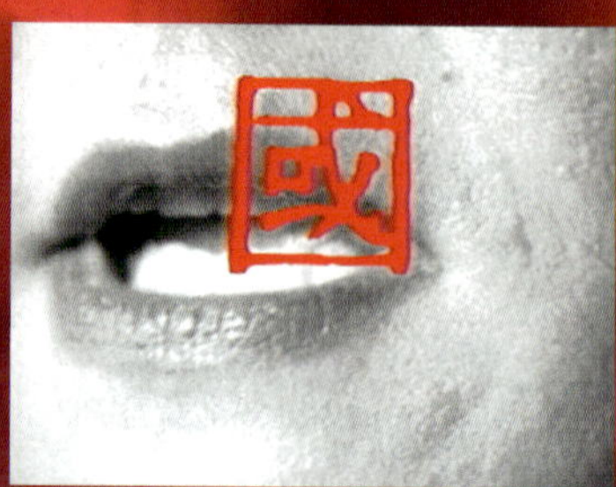
00:06

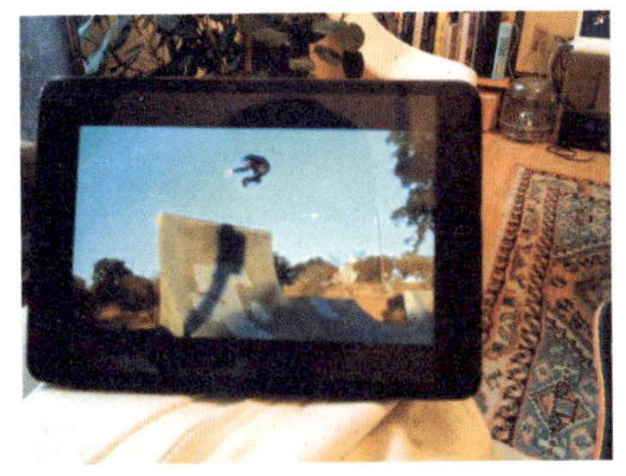
04:04

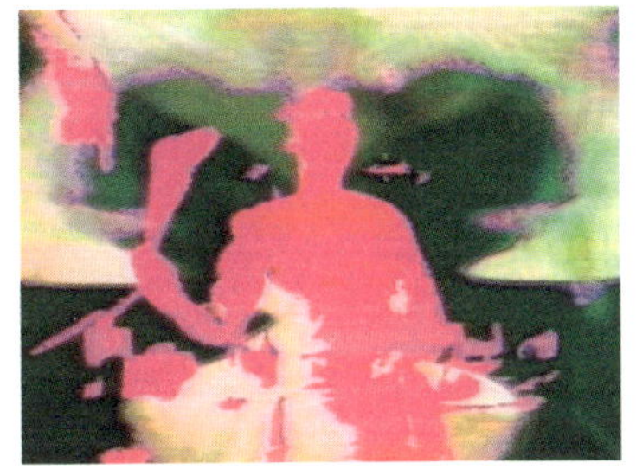
14:35

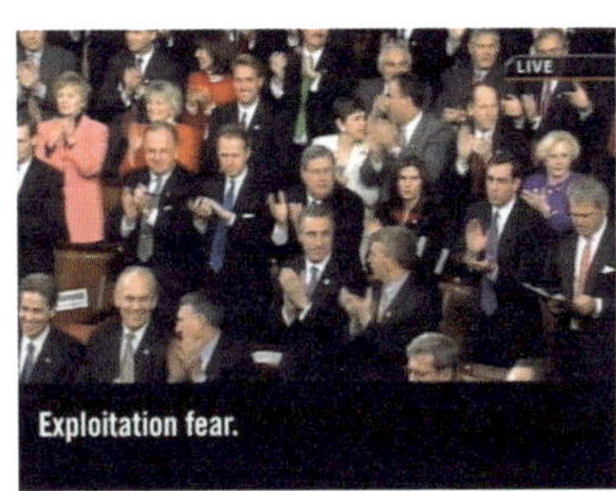

04:37

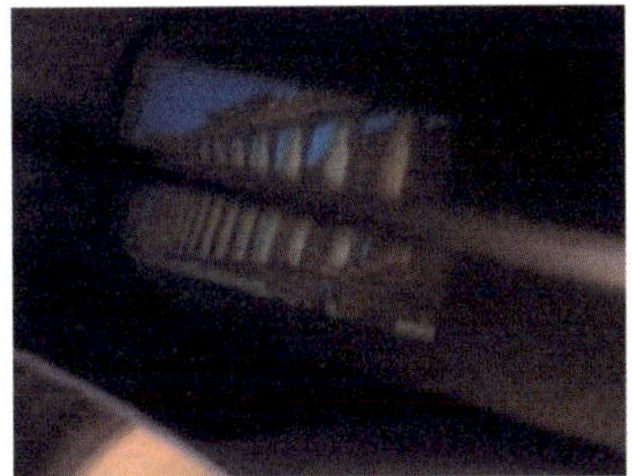
00:24

TOUCHING FROM A DISTANCE: MEDIA MIGRATION & ARTISTIC TRANSMISSION AT EAI

ALEX KLEIN

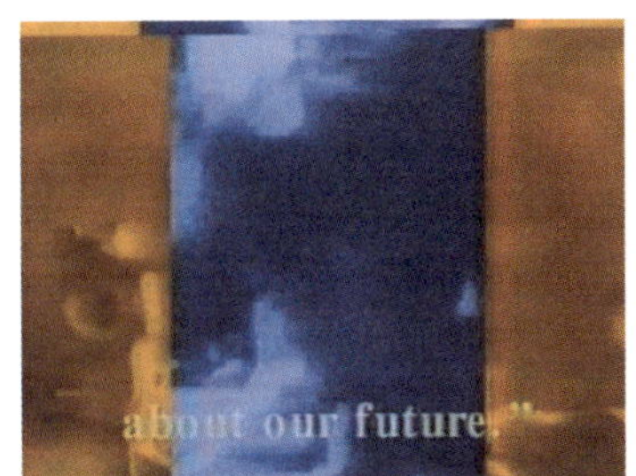

00:41

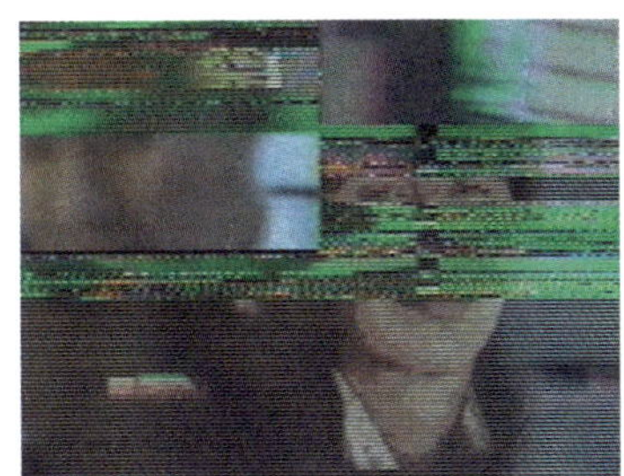
21:18

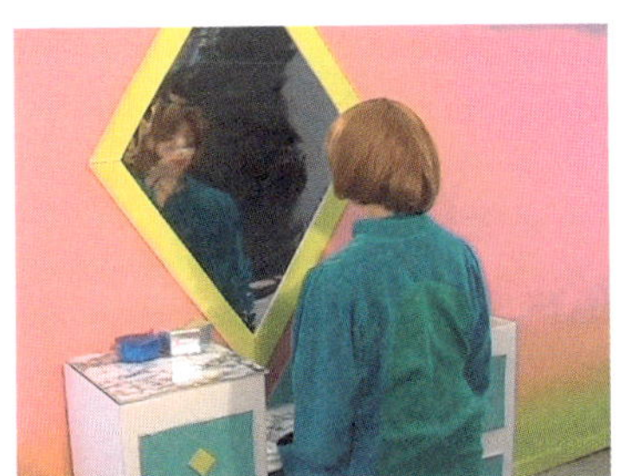
01:30

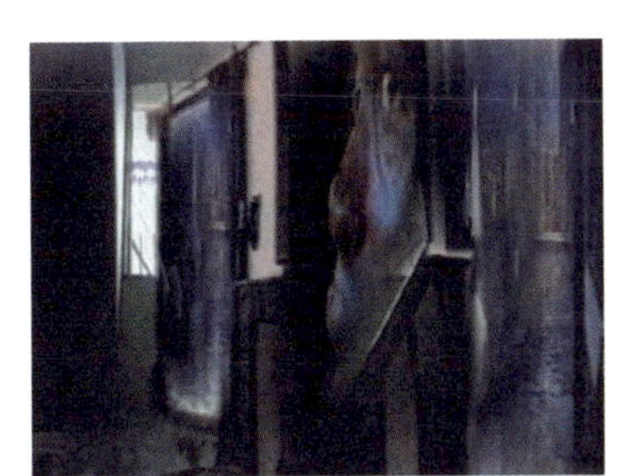
00:27

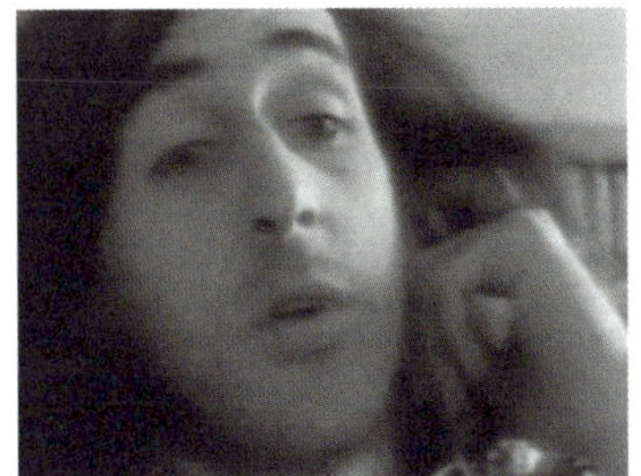
04:30

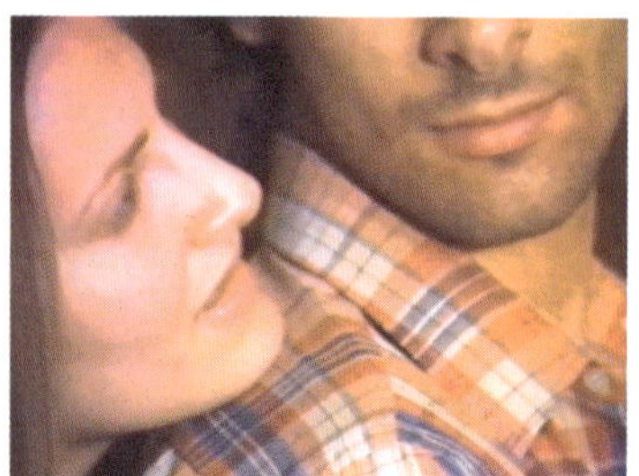

01:20

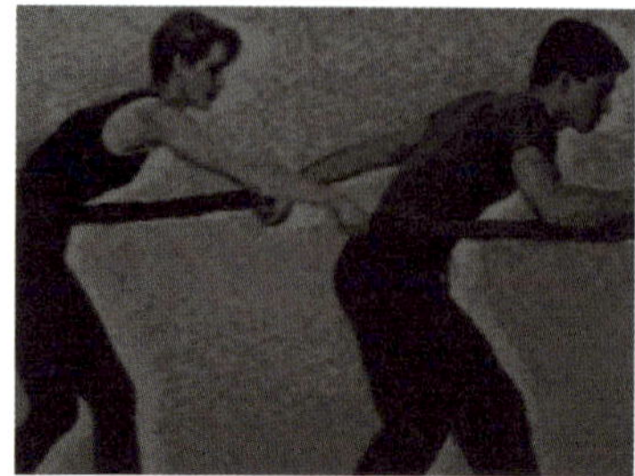

01:40

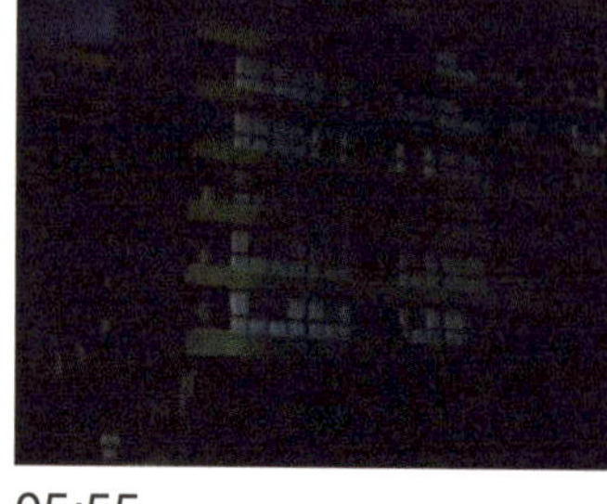

05:55

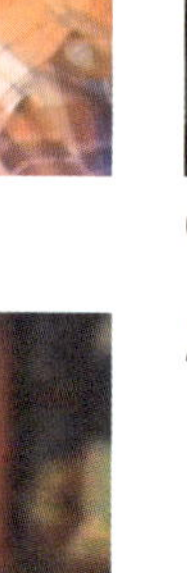

14:04

> *What I find remarkable—and gratifying—is that this "alternative paradigm" that was founded in 1971 is still relevant to artists and their art almost fifty years later.*[1]
> —Lori Zippay, Director Emerita, Electronic Arts Intermix

Today, it is taken as a given that we have shifted from an era of "broadcast" to an "on demand" culture. And yet, broadcast remains deeply embedded in our conceptions of media. One need only think of the acronyms of major television networks such as the BBC (British Broadcasting Corporation) and NBC (National Broadcasting Company), or the online channels that now complement them, CBS All Access (Columbia Broadcasting System) being just one example. Despite the allusion to a seemingly antiquated mode of technology embedded in these names, such terminology speaks to the stringent demands of brand recognition, while symbolically functioning as the hauntological residue of a previous media ecology. In this sense, broadcast can be understood as something of

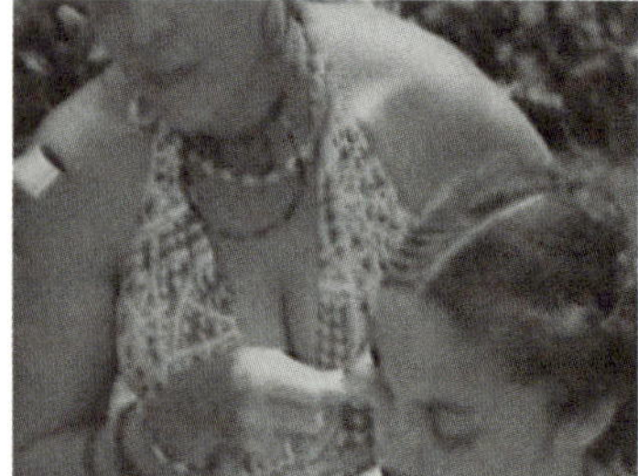

17:28

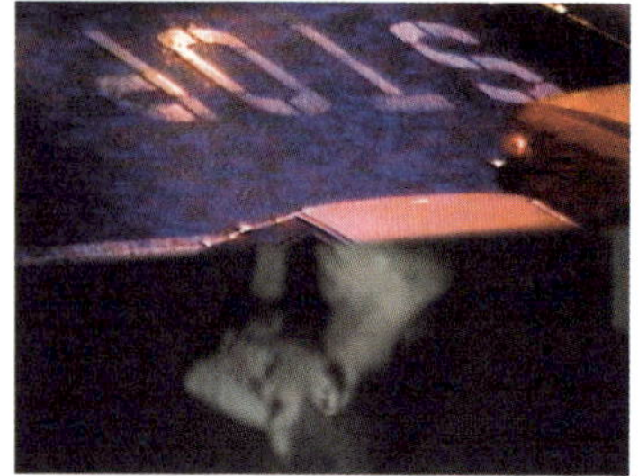

07:16

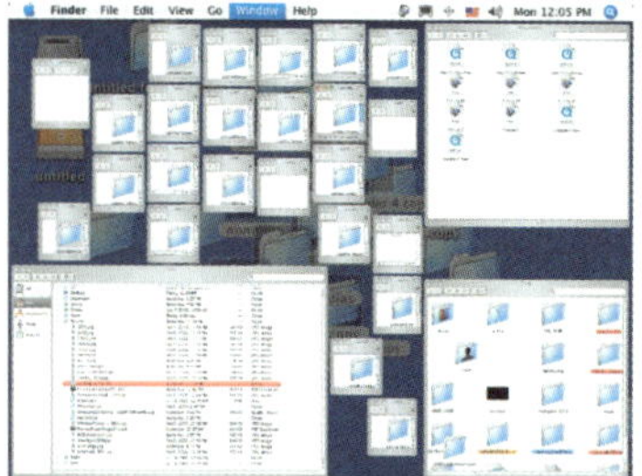

00:51

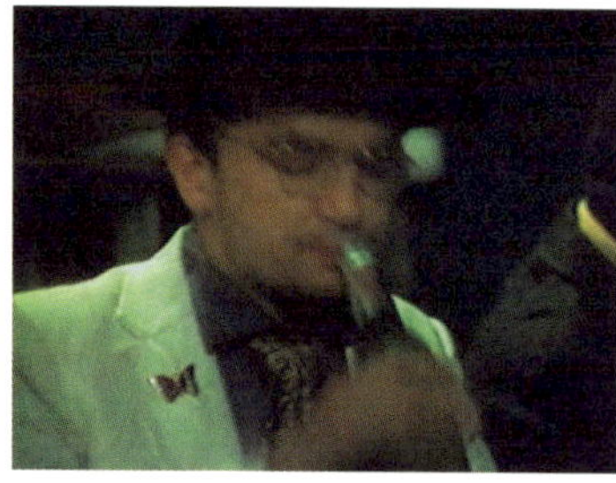

08:22

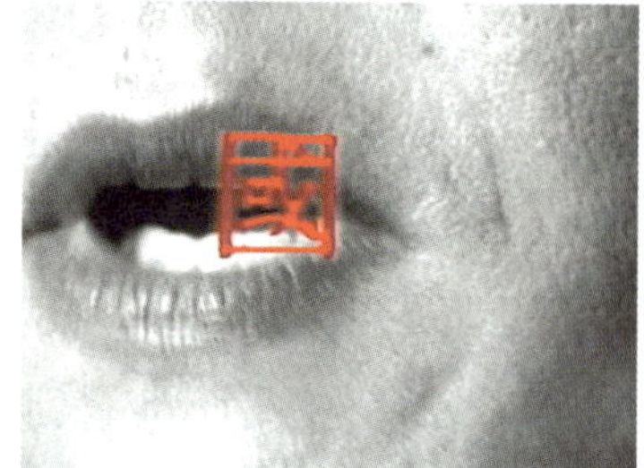

00:06

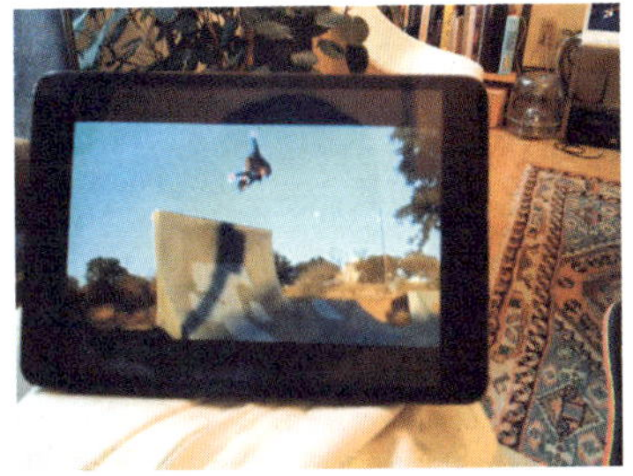
04:04

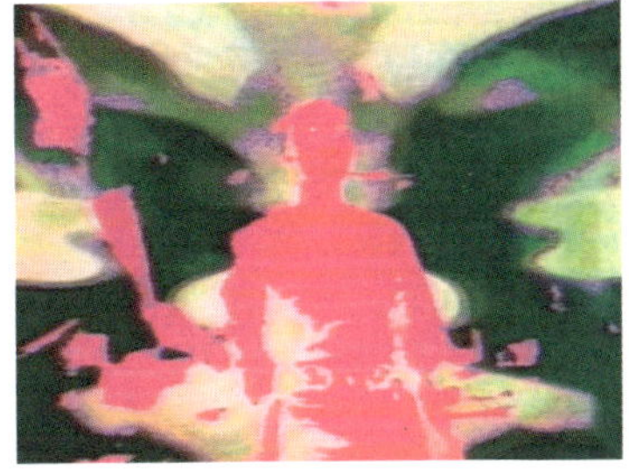
14:35

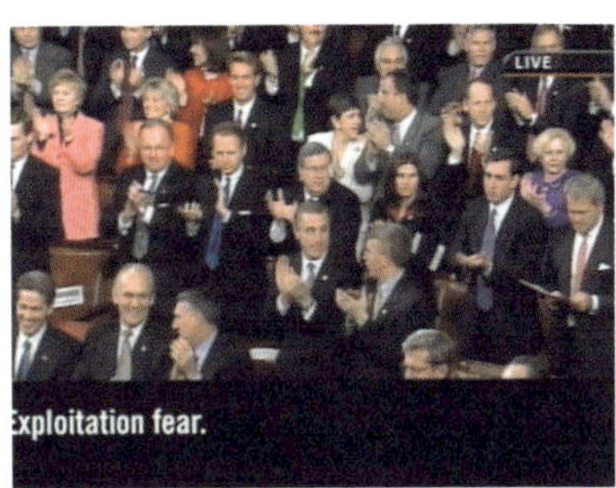

04:37

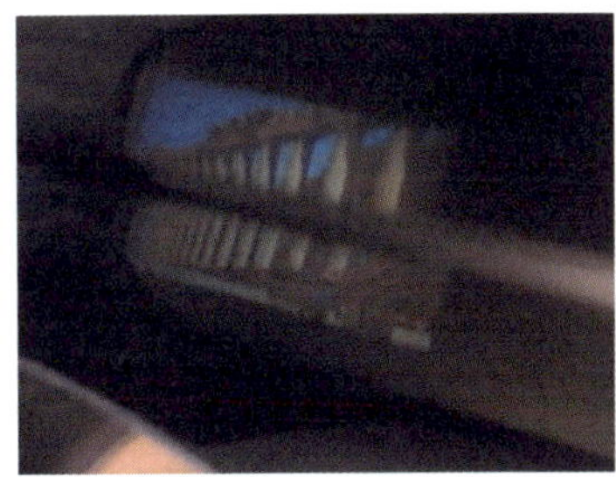
00:24

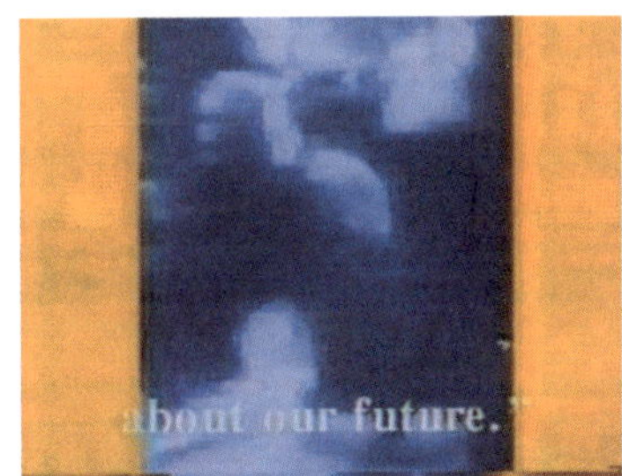

00:41

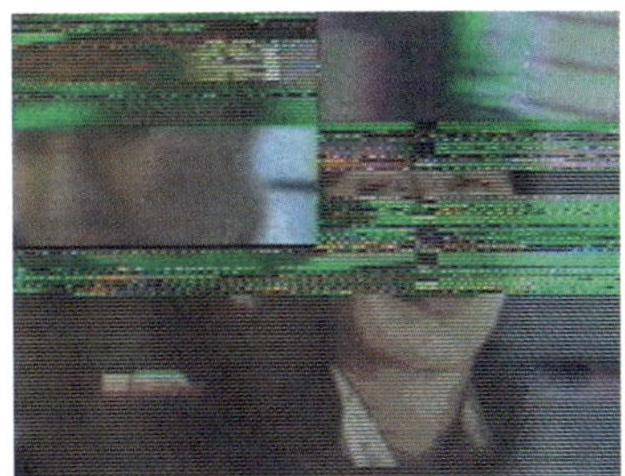
21:18

an oxymoron: it simultaneously describes a one-directional flow of information, and yet it is also imagined as an interactive platform, a site of exchange and the space of the social. In many ways, this hybridized understanding of broadcast is intrinsic. The communicative potential of media formats has been of particular interest to artists working throughout the last century, from the advent of radio and the introduction of portable video equipment to the consumer market to the current prevalence of digital tools, smartphones, and the internet.[2] In the late 1960s, when artists first gained access to the Sony Portapak camera, there was a new and direct way to experiment with the alternative possibilities embedded in mass media, whether through public interventions or private meditations. An early acknowledgment of this potential for artists to engage with the medium of video in an expanded sense was brought together and displayed in the 1969 exhibition, *TV as a Creative Medium*, organized by Howard Wise at his eponymous gallery.[3] Electronic Arts Intermix (EAI)—an

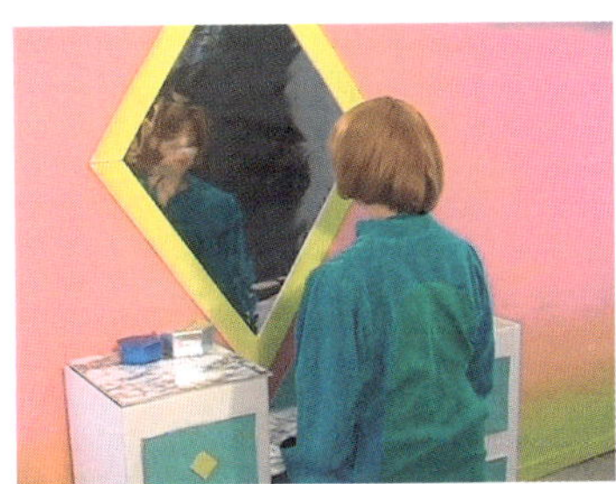
01:30

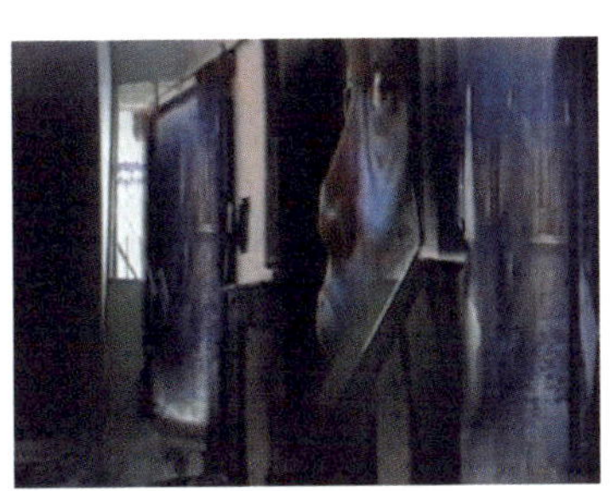
00:27

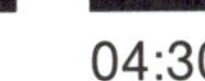
04:30

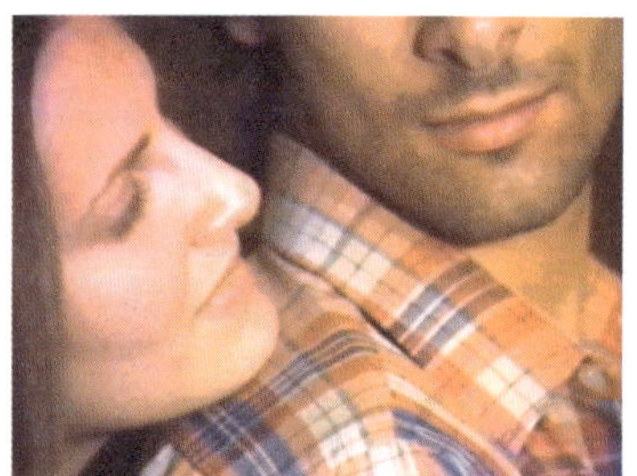
01:20

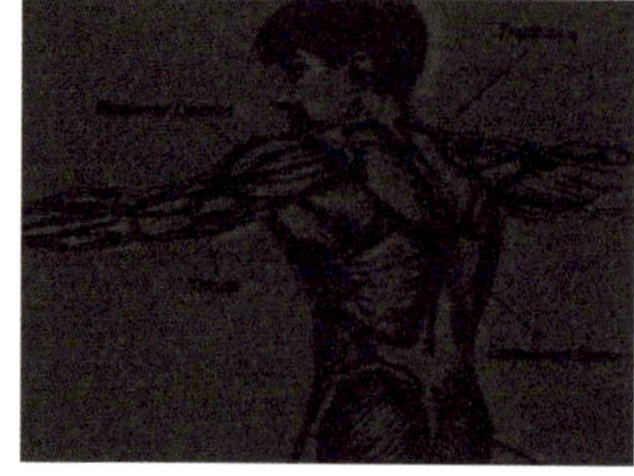
01:40

05:55

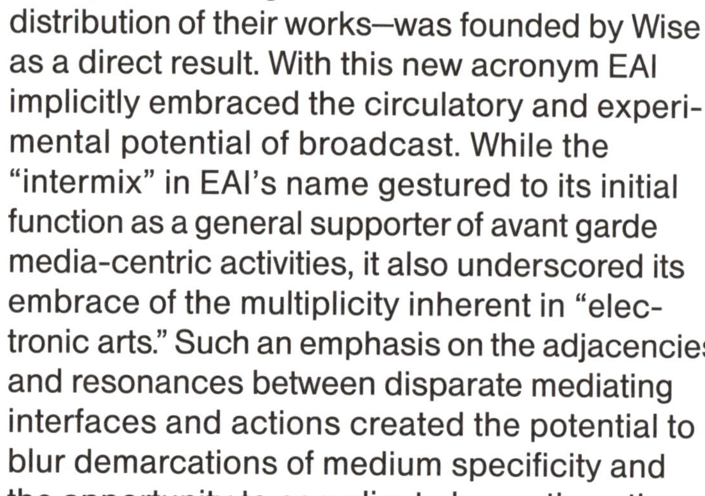

organization devoted to advocacy for artists engaged with single-channel video and the distribution of their works—was founded by Wise as a direct result. With this new acronym EAI implicitly embraced the circulatory and experimental potential of broadcast. While the "intermix" in EAI's name gestured to its initial function as a general supporter of avant garde media-centric activities, it also underscored its embrace of the multiplicity inherent in "electronic arts." Such an emphasis on the adjacencies and resonances between disparate mediating interfaces and actions created the potential to blur demarcations of medium specificity and the opportunity to complicate hermetic notions of artistic innovation.

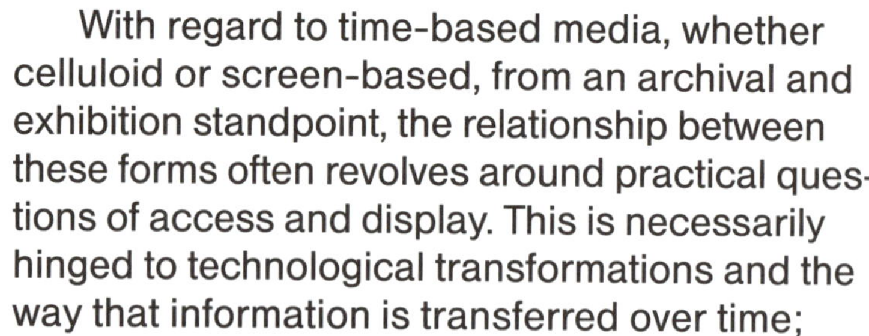
With regard to time-based media, whether celluloid or screen-based, from an archival and exhibition standpoint, the relationship between these forms often revolves around practical questions of access and display. This is necessarily hinged to technological transformations and the way that information is transferred over time;

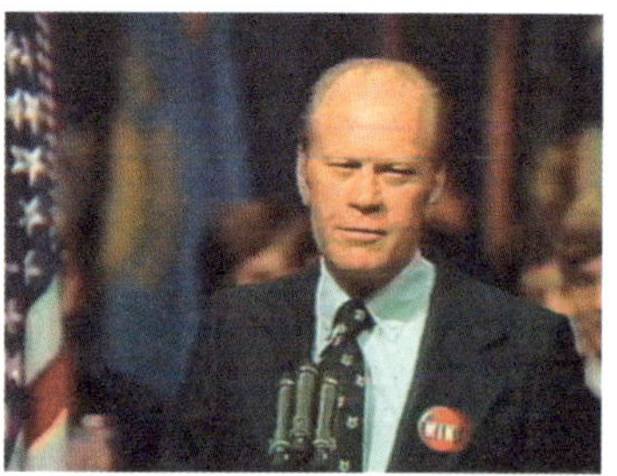
14:04

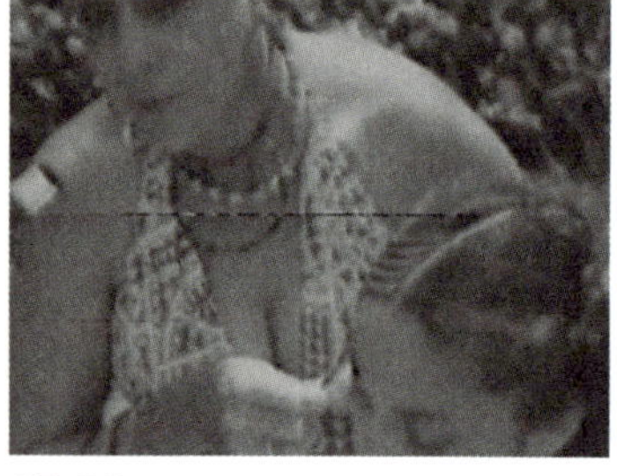
17:28

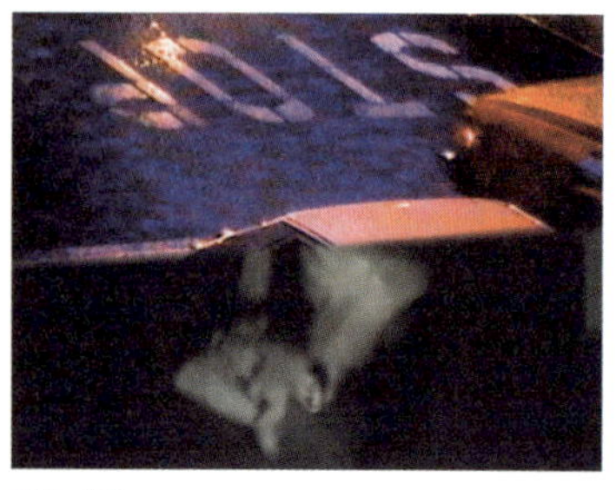
07:16

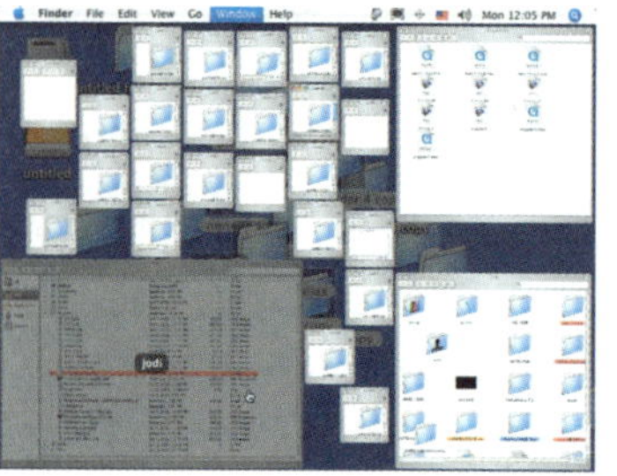
00:51

08:22

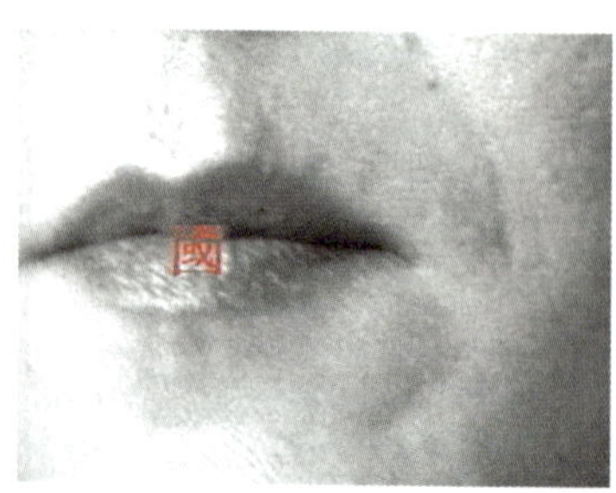
00:06

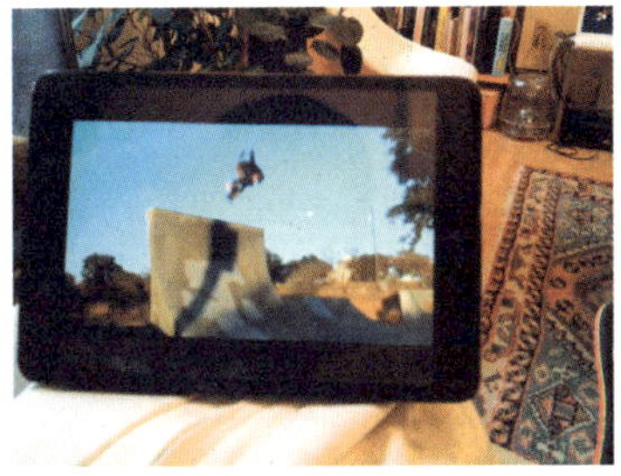
04:04

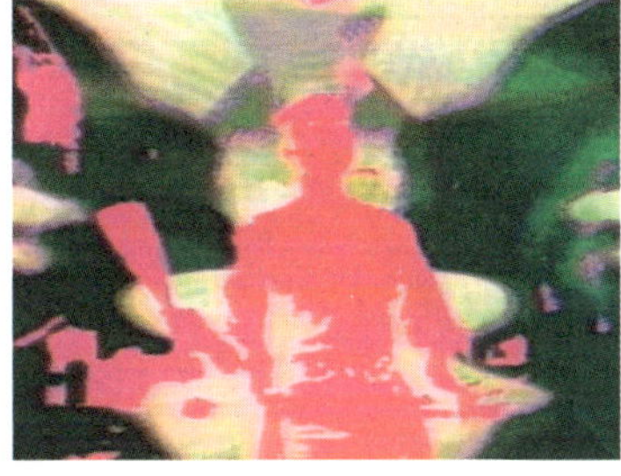
14:35

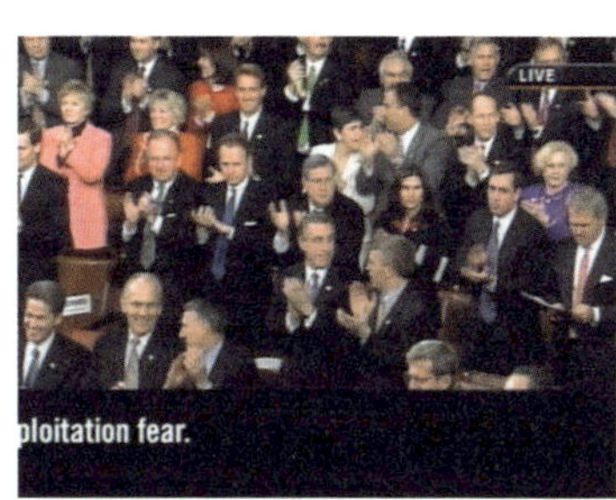

04:37

for example, the migration of a DigiBeta tape to a DVD, or the transfer of a 16 mm film to a digital file.[4] However, "migration," like "broadcast," holds another meaning. As scholar Ina Blom has observed, "Emphasis on the specific media channels of storage reformulates the concepts of cultural tradition and collective memory as a non-anthropocentric and technomathematical theory of transmission."[5] Thus, to migrate, or transfer, interweaves elements of different technological and material substrates—think of the analog stretch marks that permeate YouTube videos—while also providing an opportunity for the artistic strategies of one generation to intermingle with another.

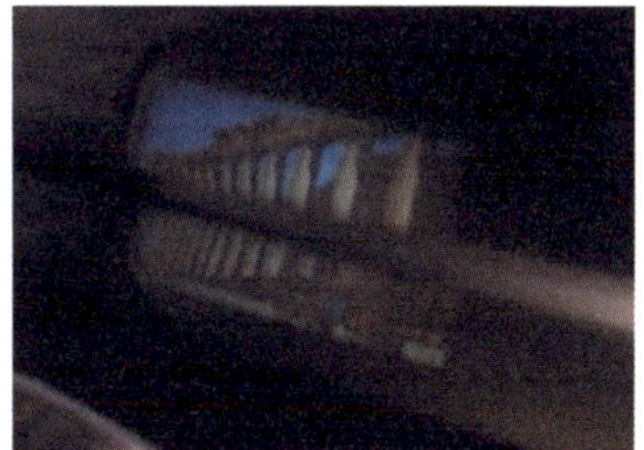
00:24

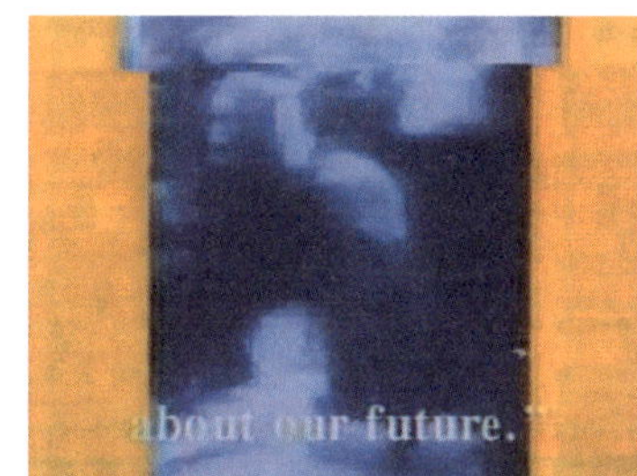

00:41

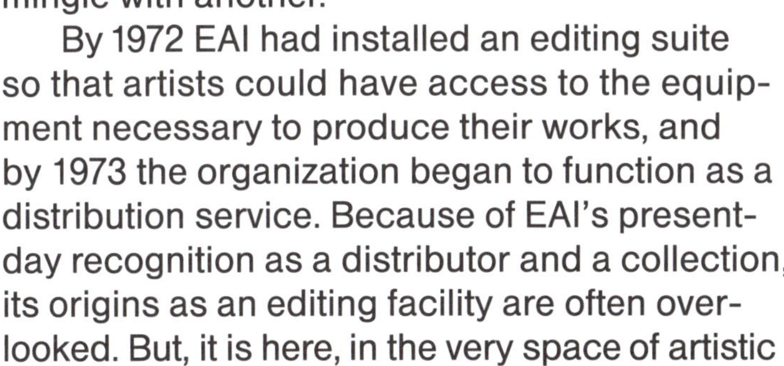

By 1972 EAI had installed an editing suite so that artists could have access to the equipment necessary to produce their works, and by 1973 the organization began to function as a distribution service. Because of EAI's present-day recognition as a distributor and a collection, its origins as an editing facility are often overlooked. But, it is here, in the very space of artistic

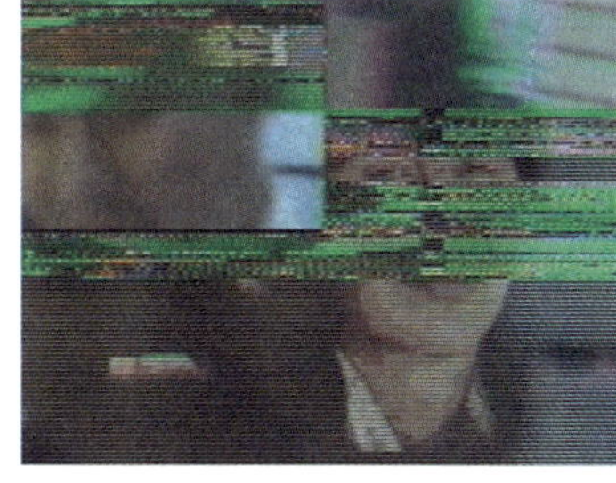
21:18

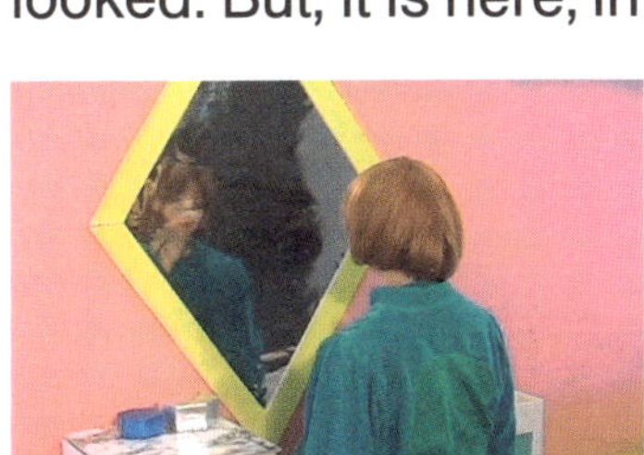
01:30

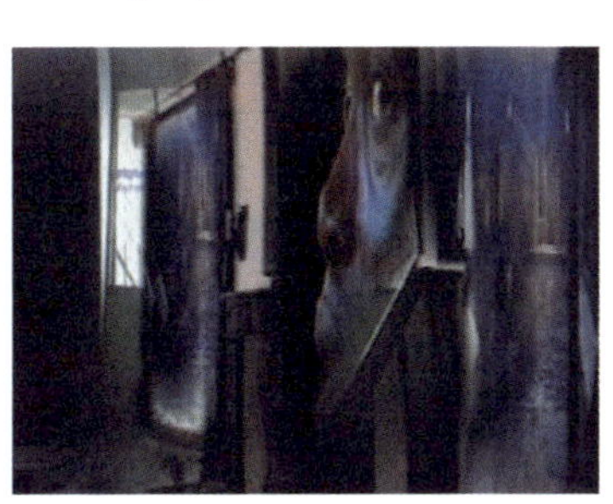
00:27

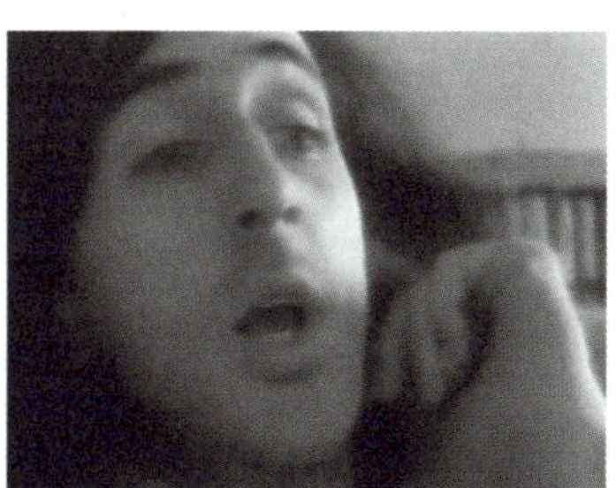
04:30

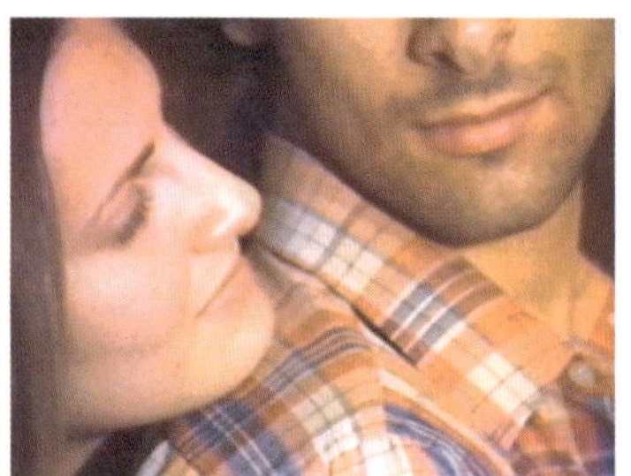
01:20

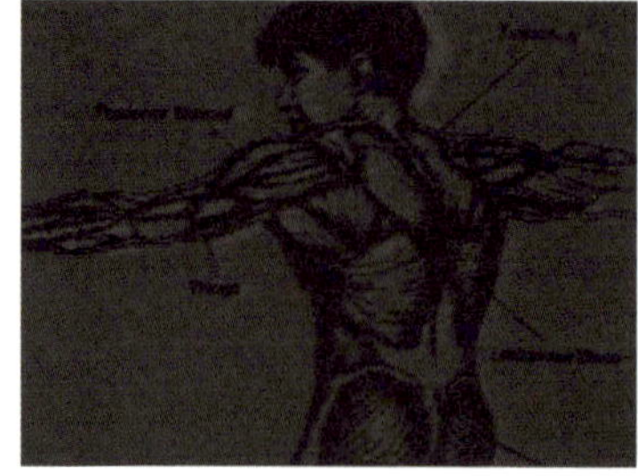
01:40

05:55

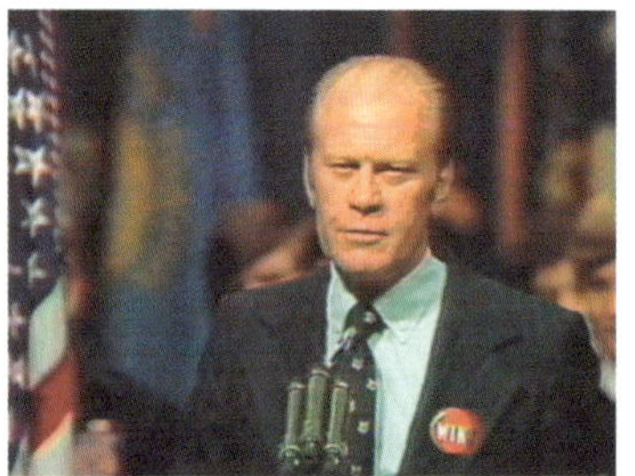
14:04

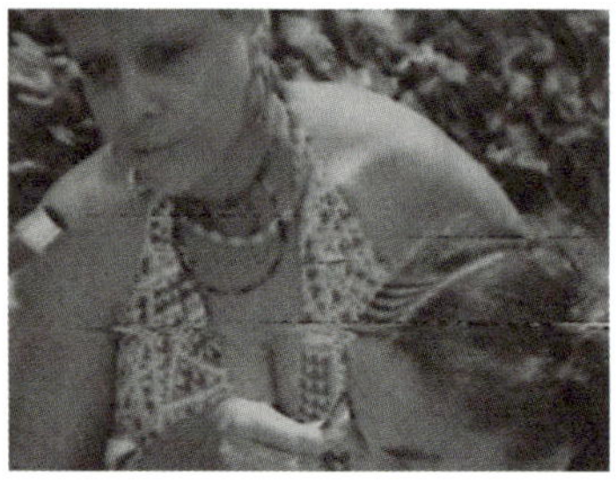
17:28

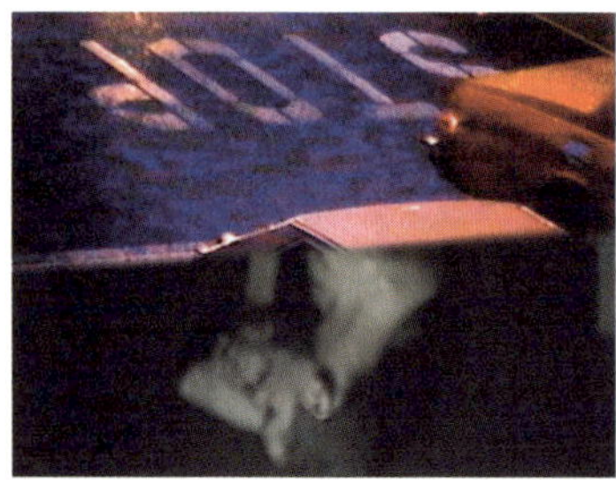
07:16

production and technological evolution, that EAI provided another kind of transmission that connected the material and machinic tools of video making with intergenerational dialogue and peer-to-peer relationships. As an archive, EAI is tasked with keeping the formats of the works under its care up-to-date and available for preservation, while staying true to the artists' original intent with regard to display in museums, galleries, and access to pedagogic platforms. And yet to do this, and maintain relevance, it must engage with younger artists familiar with the tools and technologies of the present. Film historian Erika Balsom has discussed the vogue within contemporary art for analog modes as an occasion to highlight "the need to conceive of 'new media' and 'old media' as relational categories rather than fixed essences, and signal the extent to which our understandings of media are culturally and discursively determined rather than dictated solely by material or ontological characteristics."[6] Similarly, this observation can be applied to the way in which art histories

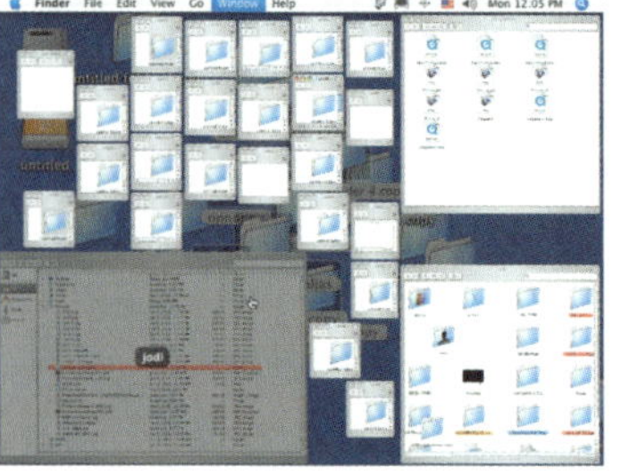
00:51

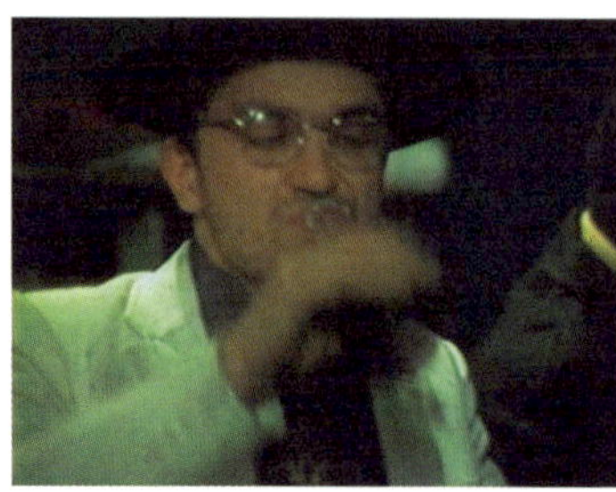
08:22

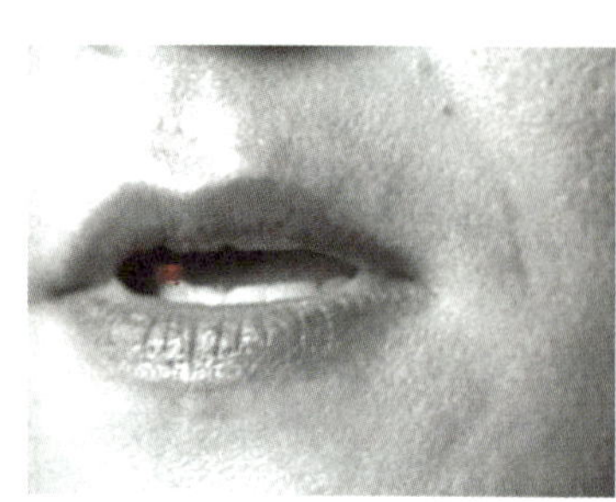
00:06

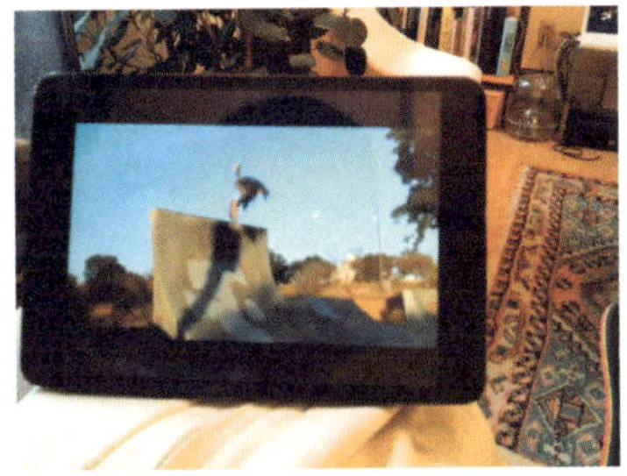
04:04

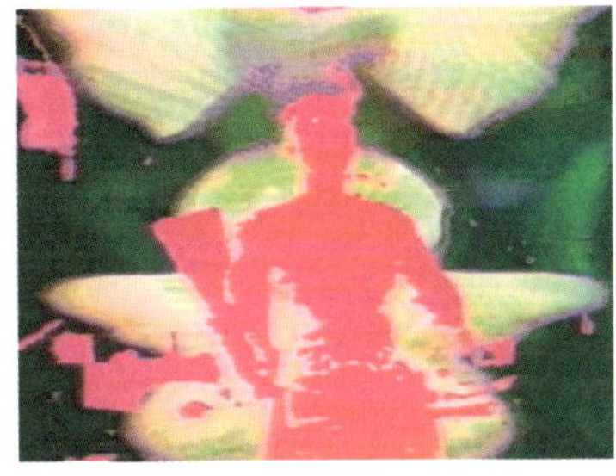
14:35

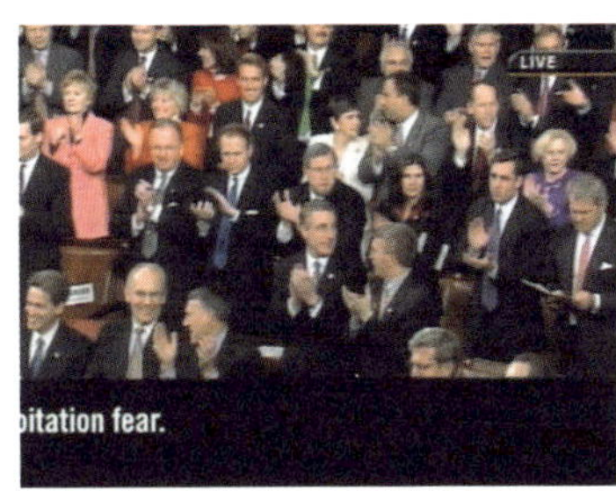

04:37

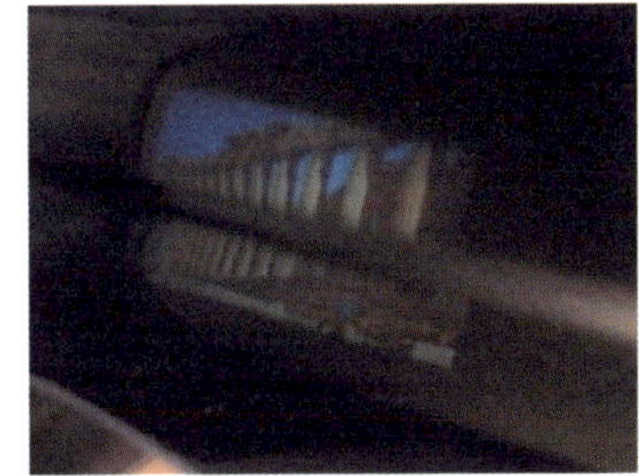
00:24

are rarely representative of the relational aspects of artistic influence and, in the case of EAI, the instrumental exchanges that take place between artists in an editing bay.

Artist Robert Buck (formerly Beck), who worked on and off at EAI in various capacities from 1982 to 2004, remembers that when he first joined the organization right out of the NYU BFA program he would come into regular contact with video pioneers such as Shigeko Kubota, Nam June Paik, Joan Jonas, Dan Graham, Antoni Muntadas, and Charlie Atlas. There were also younger artists such as Dara Birnbaum, Fitzgerald and Sanborn, Michael Smith, Gary Hill, and Tony Oursler, who were beginning to make some of their best-known videos. And in later years, Tony Cokes and X-PRZ, his collective alongside Doug Anderson, Kenseth Armstead, and Mark Pierson, at times included Buck as editor.[7] While many of these figures might have come to EAI for editing assistance, they were equally likely to swing by to discuss the latest video festivals, review the details of the distribution

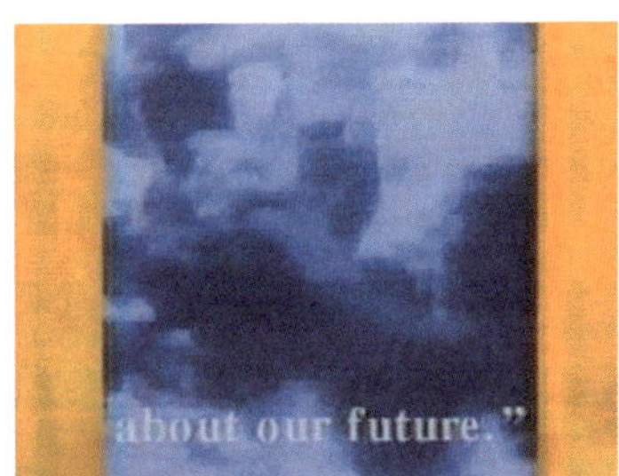

00:41

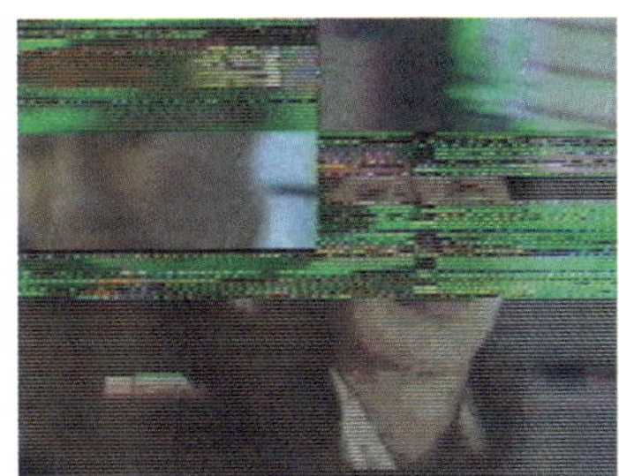
21:18

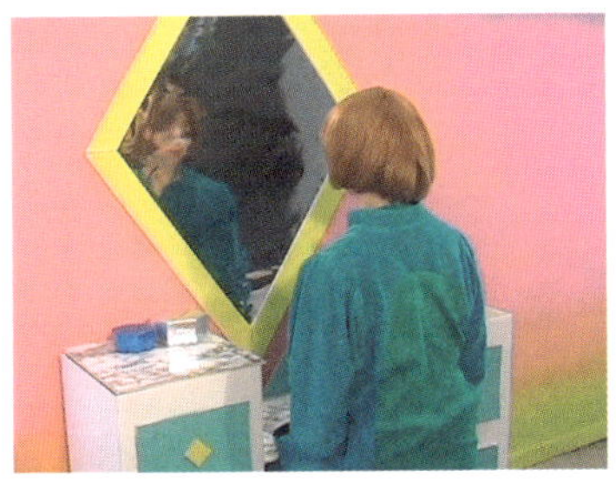
01:30

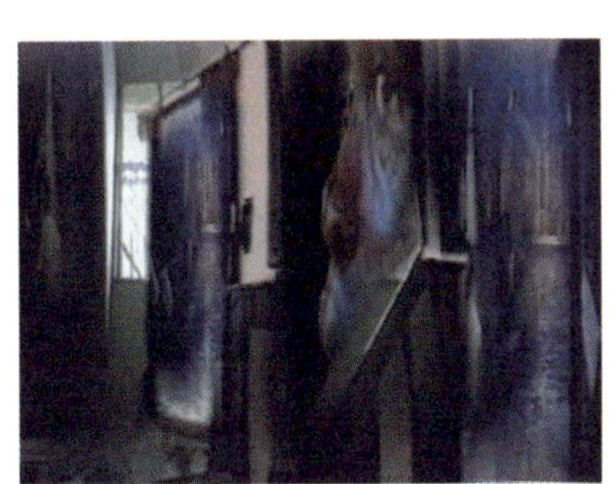
00:27

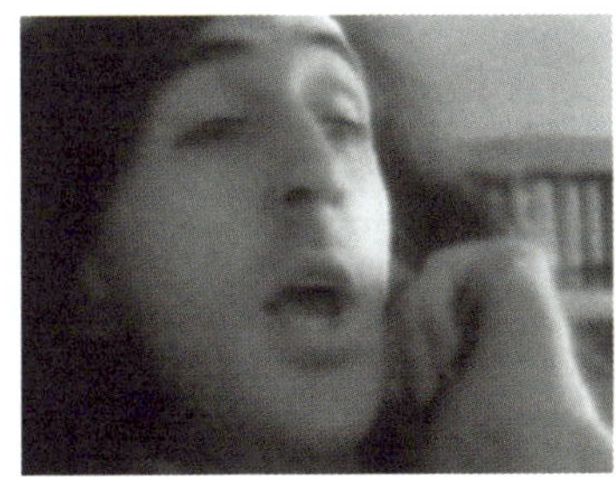
04:30

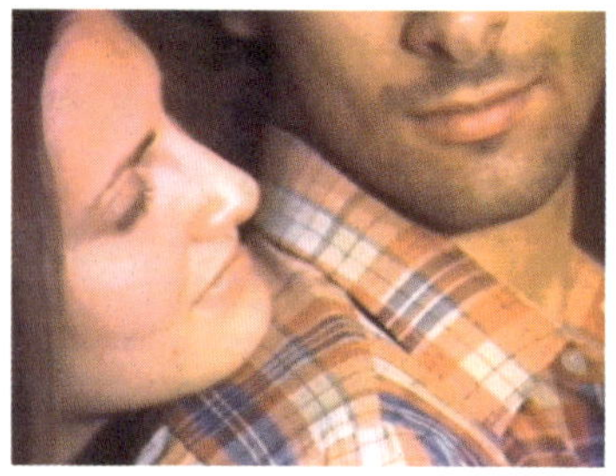

01:19

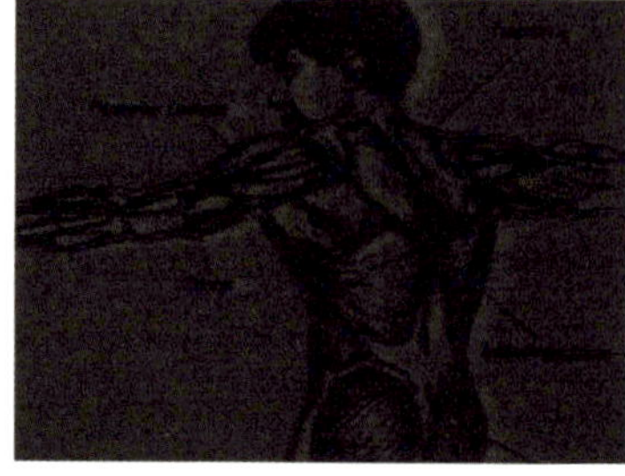

01:39

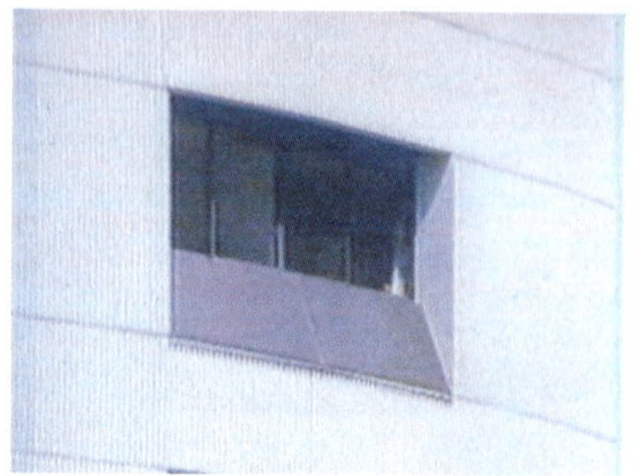

05:54

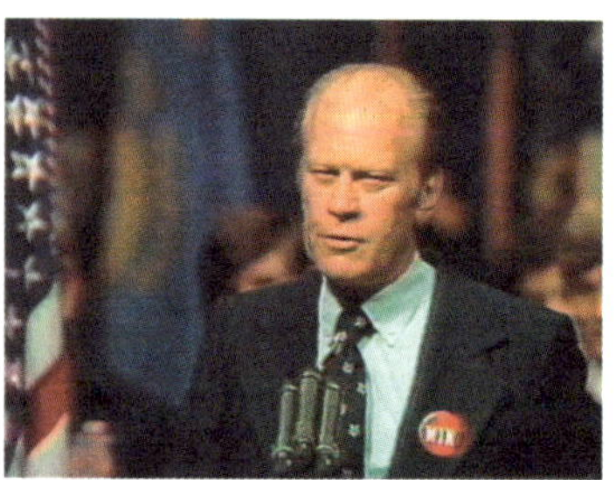

14:03

of their videos, get advice about funding for projects—a necessity in the absence of a commercial gallery system that supported video art at the time—or gossip about the art world. In the early 1980s, especially, as the downtown club and art scenes intermingled, Buck remembers the fluidity between working a job, making art, and socializing: "Good times included going to EAI, going to see a band like The Smiths, and then coming back to EAI to make a tape…There was no division between work and life."[8] Former director Lori Zippay also remembers the frenetic activity of the time: "It was around-the-clock editing. There were waiting lists. It was a staff of up to five editors at any one time, it was amazing. It was club scene video, it was music video, etc."[9]

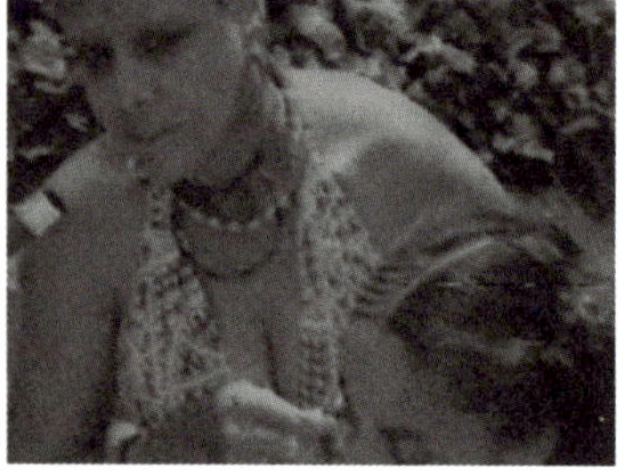

17:27

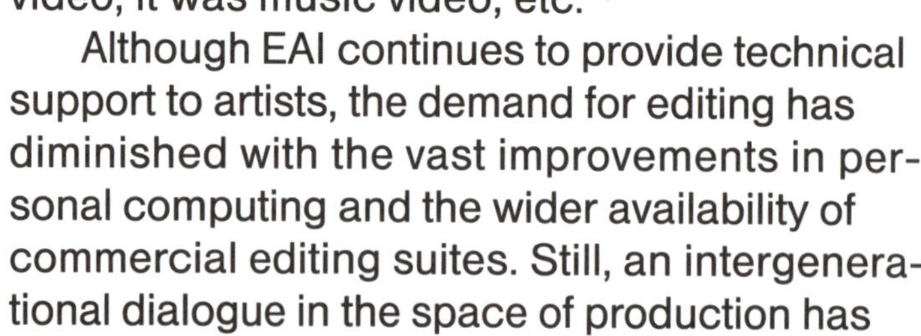

Although EAI continues to provide technical support to artists, the demand for editing has diminished with the vast improvements in personal computing and the wider availability of commercial editing suites. Still, an intergenerational dialogue in the space of production has

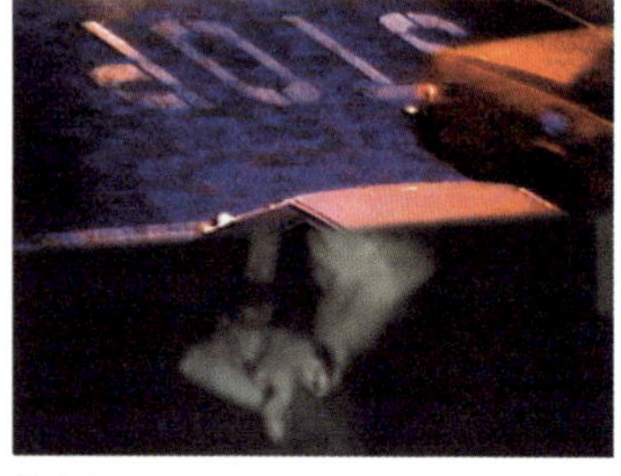

07:15

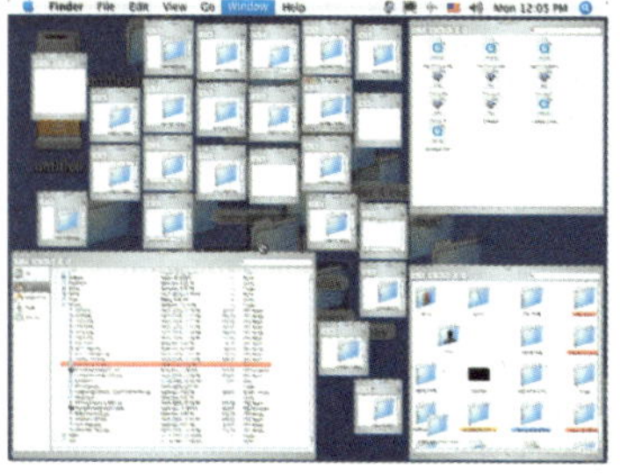

00:50

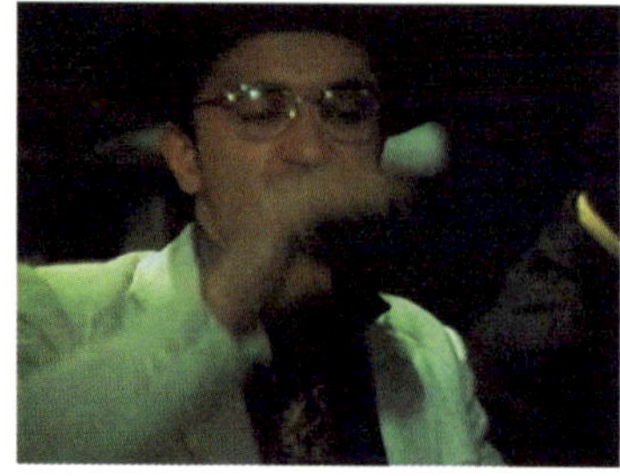

08:21

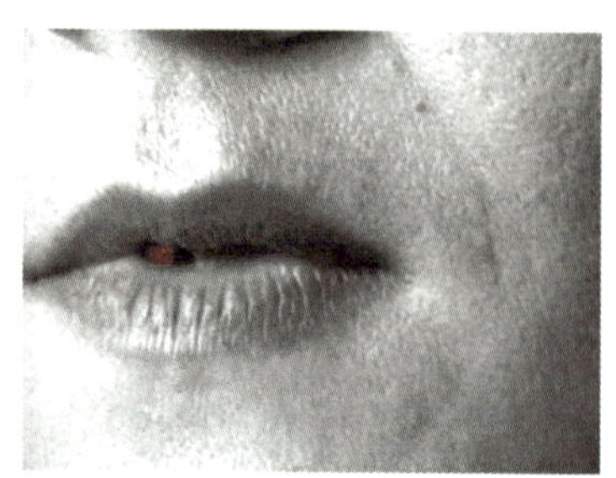

00:05

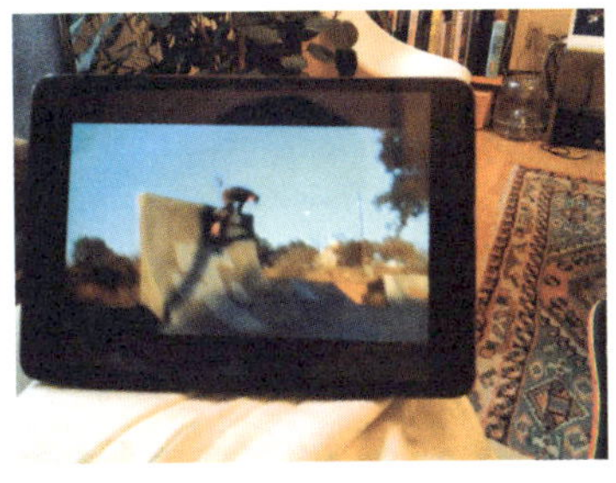

04:04

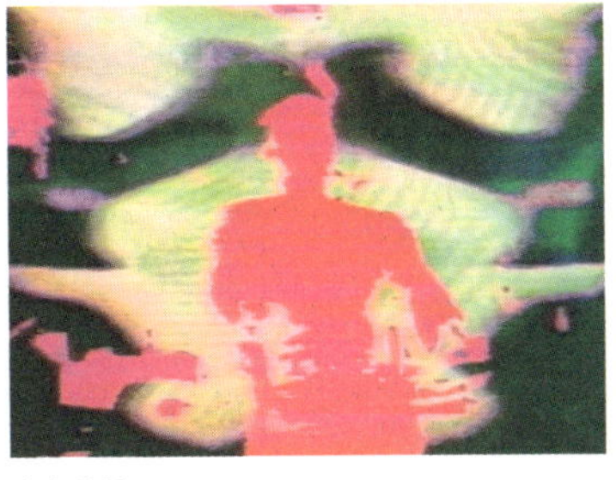

14:35

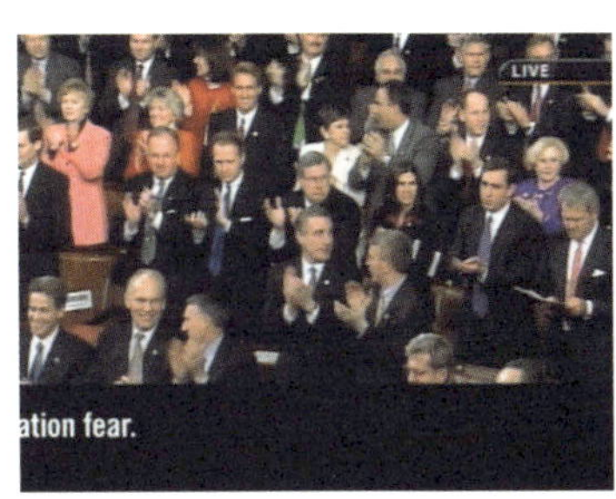

04:37

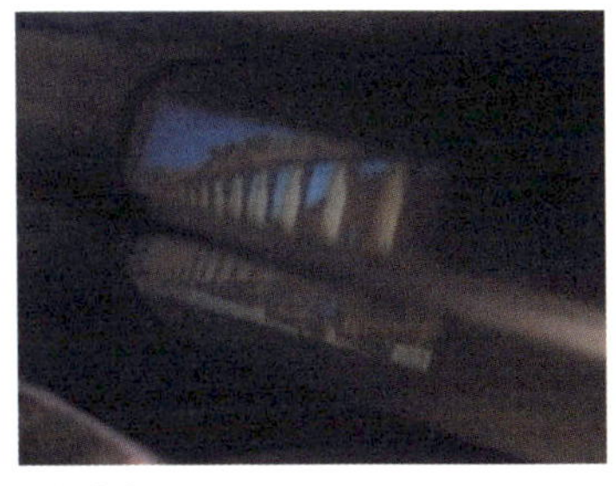

00:24

continued into the present as older artists have engaged with younger artists employed by EAI to help coordinate newer digital formats. For this younger generation, EAI has been a resource to learn about media histories that are rarely discussed in-depth in art school and an opportunity to connect with the ethos of a previous New York art world. Relationships and friendships have been forged by means of employment, internships, and late-night editing sessions. While these artists might be more commonly associated with online interventions and digital output, their strategies are deeply informed by EAI's context, collection, and people. In this way, what is often seen as a technological break should be understood as a continuity in which one group of artists learns from the strategies of another.

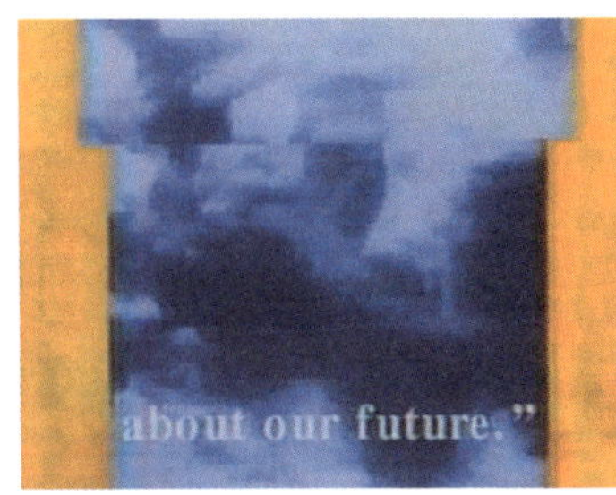

00:41

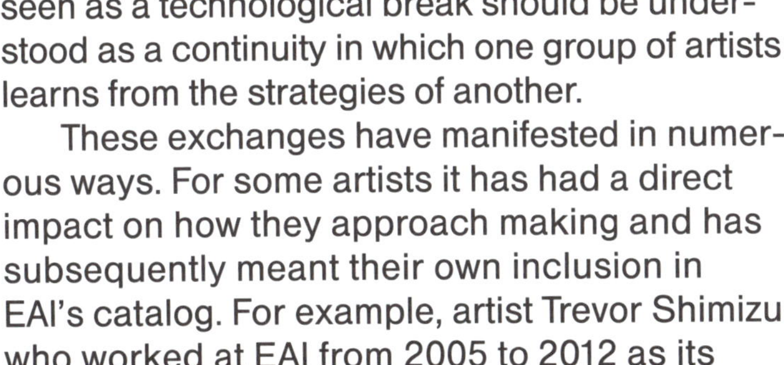

These exchanges have manifested in numerous ways. For some artists it has had a direct impact on how they approach making and has subsequently meant their own inclusion in EAI's catalog. For example, artist Trevor Shimizu, who worked at EAI from 2005 to 2012 as its

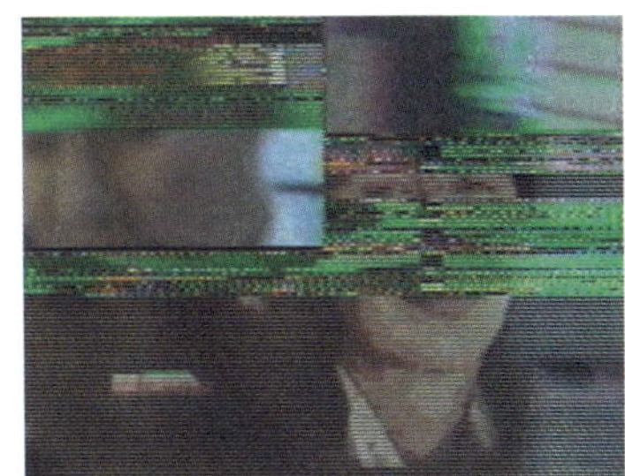

21:18

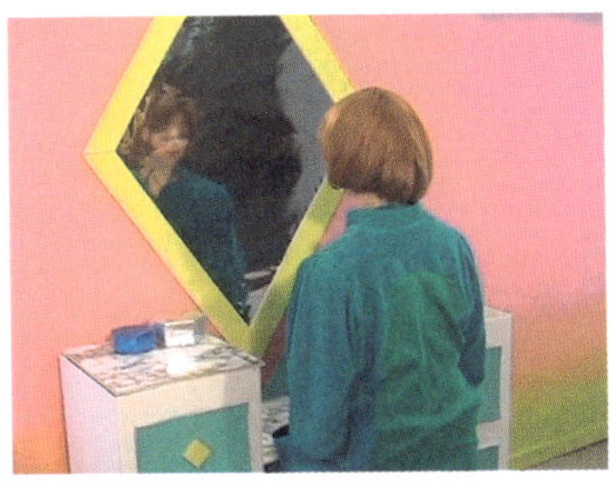

01:30

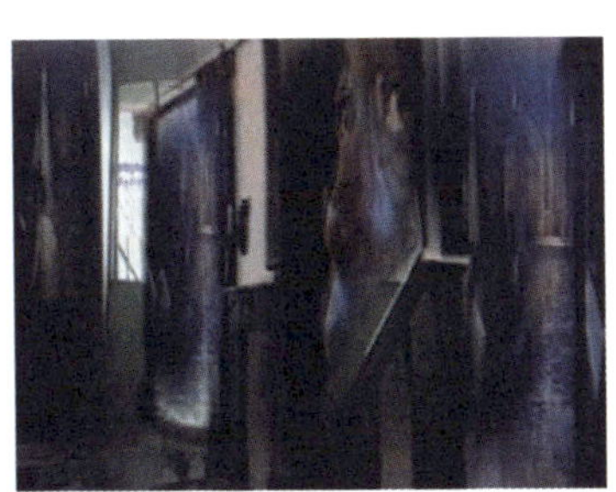

00:27

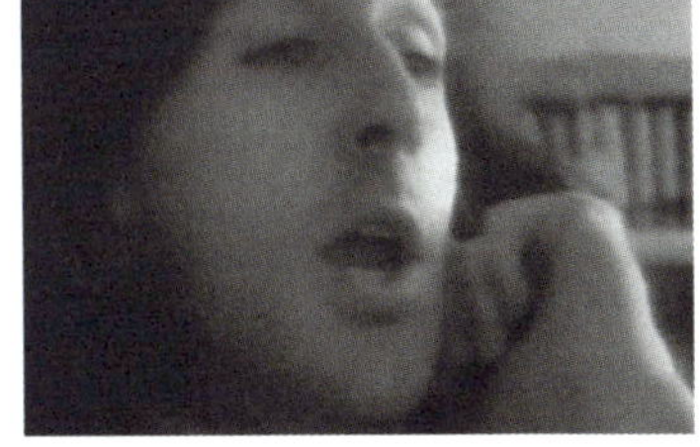

04:30

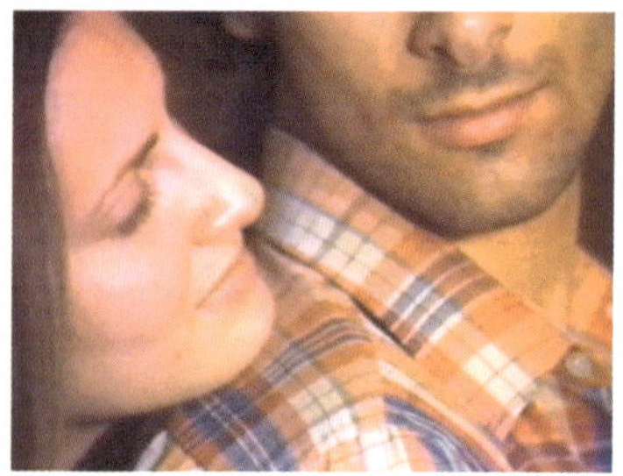

01:19

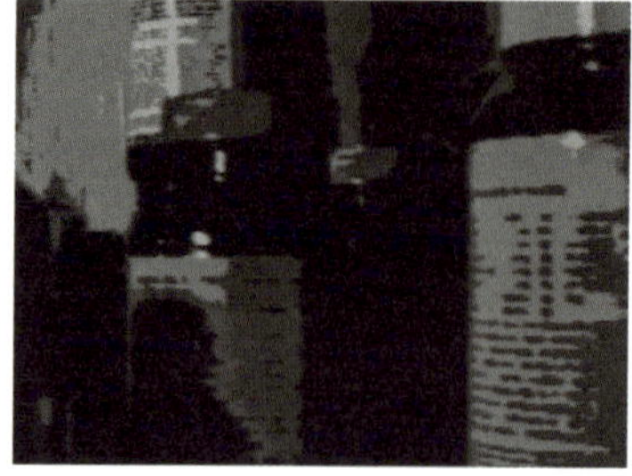

01:39

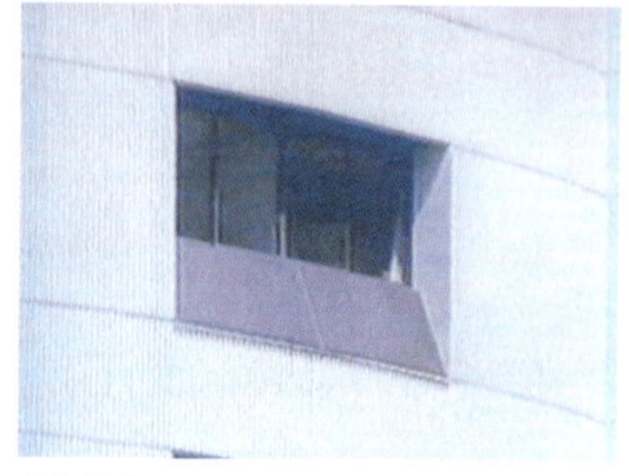

05:54

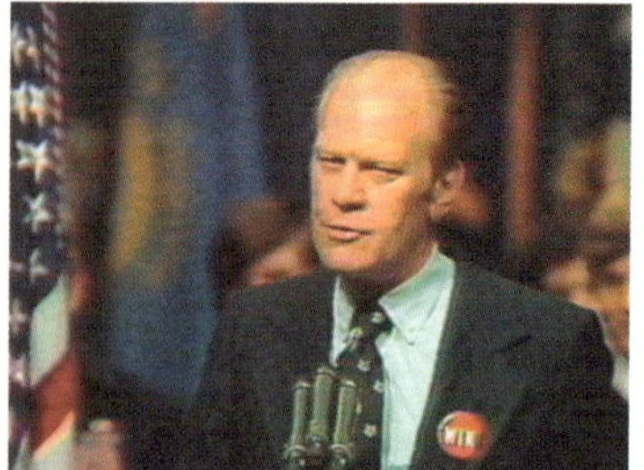

14:03

assistant technical director and later as technical director—and whose own videos have recently joined the EAI roster—recalls:

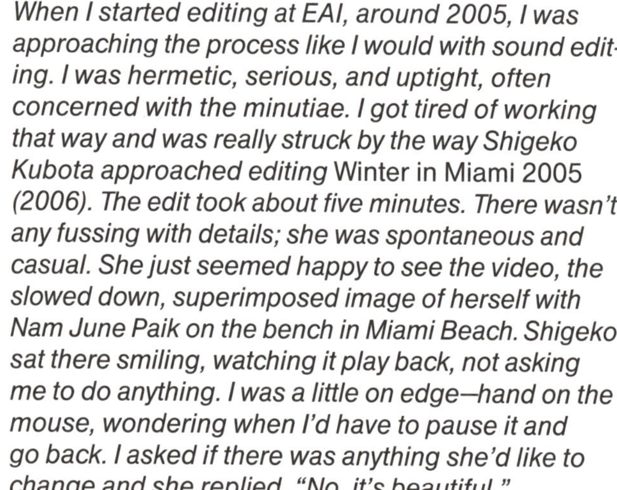

> *When I started editing at EAI, around 2005, I was approaching the process like I would with sound editing. I was hermetic, serious, and uptight, often concerned with the minutiae. I got tired of working that way and was really struck by the way Shigeko Kubota approached editing* Winter in Miami 2005 *(2006). The edit took about five minutes. There wasn't any fussing with details; she was spontaneous and casual. She just seemed happy to see the video, the slowed down, superimposed image of herself with Nam June Paik on the bench in Miami Beach. Shigeko sat there smiling, watching it play back, not asking me to do anything. I was a little on edge—hand on the mouse, wondering when I'd have to pause it and go back. I asked if there was anything she'd like to change and she replied, "No, it's beautiful."*
>
> *Dan Graham and I had a similar way of working. We worked intuitively and fast. Decisions were precise and we made only a few small changes to our edits. Making the title slates took the most work, choosing the font and color, but it was always lighthearted and fun. We'd spend thirty minutes editing at EAI and two hours eating lunch at Pepe Giallo and looking at shows.*

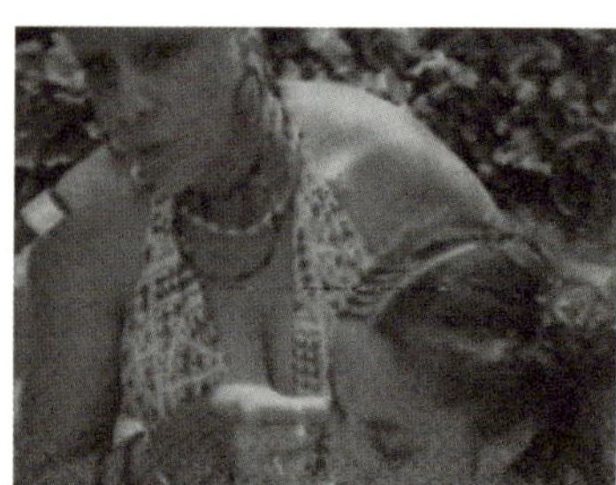

17:27

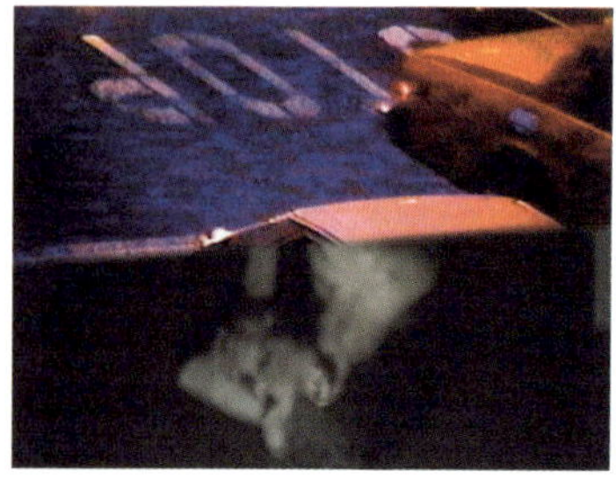

07:15

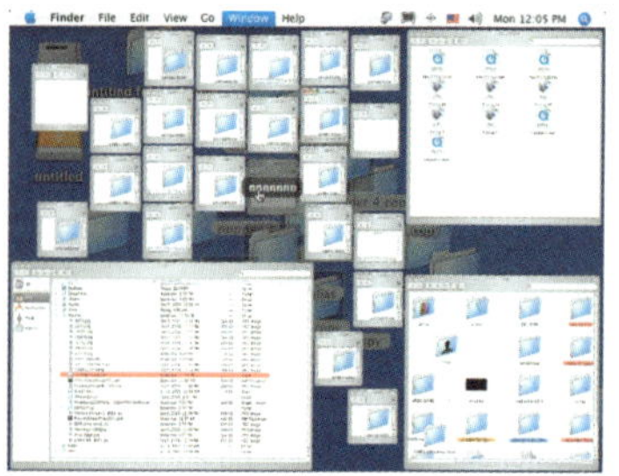

00:50

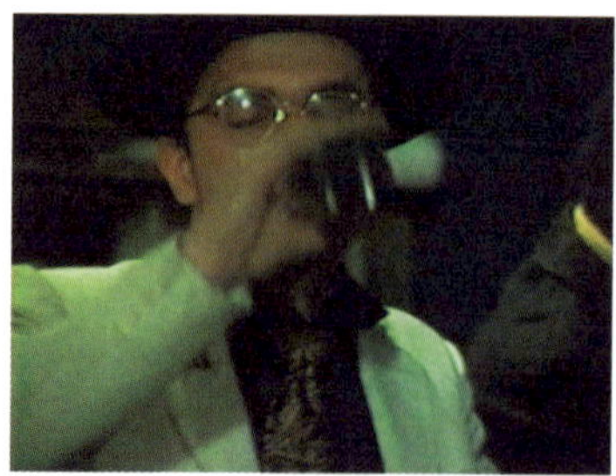

08:21

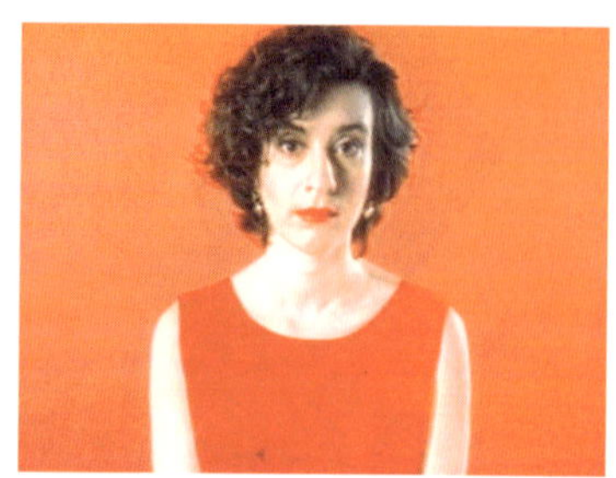

00:05

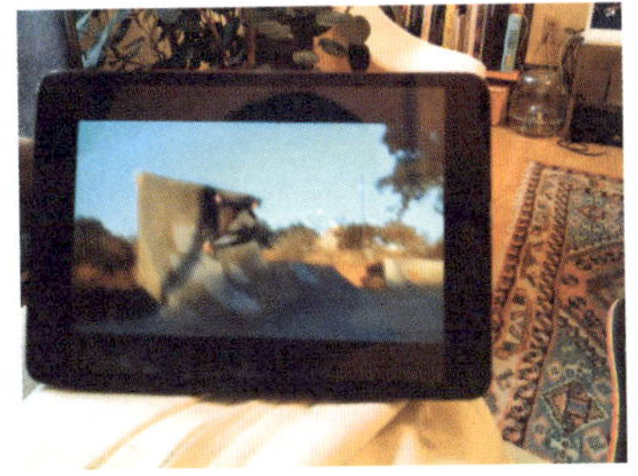

04:04

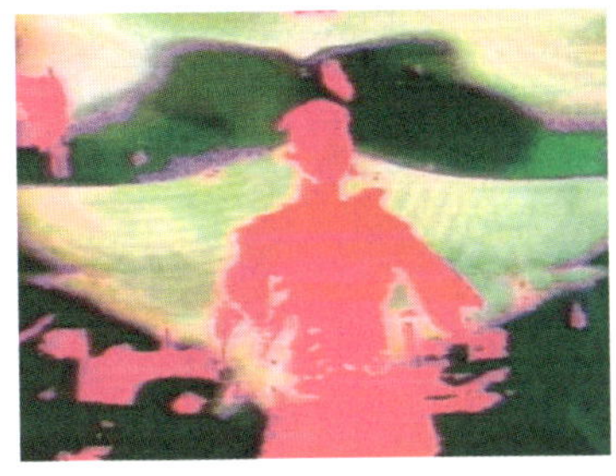

14:35

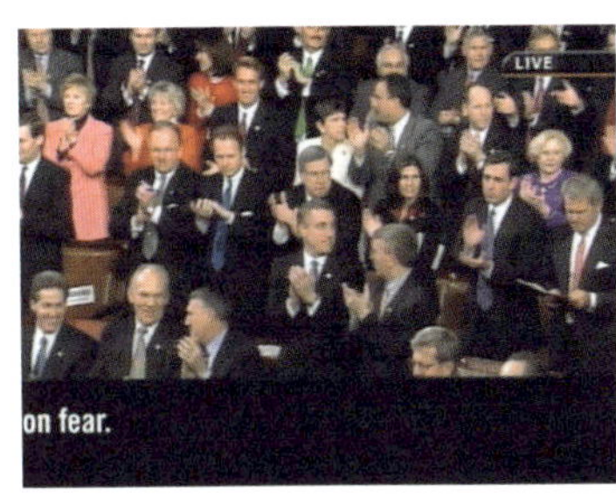

04:37

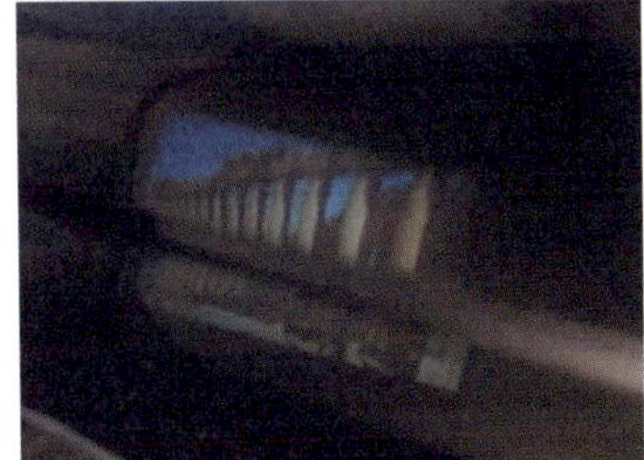

00:24

Working with Carolee [Schneemann] was a bit more involved. The process involved scanning images, digitizing "lost" tapes, frame-by-frame alterations of the image, color, and soundtrack. Editing with Carolee was often like working with her on a collage or painting. She would take existing material and want to transform it through colorizing the footage, pulling stills, superimposing existing or found material, and changing the speed of playback. Many of the videos were highly edited, but there was always a sense of fun. We'd take great lunch breaks, eating bresaola salad and apple crisp from Bottino while watching cat videos on YouTube. All of these experiences shaped how I made work then and approach pretty much everything today.[10]

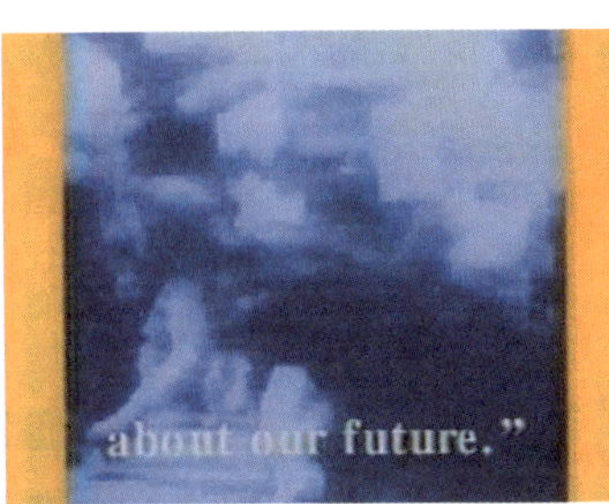

00:41

This direct learning from other artists is also bound up with an ethos of practice that is tied to the video medium having historically operated separately from market forces. Buck observes, "Part of the reason I came to EAI was to make more video and see more video. What happened in the process is that I was introduced to an alternative model for the distribution, exhibition, and sale of artwork . . . For me, and I can't stress this enough, I learned a way to work, an ethic, which

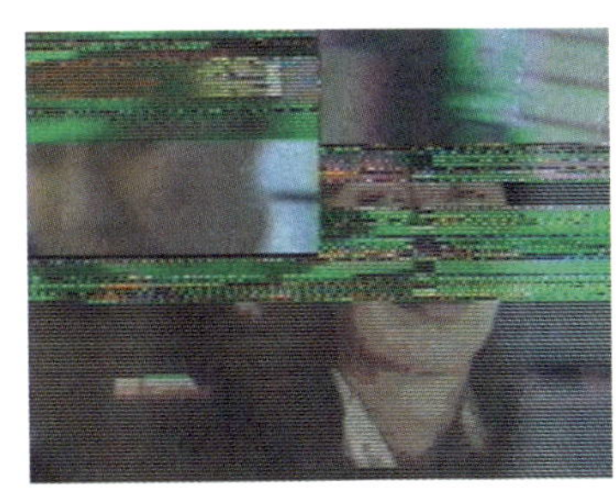

21:18

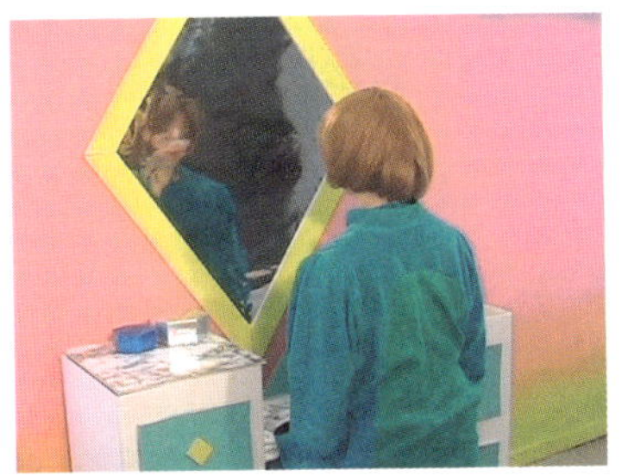

01:30

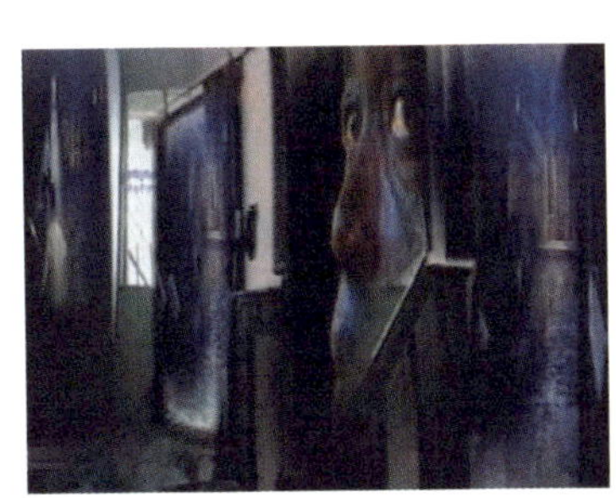

00:27

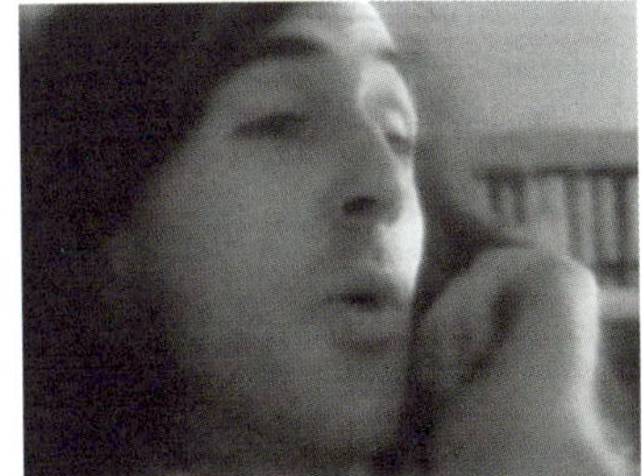

04:30

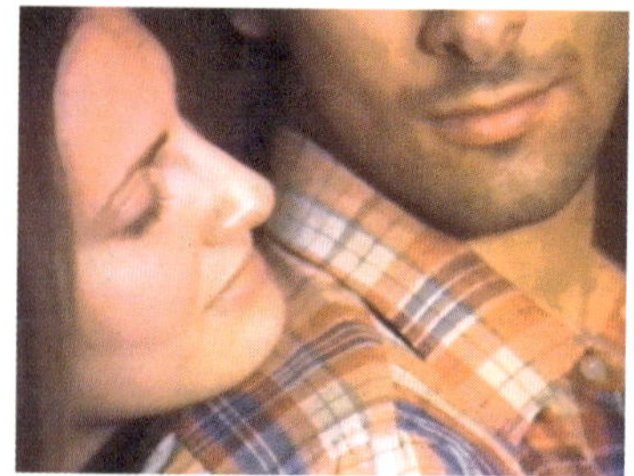

01:19

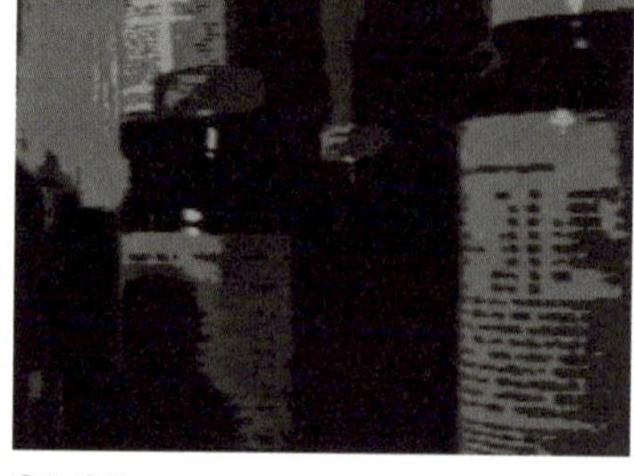

01:39

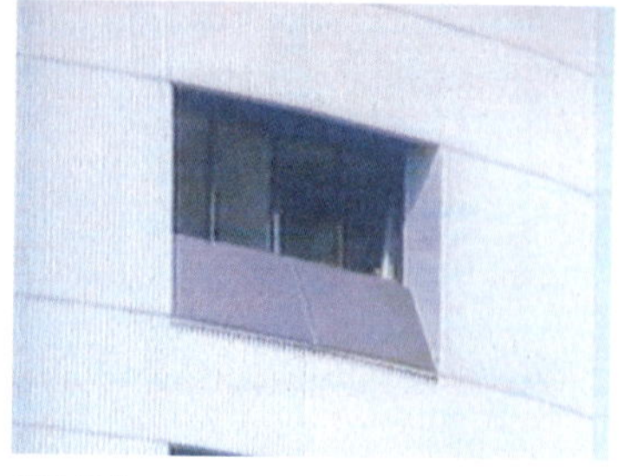

05:54

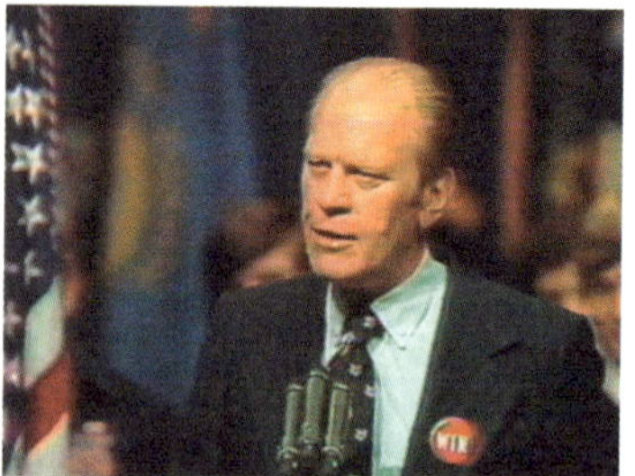

14:03

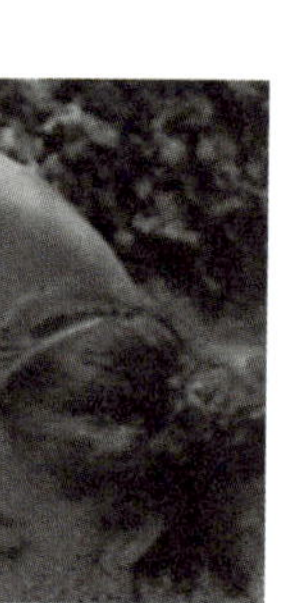

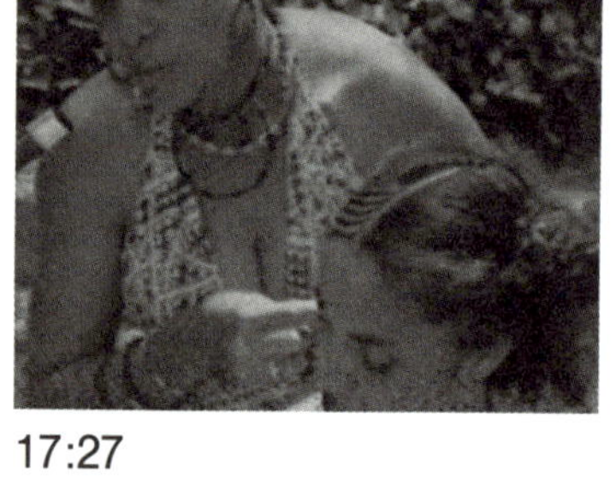

17:27

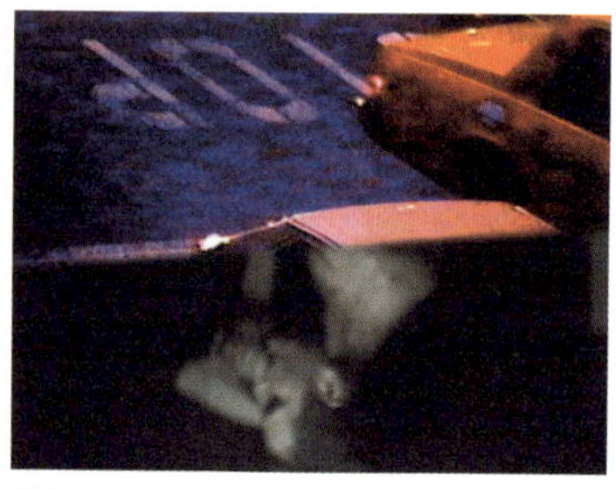

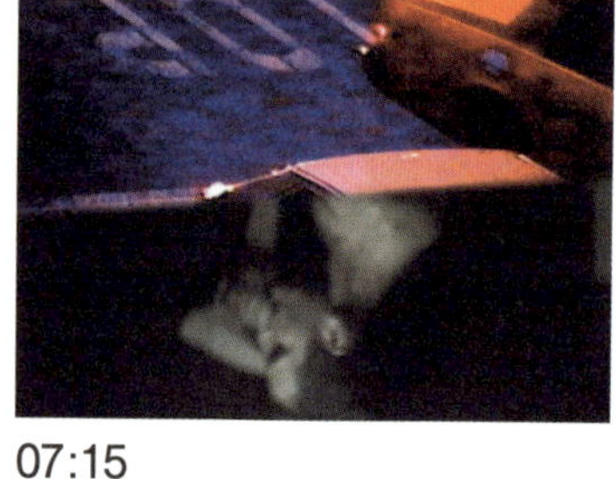

07:15

is rewarded but not in a way one would expect—not according to some transactional, capitalist model."[11] These sentiments are echoed in Seth Price's essay *Dispersion* (2002), a foundational text that ruminates on art's relationship to the readymade in the age of the internet: "An art grounded in distributed media can be seen as a political art and an art of communicative action…"[12] Indeed, it is hard not to read these words without EAI's model in mind and as being informed, at least in some part, by Price's own time working at the organization from 1998 to 2005, first as its technical assistant and later as technical director. In these roles, Price was present for some of the major institutional shifts that occurred with the nascent availability of bootlegs of artists' work online such as UbuWeb, game-changing transitions from analog to digital formats, new modes of appropriation spawned by the web, the increased interest by galleries in the commercialization of moving image works, and the recuperation of older figures. When Price writes, "With more and more

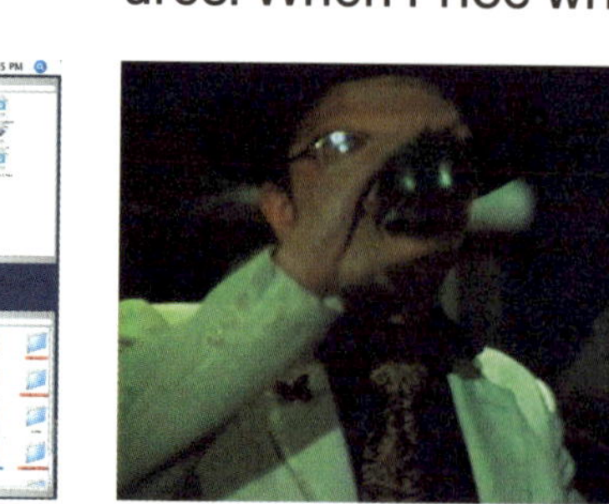

00:50

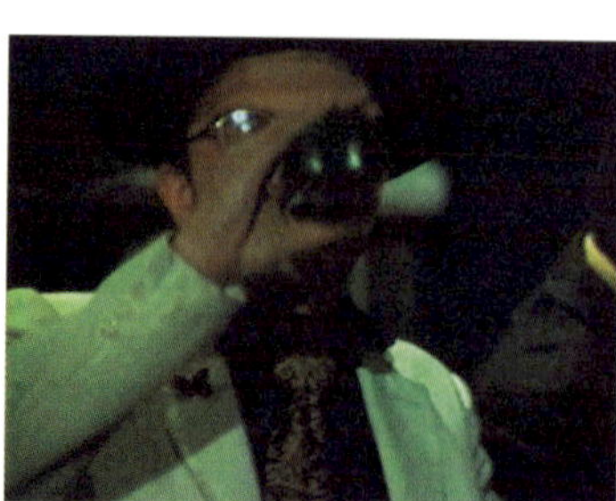

08:21

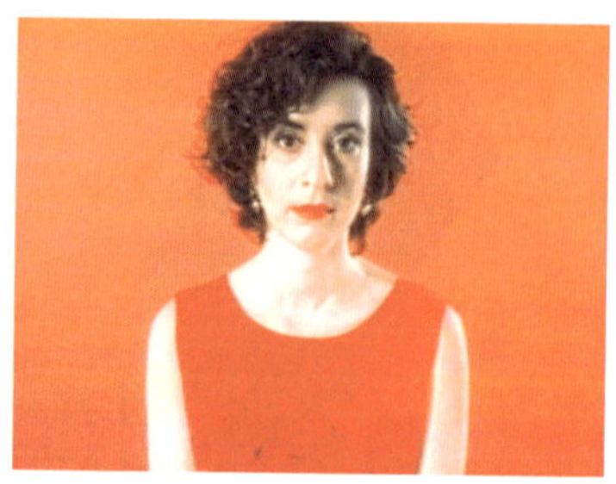

00:05

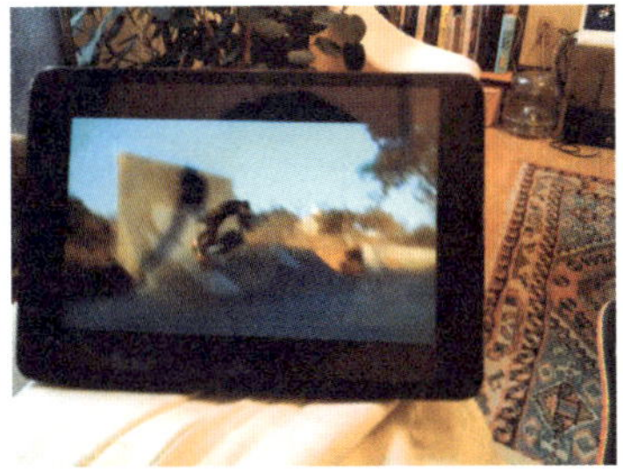
04:04

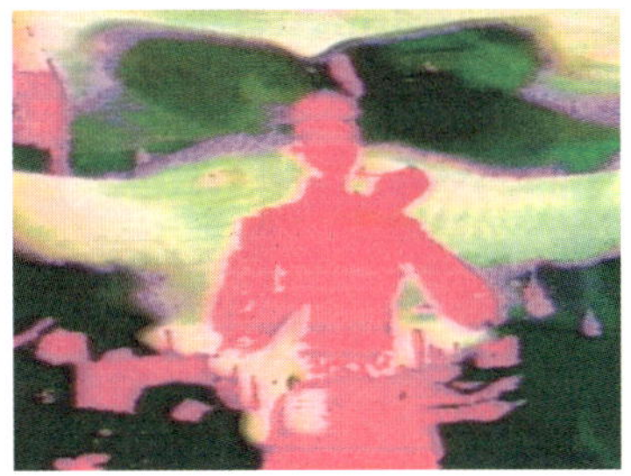
14:35

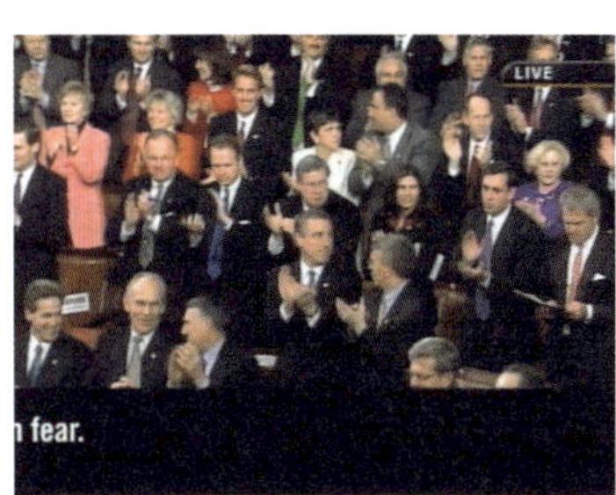

04:37

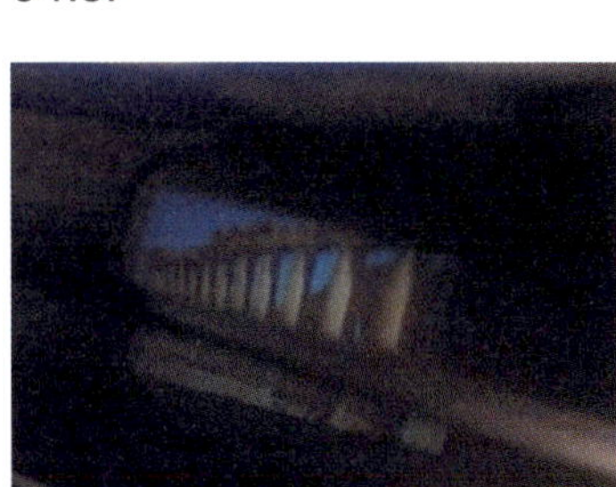
00:24

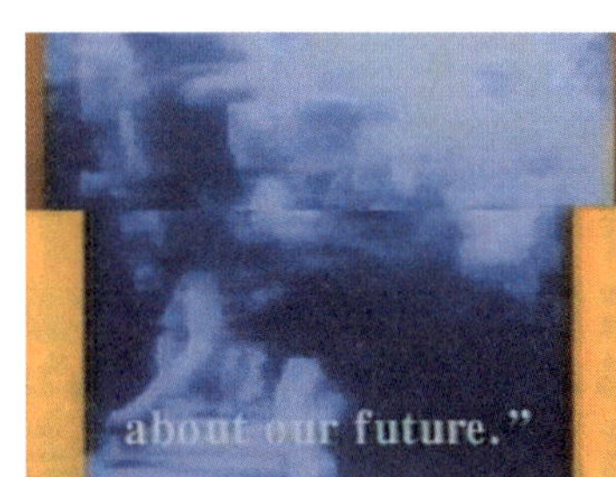

00:41

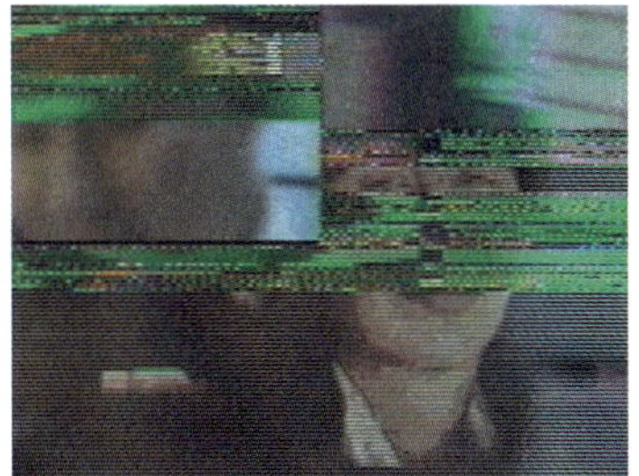
21:18

media readily available through this unruly archive, the task becomes one of packaging, producing, reframing, and distributing; a mode of production analogous not to the creation of material goods, but to the production of social contexts, using existing material," he also points to the increased stakes of EAI's operational model in the twenty-first century and the centrality of questions of distribution and circulation for artistic practice more generally.[13]

This exposure to the work of distribution and circulation has necessarily connected back to the autobiographies and activism of several artists. For Sondra Perry—who credits EAI with giving her the confidence to pursue work in video—digital fluency corresponds with the material concerns of analog production. As an intern she learned a great deal from the archive, which she viewed as a kind of network culture before the internet, and from being introduced to artists such as Tony Ramos. These experiences offered her a lineage that she could see, touch, and feel. But it was reading EAI's contracts that made

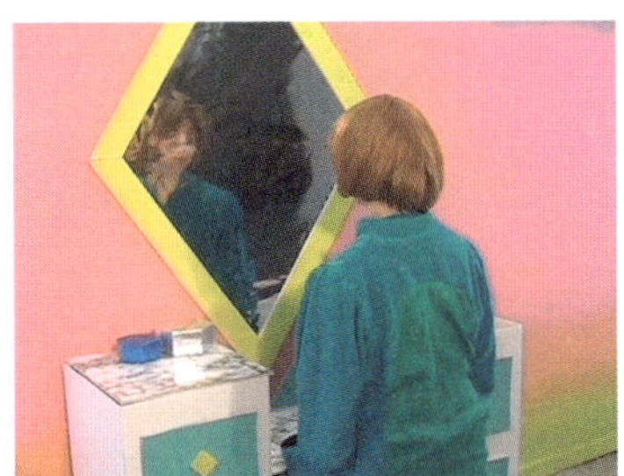
01:30

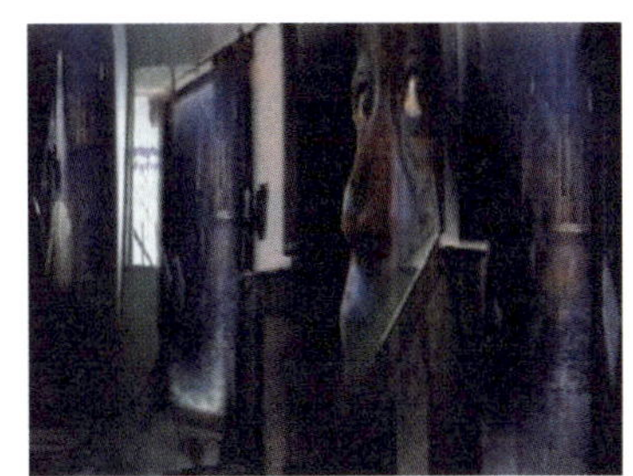
00:27

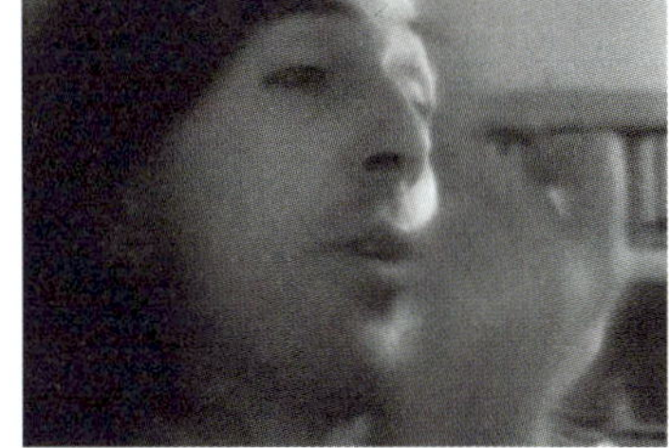
04:30

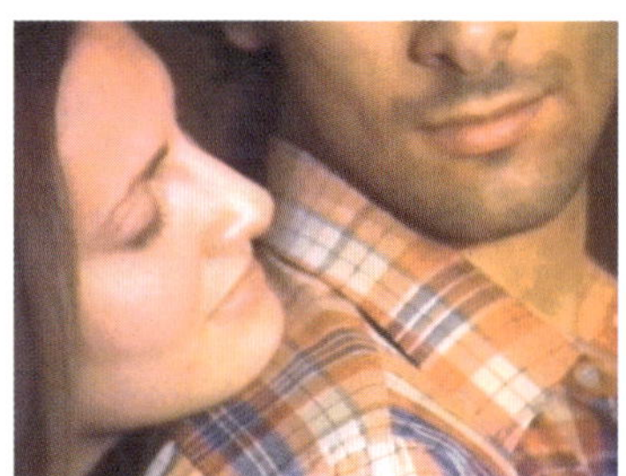

01:19

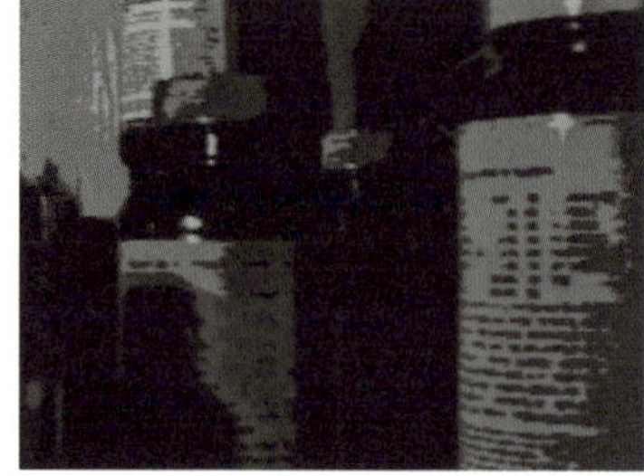

01:39

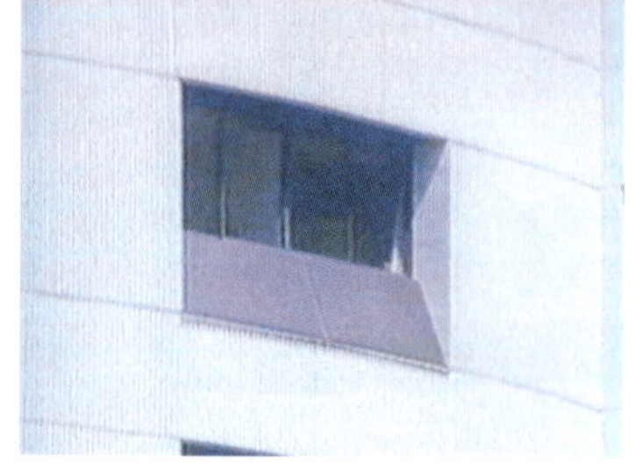

05:54

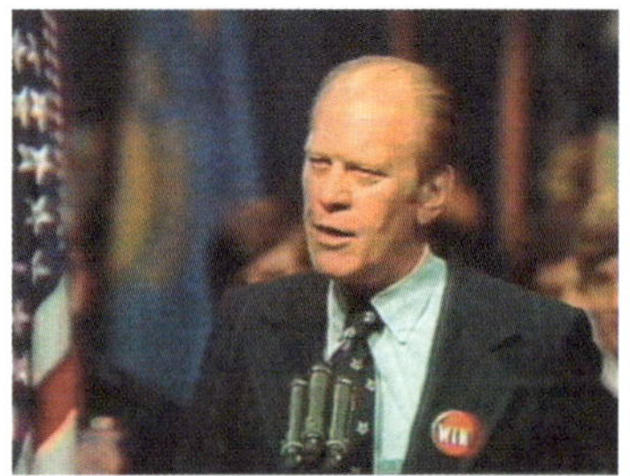

14:03

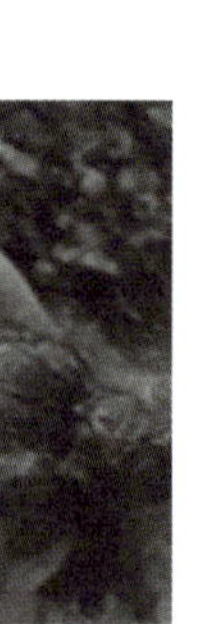

17:27

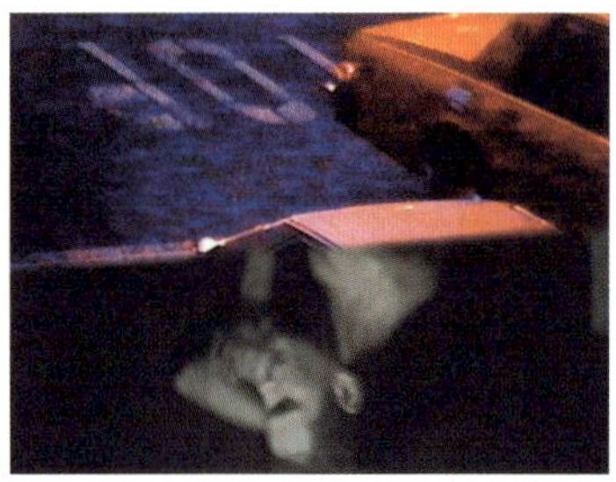

07:15

one of the biggest impressions on her. Well before initiatives such as W.A.G.E. (Working Artists and the Greater Economy), a core aspect of EAI's mission was to create a revenue stream for the artists in its collection. But for Perry, the advocacy for compensation is just one aspect of these agreements; what really hit home for her was EAI's distribution model and its engagement with the dissemination of images and the politics of ownership. She found the language especially interesting because "it didn't close down what video could do through arbitrary editions" and instead allowed the medium to move freely as it is consumed and reproduced in the multiple, while also acknowledging the need to compensate an artist's labor.[14] As her own work has developed, Perry says, "It has been helpful to go back to the EAI contracts and build in these questions about how things can circulate."[15] For Perry this is decidedly a political stance that resonates with how she often addresses the exploitation of the image of Black bodies and informs the way she provides residuals

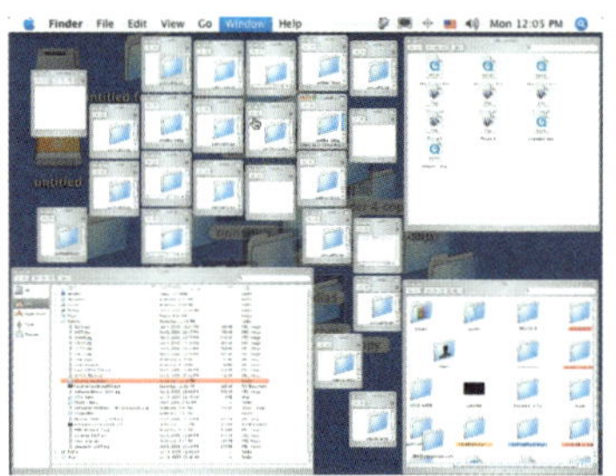

00:50

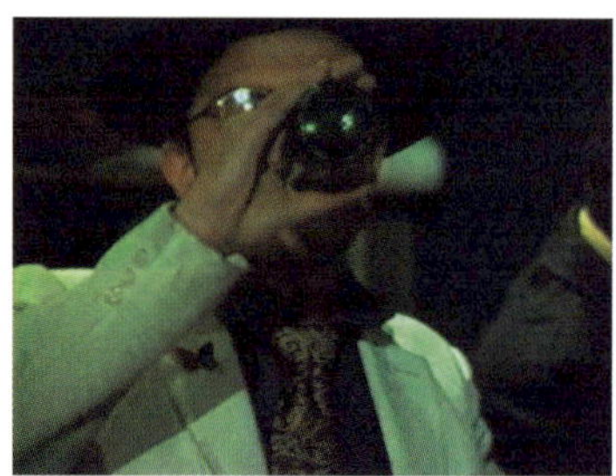

08:21

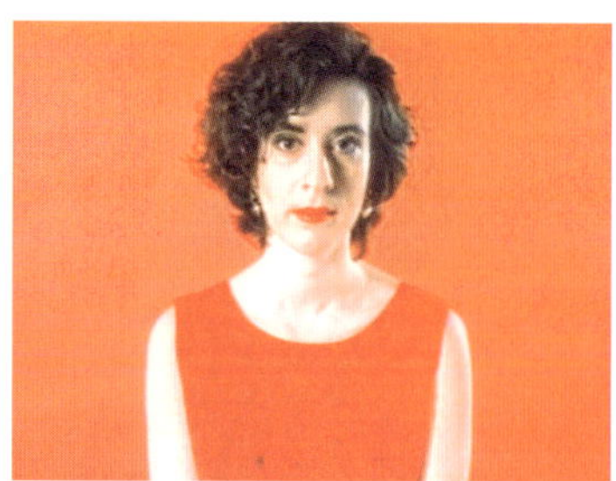

00:05

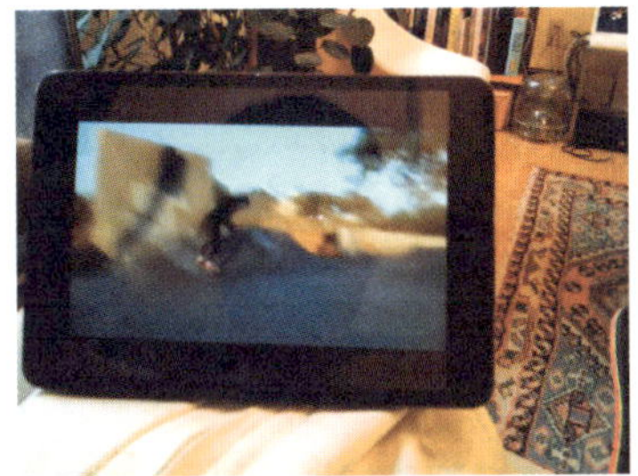

04:05

14:36

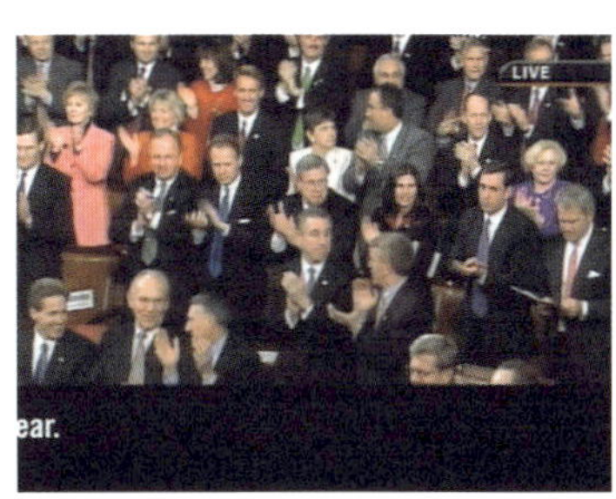

04:38

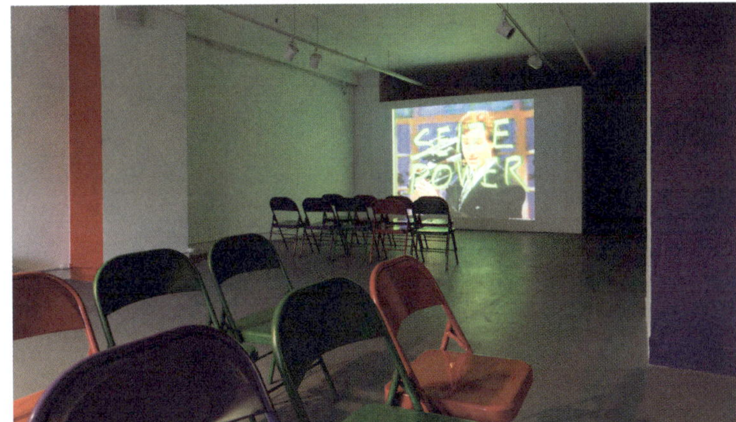

Broadcasting: Guerrilla Media, installation view, Slought

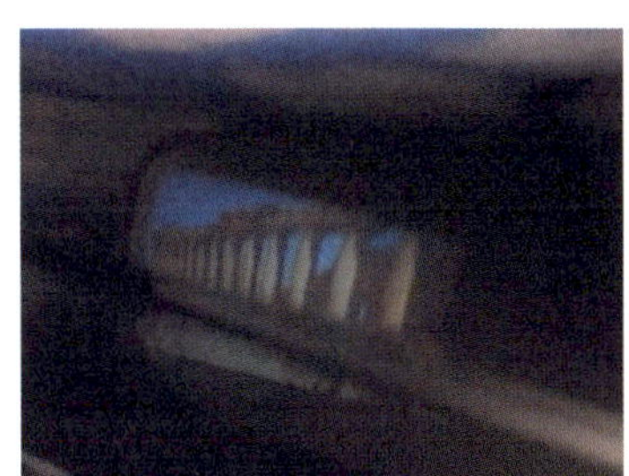

00:25

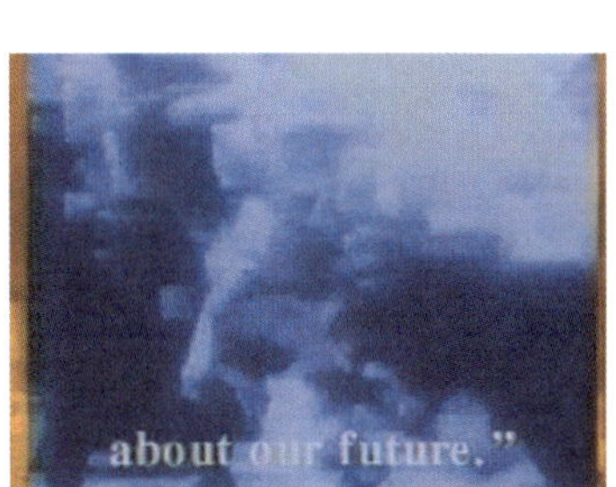

00:42

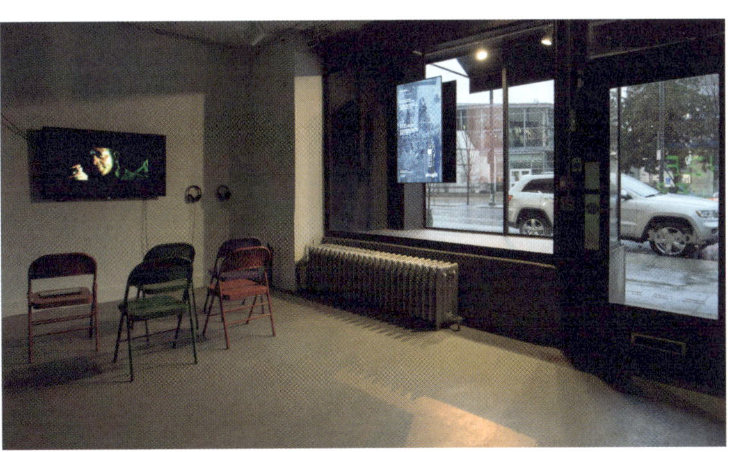

Broadcasting: Guerrilla Media, installation view, Slought

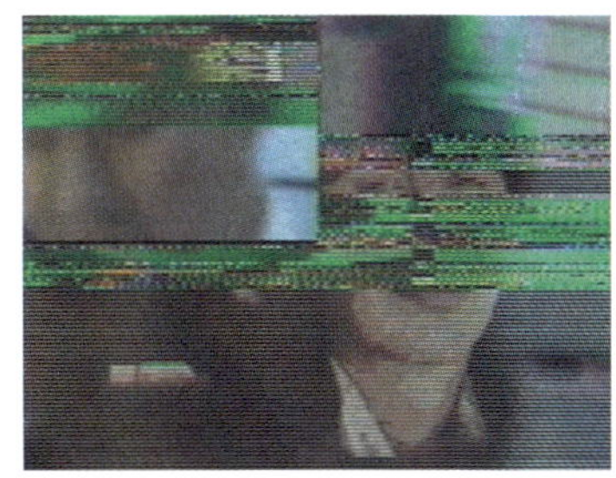

21:19

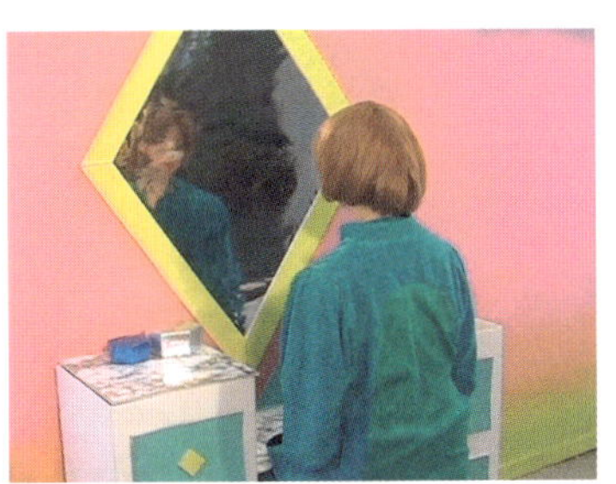

01:31

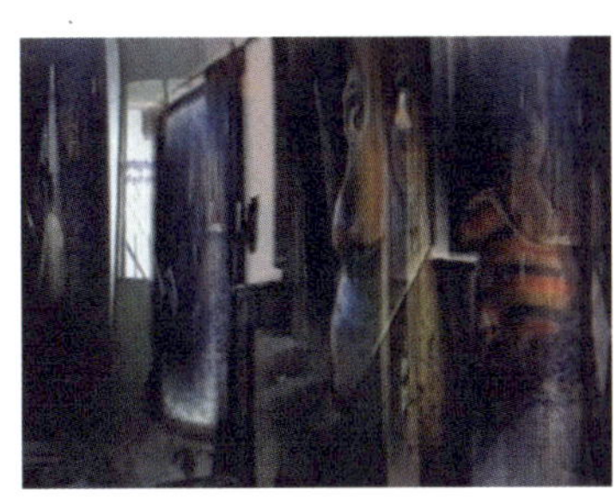

00:28

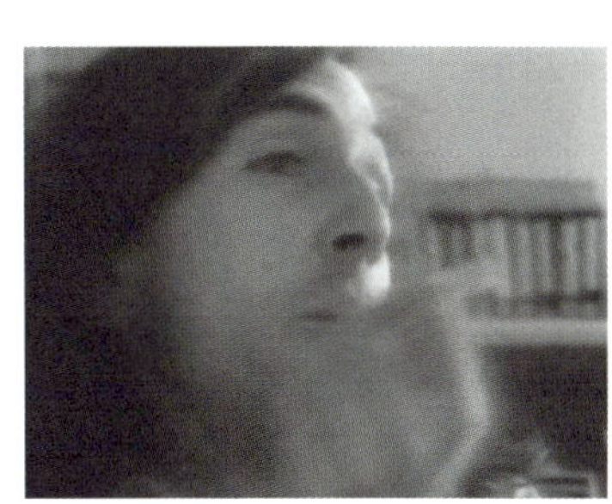

04:31

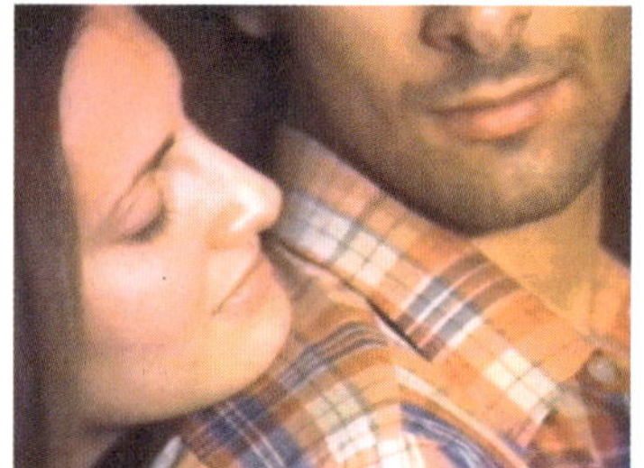

01:19

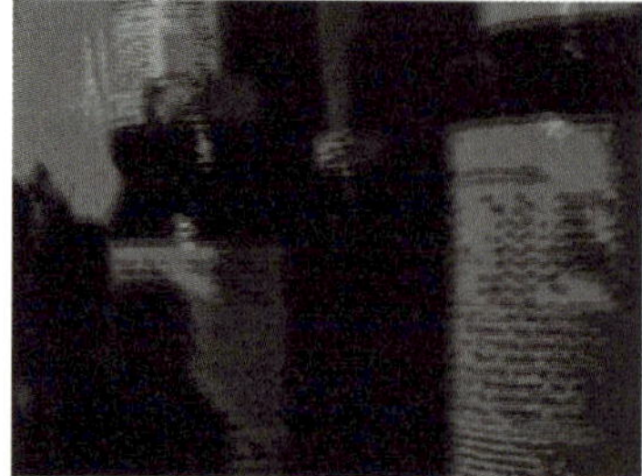

01:39

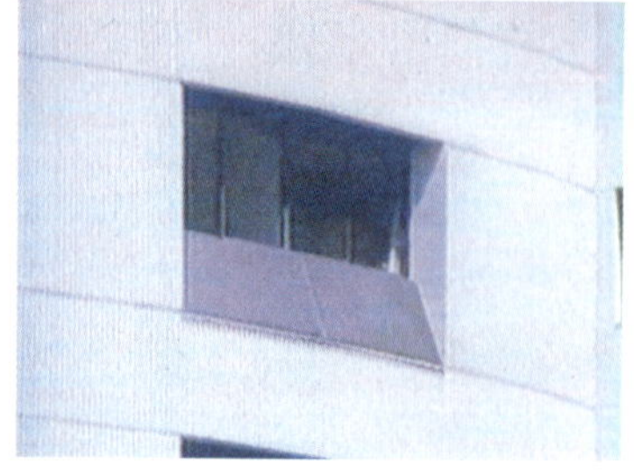

05:54

14:03

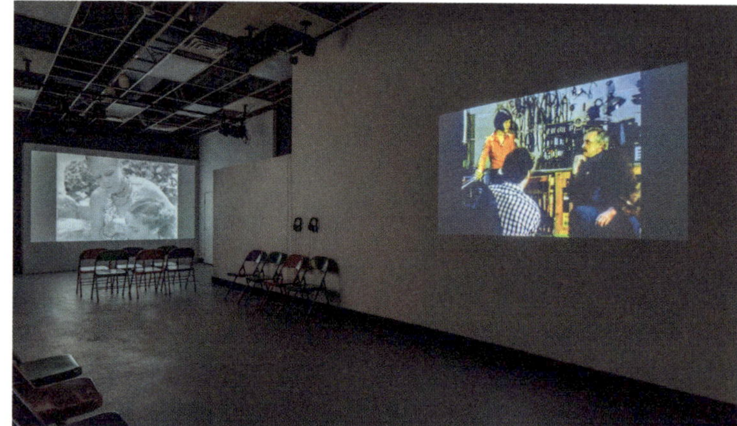

Broadcasting: Guerrilla Media, installation view, Slought

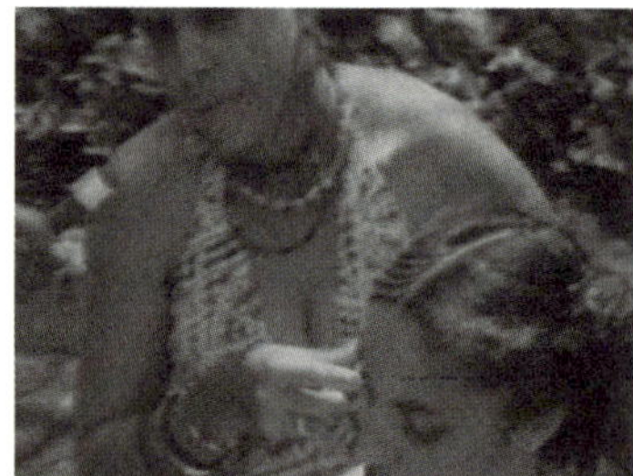

17:27

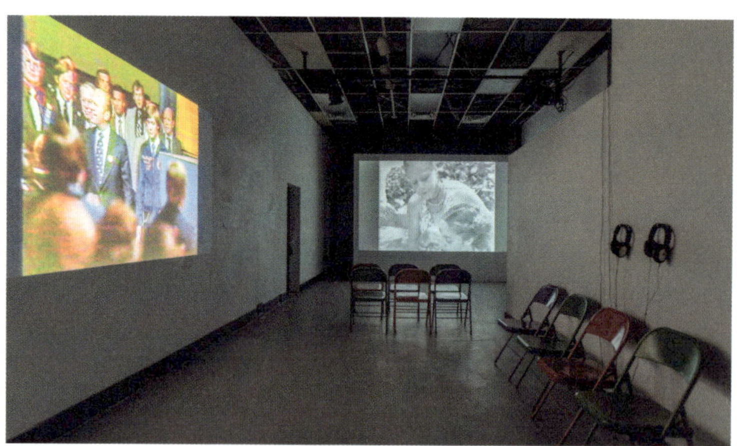

Broadcasting: Guerrilla Media, installation view, Slought

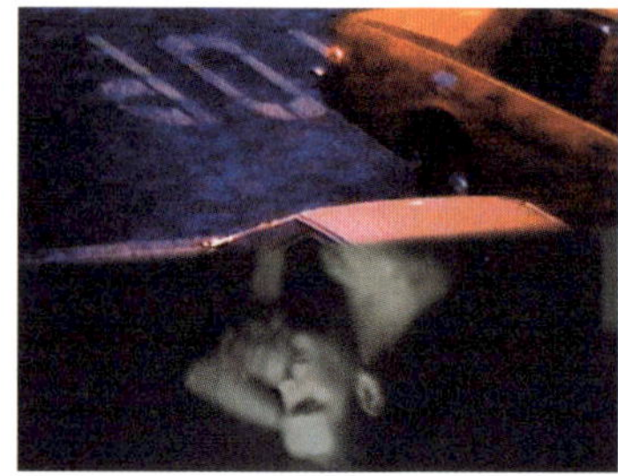

07:15

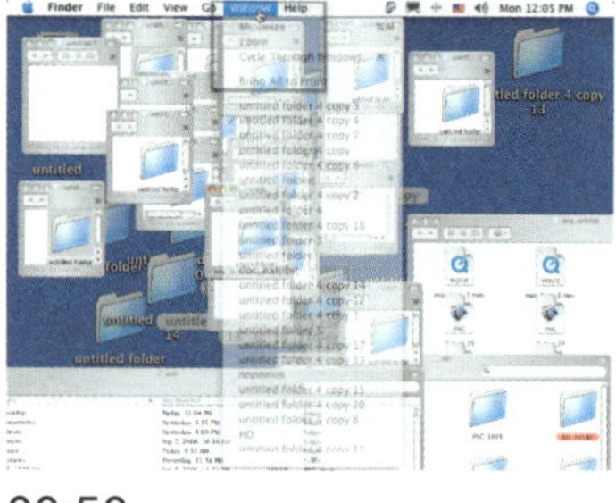

00:50

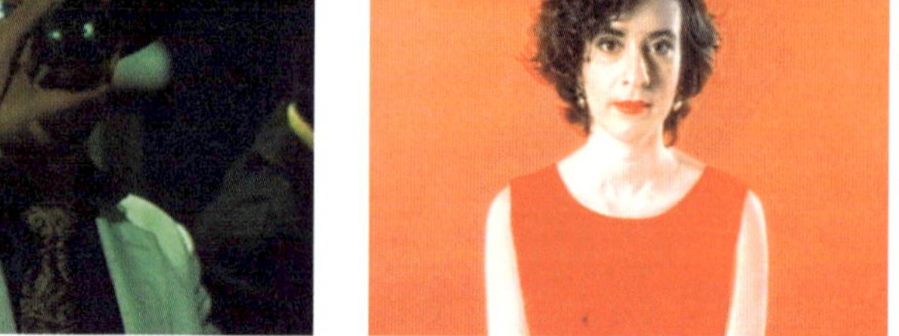

08:21

00:05

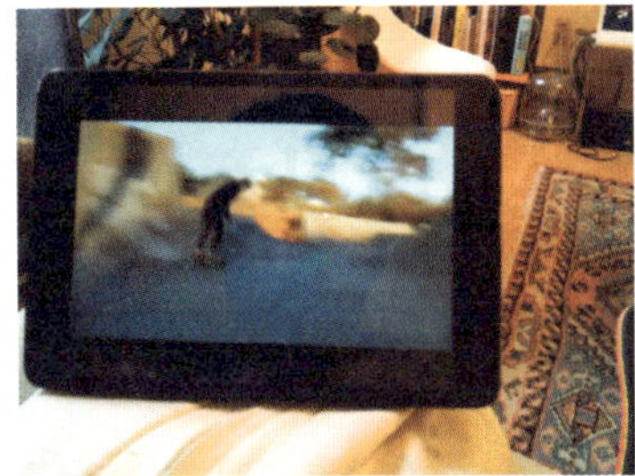

04:05

14:36

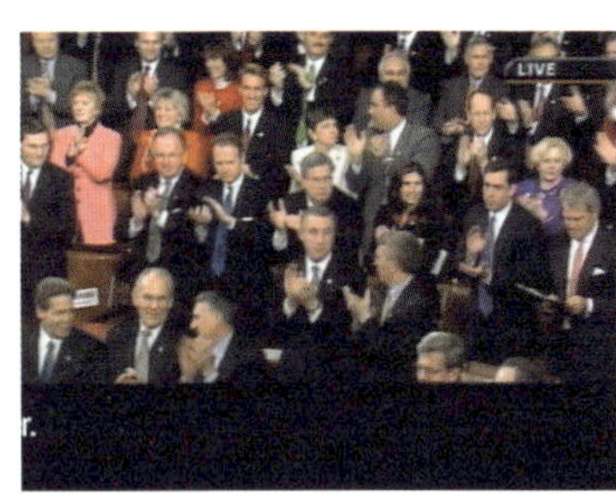

04:38

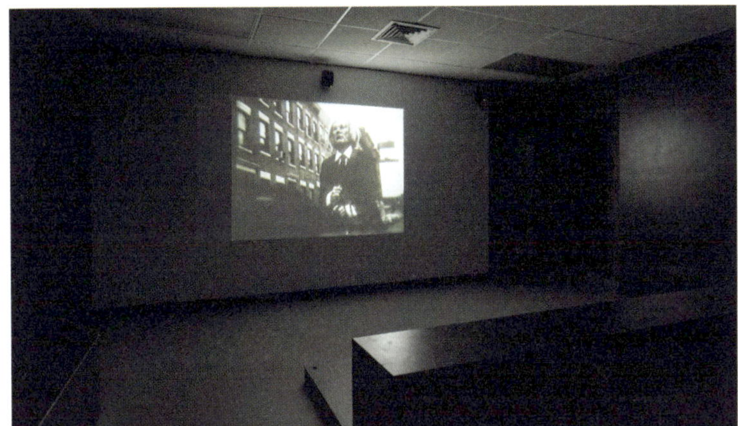

Broadcasting: Guerrilla Media, installation view, Slought

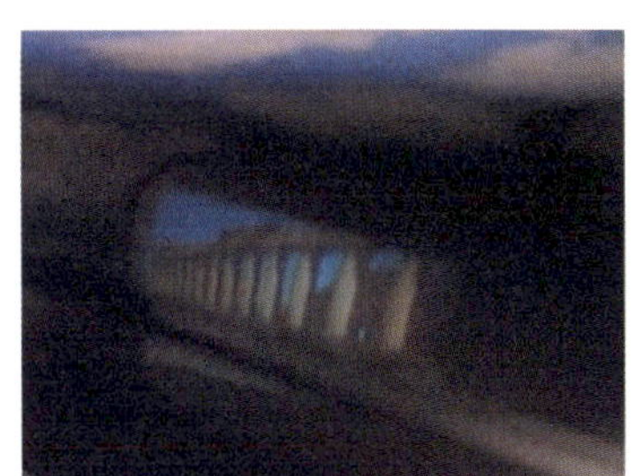

00:25

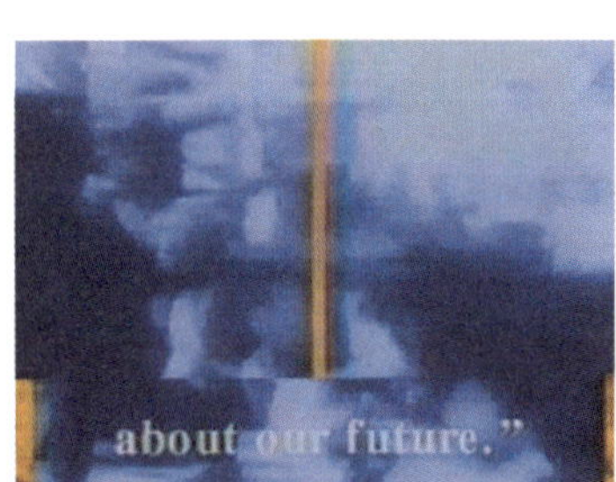

00:42

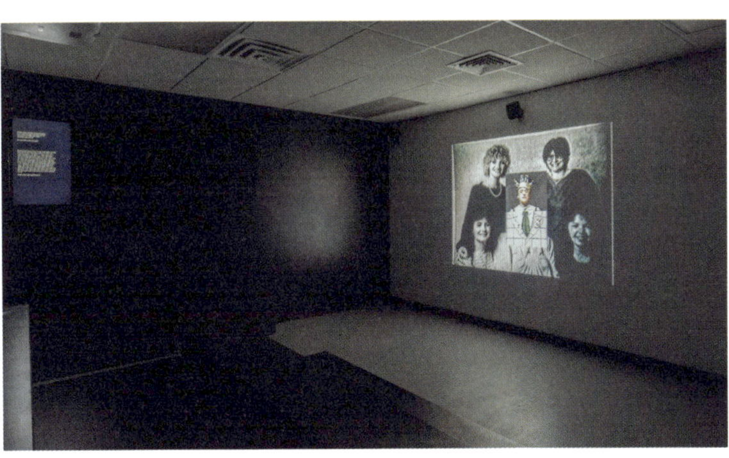

Broadcasting: Guerrilla Media, installation view, Slought

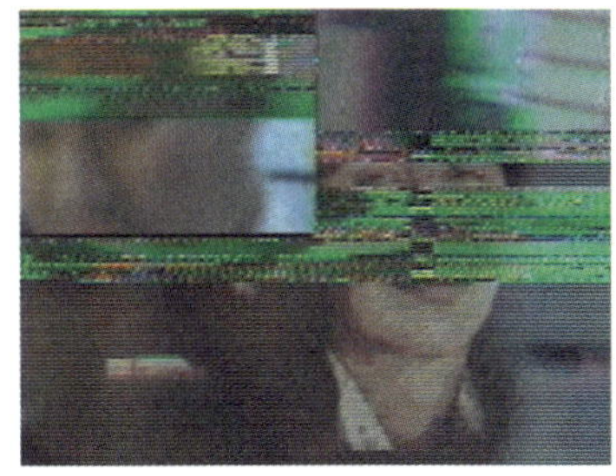

21:19

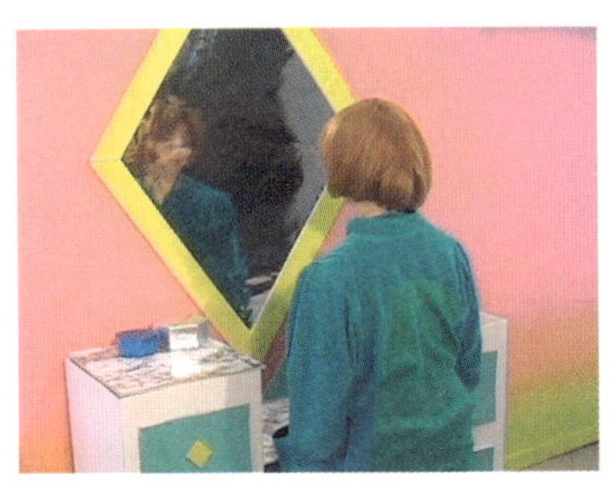

01:31

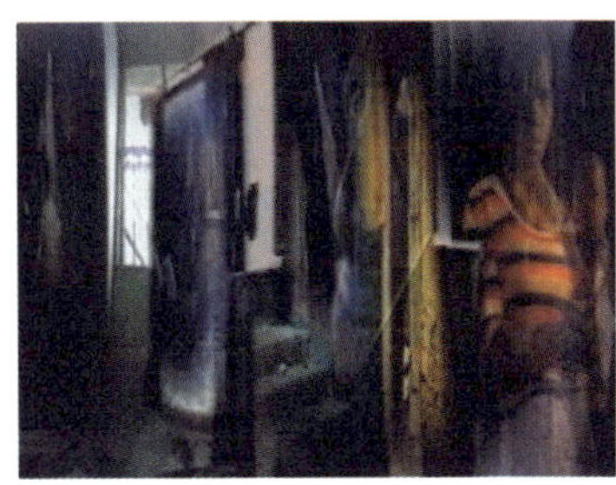

00:28

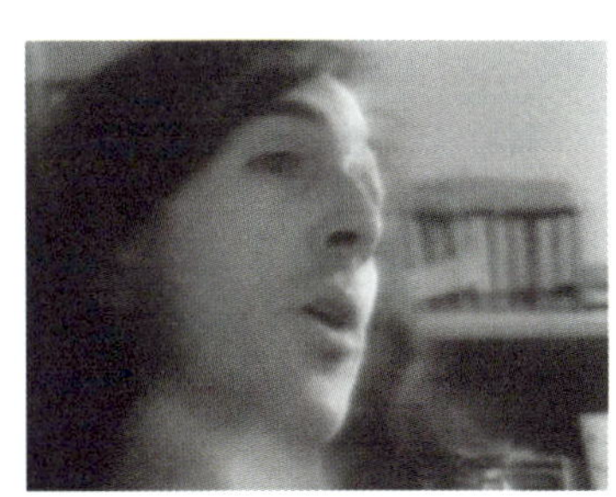

04:31

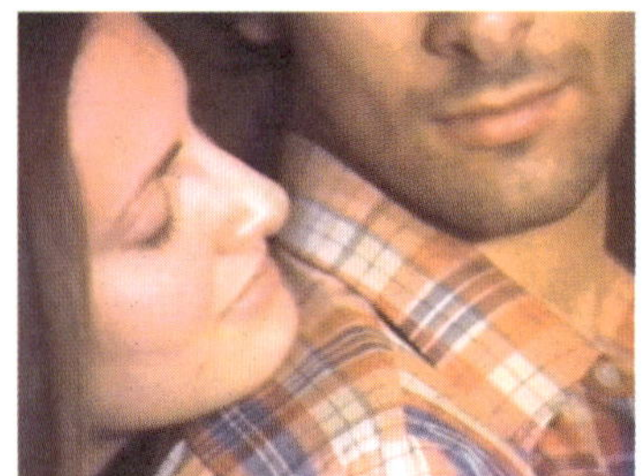

01:19

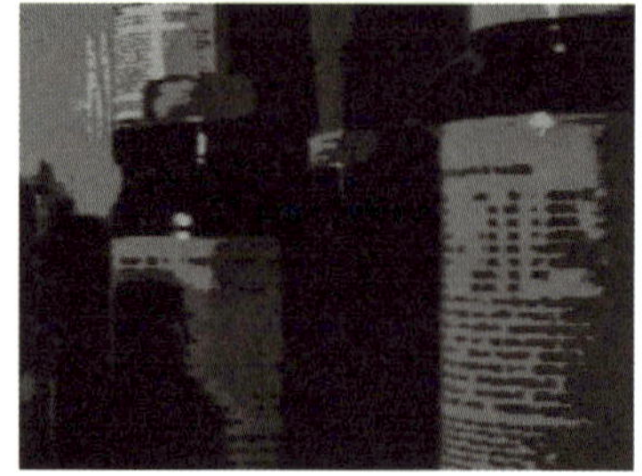

01:39

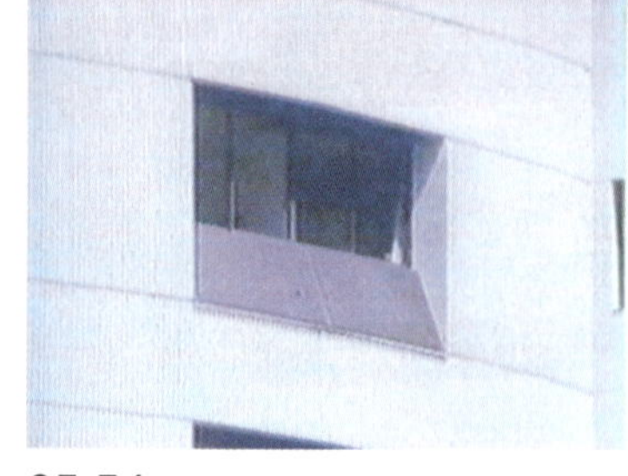

05:54

14:03

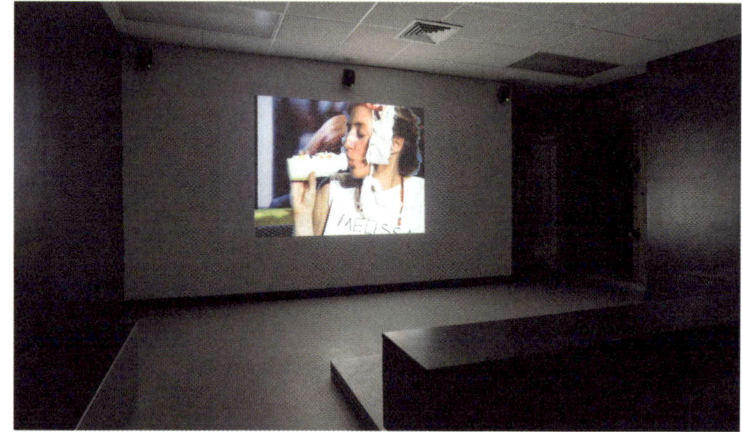

Broadcasting: Guerrilla Media, installation view, Slought

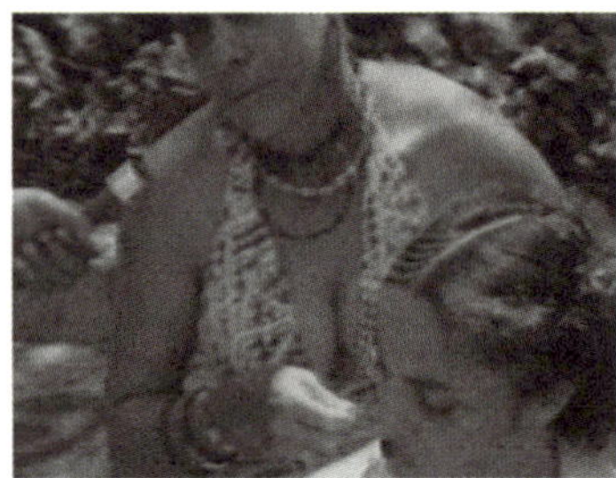

17:27

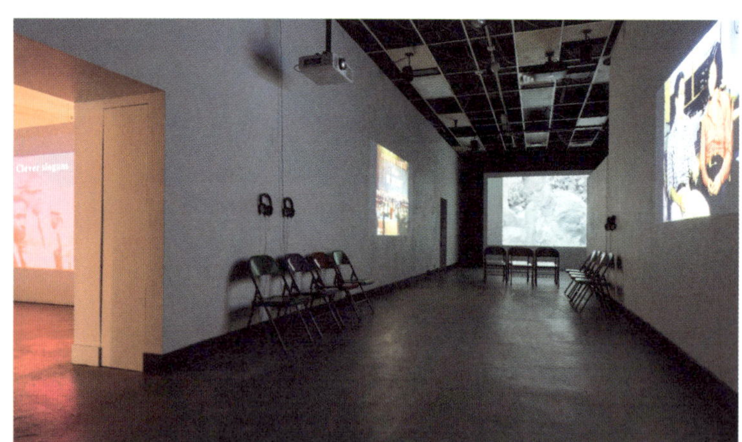

Broadcasting: Guerrilla Media, installation view, Slought

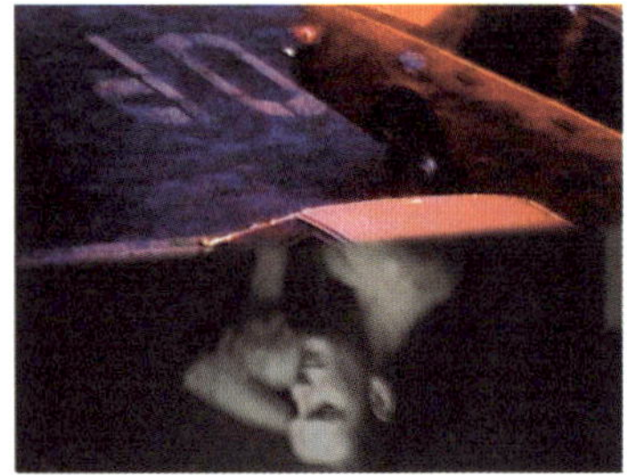

07:15

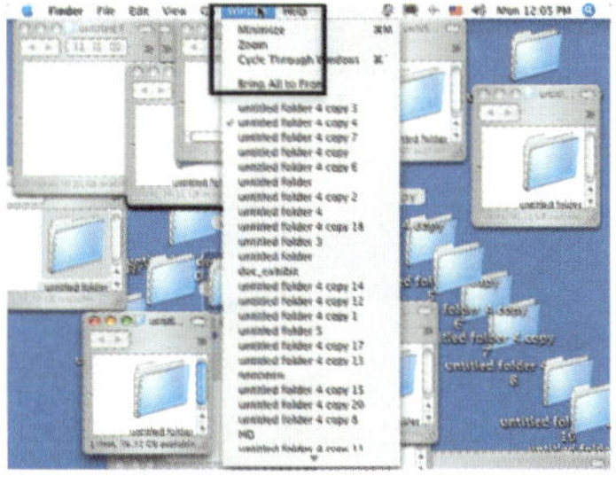

00:50

08:21

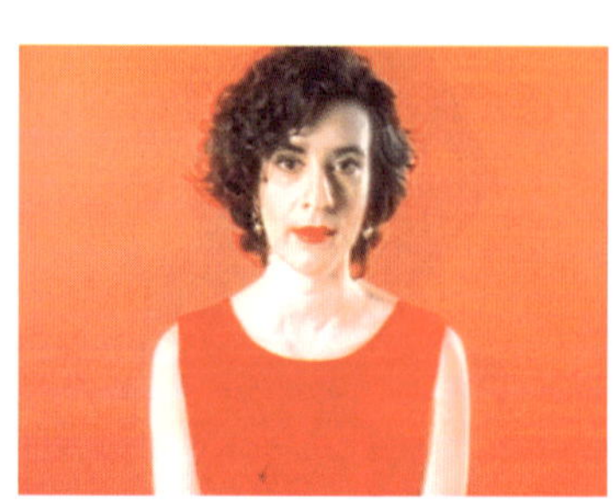

00:05

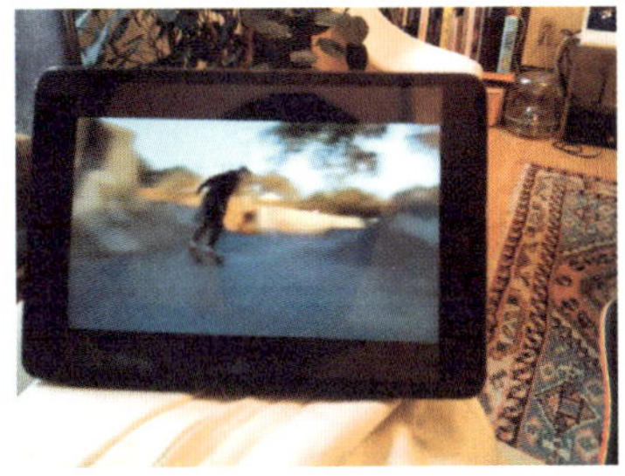
04:05

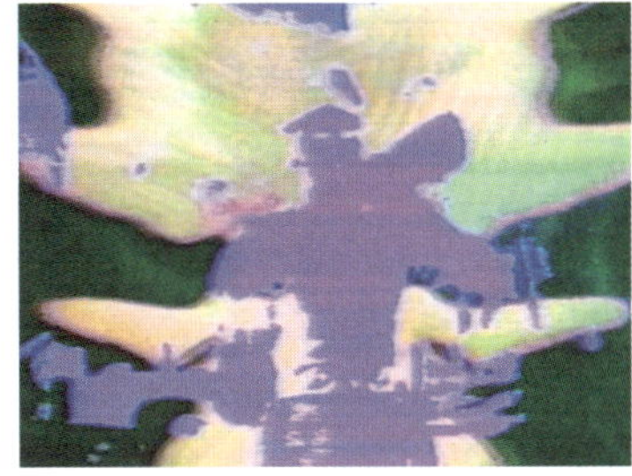
14:36

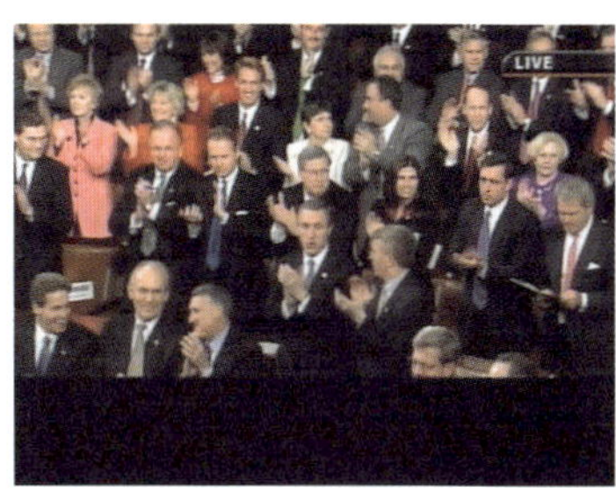

04:38

as compensation to the actors and participants featured in her videos.[16]

Similar to Perry, Josh Kline had daily encounters at EAI with DVD exhibition copies of videos being prepared to be mailed off to museums that influenced his own thinking about materiality and technological substrates. Prompted by seeing a shift in lo-res analog videos from the 1960s and 1970s being displayed on high-end plasma screens, he began to think more critically about the ephemeral nature of media formats and the endlessly duplicable and non-precious potential of the medium. This helped open up his own consideration of working with 3D printers and how they perform in an opposite manner. Instead of the low-res videos now being shown on increasingly hi-def displays, 3D printed works require hi-res files but are output on relatively lo-res 3D printers. As technology advances in the future, their resolution output will be commensurate.

For Kline, his decade working at EAI was a formative experience. He recalls applying for

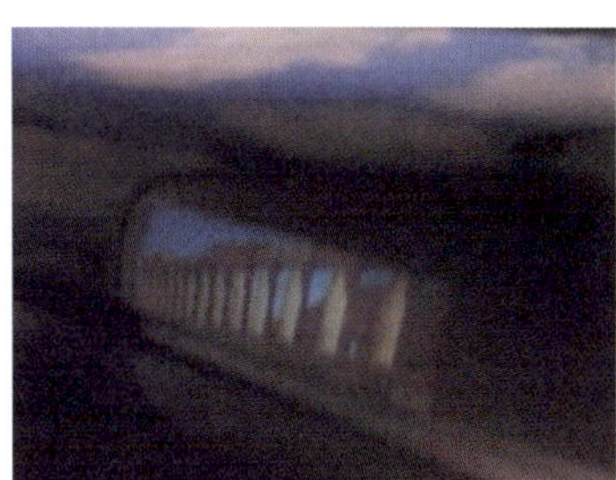
00:25

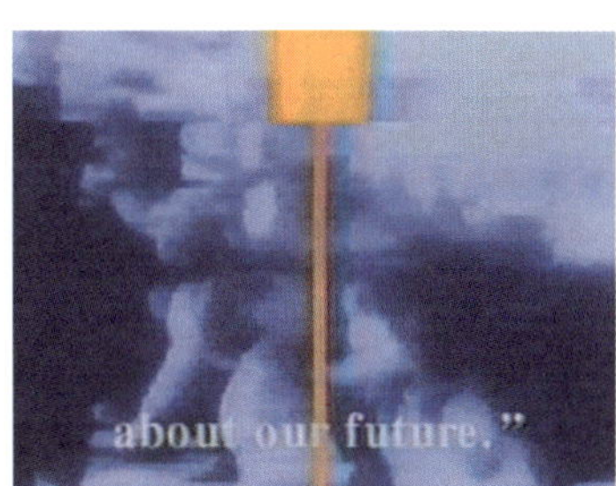

00:42

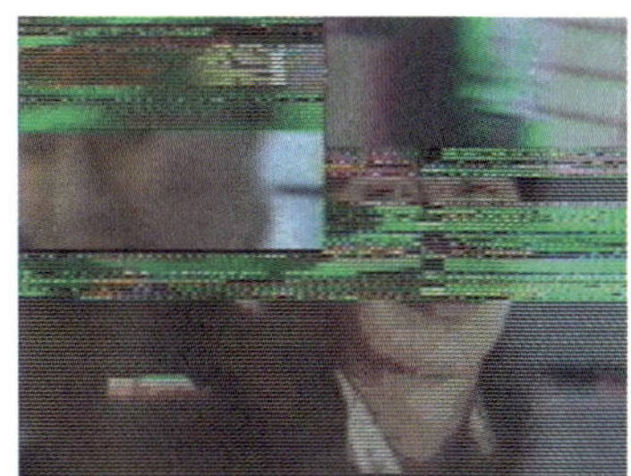
21:19

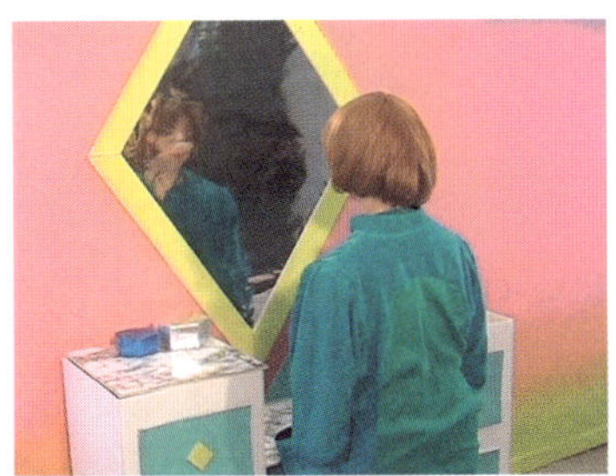
01:31

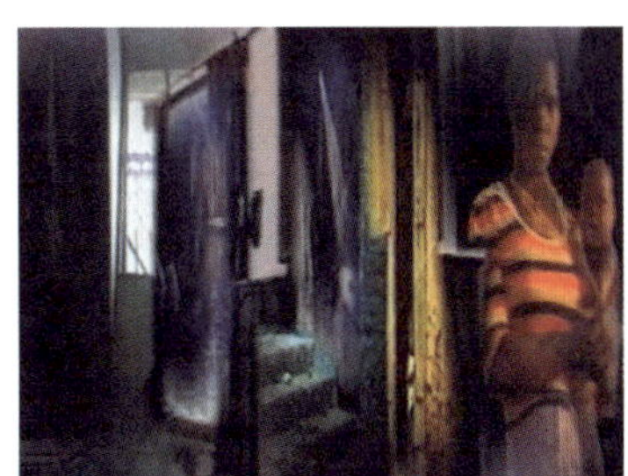
00:28

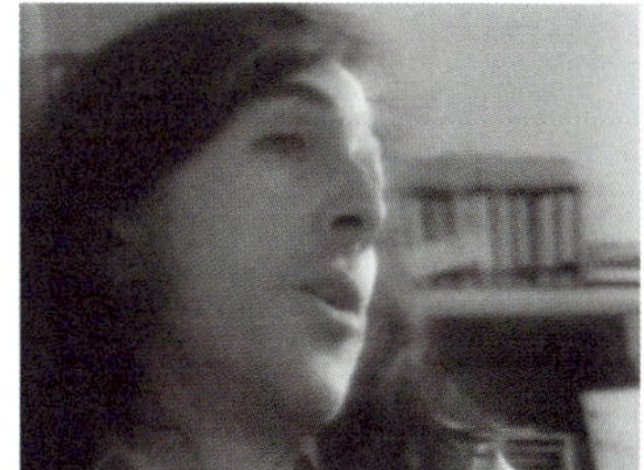
04:31

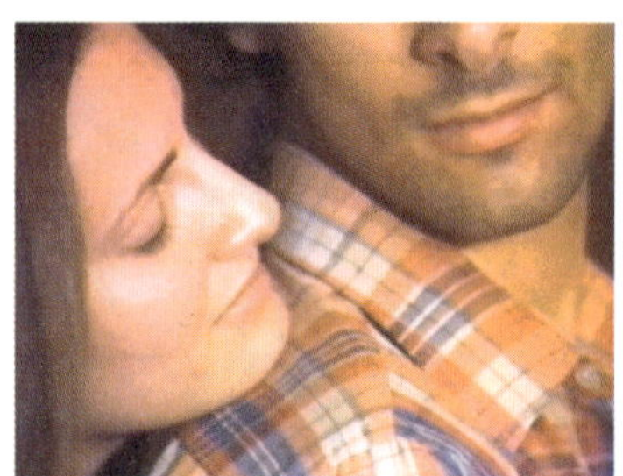

01:19

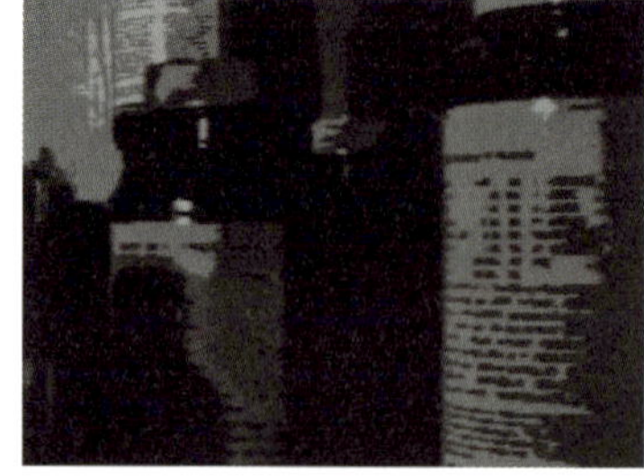

01:39

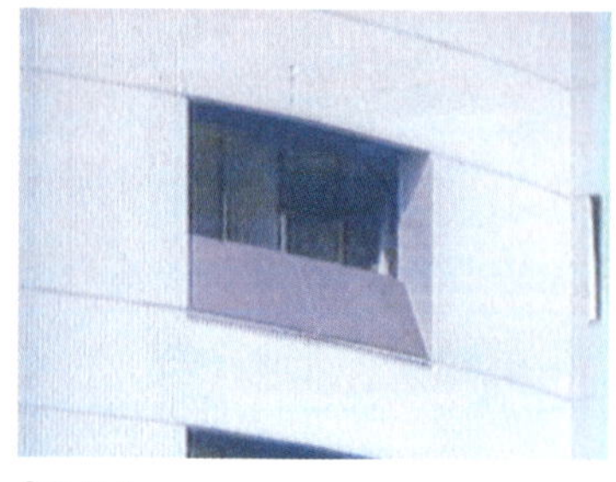

05:54

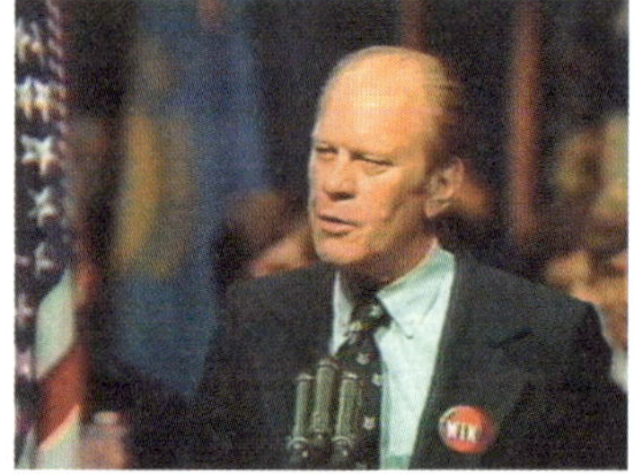

14:03

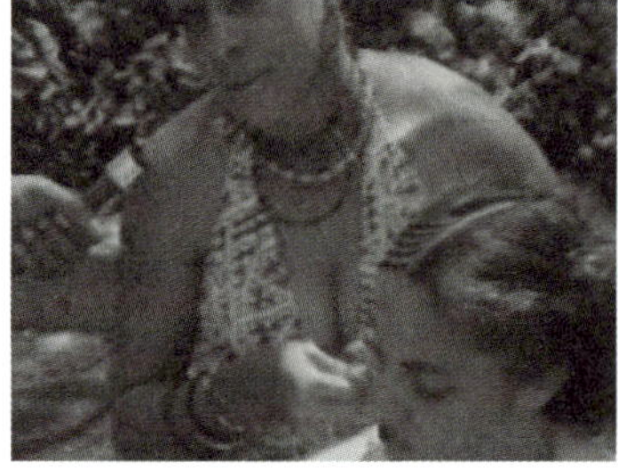

17:27

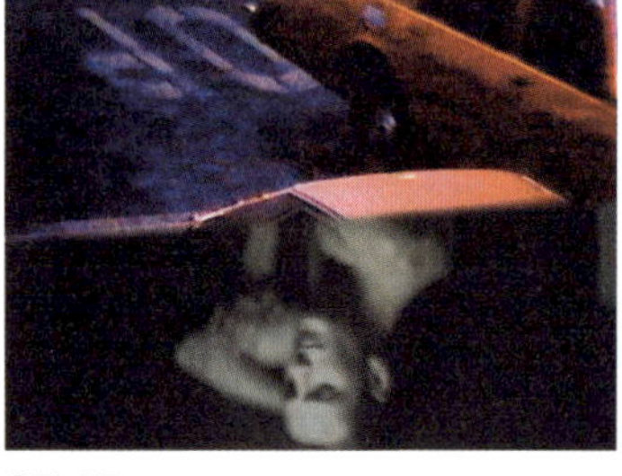

07:15

an administrative assistant position because he had been a film major who abandoned film for video art in his undergraduate studies. He soon began organizing public programming and bringing younger artists into the collection. Eventually he became the director of public programs, and in this outward-facing capacity he began to think about how curation could resonate with current political and social issues and how agency is created in the art world. At EAI he was also able to make connections between the younger New York art scene, the deep archive he encountered in EAI's collection, and his own growth as an artist. He recalls a period when he would be at the office every day curating screenings of works in the collection during business hours and then staying after work, sometimes until 5:00 am, and editing his own videos alongside his collaborators in the Circular File collective, Anicka Yi and Jon Santos, on a television show produced for Performa.

Coming into contact with an older generation underscored for Kline the difficulties of being

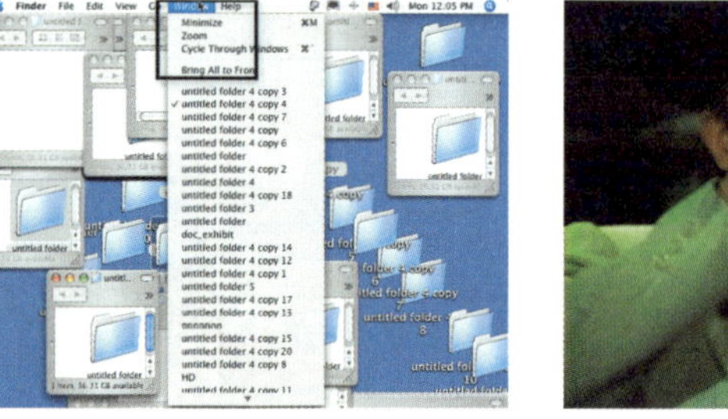

00:50

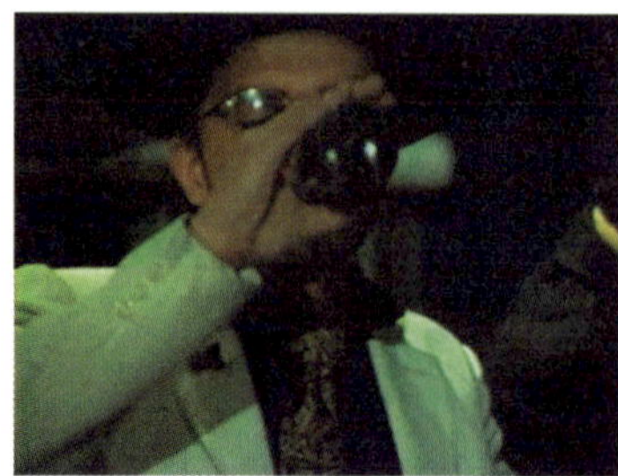

08:21

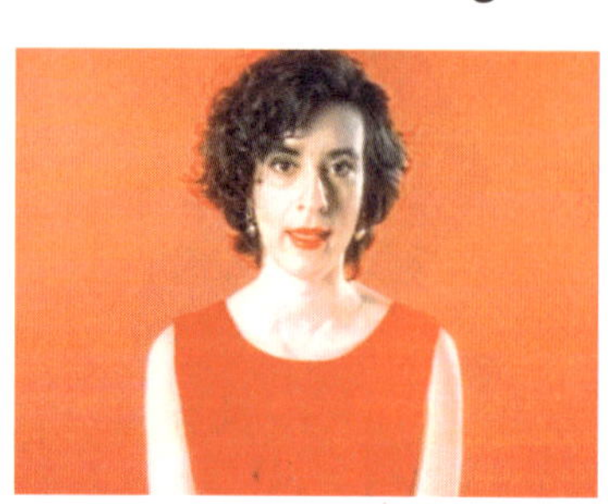

00:05

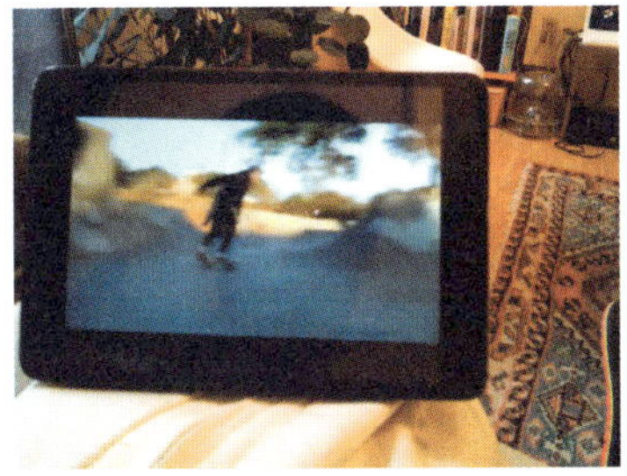
04:05

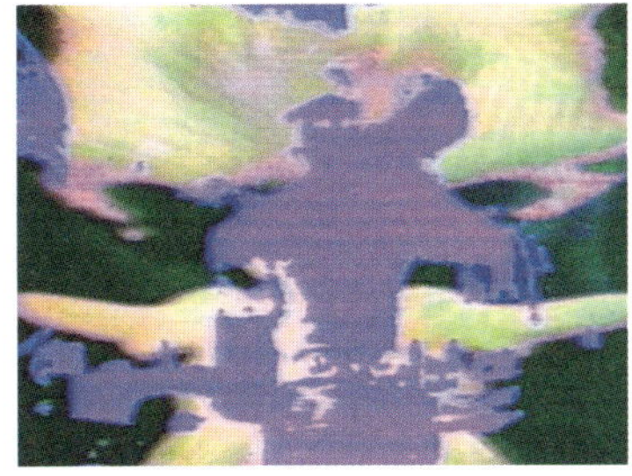
14:36

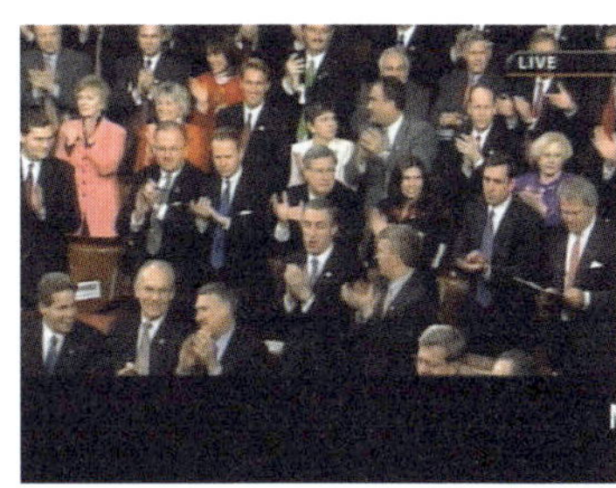

04:38

an artist, reflecting that it gave him an "overview of the life cycle of an artist and the possible life cycles of an artist. This has stuck with me over time. . .These people who are now canonical were wandering in the wilderness for so many years."[17] Ultimately, the collection and the community that shapes EAI is relational. For example, in this more horizontal and artist-centric work environment, Kline initially hired Shimizu and Antoine Catala (who would then go on to work with Dan Graham) as interns. Through Shimizu, who Kline shared a studio with for many years, he met Santos, who then introduced him to Yi. Carissa Rodriguez, who would also show alongside many of these artists at 47 Canal also worked at EAI in the 1990s. Similarly Price came to EAI as a part-time technical coordinator on the recommendation of Tony Cokes, and subsequently moved into the position of technical director upon Buck's departure. Likewise, Price was instrumental in bringing artists such as Bernadette Corporation into the catalog for distribution. This continues today with a new

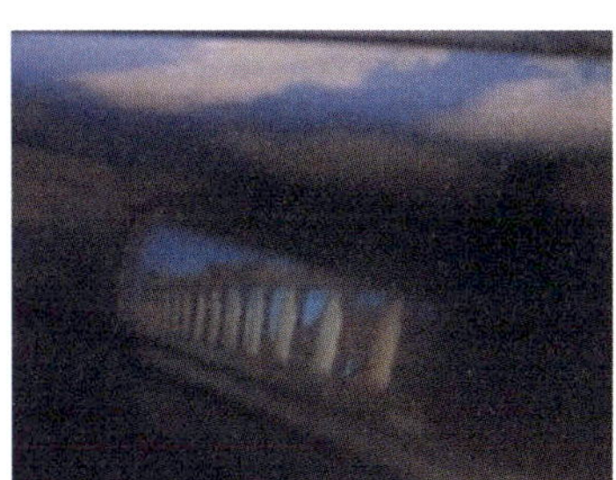
00:25

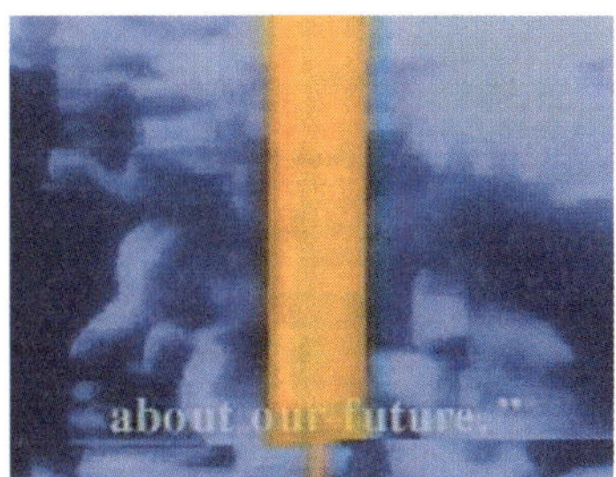

00:42

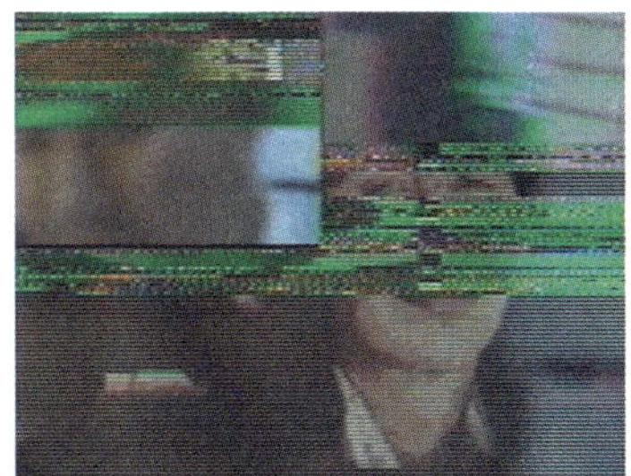
21:19

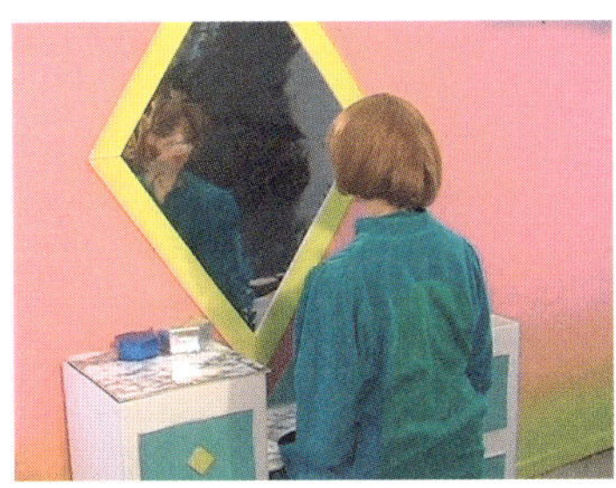
01:31

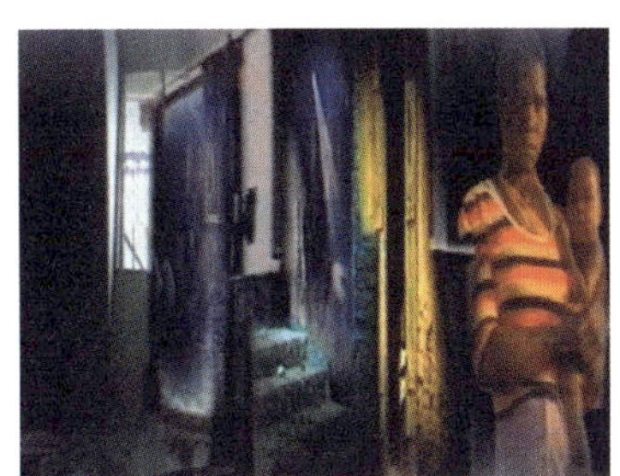
00:28

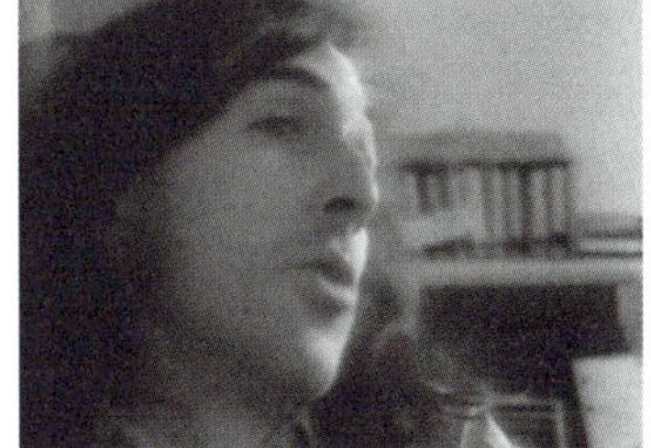
04:31

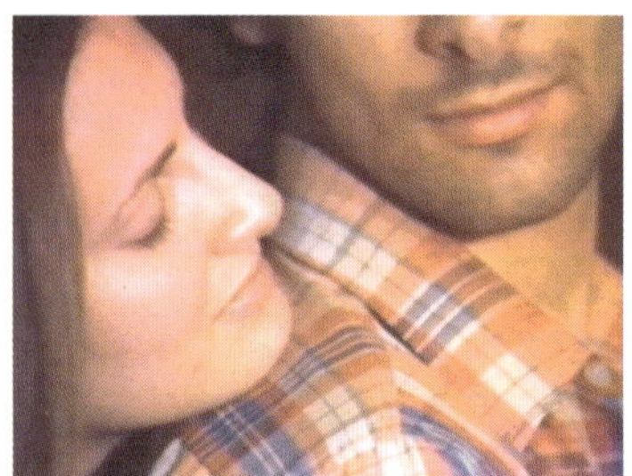

01:19

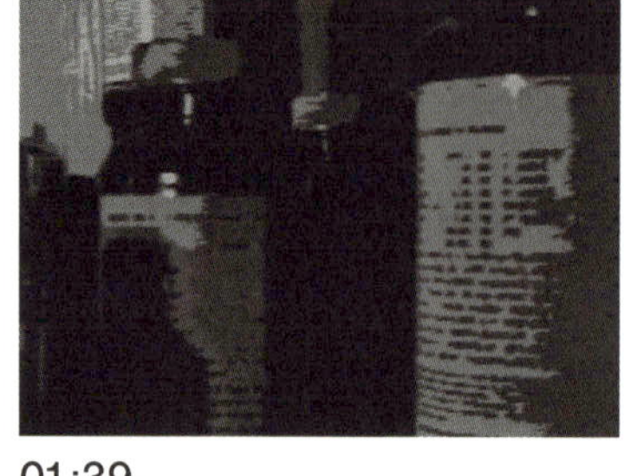

01:39

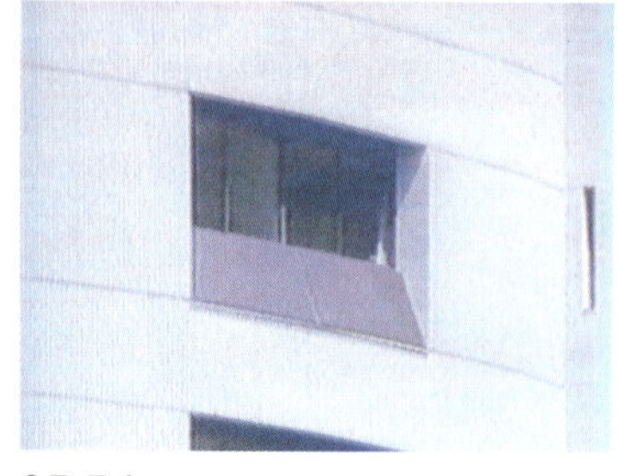

05:54

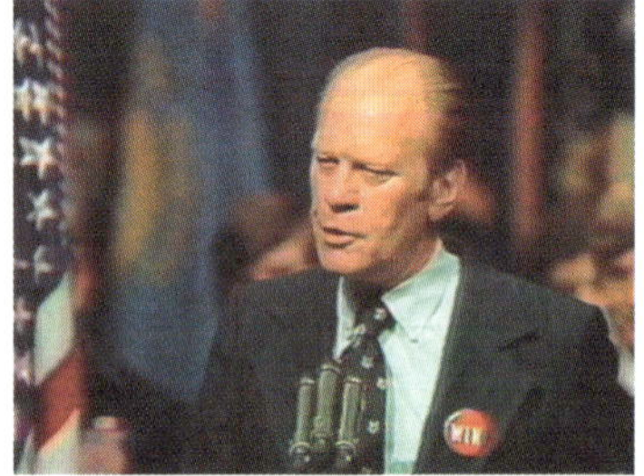

14:03

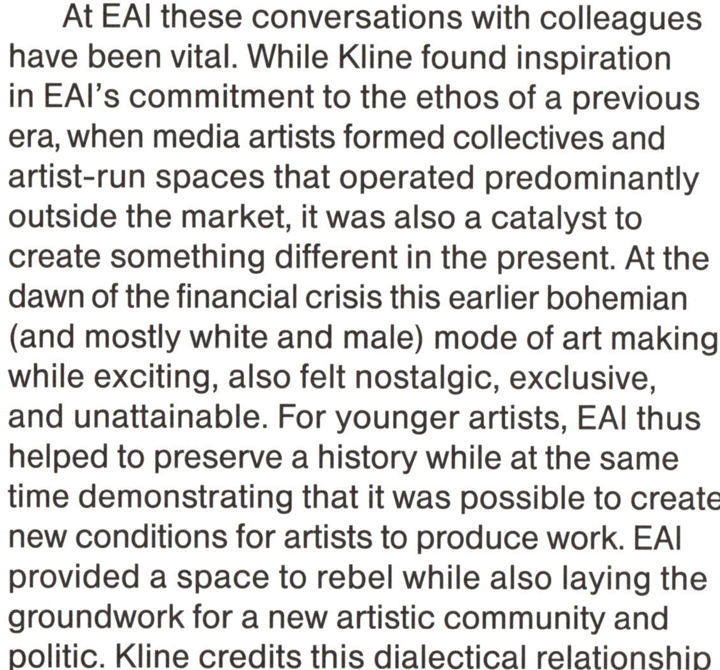

generation of artists, and former EAI employees, such as Carolyn Lazard, who found interest in EAI's licensing model in her role as distribution assistant, subsequently observing that it is partially due to EAI's impact on her that "video is my intellectual home."[18]

At EAI these conversations with colleagues have been vital. While Kline found inspiration in EAI's commitment to the ethos of a previous era, when media artists formed collectives and artist-run spaces that operated predominantly outside the market, it was also a catalyst to create something different in the present. At the dawn of the financial crisis this earlier bohemian (and mostly white and male) mode of art making, while exciting, also felt nostalgic, exclusive, and unattainable. For younger artists, EAI thus helped to preserve a history while at the same time demonstrating that it was possible to create new conditions for artists to produce work. EAI provided a space to rebel while also laying the groundwork for a new artistic community and politic. Kline credits this dialectical relationship

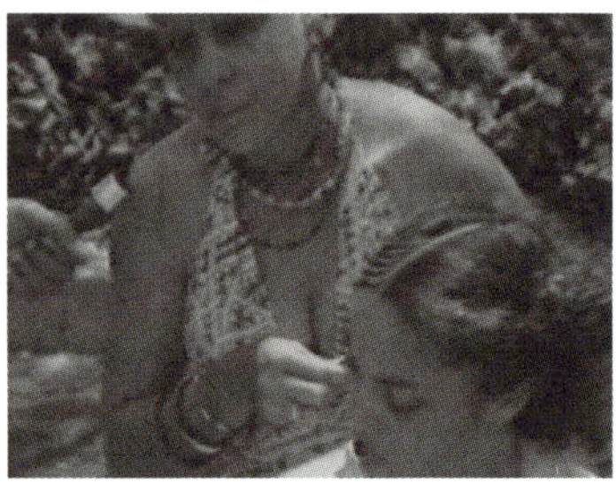

17:27

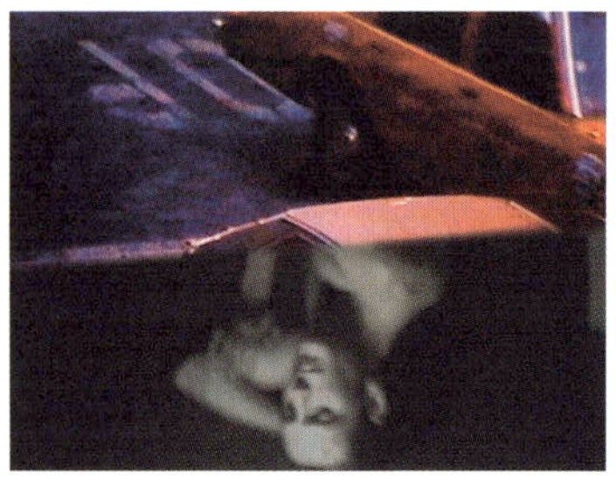

07:15

00:50

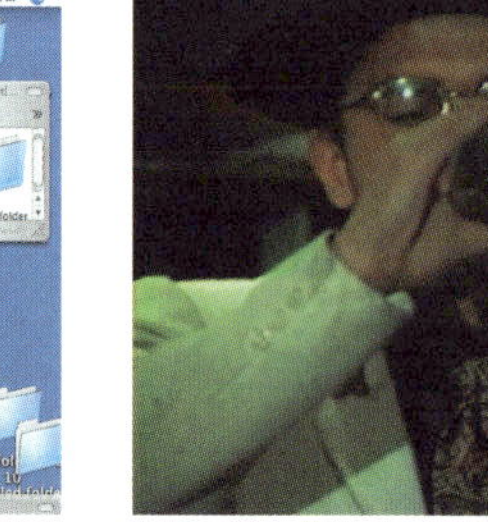

08:21

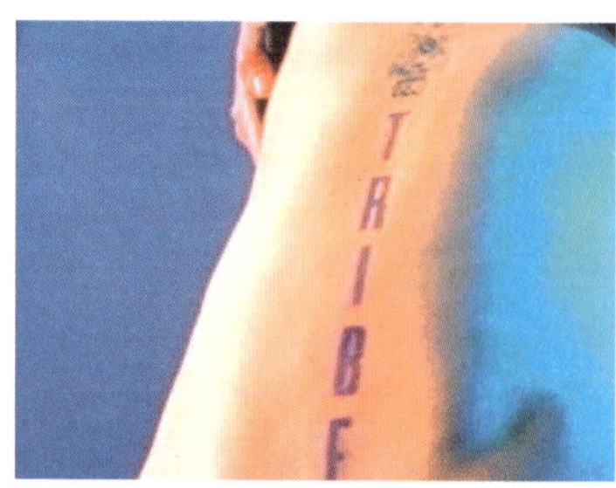

00:05

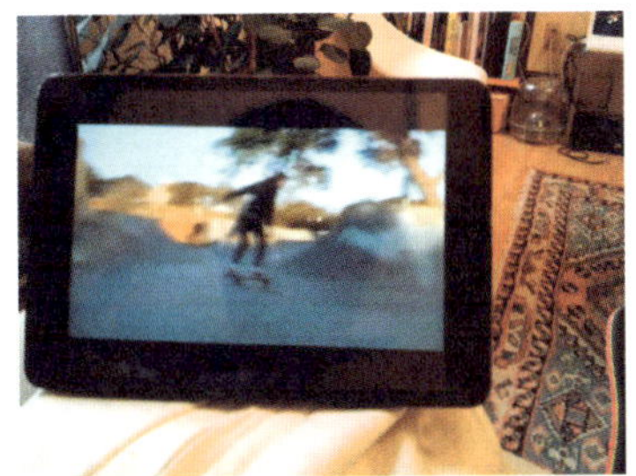

04:05

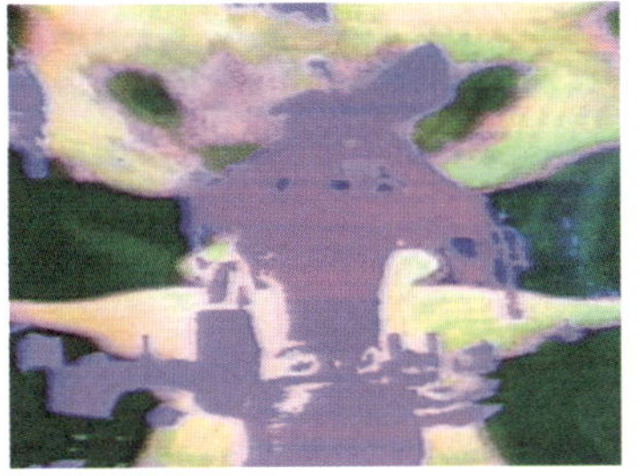

14:36

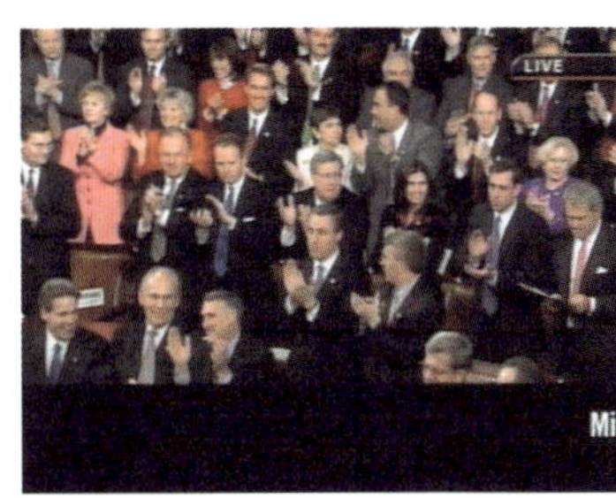

04:38

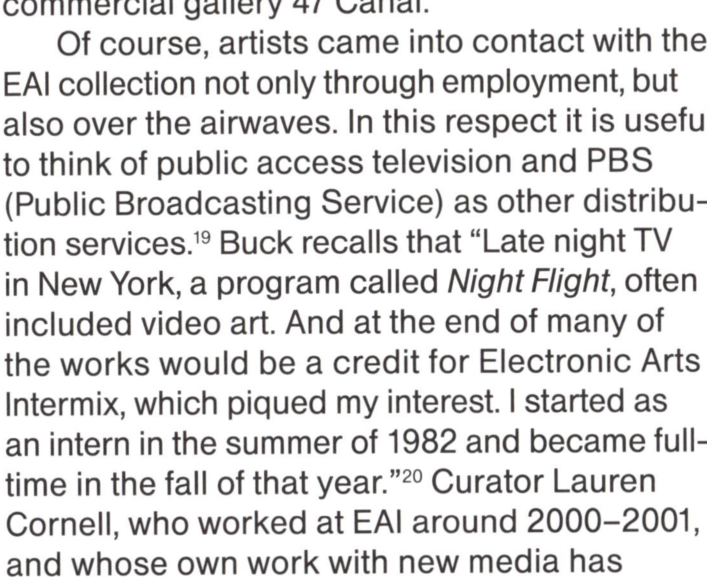

as a partial impetus behind his organization of *Nobodies New York* (May 1–3, 2009) at 179 Canal, a new, collaborative and inclusive artist-run space founded by Margaret Lee, which would eventually became formalized in 2011 as the commercial gallery 47 Canal.

Of course, artists came into contact with the EAI collection not only through employment, but also over the airwaves. In this respect it is useful to think of public access television and PBS (Public Broadcasting Service) as other distribution services.[19] Buck recalls that “Late night TV in New York, a program called *Night Flight*, often included video art. And at the end of many of the works would be a credit for Electronic Arts Intermix, which piqued my interest. I started as an intern in the summer of 1982 and became full-time in the fall of that year.”[20] Curator Lauren Cornell, who worked at EAI around 2000–2001, and whose own work with new media has been influential, recalls her experience there as “completely foundational for me” and notes that it “has had an immeasurable impact.”[21] But

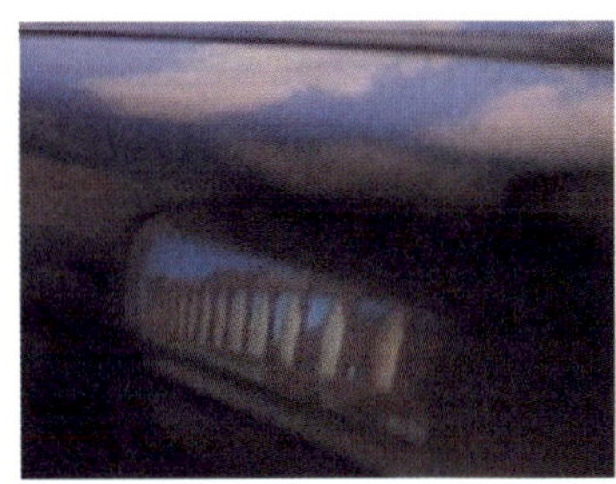

00:25

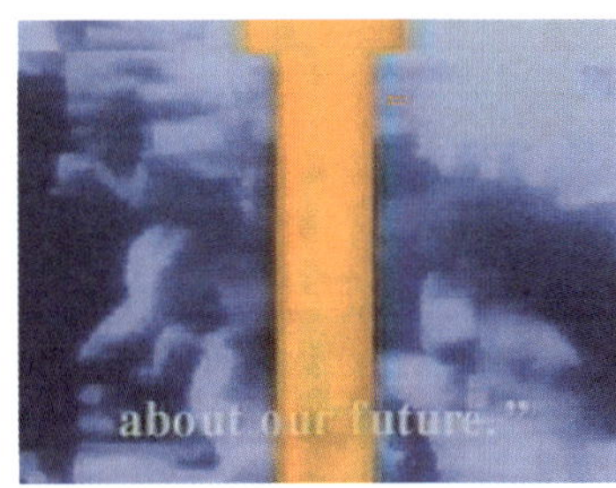

00:42

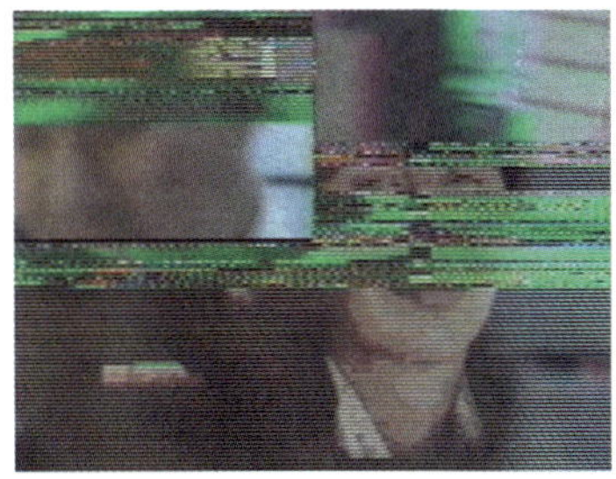

21:19

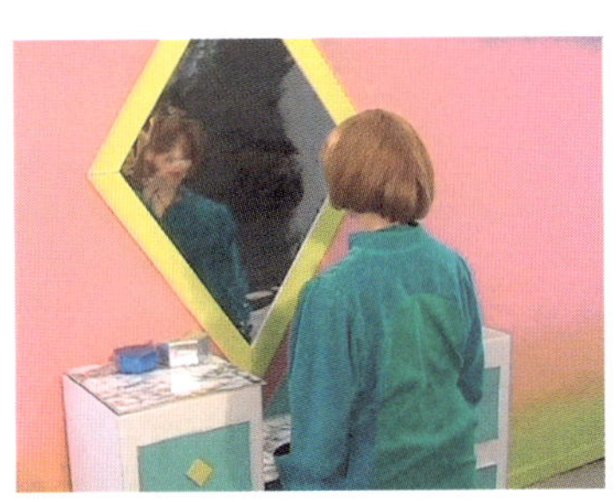

01:31

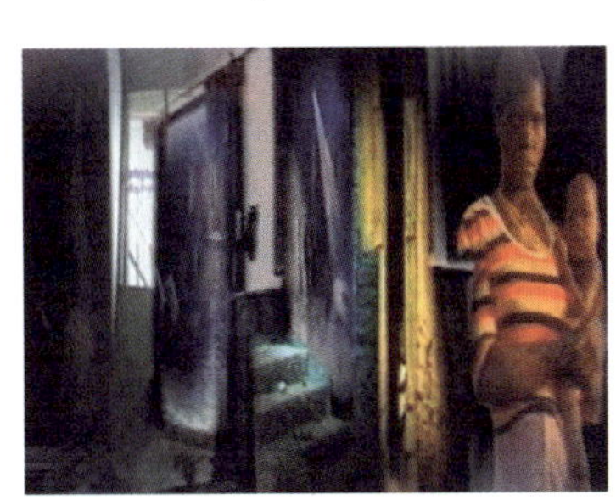

00:28

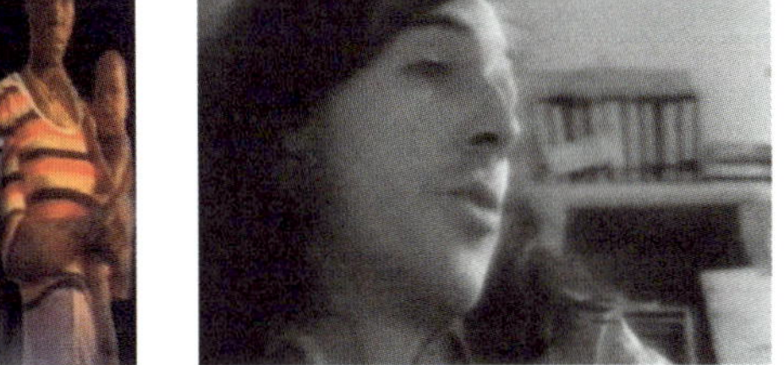

04:31

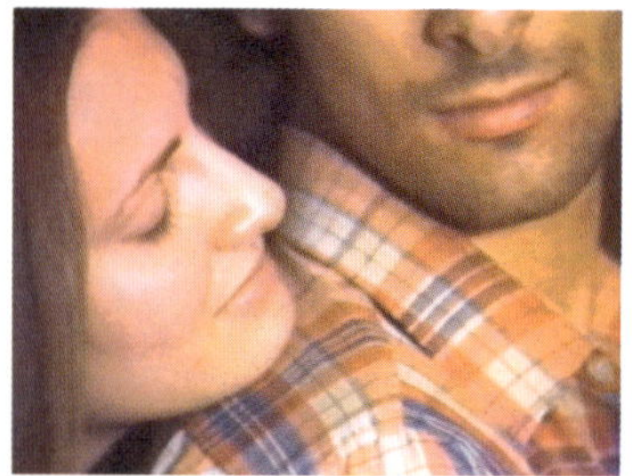
01:18

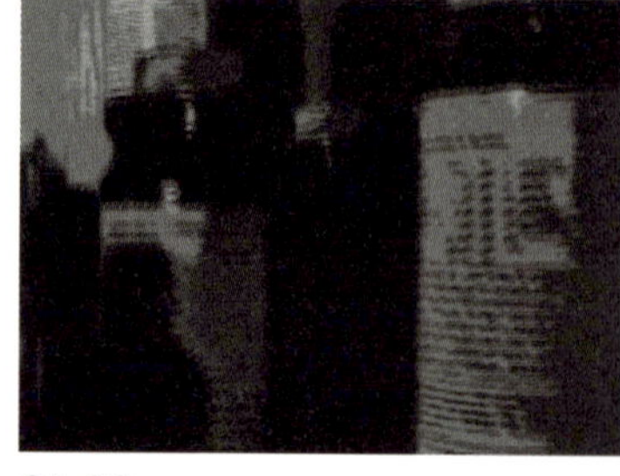
01:38

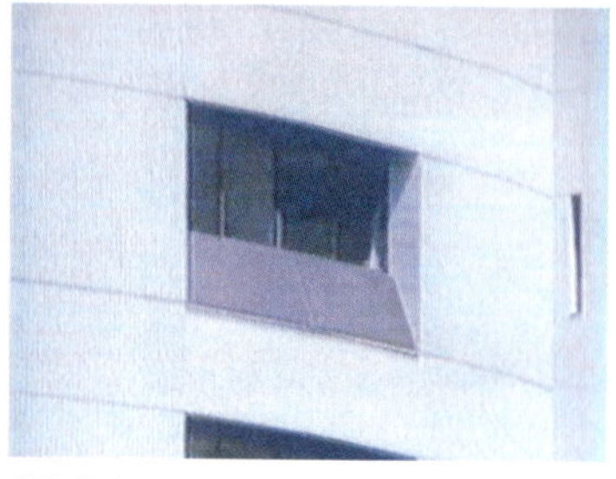
05:53

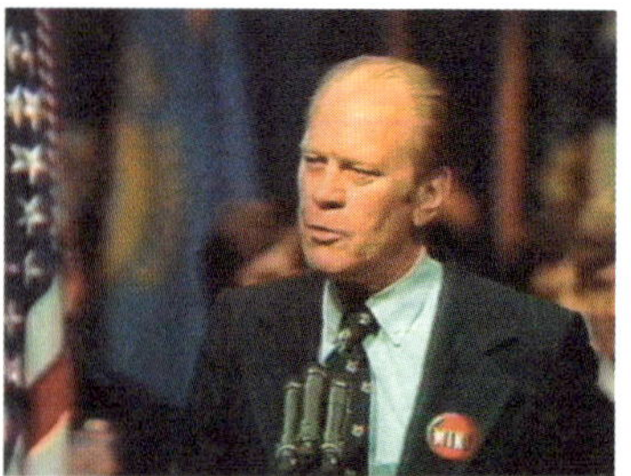
14:02

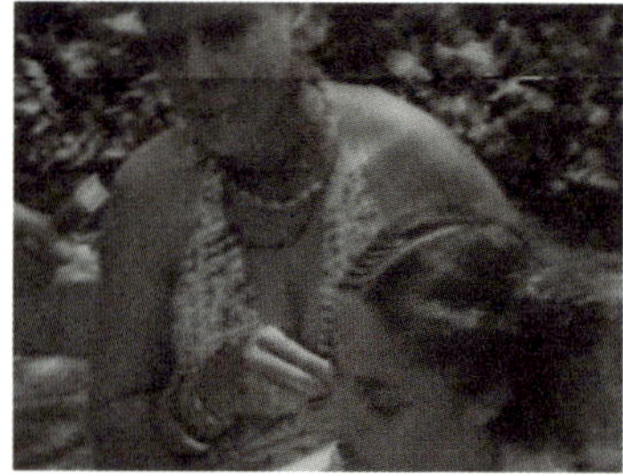
17:26

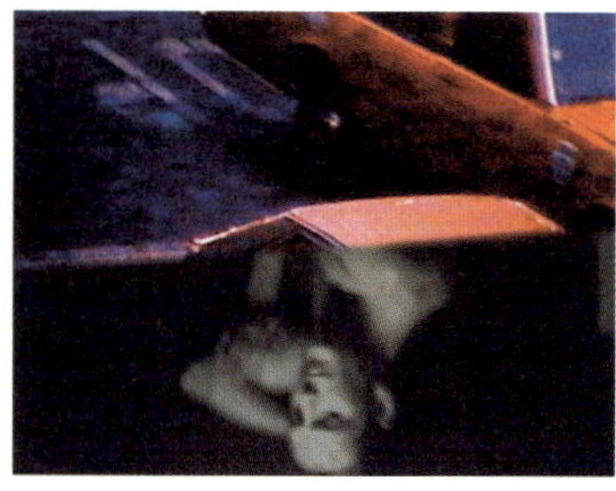
07:14

it equally had an effect on some of the younger artists who would eventually be included in EAI's distribution, such as her college friend, artist Cory Arcangel. While Cornell was working at EAI, Arcangel would often come and hang out with her in the office. Growing up in Buffalo, he was taught video art in high school and would encounter art videos on public access television through programs by EAI artist Tony Conrad like *Person in the Street* and *AxleGrease*. Arcangel recalls:

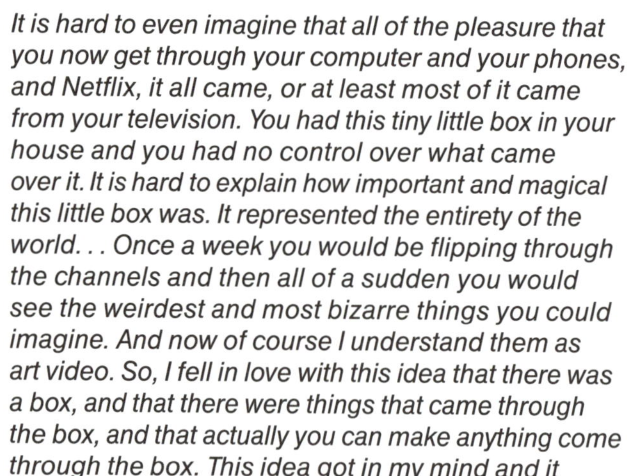

> *It is hard to even imagine that all of the pleasure that you now get through your computer and your phones, and Netflix, it all came, or at least most of it came from your television. You had this tiny little box in your house and you had no control over what came over it. It is hard to explain how important and magical this little box was. It represented the entirety of the world. . . Once a week you would be flipping through the channels and then all of a sudden you would see the weirdest and most bizarre things you could imagine. And now of course I understand them as art video. So, I fell in love with this idea that there was a box, and that there were things that came through the box, and that actually you can make anything come through the box. This idea got in my mind and it*

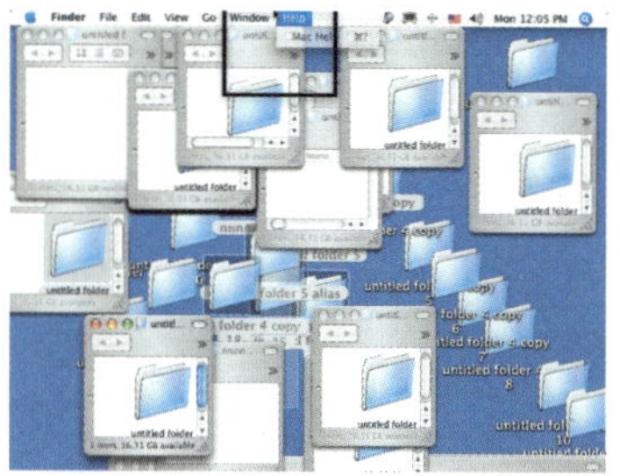
00:49

08:20

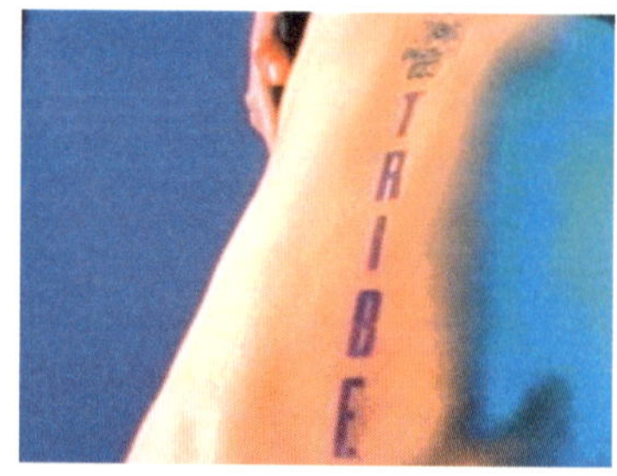

00:04

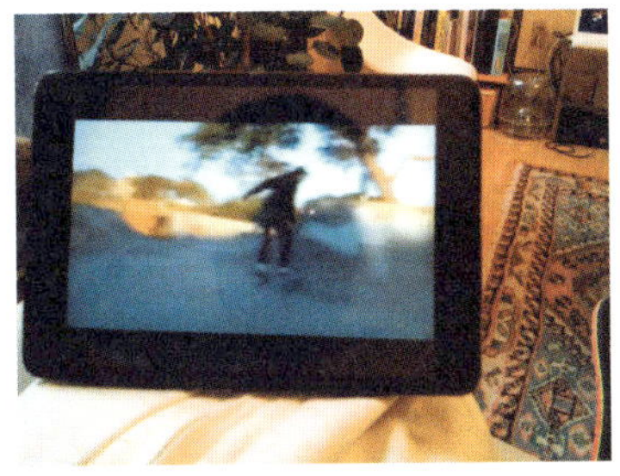

04:05

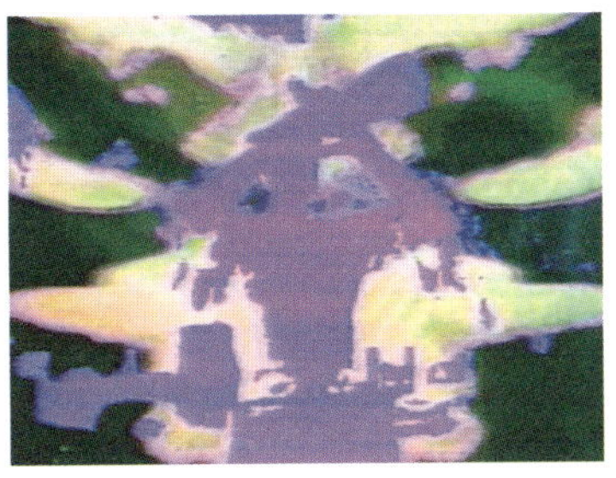

14:36

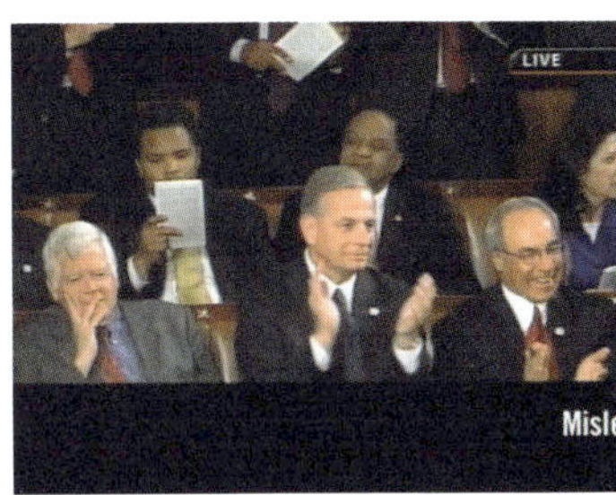

04:38

> *became a dream to have my own things come through the television, but by the time I came of age it was the internet—another box that was just as cool. And so, I started making videos for the internet in the same way that I would have done for public access.*[22]

This underscores that while television broadcast can be seen as the original distribution service, it also connects to and informs the way artists would come to work with the internet.

Through its distributable content and face-to-face interactions in the editing bay, over the years EAI has thus acted as a bridge between people, generational positions, technological dispensations, and political strategies. As EAI marks its fiftieth anniversary, the New York art world that initially produced it would appear to be an increasingly distant memory, just as the era of broadcast television would seem to have given way to a new networked society and on demand culture. And yet, our experience of both art and media is polytemporal. Like the nineteenth-century QUERTY keyboard that remains an inextricable part of every laptop, earlier modes

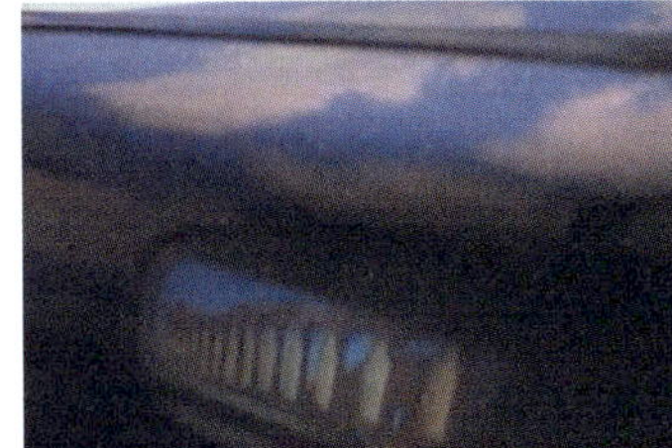

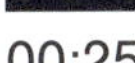

00:25

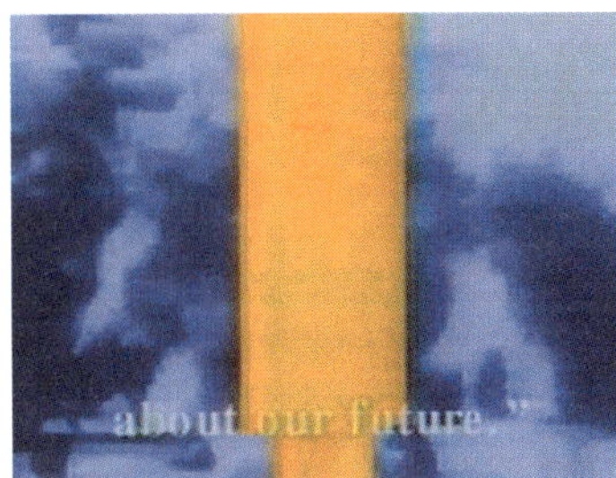

00:42

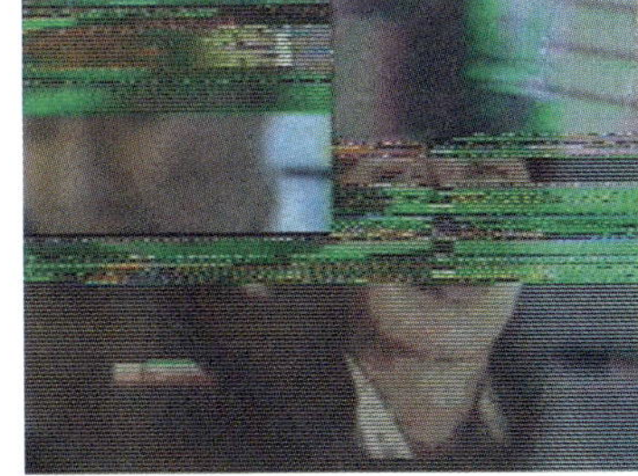

21:19

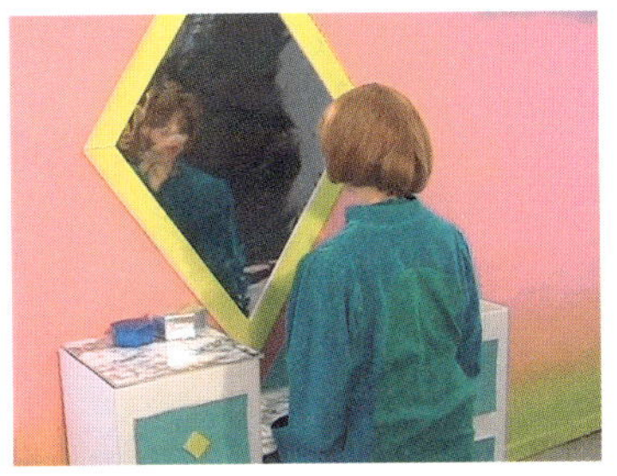

01:31

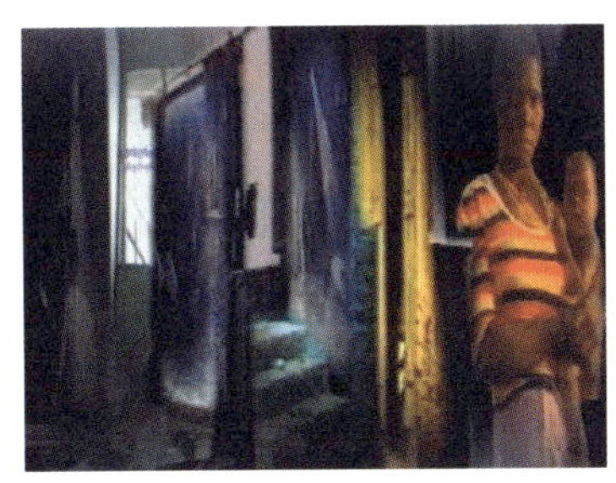

00:28

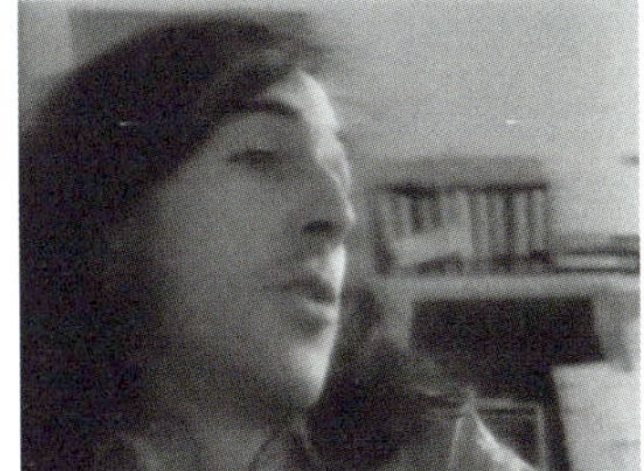

04:31

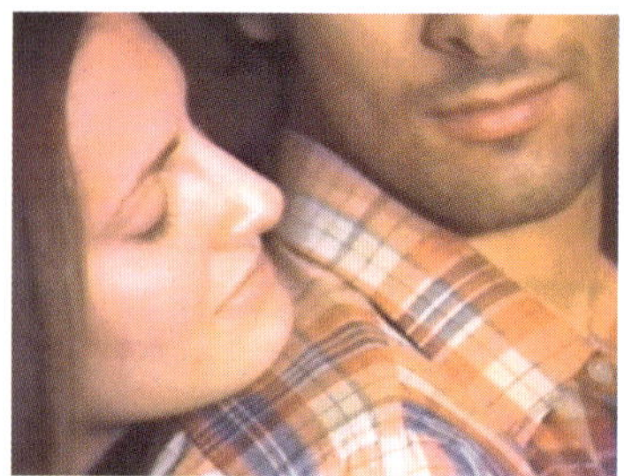
01:18

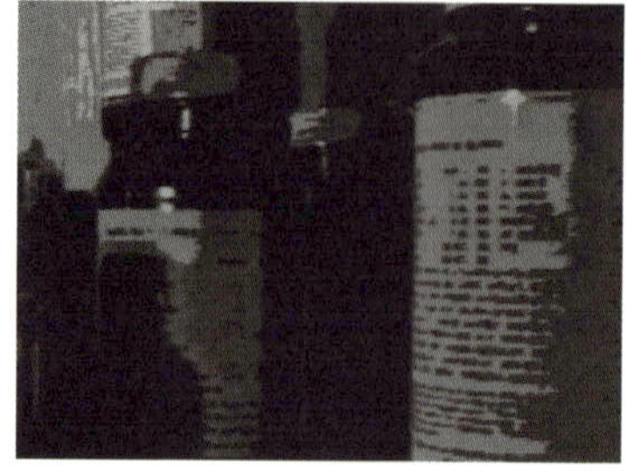
01:38

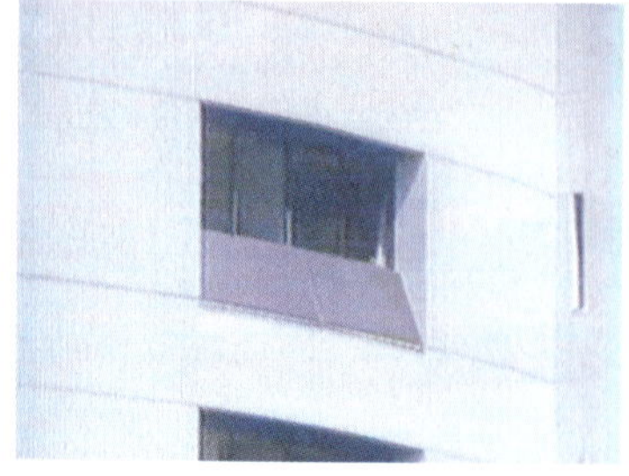
05:53

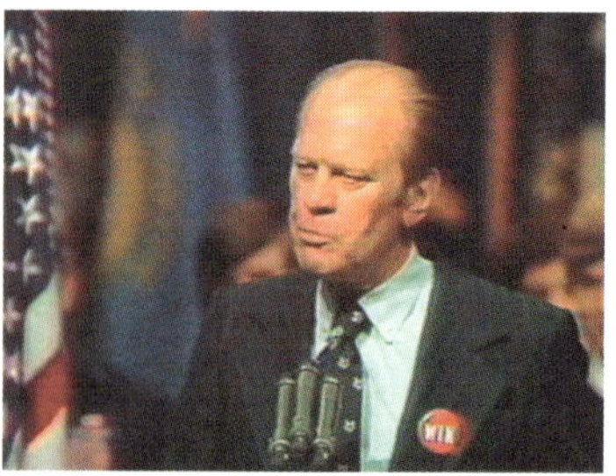
14:02

of viewership and so-called “legacy” media are still very much a part of our present, as both tools and techniques of transmission. Similarly, art historian David Joselit has employed the technologically inflected metaphor of “feedback” to discuss how artists have found ways to intervene in the anti-democratic nature of mainstream media.[23] To understand the EAI collection as representative of this relational dynamic is to propose a counter model that speaks to questions of influence that defy technologically determinist models of categorization and that resist the relentless presentism of a market-driven, professionalized art world.

17:26

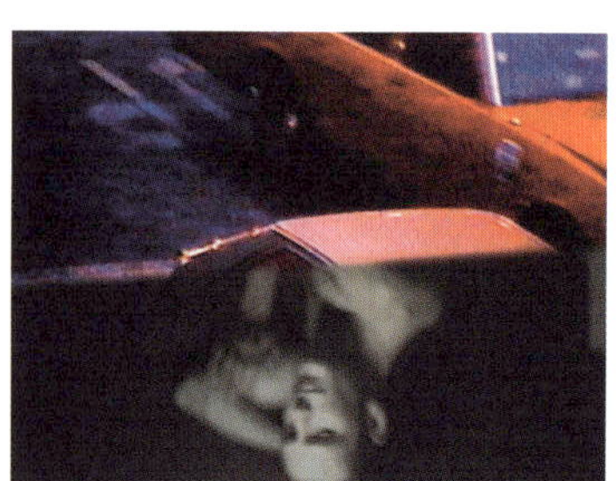
07:14

1 In-person interview with Lori Zippay, July 11, 2018.
2 Erika Balsom, *After Uniqueness: A History of Film and Video Art in Circulation* (New York: Columbia University Press, 2017), 221. “The call to disrupt the unidirectional flow of distribution with the bidirectional exchange of communication was frequently sounded in the 1960s as part of a critical project invested in disrupting the monoculture of television, often implicitly drawing on Bertolt Brecht’s 1932 text ‘The

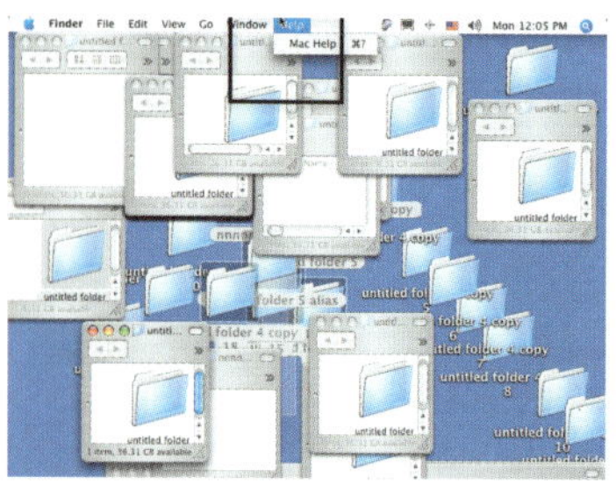

00:49

08:20

00:04

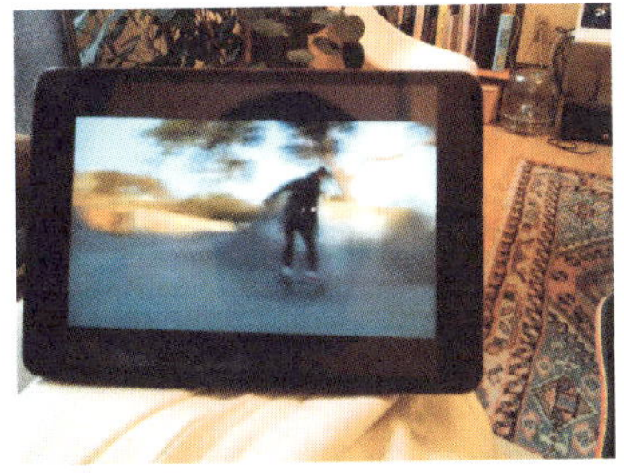
04:05

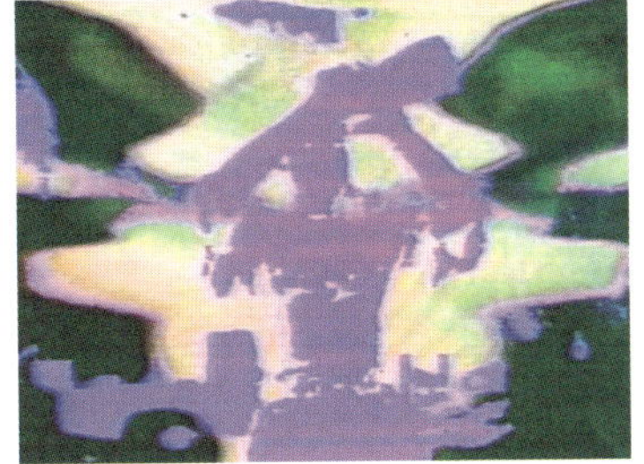
14:36

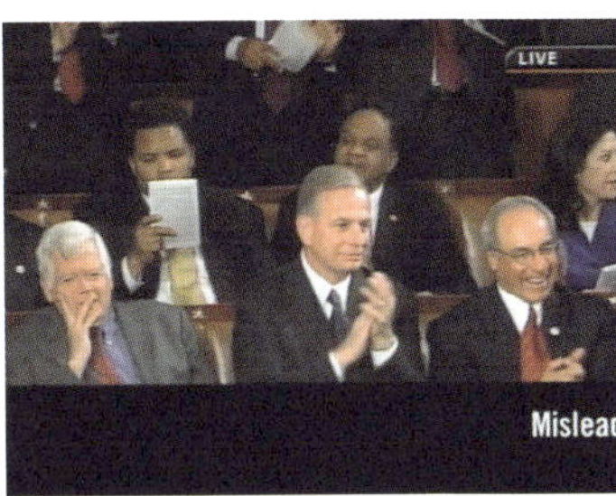

04:38

Radio as an Apparatus of Communication,' which had imagined a similar transformation in radio."

3 For more information on EAI's founding moments, see the oral history with Lori Zippay in this publication.

4 With this in mind it is crucial to resist a teleological position or advocate for a techno-determinist evolution of media in lieu of a consideration of the discrete material properties, opticalities, machinics, and historical conditions that shape them.

5 Ina Blom, *Memories in Motion. Archives, Technology, and the Social* (Amsterdam: Amsterdam University Press, 2016), 27–28.

6 Balsom, 174.

7 In 2008, Beck changed his father's name by a single vowel as a work of art. He often describes the maneuver as a "cut" and attributes it to his initial training as a film and video maker.

8 In-person interview with Robert Buck, May 3, 2019.

9 Excerpted from Lori Zippay's oral history in this publication.

10 Email exchange with Trevor Shimizu, March 5, 2019.

11 In-person interview with Robert Buck, May 3, 2019.

12 Seth Price, *Dispersion* (New York, 2002), 9.

13 Price, 11.

14 Phone interview with Sondra Perry, April 12, 2019.

15 Phone interview with Sondra Perry, April 12, 2019.

16 Phone interview with Sondra Perry, April 12, 2019.

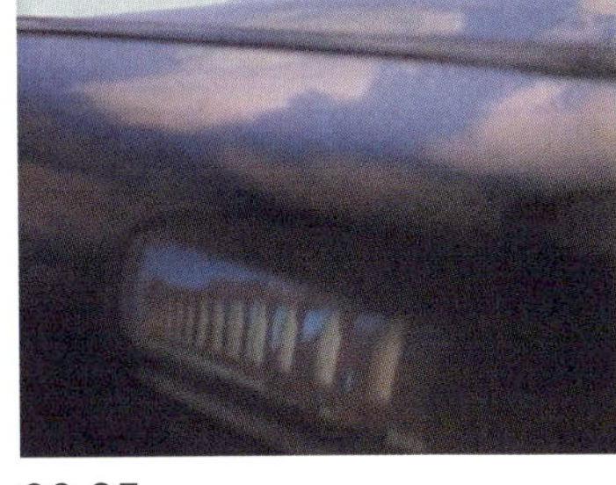
00:25

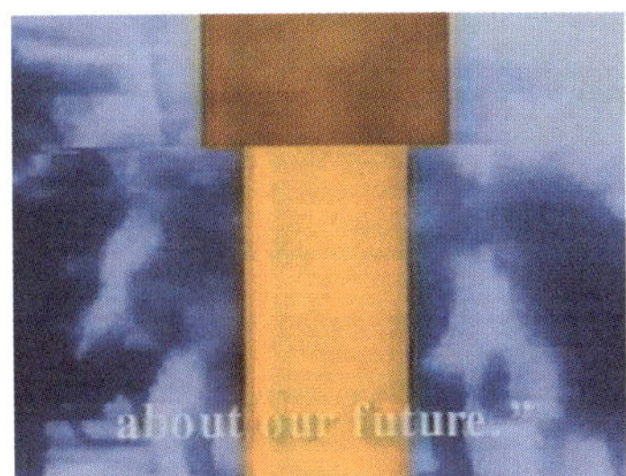
00:42

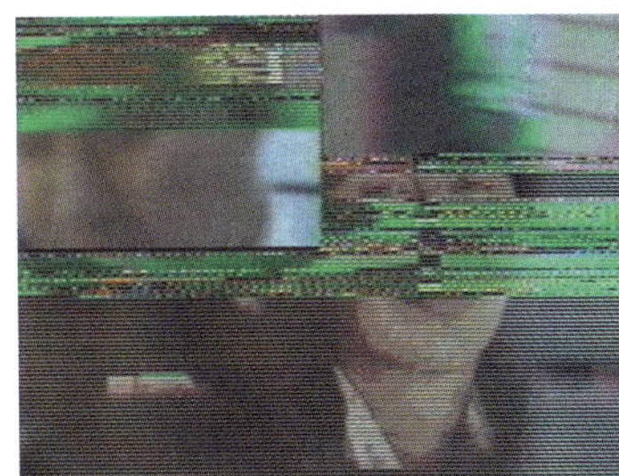
21:19

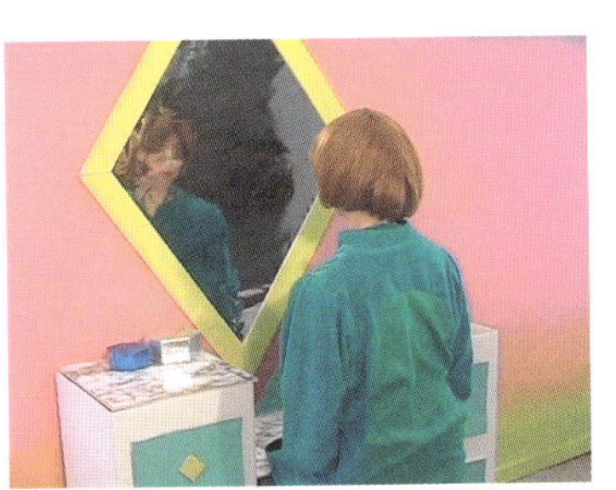
01:31

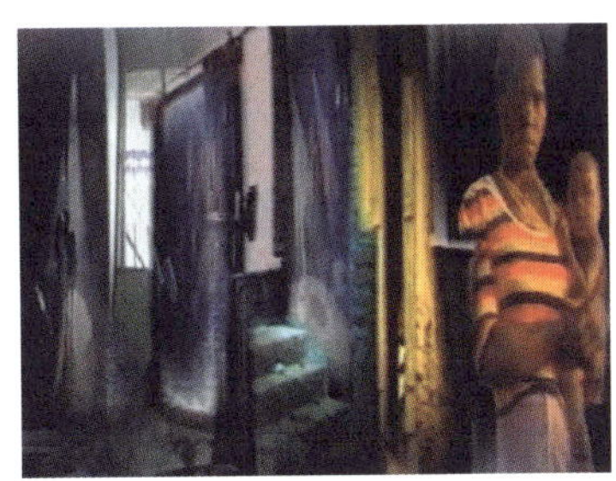
00:28

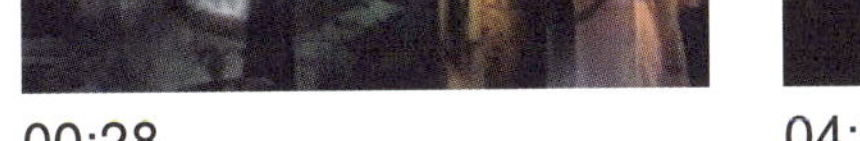
04:31

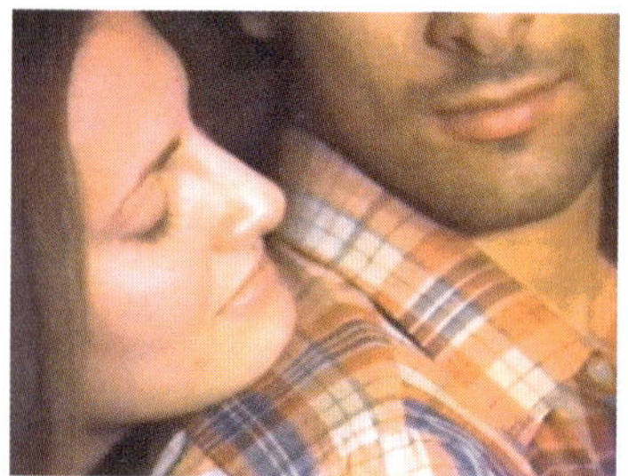

01:18

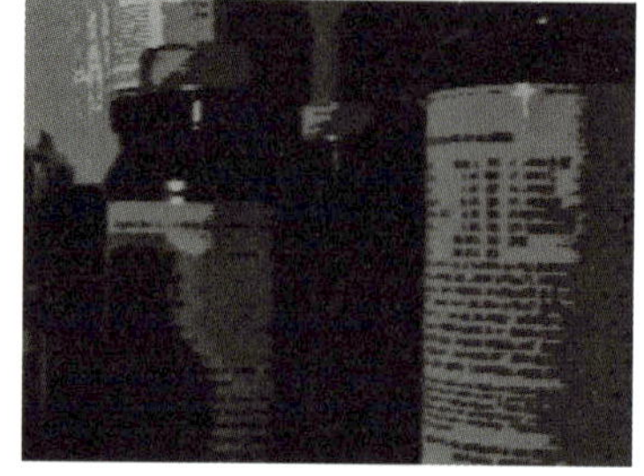

01:38

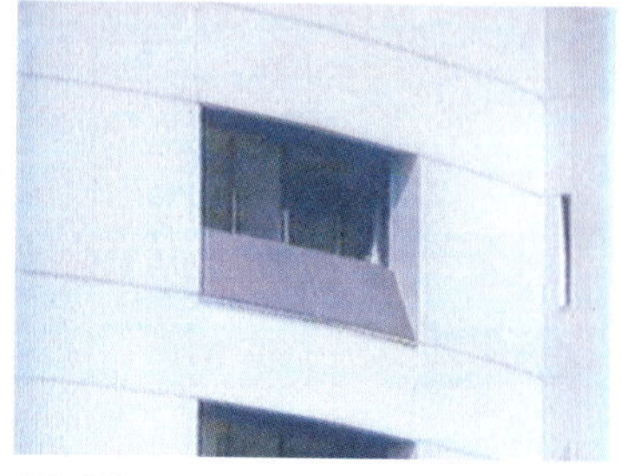

05:53

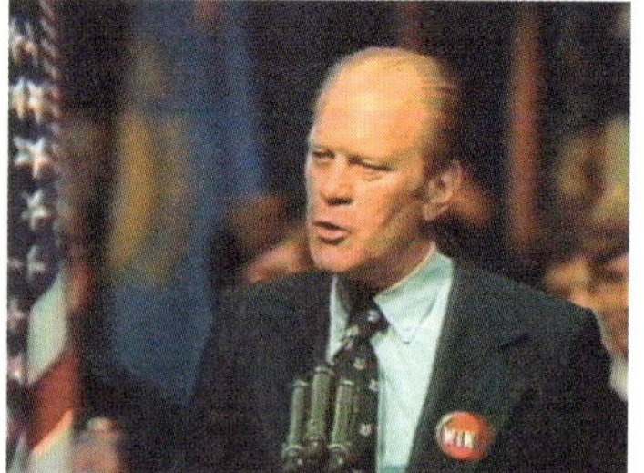

14:02

17 Phone interview with Josh Kline, April 14, 2019.

18 In-person conversation with Carolyn Lazard, March 13, 2019.

19 "PBS is not a network but a program distributor that provides television content and related services to its member stations." Wikipedia

20 In-person interview with Robert Buck, May 3, 2019.

21 Phone interview with Lauren Cornell, April 24, 2019.

22 Cory Arcangel talk at ICA, May 15, 2019.

23 See David Joselit, *Feedback: Television Against Democracy* (Cambridge: MIT Press, 2007).

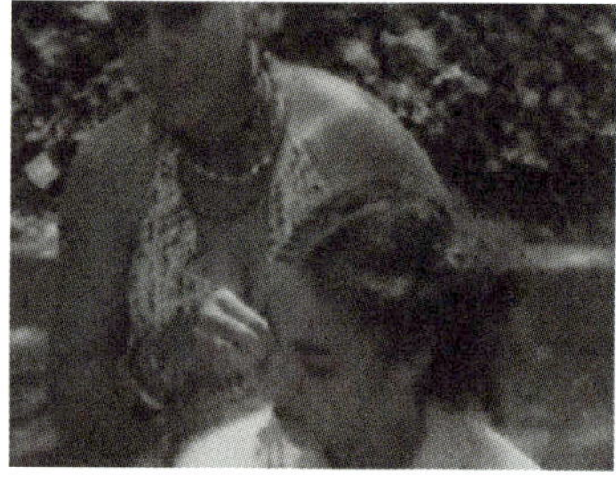

17:26

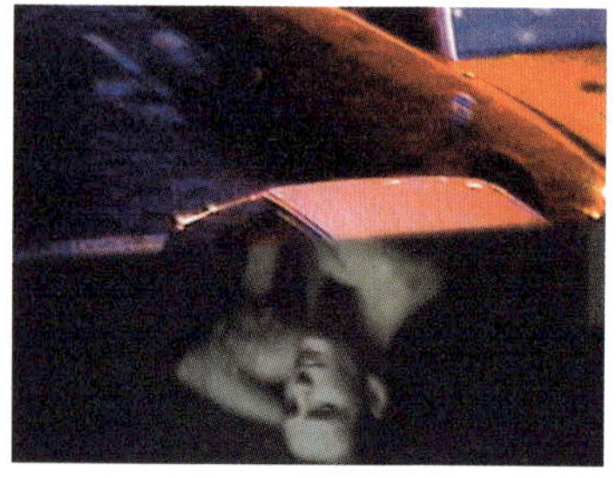

07:14

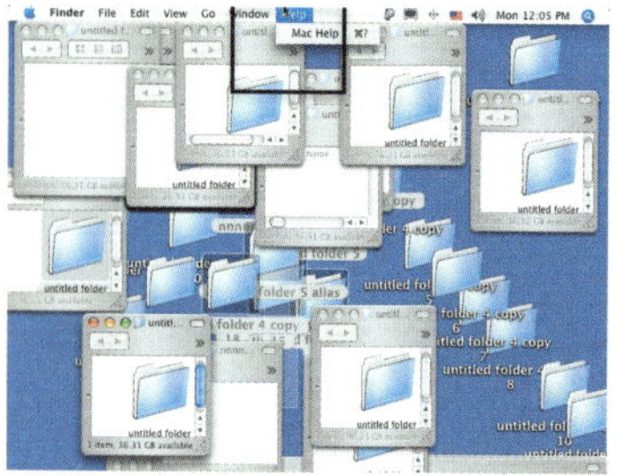

00:49

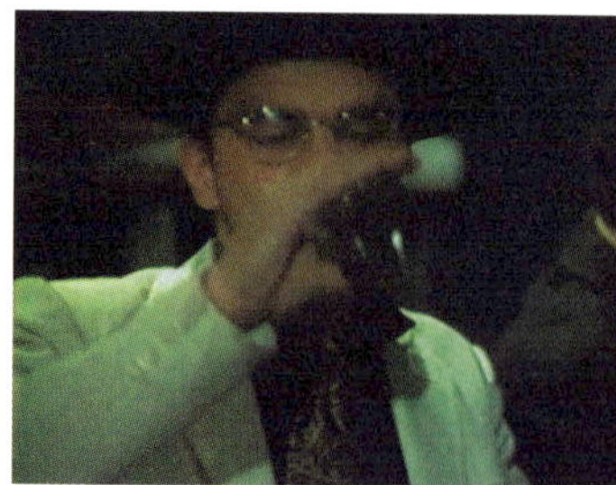

08:20

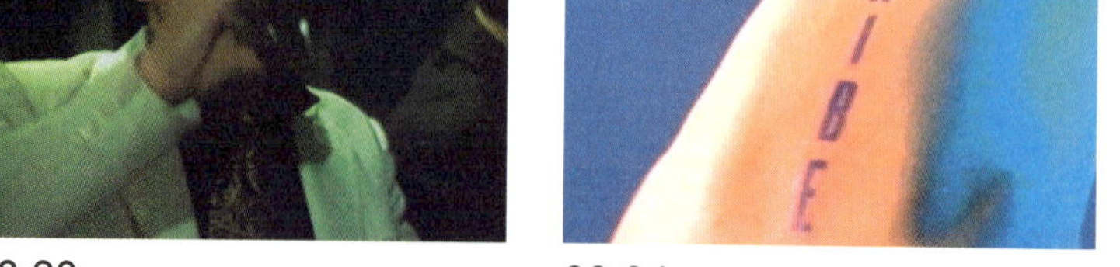

00:04

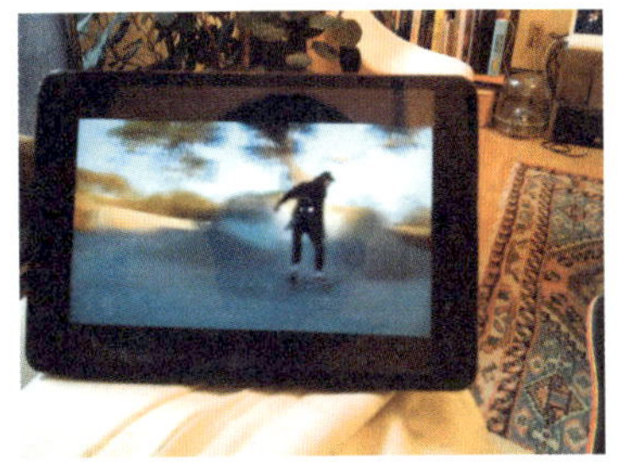
04:05

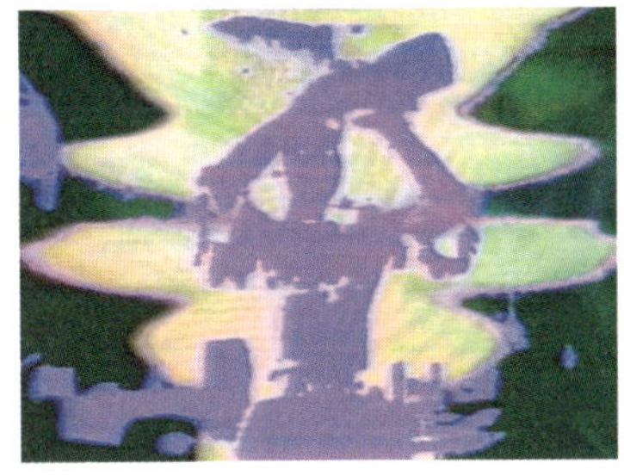
14:36

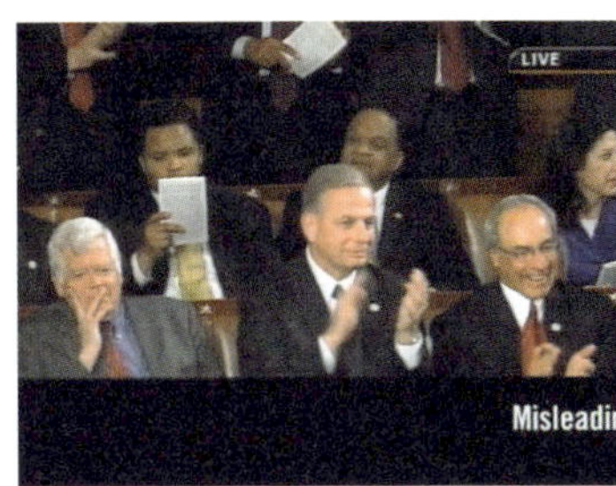

04:38

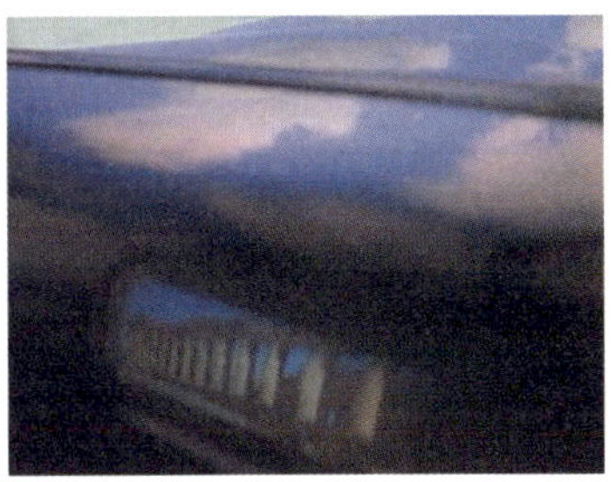
00:25

BROADCASTING: MEANS OF PRODUCTION
CONVERSATION BETWEEN
ANTOINE CATALA & TONY COKES
FEBRUARY 7, 2018

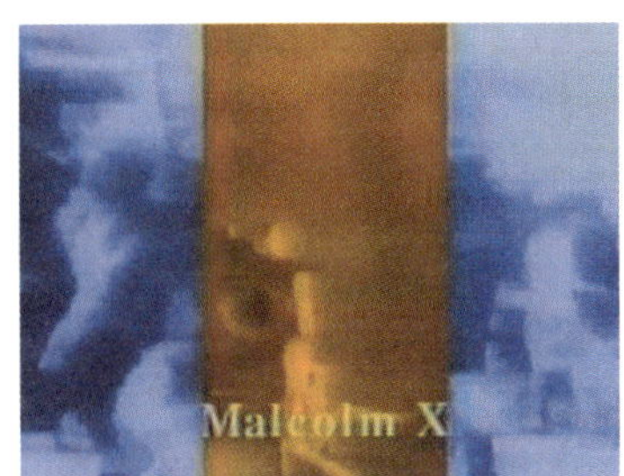

00:42

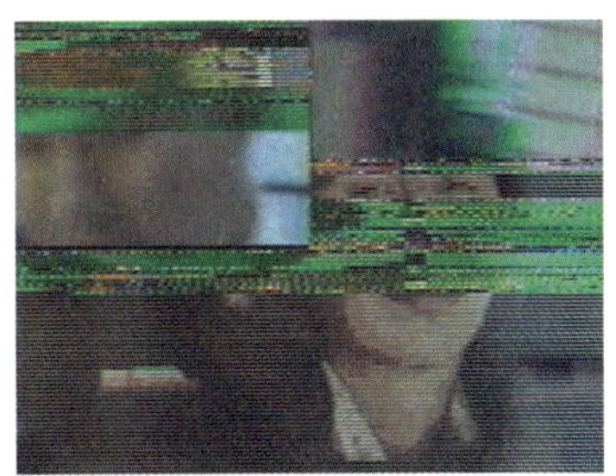
21:19

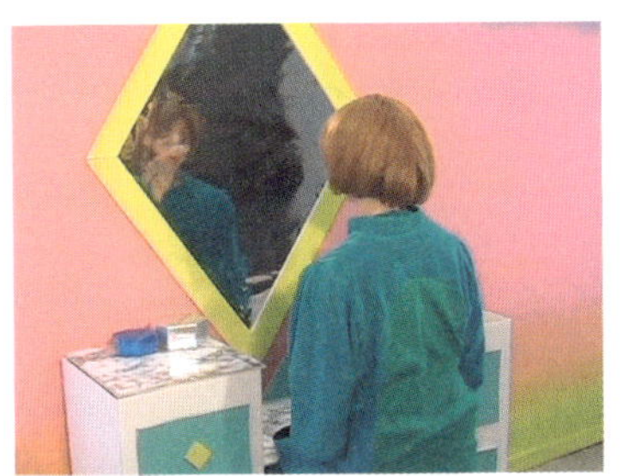
01:31

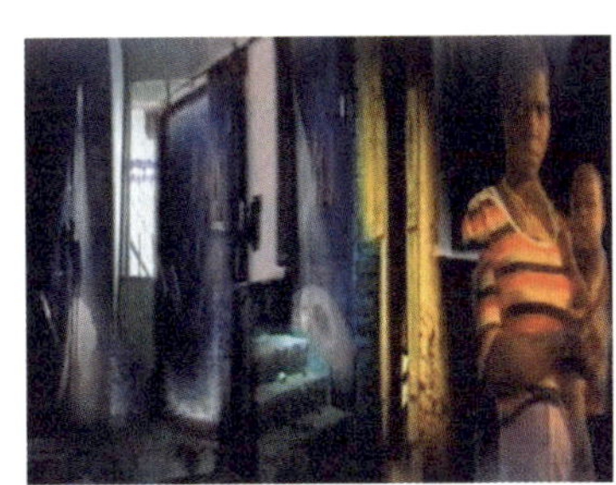
00:28

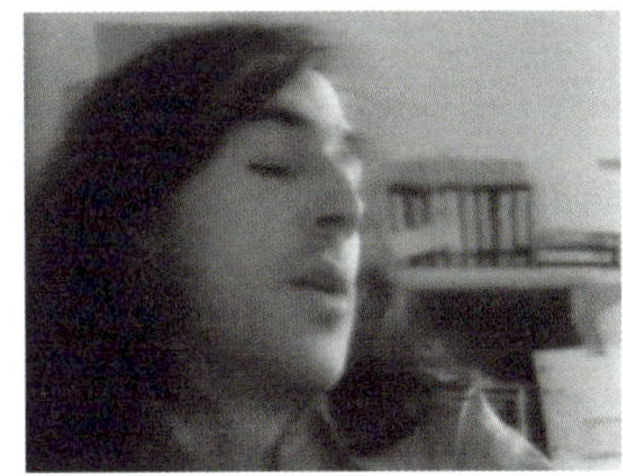
04:31

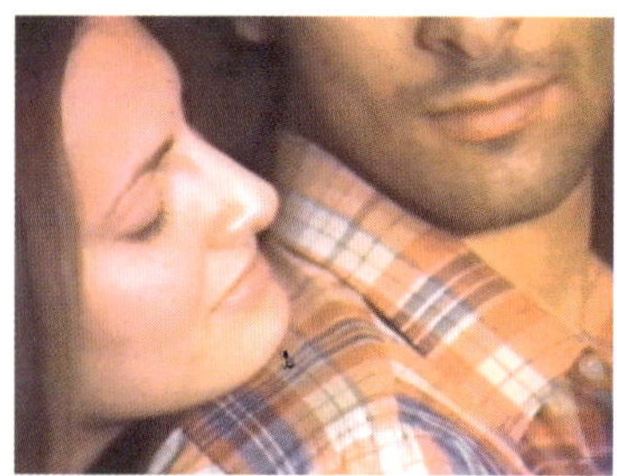

01:18

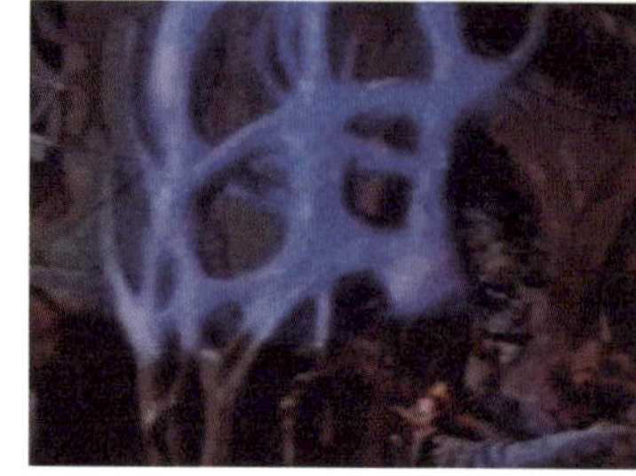

01:38

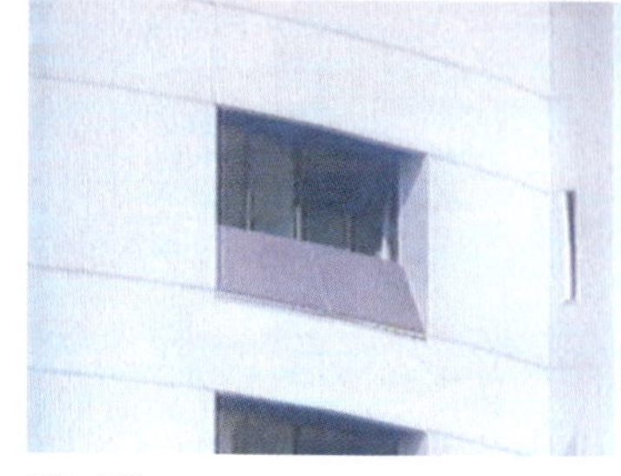

05:53

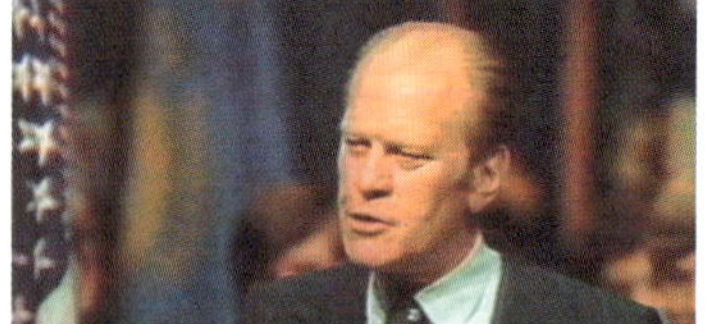

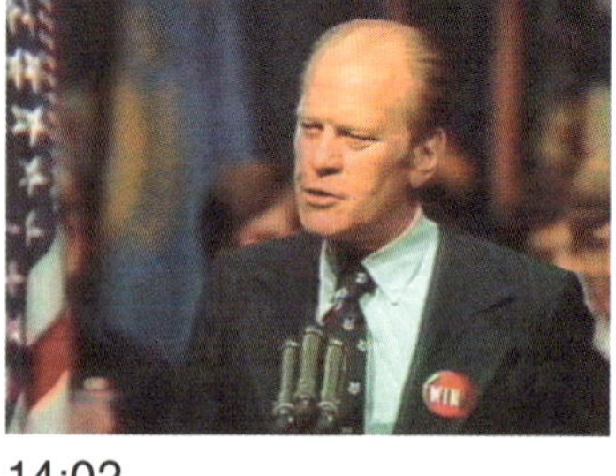

14:02

17:26

The exhibition in the gallery doubled as a television studio where intergenerational conversations between EAI-affiliated artists were staged in front of a live studio audience. Through a collaboration with PhillyCAM, a community media center and home to Philadelphia's only public access television station, the events were broadcast live on TV and streamed online. The following conversations are lightly edited transcripts of the events.

Alex Klein – It could be said that both Tony's and Antoine's work investigate modes of communication and an expanded form of textuality and messaging. As a result, we have invited both artists to come together in conversation to reflect on these concerns as they relate to the technological means of production within their respective practices.

Rebecca Cleman – Because this conversation is being broadcast live on cable access television, it's appropriate to think about the specific "environment" of mass media platforms, and how artists work in them. There's print, radio, television—in which Philadelphia played an important role from the beginning—and now the internet. The transition from one medium to the next makes me think about Marshall McLuhan's observations about what happens as one media format becomes obsolete and transitions to a new one. Here is a quote from 1964, that speaks to this transition and considers how art factors in. "The history of the arts and sciences could be written in terms of the continuing process by which new technologies create new environments for old

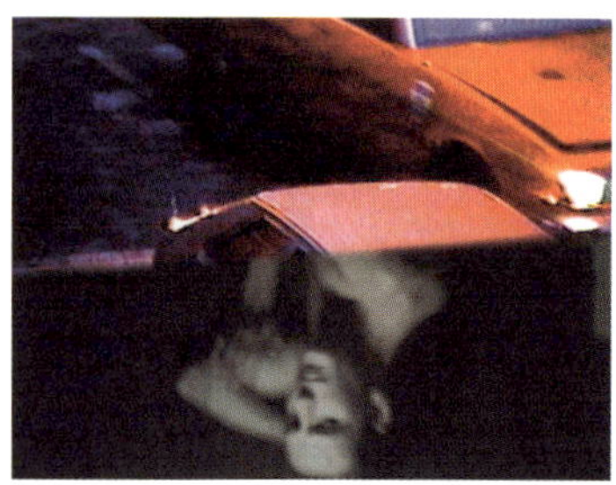

07:14

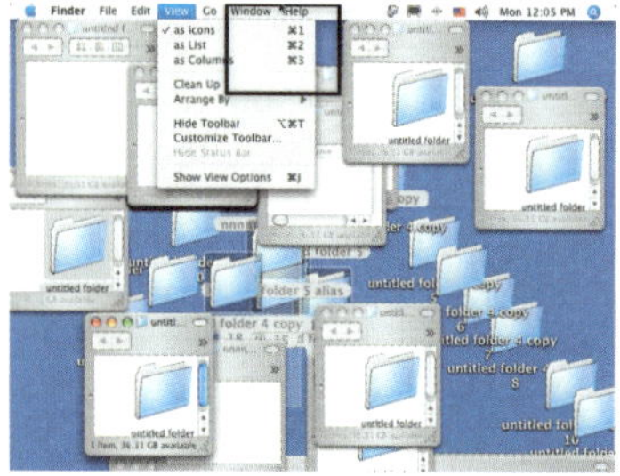

00:49

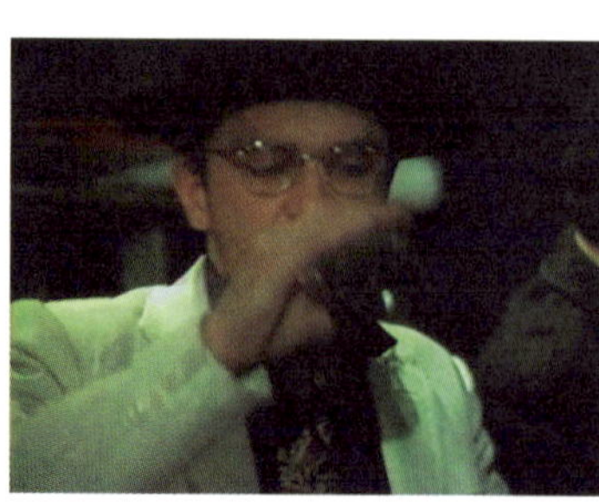

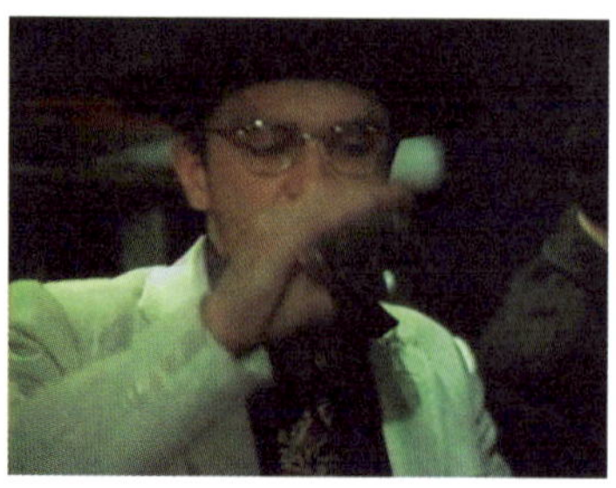

08:20

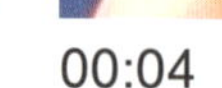

00:04

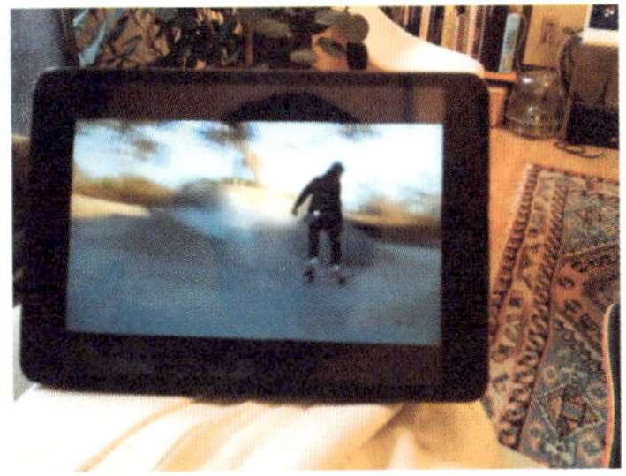
04:06

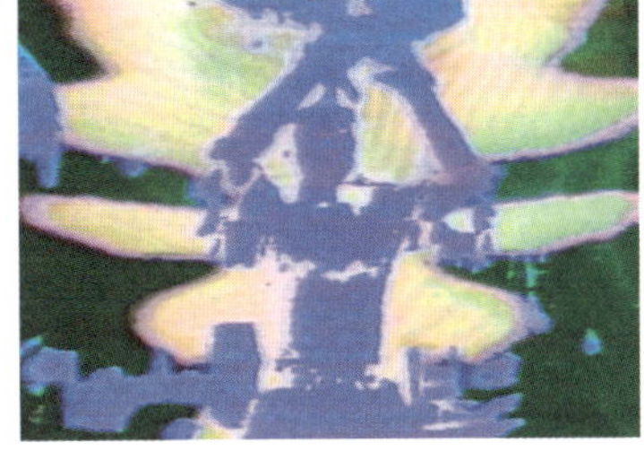
14:37

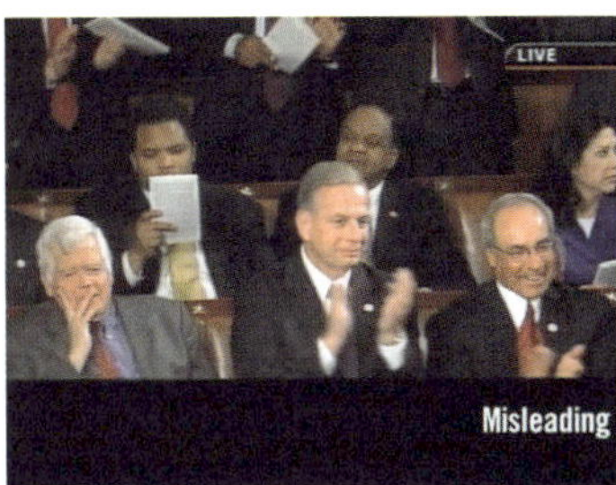

04:39

technologies. The old technology, as the content of the new, quickly becomes tidied up into an art form, such as is happening to film since it has become the content of TV.”[1] So, it makes sense to think about television as being the content of the internet because television hasn’t completely vanished, in fact, it has just adapted to the new environment. I’m reading these quotes because Tony and Antoine both make art that speaks to these transitions in media and media platforms and how they influence the public. They also both are attentive to media obsolescence and the way technology trends over time.

EAI was founded by Howard Wise in 1971, as a new paradigm to support media art which Wise understood to be in constant flux. McLuhan’s theories about the significant impact any technology shift has on culture were very influential to Wise, as they were to the larger guerrilla television, video art scene. Wise envisioned EAI as a center offering support to artists working at the intersection of art and technology, with an attention to the publicness inherent in their form. EAI has adapted from a televisual environment of broadcasts and video tapes, to an internet-based one of streaming and file formats—but distribution remains its core program.

Tony Cokes – And it also is a production site for some of my work as well.

RC – That’s right. From the beginning, EAI also functioned as a facility offering artists access to editing tools, editing equipment at a time before laptops and iBook and Apple made it

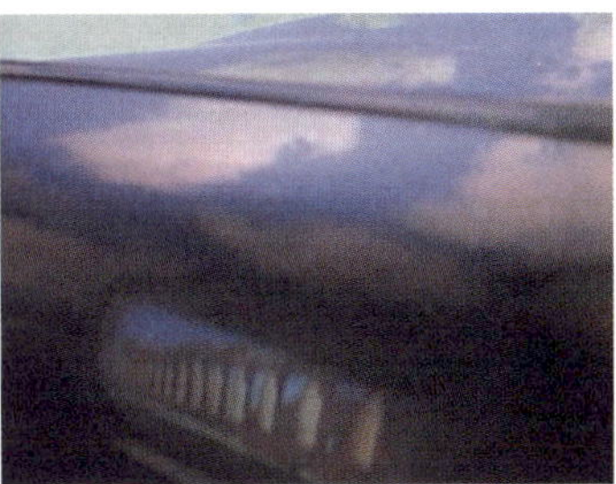
00:26

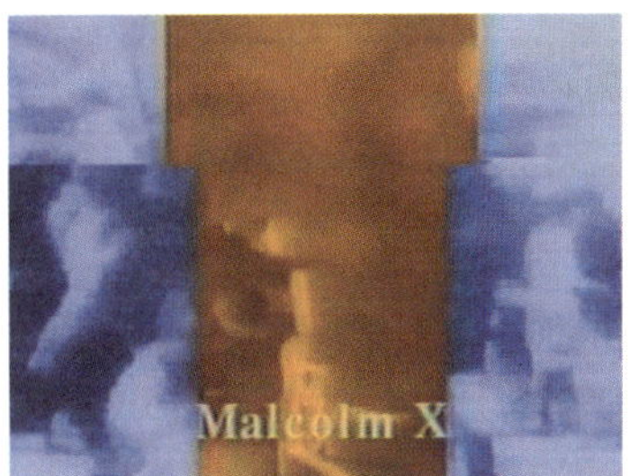

00:43

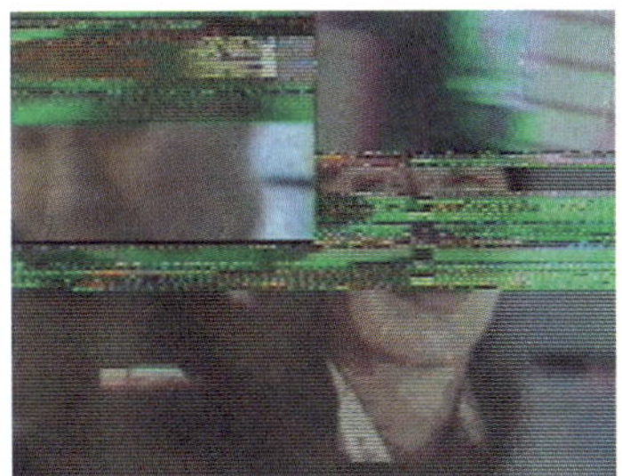
21:20

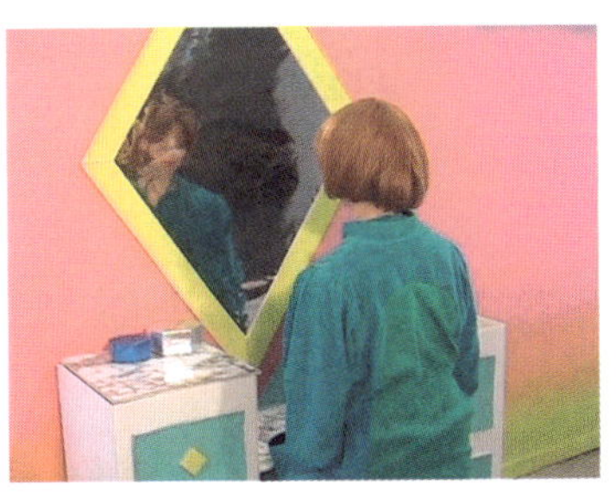
01:32

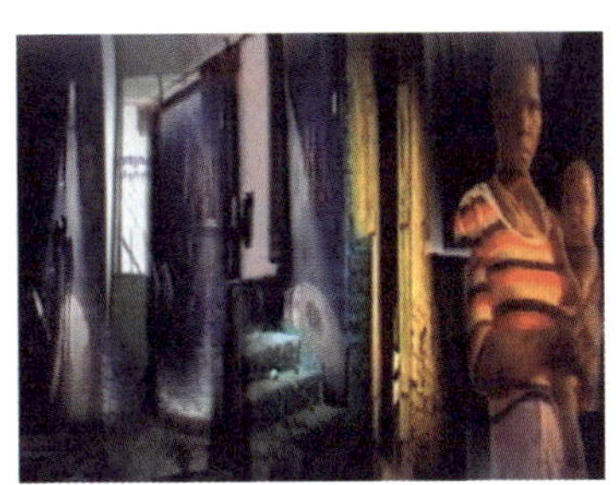
00:29

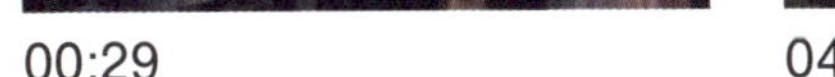
04:32

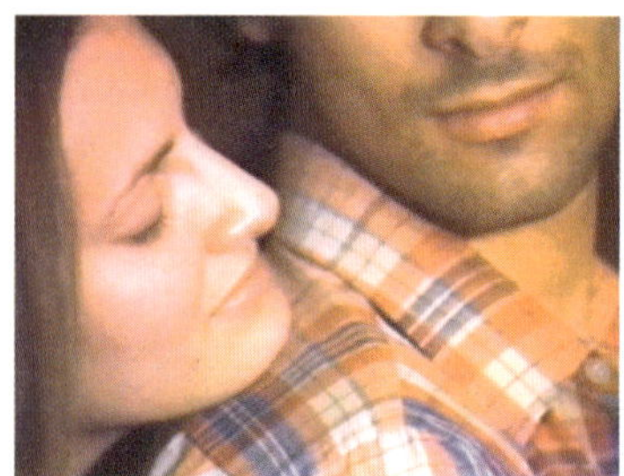
01:18

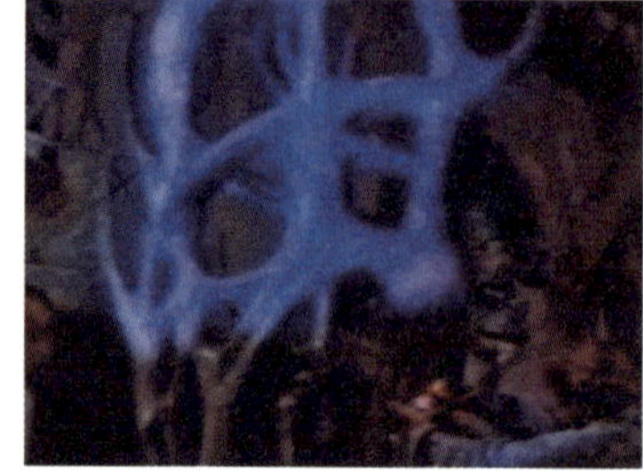
01:38

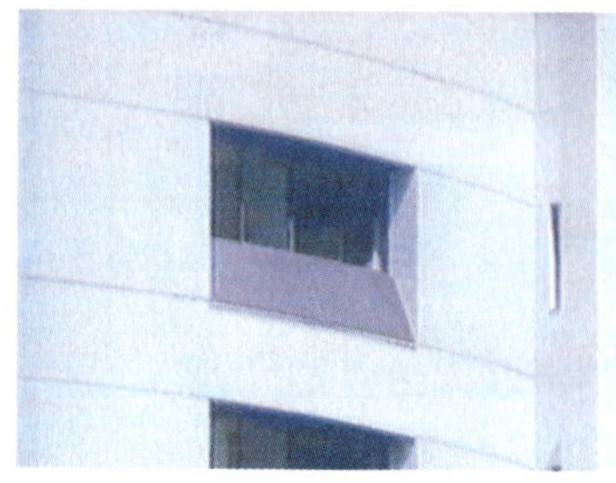
05:53

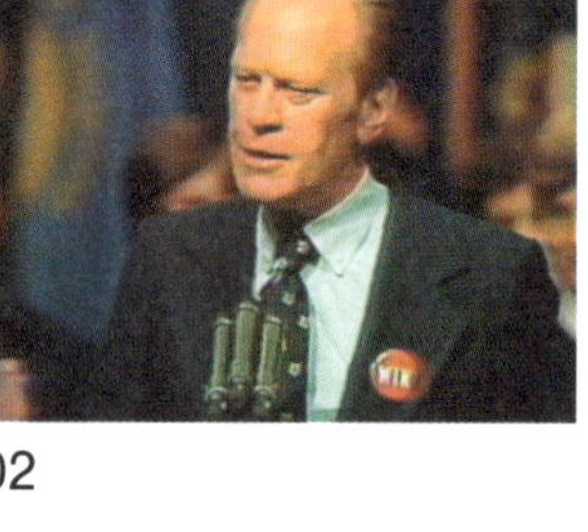
14:02

17:26

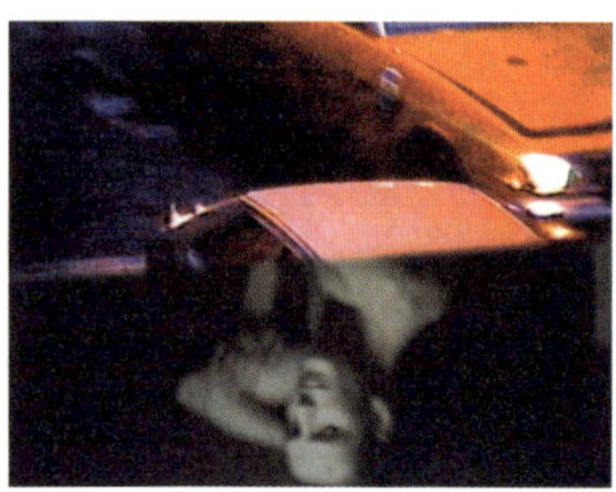
07:14

easy for you to stay at home and work as Tony now does.

TC – I stay at home.

RC – There was a time when that wasn't possible.

AK – Another thing that EAI does is you are an advocate for artists and I think that's really important in this streaming culture age where everything is kind of fluid. You find a way to compensate artists for the work that they do and for things that seem like they're "immaterial." But getting back to this idea of production, maybe even the intergenerational aspect of that, one of the things that we were really thinking about in organizing these conversations and the exhibition is the role that EAI has played as a site of dialogue between artists who have different strategies and represent different generational perspectives.

How are some of those ideas informing the works of younger artists today? For example, you might not draw a straight line between the use of the Sony Portapak in the early 1970s to some of the work that you're seeing today, but I think that some of the younger artists who are engaged with questions of the digital and the internet are also being informed by some of the conversations that may have been happening at EAI and the earlier days of video art. So, I just want to plant that seed and mention the agricultural root of broadcasting, which has really also inflected so much of our thinking about the show—planting seeds widely and seeing how things might grow and be dispersed. So thinking about EAI and ICA in that sort of dialogic terrain. ICA also had an important exhibition in 1975

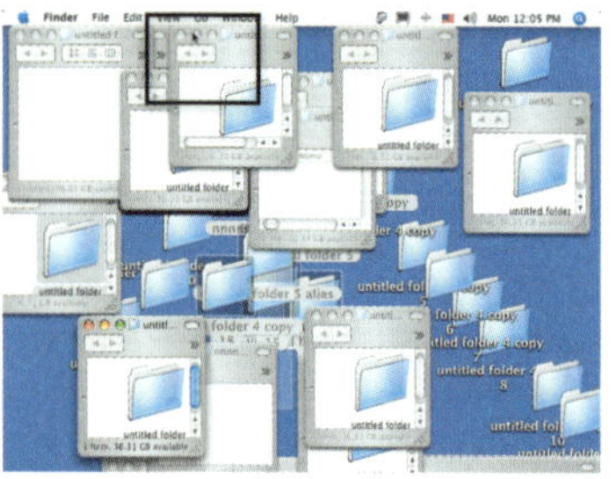
00:49

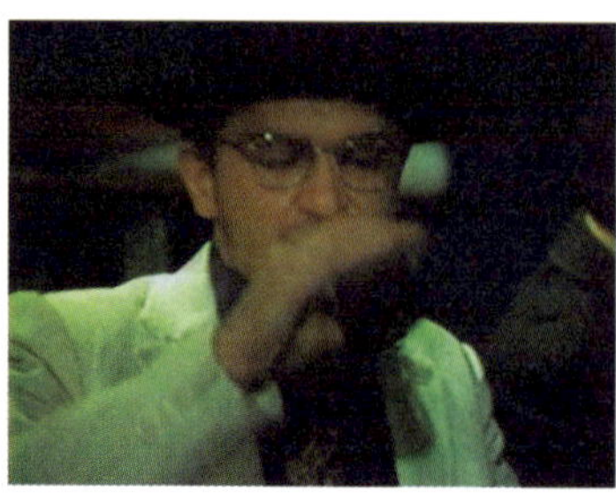
08:20

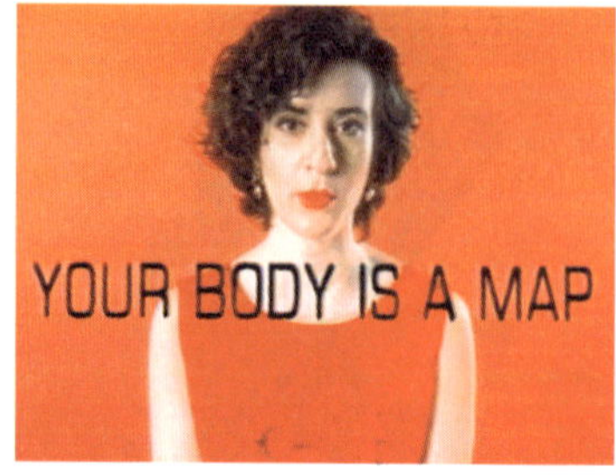

00:04

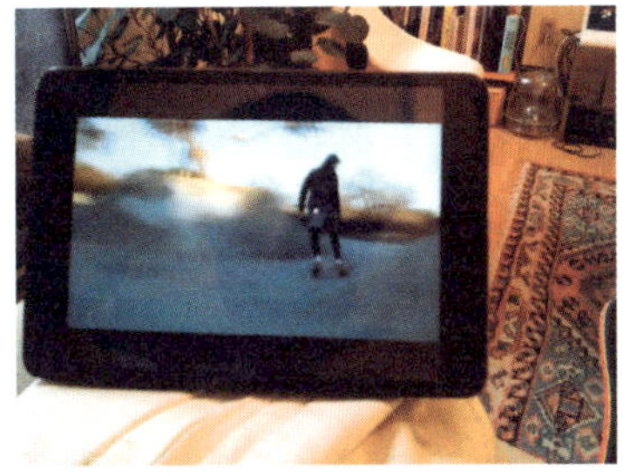
04:06

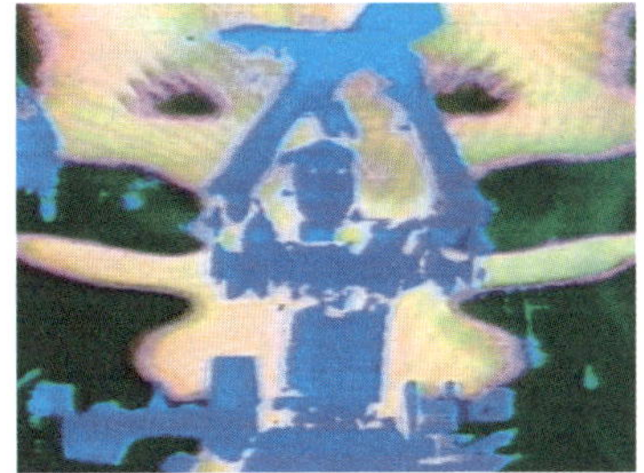
14:37

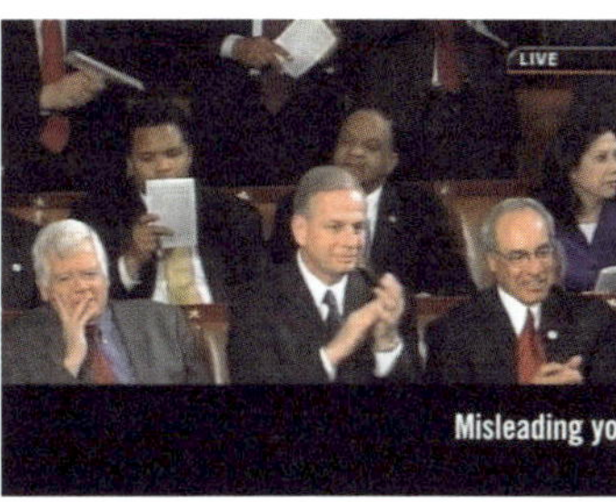

04:39

devoted to video art. It was one of the first international exhibitions devoted to the medium, which at the time was still relatively new. So again, our own history at ICA is also one of the contexts for tonight's televised show.

I think we're going to dive right into a focus on some of Tony's and Antoine's artworks. This is a very light gloss, but it will at least introduce some of terms that we're hoping to bring up this evening. We're going to begin with Tony Cokes. Tony is based in Providence, Rhode Island, where he is a professor at Brown University in the Modern Culture and Media Department, where he has been influential not just as a teacher and artist, but as a collaborator with a lot of other artists you might know such as Seth Price, Kerry Tribe, etc. He has exhibited and screened his work internationally at institutions such as REDCAT in Los Angeles, SFMOMA in San Francisco, the Whitney Museum of American Art in New York, and in the spring, he has a solo exhibition opening at Greene Naftali Gallery in Chelsea. So, we are going to begin with an older work of Tony's called *Book of Love* from 1992. I think the genesis of this was a little bit earlier. Rebecca and I were interested in asking you a bit about this work because I think it's a little atypical for people who might be familiar with your recent work, but also because it was initially intended for television.

TC – It was intended for broadcast on PBS, yes. And, of course, ultimately not used in that context. But it was an interesting process to go through and it actually made me realize that like a lot of

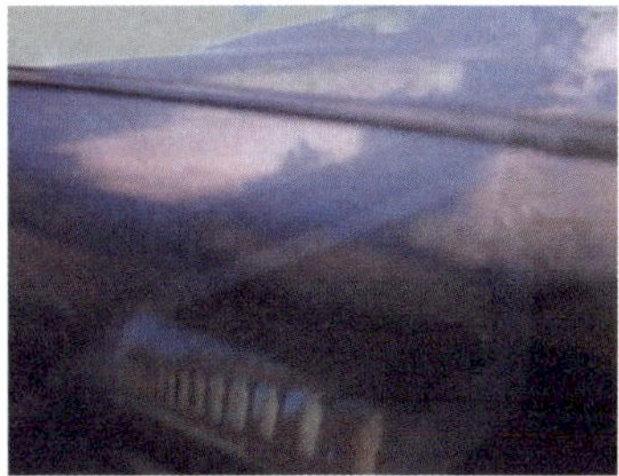
00:26

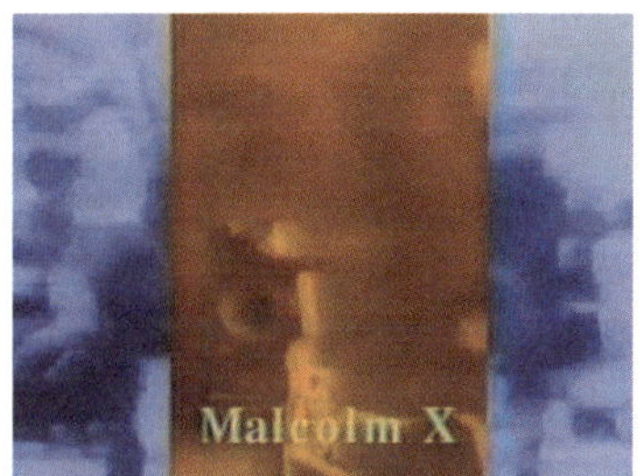

00:43

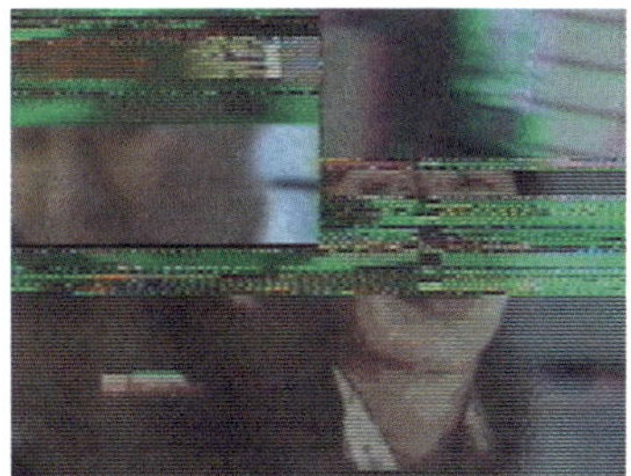
21:20

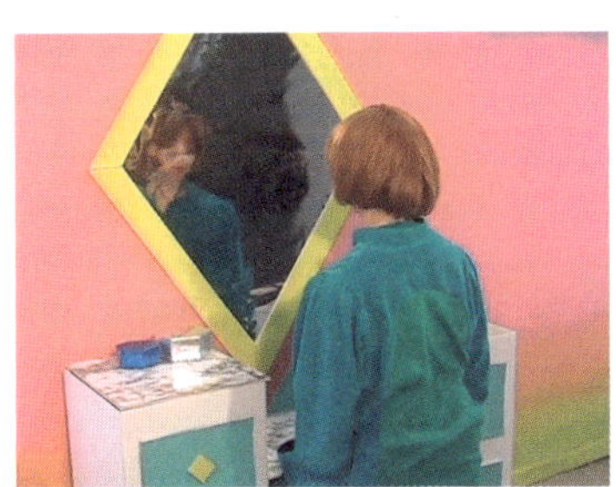
01:32

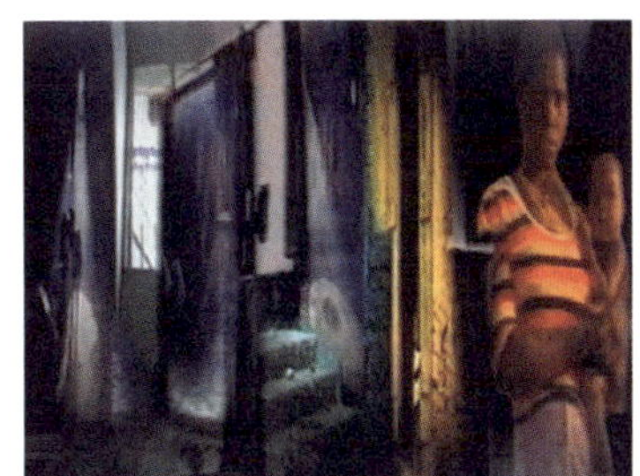
00:29

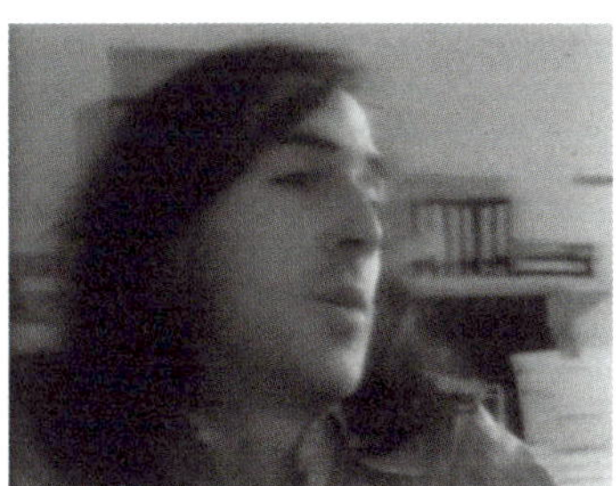
04:32

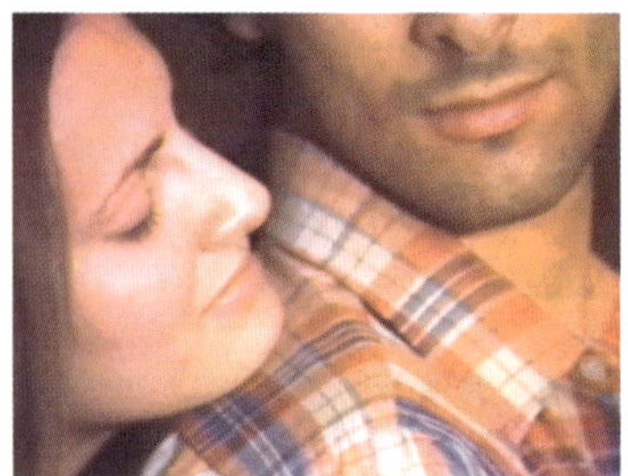
01:18

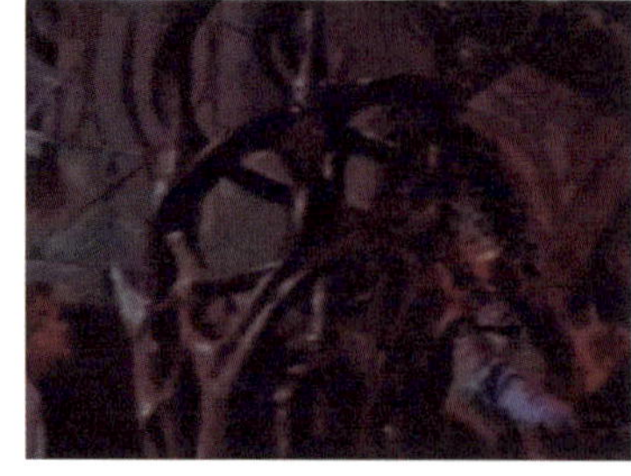
01:38

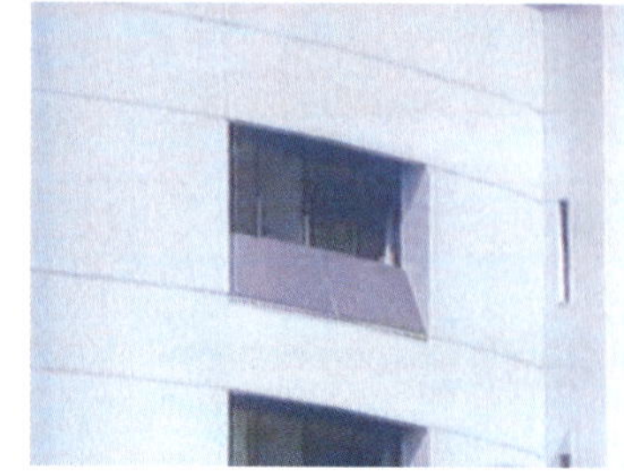
05:53

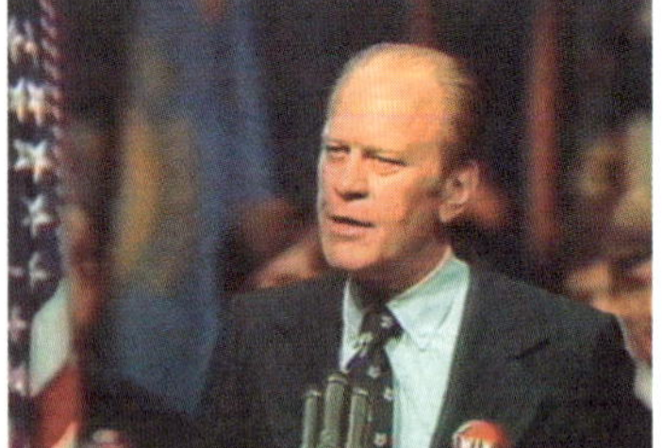
14:02

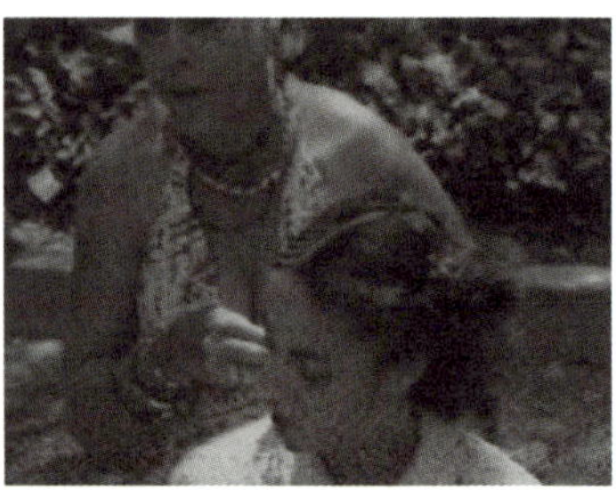
17:26

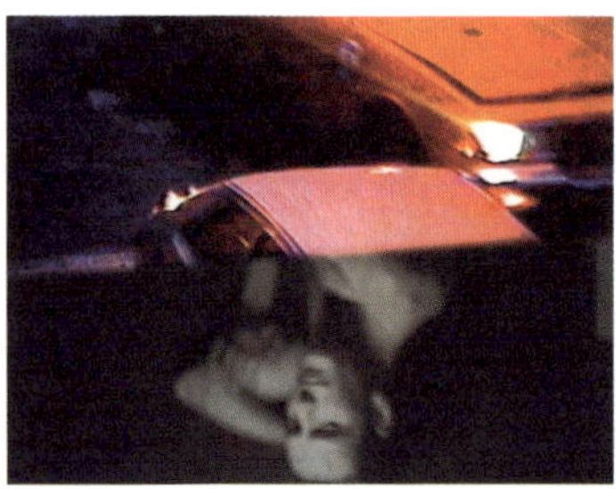
07:14

my work it had a number of different forms and points of origin. It took me a long time to actually get this thing into a form and then it kind of dispersed from there. I was interested in that trajectory as the underside of broadcast, something that was intended for one context, but never quite reached it.

AK – Can you tell us a little bit about the work? It focuses on your mother, correct?

TC – Yes it's an extended sort of documentary with my mother. I interviewed her over time in different settings and I also came up with ideas, quotations, and things that I had written related to questions around forms of representation. I displayed it, or actually workshopped it, in a strange way as a multichannel installation initially with the text elements separated from the documentary materials. But it was always intended that they interfere with each other in certain ways and I think that's of course part of what created the difficulty for broadcast; it didn't *grab* people. If it had been interview material it might have had a chance to engage with audiences in maybe a more traditional way. But I was bound and determined to not let that happen.

AK – And what is the text that is scrolling underneath the images?

TC – It's scrolling both underneath and beside the image. Some of the texts were kind of autobiographical notations, some were thoughts about the entire process of production, which is something that normally would not be foregrounded in a situation like this.

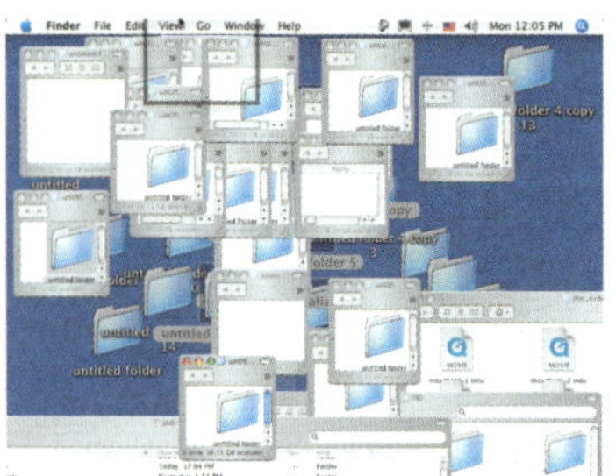
00:49

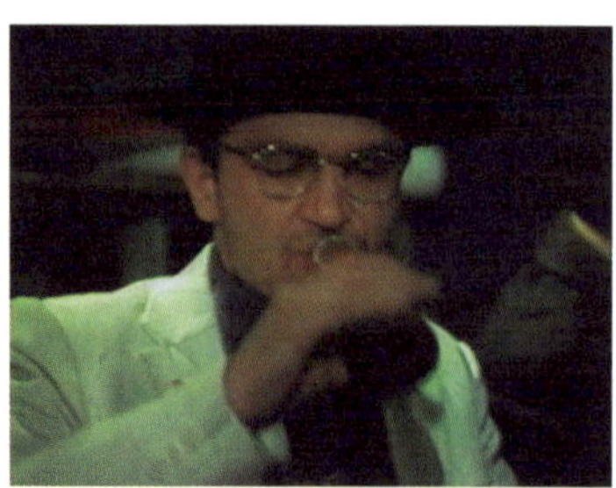
08:20

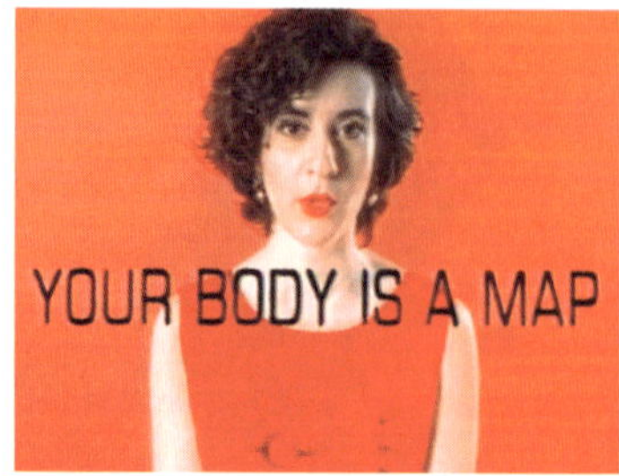

00:04

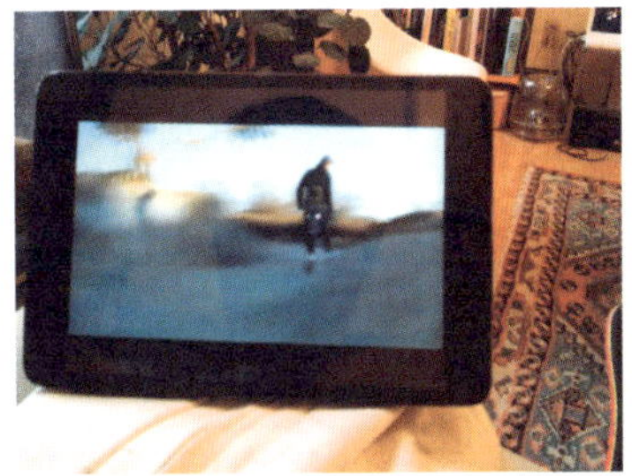
04:06

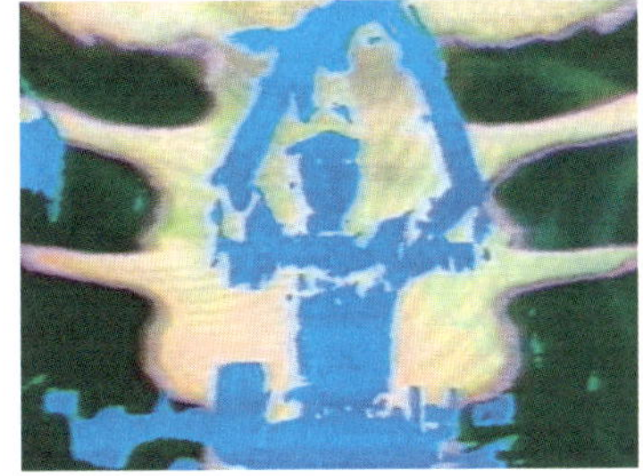
14:37

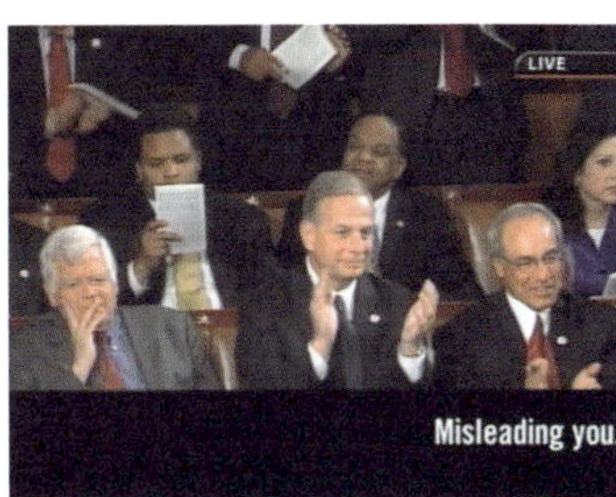

04:39

RC – I have a question in terms of time span. *Book of Love*, I think in the EAI catalog it says that the project germinated in 1984, is that correct?

TC – That is correct.

RC – You got a public broadcast grant for that; is that what the originating moment was?

TC – Yes, but the grant was later, like in 1990, from ITVS, to actually do the final version. I had done some studies in Hi8, but then we wound up shooting it I think in Betacam. I was also aware of the kind of temporality that the working process can often embody and take up. And I don't know, for me it seemed important to notate those things as opposed to simply present what appears to be a speaking subject that unpacks her whole history in a short, compressed period of time. That doesn't really happen; there has to be a relationship on the ground that informs that as a possibility.

RC – That makes me think of your video, *Black Celebration*, which is 1988, and thinking about the "re-presentation" of appropriated footage. In this case, the footage is of 1960s-era street riots such as the Watts Riot in Los Angeles in 1965 and others in Boston, Detroit, and Chicago, re-contextualized so the emphasis is not on violence and criminality, but on positive collective action, a political or racial affirmation, a "Black celebration." I also want to mention that on a monitor behind Tony is a work by Ulysses Jenkins, who started a video collective called Video Venice News. A well-known work of the collective was focused on the Watts Festival and

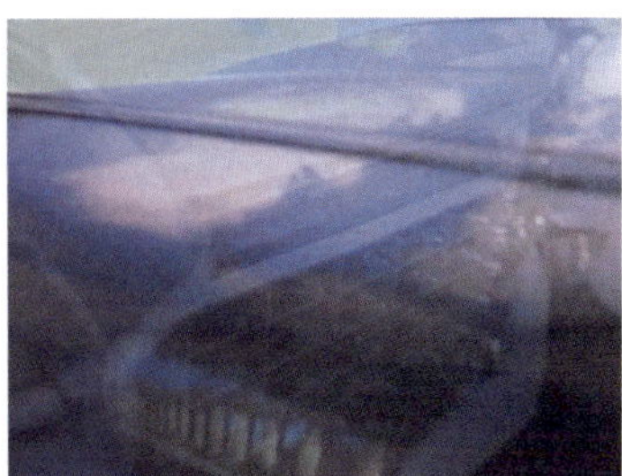
00:26

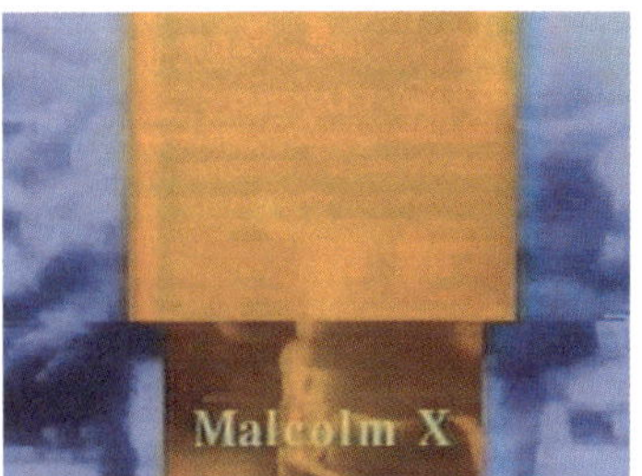

00:43

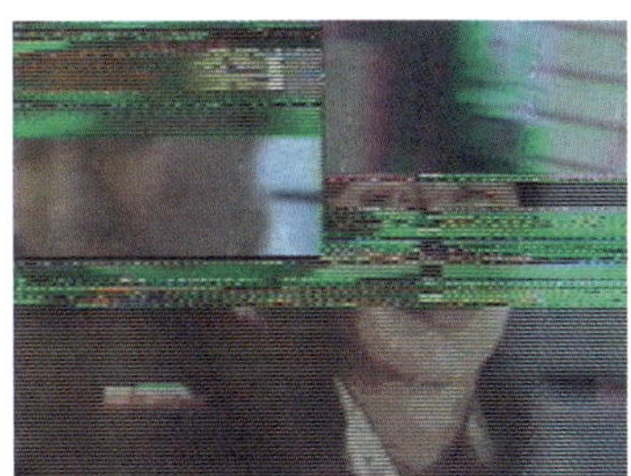
21:20

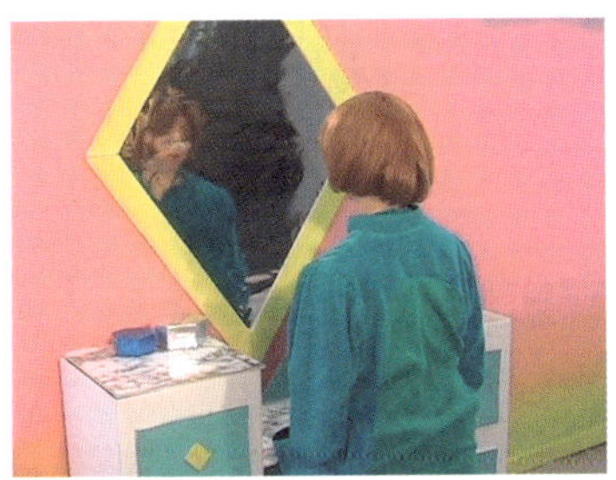
01:32

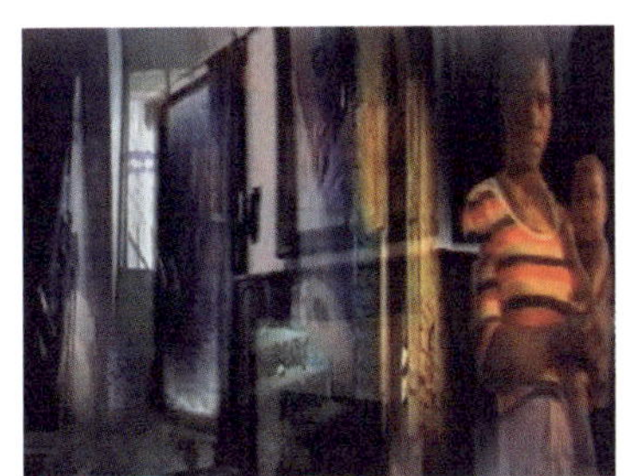
00:29

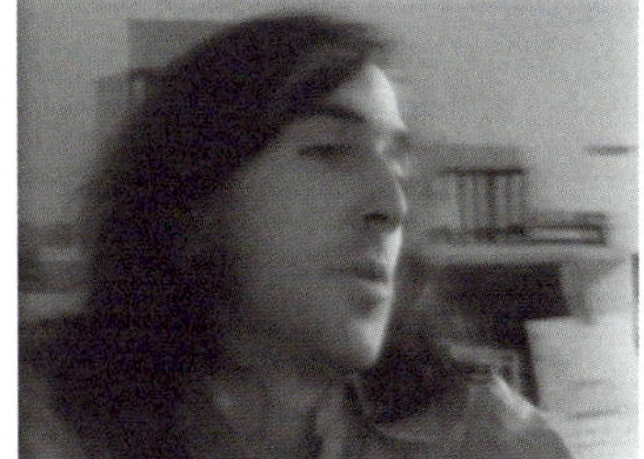
04:32

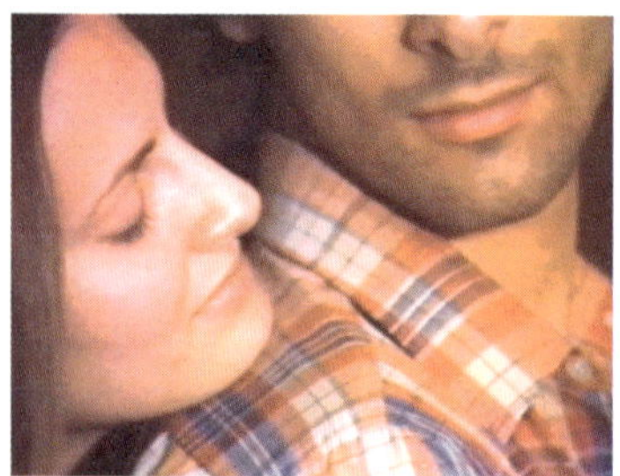

01:18

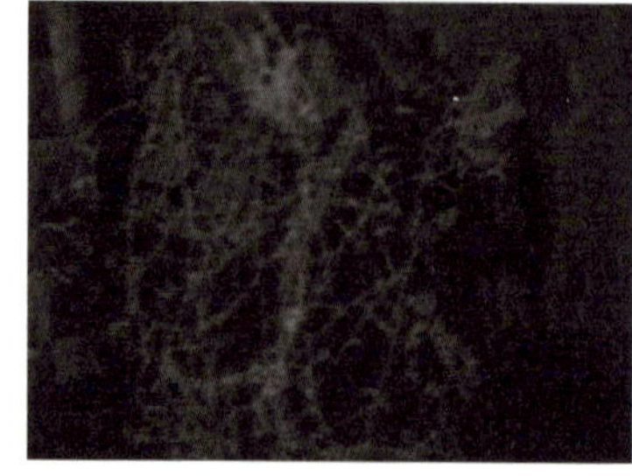

01:38

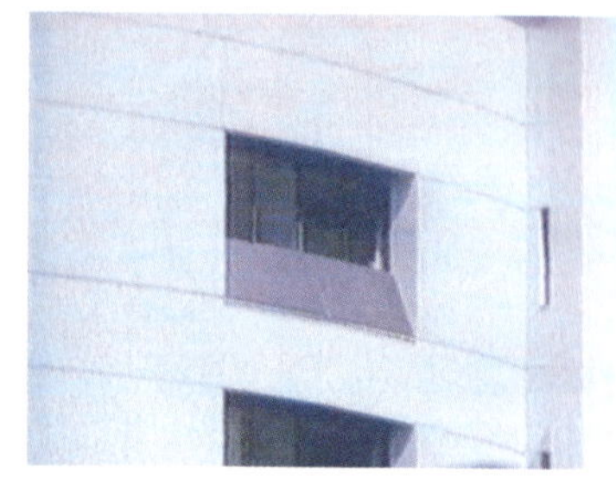

05:53

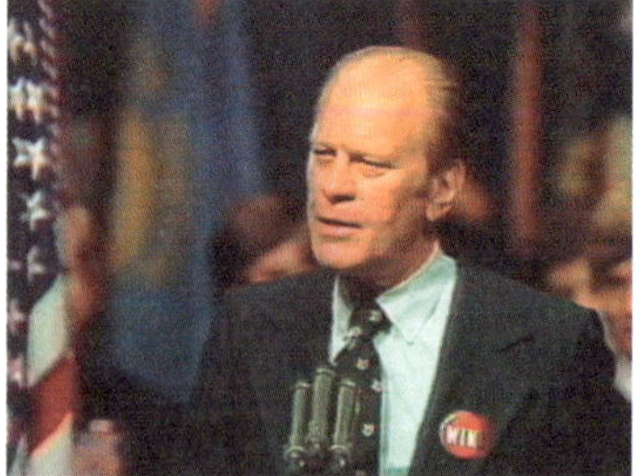

14:02

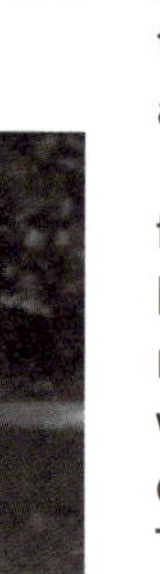

17:26

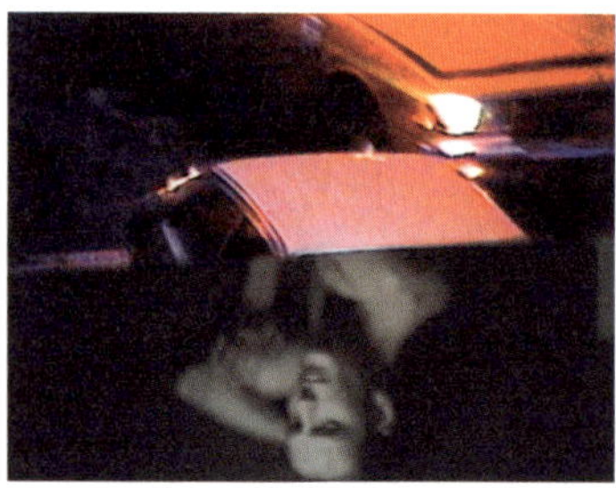

07:14

re-contextualizing that as well. So, there's a nice dialogue there.

AK – And *Black Celebration* has a soundtrack by Skinny Puppy, right? So, this is also an early example of your tactic of juxtaposing sound and image.

TC – For me it's anathema to do a period soundtrack. For instance, often in my work, not always, I'm looking at what I'm listening to while I'm composing something. There's a kind of interesting history. Of course, with this project, it was initially done as an installation where early on in the process I decided I wasn't going to have the soundtrack audible because of issues with group shows and sound bleeds, things that people should be familiar with in the context of presentations of new media art. So I still needed to edit to something and when editing usually the first thing I put down is a soundtrack. So I put down a soundtrack even though I knew I wasn't going to use it in that display condition. After that exhibition had run its course—I only presented it once in an installation format—I started to circulate it as a single-channel tape, because I liked the relationship between the sound and image. I thought that it produced certain conditions of rereading, questions around the appropriateness of the soundtrack, which were questions that maybe I had about the original source footage even initially—you know, thinking about the kind of genre of film music that was used as soundtracks for these newsreels, which perhaps didn't relate in any way to the specific place of location. To amplify that disconnect was part of the intention.

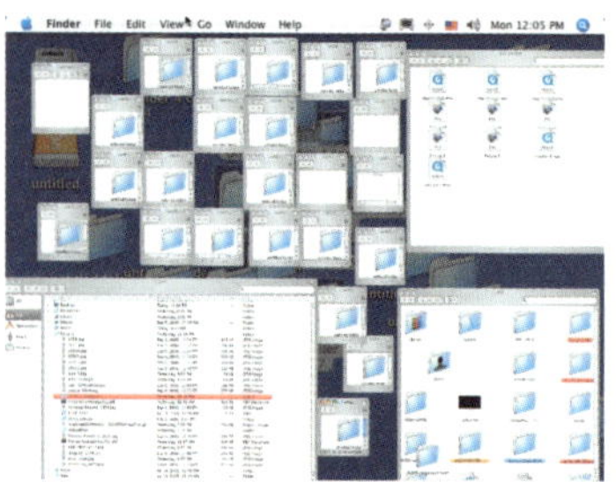

00:49

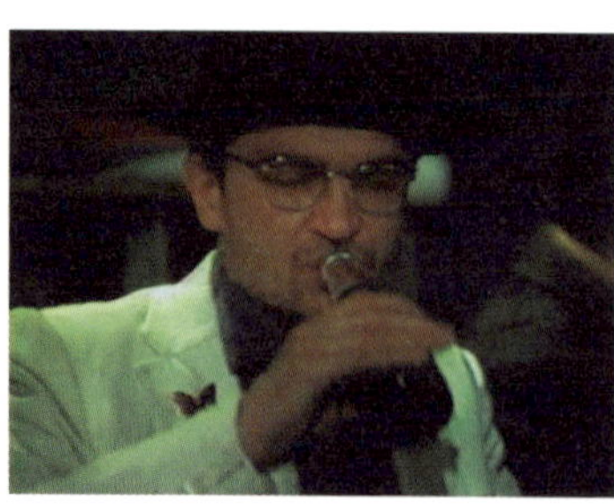

08:20

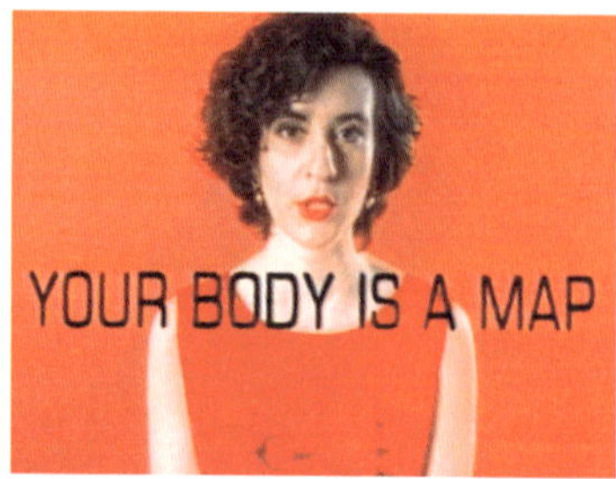

00:04

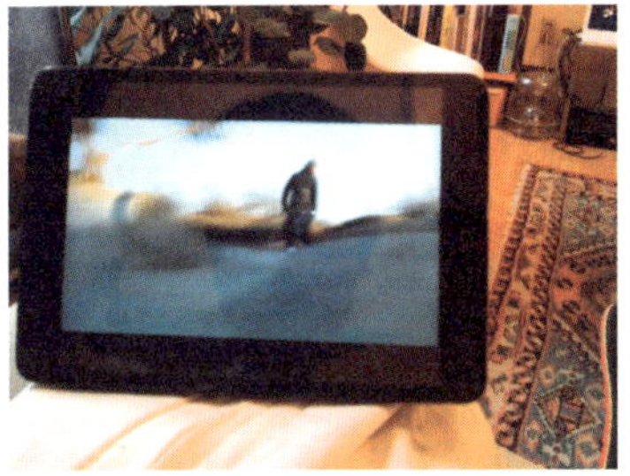
04:06

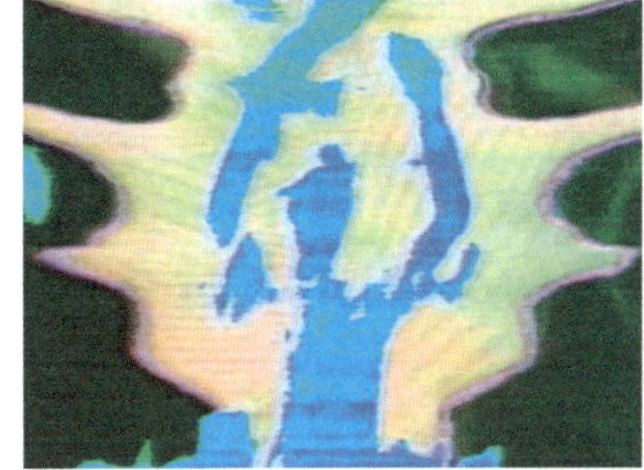
14:37

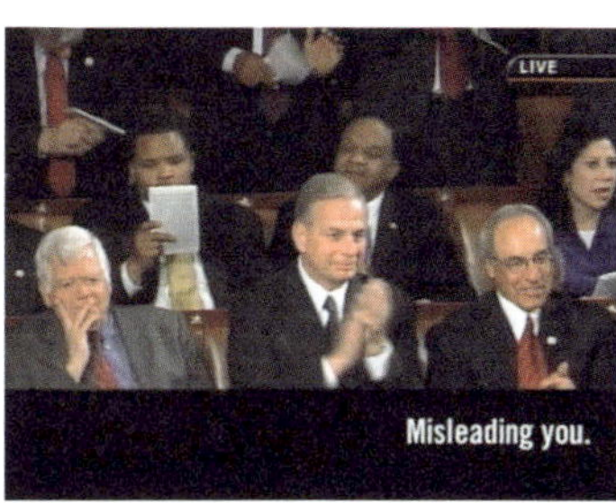

04:39

AK – So, kind of following that, I think one reason we were interested in starting with *Book of Love* is because it has an explicitly autobiographical visual that's attached to it. Earlier we were talking about questions of authorship and the dispersal of authorship. This is a still from the collaborative group that you worked with for a while, X-PRZ. Tell us a little about that collaboration and some of the strategies that it initiated in your practice with regard to classification and authorship?

TC – Yes, in some ways it's interesting to think about authorship in relation to a project like that because a lot of the actual work was done and distributed in mediated forms like a telephone call or fax or e-mail early on. So sometimes we would all be in the same room working on something, but often it would be subgroups of one or two people who would have an exchange. For us it was really important to not always go for the consensus model, but actually to kind of take differences into account. So if somebody felt very strongly about something, they could do it under the rubric of X-PRZ. And vice versa, if some of us were having a conversation about something and it was mediated, say telephonically, and we weren't reading each other in physical space, sometimes things would come out that might not have come out in any other sort of format. And we wanted to privilege those things and make using those things possible because often they were difficult things and things that none of us would do by ourselves.

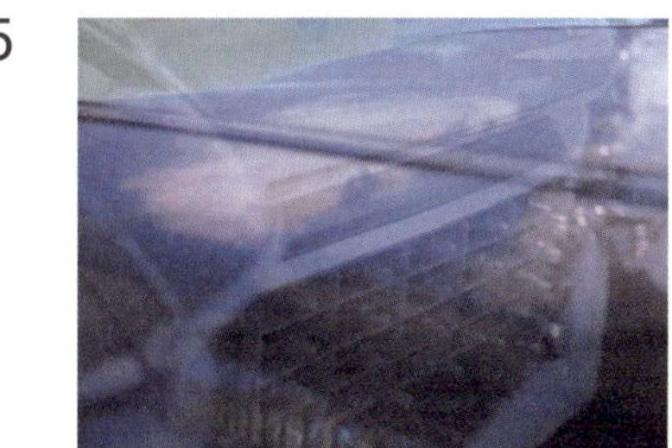
00:26

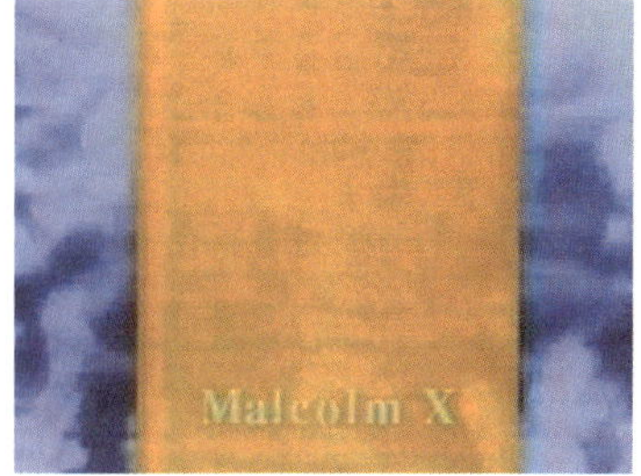

00:43

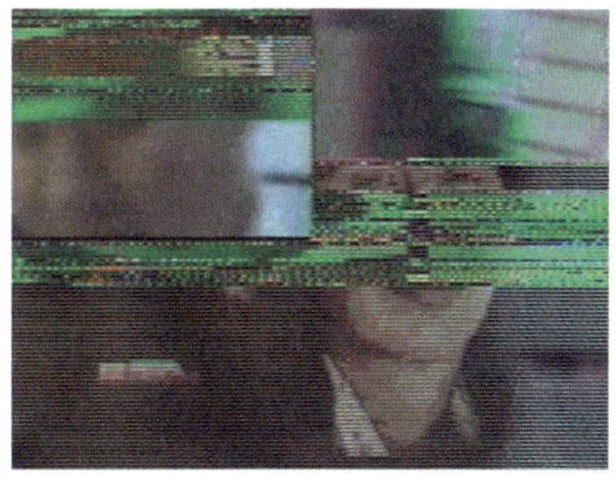
21:20

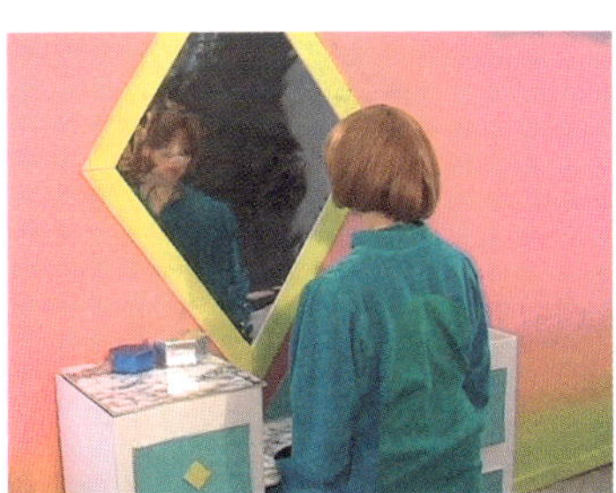
01:32

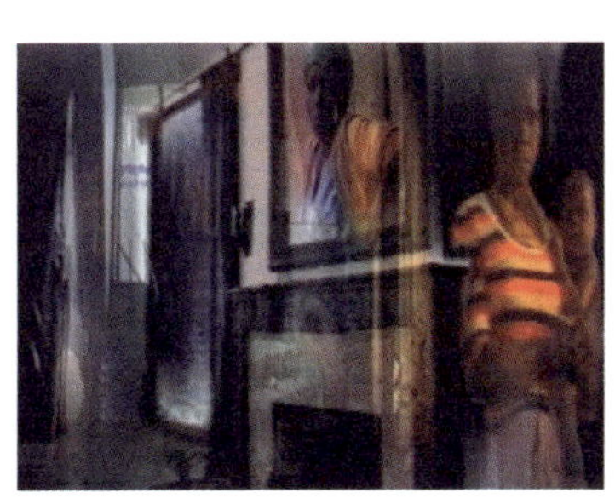
00:29

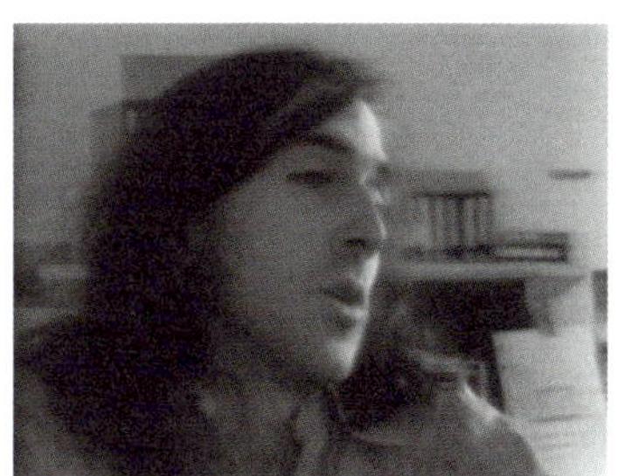
04:32

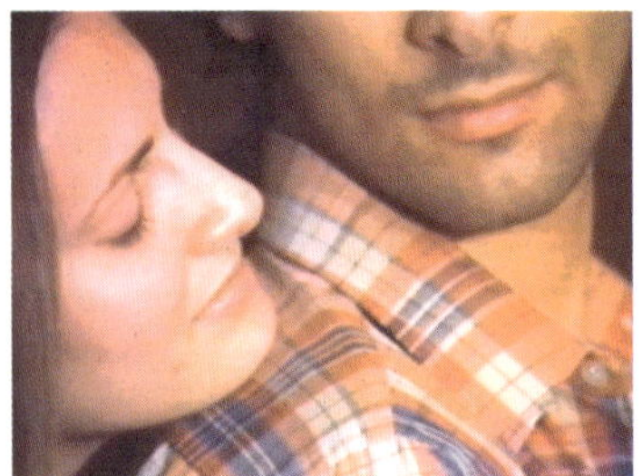

01:18

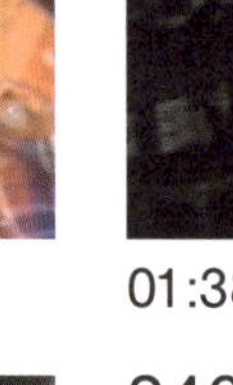

01:38

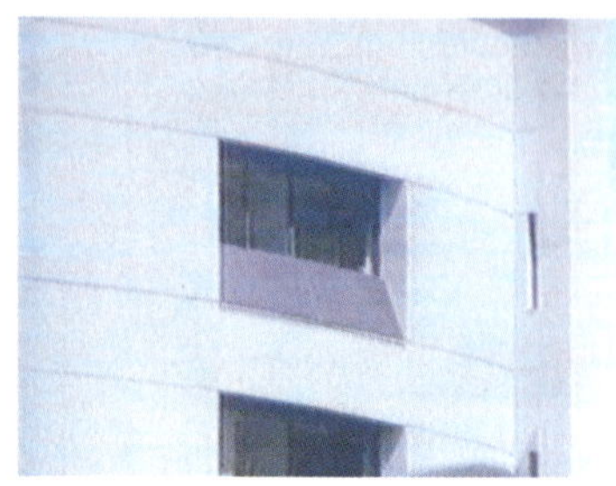

05:53

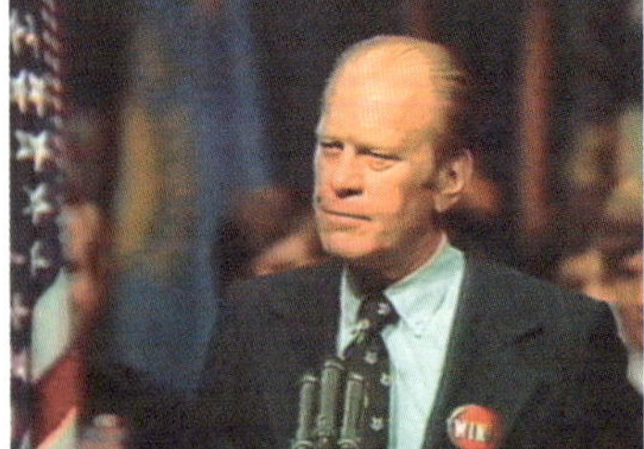

14:02

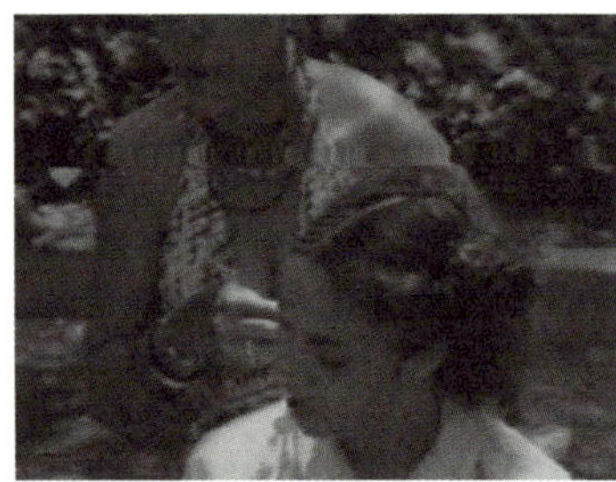

17:26

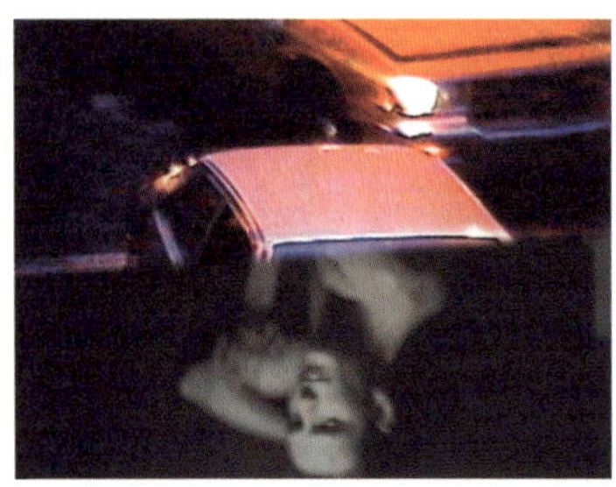

07:14

RC – So, this is a work that's in the current exhibition—in fact, it's on right now, those of you who are lucky enough to be here can turn around—*Evil.6: Making the Case/ Faking the Books*. It's from 2006. It's a really multi-layered work, incorporating a work by artist Benj Gerdes, *Intelligence Failures*, which emphasized the pauses and weird facial expressions in George W. Bush's televised State of the Union address in 2003.

TC – Right, and you know it was kind of an interesting antidote to a lot of works that were doing keyword parsings of his speeches, etc. And so I borrowed Benj's idea of tweaking that a little bit and highlighting his pauses and his awkward facial expressions.

RC – And to explain further, this is the State of the Union address where Bush is spelling out his justifications for invading Iraq. A lot of your work, the *Evil* series in particular, is responding to that administration's War on Terror, and the way its rhetoric developed and its effects, such as the color-coded warning systems.

TC – Or the flag.

RC – Or the ubiquitous American flag, which launched an aggressive and paranoid patriotic sentiment that we still experience today.

TC – And they continue. Sometimes people have asked me, "When will the *Evil* series be over?" [laughter] I wish I could tell you.

AK – I think I read somewhere that you mentioned that these are a series of case studies that have accumulated and I wanted to hear you say a little bit about that.

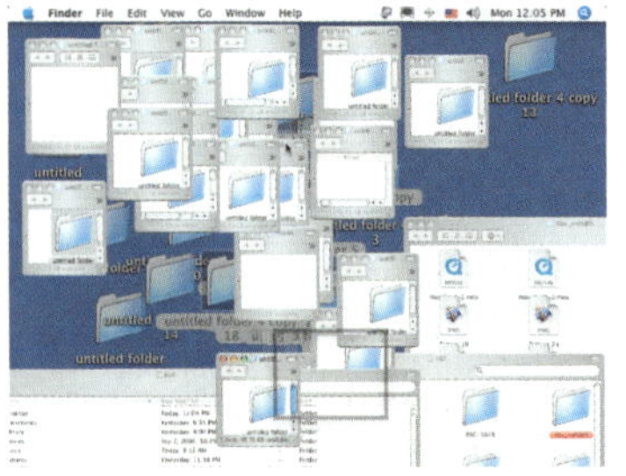

00:49

08:20

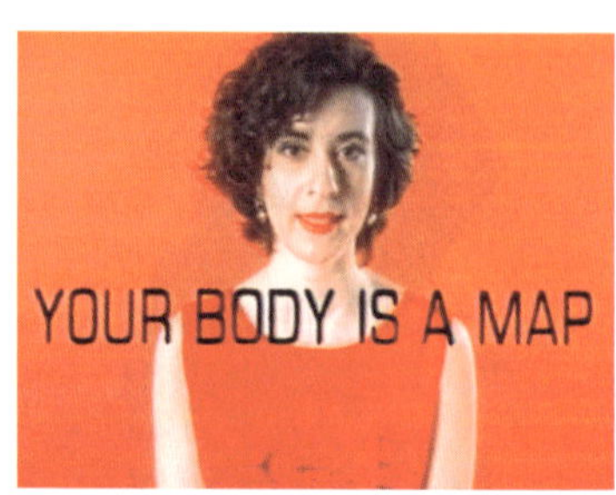

00:04

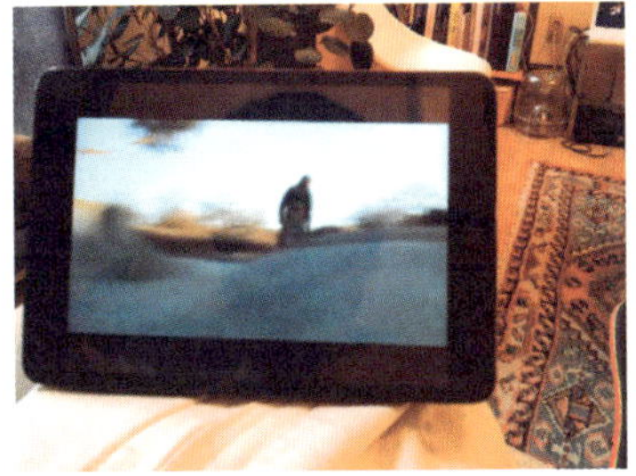
04:06

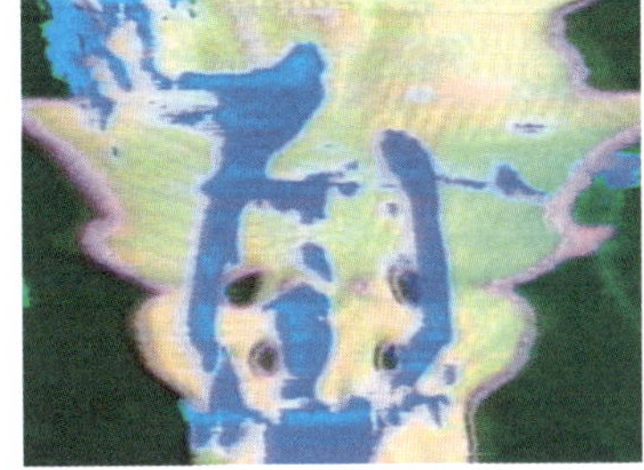
14:37

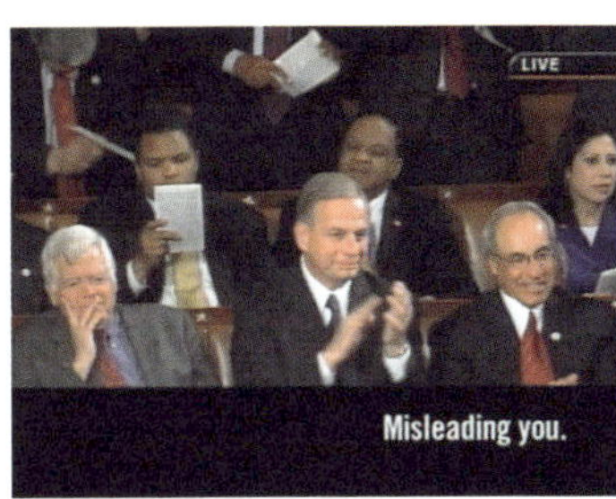

04:39

TC – They're non-chronological. I kind of work on things piecemeal. I usually have two or three different folders open at any given time. I have stuff that I accumulate: texts, ideas for things. And sometimes I go back into my archives and pull things out; other times I'll pick things that are current and contemporary, or a little bit of both. One of my responses post-9/11 was to begin accumulating things, texts that had been perhaps read well, or perhaps misread, or well circulated, but little understood. So, it was kind of important and I think we mentioned before we started that I wasn't the only person doing this. Benj's piece, for instance, is one example, like people doing keyword searches of Bush's speeches. So it was a particular sort of process and moment and I kind of like that procedure and process. I may do it in a particular way, but other people are doing it too.

RC – There's a nice term that you used once when we were talking, "iterative artwork," emphasizing art gaining different meanings as it circulates in new contexts, picking up different resonances as it rolls forward. For example, *Making the Case*, considered now. I'm assuming that when it was made you weren't thinking of it as being evidentiary. But now we can look at this 2003 address and know that his statement about weapons of mass destruction was a falsehood. But at the time of making it, you had a different relationship to the content of his speech.

AK – You mentioned that in working with other artists' work who are also mining this terrain there is a question of solidarity, which I think is

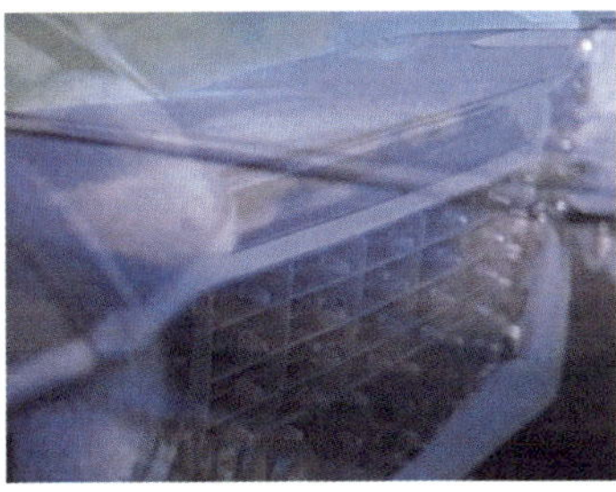
00:26

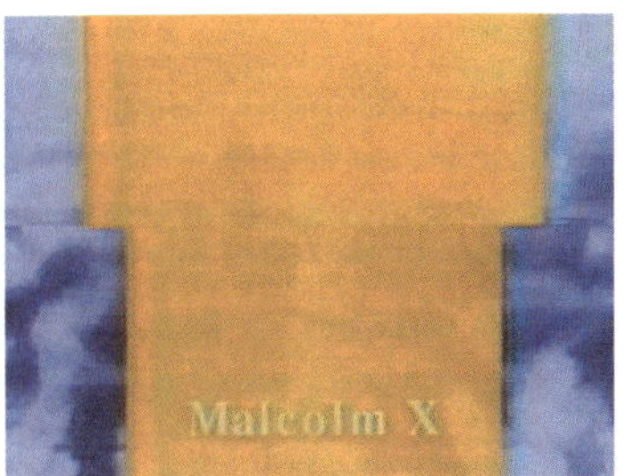

00:43

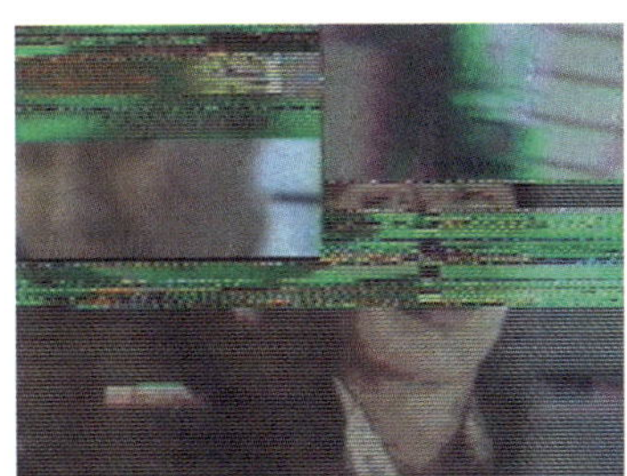
21:20

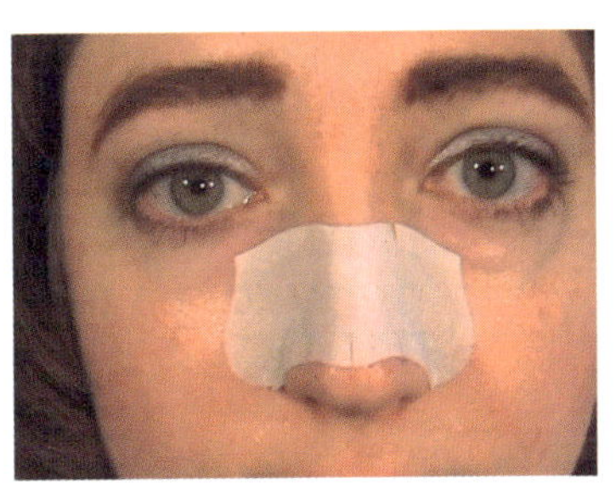
01:32

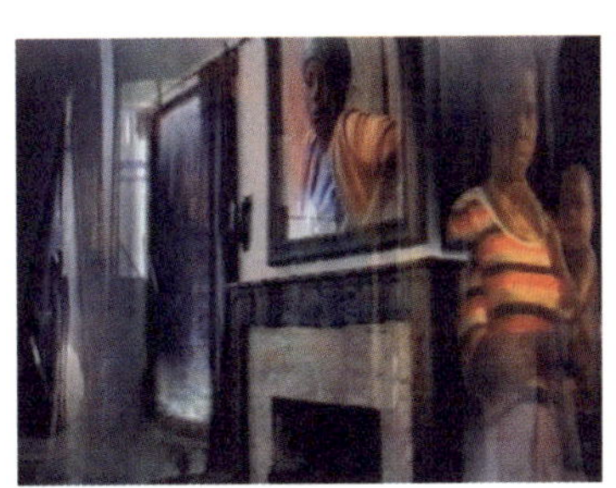
00:29

04:32

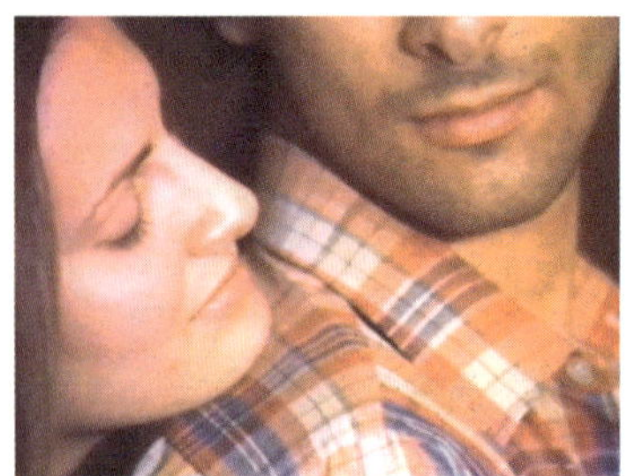
01:17

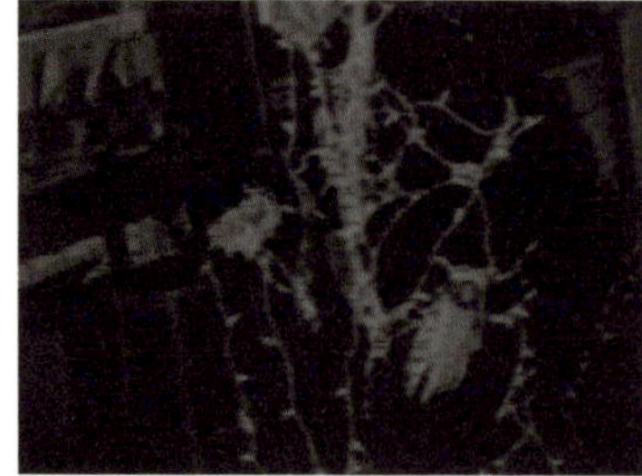
01:37

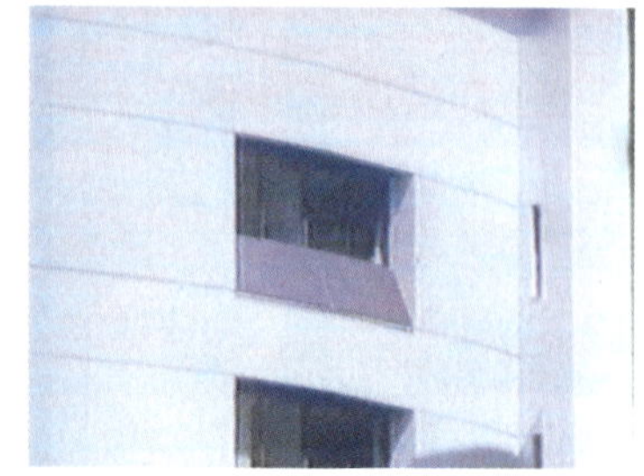
05:52

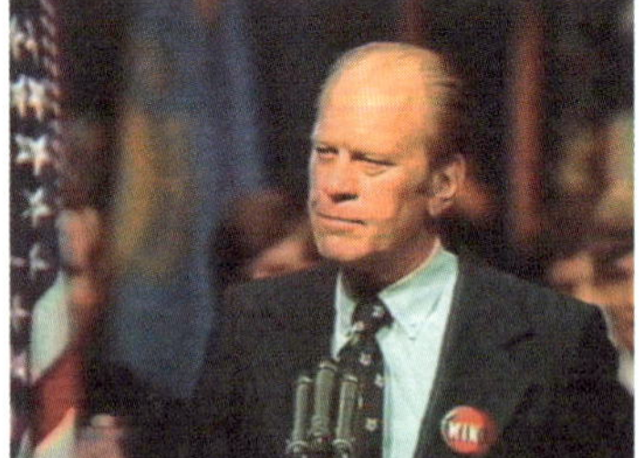
14:01

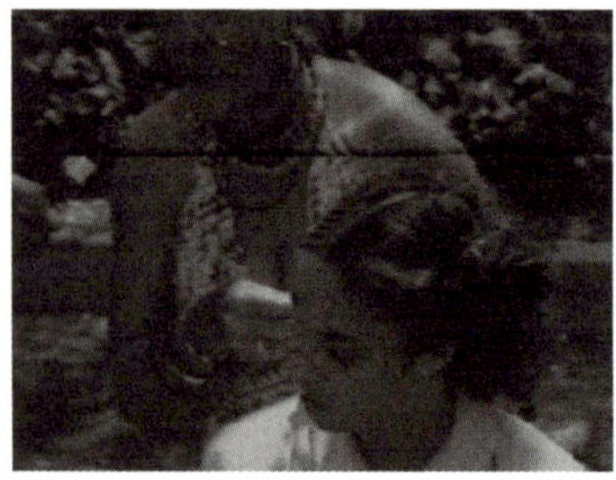
17:25

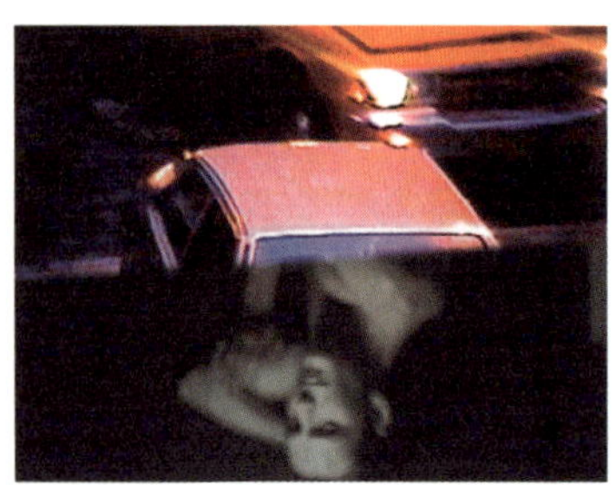
07:13

a very interesting word and has a different connotation than collaboration or appropriation. And in another work on view in the show, *Evil.27: Selma*, you're also working with the tension between audibility and visuality, and how those forms of documentation work with or against each other.

TC – I will say that it's interesting that this particular passage that we are looking at deals with questions of mediation and representation in events that may or may not have images. That question about what's visible, what's not visible, and what the audio register can do in relationship to representation is an important one. It's one that comes up consistently in my work and, to some extent, I think it will probably be a major theme of some things I am working on now.

AK – We'll dive into the next clip, which is *Evil.35: Carlin/Owners*. One thing I think that's also interesting in this question of mediation is circulation and how it is embedded in the way that you work with materials. The Carlin monologue was a piece that you found on YouTube?

TC – Yes, it was a YouTube piece. This was in 2012, during the 2012 campaign, and I guess I was reflecting on the way politics, at least in America, seems to have moved away from things that could be necessarily called "news," or "political," or "political discourse," into frameworks like comedy or news and commentary from a comedic angle. I kind of stumbled across this earlier example of the ways that say, a stand-up comedy routine could be read as a critical

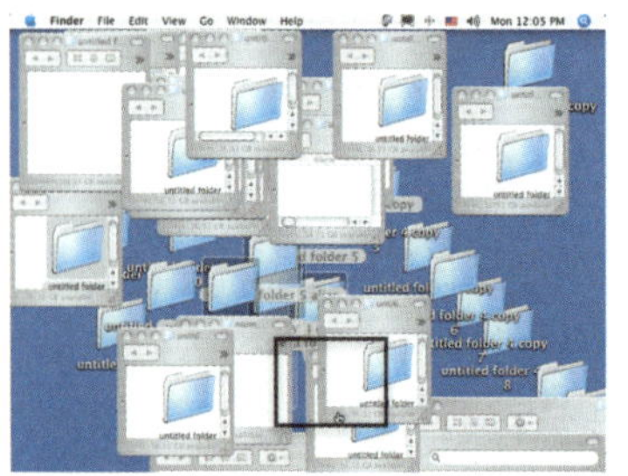
00:48

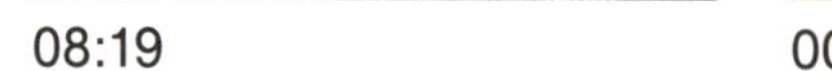
08:19

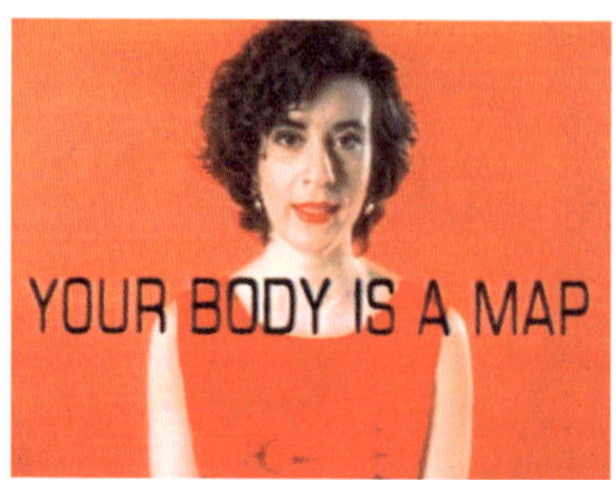

00:03

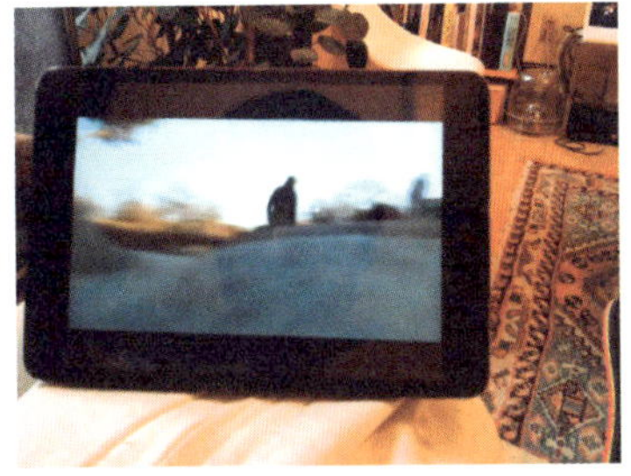
04:06

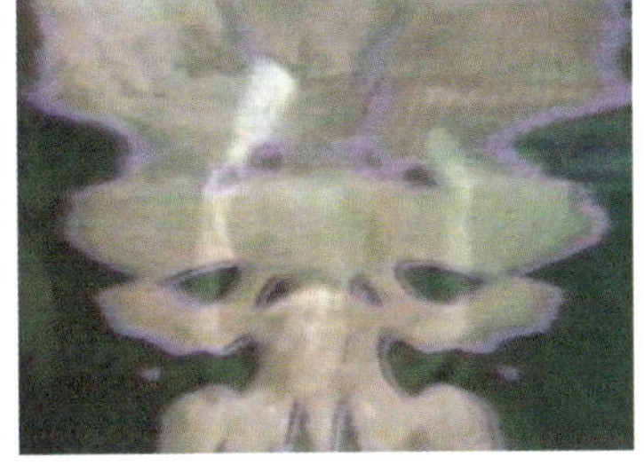
14:37

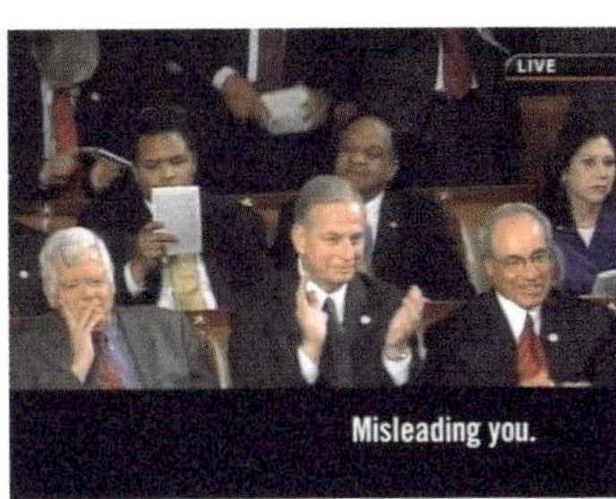

04:39

document, a way of re-framing political content or analysis.

AK – It's interesting to see this material come back into circulation, back into visibility, and seeing this piece from 2012, which in terms of its contemporary relevance feels like you made it just yesterday.

TC – Yes, these issues have a way of reverberating and resonating.

AK – So, I think we'll flesh out some more of those connections in a bit.

TC – Looking forward to that.

RC – Moving on to Antoine now.

Antoine Catala – Hello.

RC – Antoine is a French artist based in New York City. He is represented by 47 Canal and just closed an exhibition there called *Everything Is Okay*: "an opera of the everyday about small digital images used in electronic communication." His work will be featured in the upcoming Venice Biennale. There is more to say, but I think maybe we should just launch right into the first still. This is a work called *HDDH*, which was presented at AVA (Audio Visual Arts) in 2010. It was presented as a solo show called *Topologies*. Were there other works in that room?

AC – The only other work was the invitation video. So, that was part of the show but it wasn't in the show.

RC – But this was the only piece within that space: two HD monitors facing each other. I also remember seeing this in your studio, with this magical tube connecting them, this reflective tube creating this incredible optical effect where it looked like the images from the

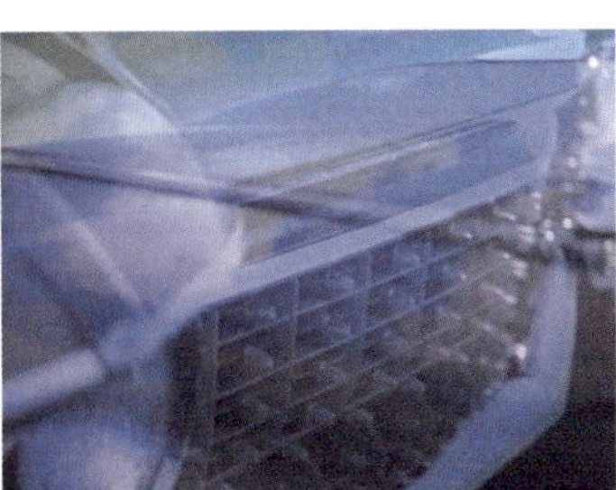
00:26

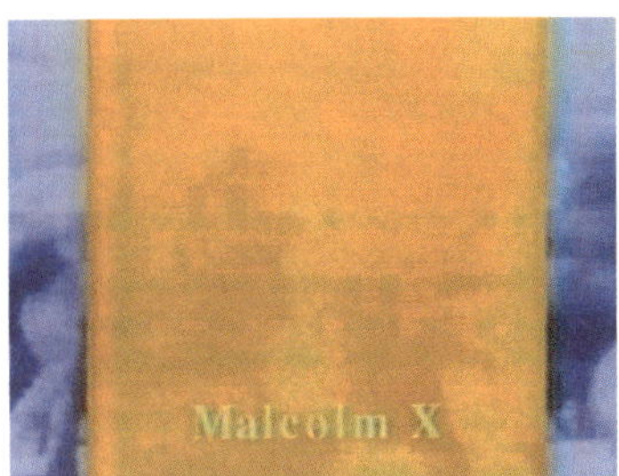

00:43

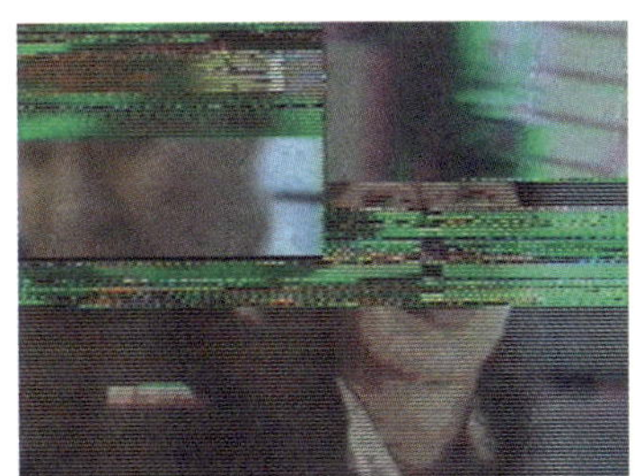
21:20

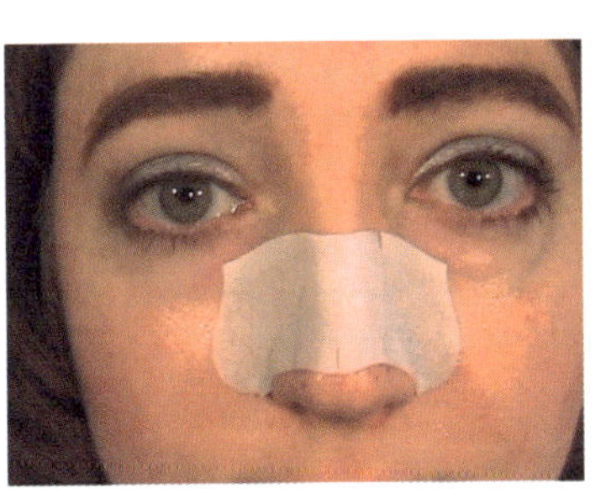
01:32

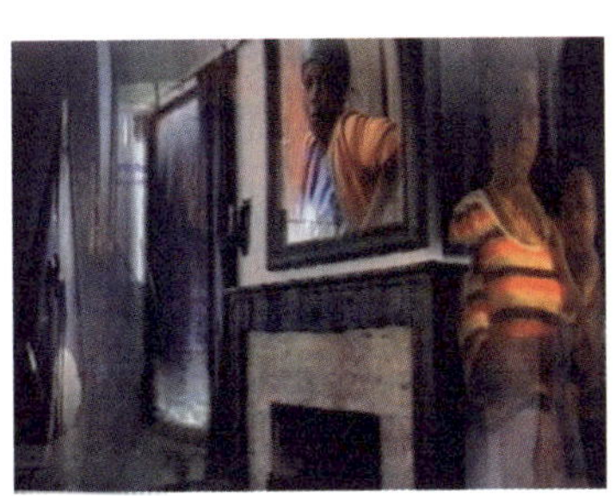
00:29

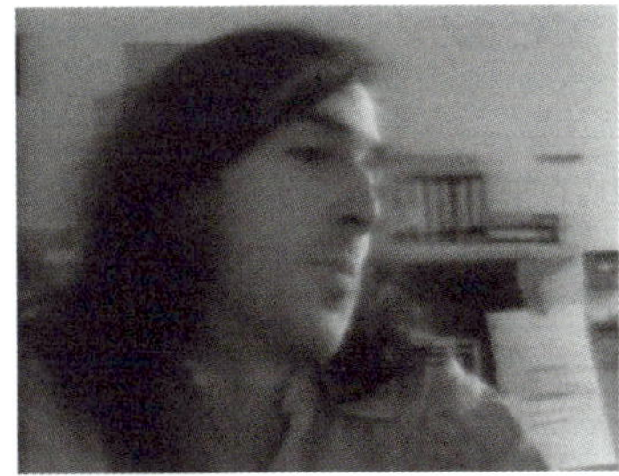
04:32

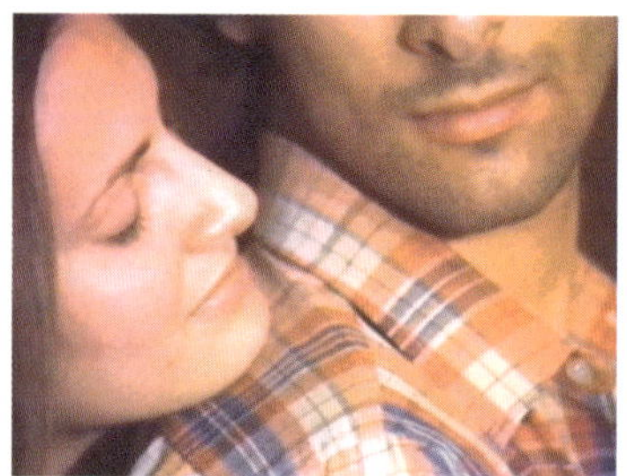

01:17

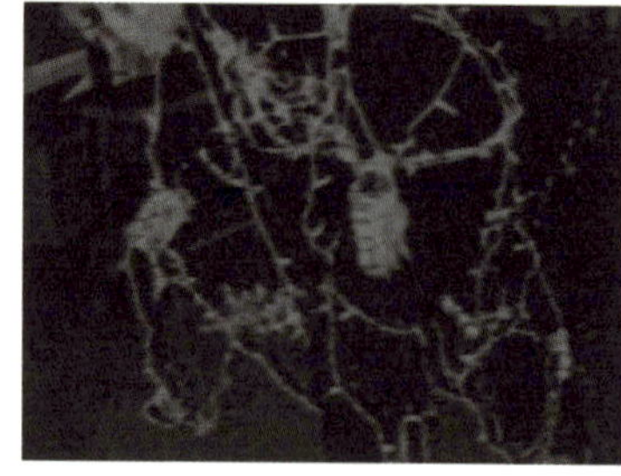

01:37

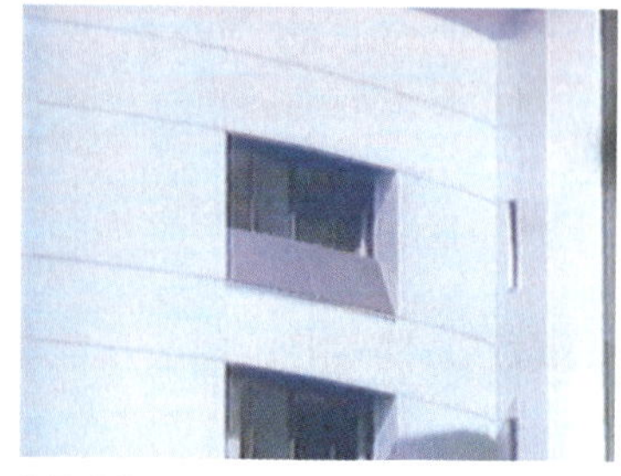

05:52

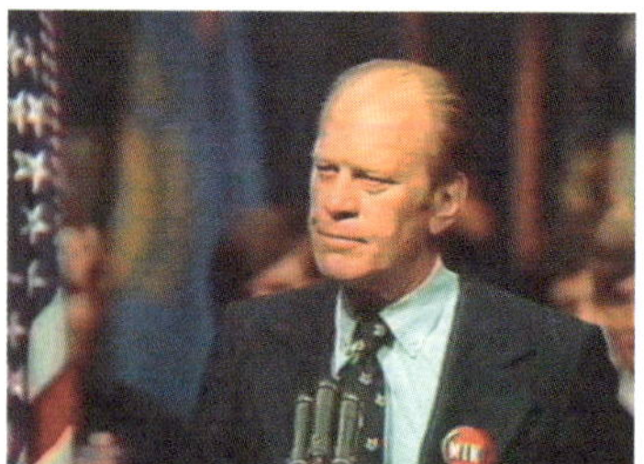

14:01

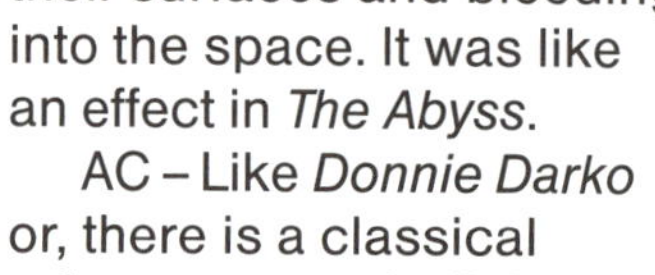

TVs were reaching out from their surfaces and bleeding into the space. It was like an effect in *The Abyss*.

AC – Like *Donnie Darko* or, there is a classical reference to a skull that appears too.

RC – Yes, exactly, the art historical reference, Holbein's anamorphic skull in *The Ambassadors*. So, this was 2010. You also had an exhibition at 179 Canal in 2009 called *TV Show* and I thought maybe you could talk a little bit about television specifically. Since obviously, it was a focus. You made other works about television at the time.

AC – A lot of it comes from the fact that I'm a foreigner and I come to the US and every time I would get in the country the first thing that I see on American soil is CNN blasted on television screens all around while I am eagerly waiting to tread foot on America. I also dated a woman named Shabd Simon-Alexander who was watching television all the time. TV is actually very different here; it's a bit of a shock coming from Europe to the US. I find it so powerful here, I wanted to do something about it, but I was thinking what is the most minimal act that I can do that can justify just putting television in the exhibition space. So, I just did a number of works where I physically distorted the television image with the idea that I could show TV in an exhibition space. And so what happens with this is that oftentimes people will ask me, *Why did you choose this ad of Dunkin' Donuts?* And I would have to explain to them this is actually just TV now.

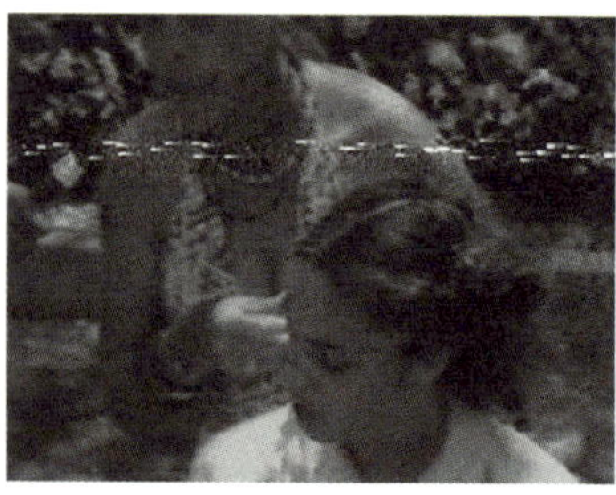

17:25

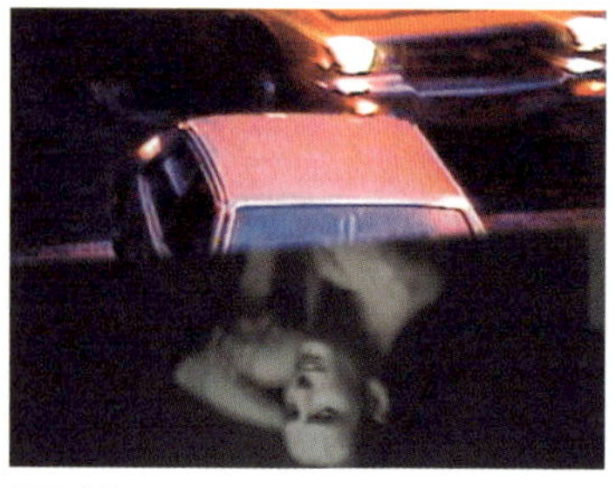

07:13

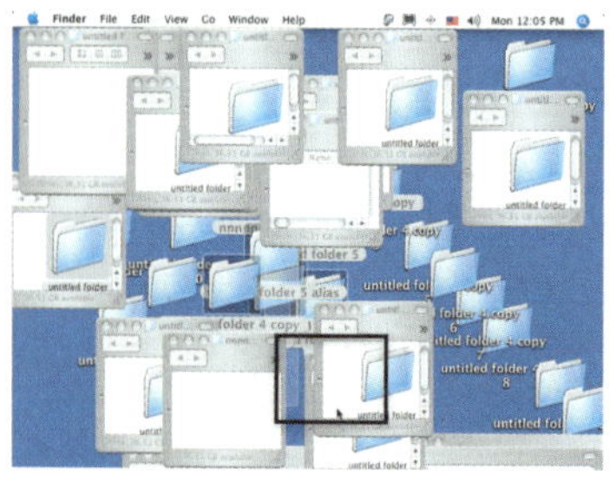

00:48

08:19

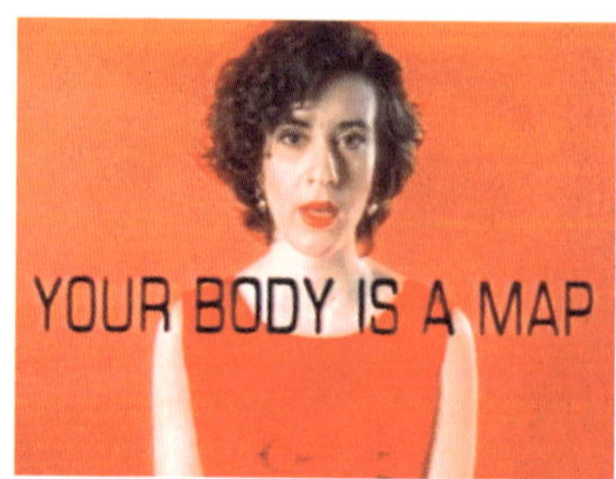

00:03

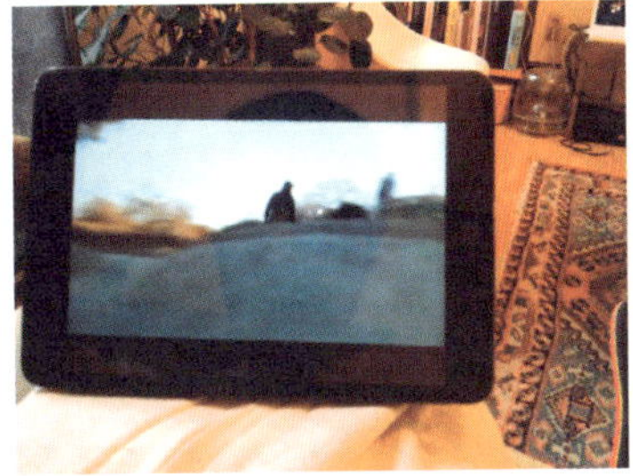

04:06

14:37

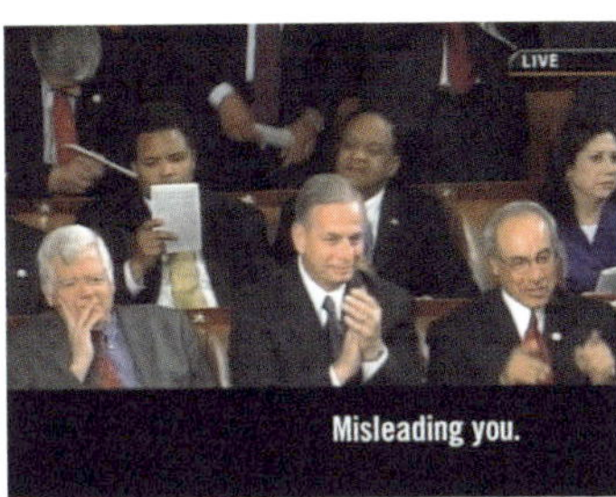

04:39

RC – It's broadcast, it's not appropriated material. It's live television.

AK – Just like this.

RC – We are all in an Antoine Catala piece right now.

AC – It was very important that it constantly renews itself. The mechanism of this is very simple but by putting this mirror tube in the middle of the televisions you can see really quickly how the faces always land in the middle of the screen. This piece works especially well with television. I tried to show movies in this display and it really doesn't work the same because the images are not formatted the same way. But with television it has something about how fast it is and how the face always lands in the middle of the screen or the thing of interest is always at the center of the screen. I have to say too, because it's important, that I added a little echo to the sound emanating from the broadcast, which added a little something that people hardly noticed. The mirror tube with the sound echo made you feel like you were in a science fiction movie and a lot of people touched this mirror tube and they were very surprised it was solid.

AK – It's quite surreal. So, one of the things we were really excited about bringing the two of you into conversation are the different ways the two of you engage with language and messaging. I think, Antoine, the first time we really got to know each other was in this exhibition in Oslo at UKS in 2013. Can you tell us a little bit about what we are looking at? It was quite a profound experience for me walking into

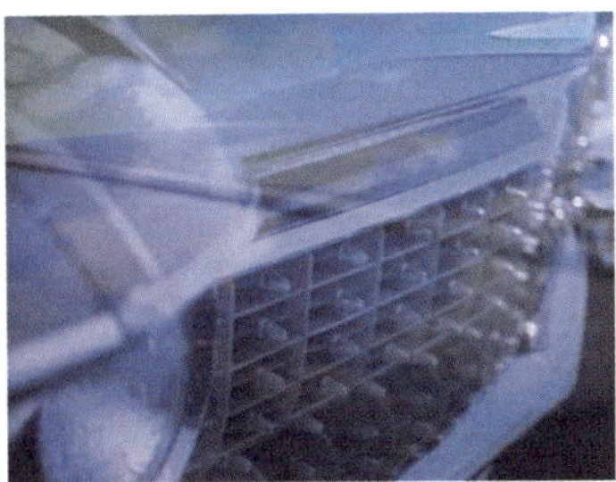

00:26

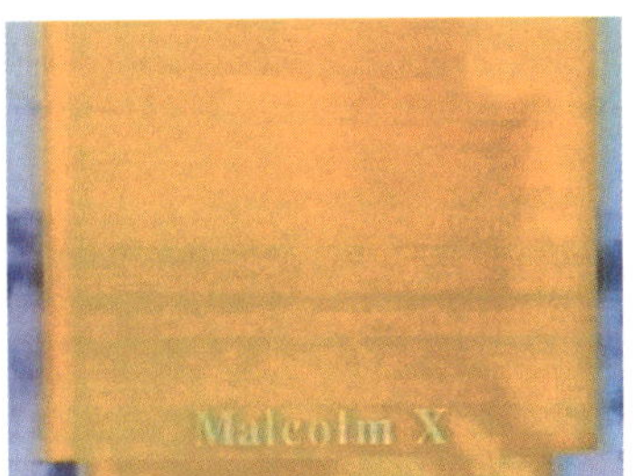

00:43

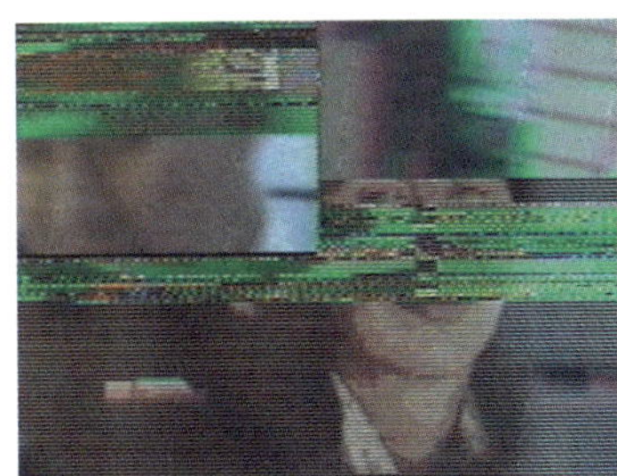

21:20

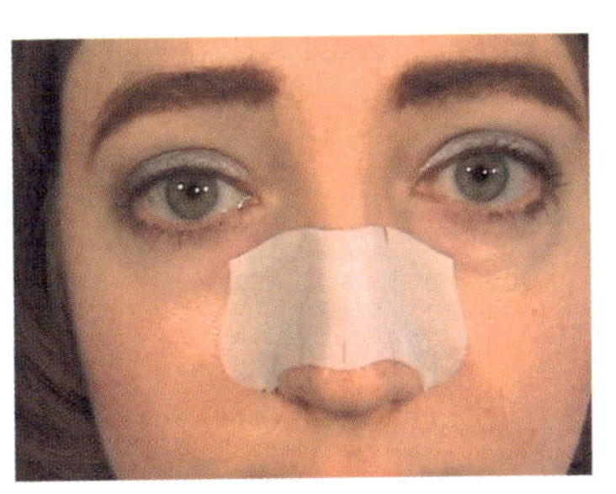

01:32

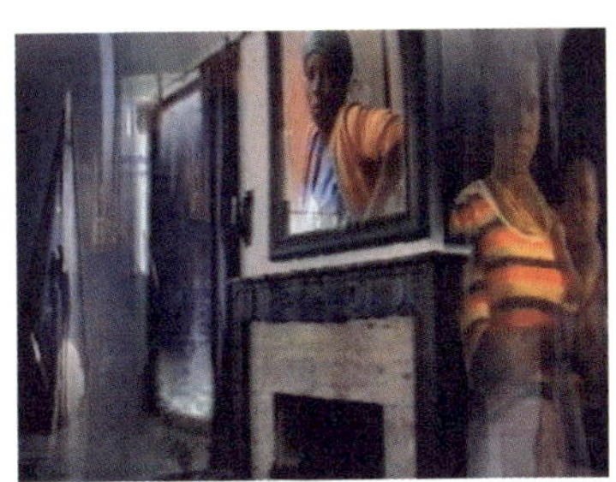

00:29

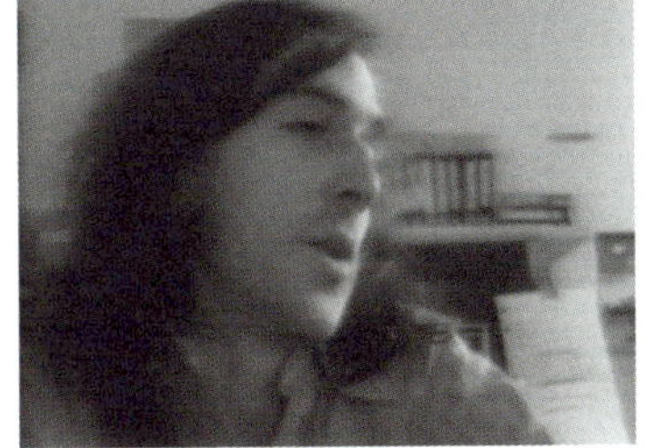

04:32

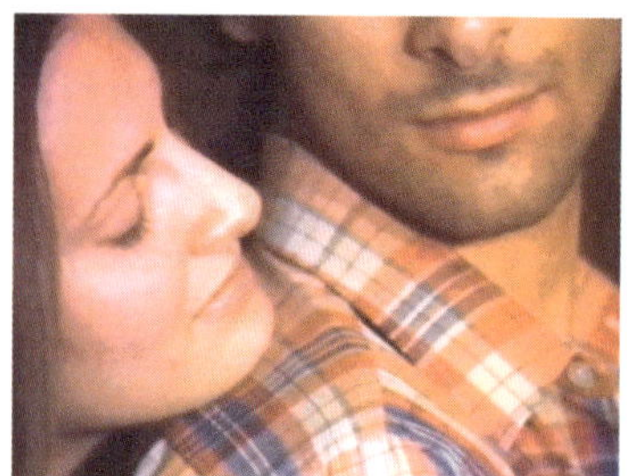

01:17

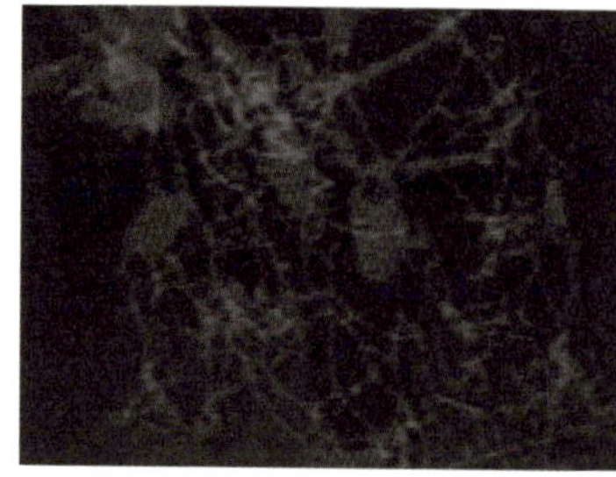

01:37

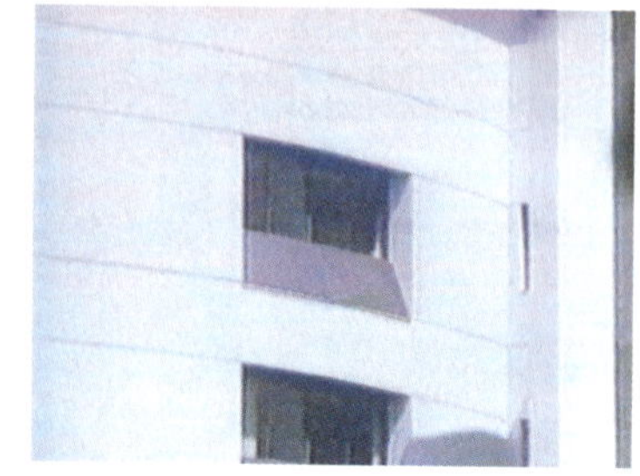

05:52

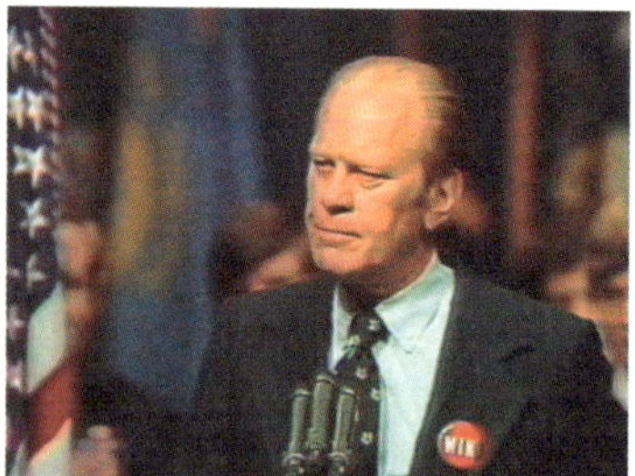

14:01

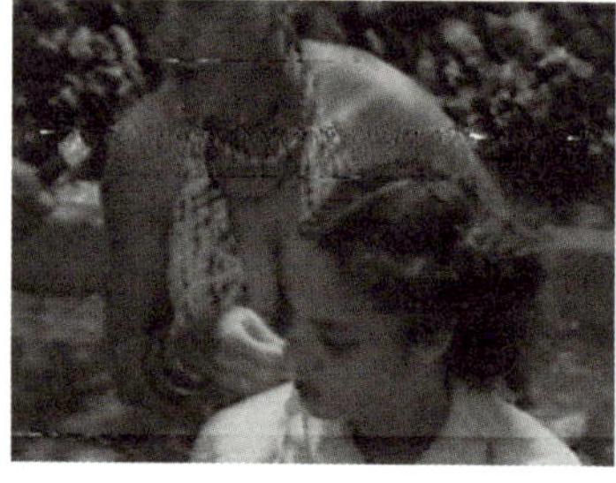

17:25

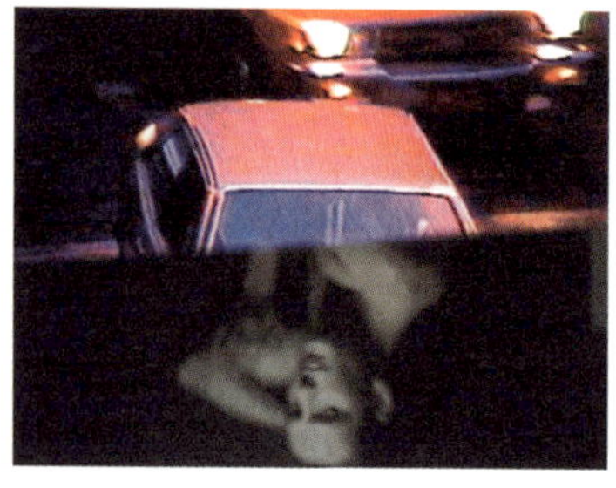

07:13

the gallery with these drones with words flying around and these advertising kiosks that are changing shape and image, messaging in different ways.

AC – This is a still from that show. It was called *Image Families*. Essentially it was a show that was completely phantasmagorical about how machines are capable of detecting what's inside images. But because of the infancy of this technology, I thought I would do a show of a machine that is only capable of detecting four things. So, if there's a cat or not a cat in the picture, or an ass or not an ass, or a pizza or not a pizza, or a car or not a car. And this kiosk image is all printed onto latex, and you have the shapes that are sucked in from the surface of the image. So here you can see a really rough head of a cat sucked into the shape of a cat, but you also have the outline of a butt sucked into the pocket of the jeans to try to determine what composes the picture.

AK – And there is a wonderful artist book that goes with it.

AC – It's like a children's book. It's this idea that technology is in its infancy of learning about ourselves, and the machine is learning about images also. It's sort of intertwined.

AK – And along these lines, let's discuss these sculptures that you've made.

AC – This sculpture is an emoticon. This one is a smiley face and the other one is a Band-Aid. It comes from this idea that the preceding show was also reflecting on: there is a technical correlation between images and words and objects. With a word, one can go online and look up tons of images. You

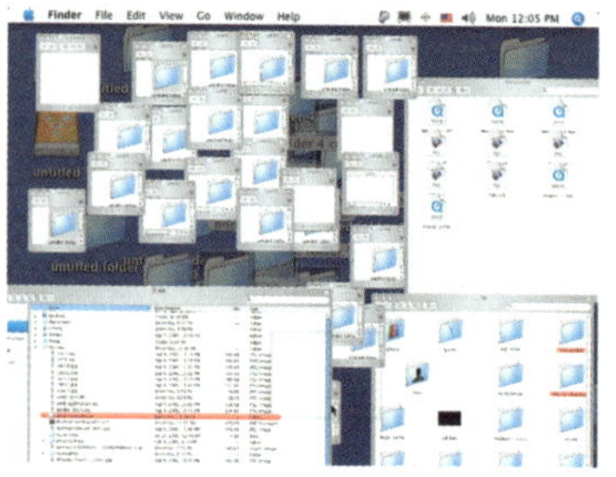

00:48

08:19

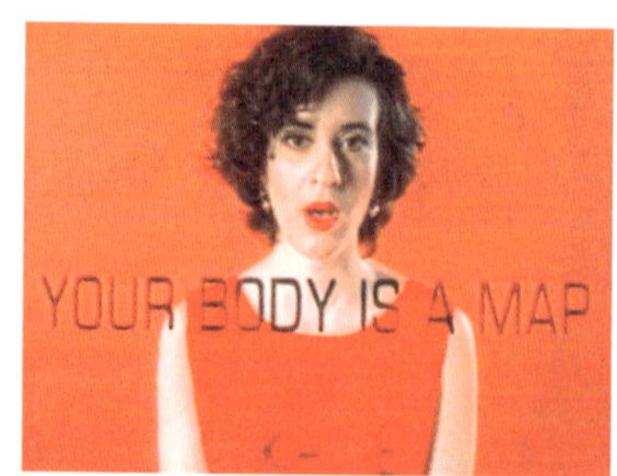

00:03

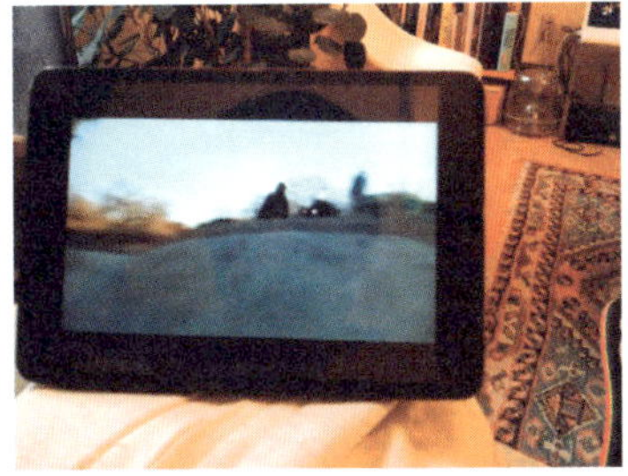

04:06

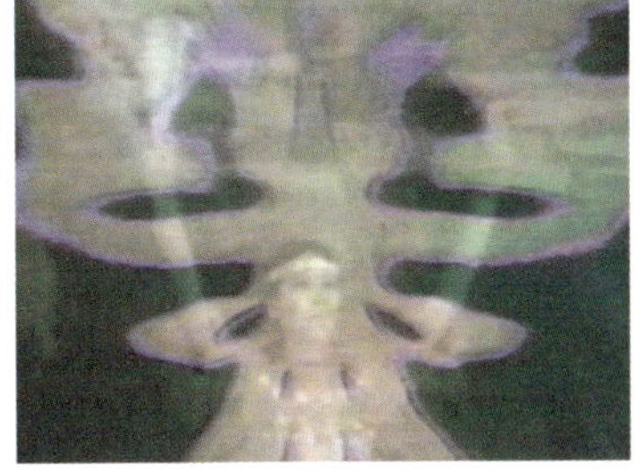

14:37

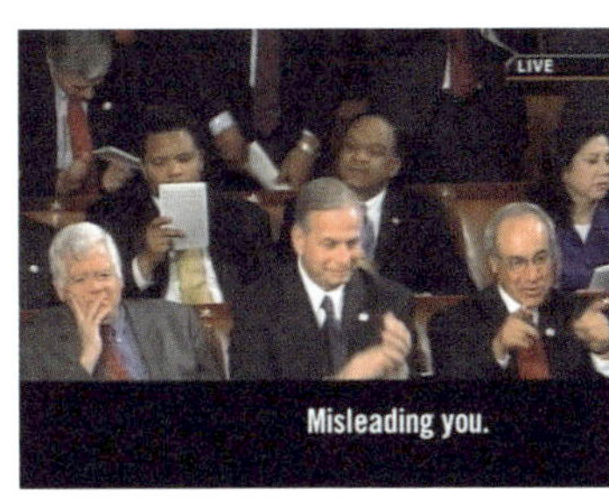

04:39

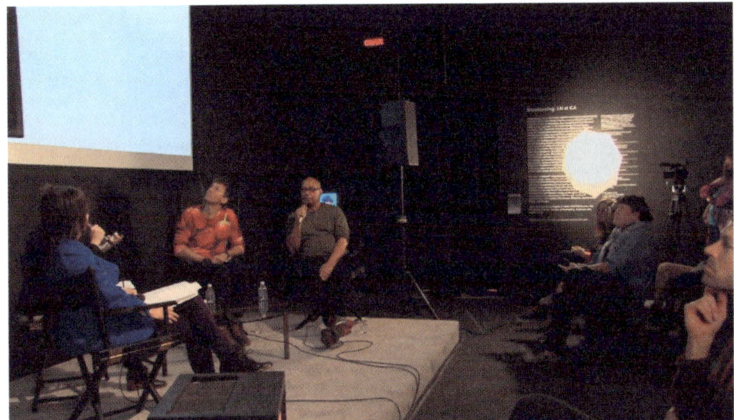

Still from PhillyCAM television broadcast

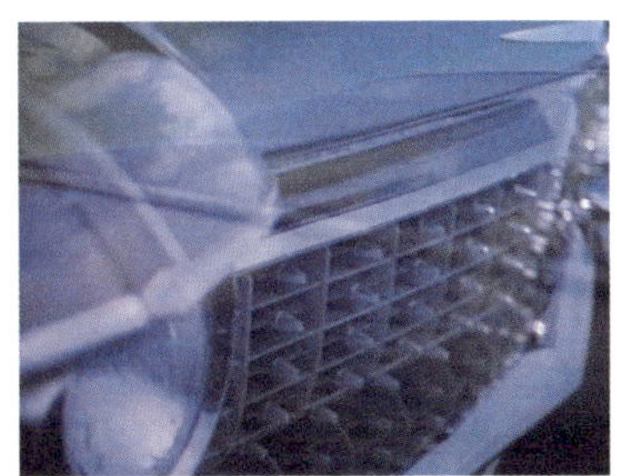

00:26

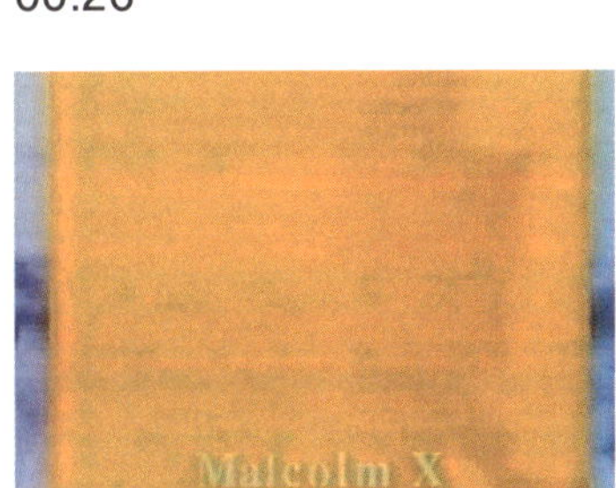

00:43

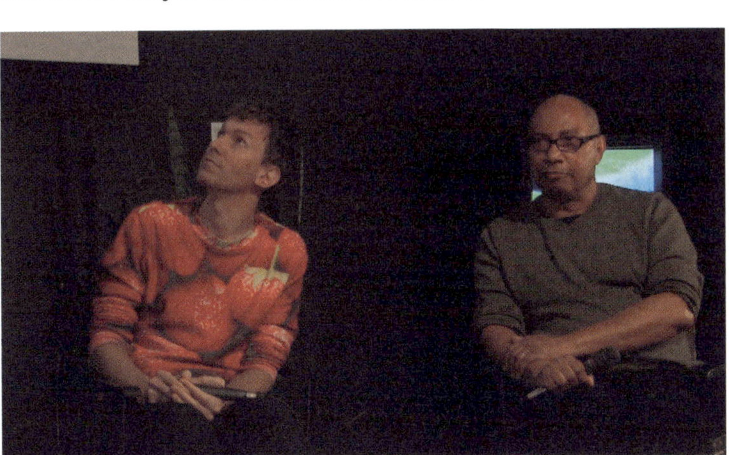

Still from PhillyCAM television broadcast

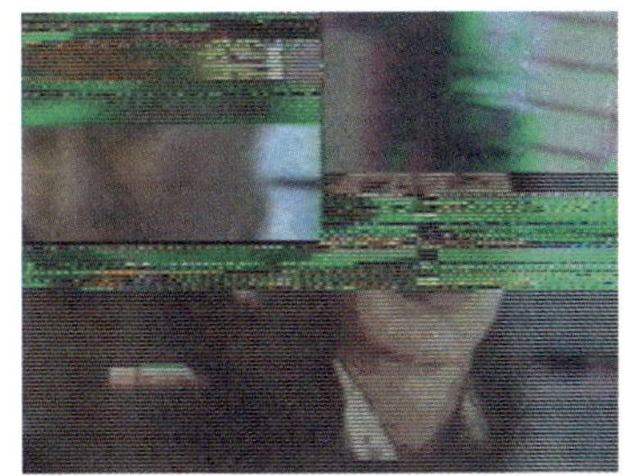

21:20

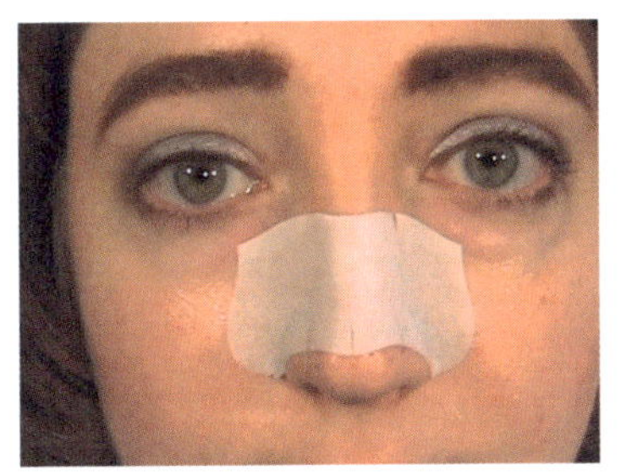

01:32

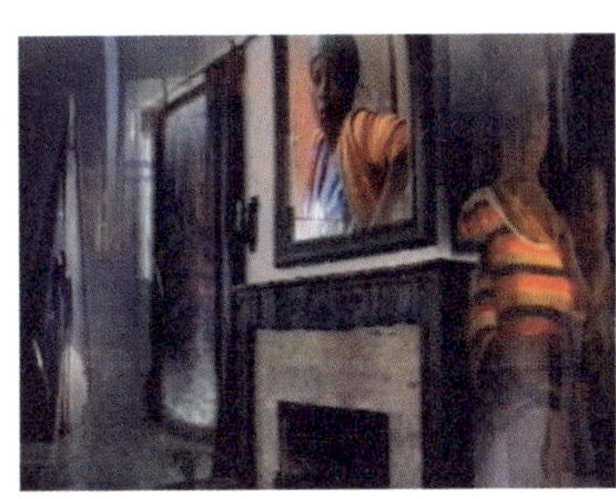

00:29

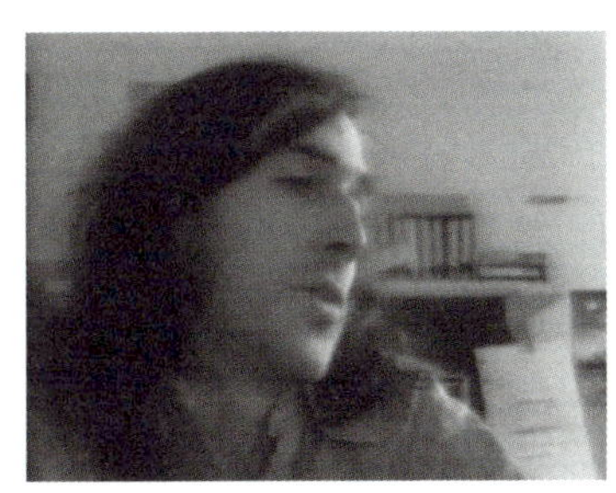

04:32

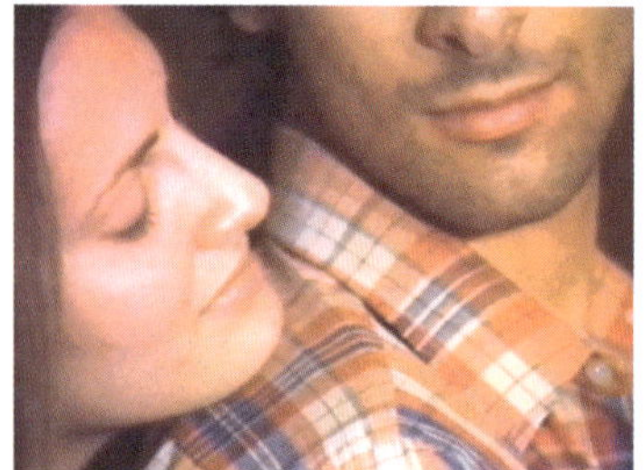

01:17

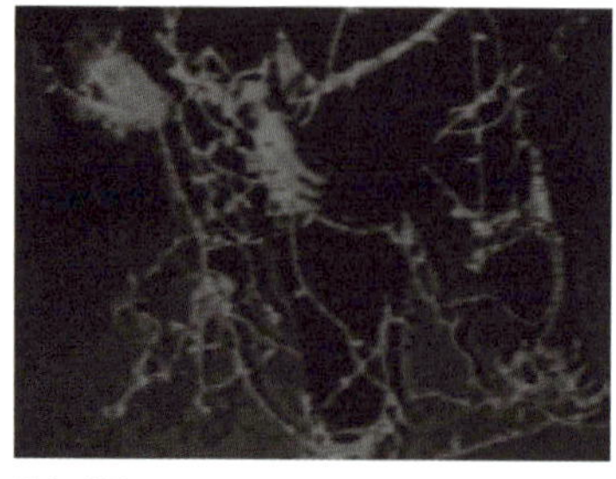

01:37

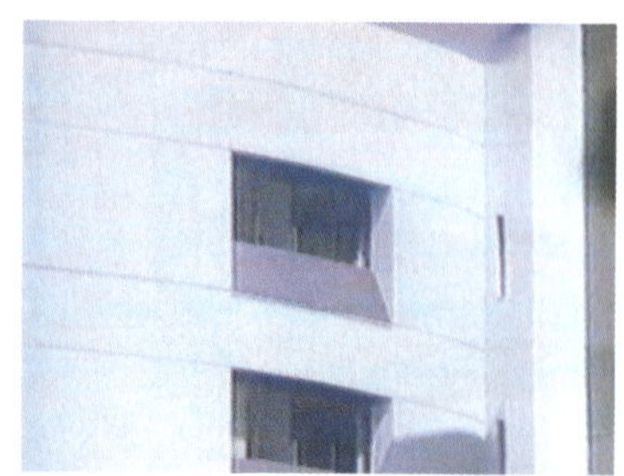

05:52

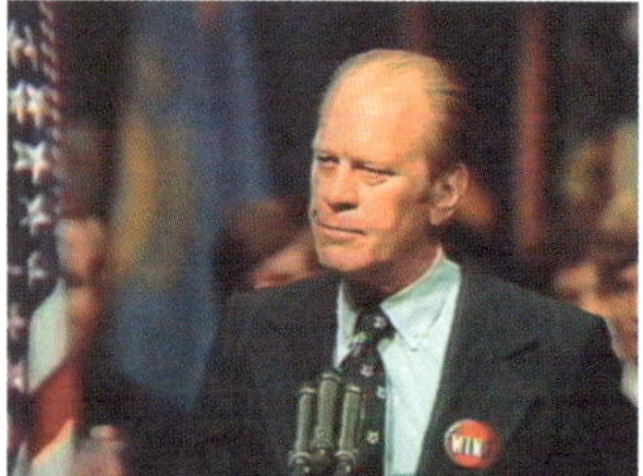

14:01

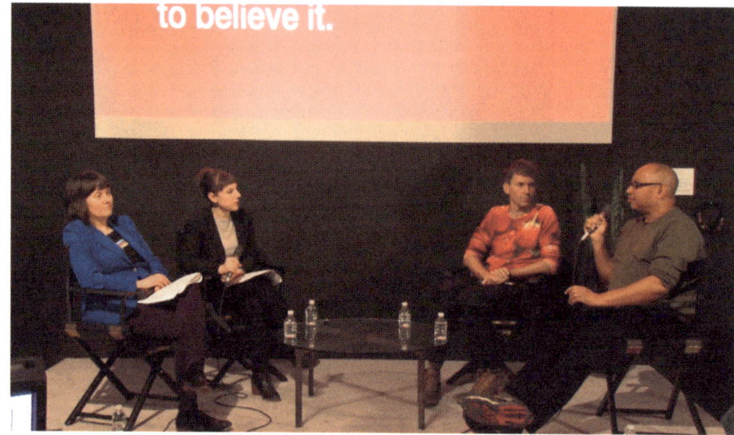

Still from PhillyCAM television broadcast

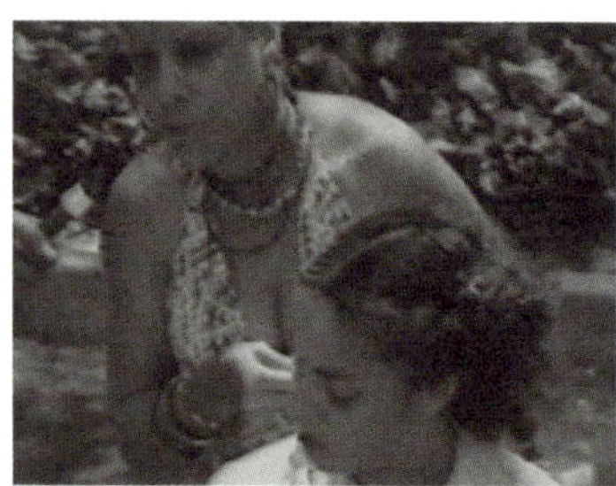

17:25

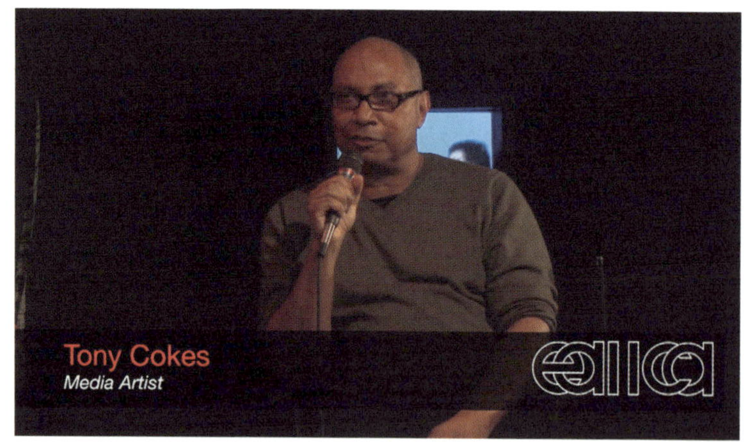

Still from PhillyCAM television broadcast

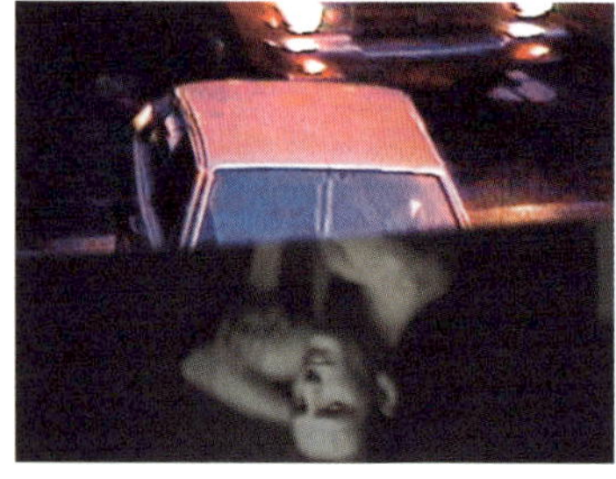

07:13

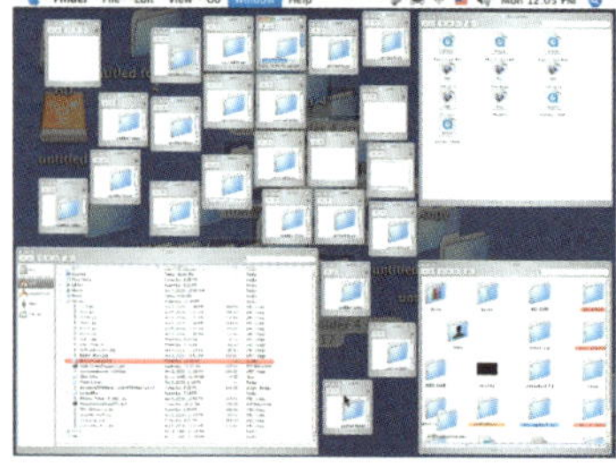

00:48

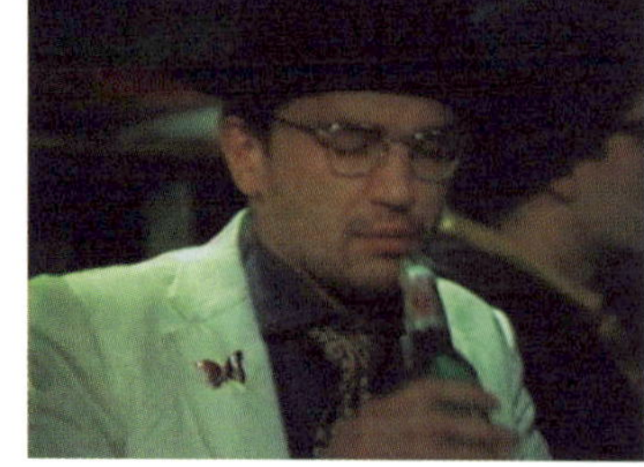

08:19

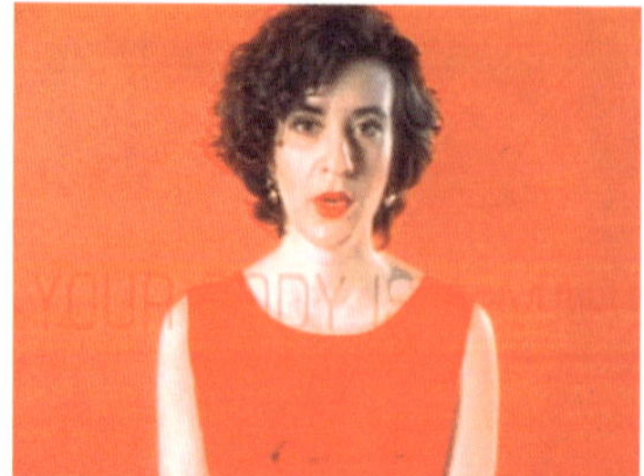

00:03

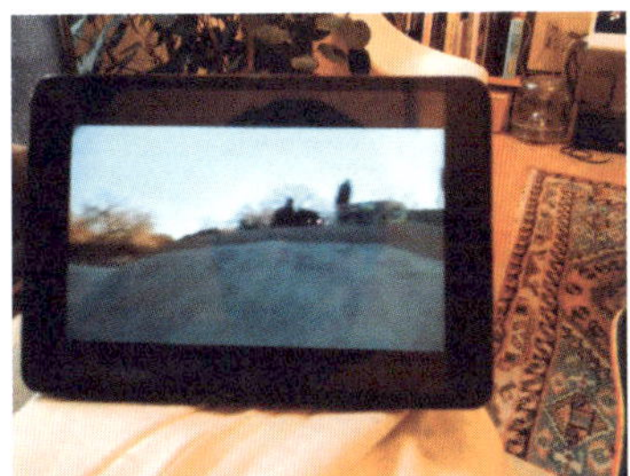
04:07

14:38

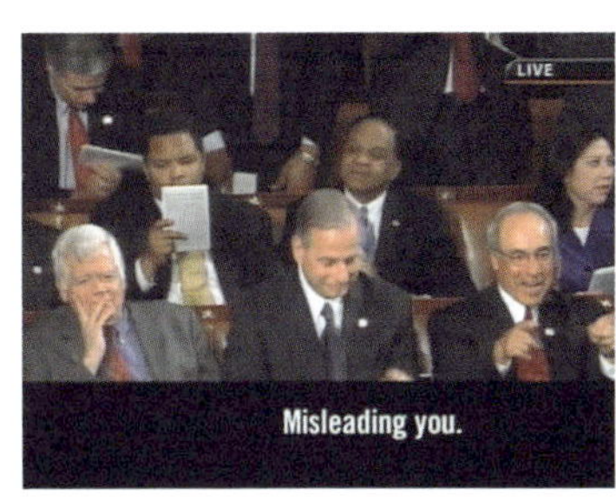

04:40

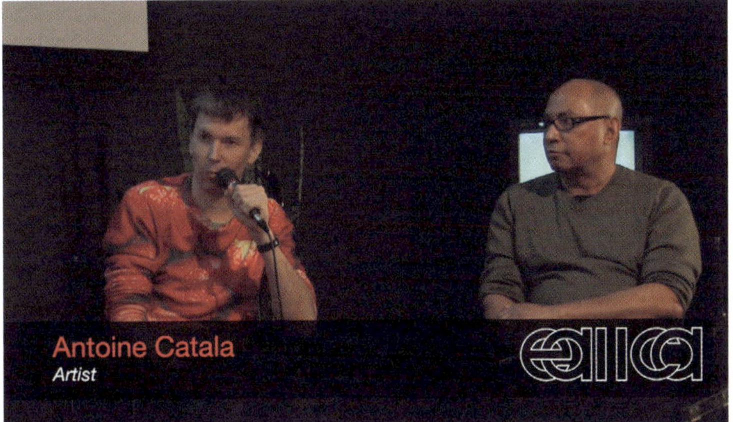

Still from PhillyCAM television broadcast

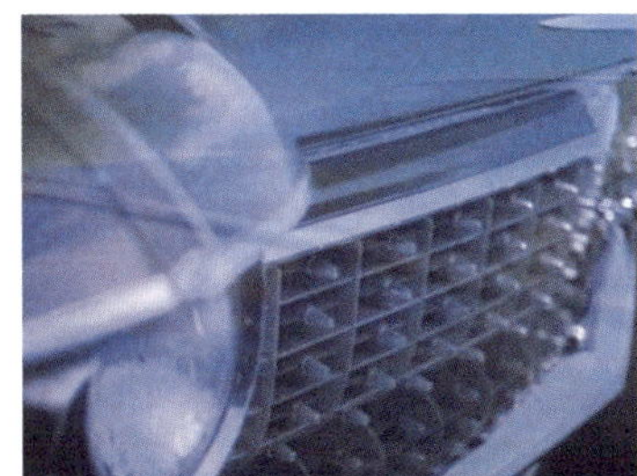
00:27

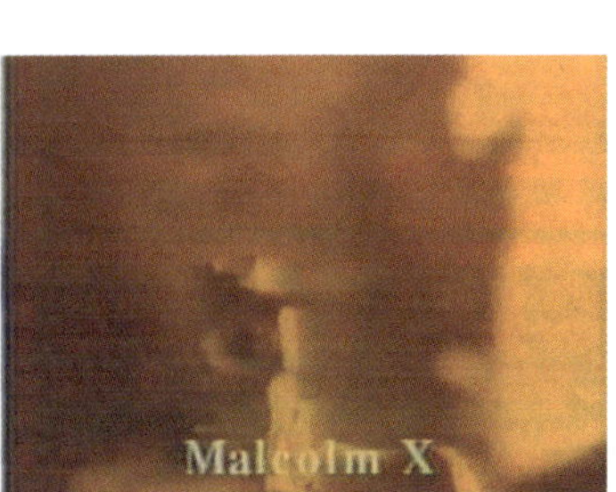

00:44

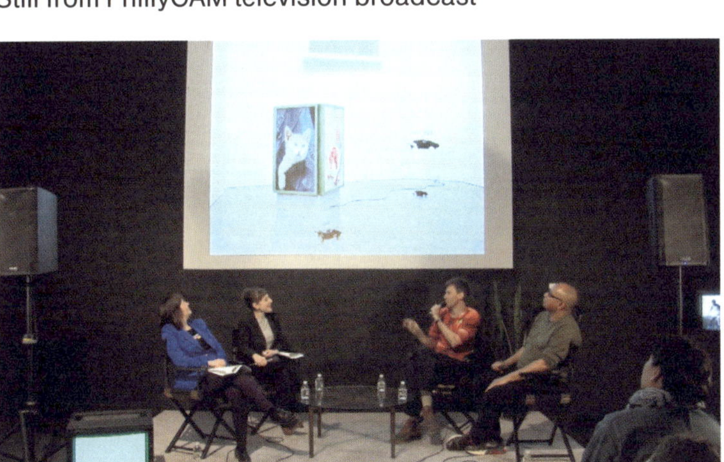
Still from PhillyCAM television broadcast

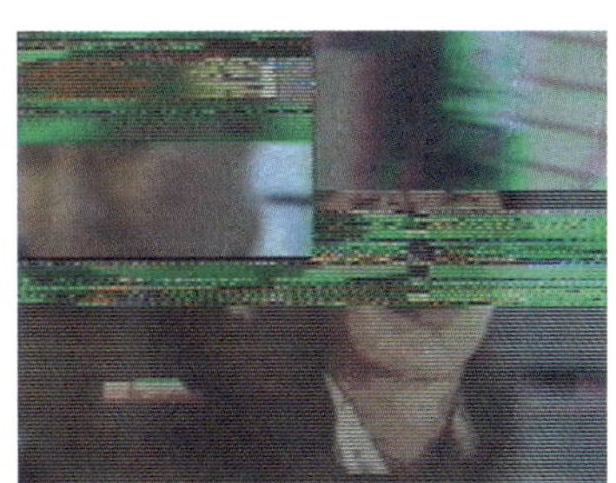
21:21

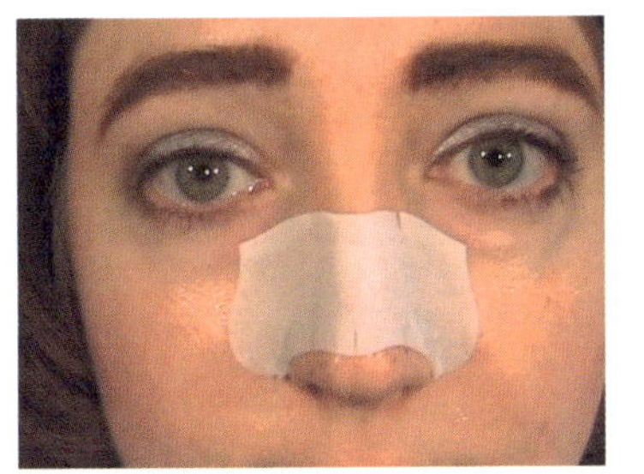
01:33

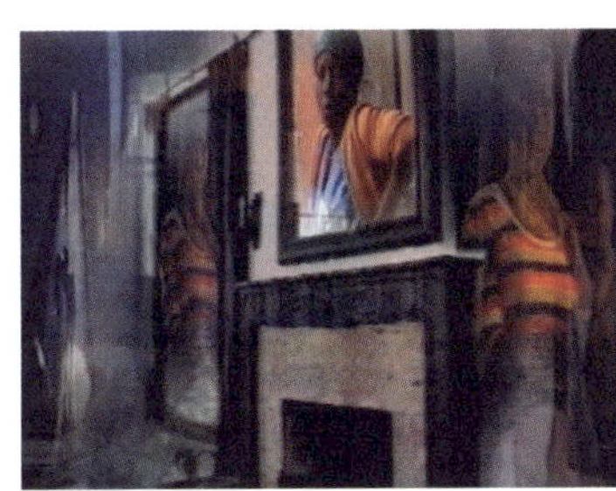
00:30

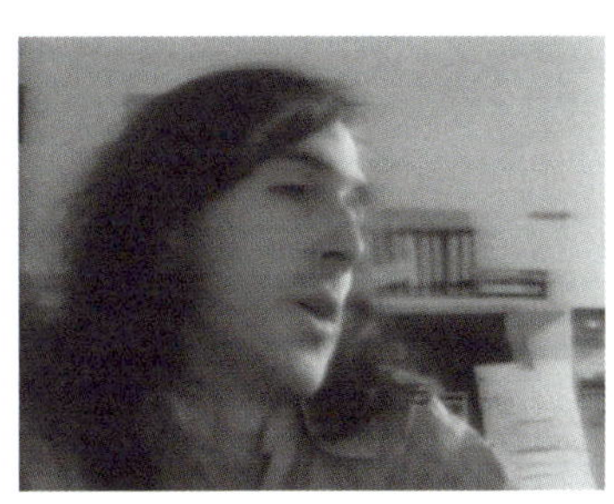
04:33

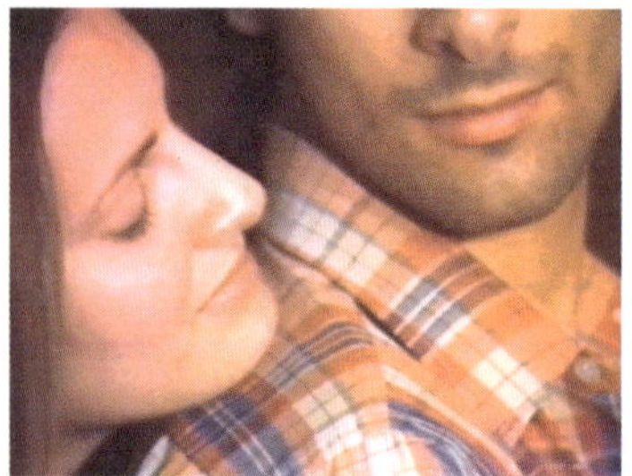

01:17

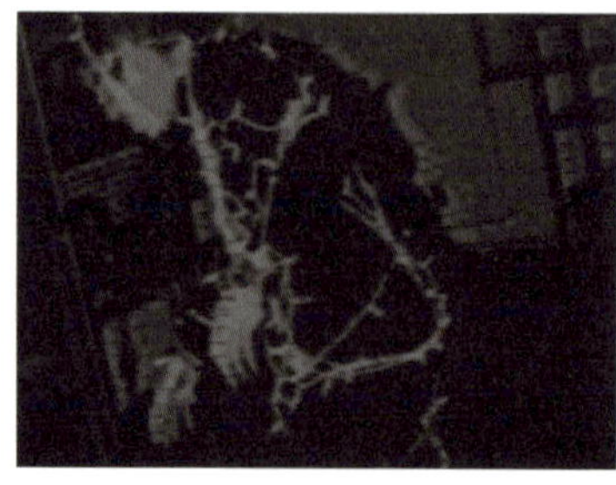

01:37

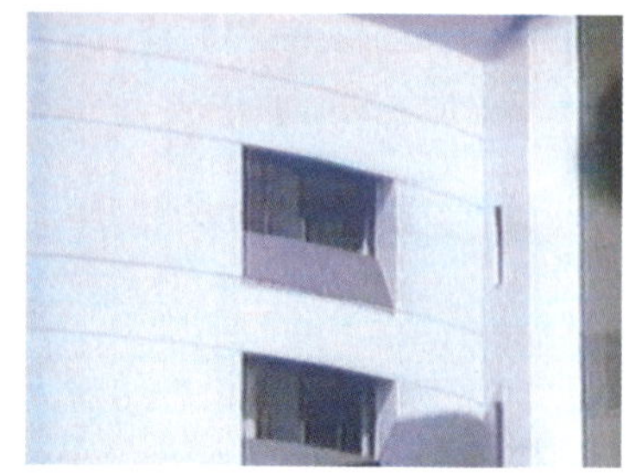

05:52

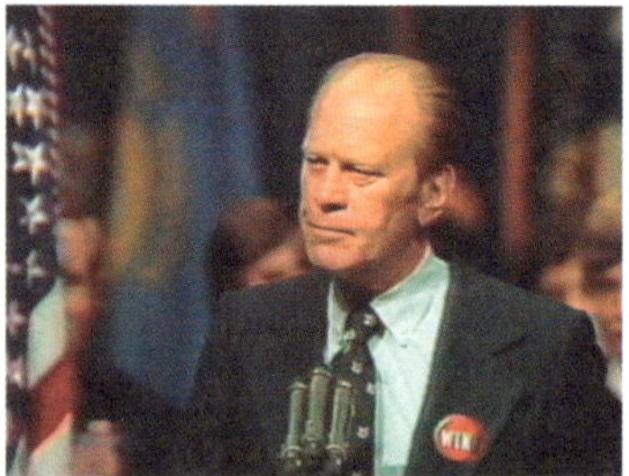

14:01

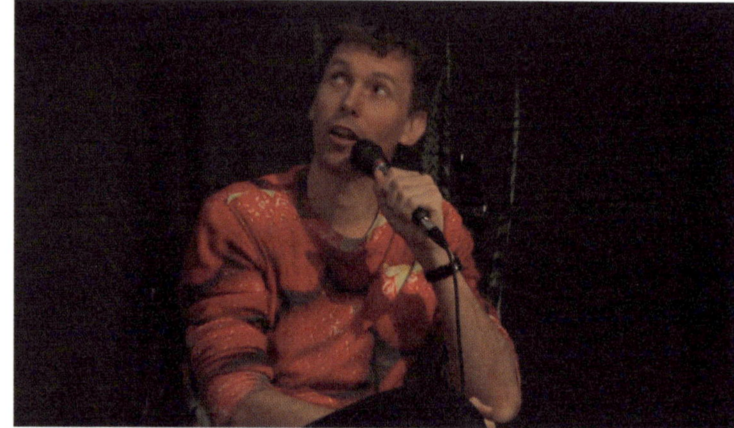

Still from PhillyCAM television broadcast

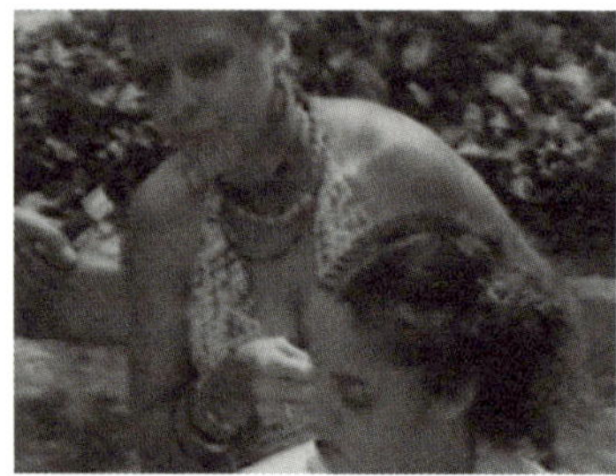

17:25

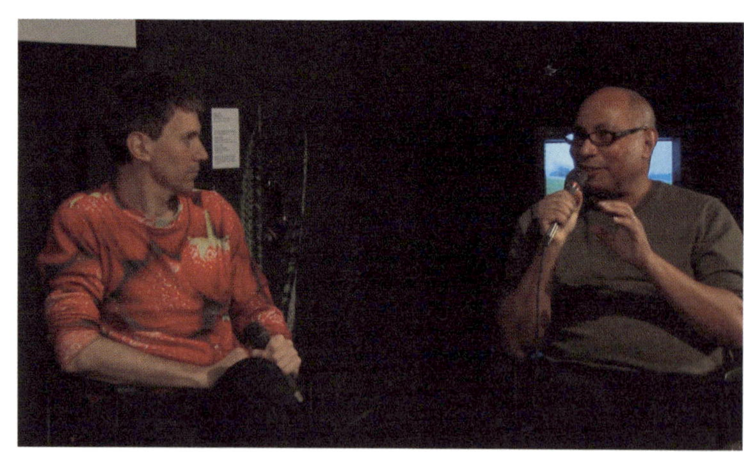

Still from PhillyCAM television broadcast

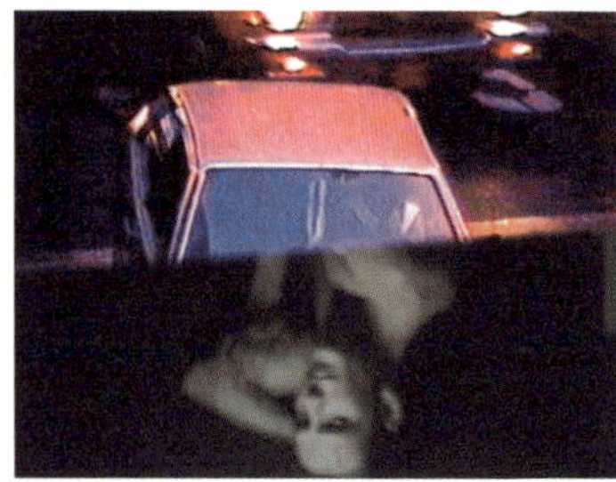

07:13

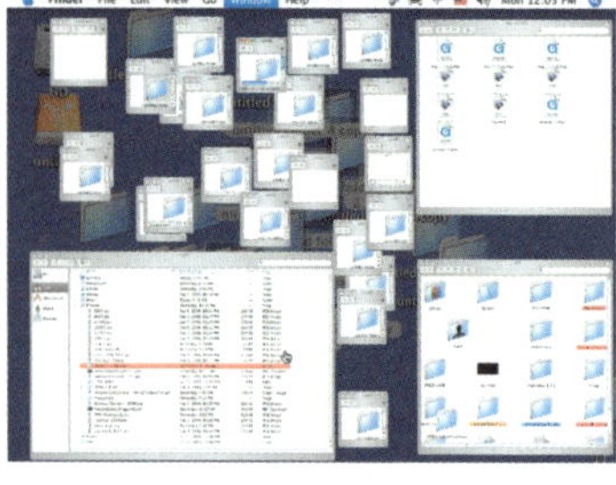

00:48

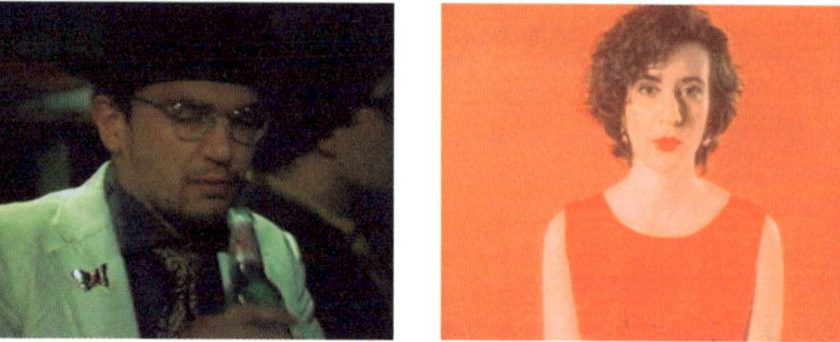

08:19

00:03

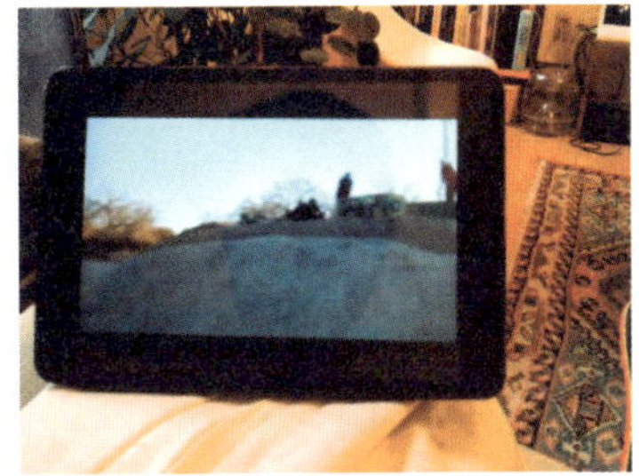

04:07

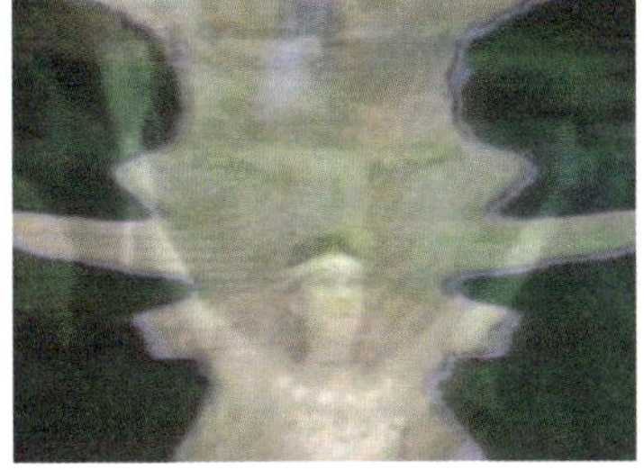

14:38

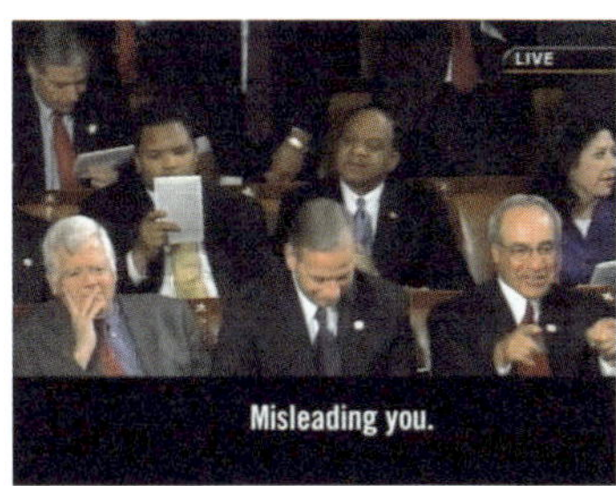

04:40

type in *cat*, and you see all these cats online, walls and walls of pictures of cats. But now you can't materialize a cat, but you can, say, materialize a teacup with a 3D printer. And I think more and more you'll be able to materialize just with words, objects. But the reverse is completely possible: you can, from an image, get a word. So there is a material correlation between these words, images, and objects. That material correlation was at the core of a series of shows. I thought that the little emoticon creatures, because they are wired and the middle part is on a roast spit which spins, so that these things crawl forward and backward. I quite like this one, the happy face becomes sad. It moves only when it's sad because this is when it touches the ground. What I liked about these guys is that they are like words, but not really, because they use characters of impressions, they don't really say anything. They are like drawings, but not really because you can't really read them very well. And they are kind of objects, but they also crawl on the floor, so not exactly. They are not really words, images, or objects, but they are also all of these things.

AK – I'm sorry we don't have a video of these because they are quite charming when they move. I should also mention that Antoine has also done exhibitions with rebuses where the sculptures in the room spell out a sentence.

RC – This is *Distant Feel*. There were many components to this work. Antoine, maybe you can talk about that. This is an ad agency's logo for empathy, or "efficient empathy."

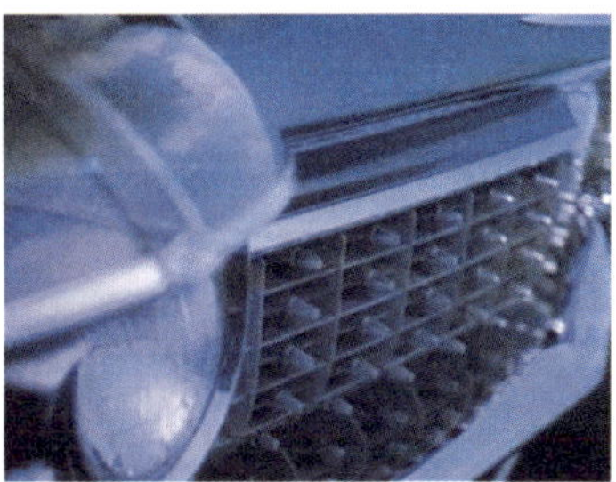

00:27

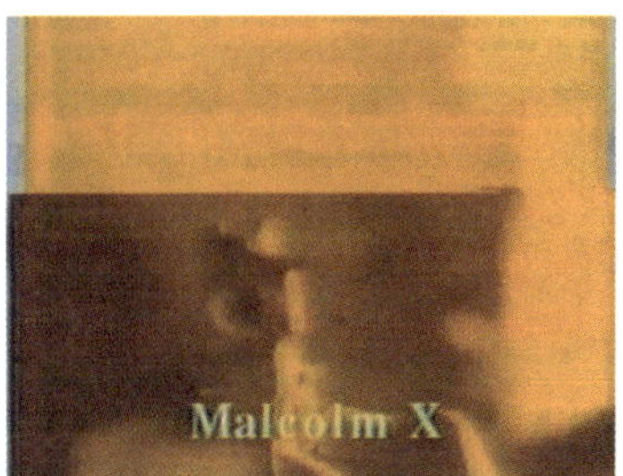

00:44

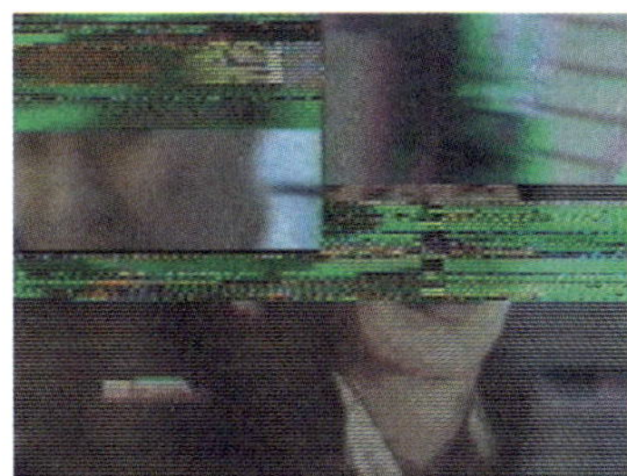

21:21

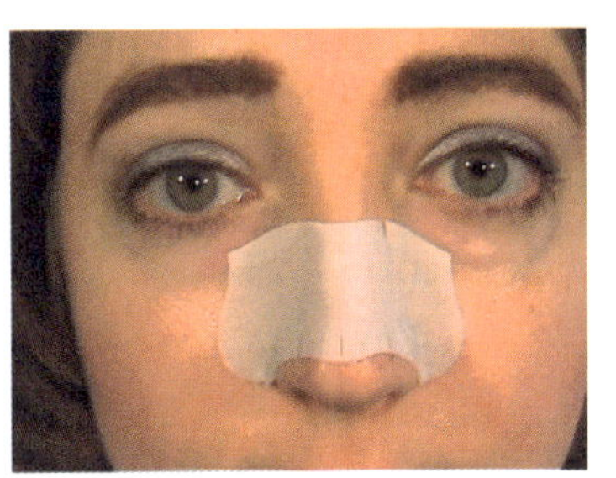

01:33

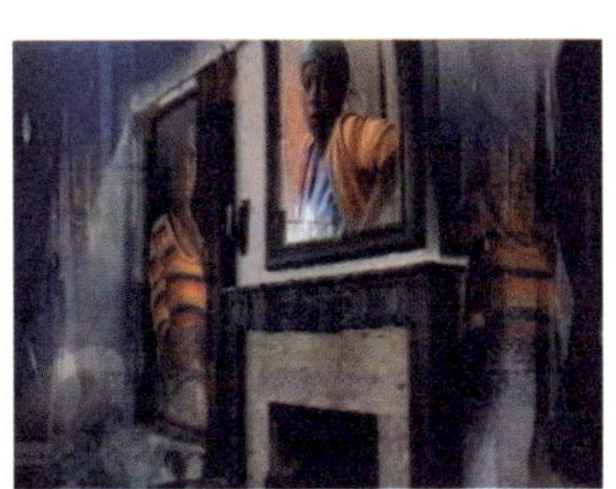

00:30

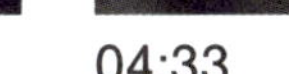

04:33

01:17

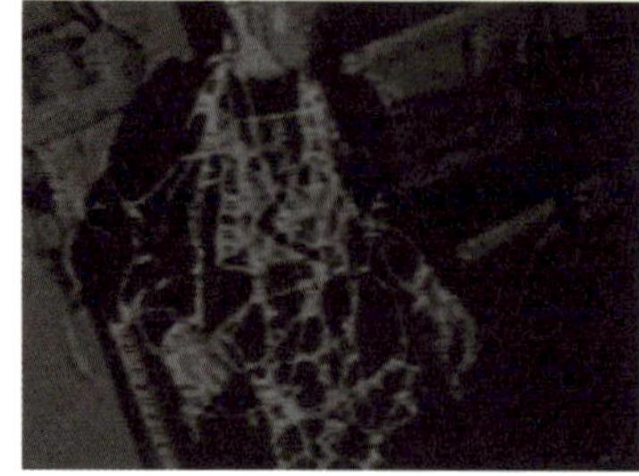

01:37

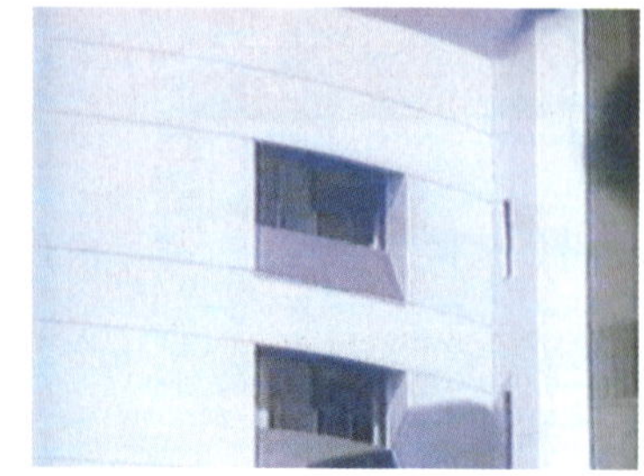

05:52

14:01

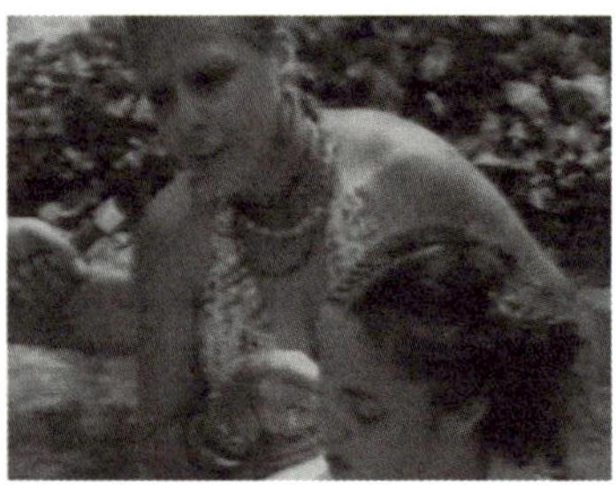

17:25

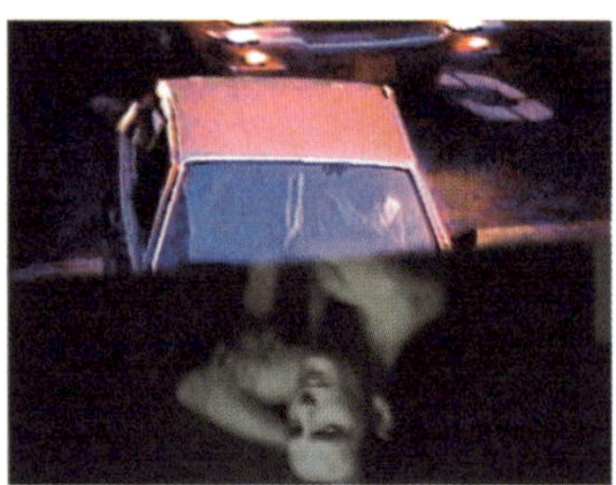

07:13

AC – “Efficient empathy,” yes. This is a show that Alex and I worked on together at the Carnegie Museum of Art in Pittsburgh, with Tina Kukielski. I always ask myself what content will I put in my work? It started with television where I appropriate content and distort it physically. I thought, OK, it would be interesting to get someone else’s content. I was interested in a naive idea of projecting something positive into the world. I thought it would be nice to revamp the peace symbol, and I would need help with that. I figured it would be interesting to work with an ad agency, a force of evil to create something good in the world. I enrolled an ad agency in New York called Droga5 and we worked on an idea of empathy. We came up with this double E. They coined it “effective empathy” and the whole project is called *Distant Feel*. This particular logo is a rather large aquarium filled with two E’s facing each other, symbolizing people in a mirror, like unspoken communication. Each E is covered in living and dancing corals. A fragile ecosystem.

AK – And this video still is a doppelgänger of a young Antoine with the logo morphing over your face, or the actor’s face I should say, as different emotions are being acted out. One thing that came up when we were talking earlier is how technology affects our emotions and our ability to communicate, and you said this interesting thing about maybe we get the technology that fits us.

AC – I often get asked, “Do you think technology has changed the way we communicate? Has it

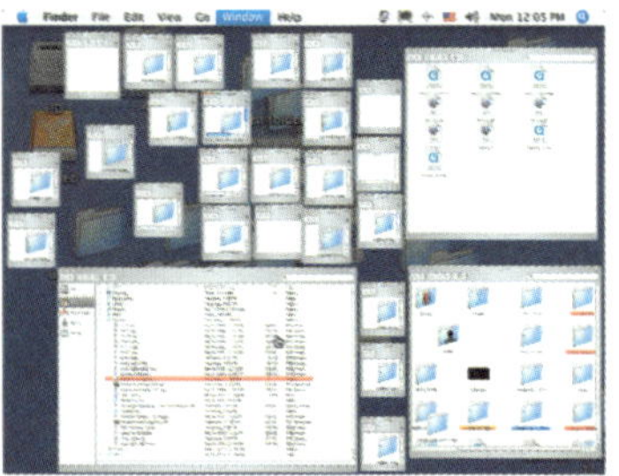

00:48

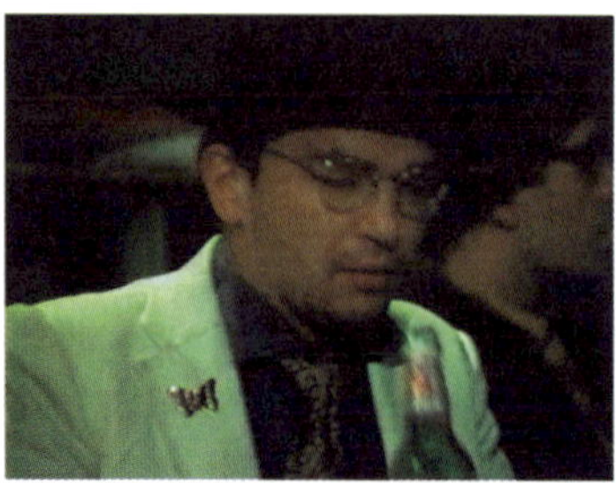

08:19

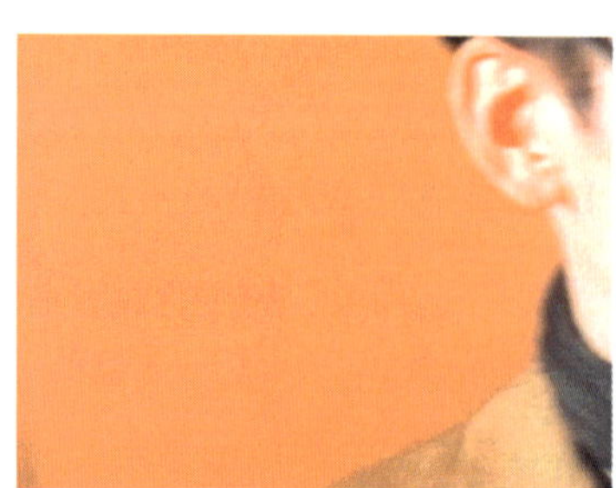

00:03

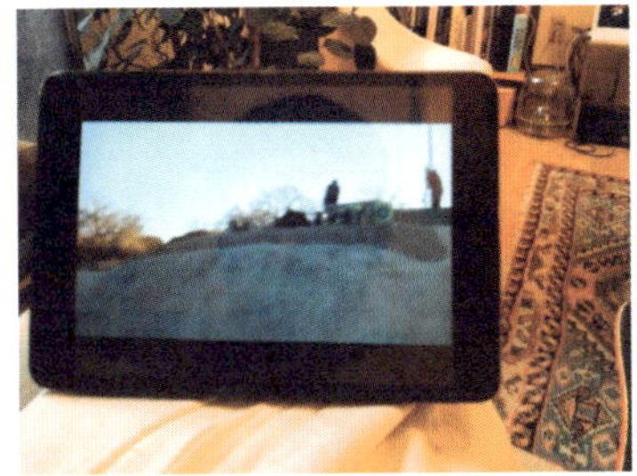
04:07

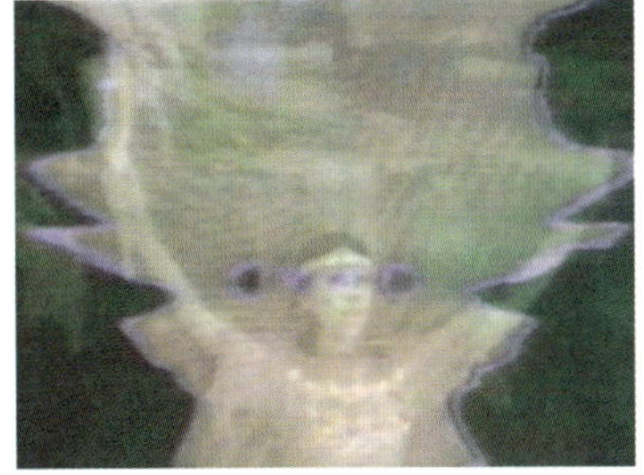
14:38

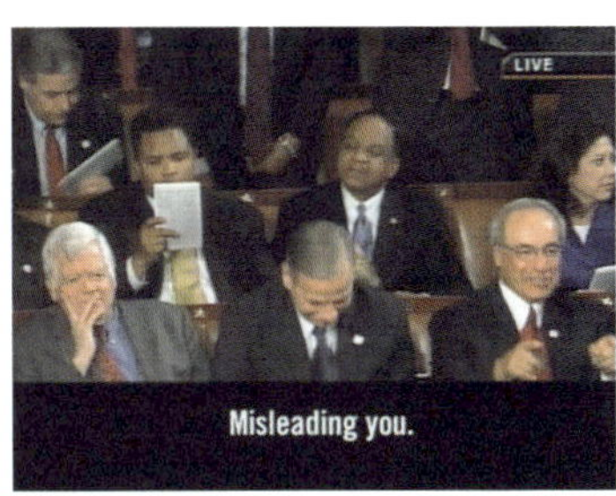

04:40

degraded or enhanced the way we talk to one another?" And I actually think more and more that it changes slightly on the surface, it looks like it's changing, but really it's the same from the beginning of time, and we do get technology to fit the way we are as humans. Technology wouldn't be adopted if it didn't fit the way we communicate, which is also full of miscommunication.

AK – And maybe that is a great segue into your most recent show at 47 Canal, *Everything Is Okay*. Do you want to give a brief introduction before we go into one of the video clips?

AC – The show was designed as an opera. Everything was dynamic, kinetic, and activated over time. And the underlying idea was pretty simple. It was based on the use of emojis in text messages. I think one key point is that emojis were used both by the companies that create the platform to message, and by the people that use the messaging to reassure their interlocutor. So you use a little banana or a happy face to make sure the message you are sending is not misinterpreted and is read as a welcoming message. It is sent as this thing that essentially says, "It's OK, don't worry." And what it says in the background if we really think about it is what does that say about the state of communication. What if we don't use emojis? Is it really going to go to shit? Also, you have the other fear from the people that create this platform. If you don't really keep up with the trends then your customers are going to go away, so you are always feeling a constant fear from the platforms who offer these services, if you

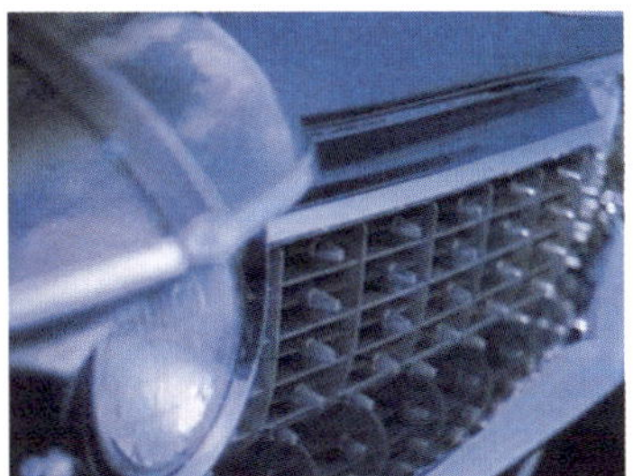
00:27

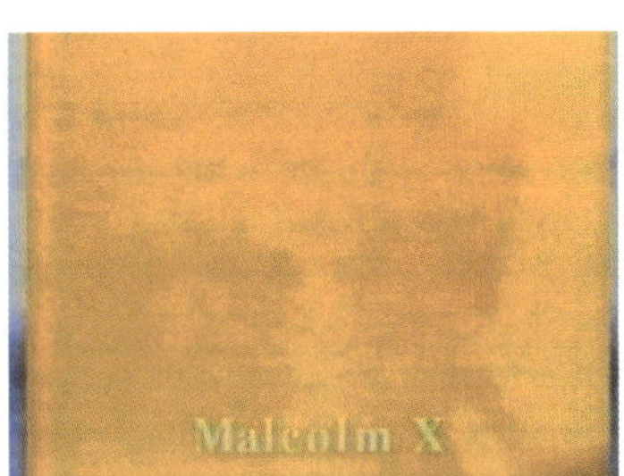

00:44

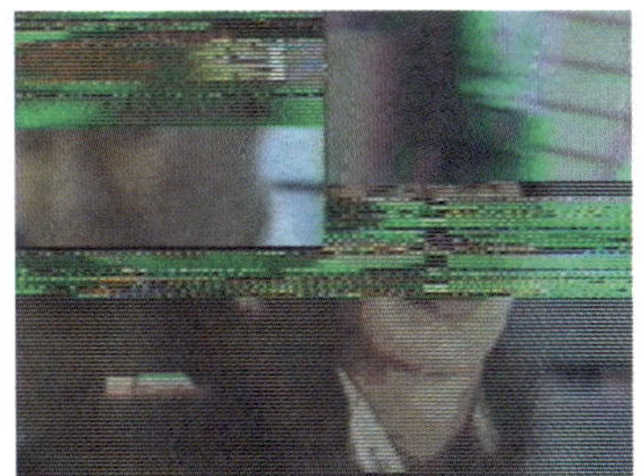
21:21

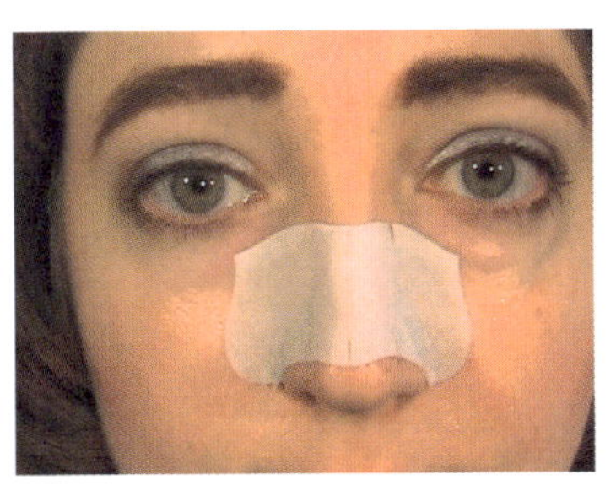
01:33

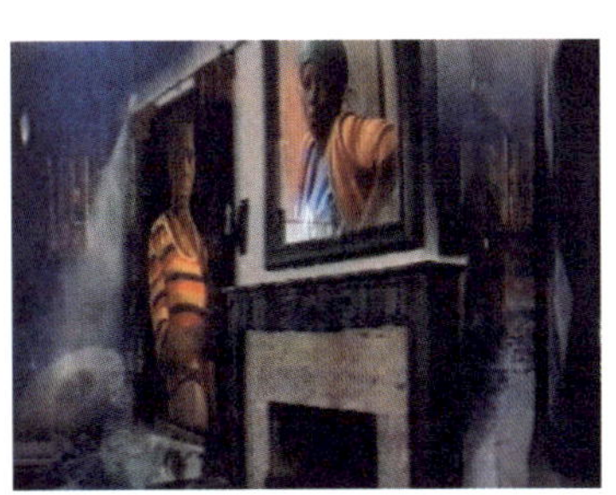
00:30

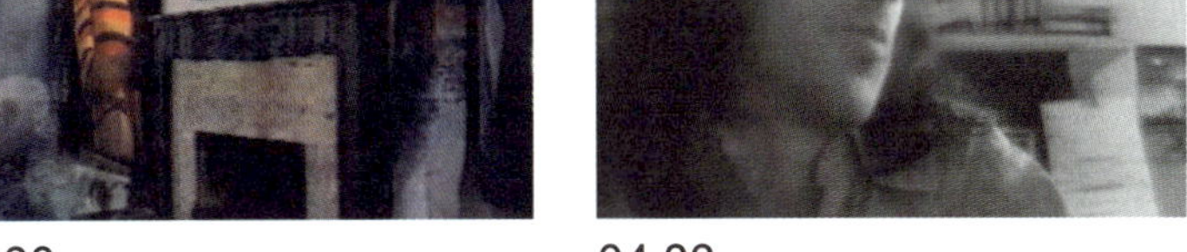
04:33

01:17

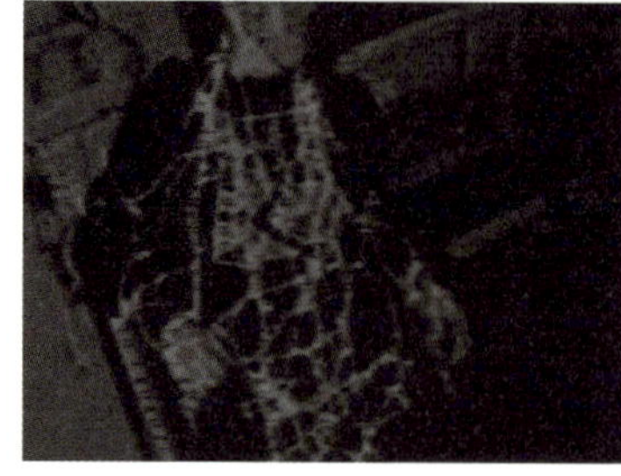

01:37

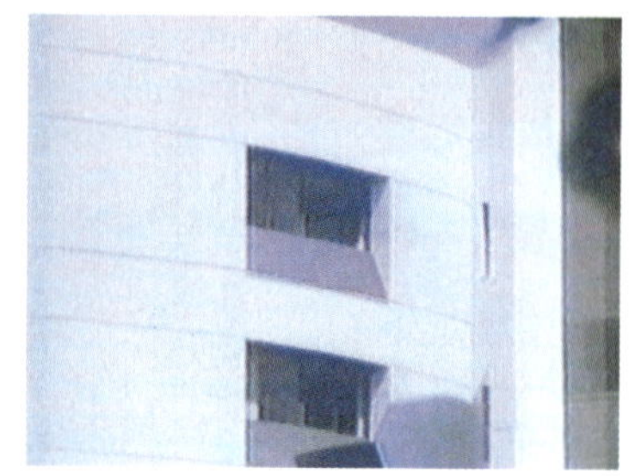

05:52

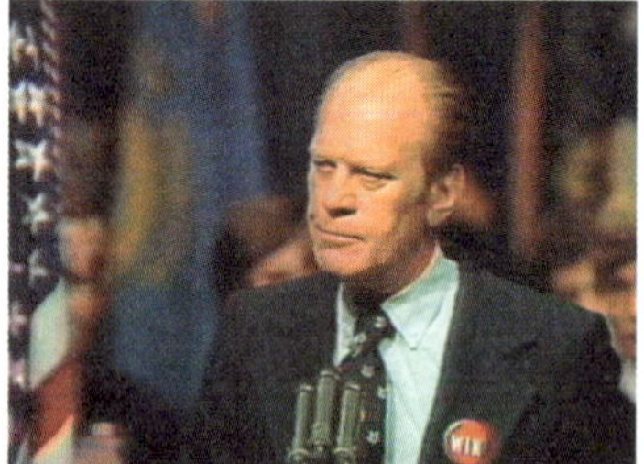

14:01

don't update your game then your users are going to run away from your platform. Internet giants are really afraid of becoming the new AOL or Myspace.

AK – So there were these pneumatic sculptures that would breathe in and out and there was a soundtrack that you commissioned.

AC – Most of the time it was just a blank canvas, and a song would come on. (By the way, my friend Olivier Alary wrote the song for the show.) The chorus is "everything is okay." When the song comes on, text appears on the surface of the canvas.

RC – It was very creepy.

AK – Do you want to tell us a little bit more about those before we jump into the conversation?

AC – I think of machines before I think of content. My struggle is always content. Thus I was wondering: what content should I put inside these new machines? My friend Micaela Durand suggested an app that teenagers are hooked on—it's actually called Hooked. It's stories distributed as text messages. Each story functions with an ongoing, underlying terror. So in this story, for instance, two people text. There is a noise in the basement—should I go, no don't go, I tell you not to go, and it just carries on and on. I used the mechanisms of Hooked to create this tension in my video. And thus to build up a tension and to have this release where "everything is OK," and to have this gentle song coming on. I call them flat sitcoms. Throughout the show there were three of those conversations with different types of tensions between two people.

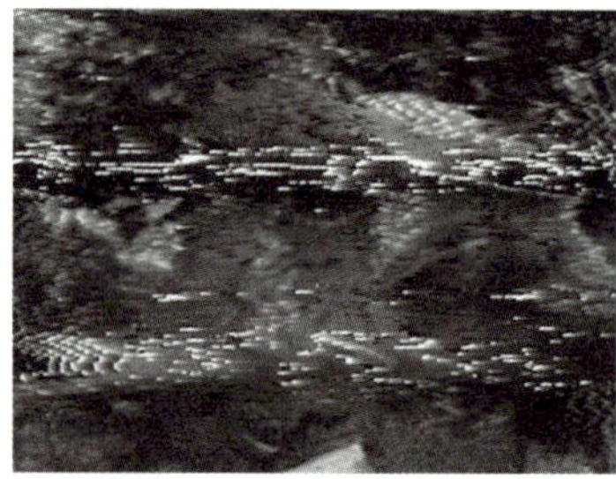

17:25

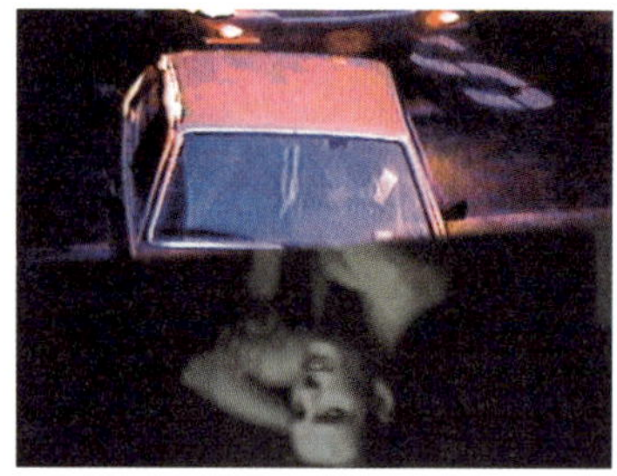

07:13

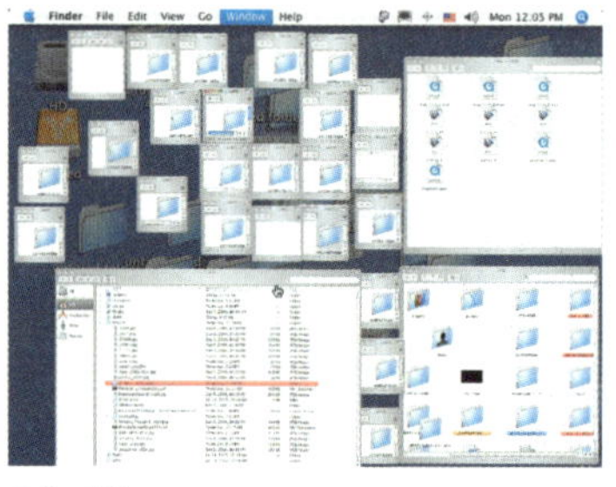

00:48

08:19

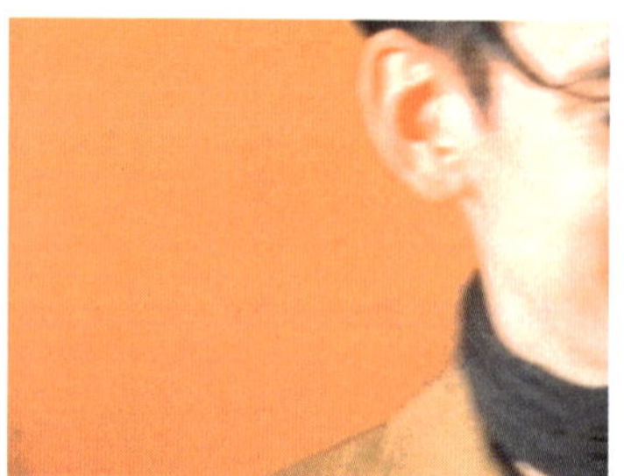

00:03

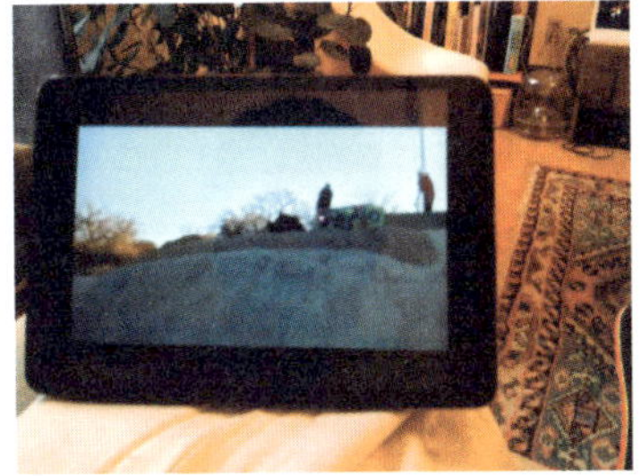
04:07

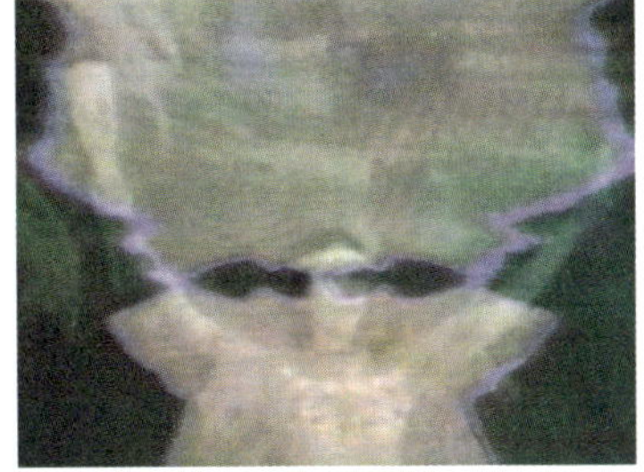
14:38

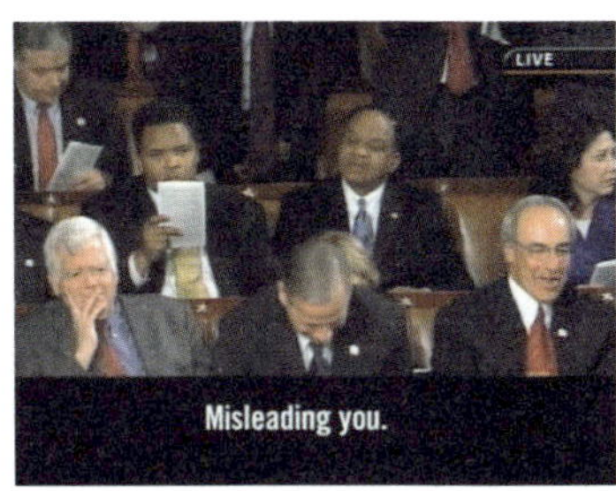

04:40

RC – I think we talked about the film *Personal Shopper* (2016) as a potential reference there. Not just the horror trope, but using devices, new-fangled technology, the latest communication tool within the horror trope.

AC – Yeah, I really love that film.

AK – But maybe that's a good transition into formats. Because I think that is something you are both interested in in different ways. Tony, you have talked about the music video or the propagandistic missive and Antoine, you just mentioned the sitcom. Both of those have roots in television, too.

RC – Also, related to storytelling and narratives, because that is maybe not such a usual reference within a contemporary visual art context. Tony, I know you have a background in creative writing.

TC – I was actually talking to Antoine a little about this earlier today, I wasn't thinking so much in terms of narrative tropes as I was in the relationship between text and image in other popular forms like the magazine. And the fact that when I was being trained it was the tail end of modernism; people were really concerned about my desire to do both text and image simultaneously, but it's ubiquitous, it's all around us. And it seems like something that would also be worth talking about and focusing on in work. To some extent it was a gesture toward the fact that these things were always already happening in popular cultures, and why shouldn't we be examining these kinds of relations in art? I put a little bit of a point on

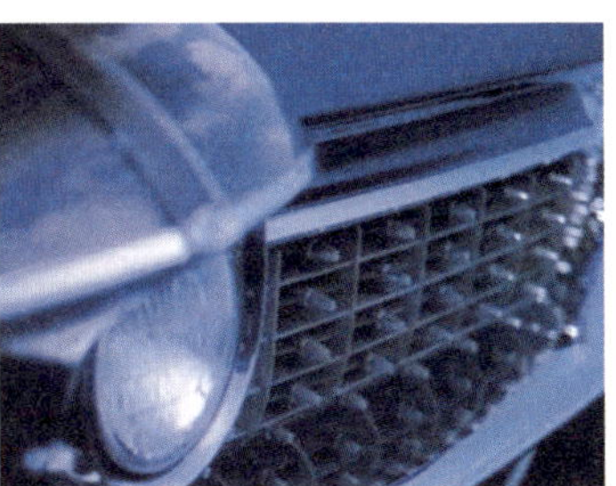
00:27

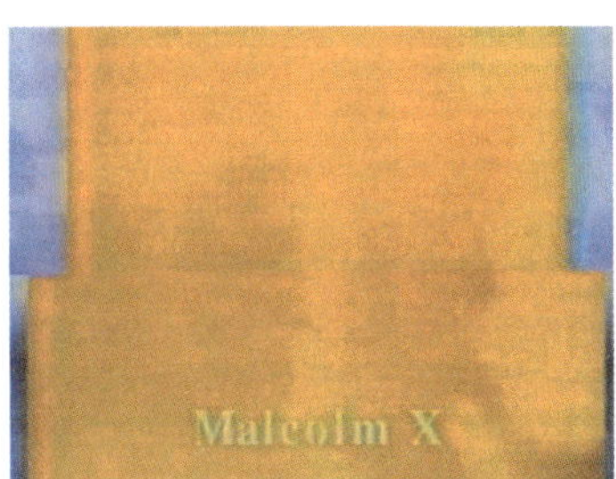

00:44

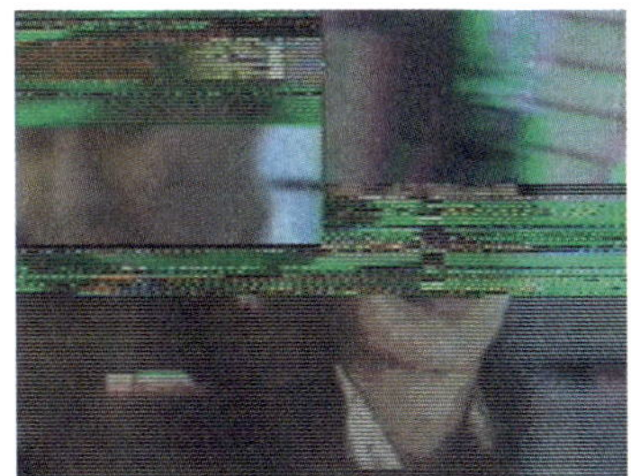
21:21

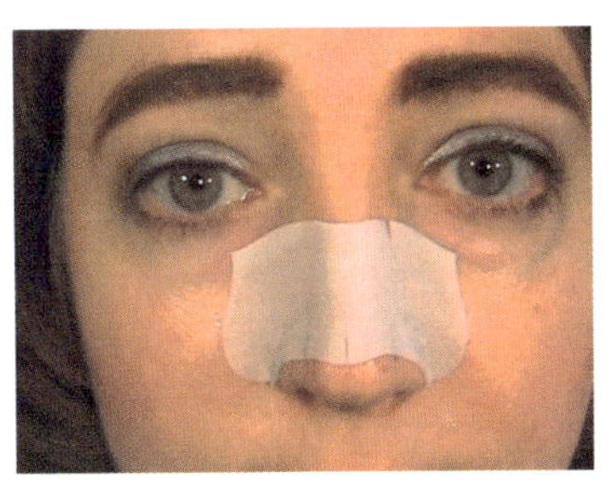
01:33

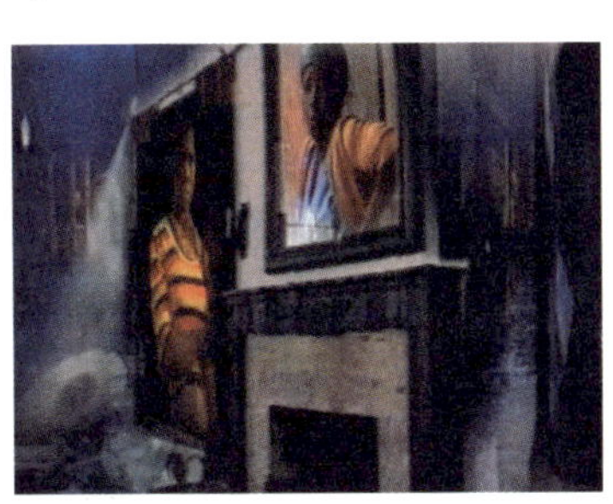
00:30

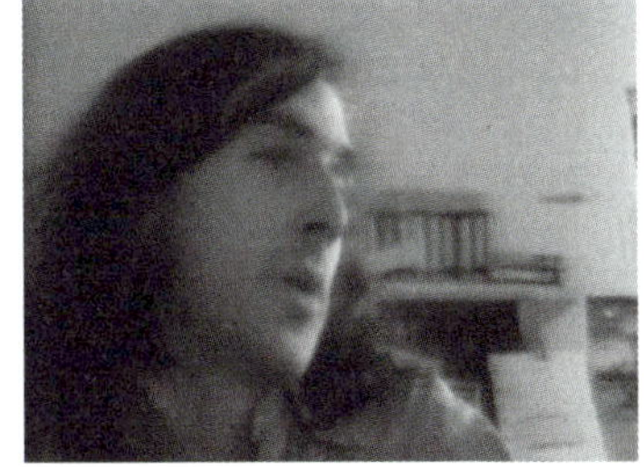
04:33

01:17

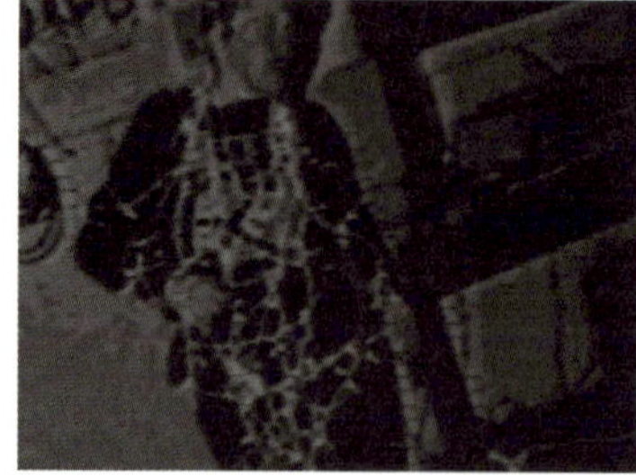
01:37

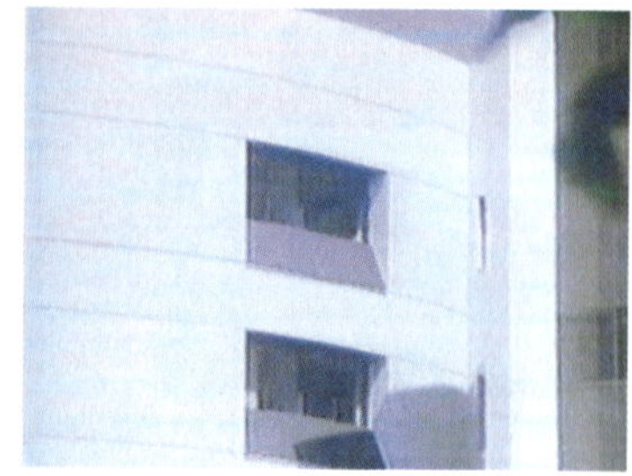
05:52

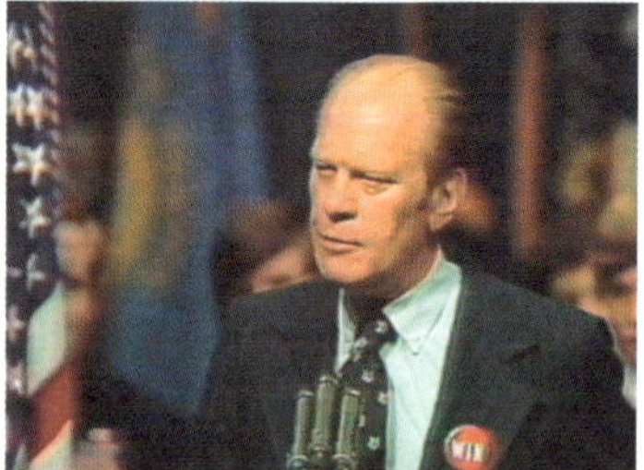
14:01

17:25

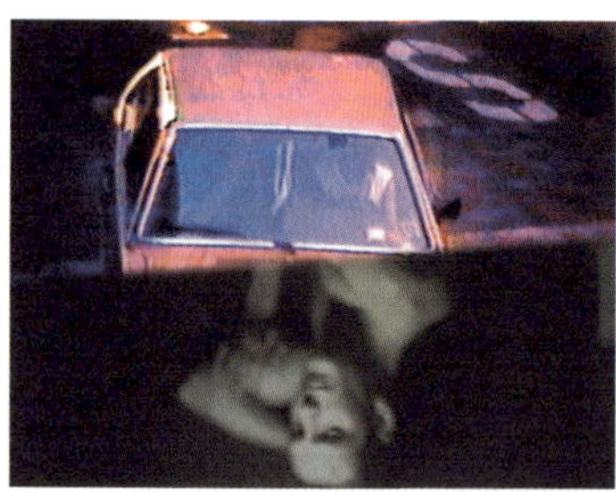
07:13

it, then went further and further into the textual as opposed to the traditionally visual. It wasn't just a simple détournement or gesture of appropriation, it was also done with a knowledge in the back of my mind that music video always was a kind of appropriation of avant-garde codes and a history of traditional and untraditional modes of putting sound and image together. And it's like, "Oh, wow, I'm being accused of making music videos, isn't that interesting?" But it's like, "Well, what are music videos? Where do they come from?"

AC – I had a question about the last work we showed of yours with George Carlin. Would you say it was a comedy?

TC – It was a stand-up routine. A comic presents a monologue on a subject, except this subject is class and educational policy.

AC – So it is super political, but it's not a political text per se?

TC – That's a good question. In fact, that is maybe one part of my strategy. To take something that could be read in a particular way and suspend it a little bit. Instead of having George Carlin pacing the stage, doing his vocal and physical gestures, to just present what he says. And we were also talking about wondering, "Who's saying this and in what context?" So maybe that's also part of the friction in it.

AC – And listening to it is also another layer, another dimension. I think of it as a kind of karaoke, but the text is misplaced.

TC – That is funny that you would mention that, because it's an idea that has occurred to me. In fact, I've

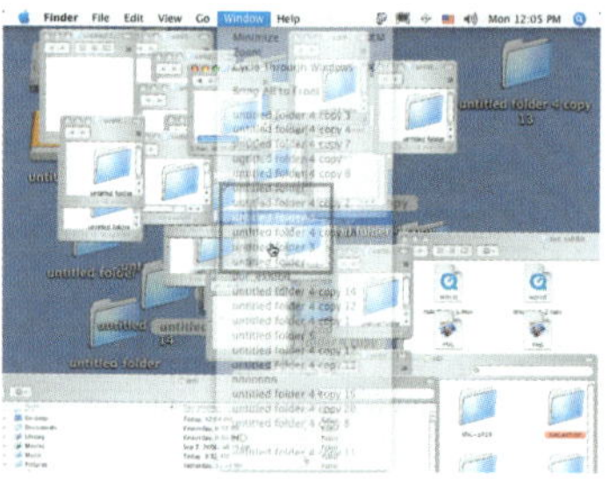
00:48

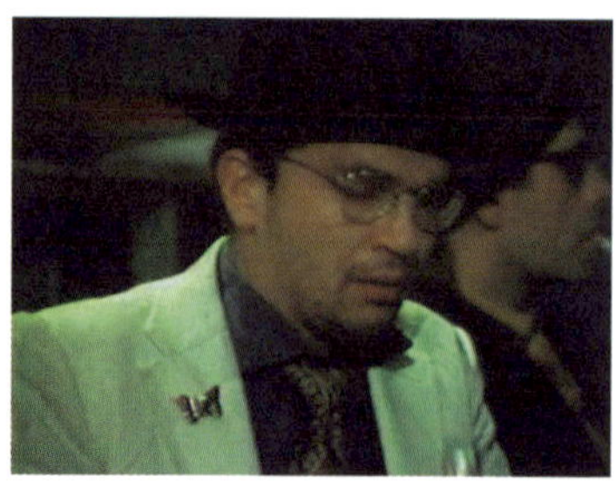
08:19

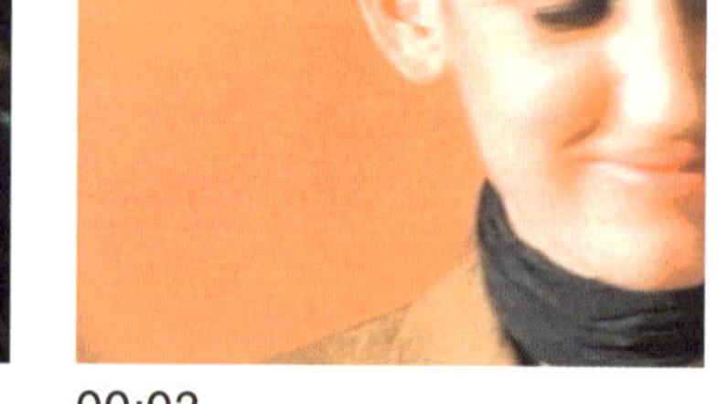
00:03

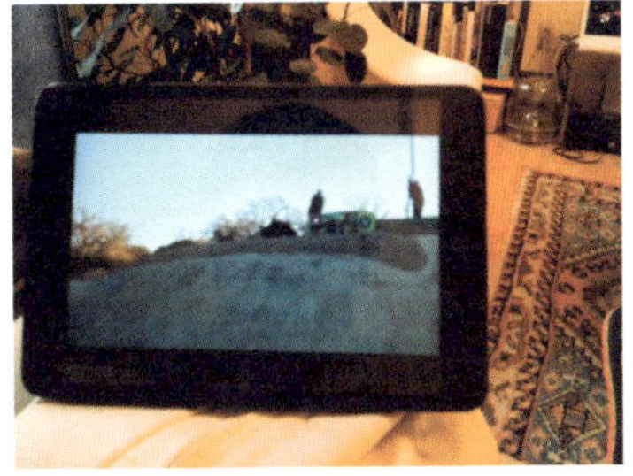
04:07

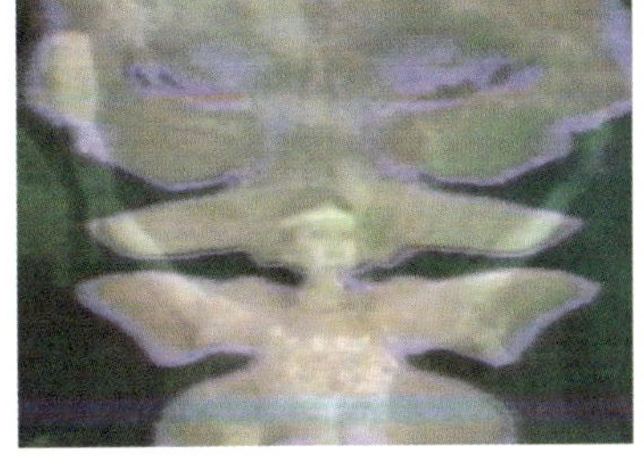
14:38

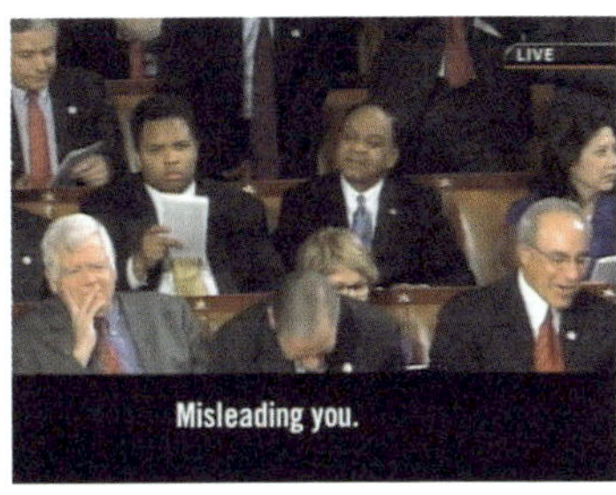

04:40

done a couple pieces that function that way. I take a song and I do the lyric in time. And it's sort of "Wow, that is something I normally wouldn't do" because they coincide. But what happens when you actually physically double the thing. But one of the things that did occur to me is, "what would it be like to just have the lyric?" Have, for instance, as was happening before we got going tonight, someone just reading the text aloud. Or a performer who on occasion appears and just reads the text that appears on screen, as opposed to just having it only be the visual signs that it is. Or having the text directly relate to the music, which would tend to normalize it and make it like all those YouTube videos with the lyrics of the songs being presented. But yes, I think about things like that.

AK – Not to change the subject entirely, but because the title of tonight's event is "Means of Production"—and thinking about being here with PhillyCAM, an organization that puts the tools of production in people's hands in a really profound way and what it means for us all to the have the media in our own hands with iPhones, etc. in this day and age—can you talk a little bit about your process as artists and how you come to the forms that you work with, and the accessibility of those tools?

RC – I was going to ask you about the transformation from the process of working privately or in an interior space and anticipating the public. I know that is a long-standing consideration in the arts, but to bring that into the conversation tonight would be interesting.

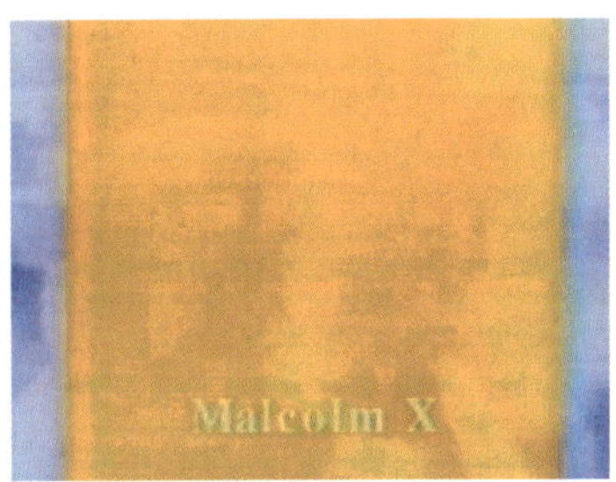
00:27

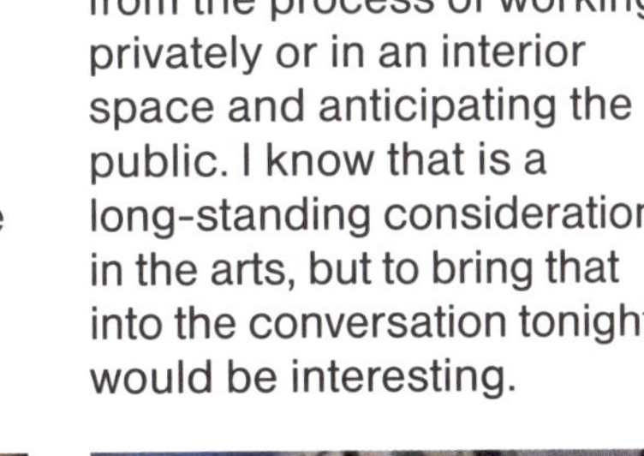

00:44

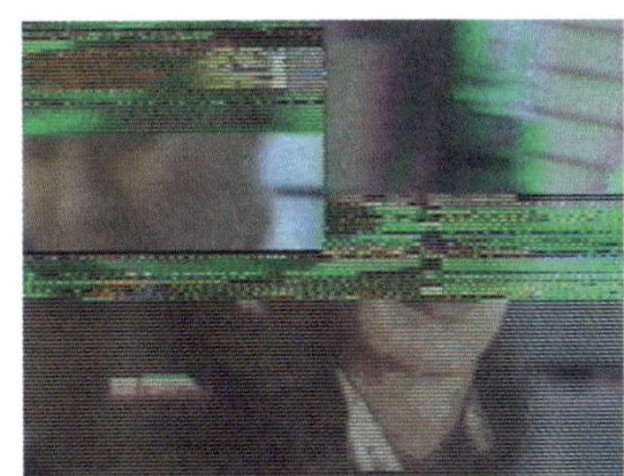
21:21

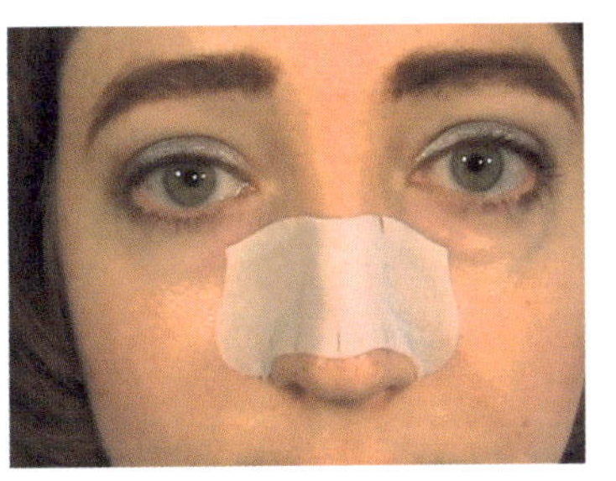
01:33

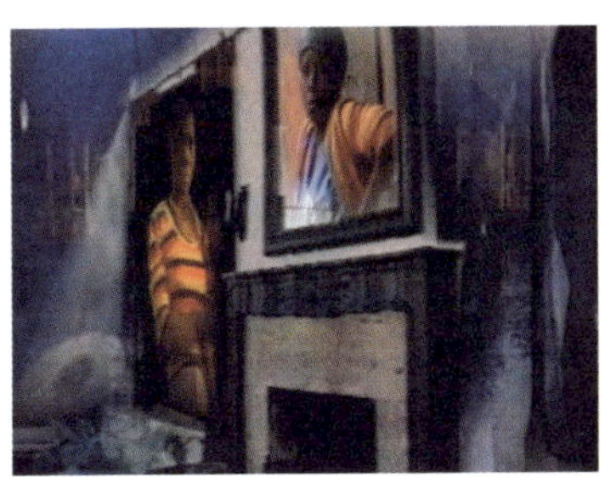
00:30

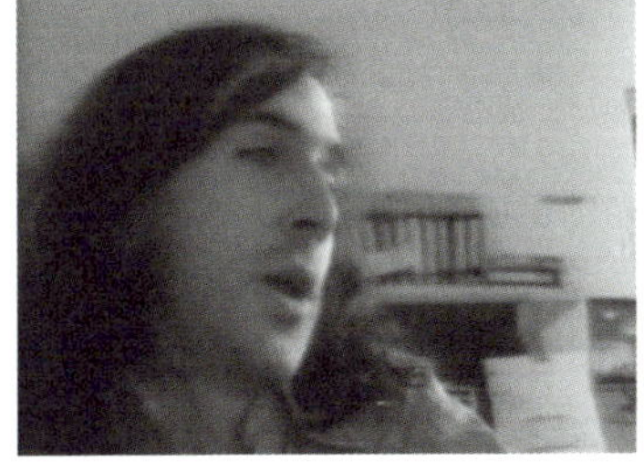
04:33

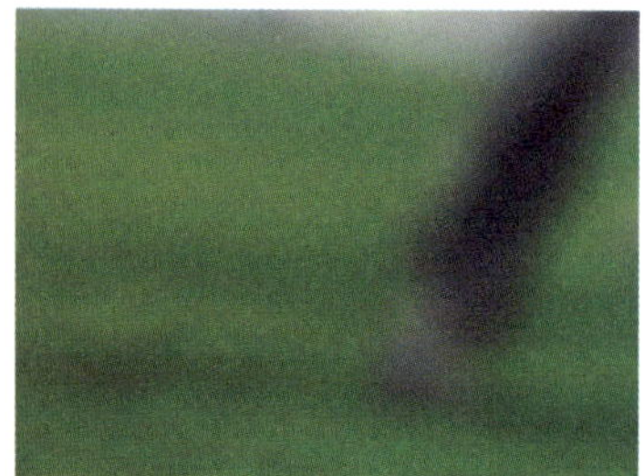

01:16

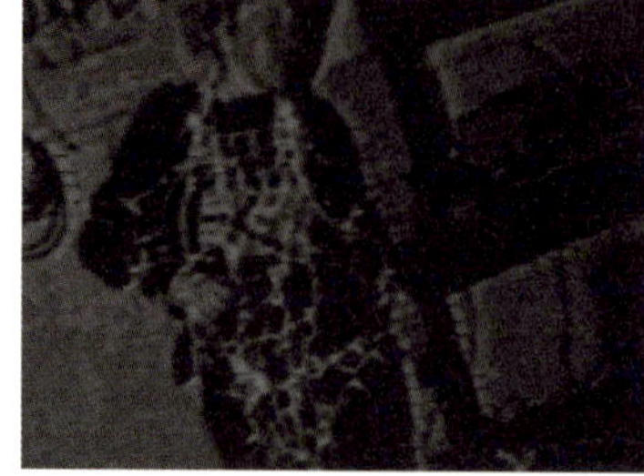

01:36

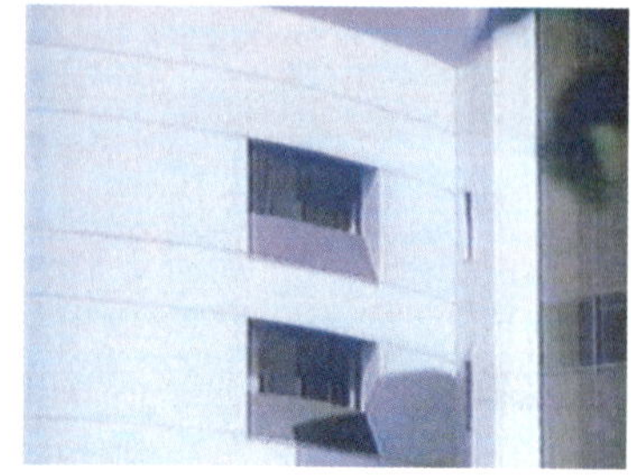

05:51

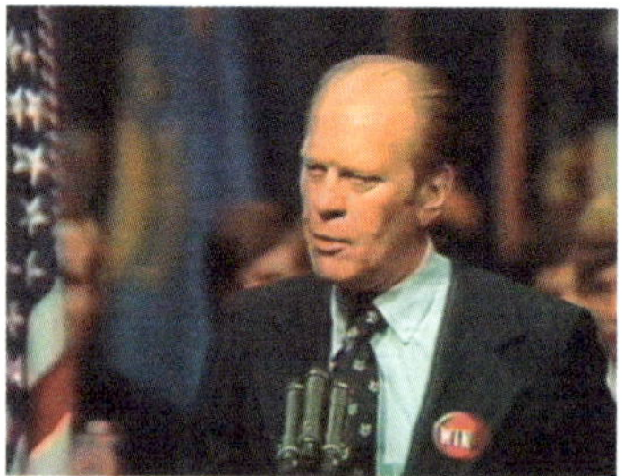

14:00

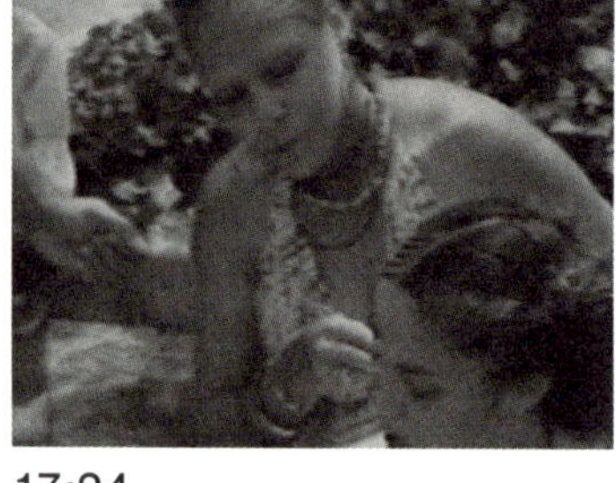

17:24

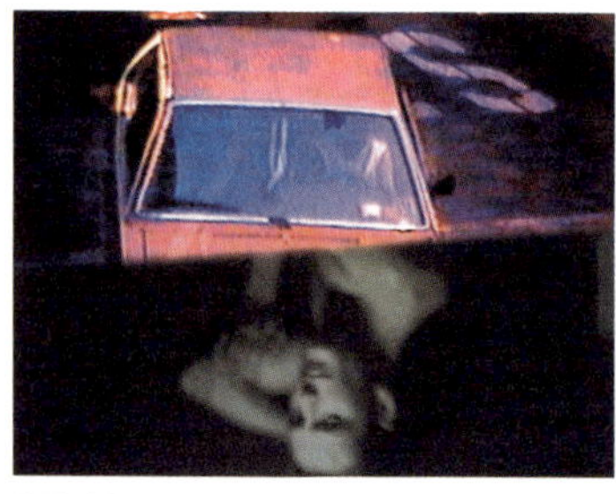

07:12

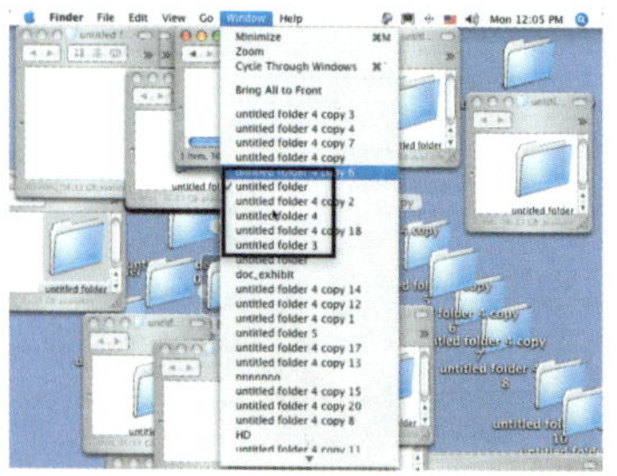

00:47

08:18

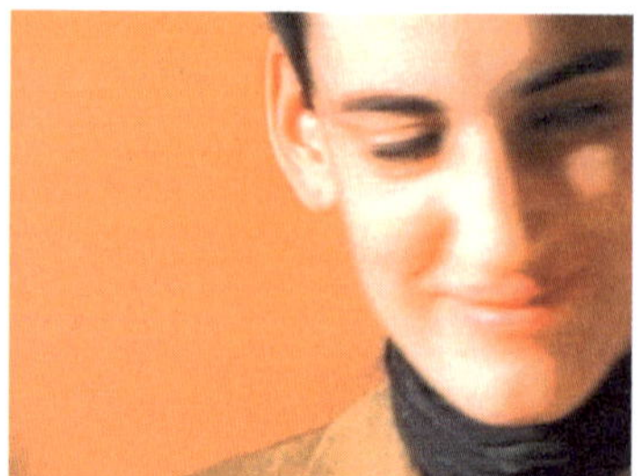

00:02

AC – For me, I work with other people because I have limited knowledge about how to create what I do, which is, a lot of the time, kinetic machines. It really is about having an idea of doing something, then going at it, then seeing how it comes to form, then navigating, renegotiating the ideas all the time. It is very much a physical response to the work itself, to what comes to life itself. I tend to get people to come to see what I'm doing, at some point, when I am set on what I want to do. So I get their response and try to incorporate it into the whole thing.

AK – In terms of some of the technologies you are working with, for some viewers it seems very much like, "Wow, how was this made?" but you often show the tentacles. You'll show how some of the machines are working, or maybe in that early television sculpture, thinking about how actually that is a very simple device in some ways. Something that looks very high tech is actually a readymade solution of some kind that you've come up with.

AC – That is always a part of the reflection. We have all of these mechanisms, but I'm more interested in the platform of presentation of images than the images themselves. I want to reflect on these platforms, so this is why I work as much as possible with banal images. I want to make something magical on the one hand, and display, "Oh, look how it's made, it's actually not that clever."

AK – And earlier, Tony, we were talking about the studio space.

TC – Yeah, my studio space, which sometimes

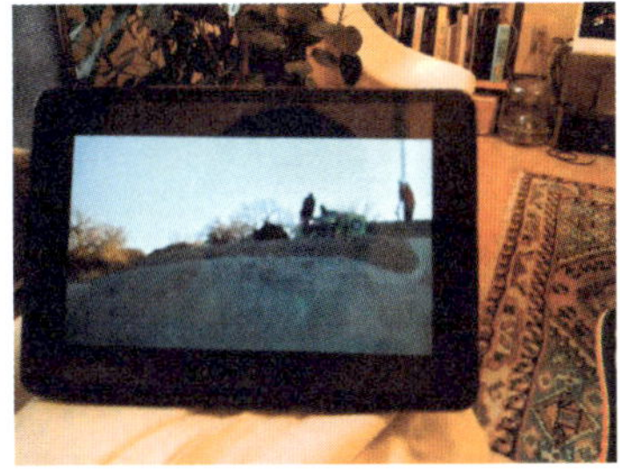

04:07

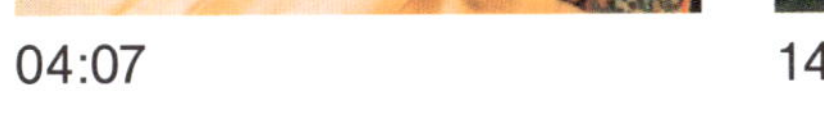

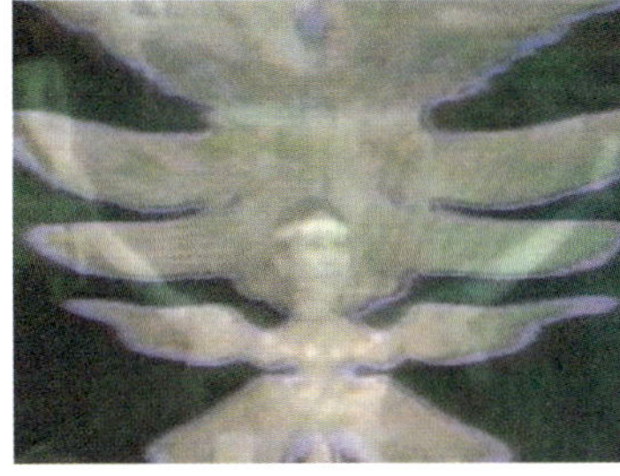

14:38

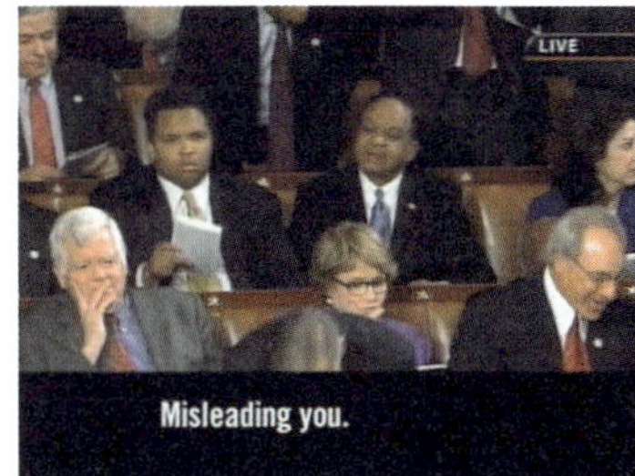

04:40

people want to see images of. Well, mine looks very much like yours: it's a little device that unfolds and there's text and sound and image.

RC – And a cup of coffee.

TC – Yes, a cup of coffee. Sometimes it's much better in a place that's non-normative like a coffee place or a hotel room. I can work just as well in a space like that as in a space in which I'm allegedly comfortable. But I'm kind of interested in that "special creative place" as a persistent image and representation, so I've been thinking and working on some things about the image of the studio and why it is so persistent. And maybe some of the things that it has come to represent and ways that ideas about the artist's studio create notions about what living spaces should be like, and what cultural practices should be like. The idea that everything has to be creative and everything has to have an economic value and function even though it is allegedly autonomous. I am fascinated by ideas like that and their persistence. Like I say, I run up against them often, though they don't really make sense. People want to see my studio. Do you want to see my living room? My office? The hotel I'm staying in tonight? How is it different than where you are? I guess that can be linked to the question of technologies.

I sketch most of my work out in Keynote or PowerPoint, sometimes with unfancy and ugly transitions and standard fonts. Then people ask, "Why would you use that?" Sometimes I may do something custom but I try to keep it as simple as possible, at least on the front end, mainly because, as you

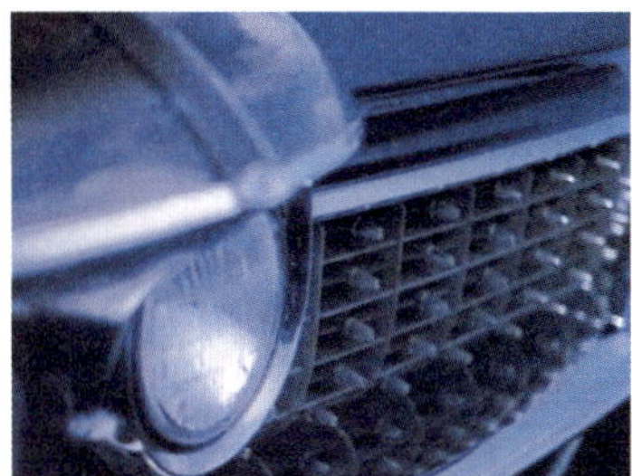

00:27

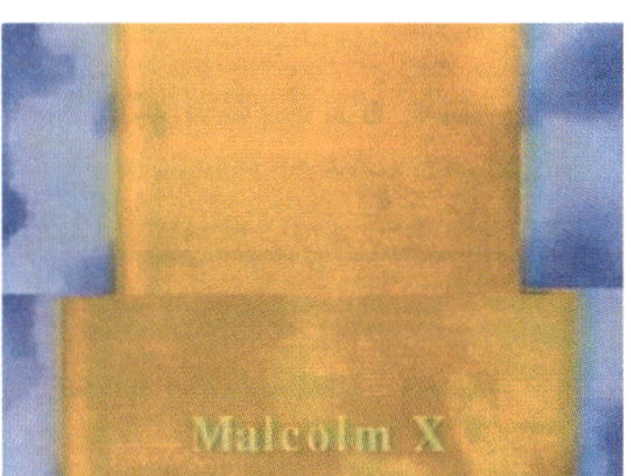

00:44

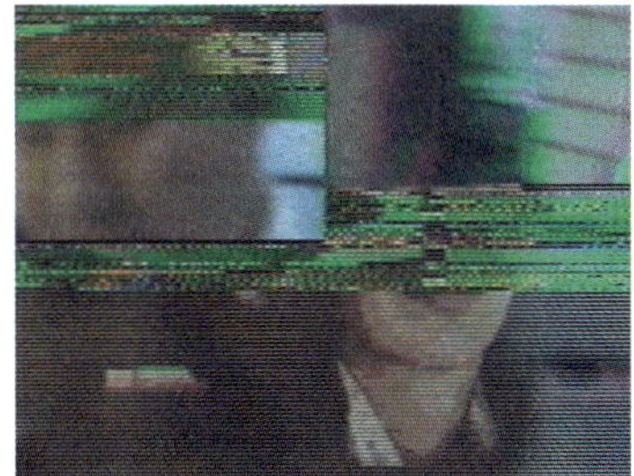

21:21

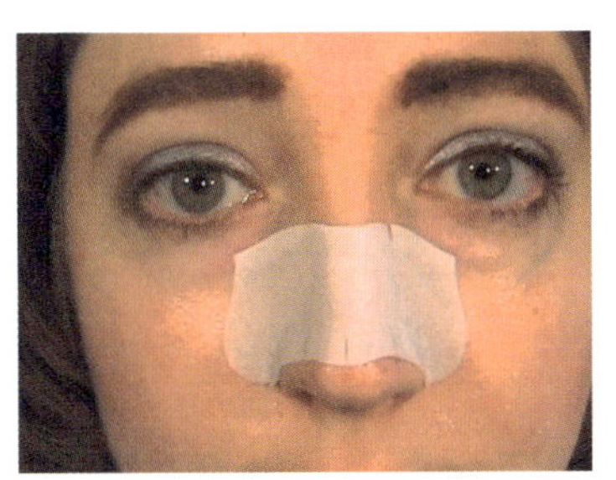

01:33

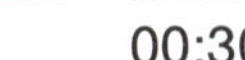

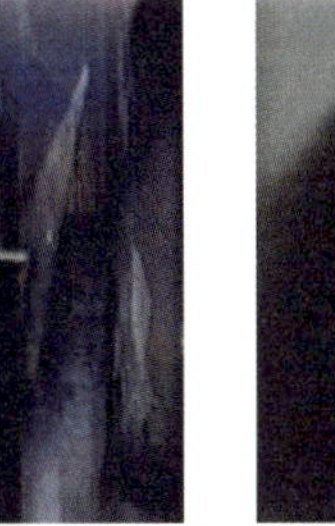

00:30

04:33

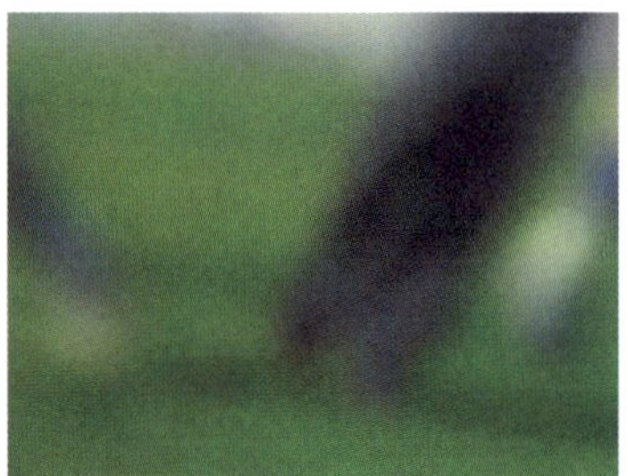
01:16

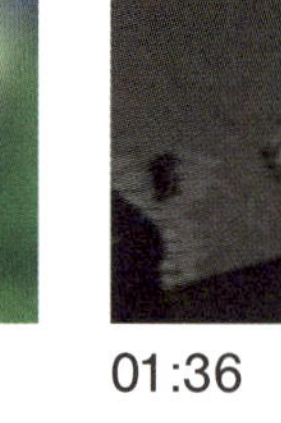
01:36

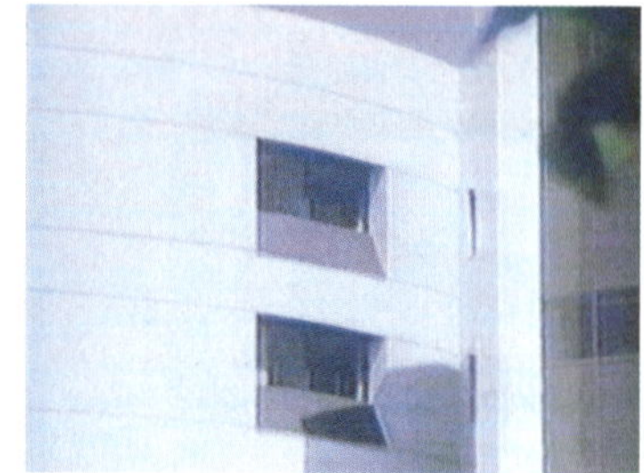
05:51

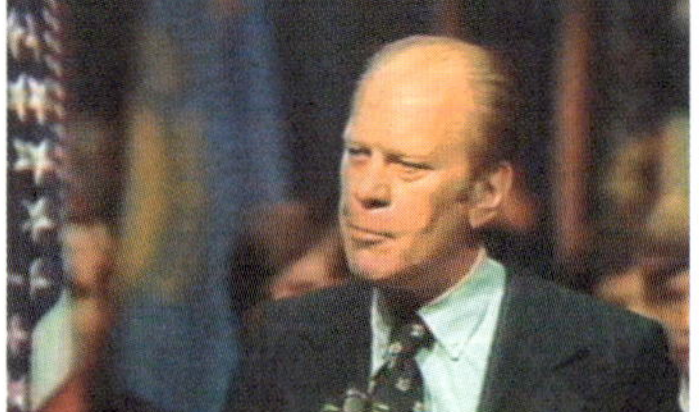
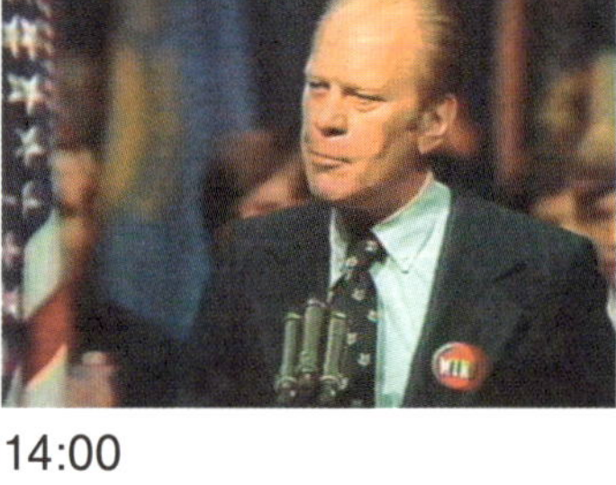
14:00

17:24

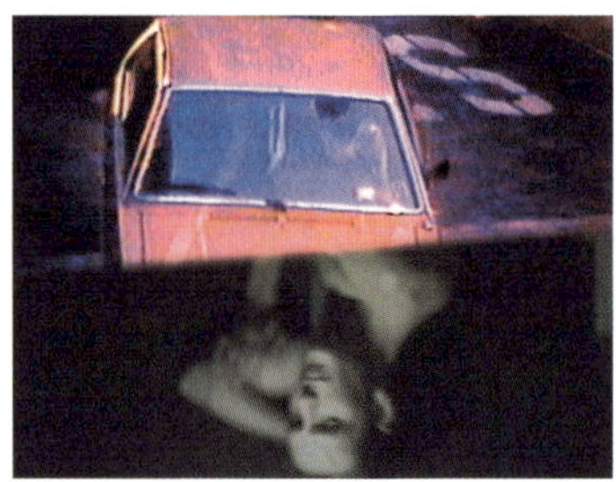
07:12

were observing earlier, it is largely iterative. There are versions and versions and I repeat and repeat and repeat. So trying to keep the technology a little bit out of the way so I can think about things while I'm doing it. As opposed to obsessing over the minutiae of the technology itself. There is nothing to obsess over in that way. There are simpler paradigms and lower stakes. For me it is both important to think about structure, historical and cultural relationships, but also to get things done and out. Nothing too fancy. I like the idea of the stupid or the simple. It's kind of like, *you* can do this! *You* really could!

AK – And we didn't even get to the banal in both of your work, which would've been a wonderful place to go. But I think we are ending on the desktop, which is actually a really great place to conclude.

RC – It's appropriate.

1 Marshall McLuhan, "New Media and the Arts," in Arts in Society 3(2): "The Avant-Garde Today" (Madison: University of Wisconsin Press, Sept 1964), 239.

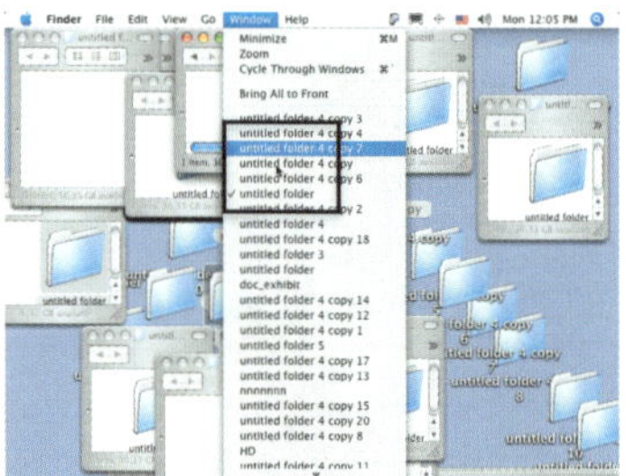
00:47

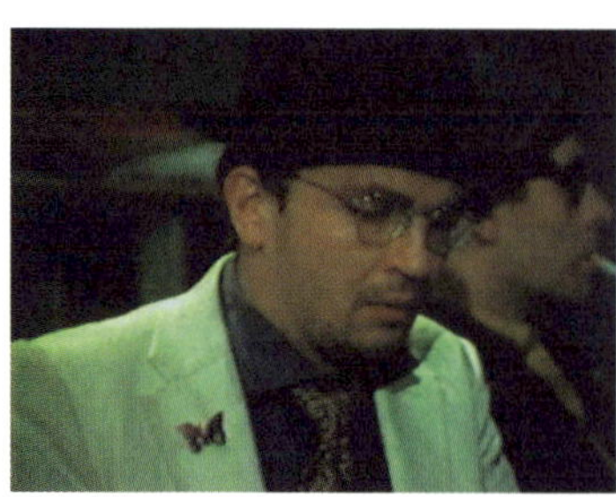
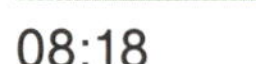
08:18

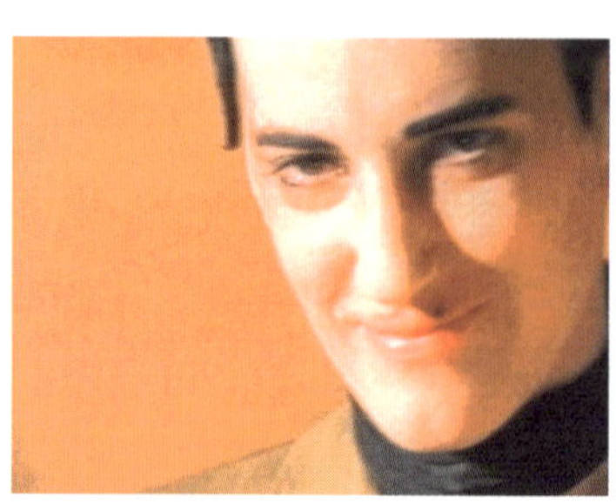
00:02

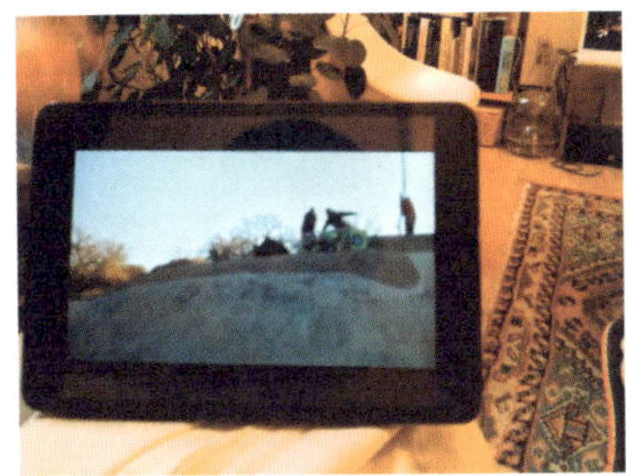
04:07

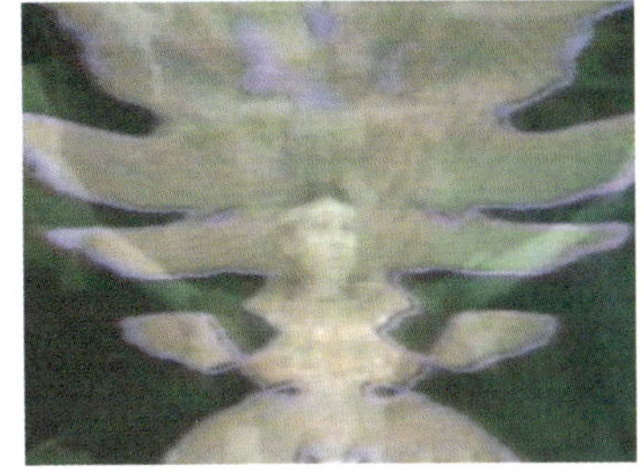
14:38

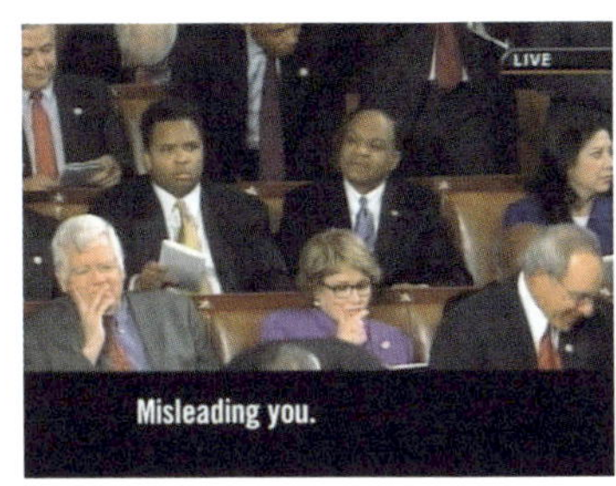

04:40

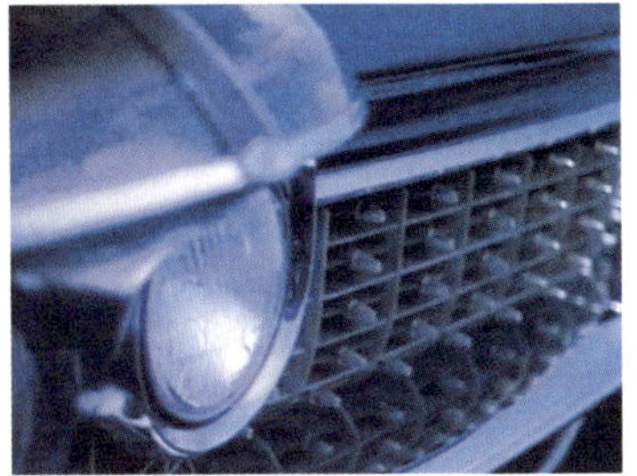
00:27

BROADCASTING: TRANSMISSION
CONVERSATION BETWEEN ULYSSES JENKINS & SONDRA PERRY
MARCH 28, 2018

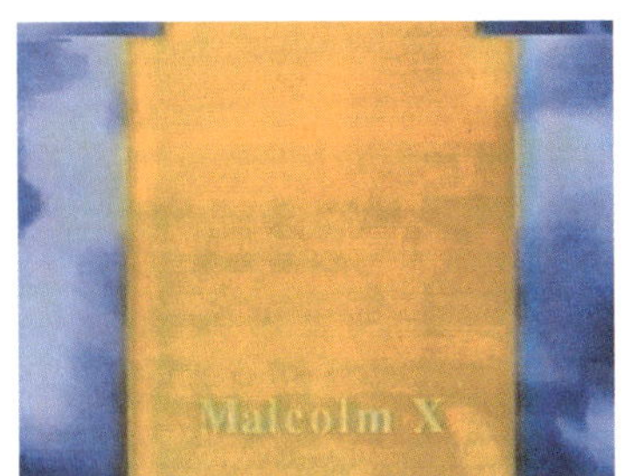

00:44

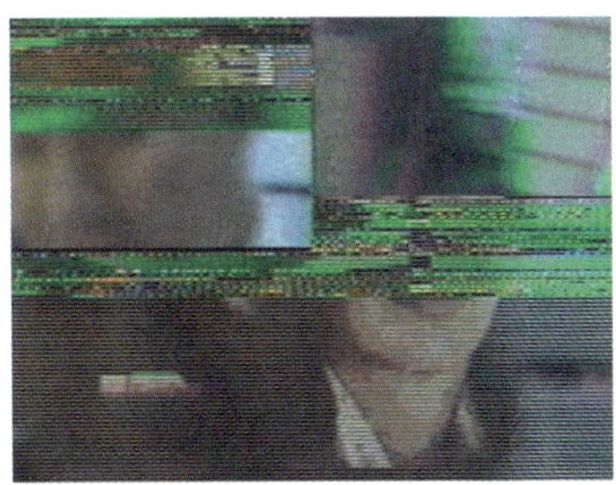
21:21

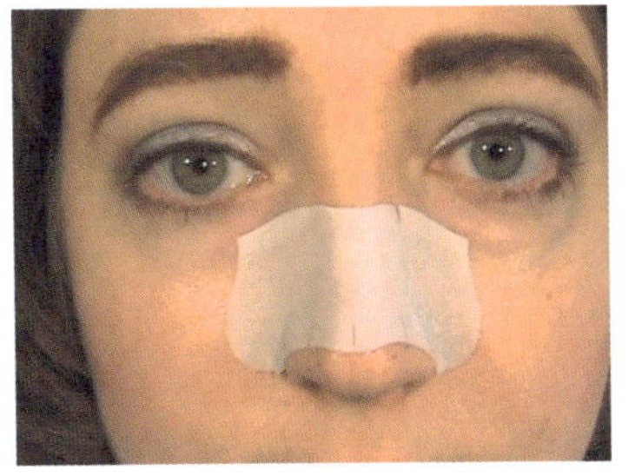
01:33

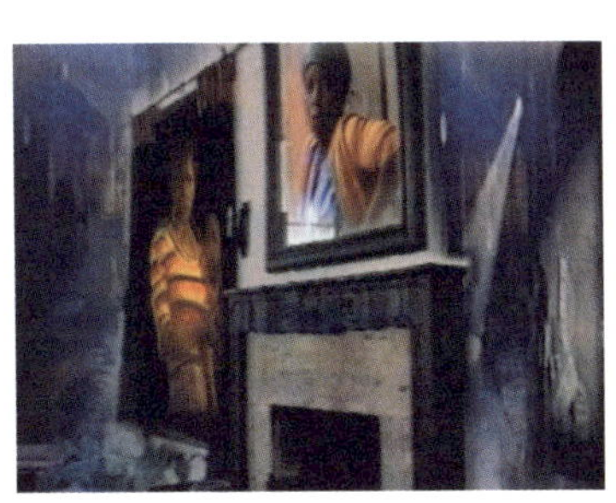
00:30

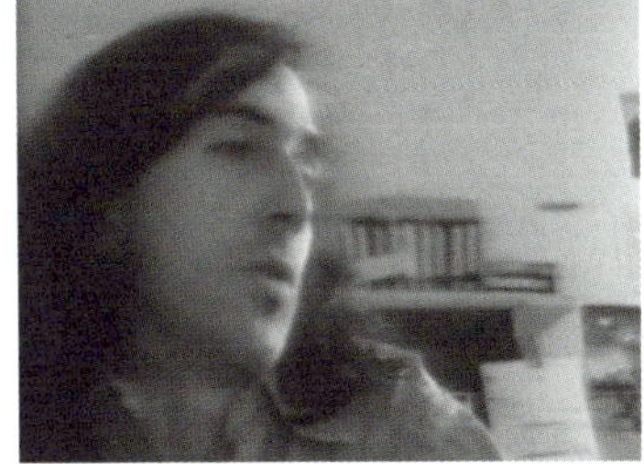
04:33

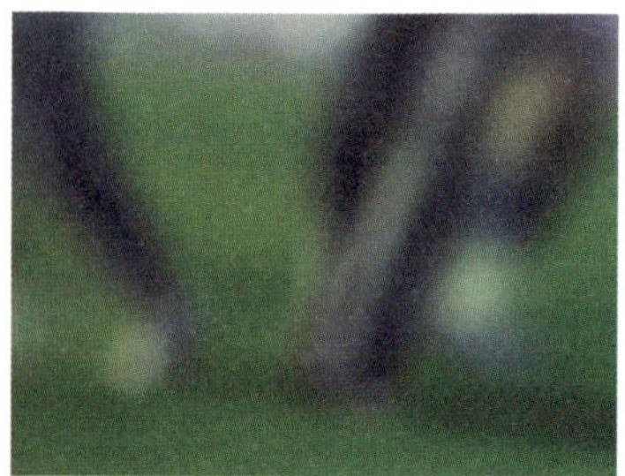
01:16

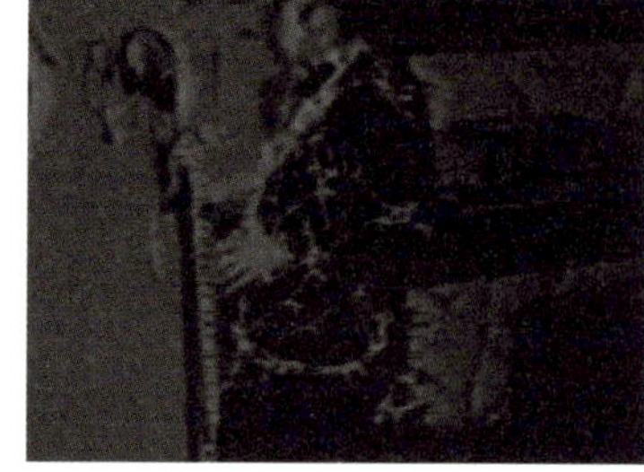
01:36

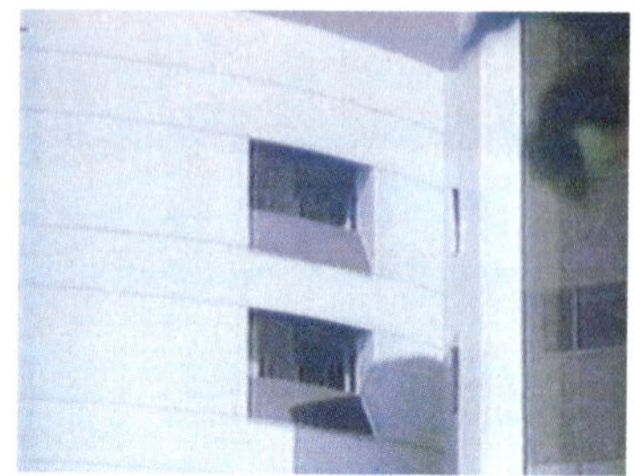
05:51

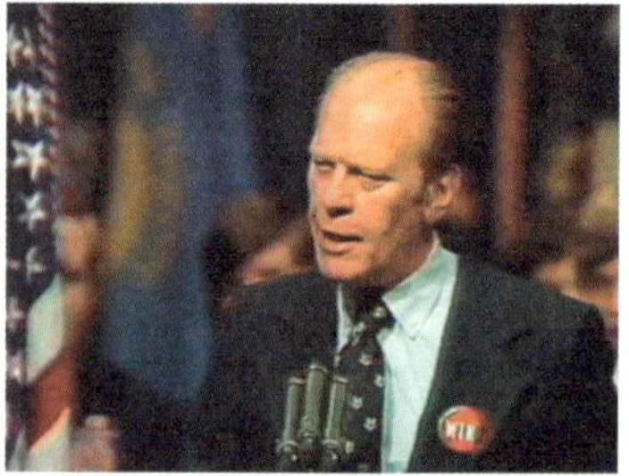
14:00

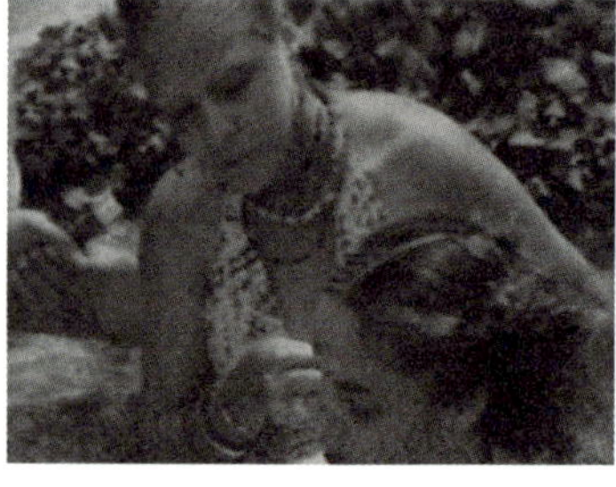
17:24

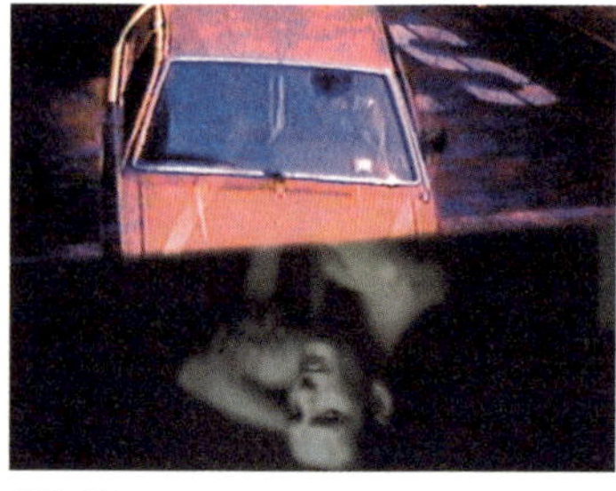
07:12

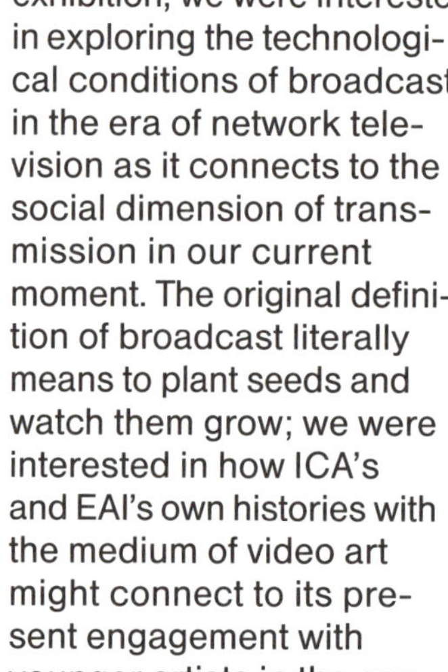

Alex Klein – When Rebecca and I first conceived of this exhibition, we were interested in exploring the technological conditions of broadcast in the era of network television as it connects to the social dimension of transmission in our current moment. The original definition of broadcast literally means to plant seeds and watch them grow; we were interested in how ICA's and EAI's own histories with the medium of video art might connect to its present engagement with younger artists in the age of social media.

Rebecca Cleman – EAI was founded in 1971 by a then-gallerist named Howard Wise who was excited by what artists were doing with technology in the 1950s and 1960s, especially around video and television. Video cameras were available on the consumer-market for the first time and artists and activists were taking advantage of this technology specifically to have a connection to and participation with television. That was an important connection that Howard made in his exhibition *TV as a Creative Medium* in 1969. It was the first exhibition of its kind in the United States. That exhibition inspired him to close his gallery and found EAI as a nonprofit organization dedicated to supporting media artists. Our primary function now is as a distributor of artists' video and media, but for the first few years, EAI helped sponsor various projects and events, such as Charlotte Moorman's annual Avant-Garde Festival, and offered access to equipment and editing facilities. Artists

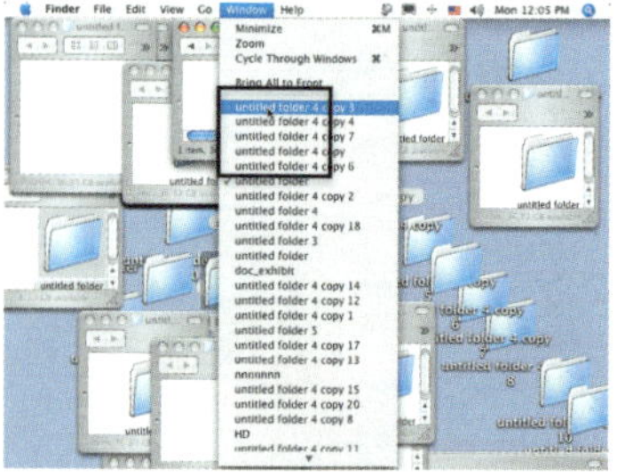
00:47

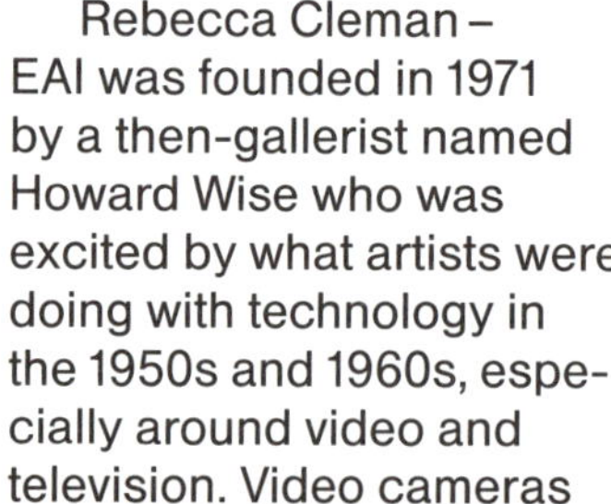
08:18

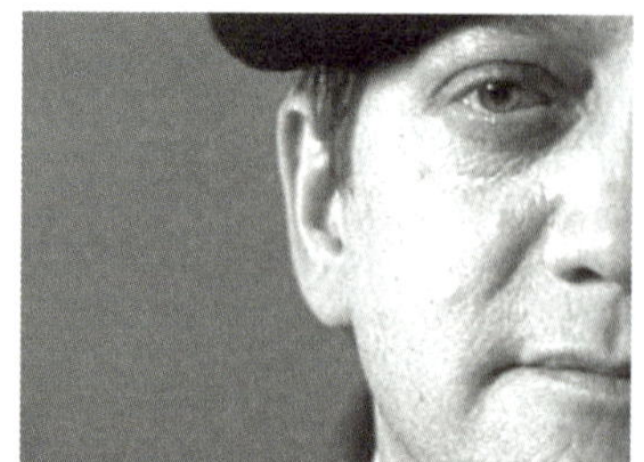
00:02

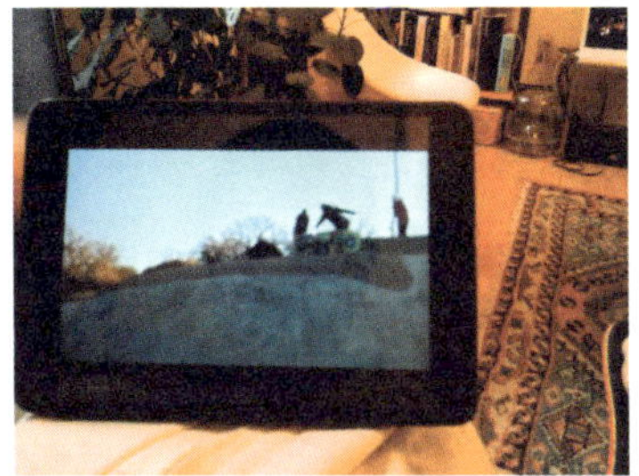

04:07

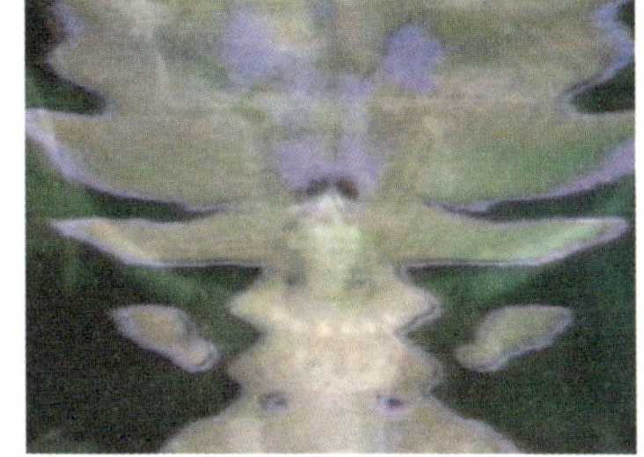

14:38

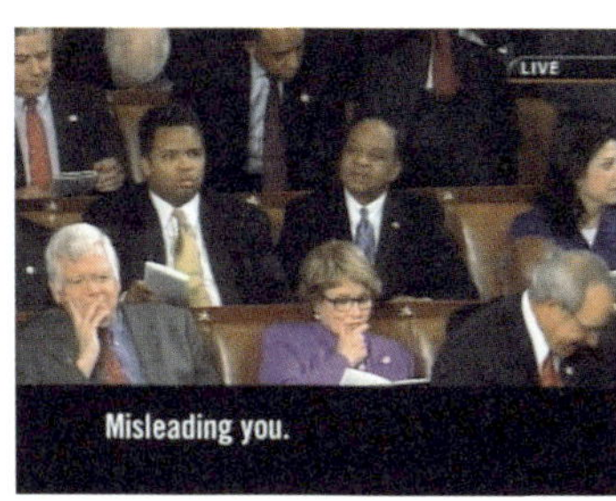

04:40

continue to use the editing facility, actually. In fact, Sondra Perry recently used the facility to finish a work for her *Resident Evil* exhibition at the Kitchen, an organization that Howard and EAI had helped sponsor when the Vasulkas opened it in the 1970s. So EAI remains true to its founding mission, and continues to be actively involved in the production and exhibition of media art.

AK – In this respect, EAI is not just a distribution service, but a crucial site of intergenerational conversation and production. With that in mind, we'll begin by introducing our guests tonight.

RC – I'll begin with Ulysses. It's really an honor to have Ulysses Jenkins visiting us tonight from Los Angeles. Ulysses is a visual artist who has consistently interrogated questions of race and gender as they relate to ritual, history, and the power of the state. In addition to his solo work, he was a founder of Video Venice News, a Los Angeles media collective in the early 1970s, and he had an association with the artist group Studio Z alongside figures such as David Hammons, Frank Parker, Senga Nengudi, and Maren Hassinger. He has done many collaborations with Nengudi and Hassinger in particular. Through his media work, Jenkins explicitly comments on the racism embedded in our culture and its effects on subjectivity. Group exhibitions include *Now Dig This! Art and Black Los Angeles 1960–1980*, which was at the Hammer Museum and came to MoMA PS1; *VideoStudio: Playback* at the Studio Museum in

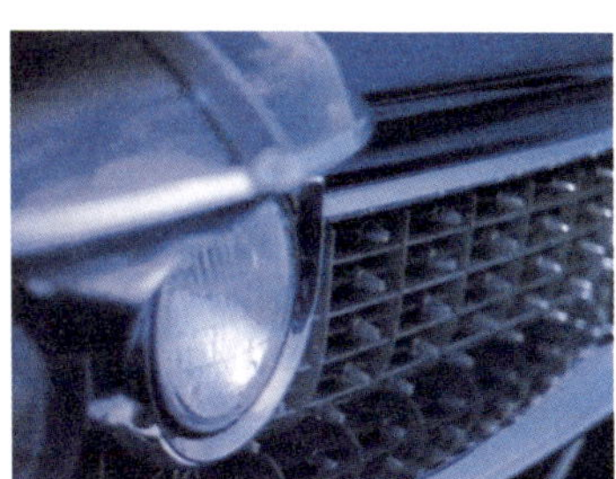

00:27

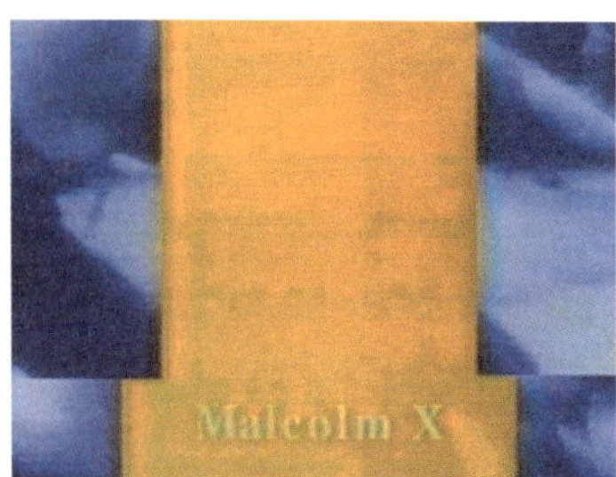

00:44

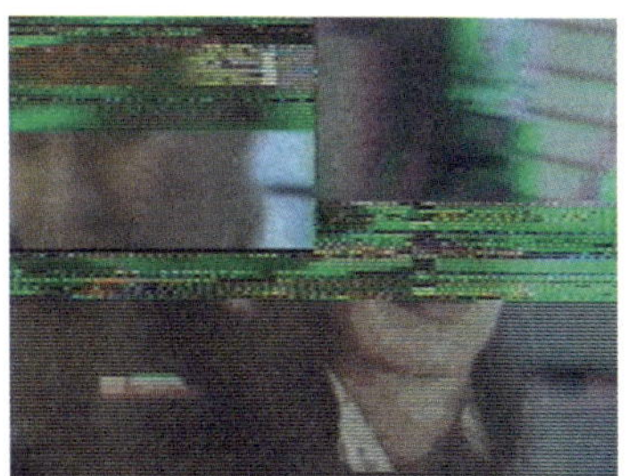

21:21

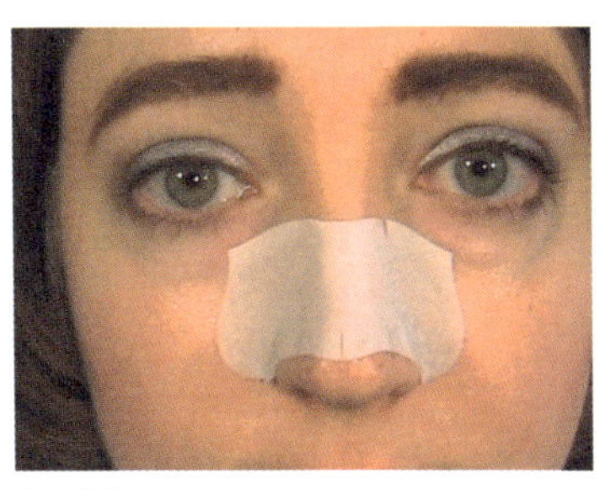

01:33

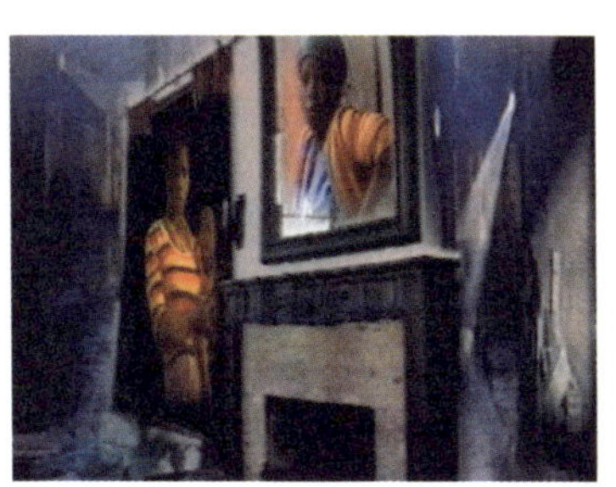

00:30

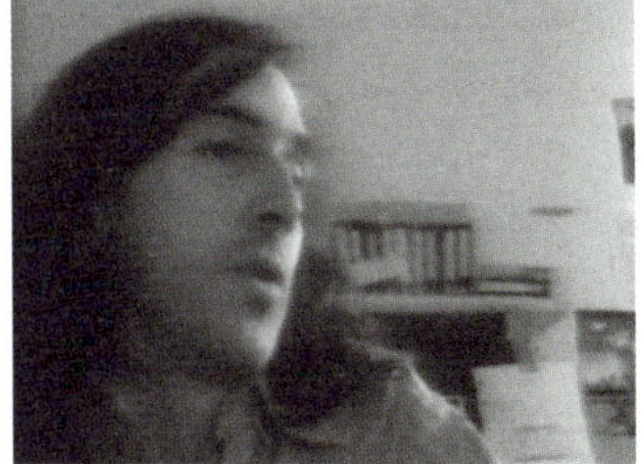

04:33

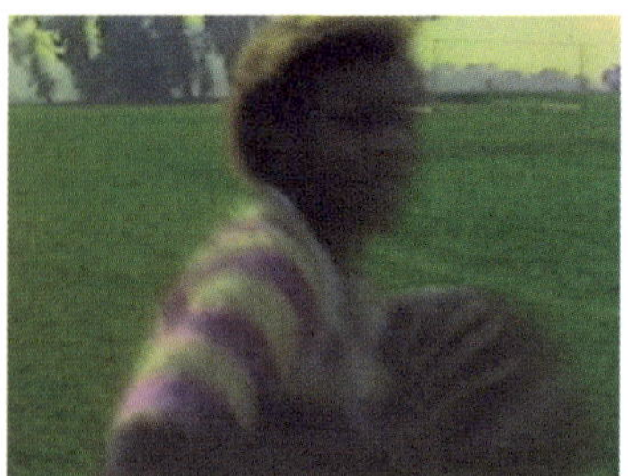

01:16

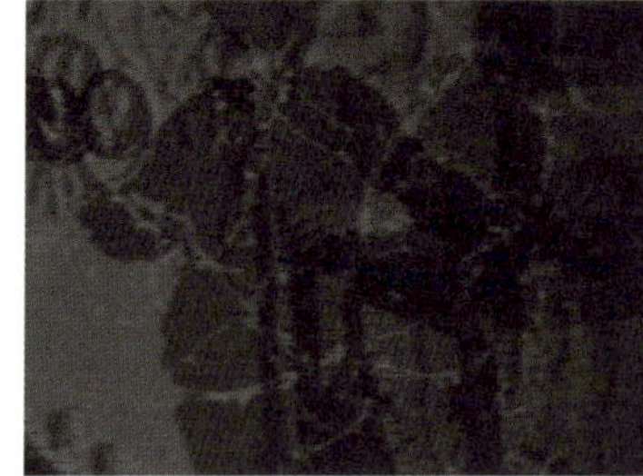

01:36

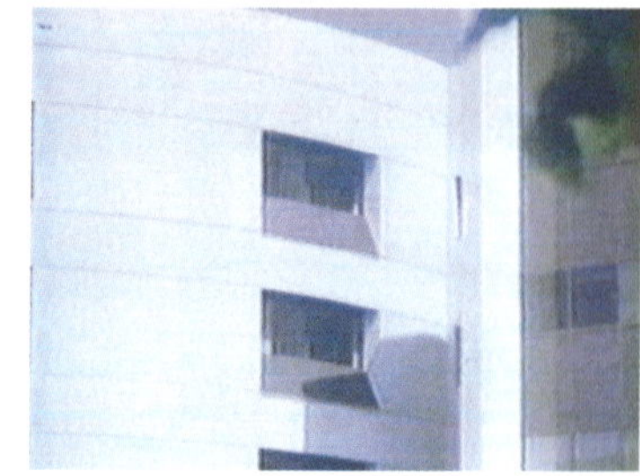

05:51

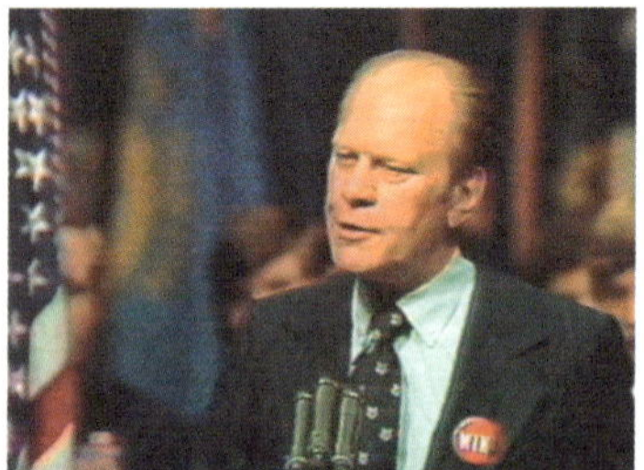

14:00

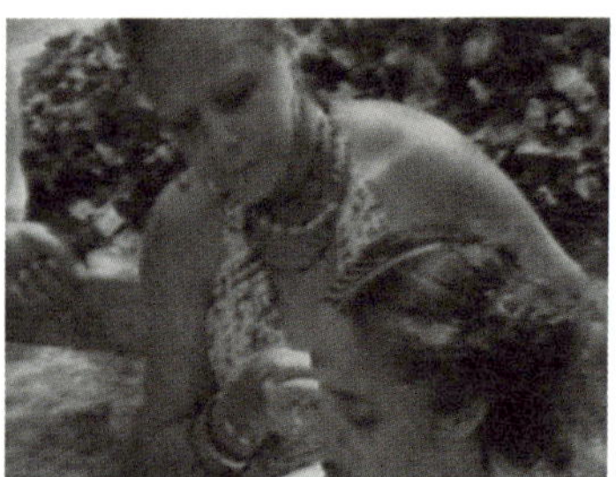

17:24

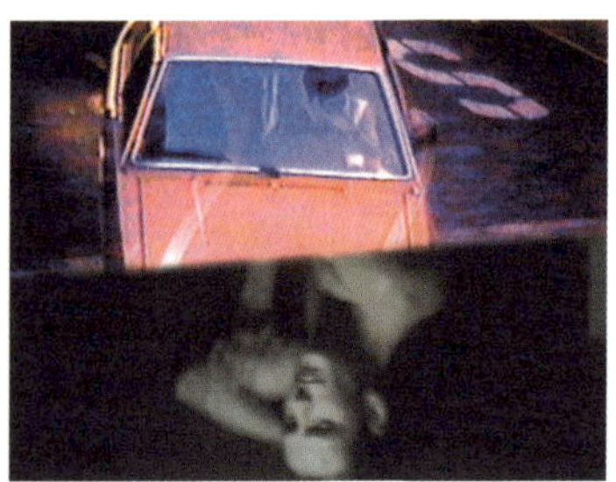

07:12

Harlem, New York; *Sympathetic Magic: Video Myths and Rituals* at the Armory Center for the Arts Pasadena, California; and *California Video* at the J. Paul Getty Museum in Los Angeles. He was born in Los Angeles and still lives there, and is Professor of Art in the Claire Trevor School of the Arts and an affiliate professor of the African American Studies program at University of California, Irvine. We are really thrilled that he is here tonight.

Ulysses Jenkins – Thank you.

AK – We will get the introductions out of the way. It is my absolute pleasure to welcome Sondra Perry back to ICA. Sondra is an artist based in Perth Amboy. Her work mobilizes the digital tools of production to critique questions of representation while unveiling the seams within our technologies. In her work she often uses her own body, sites of community, and family narratives to question what we see, how we see it, and how those images that we consume in mass culture are produced and how they might be torn apart. Recent solo exhibitions include *Typhoon coming on*, at Serpentine Gallery in London and Bridget Donahue in New York in 2018, as well as *Eclogue for [in]HABITABILITY* at the Seattle Art Museum in 2017, and her phenomenal *Resident Evil* at the Kitchen in New York in 2016. She has been included in numerous group exhibitions: most recently, *Trigger: Gender as a Tool and a Weapon* at the New Museum in New York, and we can look back also to the *Greater New York*

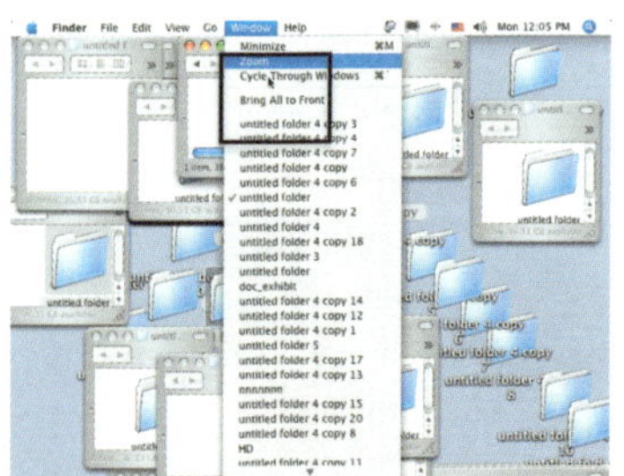

00:47

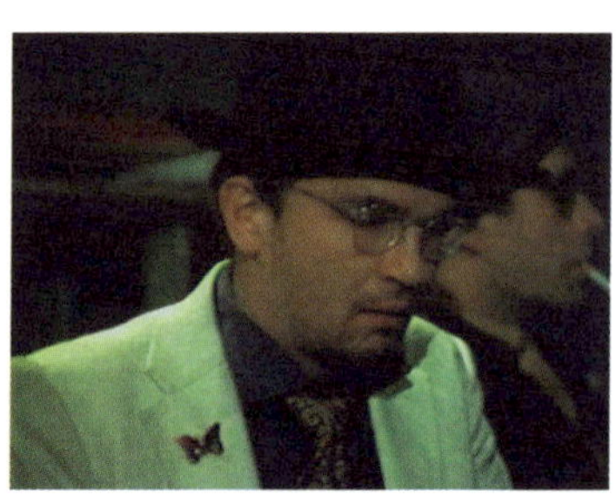

08:18

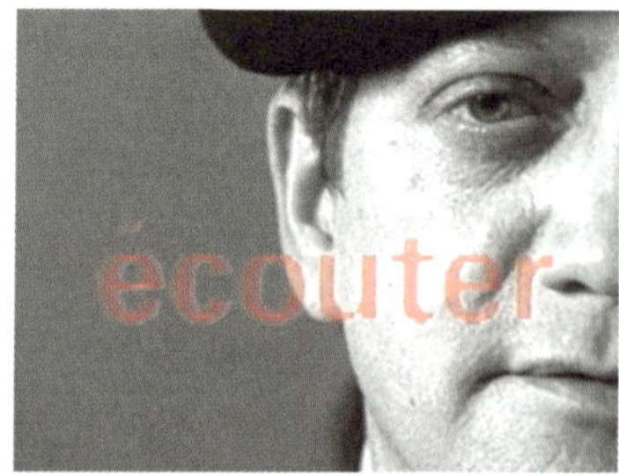

00:02

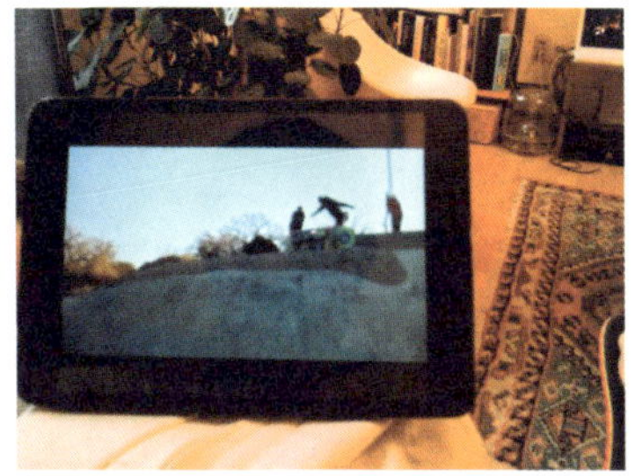

04:08

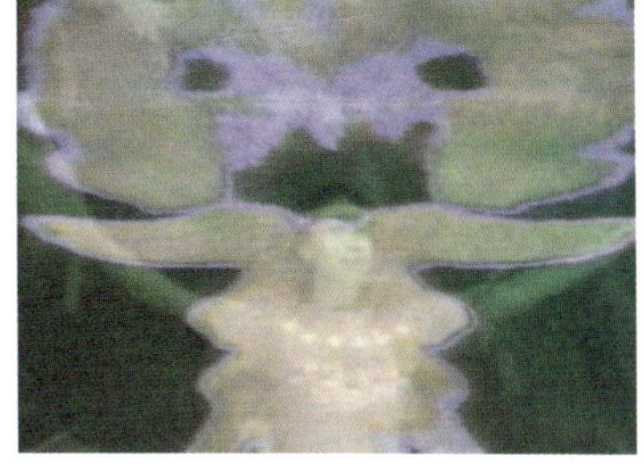

14:39

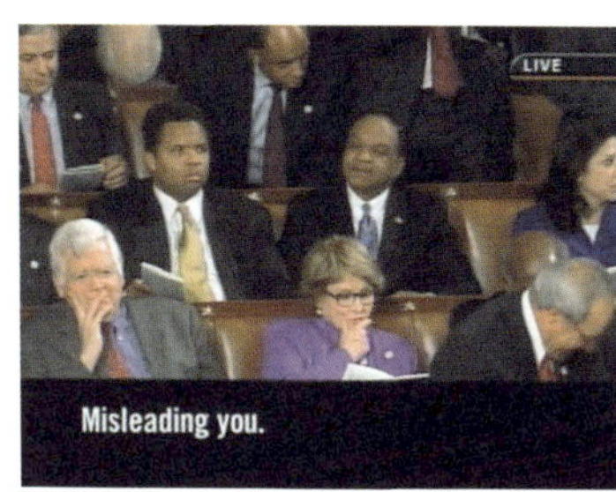

04:41

exhibition at MoMA PS1 in 2015, and, of course, the exhibition that we produced here at ICA in collaboration with the Henie Onstad Kunstsenter, Norway, in 2017, *Myths of the Marble*.

We realize these are just brief overviews, so let's take this opportunity to dive into a more substantial conversation. Ulysses, even though many people might know you first and foremost as a media artist working in video, you really have a background in painting. It was really interesting for us to discover your early work in mural making.

UJ – I began my undergraduate studies as a painting and drawing graduate. When I got out of school, I began painting murals. As you can see, the mural that is featured here is one that I did on a DMV in Los Angeles. You can't tell the scale: that's three stories high, painted by myself. The title of that piece was *Transportation Brought Art to the People* and the picture here is me being congratulated by Los Angeles's first and only African American mayor, Mayor Tom Bradley. As you can see, there I am on the scaffolding. It was quite an adventure to say the least, scale and what have you.

AK – Can you talk a little bit about how, in the culture of Venice at that time, you began working with video?

UJ – Well, I was painting murals and one of the gentlemen who was in Video Venice News, Michael Zingale, asked me about this video workshop that was happening on the boardwalk and he said, "Are you interested?" Independent video was very new and the beginnings of independent filmmaking were also on the

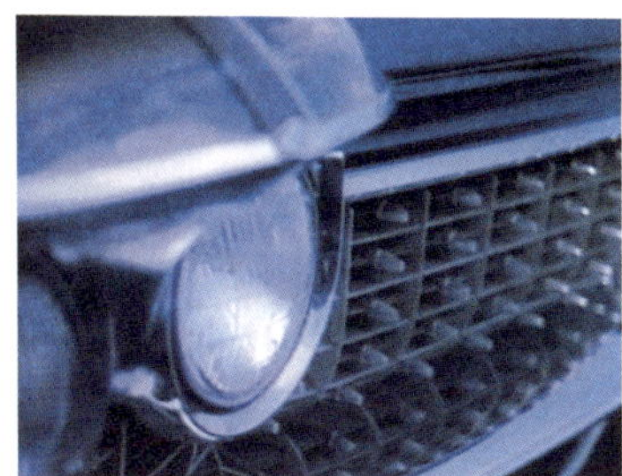

00:28

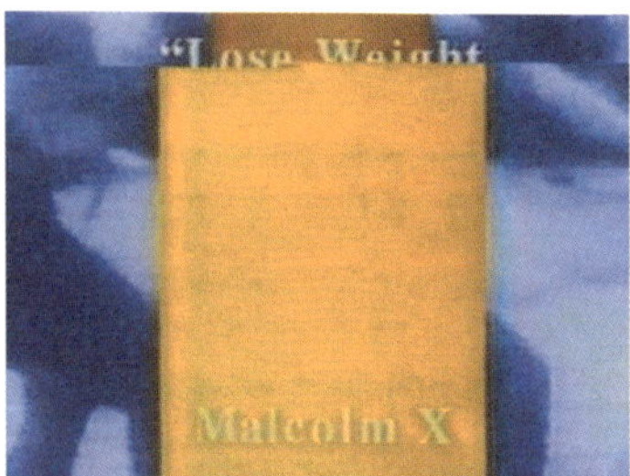

00:45

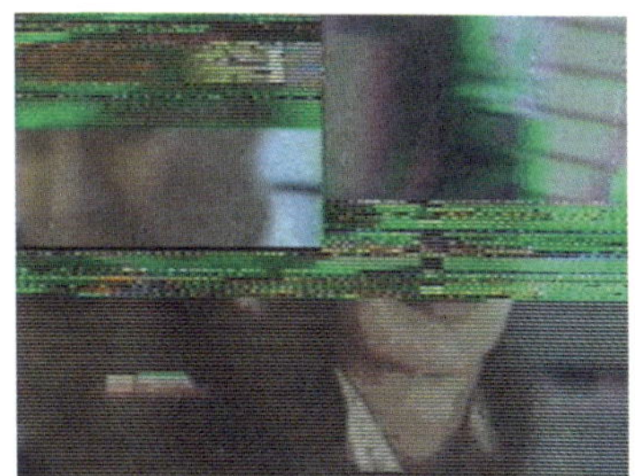

21:22

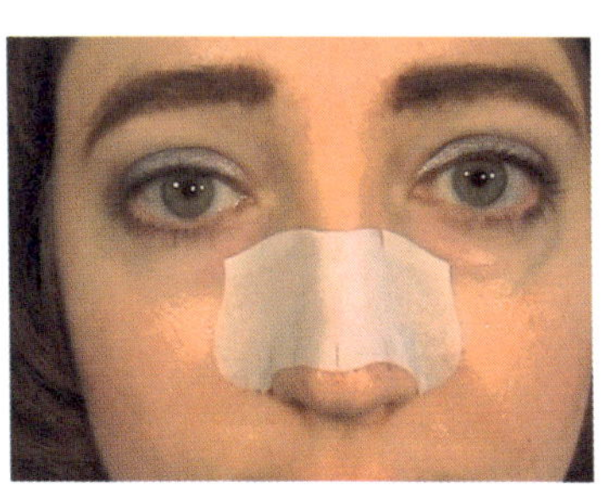

01:34

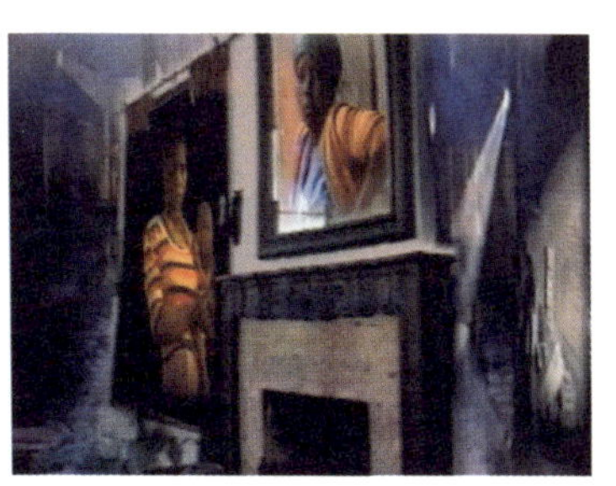

00:31

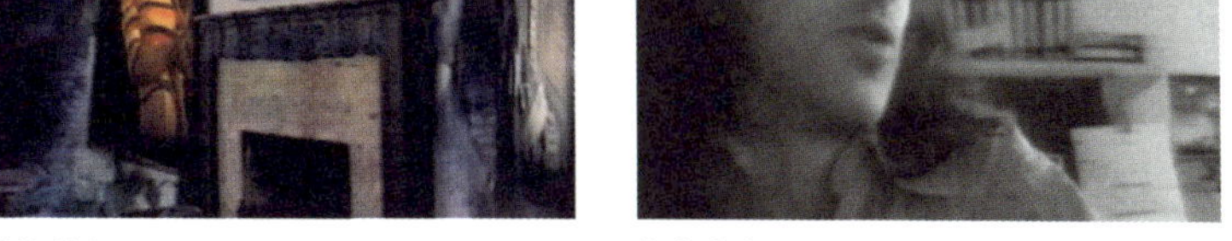

04:34

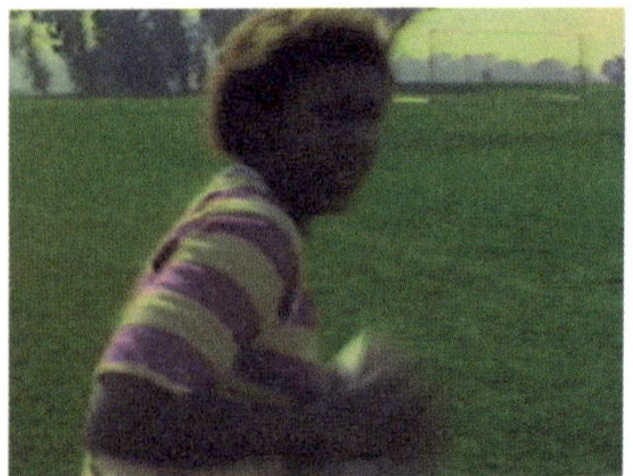

01:16

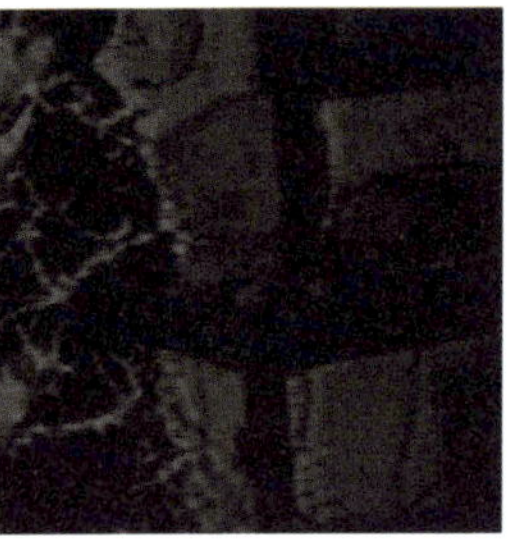

01:36

05:51

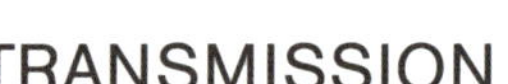

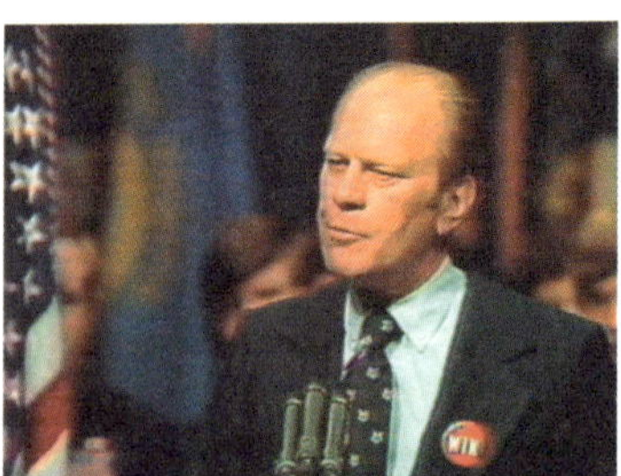

14:00

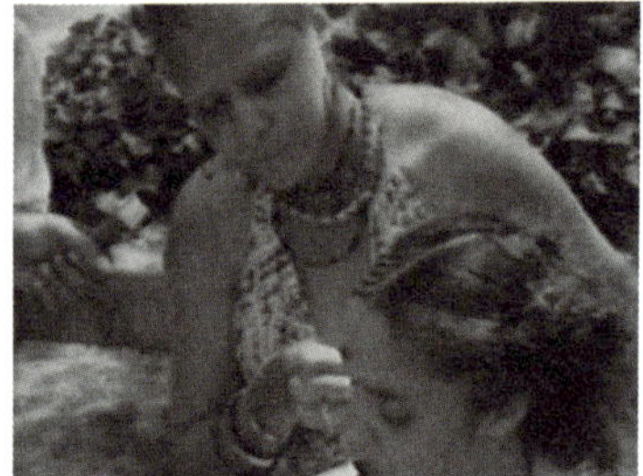

17:24

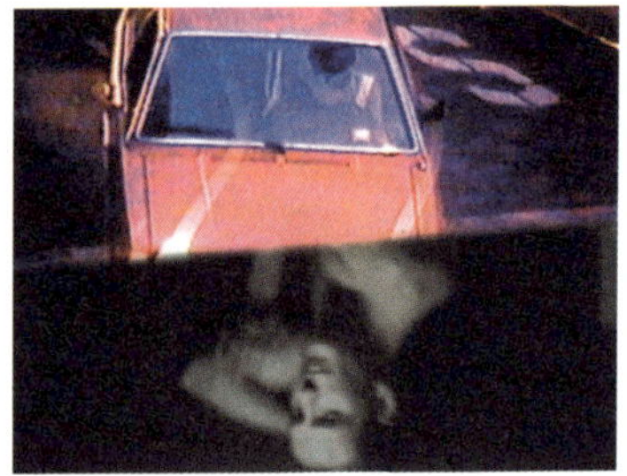

07:12

horizon. For example, *Easy Rider* (1968, produced by Peter Fonda and directed by Dennis Hopper) and *Sweet SweetBack's Baadasssss Song* (1971, produced and directed by Melvin Van Peebles).

I was very curious about it, and at first I said, "I've got my wall to keep me warm, so I think I'll take a pass." But eventually my curiosity got the best of me and I went down, and I was fascinated. The whole thing with early video, of course, was that you could record things and immediately play back, then erase them, and at the same time you could become your own producer. From that standpoint, I was very curious about what you could do. Meanwhile, there was this event that you will see here called the Watts Festival, commemorating the Watts riots in the mid-1960s. The local news media was telling everyone, "Don't come to this event." This was I think a ploy by the police to not only maintain crowd control, but also keep people from outside the community from coming to this event. You could check out this equipment from the video workshop on a personal usage basis, so I said, "Let's go to the festival and we'll show what really is going on." So that's how that documentary came to be.

AK – And the advent in the late 1960s of the Sony Portapak made the technology more accessible and less cumbersome.

UJ – Yes, because of the Portapak we ended up having the opportunity to be on stage with this group. Have you ever heard of a group called War? Actually the recording in this video is one of the few recordings of them performing live.

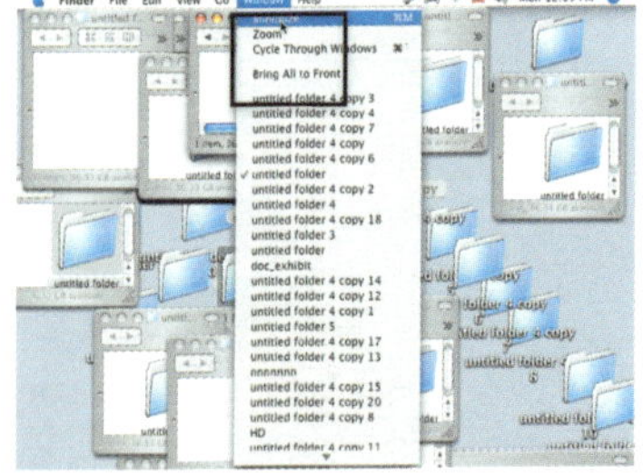

00:47

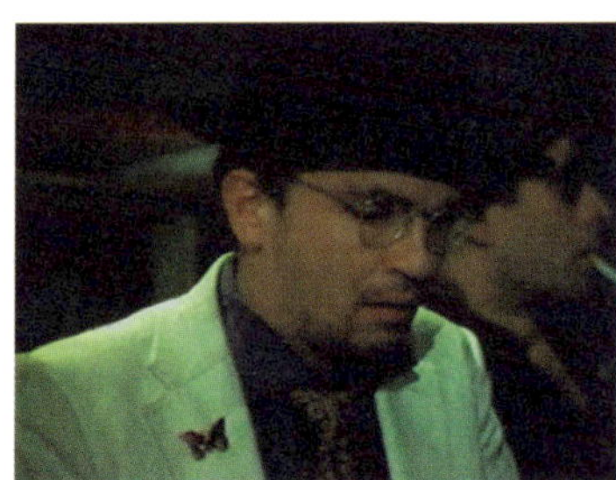

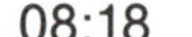

08:18

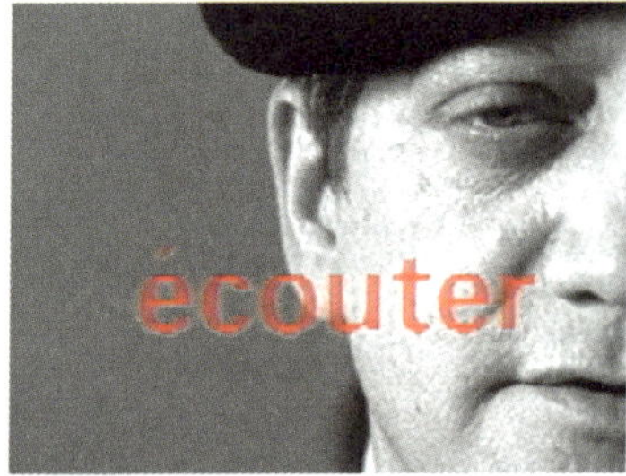

00:02

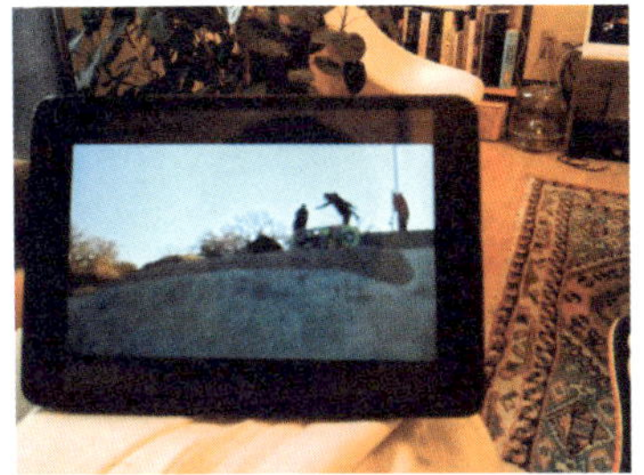
04:08

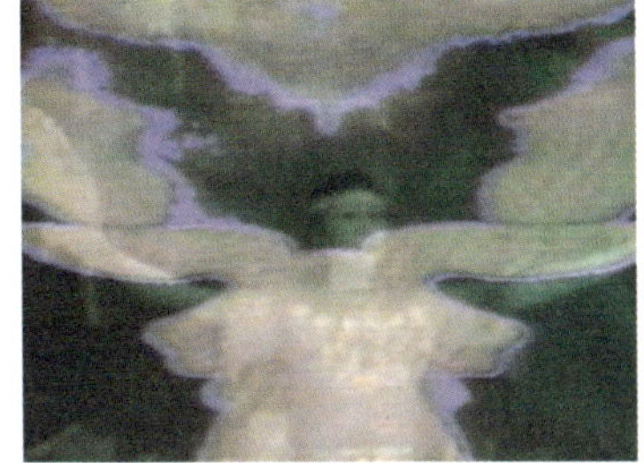
14:39

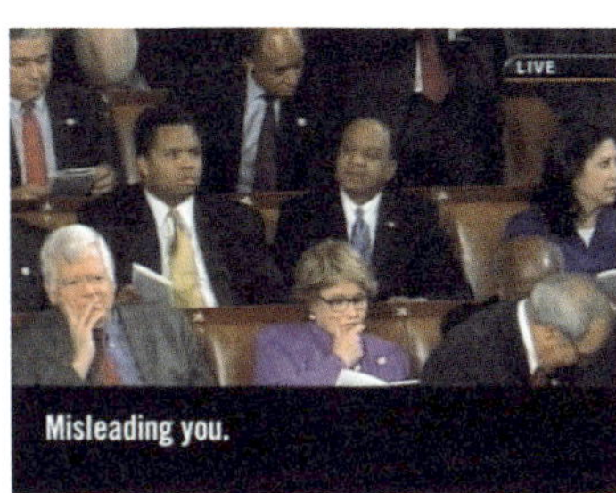

04:41

AK – So in addition to this intervention in mass media and making your own images, it also stands as an important document. It has this double function of preserving these performances and important people like Cecil Ferguson who you interview.

UJ – For the most part, for those people who know the history of this medium, a lot of what was being recorded for the first time were documentaries of this sort: community-based and of course with Cecil, who started out as a janitor at the Los Angeles County Museum of Art and eventually became a curator through his interest and what he was trying to do—especially for the African American community. When I shot this footage of the festival, I was able to get him and his wife, Miriam Ferguson, to have a conversation with me since he was an original resident and create a vocal narrative based on the Watts community point of view.

AK – So, fast forward a few years. In this early work you take a different approach from documenting to reclaiming images. Do you want to set this up? We have a short clip we are going to play.

UJ – This is *Mass of Images* (1978). For the most part I was very curious about the notion of the Black image in Western art. To whatever degree, most of the time in the Western art context, the Black image was presented in a context of servitude. I thought, well, they are carrying this premise over. They carried it over in radio, they carried it over in television. Anyone know *Amos 'n' Andy*? So, I said, if I am going to be in this medium I need to recontextualize how people understand

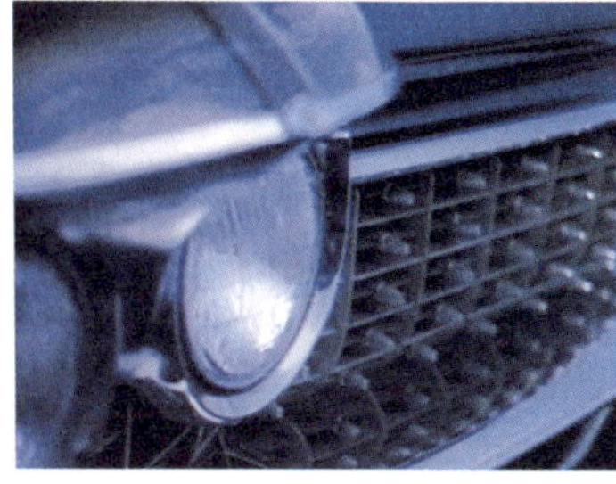
00:28

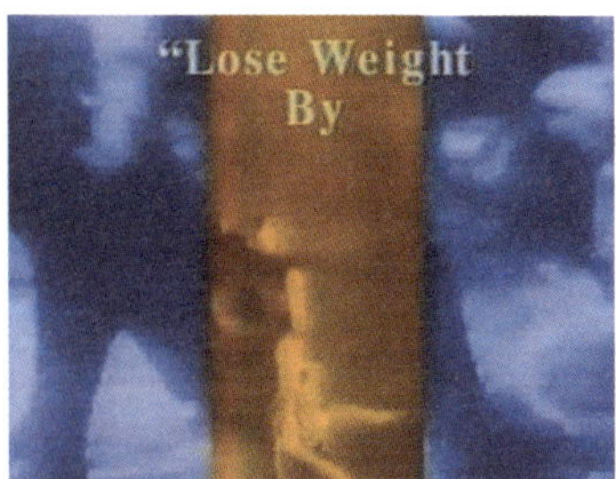

00:45

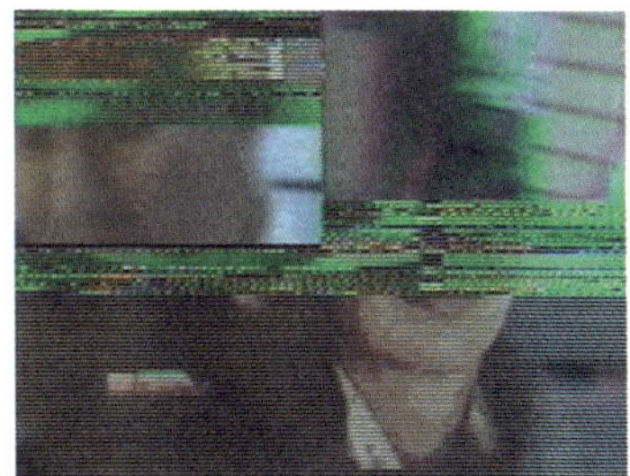
21:22

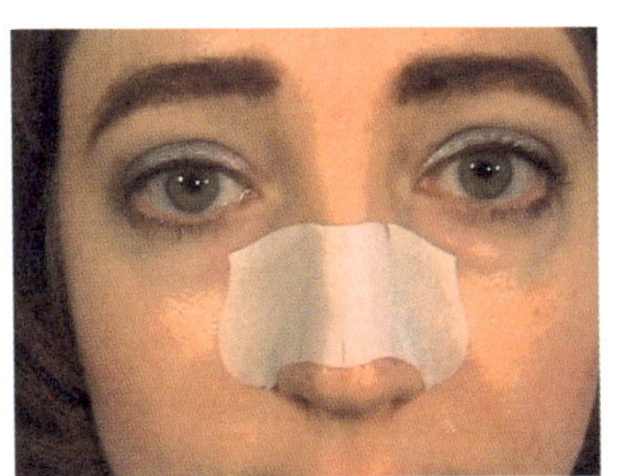
01:34

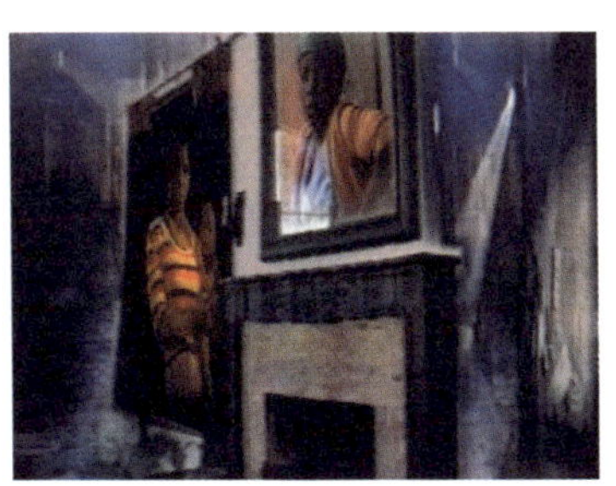
00:31

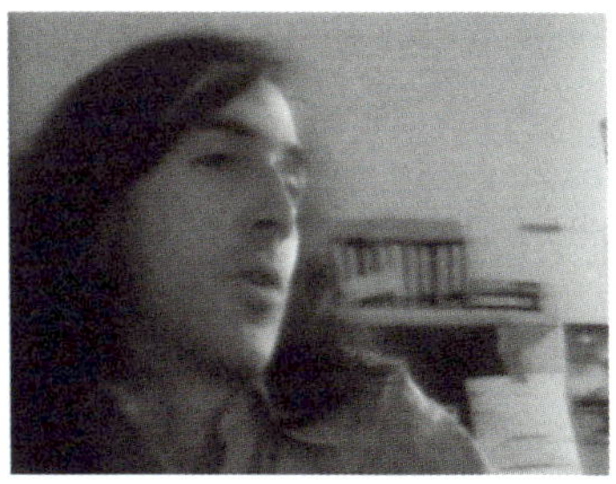
04:34

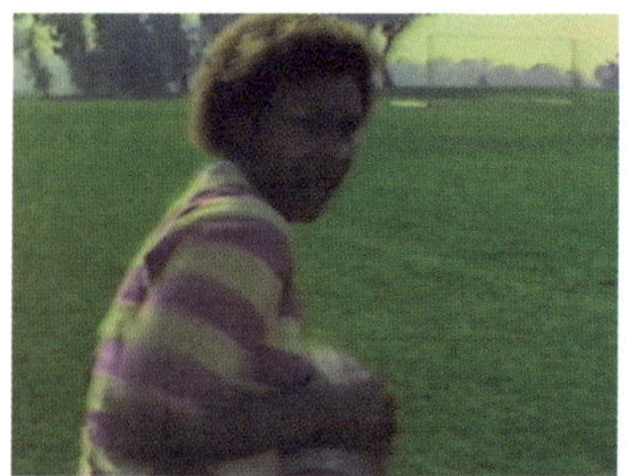

01:16

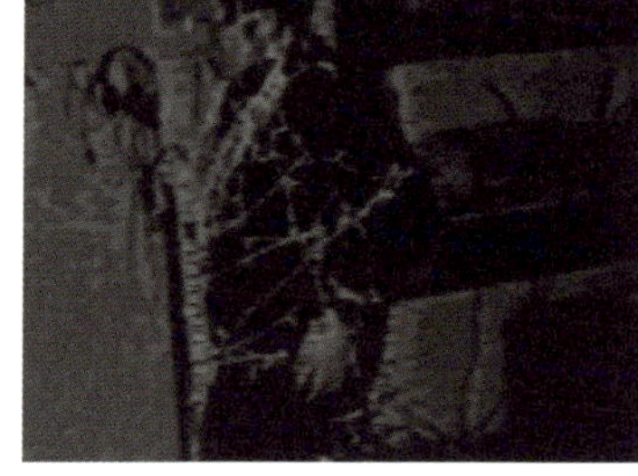

01:36

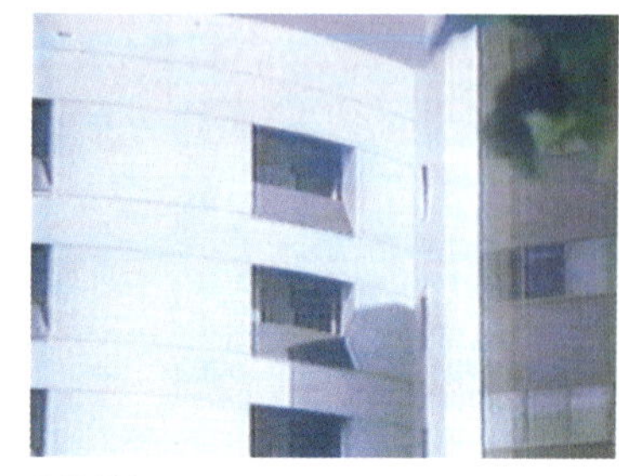

05:51

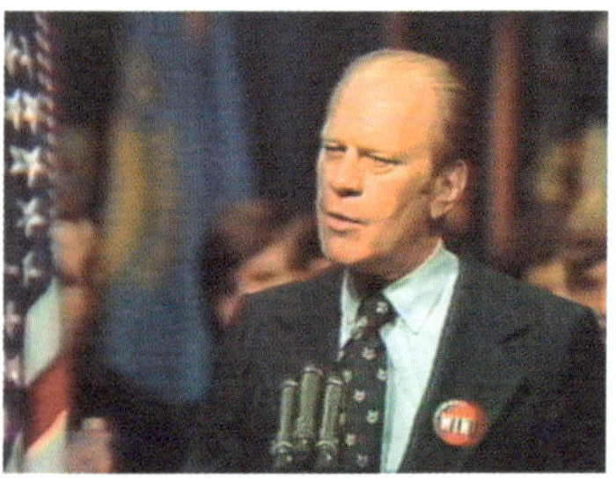

14:00

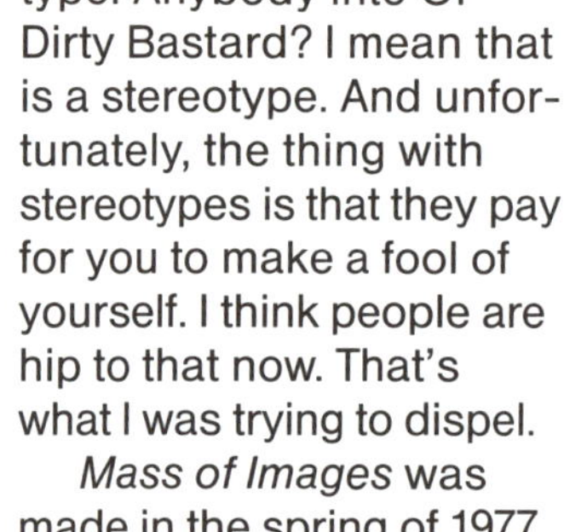

this established stereotype. Anybody into Ol' Dirty Bastard? I mean that is a stereotype. And unfortunately, the thing with stereotypes is that they pay for you to make a fool of yourself. I think people are hip to that now. That's what I was trying to dispel.

Mass of Images was made in the spring of 1977. I was preparing to go to graduate school. I wanted to make a piece of work that I could give the faculty at the time at the college I was going to an indication of what I wanted to study. For the most part, what a lot of people today maybe don't think about is that there wasn't necessarily a path for me to follow. There weren't a lot of other African American video artists. Although I found out there was another gentleman named Tony Ramos out here on the East Coast who had been working in video and another guy named Ed Bereal who was working in LA. Anyone heard of Bodacious Buggerrilla? That was the name of a performance group and he was doing a Black version of *Laugh-In*. So as a matter of fact, when I saw that piece it influenced me to make this piece, *Two-Zone Transfer* (1979), which again, back to the study that I was pursuing, was trying to dispel the misnomers of the Black image in television at this point and Western art. *Two-Zone Transfer*, the title comes from in LA, if you're taking a bus from one side of town to another, which would geographically put you in two different neighborhoods, you had to ask for a two-zone transfer.

AK – And Kerry James Marshall is in this video.

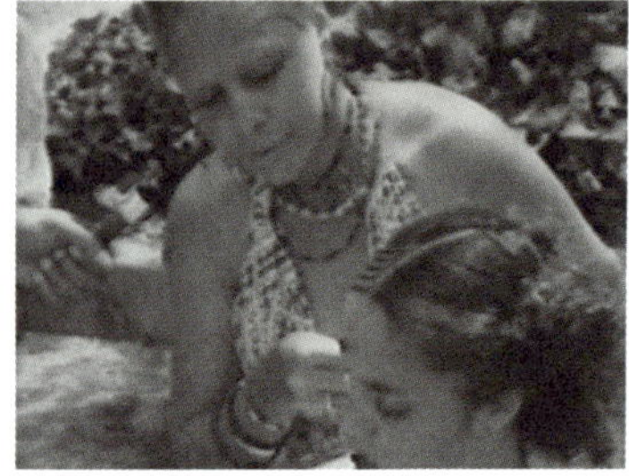

17:24

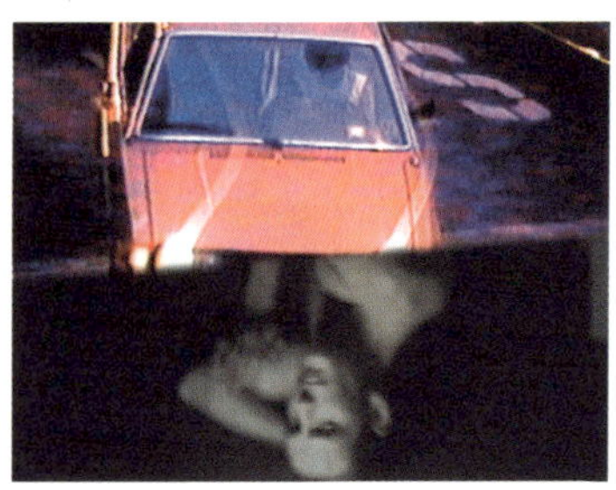

07:12

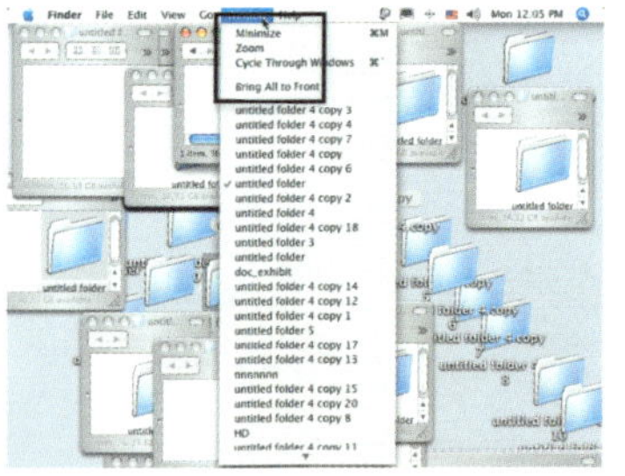

00:47

08:18

00:02

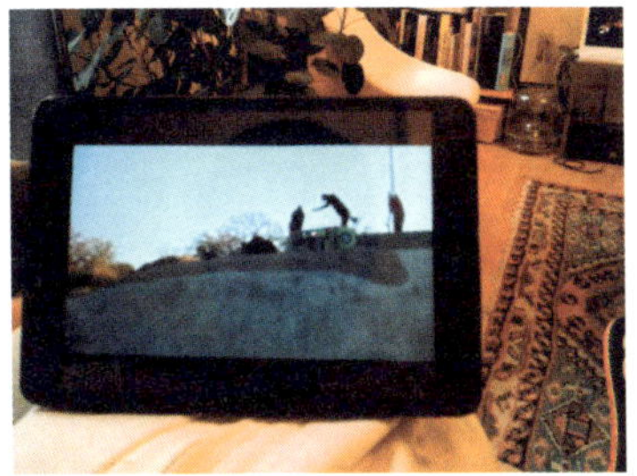
04:08

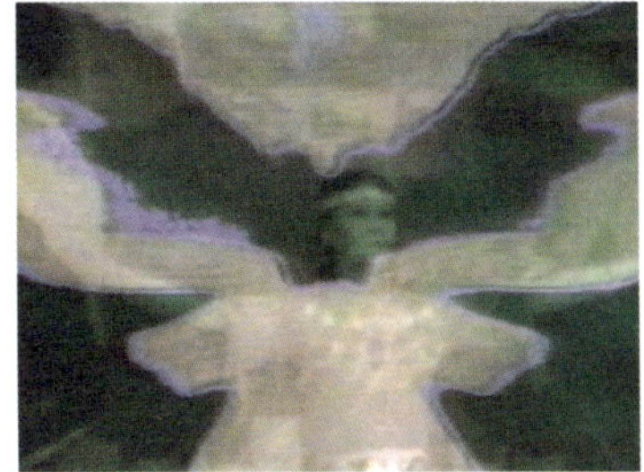
14:39

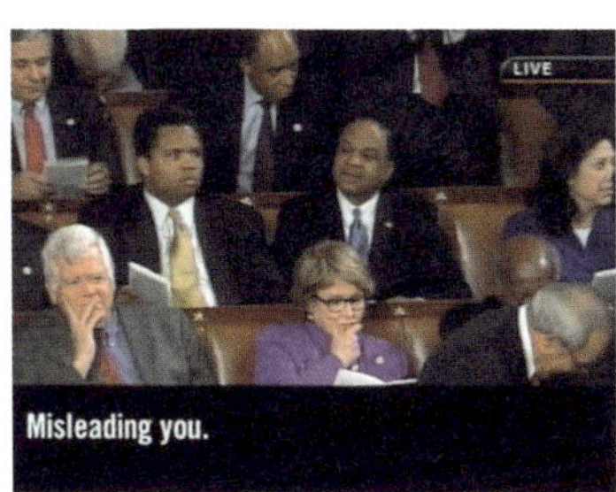

04:41

UJ – Yes, I went to school with him and we had a lot of interesting conversations along these lines. I came up with this idea that I wanted to make this project and he actually was kind enough to perform in it.

RC – Specifically, as a minstrel wearing a Richard Nixon face mask. Maybe you can say a little more about the iconography in *Two-Zone Transfer*. For me, *Two-Zone Transfer* also speaks a little to the *Twilight Zone*. Maybe I'm making too literal a connection?

UJ – See the minstrel show was created in a way to bring Black characters into the entertainment business by the Barnum & Bailey Circus kind of sphere. At that time the industrial revolution was occurring, they had all the immigrants from Europe coming into New York, but they did not have any kind of representation for the Black people who were living in New York. So this blackface character was invented, and at the time minstrel shows became supposedly the moniker of Black people. So we use this notion in this performance to tell the story of the black minstrel and how that disenfranchisement had been the way in which Black people were to be considered as a stereotype and we see it go onward into cartoons and all this stuff. For the most part this whole notion, as they say in the video, of "blackening up" so you have Bert Williams, who is a very light-skinned Black having to put cork on his face to be in this particular entertainment field. He was making more money than the president by "blackening up." So what does that say to a person's

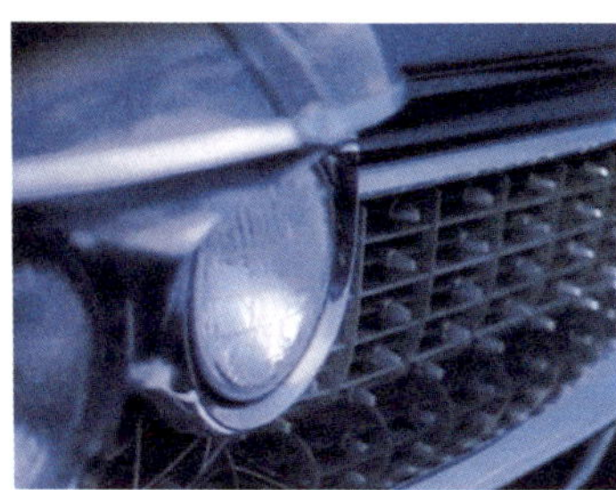
00:28

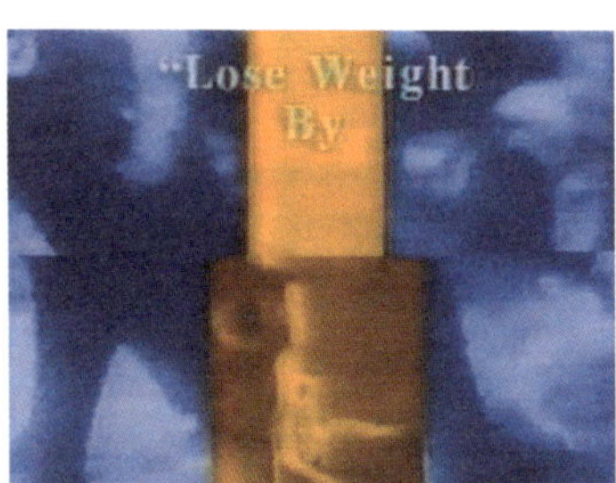

00:45

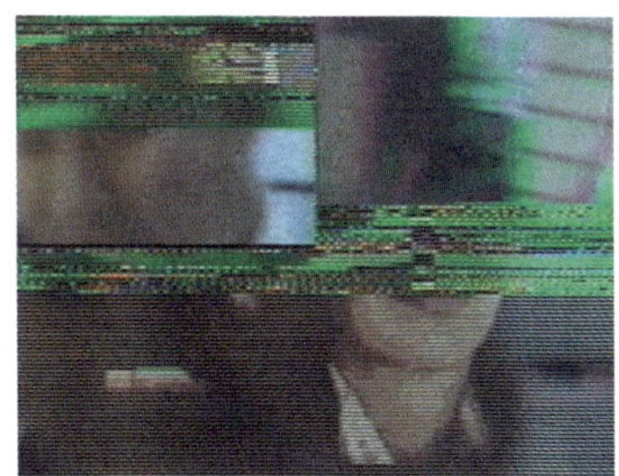
21:22

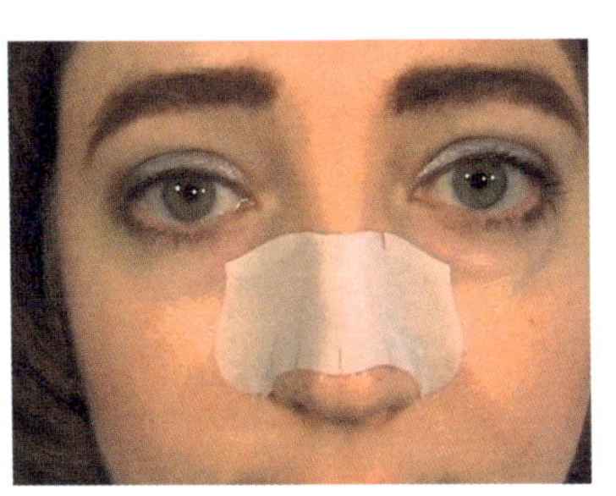
01:34

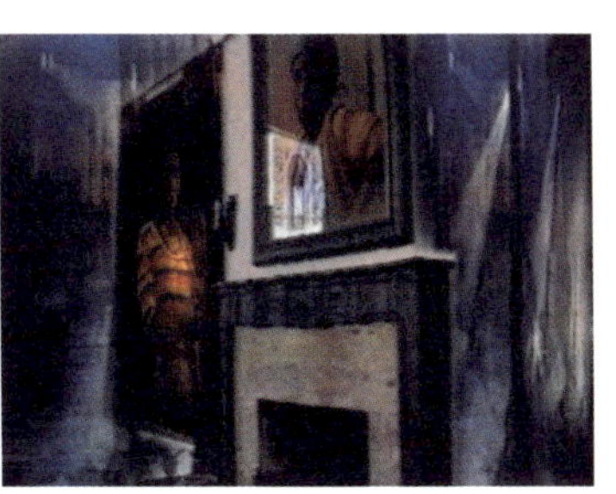
00:31

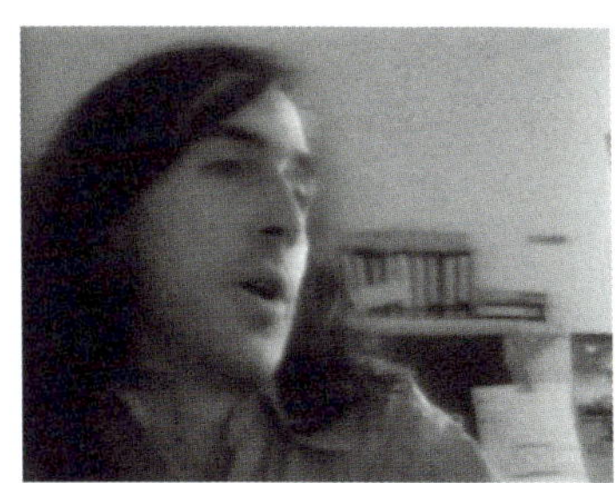
04:34

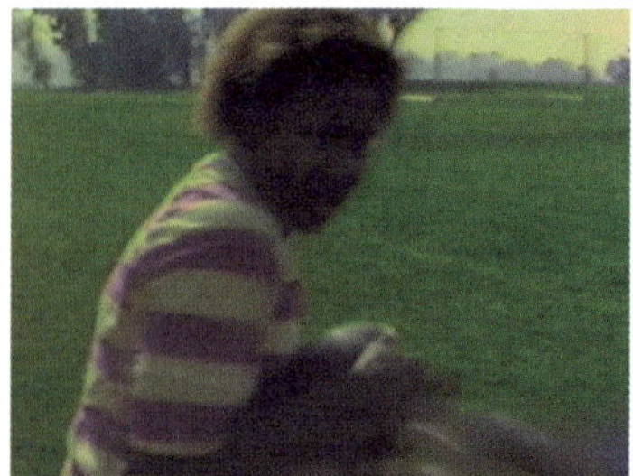
01:16

01:36

05:51

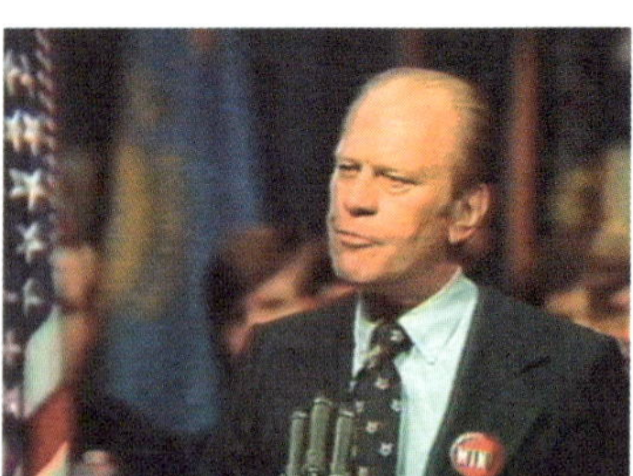
14:00

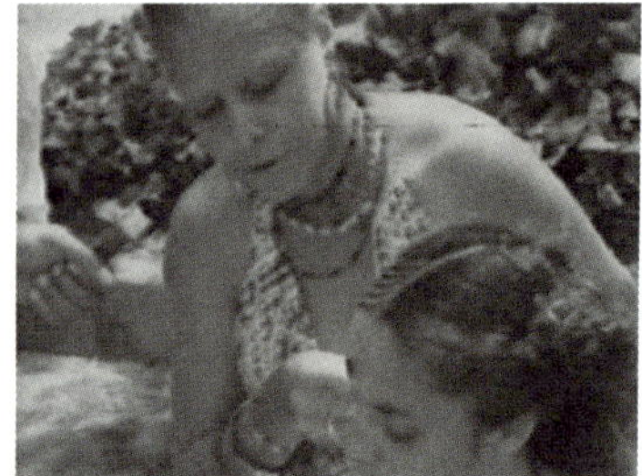
17:24

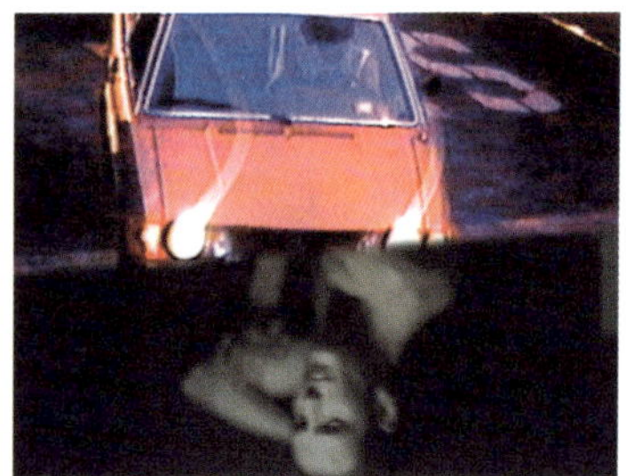
07:12

character? That's basically what it is: disenfranchising yourself. That's generally what happens when you play a stereotype.

AK – You performed a lot in your work, especially early on. Can you elaborate on your interest in "doggereal" (pronounced doggerel), especially in light of your video *Inconsequential Doggereal* (1981), which was on view during the run of this exhibition?

UJ – *Inconsequential Doggereal* was a change I wanted to make earlier on in my career, but I had to hold off while I was in grad school. Actually, for those of you who may not have had this experience I'm about to describe to you, when I was in grad school, the students—my Caucasian friends—told me I could forget about having a career in the art world because I was going to have to copy their culture. That kind of disturbed me from a standpoint where I said, "Well, why is that?" That is because the notion of what an African American cultural identity could be at that time. Timewise this is 1977, 1978, 1979. The whole thing of identity politics and multiculturalism was about to break open. For the most part, I said, "Okay, I am going to have to show you." But the thing that indicated to me was that I still needed a form or a forum to present what I was thinking. From my then instructors Charles White and Betye Saar I gleaned insights that I needed to proclaim my own conceptual notions. And so I turned to the notion of ritual. That's what *Inconsequential Doggereal*, my first video conceptual performance foremost is: a

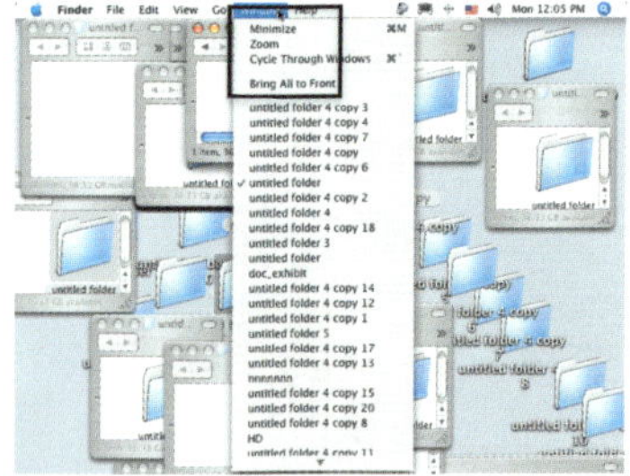
00:47

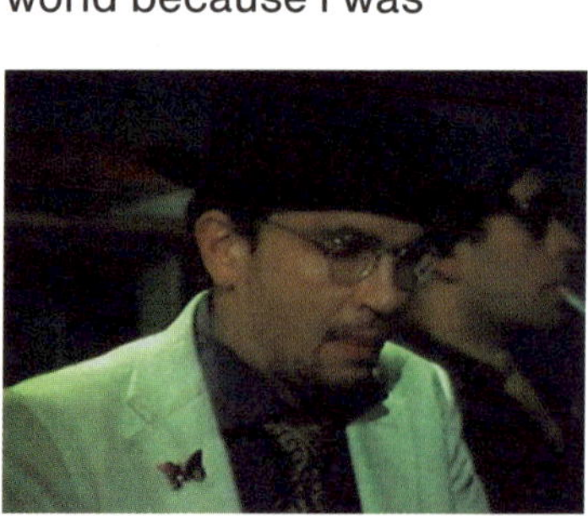
08:18

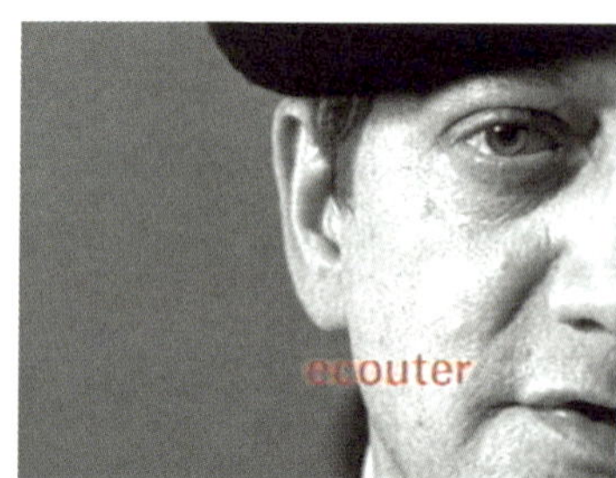

00:02

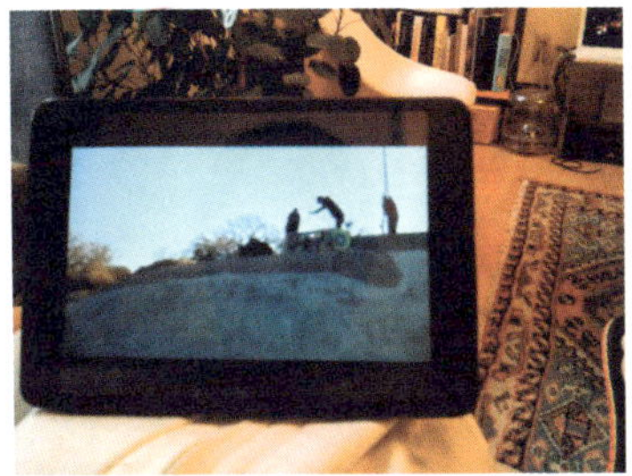

04:08

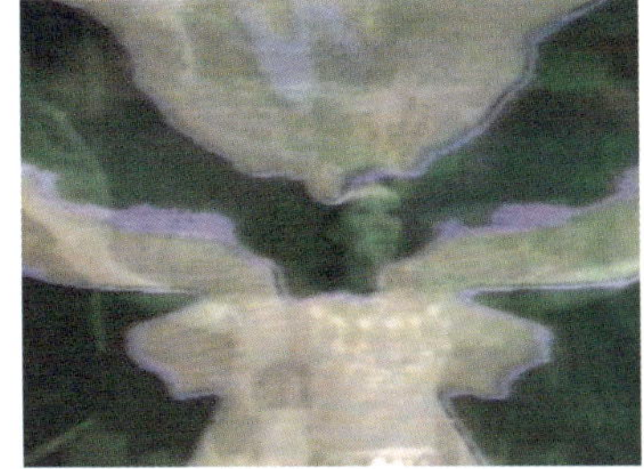

14:39

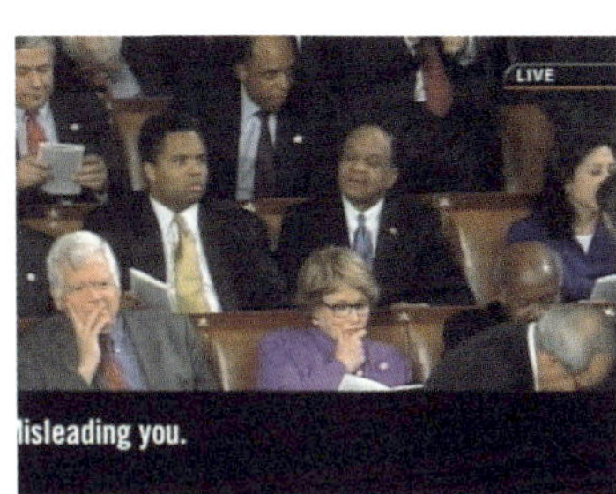

04:41

ritual. But I had done another conceptual performance ahead of *Inconsequential* entitled *Columbus Day: A Doggereal* (1980) at a then new independent gallery called LACE in downtown LA.

A lot of my friends that I made at that time were also doing rituals, such as Maren Hassinger and Senga Nengudi. I think you might have heard of David Hammons? So that became the language among us, at least by which we spoke to the public and to another degree amongst ourselves in terms of ritual. So, in terms of doing that, that's what *Inconsequential Doggereal* is. I made up the misspelling of *doggereal*, which became the form that I empowered myself with the capability to speak from. Therefore with my own means of speaking to a public, a regular variation on a theme, sometimes a comedic verse, a regular measure—I got that definition from Marlon Brando. You know, the guy who didn't accept his Oscar because of the way the Hollywood industry was treating Native American people. There was an article in the *LA Times* in the entertainment section and he discussed the character he was playing in the film *Superman*, and for the most part the interviewer was asking him what it was like playing Superman's father, and Brando said: "Well, I liked it, but what I really liked were those doggerel moments." And I thought, what are those doggerel moments? And he said, "The space in between when dialogue was being delivered." As an actor you can interpret that space in one way or another, which is what actors do. And right

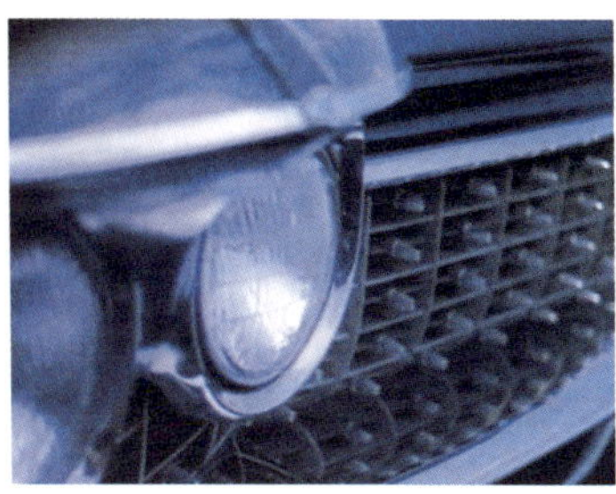

00:28

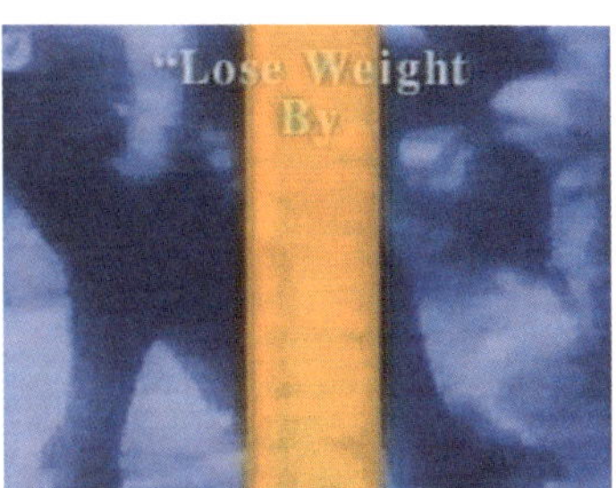

00:45

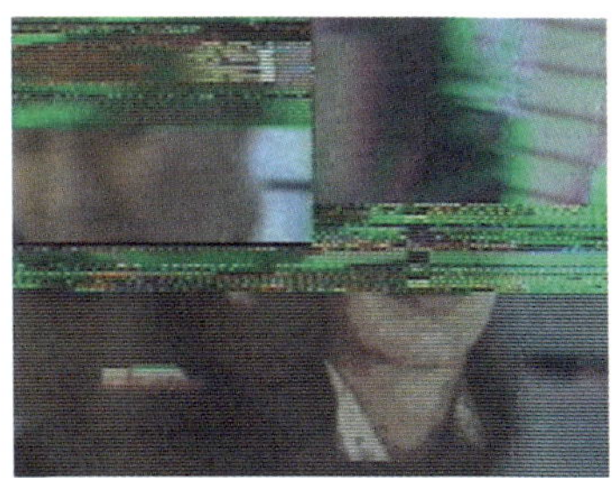

21:22

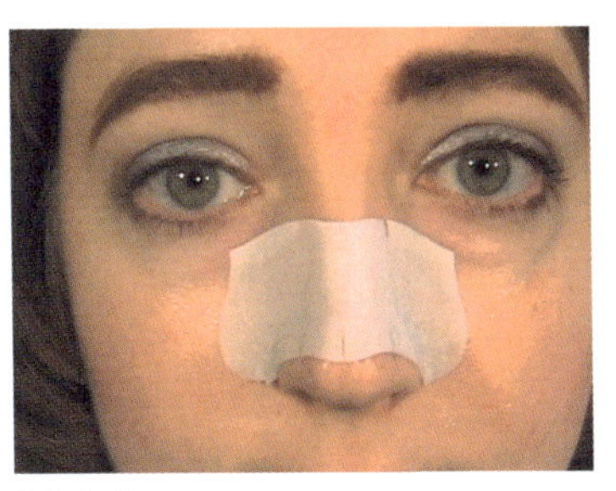

01:34

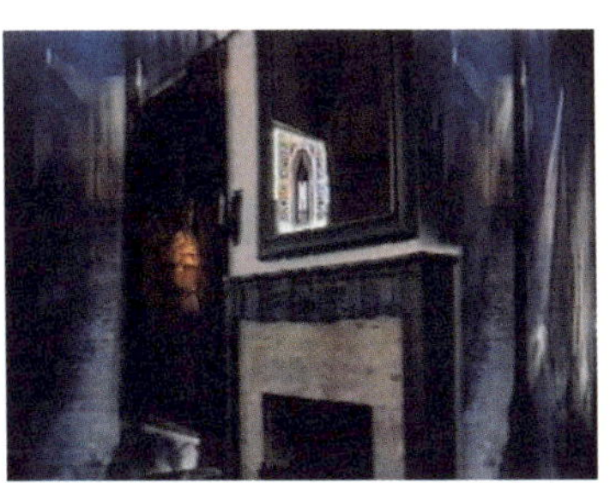

00:31

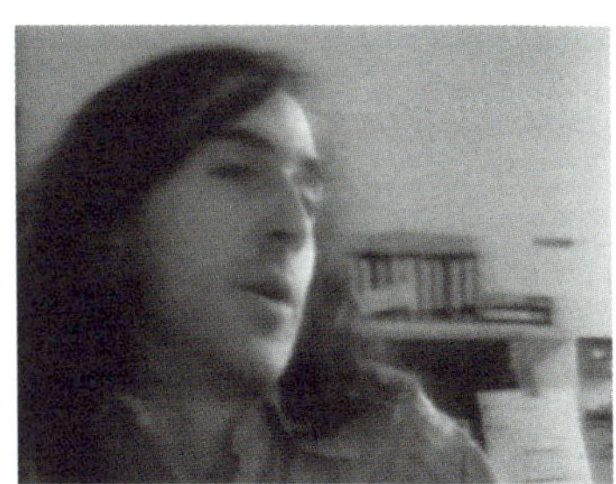

04:34

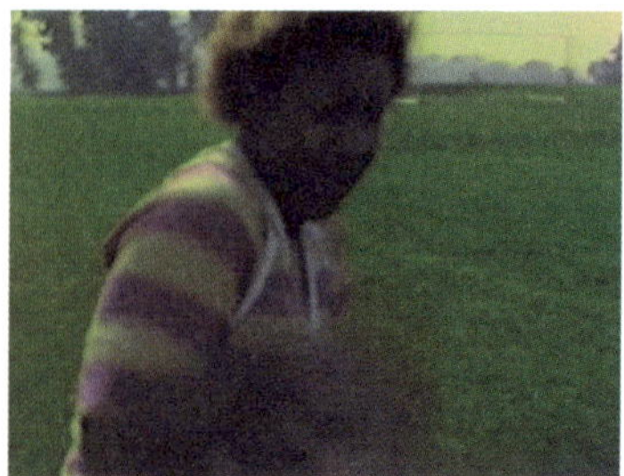
01:16

01:36

05:51

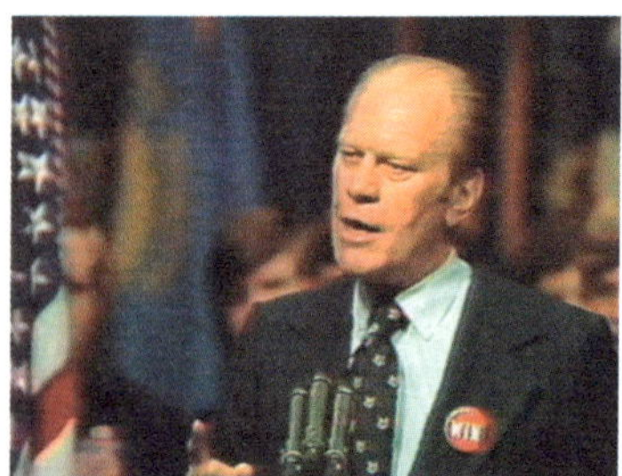
14:00

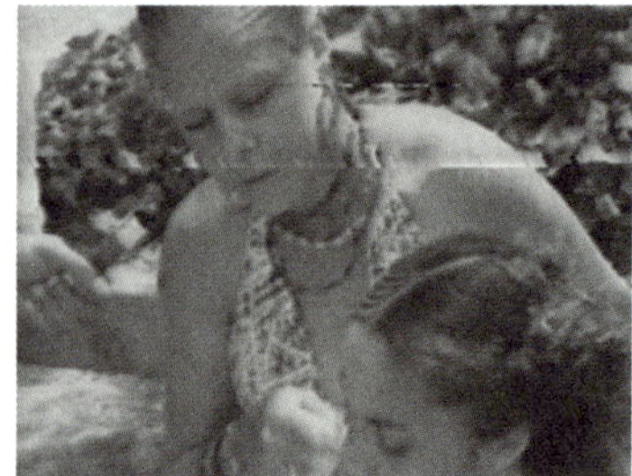
17:24

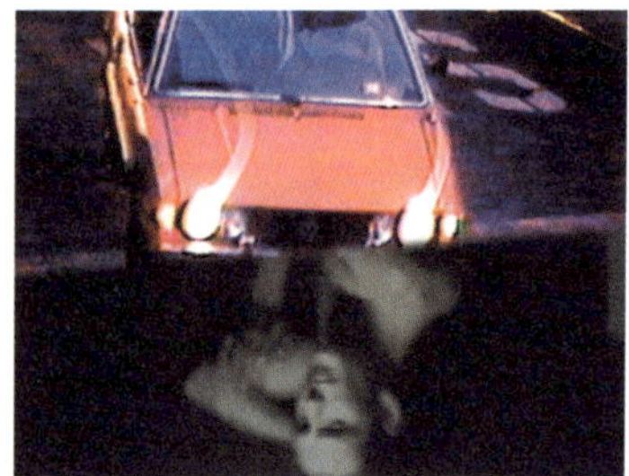
07:12

then I realized, Jesus that's what we as Black people have been doing all our lives: interpreting this irregular space. And I began using this word *doggereal* as a way of defining my work and as a way of seeing culture and this context. So *Inconsequential Doggereal* is what this video is describing. And you can see this not only in the manner of how you'd view the character, but also in the process of my productions. This is how you should view my video.

AK – For the purpose of time, we are going to focus on one more work, *Bay Windows* (1991), because this was a particularly revelatory work for us within the exhibition.

RC – And it really conveys this idea of transmission that we want to focus on tonight, so maybe if you can say a little bit about the project and the videophone technology that is being demonstrated.

UJ – This was a piece that I did when I moved to the Bay Area and it was made at the Exploratorium. I called it *Bay Windows* because in a way it's describing a portal into a technological view of how we saw the world, but at the same time it really was a multilocation kind of construct. We were using long-distance conference phone calls to link up five locations simultaneously and in that sense, I mean I don't want to describe to you the whole technical structure of it, but in doing such a thing we were able to establish what was going on in these various locations. We had discussions about the social circumstances of that time, in a way it was like my *Inconvenient Truth*

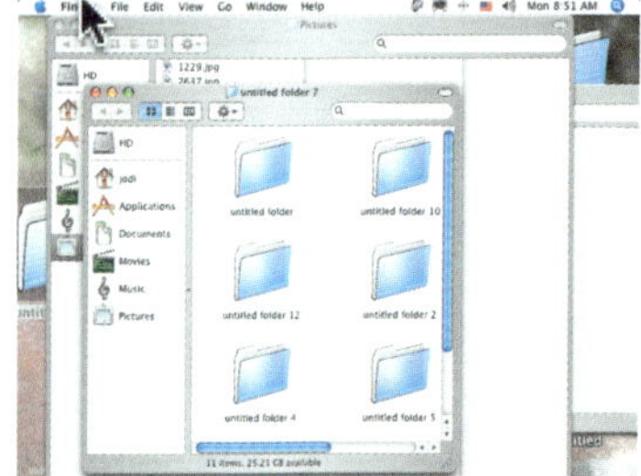
00:47

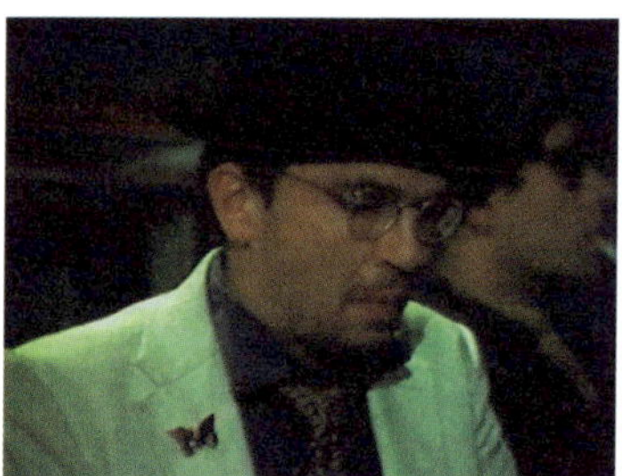
08:18

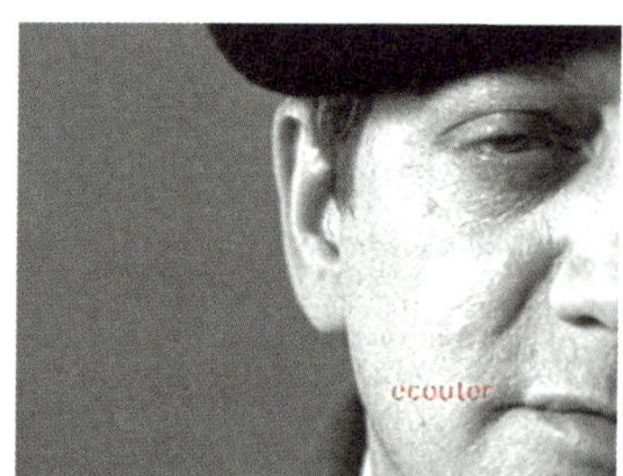

00:02

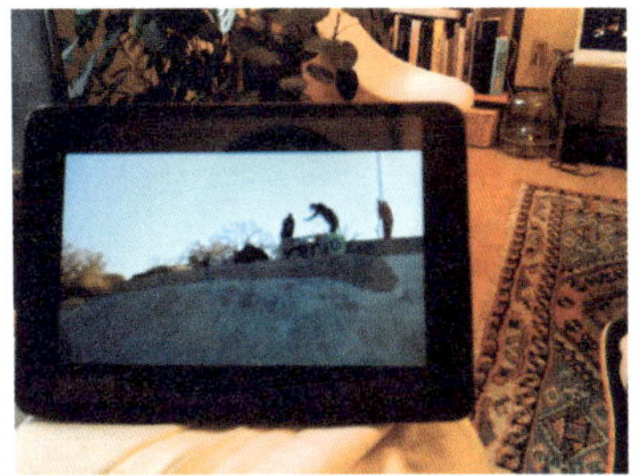
04:08

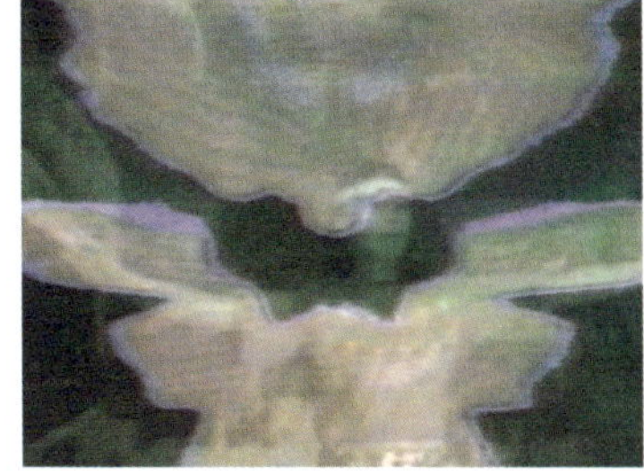
14:39

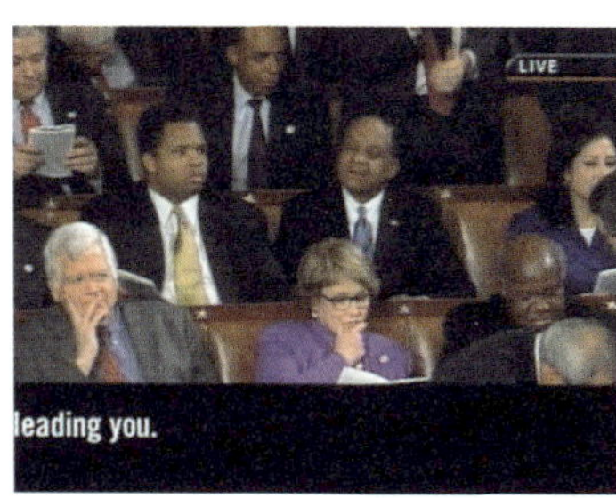

04:41

piece of that time. Because this one guy Fred who was in it from Baker Lake, in Canada, was telling us that at the time in the 1990s the Native American people were having problems with water rights and of course our wonderful oil companies were trying to take the rights of this lake that would just end up destroying their fishing rights.[1]

And so when they said that over those phone lines it's within that construct. There's basically a dualism that I must explain to you. You had to have at least two phone lines: one for the visual and one for the audio. And I have given Rebecca a picture of the Panasonic black-and-white videophone, but you know those different kinds of devices that you see in the news where you see somebody who's robbing the 7-Eleven and this picture is in a quadrant? We started using those to use as a videophone distributor because you could have color video. So back in those days, it was in the early 1990s, Amiga made the only computer that you could have color video and with computer software. So we would just disorient or orient the image, however you want to look at it, and then send that signal to the videophone and then send it back out to other people so that's a brief description of the window.

AK – This was happening in different media centers up and down the coast: Northern California, Southern California, and Canada. I'm just thinking about how different it is from the present where technological immediacy is a given.

UJ – I just remembered the guy's name who I worked

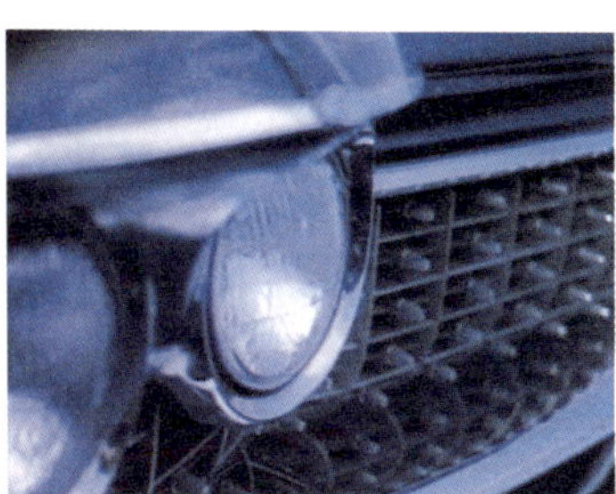
00:28

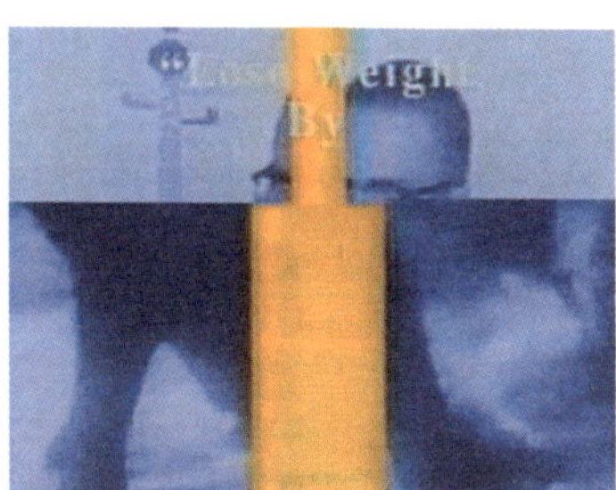
00:45

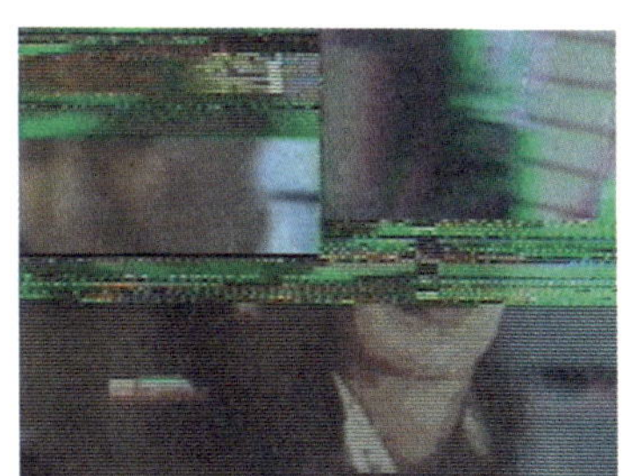
21:22

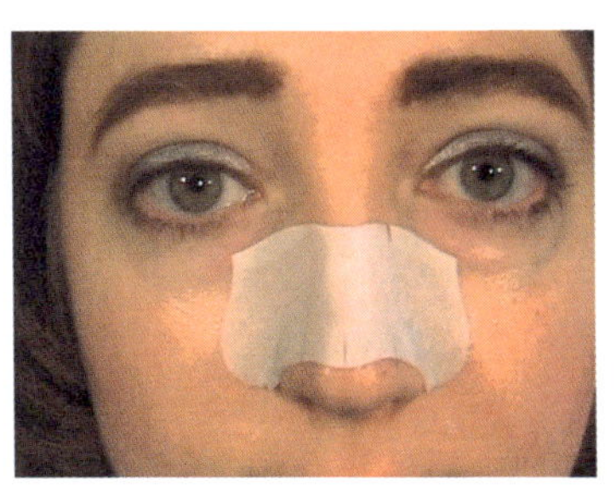
01:34

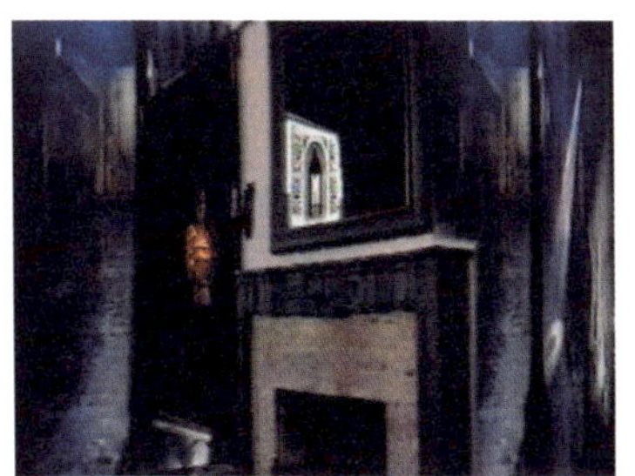
00:31

04:34

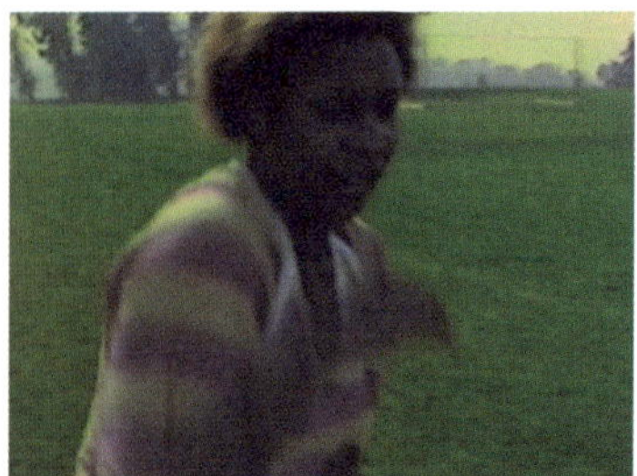

01:15

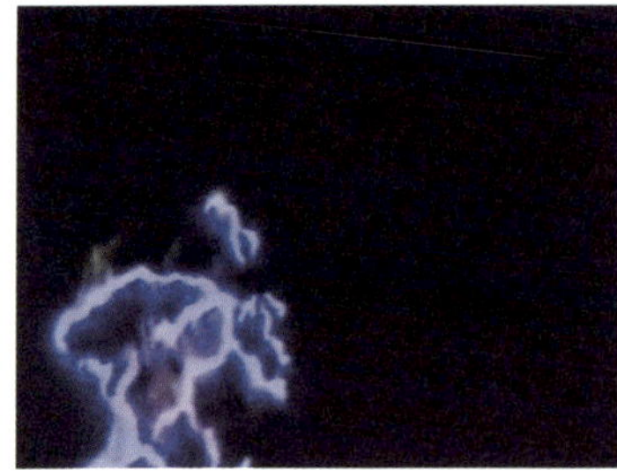

01:35

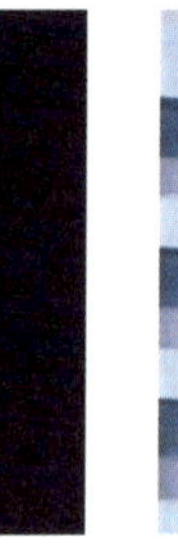

05:50

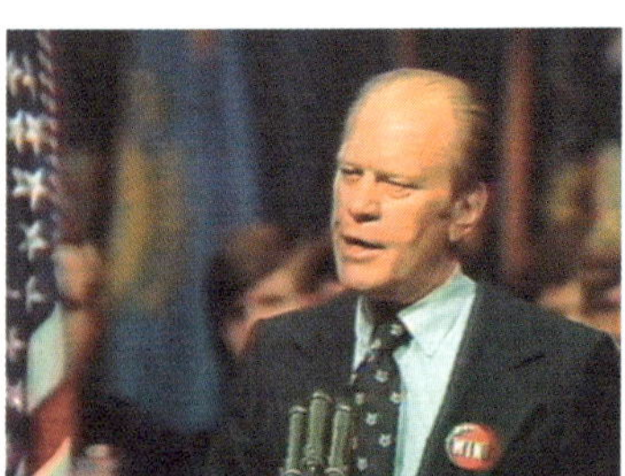

13:59

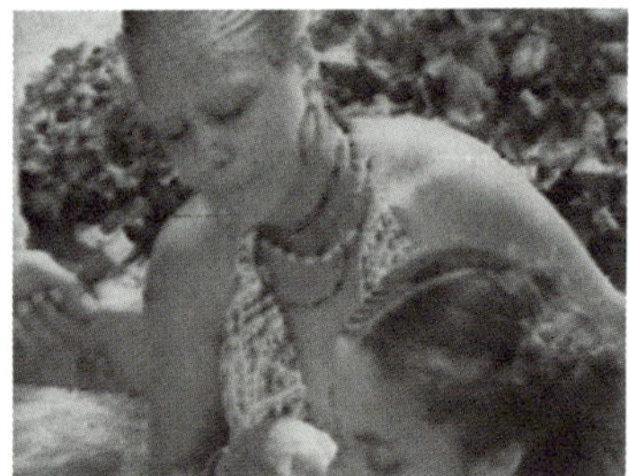

17:23

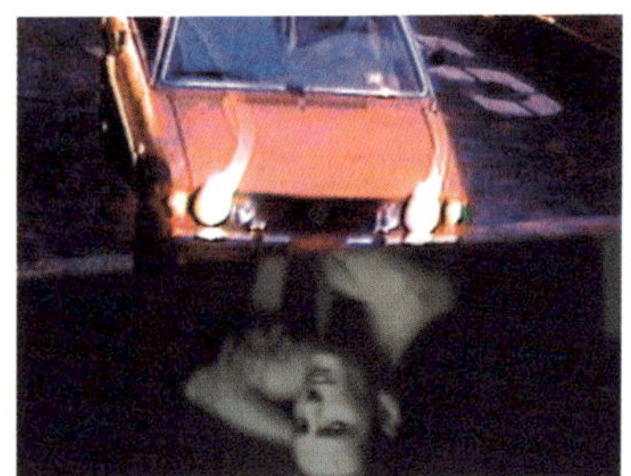

07:11

with in Vancouver: Hank Bull.

RC – Alright. So we're going to proceed to Sondra now, so you two can have a dialogue. Sondra interned at EAI in 2011, so I've known her for a long time, and she's been in my life for a while, making it even more of a thrill to be sitting here talking about her work. We could begin with *Double Quadruple Etcetera Etcetera I* and *II* from 2013, which was recently exhibited at The Kitchen. Sondra, could say something about this work?

SP – Thank y'all. Happy to be here. So this is a frame-by-frame animation of two of my friends, Joiri Minaya and Danny Giles moshing in the studio. I asked if they could do these thirty-second performances, which is kind of like a layover from the last pieces that I was doing in undergrad, which were performances that were shot face forward and then slowed down. So there is no manipulation other than the content-aware tool in Photoshop. Each frame covers the body with the rest of the space, that's how that tool works. It accumulates pixels from the area surrounding what you're covering.

RC – How is the work exhibited? Do you have a preference for how it would be displayed?

SP – I prefer these things to be projected because I'm really into psychic spaces and intentionality. And I think that there's something interesting that happens when they're across from each other, projected in a space where your body is encompassed by the movement. The reason why I chose Danny and Joiri is because we were at a residency together and all

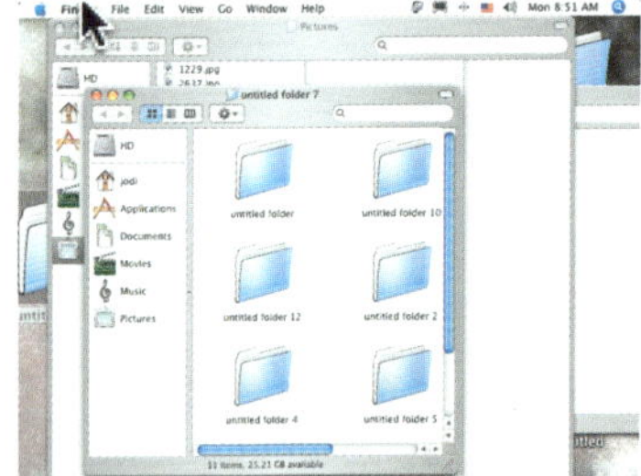

00:46

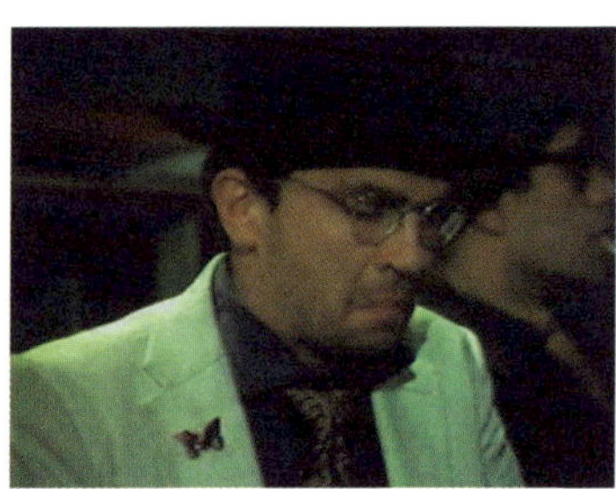

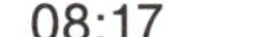

08:17

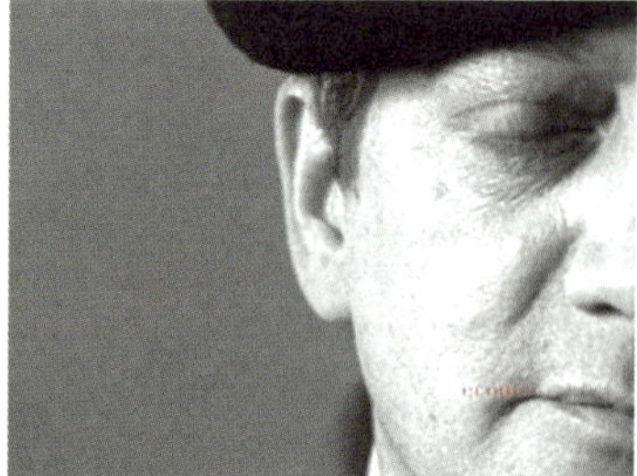

00:01

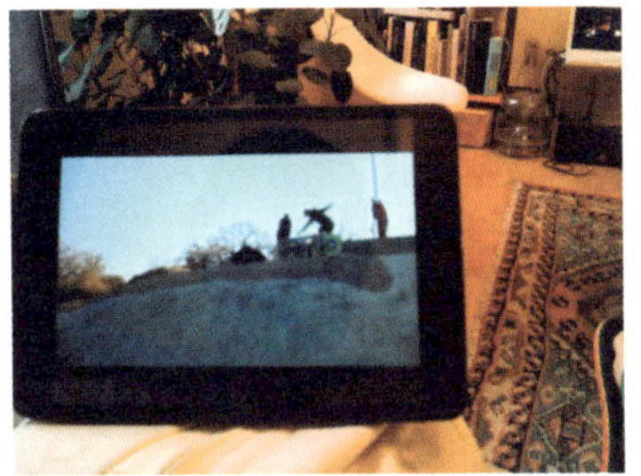
04:08

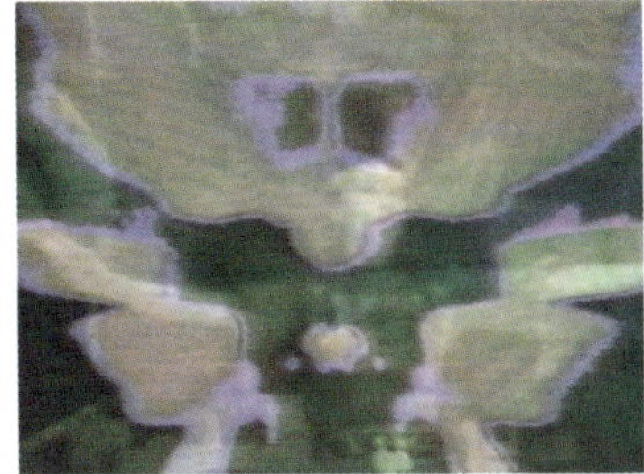
14:39

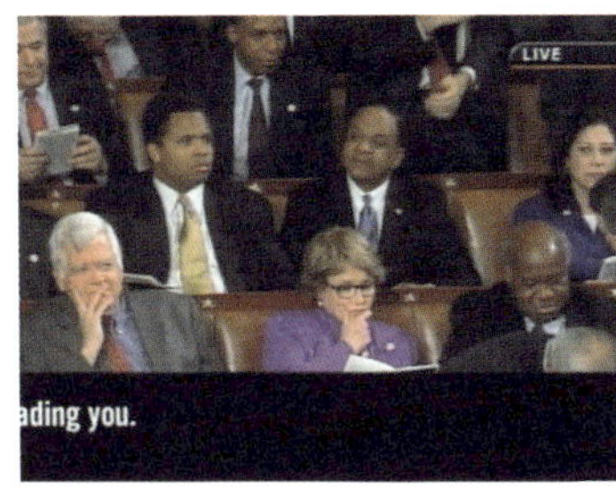

04:41

summer we drank and danced at night, and I was seeing them move on a daily basis. There was just something in their movements that felt really present and urgent all of the time. So I wanted to capture that ability to move through space while also thinking about an energy imprint onto the digital space, instead of maybe their body is telling you something about them.

AK – Maybe because we also asked Ulysses this question about his early work in another medium, can you talk a bit about how you began as a ceramicist, and what led you to embrace the medium of the video?

SP – Sure. I went to school for ceramics. It's like I'm one of those people who shouldn't have graduated from high school. It was just all of this luck stuff and other things I suppose. I didn't go to museums or galleries or anything during that time, and on the second day of college we saw Art 21 and we saw the Kara Walker section and it messed me up in many, many, many, ways. At that moment I was like, "Oh, there are so many things I can do. Like art is so full." So I ended up doing a lot and landing on sound work and moving into video later.

I think the transition was really easy for me because the program I went to was still very interested in analog processes. So we were learning to make video first in the studio with these security cameras that you'd patch into the bay, you'd make sure the image was stabilized. And then you'd fix the color; and then you would get your signal, it was all process-based, something I was very

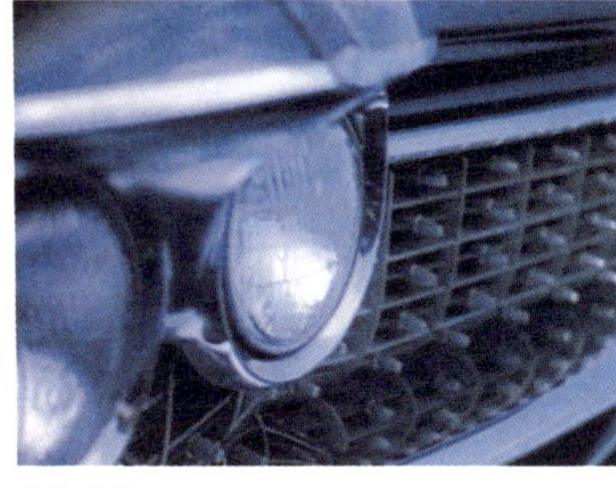
00:28

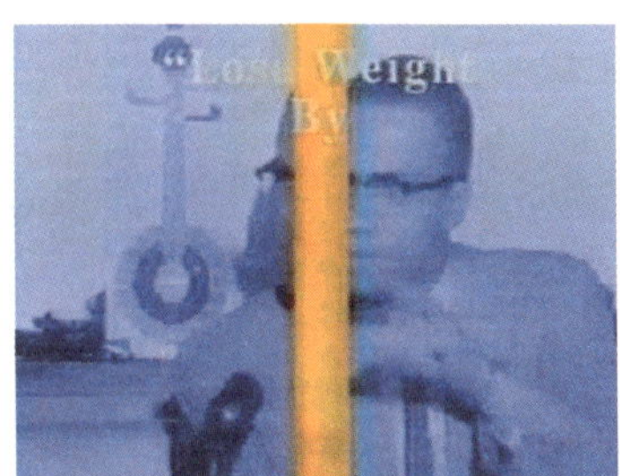
00:45

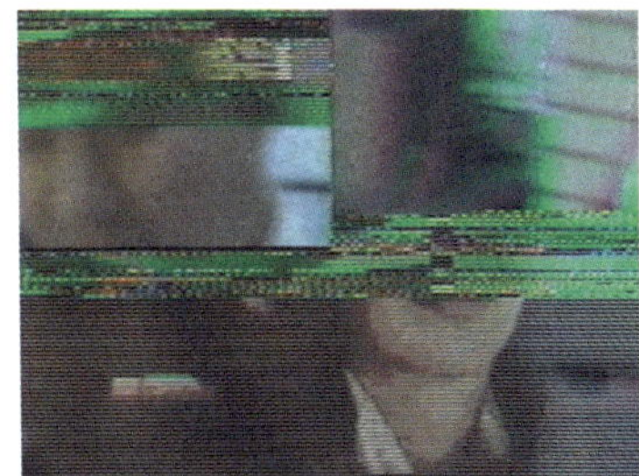
21:22

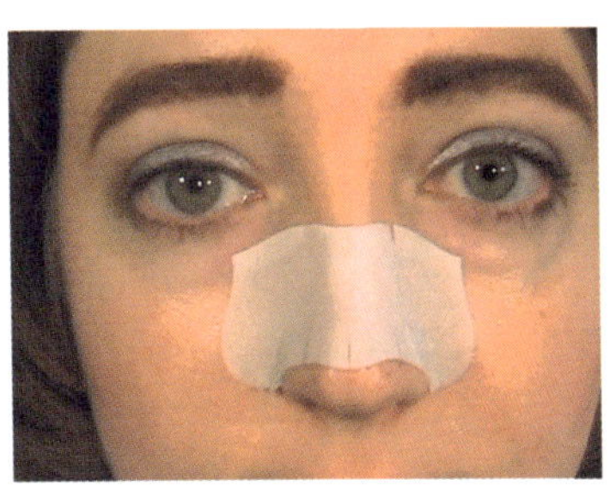
01:34

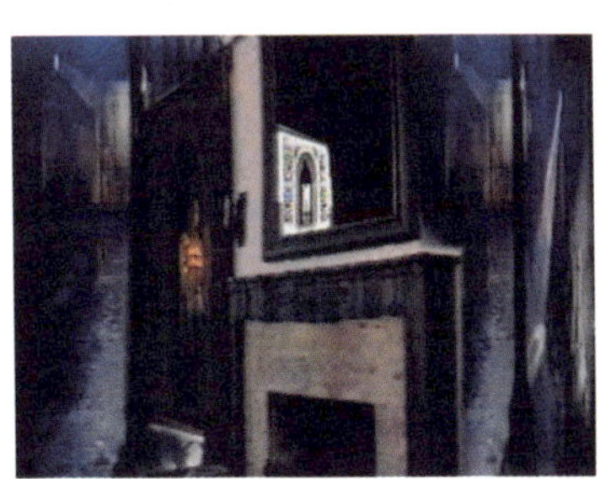
00:31

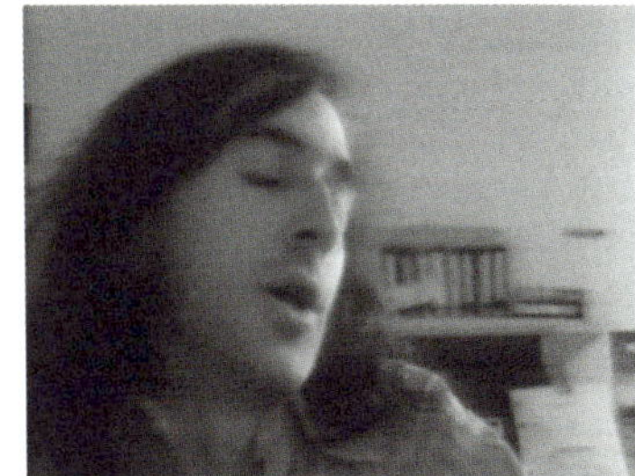
04:34

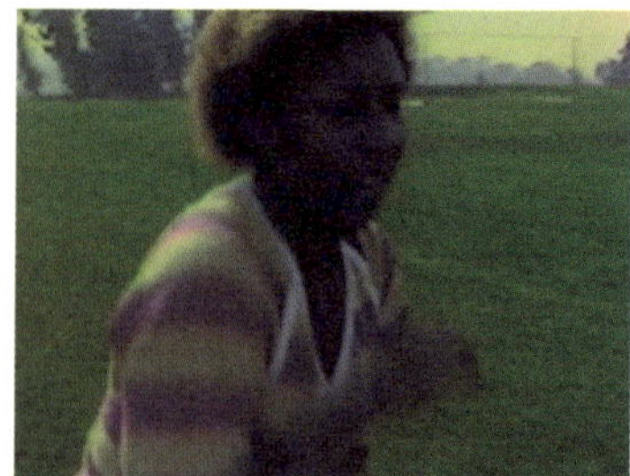
01:15

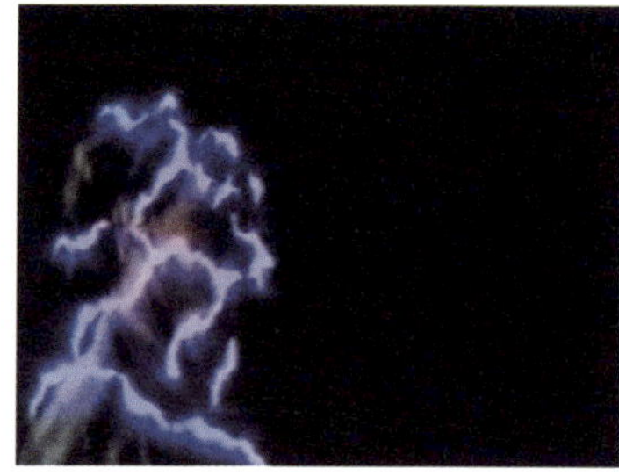
01:35

05:50

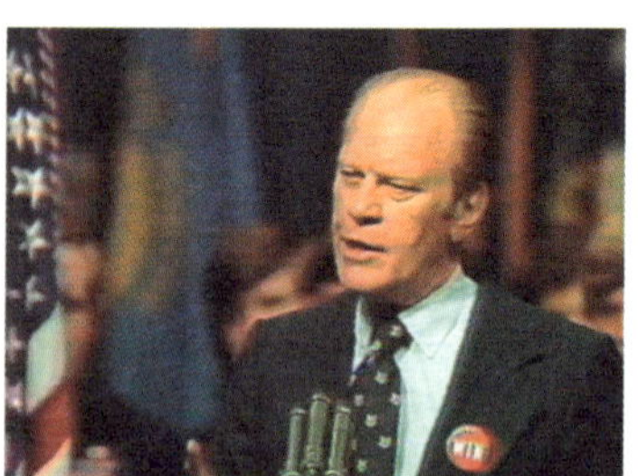
13:59

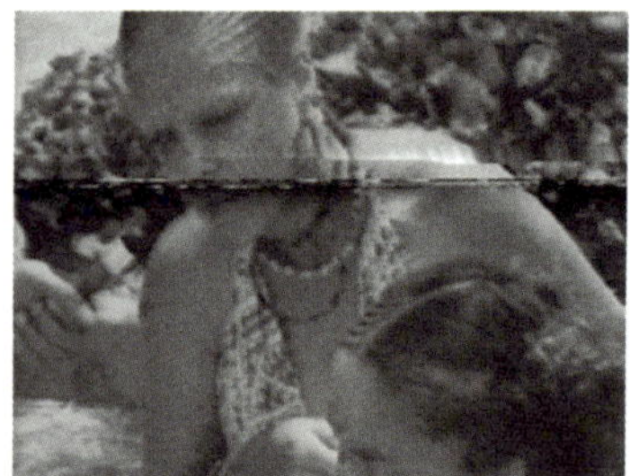
17:23

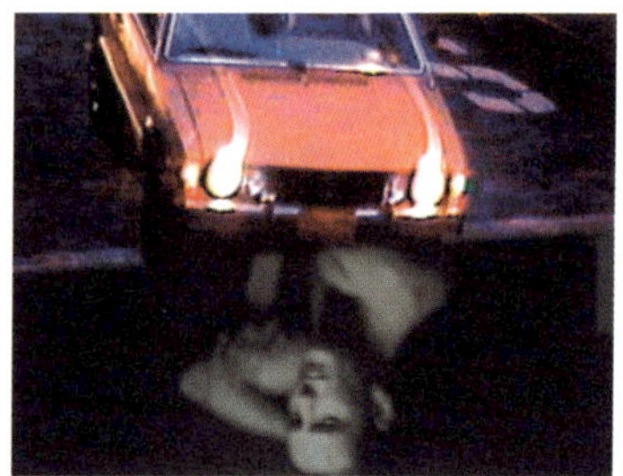
07:11

familiar with from the ceramics process. So I think that my interest in the tangibility of video, of signal, of these things that are very much based in the physical as well as having this ephemeral kind of thing, I got there sooner because of how I was taught video in the first place.

RC – The connection of media processing to ceramics is really interesting. What we're showing now is another performance work, a public project in Harlem, *42 Black Panther Balloons* from 2014.

SP – I was collecting all of these civil rights pins on my own time on eBay and I was on the homepage on which they place posts with the same terms that you search over and over again. So "Black Panther" was a term on my page and I was scrolling and there was just this balloon that said "Black Panther Balloon" on it. So it's one of these things that's made somewhere with terrible labor practices, all the balloons of animals look the same except the coloring is different. I bought as many as I could and got them filled on 125th Street and walked down the street. It was a really lovely time, it made a lot of people smile. It took about two hours.

RC – You have a different relationship to it now—yes, we have a lot we could say about it, but let's move on. This is *Young Women Sitting and Standing and Talking and Stuff (No, No, No)* from 2015.

SP – So this was a performance with my friends Joiri, Ilana, and Victoria. Ilana and Victoria were first year grads in the visual arts program at Columbia University. That's like the big deal. So many

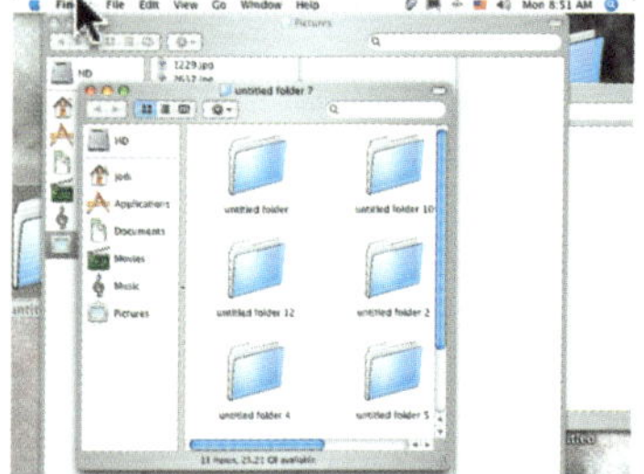
00:46

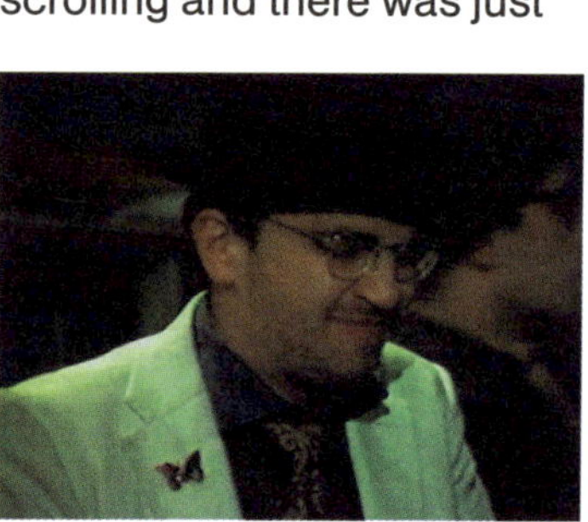
08:17

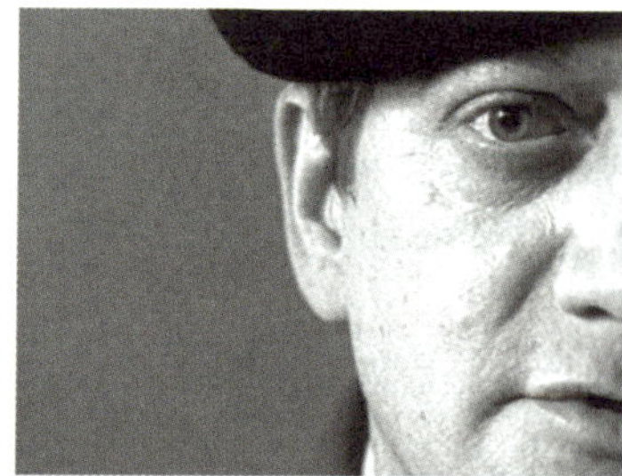
00:01

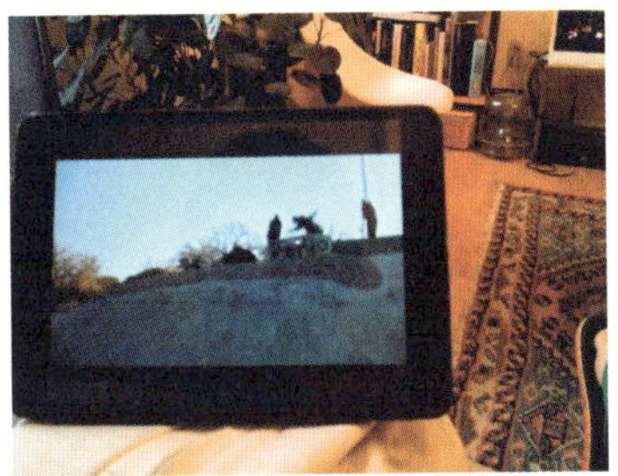

04:08

14:39

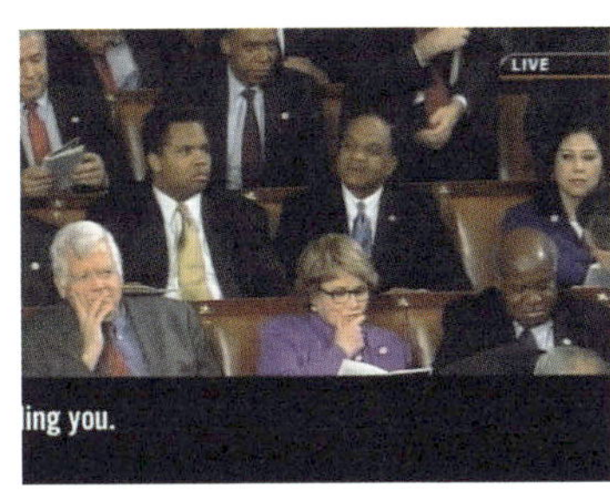

04:41

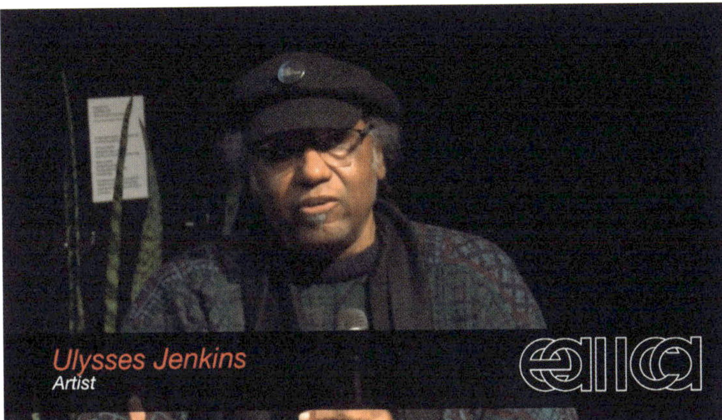

Still from PhillyCAM television broadcast

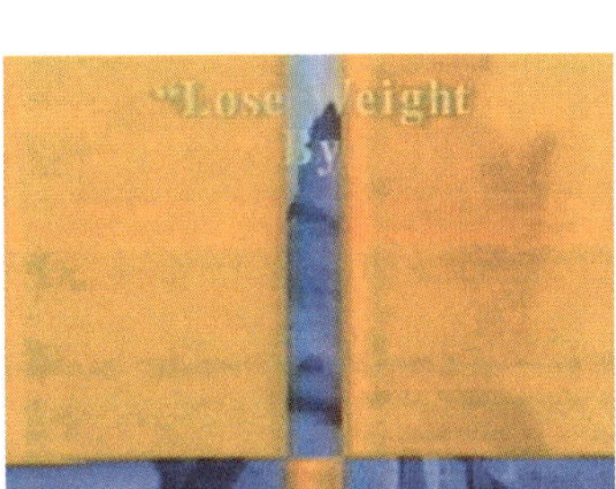

00:28

00:45

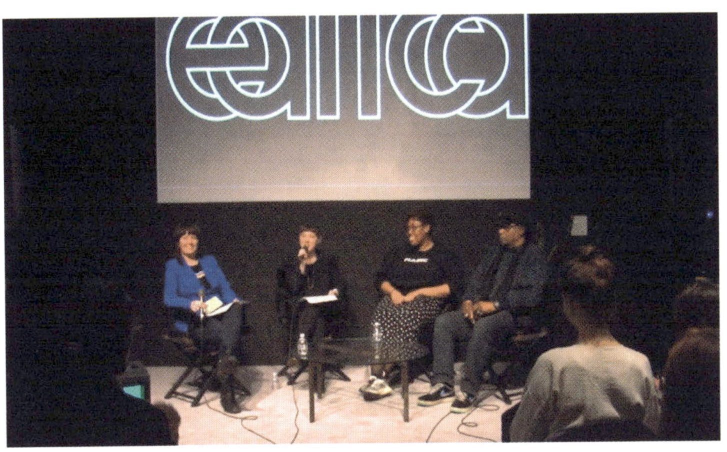

Still from PhillyCAM television broadcast

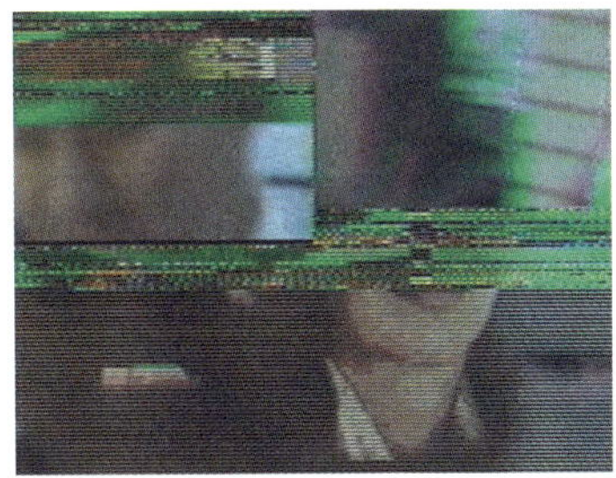

21:22

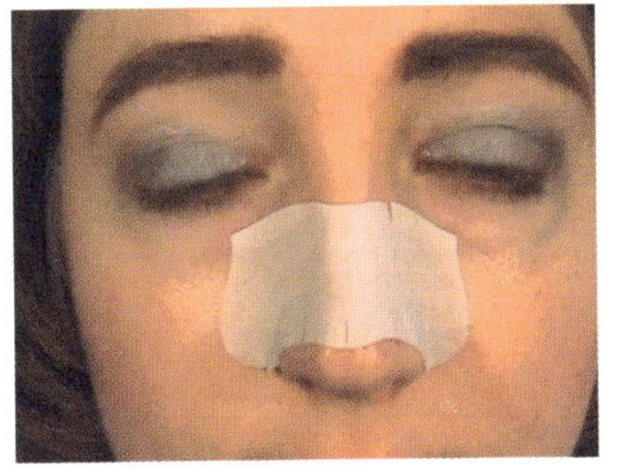

01:34

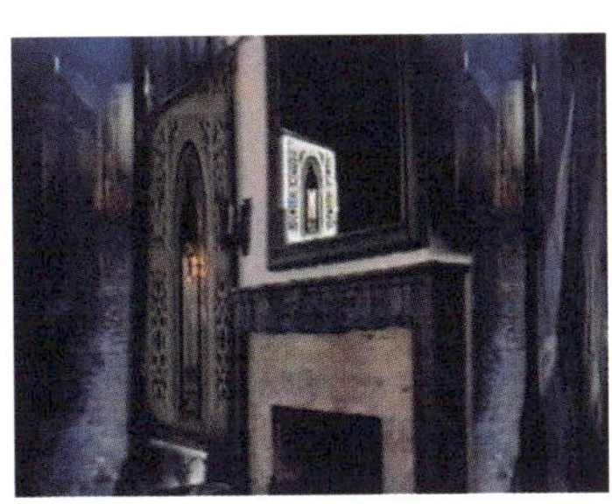

00:31

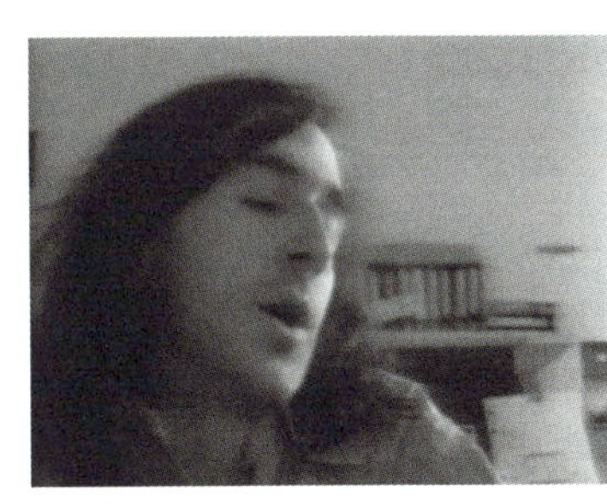

04:34

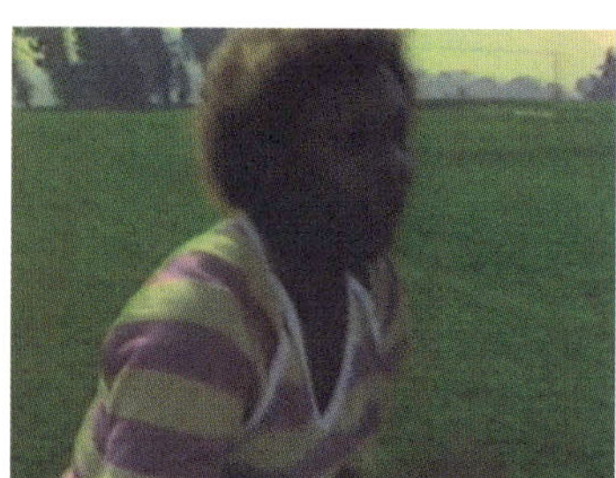

01:15

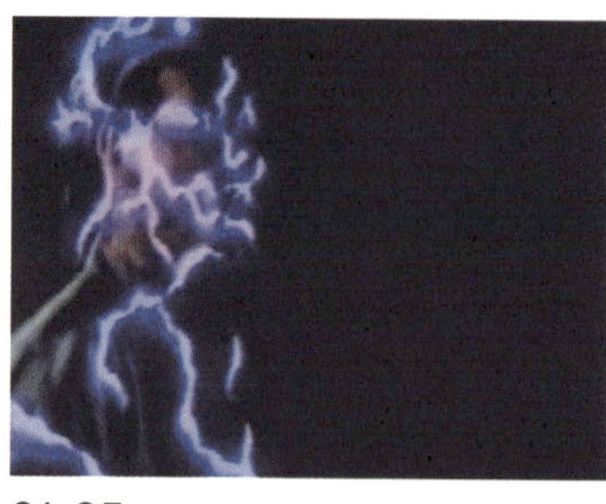

01:35

05:50

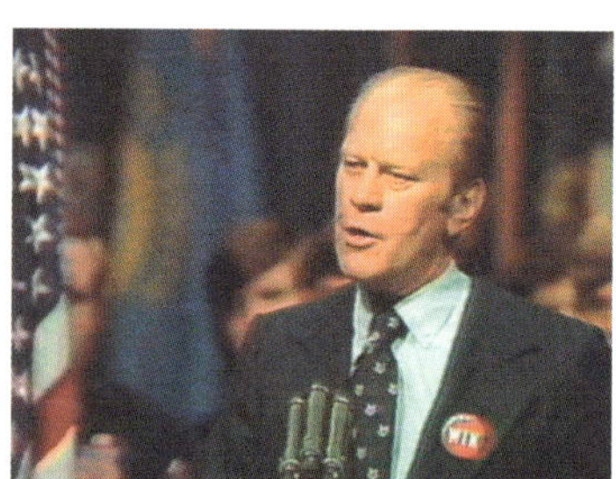

13:59

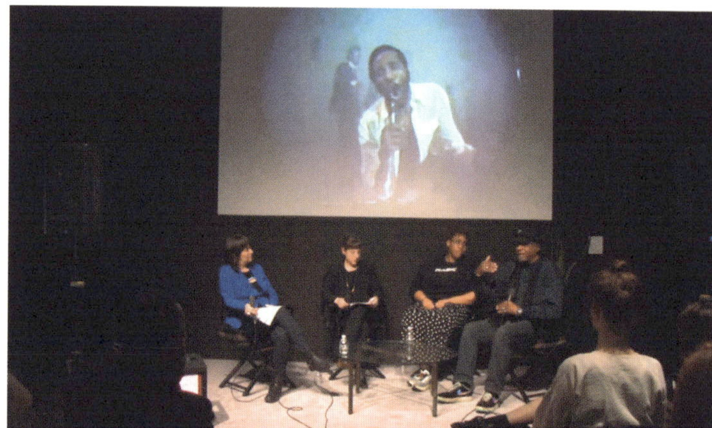

Still from PhillyCAM television broadcast

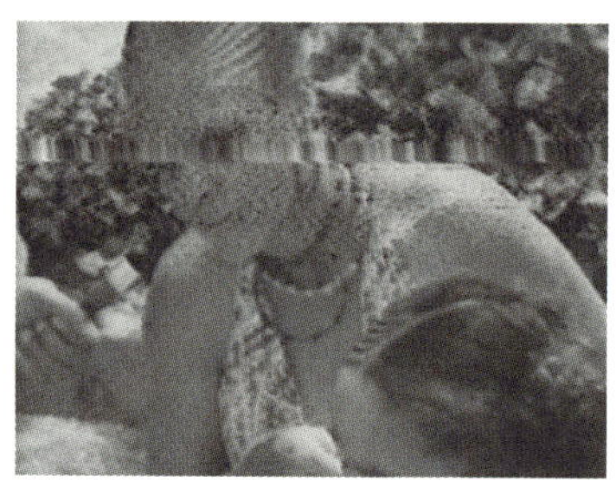

17:23

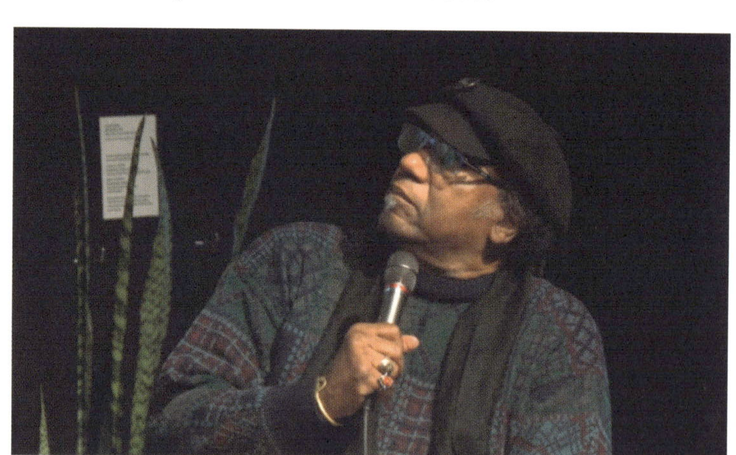

Still from PhillyCAM television broadcast

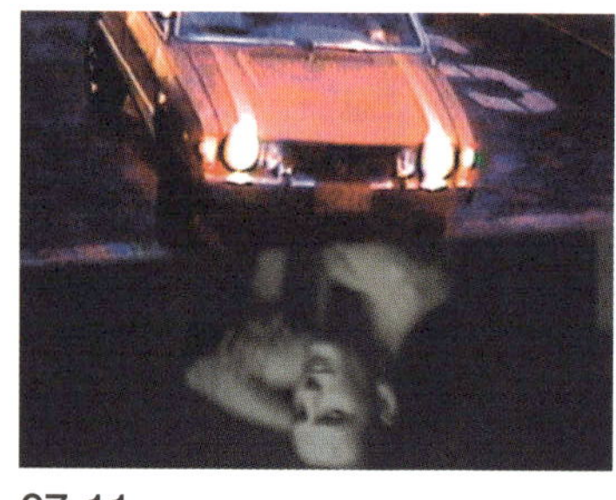

07:11

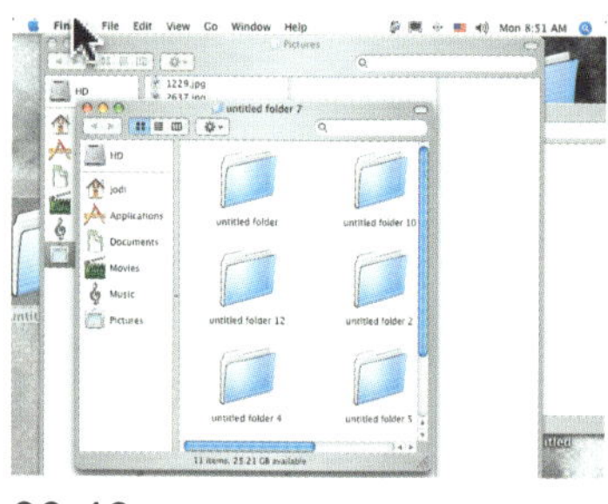

00:46

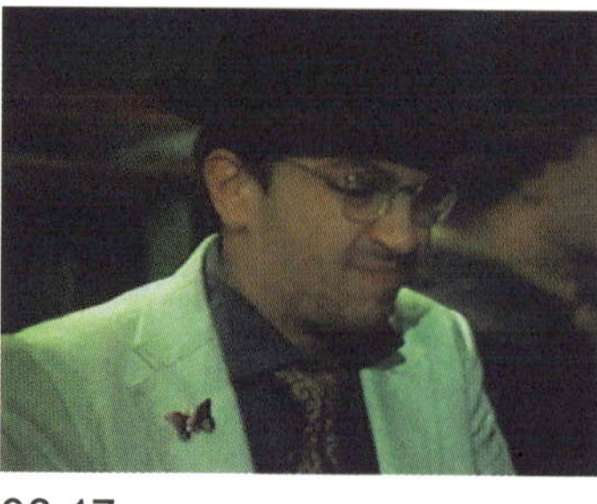

08:17

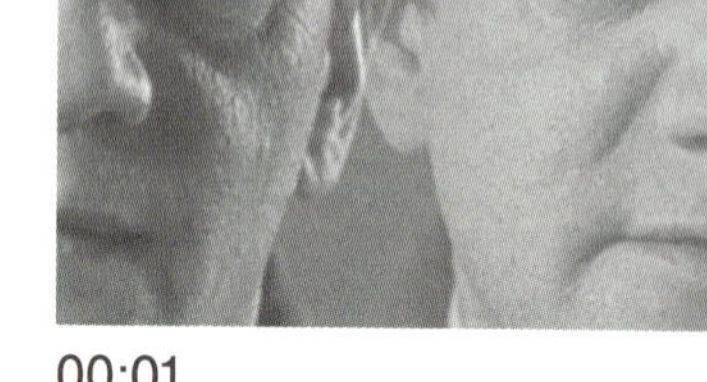

00:01

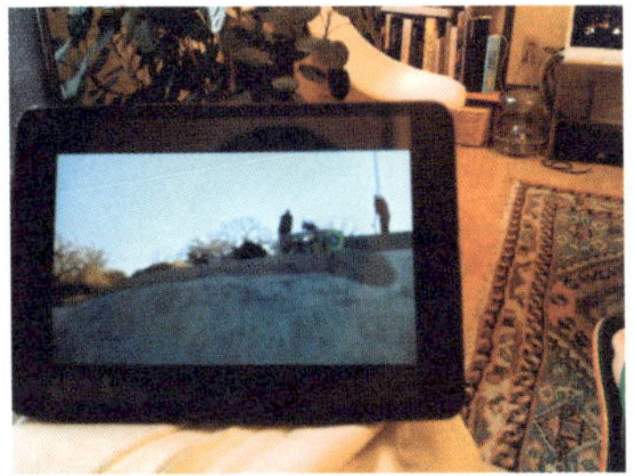

04:08

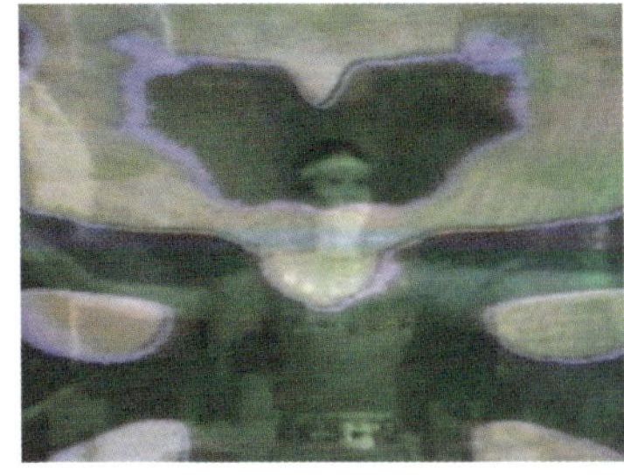

14:39

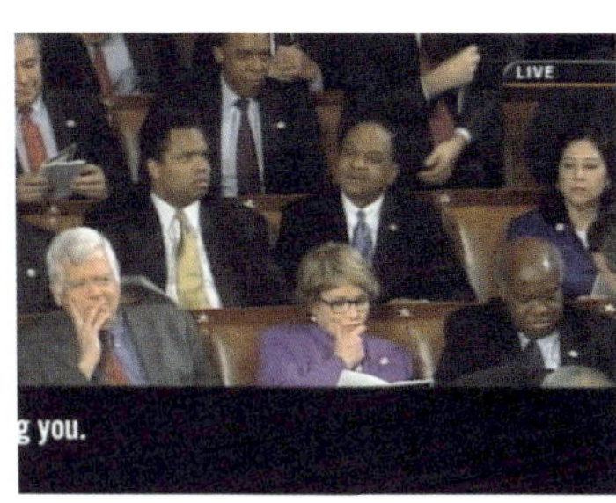

04:41

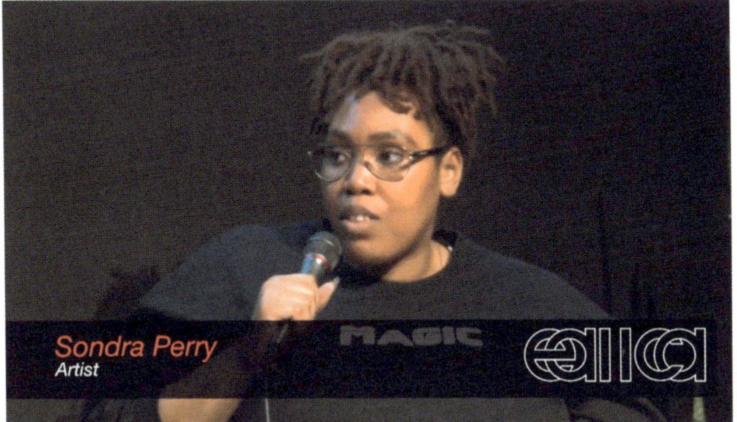

Still from PhillyCAM television broadcast

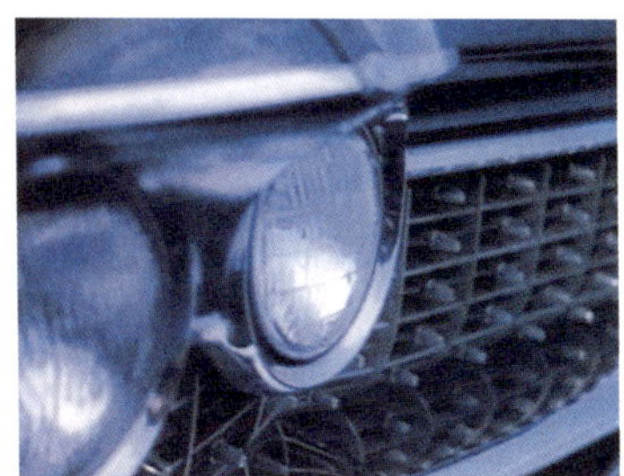

00:28

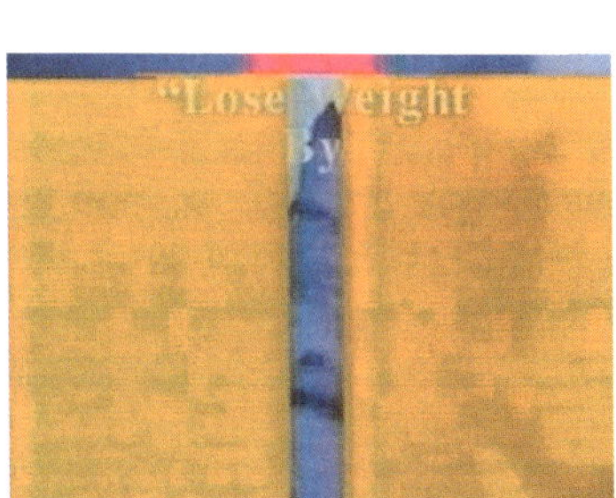

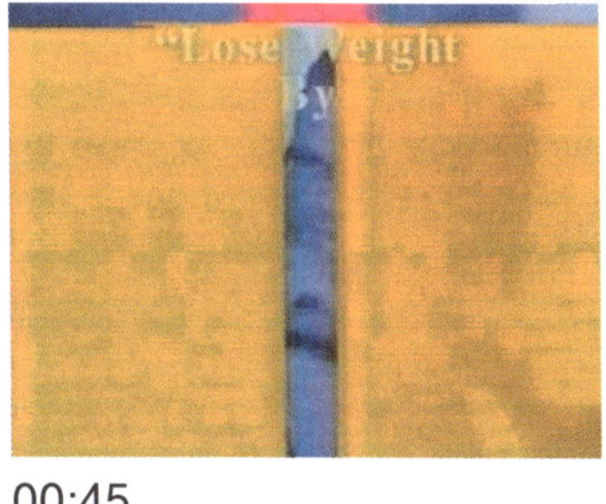

00:45

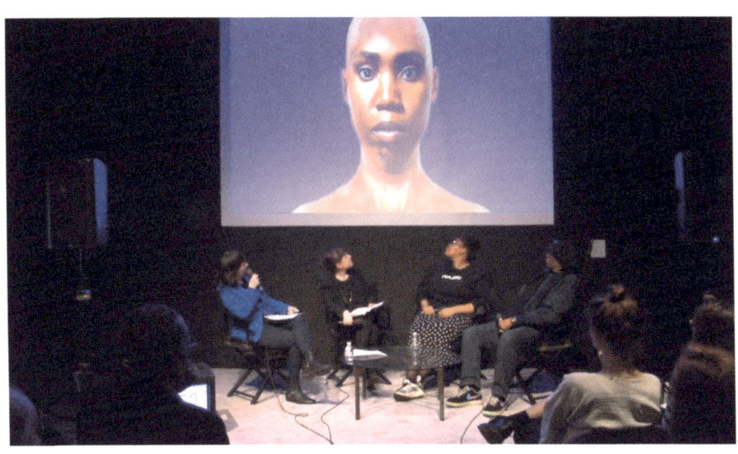

Still from PhillyCAM television broadcast

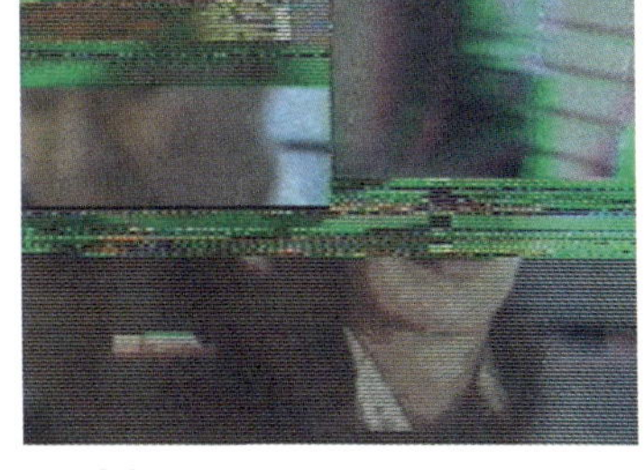

21:22

01:34

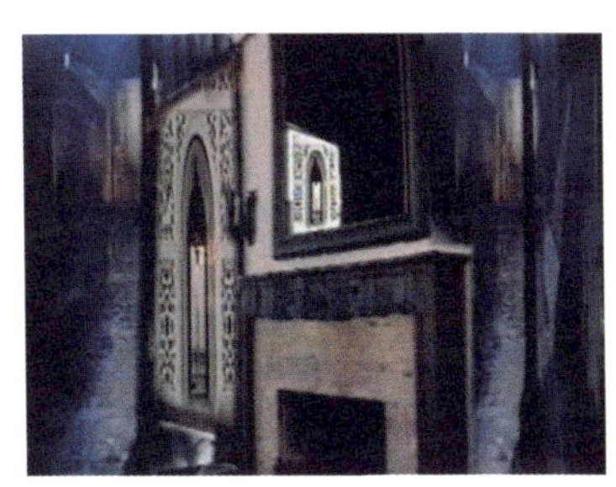

00:31

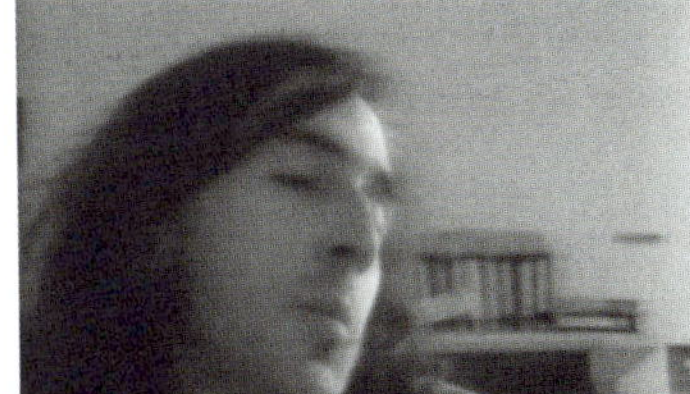

04:34

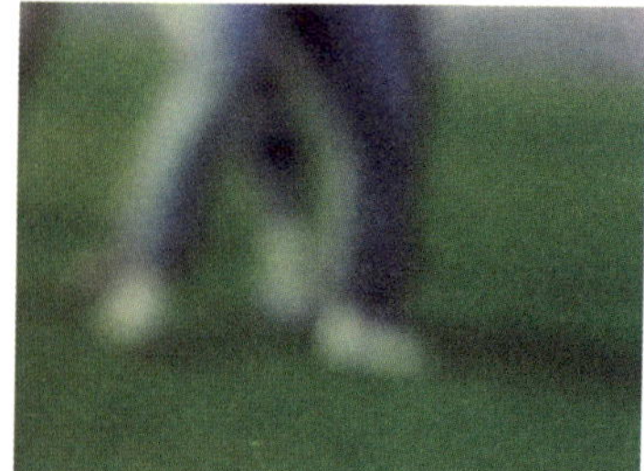

01:15

01:35

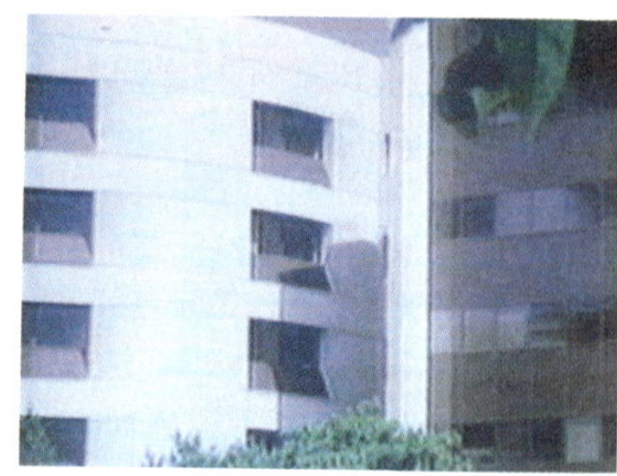

05:50

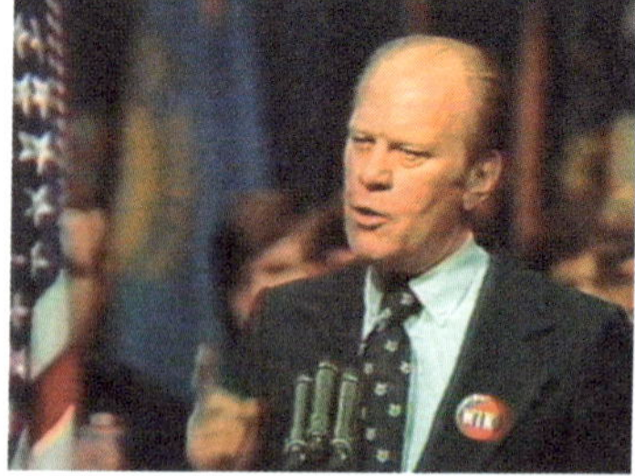

13:59

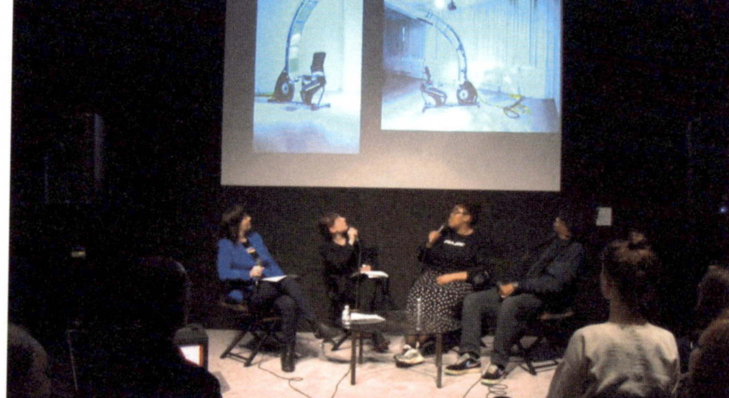

Still from PhillyCAM television broadcast

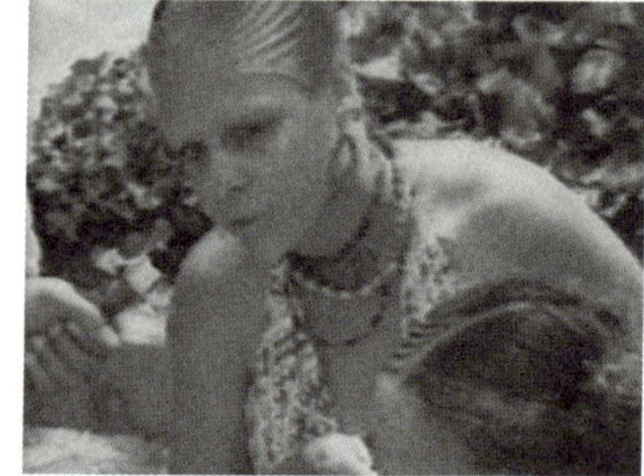

17:23

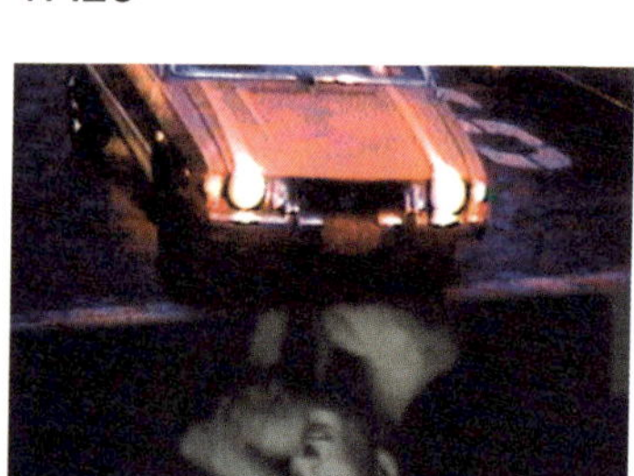

07:11

Still from PhillyCAM television broadcast

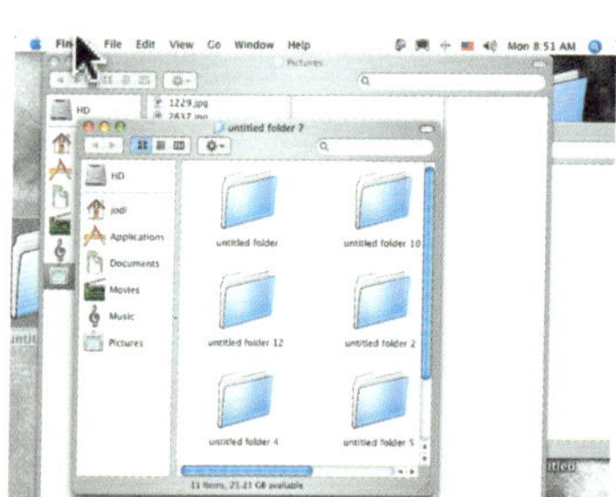

00:46

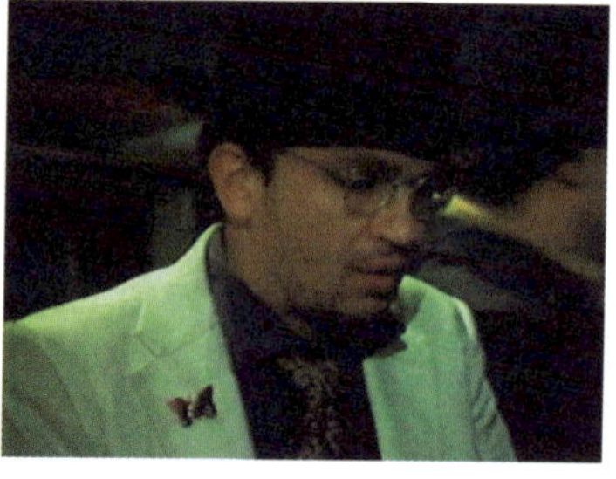

08:17

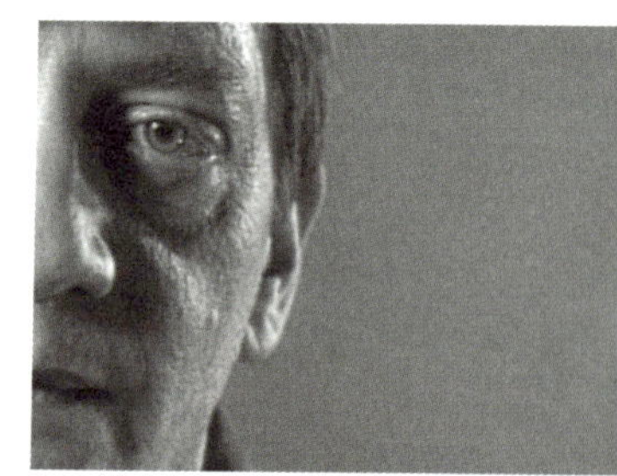

00:01

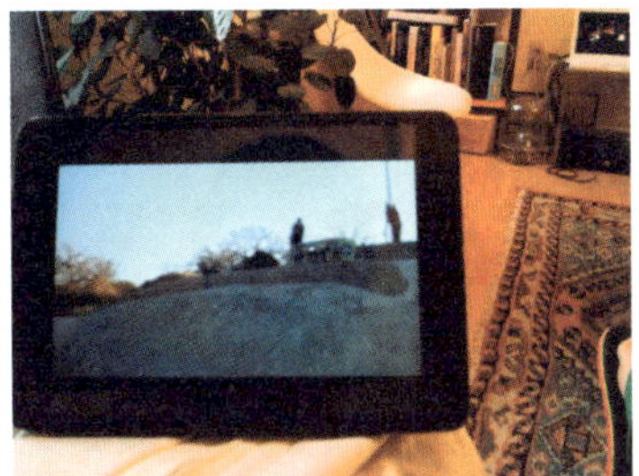
04:09

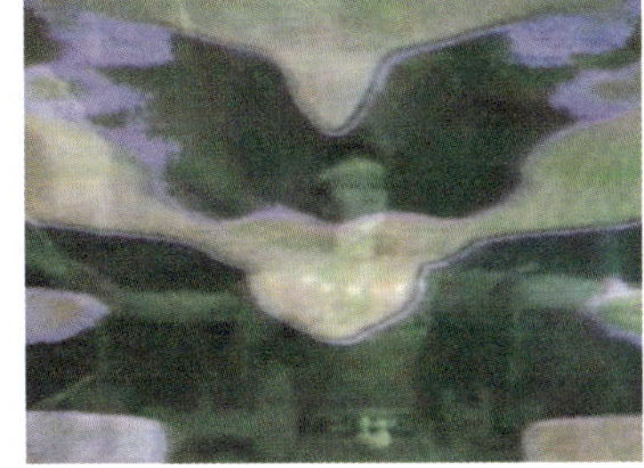
14:40

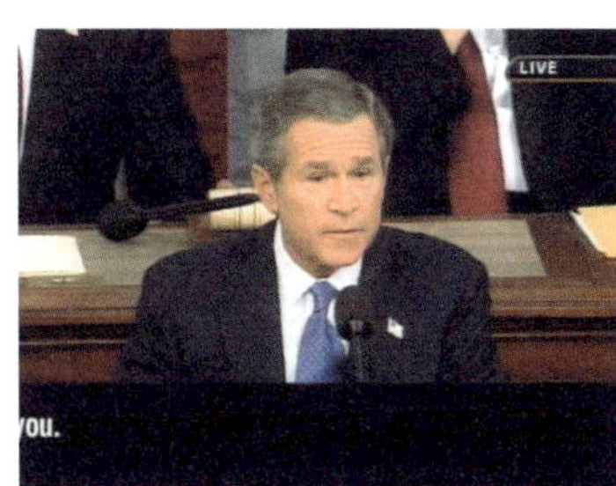

04:42

Black women were there. That was nice. I've done several performances with these masks. These rolling eyes were used during performance where I was making pancakes in an elaborate DIY not quite working the right way-like mechanism, so we'd make the pancake mix in a bucket that was suspended from the ceiling and then try to pour the pancake mix on a rolling cooking surface. We were wearing these glasses. I was really and am still so into these ways that labor happens and the ways that you can, I'm not sure if subvert is the right word, but like do some trickery inside of that labor. So I was thinking through this kind of never-ending eye roll. I had to work all through school and I had many kinds of jobs, but I worked as a fry cook for some time. So the first iteration of this work wound up happening there while I was an undergrad making pancakes in the gallery and then slowly pulling pieces of my hair out and putting it into the mix as well as, splitting the mix out, cooking and serving them knowing there were classmates who I'd made food for at the cafe during the day who would see the performance. It's like being nice to the people who are making your food *or else*. You wound up being abstracted or made invisible because of the kind of labor you had to do, but I wanted to become visible again; this is a video where there are a bunch of these amazing folks who are—Joiri didn't go to school with us, but yes she was there. I just asked them to come together for an hour and put on the masks and I thought they would get

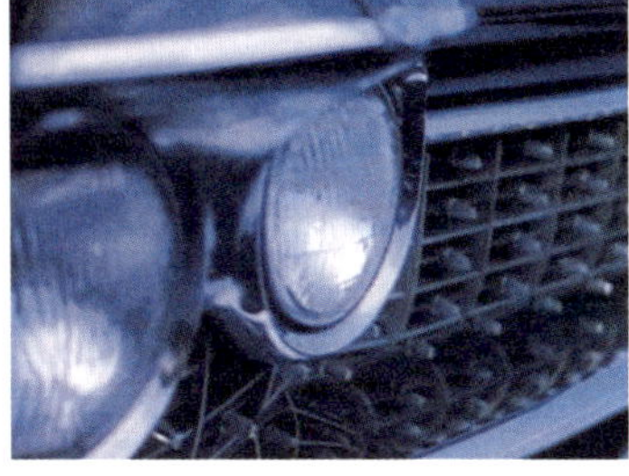
00:29

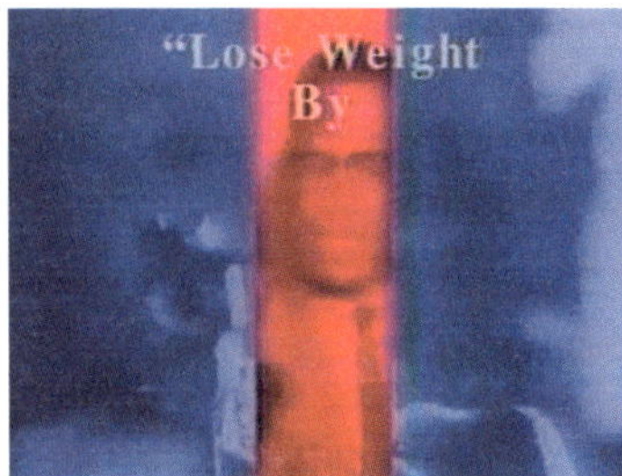

00:46

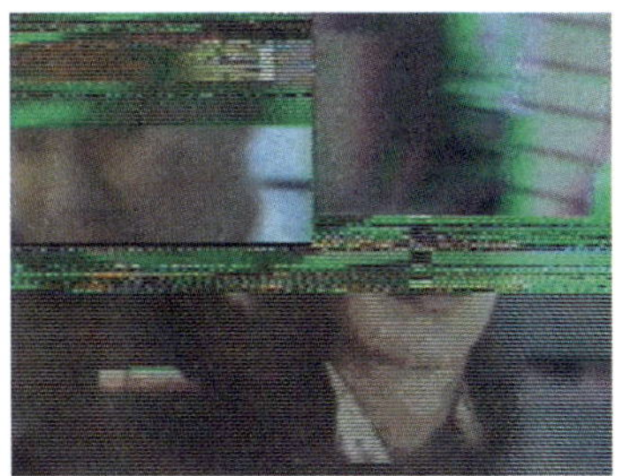
21:23

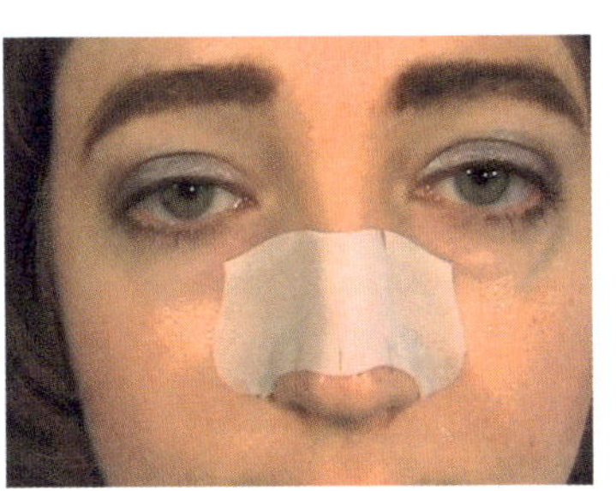
01:35

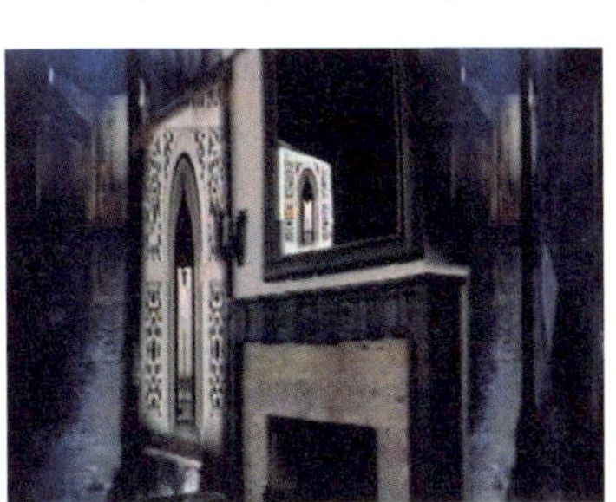
00:32

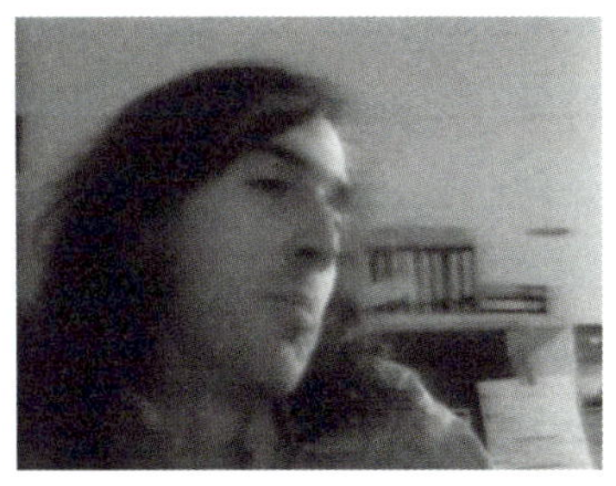
04:35

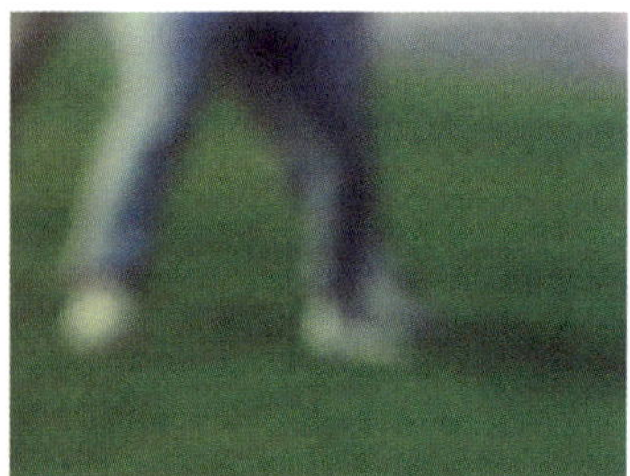

01:15

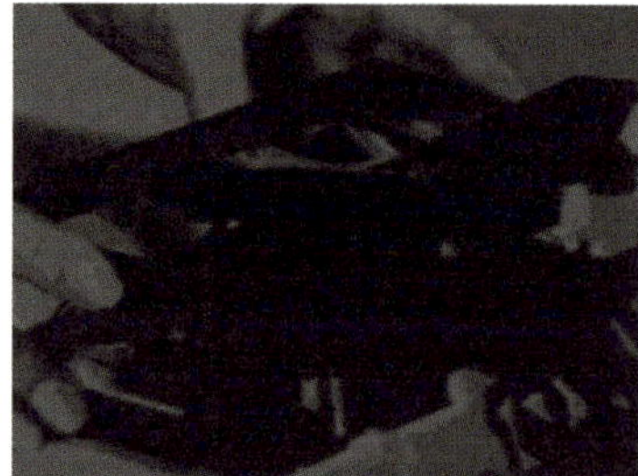

01:35

05:50

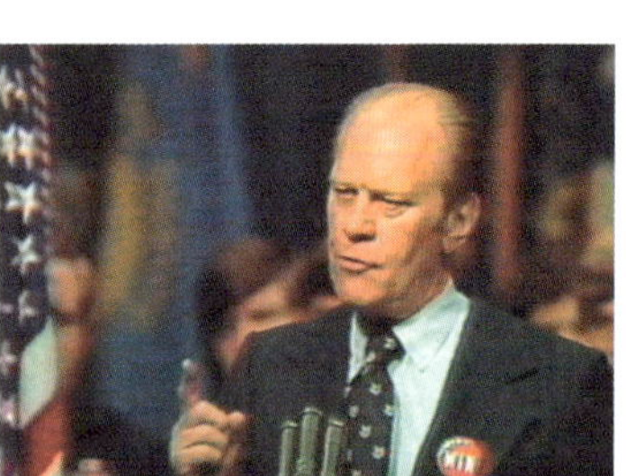

13:59

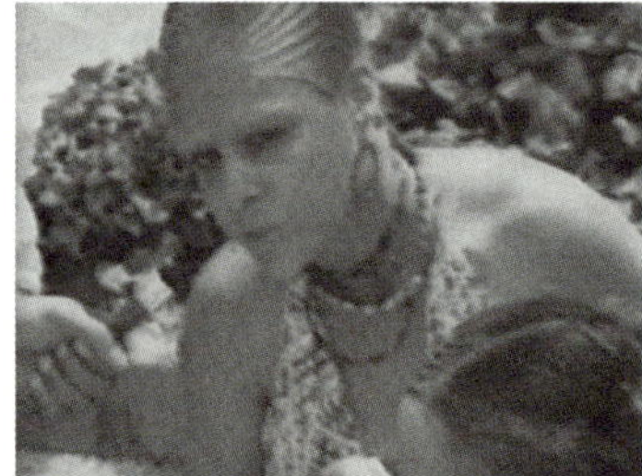

17:23

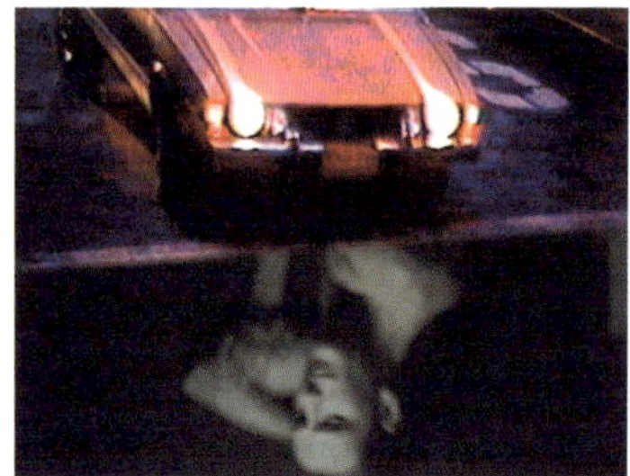

07:11

along and they did. And they wound up talking about being first-generation immigrants and what it meant to be here at Columbia and there was a lot of conversation about paperwork and interfacing with the government, your papers. A bunch of conversations just ended up flowing pretty naturally.

RC – I'm going to jump ahead a little bit so we have time. Just to make mention, this is *My Twilight Zone Thing* from 2014. But if you could maybe speak to this work, *Lineage for a Multiple-Monitor Workstation: Number One*, from 2015.

SP – This is my first dive back into Chroma Key, which is just a post-production technique where the foreground and background are separated. I went home to Perth Amboy and asked several of my family members to do a series of things that felt ritualistic. None of them were really true or things that we did on a regular basis. But I was trying to think through what it is to make portraits and what I found is that that's an impossibility and so what happens when you make images of people. And part of this, is they have these masks approximating the chroma key green color. I was trying to think through the communal or what we assume we know about a group of people, and from there the piece unfolds into familial absurdity. I, of course, know my mom and grandmother pretty well, but how can you leave some type of representational space for people who you think you know intimately to be who they are? To make that space through images you sometimes need to annihilate part of the image all

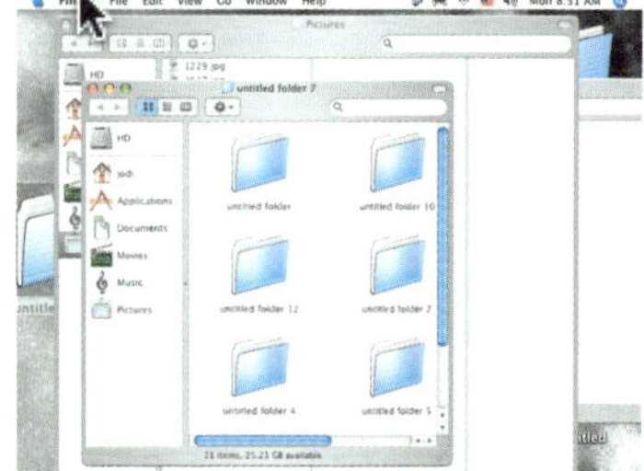

00:46

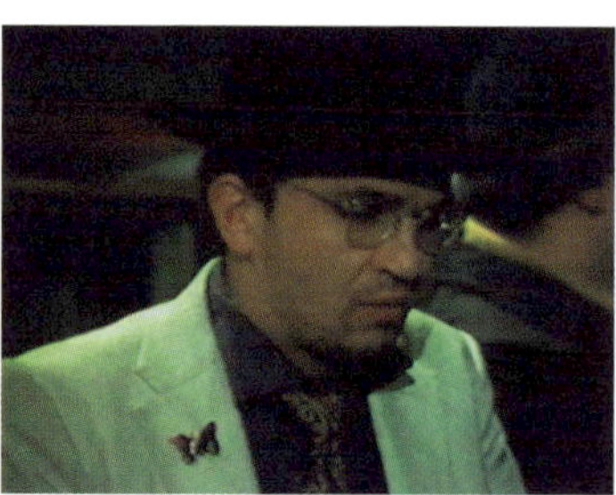

08:17

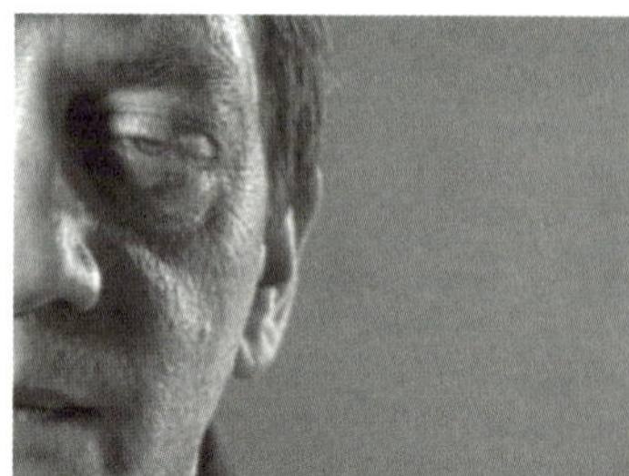

00:01

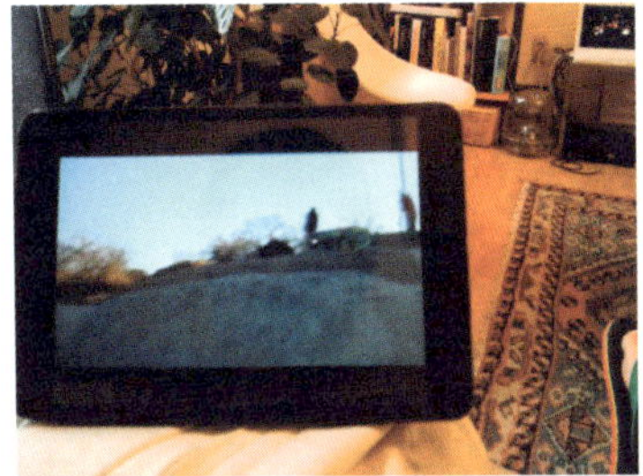

04:09

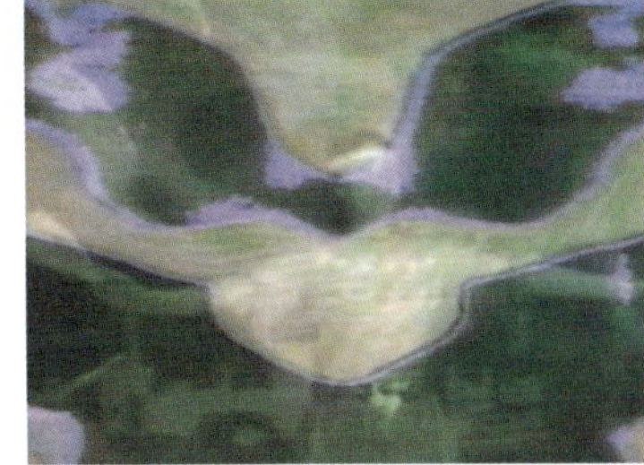

14:40

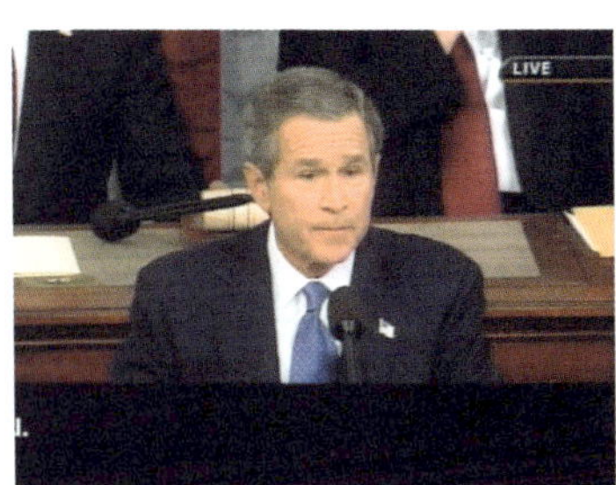

04:42

together. I think that's what the green screen does.

RC – And then maybe you could speak to this composite version, which does not reflect the installation aspect that is key to this work.

SP – Yeah it's a two-channel work. I've been really into a kind of multichannel video just because it gets people literally like moving through a space. I think it's expanding the narrative through these multiple channels, allowing a bit of the understanding even if you're not getting the thing or you're not getting a complete vision. There's still some type of pleasurableness or something that doesn't feel like a loss because you know you are not consuming the image of these people.

RC – That sounds great. So this is *Graft and Ash for a Three-Monitor Workstation* from 2016. And we do have a clip to show. I don't know if you want to say something before showing the clip.

SP – This was made in a program where you graft an image of a face on an avatar. So something went wrong in that application leaving a white mark on the cheek and I just thought it looked ashy, like it needs lotion. So I call it "graft and ash" for a three-monitor workstation. That's a joke, you laugh. And it's actually, I don't know if you have an image, but it's couched inside of a workstation. It's a machine that has pedals and a desk attached to it.

I'm interested in what self-actualization means, and I don't think it's real. So I was trying to make myself in a program that makes 3D models, just playing around and I realized that if I tried to create myself, a big part of that

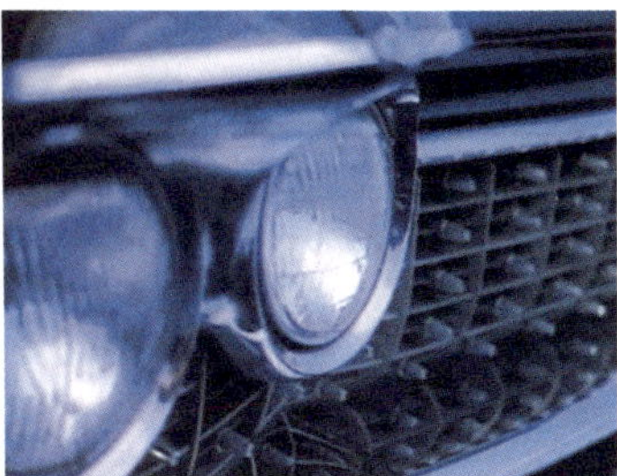

00:29

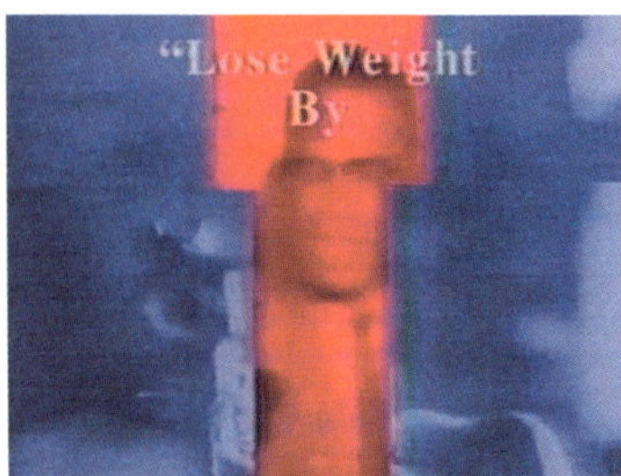

00:46

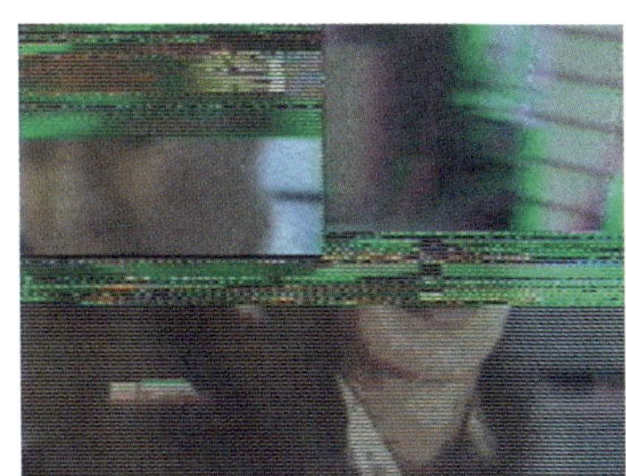

21:23

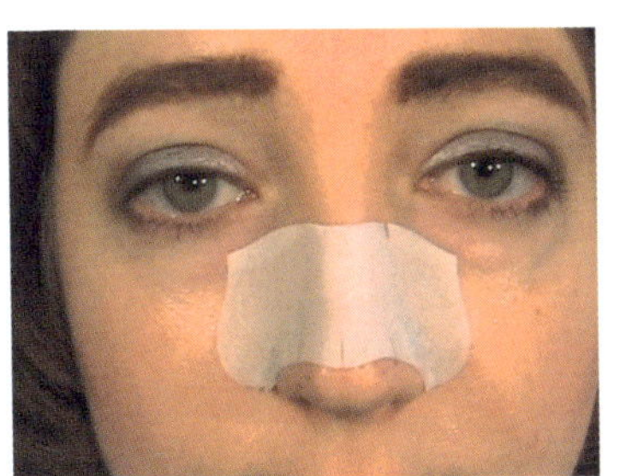

01:35

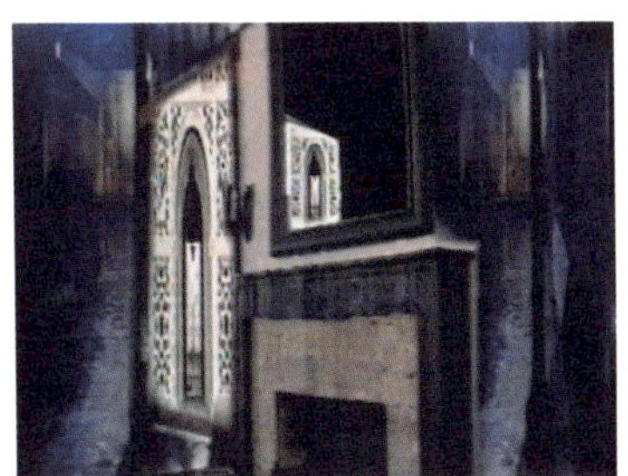

00:32

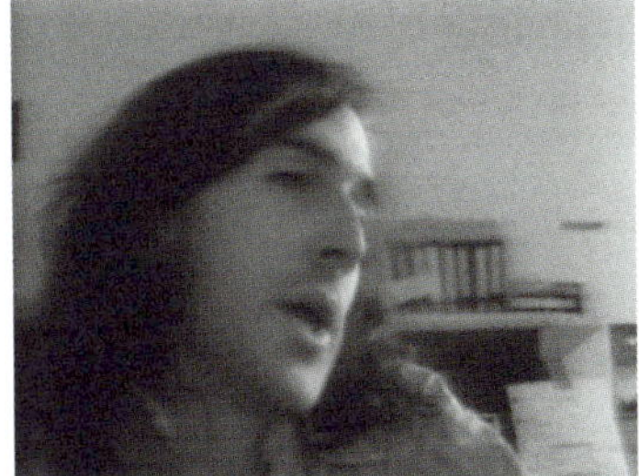

04:35

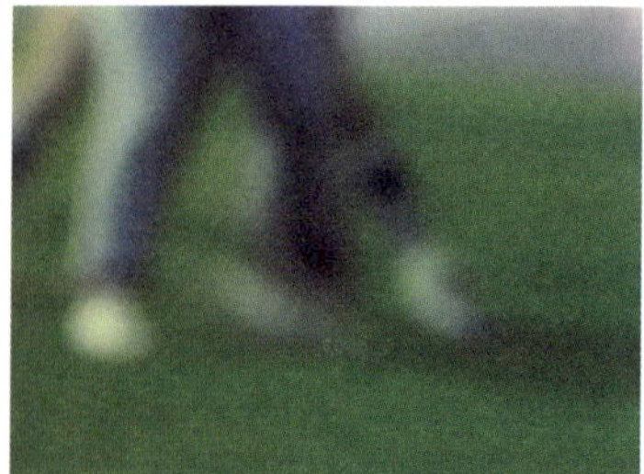

01:15

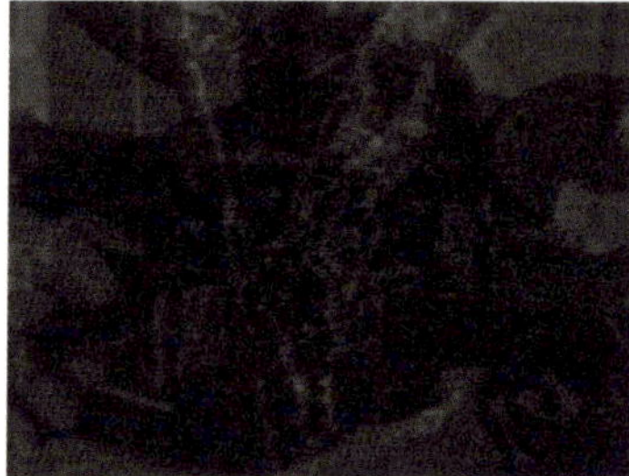

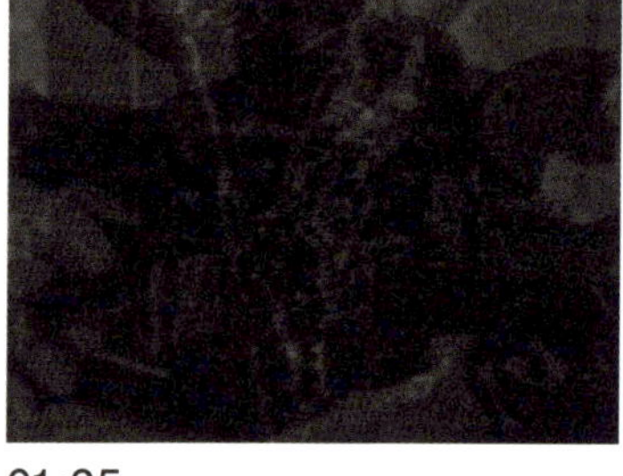

01:35

05:50

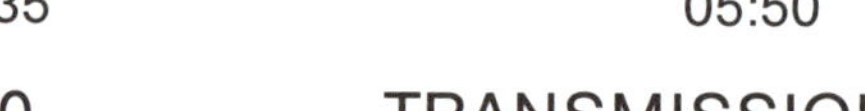

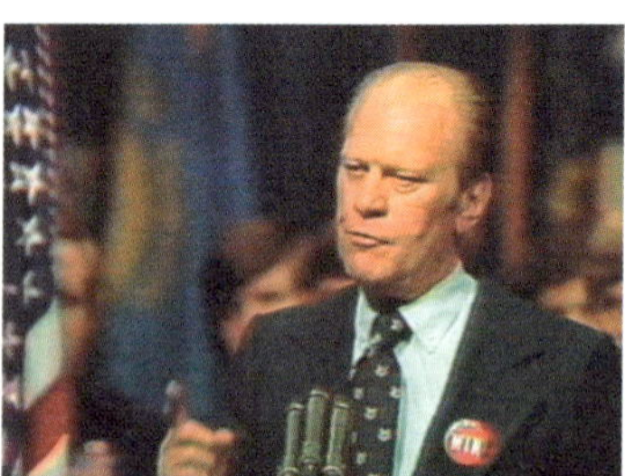

13:59

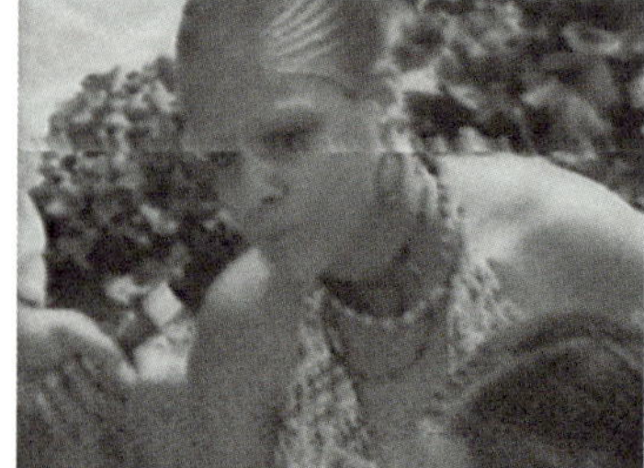

17:23

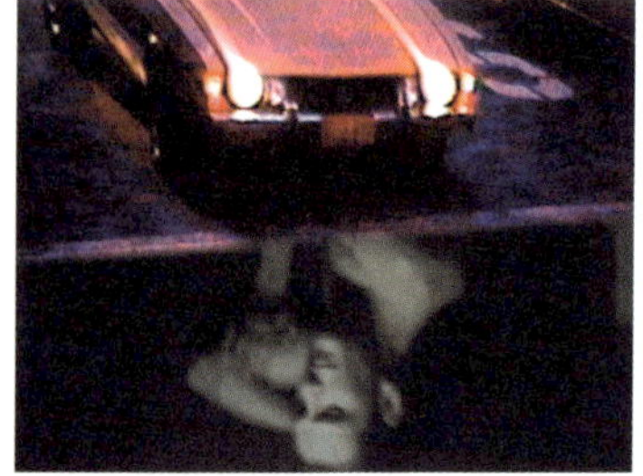

07:11

was my fatness. You can't make a fat body in the program. In the video, the machine/avatar has gone through the internet and found this real study from VCU about the just-world theory, which basically says if you're a good person, good things happen to you. But the inverse is also adopted as a belief, which is if you're a bad person, bad things happen to you. These are beliefs held widely by people of every race and class. And so it was found in the study that if the African American participants believed in just-world theory, they had higher instances of heart problems and stress. So I concluded that if you believe the world is a good place then you are likely to die faster, especially if you're a Black person or marginalized. And so this machine/avatar that is made to labor, that's made to actualize bodies has realized that what it's been built to do is impossible. And so what it's decided is that being grumpy and cynical is actually necessary for survival. It also has its modifications made to my body just so I can get in and out of it without breaking it but it's incredibly uncomfortable and the pedals are backwards, so it makes it harder to actually get it to work out.

AK – I'm going to skip over this work that we commissioned here at ICA, *IT'S IN THE GAME '17 or Mirror Gag for Vitrine and Projection* (2017), but maybe this is a good entry point to talk about both of your interests in images that are out circulating in the world and how you can reclaim them or complicate them.

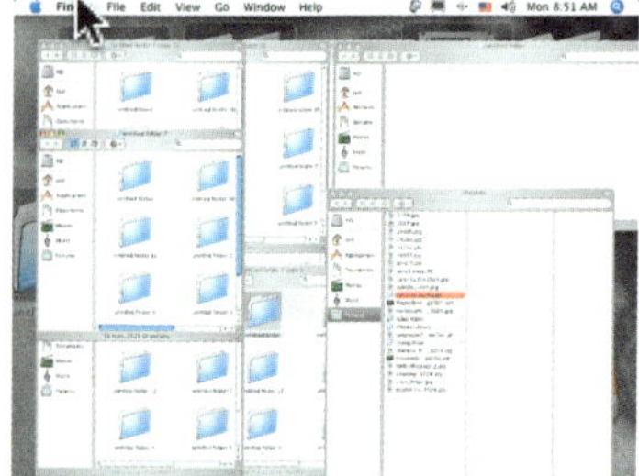

00:46

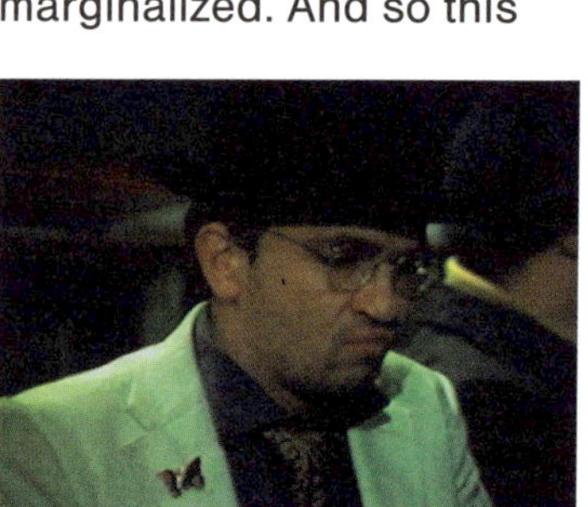

08:17

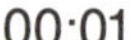

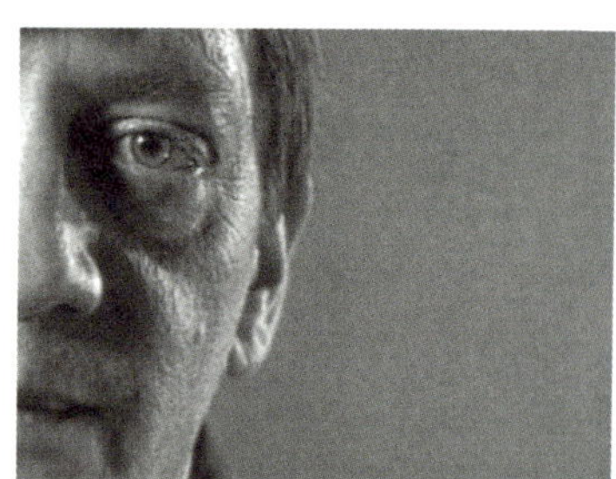

00:01

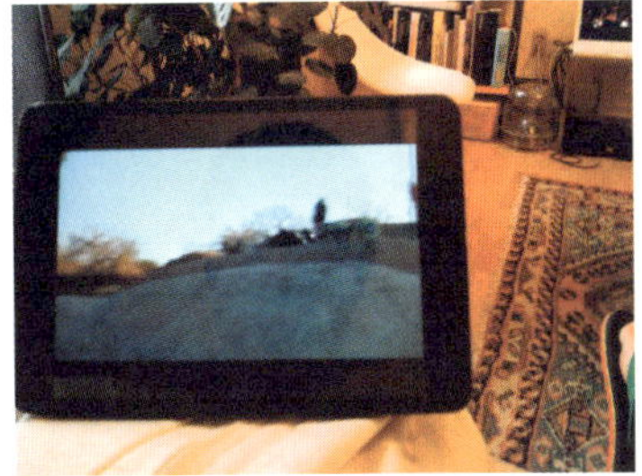
04:09

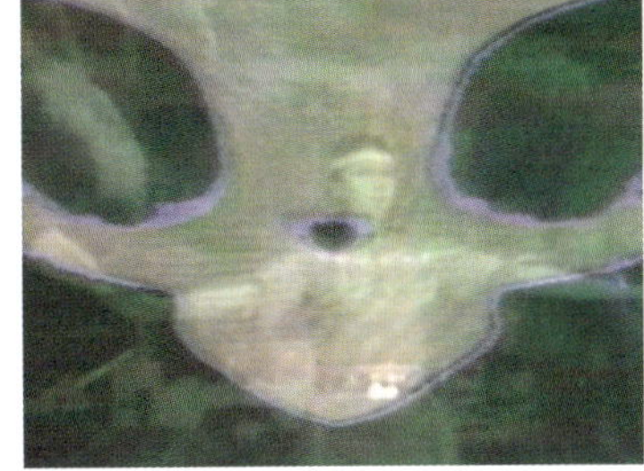
14:40

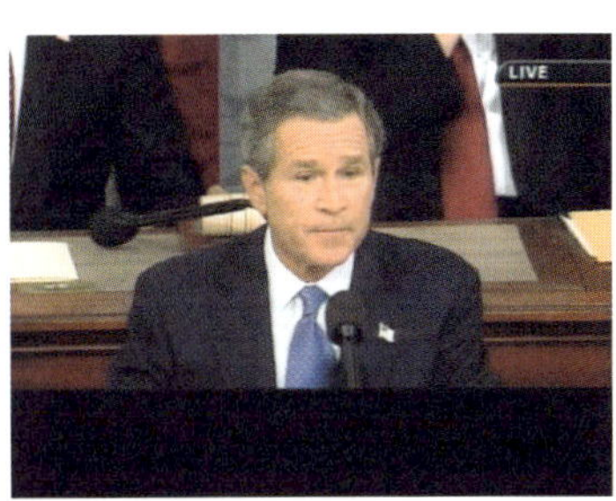

04:42

UJ – Well, Sondra, I find your work fascinating actually, the way that you are exploring using the green screen technology in particular. You said you were in ceramics and I'm coming from a painting background. For me the green screen provided me with this technique in painting that's called glazing. So when I was a painter I learned that with glazing I could superimpose images on top of another layer of imagery, which I thought was "wow." We were talking earlier about surrealism—now I can get surreal with the context of what I wanted to make, which you see a little bit of in *Planet X* (2006), and some other works where I use more green screen technique. But you're taking the whole thing. I'm looking at some point like, "Can you work out on that technology?"

SP – You could, I wouldn't. It's not enjoyable and that's like the point to make it a little difficult.

UJ – Because I thought "wow" you can really transpose yourself with what you're up to.

SP – So yeah, I think with the green screen and blue screen I'm interested in the ghosts of the space before anything even happens in there. All of these decisions that are made before and after production are really about before and after culture. The remnants and what has yet to come really meditate on all of these decisions that get made, and the possibilities that arise when people do things in groups. So I don't think they are utopian spaces, like beautiful projections of what the future can be. Who said white supremacy is basically solidarity? It's like lots of things happen

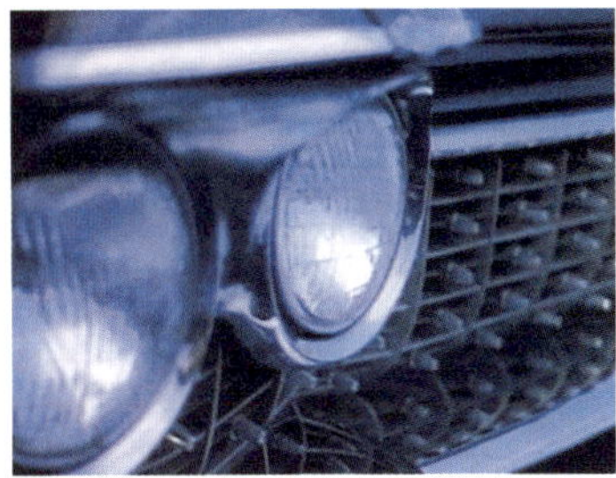
00:29

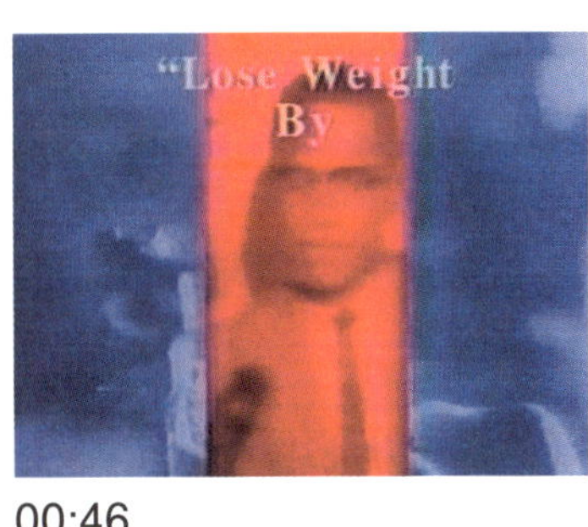

00:46

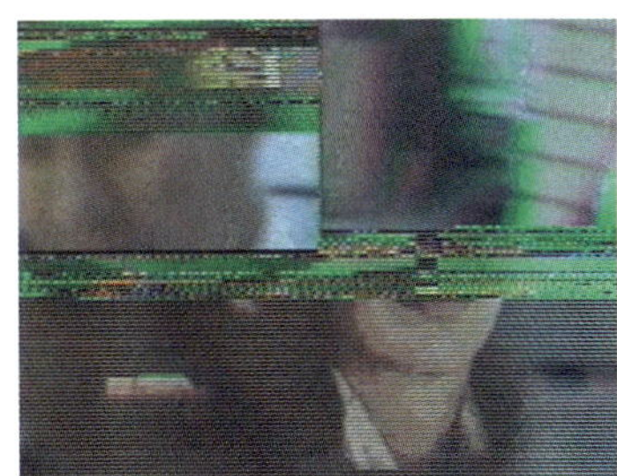
21:23

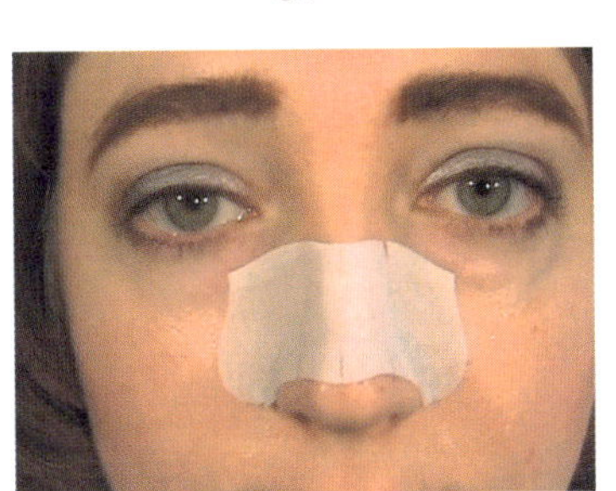
01:35

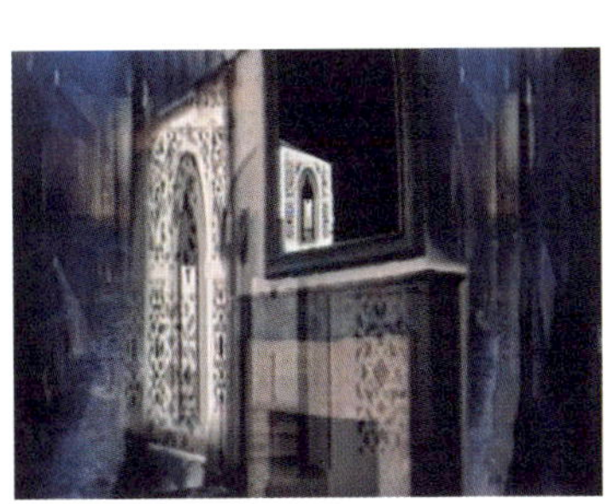
00:32

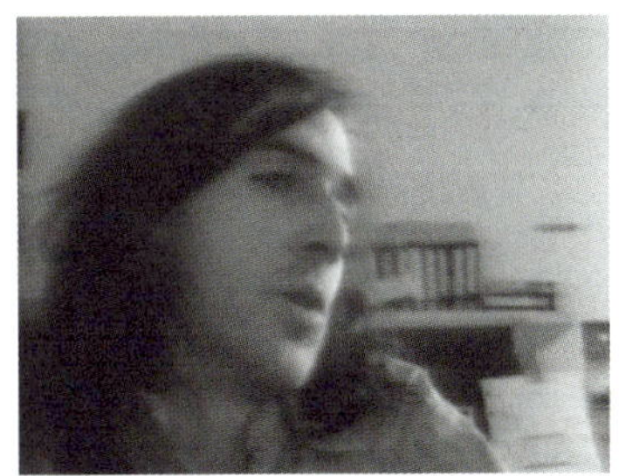
04:35

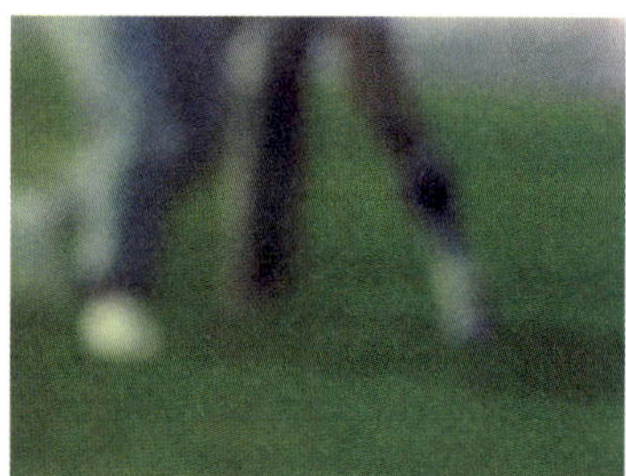
01:15

01:35

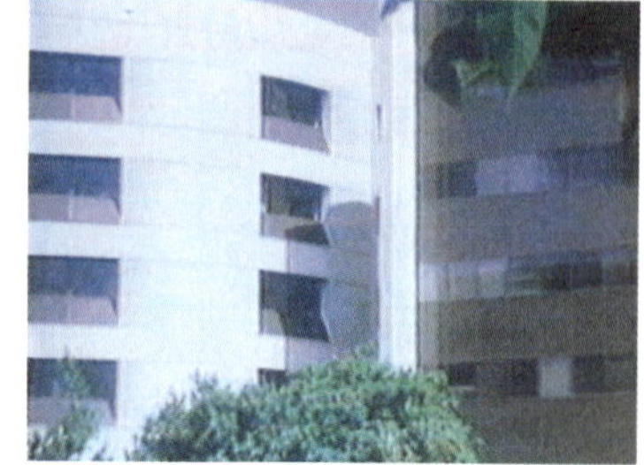
05:50

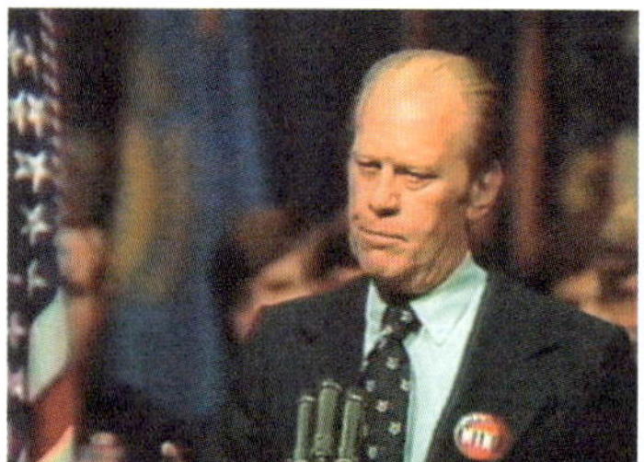
13:59

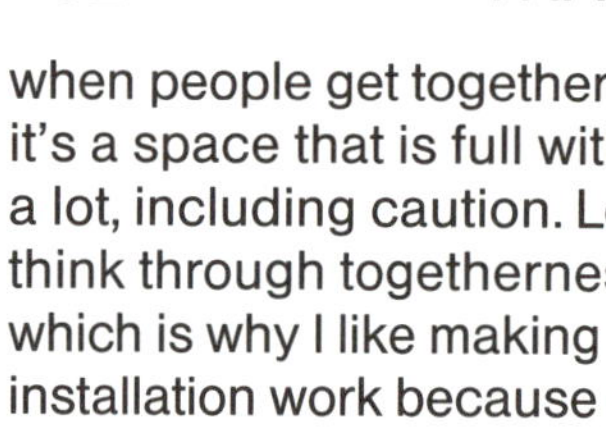

when people get together so it's a space that is full with a lot, including caution. Let's think through togetherness, which is why I like making installation work because it's likely you're going to be there with people.

UJ – See, it also reminds me of *Avatar* (2009). Because if you've ever got a chance to see the production of *Avatar*, I mean it's a total green screen world and what happens in the production of that or for that matter most science fiction films of today you can have the kind of effects that you see in *Star Wars* or *Star Trek*, and it's funny because of the political atmosphere we're living in today you've got lots of sci-fi TV shows now to get you away from thinking about now because you could escape. Do you feel you can escape in your work?

SP – No, I mean I feel like if I wanted to escape I'd make those exercise machines a little bit easier for me to use. I think sci-fi is super interesting because good sci-fi comments on now but is also generous with potential for the future. I haven't seen like *Ready Player One*—it's sci-fi but it's still like a white man saving the world—these reproductions are the same stuff over and over again and so I think that's definitely an escapism. One person saving the world and remaking it in their image. That's Elon Musk right there. That's the lineage of these Eurocentric, patriarchal, white supremacist media, that is it. I'm listening to his biography right now and like that was his thing since he was twelve years old because he's been watching these films and all of this stuff

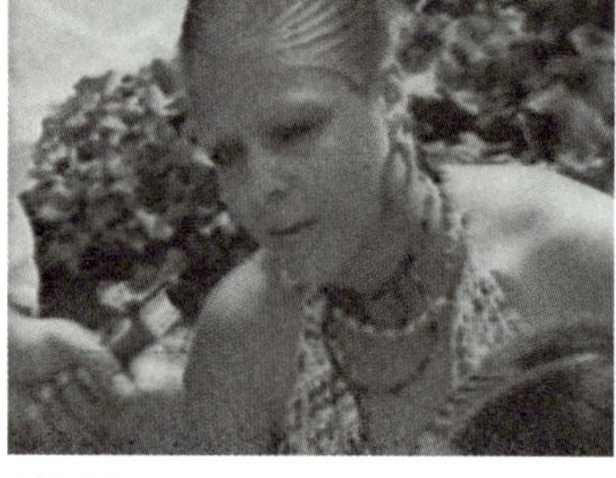
17:23

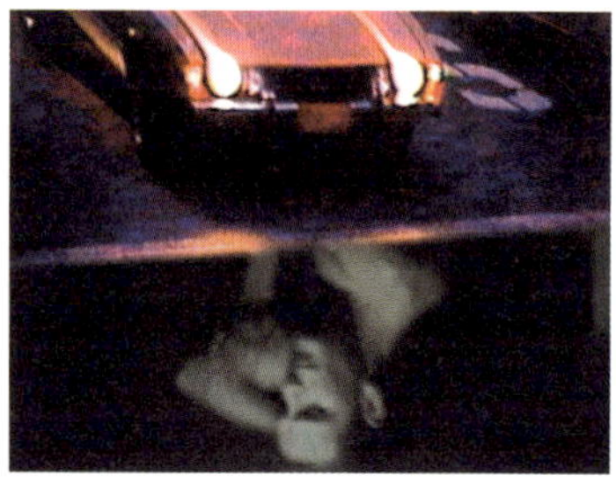
07:11

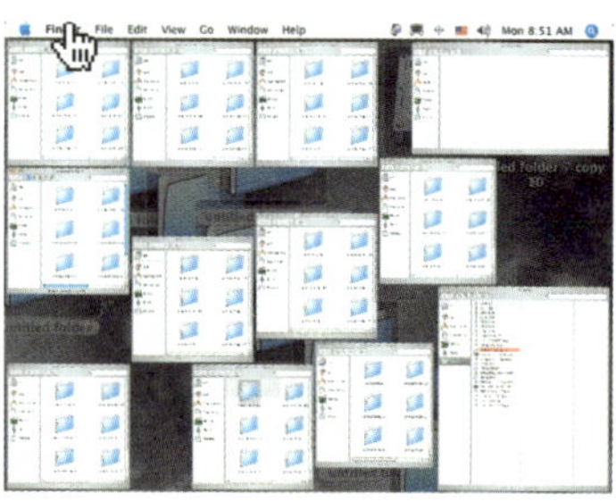
00:46

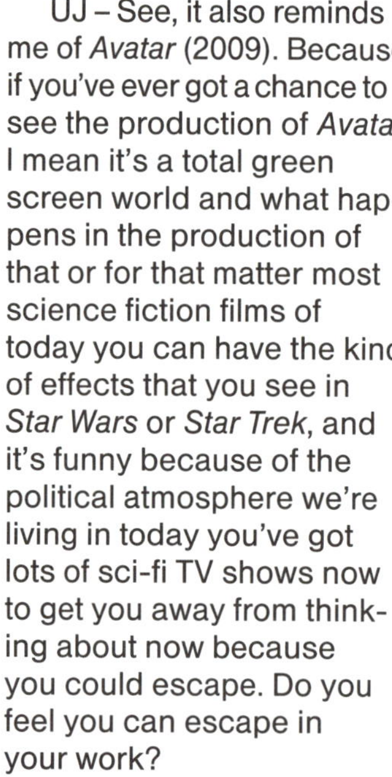

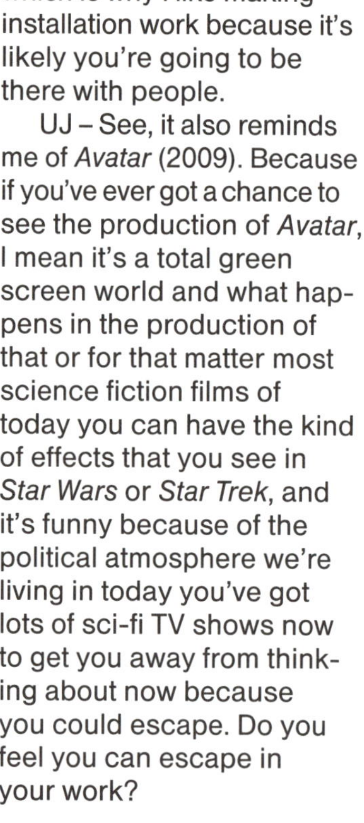
08:17

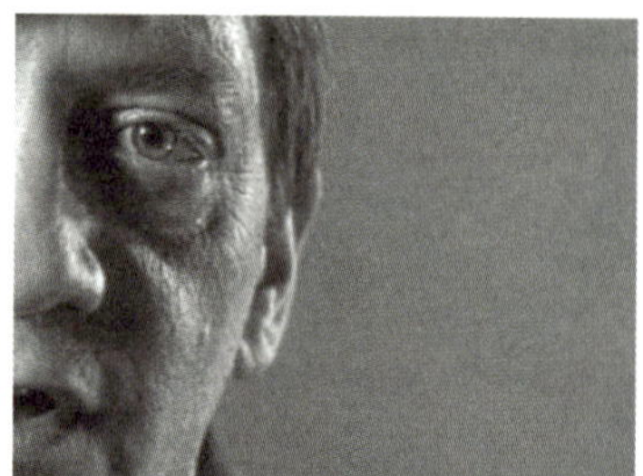
00:01

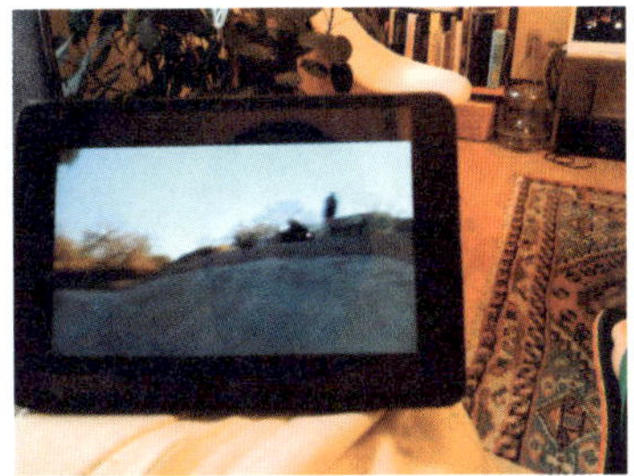
04:09

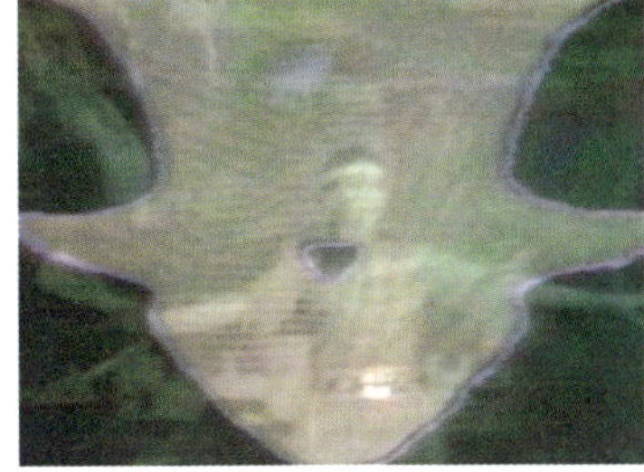
14:40

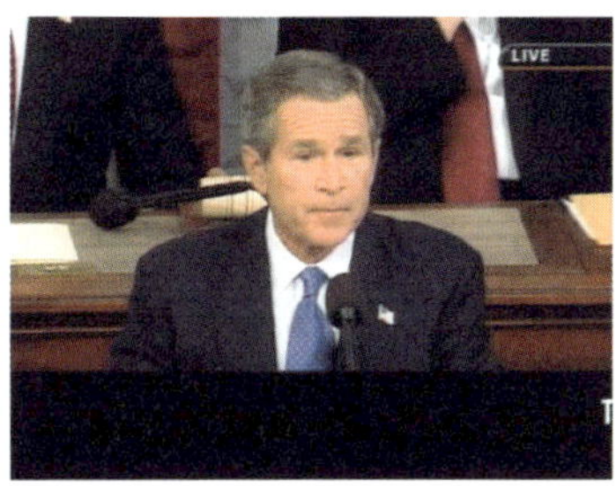

04:42

and he actually knows how to make rockets. So this is the stuff that happens. It's a disparate example but we can…

UJ – Well, I mean, just to bring a little into the context of what you were saying, which I said may add another speaking engagement here. I mean you guys are familiar with gravity, not the movie but the essence of gravity. And the fact that the people on the space station have problems having to be up there, you know the guy Scott Kelly who had stayed up there for a whole year and his twin who was down here on the earth, they've got different DNA now. That's sort of interesting I thought, but also the thing that you care so dearly for which we were talking about. It was vision—your eyes don't stay in the same place if you stay in outer space because there's no gravity and your eyeballs will shift and your internal organs move around inside this cavity you call your body. So now how are we going to go to all these other places they're talking about and maintain full body functions in space?

SP – I'm totally into that. That's the potential right there.

AK – Maybe this also relates to what you were talking about earlier about doggereal trying to reposition these things. I mean just the Eurocentric dominance that you were talking about within science fiction. That was where the impulses behind doggereal were coming from too.

UJ – Doggereal in that sense, because you know what is defined as: irregular and on a variation. I mean now to one degree I'll make

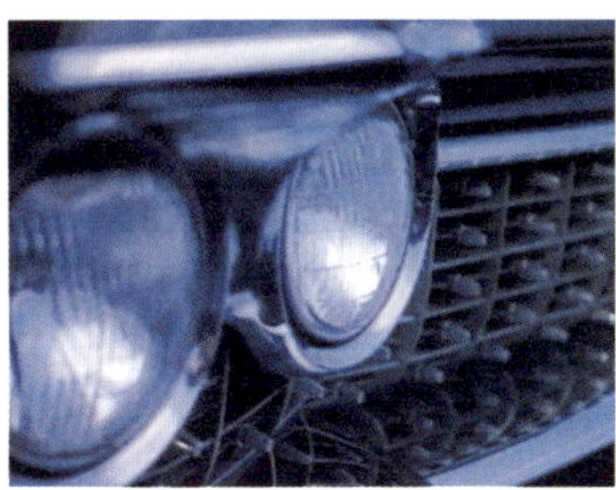
00:29

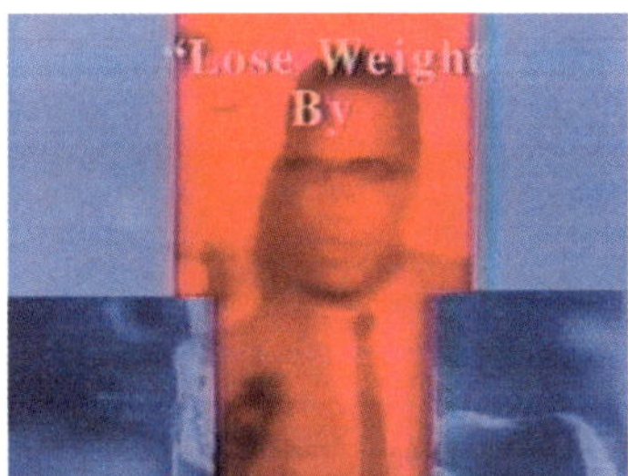

00:46

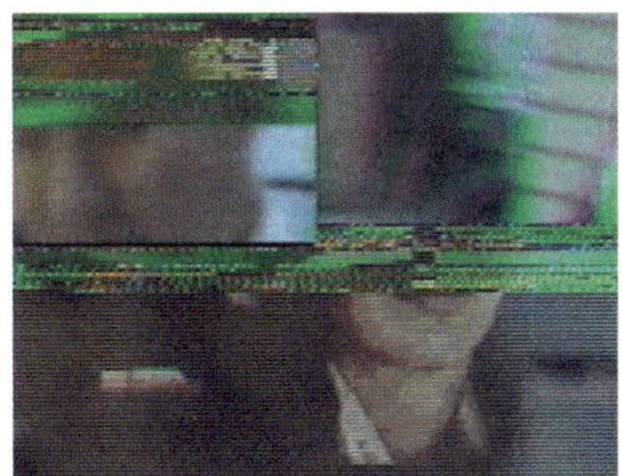
21:23

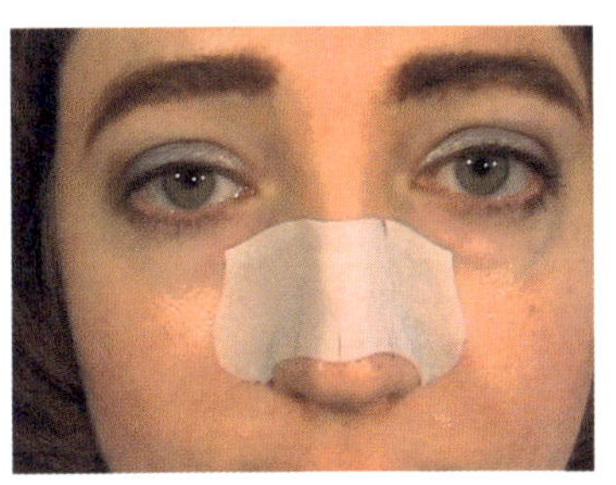
01:35

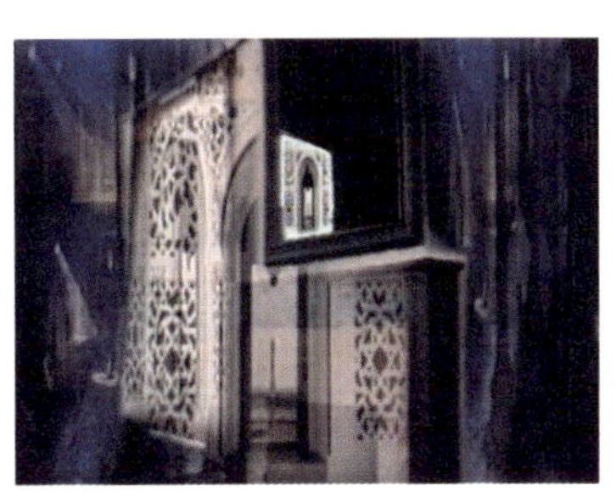
00:32

04:35

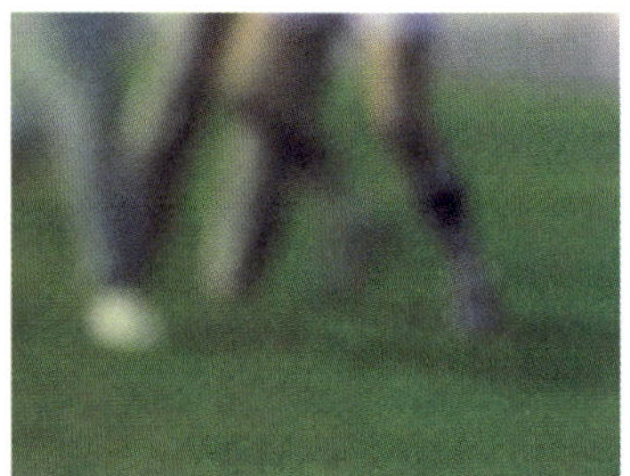

01:15

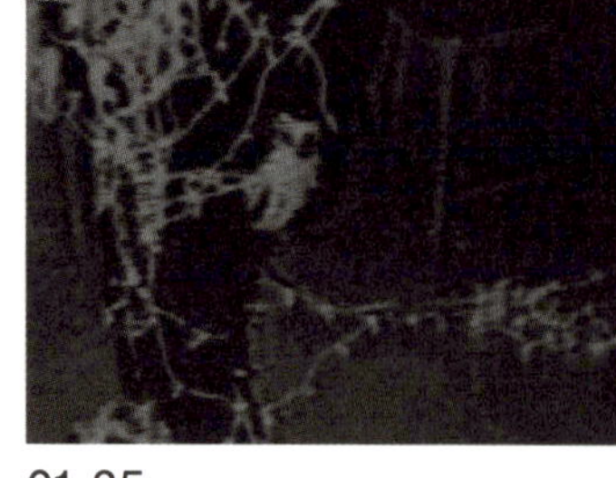

01:35

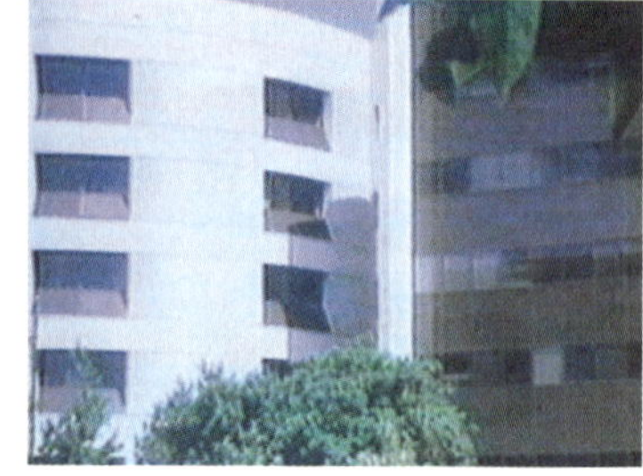

05:50

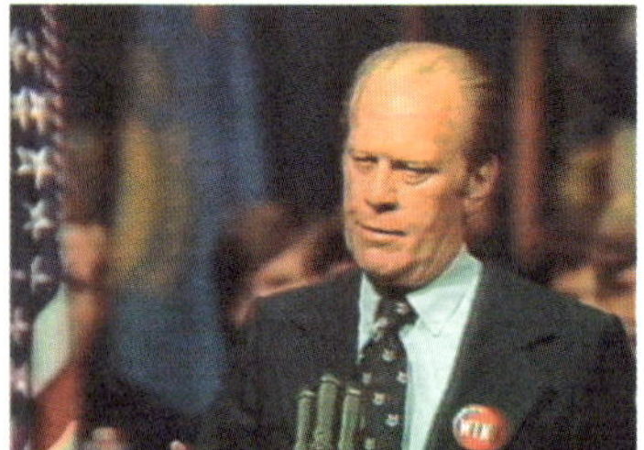

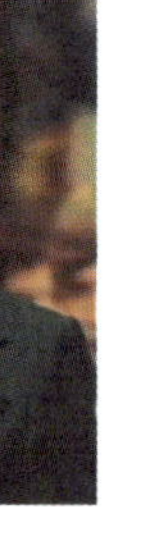

13:59

17:23

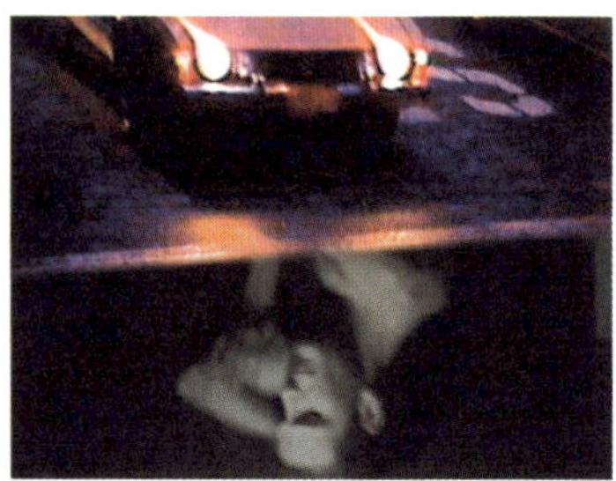

07:11

it very simple: If you're on a date and the person that you're with does something that is unrecognizable, how do you react to it? Okay? Because we have doggereal moments all the time that we don't pay attention to. As a matter of fact, sometimes we excuse them and say oh that's OK they'll be alright. They won't do that again, you think. And to whatever degree that doggereal moment, if you will, gets extended. To some degree that's what I'm playing within my narrative constructs, that some of my videos—the narrative or the doggereal moment, if you will—gets extended, and it goes on and on and as it says sometimes it's defined as a comedic verse so then you're laughing. You're laughing at something irregular but you don't question why you're laughing, so that's how I got into doggereal.

SP – I guess my question is what do you think about the doggereal moment that then becomes recognizable—is it still irregular? Because you are doing these video assemblage types of moments of recreating or the reimaging over and over again. And so these irregular things wound up becoming solid in a lot of ways, they feel like that sometimes.

UJ – You're hitting on a point. That's just like taking a nail and hitting it on me, you know hitting and hitting and hitting the nail with the hammer. I think there's a guy who's a president that keeps doing that. We got a doggereal president actually. This whole notion of something that happens again and again. And whether or not you recognize it as your regular or

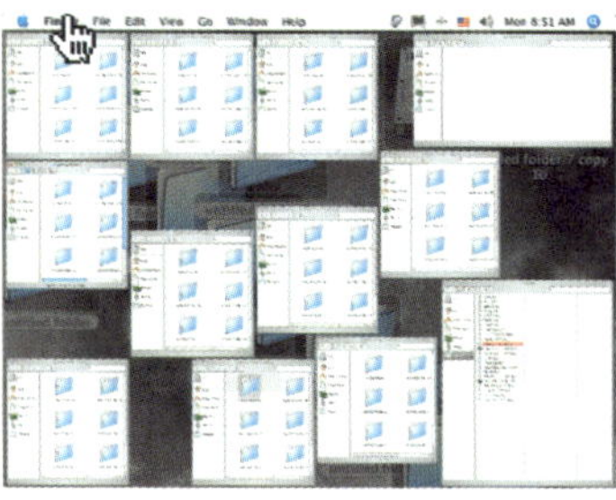

00:46

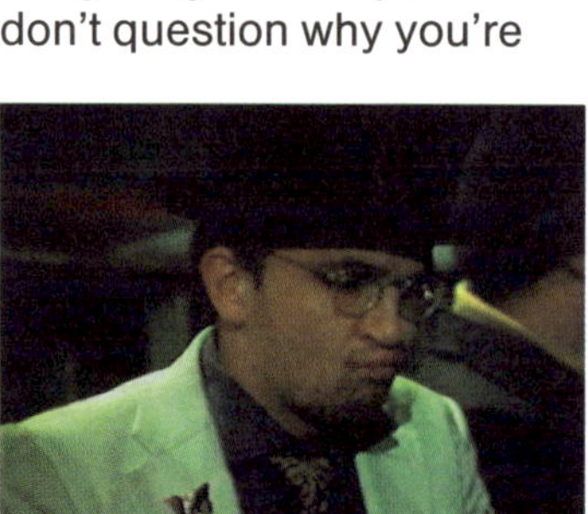

08:17

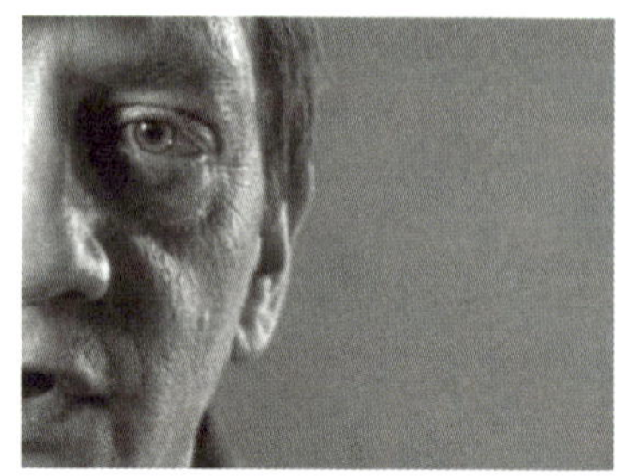

00:01

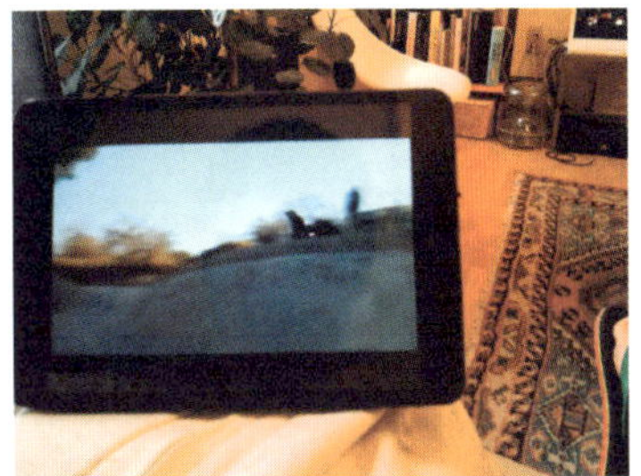

04:09

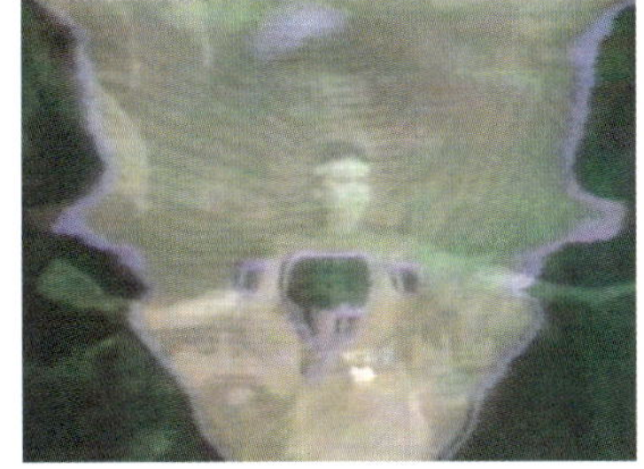

14:40

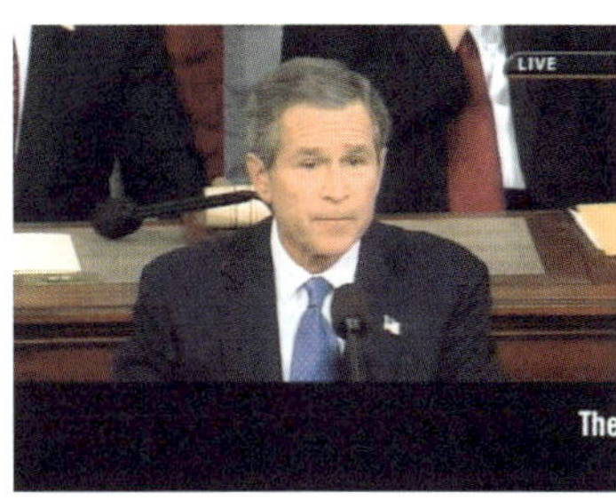

04:42

did you excuse it and say OK I'm going to embrace that now because I see the regularity in the concept of becoming again and again. I think that's what you're getting at and I recognized that that's what I said. When I made *Inconsequential Doggereal* the first time, it was considered very fast. That was 1980. Fast editing. This was actually in some ways pre-MTV, so nowadays you see things edited in such a fast motion. The thing is when you go to a gallery, how much time do you spend in front of an actual painting (since I come from a painting background)? Two or three seconds? You make the registration of that image and move on, and if the image had that kind of strength that makes you stay there longer than a few seconds, the artist is successful. They've got you concentrating on the concept, okay? So in that sense when you edit fast, the premise I was thinking of is called paramnesia, and to that extent if you're driving down the highway and you see an image and you do this all the time, maybe not on the highway, just on a subway or something. You see this image and then later on down the road that imagery comes back to you in your memory. That is the premise that I recognize back then that I wanted to establish about this collage if you were calling it, or montage of images, because I said if they're going fast enough sooner or later one of them is going to stick.

AK – I don't know where the time has gone but we are in our remaining couple of minutes and Sondra, I know we haven't even talked about Superman or the performance class

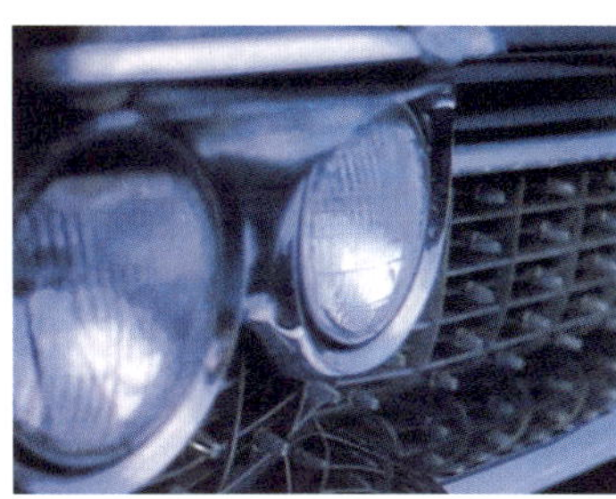

00:29

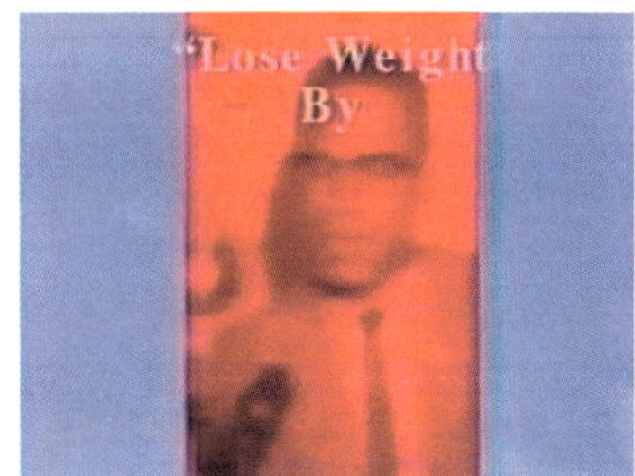

00:46

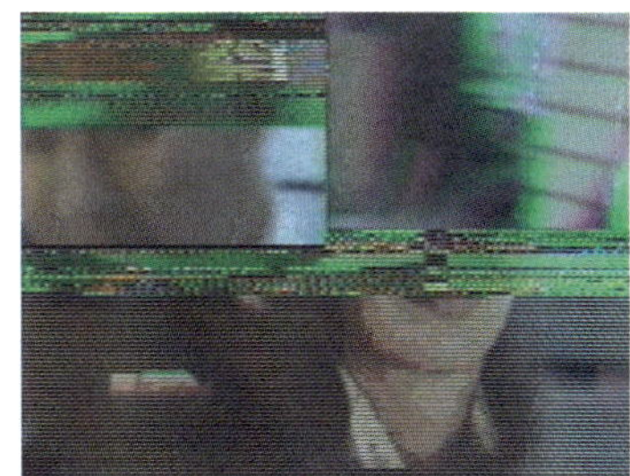

21:23

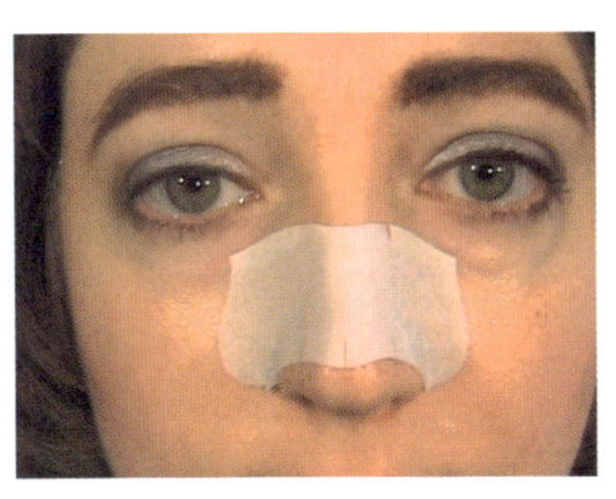

01:35

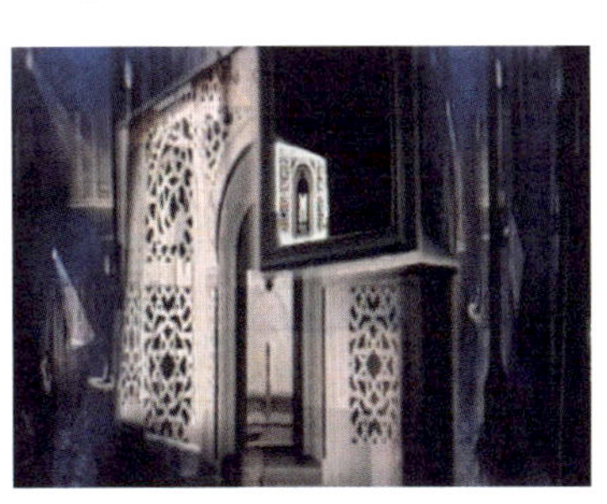

00:32

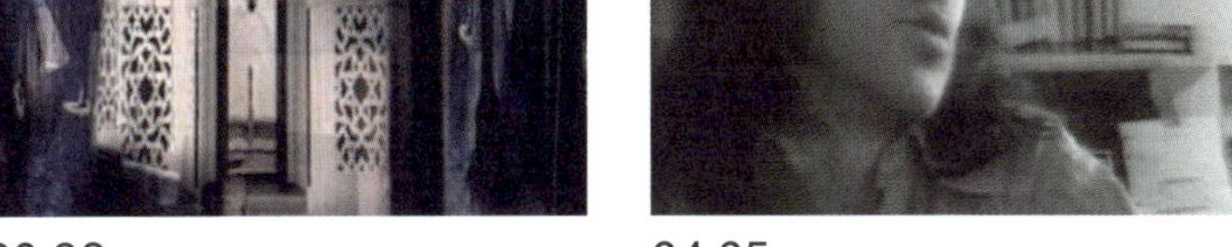

04:35

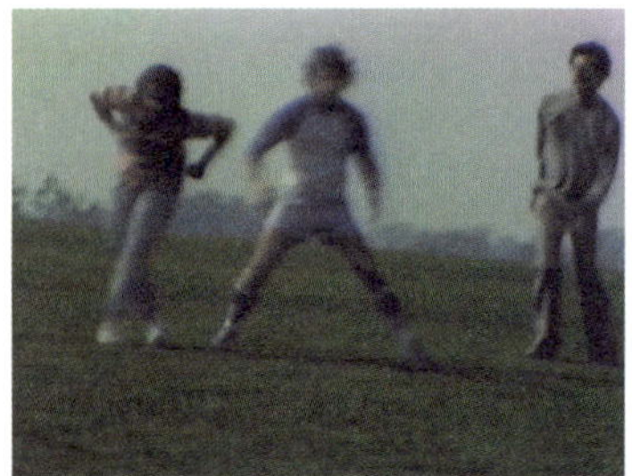
01:14

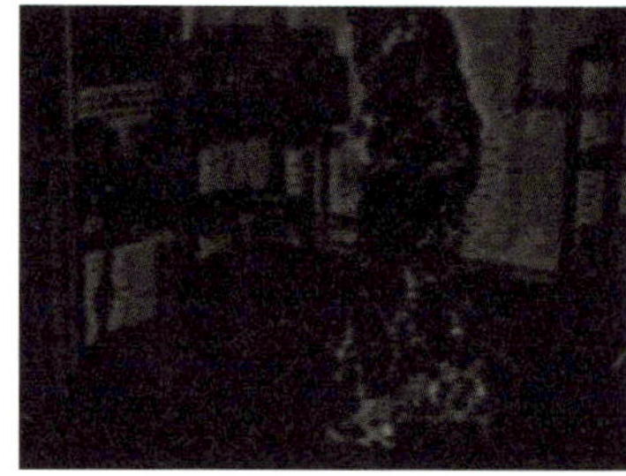
01:34

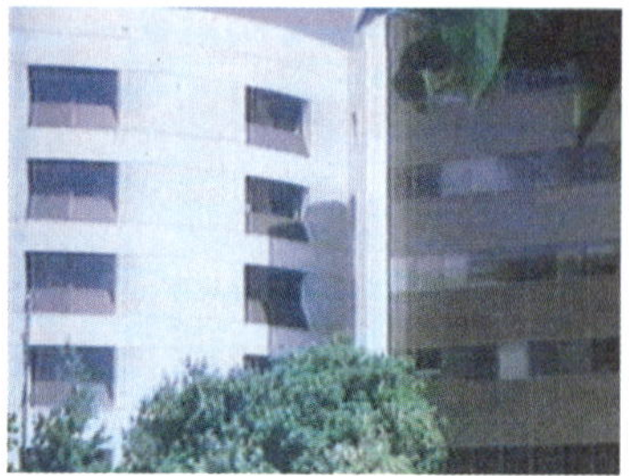
05:49

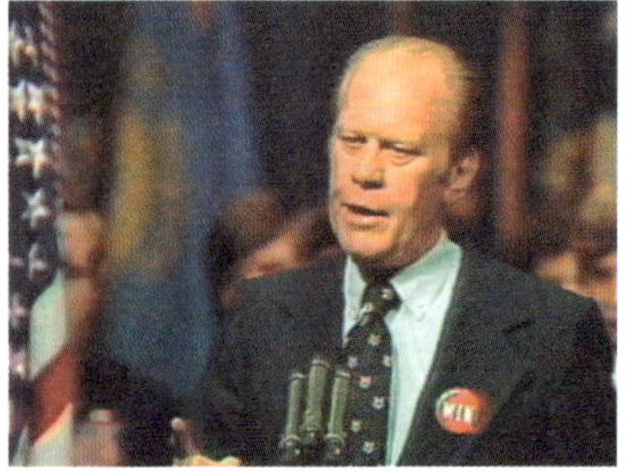
13:58

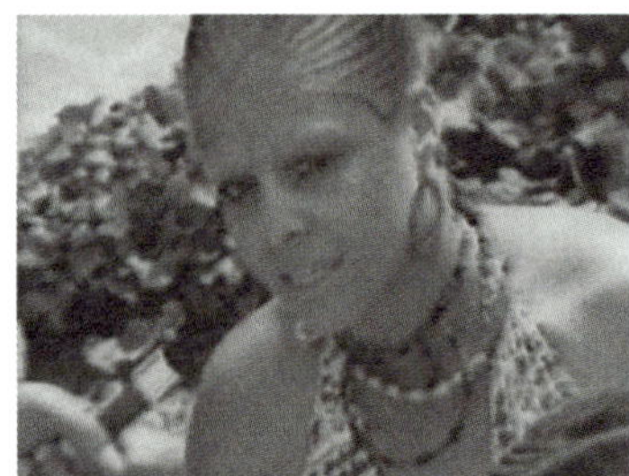
17:22

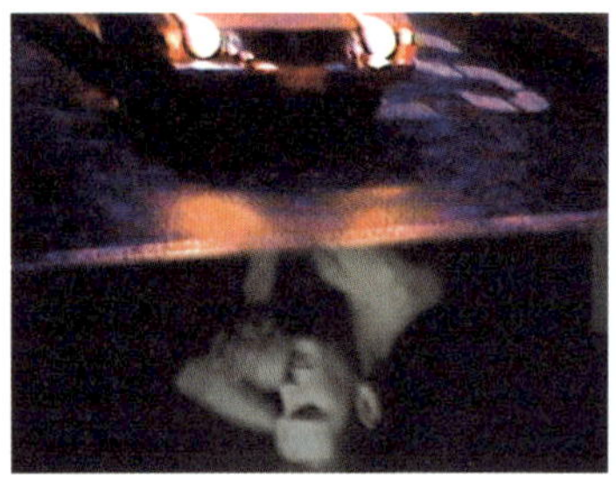
07:10

Ulysses took with Chris Burden or studying with Charles White and Betye Saar or the role of ritual in both of your work. I mean we could be here for many days and it would not get boring. But you were talking, Sondra, about this interest in the edit and I think that relates a lot to the way that you foreground the kind of tools of production and make those visible. I don't know if there's something you want to say on that.

SP – I think Ulysses touched on that really well.

AK – Well, we just got the signal actually. Rebecca, any concluding remarks?

RC – No, I just love to hear the two of you in conversation. I mean this has been doggereal—I think you've made a real impact here.

UJ – Thank you!

1 See "Bay Window 11 Fred in Baker Lake, Canada Bay Window Excerpts H 264" https://www.youtube.com/watch?v=BX6myB3s2Kw

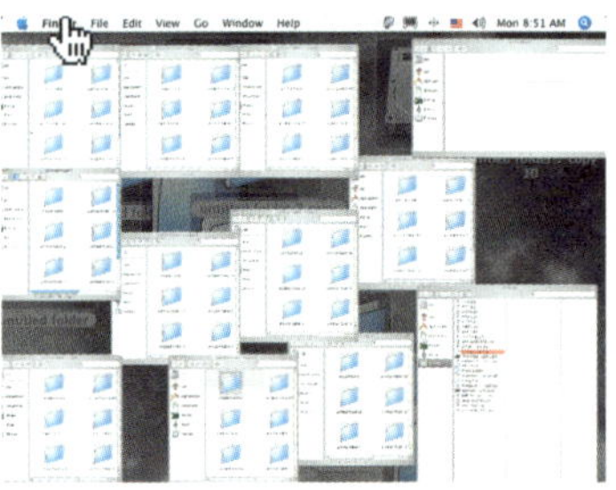
00:45

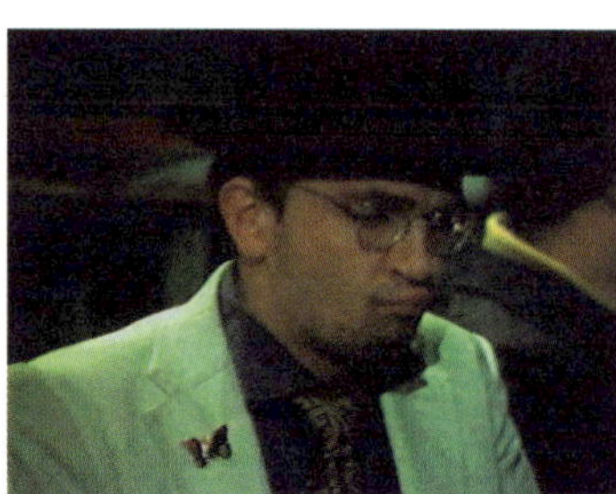
08:16

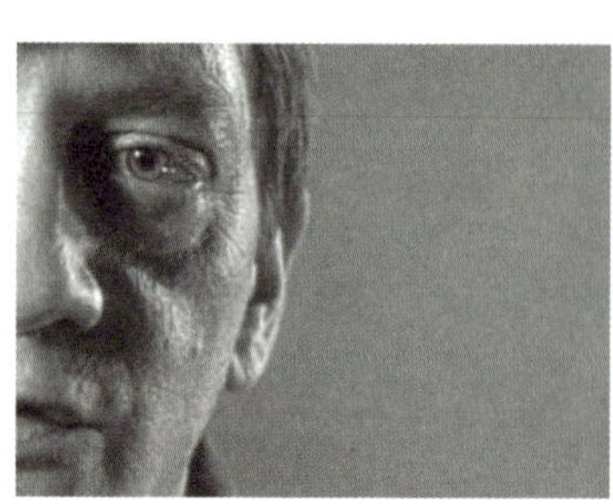
00:00

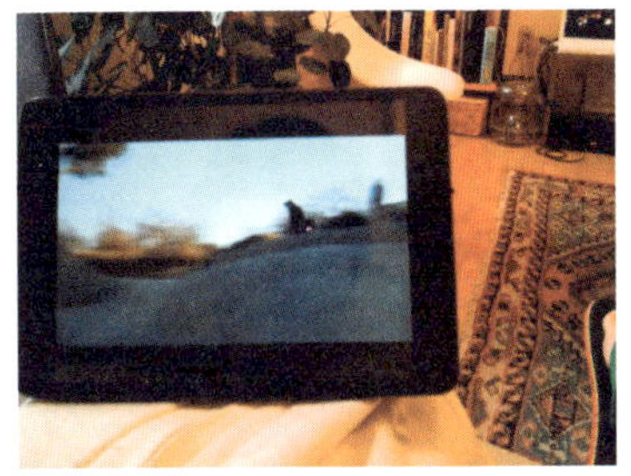

04:09

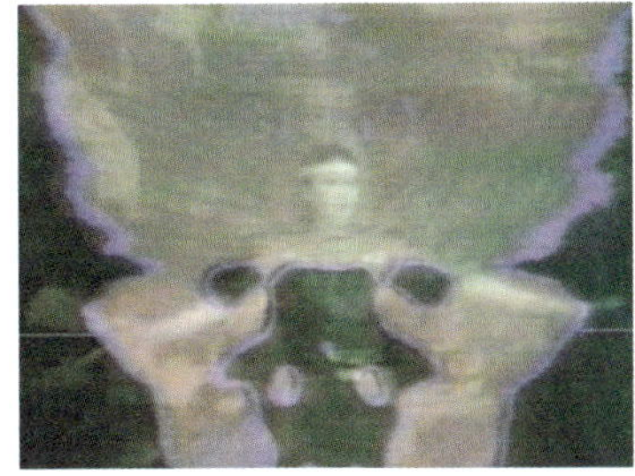

14:40

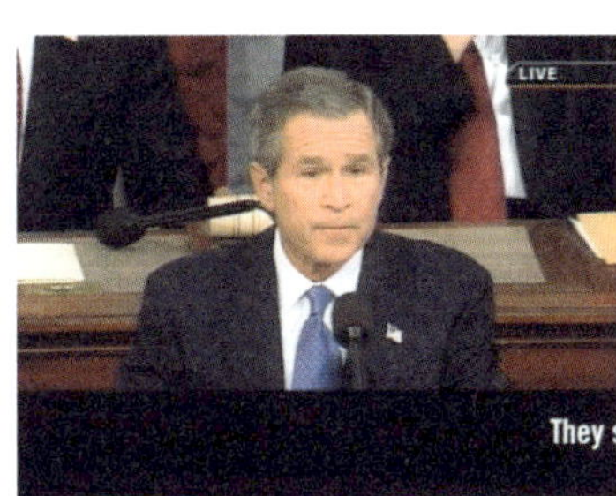

04:42

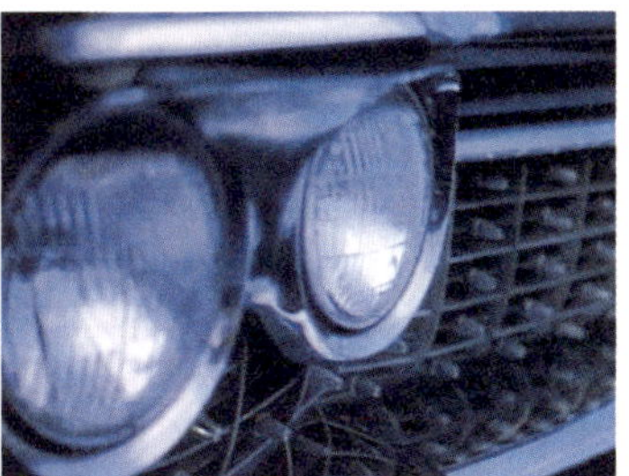

00:29

END MATTER

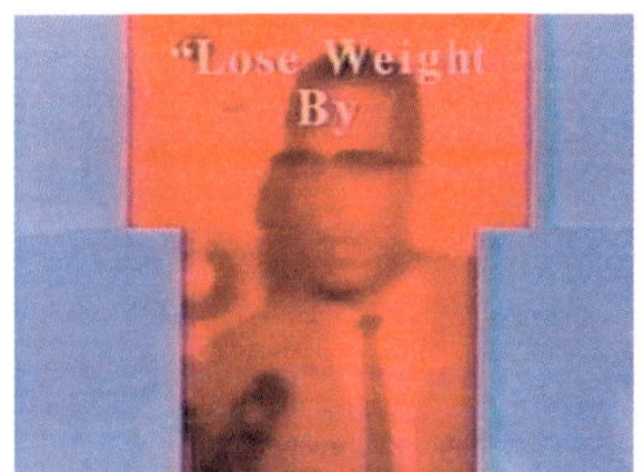

00:46

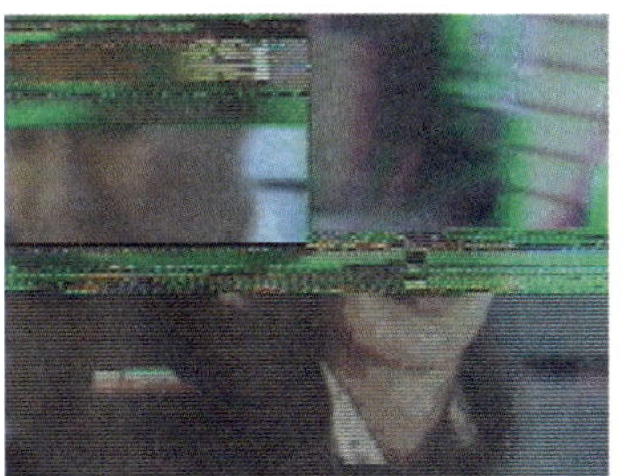

21:23

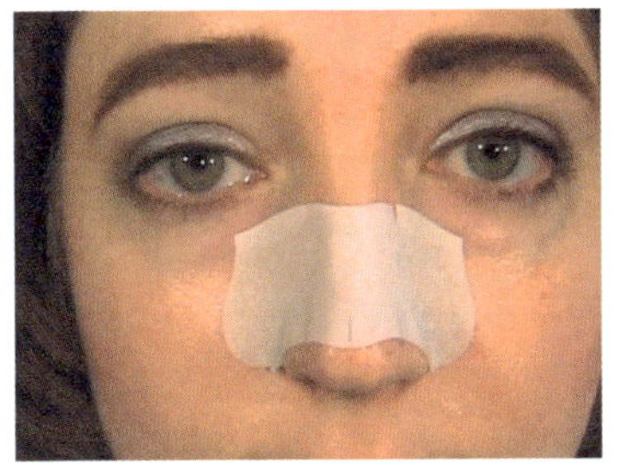

01:35

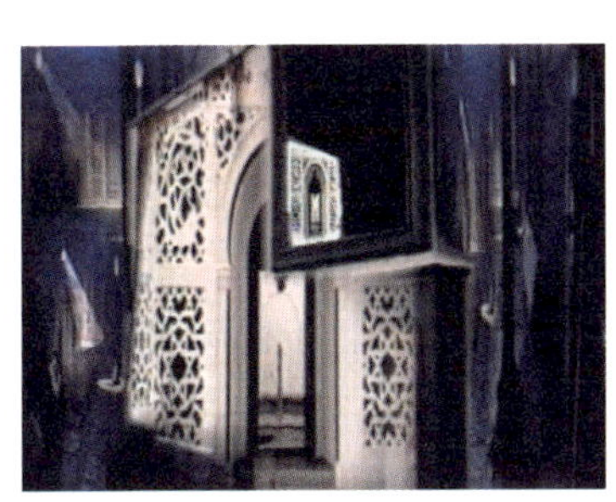

00:32

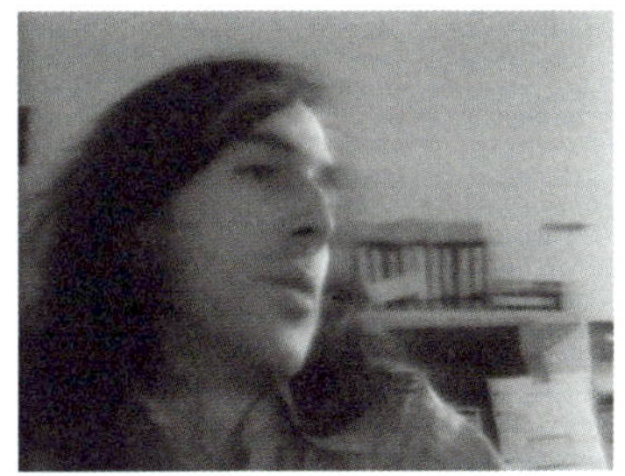

04:35

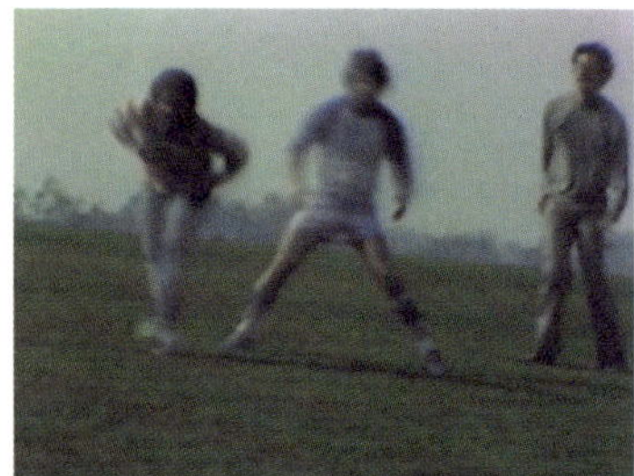

01:14

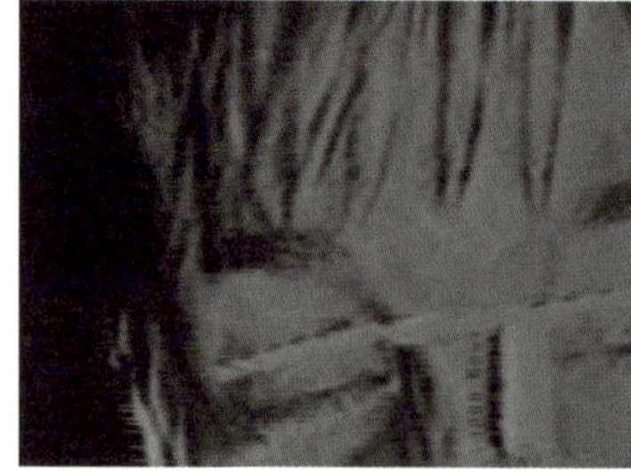

01:34

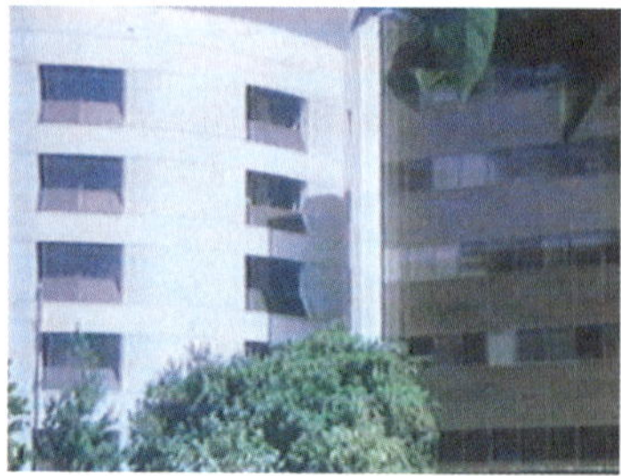

05:49

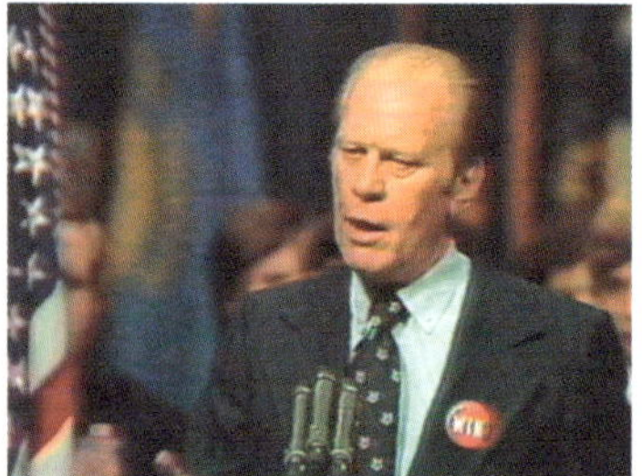

13:58

17:22

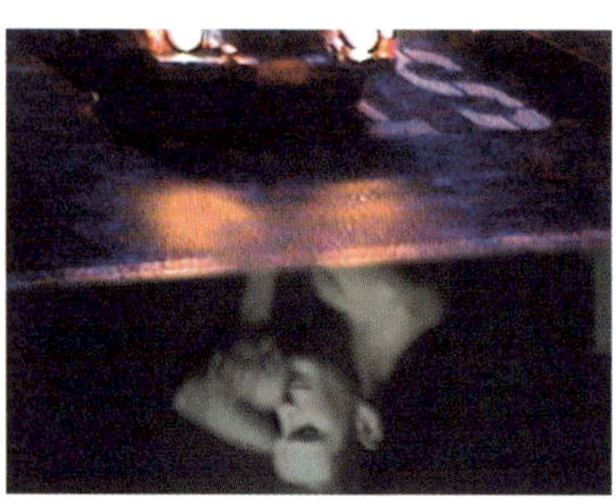

07:10

298 EAI ARCHIVAL MATERIAL

p. 35: Fish-eye photograph of the EAI editing facility. Photograph: Matthew Danowski. Circa 1986

p. 35: Back of fish-eye postcard advertising the EAI editing facility, circa 1985

p. 36: Ad for EAI's services, spring 1984

p. 37: *The New Television: A Public/Private Art*. The MIT Press, March, 1977

p. 38: Invitation card for the premiere of Bruce and Norman Yonemoto and Jeffrey Vallance's Blinky, April 1989

p. 39: Ad for EAI, College Art Association program, 1984

p. 57: Drawing of equipment in the early EAI Editing Suite

p. 58: Cover of the 1982 artists videotapes catalog, designed by Tucker Viemeister

p. 59: Cover of the 1976 artists videotapes catalog, designed by Jim McWilliams

p. 60: Postcard advertising EAI's 15th anniversary, 1986

p. 60: U-Matic & Beta Edit ad Flyer advertising U-Matic and Beta editing services, featuring former EAI editor David Riebman, 1979

p. 79: Organizational press release, circa 1977

p. 80: *At the Leading Edge*, a "manifesto" written by Howard Wise about the founding mission of EAI, 1973

p. 81: Rules for proper use of the Editing and Post Production Facilities, 1978

p. 82: Ad for EAI workshop teaching editing on the Apple II

p. 101: Howard Wise at 50 West 57th Street, June 1969. Photograph by Thomas Tadlock

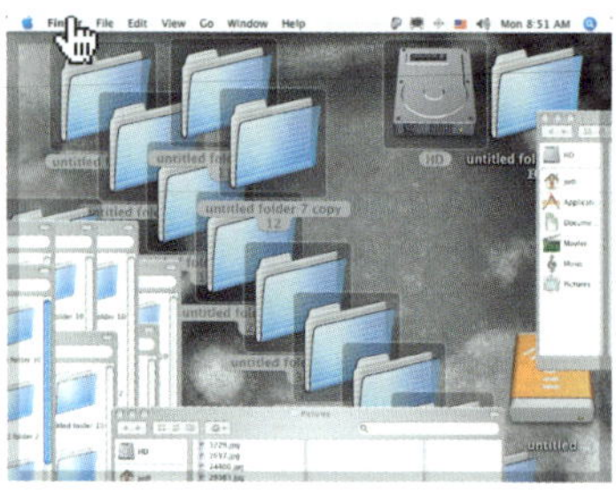

00:45

08:16

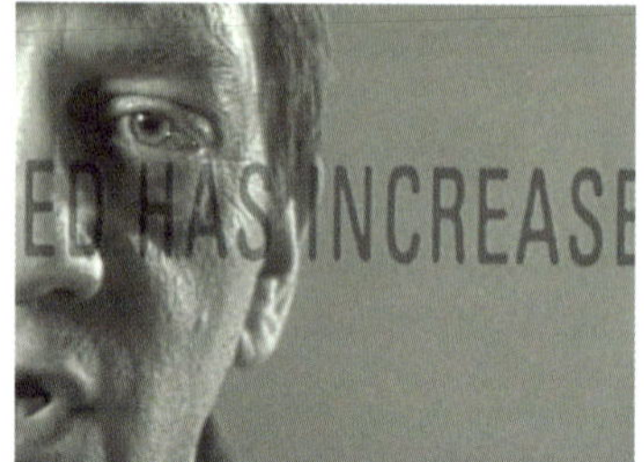

00:00

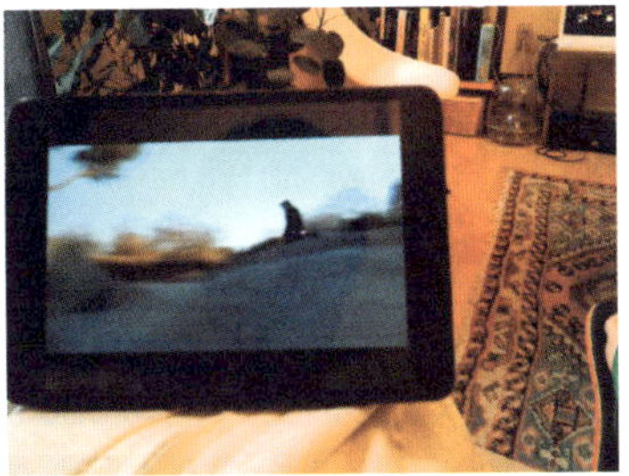

04:09

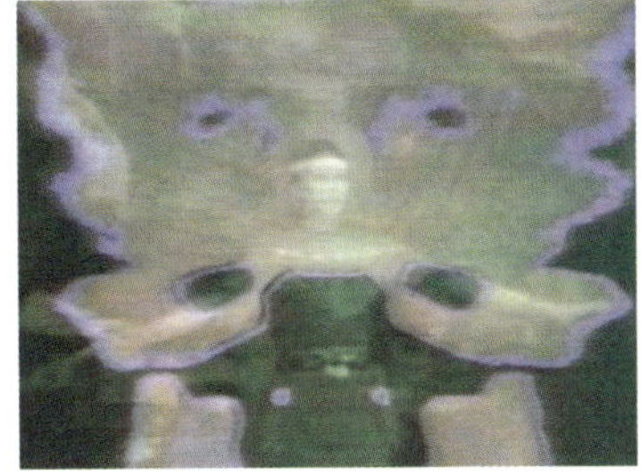

14:40

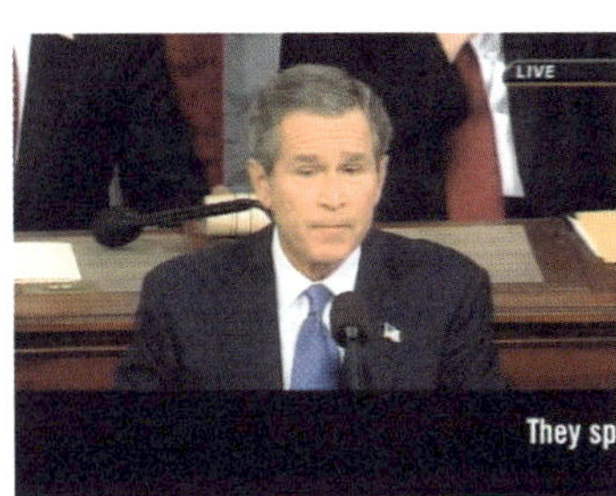

04:42

EXTENDED IMAGE CAPTIONS

p. 101: Howard Wise and Operations Engineer John Trayna at the EAI Video Editing Facility, 1972. Photo: Davidson Gigliotti

p. 102: Letter by Howard Wise announcing the closure of his gallery. December 16, 1970

p. 103: Lori Zippay, Executive Director of EAI (1985-2019). Photo by Robert Beck, 2009

p. 103: Anthony Ramos and Trevor Shimizu in the EAI editing facility, 2013

p. 104: Technical director Jon Dieringer and Emir West, 2017. Photograph: Tyler Maxin

p. 104: Drawing by Eric Siegel demonstrating an electronic video synthesizer, circa 1971

*All images courtesy Electronic Arts Intermix

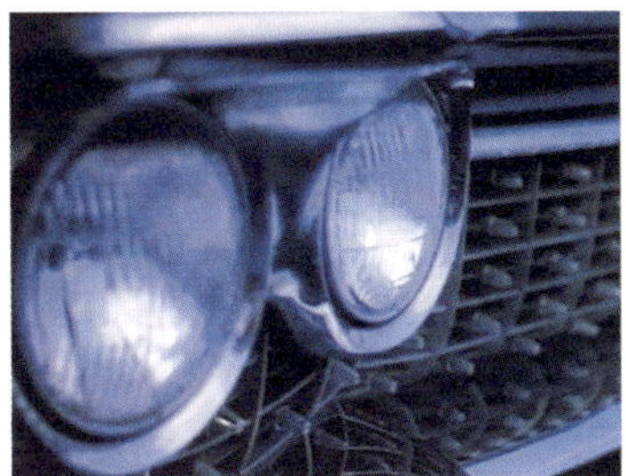

00:29

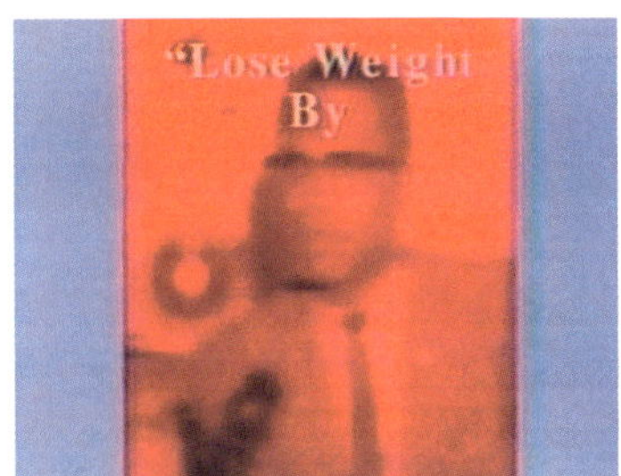

00:46

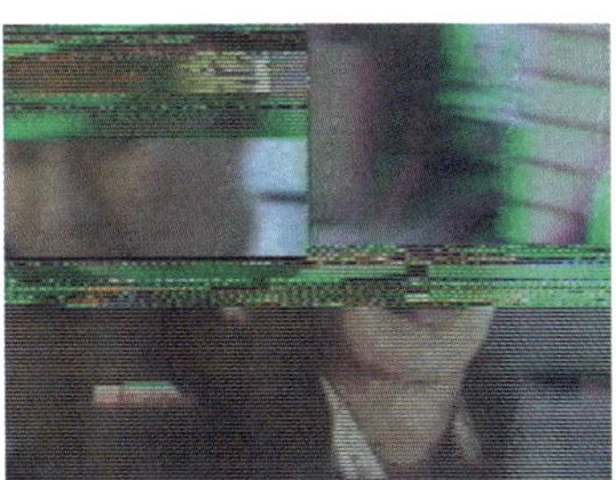

21:23

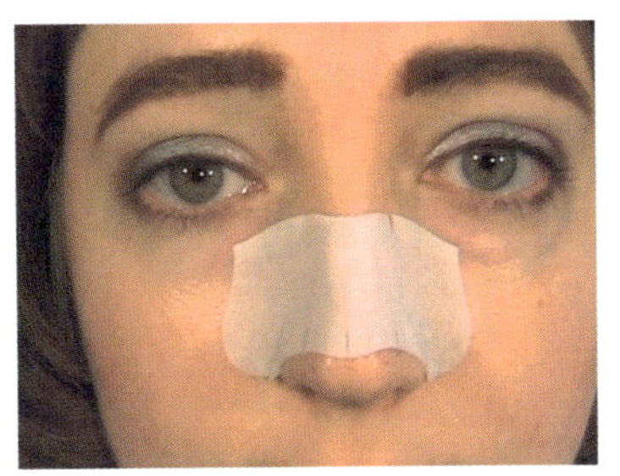

01:35

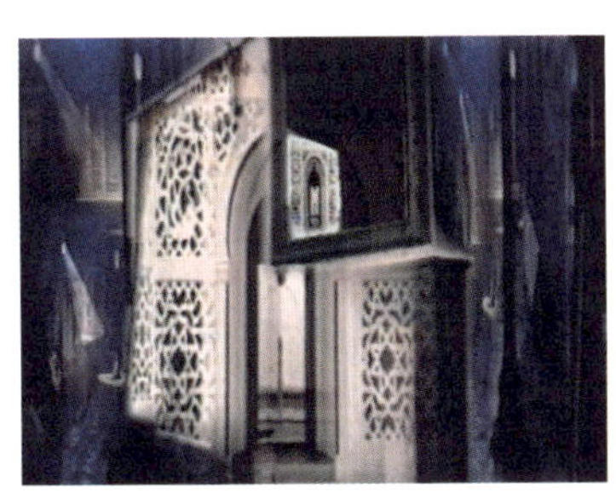

00:32

04:35

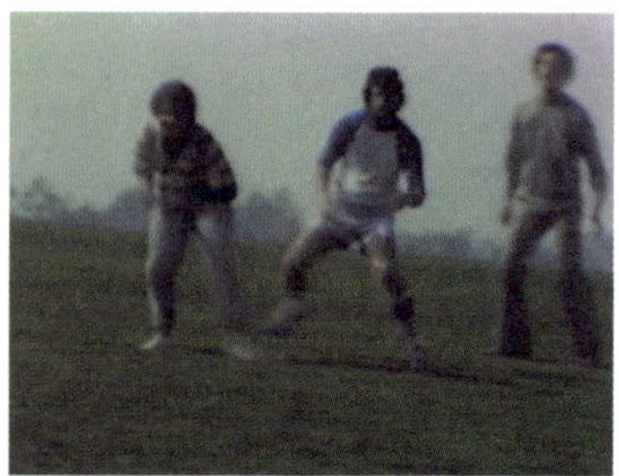

01:14

01:34

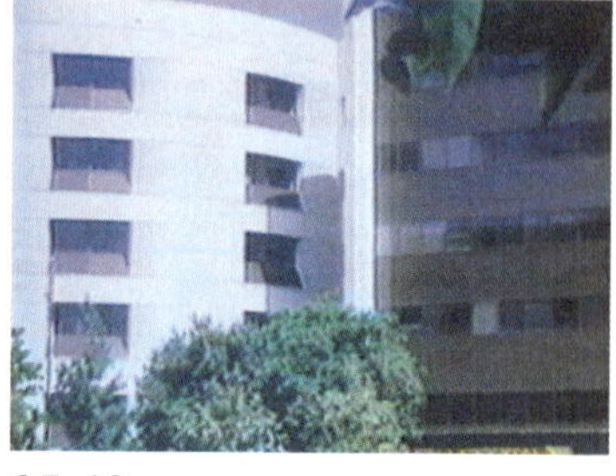

05:49

IMAGE CREDITS

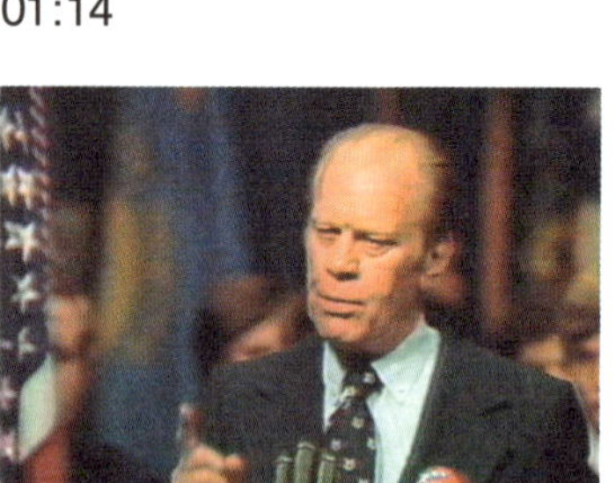

13:58

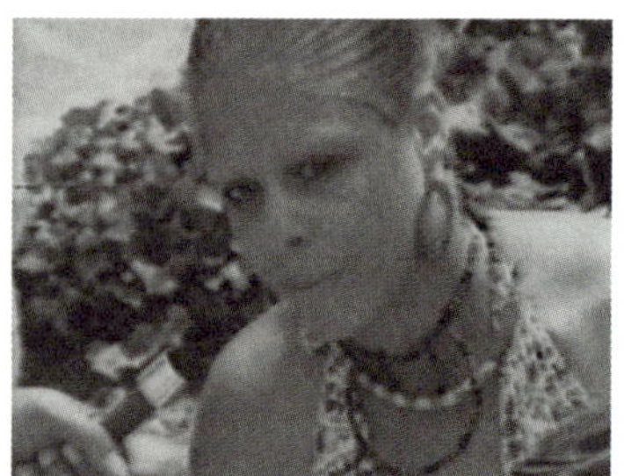

17:22

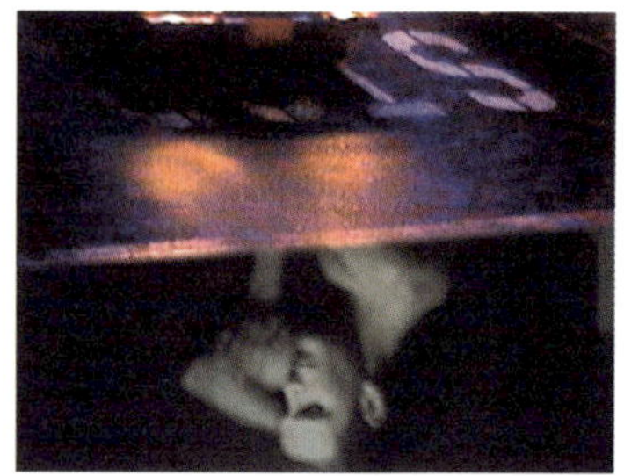

07:10

ANIMATING VIDEO STILLS
IMAGES CLOCKWISE
FROM UPPER LEFT

1 Ulysses Jenkins
Inconsequential Doggereal, 1981
video, color, sound,
15:13 minutes

2 Kristin Lucas
Cable Xcess, 1996
video, color, sound,
4:48 minutes

3 Robert Beck/Buck
The Space Program: TV Architecture, 1986
video, color, sound,
28 minutes

4 Trevor Shimizu
The Lonely Loser Trilogy: Skate Videos, 2013
video, color, sound,
14:02 minutes

5 Shigeko Kubota
Video Girls and Video Songs for Navajo Sky, 1973
video, black-and-white and color, sound,
31:56 minutes

6 Tony Cokes
Evil.6: Making the Case/ Faking the Books, 2006
video, color, sound,
9:55 minutes

7 Bruce and Norman Yonemoto
TRANS-VOICES: ahistory, 1992
video, color, sound,
1 minute

8 X-PRZ
No Sell Out… or I wnt 2 b th ultimate commodity/ machine (Malcolm X Pt. 2), 1995
video, color, sound,
5:37 minutes

9 Ulysses Jenkins
Bay Windows, 1991
video, color, sound,
84:45 minutes

10 TVTV
VTR: TVTV, 1975
video, black-and-white and color, sound, 28:30 minutes

11 Philip Mallory Jones
TRANS-VOICES: Paradigm Shift, 1992

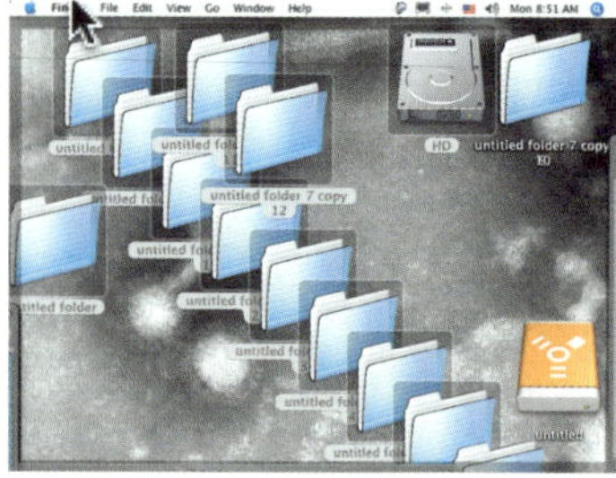

00:45

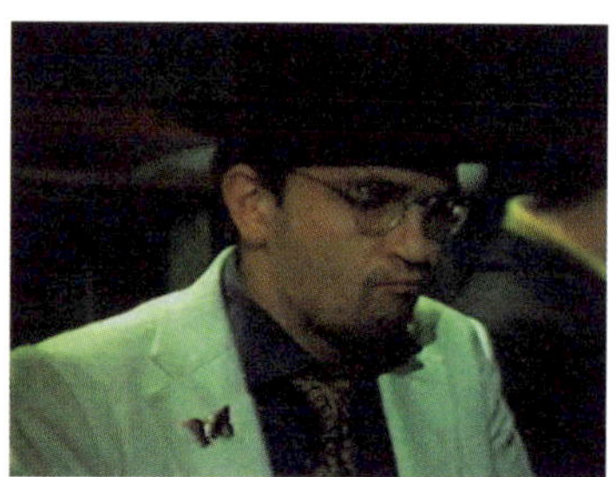

08:16

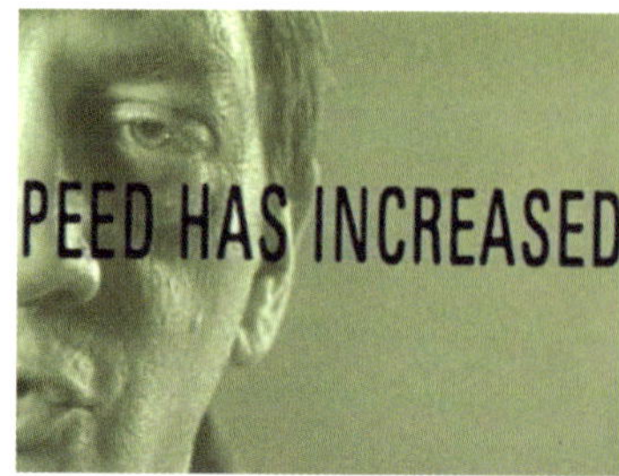

00:00

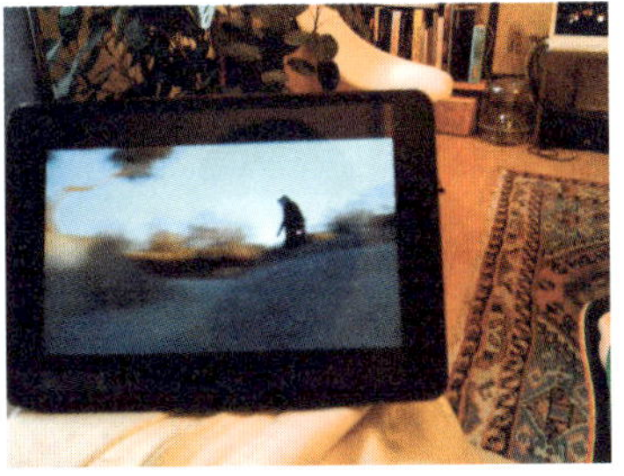

04:09

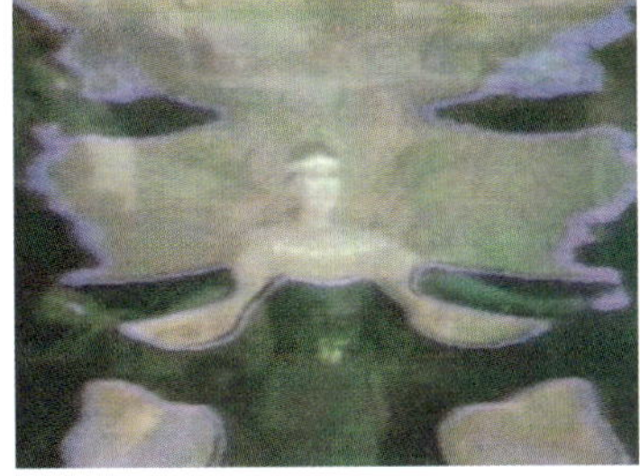

14:40

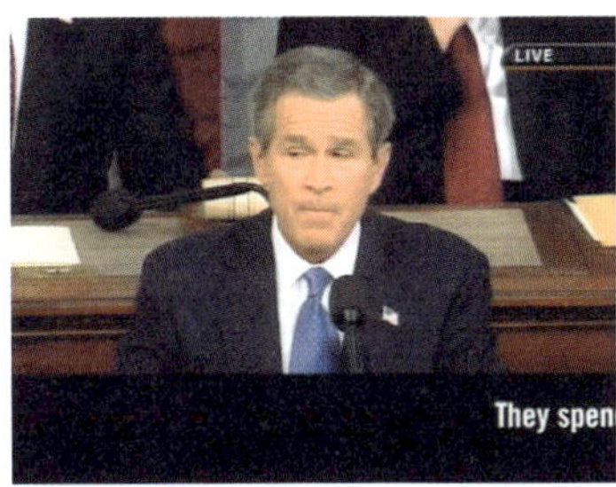

04:42

video, color, sound,
1 minute

12 Shana Moulton
Whispering Pines 7, 2006
video, color, sound,
4:43 minutes

13 Tom Kalin
TRANS-VOICES: Nation, 1992
video, color, sound,
1 minute

14 Squat Theatre
Andy Warhol's Last Love, 1978-81
video, black-and-white and color, sound,
60 minutes

15 JODI
My Desktop OS X 10.4.7, 2007
video, color, sound,
7:53 minutes

16 Robert Beck/Buck
The Space Program: STOP, 1985
video, color, sound,
28 minutes

17 Video Venice News
Remnants of the Watts Festival, 1972-73, compiled 1980
video, black-and-white, sound, 60 minutes

18 TVTV
Gerald Ford's America: WIN, 1975
video, color, sound,
28 minutes

CHECKLIST
BACKGROUND IMAGES

p. 169: Shigeko Kubota, *Video Girls and Video Songs for Navajo Sky*, 1973, video, black-and-white and color, sound, 31:56 minutes

p. 170–171: Robert Beck/Buck, *The Space Program: TV Architecture*, 1986, video, color, sound, 28 minutes

p. 172–173: Tony Cokes, *Evil.6: Making the Case/Faking the Books*, 2006, video, color, sound, 9:55 minutes

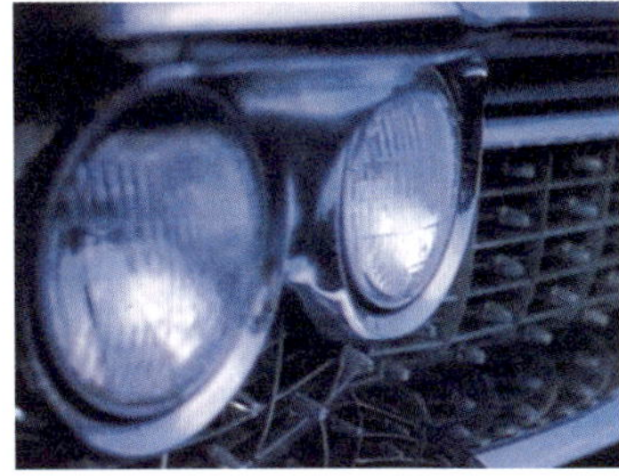

00:29

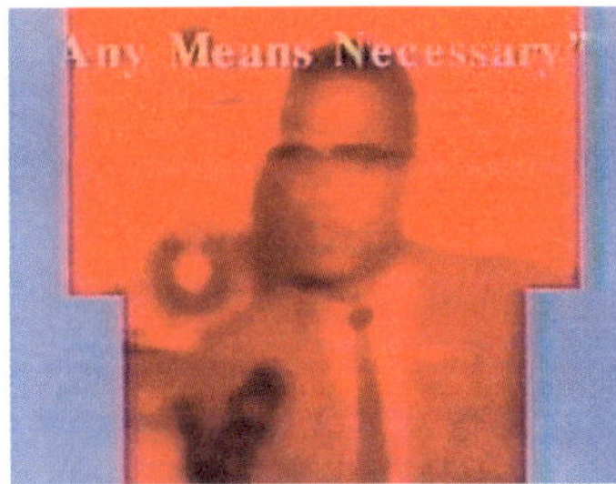

00:46

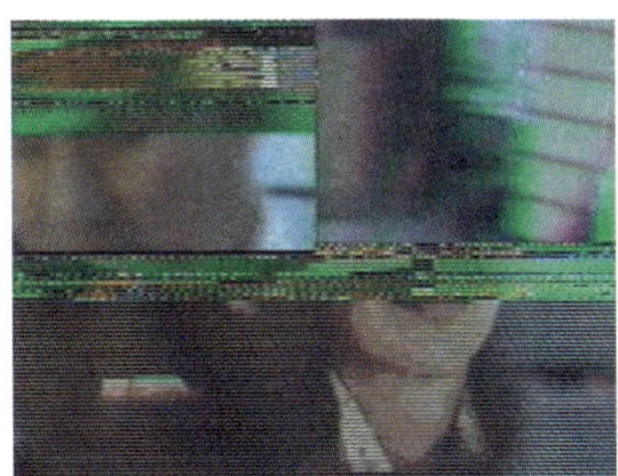

21:23

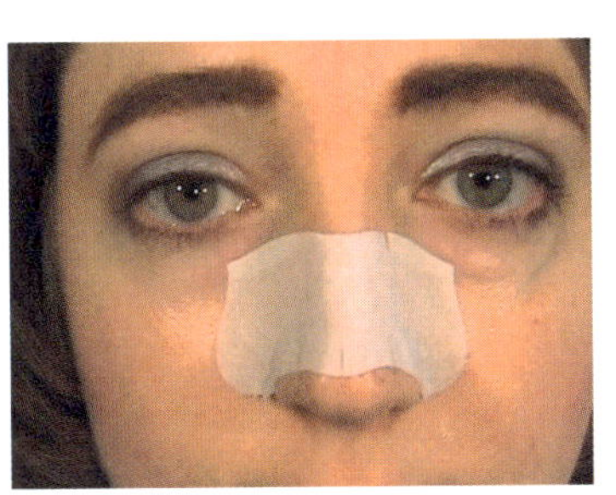

01:35

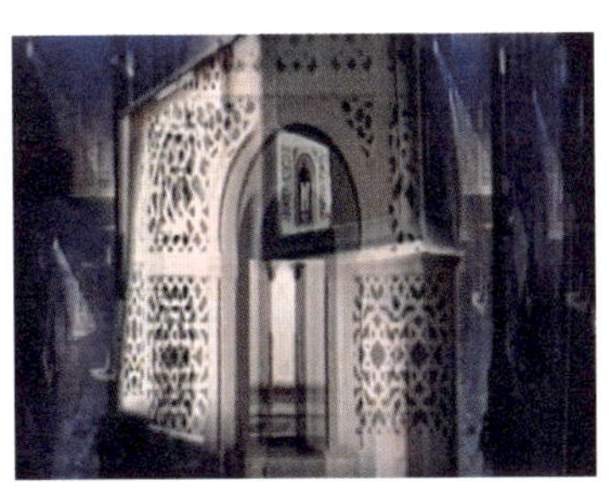

00:32

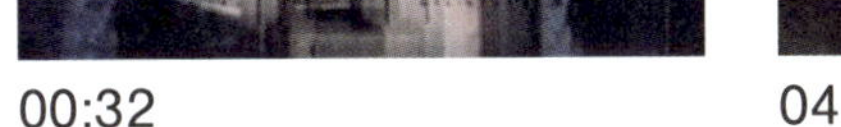

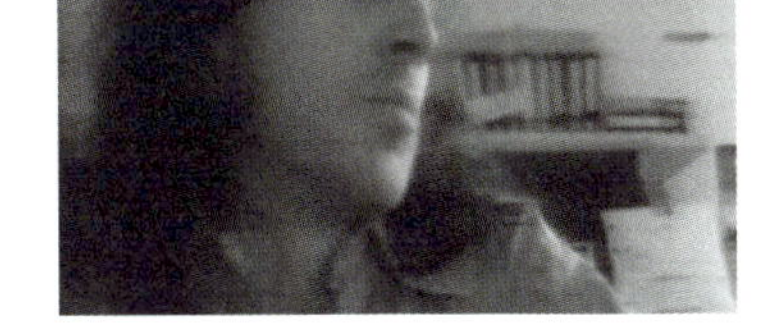

04:35

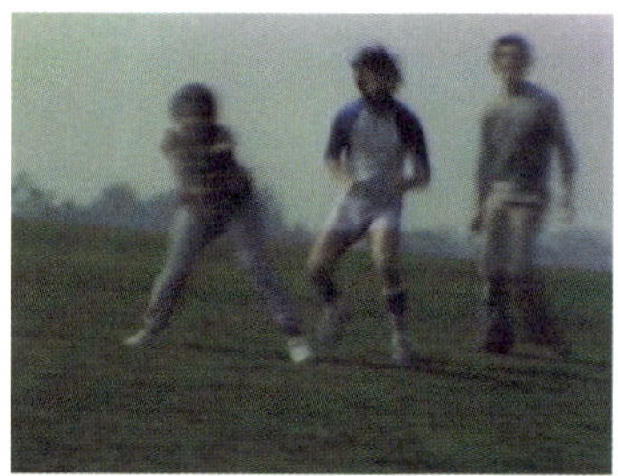

01:14

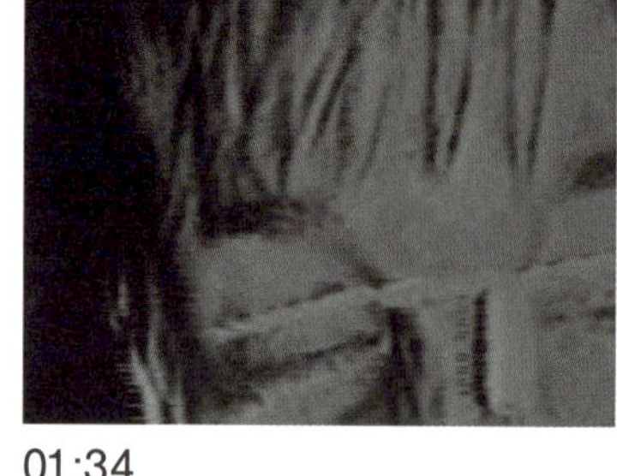

01:34

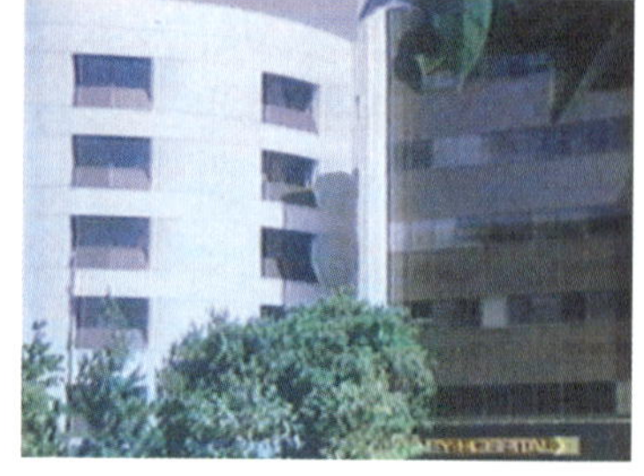

05:49

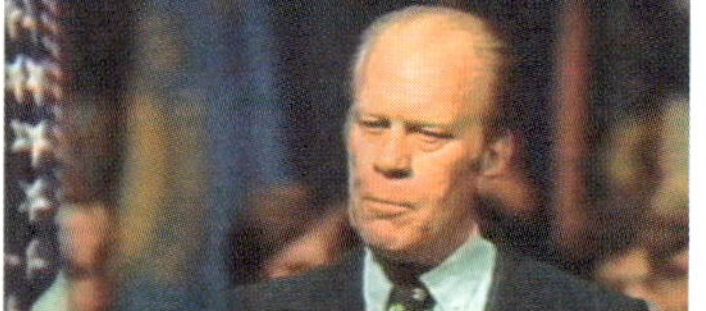

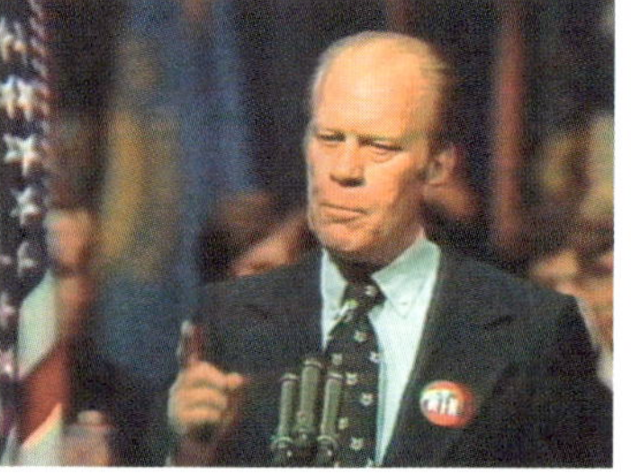

13:58

17:22

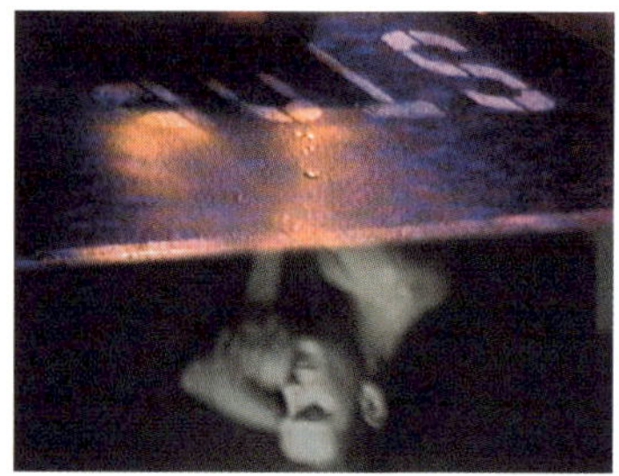

07:10

p. 174–175: Ulysses Jenkins, *Bay Windows*, 1991, video, color, sound, 84:45 minutes

p. 176–177: Ulysses Jenkins, *Inconsequential Doggereal*, 1981, video, color, sound, 15:13 minutes

p. 178–179: Shigeko Kubota, *Video Girls and Video Songs for Navajo Sky*, 1973, video, black-and-white and color, sound, 31:56 minutes

p. 180–181: Kristin Lucas, *Cable Xcess*, 1996, video, color, sound, 4:48 minutes

p. 182–183: Shana Moulton, *Whispering Pines 7*, 2006, video, color, sound, 4:43 minutes

p. 184–185: Trevor Shimizu, *The Lonely Loser Trilogy: Skate Videos*, 2013, video, color, sound, 14:02 minutes

p. 186–187: Tom Kalin, *TRANS-VOICES: Nation*, 1992, video, color, sound, 1 minute

p. 188–189: Nam June Paik and Paul Garrin, *TRANS-VOICES: A Tale of Two Cities*, 1992, video, color, sound, 1 minute

p. 190–191: DCTV, *VTR: Downtown Community Television Center*, 1975, video, black-and-white and color, sound, 29:08 minutes

p. 192–193: Martha Rosler and Paper Tiger Television, *Born to Be Sold: Martha Rosler Reads the Strange Case of Baby $/M*, 1988, video, color, sound, 35:18 minutes

p. 194–195: Radical Software Group (RSG), *RSG-BLACK-1, 2005*, video, color, sound, 22:04 minutes

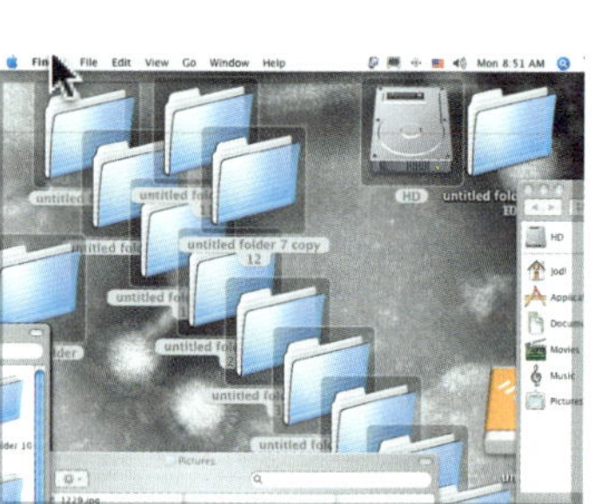

00:45

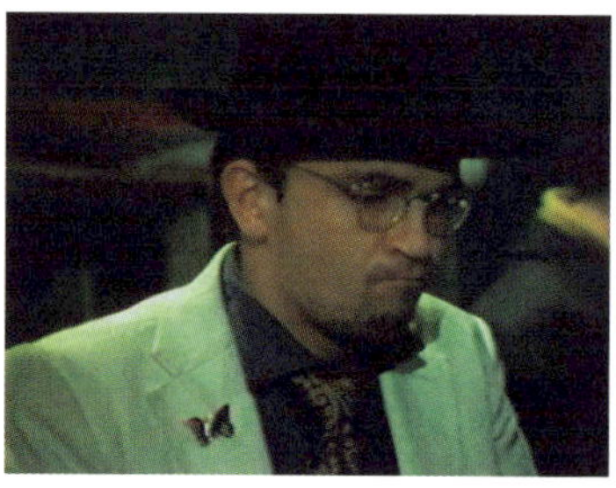

08:16

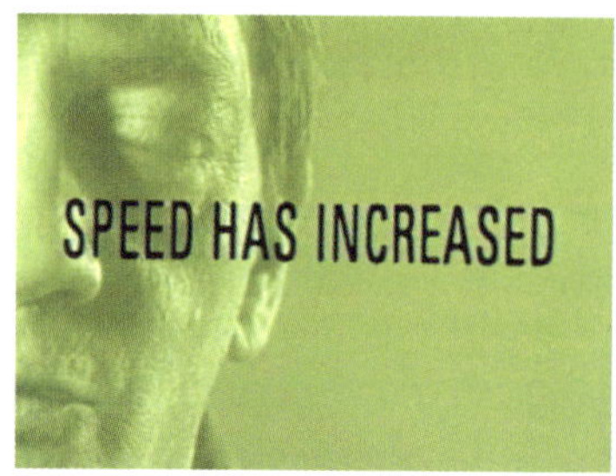

00:00

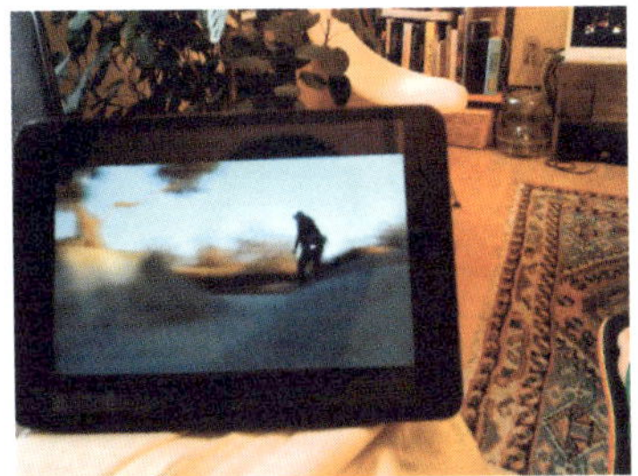
04:10

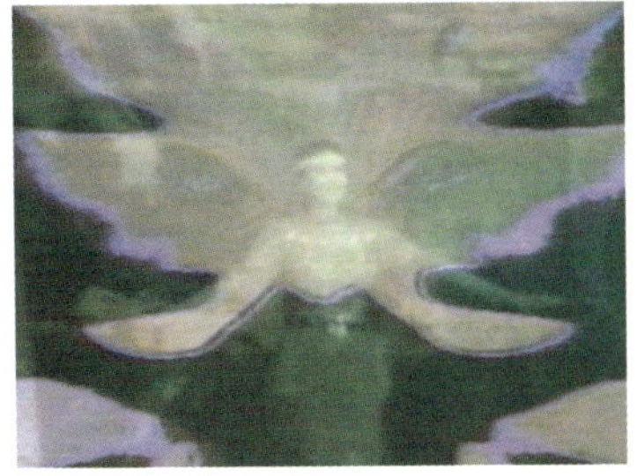
14:41

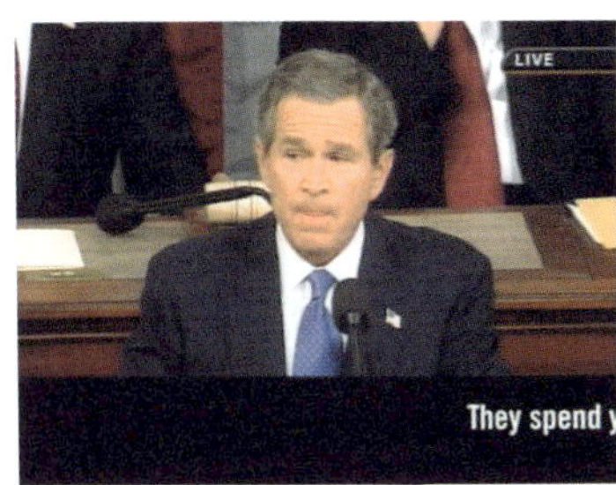

04:43

IMAGE CREDITS

p. 196–197: Robert Beck/ Buck and DIVA TV, *The Feeling of Power*, 1990, video, color, sound, 9 minutes

p. 198–199: Squat Theatre, *Andy Warhol's Last Love*, 1978-81, video, black-and-white and color, sound, 60 minutes

p. 200–201: TVTV, *Gerald Ford's America: Chic to Sheik*, 1975, video, black-and-white and color, sound, 28 minutes

p. 202–203: TVTV, *Gerald Ford's America: WIN*, 1975, video, color, sound, 28 minutes

p. 204–205: TVTV, *VTR: TVTV*, 1975, video, black-and-white and color, sound, 28:30 minutes

p. 206–207: Video Venice News, *Remnants of the Watts Festival*, 1972-73, compiled 1980, video, black-and-white, sound, 60 minutes

p. 208: X-PRZ, *No Sell Out . . . or i wnt 2 b th ultimate commodity/ machine, (Malcolm X Pt. 2)*, 1995, video, color, sound, 5:37 minutes

EXTERIOR COVER
Shigeko Kubota, *Video Girls and Video Songs for Navajo Sky*, 1973, video, black-and-white and color, sound, 31:56 minutes

INTERIOR COVER
Ulysses Jenkins, *Bay Windows*, 1991, video, color, sound, 84:45 minutes

*All images courtesy the artists and Electronic Arts Intermix

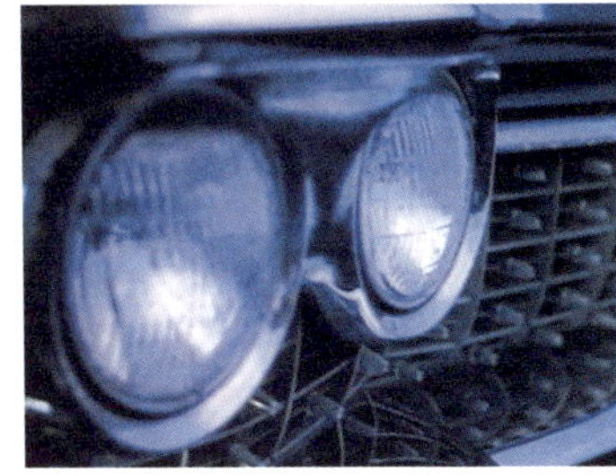
00:30

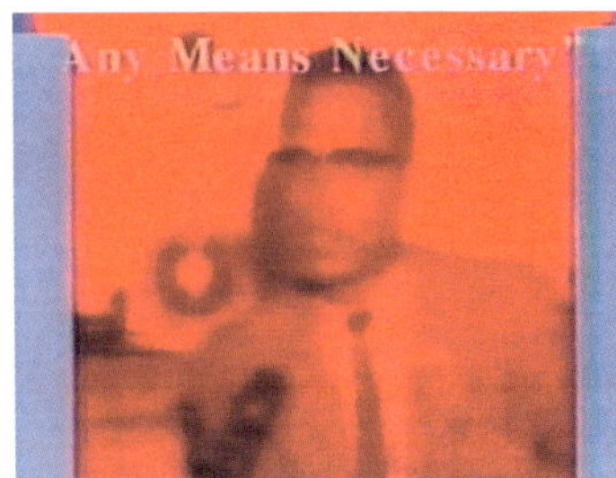

00:47

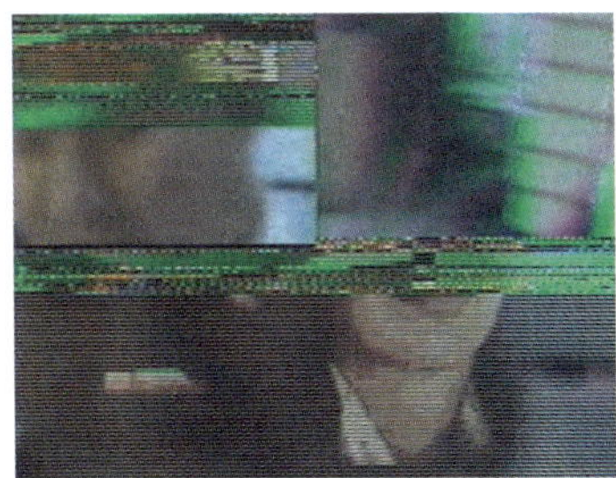
21:24

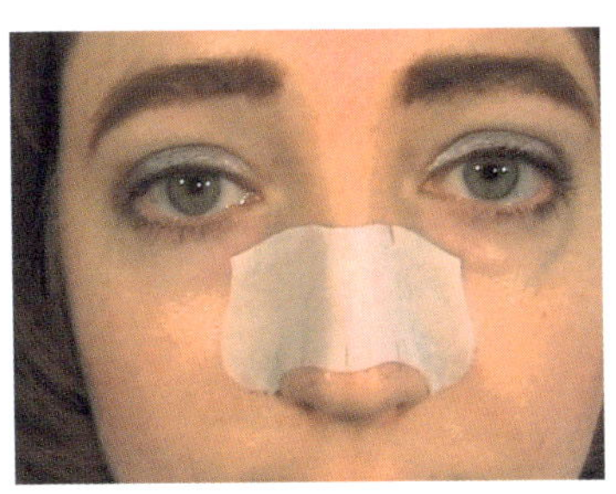
01:36

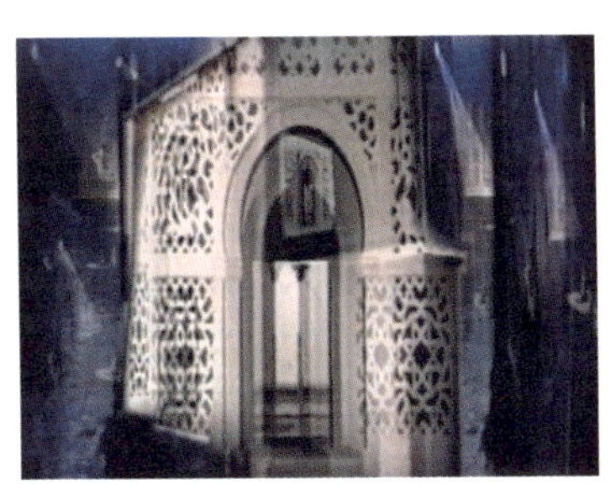
00:33

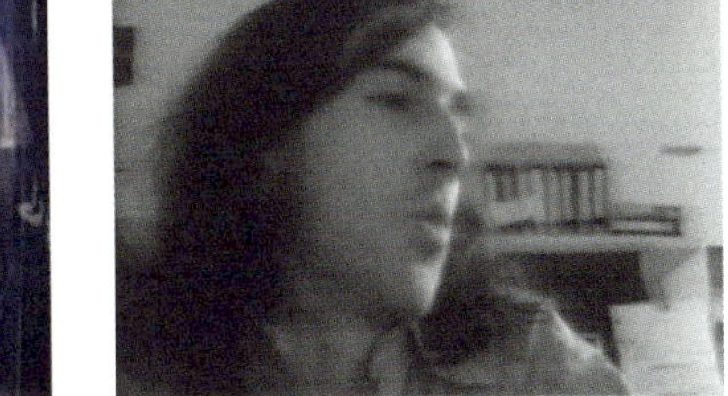
04:36

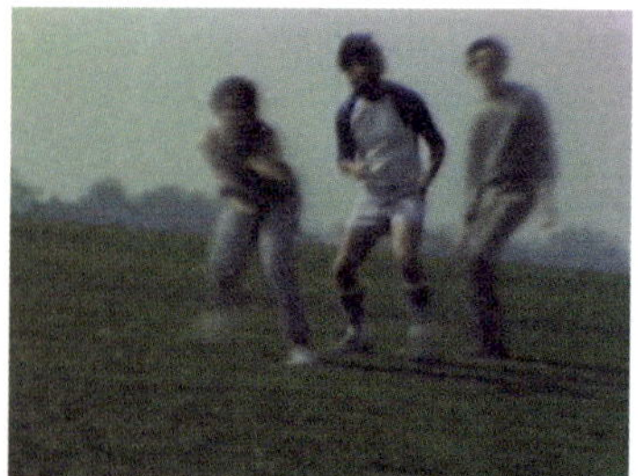

01:14

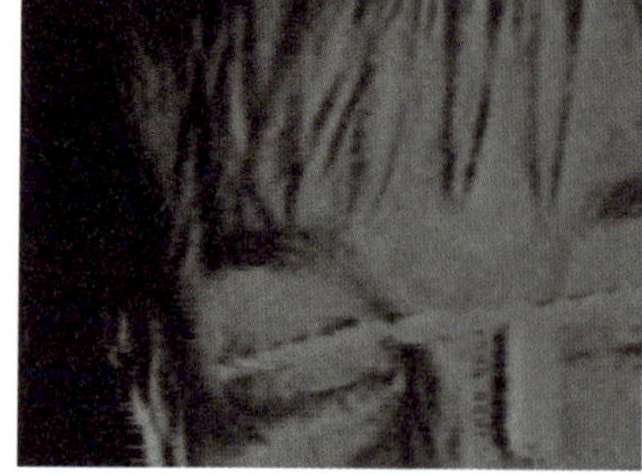

01:34

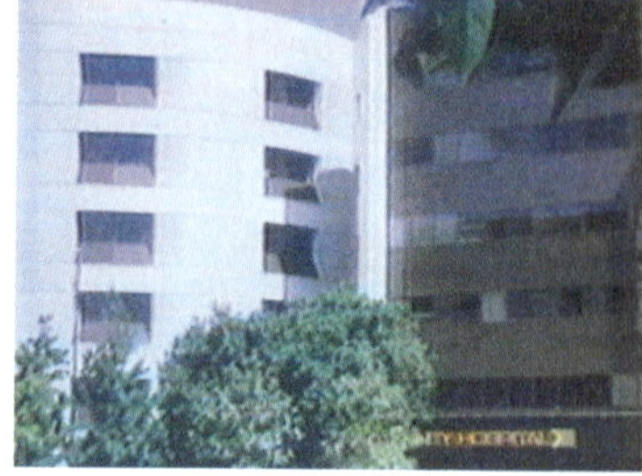

05:49

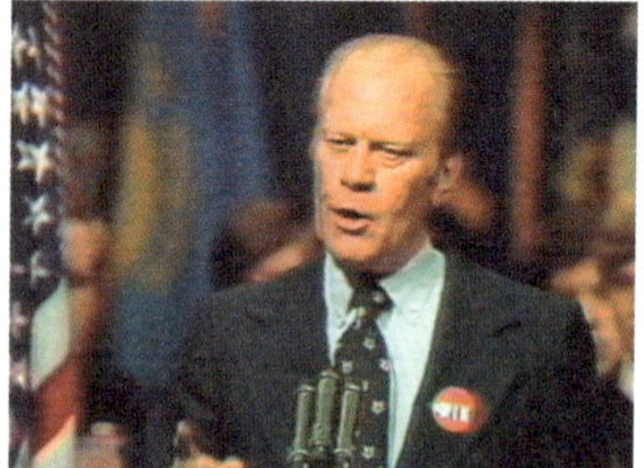

13:58

ICA BOARD OF ADVISORS

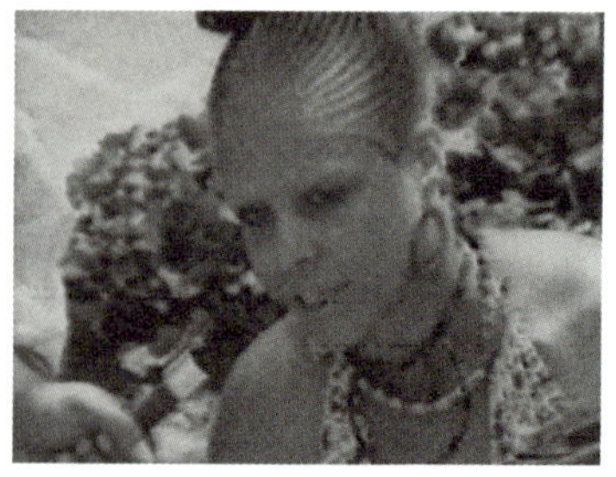

17:22

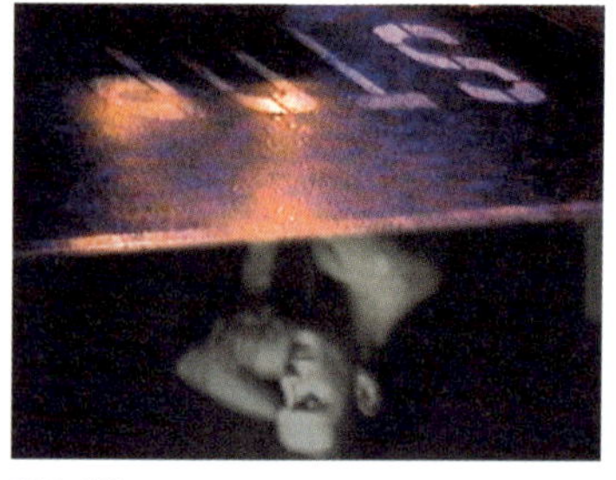

07:10

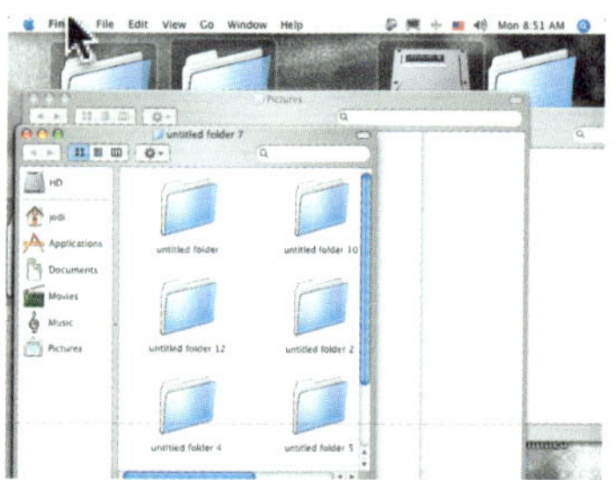

00:45

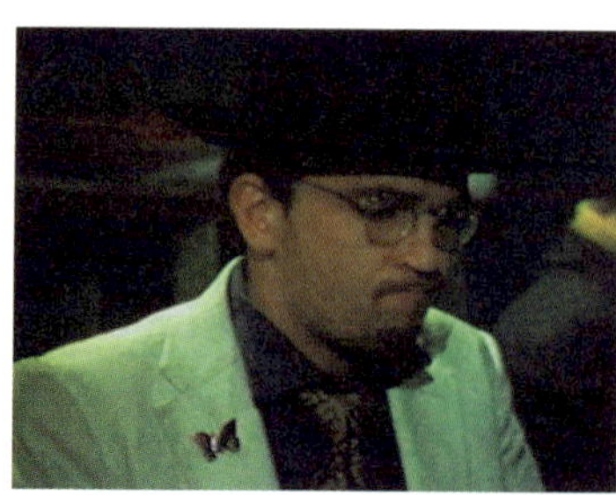

08:16

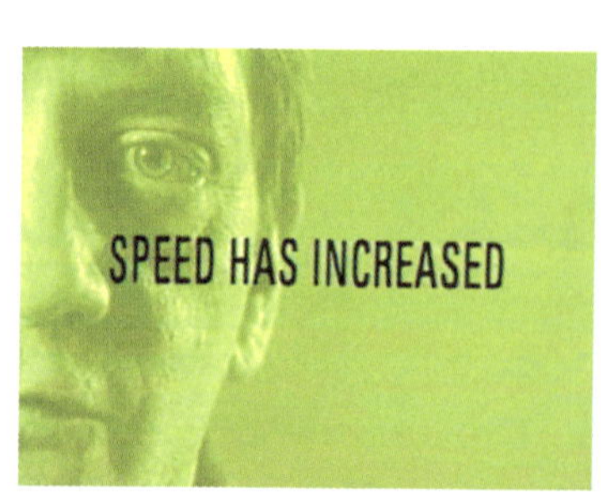

00:00

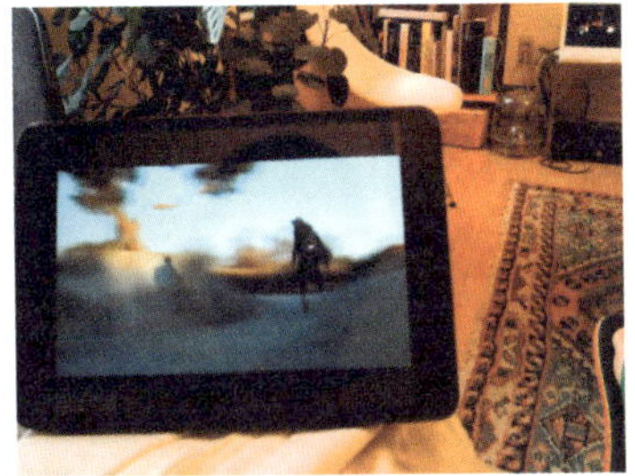
04:10

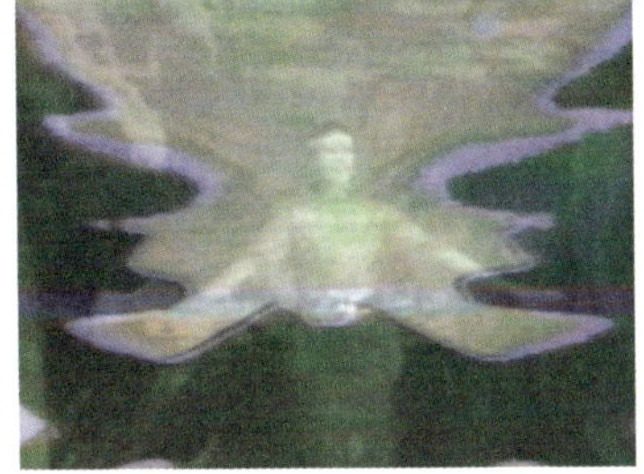
14:41

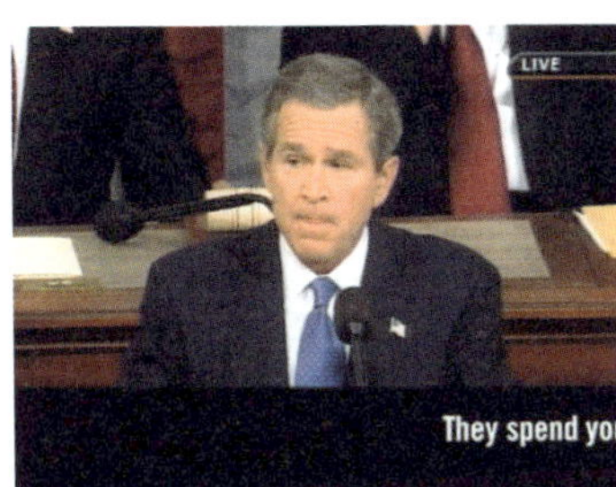

04:43

ICA STAFF LIST

Zoë Ryan, Daniel W. Dietrich, II Director
Kate Abercrombie, Registrar
James E. Britt, Jr., DAJ Director of Public Engagement
Robert Chaney, Marc J. Leder Director of Curatorial Affairs
Elizabeth Chong, Visitor Services Coordinator
Lauren Downing, Executive Assistant to the Director
Anthony Elms, Daniel and Brett Sundheim Chief Curator
Shannon Freitas, Director of Administration
Taja Jones, Associate Director of Development & Alumni Relations
Jes Kaminski, Administrative Coordinator
Jill Katz, Director of Marketing & Communications
Alex Klein, Dorothy and Stephen R. Weber (CHE '60) Curator
Ali Abdel Mohsen, Digital Content Editor
Bruno Nouril, Director of Development & Alumni Relations
Meg Onli, Andrea B. Laporte Associate Curator
Derek Rigby, Audio Visual Coordinator
Natalie Sandstrom, Programs Coordinator
Paul Swenbeck, Chief Preparator & Building Administrator
Christina Yu, Assistant Director of Development & Alumni Relations

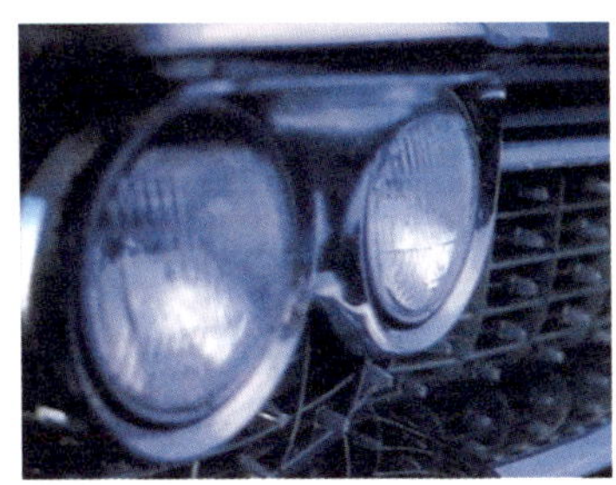
00:30

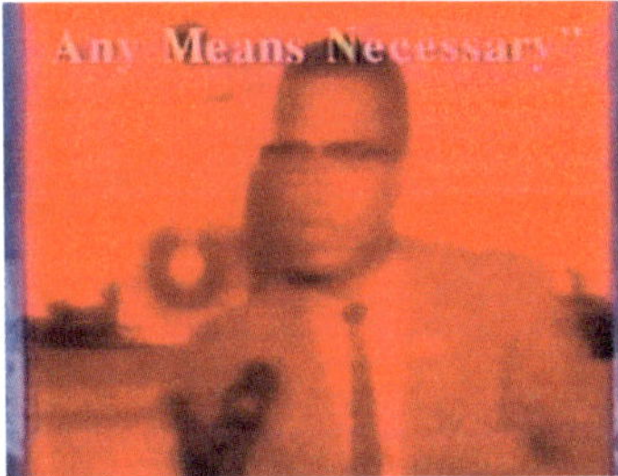

00:47

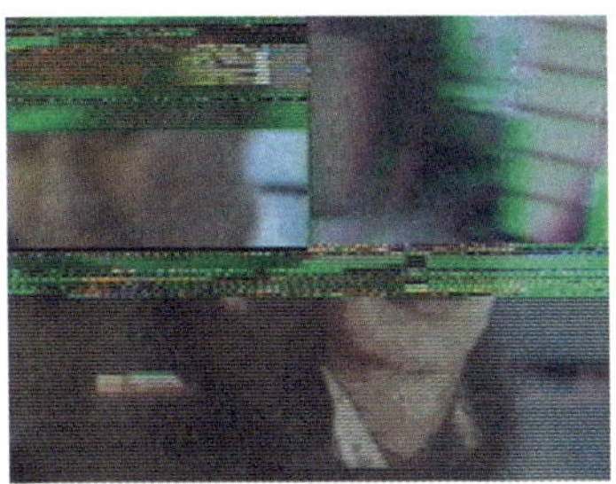
21:24

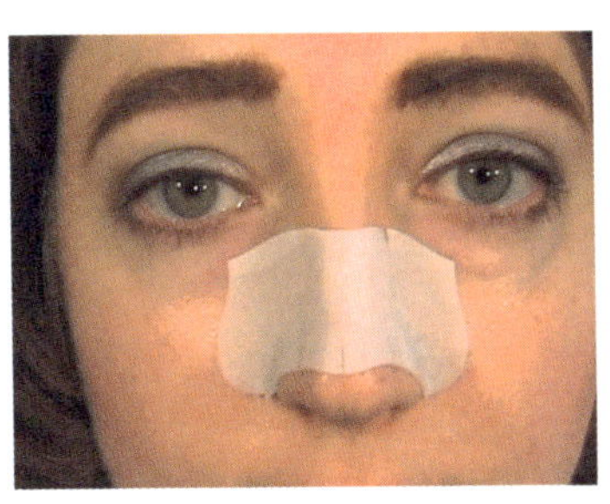
01:36

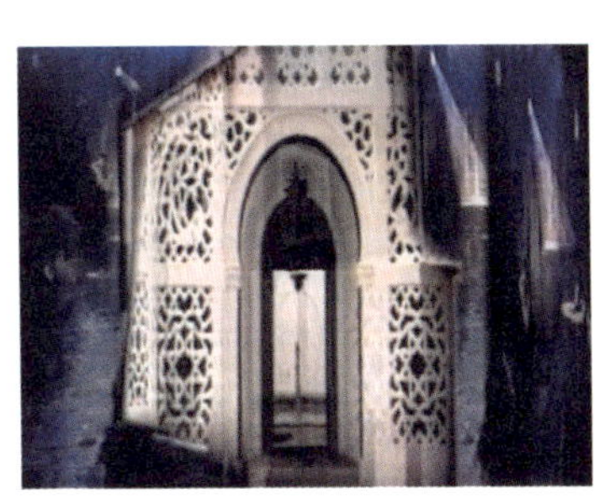
00:33

04:36

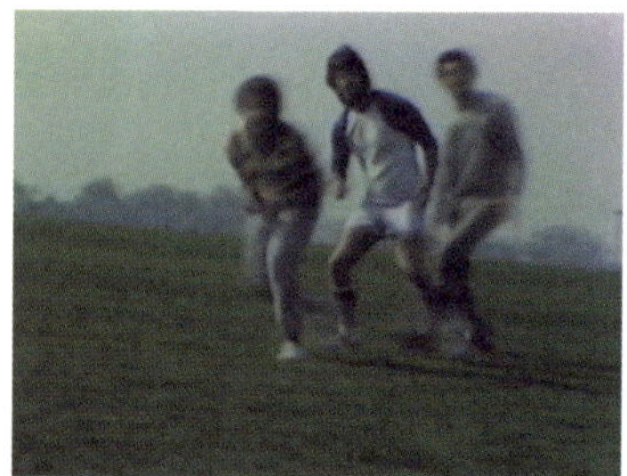
01:14

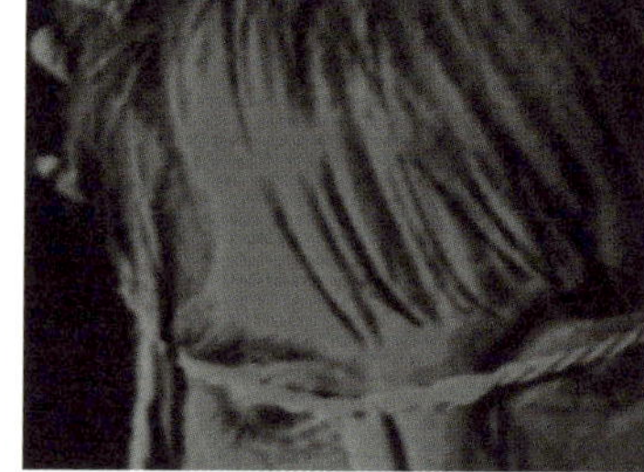
01:34

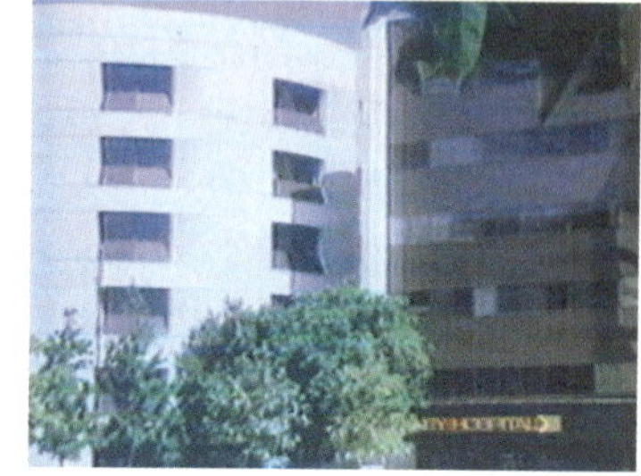
05:49

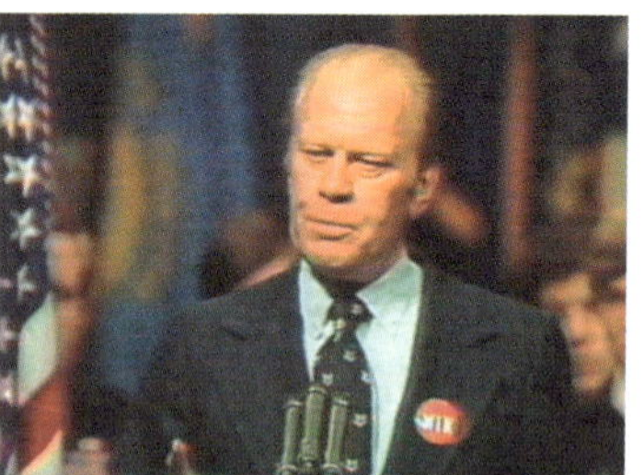
13:58

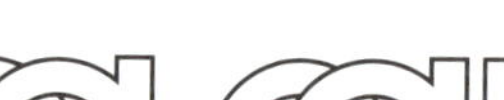

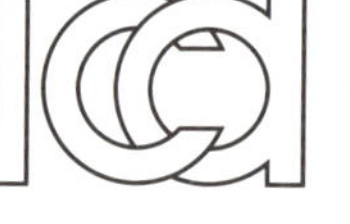

BROADCASTING:
EAI AT ICA
FEBRUARY 2–
MARCH 25, 2018

BROADCASTING:
GUERRILLA MEDIA
FEBRUARY 17–
APRIL 25, 2018

Broadcasting: EAI at ICA is co-curated by ICA's Dorothy and Stephen R. Weber (CHE '60) Curator Alex Klein and Electronic Arts Intermix Executive Director Rebecca Cleman. Support for *Broadcasting: EAI at ICA* has been provided by The Sachs Program for Arts Innovation and The Keith L. and Katherine Sachs Program in Contemporary Art.

ICA is always Free. For All. Free admission is courtesy of Amanda and Glenn Fuhrman.

ICA acknowledges the generous sponsorship of Barbara B. & Theodore R. Aronson for exhibition publications. Programming at ICA has been made possible in part by the Emily and Jerry Spiegel Fund to Support Contemporary Culture and Visual Arts and the Lise Spiegel Wilks and Jeffrey Wilks Family Foundation, and by Hilarie L. & Mitchell Morgan. Marketing is supported by Brett & Daniel Sundheim. Public and Student Engagement is supported by the Bernstein Public Engagement Fund and by Suzanne Weiss Doft & Jacob W. Doft. Exhibitions at ICA are supported by Laura Tisch Broumand & Stafford Broumand,

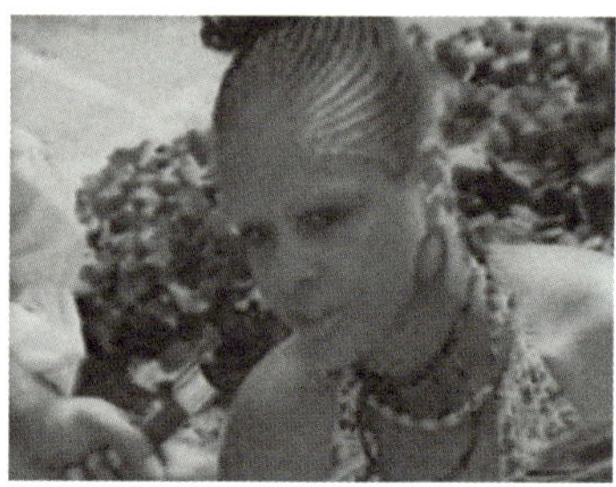
17:22

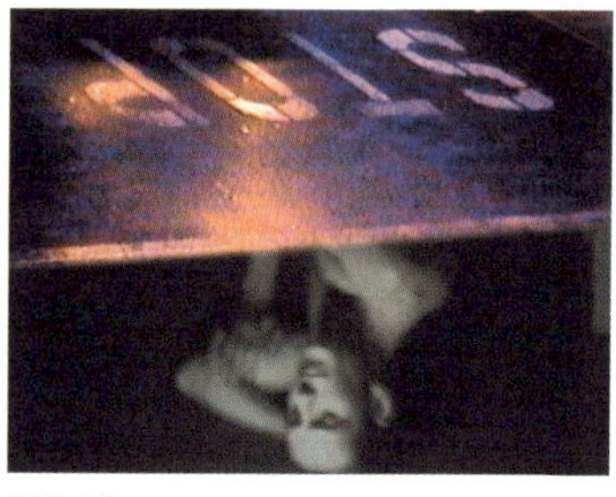
07:10

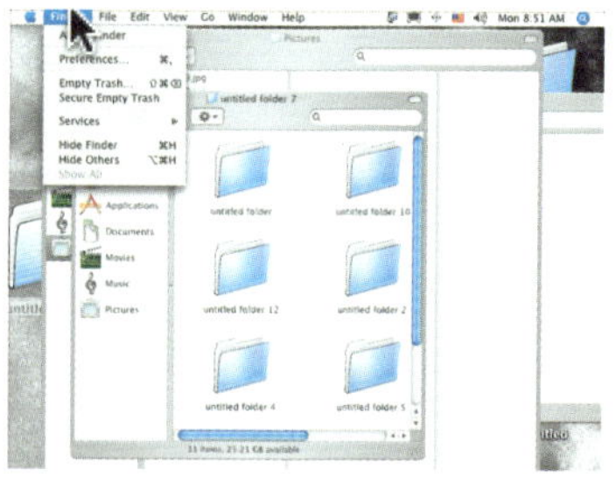
00:45

08:16

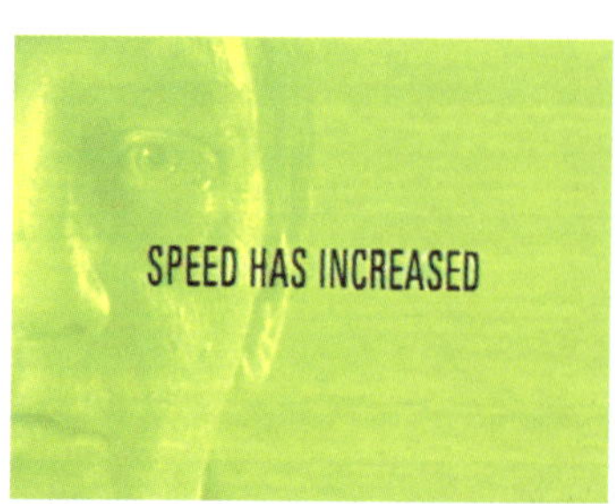

00:00

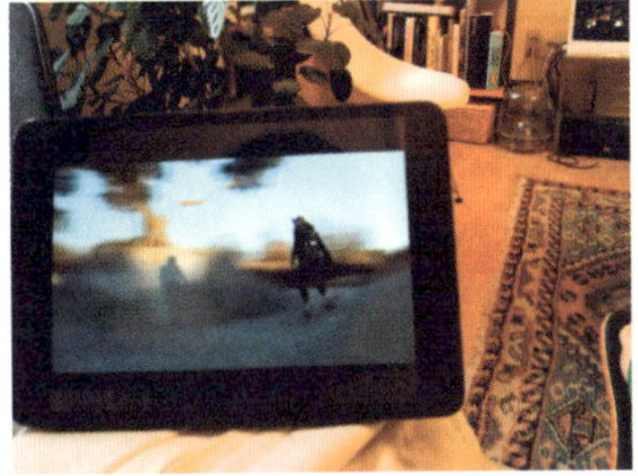

04:10

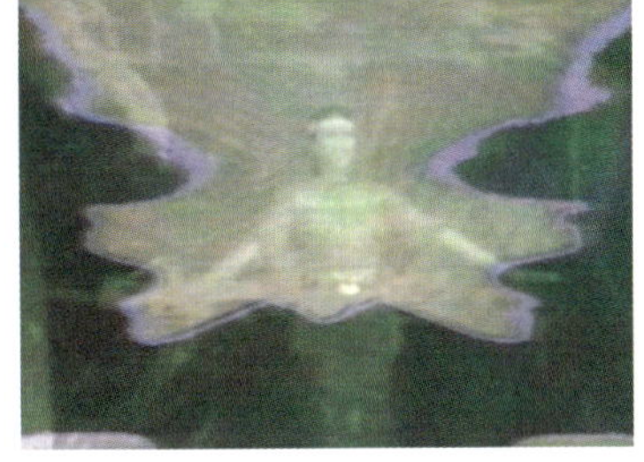

14:41

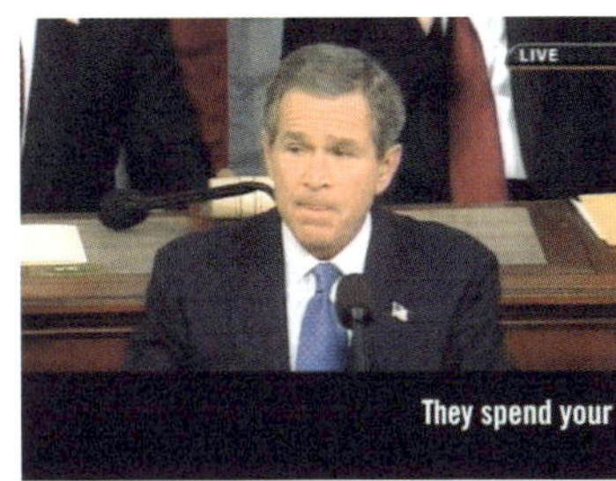

04:43

Catherine O'Connor Carrafiell & John Carrafiell, Stacey Burke Frost & Benjamin Marc Frost, Jennifer Otto-Klein & John Klein, and by Stephanie & David Simon. Additional funding has been provided by The Horace W. Goldsmith Foundation, ICA's Board of Advisors, friends and members of ICA, and the University of Pennsylvania. ICA receives state arts funding support through a grant from the Pennsylvania Council on the Arts, a state agency funded by the Commonwealth of Pennsylvania and the National Endowment for the Arts, a federal agency.

ARTS pennsylvania
COUNCIL ON THE ARTS

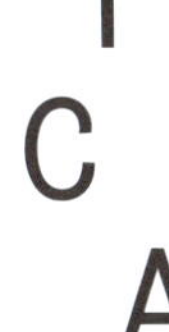

Institute of Contemporary Art,
University of Pennsylvania
118 S. 36th Street
Philadelphia, PA 19104
www.icaphila.org

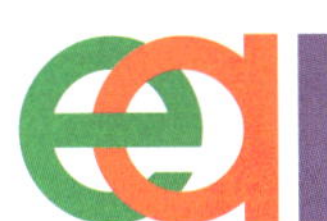

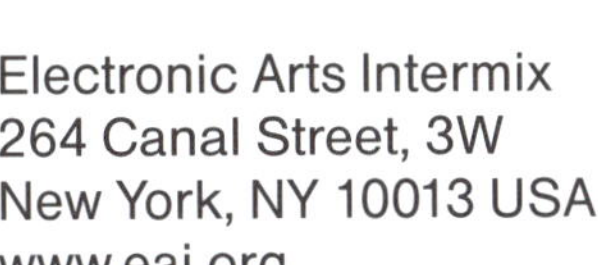

Electronic Arts Intermix
264 Canal Street, 3W
New York, NY 10013 USA
www.eai.org

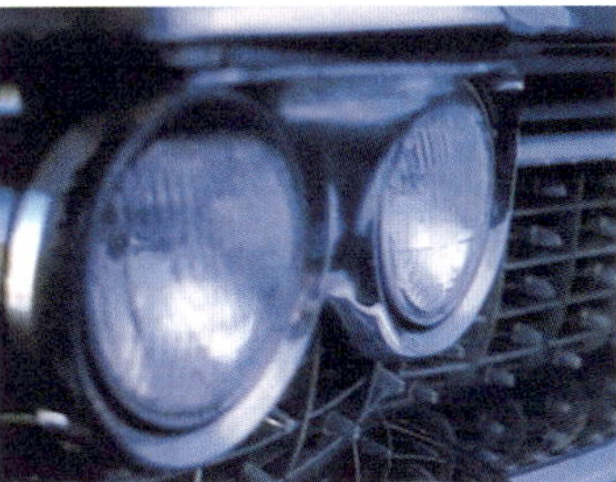

00:30

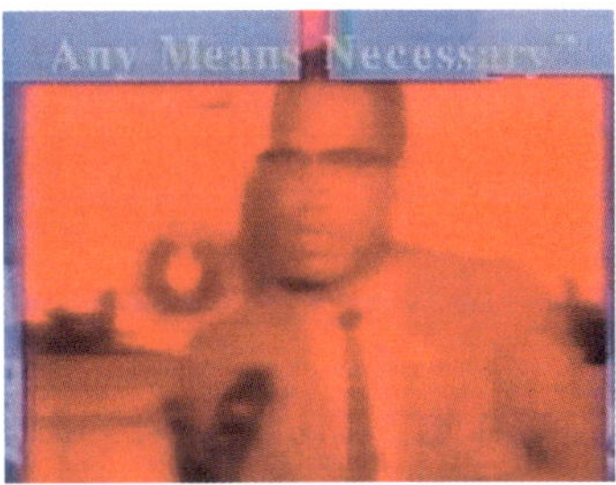

00:47

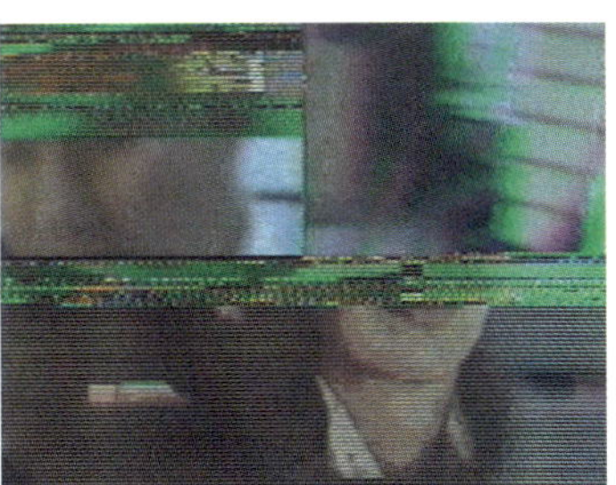

21:24

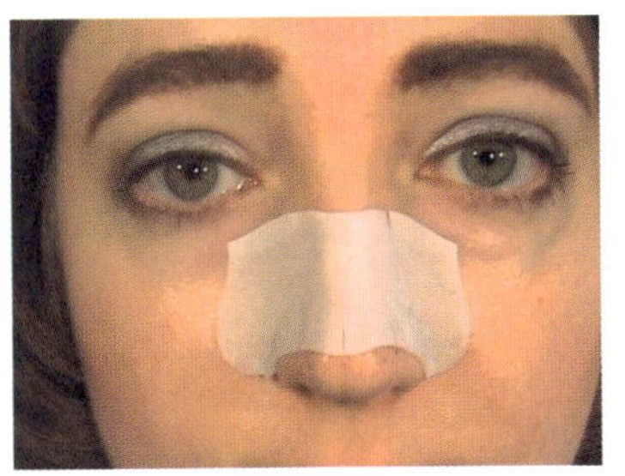

01:36

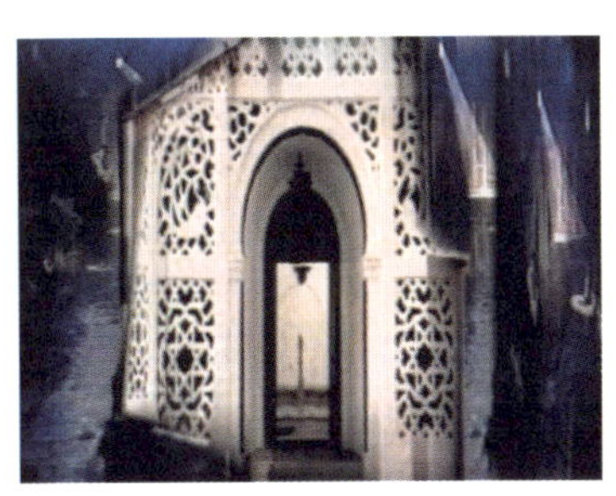

00:33

04:36

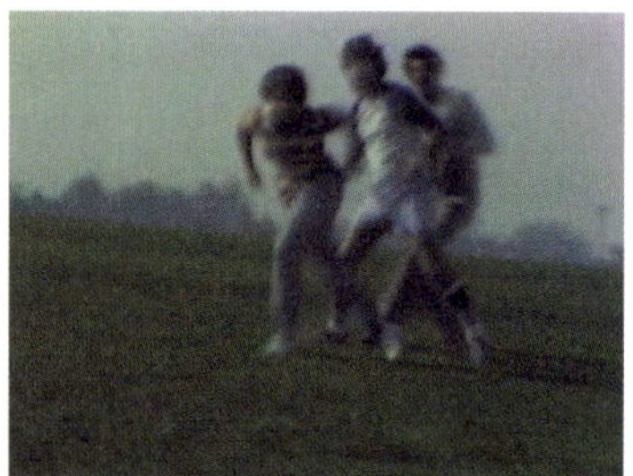

01:14

01:34

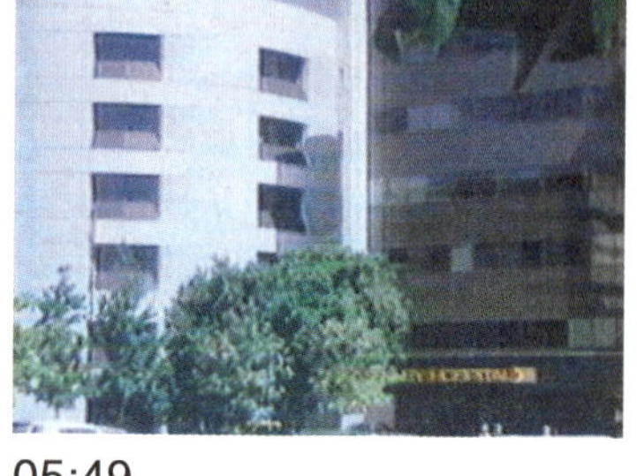

05:49

COLOPHON

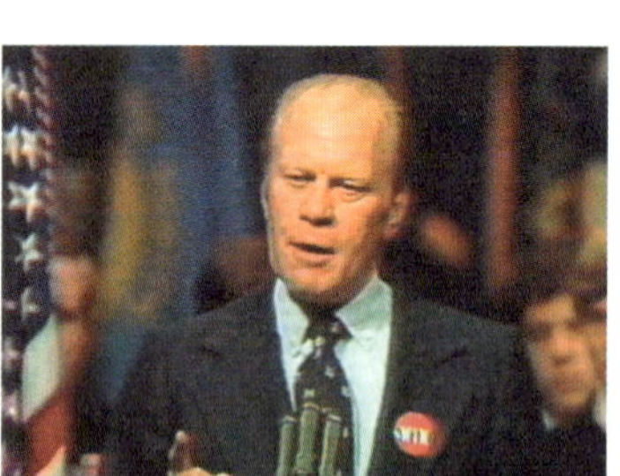

13:58

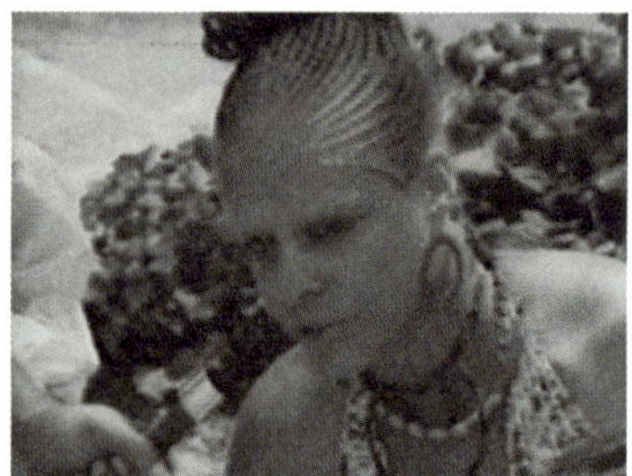

17:22

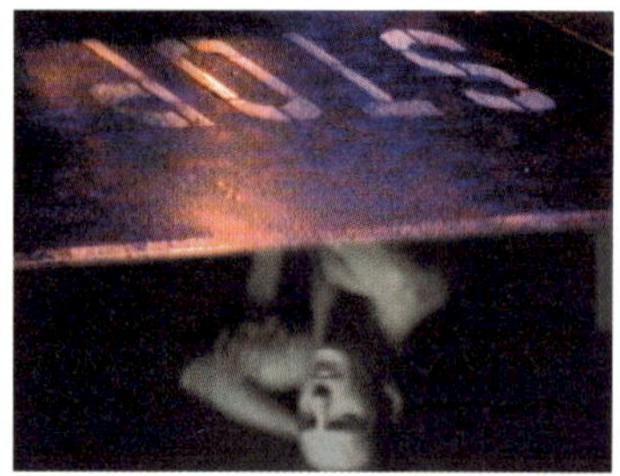

07:10

Design: Geoff Han & Anna Feng
Design Assistance: Immanuel Yang
Copy Editor: Gretchen Dykstra
Photography: Constance Mensh

Printed by Printon, Estonia
ISBN 978-0-88454-148-6

Library of Congress Cataloging-In-Publication Data can be obtained at the Library of Congress.

All images courtesy the Institute of Contemporary Art, University of Pennsylvania, Electronic Arts Intermix, and the artists.

Installation photography of *Broadcasting: EAI at ICA* and *Broadcasting: Guerrilla Media* by Constance Mensh.

Every reasonable attempt has been made to locate the owners of copyrights in the book and to ensure the credit information supplied is accurately listed. We welcome any uncredited creators to come forward so that we may acknowledge them and correct any errors or omissions in future editions.

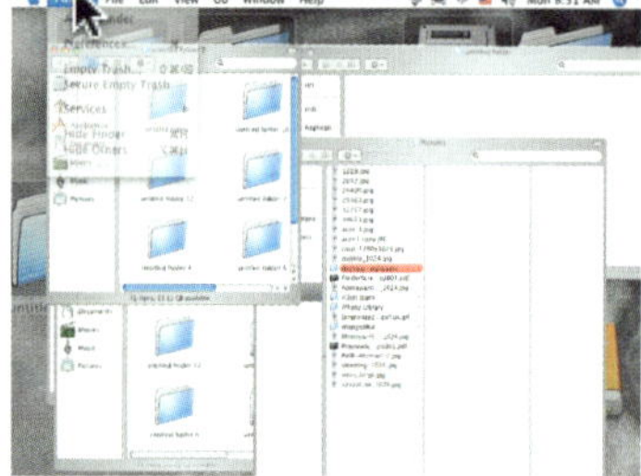

00:45

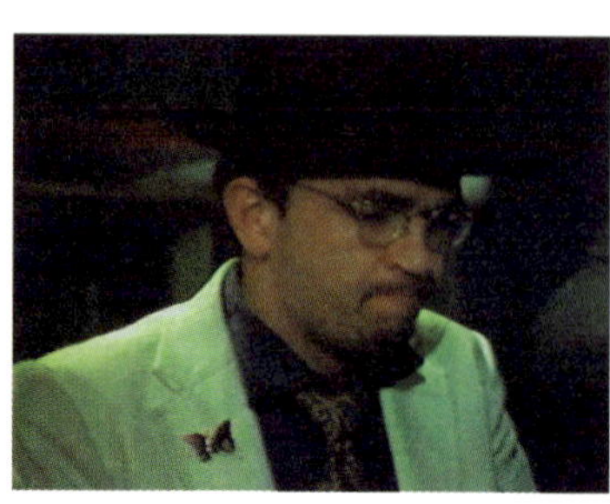

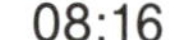

08:16

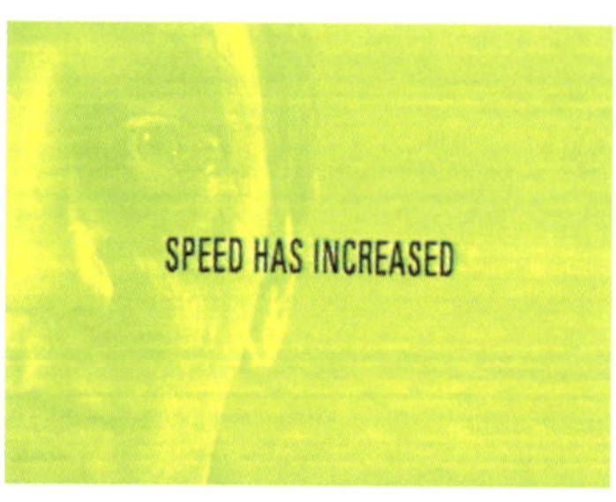

00:00